THE
FORTUNE®
ENCYCLOPEDIA
OF
ECONOMICS

THE FORTUNE®

ENCYCLOPEDIA OF ECONOMICS

EDITED BY

DAVID R. HENDERSON, PH.D.

WARNER BOOKS

A Time Warner Company

Grateful acknowledgment is made to the following for permission to reprint previously published material:

Economic Record: "Keynesian Economics" is adapted from Alan S. Blinder, "The Rise and Fall of Keynesian Economics," *Economic Record*, December 1988. Used with permission.

Regulation: "Airline Deregulation" is adapted from Alfred E. Kahn, "I Would Do It Again," *Regulation*, 1988, Number 2. Used with permission.

National Review: "Monetarism" is adapted from Allan H. Meltzer, "Is Monetarism Dead?" *National Review*, November 4, 1991. Used with permission.

Addison-Wesley Publishing Company, Inc.: "Free Trade" is adapted from Alan S. Blinder, *Hard Heads, Soft Hearts*, copyright © 1988 by Alan S. Blinder. Reprinted by permission of Addison-Wesley Publishing Company, Inc. Used with permission.

American Economic Review: "Greenhouse Effect" is adapted from Thomas C. Schelling, "Some Economics of Global Warming," *American Economic Review*, March 1992. Used with permission.

The Economist Newspaper Group, Inc.: "Third World Economic Development" is adapted from Clive Crook, "A Survey of the Third World," *The Economist*, September 23, 1989. Used with permission.

Cambridge University Press: "Marginalism" is adapted from Steven E. Rhoads, *The Economist's View of the World*, copyright © 1985 by Cambridge University Press. Reprinted with the permission of Cambridge University Press.

Warner Books, Inc., 1271 Avenue of the Americas, New York, NY 10020

 A Time Warner Company

Printed in the United States of America
First Printing: August 1993
10 9 8 7 6 5 4 3 2 1

Library of Congress Cataloging-in-Publication Data

The Fortune encyclopedia of economics / edited by David R. Henderson.
    p. cm.
  Includes bibliographical references and index.
  ISBN 0-446-51637-6
  1. Economics—Encyclopedias. I. Henderson, David R.
II. Fortune.
HB61.F67 1993
330'.03—dc20   92-50535
                                       CIP

Book design by Giorgetta Bell McRee

In loving memory of
Paul Corbett Henderson (1947–1970)
and
Roy A. Childs, Jr. (1949–1992)

ACKNOWLEDGMENTS

The main person I want to thank is my wonderful wife, Rena, who regularly reassured me that I could pull this off. Moreover, Rena was involved in the details: after I had edited each article, she used her prodigious editing skills to make the articles more understandable to someone like herself, an intelligent reader with no background in economics. I also thank my daughter Karen who was always proud and excited that "Dad's book will be in the bookstore."

Next, I thank my other friends who encouraged me and believed in me throughout this whole massive project. So many friends gave me so much support, especially Tom Nagle, the late Roy Childs, Frank Barrett, Doug Adams, Bill Haga, Paul Gerner, Jimmy Koo, Janet Beales, Mark Weston, Allen Tegtmeier, Greg De Young, Matt Johns, Barbara Glover, Bob Hessen, Marty Anderson, Lee Mairs, and Sylvia Nasar. I apologize to those friends whose names I may have overlooked.

Warner editors Al Ehrbar and Mel Minter also contributed to this book. I especially thank Al, not only for making deft edits that cut words and clarified issues further, but also for recommending about ten to fifteen important topics.

Thanks also to Bob Samuelson of *Newsweek*, Sylvia Nasar of the *New York Times*, Dan Seligman of *Fortune*, and Steve Cylke, who all made good suggestions for further topics or for authors. Tyler Cowen of George Mason University let me pick his brain for two hours and helped me think of about twenty authors whom I might not have thought of.

I thank Marshall Loeb and Ann Morrison of *Fortune* and Maureen Mahon Egen, Anne Hamilton, Harvey-Jane Kowal, Dennis Dalrymple, and Larry Kirshbaum of Warner Books. Larry deserves credit for having the idea of a readable encyclopedia of economics. I appreciate Anne Hamilton's ability to handle complicated details professionally.

I thank Jimmy Koo, my research assistant at the beginning, and again at the end, of the project. I also thank Janet Beales, my assistant editor during the summer of 1991 on an internship generously paid for by the Institute for Humane Studies. Marty Zupan of IHS suggested Janet and persuaded the institute to make her my intern. Dianne Kelsey and Barbara Glover not only provided secretarial services, but also believed in the project. Guy Cunningham, one of my students, found an important numerical error in one of the articles.

Thanks also to the Hoover Institution for lending financial support to this project.

Finally, I thank the authors of these excellent articles. They were willing to share their knowledge with a wider audience and to do so for not a very large fee. I enjoyed working with them, getting to know them, and learning from them, particularly Garrett Hardin, Bob Hessen, Jack Hirshleifer, Saul Hymans, Larry Kotlikoff, Stan Lebergott, Fred McChesney, Bob Michaels, Joe Minarik, Barry Nalebuff, June O'Neill, the late George Stigler, Jim Tobin, Kip Viscusi, and Aaron Wildavsky.

David R. Henderson
Monterey, January 1993

CONTENTS

PREFACE
xvii

CHAPTER ONE: BASIC CONCEPTS
1

Benefit Cost Analysis   3
Paul R. Portney

Demand   7
David R. Henderson

Efficiency   9
Paul Heyne

Industrial Revolution and the Standard
  of Living   12
Clark Nardinelli

Information   16
Joseph E. Stiglitz

Insurance   22
Richard Zeckhauser

Liability   27
W. Kip Viscusi

Marginalism   31
Steven E. Rhoads

Microeconomics   34
Arnold C. Harberger

Natural Resources   39
William J. Baumol and
  Sue Anne Batey Blackman

Opportunity Cost   44
David R. Henderson

Political Behavior   45
Richard L. Stroup

Population   51
Ronald Demos Lee

Poverty in the United States   56
Isabel V. Sawhill

Prisoners' Dilemma   61
Avinash Dixit and Barry Nalebuff

Profits   64
Lester C. Thurow

Property Rights   69
Armen A. Alchian

Public Goods and Externalities   74
Tyler Cowen

Research and Development   78
David M. Levy

Spatial Economics   82
Wolfgang Kasper

Supply   86
Al Ehrbar

The Tragedy of the Commons   88
Garrett Hardin

Unintended Consequences   92
Rob Norton

———— CHAPTER TWO: ECONOMIC SYSTEMS AND SCHOOLS OF ECONOMIC THOUGHT ————
95

Apartheid   97
Thomas W. Hazlett

Austrian Economics   105
Deborah L. Walker

Capitalism   110
Robert Hessen

Fascism   115
Sheldon Richman

Keynesian Economics   118
Alan S. Blinder

Marxism   123
David L. Prychitko

Monetarism   128
Allan H. Meltzer

Neoclassical Economics   135
E. Roy Weintraub

New Classical Macroeconomics   139
Robert King

New Keynesian Economics   145
N. Gregory Mankiw

Public Choice Theory   150
Jane S. Shaw

Rational Expectations   155
Thomas J. Sargent

Socialism   161
Robert Heilbroner

Supply-Side Economics   165
James D. Gwartney

———————————— CHAPTER THREE: MACROECONOMICS ————————————
171

Business Cycles   173
Christina D. Romer

Distribution of Income   177
Frank Levy

Economic Growth   183
Paul M. Romer

Forecasting and Econometric Models   190
Saul H. Hymans

Great Depression   196
Robert J. Samuelson

Gross Domestic Product   203
Lincoln Anderson

Hyperinflation   208
Michael K. Salemi

Inflation   211
David Ranson

Investment   217
Alan J. Auerbach

Productivity   222
Sylvia Nasar

Recessions   226
Geoffrey H. Moore

Saving   230
Laurence J. Kotlikoff

Unemployment   236
Lawrence H. Summers

—————————— CHAPTER FOUR: ECONOMIC POLICY ——————————
241

Federal Budget   243
John F. Cogan

Federal Debt   248
Robert Eisner

Federal Deficit   253
Laurence J. Kotlikoff

Fiscal Policy   257
David N. Weil

Government Spending   262
Gordon Tullock

Industrial Policy   265
Richard B. McKenzie

Monetary Policy   272
James Tobin

Phillips Curve   279
Kevin D. Hoover

Privatization   285
Madsen Pirie

Reaganomics   290
William A. Niskanen

Redistribution of Income   294
Dwight R. Lee

Social Security   298
Carolyn L. Weaver

Unemployment Insurance   302
David R. Francis

—————————————— CHAPTER FIVE: TAXES ——————————————
307

Taxation, A Preface   309
Joseph J. Minarik

Capital Gains Taxes   317
Joseph J. Cordes

Consumption Tax   321
Al Ehrbar

Corporate Taxation   325
Rob Norton

Marginal Tax Rates   329
Alan Reynolds

Negative Income Tax   333
Jodie T. Allen

Progressive Taxes   338
Joel B. Slemrod

———————————— CHAPTER SIX: MONEY AND BANKING ————————————
343

Bank Runs   345
George G. Kaufman

Competing Money Supplies   347
Lawrence H. White

Deposit Insurance   352
George G. Kaufman

Federal Reserve System   356
Manuel H. Johnson

Gold Standard   359
Michael D. Bordo

Money Supply   364
Anna J. Schwartz

Savings and Loan Crisis   369
Bert Ely

———————————— CHAPTER SEVEN: ECONOMIC REGULATION ————————————
377

Airline Deregulation   379
Alfred E. Kahn

Antitrust   385
Fred S. McChesney

Electric Utility Regulation   391
Robert J. Michaels

Industrial Concentration   395
Thomas W. Gilligan

Monopoly   399
George J. Stigler

Natural Gas Regulation   404
Robert J. Michaels

Occupational Licensing   409
S. David Young

Patents   414
David R. Henderson

Price Controls   416
Hugh Rockoff

Rent Control   421
Walter Block

Riskless Society   426
Aaron Wildavsky

Trucking Deregulation   433
Thomas Gale Moore

———————————— CHAPTER EIGHT: ENVIRONMENTAL REGULATION ————————————
439

Environmentalism, A Preface   441
David R. Henderson

Environmentalism, Free-Market   442
Richard Stroup

Greenhouse Effect   447
Thomas C. Schelling

Pollution Controls   453
Robert W. Crandall

Recycling   457
Jane S. Shaw

─────────── CHAPTER NINE: DISCRIMINATION AND LABOR ISSUES ───────────
461

Comparable Worth   463
June Ellenoff O'Neill

Conscription   467
Christopher Jehn

Discrimination   470
Linda Gorman

Gender Gap   475
Claudia Goldin

Human Capital   479
Gary S. Becker

Immigration   484
George J. Borjas

Job Safety   490
W. Kip Viscusi

Labor Unions   494
Morgan O. Reynolds

Minimum Wages   499
Linda Gorman

Wages and Working Conditions   503
Stanley Lebergott

─────────── CHAPTER TEN: INTERNATIONAL ECONOMICS ───────────
509

Balance of Payments   511
Herbert Stein

Competitiveness   514
Robert Z. Lawrence

Exchange Rates   518
Paul Krugman

Foreign Investment in the United
   States   522
Mack Ott

Free Trade   526
Alan S. Blinder

Free Trade Agreements and Customs
   Unions   530
Douglas A. Irwin

Mercantilism   534
Laura LaHaye

Protectionism   538
Jagdish Bhagwati

Sanctions   542
Kimberly Ann Elliott
   and Gary Clyde Hufbauer

─────── CHAPTER ELEVEN: CORPORATIONS AND FINANCIAL MARKETS ───────
549

Asset-Backed Securities   551
Phillip L. Zweig

Bonds   554
Clifford W. Smith

Corporate Debt   558
Annette Poulsen

Corporations   563
Robert Hessen

Efficient Capital Markets   569
Steven L. Jones and
  Jeffry M. Netter

Futures and Options Markets   575
Gregory J. Millman

Insider Trading   580
David D. Haddock

Interest   584
Paul Heyne

Junk Bonds   588
Glenn Yago

Pensions   591
Henry McMillan

Present Value   596
David R. Henderson

Program Trading   597
Dean Furbush

Stock Prices   602
Jeremy J. Siegel

Takeovers and Leveraged Buyouts   605
Gregg A. Jarrell

─────── CHAPTER TWELVE: THE MARKETPLACE ───────
611

Advertising   613
George Bittlingmayer

Brand Names   618
Benjamin Klein

Competition   622
Jack High

Disaster and Recovery   625
Jack Hirshleifer

Entrepreneurship   631
Mark Casson

Free Market   636
Murray N. Rothbard

Game Theory   640
Avinash Dixit and Barry Nalebuff

——————— CHAPTER THIRTEEN: THE ECONOMICS OF SPECIAL MARKETS ———————
645

Agricultural Price Supports   647
Robert L. Thompson

Computer Industry   652
George Gilder

Crime   657
David D. Friedman

Defense   661
Benjamin Zycher

Drug Lag   668
Daniel Henninger

Energy   672
Robert A. Leone

Health Care Industry   677
Patricia M. Danzon

Health Insurance   684
John C. Goodman

Housing   689
Peter D. Salins

Law and Economics   694
David D. Friedman

OPEC   697
Benjamin Zycher

Public Schools   702
John E. Chubb

Sportometrics   709
Robert D. Tollison

Sports   712
Gerald W. Scully

Telecommunications   716
John Haring

——————— CHAPTER FOURTEEN: ECONOMIES OUTSIDE THE UNITED STATES ———————
721

Capital Flight   723
Darryl McLeod

Eastern Europe   727
David Lipton

European Economic Community   733
Barry Eichengreen

German Economic "Miracle"   738
David R. Henderson

Japan and the Myth of MITI   743
David R. Henderson

Perestroika   747
Marshall I. Goldman

Third World Debt   751
Kenneth Rogoff

Third World Economic
   Development   755
Clive Crook

BIOGRAPHIES
767

Nobel Memorial Prize Winners in Economic Science   769
Chairmen of the Council of Economic Advisers   770
Presidents of the American Economic Association   771
Biographies   773

INDEX
851

PREFACE

An old joke says that if you laid all the economists in the world end to end, they would not reach a conclusion. The popular perception behind the joke is that economists never agree. Implicit in that perception is the belief that economics is largely a matter of opinion and that economists (unlike biologists or the practitioners of any other science) do not share a common set of beliefs. Given all the conflicting pronouncements by economists that appear almost daily in the press, that perception is very understandable. It also is dead wrong. While economists disagree on many matters, they have reached virtually unanimous agreement on a multitude of others. One purpose of this book is to illuminate the many, many areas where economists agree (while also describing where and why they disagree). Another is to show how economic analysis can enhance our understanding of the world.

Most of the disagreement among economists concerns ''macroeconomics,'' which deals with nationwide or worldwide phenomena such as inflation, unemployment, and economic growth. Adherents of the various ''schools'' (Keynesians, monetarists, supply-siders, rational expectationists, etc.) disagree a lot. Some of their disagreements reflect different judgments about the relative importance of, say, inflation versus unemployment. Others stem from basic disagreement on the ability of government policy to affect the total economy in predictable ways. This encyclopedia reflects those disagreements, with authors chosen from each school to explain and attempt to justify their views of how the ''macro'' world works.

Macroeconomics, however, is only a small part of the total science of economics. The vast majority of economic questions (and public policy issues) fall in the realm of what is called microeconomics. And the vast majority of economists agree on the underlying economics of most micro issues, including rent controls, minimum wages, and the need to reduce pollution. Some may disagree on the policy implications of the analysis, but remarkably few disagree on the analysis itself.

That economists agree on most micro issues became clear in the late seventies when the *American Economic Review*, the world's largest-circulation economics journal, published an opinion poll of 211 economists. The poll found that 98 percent agreed with the statement ''A ceiling on rents reduces the quantity and quality of housing available.'' Similarly, 90 percent of economists agreed that ''a minimum wage increases unemployment among young and unskilled workers.'' And 97 percent agreed with the statement ''Tariffs and import quotas reduce general economic welfare.'' The entries on those topics in this encyclopedia explain why economists are in such startling agreement on these and many other issues.

So why do people think economists disagree about everything? One reason is that the media present all economic issues as if they are inherently controversial. The issues themselves are controversial, but the economics of the issues more often are not. A journalist writing a piece on free trade versus protectionism, for example, would be hard put to find an economist who will defend protectionism (economists know that free trade virtually always improves a nation's economic well-being). But many journalists feel compelled to get "the other side" and present a "balanced view." So they go to economists who work for protectionist interest groups like the National Association of Manufacturers or the AFL-CIO to get an opinion against free trade. Or they turn to a business person or labor leader whose industry faces tough competition from imports. The result is that readers and viewers get the false impression that economists are divided on free trade.

Another equally important source of the misimpression about economics comes from the often overlooked distinction that economists make between "positive" and "normative" analysis. Positive analysis is the application of economic postulates and principles to a question—in other words, finding out the way things *are* and why the world behaves as it does. Normative analysis, in contrast, deals with the way things *ought to be*, and unavoidably involves the noneconomic value judgments of the analyst. For example, positive analysis says that licensing physicians will result in there being fewer doctors in society and higher prices for medical care. Whether states should license doctors to protect patients from quacks is a normative matter. In other words, there are no "shoulds" in purely positive economic analysis, but every economist has views on how things should be done.

In preparing this encyclopedia, we strived to separate positive and normative positions, to emphasize the areas where economists agree, while also specifying where and why they disagree. The goal is to communicate just how much economic analysis can teach us about the important issues we face as voters, consumers, employees, and as people who care about the world. As such, the encyclopedia gives a comprehensive yet readable and engaging survey of mainstream economic thought. I have chosen topics that will interest noneconomists, written by economists who can make their ideas accessible to the general reader. The entries on apartheid, discrimination, and insider trading, for example, cover issues whose important economic aspects often are overlooked.

As this book goes to press, economic issues dominate the news more than at any time since Ronald Reagan became president in 1981. This is due both to objective circumstances (the high federal budget deficit and rising costs of medical care) and to President Bill Clinton's attempt to shift economic policy in major ways. Although no one can know the actual policies that will emerge from Congress, the broad outlines of "Clintonomics" have become clear. In brief, Clinton would have the government take a larger role in the economy, both as taxer and as regulator.

To reduce deficits, Clinton wants to increase taxes, especially on high-income earners, on some of the elderly, and on corporations. Clinton wishes to cut government spending somewhat as a share of gross domestic product, but his proposals appear to shift the composition of spending more than they actually decrease it. He would cut defense spending further, along with spending in other domestic programs. At the same time, Clinton would increase domestic spending in many areas, especially on infrastructure and education. He also wants the government to spend money or require employers to spend money to make medical care available at low prices to all who want it.

Clinton wishes a larger role for government in the labor market, having appointed the most activist secretary of labor since the thirties, Robert Reich. He would increase the minimum wage and give unions more power in the workplace.

On environmental policy, Vice President Al Gore would increase regulations on polluters, while stemming some of the movement to incentive-based pollution control that began with President Jimmy Carter and continued through the Reagan and Bush administrations.

On trade policy, Clinton appears at this writing to be less in favor of free trade than was his immediate predecessor. He has raised doubts about whether he will sign the North American Free Trade Agreement. The position of chairman of the Council of Economic Advisers, in Republican and Democratic administrations, has traditionally gone to an economist who avidly favors free trade. Clinton, however, has appointed Laura Tyson, who has expressed strong reservations about it. On the other hand, Clinton has named Alan S. Blinder, an outspoken free trader, as one of the members of the Council of Economic Advisers.

This encyclopedia contains articles on all the above issues. Here you will find facts and economic analysis that are vital to understanding current economic controversies. All of the articles on taxes in chapter 5 are relevant to today's discussions, especially ''Taxation, A Preface,'' ''Corporate Taxation,'' ''Marginal Tax Rates,'' and ''Progressive Taxes.'' Indeed, that chapter's lead article, ''Taxation, A Preface,'' is written by the chief economist of the Office of Management and Budget, Joseph J. Minarik. On budgets, deficits, and debts, the chapter 4 articles ''Federal Budget,'' ''Federal Debt,'' ''Federal Deficit,'' and ''Government Spending'' are especially relevant.

On health care, two articles in chapter 13, ''Health Care Industry'' and ''Health Insurance,'' give important context and analysis that are often missing from, or at least unstated in, current discussions. On education, the article ''Public Schools,'' in chapter 13, addresses many of the same concerns that Clinton dealt with while governor of Arkansas.

On labor policy, all of the articles in chapter 9 are highly relevant, especially ''Minimum Wages,'' ''Labor Unions,'' and ''Job Safety.'' All of chapter 8 helps clarify the ongoing debate about the environment. On trade policy, the articles in chapter 10 apply to current discussion, especially ''Free Trade,'' ''Free Trade Agreements and Customs Unions,'' and ''Protectionism.'' ''Free Trade'' is written by Alan S. Blinder. The chapter 4 article ''Industrial Policy'' tells how the industrial policy debate developed in the eighties and of Robert Reich's role in that debate.

Not to be missed either are other articles by economists who are members of or advisers to the Clinton administration. Most notable are ''Keynesian Economics'' (in chapter 2) by Blinder, and ''Unemployment'' (in chapter 3) by Lawrence H. Summers, who is the undersecretary of the treasury for international affairs. Also in this encyclopedia are articles by economists who are critical of the Clinton administration. Most notable here are ''Monetarism'' (in chapter 2) by Allan H. Meltzer, ''Trucking Deregulation'' (in chapter 7) by Thomas Gale Moore, and ''Defense'' (in chapter 13) by Benjamin Zycher.

Finally, some of the world's leading economic journalists, whose job has always been to follow economic discussion closely and to make it understandable to a wide audience, have important articles in this encyclopedia. These journalists include Sylvia Nasar of *The New York Times*, Robert J. Samuelson of *Newsweek*, Al Ehrbar of the *Wall Street Journal*, Clive Crook of *The Economist*, Jodie T. Allen of the *Washington Post*, Rob Norton of *Fortune*, and David R. Francis of the *Christian Science Monitor*.

So whatever happens with the economy or with economic policy this year, or even this century, *The Fortune Encyclopedia of Economics* is an indispensable guide to help you follow and understand the continuing debates.

Producing this book was a labor of love for nearly three years. I hope you enjoy reading these articles as much as I have.

—**David R. Henderson**
March 1993

CHAPTER ONE

BASIC CONCEPTS

Benefit-Cost Analysis

Paul R. Portney

■ Whenever people decide whether the advantages of a particular action are likely to outweigh its drawbacks, they engage in a form of benefit-cost analysis (BCA). In the public arena, formal BCA is a sometimes controversial technique for thoroughly and consistently evaluating the pros and cons associated with prospective policy changes. Specifically, it is an attempt to identify and express in dollar terms all of the effects of proposed government policies or projects. While never intended to be the only basis for decision making, BCA can be a valuable aid to policymakers.

Although conceived nearly 150 years ago by the French engineer Jules Dupuit, BCA saw its first widespread use in the evaluation of federal water projects in the United States in the late 1930s. Since then, it has also been used to analyze policies affecting transportation, public health, criminal justice, defense, education, and the environment. Because BCA has had some of its most important and controversial applications in environmental policy, this discussion of key issues in BCA is illustrated with examples from the environmental arena.

To ascertain the net effect of a proposed policy change on social well-being, we must first have a way of measuring the gains to the gainers and the losses to the losers. Implicit in this statement is a central tenet of BCA: the effects of a policy change on society are no more or no less than the aggregate of the effects on the individuals who comprise society. Thus, if no individual would be made better off by a policy change, there are no benefits associated with it; nor are there costs if no one is made worse off. In other words, BCA counts no values other than those held by the individual members of society.

It is equally important to note that benefits and costs, even though they are almost always expressed in dollar terms in BCA, go well beyond changes in individuals' incomes. If someone's well-being is improved because of cleaner air—through improved visibility, for instance—he experiences a benefit even though his income may not change. Similarly, an increase in pollution that puts people at higher risk of disease imposes a cost on them even though their incomes may not fall. Indeed, a person would bear a cost (be made worse off) if the pollution posed a threat to an exotic and little-known species of animal that he cared about. Some criticize BCA on the grounds that it supposedly enshrines the free market and discourages government intervention. However, BCA exists precisely because economists recognize that free markets sometimes allocate resources inefficiently, causing problems such as dirty air and water.

How, then, are benefits and costs estimated? While it is generally assumed that they are measured differently, benefits and costs are actually flip sides of the same coin. Benefits are measured by the willingness of individuals to pay for the outputs of the policy or project in question. The proper calculation of costs is the amount of compensation required to exactly offset negative consequences. Willingness to pay or compensation required should each be the dollar amount that would leave every individual just as well off following the implementation of the policy as before it.

Suppose, for example, we wished to evaluate the benefits and costs of a proposal to control air pollution emissions from a large factory. On the positive side, pollution abatement will mean reduced damage to exposed materials, diminished health risks to people living nearby, improved visibility, and even new jobs for those who manufacture pollution control equipment. On the negative side, the required investments in pollution control may cause the firm to raise the price of its products, close down several marginal operations at its plant and lay off workers, and put off other planned investments designed to modernize its production facilities.

How do we determine the willingness to pay for the favorable effects? First, it is relatively easy to value the reduced damage to materials. If, say, awnings will now last ten years rather than five years, it is straightforward to multiply the number of awnings times their price to get an idea of savings to consumers—so long as the price of awnings is not affected by the policy. If reduced pollution meant more agricultural output, it would be similarly easy to value because crops have well-defined market prices. In other words, when benefits involve marketed outputs, valuing them is not terribly difficult.

But what about reduced health risks or improved visibility? Because these are not things that people buy and sell directly, it is much less clear how to estimate the willingness to pay (the value of the benefits). Two major techniques are available. One, called the contingent valuation method, involves asking people directly, via sophisticated questionnaires, how much they would pay for reduced health risks or improved visibility. This approach makes it possible to estimate the benefits of programs—for example, the preservation of a remote wilderness area—for which other techniques generally are inapplicable. However, this approach has its limitations. One is that it often requires individuals to place dollar values on things they are unused to viewing in economic terms. As a result, their responses may not be as reliable as we would like. Also, responses to surveys are hypothetical; economists prefer values revealed in actual market transactions.

Another approach is to observe how much people are willing to pay for goods that have an environmental quality component. For example, houses in unpolluted neighborhoods sell for more than those in polluted areas. Using statistical techniques to hold constant the other characteristics of houses and the neighborhoods in which they are located, it is possible to identify a "clean air premium." This provides important information on the value to individuals of air quality improvements. A similar approach for estimating how much people value pollution control and other public policies that reduce health risks is to estimate how much of a wage premium they are paid to work in jobs that pose health risks. Still other techniques infer values from such things as the time and money people spend traveling to and from desirable recreation sites.

It is generally assumed that cost estimation involves a mere toting up of the expenditures that affected parties must make, as in our example of the firm controlling air pollution. As suggested above, however, matters are more complicated than this. Some firms not initially affected by regulation will incur higher costs—those purchasing the product of the regulated firm, for example. These "ripple" effects must be taken into account. Or if the polluting firm closes down some operations rather than purchasing pollution control devices, its expenditures will be zero, but the social costs are still positive. In such cases the costs are borne by employees, shareholders, and purchasers of its output. Unfortunately, techniques for making these more sophisticated cost estimates are still in their infancy; for this reason, virtually all BCAs still use direct expenditures as rough measures of true social costs.

Three additional issues in BCA bear mention. First, government policies or projects typically produce streams of benefits and costs over time rather than in one-shot increments. Commonly, in fact, a substantial portion of the costs are incurred early in the life of a project, while benefits may extend for many years (perhaps beginning only after some delay). Yet, because people prefer a dollar today to one ten years from now (see INTEREST), BCA typically discounts future benefits and costs back to present values. Not only are there technical disagreements among economists about the interest rate (or rates) at which these future impacts should be discounted, but discounting raises ethical problems as well. At a discount rate of 10 percent, for instance, $1 million in benefits to people fifty years from now has a present value of only $8,500. This powerful effect of discounting is of concern when BCA is applied to the evaluation of policies with significant intergenerational effects, such as those pertaining to the prevention of global climate change or the disposal of high-level radioactive wastes (which will be lethal for hundreds of thousands of years).

A second sticking point in BCA is the fact that the willingness to pay for the favorable effects of a project or policy depends on the distribution of income: a billionaire would be able—and therefore willing—to pay more than a pauper for the same improvement in environmental quality, even though both cared about it with equal intensity. Some critics dislike BCA because it reduces benefits to pure dollar amounts. But BCA analysts use dollars to estimate benefits because there simply is no other way to directly measure the intensity with which people desire something.

Third, suppose that the aforementioned problems were to disappear, and that benefits and costs could be easily expressed in dollar terms and converted to present values. According to modern BCA, a project or policy would be attractive if the benefits it would produce exceed the costs. This is because, in theory, those gaining from the project could compensate those made worse off and still be better off themselves. In our factory example, for instance, those enjoying the benefits of cleaner air gain more than the losses to consumers who must pay more for the factory's output or to workers whose jobs are eliminated. Thus, the winners could compensate the losers and still come out ahead. In practice, of course, this compensation is seldom paid. Therefore, even the most efficient projects create some losers. This can undermine support for BCA in general and often makes it politically difficult to enact efficient policies, or, conversely, to block very inefficient projects, whose costs exceed benefits.

In spite of these sticking points, BCA seems to be playing a more important role in government decision making. One reason may be that shunning a comprehensive, analytical approach to decision making simply because it has flaws inevitably pushes decisions back into the realm of the ad hoc and purely political. While BCA does have very real shortcomings, it appears preferable to smoke-filled rooms.

—**Paul R. Portney**

Biography: Paul R. Portney is vice president and senior fellow at Resources for the Future, an environmental think tank in Washington, D.C. He was previously a senior staff economist with President Carter's Council on Environmental Quality.

Further Reading

Gramlich, Edward M. *Benefit-Cost Analysis of Government Programs.* 1981.

Hammond, P. Brett, and Rob Coppock, eds. *Valuing Health Risks, Costs, and Benefits for Environmental Decision Making.* 1990.

Kneese, Allen V. *Measuring the Benefits of Clean Air and Water.* 1984.

Kopp, Raymond, and Michael Hazilla. "Social Cost of Environmental Quality Regulations." *Journal of Political Economy* 98 (1990): 853–73.

Demand

David R. Henderson

◼ One of the most important building blocks of economic analysis is the concept of demand. When economists refer to demand, they usually have in mind not just a single quantity demanded, but what is called a demand curve. A demand curve traces the quantity of a good or service that is demanded at successively different prices.

The most famous law in economics, and the one that economists are most sure of, is the law of demand. On this law is built almost the whole edifice of economics. The law of demand states that when the price of a good rises, the amount demanded falls, and when the price falls, the amount demanded rises.

Some of the modern evidence for the law of demand is from econometric studies which show that, all other things being equal, when the price of a good rises, the amount of it demanded decreases. How do we know that there are no instances in which the amount demanded rises and the price rises? A few instances have been cited, but they almost always have an explanation that takes into account something other than price. Nobel Laureate George Stigler responded years ago that if any economist found a true counterexample, he would be "assured of immortality, professionally speaking, and rapid promotion." And because, wrote Stigler, most economists would like either reward, the fact that no one has come up with an exception to

the law of demand shows how rare the exceptions must be. But the reality is that if an economist reported an instance in which consumption of a good rose as its price rose, other economists would assume that some factor other than price caused the increase in demand.

The main reason economists believe so strongly in the law of demand is that it is so plausible, even to noneconomists. Indeed, the law of demand is ingrained in our way of thinking about everyday things. Shoppers buy more strawberries when they are in season and the price is low. This is evidence for the law of demand: only at the lower, in-season price are consumers willing to buy the higher amount available. Similarly, when people learn that frost will strike orange groves in Florida, they know that the price of orange juice will rise. The price rises in order to reduce the amount demanded to the smaller amount available because of the frost. This is the law of demand. We see the same point every day in countless ways. No one thinks, for example, that the way to sell a house that has been languishing on the market is to raise the asking price. Again, this shows an implicit awareness of the law of demand: the number of potential buyers for any given house varies inversely with the asking price.

Indeed, the law of demand is so ingrained in our way of thinking that it is even part of our language. Think of what we mean by the term *on sale*. We do not mean that the seller raised the price. We mean that he or she lowered it. The seller did so in order to increase the amount of goods demanded. Again, the law of demand.

Economists, as is their wont, have struggled to think of exceptions to the law of demand. Marketers have found them. One of the best examples was a new car wax. Economist Thomas Nagle points out that when one particular car wax was introduced, it faced strong resistance until its price was raised from $.69 to $1.69. The reason, according to Nagle, was that buyers could not judge the wax's quality before purchasing it. Because the quality of this particular product was so important—a bad product could ruin a car's finish—consumers "played it safe by avoiding cheap products that they believed were more likely to be inferior."

Many noneconomists are skeptical of the law of demand. A standard example they give of a good whose quantity demanded will not fall when the price increases is water. How, they ask, can people reduce their use of water? But those who come up with that example think of drinking water, or using it in a household, as the only possible uses. Even for such uses, there is room to reduce consumption when the price of water rises. Households can do larger loads of laundry, or shower instead of bathe, for ex-

ample. The main users of water, however, are agriculture and industry. Farmers and manufacturers can substantially alter the amount of water used in production. Farmers, for example, can do so by changing crops or by changing irrigation methods for given crops.

It is not just price that affects the quantity demanded. Income affects it too. As real income rises, people buy more of some goods (which economists call normal goods) and less of what are called inferior goods. Urban mass transit and railroad transportation are classic examples of inferior goods. That is why the usage of both of these modes of travel declined so dramatically as postwar incomes were rising and more people could afford automobiles. Environmental quality is a normal good, which is a major reason that Americans have become more concerned about the environment in recent decades.

Another influence on demand is the price of substitutes. When the price of Toyota Tercels rises, all else being equal, demand for Tercels falls and demand for Nissan Sentras, a substitute, rises. Also important is the price of complements, or goods that are used together. When the price of gasoline rises, the demand for cars falls.

—**David R. Henderson**

Biography: David R. Henderson is the editor of this encyclopedia. He is a senior research fellow with Stanford University's Hoover Institution and an associate professor of economics at the Naval Postgraduate School in Monterey, California. He was formerly a senior economist with the President's Council of Economic Advisers.

Further Reading

Nagle, Thomas T. *The Strategy and Tactics of Pricing*. 1987.
Stigler, George J. *The Theory of Price*, 3d ed. 1966.

Efficiency

Paul Heyne

■ To economists, efficiency is a relationship between ends and means. When we call a situation inefficient, we are claiming that we could achieve the desired ends with less means, or that the means employed could produce more of the ends desired. *Less* and *more* in this context necessarily refer to less and more value. Thus, economic efficiency is measured not by the relationship between the physical quantities of ends and means, but by the relationship between the value of the ends and the value of the means.

Terms such as *technical efficiency* or *objective efficiency* are meaningless. From a strictly technical or physical standpoint, every process is perfectly efficient. The ratio of physical output (ends) to physical input (means) necessarily equals one, as the basic law of thermodynamics reminds us. Consider an engineer who judges one machine more efficient than another because one produces more work output per unit of energy input. The engineer is implicitly counting only the useful work done. *Useful,* of course, is an evaluative term.

The inescapably evaluative nature of the concept raises a fundamental question for every attempt to talk about the efficiency of any process or institution: whose valuations do we use, and how shall they be weighted? Economic efficiency makes use of monetary evaluations. It refers to the relationship between the monetary value of ends and the monetary value of means. The valuations that count are, consequently, the valuations of those who are willing and able to support their preferences by offering money.

From this perspective a parcel of land is used with maximum economic efficiency when it comes under the control of the party who is willing (which implies able) to pay the largest amount of money to obtain that control. The proof that a particular resource is being used efficiently is that no one is willing to pay more in order to divert it to some other use.

Those who object that this is an extremely narrow definition of efficiency often fail to recognize that every concept of efficiency has to employ some measure of value. The monetary measure used by economics turns out to be both broad and useful. It enables us to take account of and compare the evaluations made by many different persons and to respond appropriately.

What kind of structure should sit on the corner lot at Fifth and Main? A gas station, a condominium, a florist shop, a restaurant? The owner can make a defensible decision even if everyone in town has a slightly different preference. The owner simply accepts the highest money bid that various prospective users of the land (the florist, the restaurateur) make for it. Effective social cooperation requires interpersonal comparisons of value, and monetary values supply us with a common denominator that works remarkably well.

The crucial prerequisites for the generation of these monetary values are private ownership of resources and relatively unrestricted rights to exchange ownership. When these conditions are satisfied, competing desires to use resources establish money prices that indicate each resource's value in its current use. Those who believe that particular resources would be more valuably (more efficiently) employed in some other way can raise the price and bid them away from the current users.

In the thirties, for example, a small group of people who placed a high value on hawks bought a mountain in Pennsylvania and thereby converted it from a hawk-hunting area to a hawk sanctuary. Today our laws protect hawks and other predators, but in the thirties hawks were in danger of extinction because they were hunted as vermin that ate chickens. If the only option for those who formed the Hawk Mountain Sanctuary Association in 1934 had been to persuade politicians and the public to change the laws, hawks could well be extinct today in that area. The association was able to save the hawks because its members demonstrated, through competing money bids, that a sanctuary was the most efficient (that is, the monetarily most valuable) use for the mountain.

Perhaps the importance of private ownership to achieving economic efficiency can be seen most clearly by looking at what happens when we try to work together without an effective system for assigning monetary value to resources. Take the example of urban automobile traffic. How can we arrive at a judgment about the overall efficiency or inefficiency of the commuting process when we have to compare one person's convenience with another's delay, time saved for some with carbon monoxide inhaled by others, one person's intense dissatisfactions with another person's pleasures? To find out whether Jack values clean air more than Jill values a speedy commute requires a large set of interpersonal value indicators. Urban commuting creates congestion as well as air-pollution problems in our society because we have not developed a workable procedure for weighing and comparing the positive and negative evaluations of different people.

The crucial missing element is private

property. Because so many of the key resources employed by commuters are not privately owned, commuters are not required to bid for their use and to pay a price that reflects their value to others. Users pay no money prices for resources such as urban air and urban streets. Therefore, those goods are used as if they were free resources (see THE TRAGEDY OF THE COMMONS). But their use imposes costs on all the others who have been deprived of their use. In the absence of money prices on such scarce resources as streets and air, urban dwellers ''are led by an invisible hand to promote an end that was no part of their intention,'' to apply Adam Smith's famous generalization. In this case, however, the end is not the public interest but a result that no one wants.

Critics of economic efficiency contend that it is a poor guide to public policy because it ignores important values other than money. They point out, for example, that the wealthy dowager who bids scarce milk away from the mother of an undernourished infant in order to wash her diamonds is promoting economic efficiency. The example is strained, not least because the pursuit of economic efficiency almost always makes milk available to the infant as well as the dowager. Most economists would agree that such dramatic examples can remind us that economic efficiency is not the highest good in life, but that does not mean that we should discard the concept.

The moral intuitions that enable us to arbitrate easily between the child's hunger and the dowager's vanity cannot begin to resolve the myriad issues that arise every day as hundreds of millions of people attempt to cooperate in using scarce means with varied uses to achieve diverse ends. Moreover, the remarkable feats of social cooperation that actually make wholesome milk available to hungry infants far removed from any cows would be impossible in the absence of the monetary values that express and promote economic efficiency.

The social usefulness of well-defined property rights, free exchange, and the system of relative money prices that emerges from these conditions has perhaps been demonstrated most convincingly by the catastrophic failure in the twentieth century of those societies that tried to function without them.

—**Paul Heyne**

Biography: Paul Heyne, who holds graduate degrees in both theology and economics, is currently a senior lecturer in economics at the University of Washington in Seattle.

Further Reading

Hayek, Friedrich A. ''The Use of Knowledge in Society.'' *American Economic Review* 35, no. 4 (September 1945): 519–30. Reprinted in Hayek. *Individualism and Economic Order*, 1948.

Jouvenel, Bertrand de. "Efficiency and Amenity." Earl Grey Memorial Lecture, delivered at King's College,
    Newcastle upon Tyne, England, 1960. Reprinted in *Readings in Welfare Economics,* edited by Kenneth
    J. Arrow and Tibor Scitovsky. 1969.
Knight, Frank H. "The Ethics of Competition." *Quarterly Journal of Economics* 37 (1923): 579–624.
    Reprinted in Knight. *The Ethics of Competition and Other Essays.* 1935.
Stroup, Richard L., and Jane S. Shaw. "The Free Market and the Environment." *The Public Interest* 97
    (Fall 1989): 30–43.

Industrial Revolution and the Standard of Living
Clark Nardinelli

■ Between 1760 and 1860, technological progress, education, and an increasing capital stock transformed England into the workshop of the world. The industrial revolution, as the transformation came to be called, caused a sustained rise in real income per person in England and, as its effects spread, the rest of the Western world. Historians agree that the industrial revolution was one of the most important events in history, marking the rapid transition to the modern age, but they disagree vehemently about various aspects of the event. Of all the disagreements, the oldest one is over how the industrial revolution affected ordinary people, usually called the working classes. One group, the pessimists, argues that the living standards of ordinary people fell. Another group, the optimists, believes that living standards rose.

The debate over living standards is important because it represents a place where the critics and defenders of capitalism meet head-on. It is no coincidence that the debate heated up during the Cold War. The pessimists wanted to show that the English industrial revolution, which took place within a capitalist economy, necessarily made working people worse off. Optimists defended capitalism by showing that the industrial revolution made everyone better off.

This disagreement over the standard of living is confined almost entirely to academicians. Most other people, if they think about it at all, consider it well established that the industrial revolution was a disaster for the working classes. Indeed, the ghastly images of Dickens's Coketown or Blake's "dark, satanic mills" dominate popular perceptions of what life was like during the early years of English industrialization. Economic historians, however, have gone beyond popular perceptions to try to find out what really happened to ordinary people.

First, we must consider what "standard of living" means. Economic historians would like it to mean happiness. But the impossibility of measuring happiness forces them to equate the standard of living with real income. Real income is money income adjusted for the cost of living and for the effects of things such as health, unemployment, pollution, the condition of women and children, urban crowding, and amount of leisure time.

Because a rise in real income was precisely what made England's transformation "revolutionary," it would seem that, by definition, the industrial revolution led to a rise in the standard of living. According to the estimates of economist N. F. R. Crafts, British income per person (in 1970 U.S. dollars) rose from $333 in 1700 to $399 in 1760, to $427 in 1800, to $498 in 1830, and then jumped to $804 in 1860. (For many centuries before the industrial revolution, in contrast, periods of falling income offset periods of rising income.) Both sides in the debate accept Crafts's estimates. But if the distribution of income became more unequal and if pollution, unemployment, and crowding increased, the real incomes of ordinary people could have fallen despite the rise in average income.

If significant economic growth is sustained over a century or so, the only way the poor become worse off is if inequality increases dramatically. Crafts's estimates indicate that real income per person doubled between 1760 and 1860. Therefore, the share of income going to the lowest 65 percent of the population would have had to fall by half for them to be worse off after all that growth. It didn't. In 1760 the lowest 65 percent received about 29 percent of total income in Britain; in 1860 they got about 25 percent. So the lowest 65 percent were substantially better off. Their average real income had increased by over 70 percent.

This evidence means that the optimists have won the debate on the big issue of whether the industrial revolution helped or hurt ordinary people. It helped. But smaller debates remain. Did the working class become worse off during the early years of England's industrialization, 1790 to 1840, when real income per person grew at only about 0.3 percent per year? Growth at such a slow rate made a deterioration in the lot of the working classes possible. A simple numerical illustration will show why. If we take 0.3 percent per year as the annual rate of growth of real income, average real income in 1840 would have been about 16 percent higher than in 1790. The share of total income going to the lowest 65 percent of the income distribution need only have fallen to 86 percent of its 1790 level to negate the benefit of rising average income. Although they do not agree on how much, most economic historians agree that the distribution of income became more unequal between 1790 and 1840. Moreover, if we add the effects of unemployment, pollution, urban crowding, child labor, and other social ills, the modest rise in average income could well have been accompanied by a fall in the standard of living of the working classes.

The modern debate over this issue, which began with a 1949 paper by T. S. Ashton, has focused on other measures of living standards, especially wages. Ashton himself used changes in the cost of living—measured by the prices of basic commodities—to conclude that real wages rose after 1820.

The debate heated up considerably during exchanges between the pessimist Eric Hobsbawm and the optimist Max Hartwell in the late 1950s and early 1960s. According to Hobsbawm, Ashton's evidence on real wages was inconclusive. He argued that high unemployment indicated that living standards may have deteriorated before 1840. Hobsbawm stressed that evidence on consumption also implied that living standards did not rise and may have fallen between 1790 and 1840. He placed particular emphasis on these estimates of consumption, reasoning that a decline in food consumption per person indicated a decline in the standard of living. He noted that the number of beef and sheep slaughtered at various markets failed to keep pace with the growth of population before 1840.

Hartwell criticized Hobsbawm's use of evidence. The problem with looking at the volume of beef and sheep sold at particular markets, he noted, was that new markets were appearing. Hartwell also emphasized the appearance of new, previously unavailable consumer goods after 1820, such as popular periodicals, inexpensive cotton clothing, and the exotic fruits made available by improved transportation. But Hartwell's main point was that few theories can explain falling real wages in the face of economic growth—particularly when rising labor productivity accompanied that growth. He emphasized that it would take implausibly high increases in unemploy-

ment or inequality for living standards to fall when average income was rising.

The debate gradually receded into the background until a 1983 paper by Peter Lindert and Jeffrey Williamson brought new life to the controversy. Lindert and Williamson produced new estimates of real wages for the years 1755 to 1851. Their estimates were based on money wages for workers in several broad categories, including both blue-collar and white-collar occupations. Their cost of living index attempted to represent actual working-class budgets.

The Lindert-Williamson series produced two striking results. First, real wages grew slowly between 1781 and 1819. Second, after 1819 real wages grew rapidly for all groups of workers. For all blue-collar workers—a good stand-in for the working classes—the Lindert-Williamson index number for real wages rose from 50.19 in 1819 to 100 in 1851. That is, real wages doubled in just thirty-two years.

Lindert and Williamson's findings were reinforced by estimates that economist Charles Feinstein made of consumption per person for each decade between the 1760s and 1850s. He found a small rise in consumption between 1760 and 1820 and a rapid rise after 1820. Other evidence that supported the hypothesis of rising real wages came from statistics on life expectancy at birth and on literacy rates. According to historians E. A. Wrigley and Roger S. Schofield's population history of England, life expectancy at birth rose from thirty-five years to forty years between 1781 and 1851. A modest increase in literacy in the generation before 1840 also supported Lindert and Williamson.

Although the evidence favors the optimists, doubts remain. For example, pessimists have long maintained that the largely unmeasurable effects of environmental decay more than offset any gains in well-being attributable to rising wages. Wages were higher in English cities than in the countryside, but rents were higher and the quality of life was lower. What proportion of the rise in urban wages reflected compensation for worsening urban squalor rather than true increases in real incomes? Williamson—using methods developed to measure the ill effects of twentieth-century cities—found that between 8 and 30 percent of the higher urban wages could be attributed to compensation for the inferior quality of life in English cities. Yet even the 30 percent estimate was much too small to fully offset the rise in real wages before 1850.

Another criticism of Lindert and Williamson's optimistic findings is that their results hold only for workers who earned wages. We do not know what happened to people who worked at home or were self-employed. Because the consumption per person of tea and sugar failed to rise along with real wages, Joel Mokyr has suggested that workers who were not in the Lindert-Williamson sample may have suffered sufficiently deteriorating real incomes to offset rising wage income and leave the average person no better off.

Contemporary pessimists argue that for at least some part of the industrial revolution the happiness and well-being of the lower classes was not rising much, if at all. Even if one accepts their argument, however, it is not necessary to abandon the optimists' position. For example, the industrial revolution had a positive effect on real income, but its positive effect may well have been offset by the negative effect of frequent wars (the American Revolution, the Napoleonic wars, the War of 1812). Some economic historians include bad harvests, rapid population growth, and the costs of transforming preindustrial workers into a modern labor force as additional causes of slow growth before 1820.

So careful economic research has narrowed the debate. Whether one is an optimist or pessimist today depends on whether one believes that the sustained rise in real wages began in the 1820s or the 1840s. Virtually all participants agree that growth was slow at best before 1820 and rapid after 1840.

—Clark Nardinelli

Biography: Clark Nardinelli is an economics professor at Clemson University.

Further Reading

Ashton, Thomas S. *The Industrial Revolution: 1760–1830.* 1948.
———. "The Standard of Life of the Workers in England, 1790–1830." In *Capitalism and the Historians,* edited by Friedrich A. Hayek. 1954.

Cannadine, David. "The Past and the Present in the English Industrial Revolution 1880–1980." *Past & Present* 103 (May 1984): 131–72.

Crafts, Nicholas F. R. *British Economic Growth During the Industrial Revolution.* 1985.

Deane, Phyllis. *The First Industrial Revolution.* Chap. 15. 1979.

Flinn, Michael W. "Trends in Real Wages, 1750–1850." *Economic History Review* 27 (August 1974): 395–413.

Floud, Roderick, and Donald McCloskey, eds. *The Economic History of Britain since 1700.* Vol. 1: *1700–1860.* Chaps. 2, 6, 7, 9, 11. 1981.

Hartwell, Ronald Max. *The Industrial Revolution and Economic Growth.* 1971.

Hobsbawm, Eric. *Labouring Men.* 1964.

Mokyr, Joel. *The Economics of the Industrial Revolution.* Chaps. 1, 2, 9, 10, 11. 1985.

Nardinelli, Clark. *Child Labor and the Industrial Revolution.* 1990.

Taylor, Arthur J., ed. *The Standard of Living in Britain in the Industrial Revolution.* 1975.

Williamson, Jeffrey G. *Did British Capitalism Breed Inequality?* Chaps. 1–4. 1985.

Information

Joseph E. Stiglitz

◼ In the past two decades, an important strand of economic research, sometimes referred to as information economics, has explored the extent to which markets and other institutions process and convey information. Many of the problems of markets and other institutions result from costly information, and many of their features are responses to costly information.

Many of the central theories and principles in economics are based on assumptions about perfect information. Among these, three stand out: efficiency, full employment of resources, and uniform prices.

Efficiency

At least since Adam Smith, most economists have believed that competitive markets are efficient, and that firms, in pursuing their own interests, enhance the public good "as if by an invisible hand." A major achievement of economic science during the first half of the twentieth century was finding the precise sense in which that result is true. This result, known as the Fundamental Theorem of Welfare Economics, provides a rigorous analytic basis for the presumption that competitive markets allocate resources efficiently. In the eighties economists made clear the hidden information assumptions underlying that theorem. They showed that in a wide variety of situations where information is costly (indeed, almost always), government interventions could make everyone better off if government officials had the right incentives. At the very least these results have undermined the long-standing presumption that markets are necessarily efficient.

Full Employment of Resources

A central result (or assumption) of standard economic theory is that resources are fully employed. The economy has a variety of mechanisms (savings and inventories provide buffers; price adjustments act as shock absorbers) that are supposed to dampen the effects of any shocks that the economy experiences. In fact, for the past two hundred years economies have experienced large fluctuations, and there has been massive unemployment in the slumps. Though the Great Depression of the thirties was the most recent prolonged and massive episode, the American economy suffered major recessions from 1979 to 1982, and many European economies experienced prolonged high unemployment rates during the eighties. Information economics has provided explanations for why unemployment may persist and for why fluctuations are so large.

The failure of wages to fall so that unemployed workers can find jobs has been explained by efficiency wage theories, which argue that the productivity of workers increases with higher wages (both because

they work harder and because employers can recruit a higher-quality labor force). If information about their workers' output were costless, employers would not pay such high wages because they could costlessly monitor output and pay accordingly. But because monitoring is costly, employers pay higher wages to give workers an incentive not to shirk.

While efficiency wage theory helps explain why unemployment may persist, other theories that focus on the implications of imperfect information in the capital markets can help explain economic volatility.

One strand of this theory focuses on the fact that many of the market's mechanisms for distributing risk, which are critical to an economy's ability to adjust to economic shocks, are imperfect because of costly information. Most notable in this respect is the failure of equity markets. In recent years less than 10 percent of new capital has been raised via equity markets. Information economics explains why. First, issuers of equity generally know more about the value of the shares than buyers do, and are more inclined to sell when they think buyers are overvaluing their shares. But most potential buyers know that this incentive exists and, therefore, are wary of buying. Second, shareholders have only limited control over managers. Information about what management is doing, or should be doing, to maximize shareholder value is costly. Thus, shareholders often limit the amount of "free cash" that managers have to play with. They do so by imposing sufficient debt burdens to put managers' "backs to the wall" so that managers must exert strong efforts to meet those debt obligations, and so that lenders will carefully scrutinize firms' behavior.

The fact that firms cannot (or choose not to) raise capital via equity markets means that if firms wish to invest more than their cash flow allows—or if they wish to produce more than they can finance out of their current working capital—they must turn to credit markets, and to banks in particular. From the firm's perspective borrowing has one major disadvantage: it imposes a fixed obligation on the firm. If it fails to meet that obligation, the firm can go bankrupt. (By contrast, an all-equity firm cannot go bankrupt.) Firms normally take actions to reduce the likelihood of bankruptcy by acting in a risk-averse manner.

Risk-averse behavior, in turn, has two important consequences. First, it means that a firm's behavior is affected by its net-worth position. When its financial position is adversely affected, it cuts back on all its activities (since there is some risk associated with virtually all activities); activities that are particularly risky—such as long-term investments—are cut the most.

Second, it means that if a firm perceives an increase in the risk associated with production or investment—such as when the economy appears to be going into a recession—it cuts back on those activities. Since risk perceptions are notoriously volatile, this too helps explain the economy's volatility.

Similarly, costly information explains why banks ration credit. Why ration rather than simply charge higher interest rates to higher-risk borrowers? Because often the only borrowers who will borrow at high rates are those who are the highest risk, and on whom, therefore, the lenders are most likely to lose. Also, higher interest rates may even induce borrowers to undertake greater risks.

Banks, in turn, can be viewed as highly leveraged firms that borrow from depositors. Their "production" activity is making loans (screening loan applicants, monitoring loans, etc.). When their net worth is reduced, or when they perceive that the risk from lending has increased, they (like any other risk-averse firm) cut back on their activities: they make fewer loans. But this in turn has strongly adverse effects on producing firms, particularly as the economy goes into a recession. Firms' cash flows are reduced. To maintain their production and investment levels, given their reluctance to issue equity, they turn to banks for credit. And it is precisely when they need the credit the most that banks may be cutting back their credit rather than expanding it. Thus, the recessionary pressures are exacerbated. As one might expect, these effects are particularly important for small and medium-size firms, for which the issuing of commercial paper is not a viable alternative.

Thus, the characteristics of credit and equity markets—characteristics that can be explained by imperfect, costly, and asymmetric information—help us understand the volatility of the economy. Information economics helps explain economic volatility in another important way. In standard theory, changes in economic circumstances lead to changes in wages, prices, and interest rates. Adjustments in these variables act as "shock absorbers." In fact, Keynes noted that prices, wages, and interest rates are not so flexible, and a major strand of Keynesian research has placed these rigidities at the center of macroeconomic fluctuations.

The explanation of such rigidities remains controversial, however. Perhaps the most convincing explanation is that firms are uncertain of the consequences of their actions, and the larger the change in any action, the more uncertain they feel. The greater their perceived uncertainty, the more conservative their actions. They change prices and wages only slowly because the consequences of changing them are so uncertain.

Uniform Prices

A third major principle of economics (besides the efficiency of market economies and the fact that resources, including labor, are fully utilized) is referred to as the Law of the Single Price. Under this law, there is a uniform price in the market, and price differences are quickly eliminated by arbitrage. In fact, many markets are marked by noticeable differences in prices. The differences in observed prices and wages are far larger than can be accounted for simply by differences in attributes of, say, location, differences in quality, and nonpecuniary characteristics of jobs. As George Stigler pointed out in a seminal article in 1962, costly information provides a ready explanation: arbitrage is costly. It is costly for consumers to search for the lowest price or the highest-paying jobs.

But the consequences of imperfect information are even more fundamental. Firms recognize that consumers and workers face costly search. In some special cases this may lead each firm, less concerned about losing customers or workers to rivals, to raise its price or lower its wage.

In some cases it has been shown that even though there are many firms, prices might be raised to the monopoly level, even when search costs are very small. To see why, consider a case where all firms charged the same price. If any firm were to raise its price just a little—by an amount less than the cost to customers of switching to another firm—that firm would lose no customers. Thus, so long as the price is below the monopoly price, it pays that firm to raise its price by a little. But it pays each firm to do so. They thus all raise their prices—and the process continues until the monopoly price is reached.

In other cases it has been shown that markets create their own "noise," so that an equilibrium in which all firms charge the same price cannot exist. If all firms were charging the same price (and there was, accordingly, no need to search for the store with the lowest price), it would pay some firm to raise its price to exploit those who are particularly price insensitive because their search costs are high.

Many market institutions, practices, and structures can be viewed as the economy's responses to these informational problems. We have already noted three of these: the prevalence of the use of credit rather than equity as a source of finance for new investment; the widespread occurrence of credit rationing; and the fact that firms pay wages higher than strictly necessary in order to obtain workers, both to enable them to acquire a higher-quality labor force and to induce workers to work harder.

Three other market responses to costly information are particularly important. First, firms need to have reputations so that customers know they won't be cheated, and workers need reputations so firms know that they won't shirk (see BRAND NAMES). This means that firms and workers must have an incentive to maintain their reputations. Usually, the most severe punishment that a customer can impose on a firm that has sold her a shoddy product is to stop dealing with the firm and to tell one's friends and associates. The most severe punishment a firm can impose on a worker who has shirked in performing duties is to fire the worker. But in traditional economic theory neither of these acts would make much difference: firms make zero profits at the margin, and workers are paid their opportunity cost (that is, the amount they could earn elsewhere). Therefore, there is no difference between the wage paid by the firm and what they could obtain elsewhere.

Thus, for reputation mechanisms to work, firms must at the margin receive some profits, and workers must receive wages in excess of their opportunity costs. The presence and importance of these higher-than-normal profits and wages, though long recognized, had not been previously explained.

A second response to imperfect information is advertising. Because information is costly, both suppliers and demanders must spend resources to acquire and disseminate information. Just as customers search for the lowest price and workers search for the highest wage, stores advertise to provide information to potential customers concerning the location, price, availability, and qualities of their products (see ADVERTISING).

Middlemen are a third example of a market response to costly information. Much popular literature vilifies the role of the middleman. Press reports point out the huge difference between the prices received by farmers and the prices paid by customers, suggesting that evil middlemen are engaged in robbing farmers and consumers. But middlemen provide a vital function in ensuring that goods are delivered to where they are wanted. They are in the business of ensuring the efficient allocation of the economy's scarce resources. For the most part competition in this sector is keen. The fact that so much is paid for these services reflects their value in allocating resources efficiently. The fact that there are often high profits simply reflects that some individuals are able to perform those services much better than others.

The standard theorems that underlie the presumption that markets are efficient are no longer valid once we take into account the fact that information is costly and imperfect. To some, this has suggested a switch to the Austrian approach, most forcefully developed during the forties and later by Friedrich Hayek and his followers. They have not attempted to "defend" markets by the use of theorems. Instead, they see markets as institutions that have evolved to solve information problems. According to Hayek, neoclassical economics got itself into trouble by assuming perfect information to begin with. A much better approach, wrote Hayek, is to assume the world we have, one in which everyone has only a little information. The great virtue of free markets, he wrote, is that they allow each person to efficiently use his own information, and do not require that anyone have all the information. According to Hayek, government planning requires the impossible—that a small body of officials have all this information.

The new information economics substantiates Hayek's contention that central planning faces problems because it requires an impossible agglomeration of information. It agrees with Hayek that the virtue of markets is that they make use of the dispersed information held by different participants in the market. But information economics does not agree with Hayek's assertion that markets act efficiently.

The fact that markets with imperfect information do not work perfectly provides a rationale for potential government actions. The older theory said that no government, no matter how well organized, could do better than markets. If that was true, then we had little need to inquire into the nature of government. The modern theory says that government might improve upon matters, but to ascertain whether or not this is the case requires a closer examination of how governments actually behave, or might behave under various rules.

The modern study of political economy has uncovered many inefficiencies associated with government behavior, just as the modern study of firms has uncovered many inefficiencies associated with market behavior. An important line of research has focused on identifying how government differs intrinsically from other organizations in the economy (their powers and constraints, including the limitations on information that they face and their powers and incentives to acquire information) and, based on these distinctive features, on determining the appropriate economic roles of governments and markets.

—Joseph E. Stiglitz

Biography: Joseph E. Stiglitz has been nominated to be a member of President Clinton's Council of Economic Advisers. He is on leave from Stanford University, where he is a professor of economics. He was previously a professor at Princeton and Yale. In 1979 he received the American Economic Association's John Bates Clark Award, given every two years to the economist under age forty who is judged to have made the most significant contribution to economics. He is a founding editor of the AEA's *Journal of Economic Perspectives*.

Further Reading

Hayek, Friedrich A. "The Use of Knowledge in Society." *American Economic Review* 35 (1945): 519–53.
Stiglitz, Joseph E. "The Causes and Consequences of the Dependence of Quality on Prices." *Journal of Economic Literature* 25 (March 1987): 1–48.
———. "Information and Economic Analysis." In *Current Economic Problems*, edited by Parkin and Nobay. 1975.
———. "Information and Economic Analysis: A Perspective." *Economic Journal* (1985): 21–41.
———. "On the Economic Role of the State." In *The Economic Role of the State*, edited by A. Heertze. 1989.

Insurance

Richard Zeckhauser

■ Insurance plays a central role in the functioning of modern economies. Life insurance offers protection against the economic impact of an untimely death; health insurance covers the sometimes extraordinary costs of medical care; and bank deposits are insured by the federal government. In each case a small premium is paid by the insured to receive benefits should an unlikely but high-cost event occur.

Insurance issues, traditionally a stodgy domain, have become subjects for intense debate and concern in recent years. The impact of the collapse of savings and loan institutions on the solvency of the deposit-insurance pool will burden the federal budget for decades. How to provide health insurance for the significant portion of Americans not now covered is a central political issue. Various states, attempting to hold back the tides of higher costs, have placed severe limits on auto insurance rates and have even sought refunds from insurers.

The Basics

An understanding of insurance must begin with the concept of risk, or the variation in possible outcomes of a situation. A's shipment of goods to Europe might arrive safely or might be lost in transit. C may incur zero medical expenses in a good year, but if she is struck by a car, they could be upward of $100,000. We cannot eliminate risk from life, even at extraordinary expense. Paying extra for double-hulled tankers still leaves oil spills possible. The only way to eliminate auto-related injuries is to eliminate automobiles.

Thus, the effective response to risk combines two elements: efforts or expenditures to lessen the risk, and the purchase of insurance against the risk that remains. Consider A's shipment of, say, $1 million in goods. If the chance of loss on each trip is 3 percent, on average the loss will be $30,000 (3 percent of $1 million). Let us assume that A can ship by a more costly method and cut the risk by 1 percentage point, thus saving $10,000 on average. If the additional cost of this shipping method is less than $10,000, it is a worthwhile expenditure. But if cutting risk by a further percentage point will cost $15,000, it is not worthwhile.

To deal with the remaining 2 percent risk of losing $1 million, A should think about insurance. To cover administrative costs, the insurer might charge $25,000 for a risk that will incur average losses of no more than $20,000. From A's standpoint, however, the insurance may be worthwhile because it is a comparatively inexpensive way to deal with the potential loss of $1 million. Note the important economic role of such insurance. Without it A might not be willing to risk shipping goods in the first place.

In exchange for a premium, the insurer

will pay a claim should a specified contingency, such as death, medical bills, or shipment loss, arise. The insurer is able to offer such protection against financial loss by pooling the risks from a large group of similarly situated individuals. With a large pool, the laws of probability assure that only a tiny fraction of insured shipments is lost, or only a small fraction of the insured population will be hospitalized in a year. If, for example, each of 100,000 individuals independently faces a 1 percent risk in a year, on average 1,000 will have losses. If each of the 100,000 people paid a premium of $1,000, the insurance company would collect a total of $100 million, enough to pay $100,000 to anyone who had a loss. But what would happen if 1,100 people had losses? The answer, fortunately, is that such an outcome is exceptionally unlikely. Insurance works through the magic of the Law of Large Numbers. This law assures that when a large number of people face a low-probability event, the proportion experiencing the event will be close to the expected proportion. For instance, with a pool of 100,000 people who each face a 1 percent risk, the law of large numbers dictates that 1,100 people or more will have losses only one time in 1,000.

In many cases, however, the risks to different individuals are not independent. In a hurricane, airplane crash, or epidemic, many may suffer at the same time. Insurance companies spread such risks not only across individuals but also across good years and bad, building up reserves in the good years to deal with heavier claims in bad ones. For further protection they also diversify across lines, selling health insurance as well as homeowners' insurance, for example.

The Identity and Behavior of the Insured

To an economist insurance is like most other commodities. It obeys the laws of supply and demand, for example. However, it is unlike many other commodities in one important respect: the cost of providing insurance depends on the identity of the purchaser. A year of health insurance for an eighty-year-old costs more to provide than one for a fifty-year-old. It costs more to provide auto insurance to teenagers than to middle-aged people. If a company mistakenly sells health policies to old folks at a price that is appropriate for young folks, it will assuredly lose money, just as a restaurant will lose if it sells twenty-dollar steak dinners for ten dollars. The restaurant would lure lots of steak eaters. So, too, would the insurance company attract large numbers of older clients. Because of this differential cost of providing coverage, and because customers search for their lowest price, insurance companies go to great pains to set different premiums for different groups, depending on the risks they will impose.

Recognizing that the identity of the purchaser affects the cost of insurance, insurers must be careful to whom they offer insurance at a particular price. High-risk individuals, with superior knowledge of the risks they impose, will step forth to purchase, knowing that they are getting a good deal. This is a process called adverse selection, which means that the mix of purchasers will be adverse to the insurer.

In effect, the potential purchasers have "hidden" information that relates to their particular risk. Those whose information is unfavorable are most likely to be the purchasers. For example, if an insurer determines that 1 percent of fifty-year-olds would die in a year, it might establish a premium of $11 per $1,000 of coverage, $10 to cover claims and $1 to cover administrative costs. The insurer might expect to break even. However, insureds who ate poorly or who engaged in high-risk professions or whose parents had died young might have an annual risk of mortality of 3 percent. They would be most likely to insure. Health fanatics, by contrast, might forgo insurance because for them it is a bad deal. Through adverse selection, the insurer could end up with a group whose expected costs were, say, $20 per $1,000 rather than the $10 per $1,000 for the population as a whole.

The traditional approach to the adverse selection problem is to inspect each potential insured. Individuals taking out substantial life insurance must submit to a medical exam. Fire insurance might be granted only after a check of the alarm and sprinkler system. But no matter how careful the inspection, some information will remain hidden, and those choosing to insure will be selected against the insurer. So insurers routinely set rates high to cope with adverse selection. One consequence is that high rates discourage ordinary-risk buyers from buying insurance.

Moral Hazard or Hidden Action

Once insured, an individual has less incentive to avoid risky behavior. With automobile collision insurance, for example, one is more likely to venture forth on an icy night. Federal deposit insurance made S&Ls more willing to take on risky loans. Federally subsidized flood insurance encourages citizens to build homes on flood plains. Insurers use the term "moral hazard" to describe this phenomenon. It means, simply, that insured people undertake actions they would otherwise avoid. In less judgmental language, people respond to incentives.

Ideally, the insurer would like to be able to monitor the insured's behavior and take appropriate action. Flood insurance might not be sold to new residents of a flood plain. Collision insurance might not pay off if it can be proven that the policyholder had been drinking or otherwise engaged in reckless behavior. But given the difficulty of monitoring many actions, insurers merely take into account that once policies are issued, behavior will change and more claims will be made.

The moral hazard problem is often encountered in areas that at first glance do not seem associated with traditional insurance. Products covered under optional warranties tend to get abused, as do autos that are leased with service contracts. And if all students are ensured a place in college, they are, in effect, insured against bad grades. Academic performance may suffer.

Equity Issues

The same insurance policy will have different costs for serving individuals whose behavior or underlying characteristics may differ. This introduces an equity dimension to insurance, since these cost differences will influence pricing. Is it fair that urban drivers should pay much more than rural drivers to protect themselves from auto liability? In some sense, perhaps not, but what is the alternative? If prices are not allowed to vary in relation to risk, insurers will seek to avoid various classes of customers altogether and availability will be restricted. When sellers of health insurance are not allowed to find out if potential clients are HIV positive, for example, insurance companies often respond by refusing to insure people in occupations in which an unusually large proportion of the population is gay. One way they do so is by refusing to cover males who are florists or hairdressers.

Equity issues in insurance are addressed in a variety of ways in the real world. Most employers cross-subsidize health insurance, providing the same coverage at the same price to older, higher-risk workers and younger, lower-risk ones. Sometimes the government provides the insurance itself, as the federal government does with Medicare and Social Security (an insurance policy that pays off heavily if one lives long), or it may set the rates, as many states do with auto insurance. The traditional public-interest argument for government rate regulation is to control a monopoly. But this argument ignores the fact that there are dozens of competing insurers in most regulated insurance markets. Insurance rates are regulated to help some groups, usually those imposing high risks, at the expense of others. The Massachusetts auto insurance market provides an example. In 1988, 63 percent of drivers were in a subsidized pool. To fund this subsidy, unsubsidized drivers, whose claims averaged $323, paid premiums that averaged $750.

Such practices raise a new class of equity issues. Should the government force people who live quiet, low-risk lives to subsidize the daredevil fringe? Most people's response to this question depends on whether they think people can control risks. Because most of us think we should not encourage people to engage in behavior that is costly to the system, we conclude, for example, that nonsmokers should not have to pay for smokers. The question becomes more complex when it comes to health care premiums for, say, gay men or recovering alcoholics, whose health care costs are likely to be greater than average. Moral judgments inevitably creep into such discussions. And sometimes the facts lead to disquieting considerations.

For example, smokers tend to die early, reducing expected costs for Social Security. Should they therefore pay lower Social Security taxes?

Conclusion

The traditional role of insurance remains the essential one recognized in ancient civilizations, that of spreading risk among similarly situated individuals. Insurance works most effectively when losses are not under the control of individuals (thus avoiding moral hazard) and when the losses are readily determined (lest significant transactions costs associated with lawsuits become a burden).

Individuals and firms insure against their most major risks—high health costs, the inability to pay depositors—which often are politically salient issues as well. Unsurprisingly, government participation—as a setter of rates, as a subsidizer, and as a direct provider of insurance services—has become a major feature in insurance markets. Political forces may sometimes triumph over sound insurance principles, but only temporarily. In a sound market, we must recognize that with insurance, as with bread and steel, the cost of providing it must be paid.

—Richard Zeckhauser

Biography: Richard Zeckhauser is the Frank P. Ramsey Professor of Political Economy at Harvard University.

Further Reading

Arrow, Kenneth J. ''The Economics of Agency.'' In *Principals and Agents: The Structure of Business,* edited by John W. Pratt and Richard J. Zeckhauser. 1985.
———. *Essays in the Theory of Risk-Bearing.* 1974.
Denenberg, Herbert S., Robert D. Eilers, Joseph J. Melone, and Robert A. Zelten. *Risk and Insurance,* 2d ed. 1974.
Huber, Peter W. *Liability: The Legal Revolution and Its Consequences.* 1988.

Liability

W. Kip Viscusi

■ Until recently, property and liability insurance was a small cost of doing business. But the substantial expansion in what legally constitutes liability over the past thirty years has greatly increased the cost of liability insurance for personal injuries. For U.S. producers of private aircraft, liability insurance expenses now average $100,000 per plane produced, leading Cessna to cease production and Beech Aircraft to all but eliminate private aircraft production as well. These substantial costs arise because accident victims or their survivors sue aircraft companies in 90 percent of all crashes, even though pilot error is responsible for 85 percent of all accidents.

Riders on the Philadelphia Mass Transit system pay 17 percent of every fare dollar to cover liability insurance costs for passenger injuries. Similarly, 15 to 25 percent of the cost of every ladder purchased is used to defray liability expenses. Major firms, such as A. H. Robins, and entire industries, such as the asbestos industry, have been shut down by the rising liability burden. Ten of the thirteen companies manufacturing vaccines for the five serious childhood diseases exited the market because of rising liability costs.

The dominant legal criterion for determining a firm's liability had traditionally been that of negligence. Firms were responsible for accidents arising from their products only if they did not provide an efficient level of safety (see LAW AND ECONOMICS for an explanation of how the term *efficient* is used in this case). Over the past three decades, however, broader liability doctrines, some of which have nothing to do with negligence, have placed greater responsibilities on product manufacturers. The adoption of what is called strict liability in the sixties required producers to pay for accident costs in a much broader range of circumstances. One of the stated rationales that the courts have given for this expansion was that producers could serve as the insurers of the accident victims' costs and spread these costs among all consumers through a higher product price.

Another expansion in liability has occurred through a broader concept of what constitutes a design defect. This had been reflected in, for example, a surge of litigation claiming that an inadequate warning— a warning that does not fully inform the user of a product's risks—is enough to deem a product's design to be defective. A federal appeals court found Uniroyal liable for the death of a professional truck driver because it failed to warn of the risks from underinflated tires. FMC lost a product-liability suit involving a crane because there was no warning in the cab about hitting power lines with the machine. Many asbestos cases have focused on whether companies properly informed workers of the cancer risk and the need to avoid breathing asbestos dust.

Increases in liability enhance the incentives to provide safer products. But liability costs also discourage product innovation. In a 1990 report the National Academy of Sciences concluded that the United States had fallen a decade behind Europe in the development of new contraceptives, partly because of the chilling effect of rising liability costs. In one case, G. D. Searle and Company spent $1.5 million in a single year to successfully defend itself against four lawsuits for its intrauterine device Copper-7. Since annual sales of the product were only $11 million, the company chose to discontinue it.

The substantial increase in liability is reflected in the extent of litigation. Between 1974 and 1989, product-liability lawsuits in the federal courts increased sixfold. The product-liability share of all federal civil litigation rose from 2 percent in 1975 to 6 percent in 1989. These increases cannot be accounted for by greater product riskiness. For the period 1977 to 1987, federal product-liability lawsuits increased by 400 percent, whereas total U.S. accident rates *declined* by 20 percent, motor vehicle accidents by 11 percent, work accident rates by 25 percent, and home accident rates by 26 percent.

The price tag associated with liability suits is also substantial. Million-dollar liability awards have become increasingly common, even for less highly publicized accidents. The median verdict in product-liability cases doubled in nominal terms from 1980 to 1988. Whereas the median product-liability verdict was under $100,000 in 1971, it had risen to $405,000 in 1988, a 48 percent increase after adjustment for inflation.

The principal components of these awards are economic damages (lost earnings and medical expenses) and compensation for pain and suffering. Economic damages have risen in part because the cost of medical care has risen. Pain and suffering damages have attracted the most attention from product-liability reformers because their conceptual basis remains ill defined. The legal criteria for such compensation are not well articulated. On an economic basis pain and suffering represents an economic loss that one would generally not choose to insure.

The result of this lack of a conceptual base has been substantial uncertainty in the determination of compensation for pain and suffering. But juries seem willing to see pain and suffering almost anywhere. After an Illinois refinery explosion, for example, a jury awarded $700,000 to the victim's survivors, even though there was no evidence that the comatose victim was conscious and would have experienced any pain. (The award was overturned on appeal.) Nevertheless, the fact that such awards are granted is one reason why the U.S. Department of Justice and various legal reform groups advocate schedules and limits for compensating pain and suffering. Most recently, there has been a tremendous expansion of the pain-and-suffering concept as passengers on a plane that never crashed have successfully sued for the "fear of death," and witnesses of the death of a stranger have successfully sued for the emotional trauma they experienced by witnessing this death.

Perhaps the most dramatic change in the character of product-liability litigation has been the emergence of mass toxic torts. Agent Orange, asbestos, and the Dalkon Shield cases are the three most notable examples of such litigation. Each of these lines of litigation has involved more than 100,000 injury claimants—190,000 claimants against the Manville Corporation for asbestos exposures, 150,000 claimants in other asbestos cases, 210,000 claimants against the Dalkon Shield, and 125,000 claimants in the Agent Orange litigation. Asbestos litigation comprised 2 percent of federal product-liability litigation in 1975, but by 1989 the asbestos share had risen to 61 percent. The surge in mass toxic torts had overwhelmed the courts' capacity to process these claims.

These cases are distinguished not only by their number, but also by the difficulties they create for the liability system. Due to the substantial time lags involved, causality has been difficult to determine. It is noteworthy that in the Agent Orange case, legal doctrine (*Feres* v. *United States*) prevented soldiers from suing the actor primarily responsible for their injuries—the federal government. Consequently, they sought compensation from the deep and more readily available pockets of Dow Chemical Company and other Agent Orange producers. The judge who presided over the Agent Orange litigation could not find any clear-cut causality between Agent Orange and the veterans' ailments and, as a result, fashioned a ''compromise'' settlement for $180 million.

Moreover, in the asbestos cases liability was imposed retroactively on firms that could not have anticipated the extent of the risks or the likely litigation costs. This means that one of the main modern rationales for expanded liability—that it gives companies an incentive to avoid accidents—does not apply in the asbestos cases.

The viability of insuring these losses by shifting accident costs onto companies has also come under fire as the Manville Corporation and others have reorganized under federal bankruptcy law and set up trust funds in excess of $3 billion (in the case of Manville) to cover losses that will inevitably exceed that amount.

The costs of liability are reflected in the liability-insurance costs that firms must pay. Many of the largest firms self-insure. The Ford Motor Company, which insures itself, faced $4 billion in product-liability damages claims in 1986. Liability costs have also exploded for those who still buy liability insurance. General liability premiums more than quintupled—from $1.13 billion to $6.49 billion—between 1968 and 1978. Then between 1978 and 1988, they tripled to $19.1 billion. What is particularly remarkable is that virtually all of this tripling occurred between 1984 and 1986. Not surprisingly, during the mideighties people began to talk of an emerging liability crisis.

A number of explanations have been offered for this crisis. One is that it may have been caused by the so-called insurance underwriting cycle. Over the decades, insurance companies have periodically underpriced insurance as they competed for more business. Then, as the claims on these underpriced policies generated large losses, the insurers responded by raising prices substantially. Another explanation offered is that the insurance industry may have had a capital shortfall, causing it to decrease the amount of coverage it would write. It did so, according to this explanation, by raising prices. A third explanation is that the crisis was caused by changes in liability—the rise in liability costs, the increased uncertainty of the liability system, and the presence of highly correlated risks that decrease the ability of insurers to pool offsetting risks in their portfolio. The long-run nature of the rise in insurance premiums and the linkage of this increase to the surge in litigation suggest that shifts in liability doctrine are the major contributors to the rise in liability costs.

Although the short-run crisis has abated, a broad array of tort-reform groups, ranging from the U.S. Department of Justice to the American Law Institute, has concluded that the liability system must be restructured to provide an efficient level of deterrence, to provide appropriate incentives for the introduction of new products, and to meet the legitimate needs of accident victims.

—W. Kip Viscusi

Biography: W. Kip Viscusi is the George G. Allen Professor of Economics at Duke University. He served as associate reporter for the American Law Institute Study of Enterprise Responsibility for Personal Injury. While a student at Harvard, he spent two summers working for Ralph Nader.

Further Reading

American Law Institute. *Reporters' Study, Enterprise Liability for Personal Injury*. 1991.
Huber, Peter. *Liability: The Legal Revolution and Its Consequences*. 1988.
Litan, Robert, and Clifford Winston. *Liability: Perspectives and Policy*. 1988.
National Academy of Science. *Developing New Contraceptives, Obstacles and Opportunities*. 1990.
Viscusi, W. Kip. *Reforming Products Liability*. 1991.

Marginalism

Steven E. Rhoads

■ Adam Smith struggled with what came to be called the paradox of "value in use" versus "value in exchange." Water is necessary to existence and of enormous value in use. Diamonds are frivolous and clearly not essential. But the price of diamonds their value in exchange—is far higher than that of water. What perplexed Smith is now rationally explained in the first chapters of every college freshman's introductory economics text. Smith had failed to distinguish between "total" utility and "marginal" utility. The elaboration of this insight transformed economics in the late nineteenth century, and the fruits of the marginalist revolution continue to set the basic framework for contemporary microeconomics.

The marginalist explanation is as follows: The total utility or satisfaction of water exceeds that of diamonds. We would all rather do without diamonds than without water. But almost all of us would prefer to win a prize of a diamond rather than an additional bucket of water. To make this last choice, we ask ourselves not whether diamonds or water give more satisfaction in total, but whether more of one gives greater additional satisfaction than more of the other. For this marginal utility question, our answer will depend on how much of each we already have. Though the first units of water we consume every month are of enormous value to us, the last units are not. The utility of additional (or marginal) units continues to decrease as we consume more and more.

Economists believe that sensible choice requires comparing marginal utilities and marginal costs. They also think that most people apply the marginalism concept regularly, even if subconsciously, in their private decisions. In southern states, for example, a much lower fraction of people buy snow shovels than in northern states. The reason is that although snow shovels cost about the same from state to state, the marginal benefit of a snow shovel is much higher in northern states. But in discussions of public policy issues, where most of the benefits and costs do not accrue to the individual making the policy decision (e.g., subsidies for health care), the appeal of total utility and intrinsic worth as the basis for decision can mask the insights of marginalism.

Even good answers to certain grand questions give little guidance for rational public policy choices. For example, what is more important, health or recreation? If forced to choose, everyone would find health more important than recreation. But marginalism suggests that our real concern should be with proportion, not rank. Finding health in total to be more important than recreation in total does not imply that all diving boards should be removed from swimming pools just because a few people die in diving accidents. Similarly, we clearly want cleaner air and economic growth. And we want recreational opportunities in natural settings and in developed ones. Reasonable policy choices require knowledge of how well we are now doing in all of these areas and of the alternative opportunities available.

In addition, costs must be determined. Even the biggest remaining problem may not deserve most of the extra money. One writer, for example, argues that early deaths of the young are our greatest life-saving problem, and therefore the health budget should emphasize preventing the largest killers of the young, such as accidents and suicides. But even if one accepts this writer's values, his policy conclusions do not follow. We may not know how to prevent suicides at reasonable cost, but perhaps a medical breakthrough has made possible a low-cost cure for a disease that is the sixth-leading cause of death among the young. We would then save more lives among the young if we devoted more of our resources to their sixth-largest health problem rather than their first or second. Marginalism thus requires looking at the details—looking at the costs and benefits of particular opportunities.

The marginalist insight also illuminates some weaknesses in the health-policy outlook of those who base their position on the idea of medical needs. Because health is an essential need, many think that those with medical complaints should have free and quick access to physicians. When they think of health demand, such people think of serious, medically treatable illness. But from the viewpoint of the consumer, at least, a significant portion of demand for medical care gives very small benefits. These benefits are poorly indicated by thinking about total utility (that is, how important health is).

In studying a number of small groups,

scholars have observed the effects of insurance policy changes on the demand for health care. A few actual experiments have also been conducted. One required a group of California Medicaid beneficiaries to pay one dollar for their first two office visits each month, while a similar group continued to receive completely free service. This modest charge reduced office visits by 8 percent, and it seems unlikely that those who stopped going to doctors could not afford the one-dollar charge.

Other studies have found that even small changes in time cost can have an effect. For example, when the health facility at one college was moved so that it took twenty minutes rather than five to ten to walk there, student visits fell by nearly 40 percent. Similarly, a 10 percent increase in the travel time to outpatient clinics among a low-income urban group caused an estimated 10 percent decrease in demand for visits to physicians. Whether the health services forgone in these cases were necessary remains an open question, but surely the potential patients did not act as if they had no option other than to obtain care.

Marginalism also leads one to question the old maxim that anything worth doing at all is worth doing well. Nobel Laureate James Buchanan has suggested that an economist can be distinguished from a noneconomist by his reaction to that statement. Another economist actually polled a group of his fellows to judge their agreement or disagreement with this and four other maxims. "Anything worth doing . . ." was by far the least popular, with 74 percent of respondents disagreeing. A careful weighing of marginal cost implies that we should use well the money we devote to a task, but we should rarely do as much as interested professionals think necessary.

These examples apply marginalism to government expenditures directed at specific policy areas such as health care. The tax side of the budgetary equation also calls for the concept. Marginalism reminds us that when contemplating the effect of tax rates on the incentive to work, we are usually less interested in the average tax rate paid on a family's entire income than in the marginal tax rate—the proportion of added (marginal) income that the husband or wife will pay in taxes if either works a little more. Similarly, when considering the effect of a tax cut on savings, it reminds us that we should not look at the percentage of a family's total income that is saved but rather the percentage of any additional income received (in this case from the tax cut). Though the average national savings rate is less than 5 percent, the long-run marginal savings rate is more than double the 5 percent average rate even at the lowest income levels. In the highest income brackets the long-run marginal savings rate has been estimated at over 50 percent.

—Steven E. Rhoads

Biography: Steven E. Rhoads is a professor of government and foreign affairs at the University of Virginia.

Further Reading

Anderson, Douglas. *Regulating Politics and Electric Utilities*. Chap. 4. 1981.
Cooper, Michael. "Economics of Need: The Experience of the British Health Service." In *The Economics of Health and Medical Care,* edited by Mark Perlman, esp. 89–99, 105. 1973.
Kahn, Alfred. "Applications of Economics to an Imperfect World." *American Economic Review* 69 (1979): esp. 1–3.
McKenzie, Richard, and Gordon Tullock. *The New World of Economics*. Chaps. 2, 20. 1981.
Rhoads, Steven E. *The Economist's View of the World: Government, Markets and Public Policy*. Chap. 3. 1985.

Why Repairmen Earn More Than Child-Care Workers

Child-care workers perform important work. The total utility of their work is probably much higher than the total utility of the work performed by workers who repair air conditioning. So why do air-conditioning repairmen earn more than child-care workers? Marginalism has the answer. Suppose that there are fewer children and more air conditioners than there used to be. Suppose also that for the same wage there is a surplus of child-care workers and a shortage of people who repair air conditioners. Then the wage cannot be the same. If it were, the only way to get enough air-conditioning repairmen would be to conscript them. So the only peaceful way to get the right number of child-care workers and the right number of air-conditioning workers is to let the market work. This means letting the higher supply of child-care workers drive down their wage and the lower supply of air-conditioning repairmen drive up their wage. Although the total utility of work performed by child-care workers exceeds the total utility of work performed by air-conditioning repairmen, the marginal value of the latter's utility exceeds the marginal value of the former's.   **—DRH**

Microeconomics

Arnold C. Harberger

■ Until the so-called Keynesian revolution of the late thirties and forties, the two main parts of economic theory were typically labeled monetary theory and price theory. Today, the corresponding dichotomy is between macroeconomics and microeconomics. The motivating force for the change came from the macro side, with modern macroeconomics being far more explicit than old-fashioned monetary theory about fluctuations in income and employment (as well as the price level). In contrast, no revolution separates today's microeconomics from old-fashioned price theory; one evolved from the other naturally and without significant controversy.

The strength of microeconomics comes from the simplicity of its underlying structure and its close touch with the real world. In a nutshell, microeconomics has to do with supply and demand, and with the way they interact in various markets. Microeconomic analysis moves easily and painlessly from one topic to another and lies at the center of most of the recognized subfields of economics. Labor economics, for example, is built largely on the analysis of the supply and demand for labor of different types. The field of industrial organization deals with the different mechanisms (monopoly, cartels, different types of competitive behavior) by which goods and services are sold. International economics worries about the demand and supply of individual traded commodities, as well as of a country's exports and imports taken as a whole, and the consequent demand for and supply of foreign exchange. Agricultural economics deals with the demand and supply of agricultural products, and of farmland, farm labor, and the other factors of production involved in agriculture.

Public finance looks at how the government enters the scene. Traditionally, its focus was on taxes, which automatically introduce ''wedges'' (differences between the price the buyer pays and the price the seller receives) and cause inefficiency. More recently, public finance has reached into the expenditure side as well, attempting to analyze (and sometimes actually to measure) the costs and benefits of different public outlays and programs.

Applied welfare economics is the fruition of microeconomics. It deals with the costs and benefits of just about anything—public projects, taxes on commodities, taxes on factors of production (corporation income taxes, payroll taxes), agricultural programs (like price supports and acreage controls), tariffs on imports, foreign exchange controls, different forms of industrial organiza-

tion (like monopoly and oligopoly), and various aspects of labor market behavior (like minimum wages, the monopoly power of labor unions, and so on).

It is hard to imagine a basic course in microeconomics failing to include numerous cases and examples drawn from all of the fields listed above. This is because microeconomics is so basic. It represents the trunk of the tree out of which all the listed subfields have branched.

At the root of everything is supply and demand. It is not at all farfetched to think of these as basically human characteristics. If human beings are not going to be totally self-sufficient, they will end up producing certain things that they trade in order to fulfill their demands for other things. The specialization of production and the institutions of trade, commerce, and markets long antedated the science of economics. Indeed, one can fairly say that from the very outset the science of economics entailed the study of the market forms that arose quite naturally (and without any help from economists) out of human behavior. People specialize in what they think they can do best—or more existentially, in what heredity, environment, fate, and their own volition have brought them to do. They trade their services and/or the products of their specialization for those produced by others. Markets evolve to organize this sort of trading, and money evolves to act as a generalized unit of account and to make barter unnecessary.

In this market process people try to get the most from what they have to sell, and to satisfy their desires as much as possible. In microeconomics this is translated into the notion of people maximizing their personal "utility," or welfare. This process helps them to decide what they will supply and what they will demand.

When hybrid corn first appeared in the United States, it was in experiment stations, not on ordinary farms. But over a period of decades, it became the product of choice of hundreds of thousands of farmers. At the beginning of the process, those who adopted the new hybrids made handsome profits. By the time the transition was complete, any farmer who clung stubbornly to the old nonhybrid seed was likely to be driven out of business. So what was left was farmers who acted as if they were profit-maximizing; the ones who did not had failed. By a very similar process new varieties of wheat spread through the Punjab and other parts of India in the sixties, and new varieties of rice through the Philippines and the rest of East Asia. What economists call "maximizing behavior" explains the real-world behavior of these millions of farmers, whose actions increased the supply of corn, wheat, and rice, making much more of these products available to the consumers of the world at a lower cost.

Similar scenarios reveal how maximizing behavior works on the demand side. Today's textiles include vast amounts of artificial fibers, nearly all of them unknown a century ago. They conquered markets for themselves, at the expense of the older natural fibers, because consumers perceived them to be either better or cheaper, or both. In the end, when old products end up on the ash heap of history, it is usually because consumers have found new products that they greatly prefer to the old ones.

The economics of supply and demand has a sort of moral or normative overtone, at least when it comes to dealing with a wide range of market distortions. In an undistorted market, buyers pay the market price up to the point where they judge further units not to be worth that price, while competitive sellers supply added units as long as they can make money on each increment. At the point where supply just equals demand in an undistorted market, the price measures both the worth of the product to buyers and the worth of the product to sellers.

That is not so when an artificial distortion intervenes. With a 50 percent tax based on selling price, an item that costs $1.50 to the buyer is worth only $1.00 to the seller. The tax creates a wedge, mentioned earlier, between the value to the buyer and the return to the seller. The anomaly thus created could be eliminated if the distortion were removed; then the market would find its equilibrium at some price in between (say, $1.20) where the product's worth would be the same to buyers and to sellers. Whenever we start with a distortion, we can usually assert that society as a whole can benefit from its removal. This is epitomized by the fact that buyers gain as they get extra units at less than $1.50, while sellers gain as they get to sell extra units at more than $1.00.

Many different distortions can create similar anomalies. If cotton is subsidized, the price that farmers get will exceed, by the amount of the subsidy, the value to consumers. Society thus stands to gain by eliminating the subsidy and moving to a price that is the same for both buyers and sellers. If price controls keep bread (or anything else) artificially cheap, the predictable result is that less will be supplied than is demanded. Nine times out of ten, the excess demand will end up being reflected in a gray or black market, whose existence is probably the clearest evidence that the official price is artificially low. In turn, economists are nearly always right when they predict that pushing prices down via price controls will end up reducing the market supply and generating black market prices not only well above the official price, but also above the market price that would prevail in the absence of controls.

Official prices that are too high also produce curious results. In the thirties the United States adopted so-called parity prices for the major grains and a few other farm products. Basically, if the market price was below the parity price, the government would pay farmers the difference or buy any unsold crops at the parity price. The predictable result was production in excess of demand—leading to surpluses that were bought up (and idly stored) by the government. Then, in an effort to eliminate the purchase of surpluses (but without reducing the parity price), the government instituted acreage controls under which it paid farmers to take land out of production. Some people were surprised to see that a 20 percent cut in wheat acreage did not lead to a 20 percent fall in the production of wheat. The reason was that other factors of production could be (and were) used more intensively, with the result that in order to get a 20 percent cut in wheat, acreage "had to" be cut by 30 to 40 percent.

Economists have a better solution. Had the government given wheat farmers coupons, each of which permitted the farmer to market one bushel of wheat, wheat marketings could have been cut by the desired amount. Production inefficiencies could be avoided by allowing the farmers to buy and sell coupons among themselves. Low-cost farmers would buy coupons from high-cost farmers, thus ensuring efficient production. This is known as a "second-best" solution to a policy problem. It is second rather than first best because consumers would still be paying the artificially high parity price for wheat.

Monopoly represents the artificial restriction of production by an entity having sufficient "market power" to do so. The economics of monopoly are most easily seen by thinking of a "monopoly markup" as a privately imposed, privately collected tax. This was, in fact, a reality not too many centuries ago when feudal rulers sometimes endowed their favorites with monopoly rights over certain products. The recipients need not ever "produce" such products themselves. They could contract with other firms to produce the good at low prices and then charge consumers what the traffic would bear (so as to maximize monopoly profit). The differences between these two prices is the "monopoly markup," which functions like a tax. In this example it is clear that the true beneficiary of monopoly power is the one who exercises it; both producers and consumers end up losing.

Modern monopolies are a bit less transparent, for two reasons. First, even though governments still grant monopolies, they usually grant them to the producers. Second, some monopolies just happen without government creating them, although these are often short-lived. Either way, the proceeds of the monopoly markup (or tax) are commingled with the return to capital of the monopoly firms. Similarly, labor monopoly is usually exercised by unions, which are able to charge a monopoly markup (or tax), which then becomes commingled with the wages of their members. The true effect of labor monopoly on the competitive wage is seen by looking at the nonunion segment of the economy. Here, wages end up lower, because the union wage causes fewer workers to be hired in the unionized firms, leaving a larger labor supply (and a consequent lower wage) in the nonunion segment.

A final example of what occurs with official prices that are too high is the phenomenon of "rent-seeking." Rent-seeking occurs when someone enters a business to earn a profit that the government has tried to make unusually high. A simple example is a city that imposes a high official meter rate for taxis but allows free entry into the taxi business. The fare must cover the cost of paying a driver plus a market rate of return on the capital costs involved. Labor and capital will flow into the cab industry until each ends up getting its expected, normal return instead of the high returns one would expect with high fares. What will adjust is simply the number of cabs and the fraction of the time they actually carry passengers. Cabs will get more for each rider, but each cab will have fewer riders.

Other situations of rent-seeking occur when artificially high urban wages attract migrants from rural areas. If the wage does not adjust downward to equate supply and demand, the rate of urban unemployment will rise until further migration is deterred. Still other examples are in banking and drugs. When the "margin" in banking is set too high, new banks enter and/or branches of old ones proliferate until further entry is deterred. Artificially maintained drug prices lead, in some countries, to a pharmacy on almost every block.

Rent-seeking also occurs in circumstances where something of value (like import licenses or radio/TV franchises) is being given away or sold below its true value. In such cases potential buyers often spend large amounts in "lobbying" to improve their chances of getting the prize. Indeed, a broad view of rent-seeking easily covers most cases of lobbying (using real resources in efforts to gain legislative or executive "favors").

The great unifying principles of microeconomics are, ever and always, supply and demand. The normative overtone of microeconomics comes from the fact that competitive supply price represents value as seen by suppliers, and competitive demand price represents value as seen by demanders. The motivating force is that of human beings, always gravitating toward choices and arrangements that reflect their tastes. The miracle of it all is that on the basis of such simple and straightforward underpinnings, a rich tapestry of analysis, insights, and understanding can be woven. This brief article can only give its readers a glimpse—hopefully a tempting one—of the richness, beauty, and promise of that tapestry.

—Arnold C. Harberger

Biography: Arnold C. Harberger is a professor of economics at the University of California in Los Angeles. He is also the Gustavus F. and Ann M. Swift Distinguished Service Professor Emeritus at the University of Chicago. He has consulted extensively on microeconomic issues for many international organizations, including the International Monetary Fund, the World Bank, and the Inter-American Development Bank; governments, including Argentina, Bolivia, Brazil, Canada, Chile, India, and Mexico; and corporations, including Bechtel International, Republic Steel, and Ontario Hydro. He was special ambassador, U.S. Department of State, in 1984 and was on a presidential mission to Poland in 1989. He was president of the Western Economic Association from 1989 to 1990 and was vice president of the American Economic Association in 1992.

Further Reading

Alchian, Armen, and William R. Allen. *Exchange and Production*, 3d ed. 1983.
Breit, William L., Harold M. Hochman, and Edward Saueracker. *Readings in Microeconomics*, 3d ed. 1986.
Friedman, David D. *Price Theory*, 2d ed. 1990.
Hirshleifer, Jack, and Amihai Glazer. *Price Theory and Applications*, 5th ed. 1992.
Layard, Richard R., and Alan Walters. *Introduction to Microeconomics*. 1978.
Watson, Donald S., and Malcolm Getz. *Price Theory in Action*, 4th ed. 1981.

Natural Resources
William J. Baumol and Sue Anne Batey Blackman

■ The earth's natural resources are finite, which means that if we use them continuously, we will eventually exhaust them. This basic observation is undeniable. But another way of looking at the issue is far more relevant for assessing social welfare. Our exhaustible and unreproducible natural resources, if measured in terms of their prospective contribution to human welfare, can actually increase year after year, perhaps never coming anywhere near exhaustion. How can this be? The answer lies in the fact that the *effective* stocks of natural resources are continually expanded by the same technological developments that have fueled the extraordinary growth in living standards since the industrial revolution.

Innovation has increased the productivity of natural resources (increasing the gasoline mileage of cars, for example). Innovation also increases the recycling of resources and reduces waste in their extraction or processing. And innovation affects the prospective output contribution of natural resources (for example, the coal still underneath the ground). If a scientific breakthrough in a given year increases the prospective output contribution of the unused stocks of a resource by an amount greater than the reduction (via resources actually used up) in that year, then, in terms of human economic welfare, the stock of that resource will be larger at the end of the year than at the beginning. Of course, the remaining physical amount of the resource must continually decline, but it need never be exhausted completely, and its effective quantity can rise for the indefinite future. The exhaustion of a particular resource, though not impossible, is also not inevitable.

Ever since the industrial revolution, world demand for power and raw materials has grown at a fantastic rate. Some observers (see Darmstadter, Teitelbaum, and Polach; and United Nations) estimate that humankind consumed more energy between 1900 and 1920 than in all previously recorded time. In the following two decades, 1920 to 1940, people again used more power than in the totality of the past (including the preceding twenty years), and each twenty-year period since has experienced a similar rate of increase in energy demands.

Are our natural resources truly being gobbled up by an insatiable industrial world? Table 1 presents some estimates of known world reserves of four important nonfuel minerals (aluminum, copper, iron, and lead). Clearly, even though the mining of these minerals between 1950 and 1980

all but used up the known 1950 reserves, by 1980 the known supplies of these minerals were much greater than in 1950. This increase in presumably finite stocks is explained by the way data on natural resources are compiled. Each year the U.S. Bureau of Mines estimates the amounts of "proven reserves," or quantities of mineral that have actually been located and evaluated (as in table 1). Those quantities can and do rise in response to price rises and anticipated increases in demand. As previously discovered reserves of a resource grow scarce, the price rises, stimulating exploration that frequently adds new reserves faster than the previously proven reserves run out.

Clearly, data on "proven reserves" do not show whether a resource is about to run out. There is, however, another indicator of the scarcity of a resource that is more reliable: its price. If the demand for a resource is not falling, and if its price is not distorted by interferences such as government intervention or international cartels, then the resource's price will rise as its remaining quantity declines. So any price rises can be interpreted as a signal that the resource is getting scarcer. If, on the other hand, the price of a resource actually falls, consistently and without regulatory interference, it is very unlikely that its effective stock is growing scarce.

One group of researchers (Barnett and Morse) found that the real cost (price) of extraction for a sample of thirteen minerals had declined for all but two (lead and zinc) between 1870 and 1956. More recently, Baumol et al. calculated the price of fifteen resources for the period 1900 to 1986 and showed that until the "energy crises" of the seventies, there was a negligible upward

TABLE 1

World Reserves and Cumulative Production of Selected Minerals: 1950–1980
(millions of metric tons of metal content)

Mineral	1950 Reserves	Production 1950–1980	1980 Reserves
Aluminum	1,400	1,346	5,200
Copper	100	156	494
Iron	19,000	11,040	93,466
Lead	40	85	127

SOURCE: *Repetto, p. 23.*

trend in the real (inflation-adjusted) prices of coal and natural gas, and virtually no increase in the price of crude oil. Petroleum prices catapulted in the seventies under the influence of the Organization of Petroleum Exporting Countries but have since returned to their historical levels. The longer-term prospects for these prices are uncertain, but new energy-producing techniques such as nuclear fusion may be able to keep energy prices at their long-term real levels, or even lower.

The price history of nonfuel minerals is even more striking. Some, like iron, have experienced a very slow rise over the last hundred years or so. The prices of others, like lead, have remained stable. And for some, including aluminum and magnesium, real prices today are far lower than they were seventy years ago. The prices of about half of the mineral resources investigated actually fell after correction for inflation. None of the price rises, aside from those of fuels in the seventies, was very large; in constant dollars most of them rose less than 1 percent per year. While the price de-

creases tended to be concentrated toward the beginning of the period, perhaps suggesting increasing scarcity (particularly since 1960), this is hardly evidence of imminent exhaustion.

The effective stocks of a natural resource can be increased in at least three ways:

1. A technological innovation that reduces the amount of iron ore lost during mining or smelting clearly increases the effective stock of that resource. Likewise, a new technique may make it economical to force more oil out of previously abandoned wells. This decrease in waste translates directly into a rise in the effective supplies of oil. For example, say that in 1960, with known drilling techniques, only 40 percent of the oil at a site in Borger, Texas, could have been extracted at a cost ever likely to be acceptable, but by 1990 improved technology had raised this figure to 80 percent. Assume, for simplicity, that the amount of oil in Borger was 10 million barrels. Let's say that between 1960 and 1990,

5 percent of the originally available oil—0.5 million barrels—has been used up. Then, by 1990, the effective supply of oil in that part of the Texas Panhandle will have risen from its initial level of 4 million barrels (40 percent of 10 million) to 7.6 million barrels (80 percent of 9.5 million), which yields a net rise of effective supply equal to 90 percent! In other words, there has occurred not a rise in the physical quantity of oil, but an increase in the productivity of the remaining supply.

2. The (partial) substitutability within the economy of virtually all resources for others is at the heart of the second method for increasing the effective stocks of natural resources. The energy crises of the seventies provided some dramatic illustrations of the substitutability of resources. Homeowners increased their expenditures on insulation to save on fuel costs, thus substituting fiberglass for heating oil. Newspapers reported that the cattle drives of earlier eras were being revived, with cowhand labor substituting for gasoline. Technological innovation can reduce the cost of extracting or processing a resource. Because of technological breakthroughs, a new oil rig, for example, may require fewer labor hours to operate and use less electricity and less steel in its manufacture. Those savings of other resources can translate into savings of oil, because those other resources are thus freed up to be used elsewhere in the economy, and some of the alternative uses will entail substitution for oil.

3. The third way we can increase our effective stocks of a natural resource is, of course, by technological changes that facilitate recycling. Say, for example, that a new recycling technique allows copper to be reused before it is scrapped, and that no such reuse was economical before. Then this technique has doubled the effective reserves of copper (aside from any resources used up in the recycling process). It is important to note, however, that recycling adopted without regard for economic considerations can actually waste resources rather than save them. For example, some researchers have found that combustion of municipal garbage to generate electricity sometimes actually uses up more energy than it produces.

These three means can all increase the effective supplies of exhaustible resources and can augment the prospective economic contribution of the current inventory of resources, perhaps more than enough to offset the consumption of resources during the same period.

Some people believe that the burst of productivity and increase in living standards that has occurred since the industrial revolution can be attributed to our willingness to deplete our natural heritage at the expense of future generations. But as we have seen here, rising productivity (the source of the great leap in economic growth) may, in a real sense, actually augment humanity's stock of natural resource capital, instead of depleting it, and may be able to do so, for all practical purposes, "forever." Can we expect such technological innovation to continue indefinitely? The evidence of trends in the prices of natural resources suggests that technological innovation has indeed provided continuing increases in the effective stocks of finite resources. But is there a limit to this process—can we expect the wonders of technology to continue to wring ever more out of the earth's resources? Unfortunately, no one knows the answer.

**—William J. Baumol and
Sue Anne Batey Blackman**

Biography: William J. Baumol is the director of the C. V. Starr Center for Applied Economics at New York University and professor emeritus at Princeton University. Sue Anne Batey Blackman is the senior research assistant in Princeton's economics department.

Further Reading

Barnett, H. J., and Chandler Morse. *Scarcity and Growth*. 1963.

Baumol, William J., Sue Anne Batey Blackman, and Edward N. Wolff. *Productivity and American Leadership: The Long View*. 1989. (Earlier estimates in this entry are taken from Baumol, William J., and Wallace E. Oates, with Sue Anne Batey Blackman. *Economics, Environmental Policy and the Quality of Life*. 1979.)

Darmstadter, Joel, Perry D. Teitelbaum, and Jaroslav G. Polach. *Energy in the World Economy, A Statistical Review of Trends in Output, Trade and Consumption since 1925*. 1971.

Repetto, Robert. "Population, Resources, Environment: An Uncertain Future." *Population Bureau* 42, no. 2 (July 1987).

United Nations. *Yearbook of World Energy Statistics*. 1979, 1983, and 1986.

Are We Running Out of Oil?

No resource has inspired so great a fear of running out as oil has. This fear is not new. And every time in the last hundred years that an expert predicted we would run out, that prediction has been wrong—and not just wrong, but wrong by a huge margin. In 1891, for example, the U.S. Geological Survey stated that there was little chance that oil would be found in Kansas or Texas. Since then, 14 billion barrels of oil have been produced from just those two states. In 1914 an official of the U.S. Bureau of Mines claimed that the total future U.S. production would be 5.7 billion barrels. In fact, production has already been six times that figure. In 1920 the director of the Geological Survey said that peak annual crude production had almost been reached. By 1948 annual U.S. production was four times its 1920 level.

Finally, in one of the most astoundingly wrong predictions, the Interior Department stated in 1939 that U.S. oil supplies would run out in thirteen years. Of course, over fifty years later, the United States is still producing oil.

—DRH

Source: Baumol, Blackman, and Wolff, p. 214.

Opportunity Cost

David R. Henderson

■ When economists refer to the "opportunity cost" of a resource, they mean the value of the next-highest-valued alternative use of that resource. If, for example, you spend time and money going to a movie, you cannot spend that time at home reading a book, and you can't spend the money on something else. If your next-best alternative to seeing the movie is reading the book, then the opportunity cost of seeing the movie is the money spent plus the pleasure you forgo by not reading the book.

The word *opportunity* in *opportunity cost* is actually redundant. The cost of using something is already the value of the highest-valued alternative use. But as contract lawyers and airplane pilots know, redundancy can be a virtue. In this case, its virtue

is to remind us that the cost of using a resource arises from the value of what it could be used for instead.

This simple concept has powerful implications. It implies, for example, that even when governments subsidize college education, most students still pay more than half of the cost. Take a student who pays $2,000 in tuition at a state college. Assume that the government subsidy to the college amounts to $5,000 per student. It looks as if the cost is $7,000 and the student pays less than half. But looks are deceiving. The true cost is $7,000 plus the income the student forgoes by attending school rather than working. If the student could have earned $15,000 per year, then the true cost of the education is $7,000 plus $15,000. Of this

$22,000 total, the student pays $17,000 ($15,000 plus $2,000).

What about the cost of room and board while attending school? This is not a true cost of attending school at all, because whether or not the student attends school, someone must pay room and board.

—David R. Henderson

Biography: David R. Henderson is the editor of this encyclopedia. He is a senior research fellow with Stanford University's Hoover Institution and an associate professor of economics at the Naval Postgraduate School in Monterey, California. He was formerly a senior economist with the President's Council of Economic Advisers.

Political Behavior

Richard L. Stroup

■ The fact of scarcity, which exists everywhere, guarantees that people will compete for resources. Markets are one way to organize and channel this competition. Politics is another. People use both markets and politics to get resources allocated to the ends they favor. Political activity, however, is startlingly different from voluntary exchange in markets. In a democracy groups can accomplish many things in politics that they could not in the private sector. Some of these are vital to the broader community's welfare, such as control of health-threatening air pollution from myriad sources affecting millions of individuals, or the provision of national defense. Other public-sector actions provide narrow benefits that fall far short of their costs.

In democratic politics, rules typically give a majority coalition power over the entire society. These rules replace the rule of willing consent and voluntary exchange that exists in the marketplace. In politics, people's goals are similar to the goals they have as consumers, producers, and resource suppliers in the private sector, but people participate as voters, politicians, bureaucrats, and lobbyists. In the political system, as in the marketplace, people are sometimes (but not always) selfish. In all cases, they are narrow: how much they know and how much they care about other people's goals are necessarily limited.

A Mother Teresa or an advocate of the homeless, working in the political arena, typically lobbies for a shift of funding to help the poor and the sick. The views of such a person, while admirable, are surely narrow. He or she prefers that the government allocate more resources to meet his or her goals even if it means less for the goals of others who are also lobbying. Similarly, a dedicated professional, such as the director of the National Park Service, however unselfish, pushes strongly for shifting government funds away from other uses and toward expanding and improving the national park system. His priority is to get land and dollars allocated to parks, even if goals espoused by others, such as helping the poor and the sick, necessarily suffer. Those favoring other expenditures—on space exploration, retraining workers, the arts, preventing disease, and defense—feel just as strongly. Passionate demands for funding and for legislative favors (inevitably at the expense of other people's goals) come from every direction.

Political rules determine how these competing demands, which far exceed government's (or even the whole society's) ability to provide, are arbitrated. The rules of the political game are critical. Is the government democratic? Is it a representative democracy? Who can vote? Over what

domain of issues can the government make decisions? How much of the society's output is taken for political allocation? The rules provide answers to these questions, influencing not only who gets what from society's product, but also how big the product itself is and how much of it is devoted to influencing the game.

Why do individuals and groups often seek their aims in the political sector rather than in markets? There are several reasons:

- Political solutions can compel people, on threat of prison, to support politically chosen community goals. This solves the financial "free rider" problem caused by the fact that even citizens who don't voluntarily pay for national defense or for, say, a sculpture in the town square can benefit from the expenditures of those who do.
- Political action can allow one group to benefit at the expense of others. This does not happen in a free market, where those who pay are the ones who benefit. (Of course, political victories may themselves be costly.)
- Imperfections in the legal protection of one's rights—such as one's right to be safe from harmful air pollutants, or even one's civil rights—can be addressed politically. Some aspects of the political process, however, work against those who pursue their goals via the political route:
  –One Congress or legislature cannot bind the next, so a political solution—other than the grant or sale of private rights— lasts only as long as the political muscle of those who push it. Any political program, land allocation, or treaty can be

reversed as political pressures change. In other words, a political solution cannot be purchased—only rented. A political act is inherently less secure than a private purchase or trust arrangement.

–Truly innovative activity is often difficult to sell to the majority of the political group, such as the Congress or a specific committee, that must agree to the proposed action. In the free market, on the other hand, innovations typically are funded when only a few entrepreneurs and capitalists believe in them.

For the ordinary citizens who are not politically active, political activity has very different consequences from market activity. Although such citizens benefit from some political action achieved by active groups, they are bound by (and must pay for) all political actions. They are outside the political process except when they vote and when they have concentrated, or special, interests. Dairy farmers, for example, typically know nothing about the costs to them of the space program. However, they are keenly informed about the federal milk program, which restricts milk production and keeps milk prices high.

Small groups whose members inordinately benefit or suffer from proposed legislation are often quite powerful politically. Consider the case of wool and mohair growers in the United States. During World War II military planners found that U.S. wool producers could supply only half the wool wanted by the military. Partly for this reason, and partly to give added income to wool growers, Congress passed the National Wool Act in 1954. Mohair, produced by Angora goats, had no military use but

was included as an offshoot of the wool industry. Although wool was removed from the military's list of strategic materials in 1960, the program survives and continues to grow.

Under the Wool Act, growers are given subsidy checks to supplement what they receive in the market for their wool. In 1990 the wool subsidy rate was 127 percent. The farmer who got $1,000 for selling wool in the market also got a $1,270 check from the government. Selling twice as much would have brought a check for $2,540 from the government. The subsidy rate for mohair was a much larger 387 percent. The subsidies are paid for by tariffs on imported wool. The tariffs cause consumers to pay more for imported wool, and also drive up the market price they pay for domestic wool, which is a close substitute. The economy operates less efficiently, since less wool is imported even though the imported wool costs less. The subsidy program, together with the higher price caused by the wool tariff, means that domestic land, labor, and capital resources are applied to the production of wool and mohair instead of more highly valued goods.

Nevertheless, Congress continues to support the program. Thousands of very small checks are sent to small growers in every state. Almost half of the 1990 payments were less than $100. Many of those who receive them are willing to write letters and to vote for those who support the program. Nearly half of the money, though, goes to the 1 percent of the growers who are the largest producers. The largest checks—nearly three hundred of them—averaged $98,000 and accounted for 27 percent of the program's 1990 cost. Recipients of these large checks can be counted on to contribute to organizing costs, and to give campaign donations to members of congressional committees critical to the continuation of the subsidy program. By contrast, because American taxpayers pay only a few dollars per family (Wool Act subsidies were $104 million in 1990), most are unaware of the program and of how their elected representatives voted on it. Even though taxpayers are numerous, and the Wool Act costs them a lot, each taxpayer loses so little that they do not become organized or knowledgeable on the topic. Thus the Wool Act, which harms the interests of the great majority of voters, has survived.

Although such special interest groups are sometimes in line with more general citizen interests, there is little to confine them to general interests. For example, the general public wants national defense, and weapons contractors have an interest in providing the means to obtain defense. But the contractors and the government's military itself will push for far more elaborate means of defense than would a knowledgeable citizen with broader interests.

So although political activity has benefits as well as costs, political behavior causes some predictable problems for citizens in general:

- One-to-a-citizen ballot votes, which are the currency of the formal democratic marketplace, do not allow voters to show the intensity of their preferences, as dollar votes do when citizens focus their budgets—some spending more on housing, others on entertainment, education, or their favorite charity.

- The voter is purchasing a large bundle of policies and cannot pick and choose. In a representative government the voters select a single candidate—the "bundle"—to represent them on many different issues. Voters cannot vote for the position of one candidate on issue A, the position of another on issue B, and so on, as they do routinely when shopping for thousands of items in the marketplace. In a representative democracy fine-tuning one's expression at the ballot box is impossible.

- An individual voter has virtually no chance of casting the decisive vote in an election. Even among the more than four thousand elections held each decade to fill the U.S. House of Representatives, a race decided by less than one hundred votes is newsworthy at the national level, and a recount is normally conducted. Moreover, the cost of an uninformed or mistaken vote that did make a difference would be spread among other citizens. This differs from the cost of a mistaken purchase, the full burden of which the buyer pays. People, thus, have little incentive to spend scarce time and effort learning about election issues, monitoring politicians, or even voting; instead, they tend to be "rationally ignorant" on most issues. Thus, it makes sense for a politician to pay attention primarily to special interests on most issues, and to use the financial support of special interests to campaign on "image" issues at election time.

- Because politicians do not sell their interests to their successors (the way the owners of companies, farms, and houses do), they have an incentive to provide current benefits while delaying costs into the future whenever possible. They have less incentive to invest today for the benefit of the future. Future voters cannot affect elections now but will simply inherit what current voters leave to them—both debts and assets. In contrast, private assets can either be sold or given by bequest. Only charitable instincts among voter-taxpayers (and perhaps the lobbying of special interest groups such as weapons system suppliers, or owners of real estate that may go up in value) will push for a costly project with benefits mainly in the future. Charitable instincts toward the future are present in the private sector, too (especially in private charities), and in the market they are reinforced by the fact that future productivity and profits are reflected in today's asset prices, including the stock price of a corporation.

Political activity is often seen as a way to solve problems not handled well by the private sector—everything from pollution problems and national defense to the redistribution of income to the poor. Clearly, private sector results in each of these areas are unsatisfactory to many, and there are massive, growing political programs aimed at each of these goals. But the problems just described reduce the ability of the political system to reach the sought-after goals.

A growing portion of government expenditures is simply to transfer income from the politically disadvantaged to the politically advantaged. In fact, since the early fifties all of the growth in federal spending, as a percentage of GNP, has been in transfer programs. Federal spending for goods and services as a percentage of GNP has been constant. However, only one of every six dollars transferred is in programs that are targeted to low-income people. The rest, such as the very large funding for Social Security and for farm subsidies, goes to members of groups that are politically better organized than most.

Pollution control programs, from the Clean Air and Clean Water acts to the Superfund program, have received great political support. The cost to the economy of environmental programs is generally agreed to be about $100 billion per year. Yet political manipulation of each program is widely recognized to have led to large imperfections in handling these problems. A classic case has been the political uses of the 1977 amendments to the Clean Air Act. Careful policy analysis by Bruce Ackerman and William Hassler has shown that by requiring the use of expensive scrubbers on coal-fired power plants, the amendments effectively protected eastern coal interests while harming both the health and the pocketbooks of millions of Americans. Robert Crandall of Brookings has shown that the same amendments were used by eastern and midwestern manufacturing interests to stifle competition from new Sunbelt factories.

Bureaucratic performance is also a serious concern. Bureaucracies often can achieve their ends with a "can't do" stance in place of the "can do" attitude that is needed for market success. A perennial case in point is the "Washington Monument strategy" of the National Park Service. At budget time the service frequently threatens to curtail visiting hours at its most popular attraction, the Washington Monument, if its budget request isn't met, and it threatens to blame Congress and the budget process when tourists complain.

It is hard to imagine a private firm, facing hard budget times, curtailing its most popular product or service. The private firm would lose too much business to the competition. But politically controlled agencies are different: they typically are monopolies. One result is that perverse behavior, such as cutting the most valued services first, is a time-honored way to expand a budget.

Political behavior in a democracy has both prospects and problems that differ from those of private, voluntary activity. Political action can force all citizens to comply with decisions made by their elected representatives. Because these political decisions are intended to be for the benefit of all, the support of all is commanded. But because each citizen's ballot is not decisive, voter monitoring of both the intent and the efficiency of political action is not very effective. Voter turnout is often low, and voters, though quite intelligent, are notoriously uninformed. Americans of voting age cannot, on average, even name their congressional representative. Such results are not as strange as they may sound when the impact of political rules on individual incentives is examined.

—Richard L. Stroup

Biography: Richard L. Stroup is an economics professor at Montana State University and senior associate at the Political Economy Research Center, both in Bozeman, Montana. From 1982 to 1984 he was director of the Office of Policy Analysis, U.S. Department of the Interior.

Further Reading

Ackerman, Bruce A., and William T. Hassler. *Clean Coal/Dirty Air or How the Clean Air Act Became a Multibillion Bail-Out for the High-Sulfur Coal Producers and What Should Be Done About It*. 1981.
Buchanan, James, and Gordon Tullock. *The Calculus of Consent*. 1962.
Crandall, Robert W. "Economic Rents as a Barrier to Deregulation." *The Cato Journal* 6, no. 1 (Spring/Summer 1986): 186–89.
Downs, Anthony. *An Economic Theory of Democracy*. 1957.
Gwartney, James, and Richard L. Stroup. *Economics: Private and Public Choice*, 6th ed. Chaps. 4, 30. 1992.
Mark Zupan. "An Economic Explanation for the Existence and Nature of Political Ticket Splitting." *Journal of Law and Economics* 34, issue 2, part I (October 1991): 343–69.

See also PUBLIC CHOICE THEORY, REDISTRIBUTION OF INCOME.

Population

Ronald Demos Lee

■ The world's population has doubled since 1950, from 2.515 billion people then to 5.292 billion in 1990. Of the 2.777 billion increase, only 13.4 percent was in developed countries, with 86.6 percent in less developed countries (LDCs). The main reasons for this growth were fertility and age distribution in developed countries and both higher life expectancies and high birthrates in less developed countries. Life expectancy in developed countries has risen from 65.7 years in 1950 to 1954, to 74.0 years today. For LDCs, life expectancy rose from only 41.0 years in 1950 to 1954, to 62.0 years today. Over that same time the number of births per woman fell from 2.84 to 1.9 in developed countries. In LDCs the rate is down from 6.18 births per woman to 3.9. But birthrates in LDCs are still high enough to contribute substantially to population growth.

Population Aging

Lower birthrates and longer life lead to "population aging" (i.e., more elderly people and fewer children). Population aging is most rapid, and has gone farthest, in the developed world. The median age in developed countries has risen from 28.2 in 1950 to 33.8. In LDCs, by contrast, the median age is only 21.9. Of course, individual countries vary. The median age in Sweden is 39, whereas in Kenya it is just 14. In Kenya there are only six people age 65 and over per hundred working-age persons (age 15 to 64), while in Sweden there are twenty-eight, or almost five times as many. The United States is typical of developed countries in having a median age of 33.

Population aging matters for many reasons, but first and foremost because of the costs of retirement (pensions and health care). In the developed countries these costs are borne principally by the central government and funded through taxes on the working-age population. In the United States in 1940, there were eleven elderly per hundred working-age people. Today there are twenty. Projections indicate that by the middle of the next century, there will be more than forty elderly per hundred working-age people, and under "pessimistic" scenarios there may be fifty. Other things being equal, the tax rate for pensions will be proportional to this ratio. Therefore, unless benefits are cut, the tax rate for pensions and health care will double in forty years, even if costs of health care do not continue to rise. Similar or more striking changes are projected for other developed countries.

Those paying for the current retirees do so with the understanding that they, in turn, will collect from the next generation of workers. Population aging generates intense political pressures to modify this implicit social contract by such devices as delaying the age of retirement or reducing the size of the benefit. The fear of population aging is a strong political force in many developed countries, leading to policies to induce people to have larger families. Such policies include banning abortion and contraception, offering prizes and financial incentives for births, and instituting generous paid-leave policies for women who stay home to care for their babies.

To some degree, however, the increased costs of the elderly are offset by declining public and private costs of raising children, since a lower birthrate is actually the prime cause of population aging. In LDCs, for example, there are fifty-nine children per hundred working-age people, while in developed countries there are only thirty-two.

Only a few years ago, concern with aging seemed ridiculous for LDCs, but with falling fertility and lengthening life, it is now taken seriously indeed. In East Asia the elderly dependency burden—the ratio of population aged sixty-five or more to the population aged twenty to sixty-four—is projected to be higher in 2025 than it now is in Europe. Not only is population aging projected for LDCs, but at the same time economic development and urbanization are weakening the traditional family-based support systems for the elderly.

Fluctuations in Generation Size

Fluctuations in generation size also cause problems. When a small generation pays high taxes to support a large retired one, as will soon happen in the United States, issues of fairness arise. Changes in generation size also affect the labor market. When the small U.S. generation born in the depressed thirties reached the labor market in the fifties, its small size relative to the demand for new workers brought it easy employment, high wages, and rapid advancement. But when the baby-boom generation reached the labor market in the seventies, it experienced relatively high unemployment, low wages, and slow promotion. This picture is complicated by immigration, as well as changing patterns of international trade and education. If the future imitates the past, however, the baby-bust generation entering the labor market in the nineties may again do relatively well.

Population and Development

Although population aging and bulging age distributions are real concerns, many people's greater fear is that global population growth will overwhelm the capacity of economies and of the global ecosystem.

This fear of population growth is not new. Thomas Malthus (see MALTHUS in Biographies section) and other classical economists believed that as growing population made land increasingly scarce, rising food prices would eventually choke off further economic and population growth, leading to the "stationary state." For classical economists, natural resource constraints, particularly of land, were at the heart of the problem. But the economic importance of land has dwindled in the modern world. The share of the labor force in agriculture has declined from around 80 percent to around 5 percent in many developed countries, while the share of output generated in agriculture has declined even more with industrialization.

Even within agriculture, land has become

less important as productivity has been boosted by other inputs, including labor, fertilizer, pesticides, insecticides, new seed varieties, irrigation, mechanical or animal draft power, and education. Contrary to the predictions of the classical economists, real food prices have historically fallen somewhat. In the United States, for example, the price of wheat in 1980 (adjusted for increases in the consumer price index) was about one-third below the price around 1800. Also contrary to the classicals' predictions, from 1950 to 1980 the world's per capita food production increased by about 1 percent per year, for a total increase of about 35 percent. The incidence of famines has diminished, not increased, and modern famines often arise from wars or mistaken policies rather than from population growth. Although hunger and malnutrition are serious problems in many parts of the world, they result more from poverty and uneven income distribution than from deficiencies of agricultural production due to population growth.

So the classical economists' emphasis on land as the critical limiting factor was undermined by the ability of technical progress and capital accumulation to expand output from the industrial revolution until the 1970s. Economists came to view natural resource constraints as unimportant. Instead, investment and capital accumulation, and the creation and transfer of technology, were seen as the keys to economic development.

In the forties and fifties economists who studied population had a new concern. They argued that when population grows more rapidly, a greater proportion of current output must be set aside to create capital—housing, tools, machinery, and schools—for new members of the population. All these investments must increase, they noted, at the same time that more children per family tend to reduce domestic savings rates. If the additional investment does not take place, they claimed, then capital will be diluted: new generations will be less well equipped than older ones.

Economists who have used data to simulate the effects of population growth on the capital stock have, however, concluded that "capital dilution" should have relatively small effects: an increase in the population growth rate from 2 percent per year to 3 percent per year, for example, would eventually reduce per capita output by about 7 percent. More important, though, is the problem of providing adequate housing and sanitary infrastructure in the rapidly growing urban areas of Third World countries.

This analysis, with its emphasis on investment and age distribution, was challenged during the sixties and seventies. Empirical studies provided only mixed support for the view that high fertility reduced savings. Second, the role of capital itself in economic growth was questioned. Empirical studies attributed more importance to other factors such as education and technology. For the United States between 1929 and 1969, for example, capital accounted for only 11 percent of the growth in per capita income. Third, two economists, Ester Boserup and Julian Simon, argued forcefully that population growth had many positive economic effects. These included stimulating investment demand, breaking down traditional barriers to the market economy, spurring technological progress, and leading to harder work (the latter because the presence of more dependents in the household raises the marginal utility of income relative to leisure and leads to longer hours of work). They noted also that a larger population can also more easily bear the costs of providing certain kinds of social infrastructure—transportation, communications, water supply, government, research—for which the need increases less than proportionately with population.

By the eighties policymakers were confused. Was population growth good? Was it bad? Did it matter at all? Systematic debate and reassessment in the eighties revealed a surprising degree of agreement among economists. While few economists accepted Julian Simon's view that population growth was actually good for development, the consensus was that population growth mattered less than had been thought. Most economists had failed to appreciate how flexible competitive market economies are. In market economies, when population growth makes resources more scarce, the prices of those resources rise. This leads consumers to reduce their demand for those resources and to find substitutes. The higher prices of resources also give producers an incentive to find new supplies. But more important, technological progress often reduces prices of resources, even in the face of higher demand (see NATURAL RESOURCES).

As Julian Simon has shown, the real prices of most minerals have been falling historically, not rising. The total costs of natural resources as a share of national output have not been rising. The one exception is petroleum prices, but that is due to OPEC, not to rising population. Before OPEC exerted control on the world oil mar-

ket in 1973, the real price of oil had been falling. And even now the world price of oil is less than half the level it reached in 1980. (See OPEC.) In 1980 Simon wagered environmentalist Paul Ehrlich that mineral prices would decline in real terms during the following decade. They agreed on five minerals—copper, chrome, nickel, tin, and tungsten. In 1990 Simon won the well-publicized bet and collected his money. Between 1980 and 1990 the inflation-adjusted prices of all five minerals fell, copper by 18 percent, chrome by 40, nickel by 3, tin by 72, and tungsten by 57.

But while economists were concluding that population growth was relatively unimportant, ecologists and environmentalists like Paul Ehrlich and Garrett Hardin were sounding the population alarm. They pointed out that the biosphere provided essential, although uncounted, inputs to economic activity, and warned that its limits and fragility placed bounds on sustainable levels of production. These bounds, they said, had already been surpassed. The global economy, they thought, was profligately consuming ecological capital, rather than living off the "interest" it yielded.

Like Malthus, the ecologists warned about the impending exhaustion of minerals. Although mineral depletion is probably not the real problem, many of the ecologists' most important warnings appear correct and persuasive. The reason is that many renewable resources—air, water, fisheries, land, forest cover, ozone layer, and species—are not privately owned. Instead, they are held in common. Therefore, as Garrett Hardin pointed out (see TRAGEDY OF THE COMMONS, THE), no person who uses these resources takes account of the damage he or she imposes on others. Individuals and companies, for example, can dump pollution into the air and water without being made to bear the full cost of environmental degradation. The costs are passed on to society as a whole. Consequently, economic incentives encourage overuse. The automatic signaling mechanism of market prices is absent. Therefore, price changes serve neither as an incentive for preservation nor as a signal of increasing scarcity.

Worries about population growth have now come full circle: from the classical concern for limited land, to the emphasis on physical capital, to more recent emphasis on human capital and the ameliorative influence of competitive markets, to beneficial aspects of population growth, and back once again to the natural constraints urged by ecologists. This time, however, the concern is for renewable natural resources, most of which fall outside the market. For some the urgency of population control on ecological grounds is obvious. Others remain skeptical.

As for the more narrowly economic reasons for restraining population growth, decades of research are still inconclusive. For a few countries with very dense populations, like Bangladesh, China, and Egypt, the case is quite clear. For a few others with exceptionally rapid population growth, like Kenya, the case is also clear. But for others the national gains from reducing fertility may be modest.

—Ronald Demos Lee

Biography: Ronald Demos Lee is a professor of demography and economics at the University of California, Berkeley. He is a past president of the Population Association of America and received the Mindel Shepps Award for outstanding research in mathematical demography and demographic methods. He cochaired the National Academy of Sciences working group on population and economic development that produced a widely cited report in 1986.

Further Reading

Ehrlich, Paul, and Ann Ehrlich. *The Population Explosion.* 1990.
Kelley, Allen. "Economic Consequences of Population Change in the Third World." *Journal of Economic Literature* 26 (September 1988), no. 4: 1685–1728.
Menken, Jane, ed. *World Population and U.S. Policy: The Choices Ahead.* 1986.
National Academy of Sciences. *Population Growth and Economic Development: Policy Questions.* 1986.
Simon, Julian. *The Ultimate Resource.* 1981.
World Bank. *World Development Report.* 1984.

See also NATURAL RESOURCES.

Poverty in the United States

Isabel V. Sawhill

■ Poverty is one of America's most persistent and serious problems. The United States produces more per capita than any other industrialized country, and in recent years has devoted more than $500 billion per year, or about 12 percent of its gross national product, to public assistance and social insurance programs like Social Security, Medicare, Aid to Families with Dependent Children (AFDC), food stamps, and Medicaid. Despite our wealth and these efforts to reduce income inequality, poverty is more prevalent in the United States than in most of the rest of the industrialized world. It is also more prevalent now than it was in the early seventies, when the incidence of poverty in America reached a postwar low. According to the most recent Census Bureau figures, 33.6 million Americans were poor in 1990, almost 14 percent of the population.

These official figures represent the number of people whose annual family income is less than an absolute "poverty line" developed by the federal government in the midsixties. The poverty line equals roughly three times the annual cost of a nutritionally adequate diet. It varies by family size and is updated every year to reflect changes in the consumer price index. In 1990 the poverty line for a family of four was $13,359.

Many researchers believe that the official method of measuring poverty is flawed. Some argue that poverty is a state of relative economic deprivation, that it depends not on whether income is lower than some arbitrary level, but whether it falls far below the incomes of others in the same society. But if we define poverty to mean relative economic deprivation, then no matter how wealthy everyone is, there will always be poverty. Others believe the official method is conceptually correct but errs by omission. For example, official poverty figures take no account of the value of noncash government transfers like food stamps and housing vouchers, which serve as income for certain purchases. The Census Bureau estimates that the inclusion of the market value of these benefits in family income would have reduced the measured poverty rate by 1.4 percentage points (or by approximately 10 percent) in 1990.

The official definition also ignores the value of assets like owner-occupied housing and consumer durables that do not generate money income but increase household resources nonetheless. According to one study based on data from the early eighties, 31 percent of the poor owned their own homes and 48 percent owned a motor vehicle, and the average net worth of poor families was thirty thousand dollars. The Census Bureau estimates that if the net imputed return on equity in owner-occupied housing were included in income, the poverty rate would have been 1.2 percentage points lower in 1990.

Another problem with the poverty measure arises from the dramatic shift in household composition since World War II. Smaller, more fragmented households are more common today than ever before. This suggests that some poor households were formed voluntarily for the sake of privacy and autonomy for their members. To the extent that some people have willingly sacrificed their access to the economic resources of parents, spouses, or adult children, some of the increase in poverty may actually represent an improvement in well-being. Such inaccuracy is inherent in a poverty measure based solely on a household's money income.

Whatever their flaws, the official figures are widely used as a simple gauge of the trends in poverty. According to the official Census Bureau figures, the poverty rate declined from 22.2 percent in 1960 to 12.8 percent in 1989. Most of this decline occurred in the sixties. By 1969 the poverty rate had fallen to 12.1 percent. It then hovered between 11.1 and 12.6 percent in the seventies, increased to a recent peak of 15.2 percent in 1983, and then decreased to 12.8 percent in 1989. Although the lack of rapid progress in recent years is discouraging, a longer-term perspective leaves a net positive impression. For example, according to one estimate by Christine Ross, Sheldon Danziger, and Eugene Smolensky, more than two-thirds of the population in 1939 was poor by today's standards.

The trend in poverty masks the divergent incidence of poverty among various demographic groups. The poverty rate among the elderly, for example, after declining dramatically from 35.2 percent in 1959 to 12.2 percent in 1990, is now lower than for the rest of the population. The poverty rate among children also declined after 1959, but only through the early seventies. It has swung up sharply since that time, and at 20.6 percent in 1990 remains higher than poverty rates among other age groups. The poverty rate among black households has also declined over the last thirty years, but at 31.9 percent in 1990 remains three times as high as the rate among white households.

The incidence of poverty also is higher among households headed by women. Although the poverty rate among these households declined from 49.4 percent in 1959 to 37.2 percent in 1990, they remain far more likely to be poor than other types of households. This higher incidence of poverty, together with the rising share of households headed by women, has led to what researchers call the "feminization of poverty," with an increasing fraction of the poor in female-headed households. Between 1959 and 1990 this fraction rose from 17.8 percent to 37.5 percent.

The failure of the aggregate poverty rate to decline in the seventies, and its subsequent rise in the eighties, suggest to some that the War on Poverty launched by the federal government in the midsixties failed. Indeed, the incidence of poverty was as high in the late eighties as it was in the late sixties, and the average poverty rate for the eighties was 2 percentage points higher than the average for the seventies. Researchers have suggested a number of plausible explanations for these trends, including changes in the composition of households, slower economic growth, the failure of government training programs to increase the skills of the poor, and the rise of a permanently poor urban underclass. Some also argue that the income transfer policies designed to alleviate poverty have themselves helped perpetuate it. Although all of these factors have likely contributed to the problem, the relative importance of each remains somewhat unclear.

The rapid growth of households headed by women and unrelated individuals, who typically cannot earn as much as married-couple families, has left a larger share of the population in poverty. This demographic trend appears to have put especially strong upward pressure on the poverty rate in the seventies, when the share of female-headed households rose most rapidly. Decennial census data indicate that if demographic characteristics such as the age, race, and gender composition of households had not changed between 1950 and 1980, the poverty rate would have been 3 percentage points lower in 1980 than it actually was.

Trends in economic growth also influence the incidence of poverty. Researchers have found that recessions have a disproportionate impact on the poor because they cause rising unemployment, a reduction in work hours, and the stagnation of family incomes. The link between macroeconomic conditions and the incidence of poverty was clearly visible during the 1982 recession, when the poverty rate rose to 15.2 percent, up from 13.0 percent in 1980. It was likewise with structural unemployment—the unemployment that results not from temporary declines in aggregate demand, but from a long-term mismatch between the skills demanded by employers and those supplied by workers. The rising trend in structural unemployment that started in the sixties appears to have contributed to the persistence of poverty. One study by Rebecca Blank and Alan Blinder finds that each 1-point

increase in the unemployment rate of males aged twenty-five to sixty-four increases poverty by 0.7 percentage point. It should not be terribly surprising, then, that poverty was almost as high in the second half of the eighties, when unemployment averaged 6.2 percent, as it was in the second half of the sixties, when unemployment averaged only 3.8 percent.

Training and compensatory education programs like the Job Corps and Head Start, designed as part of the War on Poverty to increase the skills of the poor, may also have influenced trends in poverty. One study, by Gary Burtless of the Brookings Institution, estimates that the federal government spent $282 billion in 1986 dollars on these programs between 1963 and 1985. Most of these programs have not been carefully evaluated, but of those that have, some have been successful. For example, some education programs like Head Start have had a positive effect on poor children, and some employment and training programs have raised the earnings of adult women but were generally less helpful to adult men.

Some researchers believe that the growth of an urban underclass locked in a cycle of welfare dependency, joblessness, crime, and out-of-wedlock pregnancy has also contributed to the persistence of poverty. Although researchers define the underclass in numerous ways, one common definition is the number of poor who live in inner-city neighborhoods where poverty rates are 40 percent and above. By this definition the underclass grew by 36 percent between 1970 and 1980 to 1.8 million people but is still only about 7 percent of the poor population nationwide. The fact that the underclass is a relatively small group means that its growth cannot explain much of the trend in aggregate poverty.

Finally, some researchers blame the persistence of poverty on income-transfer policies. These are typically divided into two categories: public assistance programs, like AFDC, food stamps, and Medicaid, which were designed to help people who are already poor; and social insurance programs, like Social Security, unemployment insurance, and Medicare, which were designed to prevent poverty when certain events like retirement or layoff threaten a household's well-being. Expenditures on these programs totaled roughly $570 billion in 1988, up 360 percent in real terms since 1965. In 1988, social insurance expenditures accounted for three-quarters of this total, with Social Security alone accounting for nearly 40 percent. Within the social insurance category, some 80 percent of expenditures were in the form of cash. In contrast, of the $137 billion spent on public assistance programs in 1988, less than one-third was paid out in cash. The rest was distributed through in-kind transfer programs like food stamps, housing vouchers, and Medicaid, which can be used only for buying food, housing, and medical care, respectively.

The antipoverty effectiveness of these programs is typically measured by counting the number of people with pretransfer incomes below the poverty line whose incomes are raised above the poverty line by the income transfers. According to government estimates, social insurance and public assistance programs moved over 40 percent of the pretransfer poor above the poverty line in 1989. This implies that the poverty rate is reduced by nearly 9 percentage points by these programs.

Economists realize, however, that by ignoring the incentive effects these programs have on recipients, this method of analysis overstates the success of transfer programs. Some critics of welfare policy argue that means-tested cash-income transfers like AFDC prevent recipients from leaving poverty by reducing their incentives to work and to form stable two-parent families. For example, when a recipient receives an AFDC payment, work becomes less necessary because the payment can be used instead of a regular paycheck to buy necessities like food and housing. In addition, work becomes less attractive because AFDC administrative rules require the reduction of benefits as the recipient's earned income rises. If a woman finds a job paying four dollars an hour but welfare rules require a fifty-cent reduction in her AFDC benefits for each dollar in wages, the woman's effective pay before taxes falls to only two dollars per hour and is even lower after taxes. As a result, she may be less willing to take the job.

Economists have found, however, that these incentive effects do not reduce the work efforts of recipients substantially. Sheldon Danziger, Robert Haveman, and Robert Plotnick estimate that if all income-transfer programs, including Social Security, disability insurance, unemployment insurance, and AFDC, had been eliminated, transfer recipients would have increased their work hours by 4.8 percent during the seventies. Roughly 80 percent of the increase would have been caused by the removal of social insurance programs, and only 20 percent by the removal of means-tested transfers.

Critics of welfare policy argue that because AFDC is more readily available to families headed by women than to married-couple families, it encourages divorce, discourages remarriage, and increases out-of-wedlock childbearing. While their point is well taken, economic research suggests that these effects are small. One study by Mary Jo Bane and David Ellwood concludes that an AFDC benefit increase of a hundred dollars per month (in 1975 dollars) to a family of four (a 38 percent increase over the median state benefit level for that year) would increase the number of female-headed families by 15 percent. The study finds that most of this increase results from the movement of single mothers out of the homes of their parents. There is little or no evidence that welfare encourages out-of-wedlock childbearing or that it has much of an influence on divorce or remarriage rates.

This body of evidence suggests that the persistence of poverty cannot be attributed to income-transfer programs themselves. Although transfer programs surely have not reduced poverty by the full 9 percentage points mentioned earlier, they clearly have reduced poverty significantly. Indeed, one of the greatest success stories is the decline in poverty among the elderly, due in large part to the growth of Social Security and Medicare.

In sum, a variety of factors have influenced the incidence of poverty. Those that have reduced the poverty rate, in rough order of importance, are the growth of cash transfers, the investments in government training and education programs, and the overall growth in the economy since the midsixties. Factors that have increased the poverty rate include, in order of importance, the increase in the unemployment rate, the growth of female-headed families, and (possibly) an increase in dysfunctional behavior associated with the rise of the underclass. All of these factors together have left the incidence of poverty much the same as it was in the late sixties.

—**Isabel V. Sawhill**

Biography: Isabel V. Sawhill is program associate director for human resources, veterans, and labor with the Office of Management and Budget. She previously was a senior fellow at the Urban Institute in Washington, D.C. From 1977 to 1979, she was the director of the National Commission for Employment Policy. This article was prepared with the assistance of Mark Condon.

Further Reading

Blinder, Alan. "The Level and Distribution of Economic Well-Being." In *The American Economy in Transition*, edited by Martin Feldstein. 1980.
Danziger, Sheldon, and Daniel Weinberg. *Fighting Poverty: What Works and What Doesn't.* 1986.
Ellwood, David. *Poor Support: Poverty in the American Family.* 1988.
Haveman, Robert. *Starting Even: An Equal Opportunity Program to Combat the Nation's New Poverty.* 1988.
Sawhill, Isabel V. "Poverty in the U.S.: Why Is It So Persistent?" *Journal of Economic Literature* 26 (September 1988): 1073–1119.

Few Are Poor Forever

For most Americans who experience poverty, poverty is temporary rather than permanent. In the ten years from 1969 to 1978, only 2.6 percent of the population was poor for eight years or more. During that same period 24.4 percent of the population was poor for at least one year.

Why is poverty temporary? For the nonelderly, 38 percent of poverty spells began when the head of the family's earnings dropped. Another 43 percent of poverty spells began when the marriage ended in divorce, when a child was born, or when someone in the family set up an independent household.

The fact that so small a percentage of the population is poor for eight out of ten years means that the number of people who are born into poverty and never escape is very small.

—DRH

Prisoners' Dilemma

Avinash Dixit and Barry Nalebuff

■ The prisoners' dilemma is the best-known game of strategy in social science. It helps us understand what governs the balance between cooperation and competition in business, in politics, and in social settings.

In the traditional version of the game, the police have arrested two suspects and are interrogating them in separate rooms. Each can either confess, thereby implicating the other, or keep silent. No matter what the other suspect does, each can improve his own position by confessing. If the other confesses, then one had better do the same to avoid the especially harsh sentence that awaits a recalcitrant holdout. If the other keeps silent, then one can obtain the favorable treatment accorded a state's witness by confessing. Thus, confession is the dominant strategy (see GAME THEORY) for each. But when both confess, the outcome is worse for both than when both keep silent. The concept of the prisoners' dilemma was developed by Rand Corporation scientists Merrill Flood and Melvin Dresher and was formalized by a Princeton mathematician, Albert W. Tucker.

The prisoners' dilemma has applications to economics and business. Consider two firms, say Coca-Cola and Pepsi, selling similar products. Each must decide on a pricing strategy. They best exploit their joint market power when both charge a high price; each makes a profit of $10 million per month. If one sets a competitive low price, it wins a lot of customers away from the rival. Suppose its profit rises to $12 million, and that of the rival falls to $7 million. If both set low prices, the profit of each is $9 million. Here, the low-price strategy is akin to the prisoner's confession, and the high-price akin to keeping silent. Call the former cheating, and the latter cooperation. Then cheating is each firm's dominant strategy, but the result when both "cheat" is worse for each than that of both cooperating.

Arms races between superpowers or local rival nations offer another important example of the dilemma. Both countries are better off when they cooperate and avoid an arms race. Yet the dominant strategy for each is to arm itself heavily.

On a superficial level the prisoners' dilemma appears to run counter to Adam Smith's idea of the invisible hand. When each person in the game pursues his private interest, he does not promote the collective interest of the group. But often a group's cooperation is not in the interests of society as a whole. Collusion to keep prices high,

for example, is not in society's interest because the cost to consumers from collusion is generally more than the increased profit of the firms. Therefore companies that pursue their own self-interest by cheating on collusive agreements often help the rest of society. Similarly cooperation among prisoners under interrogation makes convictions more difficult for the police to obtain. One must understand the mechanism of cooperation before one can either promote or defeat it in the pursuit of larger policy interests.

Can "prisoners" extricate themselves from the dilemma and sustain cooperation when each has a powerful incentive to cheat? If so, how? The most common path to cooperation arises from repetitions of the game. In the Coke–Pepsi example, one month's cheating gets the cheater an extra $2 million. But a switch from mutual cooperation to mutual cheating loses $1 million. If one month's cheating is followed by two months' retaliation, therefore, the result is a wash for the cheater. Any stronger punishment of a cheater would be a clear deterrent.

This idea needs some comment and elaboration:

1. The cheater's reward comes at once, while the loss from punishment lies in the future. If players heavily discount future payoffs, then the loss may be insufficient to deter cheating. Thus, cooperation is harder to sustain among very impatient players (governments, for example).

2. Punishment won't work unless cheating can be detected and punished. Therefore, companies cooperate more when their actions are more easily detected

(setting prices, for example) and less when actions are less easily detected (deciding on nonprice attributes of goods, such as repair warranties). Punishment is usually easier to arrange in smaller and closed groups. Thus, industries with few firms and less threat of new entry are more likely to be collusive.

3. Punishment can be made automatic by following strategies like "tit for tat," which was popularized by University of Michigan political scientist Robert Axelrod. Here, you cheat if and only if your rival cheated in the previous round. But if rivals' innocent actions can be misinterpreted as cheating, then tit for tat runs the risk of setting off successive rounds of unwarranted retaliation.

4. A fixed, finite number of repetitions is logically inadequate to yield cooperation. Both or all players know that cheating is the dominant strategy in the last play. Given this, the same goes for the second-last play, then the third-last, and so on. But in practice we see some cooperation in the early rounds of a fixed set of repetitions. The reason may be either that players don't know the number of rounds for sure, or that they can exploit the possibility of "irrational niceness" to their mutual advantage.

5. Cooperation can also arise if the group has a large leader, who personally stands to lose a lot from outright competition and therefore exercises restraint, even though he knows that other small players will cheat. Saudi Arabia's role of "swing producer" in the OPEC cartel is an instance of this.

—Avinash Dixit and Barry Nalebuff

Biography: Avinash Dixit is the John J. Sherred Professor of Economics at Princeton University. Barry Nalebuff is a professor of economics and management at Yale University's School of Organization and Management.

Further Reading

Introductory
Axelrod, Robert. *The Evolution of Cooperation*. 1984.
Dixit, Avinash, and Barry Nalebuff. *Thinking Strategically: A Competitive Edge in Business, Politics, and Everyday Life*. 1991.
Rapoport, Anatol, and A. M. Chammah. *Prisoners' Dilemma*. 1965.
Hofstader, Douglas. "Mathamagical Themas." *Scientific American* (May 1983): 16–26.
Advanced
Kreps, David, Robert Wilson, Paul Milgrom, and John Roberts. "Rational Cooperation in the Finitely Repeated Prisoners' Dilemma." *Journal of Economic Theory* 27, no. 2 (August 1982): 245–52.
Milgrom, Paul. "Axelrod's The Evolution of Cooperation." *Rand Journal of Economics* 15, no. 2 (Summer 1984): 305–9.

See also GAME THEORY, OPEC, THE TRAGEDY OF THE COMMONS.

Profits

Lester C. Thurow

■ In a capitalistic society, profits—and losses—hold center stage. Those who organize production efforts (the capitalists) do so to maximize their income (profits). Their search for profits is guided by the famous "invisible hand" of capitalism: the highest profits are to be found in producing the goods and services that potential buyers most want.

Capitalists earn a return on their efforts by providing three productive inputs. First, they are willing to delay their own personal gratification. Instead of consuming all of their resources today, they save some of today's income and invest those savings in activities (plant and equipment) that will yield goods and services in the future. When sold, these future goods and services will yield profits that can then be used to finance consumption or additional investment. Put bluntly, the capitalist provides capital by not consuming. Without capital much less production could occur. As a result some profits are effectively the "wages" paid to those who are willing to delay their own personal gratification.

Second, some profits are a return to those who take risks. Some investments make a profit and return what was invested plus a profit, but others don't. When a savings and loan or an airline goes broke (and there have been a lot of both recently), the investors in those firms lose their wealth and become poorer. Just as underground miners, who are willing to perform a dangerous job, get

paid more than those who work in safer occupations, so investors who are willing to invest in risky ventures earn more than those who invest in less risky ones. On average those who take risks will earn a higher rate of return on their investments than those who invest more conservatively.

Third, some profits are a return to organizational ability, enterprise, and entrepreneurial energy. The entrepreneur, by inventing a new product or process, or by organizing the better delivery of an old product, generates profits. People are willing to pay the entrepreneur because he or she has invented a "better mousetrap."

Economists use the word *interest* to mean the payment for delayed gratification, and use the word *profits* to mean only the earnings that result from risk taking and from entrepreneurship. But in everyday business language the owner's return on his or her capital is also called profits. (In business language the lender's return is called interest, even though most lending also entails some risks.)

Attempts have been made to organize productive societies without the profit motive. Communism is the best recent example. But in the modern world these attempts have failed spectacularly. Although ancient Egypt, Greece, and Rome were successful societies not based on the profit motive as we understand it today, since the industrial revolution began in the late eighteenth century, there have been essentially no successful economies that have not taken advantage of the profit motive.

While most profits flow to the three previously mentioned necessary inputs into the productive process, there are two other sources of profits. One is monopoly. A firm that has managed to establish a monopoly in producing some product or service can set a price higher than would be set in a competitive market and, thus, earn higher than normal returns. (Economists call these extra returns economic rents.) Historically, one can find examples of monopolies that have been able to extract large amounts of income from the average consumer. Some railroads, which were granted exclusive rights-of-way and given huge subsidies by the federal government, were such monopolies in the second half of the nineteenth century.

Although some monopoly profits obviously exist in any economy, they are a very small portion of total profits in any rich society. In rich societies most of our consumption consists of either luxuries or products that have close substitutes. As a result the twentieth-century monopolist has less power to raise prices than the nineteenth-century monopolist. If he does raise prices very much, the consumer simply buys something else. Professional football, for example, is a monopoly. But Americans have lots of ways to get pleasure without watching football. The National Football League, therefore, has some, but not much, power to raise prices above the competitive level.

The second other source of profits is "market imperfections." Suppose firm A sells a product for ten dollars while firm B sells the same product for eight dollars.

Suppose also that many customers do not know that the product can be bought for eight dollars from firm B and, therefore, pay ten dollars to firm A. Firm A gets an extra two dollars in profit. In a "perfect" market, where every consumer was completely informed about prices, this would not happen. But in real economies it often does. We all know of instances where we bought a product at one price only to find later that someone else was selling it for a slightly lower price. Profits from such "imperfections" certainly exist, but here again they are not a large fraction of total profits.

When it comes to actually measuring profits, some difficult accounting issues arise. Suppose one looks at the income earned by capitalists after they have paid all of their suppliers and workers. In 1989 this amounted to $971 billion, or 20 percent of GNP. Some of this flow of income represents a return to capital (profits). Some of it needs to be set aside, however, to replace the plant and equipment that have worn out or become obsolete during the year. It is hard to say exactly how much must be reinvested to maintain the size of the capital stock (what are called "capital consumption allowances") because it is hard to know precisely how fast equipment is wearing out or becoming obsolete. But the Department of Commerce thought that $514 billion needed to be set aside to maintain the capital stock in 1989. This left $457 billion for other purposes.

Many capitalists are small businessmen (technically known as single proprietorships) whose "profits" include their wages. No one knows how to disentangle these two streams of income. In the corporate sector, where this problem does not exist, profits

TABLE 1

Return on Stockholders' Equity

	1989	1988
Pharmaceutical	25.5%	23.6%
Beverages	23.2	22.8
Tobacco	20.1	22.5
Soaps, Cosmetics	18.4	18.5
Metal Products	18.0	12.7
Apparel	17.5	17.5
Forest Products	16.8	19.8
Metals	16.1	18.4
Publishing, Printing	15.6	17.7
Food	14.7	15.7
Electronics	14.1	16.8
Furniture	13.9	15.9
Chemicals	13.2	16.8
Scientific and Photo. Equip.	13.0	12.1
Computers (incl. off. equip.)	12.7	14.7
Aerospace	12.0	11.4
Rubber and Plastics Products	11.4	15.8
Transportation Equipment	10.9	13.4
Mining, Crude-Oil Production	10.6	2.4
Petroleum Refining	10.3	15.3
Industrial and Farm Equip.	9.3	12.7
Textiles	7.7	10.8
Motor Vehicles and Parts	6.9	14.5
Building Materials	4.0	−3.3
The 500 Median	15.0	16.2

SOURCE: *Fortune.*

after subtracting capital consumption allowances amounted to $273 billion, or 9 percent of the GNP produced in the corporate sector. Some of these profits, however, are paid to the government in corporate income taxes. After the payment of taxes, $137 billion, or 5 percent of the corporate GNP, was left as profits. Of this sum capitalists paid themselves $81 billion in dividends and put $56 billion back into their businesses as new investments.

Table 1 provides some information on profits by industry over time. In 1989 the highest profits were earned in pharmaceuticals (25.5 percent), the lowest in building materials (4 percent). Over time, profits rise and fall with the onset of booms and recessions (see table 2). After tax, corporate profits for nonfinancial corporations have ranged from over 9 percent of the GNP pro-

duced by nonfinancial corporations in boom years in the sixties and seventies to less than 5 percent in the recession of the early eighties. No matter what the year, corporate profits as a percent of GNP are far below 45 percent, the level, according to a Gallup poll, that many college graduates believe them to be.

The mideighties saw a steady decline in profits as firms acquired tremendous debt in the merger and takeover wars. They reached a low of 3.4 percent in 1986. Because the owners were effectively withdrawing their own capital from their businesses (substituting debt for equity), they were providing much less of the total capital stock and, therefore, earning less in profits. Profits went down as interest payments to lenders went up.

Capitalism requires profits, and profits

TABLE 2

After-Tax Profits as Percent of GNP for Nonfinancial Corporations

Year	%	Year	%	Year	%
1960	7.4%	1970	5.3%	1980	7.5%
1961	7.0	1971	5.9	1981	6.8
1962	7.6	1972	6.4	1982	4.7
1963	7.9	1973	7.4	1983	5.2
1964	8.8	1974	8.0	1984	5.7
1965	9.7	1975	7.7	1985	4.4
1966	9.5	1976	8.6	1986	3.4
1967	8.5	1977	9.4	1987	4.1
1968	7.9	1978	9.0	1988	4.7
1969	6.7	1979	8.9	1989	4.1

SOURCE: *U.S. Department of Commerce, Survey of Current Business.*

require ownership. Property ownership generates responsibility. A decade ago I wrote an article about communism entitled, "Who Stays Up with the Sick Cow?" Without ownership the answer was too often "No one," and the cow and communism died.

—**Lester C. Thurow**

Biography: Lester C. Thurow is dean of MIT's Sloan School of Management. In 1977 he was on the editorial board of *The New York Times*. From 1983 to 1987 he was a member of the Time Magazine Board of Economists. Shortly after graduating from Harvard, he was a staff member with President Johnson's Council of Economic Advisers.

Further Reading

Knight, Frank. *Risk, Uncertainty, and Profit.* 1921.
Thurow, Lester. "Who Stays Up with the Sick Cow?" *The New York Times Book Review.* September 7, 1986: 9.

Property Rights

Armen A. Alchian

■ One of the most fundamental requirements of a capitalist economic system—and one of the most misunderstood concepts—is a strong system of property rights. For decades social critics in the United States and throughout the Western world have complained that "property" rights too often take precedence over "human" rights, with the result that people are treated unequally and have unequal opportunities. Inequality exists in any society. But the purported conflict between property rights and human rights is a mirage—property rights are human rights.

The definition, allocation, and protection of property rights is one of the most complex and difficult set of issues that any society has to resolve, but it is one that must be resolved in some fashion. For the most part social critics of "property" rights do not want to abolish those rights. Rather, they want to transfer them from private ownership to government ownership. Some transfers to public ownership (or control, which is similar) make an economy more effective. Others make it less effective. The worst outcome by far occurs when property rights really are abolished (see THE TRAGEDY OF THE COMMONS).

A property right is the exclusive authority to determine how a resource is used, whether that resource is owned by government or by individuals. Society approves the uses selected by the holder of the property right with governmental administered force and with social ostracism. If the resource is owned by the government, the agent who determines its use has to operate under a set of rules determined, in the United States, by Congress or by executive agencies it has charged with that role.

Private property rights have two other attributes in addition to determining the use of a resource. One is the exclusive right to the services of the resource. Thus, for example, the owner of an apartment with complete property rights to the apartment has the right to determine whether to rent it out and, if so, which tenant to rent to; to live in it himself; or to use it in any other peaceful way. That is the right to determine the use. If the owner rents out the apartment, he also has the right to all the rental income from the property. That is the right to the services of the resources (the rent).

Finally, a private property right includes the right to delegate, rent, or sell any portion of the rights by exchange or gift at whatever price the owner determines (provided someone is willing to pay that price). If I am not allowed to buy some rights from you and you therefore are not allowed to sell rights to me, private property rights are reduced. Thus, the three basic elements of private property are (1) exclusivity of rights to the choice of use of a resource, (2) exclusivity of rights to the services of a resource, and (3) rights to exchange the resource at mutually agreeable terms.

The U.S. Supreme Court has vacillated

about this third aspect of property rights. But no matter what words the justices use to rationalize recent decisions, the fact is that such limitations as price controls and restrictions on the right to sell at mutually agreeable terms are reductions of private property rights. Many economists (myself included) believe that most such restrictions on property rights are detrimental to society. Here are some of the reasons why.

Under a private property system the market values of property reflect the preferences and demands of the rest of society. No matter who the owner is, the use of the resource is influenced by what the rest of the public thinks is the most valuable use. The reason is that an owner who chooses some other use must forsake that highest-valued use—and the price that others would pay him for the resource or for the use of it. This creates an interesting paradox: although property is called ''private,'' private decisions are based on public, or social, evaluation.

The fundamental purpose of property rights, and their fundamental accomplishment, is that they eliminate destructive competition for control of economic resources. Well-defined and well-protected property rights replace competition by violence with competition by peaceful means.

The extent and degree of private property rights fundamentally affect the ways people compete for control of resources. With more complete private property rights, market exchange values become more influential. The personal status and personal attributes of people competing for a resource matter less because their influence can be offset by adjusting the price. In other words, more complete property rights make discrimination more costly. Consider the case of a black woman who wants to rent an apartment from a white landlord. She is better able to do so when the landlord has the right to set the rent at whatever level he wants. Even if the landlord would prefer a white tenant, the black woman can offset her disadvantage by offering a higher rent. A landlord who takes the white tenant at a lower rent anyway pays for discriminating.

But if the government imposes rent controls that keep the rent below the free-market level, the price that the landlord pays to discriminate falls, possibly to zero. The rent control does not magically reduce the demand for apartments. Instead, it reduces every potential tenant's ability to compete by offering more money. The landlord, now unable to receive the full money price, will discriminate in favor of tenants whose personal characteristics—such as age, sex, ethnicity, and religion—he favors. Now the black woman seeking an apartment cannot offset the disadvantage of her skin color by offering to pay a higher rent.

Competition for apartments is not eliminated by rent controls. What changes is the ''coinage'' of competition. The restriction on private property rights reduces competition based on monetary exchanges for goods and services and increases competition based on personal characteristics. More generally, weakening private property rights increases the role of personal characteristics in inducing sellers to discriminate among competing buyers and buyers to discriminate among sellers.

The two extremes in weakened private property rights are socialism and ''commonly owned'' resources. Under socialism, government agents—those whom the government assigns—exercise control over resources. The rights of these agents to make decisions about the property they control are highly restricted. People who think they can put the resources to more valuable uses cannot do so by purchasing the rights because the rights are not for sale at any price. Because socialist managers do not gain when the values of the resources they manage increase, and do not lose when the values fall, they have little incentive to heed changes in market-revealed values. The uses of resources are therefore more influenced by the personal characteristics and features of the officials who control them. Consider, in this case, the socialist manager of a collective farm. By working every night for one week, he could make 1 million rubles of additional profit for the farm by arranging to transport the farm's wheat to Moscow before it rots. But if neither the manager nor those who work on the farm are entitled to keep even a portion of this additional profit, the manager is more likely than the manager of a capitalist farm to go home early and let the crops rot.

Similarly, common ownership of resources—whether in what was formerly the Soviet Union or in the United States—gives no one a strong incentive to preserve the resource. A fishery that no one owns, for example, will be overfished. The reason is that a fisherman who throws back small fish to wait until they grow is unlikely to get any benefit from his waiting. Instead, some other fisherman will catch the fish. The same holds true for other common resources, whether they be herds of buffalo, oil in the ground, or clean air. All will be overused.

Indeed, a main reason for the spectacular failure of recent economic reforms in the Soviet Union is that resources were shifted from ownership by government to de facto common ownership. How? By making the Soviet government's revenues de facto into a common resource. Harvard economist Jeffrey Sachs, who advised the Soviet government, has pointed out that when Soviet managers of socialist enterprises were allowed to open their own businesses but still were left as managers of the government's businesses, they siphoned out the profits of the government's business into their private corporations. Thousands of managers doing this caused a large budget deficit for the Soviet government. In this case the resource that no manager had an incentive to conserve was the Soviet government's revenues. Similarly, improperly set premiums for U.S. deposit insurance give banks and S&Ls an incentive to make excessively risky loans and to treat the deposit-insurance fund as a "common" resource.

Private property rights to a resource need not be held by a single person. They can be shared, with each person sharing in a specified fraction of the market value while decisions about uses are made in whatever process the sharing group deems desirable. A major example of such shared property rights is the corporation. In a limited-liability corporation, shares are specified and the rights to decide how to use the corporation's resources are delegated to its management. Each shareholder has the unrestrained right to sell his or her share. Limited liability insulates each shareholder's wealth from the liabilities of other shareholders, and thereby facilitates anonymous sale and purchase of shares.

In other types of enterprises, especially

where each member's wealth will become uniquely dependent on each other member's behavior, property rights in the group endeavour are usually salable only if existing members approve of the buyer. This is typical for what are often called joint ventures, "mutuals," and partnerships.

While more complete property rights are preferable to less complete rights, any system of property rights entails considerable complexity and many issues that are difficult to resolve. If I operate a factory that emits smoke, foul smells, or airborne acids over your land, am I using your land without your permission? This is difficult to answer.

The cost of establishing private property rights—so that I could pay you a mutually agreeable price to pollute your air—may be too expensive. Air, underground water, and electromagnetic radiations, for example, are expensive to monitor and control. Therefore, a person does not effectively have enforceable private property rights to the quality and condition of some parcel of air. The inability to cost-effectively monitor and police uses of your resources means "your" property rights over "your" land are not as extensive and strong as they are over some other resources, like furniture, shoes, or automobiles. When private property rights are unavailable or too costly to establish and enforce, substitute means of control are sought. Government authority, expressed by government agents, is one very common such means. Hence the creation of environmental laws.

Depending upon circumstances certain actions may be considered invasions of privacy, trespass, or torts. If I seek refuge and safety for my boat at your dock during a sudden severe storm on a lake, have I invaded "your" property rights, or do your rights not include the right to prevent that use? The complexities and varieties of circumstances render impossible a bright-line definition of a person's set of property rights with respect to resources.

Similarly, the set of resources over which property rights may be held is not well defined and demarcated. Ideas, melodies, and procedures, for example, are almost costless to replicate explicitly (near-zero cost of production) and implicitly (no forsaken other uses of the inputs). As a result, they typically are not protected as private property except for a fixed term of years under a patent or copyright.

Private property rights are not absolute. The rule against the "dead hand" or the rule against perpetuities is an example. I cannot specify how resources that I own will be used in the indefinitely distant future. Under our legal system, I can only specify the use for a limited number of years after my death or the deaths of currently living people. I cannot insulate a resource's use from the influence of market values of all future generations. Society recognizes market prices as measures of the relative desirability of resource uses. Only to the extent that rights are salable are those values most fully revealed.

Accompanying and conflicting with the desire for secure private property rights for one's self is the desire to acquire more wealth by "taking" from others. This is done by military conquest and by forcible reallocation of rights to resources (also known as stealing). But such coercion is antithetical to—rather than characteristic of—a system of private property rights. Forcible reallocation means that the existing rights have not been adequately protected.

Private property rights do not conflict with human rights. They are human rights. Private property rights are the rights of humans to use specified goods and to exchange them. Any restraint on private property rights shifts the balance of power from impersonal attributes toward personal attributes and toward behavior that political authorities approve. That is a fundamental reason for preference of a system of strong private property rights: private property rights protect individual liberty.

—**Armen A. Alchian**

Biography: Armen A. Alchian is an emeritus professor of economics at the University of California, Los Angeles. Most of his major scientific contributions are in the economics of property rights.

Further Reading

Alchian, Armen. "Some Economics of Property Rights." *Il Politico* 30 (1965): 816–29.
———, and Harold Demsetz. "The Property Rights Paradigm." *Journal of Economic History* (1973): 174–83.
Demsetz, Harold. "When Does the Rule of Liability Matter?" *Journal of Legal Studies* 1 (January 1972): 13–28.
Siegan, B. *Economic Liberties and the Constitution.* 1980.
Interview with Jeffrey Sachs. *Omni*, June 1991: 98.

See also PERESTROIKA, SAVINGS AND LOAN CRISIS, THE TRAGEDY OF THE COMMONS, SOCIALISM.

Property Rights for "Sesame Street"

Ever seen two children quarreling over a toy? Such squabbles had been commonplace in Katherine Hussman Klemp's household. But in the *Sesame Street Parent's Guide*, she tells how she created peace in her family of eight children by assigning property rights to toys.

As a young mother, Klemp often brought home games and toys from garage sales. "I rarely matched a particular item with a particular child," she says. "Upon reflection, I could see how the fuzziness of ownership easily led to arguments. If everything belonged to everyone, then each child felt he had a right to use anything."

To solve the problem, Klemp introduced two simple rules: First, never bring anything into the house without assigning clear ownership to one child. The owner has ultimate authority over the use of the property. Second, the owner is not required to share. Before the rules were in place, Klemp recalls, ''I suspected that much of the drama often centered less on who got the item in dispute and more on whom Mom would side with.'' Now, property rights, not parents, settle the arguments.

Instead of teaching selfishness, the introduction of property rights actually promoted sharing. The children were secure in their ownership and knew they could always get their toys back. Adds Klemp, ''[Sharing] raised their self-esteem to see themselves as generous persons.''

Not only do her children value their own property rights, they extend that respect to the property of others. ''Rarely do our children use each other's things without asking first, and they respect a 'No' when they get one. Best of all, when someone who has every right to say 'No' to a request says 'Yes,' the borrower sees the gift for what it is and says 'Thanks' more often than not,'' says Klemp.

—Janet Beales

Public Goods and Externalities

Tyler Cowen

■ Most economic arguments for government intervention are based on the idea that the marketplace cannot provide public goods or handle externalities. Public health and welfare programs, education, roads, research and development, national and domestic security, and a clean environment all have been labeled public goods.

Public goods have two distinct aspects— ''nonexcludability'' and ''nonrivalrous con-

sumption.'' Nonexcludability means that nonpayers cannot be excluded from the benefits of the good or service. If an entrepreneur stages a fireworks show, for example, people can watch the show from their windows or backyards. Because the entrepreneur cannot charge a fee for consumption, the fireworks show may go unproduced, even if demand for the show is strong.

The fireworks example illustrates the

"free-rider" problem. Even if the fireworks show is worth ten dollars to each person, no one will pay ten dollars to the entrepreneur. Each person will seek to "free-ride" by allowing others to pay for the show, and then watch for free from his or her backyard. If the free-rider problem cannot be solved, valuable goods and services, ones that people want and otherwise would be willing to pay for, will remain unproduced.

The second aspect of public goods is what economists call nonrivalrous consumption. Assume the entrepreneur manages to exclude noncontributors from watching the show (perhaps one can see the show only from a private field). A price will be charged for entrance to the field, and people who are unwilling to pay this price will be excluded. If the field is large enough, however, exclusion is inefficient because even nonpayers could watch the show without increasing the show's cost or diminishing anyone else's enjoyment. That is nonrivalrous competition to watch the show.

Externalities occur when one person's actions affect another person's well-being and the relevant costs and benefits are not reflected in market prices. A positive externality arises when my neighbors benefit from my cleaning up my yard. If I cannot charge them for these benefits, I will not clean the yard as often as they would like. (Note that the free-rider problem and positive externalities are two sides of the same coin.) A negative externality arises when one person's actions harm another. When polluting, factory owners may not consider the costs that pollution imposes on others. Policy debates usually focus on free-rider and externalities problems, which are con-

sidered more serious problems than nonrivalrous consumption.

While most people are unaware of it, markets often solve public goods and externalities problems in a variety of ways. Businesses frequently solve free-rider problems by developing means of excluding nonpayers from enjoying the benefits of a good or service. Cable television services, for instance, scramble their transmissions so that nonsubscribers cannot receive broadcasts. Both throughout history and today, private roads have financed themselves by charging tolls to road users. Other supposed public goods, such as protection and fire services, are frequently sold through the private sector on a fee basis.

Public goods can also be provided by being tied to purchases of private goods. Shopping malls, for instance, provide shoppers with a variety of services that are traditionally considered public goods: lighting, protection services, benches, and restrooms, for example. Charging directly for each of these services would be impractical. Therefore, the shopping mall finances the services through receipts from the sale of private goods in the mall. The public and private goods are "tied" together. Private condominiums and retirement communities also are examples of market institutions that tie public goods to private services. Monthly membership dues are used to provide a variety of public services.

Lighthouses are one of the most famous examples that economists give of public goods that cannot be privately provided. Economists have argued that if private lighthouse owners attempted to charge shipowners for lighthouse services, a free-rider problem would result. Yet lighthouses off the coast of nineteenth-century England *were* privately owned. Lighthouse owners realized that they could not charge shipowners for their services. So they didn't try to. Instead, they sold their service to the owners and merchants of the nearby port. Port merchants who did not pay the lighthouse owners to turn on the lights had trouble attracting ships to their port. As it turns out, one of the economics instructors' most commonly used examples of a public good that cannot be privately provided is not a good example at all.

Other public goods problems can be solved by defining individual property rights in the appropriate economic resource. Cleaning up a polluted lake, for instance, involves a free-rider problem if no one owns the lake. The benefits of a clean lake are enjoyed by many people, and no one can be charged for these benefits. Once there is an owner, however, that person can charge higher prices to fishermen, boaters, recreational users, and others who benefit from the lake. Privately owned bodies of water are common in the British Isles, where, not surprisingly, lake owners maintain quality.

Well-defined property rights can solve public goods problems in other environmental areas, such as land use and species preservation. The buffalo neared extinction and the cow did not because cows could be privately owned and husbanded for profit. Today, private property rights in elephants, whales, and other species could solve the tragedy of their near extinction. In Africa, for instance, elephant populations are growing in Zimbabwe, Malawi, Namibia, and Botswana, all of which allow commercial harvesting of elephants. Since 1979 Zimbabwe's elephant population rose from

30,000 to almost 70,000 today, and Botswana's went from 20,000 to 68,000. On the other hand, in countries that ban elephant hunting—Kenya, Tanzania, and Uganda, for example—there is little incentive to breed elephants but great incentive to poach them. In those countries elephants are disappearing. The result is that Kenya has only 16,000 elephants today versus 140,000 when its government banned hunting. Since 1970, Tanzania's elephant herd has shrunk from 250,000 to 61,000; Uganda's from 20,000 to only 1,600.

Property rights are a less effective solution for environmental problems involving the air, however, because rights to the air cannot be defined and enforced easily. It is hard to imagine, for instance, how market mechanisms alone could prevent depletion of the earth's ozone layer. In such cases economists recognize the likely necessity of a regulatory or governmental solution.

Contractual arrangements can sometimes be used to overcome other public goods and externalities problems. If the research and development activities of one firm benefit other firms in the same industry, these firms may pool their resources and agree to a joint project (antitrust regulations permitting). Each firm will pay part of the cost, and the contributing firms will share the benefits. In this context economists say that the externalities are ''internalized.''

Contractual arrangements sometimes fail to solve public goods and externalities problems. The costs of bargaining and striking an agreement may be very high. Some parties to the agreement may seek to hold out for a better deal, and the agreement may collapse. In other cases it is simply too costly to contact and deal with all the potential beneficiaries of an agreement. A factory, for instance, might find it impossible to negotiate directly with each affected citizen to decrease pollution.

The imperfections of market solutions to public goods problems must be weighed against the imperfections of government solutions. Governments rely on bureaucracy and have weak incentives to serve consumers. Therefore, they produce inefficiently. Furthermore, politicians may supply public "goods" in a manner to serve their own interests, rather than the interests of the public; examples of wasteful government spending and pork-barrel projects are legion. Government often creates a problem of "forced riders" by compelling persons to support projects they do not desire. Private solutions to public goods problems, when possible, are usually more efficient than governmental solutions.

—**Tyler Cowen**

Biography: Tyler Cowen is an economics professor at George Mason University.

Further Reading

Benson, Bruce. *The Enterprise of Law*. 1990.
Cowen, Tyler. *The Theory of Market Failure: A Critical Evaluation*. 1988.
Klein, Daniel. "Tie-ins and the Market Provision of Public Goods." *Harvard Journal of Law and Public Policy* 10 (Spring 1987): 451–74.
McCallum, Spencer Heath. *The Art of Community*. 1970.
Rothbard, Murray N. *For a New Liberty*. 1978.
Woolridge, William C. *Uncle Sam. Monopoly Man*. 1970.

See also DEFENSE, POLITICAL BEHAVIOR.

Research and Development

David M. Levy

■ Research and development (R&D) is the creation of knowledge to be used in products or processes. Table 1 gives a summary overview of postwar U.S. R&D activity performed in industry. The first column gives privately financed R&D (PR&D) conducted in industry in billions of 1982 dollars. The second column gives the ratio of PR&D to investment in plant and equipment (P&E). The third column gives the share of federally financed R&D (GR&D) as a fraction of the total R&D in industry. State government and private nonprofit financing of basic scientific research that is part and parcel of teaching in colleges and university is not considered R&D. The only financing of research at universities and colleges that is considered R&D is R&D contracts to those institutions. Total university and college R&D in the sixties was 10 percent of the total R&D conducted in industry; in the eighties it was 13 percent.

Two facts stand out in table 1. First, investment that takes the form of R&D is growing relative to investment in P&E. Investment in P&E is recognized as investment by the official economic measurements; investment in R&D is not so recognized. Second, the role of government R&D is falling in relative terms.

There are several important issues in the economic analysis of R&D:

1. Is private R&D productive?
2. Is government R&D productive?
3. Is special government treatment for private producers of R&D justified?
4. Why is some government R&D so successful, while other government R&D fails?
5. Who benefits from U.S. R&D?

Is Private R&D Productive?

Beginning in the sixties, economists performed empirical tests confirming that investment in private R&D yields a positive return. This findings holds up for studies of R&D in general and in particular industries. Recent findings by Lichtenberg and Siegel reported an estimated rate of return of 35 percent for company-funded R&D. The older literature they surveyed reported an average rate of return of 29 percent. This is evidence of remarkable stability in the estimates of the rate of return to privately funded R&D. When Lichtenberg and Siegel decomposed R&D into basic and applied, they found that the rate of return to basic R&D was 134 percent, compared to the two older findings of 178 percent and 231 percent. When the rate of return, even after falling, is still in triple digits, one suspects underinvestment.

Is Government R&D Productive?

Econometric research almost never finds government R&D productive. Yet technical

TABLE 1

U.S. R&D, Decade Averages

Decade	Private (billions of 1982 $)	PR&D/P&E	Share Government R&D
1950	8.84	0.06	0.49
1960	18.95	0.09	0.54
1970	27.29	0.09	0.37
1980	47.00	0.11	0.32

economists have long known about the remarkably high rate of return to agricultural GR&D. According to Robert Evenson, Paul Waggoner, and Vernon Ruttan, rates of return for government-financed agricultural R&D are consistently around 50 percent per annum. Ordinary people were able to see the efficacy of government-financed computers, electronics, and aviation in the Gulf War.

So why do broader studies find the opposite? One answer is as follows: Profit-maximizing companies use factors of production, whether they be labor, land, or R&D, up to the point where their marginal value equals the marginal cost to the firm. But unlike wages paid to labor, the price that people pay to use government R&D is zero: one need only buy a technical journal to learn R&D results that cost millions to produce. Because companies pay zero for government R&D results, they use them up to the point where the marginal value equals zero. Economists looking for a positive marginal value of government R&D, therefore, fail to find it. But all this means is that companies are using it a lot and that, while the marginal value of government R&D is zero, its total value is high.

There is a lively debate about whether government R&D enhances the supply of private R&D. The majority of economists, perhaps, hold that it does. Why would it? Because increasing the supply of one factor of production generally increases the marginal product of other factors. (More land, for example, makes a farm laborer more productive.) Similarly, more government R&D is likely to make private R&D more productive.

Is R&D Worthy of Special Treatment?

Knowledge epitomizes a public good. If someone produces knowledge, someone else can use it without paying for it. Therefore, the person who produced it will not be able to collect the full value of the knowledge produced. For this reason an unregulated, unsubsidized free market is likely to underproduce knowledge. As a result, most economists favor the creation of temporary monopolies through a patent system, such as the one provided for in the U.S. Constitution. With the prospect of a patent as a reward for innovation, people have more of an incentive to produce knowledge.

Need the government do more? Since some new knowledge is not patentable, perhaps special treatment is justified to encourage the provision of knowledge. The most dramatic case for special treatment is based on a famous argument made by Joseph Schumpeter. Schumpeter maintained that a monopoly—because it is able to garner more of the benefits to the industry from R&D (because a monopoly is the industry)—will have an incentive to invest more heavily in R&D than would a competitive industry. In economic jargon a monopoly can internalize more of the R&D benefits than a competitive industry can. Although Schumpeter himself did not argue for special treatment of R&D on this basis, the argument could be made. This consideration did not save the Bell system from breakup.

A much more modest argument—to give R&D tax credits—has been politically successful. But it is hard to tell whether the tax credit has been economically successful—that is, whether it has spurred private investment in R&D. One reason for not knowing the effect on R&D is that companies can get the tax credit simply by relabeling non-R&D expenditures as R&D. Nonetheless, the remarkably high rates of return to R&D that a wide range of studies report strongly suggests that there is underinvestment in R&D. Unfortunately, these studies do not allow one to suggest how to stimulate more R&D.

Why the Range of Government Experience?

If the experience with government R&D were uniformly wonderful or uniformly di-

sastrous, students of R&D could offer easy guidance. However, the experience has been mixed. As mentioned, agricultural R&D and defense R&D in computers, electronics, and aviation have been remarkable successes. Balancing the accounts, one need only mention the supersonic transport, which was financed by British and French taxpayers, and the synfuels project, financed by U.S. taxpayers. The costs for each of these projects exceeded the benefits by billions of dollars. Yet making a list of winners and losers is somewhat beside the point when one of the winners, the computer, has changed the world.

This list of failures raises a question: if the government can pick winners in defense, why not elsewhere? It is important to note that in aircraft and electronic R&D, the Defense Department was the major customer for many years. This is in the context of a political decision not to match the buildup of the late Warsaw Pact man for man and tank for tank. Rather, the Defense Department was charged with matching the Warsaw Pact with higher-quality equipment. The competing branches of the U.S. armed services could be held politically accountable for their performance. The resulting incentives seem to have made the Defense Department very sensitive to how infant technologies could be developed to serve its clearly delineated mandate. Similarly, agricultural R&D has long enjoyed a politically symbiotic relationship with agricultural interest groups. When government agencies have incentives to be competent, they are competent.

But who monitors R&D done only for the "public good"? The usual answer is no one. Simple public choice theory suggests that government responds to incentives. When the performance of government agencies is monitored carefully, one expects very different results than when no one in particular is supposed to benefit from the R&D expenditures. Thus, there is no reason to believe that the success rate of defense and agricultural R&D could be replicated in other areas.

Who Benefits from U.S. R&D?

One difference between stocks of knowledge and stocks of physical capital is that stocks of knowledge can be shared. If I build a machine, it cannot produce for you unless it stops producing for me. If I learn something, this knowledge can produce for you and for me at the same time. If this is so, then the rest of the world should be a major beneficiary of U.S. R&D. Other countries can rent the knowledge, or even get it for free, without having to create it themselves. This suggests that a program of high-tech economic nationalism is automatically self-defeating. One can, with difficulty, block the export of a machine. But the export of knowledge is much harder to impede.

—**David M. Levy**

Biography: David M. Levy is an economics professor at George Mason University.

Further Reading

Evenson, Robert E., Paul E. Waggoner, and Vernon W. Ruttan. "Economic Benefits from Research: An Example from Agriculture." *Science* 205 (1979): 1101–7.

Flamm, Kenneth. *Targeting the Computer*. 1987.

Levy, David M. "Estimating the Impact of Government R&D." *Economics Letters* 32 (1990): 169–72.

———. "Public Capital and International Labor Productivity." *Economics Letters* 39 (1992): 365–68.

Lichtenberg, Frank R., and Donald Siegel. "The Impact of R&D Investment in Productivity." *Economic Inquiry* 29 (1991): 203–29.

Nelson, Richard R., ed. *Government and Technical Progress*. 1982.

Spatial Economics

Wolfgang Kasper

■ Producers and buyers are spread throughout space, and bridging the distances between them is costly. Indeed, much commercial activity is concerned with "space bridging," and much entrepreneurship is aimed at cutting the costs of transport and communication. The study of how space (distance) affects economic behavior is called "spatial" economics.

Throughout history, space has often been a hindrance to economic growth. But improvements in transport and communications have been among the main driving forces of economic progress, as Australian economist Colin Clark pointed out. In medieval Europe and China three-quarters of the population never traveled farther than five miles from their birthplaces, and before the advent of book printing, most people knew very little about what happened beyond their narrow horizons. Since then technical and organizational progress has continually reduced the costs of transporting goods and "transporting" ideas (communication). Transport and communication have also become user-friendly. Now fax machines, satellite TV, and global computer networks are revolutionizing the world economy yet again.

Businesses locate their plants so as to economize on transport and communication costs (and reduce the risks of transport disruptions) between the locations of their inputs and the locations of their market demand. In the past, firms that depended on heavy inputs, such as steel makers, located near the source of major inputs, such as coal mines. Firms that require intensive and frequent interaction with their customers locate near the demand. Gasoline stations, for example, locate near busy intersections. Transport and communication costs normally give firms a degree of local monopoly. But concern about neighboring competitors entering their market niche tends to keep them from abusing this market power, keeping them in "creative unease" and thus forcing them to control costs and to remain innovative.

Falling transport and communication costs threaten such market niches. Producers are now often able to move away from their sources of supply or the neighborhood of their demand. Many firms have become more "footloose." Thus, we now find steel plants in Japan and Korea, far from the iron and coal mines but near ports, because the low cost of sea transport made it possible to ship coal and iron ore to locations with a favorable investment climate. Similarly, the telecommunications revolution has made many service operations footloose. The airline booking clerk one calls on an 800 number from New York, for example, may work in Omaha, and daily accounting services for a business in Chicago may be done by an office at the end of the fax line in Singapore.

Businesses combine inputs that are mobile in space, such as know-how and capital, with inputs that cannot be moved at all or only at great cost, such as land or unskilled labor. One immobile factor that must not be forgotten is government. Good government can raise the productivity of the other inputs and make certain locations attractive. Bad government—a hostile government or a confusing, complex set of regulations; high taxes; and poor public infrastructures—can lower productivity and induce the flight of mobile production factors.

The nineteenth-century German economist Johann Heinrich von Thünen, the father of spatial economics, laid out a basic principle of spatial economics. Producers who are remote from the market can succeed only if they bear the transport cost to the marketplace. But the mobile production factors have to be paid the same return, wherever they are used. Otherwise they leave. Therefore, pointed out von Thünen, the owners of immobile production factors (like land) must absorb the entire transport-cost disadvantage of remote locations.

This "Thünen principle" can be demonstrated at various levels of spatial analysis:

a. In a city or region, real estate rents drop as one moves from the center of activity. In the center, enterprises use a lot of capital to build high rises, saving on high land costs, and only space-saving offices, not large production plants, are located there. Cheap land on the periphery is devoted to land-intensive uses, such as for storage and dumps. If landowners on the periphery were to raise rents, they would soon be out of business.

b. Within a nation, landowners, workers, and the tax collector can reap high "location rents" if they operate in the central areas of economic activity, like Chicago or Los Angeles. There, mobile factors crowd in, so that intensive use is made of land, labor, and public administration, and high incomes are earned. High rental prices for the immobile inputs determine which goods and services are produced and which production methods are used. If, however, the differentials in land, labor, and tax costs between central regions and more remote locations exceed the transport costs from the remote locations to the central markets, producers migrate. That is how industry has spread out from historic centers like New York and Pittsburgh to new industrial regions.

c. On a global scale, as German economist Herbert Giersch recently pointed out, North America, Western Europe, and Japan are the central locations. World-market prices and product standards are determined there, and the highest incomes are earned. Both mobile and immobile inputs are most productive in these centers. Further away in economic space are the new industrial countries, such as Taiwan, Korea, Malaysia, and Mexico, where the immobile production factors are earning lower returns. And further still, on the periphery of the global economic system, are the underdeveloped countries with very low incomes.

The main production factors that tend

to be internationally immobile are labor and government, although some countries have also attracted high legal and illegal labor migration. Because they are internationally immobile, labor and governments in noncentral countries that want to join in intensive world trade must absorb the transport-cost disadvantages. What matters in this context is "economic distance," which cannot necessarily be equated with geographic distance. Places with efficient transport connections, like Hong Kong or Singapore, are closer economically to Los Angeles than, say, a town in southern Mexico.

Technical, organizational, and social change has reduced global transport and communications costs (see table 1). This is now leading to an unprecedented degree of mobility of human, financial, and physical capital, of entrepreneurship, and of entire firms. The owners of these mobile production factors, who wish to supply world markets, are increasingly "shopping around" the world for the labor and the style of government administration that promise them a high rate of return (and low risks). Thus, more and more companies are becoming "locational innovators."

Internationally, this has led to the phenomenon of globalization, which makes it imperative for the immobile production factors to become internationally competitive. High labor costs, adversarial industrial relations, productivity-inhibiting work practices, a costly legal system, and a high tax burden are conditions that make countries unattractive to globally mobile factors of production. By contrast, low labor-unit costs and efficient administration are market signals with which the new industrial countries (especially in East Asia) have made themselves highly attractive to mobile resources. The influx of mobile Western firms

TABLE 1

The Secular Decline in Transport and Communications Costs
(in constant 1990 dollars)

	1930 ($)	1950 ($)	1990 ($)	% Reduction per Annum 1950–1990
Average cost of freight and port handling (per ton) in international trade	60	34	29	−0.4%
Average air revenue per passenger mile	0.68	0.30	0.11	−2.5%
Cost of a New York–London call (3 min.)	244.65	53.20	3.32	−6.7%

SOURCE: G. Hufbauer, "World Economic Integration: The Long View." International Economic Insights (May/June) (1991): 26.

has raised their productivity, which further enhances the attractiveness of these locations even if hourly wage rates are gradually rising there.

Producers who are losing their locational advantage of being near the central markets can react in one of two ways. They can be defensive by, for example, "Korea-bashing" in order to obtain political patronage, tariff protection, or "voluntary" import restraints. Or they can be proactive and competitive, raising the productivity in the center and specializing on those goods and services that still incur high transport costs and therefore still enjoy a degree of spatial monopoly. The mature high-income economies at the center of the world economic system tend to have the best innovative potential, and they can use this to remain attractive in the era of globalization. They are more likely to succeed if they abandon political and social regulations that impede innovation, such as a legal system that raises the costs of innovation (see LIABILITY). In time, competitive producers in central locations of the global economy will also discover that the competitive new industrial countries will develop high import demand for many specialties produced by the advanced central economies.

Economic theory suggests, and history confirms, that defensive responses are very rarely sustainable over the long term. Indeed, economic openness to trade and factor mobility has been the most powerful antidote to "rent-seeking" (the use of restrictive political influence to secure artificial market niches). In open economies political and bureaucratic power has been channeled in support of mobile producers and to create an investment climate in which footloose production factors can thrive. This explains why modern industrialization took off in Europe, where small, open states were compelled by their citizens to develop institutions of limited government, the rule of law, property rights, and support for commercial competitors, whereas the closed economy of Imperial China stagnated under arbitrary despotism, despite the much more advanced state of Chinese technical know-how. Openness to trade and factor movements (with the help of the transport and communications industries that have made such movements increasingly feasible) have indeed been among the prime movers of economic progress.

—Wolfgang Kasper

Biography: Wolfgang Kasper, an economics professor at the University of New South Wales, Australia, previously served on the staff of the German Council of Economic Advisers, the Kiel Institute of World Economics, the Malaysian Finance Ministry, and the Organization for Economic Cooperation and Development.

Further Reading

Blaug, Mark. *Economic Theory in Retrospect*, 4th ed. Chap. on Thünen. 1985.
Clark, Colin. *Conditions of Economic Progress*, 2d ed. 1957.

Giersch, Herbert. "Labor, Wage and Productivity." In *Openness for Prosperity*. 1993 (forthcoming).

Hoover, E. M. *The Location of Economic Activity*. 1948.

Kasper, Wolfgang. "Competition and Economic Growth: The Lessons from East Asia." In *Money, Trade and Competition*, edited by Herbert Giersch. 1992.

McKenzie, Richard B., and Dwight R. Lee. *Quicksilver Capital*. 1991.

Ohlin B. *Interregional and International Trade*. Rev. ed. 1967.

Supply

Al Ehrbar

■ The most basic laws in economics are those of supply and demand. Indeed, almost every economic event or phenomenon is the product of the interaction of these two laws. The law of supply states that the quantity of a good supplied (that is, the amount that owners or producers offer for sale) rises as the market price rises, and falls as the price falls. Conversely, the law of demand says that the quantity of a good demanded falls as the price rises, and vice versa. (For reasons unknown, economists do not really have a "law" of supply, though they talk and write as though they did.)

One function of markets is to find "equilibrium" prices that balance the supplies of and demands for goods and services. An equilibrium price (also known as a "market-clearing" price) is one at which each producer can sell all he wants to produce and each consumer can buy all he demands.

Naturally, producers always would like to charge higher prices. But even if they have no competitors, they are limited by the law of demand: if producers insist on a higher price, consumers will buy fewer units. The law of supply puts a similar limit on consumers. They always would prefer to pay a lower price than the current one. But if they successfully insist on paying less (say, though price controls), suppliers will produce less and some demand will go unsatisfied.

Economists often talk of supply "curves" and demand "curves." A demand curve traces the quantity of a good that consumers will buy at various prices. As the price rises, the number of units demanded declines. That is because everyone's resources are finite; as the price of one good rises, consumers buy less of that and more of other goods that now are relatively cheaper. Similarly, a supply curve traces the quantity of a good that sellers will produce at various prices. As the price falls, so does the number of units supplied. Equilibrium is the point at which the demand and supply curves intersect—the single price at which the quantity demanded and the quantity supplied are the same.

Markets in which prices can move freely are always in equilibrium or moving toward it. For example, if the market for a good is already in equilibrium and producers raise prices, consumers will buy fewer units than they did in equilibrium, and fewer units than producers have available for sale. In that case producers have two choices. They can reduce price until supply and demand return to the old equilibrium, or they can cut production until supply falls to the lower number of units demanded at the higher price. But they cannot keep the price high and sell as many units as they did before.

Why does supply (the quantity that sellers produce) rise as the price rises and fall as the price falls? The reasons really are quite logical. First, consider the case of a company that makes a consumer product. Acting rationally, the company will buy the cheapest materials (not the lowest quality, but the lowest cost for any given level of quality). As production (supply) increases, the company has to buy progressively more expensive (i.e., less efficient) materials or labor, and its costs increase. It has to charge a higher price to offset its rising unit costs.

Or consider the case of a good whose supply is fixed, such as apartments in a condominium. If prospective buyers suddenly begin offering higher prices for apartments, more owners will be willing to sell and the supply of "available" apartments will rise. But if buyers offer lower prices, some owners will take their apartments off the market and the number of available units drops.

History has witnessed considerable controversy over the prices of goods whose supply is fixed in the short run. Critics of market prices have argued that rising prices for these types of goods serve no economic purpose because they cannot bring forth additional supply, and thus serve merely to enrich the owners of the goods at the expense of the rest of society. This has been the main argument for fixing prices, as the United States did with the price of domestic oil in the seventies and as New York City has fixed apartment rents since World War II.

Economists call the portion of a price that does not influence the amount of a good in existence in the short run an "economic quasi-rent." The vast majority of economists believe that economic rents do serve a useful purpose. Most important, they allocate goods to their highest-valued use. If price is not used to allocate goods among competing claimants, some other device becomes necessary, such as the rationing cards that the United States used to allocate gasoline and other goods during World War II. Economists generally believe that fixing prices will actually reduce both the quantity and quality of the good in question. In addition, economic rents serve as a signal to bring forth additional supplies in the future, and as an incentive for other producers to devise substitutes for the good in question.

—Al Ehrbar

Biography: Al Ehrbar is a journalist who writes about the economy for *The Wall Street Journal*. He formerly was editor of *Corporate Finance* magazine and a senior editor of *Fortune* magazine.

See also AGRICULTURAL PRICE SUPPORTS, MINIMUM WAGES, DEMAND, PRICE CONTROLS, RENT CONTROL.

The Tragedy of the Commons

Garrett Hardin

■ In 1974 the general public got a graphic illustration of the "tragedy of the commons" in satellite photos of the earth. Pictures of northern Africa showed an irregular dark patch, 390 square miles in area. Ground-level investigation revealed a fenced area inside of which there was plenty of grass. Outside, the ground cover had been devastated.

The explanation was simple. The fenced area was private property, subdivided into five portions. Each year the owners moved their animals to a new section. Fallow periods of four years gave the pastures time to recover from the grazing. They did so because the owners had an incentive to take care of their land. But outside the ranch, no one owned the land. It was open to nomads and their herds. Though knowing nothing of Karl Marx, the herdsmen followed his famous advice of 1875: ". . . to each according to his needs." Their needs were

uncontrolled and grew with the increase in the number of animals. But supply was governed by nature, decreasing drastically during the drought of the early seventies. The herds exceeded the natural "carrying capacity" of their environment, soil was compacted and eroded, and "weedy" plants, unfit for cattle consumption, replaced good plants. Many cattle died, and so did humans.

The rational explanation for such ruin was given more than 150 years ago. In 1832 William Forster Lloyd, a political economist at Oxford University, looking at the recurring devastation of common (i.e., not privately owned) pastures in England, asked: "Why are the cattle on a common so puny and stunted? Why is the common itself so bare-worn, and cropped so differently from the adjoining inclosures?"

Lloyd's answer assumed that each human exploiter of the common was guided by self-interest. At the point when the carrying capacity of the commons was fully reached, a herdsman might ask himself, "Should I add another animal to my herd?" Because the herdsman owned his animals, the gain of so doing would come solely to him. But the loss incurred by overloading the pasture would be "commonized" among all the herdsmen. Because the privatized gain would exceed his share of the commonized loss, a self-seeking herdsman would add another animal to his herd. And another. And reasoning in the same way, so would all the other herdsmen. Ultimately, the common property would be ruined.

Even when herdsmen understand the long-run consequences of their actions, they generally are powerless to prevent such damage without some coercive means of controlling the actions of each individual. Idealists may appeal to individuals caught in such a system, asking them to let the long-term effects govern their actions. But each individual must first survive in the short run. If all decision makers were unselfish and idealistic calculators, a distribution governed by the rule "to each according to his needs" might work. But such is not our world. As James Madison said in 1788, "If men were angels, no Government would be necessary." That is, if *all* men were angels. But in a world in which all resources are limited, a single nonangel in the commons spoils the environment for all.

The spoilage process comes in two stages. First, the nonangel gains from his "competitive advantage" (pursuing his own interest at the expense of others) over the angels. Then, as the once noble angels realize that they are losing out, some of

them renounce their angelic behavior. They try to get their share out of the commons before competitors do. In other words, every workable distribution system must meet the challenge of human self-interest. An unmanaged commons in a world of limited material wealth and unlimited desires inevitably ends in ruin. Inevitability justifies the epithet *tragedy*, which I introduced in 1968.

Whenever a distribution system malfunctions, we should be on the lookout for some sort of commons. Fish populations in the oceans have been decimated because people have interpreted the "freedom of the seas" to include an unlimited right to fish them. The fish were, in effect, a commons. In the seventies, nations began to assert their sole right to fish out to two hundred miles from shore (instead of the traditional three miles). But these exclusive rights did not eliminate the problem of the commons. They merely restricted the commons to individual nations. Each nation still has the problem of allocating fishing rights among its own people on a noncommonized basis. If each government allowed ownership of fish within a given area, so that an owner could sue those who encroach on his fish, owners would have an incentive to refrain from overfishing. But governments do not do that. Instead, they often estimate the maximum sustainable yield and then restrict fishing either to a fixed number of days or to a fixed aggregate catch. Both systems result in a vast overinvestment in fishing boats and equipment as individual fishermen compete to catch fish quickly.

Some of the common pastures of old England were protected from ruin by the tradition of stinting, the limitation of each herdsman to a fixed number of animals (not necessarily the same for all). Such cases are spoken of as ''managed commons,'' which is the logical equivalent of socialism. Viewed this way, socialism may be good or bad, depending on the quality of the management. As with all things human, there is no guarantee of permanent excellence. The old Roman warning must be kept constantly in mind: *Quis custodiet ipsos custodes?* ''Who shall watch the watchers themselves?''

Under special circumstances even an unmanaged commons may work well. The principal requirement is that there be no scarcity of goods. Early frontiersmen in the American colonies killed as much game as they wanted without endangering the supply, the multiplication of which kept pace with their needs. But as the human population grew larger, hunting and trapping had to be managed. Thus, the ratio of supply to demand is of critical importance.

The scale of the commons (the number of people using it) also is important, as an examination of Hutterite communities reveals. These devoutly religious people in the northwestern United States live by Marx's formula: ''From each according to his ability, to each according to his needs.'' (They give no credit to Marx, however; similar language can be found several places in the Bible.) At first glance Hutterite colonies appear to be truly unmanaged commons. But appearances are deceiving. The number of people included in the decision unit is crucially important. As the size of a colony approaches 150, individual Hutterites begin to undercontribute from their abilities and overdemand for their needs. The experience of Hutterite communities indicates that below 150 people, the distri-bution system can be managed by shame; above that approximate number, shame loses its effectiveness.

If any group could make a commonistic system work, an earnest religious community like the Hutterites should be able to. But numbers are the nemesis. In Madison's terms nonangelic members then corrupt the angelic. Whenever size alters the properties of a system, engineers speak of a ''scale effect.'' A scale effect, based on human psychology, limits the workability of commonistic systems.

Even when the shortcomings of the commons are understood, areas remain in which reform is difficult. No one owns the earth's atmosphere. Therefore, it is treated as a common dump into which everyone may discharge wastes. Among the unwanted consequences of this behavior are acid rain, the greenhouse effect, and the erosion of the earth's protective ozone layer. Industries and even nations are apt to regard the cleansing of industrial discharges as prohibitively expensive. The oceans are also treated as a common dump. Yet continuing to defend the freedom to pollute will ultimately lead to ruin for all. Nations are just beginning to evolve controls to limit this damage.

The tragedy of the commons also has arisen in the savings and loan crisis. The federal government created this tragedy by forming the Federal Savings and Loan Insurance Corporation. FSLIC relieved S&L depositors of worry about their money by guaranteeing that it would use taxpayers' money to repay them if an S&L went broke. In effect, the government made the taxpayers' money into a commons that S&Ls and their depositors could exploit. S&Ls had the incentive to make overly risky investments, and depositors did not have to care because they did not bear the cost. This, combined with faltering federal surveillance of the S&Ls, led to widespread failures. The losses were "commonized" among the nation's taxpayers, with serious consequences to the federal budget.

Congestion on public roads that don't charge tolls is another example of a government-created tragedy of the commons. If roads were privately owned, owners would charge tolls and people would take the toll into account in deciding whether to use them. Owners of private roads would probably also engage in what is called peak-load pricing, charging higher prices during times of peak demand and lower prices at other times. But because governments own roads that they finance with tax dollars, they normally do not charge tolls. The government makes roads into a commons. The result is congestion.

—**Garrett Hardin**

Biography: Garrett Hardin is professor emeritus of human ecology at the University of California at Santa Barbara.

Further Reading

Berkes, Fikret. *Common Property Resources*. 1989.
Hardin, Garrett. "The Tragedy of the Commons." *Science* 162 (1968): 1243–48.
———. "Living on a Lifeboat." *BioScience* 24 (1974): 561–68.
———. *Filters against Folly*. 1985.
———, and John Baden, eds. *Managing the Commons*. 1977.
Hiatt, Howard H. *America's Health in the Balance*. 1987.
McCay, Bonnie J., and James M. Acheson, eds. *The Question of the Commons*. 1987.
McGoodwin, James R. *Crisis in the World's Fisheries*. 1990.
Ostrom, Elinor. *Governing the Commons*. 1990.

Unintended Consequences

Rob Norton

■ The law of unintended consequences, often cited but rarely defined, is that actions of people—and especially of government—always have effects that are unanticipated or "unintended." Economists and other social scientists have heeded its power for centuries; for just as long, politicians and popular opinion have largely ignored it.

The concept of unintended consequences is one of the building blocks of economics. Adam Smith's "invisible hand," the most famous metaphor in social science, is an example of a positive unintended consequence. Smith maintained that each individual, seeking only his own gain, "is led by an invisible hand to promote an end which was no part of his intention," that end being the public interest. "It is not from the benevolence of the butcher, or the baker, that we expect our dinner," Smith wrote, "but from regard to their own self interest."

Most often, however, the law of unintended consequences illuminates the perverse unanticipated effects of legislation and regulation. In 1692 John Locke, the English philosopher and a forerunner of modern economists, urged the defeat of a parliamentary bill designed to cut the maximum permissible rate of interest from 6 percent to 4 percent. Locke argued that instead of benefiting borrowers, as intended, it would hurt them. People would find ways to circumvent the law, with the costs of circumvention borne by borrowers. To the extent the law was obeyed, Locke concluded, the chief results would be less available credit and a redistribution of income away from "widows, orphans and all those who have their estates in money."

The first and most complete analysis of the concept of unintended consequences was done in 1936 by the American sociologist Robert K. Merton. In an influential article titled "The Unanticipated Consequences of Purposive Social Action," Merton identified five sources of unanticipated consequences. The first two—and the most pervasive—were ignorance and error.

Merton labeled the third source the "imperious immediacy of interest." By that he was referring to instances in which an individual wants the intended consequence of an action so much that he purposefully chooses to ignore any unintended effects. (That type of willful ignorance is very different from true ignorance.) A nation, for example, might ban abortion on moral grounds even though children born as a result of the policy may be unwanted and likely to be more dependent on the state. The unwanted children are an unintended consequence of banning abortions, but not an unforeseen one.

"Basic values" was Merton's fourth example. The Protestant ethic of hard work and asceticism, he wrote, "paradoxically leads to its own decline through the accumulation of wealth and possessions." His final case was the "self-defeating prediction." Here he was referring to the instances when the public prediction of a social development proves false precisely because the prediction changes the course of history. For example, the warnings earlier in this century that population growth would lead to mass starvation helped spur scientific breakthroughs in agricultural productivity that have since made it unlikely that the gloomy prophecy will come true. Merton later developed the flip side of this idea, coining the phrase "the self-fulfilling prophecy." In a footnote to the 1936 article, he vowed to write a book devoted to the history and analysis of unanticipated consequences. By 1991, Merton, age eighty, had produced six hundred pages of manuscript but still not completed the work.

The law of unintended consequences provides the basis for many criticisms of government programs. As the critics see it, unintended consequences can add so much to the costs of some programs that they make the programs unwise even if they achieve their stated goals. For instance, the United States has imposed quotas on imports of steel in order to protect steel companies and steelworkers from lower-priced competition. The quotas do help steel companies. But they also make less of the cheap steel available to U.S. automakers. As a result the automakers have to pay more for steel than their foreign competitors do. So a policy that protects one industry from foreign competition makes it harder for another industry to compete with imports.

Similarly, Social Security has helped alleviate poverty among senior citizens. Many economists argue, however, that it has carried a cost that goes beyond the payroll taxes levied on workers and employers. Martin Feldstein and others maintain that today's workers save less for their old age because they know they will receive Social Security checks when they retire. If Feldstein and the others are correct, it means that less savings are available, less investment takes place, and the economy—and wages—grow more slowly than they would without Social Security.

The law of unintended consequences is at work always and everywhere. In 1968, for instance, Vermont outlawed roadside billboards and large signs in order to protect the state's pastoral vistas. One unintended consequence was the appearance of large, bizarre "sculptures" adjacent to businesses. An auto dealer commissioned a twelve-foot, sixteen-ton gorilla, clutching a real Volkswagen Beetle. A carpet store is marked by a nineteen-foot genie holding aloft a rolled carpet as he emerges from a smoking teapot. Other sculptures include a horse, a rooster, and a squirrel in red suspenders.

In the wake of the Exxon Valdez oil spill in 1989, many coastal states enacted laws placing unlimited liability on tanker operators. As a result the Royal Dutch/Shell group, one of the world's biggest oil companies, began hiring independent ships to deliver oil to the United States instead of using its own forty-six-tanker fleet. Oil specialists fretted that other reputable shippers would flee as well, rather than face such unquantifiable risk, leaving the field to fly-by-night tanker operators with leaky ships and iffy insurance. Thus, the probability of spills will increase and the likelihood of collecting damages will decrease as a consequence of the new laws.

—Rob Norton

Biography: Rob Norton is an associate editor of *Fortune* magazine.

Further Reading

Hayek, Friedrich A. *New Studies in Philosophy, Politics, Economics and the History of Ideas.* 1978.
Merton, Robert K. *Sociological Ambivalence and Other Essays.* 1979.

CHAPTER TWO

ECONOMIC SYSTEMS AND SCHOOLS OF ECONOMIC THOUGHT

Apartheid

Thomas W. Hazlett

■ The apartheid system of South Africa presents one of the most fascinating instances of interest group competition for political advantage. In light of the extreme human rights abuses stemming from apartheid, it is remarkable that so little attention has been paid to the economic foundations of that torturous social structure. The conventional view is that apartheid was devised by affluent whites to suppress poor blacks. In fact, the system sprang from class warfare and was largely the creation of white workers struggling against both the black majority and white capitalists. Apartheid was born in the political victory of radical white trade unions over both their rivals. In short, this cruelly oppressive economic system is socialism with a racist face.

The Roots of Conflict

When the British arrived in South Africa in 1796, they quickly conquered the Dutch settlement that had been established in 1652, setting up a government under the English Parliament and British common law. This liberal, individualistic regime was inherently offensive to the Afrikaners—the Dutch settlers of South Africa—who enjoyed both slavery (generally of imported Chinese and Malays) and a system of law that granted no standing to the nonwhite. The Boers, as the Afrikaners were to call themselves, abhorred the intervention of the British, whom they considered agents of an imperialist power. Following Britain's abolition of South African slavery in 1834, the Afrikaners physically escaped the rule of the British crown in the Great Trek of 1835.

Moving north from Capetown and spilling the blood of several major tribes, including the fierce Zulus, the Boers founded the Transvaal and the Orange Free State (i.e., free of British domination), and proceeded to establish racist legal institutions. The Boers treated brutally, and denied rights to, the relatively few nonwhites who resided and worked in their agricultural economy.

The Capetown of nineteenth-century British rule was markedly different. That area experienced some of the most unconstrained racial mixing in the world. A large nonwhite population, the Cape Coloureds, participated in integrated schools, churches, businesses, and government institutions. And they voted. A color-blind franchise was explicitly adopted in 1854. As a port city, Capetown became internationally famous for its laissez-faire social scene (including miscegenation), rivaling New Orleans as a haven for sea-weary sailors.

The physical separation of the two European populations, as well as the small degree of interaction between the Afrikaners and the African tribes, allowed a brief and uneasy equilibrium in the midnineteenth century. It was not to last. When gold was discovered near the Rand River in the Transvaal in 1871 (diamonds had been found beginning in 1866), the world's richest deposits exerted a powerful magnetic force upon the tribes within the subcontinent: Afrikaners, British, Xhosi, Sotho, and Zulu were all drawn to the profitable opportunities opening in the Witwatersrand basin.

Synergy and Competition: The Dynamics of the Colour Bar

The South African gold rush made the natural synergy between white-owned capital and abundant black labor overpowering. The gains from cooperation between eager British investors and thousands of African workers were sufficient to bridge gaping differences in language, customs, and geography. At first, however, the white capitalist could deal directly only with the limited number of English and Afrikaner managers and foremen who shared his tongue and work habits. But the premium such workers commanded soon became an extravagance. Black workers were becoming capable of performing industrial leadership roles in far greater numbers and at far less cost. Driven by the profit motive, the substitution of black for white in skilled and semiskilled mining jobs rose high on the agenda of the mining companies.

White workers feared the large supply of African labor as the low-priced competition that it was. Hence, white tradesmen and government officials, including police, regularly harassed African workers to discourage them from traveling to the mines and competing for permanent positions. Begin-

ning in the 1890s, the Chamber of Mines, a group of employers, complained regularly of this systematic discrimination and attempted to secure better treatment of black workers. Their gesture was not altruistic, nor founded on liberal beliefs. Indeed, the mine owners often resorted to racist measures themselves. But here they had a clear economic incentive: labor costs were minimized where rules were color-blind. This self-interest was so powerful that it led the chamber to finance the first lawsuits and political campaigns against segregationist legislation.

Nonetheless, the state instituted an array of legal impediments to the promotion of black workers. The notorious Pass Laws sought to sharply limit the supply of nonwhite workers in "white" employment centers. Blacks were not allowed to become lawful citizens, to live permanently near their work, or to travel without government passports. This last restriction created a catch-22. Since passports were issued only to those already possessing jobs, how was a nonwhite to get into the job area to procure a job so as to obtain a passport? Nonwhites also were prohibited from bringing their families while working in the mines (reinforcing the transient nature of employment).

Each restriction undercut the ability of blacks to fully establish themselves in the capitalist economy and, hence, to compete with white workers on equal terms. Confined to temporary status, blacks were robbed of any realistic chance of building up the human capital to challenge their white bosses directly in the labor market.

Yet even on this decidedly unlevel playing field, the profit motive often found ways of matching white capitalists with black workers. Whites formed labor unions in the early 1900s to guard against this persistent tendency, and the South African Labour Party (SALP) was formed in 1908 to explicitly advance the interests of European workers. The SALP, and the unions with which it allied, including the powerful Mine Workers' Union, were all white and avowedly socialist; the British Labour Party formed the model for the SALP.

These organizations opposed any degradation of "European" or "civilized" standards in the workplace, by which they meant the advancement of blacks willing to undercut white union pay scales. To discourage mine owners from substituting cheaper African labor for more expensive European labor, the trade unions regularly resorted to violence and the strike threat. They also turned to legislation: the Mines and Works Act of 1911 (commonly referred to as the First Colour Bar Act) used the premise of "worker safety" to institute a licensing scheme for labor. A government board was set up to certify individuals for work in "hazardous" occupations. The effect was to decertify non-Europeans, who were deemed "unqualified."

The legislative victory by the white unions froze African advances until the booming World War I demand for minerals raised employment and pay scales for all races. White workers did not object to black advancement per se, but only to that which they perceived to come at their expense.

The postwar recession and the plummeting price of gold ended such tranquillity. In December 1921 the Chamber of Mines announced a plan to fire two thousand highly paid whites in semiskilled occu-

pations and replace them with Africans. Even before the planned substitution took effect, the Mine Workers' Union launched a massive strike, seizing the mines and occupying the entire Rand mining region for two months.

In a full-scale assault involving seven thousand government troops complete with tanks, artillery, and air support, the government reclaimed the Rand at a reported cost of 250 lives. Several leaders of the strike were hanged. The insurrection was sensational, as was the haunting slogan of the striking miners: "Workers of the world unite, and fight for a white South Africa." The miners saw not an ounce of irony in their "V. I. Lenin meets Lester Maddox" radicalism. They saw ever so clearly that the threat to their interests lay in the mutual interests of white capital and black labor.

Although white workers shared skin color with the capitalists, the goal of mining and manufacturing capital was to hire cheap. As Africans assimilated into Western culture and the work force, the abundance of managerial, skilled, and semi-skilled talent would mushroom. The precariously privileged position of white labor would topple. These were not casual racists; they were economically vested up to their eyeballs in the policy of exclusion by skin color. Hence, the landmark election of 1924 tossed out the Smuts government—condemned by the strikers as a tool of big business—in a "white backlash" over suppression of the Rand Rebellion by Pretoria.

The Pact Government, composed of Afrikaner nationalists (in the National Party) and white unionists (SALP), set an agenda of pro forma socialism, which it dubbed the Civilized Labour Policy. Measures enacted in Western democracies as standard, off-the-shelf trade union legislation were adopted in South Africa, but with a racist twist. After the courts threw out the first Colour Bar Act in 1923, on a lawsuit by the Chamber of Mines, the Mines and Works Act of 1926 reestablished the Colour Bar. Like the earlier act, the new one used the pretext of "industrial safety" to keep blacks from moving into favorable job classifications. Despite the legalistic cover story, the government admitted its intent: to "counteract the force of economic advantages at present enjoyed by the native."

Similarly, the Industrial Conciliation Act of 1924, for the ostensible purpose of securing labor peace, authorized sector-by-sector labor-union wage setting. The following year, the Wage Act extended this to the nonunionized sector. These rules amounted to syndicalism with a racial vengeance.

The ebb and flow of the power of white trade unions to dictate terms to their bosses is graphically visible in the ethnic employment statistics. From 1910 to 1918 the ratio of blacks to whites employed in the mines ranged from 8 or 9 to 1. This was pushed down to 7.4 to 1 in the 1918 "status quo" agreement sought by the unions. After the Chamber of Mines suppressed the Rand Rebellion in 1922, it managed to up the ratio to 11.4 to 1. By 1929, however, the National-Labour government, with its "civilized labour policy," had cut it back to 8.8 to 1. In 1953—the heyday of apartheid—the ratio was further constrained to 6.4 to 1, an incredible regulatory "achievement" considering that the natural (unregulated) advance of Africans would surely have pushed the ratio progressively higher over the passing decades.

Black trade unions were not illegal per se, but no black union was registered by the Ministry of Manpower until legislation explicitly promoting African unions was enacted in the late 1970s. Thus white workers were empowered—under the guise of the Industrial Conciliation Acts of 1924, 1936, and 1956—to solely control the terms of employment via officially sanctioned union bargaining. The enormous range of state-backed union powers—setting wages, employment conditions, benefits, entry qualifications, work rules, and negotiation rights on behalf of the entire industrial economy—is staggering. But this was the level of state intervention required to supersede the profit motives of both firms and nonwhite workers. And that was the announced goal: to overrule the market forces that constantly sought to undermine "civilized standards for European workers."

The labor market rules that were intended to raise barriers against black workers ironically blocked the path for what were commonly called "poor whites," the lowest tier of the protected class. Hence, the final intervention of the "civilized labour policy" was nationalization of businesses that employed large numbers of nonwhites. In a policy of "affirmative action," state-run railways and other huge state enterprises preferentially hired and promoted less skilled whites. In fact, many industries were nationalized just to impose racial preference. Merle Lipton reports that the perverse tendency toward the employment of (more expensive) whites was evident after the proclamation of the 1924 "civilized labour policy." Between 1924 and 1933 the number of whites employed by South African Railways rose from 4,760 to 17,783, or from 10 to 39 percent of employees, while the number of blacks fell from 37,564 to 22,008, or from 75 to 49 percent. In central and local government employment the proportion of whites rose from 45 to 64 percent, while the number and percentage of blacks correspondingly fell.

From the Colour Bar to Apartheid

The Colour Bar brought labor calm because the black workers and white capitalists "taxed" by the deal lacked the requisite political muscle to disrupt the system. Moreover, a long period of South African prosperity began in the midthirties, fed by international demands for the country's mineral exports. Demand during World War II was particularly strong and led again to a large expansion of the mining and industrial sectors. This lured many thousands of new African workers into the wage economy. During the boom these new workers were not substituting for white managers; indeed, the massive influx of black industrial labor prevented severe bottlenecks that would have lowered even white working-class incomes.

But mirroring the experience of a generation earlier, the postwar contraction brought an end to the comparative tranquillity. By 1948 the first signs of white unemployment sent a shock wave through the (white) electorate, and tremors that "poor whites" would be passed up by upwardly mobile black workers excited a radical response: the National Party was elected to implement apartheid, a newly comprehensive social policy of "separate development."

The problem apartheid attacked was circular. Economic cooperation among the races led to social integration. Social integration led to further economic cooperation because industrialists, eyeing low-wage blacks anywhere in their neighborhoods, found them irresistible. Social separation enforced by law—apartheid—was seen as the essential way to shore up the economic protection of white labor.

Furthermore, white farmers, wanting an artificially large supply of cheap black labor, endorsed measures limiting industrial jobs for blacks. Farmers have been key allies of white labor in initiating and preserving apartheid. Indeed, the gerrymandering of parliamentary seats to grant overrepresentation to the rural sector gave the National Party its 1948 victory even though the party lost the popular vote by a substantial margin.

The ruthlessness with which South Africa applied apartheid is legendary. The Group Areas Act (1950) dictated where members of the various races could legally reside. To enforce this, whole communities were brutally uprooted on the orders of bureaucrats. The Population Registration Act (1950) gave the state bureaucratic control over the racial identity of its citizens, and in combination with the Pass Laws, regulated internal travel. Government spending on education was hugely biased in favor of whites. In 1952, school spending per black child was about 5 percent of spending per white child. Africans were not allowed to own real estate. All these measures attempted to buttress the economic protectionism already enjoyed by white labor under the Colour Bar legislation.

Capitalists strongly opposed apartheid, and apartheidists strongly opposed capitalism. As historian Brian Lapping notes: "The National Party had to override some of the biggest financial, commercial and industrial interests in the state. . . . Overruling the bosses, the 'capitalists', as both the National Party and the communists liked to call them, was popular with the party faithful."

The notorious Broederbond, the secret Afrikaner "brotherhood," which exercised huge influence on the racist policies of the apartheid government, stated its agenda quite succinctly in 1933: "Abolition of the exploitation by foreigners of [South Africa's] national resources . . . the nationalization of finance and the planned coordination of economic policy." White supremacy had its very own industrial policy.

Apartheid in Retreat

Beginning about 1970, the internal contradictions of apartheid finally caused its slow demise. After the massive legal discrimination of the early apartheid years, black income, relative to white, fell dramatically, and the advance of white workers was won. But much like the boom periods of the two world wars, the robust economic growth of the sixties rendered apartheid's protection increasingly obsolete (many white workers no longer required all the separateness that apartheid had wrought) and exceedingly expensive (the South African economy was continually stalled by the artificial truncation of labor supply). Necessity became the mother of reform. According to Herbert Giliomee and Lawrence Schlemmer:

As the white skilled-labor shortage worsened, the government became ever more impatient with white trade unions which were hampering the training of blacks and thus blocking black advances into skilled jobs. In 1973 it was announced that blacks, including Africans, could do skilled work in the white areas. The government did not rigorously adhere to its promise that it would consult with white trade unions before making this decision. In 1975 the defence force announced that black soldiers would enjoy the same status as whites of equal rank, and that whites would have to take orders from black officers. This broke the rule that the hierarchical structure (or ratchet) must be kept intact, with blacks always working under whites.

Postwar economic growth in South Africa has made the nonwhite population so heavily integrated within the "white" society that the very idea of "separate development" is ridiculous as a practical proposition, never mind its moral implications. Without skilled black labor, white living standards would fall precipitously. The inevitable economic magnetism between the races has drawn people physically and socially close together. Whereas the median white voter of the twenties insecurely viewed black workers as substitutes, the majority of whites in recent years have seen racial cooperation as economically beneficial. On the other hand, the dramatic growth of an educated, urban African population, including a sizable black middle class, served to enormously raise the cost of enforcing apartheid. Indeed, the old African tribal system, which was cynically manipulated by apartheid policymakers under the notorious homelands policy, was eclipsed by the rise of urban townships closely tied to industrial job centers.

The vicissitudes of apartheid can be measured by the ratio of black income to white. From 1946 to 1960, despite a decrease in the white proportion of the population, a constant 70 percent of South Africa's national income went to whites. But between 1970 and 1980, this fell to 60 percent. Apartheid's decline can also be seen in increasing expenditures on black education: the twenty-to-one ratio in white-to-black per-pupil educational spending in 1952 had shrunk to about five to one in 1987. Most evidently, reform is seen in the elimination of the apartheid laws: the Prohibition of Mixed Marriages Act (scrapped in 1985), the abolition of the Pass Laws (1986), and the widespread elimination of "petty apartheid" (whereby separate facilities for racial groups was rigidly maintained). In 1991 President F. W. de Klerk eliminated the Group Areas and Population Registration Acts, the backbone of social apartheid. The nation turned its attention to crafting "a new South Africa," as the president set a 1994 deadline for adoption of a color-blind constitution guaranteeing equal rights under law to all citizens.

Did international sanctions against South Africa force Pretoria's hand in these reforms? The evidence is virtually unanimous that progress has been only modestly correlated at best, and negatively correlated at worst, with such foreign campaigns. Not only did sanctions fail to lower South African trade flows from their previous levels, but GNP growth actually accelerated after the European Community and the U.S. sanctions (in September and October of 1986, respectively). Most astoundingly, South African businesses reaped at least $5 billion to $10 billion in windfalls as Western firms disinvested at fire sale prices in the 1984–89 period.

Whatever the economic impact, the immediate political effect of sanctions was to encourage retrenchment by the Botha regime. Right-wing (proapartheid) support rose sharply in the May 1987 parliamentary elections, and the National Party government responded by shelving all reforms and brutally suppressing antiapartheid dissent, initiating a state of emergency accompanied by sweeping press censorship. Only with a fading of sanctions pressures, a rebounding economy, and key changes in the international geopolitical environment (notably, the collapse of the Eastern bloc) did the course of reform reassert itself.

Apartheid was sought by those economically threatened by the synergies between black workers and white capitalists. That interest groups can so steer economic regulation as to achieve the social savagery of apartheid is a chilling lesson for those who take their politics—and hence their economics—seriously.

—**Thomas W. Hazlett**

Biography: Thomas W. Hazlett is an associate professor of agricultural economics at the University of California, Davis. He wrote this article while a visiting scholar at the Columbia University Graduate School of Business.

Further Reading

Doxey, G. V. *The Industrial Colour Bar in South Africa.* 1961.

Frederickson, G. M. *White Supremacy: A Comparative Study in American and South African History.* 1981.

Giliomee, Herbert, and Lawrence Schlemmer. *From Apartheid to Nation-Building.* 1989.

Hazlett, Thomas W. "Kinnock's Crowning Cheek on Apartheid." *The Wall Street Journal* (December 31, 1986): 14.

———. "The Economic Origins of Apartheid." *Contemporary Policy Issues* 6 (October 1988): 85–104.

———. "One Man, One Share: How to Privatize South Africa." *The New Republic* 203 (December 31, 1990): 14–15.

———. *The Effect of U.S. Economic Sanctions on South African Apartheid.* Davis, CA: University of California at Davis, Institute of Governmental Affairs, Applied Public Policy Research Program, working paper series no. 3, April 1992.

Hufbauer, Gary Clyde, Jeffrey J. Schott, and Kimberly Ann Elliott. *Economic Sanctions Reconsidered,* 2d ed. 1990.

Lowenberg, Anton D. "An Economic Theory of Apartheid." *Economic Inquiry* 27, no. 1 (January 1989): 57–74

Lapping, Brian. *Apartheid: A History.* 1987.

Lingle, Christopher. "Apartheid as Racial Socialism." *Kyklos* 43, no. 2 (1989): 229–47.

Lipton, Merle. *Capitalism and Apartheid.* 1986.

———. "The Challenge of Sanctions." Washington, DC: Investor Responsibility Research Center, 1989. Paper presented to the Economic Society of South Africa, Johannesburg, September 6–7, 1989.

Austrian Economics

Deborah L. Walker

History

The Austrian school of economics dates from the 1871 publication of Carl Menger's *Principles of Economics (Grundsätze der Volkswirtschaftslehre)*. Two of Menger's students, Eugen von Böhm-Bawerk and Freidrich von Wieser, carried his work forward and made considerable contributions of their own. Especially notable is Böhm-Bawerk's analysis of capital and interest. In the 1920s, 1930s, and 1940s, Ludwig von Mises and Friedrich A. Hayek continued the Austrian tradition with their works on the business cycle and on the impossibility of economic calculation under socialism.

Austrian analysis fell out of favor with the economics profession during the fifties and sixties, but the awarding of the Nobel Prize in economics to Hayek in 1974, coupled with the spread of Mises's ideas by his students and followers, led to a revival of the Austrian school.

The Cornerstones

The major cornerstones of Austrian economics are methodological individualism, methodological subjectivism, and an emphasis on processes rather than on end states.

- **Methodological individualism.** Economics, to an Austrian economist, is the study of purposeful human action in its broadest sense. Since only individuals act, the focus of study for the Austrian economist is always on the individual. Although Austrian economists are not alone in their methodological individualism, they do not stress the maximizing behavior of individuals in the same way as mainstream neoclassical economists. Austrian economists believe that one can never know if humans have maximized benefits or minimized costs. Austrian economists emphasize instead the process by which market participants gain information and form their expectations in order to lead them to their own idea of a best solution.

The most important economic problem that people face, according to Austrian economists, is how to coordinate their plans with those of other people. Why, for example, when a person goes to a store to buy an apple, is the apple there to be bought? This meshing of individual plans in a world of uncertainty is, to Austrians, the basic economic problem.

Austrian economists do not use mathematics in their analyses or theories because they do not think mathematics can capture the complex reality of human action. They believe that as people act, change occurs, and that quantifiable relationships are applicable only when there is no change. Mathematics can capture what has taken place, but can never capture what will take place.

- **Methodological subjectivism.** An individual's actions and choices are based upon a unique value scale known only to that individual. It is this subjective valuation of goods that creates economic value. Like other economists, the Austrian does not judge or criticize these subjective values but instead takes them as given data. But unlike other economists, the Austrian never attempts to measure or put these values in mathematical form. The idea that an individual's values, plans, expectations, and understanding of reality are all subjective permeates the Austrian tradition and, along with an emphasis on change or processes, is the basis for their notion of economic efficiency.
- **Processes versus end states.** An individual's action takes place through time. A person decides on a desired end, chooses a means to attain that end, and then acts to attain it. But because all individuals act under the condition of uncertainty—especially uncertainty regarding the plans and actions of other individuals—people sometimes do not achieve their desired ends. The actions of one person may interfere with the actions of another. The actual consequences of any action can be known only after the action has taken place. This does not mean that people do not include in their plans expectations regarding the plans of others. But the exact outcome of a vast number of plans being executed at the same time can never be predicted. When offering a product on the market, for example, a producer can only guess as to what price will produce the greatest demand for his product or how many, if any, new competitors will enter his market. Offering a product on the market is always a trial-and-error, never-ending process of changing one's plans to reflect new knowledge one gains from day to day.

Since the Austrian economist holds all costs and benefits to be subjective and, therefore, not measurable, only the individual can decide what actions are efficient or inefficient. Often the individual may decide, after the fact, that a decision was not efficient. In the actual process of acting to achieve an end, an individual will discover what works best. And even then, what worked best this time may not work best next time. But a person cannot know this without the process of acting.

The notion of an equilibrium state is sometimes seen as the epitome of economic efficiency: supply would equal demand, and therefore, no surplus or shortage of goods would exist. This assumes, however, that market participants know where the equilibrium price is and that moving toward it will not change it. But if the price is already known, why isn't the market already in equilibrium? Furthermore, the movement to equilibrium is a process of learning and of changing expectations, which will change the equilibrium itself. To the Austrian economist efficiency is defined within the process of acting, not as a given or known end state of affairs. Efficiency means the fulfillment of the purposes deemed most important to an individual, rather than the fulfillment of less important purposes. The Austrian economist never speaks of efficiency outside of the individual.

Policy Implications

So what do Austrian economists do? They try to understand the process by which knowledge is generated, spread, and used within the economy. They focus on the institutions that emerge because people lack perfect knowledge and try to cope with this uncertainty. Money is just one example of such institutions.

A medium of exchange, or money, spontaneously emerges because individuals engaging in trade want to decrease the uncertainty that they will be able to obtain goods that they themselves are not producing. When a commodity is generally accepted in all exchanges, people can specialize (in producing corn, for example) and can be certain that they will be able to exchange the corn for the medium of exchange. They can then use the medium to obtain other goods that they want. The existence of money enhances the benefits of specialization and division of labor. Austrian economists explain how and why money and other institutions emerge; they do not take them as given, as do many neoclassical economists.

The basic question for the Austrian economist is, Which institutions enable individuals to reach their own goals, and which do not? Therefore, their policy recommendations run to changes in the institutional framework within which a society operates. Two key public policy issues that provide good illustrations of Austrian analysis are antitrust and central planning.

- **Antitrust.** The neoclassical economic theory of perfect competition defines a competitive market as one in which there are a large number of small firms, all selling a homogeneous good and possessing perfect knowledge. The structure of the market, according to this analysis, determines the competitiveness of a market. But Austrian economists Friedrich A. Hayek and Israel M. Kirzner have rejected this theory of competition. According to Hayek there is no competition in the neoclassical theory of perfect competition. Competition to an Austrian economist is defined simply as rivalrous behavior, and to compete is to attempt to offer a better deal than one's competitors. Competition in the market arises out of one firm distinguishing its products in some way from those of other firms. And because firms in the real world do not have perfect knowledge, they do not know what a successful competitive strategy is until they try it. Competition is, therefore, as Hayek explains, a "discovery procedure." As each firm attempts to do better than all other firms, the knowledge of what consumers actually want in the market is discovered.

If the neoclassical definition of competition is accepted, many people may want antitrust laws to eliminate excessive divergences from an industry structure characterized by a large number of small firms. If the Austrian definition of rivalrous behavior is accepted, then antitrust laws are seen to be beneficial only if market structure affects rivalrous behavior. But the evidence indicates that market structure does not affect the competitiveness of a market. What matters to Austrian economists is whether governments interfere with rivalrous behavior. For example, when government imposes import quotas, domestic firms in an industry are shielded from the rivalrous competitive behavior of potential and actual foreign competitors. Or when the government prohibits entry into an industry, such as in the delivery of first-class mail, the competitive process of discovering new and more efficient ways of offering the service to the consumer is stifled.

According to Austrian economists, antitrust legislation is neither necessary nor desirable. In recent years many mainstream economists working in the area of antitrust have begun to express this view (see ANTITRUST). This is especially true of economists in the so-called Chicago school of industrial organization, such as Harold Demsetz, Armen Alchian, and George Stigler. Stigler, in his book *The Organization of Industry*, wrote: ''In economic life competition is not a goal: it is a means of organizing economic activity to achieve a goal.''

• **Central planning.** The failure of centrally planned economies to allocate resources to meet the most basic human needs is something that Mises and Hayek predicted long ago (see SOCIALISM). They pointed out that every individual in an economy possesses knowledge (about production techniques, availability of some sources of supply, etc.) only some of which is known by others. This knowledge is dispersed throughout the economy and is constantly changing. In a centrally planned economy the information available to the planners is a tiny fraction of the amount in various people's heads. Therefore, much information in a centrally planned economy is never acted on.

The socialist manager who knows of a cheap source of supply can't necessarily use it because he must get permission to do so, and even if he gets permission, it is likely to be too late to use it.

But in a free market, explain Mises and Hayek, private ownership of the means of production allows people to use their information; they don't need permission. Private ownership also allows people to bid for resources, which in turn generates market prices for these resources. People can then use these prices to decide, as producers or consumers, what goods to buy or sell, and how to use them. A market price summarizes the diverse knowledge of millions of individual human beings as they act in the market. The very act of buying a good at a particular price signals the producer to continue producing and selling this good. The producer does not have to know why consumers buy the goods they do, only that they do. And profits are also knowledge signals in the market that direct resources into one industry and out of another. This is why Austrian economists have always been highly critical of central planning and strong supporters of a free market.

Conclusion

Although the theory of competition and economic calculation are good examples of Austrian economic analysis, there are many others. The Austrian theory of the business cycle and of the inflationary process that takes place because of credit expansion through monetary policy, and the Austrian explanation of the emergence of money in a modern economy are also important contributions to economic analysis. Today, Austrian economists are also working in the areas of environmental economics, labor economics, and legal analysis. Many of the traditionally Austrian theories, and even methods, are being accepted into mainstream economic analysis.

This is especially true of the Austrian view of central economic planning. The Austrian analysis of central planning, although never stated explicitly as such, is found in the writing of many mainstream economists. Robert Heilbroner, for example, who himself advocated socialist policies in the past, attributes the collapse of the Soviet economy to a knowledge problem. He states:

> Planning thus requires that the immense map of desired national output be carved up into millions of individual pieces, like a jigsaw puzzle—the pieces produced by hundreds of thousands of enterprises, and the whole thing finally reassembled in such a way as to fit. That would be an extraordinarily difficult task even if the map of desired output were unchanged from year to year, but, of course, it is not. . . .

And Charles L. Schultze, formerly President Jimmy Carter's chief economic adviser, writes: "The first problem for the government in carrying out an industrial policy is that we actually know precious little about identifying, before the fact, a 'winning' industrial structure."

—Deborah L. Walker

Biography: Deborah L. Walker is an economics professor at Loyola University in New Orleans.

Further Reading

Dolan, Edwin G., ed. *The Foundations of Modern Austrian Economics*. 1976.
Hayek, Friedrich A. *Collectivist Economic Planning*. 1975.
———. *Individualism and Economic Order*. 1948.
Kirzner, Israel M. *Competition and Entrepreneurship*. 1973.
Menger, Carl. *Principles of Economics*. 1871. Reprint. 1981.
Mises, Ludwig von. *Human Action*. 1949.
———. *Socialism*. 1936.
Spadaro, Louis M., ed. *New Directions in Austrian Economics*. 1978.

See also BÖHM-BAWERK, HAYEK, INDUSTRIAL POLICY, MENGER, MISES, SOCIALISM.

Capitalism

Robert Hessen

■ Capitalism, a term of disparagement coined by socialists in the midnineteenth century, is a misnomer for "economic individualism," which Adam Smith earlier called "the obvious and simple system of natural liberty." Economic individualism's basic premise is that the pursuit of self-interest and the right to own private property are morally defensible and legally legitimate. Its major corollary is that the state exists to protect individual rights. Subject to certain restrictions, individuals (alone or with others) are free to decide where to invest, what to produce or sell, and what prices to charge, and there is no natural limit to the range of their efforts in terms of assets, sales and profits, or the number of customers, employees, and investors, or whether they operate in local, regional, national, or international markets.

The emergence of capitalism is often mistakenly linked to a Puritan work ethic. German sociologist Max Weber, writing in 1903, located the catalyst for capitalism in seventeenth-century England, where members of a religious sect, the Puritans, under the sway of John Calvin's doctrine of predestination, channeled their energies into hard work, reinvestment, and modest living, and then carried these attitudes to New England. Weber's thesis breaks down, however. The same attitudes toward work and savings are exhibited by Jews and Japanese, whose value systems contain no Calvinist component. Moreover, Scotland in the seventeenth century was simultaneously orthodox Calvinist and economically stagnant.

A better explanation of the Puritans' diligence is that by refusing to swear allegiance to the established Church of England, they were barred from activities and professions to which they otherwise might have been drawn—land ownership, law, the military, civil service, universities—so they focused on trade and commerce. A similar pattern of exclusion or ostracism explains why Jews and other racial and religious minorities in other countries and later centuries tended to concentrate on retail businesses and money lending.

In early nineteenth-century England the most visible face of capitalism was the textile factories that hired women and children. Critics (Richard Oastler and Robert Southey, among others) denounced the mill owners as heartless exploiters. They described the working conditions—long hours, low pay, monotonous routine—as if they were unprecedented. Believing that poverty was new, not merely more visible in crowded towns and villages, critics compared contemporary times unfavorably with earlier centuries. Their claims of increasing misery, however, were based on ignorance of how squalid life actually had been earlier. Before children began earning money working in factories, they had been sent to live in parish poorhouses, apprenticed as unpaid household servants, rented out for backbreaking agricultural labor, or became beggars, vagrants, thieves, and prostitutes. The precapitalist "good old days" simply never existed (see INDUSTRIAL REVOLUTION AND THE STANDARD OF LIVING).

Nonetheless, by the 1820s and 1830s the growing specter of child labor and "dark satanic mills" generated vocal opposition to these unbridled examples of self-interest and the pursuit of profit. Some critics urged legislative regulation of wages and hours, compulsory education, and minimum-age limits for laborers. Others offered more radical attacks and alternatives. The most vociferous were the socialists, who aimed to eradicate individualism, the name that preceded capitalism.

Socialist theorists repudiated individualism's leading tenets: that individuals possess inalienable rights, that society should not restrain individuals from pursuing their own happiness, and that economic activity should not be regulated by government. Instead, they proclaimed an organic conception of society. They stressed ideals such as brotherhood, community, and social solidarity and set forth detailed blueprints for model utopian colonies in which collectivist values would be institutionalized.

The short life span of these utopian societies acted as a brake on the appeal of socialism. But its ranks swelled once Karl Marx offered a new "scientific" version, proclaiming that he had discovered the laws of history and that socialism inevitably would replace capitalism. Beyond offering sweeping promises that socialism would create economic equality, eradicate poverty, end

specialization, and abolish money, Marx supplied no details at all about how a future socialist society would be structured or operate.

Even nineteenth-century economists—in England, America, and Western Europe—who were supposedly capitalism's defenders, did not defend capitalism effectively because they did not understand it. They came to believe that the most defensible economic system was one of "perfect" or "pure" competition. Under perfect competition all firms are small scale, products in each industry are homogeneous, consumers are perfectly informed about what is for sale and at what price, and all sellers are what economists call price takers (that is, they have to "take" the market price and cannot charge a higher one for their goods).

Clearly, these assumptions were at odds with both common sense and the reality of market conditions. Under real competition, which is what capitalism delivered, companies are rivals for sales and profits. This rivalry leads them to innovate in product design and performance, to introduce cost-cutting technology, and to use packaging to make products more attractive or convenient for customers. Unbridled rivalry encourages companies to offer assurances of security to imperfectly informed consumers, by means such as money-back guarantees or product warranties and by building customer loyalty through investing in their brand names and reputations (see ADVERTISING and BRAND NAMES).

Companies that successfully adopted these techniques of rivalry were the ones that grew, and some came to dominate their industries, though usually only for a few years until other firms found superior methods of satisfying consumer demands. Neither rivalry nor product differentiation occurs under perfect competition, but they happen constantly under real flesh-and-blood capitalism.

The leading American industrialists of the late nineteenth century were aggressive competitors and innovators. To cut costs and thereby reduce prices and win a larger market share, Andrew Carnegie eagerly scrapped his huge investment in Bessemer furnaces and adopted the open hearth system for making steel rails. In the oil-refining industry John D. Rockefeller embraced cost cutting by building his own pipeline network, manufacturing his own barrels, and hiring chemists to remove the vile odor from abundant, low-cost crude oil. Gustavus Swift challenged the existing network of local butchers when he created assembly-line meat-packing facilities in Chicago and built his own fleet of refrigerated railroad cars to deliver low-price beef to distant markets. Local merchants also were challenged by Chicago-based Sears Roebuck and Montgomery Ward, which pioneered mail-order sales on a money-back, satisfaction-guaranteed basis.

Small-scale producers denounced these innovators as "robber barons," accused them of monopolistic practices, and appealed to Congress for relief from relentless competition. Beginning with the Sherman Act (1890), Congress enacted antitrust laws that were often used to suppress cost cutting and price slashing, based on acceptance of the idea that an economy of numerous small-scale firms was superior to one dominated by a few large, highly efficient companies operating in national markets (see ANTITRUST).

Despite these constraints, which worked sporadically and unpredictably, the benefits of capitalism were widely diffused. Luxuries quickly were transformed into necessities. First, the luxuries were cheap cotton clothes, fresh meat, and white bread; then sewing machines, bicycles, sporting goods, and musical instruments; then automobiles, washing machines, clothes dryers, and refrigerators; then telephones, radios, televisions, air conditioners, and freezers; and most recently, microwave ovens, videocassette recorders, answering machines, personal computers, sophisticated cameras, and compact disc players.

That these amenities had become available to most people did not cause capitalism's critics to recant, or even relent. Instead, they ingeniously reversed themselves. Marxist philosopher Herbert Marcuse proclaimed that the real evil of capitalism is prosperity, because it seduces workers away from their historic mission—the revolutionary overthrow of capitalism—by supplying them with cars and household appliances, which he called "tools of enslavement." Some critics reject capitalism by extolling "the simple life" and labeling prosperity as mindless materialism. Critics such as John Kenneth Galbraith and Vance Packard attacked the legitimacy of consumer demand, asserting that if goods had to be advertised in order to sell, they could not be serving any authentic human needs. They charged that consumers are brainwashed robots of Madison Avenue who crave whatever the giant corporations choose to produce and advertise. They complained that the "public sector" was being starved while frivolous private desires were being satisfied. And having seen that capitalism reduced poverty, instead of intensifying it, critics such as Gar Alperovitz and Michael Harrington proclaimed equality as the highest moral value, calling for higher taxes on incomes and inheritances to massively redistribute wealth, not only nationally but also internationally.

Other critics (like Ralph Nader and Mark Green) focused their fire on giant corporations, charging that they are illegitimate institutions because they do not conform to the model of small-scale, owner-managed firms that Adam Smith extolled in 1776. In fact, giant corporations are fully consistent with capitalism, which does not imply any particular configuration of firms in terms of size or legal form. They attract capital from thousands (sometimes millions) of investors who are strangers to each other and who entrust their savings to the managerial expertise of others in exchange for a share of the resulting profits.

In an influential 1932 book, *The Modern Corporation and Private Property*, Adolf A. Berle, Jr., coined the phrase "splitting of the atom of ownership" to lament the fact that investment and management had become two distinct elements. In fact the process is merely an example of the specialization of function or division of labor that occurs so often under capitalism. Far from being an abuse or defect, giant corporations are an eloquent testimonial to the ability of individuals to engage in large-scale, long-range cooperation for their mutual benefit and enrichment.

As noted earlier, the freedoms to invest, to decide what to produce, and to decide what to charge have always been restricted. A fully free economy (true laissez-faire) never has existed, but governmental authority over economic activity has sharply increased since the eighteenth century, and especially since the Great Depression. Originally, local authorities fixed the prices of necessities, such as bread and ale, bridge and ferry tolls, or fees at inns and mills, but most products and services were unregulated. By the late nineteenth century governments were setting railroad freight rates and the prices charged by grain elevator operators, because these businesses had become "affected with a public purpose." By the 1930s the same criterion was invoked to justify price controls over milk, ice, and theater tickets.

Simultaneously, from the eighteenth century on, government began to play a more active, interventionist role in offering benefits to business, such as tax exemptions, bounties or subsidies to grow certain crops, and tariff protection so domestic firms would devote capital to manufacturing goods that otherwise had to be imported. Special favors became entrenched and hard to repeal because the recipients were organized while consumers, who bore the burden of higher prices, were not.

Once safe from foreign competition behind these barriers to free trade, some U.S. producers—steel and auto manufacturers, for example—stagnated. They failed to adopt new technologies or to cut costs until low-cost, low-price overseas rivals—the Japanese, especially—challenged them for their customers. They responded initially by asking Congress for new favors—higher tariffs, import quotas, and loan guarantees—and pleading with consumers to "buy American" and thereby save domestic jobs. Slowly, but inevitably, they began the expensive process of catching up with foreign companies so they could try to recapture their domestic customers.

Today the United States, once the citadel of capitalism, is a "mixed economy" in which government bestows favors and imposes restrictions with no clear or consistent principle in mind. As Soviet Russia and Eastern Europe struggle to embrace free-market ideas and institutions, they can learn from American (and British) experience about not only the benefits that flowed from economic individualism, but also the burden of regulations that became impossible to repeal and trade barriers that were hard to dismantle. If the history of capitalism proves one thing, it is that the process of competition does not stop at national borders. As long as individuals anywhere perceive a potential for profits, they will amass the capital, produce the product, and circumvent the cultural and political barriers that interfere with their objectives.

—Robert Hessen

Biography: Robert Hessen, a specialist in business and economic history, is a senior research fellow at Stanford University's Hoover Institution. He also teaches in Stanford's Graduate School of Business.

Further Reading

Berger, Peter. *The Capitalist Revolution*. 1988.
Hayek, Friedrich A., ed. *Capitalism and the Historians*. 1953.
Hessen, Robert. *In Defense of the Corporation*. 1979.
Mises, Ludwig von. *The Anti-Capitalistic Mentality*. 1956.
Rand, Ayn. *Capitalism: The Unknown Ideal*. 1966.
Seldon, Arthur. *Capitalism*. 1990.

See also ANTITRUST, BRAND NAMES, COMPETITION, ENTREPRENEURSHIP, INDUSTRIAL REVOLUTION AND THE STANDARD OF LIVING, MARXISM, MONOPOLY.

Fascism

Sheldon Richman

■ The best example of a fascist economy is the regime of Italian dictator Benito Mussolini. Holding that liberalism (by which he meant freedom and free markets) had "reached the end of its historical function," Mussolini wrote: "To Fascism the world is not this material world, as it appears on the surface, where Man is an individual separated from all others and left to himself. . . . Fascism affirms the State as the true reality of the individual."

This collectivism is captured in the word *fascism*, which comes from the Latin *fasces,* meaning a bundle of rods with an axe in it. In economics, fascism was seen as a third way between laissez-faire capitalism and communism. Fascist thought acknowledged the roles of private property and the profit motive as legitimate incentives for productivity—provided that they did not conflict with the interests of the state.

Fascism in Italy grew out of two other movements: syndicalism and nationalism. The syndicalists believed that economic life should be governed by groups representing the workers in various industries and crafts. The nationalists, angered by Italy's treatment after World War I, combined the idea of class struggle with that of national struggle. Italy was a proletarian nation, they said, and to win a greater share of the world's wealth, all of Italy's classes must unite. Mussolini was a syndicalist who turned nationalist during World War I.

From 1922 to 1925, Mussolini's regime pursued a laissez-faire economic policy under the liberal finance minister Alberto De Stefani. De Stefani reduced taxes, regulations, and trade restrictions and allowed businesses to compete with one another. But his opposition to protectionism and business subsidies alienated some industrial leaders, and De Stefani was eventually forced to resign. After Mussolini consolidated his dictatorship in 1925, Italy entered a new phase. Mussolini, like many leaders at this time, believed that economies did not operate constructively without supervision by the government. Foreshadowing events in Nazi Germany, and to some extent in New Deal America, Mussolini began a program of massive deficit spending, public works, and eventually, militarism.

Mussolini's fascism took another step at this time with the advent of the Corporative State, a supposedly pragmatic arrangement under which economic decisions were made by councils composed of workers and employers who represented trades and industries. By this device the presumed economic rivalry between employers and employees was to be resolved, preventing the class struggle from undermining the national struggle. In the Corporative State, for example, strikes would be illegal and labor disputes would be mediated by a state agency.

Theoretically, the fascist economy was to be guided by a complex network of employer, worker, and jointly run organizations representing crafts and industries at the local, provincial, and national levels. At the summit of this network was the National Council of Corporations. But although syndicalism and corporativism had a place in fascist ideology and were critical to building a consensus in support of the regime, the council did little to steer the economy. The real decisions were made by state agencies such as the Institute for Industrial Reconstruction (Istituto per la Ricosstruzione Industriale, or IRI), mediating among interest groups.

Beginning in 1929, in preparation for achieving the "glories" of war, the Italian government used protectionist measures to turn the economy toward autarchy, or economic self-sufficiency. The autarchic policies were intensified in the following years because of both the depression and the economic sanctions that other countries imposed on Italy after it invaded Ethiopia. Mussolini decreed that government bureaus must buy only Italian products, and he increased tariffs on all imports in 1931. The sanctions following the invasion of Ethiopia spurred Italy in 1935 to increase tariffs again, stiffen import quotas, and toughen its embargo on industrial goods.

Mussolini also eliminated the ability of business to make independent decisions: the government controlled all prices and wages, and firms in any industry could be forced into a cartel when the majority voted for it. The well-connected heads of big business had a hand in making policy, but most smaller businessmen were effectively turned into state employees contending with corrupt bureaucracies. They acquiesced, hoping that the restrictions would be temporary. Land being fundamental to the nation,

the fascist state regimented agriculture even more fully, dictating crops, breaking up farms, and threatening expropriation to enforce its commands.

Banking also came under extraordinary control. As Italy's industrial and banking system sank under the weight of depression and regulation, and as unemployment rose, the government set up public works programs and took control over decisions about building and expanding factories. The government created the Istituto Mobiliare in 1931 to control credit, and the IRI later acquired all shares held by banks in industrial, agricultural, and real estate enterprises.

The image of a strong leader taking direct charge of an economy during hard times fascinated observers abroad. Italy was one of the places that Franklin Roosevelt looked to for ideas in 1933. Roosevelt's National Recovery Act (NRA) attempted to cartelize the American economy just as Mussolini had cartelized Italy's. Under the NRA Roosevelt established industry-wide boards with the power to set and enforce prices, wages, and other terms of employment, production, and distribution for all companies in an industry. Through the Agricultural Adjustment Act the government exercised similar control over farmers. Interestingly, Mussolini viewed Roosevelt's New Deal as "boldly . . . interventionist in the field of economics." Hitler's nazism also shared many features with Italian fascism, including the syndicalist front. Nazism, too, featured complete government control of industry, agriculture, finance, and investment.

As World War II approached, the signs of fascism's failure in Italy were palpable: per capita private consumption had dropped to below 1929 levels, and Italian industrial production between 1929 and 1939 had increased by only 15 percent, lower than the rates for other Western European countries. Labor productivity was low and production costs were uncompetitive. The fault lay in the shift of economic decision-making from entrepreneurs to government bureaucrats, and in the allocation of resources by decree rather than by free markets. Mussolini designed his system to cater to the needs of the state, not of consumers. In the end, it served neither.

—Sheldon Richman

Biography: Sheldon Richman is senior editor at the Cato Institute in Washington, D.C. He is a lecturer and author of articles on the New Deal era, American foreign policy, and international trade.

Further Reading

Basch, Ernst. *The Fascist: His State and His Mind*. 1937.
Flynn, John T. *As We Go Marching*. 1944. Reprint. 1973.
Laqueur, Walter, ed. *Fascism: A Reader's Guide*. 1978.
Mussolini, Benito. *Fascism: Doctrine and Institutions*. 1935. Reprint. 1968.
Pitigliani, Fauto. *The Italian Corporative State*. 1934.

See also APARTHEID, GREAT DEPRESSION.

Keynesian Economics

Alan S. Blinder

■ Keynesian economics is a theory of total spending in the economy (called aggregate demand) and of its effects on output and inflation. Although the term is used (and abused) to describe many things, six principal tenets seem central to Keynesianism. The first three describe how the economy works.

1. A Keynesian believes that aggregate demand is influenced by a host of economic decisions—both public and private—and sometimes behaves erratically. The public decisions include, most prominently, those on monetary and fiscal (i.e., spending and tax) policy. Some decades ago, economists heatedly debated the relative strengths of monetary and fiscal policy, with some Keynesians arguing that monetary policy is powerless, and some monetarists arguing that fiscal policy is powerless. Both of these are essentially dead issues today. Nearly all Keynesians and monetarists now believe that both fiscal and monetary policy affect aggregate demand. A few economists, however, believe in what is called debt neutrality—the doctrine that substitutions of government borrowing for taxes have no effects on total demand (more on this below).
2. According to Keynesian theory, changes in aggregate demand, whether anticipated or unanticipated, have their greatest short-run impact on real output and employment, not on prices. This idea is portrayed, for example, in Phillips curves that show inflation changing only slowly when unemployment changes. Keynesians believe the short run lasts long enough to matter. They often quote Keynes's famous statement "In the long run, we are all dead" to make the point.

Anticipated monetary policy (that is, policies that people expect in advance) can produce real effects on output and employment only if some prices are rigid—if nominal wages (wages in dollars, not in real purchasing power), for example, do not adjust instantly. Otherwise, an injection of new money would change all prices by the same percentage. So Keynesian models generally either assume or try to explain rigid prices or wages. Rationalizing rigid prices is hard to do because, according to standard microeconomic theory, real supplies and demands do not change if all nominal prices rise or fall proportionally.

But Keynesians believe that, because prices are somewhat rigid, fluctuations in any component of spending—consumption, investment, or government expenditures—cause output to fluctuate. If government spending increases, for example, and all other components of spending remain constant, then output will increase. Keynesian models of economic activity also include a so-called multiplier effect. That is, output increases by a multiple of the original change in spending that caused it. Thus, a $10 billion increase in government spending could cause total output to rise by $15 billion (a multiplier of 1.5) or by $5 billion (a multiplier of 0.5). Contrary to what many people believe, Keynesian analysis does not require that the multiplier exceed 1.0. For Keynesian economics to work, however, the multiplier must be greater than zero.

3. Keynesians believe that prices and, especially, wages respond slowly to changes in supply and demand, resulting in shortages and surpluses, especially of labor. Even though monetarists are more confident than Keynesians in the ability of markets to adjust to changes in supply and demand, many monetarists accept the Keynesian position on this matter. Milton Friedman, for example, the most prominent monetarist, has written: "Under any conceivable institutional arrangements, and certainly under those that now prevail in the United States, there is only a limited amount of flexibility in prices and wages." In current parlance, that would certainly be called a Keynesian position.

No policy prescriptions follow from these three beliefs alone. And many economists who do not call themselves Keynesian—including most monetarists—would, nevertheless, accept the entire list. What distinguishes Keynesians from other economists is their belief in the following three tenets about economic policy.

4. Keynesians do not think that the typical level of unemployment is ideal—partly because unemployment is subject to the caprice of aggregate demand, and partly because they believe that prices adjust only gradually. In fact, Keynesians typically see unemployment as both too high on average and too variable, although they know that rigorous theoretical justification for these positions is hard to come by. Keynesians also feel certain that periods of recession or depression are economic maladies, not efficient market responses to unattractive opportunities. (Monetarists, as already noted, have a deeper belief in the invisible hand.)

5. Many, but not all, Keynesians advocate activist stabilization policy to reduce the amplitude of the business cycle, which they rank among the most important of all economic problems. Here Keynesians and monetarists (and even some conservative Keynesians) part company by doubting either the efficacy of stabilization policy or the wisdom of attempting it.

This does not mean that Keynesians advocate what used to be called fine-tuning—adjusting government spending, taxes, and the money supply every few months to keep the economy at full employment. Almost all economists, including most Keynesians, now believe that the government simply cannot know enough soon enough to fine-tune successfully. Three lags make it unlikely that fine-tuning will work. First, there is a lag between the time that a change in policy is required and the time that the government recognizes this. Second, there is a lag between when the government recognizes that a change in policy is required and when it takes action. In the United States, this lag is often very long for fiscal policy because Congress and the administration must first agree on most changes in spending and taxes. The third lag comes between the time that policy is changed and when the changes affect the economy. This, too, can be many months. Yet many Keynesians still believe that more modest goals for stabilization policy—coarse-tuning, if you will—are not only defensible, but sensible. For example, an economist need not have detailed quantitative knowledge of lags to prescribe a dose of expansionary monetary policy when the unemployment rate is 10 percent or more—as it was in many leading industrial countries in the eighties.

6. Finally, and even less unanimously, many Keynesians are more concerned about combating unemployment than about conquering inflation. They have concluded from the evidence that the costs of low inflation are small. However, there are plenty of anti-inflation Keynesians. Most of the world's current and past central bankers, for example, merit this title whether they like it or not. Needless to say, views on the relative importance of unemployment and inflation heavily influence the policy advice that economists give and that policymakers accept. Keynesians typically advocate more aggressively expansionist policies than non-Keynesians.

Keynesians' belief in aggressive government action to stabilize the economy is based on value judgments and on the beliefs that (a) macroeconomic fluctuations significantly reduce economic well-being, (b) the government is knowledgeable and capable enough to improve upon the free market, and (c) unemployment is a more important problem than inflation.

The long, and to some extent, continuing battle between Keynesians and monetarists has been fought primarily over (b) and (c).

In contrast, the briefer and more recent debate between Keynesians and new classical economists has been fought primarily over (a) and over the first three tenets of Keynesianism—tenets that the monetarists had accepted. New classicals believe that anticipated changes in the money supply do not affect real output; that markets, even the labor market, adjust quickly to eliminate shortages and surpluses; and that business cycles may be efficient. For reasons that will be made clear below, I believe that the "objective" scientific evidence on these matters points strongly in the Keynesian direction.

Before leaving the realm of definition, however, I must underscore several glaring and intentional omissions.

First, I have said nothing about the rational expectations school of thought (see RATIONAL EXPECTATIONS). Like Keynes himself, many Keynesians doubt that school's view that people use all available information to form their expectations about economic policy. Other Keynesians accept the view. But when it comes to the large issues with which I have concerned myself, nothing much rides on whether or not expectations are rational. Rational expectations do not, for example, preclude rigid prices. Stanford's John Taylor and MIT's Stanley Fischer have constructed rational expectations models with sticky prices that are thoroughly Keynesian by my definition. I should note, though, that some new classicals see rational expectations as much more fundamental to the debate.

The second omission is the hypothesis that there is a "natural rate" of unemployment in the long run. Prior to 1970, Keynesians believed that the long-run level of unemployment depended on government policy, and that the government could achieve a low unemployment rate by accepting a high but steady rate of inflation. In the late sixties Milton Friedman, a monetarist, and Columbia's Edmund Phelps, a Keynesian, rejected the idea of such a long-run trade-off on theoretical grounds. They argued that the only way the government could keep unemployment below what they called the "natural rate" was with macroeconomic policies that would continuously drive inflation higher and higher. In the long run, they argued, the unemployment rate could not be below the natural rate. Shortly thereafter, Keynesians like Northwestern's Robert Gordon presented empirical evidence for Friedman's and Phelps's view. Since about 1972 Keynesians have integrated the "natural rate" of unemployment into their thinking. So the natural rate hypothesis played essentially no role in the intellectual ferment of the 1975–85 period.

Third, I have ignored the choice between monetary and fiscal policy as the preferred instrument of stabilization policy. Economists differ about this and occasionally change sides. By my definition, however, it is perfectly possible to be a Keynesian and still believe either that responsibility for stabilization policy should, in principle, be ceded to the monetary authority or that it is, in practice, so ceded.

Keynesian theory was much denigrated in academic circles from the midseventies until the mideighties. It has staged a strong comeback since then, however. The main reason appears to be that Keynesian economics was better able to explain the economic events of the seventies and eighties than its principal intellectual competitor, new classical economics.

True to its classical roots, new classical theory emphasizes the ability of a market economy to cure recessions by downward adjustments in wages and prices. The new classical economists of the midseventies attributed economic downturns to people's misperceptions about what was happening to relative prices (such as real wages). Misperceptions would arise, they argued, if people did not know the current price level or inflation rate. But such misperceptions should be fleeting and surely cannot be large in societies in which price indexes are published monthly and the typical monthly inflation rate is under 1 percent. Therefore, economic downturns, by the new classical view, should be mild and brief. Yet during the eighties most of the world's industrial economies endured deep and long recessions. Keynesian economics may be theoretically untidy, but it certainly is a theory that predicts periods of persistent, involuntary unemployment.

According to new classical theory, a correctly perceived decrease in the growth of the money supply should have only small effects, if any, on real output. Yet when the Federal Reserve and the Bank of England announced that monetary policy would be tightened to fight inflation, and then made good on their promises, severe recessions followed in each country. New classicals might claim that the tightening was unanticipated (because people did not believe what the monetary authorities said). Perhaps it was in part. But surely the broad contours of the restrictive policies were anticipated, or at least correctly perceived as they unfolded. Old-fashioned Keynesian theory, which says that any monetary restriction is contractionary because firms and individuals are locked into fixed-price contracts, not inflation-adjusted ones, seems more consistent with actual events.

An offshoot of new classical theory formulated by Harvard's Robert Barro is the idea of debt neutrality. Barro argues that inflation, unemployment, real GNP, and real national saving should not be affected by whether the government finances its spending with high taxes and low deficits or with low taxes and high deficits. Because people are rational, he argues, they will correctly perceive that low taxes and high deficits today must mean higher future taxes for them and their heirs. They will, Barro argues, cut consumption and increase their saving by one dollar for each dollar increase in future tax liabilities. Thus, a rise in private saving should offset any increase in the government's deficit. Naïve Keynesian analysis, by contrast, sees an increased deficit, with government spending held constant, as an increase in aggregate demand. If, as happened in the United States, the stimulus to demand is nullified by contractionary monetary policy, real interest rates should rise strongly. There is no reason, in the Keynesian view, to expect the private saving rate to rise.

The massive U.S. tax cuts between 1981 and 1984 provided something approximating a laboratory test of these alternative views. What happened? The private saving rate did not rise. Real interest rates soared, even though a surprisingly large part of the shock was absorbed by exchange rates rather than by interest rates. With fiscal stimulus offset by monetary contraction, real GNP growth was approximately unaffected; it grew at about the same rate as it had in the recent past. Again, this all seems more consistent with Keynesian than with new classical theory.

Finally, there was the European depression of the eighties, which was the worst since the depression of the thirties. The Keynesian explanation is straightforward. Governments, led by the British and German central banks, decided to fight inflation with highly restrictive monetary and fiscal policies. The anti-inflation crusade was strengthened by the European Monetary System, which, in effect, spread the stern German monetary policy all over Europe. The new classical school has no comparable explanation. New classicals, and conservative economists in general, argue that European governments interfere more heavily in labor markets (with high unemployment benefits, for example, and restrictions on firing workers). But most of these interferences were in place in the early seventies, when unemployment was extremely low.

—Alan S. Blinder

Biography: Alan S. Blinder is a member of President Clinton's Council of Economic Advisers. He is on leave from Princeton University, where he is the Gordon S. Rentschler Memorial Professor of Economics.

Further Reading

Blinder, Alan S. *Hard Heads, Soft Hearts*. Chaps. 2, 3. 1987.
———. "Keynes after Lucas." *Eastern Economic Journal* (July–September 1986): 209–16.
———. "Keynes, Lucas, and Scientific Progress." *American Economic Review* (May 1987): 130–36. (Reprinted in *John Maynard Keynes (1833–1946)*, vol. 2, edited by Mark Blaug. 1991.
Gordon, Robert J. "What Is New-Keynesian Economics?" *Journal of Economic Literature* 28, no. 3 (September 1990): 1115–71.
Keynes, John Maynard. *The General Theory of Employment, Interest, and Money*. 1936.
Mankiw, N. Gregory. "A Quick Refresher Course in Macroeconomics." *Journal of Economic Literature* 28 (December 1990): 1645–60.

See also NEW KEYNESIAN ECONOMICS.

Marxism

David L. Prychitko

■ A century after his death, Karl Marx remains one of the most controversial figures in the Western world. His relentless criticism of capitalism, and his corresponding promise of an inevitable, harmonious socialist future, inspired a revolution of global proportions. It seemed that—with the Bolshevik revolution in Russia and the spread of communism throughout Eastern Europe—the Marxist dream had firmly taken root during the first half of the twentieth century.

Now we witness the utter collapse of that dream in Poland, Hungary, Czechoslovakia, East Germany, Romania, Yugoslavia, Bulgaria, Albania, and the USSR itself. What was it about Marxism that created such a powerful revolutionary force? And what explains its eventual demise? The answers lie in some general characteristics of Marxism—its economics, social theory, and overall vision.

Labor Theory of Value

The labor theory of value is a major pillar of traditional Marxian economics, which is evident in Marx's masterpiece, *Capital* (1867). Its basic claim is simple: the value of a commodity can be objectively measured by the average amount of labor hours that are required to produce that commodity.

If a pair of shoes usually takes twice as long to produce as a pair of pants, for example, then shoes are twice as valuable as pants. In the long run the competitive price of shoes will be twice the price of pants, *regardless of the value of the physical inputs*.

The labor theory of value is demonstrably false. But it did prevail among classical economists through the midnineteenth century. Adam Smith, for instance, flirted with a labor theory of value in his classic defense of capitalism, *The Wealth of Nations* (1776), while David Ricardo later systematized it in his *Principles of Political Economy* (1817), a text studied by generations of free-market economists.

So the labor theory of value was not unique to Marxism. Marx did attempt, however, to turn the theory against the champions of capitalism. He pushed the theory in a direction that most classical economists hesitated to follow. Marx argued that the theory is supposed to explain the value of all commodities, including the commodity that workers sell to capitalists for a wage. Marx called this commodity "labor power."

Labor power is the worker's capacity to produce goods and services. Marx, using principles of classical economics, explained that the value of labor power must depend upon the number of labor hours it takes society, on average, to feed, clothe, and shelter a worker so that he or she has the capacity to work. In other words, the long-run wage that workers receive will depend upon the number of labor hours it takes to produce a person who is fit for work. Suppose that five hours of labor are needed to feed, clothe, and protect a worker each day so that the worker is fit for work the following morning. If one labor hour equaled one dollar, the correct wage would be five dollars per day.

Marx then asked an apparently devastating question: if all goods and services in a capitalist society tend to be sold at prices (and wages) that reflect their true value (measured by labor hours), how can it be that capitalists enjoy profits? How do capitalists manage to squeeze out a residual between total revenue and total costs?

Capitalists, Marx answered, must enjoy a privileged and powerful position as owners of the means of production and are, therefore, able to ruthlessly exploit workers. Although the capitalist pays workers the correct wage, somehow—Marx was terribly vague here—the capitalist makes workers work more hours than are needed to create the worker's labor power. If the capitalist pays each worker five dollars per day, he can require workers to work, say, twelve hours per day—not uncommon during Marx's time. Hence, if one labor hour equals one dollar, workers produce twelve dollars' worth of products for the capitalist but are paid only five. The bottom line: capitalists extract "surplus value" from the workers and enjoy monetary profits.

Although Marx tried to use the labor theory of value against capitalism by stretching it to its limits, he unintentionally demonstrated the weakness of the theory's logic and underlying assumptions. Marx was correct when he claimed that classical economists failed to adequately explain capitalist profits. But Marx failed as well. Therefore, the economics profession rejected the labor theory of value by the late nineteenth century. Mainstream economists now believe that capitalists do not earn profits by exploiting workers (see PROFITS). Instead, they believe, capitalists earn profits by forgoing current consumption, by taking risks, and by organizing production.

Alienation

There is more to Marxism, however, than the labor theory of value. Marx wove economics and philosophy together to construct a grand theory of human history and social change. His concept of alienation, for example, first articulated in his *Economic and Philosophic Manuscripts of 1844*, plays a key role in his criticism of capitalism.

Marx believed that people by nature are free, creative beings who have the potential to totally transform the world. But he observed that the modern, technologically developed world is apparently beyond our full control. Marx condemned the free market, for instance, as being "anarchic," or ungoverned. He maintained that the way the market economy is coordinated—through the spontaneous purchase and sale of private property dictated by the laws of supply and demand—blocks our ability to take control of our individual and collective destinies.

Marx condemned capitalism as a system that alienates the masses. His reasoning was as follows: Although workers produce things for the market, market forces control things; workers do not. People are required to work for capitalists who have full control over the means of production and maintain power in the workplace. Work, he said, becomes degrading, monotonous, and suitable for machines rather than free, creative people. In the end people themselves become objects—robotlike mechanisms that have lost touch with human nature, that make decisions based on cold profit-and-loss considerations, with little concern for human worth and need. Marx concluded that capitalism blocks our capacity to create our own humane society.

Marx's notion of alienation rests on a crucial but, in fact, shaky assumption. It assumes that people can successfully abolish an advanced, market-based society and replace it with a democratic, comprehensively planned society. Marx claimed we are alienated not only because many of us toil in tedious, perhaps even degrading, jobs or because by competing in the marketplace, we tend to place profitability above human need. We are alienated because we have not yet designed a society that is fully planned and controlled, a society without competition, profits and losses, money, private property, and so on, a society which, Marx predicts, must inevitably appear as the world advances through history.

Here is the greatest problem with Marx's theory of alienation: even with the latest developments in computer technology, we cannot create a comprehensively planned society that puts an end to scarcity. Marx must assume that a successfully planned world is possible in order to speak of alienation under capitalism. If socialist planning fails to work in practice, Marx's notion of alienation falls apart. Alienation is a meaningful concept in this sense only if there is an alternative that does not produce the same alienation.

Scientific Socialism

A staunch antiutopian, Marx claimed his criticism of capitalism was based on the latest developments of science. He called his theory "scientific socialism" to clearly distinguish his approach from other socialists (Henri de Saint-Simon and Charles Fourier, for instance) who seemed more content to dream about some future ideal society without comprehending how existing society really worked.

Marx's scientific socialism combined his economics and philosophy—including his theory of value and the concept of alienation—to demonstrate that throughout the course of human history, a profound struggle has developed between the "haves" and the "have-nots." Specifically, Marx claimed that capitalism has ruptured into a war between two classes—the bourgeoisie (the capitalist class that owns the means of production) and the proletariat (the working class, which is at the mercy of the capitalists). Marx claimed he had discovered the laws of history, laws that expose the contra-dictions of capitalism and the necessity of the class struggle.

Marx predicted that competition among capitalists would grow so fierce that eventually most capitalists would go bankrupt, leaving only a handful of monopolists controlling nearly all production. This, to Marx, was one of the contradictions of capitalism: competition, rather than creating better-quality products at lower prices for consumers, in the long run creates monopoly, which exploits workers and consumers alike. What happens to the former capitalists? They fall into the ranks of the proletariat, creating a greater supply of labor, a fall in wages, and what Marx called a growing reserve army of the unemployed. Also, thought Marx, the anarchic, unplanned nature of a complex market economy is prone to economic crises as supplies and demands become mismatched, causing huge swings in business activity and, ultimately, severe economic depressions.

The more advanced the capitalist economy becomes, Marx argued, the greater these contradictions and conflicts. The more capitalism creates wealth, the more it sows the seeds of its own destruction. Ultimately, the proletariat will realize that it has the collective power to overthrow the few remaining capitalists and, with them, the whole system.

The entire capitalist system—with its private property, money, market exchange, profit-and-loss accounting, labor markets, and so on—must be abolished, thought Marx, and replaced with a fully planned, self-managed economic system that brings a complete and utter end to exploitation and alienation. A socialist revolution, argued Marx, is inevitable.

An Appraisal

Marx was surely a profound thinker who won legions of supporters around the world. But his predictions have not withstood the test of time. Although capitalist markets have changed over the past 150 years, competition has not devolved into monopoly. Real wages have risen and profit rates have not declined. Nor has a reserve army of the unemployed developed. We do have bouts with the business cycle, but more and more economists believe that significant recessions and depressions may be more the unintended result of state intervention (through monetary policy carried out by central banks and government policies on taxation and spending) and less an inherent feature of markets as such.

Socialist revolutions, to be sure, have occurred throughout the world, but never where Marx's theory predicted—in the most advanced capitalist countries. On the contrary, socialist revolts have occurred in poor, so-called Third World countries. Most troubling to present-day Marxism is the ongoing collapse of socialism. Revolutions in socialist countries today are against socialism and for free markets. In practice, socialism has failed to create the nonalienated, self-managed, and fully planned society. Real-world socialism in the twentieth century failed to emancipate the masses. In most cases it merely led to new forms of statism, domination, and abuse of power.

Marx's theory of value, his philosophy of human nature, and his claims to have uncovered the laws of history fit together to offer a complex, yet grand vision of a new world order. If the first three-quarters of the twentieth century provided a testing ground for that vision, the end of the century demonstrates its truly utopian nature and ultimate unworkability.

—David L. Prychitko

Biography: David L. Prychitko is an economics professor at the State University of New York in Oswego.

Further Reading

Boettke, Peter J. *The Political Economy of Soviet Socialism: The Formative Years, 1918–1928.* 1990.
Böhm-Bawerk, Eugen von. *Karl Marx and the Close of His System.* 1896. Reprint. 1975.
Elliot, John E., ed. *Marx and Engels on Economics, Politics, and Society: Essential Readings with Editorial Commentary.* 1981.
Kolakowski, Leszek. *Main Currents of Marxism.* 3 vols. 1985.
Hayek, Friedrich A. *The Fatal Conceit: The Errors of Socialism.* 1988.
Prychitko, David L. *Marxism and Workers' Self-Management: The Essential Tension.* 1991.

See also MARX, PROFITS, SOCIALISM.

Monetarism

Allan H. Meltzer

■ During early 1990, inflation rates reported by the International Monetary Fund ranged from negative numbers to an annual rate of more than 1,400 percent. Countries like Poland, Argentina, Yugoslavia, and Brazil, where the reported annual rate of inflation was above 1,000 percent, all had experienced high money growth—more than 2,000 percent in Yugoslavia and more than 4,000 percent in Argentina in 1989. A few countries, such as Togo and Ethiopia, reported falling prices. They had experienced negative rates of money growth in the recent past.

The association between money growth and inflation is evidence for one of the principal monetarist propositions: *sustained money growth in excess of the growth of output produces inflation; to end inflation or produce deflation, money growth must fall below the growth of output*. It is noteworthy that one country with low or negative money growth, Ethiopia, reports a falling price level despite a long civil war and periodic famines. Consumer prices reported for 1987 were below the level reached two years earler.

What is true across countries also is true over time in a particular country. Inflation will be sustained if the rate of money growth far exceeds the rate of output. To end inflation, money growth must be reduced permanently. Countries as diverse as Chile, Israel, Brazil, Argentina, Italy, Japan, Turkey, and the United States, to name only a few, have increased or reduced inflation at different times by speeding up or reducing the rate of money growth. In some countries the changes in money growth and inflation have ranged over hundreds or thousands of percentage points. In others the range has been narrower.

Recent decades provide many examples. In the years since World War II, almost all countries experienced inflation. Average rates of inflation differ markedly, however, both from country to country and over time within a country. For example, comparing five-year averages for the United States shows that for 1960 to 1964, the growth of money (currency and checking deposits) remained close to the average growth of output, 2.5 to 3 percent. Inflation, measured by the deflator for total output, averaged 1.6 percent. The Federal Reserve increased money growth from 1965 to 1969 to help finance government spending for the Vietnam War and for the War on Poverty. Inflation increased. By the late seventies money growth was nearly 7 percent a year on average and inflation reached an 8 percent average. At that rate prices doubled in less than a decade. Money growth slowed and remained low after the middle eighties. In the five years ending in 1991, inflation and money growth were back at the levels of 1965 to 1969. Table 1 shows these and other periods.

The table illustrates the general association between money growth and inflation,

TABLE 1

U.S. Money Growth and Inflation
(compound annual rates in percent)

	Money Growth	Inflation
1960–64	2.8	1.6
1965–69	4.9	3.7
1970–74	6.0	6.0
1975–79	6.9	7.9
1980–84	6.6	7.3
1985–89	7.2	3.5
1987–91	4.4	3.8

but it illustrates also that the relation, while generally reliable, is not mechanical. In the years 1985 to 1989, inflation fell even though average money growth remained high. Explanations for this differ. What is most important is that such exceptions can occur; money growth in excess of output growth is a necessary but not a sufficient condition for inflation.

A second monetarist proposition is that *when inflation is expected to be high, interest rates on the open market are high and the foreign-exchange value of a currency falls relative to more stable currencies.* These monetarist claims have been validated across countries and over time. Interest rates in 1989 reached 8,000 percent a year in Argentina and Yugoslavia, an almost twentyfold increase in one year. Between 1985 and 1990 the Argentine australes depreciated against the dollar from 0.80 to 1, to 6,000 to 1. In the same period the Yugoslav dinar went from 0.03 to 10.6, and Brazilian currency (under various names) fell from 0.01 to 177.

In each of these countries, as in others experiencing rapid inflation, sustained high growth of money was followed by a flight from money that left the currency worthless. Government's efforts to use price controls in order to hide these effects of past inflation and of anticipations of future inflation may succeed for a time, but they do not succeed permanently (see PRICE CONTROLS). Although inflation may not be reflected fully in official measures, black market or open-market rates on unofficial markets tell a more correct story.

Rising money growth and rising inflation after 1964 (see table 1) brought the Bretton Woods system of fixed exchange rates to an end. The dollar depreciated against major currencies by 20 percent (based on the Federal Reserve's index) between August 1971 and March 1973. Continued inflation during the seventies contributed to the further 12 percent depreciation of the dollar by the end of the decade. After 1980, disinflationary policy contributed to the appreciation of the dollar; the Federal Reserve index reached 143 percent of its 1973 value before falling again during the period of more rapid money growth from 1985 to 1987 (see table 1).

Again, there is not a one-to-one relation between inflation and currency depreciation. Other factors—such as growth of defense spending, government purchases, tax rates, productivity growth at home and abroad, and foreign decisions—affect currency values. But sustained inflation induces depreciation, and disinflation induces appreciation, as monetarist theory implies.

When inflation increases, output often rises for a time above its trend rate. Reductions of inflation have the opposite effect;

output falls or grows at less than trend rate. These temporary changes in the growth rate of output illustrate a third monetarist proposition: *the first effects of changes in money growth are on output; later, the rate of inflation changes*. The synchronous reduction in money growth in most of the industrial countries at the beginning of the 1980s produced a severe downturn in many of these countries. The size and duration of the downturn differed from country to country. The United States experienced a sharp contraction of real output; output fell by 2.5 percent in 1982 and the unemployment rate rose above 10 percent. Germany and much of Europe experienced a much longer recession; unemployment rates in France and Italy rose annually from 1981 to 1986 and were between 10 percent and 11 percent at the end of the period, while Germany's unemployment rate reached a peak above 9 percent in 1985. Japan escaped with only a modest reduction in the growth rate of output.

Not all recessions are caused by monetary change, but many are. During the past thirty years in the United States, money growth declined markedly from its previous trend in 1960, 1966, 1969, 1974, 1979, and 1989. In each instance the growth of output fell in the same year or the succeeding year, and recessions occurred in many of these years. Other countries show a similar association between reductions in money growth and reductions in the growth of output. For example, Germany slowed its money growth from a 10.4 percent average rate in 1977 to 1979, to a 1.8 percent rate in 1980 and 1981. Real output fell in 1981 and 1982. Later, inflation fell from a peak rate of 4.8 percent in 1980 to between 2 and 3 percent in the middle of the decade.

Similarly, Britain reduced its money growth from an average of 14 percent for the 1976–79 period, to a 6 percent average rate for 1979 to 1982. Output fell in 1980 and 1981. The recession in these years was the longest and deepest of the postwar years. By 1983, output was rising, and inflation had been brought from about 15 percent to 4 to 5 percent. With lower inflation, market interest rates declined and the pound sterling appreciated in value.

These monetarist propositions about inflation, interest rates, exchange rates, and output are now widely accepted by academic economists and policymakers. Many central bankers have adopted targets or guidelines for money growth. Conversations with central bank governors these days find them more alert to the risks of inflation, more conscious of the costs of slowing inflation once the inflation has become widely anticipated, and more aware of the long-term relation between money growth and inflation.

Contrast the responses of the United States and Japanese central banks to the oil shocks in 1973 to 1974 and in 1979 to 1980. Between 1973 and 1975 U.S. and Japanese money (currency plus checking deposits) rose by 10 percent and 29 percent, respectively, and consumer prices rose by 20 percent and 35 percent. In the 1979–81 period the relative positions reversed. The U.S. money stock increased by 14 percent and consumer prices rose 25 percent; in Japan money and prices rose by 5 percent and 13 percent, respectively. A lesson learned from these different approaches to the common experience, and the analyses of that experience, is that oil shocks can change the price level, but if money growth remains moderate, the surge in prices will be temporary and short-lived. In 1982, Japanese prices rose by 2.7 percent, and by the middle of the decade prices were stable.

Experience during the war over Kuwait showed again that maintaining relatively slow money growth (in the United States, Britain, and Japan, for example) assured that the one-time oil price increase had a short-lived, temporary effect on measures of inflation. Monetarists have emphasized the distinction between one-time price-level changes and the sustained rates of change that are properly called inflation.

Academic and professional opinion has now accepted several of the monetarist propositions that many once regarded as wrongheaded or even heretical. Central bankers in leading countries, including the United States, no longer offer a laundry list of important objectives. They now most often describe their principal task as the maintenance of price stability. Countries like Italy, France, and Britain, with a history of inflationary policy, tie their currencies to the German mark to borrow credibility from the successful, low-inflation policies of the Bundesbank. And the Bundesbank sets a target for the growth rate for the money stock that it achieves much of the time. Just as important, consumers and producers believe that the directors of the Bundesbank will not persistently exceed their monetary target.

Keynesians and Monetarists

The Keynesian tradition gave government the responsibility for stabilizing an unruly economy. Keynesians developed the notion of a fiscal/monetary mix to control spending and the balance of payments simultaneously. Judicious, well-timed changes in taxes and government spending were to be balanced against propitious changes in money to control the economy. The famous Phillips curve trade-off supposedly gave economists a tool for choosing between inflation and unemployment. If the choice didn't work out as intended, Keynesians relied on informal price and wage controls, jawboning (threats), and guideposts to improve the trade-off. Under flexible exchange rates they urged international policy coordination and selective exchange-market intervention to manage the global economy. In these and other ways they presented economists as engineers who adjust the controls and, when necessary, design new controls to maintain just the right mix of policies.

To know when and how much to adjust policies, Keynesian economists developed forecasting models. Some had hundreds of equations. On large-scale computers the models could simulate possible policy changes to predict their effect and more closely adjust the mix of policy actions.

Monetarists have always been critical of these models and their use in policy. They favor stable policy rules that reduce variability and uncertainty for private decision makers. They argue that government serves the economy best by enhancing stability and acting predictably, not by trying to engineer carefully timed changes in policy actions. Monetarists saw such efforts as frequently destabilizing (that is, doing the opposite of what they were supposed to do).

The attempt to apply Keynesian policies, notably in the United States and Britain, produced alternating periods of rising inflation and rising unemployment, not the finely adjusted trade-off that the Keynesians sought. As inflation increased during the late sixties and seventies (see table 1), unemployment rose from the 3½ to 4 percent range of the late sixties to the 6 to 7 percent range of the late seventies. Lower inflation in the late eighties was accompanied by lower unemployment rates, about 5½ percent in the last years of the decade.

Instead of a carefully crafted adjustment of domestic output and the balance of payments, Keynesian policies brought the world economy a surge of inflation, unprecedented in peacetime history. Later, increases in oil prices added to the problem of rising prices, but the oil price increases were themselves a reaction, at least in part, to the surge in the world price level.

Forecasting proved a weak foundation for policy actions. The best forecasts of spending, output, prices, and inflation proved to be unreliable. Systematic studies of forecasting accuracy show that on average forecasters have been unable to distinguish between booms and recessions a quarter or a year ahead, so they are as likely to mislead as to benefit policymakers. The records of the Federal Reserve that have become available show that during the period of rising inflation, annual inflation was always underpredicted. When inflation fell in the eighties, the Federal Reserve persistently predicted too high an inflation rate. A vast amount of research has shown that econometric models cannot accurately forecast interest rates and exchange rates. This research concludes that changes in interest rates and exchange rates are caused mainly by unforeseen changes in policy and in the economy.

Inflation put an end to the Bretton Woods system of fixed but adjustable exchange rates. The Bretton Woods system of fixed exchange rates required all countries to accept the inflationary consequences of U.S. economic policy. Once the system ended, countries were free to adopt independent policies. Many did just that. Of particular interest are the policies of Japan, Germany, and Switzerland. These countries undertook to lower inflation by gradual but persistent reductions in money growth. Later, several European countries adopted medium-term fiscal strategies. And although countries did not call their actions "rules" and did not always follow their rules, the general approach is much closer to the monetarist prescription for policies based on rules than to Keynesian activist intervention.

Nowhere was the change more apparent than in Britain in the eighties. A medium-term fiscal plan designed to achieve gradually lower tax rates, persistent reductions in money growth, and an end to exchange controls and wage-price guidelines were Margaret Thatcher's main macroeconomic reforms. These reforms produced a revival of growth and confidence. In the eighties, for the first time in many decades, Britain's economy outperformed most other industrial economies. Not all of the British reforms were monetarist prescriptions, but the shift toward rules or medium-term strategies and the reduction in money growth and inflation were key parts of the policy.

Later, the monetary policy was changed. Instead of controlling domestic money growth to maintain domestic price stability, the chancellor of the Exchequer, Nigel Lawson, told the Bank of England to control the exchange rate against the German mark and other European currencies.

I believe this was a poor choice. It illustrates that a fixed exchange rate does not prevent inflation at home if there is high money growth in the country (Germany in this case) to which the currency is fixed. From 1985 to 1988, the growth of German money (currency plus checking deposits) averaged 9.5 percent a year. The result for Britain was higher money growth followed by booming demand and higher inflation, then by a disinflationary policy and a recession. Trying to keep the pound level with the mark left Britain with the highest interest rates and inflation among major countries. The spending boom, the return of inflation and high interest rates, and later, the onset of recession show the familiar monetarist associations of money growth with inflation and high interest rates, unanticipated increases in money growth with booms, and unanticipated reductions of money growth with recessions. In 1989 and 1990 Germany reduced its money growth rate to 6.5 percent and 4.5 percent. Britain's money growth fell sharply from 11 percent in 1988 and 14 percent in 1989 to 7.5 percent in 1990. As monetarist theory predicts, unemployment rates rose from a low of 7 percent to more than 10 percent by 1991.

Why the Skepticism?

Although monetarism is as alive and well as ever, considerable skepticism and contrary opinions can be found.

I think there are two factors behind the skepticism. First, the Federal Reserve's "monetarist" experiment in the early eighties is generally described as a failure. The presumed reasons for the alleged failure differ, but prominent among them is a relatively large increase in the demand for money in 1982. Second, the critics and the monetarists have very different policy agendas. The critics see government policy action as a way of removing instability caused by unruly private behavior. They have long advocated activist policies to control spending.

When taxes and spending proved to be less flexible and their influence on output and prices less potent than Keynesians (and other activists) believed, many of the advocates of activist policy shifted attention to monetary policy. They hoped to use changes in money, credit, and interest rates to fine-tune the economy. Some monetarists may have encouraged this behavior by making short-term forecasts (that often proved wide of the mark) and by overstating what monetarism could deliver. Monetary relations are a basis for policy rules, not for short-run policy activism.

Leading monetarists were very critical of the Federal Reserve's experiment at the time. They pointed out that the Fed made very few of the technical changes needed to make the experiment a success. Further, using measures of the money stock and estimates of the demand for money to predict income or spending proved to be inaccurate and misleading in 1981 and 1982.

Short-term monetarist forecasts went awry as a result. Monetarists did not predict the rapid fall in inflation after 1982 or the magnitude of the decline in output in 1982. The same can be said, however, for all other systematic efforts to forecast the economy. The Congressional Budget Office (CBO), for example, substantially underestimated the recession of 1982 and the decline in inflation in 1983. In February 1982 it predicted a 0.1 percent decline in real (inflation-adjusted) gross national product for 1982. The actual change was a decline of 2.5 percent. CBO also forecast that inflation, as measured by the GNP deflator, would be 7.5 percent in 1982 and 7.3 percent in 1983. The actual inflation was 6.4 percent and 3.9 percent.

The lesson to be learned is that economics does not deliver tight forecasts of economic variables. Economists' forecasts are probably the best forecasts available. But they are not good enough to form a reliable basis for setting policies designed to stabilize the economy in the short run. An adaptive, monetarist rule that adjusts to reflect past experience reduces some of these problems. The adaptive rule calls for money growth to adjust to an average of recent changes in the growth rates of output and the demand for money. An adaptive rule of this kind would not eliminate all fluctuations. But it would do a substantially better job of stabilizing the economy and avoiding inflation than policies based on forecasts. Some countries have learned that lesson— the monetarist lesson. They have low inflation, strong currencies, and greater stability. Unfortunately ours is not yet one of them.

—**Allan H. Meltzer**

Biography: Allan H. Meltzer is the University Professor of Economics and Public Policy at Carnegie Mellon University. He is also a visiting scholar at the American Enterprise Institute.

Further Reading

Brunner, Karl, and Allan H. Meltzer. *Money and the Economy: Issues in Monetary Analysis*. 1992.
Gordon, Robert J., ed. *Milton Friedman's Monetary Framework: A Debate with His Critics*. 1974.
Modigliani, Franco. "The Monetarist Controversy or, Should We Forsake Stabilization Policies?" *American Economic Review* 67 (March 1977): 1–19.
Stein, Jerome L., ed. *Monetarism*. 1976.

Neoclassical Economics

E. Roy Weintraub

■ Economists publicly disagree with each other so often that they are easy targets for standup comedians. Yet noneconomists may not realize that the disagreements are mostly over the details—the way in which the big picture is to be focused on the small screen. When it comes to broad economic theory, most economists agree. President Richard Nixon, defending deficit spending against the conservative charge that it was "Keynesian," is reported to have replied, "We're all Keynesians now." In fact, what he should have said is "We're all neoclassicals now, even the Keynesians," because what is taught to students, what is mainstream economics today, is neoclassical economics.

By the middle of the nineteenth century, English-speaking economists generally shared a perspective on value theory and distribution theory. The value of a bushel of corn, for example, was thought to depend on the costs involved in producing that bushel. The output or product of an economy was thought to be divided or distributed among the different social groups in accord with the costs borne by those groups in producing the output. This, roughly, was the "Classical Theory" developed by Adam Smith, David Ricardo, Thomas Malthus, John Stuart Mill, and Karl Marx.

But there were difficulties in this approach. Chief among them was that prices in the market did not necessarily reflect the "value" so defined, for people were often willing to pay more than an object was "worth." The classical "substance" theories of value, which took value to be a property inherent in an object, gradually gave way to a perspective in which value was associated with the relationship between the object and the person obtaining the object. Several economists in different places at about the same time (the 1870s and 1880s) began to base value on the relationship between costs of production and "subjective elements," later called "supply" and "demand." This came to be known as the Marginal Revolution in economics, and the overarching theory that developed from these ideas came to be called neoclassical economics. (The first to use the term "neoclassical economics" seems to have been the American economist Thorstein Veblen.)

The framework of neoclassical economics is easily summarized. Buyers attempt to maximize their gains from getting goods, and they do this by increasing their purchases of a good until what they gain from an extra unit is just balanced by what they have to give up to obtain it. In this way they maximize "utility"—the satisfaction associated with the consumption of goods and services. Likewise, individuals provide labor to firms that wish to employ them, by balancing the gains from offering the marginal unit of their services (the wage they would receive) with the disutility of labor itself—the loss of leisure. Individuals make choices at the margin. This results in a theory of demand for goods, and supply of productive factors.

Similarly, producers attempt to produce units of a good so that the cost of producing the incremental or marginal unit is just balanced by the revenue it generates. In this way they maximize profits. Firms also hire employees up to the point that the cost of the additional hire is just balanced by the value of output that the additional employee would produce.

The neoclassical vision thus involves economic "agents," be they households or firms, optimizing (doing as well as they can), subject to all relevant constraints. Value is linked to unlimited desires and wants colliding with constraints, or scarcity. The tensions, the decision problems, are worked out in markets. Prices are the signals that tell households and firms whether their conflicting desires can be reconciled.

At some price of cars, for example, I want to buy a new car. At that same price others may also want to buy cars. But manufacturers may not want to produce as many cars as we all want. Our frustration may lead us to "bid up" the price of cars, eliminating some potential buyers and encouraging some marginal producers. As the price changes, the imbalance between buy orders and sell orders is reduced. This is how optimization under constraint and market interdependence lead to an economic equilibrium. This is the neoclassical vision.

Neoclassical economics is what is called a metatheory. That is, it is a set of implicit rules or understandings for constructing satisfactory economic theories. It is a scientific research program that generates economic theories. Its fundamental assumptions are

not open to discussion in that they define the shared understandings of those who call themselves neoclassical economists, or economists without any adjective. Those fundamental assumptions include the following:

1. People have rational preferences among outcomes.
2. Individuals maximize utility and firms maximize profits.
3. People act independently on the basis of full and relevant information.

Theories based on, or guided by, these assumptions are neoclassical theories.

Thus, we can speak of a neoclassical theory of profits, or employment, or growth, or money. We can create neoclassical production relationships between inputs and outputs, or neoclassical theories of marriage and divorce and the spacing of births. Consider layoffs, for example. A theory which assumes that a firm's layoff decisions are based on a balance between the benefits of laying off an additional worker and the costs associated with that action will be a neoclassical theory. A theory that explains the layoff decision by the changing tastes of managers for employees with particular characteristics will not be a neoclassical theory.

What can be contrasted to neoclassical economics? Some have argued that there are several schools of thought in present-day economics. They identify (neo-)Marxian economics, (neo-)Austrian economics, post-Keynesian economics, or (neo-)institutional economics as alternative metatheoretical frameworks for constructing economic theories. To be sure, societies and journals promulgate the ideas associated with these perspectives. Some of these schools have had insights that neoclassical economists have learned from; the Austrian insights on entrepreneurship are one example. But to the extent these schools reject the core building blocks of neoclassical economics—as Austrians reject optimization, for example—they are regarded by mainstream neoclassical economists as defenders of lost causes or as kooks, misguided critics, and antiscientific oddballs. The status of non-neoclassical economists in the economics departments in English-speaking universities is similar to that of flat-earthers in geography departments: it is safer to voice such opinions after one has tenure, if at all.

One specific attempt to discredit neoclassical economics developed from British economist Joan Robinson and her colleagues and students at Cambridge in the late fifties and early sixties. The so-called Two Cambridges Capital Controversy was ostensibly about the implications, and limitations, of Paul Samuelson and Robert Solow's aggregating "capital" and treating the aggregate as an input in a production function. However, this controversy really was rooted in a clash of visions about what would constitute an "acceptable" theory of the distribution of income. What became the post-Keynesian position was that the distribution of income was "best" explained by power differences among workers and capitalists, while the neoclassical explanation was developed from a market theory of factor prices. Eventually the controversy was not so much settled as laid aside, as neoclassical economics became mainstream economics.

How did such an orthodoxy come to prevail? In brief, the success of neoclassical economics is connected to the "scientificization" or "mathematization" of economics in the twentieth century. It is important to recognize that a number of the early Marginalists, economists like William Stanley Jevons and F. Y. Edgeworth in England, Leon Walras in Lausanne, and Irving Fisher in the United States, wanted to legitimize economics among the scholarly disciplines. The times were optimistic about a future linked to the successes of technology. Progress would be assured in a society that used the best scientific knowledge. Social goals would be attainable if scientific principles could organize social agendas. Scientific socialism and scientific management were phrases that flowed easily from the pens of social theorists.

Neoclassical economics conceptualized the agents, households and firms, as rational actors. Agents were modeled as optimizers who were led to "better" outcomes. The resulting equilibrium was "best" in the sense that any other allocation of goods and services would leave someone worse off. Thus, the social system in the neoclassical vision was free of unresolvable conflict. The very term "social system" is a measure of the success of neoclassical economics, for the idea of a system, with its interacting components, its variables and parameters and constraints, is the language of mid-nineteenth-century physics. This field of rational mechanics was the model for the neoclassical framework. Agents were like atoms; utility was like energy; utility maximization was like the minimization of potential energy, and so forth. In this way was the rhetoric of successful science linked to the neoclassical theory, and in this way economics became linked to science itself. Whether this linkage was planned by the early Marginalists, or rather was a feature of the public success of science itself, is less important than the implications of that linkage. For once neoclassical economics was associated with scientific economics, to challenge the neoclassical approach was to seem to challenge science and progress and modernity.

The value of neoclassical economics can be assessed in the collection of truths to which we are led by its light. The kinds of truths about incentives—about prices and information, about the interrelatedness of decisions and the unintended consequences of choices—are all well developed in neoclassical theories, as is a self-consciousness about the use of evidence. In planning for future electricity needs in my state, for example, the Public Utilities Commission de-velops a (neoclassical) demand forecast, joins it to a (neoclassical) cost analysis of generation facilities of various sizes and types (e.g., an 800-megawatt low-sulfur coal plant), and develops a least-cost system growth plan and a (neoclassical) pricing strategy for implementing that plan. Those on all sides of the issues, from industry to municipalities, from electric companies to environmental groups, all speak the same language of demand elasticities and cost minimization, of marginal costs and rates of return. The rules of theory development and assessment are clear in neoclassical economics, and that clarity is taken to be beneficial to the community of economists. The scientificness of neoclassical econom-ics, on this view, is not its weakness but its strength.

—**E. Roy Weintraub**

Biography: E. Roy Weintraub is an economics professor at Duke University.

Further Reading

Becker, Gary. *The Economic Approach to Human Behavior.* 1976.
Dow, Sheila. *Macroeconomic Thought: A Methodological Approach.* 1985.
Mirowski, Philip. *More Heat Than Light.* 1989.
Weintraub, E. Roy. *General Equilibrium Analysis: Studies in Appraisal.* 1985

New Classical Macroeconomics

Robert King

■ ''New classical macroeconomics'' (NCM) uses the standard principles of economic analysis to understand how a nation's total output (gross domestic product, or GDP) is determined. In the NCM view supply and demand result from the actions of economically rational households and firms. Macroeconomic quantities like GDP are the result of the general equilibrium of the markets in an economy. It is surprising that this perspective is considered revolutionary in macroeconomics when we see the current nature of economic analysis in other fields, such as public finance, international trade, and labor economics. All use standard economic principles to analyze a wide range of issues. Macroeconomics has lagged behind because Keynesian macroeconomics was dominant when these principles were systematically applied in these other fields in the forties through the sixties.

From its inception with John Maynard Keynes's *General Theory of Employment, Interest, and Money* in 1936, Keynesian macroeconomics held a leading position for three main reasons. First, its basic analytical models were simple, flexible, and easy to use and seemed broadly consistent with observed patterns of economic activity. Second, Keynes and his disciples made a strong and effective critique of the alternative school, which they called classical macroeconomics, portraying it as complicated, inflexible, and empirically irrelevant. Third, these analytical Keynesian models provided a base for detailed statistical models of macroeconomic activity, which could be used for economic forecasting and for evaluating alternative policies.

In contrast to classical macroeconomics, new and old, Keynesian macroeconomics did not begin with the assumption that an economy is made up of individually rational economic suppliers and demanders. Instead of deriving demand from individual choices that are made within specified constraints, for example, the Keynesian procedure was to directly specify a behavioral rule. Keynes claimed that aggregate spending on consumption was governed by a ''consumption function'' in which consumption depended solely on current income. More generally, Keynesian macroeconomics posited that people followed fixed rules of thumb, with no presumption that firms and households made rational choices. Partly, this grew out of a suspicion on the part of Keynesian modelers that people did not typically act rationally. Partly, it was a pragmatic modeling decision: if people's economic behavior is purposeful, the task of specifying how they will act in various situations is more complicated and, therefore, more difficult to model.

The Keynesians were right that the classical macroeconomics of the thirties could not answer important public policy questions. Classical macroeconomics at that time, like most other fields of economics, was just beginning to build formal mathematical and statistical models of economic behavior. Over the last decade an intense amount of research has largely overcome these challenges, and this body of research is now called the new classical macroeconomics. The NCM approach has become increasingly important in discussions of macroeconomic policy in the United States and other countries around the world in recent years.

The superiority of new classical or Keynesian macroeconomics will depend on which appears to provide a better understanding of macroeconomic activity. It is important to decide between these contending views because they typically imply very different consequences for public policies.

The General Differences in Perspective

Some central, repeated differences of opinion in macroeconomic policy are traceable to basic differences in Keynesian and new classical macroeconomics.

Three ideas are central to the Keynesian view. The first is that there is little presumption that market outcomes are desirable. This leaves a great deal of scope for government intervention. The second is that changes in the supply side of markets are important mainly in the long run, which is taken to be very far away in most policy situations. The third Keynesian view is that the fiscal and monetary authorities can control demand conditions for specific products and for the economy as a whole.

By contrast, three diametrically opposed ideas are central to new classical macroeconomics. First, because market supply and demand decisions are assumed to be made by economically rational agents, these decisions are presumed to be efficient for those who make them. That individual rationality in markets will generally lead to socially desirable outcomes is, of course, the message that is at the core of economic analysis from Adam Smith's *Wealth of Nations* to modern welfare economics. Thus, the case for government intervention, in the NCM view, requires two key steps: (1) identifying a "market failure" and (2) demonstrating that the government can actually follow policies that will lead to social improvements.

Second, the NCM view systematically stresses the importance of supply behavior to market outcomes even in the very short run. Third, the NCM view questions whether typical policy instruments can be manipulated to accomplish specific policy objectives.

Current Policy Discussions

Keynesian and new classical macroeconomics lead to very different conclusions about three economic policies that were often suggested, for example, during the election campaign of 1992:

1. a temporary tax cut for the middle class
2. a temporary revival of the investment tax credit
3. expansionary policies by the Federal Reserve (i.e., increases in the rate of growth of the money supply and reductions in the discount rate)

Investigating the first two topics requires an understanding of how consumer spending and investment spending are determined, so we begin by discussing how Keynesian and new classical macroeconomics view each of these.

Determinants of Consumption and Investment

In the Keynesian view, consumption (consumer spending) is determined primarily by changes in current disposable income (i.e., national income minus taxes). The new classical perspective is quite different. In the NCM view a household's consumption in a specific time period depends on its current income and on the income it expects in the future, as well as on the interest rates at which it can borrow or lend.

The Keynesian and new classical perspectives regarding investment also differ. Keynesian macroeconomists typically stress current cash flows to a firm and its current cost of capital as the main determinants of investment spending. NCM agrees that these matter, but stresses the role of expected future cash flows and expected future costs of capital as well.

For both consumption and investment, then, a key difference between the Keynesian and new classical views is the importance each puts on expectations about future economic conditions. While many Keynesian macroeconomists might accept some role for expectations, they do not think expectations are important. Further, many Keynesian macroeconomists view expectations about the future as having little systematic relationship to actual future outcomes. Therefore, in the Keynesian view, expectations change only gradually or are governed by what Keynes called "an-

imal spirits." By contrast, NCM sees individuals as regularly trying to determine what will actually happen in the future and using new information efficiently in gauging the relative likelihood of different economic outcomes.

Temporary Tax Cuts for the Middle Class

The traditional Keynesian analysis of tax reductions is very simple and direct. Because tax cuts leave households with more funds, households increase their spending as a result. With higher demand for products, there is an increase in the output of domestic business. Thus tax cuts stimulate the economy, leading to more income and more jobs.

In this view there are only two problems. First, consumers may save their tax cut instead of spending it. Second, consumers may spend their tax cut on imported goods rather than domestic ones. Either way, demand would not rise by the full amount of the tax cut, and the tax cut would be less effective than otherwise at raising domestic production and creating jobs.

But Keynesian macroeconometric models suggest that these two problems are not very important. Following Keynes, economists describe the coefficient linking consumption changes to income changes as "the marginal propensity to consume [MPC] out of income." In a typical Keynesian econometric model the MPC is about .6, which means that 60 percent of a tax cut is spent. Further, standard Keynesian econometric models suggest that only a very small portion of changes in income is spent on imports. So the Keynesian policy of stimulating the economy looks pretty effective on these grounds.

NCM challenges this logic directly and concludes that a one-time tax cut would have a minimal effect on consumption. From the NCM perspective the key point is that the tax change is temporary and thus will add little to the household's ability to finance consumption expenditures on a sustained basis. Therefore, the NCM view is that about 95 percent of the tax reduction will be saved. In other words, the marginal propensity to consume out of this type of income is only .05.

But isn't this NCM view inconsistent with the estimates of Keynesian models, which have found that changes in income brought about sizable changes in consumption? The surprising answer is no. As Milton Friedman first explained and Robert Lucas subsequently emphasized, Keynesian macroeconomic models confuse the response of private consumption to permanent changes in income—such as those that often happen when someone changes jobs—with other, more transitory variations. Consumption responds a lot to permanent changes, which are the dominant influence, and little to temporary ones. By failing to distinguish between these different types of income changes, NCM followers believe, Keynesian modelers overestimate the effect of a temporary tax cut on consumption spending.

Moreover, when there is a tax cut now, the government must raise its borrowing and, ultimately, raise taxes in the future. The recognition that more taxes will come later can actually cause current overall demand to decrease. Thus, the NCM view questions the idea that a temporary tax cut will stimulate the total demand for products.

On-Again–Off-Again Investment Tax Credits

The investment tax credit (ITC), which was abolished in the 1986 tax reform, permitted a company to deduct a fraction of the purchase price of a new investment good from its corporate income tax payments. For this reason it provided a powerful incentive for investment. Most Keynesian macroeconomic models predict that a restoration of the tax credit would cause large, immediate increases in investment spending. The reasoning is that reducing a tax on any activity increases the amount of that activity.

But Keynesian models typically miss a key feature of the investment tax credit— its on-again–off-again nature. An ITC that is temporarily high in one year makes it desirable for firms to delay investment they had scheduled for the prior year and move forward investment that would otherwise have been made in later years. Therefore, a temporary ITC, unlike a temporary income tax cut, can have very powerful effects on demand precisely because it is temporary. But the effects are likely to be perverse.

Take the slowdown in the U.S. economy that started in the summer of 1990 and developed gradually through the subsequent year. By summer 1991 there was intense speculation in the financial press that the ITC would be restored. Such speculation was reasonable because the ITC was raised during many other post–World War II recessions. But subsequent to each recession, Congress typically reduced the ITC. Consider a company thinking of upgrading a photocopying machine during the summer of 1991. Suppose that the company would have to pay thirty thousand dollars for this machine. If there was a temporary ITC of 10 percent during 1992, then the company could save three thousand dollars just by delaying its purchase until the beginning of 1992. This is very likely a desirable strategy for the company. But for the economy it is perverse: lower investment occurs just when the economy needs high demand for investment goods.

Note the irony. In 1991 the administration considers an ITC for 1992 partly because of low investment in 1991. But part of the reason for low investment is that firms anticipate an ITC for 1992. Thus, the on-again–off-again ITC destabilizes the economy during 1991.

Investment and the Middle-Class Tax Cut

In considering the temporary income tax cut, we focused entirely on the implications for consumption and ignored investment. Did we miss something? It depends critically on how the government plans to pay for the tax cut. If it plans to increase taxes on business, then there could well be effects like those for the investment tax credit. A personal income tax cut for the middle class could signal higher future taxes on capital income and lower rewards to the current investments that are necessary to generate those incomes. The link is an indirect one,

but one that could easily overwhelm the small positive effect on consumption.

Monetary Policy and Macroeconomic Activity

In the fifties and sixties the orthodox Keynesian view was that permanently high inflation—brought about by expansionary monetary and fiscal policy—would lead to permanent increases in GDP. Correspondingly, monetary policies that reduced the long-run rate of inflation would cause a long-run reduction in GDP. In the United Kingdom such a trade-off was suggested by the empirical work of A. W. Phillips, who was careful to avoid indicating whether the trade-off was short run or long run. But other economists in the United States and United Kingdom were less cautious. The importance of this trade-off in the United States was stressed by leading theoretical macroeconomists such as Paul Samuelson and Robert Solow of MIT and built into most major econometric models, such as the Data Resources model developed by Otto Eckstein and his colleagues.

But few economists now believe that higher inflation has any important long-run benefits. The shift in thinking has occurred because of two related events. First, work in the classical tradition by Milton Friedman, Edmund Phelps, and Robert Lucas suggested that little or no long-run trade-off should exist, even if macroeconometric models predicted their existence. Second, the coexistence of high inflation and low growth in the United States during the seventies led to a questioning of this trade-off.

Economists devoted increased attention to other episodes of high inflation, like those in Latin America in recent decades and in Europe between the wars. In those episodes very high inflation rates proved unambiguously bad for real GDP.

Thus, if a U.S. recession is due in part to real factors—such as a decline in U.S. competitiveness in world markets—monetary policy has limited ability to make things better. Although expansionary monetary policy may work to increase real activity over one or two years, it cannot deal with the systematic long-run challenges that the United States faces. And the expansionary monetary policy risks igniting higher inflation.

Conclusion

New classical macroeconomics applies standard principles of economics to the behavior of the economy as a whole. Thus, it means that macroeconomists and other economists—such as public finance economists—can use broadly similar models to discuss what public policies are best for the United States and for other countries. As a result NCM has begun to refocus the debate about the appropriate choice of macroeconomic policies. In particular, since NCM now enjoys an increasingly wide following among economists, there is less discussion of policies that seek to "fine-tune" the economy in the short run—like the temporary middle-class tax cut or the countercyclical manipulation of the ITC—which were stressed by Keynesian macroeconomics. More attention is being given to developing macroeconomic policies that promote the long-run health of the economy.

—**Robert King**

Biography: Robert King is a professor of economics at the University of Rochester in Rochester, New York. He is also the editor of the *Journal of Monetary Economics* and a consultant to the Research Department at the Federal Reserve Bank of Richmond.

Further Reading

Barro, Robert J. *Macroeconomics*. 1985.
King, Robert G. "Will the New Keynesian Macroeconomics Resurrect the IS-LM Model?" *Journal of Economic Perspectives* 7, no. 1 (Winter 1993): 67–82.
Lucas, Robert E., Jr. "Econometric Policy Evaluation: A Critique." In *The Carnegie-Rochester Conference Series on Public Policy*. Vol. 1, *The Phillips Curve and Labor Markets*, edited by Karl Brunner and Alan Meltzer. 1976. (A classic article articulating the NCM view that central failures of Keynesian econometric models could be traced to the fact that these models did not build on standard principles of economics.)
McCallum, Bennett T. *Monetary Economics: Theory and Policy*. 1989.

New Keynesian Economics

N. Gregory Mankiw

■ New Keynesian economics is the school of thought in modern macroeconomics that evolved from the ideas of John Maynard Keynes. Keynes wrote *The General Theory of Employment, Interest, and Money* in the thirties, and his influence among academics and policymakers increased through the sixties. In the seventies, however, new classical economists such as Robert Lucas, Thomas J. Sargent, and Robert Barro called into question many of the precepts of the Keynesian revolution. The label "new Keynesian" describes those economists who, in the eighties, responded to this new classical critique with adjustments to the original Keynesian tenets.

The primary disagreement between new classical and new Keynesian economists is over how quickly wages and prices adjust. New classical economists build their macroeconomic theories on the assumption that wages and prices are flexible. They believe that prices "clear" markets—balance supply and demand—by adjusting quickly. New Keynesian economists, however, believe that market-clearing models cannot explain short-run economic fluctuations, and so they advocate models with "sticky" wages and prices. New Keynesian theories rely on this stickiness of wages and prices to explain why involuntary unemployment exists and why monetary policy has such a strong influence on economic activity.

A long tradition in macroeconomics (including both Keynesian and monetarist perspectives) emphasizes that monetary policy affects employment and production in the short run because prices respond sluggishly to changes in the money supply. According to this view, if the money supply falls, people spend less money, and the demand for goods falls. Because prices and wages are inflexible and don't fall immediately, the decreased spending causes a drop in production and layoffs of workers. New classical economists criticized this tradition because it lacked a coherent theoretical explanation for the sluggish behavior of prices. Much new Keynesian research attempts to remedy this omission.

Menu Costs and Aggregate-Demand Externalities

One reason that prices do not adjust immediately to clear markets is that adjusting prices is costly. To change its prices, a firm may need to send out a new catalog to customers, distribute new price lists to its sales staff, or in the case of a restaurant, print new menus. These costs of price adjustment, called "menu costs," cause firms to adjust prices intermittently rather than continuously.

Economists disagree about whether menu costs can help explain short-run economic fluctuations. Skeptics point out that menu costs usually are very small. They argue that these small costs are unlikely to help explain recessions, which are very costly for society. Proponents reply that small does not mean inconsequential. Even though menu costs are small for the individual firm, they could have large effects on the economy as a whole.

Proponents of the menu-cost hypothesis describe the situation as follows. To understand why prices adjust slowly, one must acknowledge that changes in prices have externalities—that is, effects that go beyond the firm and its customers. For instance, a price reduction by one firm benefits other firms in the economy. When a firm lowers the price it charges, it lowers the average price level slightly and thereby raises real income. (Nominal income is determined by the money supply.) The stimulus from higher income, in turn, raises the demand for the products of all firms. This macroeconomic impact of one firm's price adjustment on the demand for all other firms' products is called an "aggregate-demand externality."

In the presence of this aggregate-demand externality, small menu costs can make prices sticky, and this stickiness can have a large cost to society. Suppose that General Motors announces its prices and then, after a fall in the money supply, must decide whether to cut prices. If it did so, car buyers would have a higher real income and would, therefore, buy more products from other companies as well. But the benefits to other companies are not what General Motors cares about. Therefore, General Motors would sometimes fail to pay the menu cost and cut its price, even though the price cut is socially desirable. This is an example in which sticky prices are undesirable for the economy as a whole, even though they may be optimal for those setting prices.

The Staggering of Prices

New Keynesian explanations of sticky prices often emphasize that not everyone in the economy sets prices at the same time. Instead, the adjustment of prices throughout the economy is staggered. Staggering complicates the setting of prices because firms care about their prices relative to those charged by other firms. Staggering can make the overall level of prices adjust slowly, even when individual prices change frequently.

Consider the following example. Suppose, first, that price setting is synchronized: every firm adjusts its price on the first of every month. If the money supply and aggregate demand rise on May 10, output will be higher from May 10 to June 1 because prices are fixed during this interval. But on June 1 all firms will raise their prices in response to the higher demand, ending the three-week boom.

Now suppose that price setting is staggered: Half the firms set prices on the first of each month and half on the fifteenth. If the money supply rises on May 10, then half the firms can raise their prices on May 15. Yet because half of the firms will not be changing their prices on the fifteenth, a price increase by any firm will raise that firm's relative price, which will cause it to lose customers. Therefore, these firms will probably not raise their prices very much. (In contrast, if all firms are synchronized, all firms can raise prices together, leaving relative prices unaffected.) If the May 15 price setters make little adjustment in their prices, then the other firms will make little adjustment when their turn comes on June 1, because they also want to avoid relative price changes. And so on. The price level rises slowly as the result of small price increases on the first and the fifteenth of each month. Hence, staggering makes the price level sluggish, because no firm wishes to be the first to post a substantial price increase.

Coordination Failure

Some new Keynesian economists suggest that recessions result from a failure of coordination. Coordination problems can arise in the setting of wages and prices because those who set them must anticipate the actions of other wage and price setters. Union leaders negotiating wages are concerned about the concessions other unions will win. Firms setting prices are mindful of the prices other firms will charge.

To see how a recession could arise as a failure of coordination, consider the following parable. The economy is made up of two firms. After a fall in the money supply, each firm must decide whether to cut its price. Each firm wants to maximize its profit, but its profit depends not only on its pricing decision but also on the decision made by the other firm.

If neither firm cuts its price, the amount of real money (the amount of money divided by the price level) is low, a recession ensues, and each firm makes a profit of only fifteen dollars.

If both firms cut their price, real money balances are high, a recession is avoided, and each firm makes a profit of thirty dollars. Although both firms prefer to avoid a recession, neither can do so by its own actions. If one firm cuts its price while the other does not, a recession follows. The firm making the price cut makes only five dollars, while the other firm makes fifteen dollars.

The essence of this parable is that each firm's decision influences the set of outcomes available to the other firm. When one firm cuts its price, it improves the opportunities available to the other firm, because the other firm can then avoid the recession by cutting its price. This positive impact of one firm's price cut on the other firm's profit opportunities might arise because of an aggregate-demand externality.

What outcome should one expect in this economy? On the one hand, if each firm expects the other to cut its price, both will cut prices, resulting in the preferred outcome in which each makes thirty dollars. On the other hand, if each firm expects the other to maintain its price, both will maintain their prices, resulting in the inferior solution, in which each makes fifteen dollars. Hence, either of these outcomes is possible: there are multiple equilibria.

The inferior outcome, in which each firm makes fifteen dollars, is an example of a coordination failure. If the two firms could coordinate, they would both cut their price and reach the preferred outcome. In the real world, unlike in this parable, coordination is often difficult because the number of firms setting prices is large. The moral of the story is that even though sticky prices are in no one's interest, prices can be sticky simply because people expect them to be.

Efficiency Wages

Another important part of new Keynesian economics has been the development of new theories of unemployment. Persistent unemployment is a puzzle for economic theory. Normally, economists presume that an excess supply of labor would exert a downward pressure on wages. A reduction in wages would, in turn, reduce unemployment by raising the quantity of labor demanded. Hence, according to standard economic theory unemployment is a self-correcting problem.

New Keynesian economists often turn to theories of what they call efficiency wages to explain why this market-clearing mechanism may fail. These theories hold that high wages make workers more productive. The influence of wages on worker efficiency may explain the failure of firms to cut wages despite an excess supply of labor. Even though a wage reduction would lower a firm's wage bill, it would also—if the theories are correct—cause worker productivity and the firm's profits to decline.

There are various theories about how wages affect worker productivity. One efficiency-wage theory holds that high wages reduce labor turnover. Workers quit jobs for many reasons—to accept better positions at other firms, to change careers, or to move to other parts of the country. The more a firm pays its workers, the greater their incentive to stay with the firm. By paying a high wage, a firm reduces the frequency of quits, thereby decreasing the time spent hiring and training new workers.

A second efficiency-wage theory holds that the average quality of a firm's work force depends on the wage it pays its employees. If a firm reduces wages, the best employees may take jobs elsewhere, leaving the firm with less productive employees who have fewer alternative opportunities. By paying a wage above the equilibrium level, the firm may avoid this adverse selection, improve the average quality of its work force, and thereby increase productivity.

A third efficiency-wage theory holds that a high wage improves worker effort. This theory posits that firms cannot perfectly monitor the work effort of their employees and that employees must themselves decide how hard to work. Workers can choose to work hard, or they can choose to shirk and risk getting caught and fired. The firm can raise worker effort by paying a high wage. The higher the wage, the greater is the cost to the worker of getting fired. By paying a higher wage, a firm induces more of its employees not to shirk and, thus, increases their productivity.

Policy Implications

Because new Keynesian economics is a school of thought regarding macroeconomic theory, its adherents do not necessarily share a single view about economic policy. At the broadest level new Keynesian economics suggests—in contrast to some new classical theories—that recessions do not represent the efficient functioning of markets. The elements of new Keynesian economics, such as menu costs, staggered prices, coordination failures, and efficiency wages, represent substantial departures from the assumptions of classical economics, which provides the intellectual basis for economists' usual justification of laissez-faire. In new Keynesian theories recessions are caused by some economy-wide market failure. Thus, new Keynesian economics provides a rationale for government intervention in the economy, such as countercyclical monetary or fiscal policy. Whether policymakers should intervene in practice, however, is a more difficult question that entails various political as well as economic judgments.

—N. Gregory Mankiw

Biography. N. Gregory Mankiw is a professor of economics at Harvard University.

Further Reading

Mankiw, N. Gregory, and David Romer, eds. *New Keynesian Economics*. 2 vols. 1991.
Rotemberg, Julio. "The New Keynesian Microfoundations." *NBER Macroeconomics Annual 1987,* edited by Stanley Fischer. 1987.

Public Choice Theory

Jane S. Shaw

■ Public choice theory is a branch of economics that developed from the study of taxation and public spending. It emerged in the fifties and received widespread public attention in 1986, when James Buchanan, one of its two leading architects (the other was his colleague Gordon Tullock), was awarded the Nobel Prize in economics. Buchanan started the Center for Study of Public Choice at George Mason University, now headed by Robert Tollison, and it remains the best-known locus of public choice research. Others include Florida State University, Washington University (St. Louis), Montana State University, the California Institute of Technology, and the University of Rochester.

Public choice takes the same principles that economists use to analyze people's actions in the marketplace and applies them to people's actions in collective decision making. Economists who study behavior in the private marketplace assume that people are motivated mainly by self-interest. Although most people base some of their actions on their concern for others, the dominant motive in people's actions in the marketplace—whether they are employers, employees, or consumers—is a concern for themselves. Public choice economists make the same assumption—that although people acting in the political marketplace have some concern for others, their main motive, whether they are voters, politicians, lobbyists, or bureaucrats, is self-interest. In Bu-

chanan's words the theory "replaces . . . romantic and illusory . . . notions about the workings of governments [with] . . . notions that embody more skepticism."

In the past many economists have argued that the way to rein in "market failures" such as monopolies is to introduce government action. But public choice economists point out that there also is such a thing as "government failure." That is, there are reasons why government intervention does not achieve the desired effect. For example, the Justice Department has responsibility for reducing monopoly power in noncompetitive industries. But a 1973 study by William F. Long, Richard Schramm, and Robert Tollison concluded that actual anticompetitive behavior played only a minor role in decisions by the Justice Department to bring antimonopoly suits. Instead, they found, the larger the industry, the more likely were firms in it to be sued. Similarly, Congress has frequently passed laws that are supposed to protect people against environmental pollution. But Robert Crandall has shown that congressional representatives from northern industrial states used the 1977 Clean Air Act amendments to reduce competition by curbing economic growth in the Sunbelt. The amendments required tighter emissions standards in undeveloped areas than in the more developed and more polluted areas, which tend to be in the East and Midwest.

One of the chief underpinnings of public

choice theory is the lack of incentives for voters to monitor government effectively. Anthony Downs, in one of the earliest public choice books, *An Economic Theory of Democracy,* pointed out that the voter is largely ignorant of political issues and that this ignorance is rational. Even though the result of an election may be very important, an individual's vote rarely decides an election. Thus, the direct impact of casting a well-informed vote is almost nil; the voter has virtually no chance to determine the outcome of the election. So spending time following the issues is not personally worthwhile for the voter. Evidence for this claim is found in the fact that public opinion polls consistently find that less than half of all voting-age Americans can name their own congressional representative.

Public choice economists point out that this incentive to be ignorant is rare in the private sector. Someone who buys a car typically wants to be well informed about the car he or she selects. That is because the car buyer's choice is decisive—he or she pays only for the one chosen. If the choice is wise, the buyer will benefit; if it is unwise, the buyer will suffer directly. Voting lacks that kind of direct result. Therefore, most voters are largely ignorant about the positions of the people for whom they vote. Except for a few highly publicized issues, they do not pay a lot of attention to what legislative bodies do, and even when they do pay attention, they have little incentive to gain the background knowledge and analytic skill needed to understand the issues.

Public choice economists also examine the actions of legislators. Although legislators are expected to pursue the "public in-

terest," they make decisions on how to use other people's resources, not their own. Furthermore, these resources must be provided by taxpayers and by those hurt by regulations whether they want to provide them or not. Politicians may intend to spend taxpayer money wisely. Efficient decisions, however, will neither save their own money nor give them any proportion of the wealth they save for citizens. There is no direct reward for fighting powerful interest groups in order to confer benefits on a public that is not even aware of the benefits or of who conferred them. Thus, the incentives for good management in the public interest are weak. In contrast, interest groups are organized by people with very strong gains to be made from governmental action. They provide politicians with campaign funds and campaign workers. In return they receive at least the "ear" of the politician and often gain support for their goals.

In other words, because legislators have the power to tax and to extract resources in other coercive ways, and because voters monitor their behavior poorly, legislators behave in ways that are costly to citizens. One technique analyzed by public choice is log rolling, or vote trading. An urban legislator votes to subsidize a rural water project in order to win another legislator's vote for a city housing subsidy. The two projects may be part of a single spending bill. Through such log rolling both legislators get what they want. And even though neither project uses resources efficiently, local voters know that their representative got something for them. They may not know that they are paying a pro-rata share of a bundle of inefficient projects! And the total expenditures may well be more than individual taxpayers would be willing to authorize if they were fully aware of what is going on.

In addition to voters and politicians, public choice analyzes the role of bureaucrats in government. Their incentives explain why many regulatory agencies appear to be "captured" by special interests. (The "capture" theory was introduced by the late George Stigler, a Nobel Laureate who did not work mainly in the public choice field.) Capture occurs because bureaucrats do not have a profit goal to guide their behavior. Instead, they usually are in government because they have a goal or mission. They rely on Congress for their budgets, and often the people who will benefit from their mission can influence Congress to provide more funds. Thus interest groups—who may be as diverse as lobbyists for regulated industries or leaders of environmental groups—become important to them. Such interrelationships can lead to bureaucrats being captured by interest groups.

Although public choice economists have focused mostly on analyzing government failure, they also have suggested ways to correct problems. For example, they argue that if government action is required, it should take place at the local level whenever possible. Because there are many local governments, and because people "vote with their feet," there is competition among local governments, as well as some experimentation. To streamline bureaucracies, Gordon Tullock and William Niskanen have recommended allowing several bureaus to supply the same service on the grounds that the resulting competition will improve efficiency. Forest economist Randal O'Toole recommends that the Forest

Service charge hikers and backpackers more than token fees to use the forests. This, he argues, will lead Forest Service personnel to pay more attention to recreation and reduce logging in areas that are attractive to nature lovers. And Rodney Fort and John Baden have suggested the creation of a "predatory bureau" whose mission is to reduce the budgets of other agencies, with its income depending on its success.

Public choice economists have also tried to develop rule changes that will reduce legislation that caters to special interests and leads to ever-expanding government expenditures. In the late eighties James C. Miller, a public choice scholar who headed the Office of Management and Budget during the Reagan Administration, helped pass the Gramm-Rudman law, which set a limit on annual spending and backed it with automatic cuts if the ceiling was not met. The law had at least a temporary effect in slowing spending. Support for term limits and for a line-item veto also reflects the public choice view that additional legislative rules are needed to limit logrolling and the power of special interests. Public choice scholars, however, do not necessarily agree on the potential effectiveness of specific rules.

Because of its skepticism about the supposedly benign nature of government, public choice is sometimes viewed as a conservative or libertarian branch of economics, as opposed to more "liberal" (that is, interventionist) wings such as Keynesian economics. This is partly correct. The emergence of public choice economics reflects dissatisfaction with the implicit assumption, held by Keynesians, among others, that government effectively corrects market failures.

But not all public choice economists are conservatives or libertarians. Mancur Olson is an important counterexample. Olson is known in public choice for his path-breaking book *The Logic of Collective Action,* in which he pointed out that large interest groups have trouble gaining and maintaining the support of those who benefit from their lobbying. That is because it is easy for individuals to ''free-ride'' on the efforts of others if they benefit automatically from those efforts. That is why, Olson explained, nineteenth-century farmers' groups, which were organized to be political lobbying groups, also sold insurance and other services. These provided a direct incentive for the individual farmer to stay involved. (As the number of farmers has declined in recent decades, they have become more politically powerful, an observation that supports Olson's contention.)

More recently, Olson wrote *The Rise and Decline of Nations,* which concludes that Germany and Japan thrived after World War II because the war destroyed the power of special interests to stifle entrepreneurship and economic exchange. But Olson still favors a strong government.

Many public choice economists take no political or ideological position. Some build formal mathematical models of voting strategies and apply game theory to understand how political conflicts are resolved. Economists at the California Institute of Technology, for example, have pointed out that ''agenda-setting''—that is, identifying the options that voters choose from, and even specifying the order of voting on the options—can influence political outcomes. This explains the role of initiatives and referenda as ways for voters to set agendas,

opening up options that legislatures otherwise would ignore or vote down.

Some of these economists have developed a separate and quite mathematical discipline known as ''social choice.'' Social choice traces its roots to early work by Nobel Prize–winning economist Kenneth Arrow. Arrow's 1951 book, *Social Choice and Individual Values,* attempted to figure out through logic whether people who have different goals can use voting to make collective decisions that please everyone. He concluded that they cannot, and thus his argument is called the ''impossibility theorem.''

In addition to providing insight into how public decision making occurs today, public choice analyzes the rules that guide the collective decision-making process itself. These are the constitutional rules that are made before political activity gets underway. Consideration of these rules was the heart of *The Calculus of Consent,* by James Buchanan and Gordon Tullock, one of the classics of public choice.

Buchanan and Tullock began with the view that a collective decision that is truly just—that is, a decision in the public interest—would be one that all voters would support unanimously. While unanimity is largely unworkable in practice, the book effectively challenged the widespread assumption that majority decisions are inherently fair. The approach reflected in *The Calculus of Consent* has led to a further subdiscipline of public choice, ''constitutional economics,'' which focuses exclusively on the rules that precede parliamentary or legislative decision making and limit the domain of government.

—**Jane S. Shaw**

Biography: Jane S. Shaw is a senior associate at the Political Economy Research Center in Bozeman, Montana. She was formerly associate economics editor with *Business Week*.

Further Reading

Buchanan, James M., and Gordon Tullock. *The Calculus of Consent*. 1962.
Downs, Anthony. *An Economic Theory of Democracy*. 1957.
Gwartney, James D., and Richard L. Stroup. *Economics: Private and Public Choice,* 6th ed. Especially chaps. 4, 30. 1992.
Gwartney, James D., and Richard E. Wagner, eds. *Public Choice and Constitutional Economics*. 1988.
Henderson, David R. ''James Buchanan and Company.'' *Reason* (November 1987): 37–43.

Growing Skepticism

One sure sign of the impact of a school of thought is whether and how it shows up in popular textbooks. By that criterion public choice thinking has had a big impact. Consider the famous textbook by noted MIT economist and Nobel Prize winner Paul Samuelson. In the book's early editions, starting in 1948, Samuelson showed little skepticism about the efficacy of government solutions. But by 1985 Samuelson's text, coauthored with Yale University's William Nordhaus, had become more critical of government. Their skepticism was explicitly based on public choice reasoning. Indeed, in ''Public Choice,'' an eleven-page section of the 1985 text, they explain some of the points made in this article. ''Often,'' they write, ''a logrolling process may end up as a redistributive scheme, where the winning coalition takes a bad initial proposal, and loads it with enough provisions that appeal to special-interest groups, until a solid majority has been obtained for a legislative dog.'' Samuelson and Nordhaus conclude: ''Before we race off to our federal, state, or local legislature, we should pause to recognize that *there are government failures as well as market failures*.'' [Italics theirs.]

—DRH

See also POLITICAL BEHAVIOR, PUBLIC GOODS AND EXTERNALITIES.

Rational Expectations

Thomas J. Sargent

■ The theory of rational expectations was first proposed by John F. Muth of Indiana University in the early sixties. He used the term to describe the many economic situations in which the outcome depends partly upon what people expect to happen. The price of an agricultural commodity, for example, depends on how many acres farmers plant, which in turn depends on the price that farmers expect to realize when they harvest and sell their crops. As another example, the value of a currency and its rate of depreciation depend partly on what people expect that rate of depreciation to be. That is because people rush to desert a currency that they expect to lose value, thereby contributing to its loss in value. Similarly, the price of a stock or bond depends partly on what prospective buyers and sellers believe it will be in the future.

The use of expectations in economic theory is not new. Many earlier economists, including A. C. Pigou, John Maynard Keynes, and John R. Hicks, assigned a central role in the determination of the business cycle to people's expectations about the future. Keynes referred to this as "waves of optimism and pessimism" that helped determine the level of economic activity. But proponents of the rational expectations theory are more thorough in their analysis of—and assign a more important role to—expectations.

The influences between expectations and outcomes flow both ways. In forming their expectations, people try to forecast what will actually occur. They have strong incentives to use forecasting rules that work well because higher "profits" accrue to someone who acts on the basis of better forecasts, whether that someone be a trader in the stock market or someone considering the purchase of a new car. And when people have to forecast a particular price over and over again, they tend to adjust their forecasting rules to eliminate avoidable errors. Thus, there is continual feedback from past outcomes to current expectations. Translation: in recurrent situations the way the future unfolds from the past tends to be stable, and people adjust their forecasts to conform to this stable pattern.

The concept of rational expectations asserts that outcomes do not differ systematically (i.e., regularly or predictably) from what people expected them to be. The concept is motivated by the same thinking that led Abraham Lincoln to assert, "You can fool some of the people all of the time, and all of the people some of the time, but you cannot fool all of the people all of the time." From the viewpoint of the rational expectations doctrine, Lincoln's statement gets things right. It does not deny that people often make forecasting errors, but it does suggest that errors will not persistently occur on one side or the other.

Economists who believe in rational expectations base their belief on the standard economic assumption that people behave in ways that maximize their utility (their enjoyment of life) or profits. Economists have used the concept of rational expectations to understand a variety of situations in which speculation about the future is a crucial factor in determining current action. Rational expectations is a building block for the ''random walk'' or ''efficient markets'' theory of securities prices, the theory of the dynamics of hyperinflations, the ''permanent income'' and ''life-cycle'' theories of consumption, the theory of ''tax smoothing,'' and the design of economic stabilization policies.

The Efficient Markets Theory of Stock Prices

One of the earliest and most striking applications of the concept of rational expectations is the efficient markets theory of asset prices. A sequence of observations on a variable (such as daily stock prices) is said to follow a random walk if the current value gives the best possible prediction of future values. The efficient markets theory of stock prices uses the concept of rational expectations to reach the conclusion that, when properly adjusted for discounting and dividends, stock prices follow a random walk. The chain of reasoning goes as follows. In their efforts to forecast prices, investors comb all sources of information, including patterns that they can spot in past price movements.

Investors buy stocks that they expect to have a higher-than-average return and sell those that they expect to have lower returns. When they do so, they bid up the prices of stocks expected to have higher-than-aver-

age returns and drive down the prices of those expected to have lower-than-average returns. The prices of the stocks adjust until the expected returns, adjusted for risk, are equal for all stocks. Equalization of expected returns means that investors' forecasts become built into or reflected in the prices of stocks. More precisely, it means that stock prices change so that after an adjustment to reflect dividends, the time value of money, and differential risk, they equal the market's best forecast of the future price. Therefore, the only factors that can change stock prices are random factors that could not be known in advance. Thus, changes in stock prices follow a random walk.

The random walk theory has been subjected to literally hundreds of empirical tests. The tests tend to support the theory quite strongly. While some studies have found situations that contradict the theory, the theory does explain, at least to a very good first approximation, how asset prices evolve (see EFFICIENT CAPITAL MARKETS).

The Permanent Income Theory of Consumption

The Keynesian consumption function holds that there is a positive relationship between people's consumption and their income. Early empirical work in the forties and fifties encountered some discrepancies from the theory, which Milton Friedman successfully explained with his celebrated ''permanent income theory'' of consumption. Friedman built upon Irving Fisher's insight that a person's consumption ought not to depend on current income alone, but also on prospects of income in the future. Friedman posited that people consume out of their "permanent income," which can be defined as the level of consumption that can be sustained while leaving wealth intact. In defining "wealth," Friedman included a measure of "human wealth"—namely, the present value of people's expectations of future labor income.

Although Friedman did not formally apply the concept of rational expectations in his work, it is implicit in much of his discussion. Because of its heavy emphasis on the role of expectations about future income, his hypothesis was a prime candidate for the application of rational expectations. In work subsequent to Friedman's, John F. Muth and Stanford's Robert E. Hall imposed rational expectations on versions of Friedman's model, with interesting results. In Hall's version, imposing rational expectations produces the result that consumption is a random walk: the best prediction of future consumption is the present level of consumption. This result encapsulates the consumption-smoothing aspect of the permanent income model and reflects people's efforts to estimate their wealth and to allocate it over time. If consumption in each period is held at a level that is expected to leave wealth unchanged, it follows that wealth and consumption will each equal their values in the previous period plus an unforecastable or unforeseeable random shock—really a forecast error.

The rational expectations version of the permanent income hypothesis has changed the way economists think about short-term stabilization policies (such as temporary tax cuts) designed to stimulate the economy. Keynesian economists used to believe that tax cuts would boost disposable income and thus cause people to consume more. But according to the permanent income model, temporary tax cuts would have much less of an effect on consumption than Keynesians had thought. The reason is that people are basing their consumption decisions on their wealth, not their current disposable income. Because temporary tax cuts are bound to be reversed, they have little or no effect on wealth, and therefore, they have little or no effect on consumption. Thus, the permanent income model had the effect of diminishing the expenditure "multiplier" that economists ascribed to temporary tax cuts.

The rational expectations version of the permanent income model had been extensively tested, with results that are quite encouraging. The evidence is that the model works well but imperfectly. Economists are currently extending the model to take into account factors such as "habit persistence" in consumption and the differing durabilities of various consumption goods. Expanding the theory to incorporate these features alters the pure "random walk" prediction of the theory (and so helps remedy some of the empirical shortcomings of the model), but it leaves the basic permanent income insight intact.

Tax-Smoothing Models

How should a government design tax policy when it knows that people are making decisions partly in response to the government's plans for setting taxes in the future? That is, when participants in the private sector have rational expectations about the government's rules for setting tax rates, what rules should the government use to set tax rates? Robert Lucas and Nancy Stokey, as well as Robert Barro, have studied this problem under the assumption that the government can make and keep commitments to execute the plans that it designs. All three authors have identified situations in which the government should finance a volatile (or unsmooth) sequence of government expenditures with a sequence of tax rates that is quite stable (or smooth) over time. Such policies are called "tax-smoothing" policies. Tax smoothing is a good idea because it minimizes the supply disincentives associated with taxes. For example, workers who pay a 20 percent marginal tax rate every year will reduce their labor supply less (that is, will work more at any given wage) than they would if the government set a 10 percent marginal tax rate in half the years and a 30 percent rate in the other half.

During "normal times" a government operating under a tax-smoothing rule typically has close to a balanced budget. But during times of extraordinary expenditures—during wars, for example—the government runs a deficit, which it finances by borrowing. During and after the war the government increases taxes by enough to service the debt it has occurred; in this way the higher taxes that the government imposes to finance the war are spread out over time. Such a policy minimizes the cumulative distorting effects of taxes—the adverse "supply-side" effects.

Barro's tax-smoothing theory helps explain the behavior of the British and U.S. governments in the eighteenth and nineteenth centuries, when the standard pattern was to finance wars with deficits but to set taxes after wars at rates sufficiently high to service the government's debt.

Expectational Error Models of the Business Cycle

A long tradition in business cycle theory has held that errors in people's forecasts are a major cause of business fluctuations. This view was embodied in the Phillips curve (the observed inverse correlation between unemployment and inflation), with economists attributing the correlation to errors that people made in their forecasts of the price level. Before the advent of rational expectations, economists often proposed to "exploit" or "manipulate" the public's forecasting errors in ways designed to generate better performance of the economy over the business cycle. Thus, Robert Hall aptly described the state of economic thinking in 1973 when he wrote:

> The benefits of inflation derive from the use of expansionary policy to trick economic agents into behaving in socially preferable ways even though their behavior is not in their own interest. . . . The gap between actual and expected inflation measures the extent of the trickery. . . . The optimal policy is not nearly as expansionary [inflationary] when expectations adjust rapidly, and most of the effect of an inflationary policy is dissipated in costly anticipated inflation.

Rational expectations undermines the idea that policymakers can manipulate the economy by systematically making the public have false expectations. Robert Lucas showed that if expectations are rational, it simply is not possible for the government to manipulate those forecast errors in a predictable and reliable way for the very reason that the errors made by a rational forecaster are inherently unpredictable. Lucas's work led to what has sometimes been called the "policy ineffectiveness proposition." If people have rational expectations, policies that try to manipulate the economy by inducing people into having false expectations may introduce more "noise" into the economy but cannot, on average, improve the economy's performance.

Design of Macroeconomic Policies

The "policy ineffectiveness" result pertains only to those economic policies that have their effects solely by inducing forecast errors. Many government policies work by affecting "margins" or incentives, and the concept of rational expectations delivers no "policy ineffectiveness" result for such policies. In fact, the idea of rational expectations is now being used extensively in such contexts to study the design of monetary, fiscal, and regulatory policies to promote good economic performance.

For example, extensions of the tax-smoothing models are being developed in a variety of directions. The tax-smoothing result depends on various special assumptions about the physical technology for transferring resources over time, and also on the sequence of government expenditures assumed. These assumptions are being relaxed, with interesting modifications of the tax-smoothing prescription being a con-

sequence. Christophe Chamley reached the striking conclusion that an optimal tax scheme involves eventually setting the tax rate on capital to zero, with labor bearing the entire tax burden. To get his result, Chamley assumed that "labor" and "capital" are very different factors, with the total availability of labor being beyond people's control while the supply of capital could be affected by investment and saving. When Chamley's assumptions are altered to acknowledge the "human capital" component of labor, which can be affected by people's decisions, his conclusion about capital taxation is different.

The idea of rational expectations has also been a workhorse in developing prescriptions for optimally choosing monetary policy. Important contributors to this literature have been Truman Bewley and William A. Brock. Bewley and Brock's work describes precisely the contexts in which an optimal monetary arrangement involves having the government pay interest on reserves at the market rate. Their work supports, clarifies, and extends proposals to monetary reform made by Milton Friedman in 1960 and 1968.

Rational expectations has been a working assumption in recent studies that try to explain how monetary and fiscal authorities can retain (or lose) "good reputations" for their conduct of policy. This literature is beginning to help economists understand the multiplicity of government policy strategies followed, for example, in high-inflation and low-inflation countries. In particular, work on "reputational equilibria" in macroeconomics by Robert Barro and by David Gordon and Nancy Stokey has shown that the preferences of citizens and policymakers and the available production technologies and trading opportunities are not by themselves sufficient to determine whether a government will follow a low-inflation or a high-inflation policy mix.

Instead, reputation remains an independent factor even after rational expectations have been assumed.

—Thomas J. Sargent

Biography: Thomas J. Sargent is a senior fellow at Stanford's Hoover Institution and an economics professor at the University of Chicago. He is one of the pioneers in the theory of rational expectations.

Further Reading

Fischer, Stanley, ed. *Rational Expectations and Economic Policy*. 1980.
Lucas, Robert E., Jr. *Models of Business Cycles*. 1987.
Muth, John A. "Rational Expectations and the Theory of Price Movements." *Econometrica* 29, no. 6 (1961): 315–35.
Sargent, Thomas J. *Rational Expectations and Inflation*. 1986.

Socialism

Robert Heilbroner

■ Socialism—defined as a centrally planned economy in which the government controls all means of production—has been the tragic failure of the twentieth century. Born of a commitment to remedy the economic and moral defects of capitalism, it has far surpassed capitalism in both economic malfunction and moral cruelty. Yet the idea and the ideal of socialism linger on. Whether socialism in some form will eventually return as a major organizing force in human affairs is unknown, but no one can accurately appraise its prospects who has not taken into account the dramatic story of its rise and fall.

The Birth of Socialist Planning

It is often thought that the idea of socialism derives from the work of Karl Marx. In fact, Marx wrote only a few pages about socialism, as either a moral or a practical blueprint for society. The true architect of a socialist order was Lenin, who first faced the practical difficulties of organizing an economic system without the driving incentives of profit seeking or the self-generating constraints of competition. Lenin began from the long-standing delusion that economic organization would become less complex once the profit drive and the market mechanism had been dispensed with— "as self-evident," he wrote, as "the extraordinarily simple operations of watching,

recording, and issuing receipts, within the reach of anybody who can read and write and knows the first four rules of arithmetic."

In fact, economic life pursued under these first four rules rapidly became so disorganized that within four years of the 1917 revolution, Soviet production had fallen to 14 percent of its prerevolutionary level. By 1921 Lenin was forced to institute the New Economic Policy (NEP), a partial return to the market incentives of capitalism. This brief mixture of socialism and capitalism came to an end in 1927 after Stalin instituted the process of forced collectivization that was to mobilize Russian resources for its leap into industrial power.

The system that evolved under Stalin and his successors took the form of a pyramid of command. At its apex was Gosplan, the highest state planning agency, which established such general directives for the economy as the target rate of growth, the allocation of effort between military and civilian outputs, between heavy and light industry, or among various regions. Gosplan transmitted the general directives to successive ministries of industrial and regional planning, whose technical advisers broke down the overall national plan into directives assigned to particular factories, industrial power centers, collective farms, or whatever. These thousands of individual subplans were finally scrutinized by the factory managers and engineers who would eventually have to implement them. Thereafter, the blueprint for production reascended the pyramid, together with the suggestions, emendations, and pleas of those who had seen it. Ultimately, a completed plan would be reached by negotiation, voted on by the Supreme Soviet, and passed into law.

Thus, the final plan resembled an immense order book, specifying the nuts and bolts, steel girders, grain outputs, tractors, cotton, cardboard, and coal that, in their entirety, constituted the national output. In theory such an order book should enable planners to reconstitute a working economy each year—provided, of course, that the nuts fitted the bolts, the girders were of the right dimensions, the grain output was properly stored, the tractors operable, and the cotton, cardboard, and coal of the kinds needed for their manifold uses. But there was a vast and widening gap between theory and practice.

Problems Emerge

The gap did not appear immediately. In retrospect, we can see that the task facing Lenin and Stalin in the early years was not so much economic as quasi-military—mobilizing a peasantry into a work force to build roads and rail lines, dams and electric grids, steel complexes and tractor factories. This was a formidable assignment, but far less formidable than what would confront socialism fifty years later, when the task was not so much to create enormous undertakings, but relatively self-contained ones, and to fit all the outputs into a dovetailing whole.

Through the sixties the Soviet economy continued to report strong overall growth—roughly twice that of the United States—but observers began to spot signs of impending trouble. One was the difficulty of specifying outputs in terms that would maximize the well-being of everyone in the economy, not merely the bonuses earned by individual factory managers for "overfulfilling" their assigned objectives. The problem was that the plan specified outputs in physical terms. One consequence was that managers maximized yardages or tonnages of output, not its quality. A famous cartoon in the satirical magazine *Krokodil* showed a factory manager proudly displaying his record output, a single gigantic nail suspended from a crane.

As the economic flow became increasingly clogged and clotted, production took the form of "stormings" at the end of each quarter or year, when every resource was pressed into use to meet preassigned targets. The same rigid system soon produced expediters, or *tolkachi,* to arrange shipments to harassed managers who needed unplanned—and therefore unobtainable—inputs to achieve their production goals. Worse, in the absence of the right to buy their own supplies or to hire or fire their own workers, factories set up fabricating shops, then commissaries, and finally their own worker housing to maintain control over their own small bailiwicks.

It is not surprising that this increasingly Byzantine system began to create serious dysfunctions beneath the overall statistics of growth. During the sixties the Soviet Union became the first industrial country in history to suffer a prolonged peacetime fall in average life expectancy, a symptom of its disastrous misallocation of resources. Military research facilities could get whatever they needed, but hospitals were low on the priority list. By the seventies the figures clearly indicated a slowing of overall production. By the eighties the Soviet Union officially acknowledged a near end to growth that was, in reality, an unofficial decline. In 1987 the first official law embodying *perestroika*—restructuring—was put into effect. President Mikhail Gorbachev announced his intention to revamp the economy from top to bottom by introducing the market, reestablishing private ownership, and opening the system to free economic interchange with the West. Seventy years of socialist rise had come to an end.

Socialist Planning in Western Eyes

Understanding of the difficulties of central planning was slow to emerge. In the midthirties, while the Russian industrialization drive was at full tilt, few voices were raised about its problems. Among those few were Ludwig von Mises, an articulate and exceedingly argumentative free-market economist, and Friedrich Hayek, of much more contemplative temperament, later to be awarded a Nobel Prize for his work in monetary theory. Together, Mises and Hayek launched an attack on the feasibility of socialism that seemed at the time unconvincing in its argument as to the functional problems of a planned economy. Mises in particular contended that a socialist system was "impossible" because there was no way for the planners to acquire the information—"produce this, not that"—needed for a coherent economy. This information, Hayek emphasized, emerged spontaneously

in a market system from the rise and fall of prices. A planning system was bound to fail precisely because it lacked such a signaling mechanism.

The Mises-Hayek argument met its most formidable counterargument in two brilliant articles by Oskar Lange, a young economist who would become the first Polish ambassador to the United States after World War II. Lange set out to show that the planners would, in fact, have precisely the same information as that which guided a market economy. The information would be revealed as inventories of goods rose and fell, signaling either that supply was greater than demand or demand greater than supply. Thus, as planners watched inventory levels, they were also learning which of their administered (i.e., state-dictated) prices were too high and which too low. It only remained, therefore, to adjust prices so that supply and demand balanced, exactly as in the marketplace.

Lange's answer was so simple and clear that many believed the Mises-Hayek argument had been demolished. In fact, we now know that their argument was all too prescient. Ironically, though, Mises and Hayek were right for a reason that they did not foresee as clearly as Lange himself. *"The real danger of socialism,"* Lange wrote, in italics, *"is that of a bureaucratization of economic life."* But he took away the force of the remark by adding, without italics, "Unfortunately, we do not see how the same or even greater danger can be averted under monopolistic capitalism."

The effects of the "bureaucratization of economic life" are dramatically related in *The Turning Point,* a scathing attack on the realities of socialist economic planning by two Soviet economists, Nikolai Smelev and Vladimir Popov, that gives examples of the planning process in actual operation. In 1982, to stimulate the production of gloves from moleskins, the Soviet government raised the price it was willing to pay for moleskins from twenty to fifty kopecks per pelt. Smelev and Popov noted:

> State purchases increased, and now all the distribution centers are filled with these pelts. Industry is unable to use them all, and they often rot in warehouses before they can be processed. The Ministry of Light Industry has already requested Goskomtsen [the State Committee on Prices] twice to lower prices, but "the question has not been decided" yet. This is not surprising. Its members are too busy to decide. They have no time: besides setting prices on these pelts, they have to keep track of another 24 million prices. And how can they possibly know how much to lower the price today, so they won't have to raise it tomorrow?

This story speaks volumes about the problem of a centrally planned system. The crucial missing element is not so much "information," as Mises and Hayek argued, as it is the motivation to act on information. After all, the inventories of moleskins did tell the planners that their production was at first too low and then too high. What was missing was the willingness—better yet,

the necessity—to respond to the signals of changing inventories. A capitalist firm responds to changing prices because failure to do so will cause it to lose money. A socialist ministry ignores changing inventories because bureaucrats learn that doing something is more likely to get them in trouble than doing nothing, unless doing nothing results in absolute disaster.

Absolute economic disaster has now been reached in the Soviet Union and its Eastern former satellites, and we are watching efforts to construct some form of economic structure that will no longer display the deadly symptoms of inertia and indifference that have come to be the hallmarks of socialism. It is too early to predict whether these efforts will succeed. The main obstacle to real perestroika is the impossibility of creating a working market system without a firm basis of private ownership, and it is clear that the creation of such a basis encounters the opposition of the former state bureaucracy and the hostility of ordinary people who have long been trained to be suspicious of the pursuit of wealth. In the face of such uncertainties, all predictions are foolhardy save one: no quick or easy transition from socialism to some form of nonsocialism is possible. Transformations of such magnitude are historic convulsions, not mere changes in policy. Their completion must be measured in decades or generations, not years.

—Robert Heilbroner

Biography: Robert Heilbroner is the Norman Thomas Professor of Economics (emeritus) at the New School for Social Research. He is the author of the best-seller *The Worldly Philosophers*.

Further Reading

Hayek, Friedrich A. "Socialist Economic Calculation: The Present State of the Debate." In Hayek. *Individualism and Economic Order*. 1942. Reprint. 1972.

Lange, Oskar, and Fred Taylor. *On the Economic Theory of Socialism*. 1938.

Mises, Ludwig von. "Economic Calculation in the Socialist Commonwealth." In *Collectivist Economic Planning*, edited by Friedrich A. Hayek. 1935.

Smelev, Nikolai, and Vladimir Popov. *The Turning Point*. 1990.

Supply-Side Economics

James D. Gwartney

■ Supply-side economics provided the political and theoretical foundation for a remarkable number of tax cuts in the United States and other countries during the eighties. Supply-side economics stresses the impact of tax rates on the incentives for people to produce and to use resources efficiently. A person's marginal tax rate—the tax rate she pays on an additional dollar of income—determines the breakdown between taxes, on the one hand, and income available for personal use, on the other. Since they directly affect the incentive of people to work, to save and invest, and to avoid and evade taxes, marginal tax rates are central to supply-side analysis.

An increase in marginal tax rates reduces the share of additional income that earners are permitted to keep. This adversely affects output for two major reasons. First, the higher marginal rates reduce the payoff that people derive from work and from other taxable productive activities. When people are prohibited from reaping much of what they sow, they will sow more sparingly. Thus, when marginal tax rates rise, some people, those with working spouses for example, will opt out of the labor force. Others will decide to take more vacation time, retire earlier, or forgo overtime opportunities. Still others will decide to forgo promising but risky business opportunities. These reductions in productive effort shrink the effective supply of resources and thereby retard output.

Second, high marginal tax rates also encourage tax shelter investments and other forms of tax avoidance. As marginal tax rates rise, investments that generate paper losses from depreciable assets become more attractive. So, too, do business activities that present opportunities to deduct expenditures on hobbies (for example, collecting antiques, raising horses, or traveling) and personal amenities (luxury automobiles, plush offices, and various fringe benefits). Thus, people are directed into activities because of tax advantages rather than profitability. Similarly, they are encouraged to substitute less desired tax-deductible goods for more desired nondeductible goods. Waste and inefficient use of valuable resources are a by-product of this incentive structure.

It is important to distinguish between a change in tax *rates* and a change in tax *revenues*. Because higher tax rates discourage work effort and encourage tax avoidance and even tax evasion, the tax base will shrink as the rates increase. When something is taxed more heavily, you will get less of it. Therefore, an increase in a tax rate causes a less than proportional increase in tax revenue. Indeed, economist Arthur Laffer (of ''Laffer curve'' fame) popularized the notion that higher tax rates may actually cause the tax base to shrink so much that tax revenues will decline.

This inverse relationship between a change in tax rates and the accompanying change in tax revenues is quite likely when marginal tax rates are high, but unlikely when rates are low. An analysis of the incentive effects for different tax brackets illustrates why this is true. Suppose that a government with progressive income tax rates ranging from a low of 15 percent to a high of 75 percent cuts tax rates by one-third. The top tax rate would then fall from

75 percent to 50 percent. After the tax cut, taxpayers in the highest tax bracket who earn an additional $100 would get to keep $50 rather than $25, a 100 percent increase in the incentive to earn. Predictably, these taxpayers will earn more taxable income after the rate reduction, and the revenues collected from them will decline by substantially less than a third. In fact, given the huge increase in their incentive to earn, the revenues collected from taxpayers confronting such high marginal rates may actually increase.

The same 33 percent rate reduction will cut the bottom tax rate from 15 percent to 10 percent. Here, take-home pay per $100 of additional earnings will rise from $85 to $90, only a 5.9 percent increase in the incentive to earn (compared to the 100 percent increase in the top bracket). Because cutting the 15 percent rate to 10 percent exerts only a small effect on the incentive to earn, the rate reduction has little impact on the tax base. Therefore, in contrast with the revenue effects in high tax brackets, tax revenue will decline by almost the same percent as tax rates in the lowest tax brackets. The bottom line is that cutting all rates by a third will lead to small revenue losses (or even revenue gains) in high tax brackets and large revenue losses in the lowest brackets. The share of the income tax paid by high-income taxpayers will rise.

The inflationary seventies created a receptive environment for the supply-side view. As inflation pushed numerous taxpayers into higher and higher marginal tax brackets, supply-side economists argued that high taxes were a major drag on economic growth. Furthermore, according to the supply-side view, the top rates could be reduced without a significant loss in revenue.

During the great tax debate of 1975 to 1986, the opponents of the supply-side view argued that it was unrealistic to expect lower tax rates to lead to increased tax revenues. According to the critics an increase in the tax base that was large enough to increase revenues would require an unrealistically large elasticity of labor supply (increase in hours worked due to higher after-tax wages). In response the supply-side proponents stressed that reductions in tax avoidance activities, as well as labor-supply effects, would enlarge the tax base when the rates were reduced. According to the supply-side view the combination of a decline in tax avoidance and increase in business activities would permit lower rates with little or no loss of revenues in the top tax brackets. At the same time, most supply-side economists, though perhaps not all, noted that reductions in low tax rates would lead to revenue losses.

Empirical studies of tax cuts that happened during the twenties and sixties buttressed the supply-side position. Prodded by Secretary of the Treasury Andrew Mellon, three major tax cuts reduced the top marginal tax rate from 73 percent in 1921 to 25 percent in 1926. In addition, the tax cuts eliminated or virtually eliminated the personal income tax liability of low-income recipients. The results were quite impressive. The economy grew rapidly from 1921 through 1926. After the rates were lowered, the real tax revenue (in 1929 dollars) collected from taxpayers with incomes above $50,000 rose from $305.1 million in 1921 to $498.1 million in 1926, an increase of 63 percent. In contrast, the real tax liability

of those with less than $50,000 of income declined by 45 percent. Thus, as the tax rates were cut, the revenues collected from high-income taxpayers rose, while those collect from lower-income taxpayers declined. The tax cuts of the twenties substantially increased the percent of taxes paid by the wealthy.

The results of the Kennedy-Johnson tax cuts of the midsixties were similar. Between 1963 and 1965, tax rates were reduced by approximately 25 percent. The top marginal tax rate was cut from 91 percent to 70 percent. Simultaneously, the bottom rate was reduced from 20 percent to 14 percent. For most taxpayers the lower rates reduced tax revenues. In real 1963 dollars the tax revenues collected from the bottom 95 percent of taxpayers fell from $31.0 billion in 1963 to $29.6 billion in 1965, a 4.5 percent reduction. In contrast, the real tax revenues collected from the top 5 percent of taxpayers rose from $17.2 billion in 1963 to $18.5 billion in 1965, a 7.6 percent increase. As in the case of the tax cuts of the twenties, the rate reductions of the sixties reduced the tax revenue collected from low-income taxpayers while increasing the revenues collected from high-income taxpayers.

Major tax legislation passed in 1981 and 1986 reduced the top U.S. federal income tax rate from 70 percent to approximately 33 percent. The performance of the U.S. economy during the eighties was impressive. The growth rate of real GNP accelerated from the sluggish rates of the seventies. U.S. economic growth exceeded that of all other major industrial nations except Japan.

The critics of the eighties tax policy argue that the top rate reductions were a bonanza for the rich. The taxable income in the upper tax brackets did increase sharply during the eighties. But the taxes collected in these brackets also rose sharply. Measured in 1982–84 dollars, the income tax revenue collected from the top 10 percent of earners rose from $150.6 billion in 1981 to $199.8 billion in 1988, an increase of 32.7 percent. The percentage increases in the real tax revenue collected from the top 1 and top 5 percent of taxpayers were even larger. In contrast, the real tax liability of other taxpayers (the bottom 90 percent) declined from $161.8 billion to $149.1 billion, a reduction of 7.8 percent. These findings confirm what the supply-siders predicted: the lower rates, by increasing the tax base substantially in the upper tax brackets, caused high-income taxpayers to pay more taxes. In effect, the lower rates soaked the rich.

Probably the most detailed study of the tax changes in the eighties was conducted by Lawrence Lindsey of Harvard University. Lindsey used a computer simulation model to estimate the impact of the eighties' tax-rate changes on the various components of income. He found that after the tax rates were lowered, the wages and salaries of high-income taxpayers were approximately 30 percent larger than projected. Similarly, after the rate cuts capital gains were approximately 100 percent higher than projected, and high-income taxpayers' business income was a whopping 200 percent higher than expected. Lindsey concluded that the main supply-side effects resulted from (a) people paying themselves more in the form of money income rather than fringe benefits and amenities, (b) increases in business activity, and (c) a reduction in tax shelter activities. His findings undercut the position of those supply-side critics who had as-

sumed that substantial supply-side effects were dependent on a large increase in labor supply.

Studies linking rate changes with changes in tax revenue measure the short-term effects of tax policy. But because taxpayers take time to adjust, revenues are even more responsive to rate changes in the long run. James Long and I conducted a study that found that taxpayers in states with lower marginal tax rates had much lower deductions and much lower expenditures on tax shelters than taxpayers in states with higher marginal rates. We found that when the combined federal-state marginal tax rate rises above 50 percent, the government's tax revenues decline. Lindsey estimates that the government's revenue begins declining at even lower tax rates, approximately 35 percent.

Supply-side economics influenced tax policy throughout the world in the late eighties. Of eighty-six countries with a personal income tax, fifty-five reduced their top marginal tax rate during the 1985–90 period, while only two (Luxembourg and Lebanon) increased their top rate. Countries that substantially reduced their top marginal tax rates include Australia, Brazil, France, Italy, Japan, New Zealand, Sweden, and the United Kingdom.

Reflecting the dominant Keynesian view at the beginning of the eighties, most economists thought that tax changes influenced output and revenue primarily by changing the demand for goods and services. Both research and the tax policy changes of the eighties, however, indicate that supply-side incentive effects are quite important. While controversy continues about the precise magnitude of the supply-side effects, the view that marginal tax rates in excess of 40 percent exert a destructive influence on the incentive of people to work and use resources wisely is now widely accepted among economists. This was not true prior to the eighties. An important piece of evidence for the shift in thinking is a 1987 statement by the Congressional Budget Office (CBO), which had been critical of the supply-side claims and had always assumed in its revenue projections that taxpayers did not respond at all to changes in tax rates. The CBO wrote: "The data show considerable evidence of a very significant revenue response among taxpayers at the highest income levels." This change in thinking is the major legacy of supply-side economics.

—James D. Gwartney

Biography: James D. Gwartney is a professor of economics at Florida State University.

Further Reading

Canto, Victor A., Douglas H. Joines, and Arthur B. Laffer. *Foundations of Supply-Side Economics*. 1983.
Federal Reserve Bank of Atlanta. *Supply-Side Economics in the 1980s*. 1982.
Henderson, David R. "Are We All Supply-Siders Now?" *Contemporary Policy Issues* 7, no. 4 (October 1989): 116–28.
Lindsey, Lawrence. *The Growth Experiment: How the New Tax Policy Is Transforming the U.S. Economy*. 1990.
Long, James, and James D. Gwartney. "Income Tax Avoidance: Evidence from Individual Tax Returns." *National Tax Journal* 50 (December 1987): 517–32.

See also MARGINAL TAX RATES; PROGRESSIVE TAXES; TAXATION, A PREFACE.

CHAPTER THREE

MACROECONOMICS

Business Cycles

Christina D. Romer

■ The United States and all other modern industrial economies experience significant swings in economic activity. In some years most industries are booming and unemployment is low; in other years most industries are operating well below capacity and unemployment is high. Periods of economic expansion are typically called booms; periods of economic decline are called recessions or depressions. The combination of booms and recessions, the ebb and flow of economic activity, is called the business cycle.

Business cycles as we know them today were first identified and analyzed by Arthur Burns and Wesley Mitchell in their 1946 book, *Measuring Business Cycles*. One of their key insights was that many economic indicators move together. During a boom, or expansion, not only does output rise, but also employment rises and unemployment falls. New construction and prices typically rise during a boom as well. Conversely, during a downturn, or depression, not only does the output of goods and services decline, but employment falls and unemployment rises as well. New construction also declines. In the era before World War II, prices also typically fell during a recession; since the fifties, prices have risen during downturns, though usually more slowly than during booms.

Business cycles are dated according to when the direction of economic activity changes. The peak of the cycle refers to the last month before several key economic indicators, such as employment, output, and new housing starts, begin to fall. The trough of the cycle refers to the last month before the same economic indicators begin to rise. Because key economic indicators often change direction at slightly different times, the dating of peaks and troughs necessarily involves a certain amount of subjective judgment. The National Bureau of Economic Research, an independent research institution, determines the official dates of peaks and troughs in U.S. business cycles. Table 1 shows the NBER monthly dates for peaks and troughs of U.S. business cycles since 1890.

In many ways the term *business cycle* is misleading. "Cycle" seems to imply that there is some regularity in the timing and duration of upswings and downswings in economic activity. Most economists, however, believe otherwise. Booms and recessions occur at irregular intervals and last for varying lengths of time. For example, economic activity hit low points in 1975, 1980, and 1982. The 1982 trough was then followed by eight years of uninterrupted expansion. For describing the swings in economic activity, therefore, most modern economists prefer the term *economic fluctuations*.

Just as there is no regularity in the timing of business cycles, there is no reason why cycles have to occur at all. The prevailing view among economists is that there is a

TABLE 1

Business Cycle Peaks and Troughs in the United States
1890–1992

Peak		Trough		Peak		Trough	
July	1890	May	1891	Aug.	1929	Mar.	1933
Jan.	1893	June	1894	May	1937	June	1938
Dec.	1895	June	1897	Feb.	1945	Oct.	1945
June	1899	Dec.	1900	Nov.	1948	Oct.	1949
Sep.	1902	Aug.	1904	July	1953	May	1954
May	1907	June	1908	Aug.	1957	Apr.	1958
Jan.	1910	Jan.	1912	Apr.	1960	Feb.	1961
Jan.	1913	Dec.	1914	Dec.	1969	Nov.	1970
Aug.	1918	Mar.	1919	Nov.	1973	Mar.	1975
Jan.	1920	July	1921	Jan.	1980	July	1980
May	1923	July	1924	July	1981	Nov.	1982
Oct.	1926	Nov.	1927	July	1990	Mar.	1991

level of economic activity, often referred to as full employment, at which the economy theoretically could stay forever. Full employment refers to a level of production at which all the inputs to the production process are being used, but not so intensively that they wear out, break down, or insist on higher wages and more vacations. If nothing disturbs the economy, the full-employment level of output, which naturally tends to grow as the population increases and new technologies are discovered, can be maintained forever. There is no reason why a time of full employment has to give way to either a full-fledged boom or a recession.

Business cycles do occur, however, because there are disturbances to the economy of one sort or another. Booms can be generated by surges in private or public spending.

For example, if the government spends a lot of money to fight a war but does not raise taxes, the increased demand will cause not only an increase in the output of war materiel, but also an increase in the take-home pay of government plant workers. The output of all the goods and services that these workers want to buy with their wages will also increase. Similarly, a wave of optimism that causes consumers to spend more than usual and firms to build new factories will cause the economy to expand. Recessions or depressions can be caused by these same forces working in reverse. A substantial cut in government spending or a wave of pessimism among consumers and firms may cause the output of all types of goods to fall.

Another cause of recessions and booms

is monetary policy. The Federal Reserve System determines the size and growth rate of the money stock and, thus, the level of interest rates in the economy. Interest rates, in turn, are a crucial determinant of how much firms and consumers want to spend. A firm faced with high interest rates may decide to postpone building a new factory because the cost of borrowing is so high. Conversely, a consumer may be lured into buying a new home if interest rates are low and mortgage payments are, therefore, more affordable. Thus, by raising or lowering interest rates, the Federal Reserve is able to generate recessions or booms.

This description of what causes business cycles reflects the Keynesian or New Keynesian view that cycles are the result of imperfections in the economy. Only when prices and expectations are not fully flexible can fluctuations in government spending or the money stock cause large swings in real output. An alternative framework, referred to as the New Classical view, holds that modern industrial economies are quite flexible. As a result a change in government policy does not necessarily affect real output and employment. In the New Classical view, for example, a change in the stock of money will change only prices; it will have no effect on real interest rates and thus on people's willingness to invest. According to this view business cycles are largely the result of disturbances in productivity and tastes, not of changes in government economic policy. One implication of this view would be that there is nothing inherently wrong with an economic downturn.

The empirical evidence, I believe, is strongly on the side of the New Keynesian view that cycles are often the result of changes in economic policy. Monetary policy, in particular, appears to have played a crucial role in causing business cycles in the United States since World War II. The severe recessions of both the early seventies and the early eighties, for example, were directly attributable to the Federal Reserve's decisions to raise interest rates. On the positive side, the booms of the mid-sixties and the mideighties were both at least partly due to monetary ease and falling interest rates.

The role of money in causing business cycles is even stronger if one considers the era before World War II. Many of the worst prewar depressions, including the recessions of 1908, 1921, and the Great Depression, were to a large extent the result of declines in the money supply and the related high real interest rates. In this earlier era, however, most monetary swings were engendered not by conscious monetary policy, but by financial panics and international monetary developments.

If one accepts that cycles are the result of market imperfections and not the result of the optimal adjustment of the economy to productivity shocks, then cycles are costly. Every recession in which workers are involuntarily unemployed results in a loss of output that cannot be regained. This fact naturally leads to the question of what can be done to eliminate swings in economic activity. If government spending and monetary policy can cause booms and recessions, it seems obvious that they could be used to cure economic fluctuations. Indeed, the Employment Act of 1946 mandated that the U.S. government use its control of spending, taxation, and the money supply to stabilize output and employment.

Such policies appear to have reduced the amplitude and duration of recessions. A comparison of the traditional prewar unemployment statistics with the official postwar statistics, for example, suggests that the average rise in the unemployment rate during a recession was twice as large in the years 1900 to 1930 as it has been in the period since 1947. Recessions also appear to have occurred more frequently and lasted longer in the prewar era than in the postwar era.

But appearances are deceiving. The kind of statistics that economists use to measure the severity of business cycles, such as data on the unemployment rate, real gross national product, and industrial production, have been kept carefully and consistently only since World War II. Therefore, the conclusion that government policy has smoothed business cycles is based on a comparison of fragmentary prewar evidence with sophisticated postwar statistics.

In some recent research, I have tried to avoid the problem of inconsistent data by comparing the crude prewar statistics with equally crude postwar statistics. That is, I have compared the existing prewar series with modern data that are constructed using the same assumptions and data fragments that were used to piece together the prewar series. These comparisons show essentially no decline in the severity of cycles between the prewar and postwar eras. They also show little change in the duration and frequency of cycles over time. Thus, much of our apparent success at eliminating the business cycle seems to be a figment of the data.

Why has public policy failed to cure business cycles in the United States? One reason is that monetary and fiscal policy are difficult to use with any precision. There are long lags in the implementation and effect of changes in spending, taxes, and monetary stance. There is also significant uncertainty about how much of a monetary or fiscal stimulus is needed to end a recession of a particular severity. Finally, policymakers also often have conflicting goals. Because inflation tends to slow down in recessions and speed up in booms, policymakers cannot cure the dual problems of inflation and unemployment with the same policy tools. As a result they often seem to adopt the strategy of fighting inflation with tight policy and then reducing unemployment with a switch to loose policy.

While government policy may not have cured the business cycle, the effects of cycles on individuals in the United States and other industrialized countries almost surely have been lessened in recent decades. The advent of unemployment insurance and other social welfare programs means that recessions no longer wreak the havoc on individuals' standards of living that they once did.

—**Christina D. Romer**

Biography: Christina D. Romer is an economics professor at the University of California, Berkeley, and a research associate of the National Bureau of Economic Research. She has served as a member of the Brookings Panel on Economic Activity and has earned the National Science Foundation's Presidential Young Investigator Award.

Further Reading

Burns, Arthur F., and Wesley C. Mitchell. *Measuring Business Cycles*. 1946.

Friedman, Milton, and Anna J. Schwartz. "Money and Business Cycles." *Review of Economics and Statistics* 45 (February 1963): 32–64.

Gordon, Robert J., ed. *The American Business Cycle: Continuity and Change*. 1986.

Romer, Christina D. "Is the Stabilization of the Postwar Economy a Figment of the Data?" *American Economic Review* 76 (June 1986): 314–34.

Distribution of Income

Frank Levy

■ The distribution of income is central to one of the most enduring issues in political economics. On one extreme are those who argue that all incomes should be the same, or as nearly so as possible, and that a principal function of government should be to redistribute income from the haves to the have-nots. On the other extreme are those who argue that any income redistribution by government is bad.

Whether government should redistribute more or less income is, of course, a normative question. Each person's answer depends on his values. But for many people, answering the normative question requires an understanding of just how income is distributed now, and how—and why—the distribution has changed over the decades. To start, here is what the basic numbers tell us.

A statistical summary of U.S. family income distribution since World War II shows the following:

1. The U.S. family income distribution is highly unequal.
2. The degree of income inequality is not much greater today than it was at the end of World War II.
3. Family income inequality declined slowly from 1946 through 1969, increased slowly from 1970 through 1979, and has increased somewhat faster since then.

Data for the summary comes from the U.S. Census Bureau's Current Population Survey (CPS), a monthly survey of sixty-five thousand households that includes both families and unrelated individuals. Every March the CPS collects data on household income in the previous year. To keep interviews simple, the questions focus on gross money income (excluding capital gains but including interest and dividends). This means that census statistics—the standard source of income data—measure income before taxes and do not count nonmoney income like Medicare coverage and employer-paid health insurance.

The census constructs the family income distribution by listing CPS sample families in order of increasing income. The distribution is described by computing the share of total family income going to the poorest one-fifth of families, the second fifth, and so on. Part A of table 1 contains these data for selected years since World War II.

In 1929, on the eve of the Great Depression, the richest one-fifth of families received over half of all income going to families. The depression and World War II reduced that figure so that in 1949, the richest one-fifth of families received 42.7 percent of all family income while the poorest

TABLE 1

The Shape of the Family Income Distribution

A. Percent of Total Family Income Going to Each Fifth of Families

	1st (poorest)	2nd	3rd	4th	5th (richest)	Total	Median Family Income ($1990)
1949	4.5%	11.9	17.3	23.5	42.7	100%	$16,712
1959	4.9%	12.3	17.9	23.8	41.1	100%	$23,057
1969	5.6%	12.4	17.7	23.7	40.6	100%	$31,912
1979	5.2%	11.6	17.5	24.1	41.7	100%	$33,454
1989	4.6%	10.6	16.5	23.7	44.6	100%	$34,213

B. Income Cutoffs in the 1989 Family Income Distribution ($1989)

1st fifth (poorest) ends at	2nd fifth ends at	3rd fifth ends at	4th fifth ends at*	5th fifth (richest) begins at*
$16,003	$28,000	$40,800	$59,550	$59,551

*$59,500 is the dividing line between the fourth and top fifths of families. The highest-income 5% of families had incomes beginning at $98,963.

SOURCE: *U.S. Bureau of the Census*, Current Population Reports, *various issues.*

one-fifth received 4.5 percent. Put differently, in the late forties the top fifth of families received about $9.50 in income for every $1.00 received by the bottom fifth. Inequality continued to decline slowly through the fifties and sixties. By 1969 the top fifth of families received $7.25 for every $1.00 received by the bottom fifth.

But 1968 and 1969, when unemployment averaged 3.5 percent, marked the high point of family income equality. Beginning in 1970, inequality began to grow again at a moderate rate. Through much of the seventies, the slow rise of inequality seemed to reflect the economy's general weakness. Yet contrary to expectations, inequality increased even more rapidly in the post-1982 recovery. In 1989 the top fifth of families received $9.69 in gross money income for every $1.00 received at the bottom, roughly the same as in the late forties.

Family income inequality is now high not only by our own post–World War II standards, but also when compared to other industrialized countries. Detailed comparisons from the Luxembourg Income Study show that in the United States, West Germany, and Israel, the richest fifth of families receives about 45 percent of all family income, compared to 39 percent in Sweden and 41 percent in Canada, the United Kingdom, and Norway. One reason for greater U.S. inequality is the large number of female-headed families, which comprise about two-fifths of the bottom quintile. These female-headed families, in turn, reflect the nation's high divorce rate and high rate of out-of-wedlock births. Partially because of these single-parent families, there are only eight earners for every ten families in the distribution's bottom fifth, while there are twenty-three earners for every ten families in the top fifth. In recent years U.S. income inequality has also been driven by falling wages for less skilled workers and relatively limited cash benefits for the poor.

A Vanishing Middle Class?

Although many people have claimed that the United States is losing its middle class, the 1989 distribution of income was not radically less equal than the distribution of 1949 or 1959, a period when the middle class was perceived to be growing rapidly. Moreover, the whole concept of a middle class is vague. In 1989 the top fifth of families (with 44.6 percent of all income) included every family with income above $59,500, many of whom saw themselves as middle class. Because the concept is vague, it follows that inequality statistics cannot, by themselves, say whether the middle class is vanishing. They must be supplemented with data on both economic growth and demographics.

Begin with economic growth. In 1947, median family income—the midpoint of the income distribution—stood at $16,712 (all income figures are in 1990 dollars). By 1973 it had doubled to $33,398. During these years income inequality had declined modestly. But more important, the whole income distribution had moved to much higher real incomes. The poor and the rich were both getting richer and an increasing proportion of all families could afford a middle-class life, including a single-family home, two cars, and so forth.

Since 1973, median family income has grown very little. Income growth fell victim to oil price shocks and to the productivity slowdown (the slow growth of output per worker that has plagued most industrialized countries). This slow growth has affected our outlook on economic life. When incomes grow rapidly, more inequality means that the poor get richer but the rich get richer faster. But when inequality increased in the slow-growth eighties, some groups' incomes fell in real terms. Between the business cycle peak of 1979 and the next business cycle peak of 1989, the average income of the poorest fifth of families fell from $10,900 to $10,200, while the average income of the top fifth grew from $89,600 to $97,600. Moreover, the price of two key pieces of a middle-class life—a single-family home and a college education—grew faster than the general rate of inflation and faster than average incomes. For all of these reasons, slow income growth played a key role in perceptions of a vanishing middle class.

Turn next to demographics, where movements of families within the income distribution add to perceptions of a vanishing middle class. In popular culture the middle class usually appears as urban families with children. In the late forties these families were concentrated in the top four-fifths of the distribution. The poorest fifth contained mainly farm families, other rural families, and elderly families, most of whom were not yet eligible for Social Security benefits. Put differently, those families that "should have been" in the middle class were relatively unlikely to have incomes in the lowest quintile.

Today the situation is reversed. Farm and rural families are far fewer in number. Many elderly families have moved from the bottom of the distribution to the lower middle, the result of a mature Social Security program and better private pensions. Now the poorest fifth does contain urbanized families with children. Included in the group are a significant number of families headed by single women and, since the early eighties, husband-wife families hurt by a sharp drop in the wages of men with a high school education or less. A higher proportion of families that "should be" in the middle class are now in the lowest quintile. For urban families with children, the picture of a distribution with a shrinking middle has some validity.

In sum, slow income growth and movements within the income distribution have led to a sense of a vanishing middle class even though overall family income inequality has not increased very much.

Does Measurement Matter?

All the data on family income discussed so far are on a pretax, money-only basis. Would a different income definition lead to a different story?

Consider three reasons why it might. First, increases in aid to the poor over the last two decades have been concentrated in nonmoney benefits like food stamps and Medicaid, neither of which is counted in standard census statistics. Second, an increasing proportion of wage earners' total compensation over the same period is for health insurance and other nonmoney benefits (again not counted). Third, taxes modify the income distribution.

The Census Bureau has attempted to answer this question for recent years by estimating the household income distribution under a number of alternative income definitions. Households include both families and unrelated individuals. Table 2 shows the impact in 1989 of moving from the standard census income (pretax money only) to an adjusted census income that subtracts taxes paid from gross income and adds to income the cost of benefits provided by the government and the employers. Improving the measure of income in this way reduces the level of inequality by shrinking the numbers of households at the highest and lowest ends of the income spectrum. In 1988 the percent of households with income over $100,000 falls by almost half, and the proportion with incomes under $10,000 falls by almost one-fourth.

Better income measurement reduces the estimated level of income inequality, but it does not appear to alter the trend in inequality over time. While the Census Bureau has produced adjusted income distributions for only a few years, these data and such other evidence as exists suggest that the trend toward greater inequality in the eighties would exist under any plausible definition of income.

A different kind of adjustment changes our picture of income growth: an adjustment of family income for family size. Over the last two decades average family size has declined by 12 percent, largely reflecting fewer children per family. As a result, even though family income has been largely stagnant, income per family member, a rough measure of living standards, has increased by about 15 percent. If we look beyond families to all households—including the growing number of young singles who have

TABLE 2

The Shape of the *Household* Income Distribution under Alternative Income Definitions, 1989*

Percent of Households in Income Class (classes in thousands)

	<$10	$10–$20	$20–$30	$30–$40	$40–$50	$50–$75	$75–$100	>$100	Total
Standard census income**	16.6%	18.9	17.0	14.2	10.8	14.5	5.1	3.9	100%
Adjusted census income***	12.5%	22.7	21.2	16.4	10.9	11.5	2.6	2.1	100%

*Households include both families and unrelated individuals.
**Standard census income statistics are based on gross money income, excluding capital gains.
***Gross money income including capital gains, less all taxes paid, plus the imputed value of in-kind income from employer-provided health insurance and government nonmoney benefits like food stamps, Medicaid, and free school lunches.

SOURCE: *U.S. Bureau of the Census, September 1990.*

only themselves to support—the Congressional Budget Office estimated that living standards since the early seventies have increased by 20 percent. There are limits to this type of adjustment, however. Most people eventually form families and most families have children. In the long run living standards cannot grow faster than the general rate of economic growth.

—**Frank Levy**

Biography: Frank Levy is the Rose Professor of Urban Economics at MIT's Department of Urban Studies and Planning.

Further Reading

Congressional Budget Office. *Trends in Family Incomes: 1970–1986*. Report prepared by Robertin Williams. 1988.
Levy, Frank. *Dollars and Dreams: The Changing American Income Distribution*. 1989.
———. "Incomes, Families and Living Standards." In *American Living Standards: Threats and Challenges*, edited by Robert Litan, Robert Lawrence, and Charles Schultze. 1988.
O'Higgins, Michael, Gunther Schmaus, and Geoffrey Stephenson. "Income Distribution and Redistribution: A Microdata Analysis for Seven Countries." In *Poverty, Inequality and Income Distribution in Comparative Perspective*, edited by Timothy M. Smeeding, Michael O'Higgins, and Lee Rainwater. 1990.
U.S. Bureau of the Census. "Measuring the Effect of Benefits and Taxes on Income and Poverty: 1989." *Current Population Reports*, series P-60, no. 169. September 1990.
U.S. Bureau of the Census. "Trends in Income by Selected Characteristics." *Current Population Reports*, series P-60, no. 167. April 1990.

See also POVERTY, REDISTRIBUTION OF INCOME.

"One reason that action to limit growing income inequality in the United States is difficult is that the growth in inequality is not a simple picture. Old-line leftists, if there are any left, would like to make it a single story—the rich becoming richer by exploiting the poor. But that's just not a reasonable picture of America in the 1980s. For one thing, most of our very poor don't work, which makes it hard to exploit them. For another, the poor had so little to start with that the dollar value of the gains of the rich dwarfs that of the losses of the poor. (In constant dollars, the increase in per family income among the top tenth of the population in the 1980s was about a dozen times as large as the decline among the bottom tenth.)"

—Paul Krugman
The Age of Diminished Expectations, 1990, p. 22.

Economic Growth

Paul M. Romer

Compound Rates of Growth

In the modern version of an old legend, an investment banker asks to be paid by placing one penny on the first square of a chess board, two pennies on the second square, four on the third, etc. If the banker had asked that only the white squares be used, the initial penny would double in value thirty-one times, leaving $21.5 million on the last square. Using both the black and the white squares makes the penny grow to $92,000,000 billion.

People are reasonably good at forming estimates based on addition, but for operations such as compounding that depend on repeated multiplication, we systematically underestimate how fast things grow. As a result we often lose sight of how important the average rate of growth is for an economy. For an investment banker the choice between a payment that doubles with every square on the chess board and one that doubles with every other square is more important than any other part of the contract. Who cares whether the payment is in pennies, pounds, or pesos? For a nation the choices that determine whether income doubles with every generation, or instead with every other generation, dwarf all other policy concerns.

Growth in Income Per Capita

Starting at one-third the level in the United States, income per capita in Japan grew at the rate of 5.8 percent per year from 1960 to 1985. Starting at one-fifteenth of the level in the United States, income per capita in India grew at the rate of 1.5 percent per year. Because income per person grew at an annual rate of 2.1 percent in the United States, Japan was catching up and India was falling farther behind.

You can figure out how long it takes income to double by dividing the growth rate into the number 72. If growth in the United States continues at the annual rate of 2.1 percent, income per capita will double every 34 years (72/2.1 = 34). In 102 years, income will increase eightfold. This increase is large, but not unprecedented.

In the United States, income per person grew by about this factor over the last 100 years. At the Japanese rate of 5.8 percent, income will double every 12 years. If this were sustained for 96 years, average income in Japan would increase by a factor of 256.

One reason Japan grew so fast is that it started from so far behind. Rapid growth could be achieved in large part by copying industrial practices in the leading countries of the world. The interesting question is why India did not manage the same trick (see THIRD WORLD ECONOMIC DEVELOPMENT). As Japan catches up with the leading countries, growth will inevitably slow. Over the course of the next century, an increase by a factor of 8 in per capita income is believable, but an increase by a factor of 256 is not.

After correcting for the cost of living, North America is still the most prosperous region in the world, but it may not remain so for long. Even if growth in Japan slows dramatically, Japan may still take the lead, just as North America surpassed England at the beginning of this century.

Suppose that the rate of increase in Japan is 2.6 percent, half a percentage point higher than the recent rate in the United States, and suppose that the rate in North America falls by half a percentage point to 1.6 percent. In a hundred years income per person would be more than twice as large in Japan as it is in North America.

Growth and Recipes

Economic growth occurs whenever people take resources and rearrange them in ways that are more valuable. A useful metaphor for production in an economy comes from the kitchen. To create valuable final products, we mix inexpensive ingredients together according to a recipe. The cooking one can do is limited by the supply of ingredients, and most cooking in the economy produces undesirable side effects. If economic growth could be achieved only by doing more and more of the same kind of cooking, we would eventually run out of raw materials and suffer from unacceptable levels of pollution and nuisance. Human history teaches us, however, that economic growth springs from better recipes, not just from more cooking. New recipes generally produce fewer unpleasant side effects and generate more economic value per unit of raw material (see NATURAL RESOURCES).

Every generation has perceived the limits to growth that finite resources and undesirable side effects would pose if no new recipes or ideas were discovered. And every generation has underestimated the potential for finding new recipes and ideas. We consistently fail to grasp how many ideas remain to be discovered. The difficulty is the same one we have with compounding. Possibilities do not add up. They multiply.

In a branch of physical chemistry known as exploratory synthesis, chemists try mixing selected elements together at different temperatures and pressures to see what comes out. Several years ago, one of the hundreds of compounds discovered this way was found to be a superconductor at temperatures far higher than anyone previously thought possible. This discovery may ultimately have economic implications that are as far-reaching as the discovery of the transistor.

To get some sense of how much scope there is for more such discoveries, we can calculate as follows. The periodic table contains about a hundred different types of atoms, so the number of combinations made up of four different elements is about $100 \times 99 \times 98 \times 97 = 94,000,000$. A list of numbers like 1, 2, 3, 7 can represent the proportions for using the four elements in a recipe. To keep things simple, assume that the numbers in the list must lie between 1 and 10, that no fractions are allowed, and that the smallest number must always be 1. Then there are about 3,500 different sets of proportions for each choice of four elements, and $3,500 \times 94,000,000$ (or 330 billion) different recipes in total. If laboratories around the world evaluated 1,000 recipes each day, it would take nearly a million years to go through them all. (In fact, this calculation vastly underestimates the amount of exploration that remains to be done because mixtures can be made of more than four elements, fractional proportions can be selected, and a wide variety of pressures and temperatures can be used during mixing.)

Even after correcting for these additional factors, this kind of calculation only begins to suggest the range of possibilities. Instead of just mixing elements together in a disorganized fashion, we can use chemical reactions to combine elements such as hydrogen and carbon into ordered structures like polymers or proteins. To see how far this kind of process can take us, imagine the ideal chemical refinery. It would convert abundant, renewable resources into a product that humans value. It would be smaller than a car, mobile so that it could search out its own inputs, capable of maintaining the temperature necessary for its reactions within narrow bounds, and able to automatically heal most system failures. It would build replicas of itself for use after it wears out, and it would do all of this with little human supervision. All we would have to do is get it to stay still periodically so that we could hook up some pipes and drain off the final product.

This refinery already exists. It is the milk cow. And if nature can produce this structured collection of hydrogen, carbon, and miscellaneous other atoms by meandering along one particular evolutionary path of trial and error (albeit one that took hundreds of millions of years), there must be an unimaginably large number of valuable structures and recipes for combining atoms that we have yet to discover.

Objects and Ideas

Thinking about ideas and recipes changes how one thinks about economic policy (and cows). A traditional explanation for the persistent poverty of many less developed countries is that they lack objects such as natural resources or capital goods. But Japan had little of either in 1950 and still has few natural resources, so something else must be involved. Increasingly, emphasis is shifting to the notion that it is ideas, not objects, that poor countries lack. The knowledge needed to provide citizens of the poorest countries with a vastly improved standard of living already exists in the advanced countries. If a poor nation invests in education and does not destroy the incentives for its citizens to acquire ideas from the rest of the world, it can rapidly take advantage of the publicly available part of the worldwide stock of knowledge. If, in addition, it offers incentives for privately held ideas to be put to use within its borders (for example, by protecting foreign patents, copyrights, and licenses, and by permitting direct investment by foreign firms), its citizens can soon work in state-of-the-art productive activities.

Some ideas from the developed world are rapidly adopted by less developed countries. For example, oral rehydration therapy now saves the lives of hundreds of thousands of children who previously would have died from diarrhea. Yet governments in poor countries continue to impede the flow of many other kinds of ideas, especially those with commercial value. Even automobile producers in North America recognize that they can learn from ideas developed in the rest of the world. But car firms in India operate in a government-created protective time warp. The Hillman and Austin cars produced in England in the fifties continue to roll off production lines in India today. India's commitment to closing itself off and striving for self-sufficiency has been as strong as Japan's commitment to acquiring foreign ideas and participating fully in world markets. The outcomes— grinding poverty in India and opulence in Japan—could hardly be more disparate.

For a developing country like India, enormous increases in standards of living could be achieved merely by letting in the ideas held by companies from industrialized nations. But leading countries like the United States and Canada, and new leaders like Japan, cannot stay ahead merely by adopting ideas developed elsewhere. They must also offer incentives for the discovery of new ideas at home, and this is not easy to do. The same characteristic that makes an idea so valuable—everybody can use it at the same time—also means that it is hard to earn an appropriate rate of return on investments in ideas. The many people who benefit from a new idea can too easily free-ride on the efforts of others.

After the transistor was invented at Bell Labs, for example, many applied ideas had to be developed before this basic science discovery yielded any commercial value. By now, private firms have developed improved recipes that have brought the cost of a transistor down by a factor of 1 million. Yet most of the benefits from those discoveries have been reaped not by the innovating firms, but by the users of the transistors. Just a few years ago, I paid a thousand dollars per million transistors for memory in my computer. Now I pay less than a hundred per million, and yet I have done nothing to deserve or help pay for this windfall.

If the government confiscated most of the oil from major discoveries and gave it to consumers, oil companies would do much less exploration. Some oil would still be found serendipitously, but many promising opportunities for exploration would be bypassed. Both oil companies and consumers would be worse off. The leakage of benefits such as those from improvements in the transistor acts just like this kind of confiscatory tax and has the same effect on incentives for exploration. For this reason most economists support three government policies designed to encourage the production, transmission, and implementation of ideas: universal subsidies for education, competitive grants for basic research, and patents and copyrights, which offer temporary monopoly profits on ideas. Economists also recognize, however, that such policies may not provide adequate incentives to discover the many small applied ideas needed to convert a basic idea such as the transistor into a product such as computer memory, or to convert a new product such as the videocassette recorder (which was first produced in the United States) into an inexpensive consumer good.

Stimulated in part by the dramatic and continuing success of the Japanese in catching and then surpassing North American firms in many areas of manufacturing, policymakers in the United States are now considering additional ways to stimulate the production of ideas. Proposed changes range from increased funding for basic science to antitrust exemptions for research consortia, from cuts in capital gains tax rates to an explicit ''industrial policy'' whereby a government agency directly subsidizes specific industries. We should not attempt to transplant institutions from Japan into the very different social and political climate of North America, but we should learn from Japan's experience.

Through a complicated and poorly understood combination of practices that we would not want to copy—practices that seem to include collusion between firms, bid rigging, systematic exclusion of foreigners, arm twisting by the government, the isolation of managers from any effective control by shareholders, and the pursuit of growth in firms that takes precedence over shareholder returns—the Japanese have achieved a far higher level of research and development by firms than exists in the United States. In the construction industry, for example, Japanese firms spend more than five times as much on research as comparable firms in the United States. All of the top six construction firms in Japan maintain major research laboratories with facilities, budgets, and coverage of disciplines that exceed those of the largest university- or government-based construction-oriented laboratories in the United States. None of the top North American firms maintains a similar institute. In a further contrast with the United States, very little of the research done by firms in Japan is funded directly or indirectly by the government or conducted in universities. As just one indication of the success of their system, the Japanese share of the worldwide construction market has been increasing and the North American share has been falling.

The usual retort to this kind of comparison is that universities in Japan are weak and that the quantity and quality of basic research are much higher in the United States. From the perspective of our national interest, this response is doubly misleading. The benefits of pure basic science in the United States can be captured by any country in the world. For the price of a journal subscription, Japanese firms can learn the latest recipe for high-temperature superconductors. In addition, because construction is a very large fraction of GNP—9 percent in the United States and 18 percent in Japan—even small improvements in construction techniques can have effects on national income that are large compared with more exciting basic science discoveries.

The lesson from the Japanese experience is clear: mundane forms of applied research, such as design work or product and process engineering, can have large cumulative benefits for the firm that undertakes them and even larger benefits for society as a whole. Moreover, the gains from applied research are largest not when it is dictated by government agency priorities or academic interests, but instead when it is closely integrated into the operations of a firm and motivated by the problems and opportunities that the firm faces.

Meta-Ideas

Perhaps the most important ideas of all are meta-ideas. These are ideas about how to support the production and transmission of other ideas. The British invented patents and copyrights in the seventeenth century. North Americans invented the agricultural extension service in the nineteenth century and peer-reviewed competitive grants for basic research in the twentieth century. Japanese economic policy has been remarkably successful in the last three decades, but a growing number of scandals involving bribe-taking politicians warns us not to blindly imitate their institutions. The Japanese are learning the same lesson we should have learned when members of Congress intervened in the supervision of savings and loans: if the government has important discretionary power over economic affairs, members of the government can all too easily divert that power from its intended public purpose and put it to private use. The challenge facing all of the industrialized countries, including Japan, is therefore to invent new institutions that support a high level of applied, commercially relevant research in the private sector. These institutions must not impose high efficiency costs and, most important, must not be vulnerable to capture by narrow interests.

We do not know what the next major idea about how to support ideas will be. Nor do we know where it will emerge. There are, however, two safe predictions. First, the country that takes the lead in the twenty-first century will be the one that implements an innovation that supports the production of commercially relevant ideas in the private sector. Second, new meta-ideas of this kind will be found.

Only a failure of imagination, the same one that leads the man on the street to suppose that everything has already been invented, leads us to believe that all of the relevant institutions have been designed and that all of the policy levers have been found. For social scientists, every bit as much as for physical scientists, there are vast regions to explore and wonderful surprises to discover.

—Paul M. Romer

Biography: Paul M. Romer is a professor of economics at the University of California, Berkeley, a research associate with the National Bureau of Economic Research, and the Royal Bank fellow of the Canadian Institute for Advanced Research.

Further Reading

"A survey of India." *The Economist,* May 4, 1991.

"Exploring the New Material World." *Science* 252 (May 3, 1991): 644–46.

Japanese Technology Evaluation Center. "Construction Technologies in Japan." National Technical Information Service report no. PB91-100057. 1991.

North, Douglass C. *Institutions, Institutional Change, and Economic Performance.* 1990.

Romer, Paul. "Increasing Returns and New Developments in the Theory of Growth." In *Equilibrium Theory and Applications: Proceedings of the 6th International Symposium in Economic Theory and Econometrics,* edited by William Barnett et al. 1991.

Rosenberg, Nathan. *Inside the Black Box: Technology and Economics.* 1982.

World Bank. *The Challenge of Development: World Development Report 1991.*

See also JAPAN AND THE MYTH OF MITI, NATURAL RESOURCES, THIRD WORLD ECONOMIC DEVELOPMENT, WAGES AND WORKING CONDITIONS.

Forecasting and Econometric Models

Saul H. Hymans

■ An econometric model is one of the tools that economists use to forecast future developments in the economy. In the simplest terms, econometricians measure past relationships between variables such as consumer spending and gross national product, and then try to forecast how changes in some variables will affect the future course of others.

Before econometricians can make such calculations, they need what is called an economic model, or a theory of how different factors in the economy interact with one another. For instance, think of the economy as composed of households and business firms, as depicted on the left-hand side of figure 1. Households supply business firms with labor services (as tailors, accountants, engineers, etc.) and earn wages and salaries from the businesses in exchange for their labor. Using the labor services, businesses produce various outputs (clothing, cars, etc.), which are available for purchase (right-hand side of figure 1). Households, using the earnings derived from their labor services, become the customers who purchase the output. The products produced by the businesses wind up in the households, and the wage and salary payments return to the businesses in exchange for the products being sold to the households.

This chain of events, as shown by the activities numbered 1 through 5 in figure 1, is a description—or diagrammatic model—of the operation of a private enterprise economy. It is obviously incomplete. There is no central bank supplying money, no banking system, and no government levying taxes, building roads, or providing education. But the essentials of the private sector of the economy—working, producing, and buying products and services—are represented in a useful way in figure 1.

The diagrammatic model of figure 1 has certain disadvantages when it comes to representing quantities, such as the value of the wage and salary payments or the number of cars produced. To represent magnitudes more conveniently, economists employ a mathematical model, which basically is a set of equations that describe various relationships between variables. Consider household purchases of output, shown as activity number 4 in figure 1. If W is the amount of wages and salaries earned by households, and C is household expenditures on clothing, then the equation $C = .12W$ states that households spend 12 percent of their wages and salaries on clothing. An equation could also be constructed to represent household purchases of cars or any other goods and services. Indeed, each of the activities pictured in figure 1 can be represented in the form of an equation. Doing so may take a blend of economic theory, physical and institutional realities, and mathematical sophistication, but once done, the result would be a mathematical or

FIGURE 1

An Economic Model

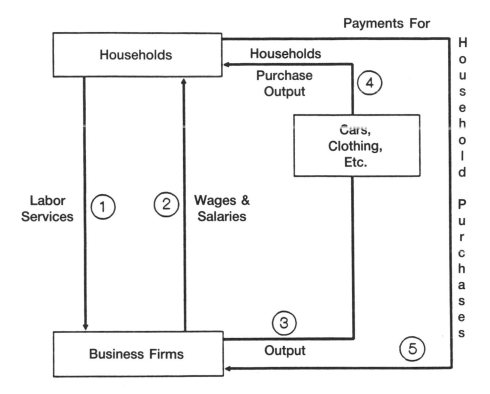

"quantitative economic model," which is but one important step away from an econometric model.

The equation for clothing purchases, $C = .12W$, asserts that 12 percent of household income is spent on clothing. That "12 percent" was selected purely for illustrative purposes. But if the model is to say anything useful about the American economy of today, the model must contain numbers (econometricians and others applying simi-

lar statistical methods refer to such numbers as parameters) that describe what really goes on in the real world. For this purpose one can turn to the relevant historical data to find out what percentage of household income Americans do, in fact, typically spend on clothing. Table 1 presents the figures for the years 1984 through 1989.

Obviously, the illustrative 12 percent figure was way off and, if left in the model, would have led to serious errors in applica-

TABLE 1

Spending on Clothing

Year	% of Household Income
1984	5.8
1985	5.8
1986	6.0
1987	6.0
1988	5.9
1989	6.0

tion to the American economy. A more appropriate value is 5.9 percent, which implies the equation $C = .059W$. Because the parameter value of .059 in the clothing equation is derived from the relevant data, the equation should say something meaningful about the economy. Using real data to determine or estimate all the parameter values in the model is the critically important step that turns the abstract mathematical economic model into an econometric model.

An econometric model is said to be complete if it contains enough equations to predict values for all of the variables in the model, such as C and W. The single equation $C = .059W$, for example, predicts C if the value of W is known. Thus, there must be an equation somewhere in the model that determines W. If all such logical connections have been made, the model is complete and can, in principle, be used to forecast the economy or to test theories about its behavior.

Actually, no econometric model is ever truly complete. All models contain variables that the model cannot predict because they are determined by forces "outside" the model. For example, a realistic model must include personal income taxes collected by the government because taxes are the "wedge" between the gross income earned by households and the net income (what economists call disposable income) available for households to spend. The taxes collected depend on the tax rates in the income tax laws. If the model is to forecast economic activity several years into the future, anticipated future tax rates must be made a part of the model's information base. That requires an assumption about whether the government will change future income tax rates and, if so, when and by how much. Similarly, the model requires an assumption about the monetary policy that will be pursued by the central bank (the Federal Reserve System in the United States), and assumptions about many other such "outside of the model" (or exogenous) variables in order to forecast all the "inside of the model" (or endogenous) variables.

The need for the econometrician to use the best available economic judgment about "outside" factors is inherent in economic forecasting. An econometrically based economic forecast can, therefore, be wrong for several reasons:

1. incorrect assumptions about the "outside," or exogenous, variables, which are called input errors
2. econometric equations that are only approximations to the truth (note that clothing purchases do not amount to exactly 5.9 percent of household income every year), which are called model errors

3. some combination of input error and model error

Most econometric forecasters believe that economic judgment can and should be used not only to determine values for exogenous variables (an obvious requirement), but also to reduce the likely size of model error. Taken literally, the equation $C = .059W$ means that "any deviation of clothing purchases from 5.9 percent of household income must be considered a random aberration from normal or expected behavior"—one of those inherently unpredictable vagaries of human behavior that continually trip up pollsters, economists, and any others who attempt to forecast socioeconomic events.

The economic forecaster must be prepared to be wrong because of unpredictable model error. But is all model error really unpredictable? Suppose the forecaster reads reports that indicate unusually favorable consumer reaction to the latest styles in clothing. Suppose that on this basis, the forecaster believes that about 6.5 percent of household income, rather than the usual 5.9 percent, will be spent on clothing next year. Should the forecaster ignore his belief that clothing sales are about to "take off," leave the model alone, and produce a forecast that he expects to be wrong?

The answer depends on the purpose of the forecast. If the purpose is the purely scientific one of determining how accurately a well-constructed model can forecast, the answer must be "Ignore the outside information and leave the model alone." If the purpose is the more pragmatic one of using the best available information to produce the most informative forecast, the answer must be "Incorporate the outside information into the model, even if that means effectively 'erasing' the parameter value .059 and replacing it with .065 while generating next year's forecast." Imposing such constant adjustments on forecasts used to be disparaged as entirely unscientific. In recent years, however, researchers have begun to regard such behavior as inevitable in the social science of economic forecasting and have begun to study how best—from a scientific perspective—to incorporate such outside information.

Much of the motivation behind trying to specify the most accurately descriptive economic model, trying to determine parameter values that most closely represent economic behavior, and combining these with the best available outside information arises from the desire to produce accurate forecasts. Unfortunately, the accuracy of an economic forecast is not easy to judge. There are simply too many dimensions of detail and interest. One user of the forecast may care mostly about gross national product (GNP), another mostly about exports and imports, and another mostly about inflation and interest rates. Thus, the same forecast may provide very useful information to some users, while being misleading to others.

For want of anything obviously superior, the most common gauge of the quality of a forecast is how accurately it predicts real GNP. Real GNP is the most inclusive summary measure of total national production. For many purposes there is much value in knowing, with some lead time, whether to expect real GNP to be increasing rapidly (a booming economy), to be slowing down or speeding up relative to recent behavior, or

CHART 1

RSQE Forecast Accuracy: 1971–1990

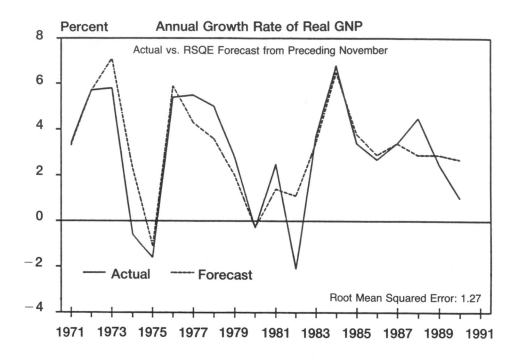

Percent   Annual Growth Rate of Real GNP

Actual vs. RSQE Forecast from Preceding November

—— Actual   ---- Forecast

Root Mean Squared Error: 1.27

to be declining (a slumping or recessionary economy). The information contained in chart 1 can be used to judge, in the summary fashion just indicated, the forecasting accuracy achieved by the econometric model I work on, that of the Research Seminar in Quantitative Economics (RSQE) of the University of Michigan.

The RSQE forecasting project, dating back to the fifties, is one of the oldest in the United States. Chart 1 compares, for each of the years from 1971 through 1990, the actual percent change in real GNP (the economy's growth rate) with the RSQE

forecast published in November of the preceding year. Although the forecast missed the actual percentage change by an average of 1.27 percentage points, the forecast was sometimes off by considerably more than that—by 3.2 percentage points for 1982, for example. Nonetheless, there was never a boom year that RSQE forecast to be a bad year, never a bad year that RSQE forecast to be a boom year, and almost never an instance in which the forecast didn't provide the right information as to whether the economy's growth rate was about to speed up or slow down. These forecast errors would be large if we were forecasting a rocket trajectory. But economics is a social science with few truly reliable laws of behavior, and chart 1 surely is suggestive of a long record of informative GNP forecasting.

Econometric forecasting is the joint product of the econometric model and the economist who uses it. Studies have shown that forecasts that combine the model and the forecaster's judgment are generally more accurate than "purely objective" forecasts that are produced with the econometric model alone. Models are, however, routinely used by themselves in the important area of econometric policy analysis and in other "what if" calculations. Thus, a baseline forecast may be calculated using the model and the best information available to the forecaster. Then some question is asked, such as "What if the income tax rate is increased by 10 percentage points?" The forecaster puts the new tax rate into the model and recalculates the projected level of, say, real GNP, to show the new tax rate's effect on the economy.

Economists commonly employ such calculations to help them advise businesses and governments. The practical validity of such applications depends on how well the model's structure represents the economic behavior that is central to the "what if" question being asked. All models are merely approximations to reality; the issue is whether a given model's approximation is good enough for the question at hand. Thus, making models more accurate is important. As long as people ask "What if . . . ?" econometric models will continue to be used and useful.

—Saul H. Hymans

Biography: Saul H. Hymans is a professor of economics and statistics and director of the Research Seminar in Quantitative Economics at the University of Michigan.

Further Reading

Howrey, E. Philip, Saul H. Hymans, and Michael R. Donihue. "Merging Monthly and Quarterly Forecasts: Experience with MQEM." *Journal of Forecasting* 10 (May 1991): 255–68

Klein, Lawrence R., ed. *Comparative Performance of U.S. Econometric Models.* Especially chaps. 1, 3, 10, 11, 12. 1991.

Klein, Lawrence R., and Richard M. Young. *An Introduction to Econometric Forecasting and Forecasting Models.* 1980.

Great Depression

Robert J. Samuelson

■ The Great Depression of the thirties remains the most important economic event in American history. It caused enormous hardship for tens of millions of people and the failure of a large fraction of the nation's banks, businesses, and farms. It transformed national politics by vastly expanding government, which was increasingly expected to stabilize the economy and to prevent suffering. Democrats became the majority party. In 1929 the Republicans controlled the White House and Congress. By 1933, the Democrats had the presidency and, with huge margins, Congress (310–117 in the House, and 60–35 in the Senate). President Franklin Roosevelt's New Deal gave birth to the American version of the welfare state. Social Security, unemployment insurance, and federal family assistance all began in the thirties.

It is hard for those who did not live through it to grasp the full force of the worldwide depression. Between 1930 and 1939 U.S. unemployment averaged 18.2 percent. The economy's output of goods and services (gross national product) declined 30 percent between 1929 and 1933 and recovered to the 1929 level only in 1939. Prices of almost everything (farm products, raw materials, industrial goods, stocks) fell dramatically. Farm prices, for instance, dropped 51 percent from 1929 to 1933. World trade shriveled: between 1929 and 1933 it shrank 65 percent in dollar value

and 25 percent in unit volume. Most nations suffered. In 1932 Britain's unemployment was 17.6 percent. Germany's depression hastened the rise of Hitler and, thereby, contributed to World War II.

The depression is best understood as the final chapter of the breakdown of the worldwide economic order. The breakdown started with World War I and ended in the thirties with the collapse of the gold standard. As the depression deepened, governments tried to protect their reserves of gold by keeping interest rates high and credit tight for too long. This had a devastating impact on credit, spending, and prices, and an ordinary business slump became a calamity. What ultimately ended the depression was World War II. Military spending and mobilization reduced the U.S. unemployment rate to 1.9 percent by 1943.

With hindsight it seems amazing that governments did not act sooner and more forcefully to end the depression. The fact that they did not attests to how different people's expectations and world politics were in the thirties. The depression can be understood only in the context of the times. Consider four huge differences between then and now:

1. **The gold standard.** Most money was paper, as it is now, but governments were obligated, if requested, to redeem that paper for gold. This "convertibil-

ity'' put an upper limit on the amount of paper currency governments could print, and thus prevented inflation. There was no tradition (as there is today) of continuous, modest inflation. Most countries went off the gold standard during World War I, and restoring it was a major postwar aim. Britain, for instance, returned to gold in 1925. Other countries backed their paper money not with gold, but with other currencies—mainly U.S. dollars and British pounds—that were convertible into gold. As a result flexibility of governments was limited. A loss of gold (or convertible currencies) often forced governments to raise interest rates. The higher interest rates discouraged conversion of interest-bearing deposits into gold and bolstered confidence that inflation would not break the commitment to gold.

2. **Economic policy.** Apart from the gold standard, economic policy barely existed. There was little belief that governments could, or should, prevent business slumps. These were seen as natural, therapeutic, and self-correcting. The lower wages and interest rates caused by slumps would spur recovery. The 1920–21 downturn (when industrial production fell 25 percent) had preceded the prosperous twenties. ''People will work harder, live a more moral life,'' Andrew Mellon, Treasury secretary under President Herbert Hoover, said after the depression started. ''Enterprising people will pick up the wrecks from less competent people,'' he claimed. One exception to the hands-off attitude was the Federal Reserve, created in 1913. It was charged with the responsibility for providing emergency funds to banks so that surprise withdrawals would not trigger bank runs and a financial panic.

3. **Production patterns.** Farming and raw materials were much more important parts of the economy than they are today. This meant that lower commodity prices could cripple domestic prosperity and world trade, because price declines destroyed the purchasing power of farmers and other primary producers (including entire nations). In 1929 farming accounted for 23 percent of U.S. employment (versus 2.5 percent today). Two-fifths of world trade was in farm products, another fifth in other raw materials. Poor countries (including countries in Latin America, Asia, and Central Europe) exported food and raw materials and imported manufactured goods from industrial nations.

4. **The impact of World War I.** Wartime inflation, when the gold standard had been suspended, raised prices and inspired fears that gold stocks were inadequate to provide backing for enlarged money supplies at the new, higher price level. This was one reason that convertible currencies, such as the dollar and pound, were used as gold substitutes. The war weakened Britain, left Germany with massive reparations payments, and split the Austro-Hungarian Empire into many countries. These countries, plus Germany, depended on foreign loans (in convertible currencies) to pay for their imports. The arrangement was unstable because any withdrawal of short-term loans would force

the borrowing countries to retrench, which could cripple world trade.

To view the Great Depression as the last gasp of the gold standard—as economic historians Barry Eichengreen and Peter Temin suggest—bridges the gap between two popular explanations. The best-known, advanced by economists Milton Friedman and Anna Schwartz in *A Monetary History of the United States, 1867–1960*, blames the Federal Reserve for permitting two-fifths of the nation's banks to fail between 1929 and 1933 (or 10,797 of the 25,568 banks in 1929). Since deposits were not insured then, the bank failures wiped out savings and shrank the money supply. From 1929 to 1933 the money supply dropped by one-third, choking off credit and making it impossible for many individuals and businesses to spend or invest. Friedman and Schwartz argue that it was this drop in the money supply that strangled the economy. They consider the depression mainly an American affair that spread abroad.

In contrast, economist Charles Kindleberger, in *The World in Depression, 1929–1939*, sees the depression as a global event caused by a lack of world economic leadership. According to Kindleberger, Britain provided leadership before World War I. It fostered global trade by keeping its markets open, promoted expansion by making overseas investments, and prevented financial crises with emergency loans. After World War II the United States played this role. But between the wars no country did, and the depression fed on itself, Kindleberger argues. No country did enough to halt banking crises, and the entire industrial world adopted protectionist measures in attempts to curtail imports. In 1930, for example, President Herbert Hoover signed the Smoot-Hawley tariff, raising tariffs on dutiable items by 52 percent. The protectionism put an extra brake on world trade just when countries should have been promoting it.

With the passage of time, both the Friedman-Schwartz and Kindleberger views seem correct. Inept monetary policy explains the depression's severity, as Friedman and Schwartz argue. But because the gold standard caused many governments to make similar errors, the effects were worldwide, as Kindleberger contends.

The start of the depression is usually dated to the spectacular stock market crash of 1929. The Dow Jones industrial average hit its peak of 381 on September 3, up from 300 at the start of the year. After sporadic declines, the roof fell in on October 24 (Black Thursday). Stock prices dropped 15 to 20 percent before being supported by buying from a pool of bankers. Although the market closed with only a small loss (down 6 to 299), trading was nearly 12.9 million shares, about triple the normal volume. The selling panic resumed the next week. On Monday the Dow fell 38 points to 260, then the biggest one-day drop ever. The next day (Black Tuesday), it slid another 30 points. By November 13, the Dow was at 198.

There had been warnings. Many commentators complained before the crash that the market was driven by speculation. A lot of stock was bought on credit. Between the end of 1927 and October 1929, loans to brokers rose 92 percent. At the start of October, loans equaled nearly a fifth of the value of all stocks. But by itself the stock market crash did not cause the depression.

By year's end the Dow Jones industrial average had actually rebounded to 248 (down 17 percent from the beginning of 1929). It continued rising in early 1930.

The depression is often blamed on the passivity of President Hoover and the Federal Reserve. This view is simplistic. True, Hoover's commitment to a balanced budget—the orthodoxy of the day—precluded big new spending programs. And his decision in 1932 to combat a budget deficit by raising taxes sharply is widely viewed as a major blunder. But it is not true that Hoover and the Federal Reserve stood idly by and did nothing as the depression worsened. After the crash Hoover instituted a tax cut equal to 4 percent of federal revenues. He urged state and local governments to raise their spending on public works projects. Hoover also created the Reconstruction Finance Corporation, which provided loans to shaky banks, utilities, and railroads. In 1931 he suspended collection of foreign-debt payments to the United States, which he thought were impeding recovery of the international economy.

Nor was the Federal Reserve entirely passive. During the crash the Fed lent liberally to banks so they could sustain securities lending. Interest rates were allowed to drop rapidly. The discount rate (the rate at which the Federal Reserve lends to commercial banks) fell from 6 percent in October 1929 to 2.5 percent in June 1930. The money supply (cash in circulation plus checking and time deposits at banks) declined only slightly in the next year. Tighter Federal Reserve policy in 1928 and early 1929—intended to check stock market speculation—may have helped trigger the economic downturn. But the Federal Reserve was not stingy in early 1930 and was not driving the economy into depression at that time. It was not until 1931 and later that the Federal Reserve failed to act as the "lender of last resort" and allowed so many banks to fail.

The truth is that, until the summer of early fall of 1930, almost everyone expected the economy to recover, just as it had in 1921. Unfortunately, almost everyone underestimated the forces pulling the economy down. One was the drop in trade that resulted from collapsing commodity prices. Kindleberger has argued that the price collapse was worsened by the stock market crash. The connection lay in a drying up of credit. Many loans used to buy stock had come from foreigners and big corporations, and they demanded repayment when stock prices plummeted. New York banks assumed some of the loans, but they cut loans to the importers of raw materials. Demand for these products (rubber, cocoa, coffee) dropped, and prices fell. Strapped for funds, countries that exported commodities reduced their imports of manufactured goods from industrial nations. The drop in trade was deepened by Smoot-Hawley, which provoked massive retaliation by other nations.

What made matters worse was a big drop in U.S. consumer spending—far more than can be explained by the stock market crash. The drop may have been a backlash to the rise of installment lending (for cars, furniture, and appliances) in the twenties. The prevailing practice allowed lenders to repossess an item if the borrower missed just one payment. People may have stopped making new purchases to reduce the risk of losing things they already had bought on credit. Whatever happened, the slump soon fed on itself. Weak spending depressed prices, which meant that many farmers, businesses, and nations couldn't repay their debts. Rising bad debts prompted banks to restrict new loans and sell financial assets, usually bonds. Scarce credit led to less borrowing, less spending, lower prices, and more bankruptcies. Trade and investment spiraled downward. Confidence crumbled, and as it did, bank runs—people clamoring to convert deposits into cash—ensued.

Why could no one stop this spiral? In the United States there were waves of bank failures in 1931 and 1932. Friedman and Schwartz maintain that the Federal Reserve could have prevented them by lending directly to weak banks and by aggressive "open market" operations (that is, by buying U.S. Treasury securities and thereby injecting new funds into banks and the economy). This action would have halted the depression, they argue. They blame the Federal Reserve's timidity on the 1928 death of Benjamin Strong, the president of the Federal Reserve Bank of New York. Strong had dominated the Federal Reserve System, which consists of twelve regional banks and a board of governors in Washington. He firmly believed that the Federal Reserve had to prevent banking panics and sustain economic growth. When he died, power in the Federal Reserve passed to officials in Washington, whose ideas were murkier. Had Strong lived, Friedman and Schwartz contend, he would have averted the banking collapse.

Maybe—and maybe not. In fact, the Federal Reserve faced conflicting demands to end the depression and to protect the gold standard. The first required easier credit,

the second tighter credit. The gold standard handcuffed governments around the world. The mere hint that a country might abandon gold prompted speculators and international depositors to change local money into gold or a convertible currency. Deposit withdrawals spread panic and squeezed lending. It was a global process that ultimately forced all governments off gold. In May 1931 there was a run against Creditanstalt, a large Austrian bank. The panic then shifted to Germany and, in late summer, to Britain, which left gold in September.

The United States was trapped by the same forces. After Britain went off gold, for instance, the Federal Reserve raised interest rates sharply to stem gold outflows. The discount rate went from 1.5 to 3.5 percent, which, considering the condition of the economy, was a huge increase. The best evidence that the gold standard fostered the depression is that once countries abandoned it, their economies usually began growing again. This happened in Germany, Britain, and, after Roosevelt left gold in March and April 1933, the United States.

Although self-defeating, the defense of gold was a product of law as well as custom. The Federal Reserve had to ensure that every dollar of paper money was backed by at least forty cents of gold. Once Congress ended the obligation to exchange gold for currency, the Fed was largely liberated from worrying about gold. This may have been the most important part of the New Deal's economic program. The economy did improve. Between 1933 and 1937, the unemployment rate dropped from 25 to 14 percent before a new recession pushed it back up to 19 percent in 1938. The 1937–38 recession is widely blamed on the Federal

Reserve's mistaken decision to raise bank reserve requirements in August 1936 and early 1937. (Reserves are funds that banks keep as vault cash or as deposits at the Federal Reserve.)

Many economists now believe that the New Deal, apart from its gold policy, probably had little impact on economic activity. At the heart of the early New Deal were the National Recovery Administration (NRA) and the Agriculture Adjustment Act (AAA). Created in Roosevelt's first hundred days, they sought to promote recovery by propping up prices. The idea was to improve incomes and halt bankruptcies. The AAA tried to eliminate agricultural surpluses (pigs were slaughtered, crops destroyed) and paid farmers not to plant. The NRA allowed companies in the same industry to set wages, prices, and working hours in an effort to check "destructive competition." This approach rested on a remarkable contradiction: the way to get recovery, which requires more production, is to have less production. There never has been much evidence that it worked, and the Supreme Court found the NRA unconstitutional in 1935.

The New Deal did relieve suffering. Perhaps 10 million to 12 million Americans worked at some time on public works or in relief jobs (through the Public Works Administration, the Works Project Administration, and the Civilian Conservation Corps). People had their bank deposits protected with the advent of deposit insurance. The Securities and Exchange Commission regulated the stock market. Roosevelt maintained faith in democracy.

But there was a cost. The New Deal also caused suffering. Sharecroppers were often thrown out of work, for example, when the AAA paid landowners not to grow. The New Deal also fostered class consciousness. Roosevelt increasingly blamed the depression on the wealthy—"economic royalists," as he called them. The loss of business confidence in government policies may have deterred new investment, offsetting any economic stimulus of higher public spending. But by 1933 the economy had been so ravaged that only a partial recovery may have been possible until the huge wartime boom.

The depression left an enormous legacy. The New Deal accustomed people to look to government, rather than to private charity, for help. After World War II, governments everywhere strove to prevent a repetition of the Great Depression. Economic policies became more active and, as a practical matter, more inflationary. With the gold standard gone, governments had more freedom to stimulate their economies with an expansion of money and credit. The political inclination was to act sooner, rather than later, to halt a slump. Likewise, the protectionism of the thirties prompted postwar efforts to reduce tariffs and other trade barriers. Finally, the wild swings of exchange rates that occurred after countries went off gold spurred the creation of the Bretton Woods system of fixed exchange rates in 1944. This system (named after a resort in New Hampshire where the agreement was finalized) stipulated that currencies were to maintain fixed exchange rates with the dollar. The system broke down in the early seventies.

It is commonly said that another depression will never occur. This is probably true, as long as "another depression" means a crude repetition of the thirties. However, crises can come in unfamiliar forms. The basic lesson from the Great Depression is that governments cannot permit massive collapses of banks or spending. The deeper lesson is that there are times when the world changes so much and events move so rapidly that even the well-informed do not know how to respond. This is the story of the depression. Now it seems preventable. Then, it was baffling. World War I made restoration of the prewar economic system difficult, maybe impossible. But that is what world leaders attempted because it was all they knew and it had worked. Only its collapse convinced them to try something different. Old ideas were overtaken and overwhelmed. It has happened before—and could again.

—Robert J. Samuelson

Biography: Robert J. Samuelson is a journalist who writes a column on economic affairs for *Newsweek*, the *Washington Post*, and other newspapers.

Further Reading

Allen, Frederick Lewis. *Since Yesterday: The 1930s in America*. 1939.

Eichengreen, Barry. *Golden Fetters: The Gold Standard and the Great Depression*. 1992.

Friedman, Milton, and Anna Jacobson Schwartz. *A Monetary History of the United States, 1867–1960*. 1963.

Kindleberger, Charles P. *The World in Depression, 1929–1939*. Revised and enlarged edition. 1986.

Lewis, W. Arthur. *Economic Survey, 1929–1939*. 1949.

Saint-Etienne, Christian. *The Great Depression, 1929–1938, Lessons for the 1980s*. 1984.

Temin, Peter. *Lessons from the Great Depression*. 1989.

Wigmore, Barrie A. *The Crash and Its Aftermath, A History of Securities Markets in the United States, 1929–1933*. 1985.

Gross Domestic Product

Lincoln Anderson

■ Gross domestic product, the official measure of total output of goods and services in the U.S. economy, represents the capstone and grand summary of the world's best system of economic statistics. The federal government organizes millions of pieces of monthly, quarterly, and annual data from government agencies, companies, and private individuals into hundreds of statistics, such as the consumer price index (CPI), the employment report, and summaries of corporate and individual tax returns. The U.S. Department of Commerce then marshals the source data into a complete set of statistics known as the National Income and Product Accounts. This set of double-entry accounts provides a consistent and detailed representation of production in the United States (GDP) and its associated income (national income).

In addition, the Commerce Department derives data on inputs to production (labor and capital) and tabulates them to form industry data on production; intermediate steps in production (input-output tables); detailed data on prices; and international and regional statistics. The theoretical development and construction of this accounting system was a major achievement requiring the services of a renowned group of accountants, business executives, economists, and statisticians. And because the economy continues to evolve, the conceptual and statistical work is never complete.

Government agencies are continuously revising the data and occasionally find sizable errors in GDP or GDP components. Keeping GDP current and accurate is no mean feat.

For the United States, GDP replaces gross national product (GNP) as the main measure of production. GDP measures the output of all labor and capital within the U.S. geographical boundary regardless of the residence of that labor or owner of capital. GNP measures the output supplied by residents of the United States regardless of where they live and work or where they own capital. Conceptually, the GDP measure emphasizes production in the United States, while GNP emphasizes U.S. income resulting from production. The difference, called net factor income received from abroad, is trivial for the United States, amounting to only $13 billion (0.2 percent of GDP) in 1991. This shift in emphasis brings the United States into conformance with the international accounting convention.

GDP measures production, not exchange. If economists, policymakers, and news commentators kept this simple truth in mind, much confusion over the interpretation of economic statistics might be avoided. Many proposals to cut taxes, for example, are aimed at ''stimulating consumer spending,'' which is expected to cause an increase in GDP. But consumer spending is a *use* of GDP, not production. A rise in consumer demand could simply crowd out investment, not raise GDP.

Unfortunately, the GDP data are usually presented in a format that emphasizes exchange (the use of GDP) rather than production (the source of GDP). GDP is represented as the sum of consumer spending, housing and business investment, net exports, and government purchases. Behind this accounting facade lurks the truth: GDP is generated by individual labor combined with both proprietors' and business capital, raw materials, energy, and technology in a myriad of different industries. The Bureau of Economic Analysis (the agency within the Department of Commerce that is responsible for GDP statistics) does show these relationships in the input-output tables and in the GDP-by-industry data tables (now produced annually). But most economists and the press focus on the uses of GDP rather than these presentations of GDP as production.

For better or worse, the different formats do influence how people think about the sources of economic growth. Which, for example, is more of a driving force in the economy—retail sales or growth in the labor force? Are inventory levels a key factor at turning points in the business cycle, or is prospective return on investment the key? Does higher government spending increase GDP, or do lower marginal tax rates? Are higher net exports a positive or a negative factor? In answering these questions, Keynesians usually emphasize the first choice while supply-siders place more weight on the second.

In the short run, in business cycles the Keynesian emphasis on demand is relevant

and alluring. But heavy-handed reliance on "demand management" policies can distort market prices, generate major inefficiencies, and destroy production incentives. India since its independence and Peru in the eighties are classic examples of the destruction that demand management can cause. Other less developed countries like South Korea, Mexico, and Argentina have shifted from an emphasis on government spending and demand management to freeing up markets, privatizing assets, and generally enhancing incentives to work and invest. Rapid growth of GDP has resulted (see THIRD WORLD ECONOMIC DEVELOPMENT).

In the United States the debate over the sources of economic growth can be informed by GDP statistics. Take three examples over the past decade. First, there has been a lot of handwringing over the supposed decline in U.S. manufacturing. Based on declining employment in manufacturing, many commentators asserted throughout the eighties that the United States was "deindustrializing." It certainly is true that employment in manufacturing fell from a peak of 21 million workers in 1979 to 19 million by 1990. But the GDP data show that the production of goods in the United States was rising rapidly after the 1982 recession and, by 1989, hit a ten-year high as a share of total GDP. The decline in manufacturing employment was more than offset by surging productivity. The rebuilding of U.S. manufacturing in the eighties occurred at the same time that many politicians and some economists were convinced we had given up our competitive position in world markets. A cursory glance at the GDP production data would have revealed the error.

Second, many people have viewed the rise in imports in the eighties with similar alarm. I believe that fear is groundless and is based on accounting rather than economics. With all other components of GDP held constant, a one-dollar increase in imports necessarily means a one-dollar drop in GDP. But—and this is something that simple accounting cannot tell us but that economics does—all other things are not equal. Rapid growth in GDP is generally associated with a large rise in imports. The reason is that high demand for foreign products coupled with high rates of return on domestic investment tends to pull foreign investment into a country and increase imports. The eighties were no exception: imports and the trade deficit surged concurrently with fast growth in GDP. Despite the lack of historical support for the proposition that imports reduce GDP, and despite strong opposition from economists stretching back to Adam Smith, protectionist trade policies were advocated and to some degree implemented in the eighties to "solve" the "problem." A closer look at the correlations between GDP and imports might have dispelled some of the mercantilist myths that protectionists raised (see MERCANTILISM).

Third, there is the controversy over the cause of the federal budget deficit. In the eighties, when the budget deficit ballooned to over $200 billion, a prolonged debate ensued over whether the rise in the deficit was caused by spending growth or tax cuts. One way to cut through the haze of numbers and get at the simple truth is to look at total federal receipts and outlays as shares of GDP. Federal tax receipts as a share of GDP did dip from a high of 21 percent in 1981

to 19 percent in the mideighties, but they have since climbed back to about 20 percent. With current tax receipts now low as a share of GDP, it is clear that major tax "cuts" have not occurred and that higher government spending is largely responsible for the budget deficit.

So-called real GDP is real only in the economist's sense that it is adjusted for inflation. The government computes real GDP for, say, 1991 by valuing production in 1991 at the relative prices that existed in a "base year." The choice of the base year used to compute the real GDP index is important. Relative prices in the base year tend to reflect relative production costs at that time. As GDP and GDP components are computed for periods further away from the base year, the accuracy deteriorates. Going forward from a base year, estimates of real GDP growth tend to be biased upward, with the bias rising as time passes. This occurs because the relative price of goods that embody rapid technical innovations, such as computers, falls, while relative prices of low-tech goods like coffee cups rise. And production moves with relative prices. Computers are a rising share of GDP while coffee cups are a falling share. So using a fixed base year that holds relative production technology constant results in an upward bias in the estimated production costs of high-tech goods in GDP.

The United States revises its base year about every five years. The base year for real GDP was recently moved up from 1982 to 1987. As a result "real" GDP growth over the eighties was revised down slightly. The Soviet Union took much longer to revise its base year. Until the sixties the Soviets used 1928 as the base year for computing

CHART 1

Federal Spending and Taxes as GDP Shares
Four-Quarter Average: 1960 to 1992

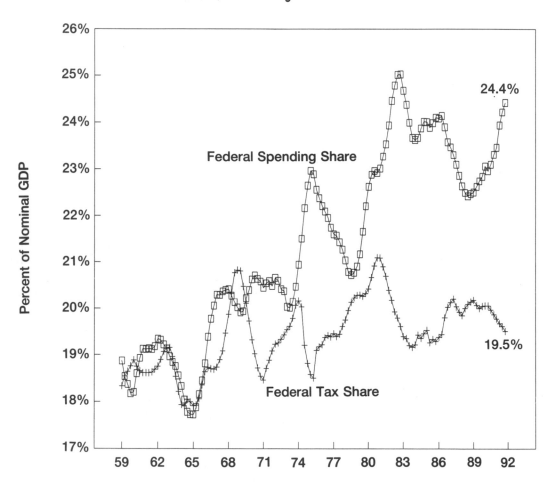

SOURCE: *Bureau of Economic Analysis.*

"real" GDP. Therefore, published data on growth rates were biased upward by a large percentage, and the underlying weakness in the Soviet economy was obscured. The Bureau of Economic Analysis (BEA) plans to publish a measure of real GDP and major components using a shifting base year. This measure will provide a more accurate representation of growth in years far from the 1987 base period. I strongly recommend sliding base (or "chain") measures in studies using a decade or more of real GDP data.

In practice BEA first uses the raw data on production to make estimates of nominal GDP, or GDP in current dollars. It then adjusts these data for inflation to arrive at real GDP. But BEA also uses the nominal GDP figures to produce the "income side" of GDP in double-entry bookkeeping. For every dollar of GDP there is a dollar of income. The income numbers inform us about overall trends in the income of corporations and individuals. Other agencies and private sources report bits and pieces of the income data, but the income data associated with the GDP provide a comprehensive and consistent set of income figures for the United States. These data can be used to address important and controversial issues such as the level and growth of disposable income per capita, the return on investment, and the level of saving.

In fact, just about all empirical issues in macroeconomics turn on the GDP data. The government uses the data to define emerging economic problems, devise appropriate policies, and judge results. Businesses use the data to forecast sales and adjust production and investment. Individuals watch GDP as an indicator of well-being and adjust their voting and investment decisions accordingly. This is not to say that the GDP data are always used or used wisely. Often they are not. Nor are the GDP data perfect. But ignoring the GDP data is as close as one can come in macroeconomics to ignoring the facts. And that is a perilous practice.

—**Lincoln Anderson**

Biography: Lincoln Anderson is the economist at Fidelity Investments in Boston. He was previously at Bear Stearns and Company in New York and, prior to that, was a senior economist at the Council of Economic Advisers from 1982 to 1986. From 1976 to 1982 he was a research economist at the Bureau of Economic Analysis.

Further Reading

Fox, Douglas R., and Robert Parker. "The Comprehensive Revision of the U.S. National Income and Product Accounts: A Review of Revisions and Major Statistical Changes." *Survey of Current Business* 71, no. 12 (December 1991): 24–42.

"Gross Domestic Product as a Measure of U.S. Production." *Survey of Current Business* 71, no. 8 (August 1991): 8.

Jaszi, George, ed. "The Economic Accounts of the U.S.: Retrospect and Prospect." *Survey of Current Business* 51, no. 7 (July 1971).

Young, Allan H. "Alternative Measures of Real GDP." *Survey of Current Business* 69, no. 4 (April 1989): 27–34.

Hyperinflation

Michael K. Salemi

■ Inflation is a sustained increase in the aggregate price level. Hyperinflation is very high inflation. Although the threshold is arbitrary, economists generally reserve the term hyperinflation to describe episodes where the monthly inflation rate is greater than 50 percent. At a monthly rate of 50 percent, an item that cost $1 on January 1 would cost $130 on January 1 of the following year.

Hyperinflations are largely a twentieth-century phenomenon. The most widely studied hyperinflation occurred in Germany after World War I. The ratio of the German price index in November 1923 to the price index in August 1922—just fifteen months earlier—was 1.02×10^{10}. This huge number amounts to a monthly inflation rate of 322 percent. On average, prices quadrupled each month during the sixteen months of hyperinflation.

While the German hyperinflation is better known, a much larger hyperinflation occurred in Hungary after World War II. Between August 1945 and July 1946 the general level of prices rose at the astounding rate of over 19,000 percent per month, or 19 percent per day.

Even these very large numbers understate the rates of inflation experienced during the worst days of the hyperinflations. In October 1923, German prices rose at the rate of 41 percent per day. And in July 1946, Hungarian prices more than tripled each day.

What causes hyperinflations? No one-time shock, no matter how severe, can explain sustained (i.e., continuously rapid) price growth. The world wars themselves did not cause the hyperinflations in Germany and Hungary. The destruction of resources during the wars can explain why prices in Germany and Hungary would be higher after them than before. But the wars themselves cannot explain why prices would continuously rise at rapid rates during the hyperinflation periods.

Hyperinflations are caused by extremely rapid growth in the supply of "paper" money. They occur when the monetary and fiscal authorities of a nation regularly issue large quantities of money to pay for a large stream of government expenditures. In effect, inflation is a form of taxation where the government gains at the expense of those who hold money whose value is declining. Hyperinflations are, therefore, very large taxation schemes.

During the German hyperinflation the number of German marks in circulation increased by a factor of 7.32×10^9. In Hungary, the comparable increase in the money supply was 1.19×10^{25}. These numbers are smaller than those given earlier for the growth in prices. In hyperinflations prices typically grow more rapidly than the money stock because people attempt to lower the amount of purchasing power that they keep in the form of money. They attempt to avoid the inflation tax by holding more of their wealth in the form of physical commodities. As they buy these commodities, prices rise higher and inflation accelerates.

Hyperinflations tend to be self-perpetuating. Suppose a government is committed to financing its expenditures by issuing money and begins by raising the money stock by 10 percent per month. Soon the rate of inflation will increase, say, to 10 percent per month. The government will observe that it can no longer buy as much with the money it is issuing and is likely to respond by raising money growth even further. The hyperinflation cycle has begun. During the hyperinflation there will be a continuing tug-of-war between the public and the government. The public is trying to spend the money it receives quickly in order to avoid the inflation tax; the government responds to higher inflation with even higher rates of money issue.

How do hyperinflations end? The standard answer is that governments have to make a credible commitment to halting the rapid growth in the stock of money. Proponents of this view consider the end of the German hyperinflation to be a case in point. In late 1923, Germany undertook a monetary reform creating a new unit of currency called the rentenmark. The German government promised that the new currency could be converted on demand into a bond having a certain value in gold. Proponents of the standard answer argue that the guarantee of convertibility is properly viewed as a promise to cease the rapid issue of money.

An alternative view held by some economists is that not just monetary reform, but also fiscal reform, is needed to end a hyperinflation. According to this view a successful reform entails two believable commitments on the part of government. The first is a commitment to halt the rapid growth of paper money. The second is a commitment to bring the government's budget into balance. This second commitment is necessary for a successful reform because it removes, or at least lessens, the incentive for the government to resort to inflationary taxation. Thomas Sargent, a proponent of this second view, argues that the German reform of 1923 was successful because it created an independent central bank that could refuse to monetize the government deficit and because it included provisions for higher taxes and lower government expenditures.

What effects do hyperinflations have? One effect with serious consequences is the reallocation of wealth. Hyperinflations transfer wealth from the general public, which holds money, to the government, which issues money. Hyperinflations also cause borrowers to gain at the expense of lenders when loan contracts are signed prior to the worst inflation. Businesses that hold stores of raw materials and commodities gain at the expense of the general public. In Germany, renters gained at the expense of property owners because rent ceilings did not keep pace with the general level of prices. Costantino Bresciani-Turroni has argued that the hyperinflation destroyed the wealth of the stable classes in Germany and made it easier for the National Socialists (Nazis) to gain power.

Hyperinflation reduces an economy's efficiency by driving agents away from monetary transactions and toward barter. In a normal economy great efficiency is gained by using money in exchange. During hyperinflations people prefer to be paid in commodities in order to avoid the inflation tax. If they are paid in money, they spend that money as quickly as possible. In Germany workers were paid twice per day and would shop at midday to avoid further depreciation of their earnings. Hyperinflation is a wasteful game of "hot potato" where individuals use up valuable resources trying to avoid holding on to paper money.

The recent examples of very high inflation have mostly occurred in Latin America. Argentina, Bolivia, Brazil, Chile, Peru, and Uruguay together experienced an average annual inflation rate of 121 percent between 1970 and 1987. One true hyperinflation occurred during this period. In Bolivia prices increased by 12,000 percent in 1985. In Peru in 1988, a near hyperinflation occurred as prices rose by about 2,000 percent for the year, or by 30 percent per month.

The Latin American countries with high inflation also experienced a phenomenon called "dollarization." Dollarization is the use of U.S. dollars by Latin Americans in place of their domestic currency. As inflation rises, people come to believe that their own currency is not a good way to store value and they attempt to exchange their domestic money for dollars. In 1973, 90 percent of time deposits in Bolivia were denominated in Bolivian pesos. By 1985, the year of the Bolivian hyperinflation, more than 60 percent of time deposit balances were denominated in dollars.

What caused high inflation in Latin America? Many Latin American countries borrowed heavily during the seventies and agreed to repay their debts in dollars. As interest rates rose, all of these countries found it increasingly difficult to meet their debt-service obligations. The high-inflation countries were those that responded to these higher costs by printing money.

The Bolivian hyperinflation is a case in point. Eliana Cardoso explains that in 1982 Hernan Siles-Suazo took power as head of a leftist coalition that wanted to satisfy demands for more government spending on domestic programs but faced growing debt-service obligations and falling prices for its tin exports. The Bolivian government responded to this situation by printing money. Faced with a shortage of funds, it chose to raise revenue through the inflation tax instead of raising income taxes or reducing other government spending.

—**Michael K. Salemi**

Biography: Michael K. Salemi is an economics professor at the University of North Carolina in Chapel Hill.

Further Reading

Bomberger, William A., and Gail E. Makinen. "The Hungarian Hyperinflation and Stabilization of 1945–1946." *Journal of Political Economy* 91 (October 1983): 801–24.

Bresciani-Turroni, Costantino. *The Economics of Inflation: A Study of Currency Depreciation in Post-War Germany.* 1937.

Cagan, Phillip. "The Monetary Dynamics of Hyperinflation." In *Studies in the Quantity Theory of Money*, edited by Milton Friedman. 1956.

Cardoso, Eliana A. "Hyperinflation in Latin America." *Challenge* January/February 1989: 11–19.

Holtfrerich, Carl-Ludwig. *The German Inflation 1914–1923: Causes and Effects in International Perspective.* 1986.

Salemi, Michael. "Hyperinflation, Exchange Depreciation, and the Demand for Money in Post World War I Germany." 1976.

———, and Sarah Leak. *Analyzing Inflation and Its Control: A Resource Guide.* 1984.

Sargent, Thomas J. "The Ends of Four Big Inflations." In Sargent. *Rational Expectations and Inflation.* 1986.

Inflation

David Ranson

◾ Inflation is the loss in purchasing power of a currency unit such as the dollar, usually expressed as a general rise in the prices of goods and services. A classic example is the Great Inflation of the Roman Empire. Successive emperors replaced a steadily increasing fraction of the silver in their ancient currency, the denarius, with base metals like bronze or copper. As a result prices rose inexorably despite repeated attempts to restrain them through legislation. Diocletian, rather than taking responsibility for the debasement, attributed the rapid inflation of his day to the avarice of his subjects. His famous edict of A.D. 301 threatened with death any vendor who charged prices exceeding official limits. But inflation ran along unhindered for another century until an alternative currency, an undepreciated gold coin known to Shakespeare as the bezant, became the customary unit of account, spreading throughout Europe and lasting well into the Middle Ages.

In modern times inflation continues to be blamed on private greed, and governments still seek to restrain it by decree, sometimes even devaluing their currencies as they do so. The United States has experienced much inflation during the twentieth century, especially since official efforts to maintain the gold price at thirty-five dollars an ounce ceased during the presidencies of Lyndon

Johnson (in the world market) and Richard Nixon (through the "gold window" open only to foreign central banks). An annual inflation rate of 4 to 5 percent, once thought to be calamitous, has become routine.

We have many measures of inflation, but none provides a truly reliable gauge of inflation at any specific time. The most widely watched measure is the consumer price index (CPI), published monthly by the Bureau of Labor Statistics. Subindexes are available for different cities and for many different classes of goods and services.

One problem with the CPI is that the weight attached to each class of goods and services is held constant for years at a time. Therefore, when consumers lower their cost of living by buying more items whose relative price has fallen and fewer items whose relative price has risen, the CPI will not show a decline in the cost of living. Moreover, the difficult problem of allowing for changing quality has never been solved. Nor can the government inspectors who collect the data from retailers track down all the sales and discounts of which consumers are so keenly aware. As a result of these and other factors, the consumer price index reflects inflation trends only with a long delay and portrays an artificially smooth path for the inflation rate.

Other popular indicators of inflation include producer prices (formerly known as wholesale prices) and unit-value indexes for imports and exports. As we move back through the distribution chain from the consumer toward the supplier of raw materials, a more jumpy picture of inflation is revealed at each step. Commodities, whose prices can be monitored continuously on centralized exchanges, and which are easy to mea-

sure, are the most volatile indicators of all. An index of commodity prices, when plotted on a graph, looks much like an index of stock prices. But its ups and downs are significant; it provides warning one or even two years ahead of movements in the consumer price index.

In the news media, discussion of inflation often takes a "bottom up" view. Each month's change in the CPI can be, and is, split up into dozens of components, such as food, energy, and housing. It is tempting to see the sectors where prices rose the most as causes of the observed inflation. Sometimes policymakers speculate that if "price pressure" in those areas could be relieved, overall inflation could be reduced.

This way of looking at inflation is mistaken. The prices of some items always are rising or falling relative to others. This is a natural feature of the way a market economy adapts to changes in supply or demand. Rapid price increases within a single sector, though often labeled "sectoral inflation," are partly the result of an adjustment in relative prices and partly a manifestation of the overall inflation rate. They may have no causative significance whatever. When we watch the tide come in at the beach, we know that it is not caused by the waves, however forceful they may be. Inflation is not simply the sum total of a collection of independent price changes, as the arithmetic of the CPI implies. It is the degree to which all of those prices move in concert.

Another popular game is to sift out the more volatile items in the basket of goods and services—often energy and food—and focus on the remainder as a truer "underlying" or "core" rate of inflation. This exercise, though it succeeds in producing a less volatile index, is dubious. The least volatile components are not necessarily the most informative. Some of them appear to be unresponsive to economic forces because of pitfalls in measurement or stickiness in their speed of adjustment to market forces. The price of rental housing, for example, is fixed month-to-month by contract. At the other end of the scale, some of the most volatile items—such as precious metals—are highly informative, to the extent that their movements anticipate a broad range of sectors where price changes have not yet been perceived.

What does inflation cost? There are polar opinions here, and a lively debate. In and of itself inflation "costs" little or nothing because it consists of nothing more than a change in the units we use to measure prices throughout our economy. It is confusing and irritating to keep requoting prices, but that's something people get used to, as recent writers like Paul Krugman and Alan Blinder have emphasized. From this point of view it is possible to see a steady inflation rate as high as 10 percent annually as nearly costless. But dwelling on this problem misses the point of the debate.

Economists who view inflation as a very serious problem point to what they call the "inflation tax." By this they mean the reduction in the purchasing power of the cash balances held by the private sector—like a wealth tax. This tax is a drag on the economy—an "efficiency loss"—because it induces people and businesses to economize on cash balances, making it more difficult to participate in the money economy.

Economic losses associated with the inflation tax and other distortions are known as the "welfare cost of inflation." At one extreme of the debate, Harvard economist Martin Feldstein has claimed that the present value of the losses that result from unending inflation may be infinite! His argument is that each year the cost to the economy grows in proportion to society's money balances. Because the rate of growth of money balances exceeds the interest rate he uses to calculate the present value, the present value is unbounded.

But the force of the inflation-tax argument has been depleted in recent years by the increasing tendency to hold cash in the form of money market mutual funds and bank deposits that pay interest. The higher the expected rate of inflation, the higher the interest rate paid by mutual funds and banks. People have shifted their cash balances to these types of accounts only recently because government regulations used to prohibit the payment of interest on checking accounts.

Quite a different problem results from the collision of inflation with the U.S. tax system, particularly the federal taxes on personal income, corporate profits, and capital gains. Progressive rate structures were intended to shift tax burdens from low- to higher-income groups. But over the years they have instead imposed on the general income-earning population high tax rates that had originally been thought appropriate only for millionaires. A family with a constant real income of $50,000 (in 1978 dollars), for example, was pushed from the 28 percent bracket in 1965 to a 46 percent rate in 1978. Its average tax rate rose from 16 percent to 23 percent. Offsetting reductions in tax rates have been extremely slow to develop, in spite of across-the-board rate cuts during the Kennedy-Johnson and

Reagan years. Instead, government spending has tended to absorb revenue unintentionally collected as a result of escalating tax brackets driven by inflation.

The increase in government spending could be claimed as either a cost or a benefit to the economy, depending on whether one wants more or less government spending. But there is a real cost that is not ambiguous. High tax rates on employment, on business investment, and on the accumulation of capital deter all these activities in favor of untaxed uses of the economy's resources and, therefore, impede output and growth.

The effects are visible in the lurching path that the economy has followed in the past few decades, coupling highs in inflation with lows in economic growth. Since 1953, as table 1 shows, there has been a consistently inverse relationship between inflation and growth in the U.S. economy. This is true not only for the 1973–74 and 1979–80 periods, when large increases in oil prices were partly responsible for both high inflation and low growth, but for other years as well. Such evidence undermines the widely held belief in the "trade-off" between inflation and unemployment.

Still more difficult than measuring inflation is the problem of identifying its root causes. In spite of its long and rich history, few subjects in the field of economics are more confused. Professional economists have still not reached broad agreement as to the origins of the inflation process. Two camps dominate the debate. Some see inflation as a malady of the currency (as was surely the case in the Roman Empire). In the words of Milton Friedman, "Inflation is always and everywhere a monetary prob-

lem." Others see nonmonetary forces at work, such as monopolies, union demands for higher wages. oil politics, or the "wage-price spiral."

Some nonmonetary ideas are illogical. The existence of monopoly power or union power might be argued to raise prices generally relative to what they otherwise would be. But a continuing price rise year-in year-out requires a continuing increase in the degree of monopoly or union power in the economy. This is neither plausible over long periods of time, nor consistent with evidence from recent decades for the United States.

Nonmonetary theories of inflation traditionally separate "demand-pull" sources from "cost-push" factors like oil, monopoly power, or wages. A surge in the demand for goods and services in general ("aggregate demand") is thought to "pull" prices up across the board, especially when "aggregate supply" is held back by inertia or capacity limitations. Skeptics rightly question how demand could constantly outstrip supply. Surely, demand must originate from purchasing power, purchasing power from wealth, wealth from income, and income from the ability to produce (and hence supply) goods and services. This contradiction was understood early in the nineteenth century by Jean-Baptiste Say and others.

Other logical objections to the idea of demand-pull inflation center on the importance of money. How could prices rise without a commensurate increase in the quantity of money in private hands? If such a thing happened, the purchasing power of the quantity of money would have declined involuntarily, and that would not be consistent with market equilibrium. Economists

TABLE 1

Inflation Versus Jobs
The Historical Record, 1953–90

	Average Increase in Consumer Prices	Average Growth of Employment		
		Same Year	Next Year	Cumulative
The Fifties (1953–62)				
4 highest-inflation years	2.3%	0.0%	0.0%	1.1%
4 lowest-inflation years	0.5	1.4	2.4	3.8
The Sixties (1962–71)				
4 highest-inflation years	4.9%	1.6%	2.0%	3.7%
4 lowest-inflation years	1.8	2.2	2.4	4.7
The Seventies (1971–80)				
4 highest-inflation years	11.3%	1.1%	1.0%	2.0%
4 lowest-inflation years	5.4	3.5	3.4	7.1
The Eighties (1980–89)				
4 highest-inflation years	6.4%	1.6%	0.7%	2.4%
4 lowest-inflation years	3.1	2.1	2.8	4.9

DATA: Consumer price index, all urban consumers; civilian employment (labor force survey).

SOURCE: *Bureau of Labor Statistics.*

of the "monetarist" school emphasize the power and discretion of government to vary the money supply, causing private markets to bring the economy's price structure into conformity.

Finally, there is strong, though surprisingly little known evidence against the demand-pull view that excessively rapid economic growth ("overheating") is an important source of inflation. The evidence in table 1 shows that the reverse is nearer the truth for the United States in recent decades. Inflation has tended to increase in periods of slow growth or recession and decrease in periods of expansion. The idea that growth risks inflation is not on as strong a footing factually as the idea that inflation hurts growth.

Among those who attribute inflation to monetary causes, at least two quite different views exist. The monetarist view is that increases in the quantity of money cause inflation. Critics of this view point out that the quantity of money is difficult to define, especially when funds can be transferred electronically and credit cards can substitute for cash balances. It can also be argued that people have freedom to choose the quantity of money they want to hold rather than merely accept the quantity the government wishes to impose upon them.

The other monetary view, held historically by opponents of fiat (i.e., government) paper money, and by advocates today of restoring the gold standard, is that the quantity of money can take care of itself. What really is needed, according to this view, is a mechanism for keeping the price of the currency stable, for providing an anchor, so to speak.

Governments have been slow to accept the recommendations of either of these camps. That probably is because either a strict monetary rule or strict adherence to a gold standard or other price rule would place strict limits on discretionary government management of the economy.

—David Ranson

Biography: David Ranson is president of H. C. Wainwright and Company, Economics, an investment research firm in Boston. He was formerly an assistant to the secretary of the Treasury in Washington.

Further Reading

Blinder, Alan. ''The Efficiency Costs of Inflation: Myth and Reality.'' In Blinder. *Hard Heads, Soft Hearts*. 1987.

Feldstein, Martin. ''The Welfare Cost of Permanent Inflation and Optimal Short-Run Economic Policy.'' *Journal of Political Economy* 87 (August 1979): 749–68.

Jones, A. H. M. ''The Anarchy.'' In Jones. *The Later Roman Empire*. 1964.

Krugman, Paul. ''Inflation.'' In Krugman. *The Age of Diminished Expectations*. 1990.

Laffer, Arthur, and David Ranson. ''Inflation, Taxes and Equity Values.'' Report prepared for H. C. Wainwright and Company, Economics. September 20, 1979.

Wanniski, Jude. ''Money and Tax Rates.'' In Wanniski. *The Way the World Works*. 1978.

Investment

Alan J. Auerbach

■ In the United States, investment accounts for about one-sixth of gross national product. It was 16.6 percent of GNP in 1990. Yet investment has occupied a much more important role in policy discussions than this share of production might suggest. The two main reasons for this are that investment is volatile and, therefore, a cause of business fluctuations and that investment contributes to economic growth.

Concern with these issues of business cycles and growth has led to very active tax policy toward investment during the postwar years, as a succession of governments has tried to influence the level, pattern, and timing of investment spending. The evidence suggests that such policies have been effective, but that many other, uncontrollable factors continue to influence investment. In the short term, investment decisions still appear to be strongly driven by the "animal spirits" to which Keynes attributed investment fluctuations. Over the longer term, the nature of investment has been affected by changes in the demographic makeup of society and in the composition of industrial production.

What Is Investment?

Although in general parlance investment may connote many types of economic activity, economists normally use the term to describe the purchase of durable goods by households, businesses, and governments. Private (nongovernmental) investment is commonly divided into three broad categories: residential investment, which accounts for about a quarter of all private investment (25.7 percent in 1990); nonresidential, or business, fixed investment, which accounts for most of the remainder; and inventory investment, which is small but volatile. Indeed, inventory investment is often negative (it was in 1990, and in three years during the eighties). Business fixed investment, in turn, is composed of equipment and nonresidential structures. Equipment now makes up over three-quarters of business investment.

Because of the decline in manufacturing and agriculture and the rise in services in the United States, the composition of private investment has changed considerably during the postwar period. The biggest single change has been the increased investment in computers and information-processing equipment. In 1953, spending on computers and related equipment was only 1 percent of nonresidential investment spending. By 1989 this figure had grown to 25 percent.

Governments invest, too—in schools, roads, and other components of economic infrastructure. But one important development in recent years has been the decline of government investment. Between 1982 and 1989, the net (of depreciation) private nonresidential capital stock rose by 20 percent, adjusted for inflation. Residential capital rose by 21 percent over the same period. In contrast, the nonmilitary government capital stock fell by 3 percent. Because, as past evidence has shown, many government capital assets (such as roads and waterways) facilitate private business activities, this decline suggests that private productivity will suffer as a result.

Investment and Business Fluctuations

One reason for so much interest in investment behavior is its apparent role in causing or exacerbating business cycles. Investment is a volatile component of GNP, falling sharply during recessions and rising just as sharply during booms. As the economy went into a deep recession in the early eighties, for example, real GNP fell 3 percent between 1981 and 1982, but investment fell in real terms by 18 percent. In the following year, as the expansion began, GNP rose 4 percent while investment rose 13 percent.

Why is investment so volatile? The key lies in the nature of the investment process. Investment decisions often require long lead times, and their consequences are as durable as the investment goods themselves. Consider, for example, the case of commercial construction, which declined in the late eighties. Office buildings planned during a period of strong demand for space may be completed during a recession, when demand even for existing space is weak. Such a shift in fortunes causes a decline in investment for two reasons. First, the need for office space has declined. Second, the amount of office space has risen, so that subsequent investment must fall not only to

keep pace with slower demand, but also to eliminate the "overhang" of empty space.

Economists call this magnification of the impact of declines in product demand the "accelerator" model of investment. As industrial production shifts away from such strongly cyclical industries as manufacturing, the strength of cycles in business fixed investment may weaken. This moderating process is also likely to be helped by the shift toward less durable investments requiring shorter planning and construction periods, such as computers.

Investment and the Cost of Capital

While fluctuations in output exert a strong influence on investment behavior, the costs of investing matter, too. These costs include the prices of capital goods themselves, as well as interest rates, required returns to equity owners, and the taxes that firms must pay on the profits that the investments generate.

A convenient summary of the effects of these different cost components is the "user cost of capital," a term introduced in the sixties by Harvard economist Dale Jorgenson. The user cost of capital shows how each of these factors influences investment, and has proved particularly useful in evaluating a variety of tax changes that have been introduced during the past few decades.

Activist tax policy toward investment began in 1954 with the introduction of accelerated depreciation. By permitting investors earlier deductions for depreciation, the 1954 changes increased the present value of these tax deductions and lowered the user cost of capital. An even more powerful incentive, the investment tax credit (ITC), was introduced in 1962. Although its provisions were frequently changed, the credit was in force for most of the period between 1962 and 1986, when it was repealed in the Tax Reform Act of 1986.

By permitting a 10 percent credit for qualifying investments (primarily in machinery and equipment), the ITC lowered the effective cost of investing, the user cost, by roughly the same percentage. The effects of this cost reduction are evident in the increasing share of equipment investment after the credit's introduction. In 1961, the year before the ITC was introduced, expenditures on equipment accounted for 51 percent of business fixed investment. This share rose to 52 percent in 1962, 54 percent in 1963, 55 percent in 1964 and 1965, and 57 percent by 1966. Although the repeal of the credit in 1986 did not cripple investment in machinery and equipment, some studies have found that the investment would have been even higher—by perhaps as much as 1 percent of GNP—had the credit not been repealed.

Other Determinants of Investment

Investment is influenced by demand conditions, the effects of which (including profitability) can be represented by the accelerator effect, and cost conditions, as summarized by the user cost of capital. Researchers have found that another independent determinant of investment behavior is liquidity—the liquid assets a company has on hand plus the cash flow it is currently generating. While the user cost of capital varies with the cost of funds in credit markets or to firms issuing equity, many firms are limited in their access to these markets. Because they must rely primarily on internal funds to finance investment, liquidity matters. The liquidity constraint seems particularly to affect smaller corporations and (along with accelerator effects) helps explain investment volatility, because cash flow itself (after-tax profits plus book depreciation) is very cyclical.

Liquidity also plays an important role in residential investment. About two-thirds of all residential investment takes the form of owner-occupied housing. The reliance of home buyers on the mortgage market has wrought havoc on residential construction during periods of tight credit that typically have accompanied recessions. As a result residential investment has often been even more cyclical than other forms of fixed investment. However, the reliance on borrowed money has, in certain periods, actually encouraged investment in owner-occupied housing, through the interaction of inflation and the tax system.

Inflation encourages housing investment in two ways. First, mortgage interest payments are tax deductible. As interest rates rise with inflation, so do tax deductions, even if the real interest rate, defined as the interest rate less the inflation rate, does not. For example, if the interest rate is 8 percent and the inflation rate 4 percent, the real interest rate is 4 percent, and an investor in the 28 percent tax bracket gains a tax reduction of 2.24 cents (28 percent of 8 percent) per dollar of debt. If the real interest rate remains at 4 percent, but the inflation rate rises to 8 percent, the nominal interest rate rises to 12 percent and the value of tax deductions rises to 3.36 cents (28 percent of 12 percent) per dollar of debt.

Second, the increased value of a home that accompanies inflation is essentially untaxed, because of provisions that allow a tax-free rollover if another house is purchased and a one-time exclusion of gain (currently $125,000) after age 55. This favors investment in owner-occupied housing over other types of investment with taxable gains. Another disadvantage of other types of fixed investment is that the depreciation allowances that investors receive are based on original asset cost, which may fall well short of true replacement cost in the presence of inflation. (This is not a problem faced by owner-occupiers, who do not receive depreciation allowances.)

The evidence in favor of the hypothesis of inflation-induced investment in owner-occupied housing comes primarily from the late seventies, when the hypothesis arose. During the economic expansion from 1976 to 1979, when inflation averaged 7.3 percent (measured using the GNP deflator, based on the prices of all goods and services included in GNP), investment in owner-occupied housing accounted for 33.5 percent of fixed investment. During the comparable expansion period of 1983 to 1986 with inflation averaging just 3.3 percent, residential investment's share fell to 29.1 percent.

An alternative explanation, for which there is evidence, is that the increase in housing investment in the late seventies was caused by the increase in family formation during the period—the coming of age of the baby boomers. If this explanation is correct, then housing prices and demand are likely to decline into the next century, well past the housing slump of the 1990–91 recession.

Why Is U.S. Investment So Low?

Investment helps increase productivity by raising the level of capital per worker and, perhaps, hastening the adoption of new technologies. As a share of GNP, gross private investment has been relatively stable over the past few decades. This stability, however, masks a disturbing trend. Because additions to the productive capital stock equal gross investment less depreciation, the shift toward equipment and, particularly, short-lived and rapidly depreciating equipment, means that the ratio of net investment to GNP has fallen over time. While gross investment's share of GNP went from 15.9 percent to 15.3 percent between 1969 and 1988 (both relatively strong investment years) net investment's share fell from 7.4 percent to 4.8 percent.

By the early nineties the dollar value of investment in the United States was less than in Japan, a country with roughly half the population. The main explanation for this difference is that U.S. investors faced a higher cost of capital than their Japanese counterparts. Comparative studies of the United States and Japan suggest that a lower Japanese cost of funds (as opposed to differences in the tax treatment of corporations, for example) is the major source of a cost-of-capital gap that appears to exist, or at least to have existed in recent decades, between the two countries. The cost of funds is higher in the United States because the low saving rate in the United States makes the supply of funds low and drives up interest rates.

The liberalization of international capital markets can offset the effects of low saving rates in particular countries. Investors living in countries with high saving rates can invest in countries, like the United States, that have low saving rates. This has happened and is the main reason for the large inflows of capital to the United States in recent years. Yet there remains a correlation across countries between levels of national saving and investment.

—Alan J. Auerbach

Biography: Alan J. Auerbach is a professor of economics and law at the University of Pennsylvania and a research associate at the National Bureau of Economic Research in Cambridge, Massachusetts.

Further Reading

Ando, Albert, and Alan J. Auerbach. "The Cost of Capital in the United States and Japan: A Comparison." *Journal of Japanese and International Economies* 1 (June 1988): 134–58.

Auerbach, Alan J. "The Tax Reform Act of 1986 and the Cost of Capital." *Journal of Economic Perspectives* 1, no. 1 (Summer 1987): 73–86.

Feldstein, Martin, ed. *The Effects of Taxation on Capital Accumulation.* 1987.

Mankiw, N. Gregory, and David N. Weil. "The Baby Boom, the Baby Bust and the Housing Market." *Regional Science and Urban Economics* 19 (May 1989): 235–58.

Munnell, Alicia H., ed. *Is There a Shortfall in Public Capital Investment?* 1990.

Productivity

Sylvia Nasar

■ Productivity—the amount of output per unit of input—is a basic yardstick of an economy's health. When productivity is growing, living standards tend to rise. When productivity is stagnating, so, generally, is well-being. "It can be said without exaggeration that in the long run probably nothing is as important for economic welfare as the rate of productivity growth," wrote Princeton economists William J. Baumol and Sue Anne Blackman, with New York University economist Edward N. Wolff, in *Productivity and American Leadership*.

Productivity can be defined in two basic ways. The most familiar, labor productivity, is simply output divided by the number of workers or, more often, by the number of hours worked. Output can be anything from tons of steel to airline miles flown, but more generally it is some very broad aggregate like gross domestic product. Measures of labor productivity, however, actually capture the contribution to output of other inputs than hours worked.

Total factor productivity, by contrast, captures the contribution to output of everything except labor and capital: innovation, managerial skill, organization, even luck.

The two productivity concepts are related. Increases in labor productivity can reflect the fact that each worker is better equipped with capital—a supermarket clerk who has an automatic scanner instead of an old-fashioned cash register—or, alterna-tively, gains in total factor productivity. Thanks to specialization, for example, Adam Smith's pin factory turned out more pins with the same number of craftsmen and identical tools. And General Motors' Fremont, California, plant—once one of the worst in the company—had a productivity turnaround when it required its workers to use Japanese manufacturing methods.

While factors of production like land will always be scarce, the potential for increasing total factor productivity is limitless. At least half, if not more, of the growth in labor productivity in the post–World War II period has been due not to the use of added capital, but to making better use of these inputs. The United States produced 65 percent more in 1981 than in 1948 from the same quantity of labor and capital resources.

Gains in living standards are tied to productivity gains. There are only three ways that a nation can enjoy a rising level of per capita consumption. First, a bigger proportion of the population can go to work. Second, a country can borrow from abroad or sell assets to foreigners to pay for extra imports. Third, the nation can boost productivity—either by investing a bigger share of national income in plant and equipment or by finding new ways to increase efficiency.

In fact, the United States has done all three at different times. But there are limits on how many Americans can join the labor force and on how much foreigners will lend.

For most countries most of the time, the "lever of riches," to use a term coined by economist Joel Mokyr, is rising output per hour of work.

In the United States, labor productivity growth has averaged about 2 percent a year for the past century. That means living standards have doubled, on average, every thirty-five years. America's place in the sun reflects its productivity. The number one country in the world at any given time has always been the productivity leader. It was northern Italy from the thirteenth to the sixteenth centuries, the Dutch republic in the seventeenth and early eighteenth, Britain in the late eighteenth and most of the nineteenth, and the United States for the entire twentieth century.

Now the United States faces two productivity problems. First, its productivity growth has slowed sharply since 1973, part of a puzzling worldwide productivity slowdown. Second, although U.S. productivity is still the highest in the world by a wide margin—$45,918 of GNP per worker in 1990, 25 percent ahead of Japan and 35 percent ahead of Germany—its productivity growth has been trailing that of other nations since World War II. That has stoked fears that the United States will eventually fall behind. After all, British productivity from 1880 to 1990 grew just 1 percentage point more slowly than that of its trading partners—hardly a huge shortfall, but enough to transform the once proud empire into a second-rate economy in little more than a lifetime.

"Compared with the problem of slow productivity growth," wrote Paul R. Krugman in *The Age of Diminished Expectations,* "all our other long-term economic concerns—foreign competition, the industrial base, lagging technology, deteriorating infrastructure and so on—are minor issues."

Economists caution that lagging productivity growth is, by its nature, a long-run problem. "The tyranny of compounding manifests its full powers only in longer periods," write Baumol, Blackman, and Wolff, who maintain that it is not yet clear whether the productivity slowdown in the United States and elsewhere since the early seventies represents a long-term shift to a lower growth path or a temporary aberration.

According to the *Economic Report of the President* [1992], U.S. productivity growth can be divided into three distinct phases. After averaging 1.9 percent a year from 1889 to 1937 and an even stronger 3 percent during the twenty-five-year boom that followed World War II, productivity growth has averaged a mere 1 percent since 1973. In spite of the supply-side revolution of the early eighties (which brought, among other things, lower inflation and lower marginal tax rates), productivity growth failed to revive in the past decade.

As a consequence of slower productivity growth in the past two decades, average compensation has edged up only slightly faster than the price level. Living standards have increased largely because more Americans, especially mothers, have been working, and because the United States has been able to attract capital from abroad to offset a persistent trade deficit. "Most of the growth slowdown [in per capita income]," states the *Economic Report of the President,* "can be traced to a slowdown of productivity growth."

Other industrial countries have also experienced a productivity slowdown, most even sharper, suggesting that worldwide forces rather than local ones are to blame. Despite two decades of speculation and study, however, the reasons for the worldwide productivity slump remain a mystery. A host of explanations have been proposed, including some that suggest that productivity growth is likely to revive spontaneously. Harvard economist Dale W. Jorgenson, for example, blames the sudden surge in oil prices in 1973, which he claims made much of the existing capital stock obsolete. His colleague Zvi Griliches points a finger at the slower growth of aggregate demand by consumers for goods and services, which, he argues, has kept a great deal of productive capacity idle and hence inputs underemployed. But Edward Denison, an emeritus fellow of the Brookings Institution who conducted a comprehensive analysis of seventeen suggested causes, has concluded that much, if not most, of the slowdown remains unexplained.

Most of the focus in recent years has been on three suspects:

1. **Lagging investment.** How much a country invests matters, many economists have decided, because more capital per worker should lift output per worker. In stock brokerage, for example, the latest computer not only lets a broker execute more trades every day, but also embodies technological breakthroughs that allow new products to be traded.

   One reason that investment received so much attention is growing evidence that countries with high productivity growth consistently save and invest more than countries with low productivity growth. Baumol writes: "A substantial part of the superior performance of Japanese growth in labor productivity may be ascribable not to increasing efficiency but to the accumulation of capital."

   By the same token, British per capita incomes in the late nineteenth and early twentieth centuries, despite the industrial revolution's dramatic breakthroughs, grew at less than one-tenth the rate of lesser developed countries during the seventies. Not coincidentally, British investment back then was very low also. Similarly, in the United States the growth of productivity has been highly correlated with the growth of capital per worker. From 1959 to 1973, productivity grew by 2.8 percent a year while capital per worker in the private sector grew by 2.4 percent a year. From 1973 to 1989, in contrast, annual productivity growth of 0.9 percent coincided with growth of capital per worker of only 0.8 percent annually.

   On the other hand, economists generally agree that most of the slowdown in productivity growth reflected factors other than investment, namely, a slowdown in total factor productivity.

2. **Innovation.** The rate of return to capital invested in research and development is very high, averaging more than 20 percent a year. But the United States spends a smaller fraction of its GDP on civilian R&D than Germany or Japan. And Zvi Griliches points out that the number of new patents granted each year began to decline as far back as the sixties.

   Some economists think the spurt of

productivity growth after World War II was due to the backlog of ideas and technology and investment projects that were put on hold during the depression and World War II. Pent-up consumer demand and the rebuilding of Japan and Germany, according to this thinking, created tremendous demand for new construction and equipment. This explanation is consistent with the decline in productivity growth that started in 1973. Thus, part of the decline may have been simply a return to more normal growth rates.

3. **Skills.** About 10 to 15 percent of the growth in productivity over the post–World War II era can be traced to more and better schooling. But average years of schooling have not increased since 1976, when it peaked at 12.9 years. Moreover, the quality of basic elementary and secondary education has stagnated or even declined in the past two decades.

Many economists have focused in the past decade on the apparently divergent behavior of productivity in manufacturing and in services. (The Bureau of Labor Statistics publishes separate measures of productivity in manufacturing despite Edward Denison's warnings that measuring productivity below the level of the economy as a whole is tricky.) From 1948 to 1973, manufacturing and services productivity grew more or less in tandem and then, from 1973 to 1979, stagnated in tandem. In the eighties productivity growth in manufacturing snapped back. Tougher foreign competition and deregulation led to a wave of mergers and acquisitions, which in turn led to plant modernizations and streamlined production processes. Productivity growth in services, by contrast, slowed even more in the eighties. Outside of manufacturing—from government to construction to retailing—productivity growth has come to a standstill despite huge investments in information-processing technology.

Some economists have concluded that industrialized countries are specializing in what they do best. While Japan and Germany have surged ahead in some industries, the United States has widened its lead in others and stayed ahead, if by a narrower margin, in still others.

Stagnating pay and greater income inequality have focused renewed public attention on slow productivity growth. Policy prescriptions range from tax cuts on capital gains and more deregulation to industrial policy and government backing for commercially promising technologies. Most economists support closing the federal budget deficit and maintaining low inflation because they believe a stable macroeconomic environment is good for productivity growth. But the major focus of current discussion is on how to raise investment in people and machines and how to get more bang for the buck from that investment.

—**Sylvia Nasar**

Biography: Sylvia Nasar is an economics reporter for *The New York Times*. She was previously a columnist for *U.S. News and World Report* and, before that, an economics writer for *Fortune*.

Further Reading

Baumol, William J., Sue Anne Batey Blackman, and Edward N. Wolff. *Productivity and American Leadership*. 1989.
Committee for Economic Development. *Productivity Policy: Key to the Nation's Economic Future*. April 1983.
Denison, Edward F. *Estimates of Productivity Change by Industry*. 1989.
Economic Report of the President. 1990.
Economic Report of the President. 1992
Mokyr, Joel. *The Lever of Riches*. 1990.
"The Slowdown in Productivity Growth: A Symposium." *Journal of Economic Perspectives* 2, no. 4 (Fall 1988): 3–97.

Recessions

Geoffrey H. Moore

■ One of the most popular definitions of recessions is that they are periods when real gross national product (GNP) has declined for at least two consecutive quarters. In 1990, real GNP declined between the third and fourth quarters and again between the fourth quarter of 1990 and the first quarter of 1991. Hence, there is general agreement that a recession did occur.

Although the definition worked quite well in this instance, there are several problems with it. One is that it does not provide monthly dates of when recessions began or ended. For this purpose the National Bureau of Economic Research (NBER), whose

chronology of recessions is widely accepted, uses monthly measures of production, employment, sales, and income, all expressed in real terms (after allowing for inflation). GNP figures are not available monthly. The NBER found that the latest recession, from business cycle peak to trough, ran from July 1990 to March 1991.

Another problem with the two-consecutive-quarters definition is that there can be serious declines in economic activity even without two consecutive quarters of negative growth. Suppose that in one period, real GNP declines 5 percent in the first quarter, rises 1 percent in the second, and de-

CHART 1

Length of Business Recessions and Expansions
United States, 1790–1991

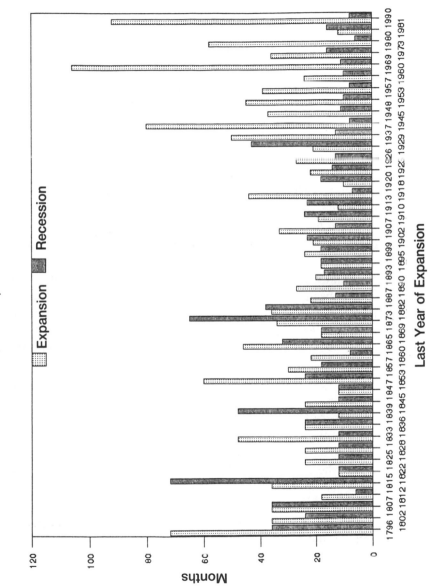

SOURCE: *Compiled from data supplied by the National Bureau of Economic Research Center for International Business Cycle Research, January 1993.*

clines 5 percent again in the third. In another period let's say real GNP declines 1 percent in each quarter. Obviously the first period shows a much more serious drop in GNP, but only the second period qualifies as a recession according to the definition.

These and other considerations have led the NBER to use a broader definition of recessions, which takes into account three dimensions of the decline in aggregate economic activity—its depth, duration, and diffusion across industries. These are known as the three Ds. Measures of this sort for several recent recessions are shown in table 1. This broader concept has also been applied to a much longer period, covering two hundred years of U.S. history (see chart 1).

One significant trend seen in the chart is that recessions have been getting shorter and expansions longer. The average recession during the past fifty years lasted eleven months, whereas the average recession was more than twice that long in the nineteenth century. Expansions, on the other hand, now last about twice as long as they did in earlier times. A number of factors account for this trend. One is the growing importance of the service industries, such as trade and transportation, where employment is usually more stable than in manufacturing. As the more stable industries have grown in importance, this has made the whole economy more stable and less susceptible to prolonged and severe recessions. Also,

the government has been playing a bigger role in moderating recessions, especially since the thirties. Unemployment insurance has helped to reduce the loss of income during recessions, and monetary policy has been used to reduce interest rates and make credit more accessible.

Recessions have a global as well as domestic dimension. Financial markets in many countries are closely watched in other countries, and many investors are making investments on an international scale. Exports and imports have become more important to business enterprises, and managements must now deal with global competition. As a result periods of recession are likely to encompass many countries at about the same time. During recessions in the United States, a majority of the industrial countries in Europe and the Pacific are apt to show signs of recession also. This, in turn, has depressing effects on the United States by slowing the foreign demand for U.S. exports.

The upshot is that even though recessions are not as severe as they used to be, they have serious consequences in many directions. Some industries, some occupations, and some areas of the country are hit much harder than others. Hence, it pays to keep close watch on them with all the daily, weekly, monthly, and quarterly data that are available for that purpose.

—Geoffrey H. Moore

Biography: Geoffrey H. Moore is the director of the Center for International Business Cycle Research, Columbia University, New York.

TABLE 1

The Three Ds of Recession: A Brief History

	Duration		Depth	Diffusion
			Unemployment Rate, maximum	Percent of Industries with Declining Employment, maximum
	Months	Percent Change in Real GNP		
Three Depressions				
Jan. 1920–July 1921	18	n.a.	11.9	97
Aug. 1929–Mar. 1933	43	−32.6	24.9	100
May 1937–June 1938	13	−18.2	20.0	97
Six Sharp Recessions				
May 1923–July 1924	14	−4.1	5.5	94
Nov. 1948–Oct. 1949	11	−1.5	7.9	90
July 1953–May 1954	10	−3.2	6.1	87
Aug. 1957–Apr. 1958	8	−3.3	7.5	88
Nov. 1973–Mar. 1975	16	−4.9	9.0	88
July 1981–Nov. 1982	16	−2.6	10.8	72
Five Mild Recessions				
Oct. 1926–Nov. 1927	13	−2.0	4.4	71
Apr. 1960–Feb. 1961	10	−1.2	7.1	80
Dec. 1969–Nov. 1970	11	−1.0	6.1	80
Jan. 1980–July 1980	6	−2.5	7.8	63
July 1990–March 1991	8	−1.2	6.9	73
Averages				
1920–1938 (5)	20	−14.2	13.3	92
1948–1991 (9)	11	−2.4	7.7	80

SOURCE: *Based on table A-2 in G. H. Moore,* Business Cycles, Inflation and Forecasting, *2nd ed., 1983. Note that the brief and mild recession of 1945 is omitted here.*

Further Reading

Burns, Arthur F., and Wesley C. Mitchell. *Measuring Business Cycles.* 1946.
Center for International Business Cycle Research. *Recession-Recovery Watch.* Monthly.
Gordon, Robert J., ed. *The American Business Cycle: Continuity and Change.* 1986.
Moore, Geoffrey H. *Business Cycles, Inflation, and Forecasting.* 1983.
Moore, Geoffrey H. *Leading Indicators for the 1990s.* 1989.
U.S. Department of Commerce. *Survey of Current Business.* Monthly.

Saving

Laurence J. Kotlikoff

■ Saving means different things to different people. To some it means putting money in the bank. To others it means buying stocks or contributing to a pension plan. But to economists, saving means only one thing—consuming less in the present in order to consume more in the future.

An easy way to understand the economist's view of saving—and its importance for economic growth—is to consider an economy in which there is a single commodity, say, corn. The amount of corn on hand at any point in time can either be consumed (literally gobbled up) or saved. Any corn that is saved is immediately planted (invested), yielding more corn in the future. Hence, saving adds to the stock of corn in the ground, or in economic jargon, the stock of capital. The greater the stock of capital, the greater the amount of future corn, which can, in turn, either be consumed or saved.

Any country that saves little—that eats a high fraction of its seed corn—does so at the price of a lower future standard of living. The United States is an example of this grim law of saving. Since 1980 the annual rate of U.S. net national saving (net national output less private consumption expenditures less government consumption expenditures, all divided by net national product) has averaged only 4.2 percent. This saving rate is 60 percent smaller than the rate observed between 1950 and 1979! In the past few years saving has fallen even more. Since 1986 the United States has saved less

than 3 percent of its net output. The saving rate in 1992 was only 2.8 percent.

The current rate of U.S. saving is remarkably low, not only by U.S. standards but also by international standards. Differences in how the statisticians in different countries define income and consumption make it difficult to compare saving rates across nations. But after correcting as well as possible for such data problems, one concludes that Americans are saving at less than one-third the rate of the Japanese and at less than half the rate of the Germans and many other Europeans. And as U.S. saving has declined, America's lead in per capita income (adjusted for purchasing power) has diminished.

Why do countries save at different rates? Economists do not know all the answers. Some of the factors that undoubtedly affect the amount people save are culture, differences in saving motives, economic growth, demographics, how many people in the economy are in the labor force, the insurability of risks, and economic policy. Each of these factors can influence saving at a point in time and produce changes in saving over time.

Motives for Saving

The famous life-cycle model of Nobel Laureate Franco Modigliani asserts that people save—accumulate assets—to finance their retirement, and they dissave—spend their assets—during retirement. The more young savers there are relative to old dissavers, the greater will be a nation's saving rate. Most economists believed for decades that this life-cycle model provided the main explanation of U.S. saving. But in the early eighties Lawrence H. Summers of Harvard and I showed that saving for retirement explains only about one-fifth of total U.S. wealth. Most of U.S. wealth accumulation—the remaining four-fifths—is saving that is ultimately bequeathed or given to younger generations. The motive for much of the substantial flow of bequests and gifts from older to younger Americans is surely altruism. But a large component of the bequests may be involuntary, and simply reflect the fact that many people do not spend all their savings before they die.

In recent years a much larger fraction of the retirement savings of the American elderly has been annuitized. That is, the savings take the form of company pensions or Social Security that pay regular checks until death, with no payments after the person dies. Having one's retirement finances come in the form of an annuity eliminates the risk of living longer than your money lasts. One possible result of the increased annuitization of retirement assets may be that people, especially those who have already retired, have less incentive to save more in case they "live too long."

That precautionary motive is one of the key reasons people save. Besides the risk of living longer than expected, people save against more mundane risks, like losing their jobs or incurring large uninsured medical expenses. Computer simulation studies show that the amount of precautionary sav-

ing can be very sensitive to the availability of insurance against these and other kinds of risks. For example, one such study that I did shows that the failure to insure low-risk, but high-cost, health expenditures such as nursing-home care can lead to a 10 percent increase in national saving.

Another issue related to motives and preferences for saving is the role of the rich in generating aggregate saving. Do rich Americans account for most of U.S. saving? Not really. Relative to their incomes, some of the rich save a lot, and some dissave. So, too, for the poor. As Donald Trump will tell you, there is considerable mobility of wealth in the United States, at least over long periods of time (see HUMAN CAPITAL). The fact that the ranks of the rich are continually changing suggests that some of those who are initially rich dissave and dissipate their wealth, while others who are not initially rich save considerable sums and become rich.

Economic Growth and Demographic Change

A country's saving rate and its economic growth are closely connected. In an economy experiencing no growth in either technology or population, one would expect, at least in the long run, saving to be zero, with the exception of the saving needed to replace depreciating capital. That an economy's overall long-run saving rate is zero doesn't mean that no one saves or dissaves. Rather, it means that the positive savings of those accumulating assets exactly balances the negative savings of those decumulating assets. For growing economies, long-run saving is likely to be positive to ensure that the stock of capital assets keeps pace with the number and technical abilities of workers.

In the United States the continuous decline in saving may be traced, in part, to a decline in technical progress. Economists measure technical progress as the increase in output that cannot be traced to increases in inputs—technical progress is a measure of the efficiency with which inputs are transformed into output. Since 1970, according to the U.S. Bureau of Labor Statistics, technology has been improving by only 0.57 percent per year, compared with 1.79 percent per year between 1950 and 1969. U.S. population growth has also declined. In combination, the slow growth in both technology and population spells a very low long-run rate of U.S. saving.

But demographic change should be causing U.S. saving to increase. In the last five years the numerous baby boomers have been reaching their primary saving years, which should have boosted the U.S. saving rate by several percentage points. That makes the fact that U.S. saving has been so low all the more surprising.

Labor-Supply Decisions

National saving is the difference between national output and national consumption. Labor income represents about three-quarters of U.S. output. So changes in labor income, if not accompanied by equivalent changes in consumption, can greatly affect an economy's saving rate. Take, for example, the recent remarkable increase in U.S. female labor force participation. In 1975

half of the women age twenty-five to forty-four participated in the labor force. In 1988 over two-thirds were in the labor force. This increase in female labor supply is the primary reason for the more than 20 percent increase in U.S. per capita income since 1975.

If this additional income had all been saved, the U.S. saving rate post-1980 would have exceeded 20 percent. Because much of the increase in labor supply was for women age eighteen to thirty-five, particularly married women, one would expect them to have saved some portion of that income for their old age. But they did not. This fact is another part of the recent U.S. saving puzzle.

Adding to the puzzle is the ongoing increase in the expected length of retirement. More and more Americans, particularly men, are retiring in their midfifties. At the same time, life expectancies continue to rise. Today's thirty-year-old male can expect to live to age seventy-four, 3.5 years longer than the typical thirty-year-old in 1960. If he retires at age fifty-five, today's thirty-year-old will spend almost half of his remaining life in retirement. Economic models of saving suggest that aggregate saving should depend strongly and positively on the length of retirement. Thus, with the retirement age coming down and life expectancy going up, economists would expect people to save a lot more—not a lot less.

Economic Policy

Government policy also can have powerful effects on a nation's saving. To begin with, governments are, themselves, large consumers of goods and services. In the United States the government accounts for over one fifth of all national consumption. More government consumption spending does not, however, necessarily imply less national saving. If the private sector responds to a one-dollar increase in government consumption by reducing its own consumption by one dollar, aggregate saving remains unchanged.

The private sector's consumption response depends critically on who pays for the government's consumption and how the government extracts these payments. If the government assigns most of the tax burden to future generations (with, for example, our current pay-as-you-go Social Security system), current generations will have little reason, other than concern for their offspring, to reduce their consumption expenditures. If current generations are forced to pay for the government's spending, the size of the private sector consumption response will vary according to who among people living today foots the bill. The older the people taxed, the larger will be the reduction in consumption. The reason is that older people consume a higher percentage of their income than younger ones. Thus, taxing dollars away from retirees, say, instead of forty-year-old workers, will bring a larger decrease in private sector consumption.

Finally, different taxes have different incentive effects. For example, the government might raise its funds with taxes on capital rather than taxes on labor income. By lowering the after-tax return to saving, taxes on capital income discourage saving for future consumption.

Alternative Explanations of the Recent Decline in U.S. Saving

What explains the recent decline in U.S. saving? One explanation that can quickly be dismissed is that increased government consumption is to blame. The ratio of government consumption to national output since 1980 has been essentially the same as it was in the previous two decades.

Another explanation is that the U.S. government, by cutting income taxes and running large deficits, shifted the burden of paying for government consumption from current to future generations and induced a spending spree by current generations. This explanation, however, ignores other policies that redistributed away from current generations, like the baby boomers, toward future generations, such as their children. One important example is the 1983 Social Security Amendments, which cut baby boomers' prospective Social Security retirement benefits by roughly 20 percent in order to limit the payroll taxes their children would have to face when they join the work force. Of course, it is possible that people in their thirties and forties do not realize that their future benefits will be lower than was promised before 1983.

The argument that cutting federal income taxes raised disposable incomes and stimulated Americans to consume excessively also ignores increases in state and local taxes, as well as federal payroll taxes. On balance, disposable income as a share of net national output was only slightly higher in the eighties than in the previous decades. For all governments—federal, state, and local—the ratio of taxes, minus transfer payments (for example, welfare and Social

Security), to U.S. output averaged .220 between 1980 and 1987. It averaged .226 for the seventies, .239 for the sixties, and .224 for the fifties.

Nor do disincentives to save appear to be responsible for the decline in U.S. saving in the eighties. Marginal personal tax rates on capital income fell through the last decade, with the top marginal rate declining from 70 percent in 1980 to 31 percent today. Individual Retirement Accounts (IRAs), intended to promote saving, probably reduced it. How could this be? Imagine that the government lets someone who invests in an IRA avoid taxes whose present value is $1,000. That person is then $1,000 wealthier. He will save some portion of this wealth and consume a portion. Say he saves $300, a generous estimate, and consumes $700. Then personal saving increases by $300. But assume that the government does not cut spending to finance this tax cut. Then the deficit rises by $1,000. The net result is that although personal saving rises, national saving falls by $700.

Most theories of consumption predict that households will increase their spending after their wealth increases. In the eighties real capital gains accruing to U.S. households on their holdings of equities were about $900 billion (measured in 1988 dollars). But in the eighties the real capital gains on the total portfolio of U.S. households, including all net assets (all assets net of all liabilities), measured in 1988 dollars was only $260 billion. It is true that most U.S. assets gained value in nominal terms—their dollar values at the end of the eighties exceeded their dollar values in 1980. But assets other than stock lost value in real terms. Their nominal appreciation

failed to keep pace with inflation. The value of residential structures, most of which were owner-occupied housing, fell by over $600 billion between 1980 and 1989. The $260 billion figure represented only 1.7 percent of total U.S. net wealth as of the end of the 1980s and is too small to account for much of the decline in net national saving.

The eighties witnessed changes in income inequality, demographics, the expected duration of retirement, and female labor force participation, but as already mentioned, these changes should have led to more, not less, saving. One possible explanation for the recent decline in saving is a reduction in saving for bequests, which may tie in with the decline in the birthrate. Only significant additional research can test the validity of this explanation. At the moment, however, there is no "smoking gun" explanation for the critically low level of U.S. saving.

The Implications of Low Saving for Baby Boomers

Americans as a group used to save more than they did in the eighties. And as a consequence the collective stock of U.S. wealth holdings is still quite large—roughly $20 trillion. This is enough to finance all Americans' consumer expenditures for over five years. But 59 percent of this wealth is owned by people who are fifty or older, who appear to be spending a good deal of it on themselves. If the elderly do end up spending rather than bequeathing the bulk of existing U.S. wealth, will younger Americans, particularly baby boomers, accumulate enough savings to maintain the standard of living they currently enjoy in their old age?

Based on current evidence, the answer appears to be no. Compared with their parents, baby boomers can expect to retire earlier, live longer, rely less on inheritances, receive less help from children, experience slower real wage growth, face higher taxes, and replace a smaller fraction of their prere-tirement earnings with Social Security retirement benefits. Unless baby boomers change their saving habits and change them quickly, they may experience much higher rates of poverty in their old age than those currently observed among U.S. elderly.

—Laurence J. Kotlikoff

Biography: Laurence J. Kotlikoff is a professor of economics at Boston University and a research associate with the National Bureau of Economic Research. He was previously a senior economist with the President's Council of Economic Advisers.

Further Reading

Auerbach, Alan J., and Laurence J. Kotlikoff. *Dynamic Fiscal Policy.* 1987.
Kotlikoff, Laurence J. *Generational Accounting: Knowing Who Pays and When for What We Spend.* 1992.
Kotlikoff, Laurence J. *What Determines Savings?* Chap. 6. 1989.
Kotlikoff, Laurence J., and Lawrence H. Summers. "The Adequacy of Saving." *American Economic Review* 72, no. 5 (1982): 1056–69.
Kotlikoff, Laurence J., and Lawrence H. Summers. "The Role of Intergenerational Transfers in Aggregate Capital Formation." *Journal of Political Economy* 89, no. 4 (1981): 706–32.

Unemployment

Lawrence H. Summers

■ Few economic indicators are of more concern to Americans than unemployment statistics. Reports that unemployment rates are dropping make us happy; reports to the contrary make us anxious. But just what do unemployment figures tell us? Are they reliable measures? What influences joblessness?

How Is Unemployment Defined and Measured?

Each month, the federal government's Bureau of Labor Statistics randomly surveys sixty thousand individuals around the nation. If respondents say they are both out of work and seeking employment, they are counted as unemployed members of the labor force. Jobless respondents who have chosen not to continue looking for work are considered out of the labor force and therefore are not counted as unemployed. Almost half of all unemployment spells end because people leave the labor force. Ironically, those who drop out of the labor force—whether because they are discouraged, have household responsibilities, or are sick—actually make unemployment rates look better; the unemployment rate includes only people within the labor force who are out of work.

Not all unemployment is the same. Unemployment can be long- or short-term. It can be frictional, meaning someone is between jobs. Or it may be structural, as when someone's skills are no longer demanded because of a change in technology or an industry downturn.

Is Unemployment a Big Problem?

Some say there are reasons to think that unemployment in the United States is not a big problem. In 1991, 32.8 percent of all unemployed people were under the age of twenty-four and presumably few of these were the main source of income for their families. One out of six of the unemployed are teenagers. Moreover, the average duration of a spell of unemployment is short. In 1991 it was 13.8 weeks. And the median spell of unemployment is even shorter. In 1991 it was 6.9 weeks, meaning that half of all spells last 6.9 weeks or less.

On the basis of numbers like the above, many economists have thought that unemployment is not a very large problem. A few weeks of unemployment seems to them like just enough time for people to move from one job to another. Yet these numbers, though accurate, are misleading. Much of the reason why unemployment spells appear short is that many workers drop out of the labor force at least temporarily because they cannot find attractive jobs. Often two short spells of unemployment mean a long spell of joblessness because the person was unemployed for a short time, then withdrew from the labor force, and then reentered the labor force.

And even if most unemployment spells are short, most weeks of unemployment are experienced by people who are out of work for a long time. To see why, consider the following example. Suppose that each week, twenty spells of unemployment lasting one week begin, and only one begins that lasts twenty weeks. Then the average duration of a completed spell of unemployment would be only 1.05 weeks. But half of all unemployment (half of the total of forty weeks that the twenty-one people are out of work) would be accounted for by spells lasting twenty weeks.

Something like this example applies in the real world. In November 1991, for example, 40 percent of the unemployed had been unemployed for less than five weeks, but 15 percent had been unemployed for six or more months.

What Causes Long-Term Unemployment?

To fully understand unemployment, we must consider the causes of recorded long-term unemployment. Empirical evidence shows that two causes are welfare payments and unemployment insurance. These government assistance programs contribute to long-term unemployment in two ways.

First, government assistance increases the *measure* of unemployment by prompting people who are not working to claim that they are looking for work even when

they are not. The work-registration requirement for welfare recipients, for example, compels people who otherwise would not be considered part of the labor force to register as if they were a part of it. This requirement effectively increases the measure of unemployed in the labor force even though these people are better described as nonemployed—that is, not actively looking for work.

In a study using state data on registrants in Aid to Families with Dependent Children and food stamp programs, my colleague Kim Clark and I found that the work-registration requirement actually increased measured unemployment by about 0.5 to 0.8 percentage points. In other words, this requirement increases the measure of unemployment by 600,000 to 1 million people. Without the condition that they look for work, many of these people would not be counted as unemployed. Similarly, unemployment insurance increases the measure of unemployment by inducing people to say that they are job hunting in order to collect benefits.

The second way government assistance programs contribute to long-term unemployment is by providing an incentive, and the means, not to work. Each unemployed person has a "reservation wage"—the minimum wage he or she insists on getting before accepting a job. Unemployment insurance and other social assistance programs increase that reservation wage, causing an unemployed person to remain unemployed longer.

Consider, for example, an unemployed person who is used to making $10.00 an hour. On unemployment insurance this person receives about 55 percent of normal earnings, or $5.50 per lost work hour. If that person is in a 15 percent federal tax bracket, and a 3 percent state tax bracket, he or she pays $0.99 in taxes per hour not worked and nets $4.51 per hour after taxes as compensation for not working. If that person took a job that paid $10.00 per hour, governments would take 18 percent for income taxes and 7.5 percent for Social Security taxes, netting him or her $7.45 per hour of work. Comparing the two payments, this person may decide that a day of leisure is worth more than the extra $2.94 an hour the job would pay. If so, this means that the unemployment insurance raises the person's reservation wage to above $10.00 per hour.

Unemployment, therefore, may not be as costly for the jobless person as previously imagined. But as Harvard economist Martin Feldstein pointed out in the seventies, the costs of unemployment to taxpayers are very great indeed. Take the example above of the individual who could work for $10.00 an hour or collect unemployment insurance of $5.50 per hour. The cost of unemployment to this unemployed person was only $2.94 per hour, the difference between the net income from working and the net income from not working. And as compensation for this cost, the unemployed person gained leisure, whose value could well be above $2.94 per hour. But other taxpayers as a group paid $5.50 in unemployment benefits for every hour the person was unemployed, and got back in taxes only $0.99 on this benefit. Moreover, they forwent $2.55 in lost tax and Social Security revenue that this person would have paid per

hour employed at a $10.00 wage. Net loss to other taxpayers: $7.06 per hour. Multiply this by millions of people collecting unemployment, each missing hundreds of hours of work, and you get a cost to taxpayers in the billions.

Unemployment insurance also extends the time a person stays off the job. Clark and I estimated that the existence of unemployment insurance almost doubles the number of unemployment spells lasting more than three months. If unemployment insurance were eliminated, the unemployment rate would drop by more than half a percentage point, which means that the number of unemployed people would fall by over 600,000. This is all the more significant in light of the fact that less than half of the unemployed receive insurance benefits.

Another cause of long-term unemployment is unionization. High union wages that exceed the competitive market rate are likely to cause job losses in the unionized sector of the economy. Also, those who lose high-wage union jobs are often reluctant to accept alternative low-wage employment. Between 1970 and 1985, for example, a state with a 20 percent unionization rate, approximately the average for the fifty states and the District of Columbia, experienced an increase in unemployment of 1.2 percentage points relative to a hypothetical state that had no unions. To put this in perspective, 1.2 percentage points is about 60 percent of the increase in normal unemployment between 1970 and 1985.

There is no question that some long-term unemployment is caused by government intervention and unions that interfere with the supply of labor. It is, however, a great mistake (made by some conservative economists) to attribute most unemployment to government interventions in the economy or to any lack of desire to work on the part of the unemployed. Unemployment was a serious economic problem in the late nineteenth and early twentieth centuries prior to the welfare state or widespread unionization. Unemployment then, as now, was closely linked to general macroeconomic conditions. The Great Depression, when unemployment in the United States reached 25 percent (see GREAT DEPRESSION) is the classic example of the damage that collapses in credit can do. Since then, most economists have agreed that cyclical fluctuations in unemployment are caused by changes in the demand for labor, not by changes in workers' desires to work, and that unemployment in recessions is involuntary.

Even leaving aside cyclical fluctuations, a large part of unemployment is due to demand factors rather than supply. High unemployment in Texas in the early eighties, for example, was due to collapsing oil prices. High unemployment in New England in the early nineties is due to declines in computer and other industries in which New England specialized. The process of adjustment following shocks is long and painful, and recent research suggests that even temporary declines in demand can have permanent effects on unemployment as workers who lose jobs are unable to sell their labor due to a loss of skills or for other reasons. Therefore, most economists who study unemployment support an active government role in training and retraining workers and in maintaining stable demand for labor.

The Natural Rate of Unemployment

Long before Milton Friedman and Edmund Phelps advanced the notion of the natural rate of unemployment (the lowest rate of unemployment tolerable without pushing up inflation) policymakers had contented themselves with striving for low, not zero, unemployment. Just what constitutes an acceptably low level of unemployment has been redefined over the decades. In the early sixties an unemployment rate of 4 percent was both desirable and achievable. Over time, the unemployment rate drifted upward and, for the most part, has hovered around 7 percent. Lately, it has fallen to 6 percent. I suspect that some of the reduction in the apparent natural rate of unemployment in recent years has to do with reduced transitional unemployment, both because fewer people are between jobs and because they are between jobs for shorter periods. A sharply falling dollar has led to a manufacturing turnaround. Union power has been eroded by domestic regulatory action and inaction, as well as by international competition. More generally, international competition has restrained wage increases in high-wage industries. Another factor making unemployment lower is a decline in the fraction of the unemployed who are supported by unemployment insurance.

What Are the Prospects for the Nineties?

Although the most recent recession has seen increased unemployment, the unemployment rates are still low by the standard of previous downturns. Recovery should bring some improvement. Over the longer term key variables affecting unemployment will include unemployment insurance, unionization, and the success of the economy in handling the reduced demand for

unskilled workers caused by technological innovation.

—Lawrence H. Summers

Biography: Lawrence H. Summers is undersecretary of the treasury for International Affairs. He was previously the vice president of Development Economics and chief economist at the World Bank. This was written while he was the Nathaniel Ropes Professor of Political Economy at Harvard University.

Further Reading

Feldstein, Martin. "The Economics of the New Unemployment." *Public Interest* 33 (Fall 1973): 3–42.

Friedman, Milton. "The Role of Monetary Policy." *American Economic Review* 58 (March 1968): 1–17.

Hall, Robert. "Employment Fluctuations and Wage Rigidity." *Brookings Papers on Economic Activity* 1 (1980): 91–141.

Summers, Lawrence H. *Understanding Unemployment.* 1990.

———. "Why Is the Unemployment Rate So Very High Near Full Employment?" *Brookings Papers on Economic Activity* 2 (1986): 339–83.

———, and Kim B. Clark. "Labor Market Dynamics and Unemployment: A Reconsideration." *Brookings Papers on Economic Activity* 1 (1979): 13–60.

See also LABOR UNIONS, PHILLIPS CURVE, UNEMPLOYMENT INSURANCE.

CHAPTER FOUR

ECONOMIC POLICY

Federal Budget

John F. Cogan

◼ Deficit spending has been a way of life for the federal government for most years since World War II. A whole generation of elected federal officials has come and gone without ever balancing the budget. The last time that federal budget expenditures were brought into balance with revenues was in 1969, and prior to that the last time was in 1960.

Since World War II the federal budget deficit has risen almost continually, regardless of which political party has occupied the White House, and regardless of which party has held a majority of seats in the House of Representatives or Senate. As table 1 indicates, in each of the last four decades, the average size of the federal budget deficit relative to GNP has approximately doubled. Due to the extraordinary string of budget deficits, the national debt is now equivalent to over forty thousand dollars for every family in the United States.

The existence of chronic budget deficits during the postwar years stands in stark contrast to the pattern of federal finances during previous periods in America's history. For most of our history prior to 1940, the federal budget was balanced, except in years of war or economic recession.

The causes of persistent federal budget deficits during the last forty years are not well understood. Many observers believe that the cause of the deficit lies in unique policy mistakes during the eighties, such as the simultaneous reduction in taxes and

increase in defense spending. But this explanation ignores the persistence of budget deficits for the three decades prior to eighties. It also ignores the fact that since 1981, expenditures on nondefense programs grew almost as rapidly as those on defense, and that the federal tax claim on the country's gross national product (GNP) is currently higher than it has averaged during any preceding decade (see table 1).

Other observers claim that deficits persist because the American public demands more in government benefits than it is willing to pay for in taxes. Although this explanation has intuitive appeal, it fails to explain why the American public's preferences have changed. Why did Americans previously want the same amount of benefits as they were willing to pay for in taxes?

The Budget Process and the Commons Problem

The congressional budget process itself has contributed mightily to persistent budget deficits. The most important feature of the current budget process is its decentralized nature. At no point in the process does anyone decide on the total amount the federal government will spend. Instead, responsibility for individual legislative bills that determine the total amount of spending is divided up among fifteen separate committees in the Senate and seventeen com-

TABLE 1

Federal Budget, 1950–90
(Percent of GNP)

	Spending	Revenues	Deficit
1950–59	18.0	17.6	0.5
1960–69	19.0	18.2	0.8
1970–79	20.5	18.3	2.1
1980–89	23.0	19.0	4.3
1990	23.2	19.1	4.1

mittees in the House of Representatives. The Appropriations Committee has jurisdiction for nonentitlement programs covering about 40 percent of the total federal spending. The remaining 60 percent is made up of entitlement programs, which are handled by various other standing committees. The agriculture committees have authority over farm price supports, food stamps, and other rural programs. The tax-writing committees in the House and Senate are responsible for Social Security and Medicare. The House Energy and Commerce Committee has jurisdiction over Medicaid and shares responsibility for Medicare with the Ways and Means Committee.

This decentralization of spending authority creates powerful incentives for deficit financing. By spreading responsibility for spending authority among so many committees, the Congress has created a situation known as "the tragedy of the commons" (see THE TRAGEDY OF THE COMMONS). This type of situation arises when numerous claimants compete for a commonly owned resource. The tragedy is that the inexorable forces of competition for the resource lead to overconsumption and eventual exhaustion of the resource.

To understand the commons problem, imagine a publicly owned forest that is open to all logging companies that desire access to it. No individual company would have any reason to restrain its logging activities. In fact, each company would have every incentive to cut down as many trees as it could before a competitor did so. On a more personal level imagine that a mother sends her family to the store, tells her husband to buy beer, her teenage daughter to buy magazines, and her ten-year old son to buy candy. Imagine, moreover, that she sets no limits on how much each can spend. Each family member would then overspend on the various items.

Congress is like that family. From the individual committee standpoint the commonly owned resource is federal revenues, raised primarily from taxes levied on individuals and corporations. The consumers of this resource are the congressional committees. The common resource is "overconsumed" when government spending repeatedly exceeds tax revenue—that is, when chronic budget deficits occur.

An Historical Sketch

An historical look at government spending and the budget process reveals the powerful role the commons problem has played in producing budget deficits. When the budget process has been highly centralized, spending has been held in check and the budget has been balanced. When the process has been decentralized, the growth in spending has outpaced the growth in revenues, and chronic budget deficits have resulted.

During the first ninety years of U.S. history, spending authority was concentrated in a single committee in each house of Congress, and budgets were balanced except during recessions and wars. But in 1885 the House stripped the Appropriations Committee of much of its spending authority and gave it to numerous authorizing commit-

tees. This period of decentralized budgeting lasted until just after World War I.

At the time, some observers recognized the consequences of decentralization. Congressman Samuel Randall, chairman of the Appropriations Committee and a former Speaker of the House, warned in 1884, "If you undertake to divide all these appropriations and have many committees where there ought to be but one, you will enter upon a path of extravagance you cannot foresee the length of or the depth of until we find the Treasury of the country bankrupt."

Randall's statement proved prophetic. Immediately after Congress splintered the budget process, federal spending grew at an unprecedented rate. By the mid-1890s federal spending (excluding interest payments) was 50 percent larger than it had been in 1886, and by 1916 it had risen an additional 45 percent.

This explosive spending growth produced deficits that were more frequent and larger than ever before in peacetime. In the five years immediately preceding the

TABLE 2

Budget Average Deficits

Time Periods	Deficits (Percent of GNP)
Centralized Budgeting	
1799–1885	0.26
1922–1931	−0.77
Decentralized Budgeting	
1886–1921	0.69
1932–1989	3.61

change to decentralized budgeting in the House, annual revenues exceeded annual expenditures by 40 percent. The subsequent expenditure growth turned this sizable budget surplus into record peacetime deficits in the mid-1890s. Deficit spending persisted throughout the remainder of the decade. During the first fifteen years of the twentieth century, the budget was in deficit half the time.

Much like today, from 1886 to 1916 all growth in spending relative to GNP occurred in programs under the jurisdiction of the authorizing committees. But unlike today, Congress recognized its problems and took decisive steps to correct them. The House acted first. In 1919 it established a select committee on the budget, which quickly recommended that the House adopt a budget process reform that "centers on one Committee . . . the authority to report all appropriations." The House accepted this recommendation and voted to strip the seven authorizing committees of their power to appropriate. The Senate followed two years later.

The corrective step worked. From 1921 until the onset of the Great Depression (1930), expenditures relative to GNP were held constant and the budget was balanced. Unfortunately, decentralization returned during the depression. The process moved slowly at first, but accelerated significantly in the sixties and seventies as Congress created new programs and placed spending jurisdiction for them in an ever increasing number of congressional committees. Deposit insurance legislation, enacted in 1934, provided a federal government guarantee for certain deposits in banks and savings and loan institutions. Social Security legis-

lation, enacted a year later, provided pensions to persons age sixty-five and older and guaranteed matching payments to state governments for the cost of welfare programs. In 1956 the Social Security disability program was created to provide federal cash assistance to disabled persons. In the sixties the food stamp program (1964), Medicare (1965), Medicaid (1965), and the Guaranteed Student Loan program (1965) were created. In 1974 the General Revenue Sharing and the Child Support Enforcement programs began.

By the midseventies the process of decentralizing budget decision making by creating new programs was largely complete. The forty-year process had a profound impact on the degree of committee spending authority. In 1932 the Appropriations Committee had jurisdiction over more than 90 percent of all programs. No other committee had more than 1 percent. By the early eighties the Appropriations Committee controlled only about 40 percent. Seven other committees shared an additional 55 percent.

This return to decentralized decision making once again introduced the "commons" problem into the congressional budget-making process as it had in the past. The inevitable forces of the commons drove government expenditures upward at a rate far in excess of government revenues. The chronic federal budget deficits described in table 1 were the result.

This two-hundred-year review of the relationship between the congressional budget process and the existence of persistent deficits demonstrates the critical role that institutional rules play in determining outcomes. Although other factors, such as a defense buildup or a savings and loan crisis, may be important in contributing to deficits, it is the institutional rules that create incentives for particular forms of behavior and drive decision making over the long run. An understanding of these rules and the way in which they affect behavior is a necessary first step toward correcting the structural problem of the budget deficits.

—John F. Cogan

Biography: John F. Cogan is a senior fellow at Stanford University's Hoover Institution. Formerly deputy director of the Office of Management and Budget, he now directs a project to build a consistent record of government spending decisions since World War II.

Further Reading

Cogan, John. ''The Evolution of Congressional Budget Decisionmaking and the Emergence of Federal Deficits.'' In *The Great Budget Puzzle*, edited by Cogan, Timothy Muris, and Allen Schick. 1993.
Demsetz, Harold. ''Toward a Theory of Property Rights.'' *American Economic Review* 57, no. 2 (May 1967): 347–59.
Wildavsky, Aaron. *The New Politics of the Budgetary Process.* 1988.

See also THE TRAGEDY OF THE COMMONS.

Federal Debt

Robert Eisner

■ Everyone talks about the federal debt, but few, literally, know what they are talking about. That is all the more true for the federal deficit, which year after year adds to the total debt outstanding.

Perhaps the first thing to know about the federal debt, some $4 trillion at the end of 1992, is that $1 trillion of it is held by government agencies or government trust funds such as those for Social Security. Excluding that amount leaves the more relevant figure of "gross federal debt held by the public" at $3 trillion.

Even that number is somewhat misleading on two counts. First, because the Federal Reserve banks are technically private corporations, the debt "held by the public" includes the Federal Reserve holdings, which come to almost a quarter of a trillion dollars, although the interest paid on Federal Reserve holdings largely goes right back to the Treasury. Second, "gross" debt does not subtract what the public owes to the federal government or its credit agencies. The net debt—the debt owed by the government to the public exclusive of the Federal Reserve, minus the debt owed by the public to the government—is some 20 percent less. Therefore, the actual net debt was on the order of $2.4 trillion in 1992, or only a little more than half the gross debt.

The debt of U.S. businesses (excluding financial institutions) and households is $7 trillion, far larger than the federal debt. But business debt, it is argued, generally fi-nances income-earning plant and equipment. And individuals borrow largely to purchase homes, which provide implicit income by saving rent that would otherwise be paid. Debt that finances income-earning assets is hardly the same as dead-weight debt that must be serviced out of unrelated income.

The federal government, though, also has real assets: interstate highways, public buildings, and federal land, water, and minerals. All these assets contribute to the national income and hence—indirectly if not directly—to the "earnings" or tax receipts of the government itself. Private businesses compute their net worth by subtracting liabilities from assets. The same should be done for the government. Most unofficial estimates suggest that assets directly owned by the federal government pretty much match the entire federal debt.

Most of the federal debt is owed to Americans. In fact, the share of privately held public debt owned by foreigners fell from 21.2 percent in 1980 to 17.6 percent in 1992. The foreign share of the total gross public debt in 1992 was 12.1 percent. And virtually all of that debt was in dollars, which means that it can be paid off or bought back by the simple device of printing money or, in more sophisticated fashion, open-market operations of the Federal Reserve.

Whether that should be done raises serious issues of economic policy. But if it

TABLE 1

Alternative Measures of Federal Debt

Gross Federal Debt Held by Public[1]

Year	Billions of Dollars	Percentage of GDP	Per Capita in 1992$
1945	235.2	110.9	15,487
1946	241.9	113.8	12,824
1947	224.3	100.6	10,244
1948	216.3	87.7	9,074
1949	214.3	81.6	8,879
1950	219.0	82.4	8,715
1951	214.3	68.4	8,000
1952	214.8	63.1	7,766
1953	218.4	60.0	7,643
1954	224.5	61.0	7,598
1955	226.6	58.9	7,300
1956	222.2	53.4	6,802
1957	219.3	50.0	6,364
1958	226.3	50.5	6,328
1959	234.7	48.9	6,262
1960	236.8	46.9	6,123
1961	238.4	46.1	6,006
1962	248.0	44.7	6,026
1963	254.0	43.5	6,016
1964	256.8	41.1	5,890
1965	260.8	38.9	5,752
1966	263.7	35.9	5,553
1967	266.6	33.6	5,398
1968	289.5	34.2	5,520
1969	278.1	30.0	4,992
1970	283.2	28.7	4,775
1971	303.0	28.8	4,773
1972	322.4	28.1	4,818

TABLE 1, *Continued*

Alternative Measures of Federal Debt

Gross Federal Debt Held by Public[1]

Year	Billions of Dollars	Percentage of GDP	Per Capita in 1992$
1973	340.9	26.8	4,752
1974	343.7	24.5	4,361
1975	394.7	26.1	4,521
1976	477.4	28.3	5,105
1977	549.1	27.8	5,318
1978	607.1	28.6	5,378
1979	639.8	28.2	5,152
1980	709.3	26.8	5,148
1981	784.8	26.5	5,144
1982	919.2	29.4	5,679
1983	1,131.0	34.1	6,665
1984	1,300.0	35.2	7,268
1985	1,499.4	37.8	8,032
1986	1,736.2	41.2	8,976
1987	1,888.1	42.4	9,372
1988	2,050.2	42.6	9,675
1989	2,189.3	42.3	9,803
1990	2,410.4	44.1	10,227

[1] End of fiscal years: June 30 to 1976; September 30, 1977–90.

SOURCES: *Office of Management and Budget*, Budget Baselines, Historical Data, and Alternatives for the Future, *January 1993, Table 7.1, p. 346*; Economic Report of the President, January 1993, *Table B-29, p. 381; Bureau of Economic Analysis, National Income and Product Series Diskette, and* Survey of Current Business, *January 1993; and author's calculations.*

wishes, the federal government can always create what money it needs to service its debt. In this fundamental sense, then, federal debt is different from private debt or, for that matter, the debt of state and local governments, which do not have the power to create money. Thus the federal government has no reason ever to default on its debt or declare bankruptcy.

The federal debt held by the public differs

in another fundamental sense from private debt. For every private creditor there is a debtor who knows he is a debtor. Therefore private debt is, from the standpoint of aggregate wealth or the net worth of the private sector, a wash; the liability of one individual or business is the asset of another. The net debt of the federal government held by the public, however, is an asset of the private sector, of state and local governments, or of the rest of the world. But few people think of themselves as the debtor when the federal government goes into further debt by selling a bond. This means that the bigger the federal debt, the wealthier citizens who own the bonds feel and, hence, the more they are likely to spend. Thus the fundamental importance, for good or for bad, of the federal debt is likely to be its effect on private spending.

If the economy is in a recession because of a lack of effective demand for what can be produced, a bigger federal debt may be useful. The greater wealth it causes in the form of Treasury notes, bills, or bonds gives people less reason to save and, therefore, induces them to consume more. Businesses, which may also feel wealthier with their holdings of Treasury securities, may be expected to produce more to meet the consumer demand and also to invest more in the capacity to meet that demand.

If, however, the economy is already at full employment, with few unused resources, consumers' attempts to spend more as a consequence of their greater financial wealth can only generate higher prices. And there's the rub! Too high a federal debt, or a deficit that increases the debt and, consequently, causes aggregate demand to rise faster than production can be increased to meet that demand, brings on inflation. Then, possibly even worse, actions by the Federal Reserve to combat the inflation will raise interest rates, thus choking off investment in new housing, new factories, and new machinery.

These arguments about the federal debt, its power for good or bad, require two major qualifications. First, the debt must be measured in a correct and relevant fashion. This means, most importantly, that it must be adjusted for inflation. A person who has $101,000 in Treasury securities is not richer than he was a year ago when he held $100,000 if inflation has reduced the value of the dollar by 3 percent. He has, in fact, lost the equivalent of $3,000 in the real value of his securities from what may be called an inflation tax. He is, on balance, $2,000 poorer than he was a year ago. Thus, he is likely to buy fewer goods, not more.

Just as with individuals, so with the federal government. The federal debt must be measured in real terms, and the real deficit must be seen as the change in the real value of the debt. By this measure the apparently huge federal debt actually declined over most of the past half-century. Even now, after a decade of relatively large deficits, the per capita federal debt is still much less than in 1945, when the country and its economy were much smaller. Inflation of only 3 percent reduces a gross debt of $3 trillion by $90 billion. This indicates a real budget deficit $90 billion less than that in official measures.

A good way of judging the size of the federal debt, and hence its likely effect on the economy, is, as for an individual, to take it as a ratio of income. The federal debt reached a peak ratio of 114 percent of GDP after World War II and declined to 26 percent by 1981, before rising again. But even with the subsequent deficits, it was still only 51 percent of GDP in 1992. True "balance" in the budget, it might be suggested, would entail not a zero deficit, but one such that the debt grows at the same percentage rate as GNP, thus keeping the debt-to-GNP ratio constant.

The second qualification is that many economists question whether federal debt is real wealth for the public as a whole. They argue that increases in the federal debt will cause people to expect future increases in taxes in order to service that debt. On the assumption that the present value of the increase in expected future taxes is equal to the increase in the debt, there is no net change in perceived wealth and, hence, no effect of the debt on overall demand for goods and services.

This argument has been severely criticized for claiming too much foresight on the part of individuals and for downplaying serious reservations. Indeed, David Ricardo, the famous early-nineteenth-century economist who first enunciated the idea, was himself skeptical of it. He argued that many people would not worry about future taxes because they might not expect to be alive when taxes were finally raised. The answer that people would still worry about their children and grandchildren is weakened by the facts that some have no children and others don't want to leave money to them anyway. Other factors that weaken the "Ricardian" argument are: lower borrowing costs for the government than the public; the uncertainty that taxes will ever be raised or who will bear them; and the possibility that debt which, in fact, brought higher employment, output, and investment might eventually pay for itself out of higher incomes. In that case tax rates would not have to increase in the future.

Finally, some economists argue that we should include in federal debt the implicit debt from the government's commitment to pay future benefits such as Social Security. If we do so, shouldn't we add assets in the form of the present value of future taxes that might be received? In principle, they are both relevant, but there is a strong argument that in view of the uncertain amounts to be projected for taxes and payments over many decades, it would be better to exclude them from our measures of the debt.

—**Robert Eisner**

Biography: Robert Eisner is the William R. Kenan Professor of Economics at Northwestern University and a past president of the American Economic Association.

Further Reading

Barro, Robert J. "Are Government Bonds Net Wealth?" *Journal of Political Economy* 82 (1974): 1095–1117.
———. "The Ricardian Approach to Budget Deficits." *Journal of Economic Perspectives* 3 (1989): 37–54.
Bernheim, B. D. "A Neoclassical Perspective on Budget Deficits." *Journal of Economic Perspectives* 3 (1989): 55–72.

Buiter, W. H., and J. Tobin. "Debt Neutrality: A Brief Review of Doctrine and Evidence." In *Social Security Versus Private Saving*, edited by George M. von Furstenberg. 1979.

Eisner, Robert. *How Real Is the Federal Deficit?* 1986.

———. "Budget Deficits: Rhetoric and Reality." *Journal of Economic Perspectives* 3 (1989): 73–93.

———, and P. J. Pieper. "A New View of the Federal Debt and Budget Deficits." *American Economic Review* 74 (1984): 11–29.

Federal Deficit

Laurence J. Kotlikoff

■ The U.S. federal budget deficit is probably the world's most cited economic statistic. In recent years U.S. debt has risen at what is widely believed to be an alarming rate and has almost tripled since 1981.

Those concerned about large deficits usually argue as follows: deficits let current generations off the hook for paying the government's bills. Therefore, current generations consume more. This reduces the amount Americans save and invest. A reduced rate of investment means less capital per worker and, therefore, lower productivity growth. When capital is scarce, its rate of return rises, causing interest rates to increase. Higher U.S. interest rates attract foreign investment to the United States and imply larger trade deficits, because increased foreign investment must increase the trade deficit (see BALANCE OF PAYMENTS).

Yet, there is very little correlation between budget deficits and interest rates, saving and investment rates, or productivity growth rates. Some economists, led by Robert Barro of Harvard, claim that the absence of a correlation is evidence for their view that deficits do not matter. They take seriously an off-the-cuff remark by David Ricardo (one of the great nineteenth-century economists) that deficits may not matter because current generations will hand future generations the means to pay off the debt. Barro argues that parents and grandparents do this by making bequests and gifts to children and grandchildren. But for such transfers to be large enough, older generations must have strong altruistic ties to younger generations. Recent studies find that, on the contrary, the ties are weak.

Other economists, who worry about

deficits, claim that the correlation between the deficit and other economic variables is so low because the deficit has been defined incorrectly. Two such economists are Robert Eisner (see FEDERAL DEBT) of Northwestern University and Stanford's Michael Boskin, chairman of the President's Council of Economic Advisers under George Bush. They point out that the government's official debt measures only the government's liabilities. It completely ignores the government's assets. Using the government's debt figures to assess its financial position is, in their view, akin to calling the owner of a $1 million property a debtor because he has a large mortgage on the property. These and other economists also fault the conventional deficit measure for failing to correct for inflation.

It is hard to know where these corrections should end. The research of Martin Feldstein, a Harvard economist and former chairman of the Council of Economic Advisers, suggests that the unfunded liabilities of government retirement programs, such as Social Security, should be included in the deficit. Including such liabilities would more than triple the measure of U.S. federal debt. But if the government's commitments to pay Social Security benefits should be included, shouldn't we also include implicit commitments to other federal expenditures, such as those for defense and national parks?

The debate over how to measure the deficit is not confined to academics. In recent years many members of Congress have noted that the traditional deficit (i.e., the one that gets reported) will, in the late nineties, be reduced because revenues from Social Security taxes will greatly exceed

Social Security payments. They worry that including Social Security in the deficit may mask the true fiscal picture. To avoid this outcome, Congress in 1990 redefined the federal deficit to exclude Social Security receipts and payments.

This is not the first time Congress redefined the deficit, nor the last. Indeed, by 1993 Congress had restored the old definition of the deficit that includes the Social Security surplus. The manipulation of the definition should not be surprising. Since everyone is sure the deficit should be zero, but no one is sure how to measure it, the deficit's definition has real implications for economic and budget policy. Choosing a definition that makes the deficit large will invite efforts to lower it by limiting spending or increasing taxes. The opposite will be true with definitions that make the deficit appear small.

The simple fact is that the deficit is not a well-defined economic concept. The current measure of the deficit, or any measure, is based on arbitrary choices of how to label government receipts and payments. The government can conduct any real economic policy and simultaneously report any size deficit or surplus it wants just through its choice of words. If the government labels receipts as taxes and payments as expenditures, it will report one number for the deficit. If it labels receipts as loans and payments as return of principal and interest, it will report a very different number.

Take Social Security, for example. Social Security "contributions" are called taxes, and Social Security benefits are called expenditures. If the government taxes Mr. X by $1,000 this year and pays him $1,500 in benefits ten years from now, this year's deficit falls by $1,000 and the deficit ten years hence will be $1,500 higher. But the taxes could just as plausibly be labeled as a forced loan to the government, and the benefits could be labeled as repayment of principal plus interest. In that case there would be no impact on the deficit.

There are real problems to be concerned about, but the federal deficit doesn't measure those problems. One thing that neoclassical economists are concerned about is intergenerational transfers. Many government programs—some of which increase the traditional deficit (because of our choice of words), and some of which, like pay-as-you-go Social Security, don't increase the deficit (again because of our choice of words)—transfer resources from one generation to another. The redistribution of resources by the government occurs between existing and future generations as well as between young and old existing generations.

According to Franco Modigliani's life-cycle model (the most famous neoclassical macroeconomic model), policies that redistribute from future generations to current generations, as well as policies that redistribute from younger people to older ones, cause national consumption to increase and national saving to fall. The reason is that older generations have larger propensities to consume than do younger generations. This reflects the fact that older people, who are closer to the end of their lives, want to spend their remaining resources more quickly.

Hence, redistribution from younger to older generations can raise consumption, lower saving, lower investment, raise interest rates, increase trade deficits—in short, do all the bad things that have been ascribed to deficits. But using the federal deficit as a measure of U.S. generational policy is like driving in Los Angeles with a map of New York. While the map may be highly detailed, with overlays and multiple colors, it will, nonetheless, get us lost.

For measuring the government's generational policies, neoclassical economics suggests an alternative to deficits: generational accounts. Generational accounts indicate in present value what the typical member of each generation can expect to pay to the government, minus benefits from the government, now and in the future. A generational account is thus a set of numbers, one for each existing generation, indicating the average remaining lifetime burden imposed by the government on members of the generation. Used properly, these accounts help assess generational policy, independent of the labels the government gives to receipts and payments.

Generational accounts indicate not only what existing generations will pay, but also what future generations are likely to pay. The burden on future generations is determined by working through the government's "intertemporal budget constraint." This constraint says that the present value of the government's spending on goods and services cannot exceed the sum of three items: (1) the government's net wealth, (2) the present value of net payments to the government by current generations, and (3) the present value of net payments by future generations. Translation: the government cannot spend more than the sum of what it has and what it can raise. At any point in time we can project the present value of the government's spending and also estimate items 1 and 2. By subtracting 1 and 2 from the present value of government spending, we can determine the aggregate present value taken from future generations. By one set of estimates, as of 1989 the present value of future government spending was $25.4 trillion, the government's net wealth was − $0.5 trillion, and the present value of net payments of current generations was $21.2 trillion. This left $4.7 trillion to be paid by future generations.

An analysis of U.S. generational accounts for 1991 indicates that unless U.S. economic policy is decisively altered, the typical member of future generations will end up paying roughly 71 percent more over his or her lifetime than will the typical member of current young generations! This figure is above and beyond the fact that future generations will pay more because their incomes will be higher due to economic growth. This 71 percent figure is extraordinarily high and indicates that U.S. economic policy is, generationally speaking, very badly out of balance.

Generational accounting leads to a radically different interpretation of postwar economic policy than does reliance on the deficit. From the perspective of generational accounts, the fifties, sixties, and seventies were periods of quite loose fiscal policy (policy that placed larger burdens on future generations). The reason was the buildup of our unfunded pay-as-you-go Social Security, civil service, and military retirement programs. The eighties, in contrast, were marked by rather tight fiscal policy. While the Reagan tax cuts did increase the burden on future generations, other policies, particularly the 1983 Social Security reform, greatly reduced the projected burden on future generations. By raising the retirement age in stages to sixty-seven from sixty-five, and by gradually subjecting all retirees' Social Security benefits to income taxation, the 1983 reforms reduced the present value of Social Security benefits to be paid to current adults by about $1.1 trillion.

Generational accounting automatically deals with each of the major concerns raised by those who think the deficit is conceptually sound but simply needs to be adjusted. By measuring all current and projected payments and receipts in inflation-adjusted (constant) dollars, the proposed accounting deals with changes in the price level. It uses the government's assets minus its liabilities to form the value of government net worth, which is ultimately used to help determine the "hit" on future generations. In considering future government payments and receipts to and from individuals, it accounts for the commitments to pay future Social Security benefits and to spend on other items, such as defense and parks. In projecting the future level of government payments and receipts, it takes into account economic growth. Finally, it considers the fiscal actions of all governments—federal, state, and local.

Generational accounting thus represents a sensible alternative to the deficit delusion that has misled postwar fiscal policy.

—Laurence J. Kotlikoff

Biography: Laurence J. Kotlikoff is an economics professor at Boston University and a research associate at the National Bureau of Economic Research. From 1981 to 1982 he was senior economist for taxation and Social Security with the Council of Economic Advisers.

Further Reading

Kotlikoff, Laurence J. "Deficit Delusion." *The Public Interest* (Summer 1986): 53–65.
———. "From Deficit Delusion to the Fiscal Balance Rule—Looking for a Meaningful Way to Describe Fiscal Policy." National Bureau of Economic Research working paper no. 2841, February 1989.
———. "Generational Accounts—A Meaningful Alternative to Deficit Accounting." In *Tax Policy and the Economy,* vol. 5, edited by David Bradford. 1991.
———. *Generational Accounting: Knowing Who Pays and When for What We Spend.* 1992.

Fiscal Policy

David N. Weil

■ Fiscal policy is the use of the government budget to affect an economy. When the government decides on the taxes that it collects, the transfer payments it gives out, or the goods and services that it purchases, it is engaging in fiscal policy. The primary economic impact of any change in the government budget is felt by particular groups—a tax cut for families with children, for example, raises the disposable income of such families. Discussions of fiscal policy, however, usually focus on the effect of changes in the government budget on the overall economy—on such macroeconomic variables as GNP and unemployment and inflation.

The state of fiscal policy is usually summarized by looking at the difference between what the government pays out and what it takes in—that is, the government deficit. Fiscal policy is said to be tight or contractionary when revenue is higher than spending (the government budget is in surplus) and loose or expansionary when spending is higher than revenue (the budget is in deficit). Often the focus is not on the level of the deficit, but on the change in the deficit. Thus, a reduction of the deficit from $200 billion to $100 billion is said to be contractionary fiscal policy, even though the budget is still in deficit.

The most immediate impact of fiscal policy is to change the aggregate demand for goods and services. A fiscal expansion, for example, raises aggregate demand through one of two channels. First, if the government increases purchases but keeps taxes the same, it increases demand directly. Second, if the government cuts taxes or increases transfer payments, people's disposable income rises, and they will spend more on consumption. This rise in consumption will, in turn, raise aggregate demand.

Fiscal policy also changes the composition of aggregate demand. When the government runs a deficit, it meets some of its expenses by issuing bonds. In doing so, it competes with private borrowers for money lent by savers, raising interest rates and "crowding out" some private investment. Thus, expansionary fiscal policy reduces the fraction of output that is used for private investment.

In an open economy, fiscal policy also affects the exchange rate and the trade balance. In the case of a fiscal expansion, the rise in interest rates due to government borrowing attracts foreign capital. Foreigners bid up the price of the dollar in order to get more of them to invest, causing an exchange rate appreciation. This appreciation makes imported goods cheaper in the United States and exports more expensive abroad, leading to a decline of the trade balance. Foreigners sell more to the country than they buy from it, and in return acquire ownership of assets in the country. This effect of fiscal policy was central to discussions of the "twin deficits" (budget and trade) of the eighties.

Fiscal policy is an important tool for managing the economy because of its ability to affect the total amount of output produced—that is, gross domestic product. The first impact of a fiscal expansion is to raise the demand for goods and services. This greater demand leads to increases in both output and prices. The degree to which higher demand increases output and prices depends, in turn, on the state of the business cycle. If the economy is in recession, with unused productive capacity and unemployed workers, then increases in demand will lead mostly to more output without changing the price level. If the economy is at full employment, by contrast, a fiscal expansion will have more effect on prices and less impact on total output.

This ability of fiscal policy to affect output by affecting aggregate demand makes it a potential tool for economic stabilization. In a recession the government can run an expansionary fiscal policy, thus helping to restore output to its normal level and to put unemployed workers back to work. During a boom, when inflation is perceived to be a greater problem than unemployment, the government can run a budget surplus, helping to slow down the economy. Such a countercyclical policy would lead to a budget that was balanced on average.

One form of countercyclical fiscal policy is known as automatic stabilizers. These are programs that automatically expand fiscal policy during recessions and contract it during booms. Unemployment insurance, on which the government spends more during recessions (when the unemployment rate is high), is an example of an automatic stabilizer. Unemployment insurance serves this function even if the federal government does not extend the duration of benefits. Similarly, because taxes are roughly proportional to wages and profits, the amount of taxes collected is higher during a boom than during a recession. Thus, the tax code also acts as an automatic stabilizer.

But fiscal policy need not be automatic in order to play a stabilizing role in business cycles. Some economists recommend changes in fiscal policy in response to economic conditions—so-called discretionary fiscal policy—as a way to moderate business cycle swings. These suggestions are most frequently heard during recessions, when there are calls for tax cuts or new spending programs to ''get the economy going again.''

Unfortunately, discretionary fiscal policy is rarely able to deliver on its promise. Fiscal policy is especially difficult to use for stabilization because of the ''inside lag''— the gap between the time when the need for fiscal policy arises and when it is implemented by the president and Congress. The tax cut proposed by President Kennedy to stimulate the economy in 1962, for example, was not enacted until 1964. If economists forecast well, then the lag would not matter. They could tell Congress in advance what the appropriate fiscal policy is. But economists do not forecast well. Most economists, for example, badly underpredicted both the rise in unemployment in 1981 and the strength of the recovery that began in late 1982. Absent accurate forecasts, attempts to use discretionary fiscal policy to counteract business cycle fluctuations are as likely to do harm as good.

The case for using discretionary fiscal policy to stabilize business cycles is further weakened by the fact that another tool, monetary policy, is far more agile than fiscal policy. Even here, though, many economists argue that monetary policy is too prone to lags to be effective, and that the best countercyclical policy is to leave well enough alone.

Whether for good or for ill, fiscal policy's ability to affect the level of output via aggregate demand wears off over time. Higher aggregate demand due to a fiscal stimulus, for example, eventually shows up only in higher prices and does not increase output at all. That is because over the long run the level of output is determined not by demand, but by the supply of factors of production (capital, labor, and technology). These factors of production determine a ''natural rate'' of output, around which business cycles and macroeconomic policies can cause only temporary fluctuations. An attempt to keep output above its natural rate by means of aggregate demand policies will lead only to ever-accelerating inflation.

The fact that output returns to its natural rate in the long run is not the end of the story, however. In addition to moving output in the short run, fiscal policy can change the natural rate, and ironically, the long-run effects of fiscal policy tend to be the opposite of the short-run effects. Expansionary fiscal policy will lead to higher output today but will lower the natural rate of output below what it would have been in the future. Similarly, contractionary fiscal policy, though dampening the level of output in the short run, will lead to higher output in the future.

Fiscal policy affects the level of output in the long run because it affects the country's saving rate. The country's total saving is composed of two parts—private saving (by individuals and corporations) and government saving (which is the same as the budget surplus). A fiscal expansion entails a decrease in government saving. Lower saving means, in turn, that the country will either invest less in new plant and equipment or increase the amount that it borrows from abroad, both of which lead to unpleasant consequences in the long term. Lower investment will lead to a lower capital stock and to a reduction in a country's ability to produce output in the future. Increased indebtedness to foreigners means that a higher fraction of a country's output will have to be sent abroad in the future rather than being consumed at home.

Fiscal policy also changes the burden of future taxes. When the government runs an expansionary fiscal policy, it adds to its stock of debt. Because the government will have to pay interest on this debt (or repay it) in future years, expansionary fiscal policy today imposes an additional burden on future taxpayers. Just as taxes can be used to redistribute income between different classes, the government can run surpluses or deficits in order to redistribute income between different generations.

Some economists have argued that this effect of fiscal policy on future taxes will lead consumers to change their saving. Recognizing that a tax cut today means higher taxes in the future, the argument goes, people will simply save the value of the tax cut they receive now in order to pay those future taxes. The extreme of this argument, known as Ricardian Equivalence, holds that tax cuts will have no effect on national saving, since changes in private saving will offset changes in government saving. But if consumers decide to spend some of the extra disposable income they receive from a tax cut (because they are myopic about future tax payments, for example), then Ricardian Equivalence will not hold; a tax cut will lower national saving and raise aggregate demand. The experience of the eighties, when private saving fell rather than rose in

response to tax cuts, is evidence against Ricardian Equivalence.

In addition to its effect on aggregate demand and on saving, fiscal policy also affects the economy by changing incentives. Taxing an activity tends to discourage that activity. A high marginal tax rate on income reduces people's incentive to earn income. By reducing the level of taxation, or even by keeping the level the same but reducing marginal tax rates and reducing allowed deductions, the government can increase output. The "supply-side" economists who were prominent early in the Reagan administration argued that reductions in tax rates would have a large effect on the amount of labor supplied, and thus on output. Incentive effects of taxes also play a role on the demand side. Policies such as the investment tax credit, for example, can greatly influence the demand for capital goods.

The greatest obstacle to proper use of fiscal policy—both for its ability to stabilize fluctuations in the short run and for its long-run effect on the natural rate of output—is that changes in fiscal policy are necessarily bundled with other changes that please or displease various constituencies. A road in Congressman X's district is all the more likely to be built if it can be packaged as part of countercyclical fiscal policy. The same is true for a tax cut for some favored constituency. This naturally leads to an institutional enthusiasm for expansionary policies during recessions that is not matched by a taste for contractionary policies during booms. In addition, the benefits from such a policy are felt immediately, whereas its costs—higher future taxes and lower economic growth—are postponed until a later date. The problem of making good fiscal policy in the face of such obstacles is, in the final analysis, not economic, but political.

—David N. Weil

Biography: David N. Weil is an economics professor at Brown University.

Further Reading

Barro, Robert. "The Ricardian Approach to Budget Deficits." *Journal of Economic Perspectives* 3, no. 2 (Spring 1989): 37–54.

Friedman, Benjamin M. *Day of Reckoning: The Consequences of American Economic Policy.* 1988.

Joint Committee on Taxation. *Tax Policy and the Macroeconomy: Stabilization, Growth, and Income Distribution.* Report no. JCS-18-91. December 12, 1991.

Lindsey, Lawrence. *The Growth Experiment: How the New Tax Policy Is Transforming the U.S. Economy.* 1990.

Mankiw, N. Gregory. "A Quick Refresher Course in Macroeconomics." *Journal of Economic Literature* 27 (December 1990): 1645–60.

Government Spending

Gordon Tullock

■ In most countries government spending has grown quite rapidly in recent decades. Chart 1 shows U.S. federal spending as a percentage of gross national product from 1790 to the present. Chart 2 shows Sweden's central government expenditures as a percent of GNP. Although not many countries have such long data series, these countries apparently are typical. As the charts show, the central government's share of the economy was remarkably stable for nearly 150 years but has grown quite rapidly throughout the latter two-thirds of this century.

In the past, government spending increased during wars and then typically took some time to fall back to its previous level. Because the effects of World War I were not totally gone by 1929, the line for the United States from 1790 to 1929 has a very slight upward slant. But in the second quarter of the twentieth century, government spending began a rapid and steady increase. While economists and political scientists have offered many theories about what determines the level of government spending, there really is no known explanation for either part of this historical record.

The data contradict several prominent economic theories about why government spending as a percent of GNP grows. One such theory is presented by British economists Alan Peacock and Jack Wiseman, who suggest a "ratchet effect." If a war, say, raises expenditures, expenditures after the war will not fall all the way back to their prewar level. Thus the name "ratchet effect." This theory cannot explain the long period of stable government expenditures before 1929. Nor can it explain the steady growth since 1953.

The "leviathan" theory holds that governments try to get control of as much of the economy as possible. Obviously, the leviathan theory is inconsistent with the early decades of stable government spending. Moreover, this theory also would imply sharp increases in government spending followed by leveling off when the maximum size of government has been reached. But this is not what we see after 1945. Wagner's law—named after the German economist Adolph Wagner (1835–1917)—states that the growing government share of GNP is simply a result of economic progress. Wagner propounded it in the 1880s. However, the forty years of stability after that time would seem to rule out his theory.

Another theory, propounded by William J. Baumol, is that productivity in the private sector increases, but public-sector productivity stagnates. Therefore, says Baumol, for the government to maintain a suitable level of services per person, government spending must grow as a percent of GNP. Even granting his view of relative efficiency, Baumol's theory certainly does not explain the nongrowth of government spending before 1929. Indeed, all theories of growth to date fail to explain either the

CHART 1

U.S. Government Spending

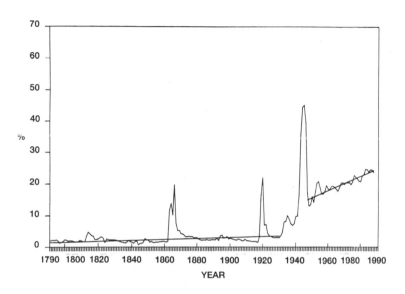

CHART 2

Swedish Government Spending

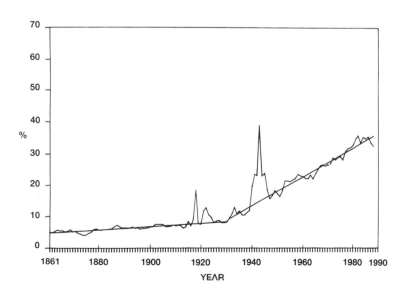

many early decades of stable government spending or the growth of government spending after 1953—or both.

The relatively smooth growth of government after 1953 is particularly hard to explain. We would anticipate that if the government took on new responsibilities, government spending would rise sharply and then stay level after these responsibilities had been fully absorbed. But in fact, spending did not rise sharply, nor did it level off.

Considering what governments spend money on may help. Government spending on so-called public goods, national defense and police, for example, is sometimes blamed. But American military expenditures have shrunk as a share of the GNP—from 13.8 percent in 1953 to 6.3 percent in 1988. Spending on police is mainly a local expenditure and, at under 1 percent of GNP, is too small in any event. Expenditures on most other public goods have also grown slowly. Of the 1991 federal budget, 43 percent is direct benefit payments to individuals, 14 percent is for interest, and 25 percent is military spending. This leaves only 18 percent for general public goods. Further, two-thirds of the remaining 18 percent is grants to local governments. This leaves only 6 percent for the rest of the federal government. Clearly we must look elsewhere.

It is frequently asserted that the government spends much in helping the poor. Although the government does do so, the bulk of all transfer payments go to people who are relatively well off.

Economists trying to explain government spending have recently attributed it to special interest coalitions lobbying the government to transfer wealth to them. The term economists use to describe such lobbying is "rent-seeking." Rent-seeking certainly has grown. The farm program, for example, did not even exist in 1929. It now absorbs about $30 billion a year. The elaborate water control projects in the West cost the general taxpayer a high multiple of the benefits to the relatively small groups of beneficiaries. Both are the result of rent-seeking.

"Rent-seeking," therefore, may explain the long, more or less steady rise in government spending as a fraction of GNP. Political rules may limit the government's ability to hand out money to more than a few new pressure groups in each session of Congress. If so, we would expect the long, gradual increase in government spending that we observe. It cannot be said, however, that the data prove this particular theory; in fact, it cannot even be said that this particular theory is a very good one. It certainly does not explain the long level period from 1790 to 1929.

The bottom line is that governments have grown in recent decades, that they did not do so earlier, and that economists do not really know why.

—**Gordon Tullock**

Biography: Gordon Tullock is the Karl Eller Professor of Economics and Political Science at the University of Arizona in Tucson. Together with James M. Buchanan, he pioneered the field of public choice economics.

Further Reading

Baumol, William J. "The Macroeconomics of Unbalanced Growth: The Anatomy of the Urban Crisis."
  American Economic Review 57 (June 1967): 415–26.
Borcherding, Thomas, ed. *Budgets and Bureaucrats*. 1977.
Higgs, Robert. *Crisis and Leviathan*. 1987.

Industrial Policy

Richard B. McKenzie

■ National industrial policy is a rubric for a broad range of proposed economic reforms that emerged as a unified political program in the early eighties. Had they been passed, these reforms would have given government officials additional authority, as well as the necessary fiscal and regulatory powers, to directly alter the country's industrial structure. Proponents of national industrial policies (NIP) across the globe have typically been harsh critics of unfettered markets and of past limited efforts of government to create economic growth simply with macroeconomic (fiscal and monetary) policies.

In the United States NIP became a major bone of contention in the 1984 presidential campaign. Democratic presidential contenders Gary Hart and Ernest Hollings and the eventual nominee, Walter Mondale, were vocal NIP advocates. The Republican incumbent and nominee, Ronald Reagan, was a staunch NIP opponent. Mondale argued that the economic policies of the country were "destroying industry—not building it," and that federal aid should be directed to "those communities and regions hit hardest by economic change."

NIP proponents believed, and some still believe, that many of the country's industrial markets had failed, causing the entire economy to come apart at its industrial seams. Harvard's Robert Reich, a leading exponent of industrial policies in the early eighties, claimed, in *The Next American Frontier,* that the U.S. economy had been "unraveling" since the sixties. He found "chronic disarray" in the political sphere, which he linked to the "growing unemployment, mounting business failures, and falling productivity" in the economy's industrial sector.

More specifically, NIP proponents claimed the following:

- The nation is in long-term economic decline, with little hope of a turnaround without greater government involvement in the restructuring of the economy.
- The country is "deindustrializing," or losing its core industrial base to plant closings and "capital flight." In *The Deindustrialization of America* economists Barry Bluestone and Bennett Harrison argued that the ongoing process of deindustrialization amounted to a "widespread, systematic disinvestment in the nation's productive capacity." Without its "core" industries—steel, textiles, rubber, shoes, and automobiles—the national economy will lose its stature in the world, and workers will lose their better-paying employment opportunities.
- Major segments of the U.S. economy are uncompetitive in the new global economic order. Many U.S. firms are gradually being destroyed by their own misguided internal policies, by their pursuit of short-term profits, and by foreign competitors that are more successful primarily because of the national industrial policies adopted by their governments. The postwar economic success of Japan was extensively credited to industrial policies orchestrated by its Ministry of International Trade and Industry (MITI). Economist Lester Thurow of MIT, in *The Zero-Sum Society*, worried that if left alone, "our economy and our institutions will not provide jobs for everyone who wants to work," and that "we have a moral responsibility to guarantee full employment."

While acknowledging that his proposed industrial policies would create "a socialized sector of the economy," Thurow maintained that "major investment decisions have become too important to be left to the private market alone. . . . Japan Inc. needs to be met with U.S.A. Inc." Reich contended that Japan and several European countries were growing relative to the United States because "these countries are organized for economic adaptation. . . . America is not."

NIP proponents generally believe that government should be directly involved in establishing national industrial goals and in assuring that the goals are achieved. Some early proponents (John Kenneth Galbraith, for example) would have had government extensively plan major sectors of the economy, dubbed the "new industrial state," if not the entire national economy. Galbraith would have had the federal government decide the industrial structure, redistribute resources and output, and reallocate income from one region of the country to another and from one income class to another. More recent NIP proponents (including Felix Rohatyn, a New York investment banker; Lester Thurow; and Robert Reich) have been more moderate. They presented less ambitious policy programs but still wanted the government to determine which industries were most likely to be competitive in the future global economy and to contribute to improved economic opportunities for workers. Government would then determine if and how the identified industries should be aided. Specifically, most modern NIP advocates pressed for some of the following:

- National and regional economic "development banks," similar to Herbert Hoover's Reconstruction Finance Corporation, which would use subsidies and federal loan guarantees to slow the contraction of declining industries and to speed the development of emerging industries.
- "Tripartite councils" at the national, regional, and firm levels, which would be composed of representatives from management, labor, and government and would seek consensus on how capital investment should be allocated.
- "Industrial (or economic) democracy," in which representatives of workers and the communities surrounding plants or offices would be given a greater say in the investment, disinvestment, and reinvestment decisions of firms.

NIP supporters also advocated federal and state expenditures for basic education and worker training and retraining that would increase the country's competitiveness, plant-closing restrictions that would slow the outflow of capital, and federal spending on day-care facilities that would enable more parents to participate in the work force. They also advocated raising the minimum wage and tying it to some average industrial wage, using tax law to discourage mergers and acquisitions, which they called "paper entrepreneurship," and using government to spread the existing capital base across states and regions.

Finally, NIP proponents generally supported protectionism, especially in the early and mideighties. They wanted tariffs, quotas, and "voluntary export restraints" for "key" industries (identified as such by the tripartite councils, for example) with the goal of "managing trade" to achieve broad industrial goals and to bring down the then-rising trade deficit.

One industrial policy advocate crystallized a common position that made the movement appealing to many industry executives: Without trade barriers, rich countries are bound to suck in cheap imports from low-wage countries, destroying the domestic industries that used to make those products. There will never be enough "high-tech" jobs to employ those who lose more traditional jobs. Therefore, unrestricted trade would eventually destroy the economies of all high-wage, developed countries.

Although the industrial policy movement created a major policy stir in the early and mideighties, it faded in the late eighties as quickly as it had emerged. Its fall from political and media grace can probably be attributed to six sources.

First, one of its leading exponents, Walter Mondale, suffered an overwhelming defeat in the 1984 presidential election, suggesting that his industrial policy agenda was not striking the expected chord with the electorate.

Second, the Reagan administration, while often conceding on protectionist proposals, maintained strong opposition to any coherent industrial policy programs, including national economic development banks, tripartite councils, and economic democracies.

Third the growing federal deficits probably choked the ability of NIP supporters in Congress to organize the necessary majority for any expensive new government programs.

Fourth, the pessimistic claims and projections for the future made by NIP proponents did not square with the economic facts brought to light in various forums. Brookings Institution economist Robert Crandall, in the *Washington Post*, pointed out that French and German readers of Reich's book (and those of other NIP supporters) would be "amazed to read of their government's success in industrial policy. Since 1975, industrial production has grown even more slowly in France and West Germany than in the United States." He continued:

The [U.S.] industrial sector did not decline markedly from the mid-1960s to 1980. In fact, basic industry accounted for roughly 22 percent of our GNP in 1980, precisely the same share as in 1947. Our output per person remains above that of all but a few countries, such as Sweden and Switzerland (which have not exactly been refuges for the world's dispossessed over the 20th century). Reich's contrary conclusions are drawn from a period ending in 1979. Were he to extend his calculations to 1981, he would find that the United States has outperformed every major industrial country in the world except Japan since 1975.

Moreover, several strategically placed researchers (including Philip Trezise at the Brookings Institution, David R. Henderson on the staff of the Reagan Administration's Council of Economic Advisers, and Katsuro Sakoh at the Heritage Foundation) reached conclusions similar to Crandall's. Regarding the economic success of his home country, Japan, Sakoh stressed, in a Heritage Foundation report, "There is no evidence that manufacturing industries in general, and any particular manufacturing sector, have been targeted [as of 1983] by the JDB [Japanese Development Bank]." Much of Japan's public funds, which in total were judged to be "negligible," were also wasted supporting "losers." Also, MITI's efforts in the sixties to discourage Honda from going into automobile production were widely cited as a "failure" of whatever Japanese industrial policy did exist.

Throughout the eighties the U.S. economy continued an upward ride on one of its longest peacetime recoveries. Rather than falling, industrial production continued to rise, peaking in 1990 (before the advent of the 1990–91 recession) at 32 percent above its 1980 level. Rather than continuing its highly advertised long-term decline relative to the rest of the world, U.S. output was the same share of world output in the mideighties as in the midseventies, and it rose slightly in the late eighties. Although the number of manufacturing jobs did fall during the eighties, manufacturing output, measured in real dollars, rose. The reason was a surge in manufacturing productivity induced in part by international competition.

Instead of wantonly destroying jobs in the eighties, the U.S. economy was, on balance, rapidly creating them. Total U.S. employment rose by about 19 million (18 percent) from 1980 to 1990. While the average real money wage (not including fringe benefits) of production workers edged downward, as did their share of the country's labor force, the average hourly payment (with both money wages and benefits included) of all American workers rose, albeit at a slower pace than prior to the early seventies.

Fifth, while Republican opposition to the NIP movement remained solid, Democratic support was badly split. Democratic economists could not support the protectionist aspects of industrial policy. They understood, as most NIP advocates did not, that free trade does not destroy jobs and that protectionism almost always makes a country worse off by hurting consumers more than it helps producers. Economists found, for example, that trade restrictions on textile imports, by increasing retail prices of clothing, destroyed far more domestic retail jobs than they saved in the domestic textile industry.

Also, Democratic economists feared that development banks and tripartite councils would give declining industries and unions undue political power. This newfound power, critics reasoned, might be exploited to the detriment of emerging industries and the competitiveness of the entire country. They also pointed out that the subsidies required to slow the decline of contracting industries would mean higher taxes, which would discourage the emergence of so-called "sunrise" industries.

Probably the most outspoken Democratic opponent of industrial policy was Charles Schultze, an economist at Brookings who was chairman of President Carter's Council of Economic Advisers. Schultze, in the *Brookings Review,* undercut the political and intellectual case for industrial policy with these salient points:

The United States does have some old-line heavy industries with deep-seated structural problems—especially the steel and automobile industries—but they are not typical of American industry generally. There is no evidence that in periods of reasonably normal prosperity, American labor and capital are incapable of making the gradual transitions that are always required in a dynamic economy, as demand and output shift from older industries to newer ones at the forefront of technological advances.

One does not have to be a cynic to forecast that the surest way to multiply unwarranted subsidies and protectionist measures is to legitimize their existence under the rubric of industrial policy. The likely outcome of an industrial policy that encompassed some elements of both "protecting the losers" and "picking the winners" is that the losers would back the subsidies for the winners in return for the latter's support on issues of trade protection.

Sixth, policy forces around the globe in the eighties were running counter to the fondest policy dreams of the NIP proponents. Rather than expanding their control over their economy, many major governments began cutting taxes, capping the growth of their expenditures, deregulating and denationalizing industries, and privatizing many government services. Yet these policies, contrary to the expectations of the NIP proponents, did not cause economic calamity.

Industrial policy proposals continued to attract a measure of political support into the early nineties. The proposals were redirected from the national to the state level and from direct support of industries to direct support for workers and the country's infrastructure. Still, the support remained subdued. By 1991 key industrial policy proponents, most notably Robert Reich, had reversed themselves or had significantly altered their positions. They began to reason that physical and financial capital had become far too mobile across national boundaries to make government subsidies pay. Former NIP enthusiasts, especially Reich, maintained that workers were the real wealth of any country. Because workers were relatively immobile and could, therefore, be counted on to repay their subsidies with future tax payments, workers—not firms—should be more extensively subsidized, through government training and retraining programs intended to develop and maintain their human capital.

Even the revised NIP agenda faces some major problems. One is that high federal and state deficits mean that few funds are available for NIP. NIP proponents advocate raising the funds by taxing the "rich." But as public finance economists know well, the only way to increase federal revenues substantially is to tax the nonrich. The "rich" are simply too few and too able to increase deductions and to reduce work effort when marginal tax rates rise for an increased tax on them to increase revenues very much. Moreover, the highly paid workers (a large component of the "rich") are almost as mobile as physical capital. NIP proposals can encourage human-capital flight.

—Richard B. McKenzie

Biography: Richard B. McKenzie is the Walter B. Gerken Professor of Enterprise and Society in the Graduate School of Management at the University of California at Irvine, and the John M. Olin Adjunct Fellow in the Center for the Study of American Business at Washington University, St. Louis.

Further Reading

Bluestone, Barry, and Bennett Harrison. *The Deindustrialization of America: Plant Closings, Community Abandonment, and the Dismantling of Basic Industry*. 1982.

Democratic Caucus, U.S. House of Representatives. *Rebuilding the Road to Opportunity: A Democratic Direction for the 1980s*. September 1982.

McKenzie, Richard B. *Competing Visions: The Political Conflict over America's Economic Future*. 1985.

Reich, Robert. *The Next American Frontier*. 1983.

Schultze, Charles. "Industrial Policy: A Dissent." *Brookings Review* (October 1983): 3–12.

Trezise, Philip. "Industrial Policy Is Not the Major Reason for Japan's Success." *Brookings Review* (Spring 1983): 13–18.

Industrial Policy: Democratic Economists Speak Out

One reason that industrial policy was never implemented in the United States was that Democratic economists opposed it. They did so, in part, on the grounds that governments cannot know which industries will be winners. In the *Brookings Review*, Brookings economist Charles Schultze, chairman of the Council of Economic Advisers under Jimmy Carter, wrote:

> The first problem for the government in carrying out an industrial policy is that we actually know precious little about identifying, before the fact, a "winning" industrial structure. There does not exist a set of economic criteria that determine what gives different countries preeminence in particular lines of business. Nor is it at all clear what the substantive criteria would be for deciding which older industries to protect or restructure.

Schultze's fellow economist Alfred Kahn, who was President Carter's chief inflation fighter, stated: "Cast a skeptical eye on glib references to the alleged success of government interventions in other countries in picking and supporting industrial winners."

And MIT's Paul Samuelson testifying, before Congress, said of industrial policy: "It's not good macroeconomics. And I don't think it's defensible social philosophy."

—DRH

Monetary Policy

James Tobin

■ Paul Volcker, while chairman of the board of governors of the Federal Reserve System (1979–87), was often called the second most powerful person in the United States. Volcker and company triggered the "double-dip" recessions of 1979–80 and 1981–82, vanquishing the double-digit inflation of 1979–80 and bringing the unemployment rate into double digits for the first time since 1940. Volcker then declared victory over inflation and piloted the economy through its long 1980s recovery, bringing unemployment below 5.5 percent, half a point lower than in the 1978–79 boom.

Volcker was powerful because he was making monetary policy. His predecessors were powerful too. At least four of the previous seven postwar recessions can be attributed to their anti-inflationary policies. Likewise, Alan Greenspan's Federal Reserve bears the main responsibility for the 1990–91 recession.

Central banks are powerful everywhere, although few are as independent of their governments as the Fed is of Congress and the White House. Central bank actions are the most important government policies affecting economic activity from quarter to quarter or year to year.

Monetary policy is the subject of a lively controversy between two schools of economics, monetarist and Keynesian. Although they agree on goals, they disagree sharply on priorities, strategies, targets, and tactics. As I explain how monetary policy works, I shall discuss these disagreements. At the outset I disclose that I am a Keynesian.

Common Goals

Few monetarists or Keynesians would disagree with this dream scenario:

- First, no business cycles. Instead, production—as measured by real (inflation-corrected) gross national product—would grow steadily, in step with the capacity of the economy and its labor force.
- Second, a stable and low rate of price inflation, preferably zero.
- Third, the highest rates of capacity utilization and employment that are consistent with a stable trend of prices.
- Fourth, high trend growth of productivity and real GNP per worker.

Monetary policies are demand-side macroeconomic policies. They work by stimulating or discouraging spending on goods and services. Economy-wide recessions and booms reflect fluctuations in aggregate demand rather than in the economy's productive capacity. Monetary policy tries to damp, perhaps even eliminate, those fluctuations. It is not a supply-side instrument.

Central banks have no handle on productivity and real economic growth.

Priorities

The second and third goals frequently conflict. Should policymakers give priority to price stability or to full employment? American and European monetary policies differed dramatically after the deep 1981–82 recession. The Fed "fine-tuned" a six-year recovery and recouped the employment and production lost in the 1979–82 downturns. Keeping a watchful eye on employment and output, and on wages and prices, the Fed stepped on the gas when the economic engine faltered and on the brakes when it threatened to overheat. During this catch-up recovery the economy grew at a faster rate than it could sustain thereafter. The Fed sought to slow its growth to a sustainable pace as full employment was restored.

European central banks, led by the German Bundesbank, were more conservative. They did little to help their economies catch up. They regarded active monetary stimulus as dangerously inflationary, even when their economies were barely emerging from recession. They were determined never to finance more than sustainable noninflationary growth, even temporarily. Europe recovered much more slowly than America, and its unemployment rates have ratcheted up from the seventies.

Priorities reflect national dreams and nightmares. German horror of inflation, for example, dates from the 1923 hyperinflation and from a second bout of inflation after World War II. Priorities also reflect divergent views of how economies work. European monetary authorities were acting like monetarists, Americans like Keynesians, although both would disavow the labels.

Here is the crucial issue: Expansionary monetary policy, all agree, increases aggregate spending on goods and services—by consumers, businesses, governments, and foreigners. Will these new demands raise output and employment? Or will they just raise prices and speed up inflation?

Keynesians say the answers depend on circumstances. Full employment means that everyone (allowing for persons between jobs) who is productive enough to be worth the prevailing real wage and wants a job at that wage is employed. In these circumstances more spending just brings inflation. Frequently, however, qualified willing workers are involuntarily unemployed; there is no demand for the products they would produce. More spending will put them to work. Competition from firms with excess capacity and from idle workers will keep extra spending from igniting inflation.

Monetarists answer that nature's remedy for excess supply in any market is price reduction. If wages do not adjust to unemployment, either government and union regulations are keeping them artificially high or the jobless prefer leisure and/or unemployment compensation to work at prevailing wages. Either way, the problem is not remediable by monetary policy. Injections of new spending would be futile and inflationary.

Experience, certainly in the Great Depression and also in subsequent recessions, indicates that downward adjustments of wages and prices cannot avoid damage to output and employment. Moreover, wage and price cuts may actually reduce demand by generating expectations of further disinflation or deflation.

A. W. Phillips's famous curve (see PHILLIPS CURVE) showed wage inflation varying inversely with unemployment. Keynesians were tempted to interpret it as a policy trade-off: less unemployment at the cost of a finite boost in inflation. Milton Friedman convinced the economics profession in 1968 that if monetary policy persistently attempts to bring unemployment below "the natural rate of unemployment" (the rate corresponding to Keynes's "full employment"), it will only boost the inflation rate explosively. Friedman's further conclusion that monetary policy should never concern itself with unemployment, production, or other real variables has been very influential. But in situations of Keynesian slack, as recent American experience again confirms, demand expansion can improve real macroeconomic performance without accelerating prices.

Strategies

Here too the monetarist-Keynesian controversy is exemplified by Federal Reserve and Bundesbank policies in the eighties. The issue is this: how actively and frequently should policymakers respond to observed and expected departures from their targets? Friedman wants them to follow the same routine regardless of the economic weather, increasing the money supply at a constant rate. In his view trying to outguess

the economy usually exacerbates fluctuations.

While not all monetarists endorse Friedman's rule, they do stress the importance of announced rules enabling the public to predict the central bank's behavior. In principle, announced rules need not blind policymakers to changing circumstances; they could specify in advance their responses to feedback information. But it is impossible to anticipate all contingencies. No central bank could have foreseen the OPEC shocks of the seventies and decided its responses in advance. Any practicable rule is bound to be simple. Any reactive policy, like the Fed's fine-tuning after 1982, is bound to allow discretion.

Relation to Fiscal Policy

In monetarists' view government budgets have important supply-side effects for good or ill but have no demand-side role unless they trigger changes in monetary policy. In Keynesian theory fiscal policy is a distinct demand-side instrument. The government affects aggregate demand directly by its own expenditures and indirectly by its taxes.

Prior to 1981, presidents and Congresses in making annual budgets considered their macroeconomic effects. In the eighties budget making became slow and cumbersome, and the explosion of deficits and debt made countercyclical fiscal policy very difficult. In the nineties the burden of stabilization policy falls almost entirely on monetary policy.

Monetary and fiscal policies are distinct only in financially developed countries, where the government does not have to cover budget deficits by printing money but can sell obligations to pay money in future, like U.S. Treasury bills, notes, and bonds. In the United States, Congress and the president decide on expenditure programs and tax codes and thus—subject to the vagaries of the economy—on the budget deficit (or surplus). This deficit (or surplus) adds to (or subtracts from) the federal debt accumulated from past budgets. The Federal Reserve decides how much, if any, of the debt is "monetized," i.e., takes the form of currency or its equivalent. The rest consists of interest-bearing Treasury securities. Those central bank decisions are the essence of monetary policy.

Mechanics of Monetary Policy

A central bank is a "bankers' bank." The customers of the twelve Federal Reserve banks are not ordinary citizens but "banks" in the inclusive sense of all depository institutions—commercial banks, savings banks, savings and loan associations, and credit unions. They are eligible to hold deposits in and borrow from Federal Reserve banks and are subject to the Fed's reserve requirements and other regulations.

At year-end 1990, federal debt outstanding was $2,569 billion, of which only 12 percent, or $314 billion, was monetized. That is, the Federal Reserve banks owned $314 billion of claims on the Treasury, against which they had incurred liabilities in currency (Federal Reserve notes) or in deposits convertible into currency on demand. Total currency in public circulation outside banks was $255 billion at year-end

1990. Banks' reserves—the currency in their vaults plus their deposits in the Fed—were $59 billion. The two together constitute the monetary base (M0), $314 billion at year-end 1990.

Banks are required to hold reserves at least equal to prescribed percentages of their checkable deposits. Compliance with the requirements is regularly tested, every two weeks for banks accounting for the bulk of deposits. Reserve tests are the fulcrum of monetary policy. Banks need "federal funds" (currency or deposits at Federal Reserve banks) to pass the reserve tests, and the Fed controls the supply. When the Fed buys securities from banks or their depositors with base money, banks acquire reserve balances. Likewise the Fed extinguishes reserve balances by selling Treasury securities. These are open-market operations, the primary modus operandi of monetary policy. These transactions are supervised by the Federal Open Market Committee (FOMC), the Fed's principal policy-making organ.

A bank in need of reserves can borrow reserve balances on deposit in the Fed from other banks. Loans are made for one day at a time in the "federal funds" market. Interest rates on these loans are quoted continuously. Central bank open-market operations are interventions in this market. Banks can also borrow from the Federal Reserve banks themselves, at their announced discount rates, in practice the same at all twelve banks. The setting of the discount rate is another instrument of central bank policy. Nowadays it is secondary to open-market operations, and the Fed generally keeps the discount rate close to the federal funds market rate. However, announcing a new discount rate is often a convenient way to send a message to the money markets. In addition to its responsibilities for macroeconomic stabilization, the central bank has a traditional safety-net role in temporarily assisting individual banks and in preventing or stemming systemic panics as "lender of last resort."

Tactics: Operating Procedures

Through open-market operations, the FOMC can set a target federal funds rate and instruct its trading desk at the Federal Reserve Bank of New York to enter the market as necessary to keep the funds rate on target. The target itself is temporary; the FOMC reconsiders it every six weeks or so at its regular meetings, or sooner if financial and economic surprises occur.

An alternative operating procedure is to target a funds quantity, letting the market move the funds interest rate to whatever level equates banks' demands to that quantity. This was the Fed's practice in 1979–82, adopted in response to monetarist complaints that the Fed had been too slow to raise interest rates in booms to check money growth and inflation. The volatility of interest rates was much greater in this regime than in the interest-rate-target regime.

How is the Fed's control of money markets transmitted to other financial markets and to the economy? How does it influence spending on goods and services? To banks, money market rates are costs of funds they could lend to their customers or invest in securities. When these costs are raised, banks raise their lending rates and become more selective in advancing credit. Their customers

borrow and spend less. The effects are widespread, affecting businesses dependent on commercial loans to finance inventories; developers seeking credit for shopping centers, office buildings, and housing complexes; home buyers needing mortgages; consumers purchasing automobiles and appliances; credit-card holders; and municipalities constructing schools and sewers.

Banks compete with each other for both loans and deposits. Before 1980 legal ceilings on deposit interest restricted competition for deposits, but now interest rates on certificates of deposits, savings accounts, and even checkable deposits are unregulated. Because banks' profit margins depend on the difference between the interest they earn on their loans and other assets and what they pay for deposits, the two move together.

Banks compete with other financial institutions and with open financial markets. Corporations borrow not only from banks but also from other financial intermediaries: insurance companies, pension funds, investment companies. They sell bonds, stocks, and commercial paper in open markets, where the buyers include individuals, nonprofit institutions, and mutual funds, as well as banks. Households and businesses compare the returns and advantages of bank deposits with those of money market funds, other mutual funds, open-market securities, and other assets.

Thanks to its control of money markets and banks, the Fed influences interest rates, asset prices, and credit flows throughout the financial system. Arbitrage and competition spread increases or decreases in interest rates under the Fed's direct control to other markets. Even stock prices are sensitive, falling when yields on bonds go up, and rising when they fall.

The Fed has less control over bond yields and other long-term rates than over money market and short-term rates. Long rates depend heavily on expectations of future short rates, and thus on expectations of future Fed policies. For example, heightened expectations of future inflation or of higher federal budget deficits will raise long rates relative to short rates, because the Fed has created expectations that it will tighten monetary policy in those circumstances.

Another mechanism for transmitting monetary policy to the demand for goods and services became increasingly important in the last two decades. Since 1973 foreign exchange rates have been allowed to float, and obstacles to international movements of funds have steadily disappeared. An increase in U.S. interest rates relative to those in Tokyo, London, and Frankfurt draws funds into dollar assets and raises the value of the dollar in terms of yen, pounds sterling, and deutsche marks. American goods become more expensive relative to foreign goods, for buyers both at home and abroad. Declines in exports and increases in imports reduce aggregate demand for domestic production. High interest rates and exchange appreciation created a large and stubborn U.S. trade deficit in 1981–85. Since 1985, as the interest advantage of dollar assets was reduced or reversed, the dollar depreciated and the U.S. trade deficit slowly fell.

Targets: Monetary Aggregates or Macroeconomic Performance?

People hold dollar currency because it is the means of payment in many transactions.

But checkable deposits are usually more convenient. They are not confined to particular denominations, cannot be lost or stolen, pay interest, and generate records most of us find useful.

The use of deposits in place of currency greatly economizes on base money. The $59 billion of bank reserves at year-end 1990 supported about $580 billion in checkable deposits. (The $521 billion of other assets behind those deposits were banks' loans and investments. In this sense banks "monetize" debts of all kinds.) These deposits plus the $255 billion in circulating currency provided a stock of transactions money (M1) of $835 billion. But time deposits and deposit certificates, though not checkable, are close substitutes for transactions deposits in many respects. So are money market funds and other assets outside banks altogether. Consequently the Fed keeps track of a spectrum of monetary aggregates, M1, M2, M3, each more inclusive than the preceding, capped by measures of liquid wealth (L) and debt. (See MONEY SUPPLY.)

The same open-market operations that move M0 up and down and interest rates down and up change the quantities of M1 and other monetary aggregates. Operations that reduce federal funds rates and related short-term interest rates add to bank reserves, thus also to bank loans and deposits. In 1990 reserve requirements averaged about 10 percent of checkable deposits. (In 1992 the Fed reduced the required reserve ratio by two percentage points.) Thus in 1990 a $1 increase in the bank reserves component of M0 meant roughly a $10 increase in the deposit component of M1. In contrast, a $1 increase in the currency component of M0 is always just a $1 increase in M1. If the public consistently held deposits and currency in the same proportion, 580/255 in the year-end 1990 example, a $1.00 increase in M0 would mean a $2.70 increase in M1. This is the "money multiplier." It does not stay constant, for several reasons. The Fed occasionally changes the required reserve ratio. Banks sometimes hold excess reserves, and sometimes borrow reserves from the Fed. The public's demand for currency relative to deposits varies seasonally, cyclically, and randomly. Thus, the Fed's control of M1 is imprecise, and its control of broader aggregates is still looser.

Monetarists urge the Fed to gear its operations to steady growth of a monetary aggregate, M1 or M2. Under congressional mandate the Fed twice a year announces target ranges for growth of monetary aggregates several quarters ahead. In the seventies the FOMC tried to stay within these ranges but often missed. Monetarist criticism became especially insistent when money growth exceeded Fed targets during the oil shocks. In October 1979 Chairman Volcker warned the public that the Fed would stick to its restrictive targets for monetary aggregates until inflation was conquered. Three years later, however, the Fed stopped taking the monetary aggregates seriously.

Monetary aggregates are not important in themselves. What matters is macroeconomic performance as indicated by GNP, employment, and prices. Monetarist policies are premised on a tight linkage between the stock of money in dollars, say Ml, and the flow of spending, GNP in dollars per year. The connection between them is the velocity of money, the number of times per year an average dollar travels around the circuit and is spent on GNP. By definition of velocity, GNP equals the stock of money times its velocity. The velocity of Ml was 6.6 in 1990. If it were predictable, control of Ml would control dollar GNP too. But Ml velocity is quite volatile. For the 1961–90 period its average annual growth was 2.1 percent. Its standard deviation was 3.0 percent. That is, the chance is about one in three in any year that velocity will either rise by more than 5.1 percent or decline by more than 0.9 percent. For the 1981–90 period the mean was -0.15, with a standard deviation of 4.0. (M2 velocity is less volatile, but M2 itself is less controllable.)

Velocity depends on the money management practices of households and businesses throughout the economy. As transactions technologies and financial institutions have evolved and an increasing array of money substitutes has arisen, velocity has become less stable and monetary aggregates have become less reliable proxies for aggregate spending and economic activity. The 1981–82 recession was deeper than the Fed intended because the FOMC stuck stubbornly to its monetary aggregates targets while velocity was precipitously falling.

Accounting for aggregate demand as the product of a money stock and its velocity is inadequate shorthand for the complex processes by which monetary policies are transmitted—via interest rates, banks, and asset markets—to spending on GNP by households, businesses, and foreigners. The Fed does better by aiming directly at desired macroeconomic performance than by binding itself to intermediate targets.

—James Tobin

Biography: James Tobin is an emeritus professor of economics at Yale University. He won the Nobel Prize in economics in 1981. He was a member of President Kennedy's Council of Economic Advisers.

Further Reading

Ando, Albert, H. Eguchi, R. Farmer, and Y. Suzuki, eds. *Monetary Policy in Our Times.* 1985.

Federal Reserve Bank of Kansas City. *Monetary Policy in the 1990s.* 1989.

Friedman, Milton. "The Role of Monetary Policy," presidential address at the 80th Annual Meeting of the American Economic Association, December 1967. *American Economic Review* 58, no. 1 (March 1968): 1–17.

Greider, William. *Secrets of the Temple: How the Federal Reserve Runs the Country.* 1987.

Meulendyke, Ann-Marie. *U.S. Monetary Policy and Financial Markets.* 1989.

Samuelson, Paul A. "Money, Interest Rates and Economic Activity: Their Interrelationship in a Market Economy." In *The Collected Scientific Papers of Paul A. Samuelson,* vol. 3, edited by Robert C. Merton. 1972. Originally published in American Bankers Association. *Proceedings of a Symposium on Money, Interest Rates, and Economic Activity.* 1967.

Phillips Curve

Kevin D. Hoover

■ The Phillips curve represents the relationship between the rate of inflation and the unemployment rate. Although several people had made similar observations before him, A. W. H. Phillips published a study in 1958 that represented a milestone in the development of macroeconomics. Phillips discovered that there was a consistent inverse, or negative, relationship between the rate of wage inflation and the rate of unemployment in the United Kingdom from 1861 to 1957. When unemployment was high, wages increased slowly; when unemployment was low, wages rose rapidly. The only important exception was during the period of volatile inflation between the two world wars.

In Phillips's analysis, when the unemployment rate was low, the labor market was tight and employers had to offer higher wages to attract scarce labor. At higher rates of unemployment there was less pressure to increase wages. Phillips's "curve" represented the average relationship between unemployment and wage behavior over the business cycle. It showed the rate of wage inflation that would result if a particular level of unemployment persisted for some time. Significantly, however, the relationship between wages and unemployment changed over the course of the business cycle. When the economy was expanding, firms would raise wages faster than "normal" for a given level of unemployment; when the economy was contracting, they would raise wages more slowly than "normal."

Economists soon estimated Phillips curves for most developed economies. Because the prices a company charges are closely connected to the wages it pays, economists also frequently used Phillips curves to relate general price inflation (as opposed to wage inflation) to unemployment rates. Chart 1 shows a typical Phillips curve fitted to data for the United States from 1961 to 1969. The individual observations appear to lie closely along the fitted curve, indicating that the cyclical behavior of inflation and unemployment is similar to the average behavior. That is, the relationship between inflation and unemployment does not seem to change much over the course of the business cycle.

This observation encouraged many economists, following the lead of Paul Samuelson and Robert Solow in 1960, to treat the Phillips curve as a sort of menu of policy trade-offs. For example, with an unemployment rate of 6.5 percent, the government might stimulate the economy to lower unemployment to 5.5 percent. Chart 1 indicates that this would entail a cost, in terms of higher inflation, of less than 0.5 percentage point. But if the government initially faced lower rates of unemployment, the costs would be considerably higher: a reduction of unemployment from 4.5 to 3.5 percent is associated with an increase in the inflation rate of about 2 percentage points.

At the height of the Phillips curve's popularity as a guide to policy, Edmund Phelps and Milton Friedman independently challenged its theoretical underpinnings. They argued that well-informed, rational employers and workers would pay attention only to real wages—the inflation-adjusted purchasing power of money wages. In their view, real wages would adjust to make the supply of labor equal to the demand for labor, and the unemployment rate would then stand at a level uniquely associated with that real wage. This level of unemployment they called the "natural rate" of unemployment.

In Friedman's and Phelps's view the government could not make a permanent trade-off between unemployment rates and inflation rates, as the Phillips curve in chart 1 suggests. Imagine that unemployment is at the natural rate. The real wage is constant: workers who expect a given rate of price inflation insist that their wages increase at the same rate to prevent the erosion of their purchasing power. Now imagine that the government uses expansionary monetary or fiscal policy in an attempt to lower unemployment below its natural rate. The resulting increase in demand encourages firms to raise their prices faster than workers had anticipated. With higher revenues firms are willing to employ more workers at the old

CHART 1

The Phillips Curve: 1961–69

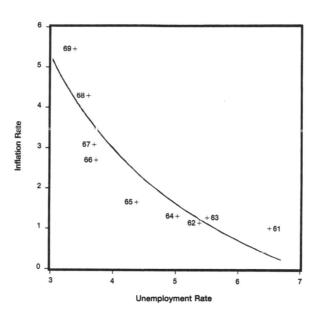

wage rates, and even to raise those rates somewhat. For a short time workers suffer from what economists call money illusion: they see that their money wages have risen, and willingly supply more labor. Thus the unemployment rate falls. They do not realize right away that their purchasing power has fallen because prices have risen more rapidly than they expected. But over time, as workers come to anticipate higher rates of price inflation, they supply less labor and insist on increases in wages that keep up with inflation. The real wage is restored to its old level, and the unemployment rate returns to the natural rate. But the price inflation and wage inflation brought on by expansionary policies continue at the new, higher rates.

Friedman's and Phelps's analysis provides a distinction between the "short-run" and "long-run" Phillips curves. So long as inflation remains fairly constant, as it did in the sixties, inflation is inversely related to unemployment. When the average rate of inflation changes, however, unemployment returns after a period of adjustment to the natural rate. That is, once worker expectations of price inflation have had time to adjust, the natural rate of unemployment is compatible with any rate of inflation. This long-run relation could be shown in chart 1 as a vertical line above the natural rate of unemployment. In other words, once unemployment falls to the natural rate, expansionary policies will not push it any lower except for brief, transitional periods. These long-run and short-run relations can be combined in a single "expectations-augmented" Phillips curve. The more quickly worker expectations of price inflation adapt to changes in the actual rate of inflation, the more quickly unemployment will return to the natural rate, and the less successful the government will be in reducing unemployment through monetary and fiscal policy.

The seventies provided striking confirmation of Friedman's and Phelps's fundamental point. The average inflation rate rose from about 2.5 percent in the sixties to about 7 percent in the seventies, while average unemployment rose from about 4.75 percent to about 6 percent. Thus, contrary to the original Phillips curve, higher inflation was associated with higher—not lower—unemployment.

Most economists now accept a central tenet of the Friedman-Phelps analysis: there is some rate of unemployment that, if maintained, would be compatible with a constant rate of inflation. Many, however, prefer to call this the "nonaccelerating inflation rate of unemployment" (NAIRU), because unlike the term "natural rate," it does not suggest an unchanging unemployment rate to which the economy inevitably returns, which policy cannot alter, and which is somehow socially optimal.

A policymaker might wish to place a value on NAIRU. To obtain a simple estimate, chart 2 plots changes in the rate of inflation (i.e., the acceleration of prices) against the level of unemployment from 1974 to 1990. The regression line (i.e., the straight line that best fits the points on the graph) summarizes the rough, inverse relationship. According to the regression line, NAIRU (i.e., the rate of unemployment for

which the change in the rate of inflation is zero) is about 7 percent. The slope of the regression line indicates the speed of price adjustment. Imagine that the economy is at NAIRU with an inflation rate of 4.5 percent, and that the government would like to reduce the inflation rate to zero. Chart 2 suggests that contractionary monetary and fiscal policies that drove the average rate of unemployment up to about 8 percent (i.e., 1 point above NAIRU) would be associated with a reduction in inflation of about 1.5 percentage points per year. Thus, if the unemployment rate were held at about 8 percent, the inflation rate of 4.5 percent would, on average, be reduced to zero in three years.

Using similar methods, estimates place NAIRU at about 5.25 percent for the twenty years before 1974 and sharply higher—at about 7 percent—after 1974. Clearly, NAIRU is not constant. It is consistent with the natural rate hypothesis for NAIRU to vary (even by considerable amounts) as a result of changes in demographics, technology, the structure of labor markets, the structure of taxation, relative prices (e.g., oil prices), and other so-called "real" factors affecting the supply of and demand for labor. But monetary and fiscal policy, which affect aggregate demand without altering these real factors, should not change the natural rate of unemployment.

The expectations-augmented Phillips curve is a fundamental element of almost every macroeconomic forecasting model now used by government and business. Nonetheless, two criticisms of the expectations-augmented Phillips curve deserve notice.

First, economists of the new classical school argue that people form expectations rationally. According to the new classicals,

CHART 2

Acceleration of Prices versus the Unemployment Rate: 1974–90

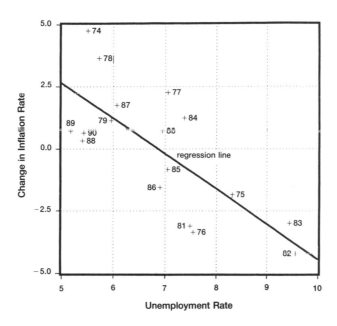

people use information efficiently, so that they find ways to eliminate every systematic mistake in their predictions. For example, if people systematically underpredicted inflation by, say, 2 percent for several years, they could simply add 2 percentage points to their forecasts to obtain more accurate results. After eliminating every systematic source of error, any remaining mistakes must be unsystematic. That is, they must be random, or inherently unpredictable, so that people are as likely to overpredict as to underpredict inflation.

The "rational expectations" hypothesis says, in effect, that people's expectations adapt so rapidly that a government using expansionary monetary and fiscal policy to engineer a higher rate of price inflation can-

not consistently push the unemployment rate below the natural rate. People will catch on too fast and demand higher wages whenever policy becomes more expansionary.

Although the rational expectations hypothesis enjoys wide currency among economic theorists, it has not affected the manner in which the expectations-augmented Phillips curve is incorporated into large macroeconomic forecasting models. This is not surprising. An expectations-augmented Phillips curve with rational expectations implies that the economy is always very close to NAIRU. But as is obvious from chart 2, unemployment has fluctuated widely over the years. This could be consistent with the new classical view only if NAIRU itself fluctuated as much as actual unemployment. And no convincing explanation has been given of why such fluctuations would occur.

Some "new Keynesian" economists offer a second criticism. They argue that there is no natural rate of unemployment in the sense of a rate to which the actual rate tends to return. Instead, when actual unemployment rises and remains high for some time, NAIRU rises as well. The dependence of NAIRU on actual unemployment is known as the hysteresis hypothesis. One explanation for hysteresis in a heavily unionized economy is that unions directly represent the interests only of those who are currently employed. Unionization undermines the ability of those outside the union to compete for employment. After prolonged layoffs employed workers inside the union may seek the benefits of higher wages for themselves, rather than moderating wage demands to promote the rehiring of

unemployed workers. The downside to the hysteresis hypothesis is that once unemployment becomes high—as it did in Europe in the recessions of the seventies—it is relatively impervious to monetary and fiscal stimulus, even in the short run. The hysteresis hypothesis appears to be more relevant to Europe, where unionization is higher and where labor laws create numerous barriers to hiring and firing, than it is to the United States, with its considerably more flexible labor markets.

The Phillips curve was hailed in the sixties as providing an account of the inflation process hitherto missing from the conventional macroeconomic model. After three decades the Phillips curve, as transformed by the natural rate hypothesis into its expectations-augmented version, remains the key to relating unemployment and inflation in mainstream macroeconomic analysis.

—**Kevin D. Hoover**

Biography: Kevin D. Hoover is an economics professor at the University of California at Davis. In 1991 and 1992 he was a fellow at the National Humanities Center. He has been on the board of editors of the *American Economic Review* since 1990.

Further Reading

Cross, Rod, ed. *Unemployment, Hysteresis, and the Natural Rate of Unemployment.* 1988.
Friedman, Milton. "The Role of Monetary Policy." *American Economic Review* 58, no. 1 (1968): 1–17.
Lucas, Robert E., Jr. "Econometric Testing of the Natural Rate Hypothesis." In *The Econometrics of Price Determination,* edited by Otto Eckstein. 1972. Reprinted in Lucas, Robert E., Jr. *Studies in Business Cycle Theory.* 1981.
Phelps, Edmund S. "Phillips Curves, Expectations of Inflation and Optimal Employment over Time." *Economica NS* 34, no. 3 (1967): 254–81.
Phillips, A. W. H. "The Relation between Unemployment and the Rate of Change of Money Wage Rates in the United Kingdom, 1861–1957." *Economica NS* 25, no. 2 (1958): 283–99.
Samuelson, Paul A., and Robert M. Solow. "Analytical Aspects of Anti-Inflation Policy." *American Economic Review* 50, no. 2 (1960): 177–94.
Sheffrin, Steven M. *Rational Expectations.* 1983.

Privatization

Madsen Pirie

■ Privatization is the process by which the production of goods or services is removed from the government sector of the economy. This has been done in a variety of ways, ranging from the public sale of shares in a previously state-owned enterprise to the use of private businesses to perform government work under contract.

The leader in this innovative strategy was the Thatcher government of Great Britain from 1979 to 1990. Previous governments had tried limited denationalization, which is the restoration of nationalized enterprises to their previous owners, but with limited success. Privatization involved totally new owners. In some cases the state enterprises that were ''privatized'' had never been in the private sector.

Governments all over the world were confronted in the seventies by the problems inherent in state ownership. Because state-owned companies have no profit motive, they lack the incentive that private companies have to produce goods that consumers want and to do so at low cost. An additional problem is that state companies often supply their products and services without direct charges to consumers. Therefore, even if they want to satisfy consumer demands, they have no way of knowing what consumers want, because consumers indicate their preferences most clearly by their purchases.

The result is misallocation of resources. Management tends to respond to political, rather than to commercial, pressures. The capital assets of state businesses are often of poor quality because, it is claimed, it is always easier for governments to attend to more urgent claims on limited resources than the renewal of capital equipment. In the absence of any effective pressure from consumers whose money is taken in taxation, state industries tend to be dominated by producer interests.

Before the British water industry was privatized in 1989, for example, analysts estimated it to be undercapitalized by over $11 billion. The result was a water supply that failed to meet European standards for quality and safety. Similarly, the post office had steadily cut back its services. First telegrams disappeared, then Sunday collection, then Saturday second delivery. These changes made life easier for producers at the expense of service to consumers. Most serious of all, the losses of state industries consume funds that are needed for private investment.

Privatization began against this background of steadily poorer performances from state industries. The Thatcher government started with the 1979 sale of a batch of shares in British Petroleum (BP), the state oil giant. The sale reduced the government's holding to below 50 percent. By British Treasury rules, this made BP a private company, and free to behave accordingly, seeking capital for investment on the market and making its own decisions on a commercial basis. The government sold more blocks of its BP shares later.

The military and civilian airplane manufacturer, British Aerospace, was sold in February 1981, followed by the radiochemicals group, Amersham International, and the state trucking group, National Freight Company, a year later. After this the pace began to accelerate. Britoil was sold in 1983, the British Ports in 1983, and Jaguar Cars in 1984, which also saw the sale of British Telecom, the state monopoly telephone service. It was sold as the largest company ever floated on a stock market, and attracted 2.3 million shareholders, many of them buying shares for the first time.

The Telecom sale demonstrated the government's desire to satisfy the various interest groups involved in public-sector operations. The previous management became the new board of the private corporation. The workers were given an allocation of free shares and were allowed to buy more from a reserved block on a basis that offered free matching shares. The telephone-using public was offered a choice if they bought shares: a share bonus if they held their shares for three years or reductions on their telephone bill. Rural dwellers were satisfied by a requirement that the new company continue its remote country services. Urban dwellers received assurances about the number of pay phones. Special services to the disabled were to be continued.

In short, the government "bid" for the support of virtually every group that might have objected. This pattern was to be repeated and refined in subsequent privatizations. The Thatcher government could take this tack because the private sector performed so much better than the state sector that the gains could be shared among many

groups while still leaving a huge bonus for the government. Not only were subsidized losses converted into taxable profits, but the revenue from the sales accrued to the public treasury.

The policy of identifying and satisfying various groups made privatization a popular strategy, and a difficult one for subsequent governments to reverse. The opposition Labour party in Britain opposed every privatization, pledging itself to reverse each one, but later abandoned its pledge. The fact that share offers to employees were taken up by over 90 percent of the work force undoubtedly contributed to this about-face.

The British government usually aimed to set the opening share price at 10 to 20 percent below its expected market price. This was done for two reasons: to deal with the difficulty of pricing companies that had never properly kept accounts, and to encourage ordinary people to invest. Over the decade the number of private stockholders in Britain more than tripled. In 1979 there were four times as many people in labor unions as there were stockholders. By 1989 the stockholders outnumbered the union members (though in many cases they were now the same people).

The British privatization of nearly four dozen major businesses and several hundred small ones set an example not only of the techniques that could be used, but also of the success that could be anticipated. The formerly underachieving state-owned British industries outperformed the market average once they entered the private sector. With the exception of the oil businesses, which were marketed to professional investors because of their high-risk nature, the privatized stocks rose in value faster than

TABLE 1

Major Sales of State Firms Completed in 1981

Country	Proceeds US$ Million	Country	Proceeds US$ Million
Argentina	1,022	Panama	23
Australia	1,620	Philippines	190
Austria	35	Poland	350
Brazil	2,189	Portugal	1,014
Canada	2,902	Singapore	67
Colombia	52	Spain	252
France	376	Sri Lanka	13
Germany	8,075	Taiwan	405
Greece	232	UK	19,348
Hungary	180	Venezuela	2,055
Ireland	489		
Jamaica	42	Total Public offers	26,498
Malaysia	190	Private sales	21,984
Mexico	9,400	Grand Total	48,482
Netherlands	150		

the stock market average, as shown by periodic surveys in London's *Financial Times* and *Privatization International*.

The sale of public housing in Britain to its tenants attracted little international attention because there was no public flotation. But the purchase of their homes by people who had been living at subsidized rents made major economic impact. In 1979, 35 percent of Britons lived in state-owned homes at rents that failed to cover the government's costs. The annual expenditure from 1979 to 1988 of $8.6 billion was not met by the income of $4.5 billion.

The homes were offered at discounts based on the number of years of residence, starting with 20 percent below market price for a two-year tenant and rising to 50 percent for those who had lived there for twenty years. The largest discount was later raised to 80 percent. Turning tenants into homeowners brought major social changes in Britain, including the upgrading of the quality of houses as people began to invest in and protect their new assets. By 1988 the total revenues that accrued to government from housing sales alone surpassed those of all other sales combined.

By the late eighties the British Treasury was receiving annual revenue from privatization sales averaging $8 billion, while total government revenue was roughly $300 billion. The revenues from privatization helped the Thatcher government cut income taxes over the decade from a bottom rate of 33 percent down to 25 percent, and from a top rate of 98 percent down to 40 percent.

Other countries were anxious to share these advantages for their own state industries. Foreign privatization ranged from massive sales in advanced countries such as France and Japan to the sale of hundreds of small enterprises in developing countries such as Bangladesh.

The French program took place in the "cohabitation" period of a socialist president and a conservative prime minister. It was passed in mid-1986, with the first sale, glassmaker Saint Gobain, in December of that year. This, like the sale of the banking group Paribas in February 1987, was a huge success, attracting so much popular support that the shares were heavily oversubscribed, like the British sales.

The first nine companies were successfully sold before the world stock market slide of 1987 brought a halt to the French program. The French copied the British idea of reserving at least 10 percent of the shares for the work force, and of keeping a "golden share," a single share retained by the government, to prevent foreigners from gaining control of strategic industries.

Japan mounted large-scale privatizations, including its tobacco and salt monopoly in 1984; its telephone service (NTT), floated in 1986; and following that, Japan National Railways (JNR), the world's biggest sale. JNR was broken into six regional passenger carriers, one freight company, one firm to lease high-speed bullet trains to four of the others, and a ninth company to sell JNR landholdings, estimated at $50 billion. No advanced economy outside Britain even approached this scale of privatization.

Following the collapse of communism in eastern and central Europe, first Poland, Hungary, and Czechoslovakia, then Romania and several of the former Soviet republics began to privatize. The problems in these economies, blighted by more than forty years of command planning and central controls, were very different from those faced by the advanced economies. Decades of low wages meant that little wealth was available for investment, and no stock markets existed on which to make sales. Very often, there were no laws to protect or even permit private ownership, much less the supporting infrastructure of contract law and financial support services such as banks and accountants.

For this reason the formerly socialist economies found themselves forced to blaze a new trail of privatization, sometimes using the distribution of "coupons" to the population as a means of spreading ownership. Very often some degree of "informal" privatization was permitted, in which management effectively expropriated what had been state property. Unlike Britain, which had about 10 percent of its economy in state hands and had sold three-fifths of it over ten years, the socialist countries were now faced with privatizing 60 to 80 percent of their economies within half that time. The scale and the problems were of altogether different proportions.

By the beginning of the nineties, hardly a country in the world did not have a privatization program. Many countries learned from the experience of the early leaders. These included the techniques of writing off past debts, allocating shares to workers, splitting monopolies into competing elements, and establishing new regulatory agencies to calm public fears about the behavior of the newly privatized operations.

By restoring market incentives and commercial reality, privatization achieved a worldwide reinvigoration of ailing state-owned industries. It diverted billions of dollars from the support of loss-making government concerns into the expansion of wealth-creating private businesses. It augmented growth rates and made tax reductions possible. Britain, which in the seventies had one of the lowest growth rates in Europe, has enjoyed one of the highest since 1981.

It went from one of the highest-taxed countries to one of the lowest. Privatization contributed, in large measure, to the revival of confidence in capitalism and the market economy, evidenced by the large number of countries which turned in that direction, and to its eventual triumph over the rival system of central planning, controls, and state ownership.

—Madsen Pirie

Biography: Madsen Pirie is president of the Adam Smith Institute in London. He took part in the development of privatization policy, first in Britain and then in other countries. He is an adviser to Prime Minister John Major on the Citizen's Charter.

Further Reading

Butler, Eamonn, and Madsen Pirie, eds. *The Manual on Privatization*. 1990.
Goodman, John C., ed. *Privatization*. 1985.
Pirie, Madsen. *Privatization: Theory, Practice and Choice*. 1988.
Poole, Robert W. *Cutting Back City Hall*. 1980.
Privatization International, monthly from Privatization International Limited, P.O. Box 863, London SE5 8JG, England.
Privatization Watch, monthly from Reason Foundation, 2716 Ocean Park Blvd., Suite 1062, Santa Monica, CA 90405.
Savas, Emanuel S. *Privatization: The Key to Better Government*. 1987.
Walker, Michael, ed. *Privatization: Tactics and Techniques*. 1988.

Reaganomics

William A. Niskanen

■ "Reaganomics" was the most serious attempt to change the course of U.S. economic policy of any administration since the New Deal. "Only by reducing the growth of government," said Ronald Reagan, "can we increase the growth of the economy." Reagan's 1981 Program for Economic Recovery had four major policy objectives: (1) reduce the growth of government spending, (2) reduce the marginal tax rates on income from both labor and capital, (3) reduce regulation, and (4) reduce inflation by controlling the growth of the money supply. These major policy changes, in turn, were expected to increase saving and investment, increase economic growth, balance the budget, restore healthy financial markets, and reduce inflation and interest rates.

Any evaluation of the Reagan economic program should thus address two general questions: How much of the proposed policy changes were approved? And how much of the expected economic effects were realized? Reaganomics continues to be a controversial issue. For those who do not view Reaganomics through an ideological lens, however, one's evaluation of this major change in economic policy will depend on the balance of the realized economic effects.

President Reagan delivered on each of his four major policy objectives, although not to the extent that he and his supporters had hoped. The annual increase in real (inflation-adjusted) federal spending declined from 4.0 percent during the Carter administration to 2.5 percent during the Reagan administration, despite a record peacetime increase in real defense spending. This part of Reagan's fiscal record, however, reflected only a moderation, not a reversal, of prior fiscal trends. Reagan made no significant changes to the major transfer payment programs (such as Social Security and Medicare), and he proposed no substantial reductions in other domestic programs after his first budget.

Moreover, the growth of defense spending during his first term was higher than Reagan had proposed during the 1980 campaign, and since economic growth was somewhat slower than expected, Reagan did not achieve a significant reduction in federal spending as a percent of national output. Federal spending was 22.9 percent of gross domestic product (GDP) in fiscal 1981, increased somewhat during the middle years of his administration, and declined to 22.1 percent of GDP in fiscal 1989. This part of the Reagan record was probably the greatest disappointment to his supporters.

The changes to the federal tax code were much more substantial. The top marginal tax rate on individual income was reduced from 70 percent to 28 percent. The corporate income tax rate was reduced from 48 percent to 34 percent. The individual tax brackets were indexed for inflation. And most of the poor were exempted from the individual income tax. These measures were somewhat offset by several tax increases. An increase in Social Security tax rates legislated in 1977 but scheduled for the eighties was accelerated slightly. Some excise tax rates were increased, and some deductions were reduced or eliminated.

More important, there was a major reversal in the tax treatment of business income. A complex package of investment incentives was approved in 1981 only to be gradually reduced in each subsequent year through 1985. And in 1986 the base for the taxation of business income was substantially broadened, reducing the tax bias among types of investment but increasing the average effective tax rate on new investment. It is not clear whether this measure was a net improvement in the tax code. Overall, the combination of lower tax rates and a broader tax base for both individuals and business reduced the federal revenue share of GDP from 20.2 percent in fiscal 1981 to 19.2 percent in fiscal 1989.

The reduction in economic regulation that started in the Carter administration continued, but at a slower rate. Reagan eased or eliminated price controls on oil and natural gas, cable TV, long-distance telephone service, interstate bus service, and ocean shipping. Banks were allowed to invest in a somewhat broader set of assets, and the scope of the antitrust laws was reduced. The major exception to this pattern was a substantial increase in import barriers. The Reagan administration did not propose changes in the legislation affecting health, safety, and the environment, but it reduced

the number of new regulations under the existing laws. Deregulation was clearly the lowest priority among the major elements of the Reagan economic program.

Monetary policy was somewhat erratic but, on net, quite successful. Reagan endorsed the reduction in money growth initiated by the Federal Reserve in late 1979, a policy that led to both the severe 1982 recession and a large reduction in inflation and interest rates. The administration reversed its position on one dimension of monetary policy: during the first term, the administration did not intervene in the markets for foreign exchange but, beginning in 1985, occasionally intervened with the objective to reduce and then stabilize the foreign-exchange value of the dollar.

Most of the effects of these policies were favorable, even if somewhat disappointing compared to what the administration predicted. Economic growth increased from a 2.8 percent annual rate in the Carter administration, but this is misleading because the growth of the working-age population was much slower in the Reagan years. Real GDP per working-age adult, which had increased at only a 0.8 annual rate during the Carter administration, increased at a 1.8 percent rate during the Reagan administration. The increase in productivity growth was even higher: output per hour in the business sector, which had been roughly constant in the Carter years, increased at a 1.4 percent rate in the Reagan years. Productivity in the manufacturing sector increased at a 3.8 percent annual rate, a record for peacetime.

Most other economic conditions also improved. The unemployment rate declined from 7.0 percent in 1980 to 5.4 percent in 1988. The inflation rate declined from 10.4 percent in 1980 to 4.2 percent in 1988. The combination of conditions proved that there is no long-run trade-off between the unemployment rate and the inflation rate (see PHILLIPS CURVE). Other conditions were more mixed. The rate of new business formation increased sharply, but the rate of bank failures was the highest since the thirties. Real interest rates increased sharply, but inflation-adjusted prices of common stocks more than doubled.

The U.S. economy experienced substantial turbulence during the Reagan years despite favorable general economic conditions. This was the "creative destruction" that is characteristic of a healthy economy. At the end of the Reagan administration, the U.S. economy had experienced the longest peacetime expansion ever. The "stagflation" and "malaise" that plagued the U.S. economy from 1973 through 1980 were transformed by the Reagan economic program into a sustained period of higher growth and lower inflation.

In retrospect the major achievements of Reaganomics were the sharp reductions in marginal tax rates and in inflation. Moreover, these changes were achieved at a much lower cost than was previously expected. Despite the large decline in marginal tax rates, for example, the federal revenue share of GDP declined only slightly. Similarly, the large reduction in the inflation rate was achieved without any long-term effect on the unemployment rate. One reason for these achievements was the broad bipartisan support for these measures beginning in the later years of the Carter administration. Reagan's first tax proposal,

for example, had previously been endorsed by the Democratic Congress beginning in 1978, and the general structure of the Tax Reform Act of 1986 was first proposed by two junior Democratic members of Congress in 1982. Similarly, the "monetarist experiment" to control inflation was initiated in October 1979, following Carter's appointment of Paul Volcker as chairman of the Federal Reserve Board. The bipartisan support of these policies permitted Reagan to implement more radical changes than in other areas of economic policy.

Reagan failed to achieve some of the initial goals of his initial program. The federal budget was substantially reallocated—from discretionary domestic spending to defense, entitlements, and interest payments—but the federal budget share of national output declined only slightly. Both the administration and Congress were responsible for this outcome. Reagan supported the large increase in defense spending and was unwilling to reform the basic entitlement programs, and Congress was unwilling to make further cuts in the discretionary domestic programs. Similarly, neither the administration nor Congress was willing to sustain the momentum for deregulation or to reform the regulation of health, safety, and the environment.

Reagan left three major adverse legacies at the end of his second term. First, the privately held federal debt increased from 22.3 percent of GDP to 38.1 percent and, despite the record peacetime expansion, the federal deficit in Reagan's last budget was still 2.9 percent of GDP. Second, the failure to address the savings and loan problem early led to an additional debt of about $125 billion. Third, the administration added more trade barriers than any administration since Hoover. The share of U.S. imports subject to some form of trade restraint increased from 12 percent in 1980 to 23 percent in 1988.

There was more than enough blame to go around for each of these problems. Reagan resisted tax increases, and Congress resisted cuts in domestic spending. The administration was slow to acknowledge the savings and loan problem, and Congress urged forbearance on closing the failing banks. Reagan's rhetoric strongly supported free trade, but pressure from threatened industries and Congress led to a substantial increase in new trade restraints. The future of Reaganomics will depend largely on how each of these three adverse legacies is resolved. Restraints on spending and regulation would sustain Reaganomics. But increased taxes and a reregulation of domestic and foreign trade would limit Reaganomics to an interesting but temporary experiment in economic policy.

The Reagan economic program led to a substantial improvement in economic conditions, but there was no ''Reagan revolution.'' No major federal programs (other than revenue sharing) and no agencies were abolished. The political process continues to generate demands for new or expanded programs, but American voters continue to resist higher taxes to pay for these programs. A broader popular consensus on the appropriate roles of the federal government, one or more constitutional amendments, and a new generation of political leaders may be necessary to resolve this inherent conflict in contemporary American politics.

—William A. Niskanen

Biography: William A. Niskanen is chairman of the Cato Institute and was a member of President Reagan's Council of Economic Advisers from 1981 to 1985. *Washington Post* columnist Lou Cannon, in his book, *President Reagan: The Role of a Lifetime*, called Niskanen's book, *Reaganomics*, ''a definitive and notably objective account of administration economic policies.''

Further Reading

Lindsey, Lawrence B. *The Growth Experiment: How the New Tax Policy Is Transforming the U.S. Economy.* 1990.
Niskanen, William A. *Reaganomics.* 1988.

See also MARGINAL TAX RATES; PRODUCTIVITY; PROGRESSIVE TAXES; SUPPLY-SIDE ECONOMICS; TAXATION, A PREFACE.

Redistribution of Income

Dwight R. Lee

■ Since the Great Depression most Americans have agreed that a principal responsibility of government is to redistribute income from the well-to-do to the impoverished and to those who are temporarily disadvantaged, most notably the unemployed. While many people complain about waste, fraud, and abuse in government income-transfer programs, or about the extent of income redistribution, few dispute the proposition that some level of redistribution is needed. Over the last twenty years, however, many economists—including some on the political left—have raised serious questions about the effectiveness of current transfer programs in helping the poor. While government policies do redistribution enormous amounts of money each year, the actual benefits to the poor may be much smaller than people presume.

Most people, of course, are certain that the government helps the poor by transferring income to them. Almost without exception academic studies and journalistic accounts of government's effect on the well-being of the poor focus exclusively on the effectiveness of transfer programs designed to redistribute income only to those in need. The fact that some government programs do indeed help the poor is taken as sufficient evidence that government helps the poor. But to know whether the net impact of all government transfer policies is really to help the poor, we need to examine government's many other transfer programs.

Such an examination quickly yields a striking fact: most redistribution by government is not from the rich to the poor. Instead, government takes from the relatively unorganized (e.g., the general taxpayer) and transfers to the relatively organized (lobbying groups with common interests or characteristics, such as the elderly and farmers). Moreover, the most important factor in determining the pattern of redistribution appears to be political power, not need. Of the more than $500 billion a year spent on public assistance and social insurance programs, only about 25 percent is allocated through means-tested programs. The other 75 percent—more than $400 billion a year—gets distributed regardless of need. Social Security payments shift approximately $270 billion of income a year to the elderly regardless of their wealth, and on average the elderly possess about twice the net worth per family as does the general population. And because qualifying for Medicare requires only that one be 65 or older, most of the more than $100 billion in annual Medicare benefits go to the nonpoor.

What's more, the direct transfer of cash and services is only one way that government transfers income. For example, government also transfers income by restricting competition among producers. The inevitable consequence—indeed, the intended consequence—of these restrictions is to enrich organized groups of producers at the expense of consumers. Here the transfers are more perverse than with Medicare and Social Security. They help relatively wealthy producers at the expense of relatively poor (and in some cases absolutely poor) consumers. Many government restrictions on agricultural production, for example, transfer billions of tax dollars to farmers annually and also allow farmers to capture billions of consumer dollars through higher food prices (see AGRICULTURAL PRICE SUPPORTS). Most of these transfers go to a relatively few large farms, whose owners are far wealthier than the average taxpayer and consumer (or the average farmer).

Restrictions on imports also transfer wealth from consumers to domestic producers of these products. Again, those who receive these transfers are typically wealthier, on average, than those who pay for them. Consider, for example, the distributional effect of the restrictions that were imposed on steel in 1984. Economist Arthur Denzau estimated that these restrictions saved 16,900 steel production jobs in the United States. Unfortunately, Denzau found, the resulting higher-priced steel raised the cost of production in U.S. industries using steel and caused a loss of 52,400 U.S. jobs. This represents a net loss of over 35,000 domestic jobs. Furthermore, according to Denzau, the workers who lost their jobs earned, on average, about 40 percent less than the steelworkers whose jobs were saved. In other words, government made many lower-paid workers poor (at least until they found new jobs) in order to help higher-paid workers.

Although transfer programs that come in the form of higher prices do not show up in the government's budget, they are just as real, and could be as large, as those that do. And the crazy-quilt pattern of subsidies, import restrictions, and the like indicates that regardless of whether or not a transfer shows up in the government budget, the size and distribution of that transfer has far less to do with the relative income of the recipients than with their relative political influence.

Not only do the poor receive a smaller percentage of income transfers than most people realize, but the transfers they do get are worth less to them, dollar for dollar, than transfers going to the nonpoor. That is because only about 30 percent of the value transferred in means-tested programs in recent years has been in cash. In contrast, well over half of the transfers to the nonpoor are cash. The remaining 70 percent of the means-tested transfers come in the form of in-kind transfers such as food stamps, housing, and medical care. Economists who study poverty point out that the value to the poor of these in-kind transfers is well below their cost to taxpayers. The reason is that the poor—like the rest of us—value cash more than in-kind transfers because if they have cash, they can choose what to buy. Therefore, a dollar taken from taxpayers and given to a poor person in the form of, say, medical care, is often worth much less than a dollar to the poor person. And it is worth much less than each dollar going to Social Security recipients.

The most important question, of course, is whether the poor have benefited from the large increase in the percentage of the national income that has been channeled through government in the name of reducing poverty. The answer, surprising as it may seem, is that we really do not know. To determine the effect of government transfer programs on the poor, we would have to know how the poor would have fared had these programs never existed, and we have no way of estimating that with any degree of confidence.

Most studies that have attempted to measure the benefit to the poor from government transfers compare the income of the recipients with what their incomes would be if all transfer income were eliminated. The assumption is that the entire transfer is an increase in the income of the recipients. Such studies conclude that government programs have significantly reduced the poverty rate.

But such studies overstate the benefits the poor receive from government transfers. For one thing, means-tested transfers that diminish as the recipient's income from working rises reduce the incentive to work. Although there is controversy over the magnitude, all economists agree that these disincentive effects exist. The late Arthur Okun, President Johnson's chief economist and a strong advocate of government transfers to the poor, compared such transfers to a leaky bucket to illustrate the fact that the increase in recipient income is less than the amount transferred.

At least to some degree, government transfers to the poor have substituted for income the poor would have earned, rather than adding to that income. Also, along with all other taxpayers and consumers, the poor have to pay for the large government transfers that go primarily to the nonpoor.

What the poor receive from some transfer programs may be largely taken away from them in the form of higher income taxes, higher Social Security taxes, and higher consumer prices to support other transfer programs.

Probably the best information on what the poor have received from the growth in transfer programs comes from examining what has happened to the distribution of income over time. If government transfers have helped the poor, as advertised, by redistributing income to them, then this should show up in a more equal distribution of income. However, studies that have investigated the trend in income distribution, after adjusting for taxes and adding in the value of all transfers, including in-kind transfers, find little if any change over the last forty years. One of the first such studies, by economists Morgan Reynolds and Eugene Smolensky, covered the period 1950 through 1970. Reynolds and Smolensky found that the households with incomes in the bottom 20 percent of the income distribution received 6.4 percent of the national net income in 1950 and 6.7 percent in 1970. Those households with incomes in the top 20 percent of the income distribution received 39.9 percent of the net national income in 1950 and 39.1 percent in 1970.

More recent studies on the trend in the after-tax/after-transfer distribution of income continue to show little evidence of redistribution from the rich to the poor. Based on these studies, economist Robert Haveman concluded that "in spite of massive increases in federal government taxes and spending, we are about as unequal in 1988 as we were in 1950."

Still, we can never know what would

have happened if government transfers had not increased. It is possible that the distribution of income would have become more unequal. The slowdown in the growth of wages since 1973, the increase in the number of female-headed households, and the aging of the population have been cited as reasons why the income distribution would have become more unequal without increased government transfers. Yet some of these very changes may have been accentuated by increases in government transfers. A partial explanation for the slowdown in the growth of wages is that governments have required private firms to increase non-wage compensation and to pay higher payroll taxes.

In sum, many economists would agree that the transfer programs designed specifically to help the poor have in fact improved their well-being. The magnitude of the improvement, however, is much less than the dollar amounts transferred—because so many of the transfers are in-kind instead of cash, and because transfers cause at least some of the poor to work less than they otherwise would. More important, looking only at transfers to the poor gives an incomplete answer—and possibly a wrong answer—to the question of whether the net impact of all government policies that affect income distribution is to help, or harm, the poor.

—Dwight R. Lee

Biography: Dwight R. Lee is the Ramsey Professor of Economics at the University of Georgia.

Further Reading

Denzau, Arthur T. *How Import Restrictions Reduce Employment.* Formal publication no. 80. Center for the Study of American Business, Washington University (St. Louis), June 1987.

Haveman, Robert. *Starting Even: An Equal Opportunity Program to Combat the Nation's New Poverty.* 1988.

Okun, Arthur M. *Equality and Efficiency: The Big Tradeoff.* 1975.

Reynolds, Morgan, and Eugene Smolensky. *Public Expenditures, Taxes, and the Distribution of Income: The United States, 1950–1970.* 1977.

Sawhill, Isabel V. "Poverty in the U.S.: Why Is It So Persistent?" *Journal of Economic Literature* 26 (September 1988): 1073–1119.

Tullock, Gordon. *Economics of Income Redistribution.* 1983.

Social Security

Carolyn L. Weaver

■ The Social Security system, including old-age and survivors insurance, disability insurance, and hospital insurance (Medicare), poses a staggering liability in the years ahead. Benefits in the year 2025, when the retirement of the baby-boom generation is in full swing, are projected to cost 23 percent of taxable payroll in the economy, up from 14 percent today. In today's dollars, that amounts to $1 trillion annually. Between now and 2065, the actuaries' official long-range measuring period, the nation's giant retirement program is slated to spend $19 trillion in present value terms. Counting Medicare, the liability is $30 trillion. How this liability is met—indeed whether it is met in full—will profoundly affect people's savings and retirement decisions, the nation's public finances, and ultimately, the amount and distribution of America's wealth.

For most of its history Social Security has been financed on a pay-as-you-go basis. With pay-as-you-go financing, benefits to retirees and other beneficiaries are met by current taxes on workers; income roughly equals outgo, and assets do not accumulate significantly. Pay-as-you-go Social Security systems have large unfunded liabilities.

Research by Harvard economist Martin Feldstein, published in 1974 (and in a follow-up article in 1982 correcting a programming error in the original study), suggested that the pay-as-you-go method of financing Social Security had depressed private saving in 1971 by a whopping one-third. His argument was simple but compelling: to the extent people view the government's promises to provide retirement benefits as a substitute for their own retirement savings, they will tend to save less. Less private saving, when not offset by increased government saving, means less new capital and ultimately lower real incomes.

Feldstein's findings touched off a major controversy in the economics profession over the determinants of private saving and the effects of government policy. Are people "life-cycle" savers, as Feldstein suggested, making choices to maximize their own financial well-being over their lifetimes, saving mainly to finance their own retirement? This is consistent with Milton Friedman's earlier discovery that an individual's spending is powerfully affected by how much he expects to earn over his entire lifetime, not simply by what he earns today. Or are people linked with their children, through financial gifts and bequests, in such as way as to neutralize the effects of Social Security? In the latter case, Social Security should increase private saving as the elderly attempt to offset, through increases in their planned gifts or bequests, the (implicit) future Social Security taxes that their children will have to pay. Harvard's Robert Barro, chief proponent of this view, argues that people adjust their private transfers to undo the compulsory transfers inherent in Social Security. If Barro is correct, the introduction or expansion of a pay-as-you-go system should reduce saving only by people who do not have surviving children or who want to transfer less than the compulsory transfers under Social Security.

While the debate is by no means resolved, most economists agree that both motives—life-cycle saving and bequests—matter. The empirical evidence, while mixed, continues to support the view that Social Security has had a significant depressing effect on private savings, although this effect does not appear to have been as large as originally believed. Economists B. Douglas Bernheim and Lawrence Levin, for example, found that Social Security depresses personal saving dollar for dollar for single individuals, but has no effect on saving by married couples.

Pay-as-you-go financing not only reduces real income through its effect on private saving, but also redistributes wealth and income over time. Those who retired in the early years of Social Security got huge wealth transfers because they paid taxes for only part of their work lives and because, as the system was being expanded and taxes were being raised, they paid these higher taxes for only a few years. According to a study by the Congressional Research Service, a worker with average earnings who retired at age 65 in 1940 got back the retirement portion of his and his employer's taxes, plus interest, in a mere two or three months. For workers who retired in 1960, the payback period was 1.1 years. For those retiring in 1980, the payback period had increased to 2.8 years.

The picture is much bleaker for future retirees. The expected payback period for today's older workers, those retiring in

2000, is 12.9 years, rising to 18.3 years for workers retiring in 2030.

This bleak long-term picture is inevitable. Average rates of return on Social Security taxes must fall as the system matures and, in the long term, cannot exceed the rate of growth of wages in the economy. Michael Boskin, chairman of President Bush's Council of Economic Advisers, and his colleagues estimated that workers with median earnings and with nonworking spouses will get a real return on taxes of only 2.1 percent if they retire in 2010, and only 1.5 percent if they retire in 2025 or later. Returns are even lower for workers with working spouses. The expected net loss for the 2025 retiree is $48,000, in present value terms, as compared to a net gain to the 1980 retiree of $63,000.

Social Security also transfers income within the same generation. For example, the weighed-benefit formula subsidizes workers with low earnings at the expense of those with higher earnings. The payback period for someone retiring in the year 2000 varies from ten years for the minimum-wage worker to twenty years for the relatively highly paid professional (1992 earnings of $55,500).

Much of the wealth redistribution that Social Security causes has little rationale. For example, Social Security subsidizes people who work in covered employment for only brief periods, even if their earnings are quite high. Also, the 50 percent benefit increase for spouses subsidizes "traditional" families, those with one breadwinner and a nonworking spouse, at the expense of two-earner couples and single people. For people born in 1945, the expected rate of return for a two-earner couple with a combined salary of $50,000 is only 0.4 percent, or less than one-fourth of the 1.74 percent return for the single-earner couple with the same salary and same total taxes paid. Finally, the retirement earnings test and actuarial adjustments for early and delayed retirement subsidize people who retire at sixty-five (and possibly earlier) at the expense of those who retire later.

Each of these transfers alters the return to work and thus distorts people's decisions about when, where, and how much to work.

There is much evidence for the view that Social Security has contributed to the sharp decline in labor force participation rates and in the average age of retirement for older men. Michael Hurd and Michael Boskin, for example, concluded that the entire 8.2 percent decline in the participation rate of men age sixty to sixty-five that occurred between 1968 and 1973 was caused by the 20 percent increase in inflation-adjusted benefits enacted during that period.

As a result of legislation in 1983 and generally healthy economic growth during the rest of the decade, Social Security is running a surplus of about $50 billion annually and accumulating assets rapidly. Trust fund assets have quadrupled in the past five years and now top $325 billion ($450 billion including Medicare). Social Security's total asset holdings are greater than those of the top fifteen private pension plans combined—including General Motors, AT&T, IBM, and Ford. According to the Social Security Board of Trustees, assets will peak in the 2020s at $5.5 trillion (roughly $2 trillion in today's dollars). Interest earned on trust fund assets is expected to defray a significant portion of the cost of future benefits.

Some economists applaud the shift from pay-as-you-go toward partial advance funding as a fiscally responsible measure that will increase national saving and lighten the tax burden when the baby boomers retire. Other economists criticize it as fiscal chicanery—a hidden redistribution of taxes over time. They argue that surplus payroll taxes are used to fund the general operations of the government today, in exchange for general fund financing of Social Security tomorrow, and that trust fund surpluses create no real saving and may result in substantial wealth losses for the economy as a whole.

Who is right depends on whether the excess payroll taxes are being (and will be) saved and productively invested, or whether they are being used to finance current consumption by the government. Presently, any surplus monies are invested in new, special-issue government bonds. The trust funds are credited with a bond—an IOU from one part of the government to another—and the Treasury gets the cash, which it can spend like any other federal receipts. Saving occurs only if the government uses the surpluses to retire outstanding government debt (or to issue less debt to the public), causing the public to buy new private securities, thus increasing the funds available for investment.

Advance funding, as currently conceived, is thus an indirect mechanism for adding to the nation's capital investment. But it can work only if Congress restrains itself from doing two things: (1) relaxing fiscal restraint in the rest of the budget— that is, increasing spending on other programs or reducing taxes—and (2) using the increase to increase Social Security benefits, bail out the financially ailing Medicare trust fund, or fund a new program like long-term health care. That's a big "if." The alternative, spending the surpluses as we go, would substantially increase the government's long-range indebtedness and undermine the economic well-being of future workers and retirees.

The budget reforms adopted in 1990 were touted for having dealt with these concerns head-on. Previously, the Social Security surpluses were counted in determining whether the government met its deficit-reduction targets. Increases in the surpluses thus reduced the savings that had to be achieved in other programs. Social Security has now been removed from the Gramm-Rudman budget targets—and from the mechanisms that enforce those targets. Also, new procedures make it more difficult to bring legislation to a vote that would undermine the financial condition of Social Security.

Economists grounded in public choice theory, and therefore skeptical of politicians, are not sanguine that these new rules can keep Congress from spending the Social Security reserves for the next forty years. The "enforcement mechanism" for Social Security is weak by design: expansions of Social Security will not trigger any automatic reductions in other spending. In addition, the procedural "fire wall" for Social Security applies only to some legislation. Moreover, enforcement mechanisms are subject to change, as evidenced by two major revisions of the Gramm-Rudman law since 1985.

Four central changes in our economic and social life since the thirties have altered the costs and benefits of Social Security, yet have had almost no effect on the design of the program. These are the great expansion in employer-provided pensions and other sources of retirement income; the steady increase in life expectancy (since 1930, life expectancy at birth has increased from 58 to 71.6 years among males, and from 61.3 to 78.6 years among females); the steady improvement in the financial well-being of the elderly relative to other age groups; and changes in federal policy itself, which have resulted in an array of programs providing assistance to the elderly poor and medical-care coverage for virtually all of the nation's elderly. U.S. retirement income policy can continue to ignore these developments only at great cost.

—**Carolyn L. Weaver**

Biography: Carolyn L. Weaver is resident scholar and director of the Social Security and Pension Project at the American Enterprise Institute in Washington, D.C.

Further Reading

Barro, Robert J. *The Impact of Social Security on Private Saving: Evidence from the U.S. Time Series.* 1978.
Board of Trustees of the Federal Old-Age and Survivors Insurance, Disability Insurance, and Hospital Insurance Trust Funds. *1992 Annual Report.* 1992.

Boskin, Michael J. *Too Many Promises: The Uncertain Future of Social Security*. 1986.

———, Laurence J. Kotlikoff, Douglas J. Puffert, and John B. Shoven. "Social Security: A Financial Appraisal across and within Generations." *National Tax Journal* 40 (March 1987), no. 1: 19–34.

Feldstein, Martin. "Social Security, Induced Retirement, and Aggregate Capital Accumulation." *Journal of Political Economy* 82, no. 5 (1974): 905–27.

———. "Social Security and Private Saving: Reply." *Journal of Political Economy* 90, no. 3 (1982): 630–41.

Hurd, Michael D., and Michael J. Boskin. "The Effect of Social Security on Retirement in the Early 1970s." *Quarterly Journal of Economics* 99 (November 1984): 767–90.

Kollman, Geoffrey. "Social Security: The Relationship of Taxes and Benefits." Congressional Research Service Report no. 92–956 EPW. December 16, 1992.

Quinn, Joseph F., Richard V. Burkhauser, and Daniel A. Myers. *Passing the Torch: The Influence of Economic   Incentives on Work and Retirement*. 1990.

Weaver, Carolyn L. *The Crisis in Social Security: Economic and Political Origins*. 1982.

———, ed. *Social Security's Looming Surpluses: Prospects and Implications*. 1991.

See also FEDERAL DEFICIT, SAVING.

Unemployment Insurance

David R. Francis

■ The United States unemployment insurance program is intended to offset income lost by workers who lose their jobs as a result of employer cutbacks. The program, launched by the Social Security Act of 1935, is the government's single most important source of assistance to the jobless.

A second goal of the program is to counter the negative impacts on the national economy, and especially on local economies, of major layoffs, seasonal cutbacks, or a recession. Unemployment benefits help sustain the level of income and hence the demand for goods and services in areas hard hit by unemployment. In short, unemployment insurance supports consumer buying power.

Not all unemployed workers are eligible for unemployment insurance. In fact, from 1984 to 1989 the proportion of the unemployed receiving benefits was at or below 34 percent every year. Benefits are not paid to employees who quit their jobs voluntarily or are fired for cause. Nor are they paid to those who are just entering the labor force but cannot find a job, nor to reentrants to the labor force who are looking for work. In February 1991, 76 percent of the target population of ''job losers''—those involuntarily laid off—received benefits.

The proportion of unemployed workers who receive benefits is always higher during recessions than during expansions. This is because during recessions a higher fraction of the unemployed are people who were laid off. By January 1991, 46 percent of total unemployed workers claimed unemployment benefits, the highest percentage for that month since 1983.

Under the joint federal-state program, most states pay a maximum of twenty-six weeks in benefits, starting after a one-week waiting period. A few extend the duration somewhat longer. These benefits replace about one-third of gross wages for people with average or below-average incomes. The average weekly benefit in 1991 was about $161. When a state's unemployment is substantially above the national average, the program provides for up to an additional thirteen weeks of benefits. Five states were paying ''extended benefits'' in the winter of 1991, but this number approximately doubled by the end of April as the recession and unemployment worsened. The state and federal government share, approximately equally, the cost of extended benefits. During the eighties many states raised their ''triggers''—the unemployment rate that must be reached—for extended benefits. As a result relatively few workers were eligible for extended benefits.

The federal government makes grants to the states for the administration of the unemployment insurance program. These grants exceeded $2 billion in fiscal 1991, ending September 30, 1991. The money helped pay the wages of about thirty-seven thousand state workers who administer the program and who dispense benefits from state unemployment insurance funds. In that fiscal year states collected about $16 billion in unemployment taxes from employers to cover the cost of the program; the federal government collected approximately $4.4 billion. Outlays on benefits were expected to run about $18.7 billion in fiscal 1991.

Federal law requires all state governments to impose a tax on employers of at least 0.8 percent on each employee's first $7,000 of pay. The tax base exceeds $7,000 in thirty-six states, with a national average of about $8,500. The highest base is $21,300 in Alaska. Most states levy a higher tax rate on businesses that have higher layoffs. However, the tax rate cannot go below the minimum even for businesses that have no layoffs. Nor do states set the maximum high enough so that employers with high layoff rates generate enough tax revenues to pay all the benefits to the workers they lay off. The result is that workers and businesses in industries with low layoff rates subsidize workers and businesses in industries, such as construction, with high layoff rates. Harvard's Martin Feldstein suggested in 1973 that this subsidization of layoffs would cause more layoffs. The evidence indicates that he was correct. Economist Robert Topel of the University of Chicago estimates that if employers could expect to repay (in taxes) the full value of unemployment benefits drawn by their laid-off workers, then the unemployment rate would fall by as much as 1 full point (e.g., from 6 percent of the labor force to 5 percent).

A basic tenet of economics is that when an activity is subsidized, people do more of it. Does unemployment insurance—a subsidy for being unemployed—increase unemployment by prompting the unemployed to delay their search for a new job or to search longer for a better position? Economists have found that it does. A 1990 study by Bruce D. Meyer, an economist at Northwestern University, found that a 10 percent boost in the "replacement ratio"—the proportion of after-tax work earnings replaced by unemployment benefits—causes unemployed people to extend their time without work by an average of 1.5 weeks. (During fiscal 1990 the average duration of benefits for the jobless was 13.6 weeks.)

Most people who receive unemployment insurance find a job or are recalled to work in the first several weeks. Meyer also found that among those who remain jobless for a longer period, the chance of a person on unemployment insurance going back to work increases rapidly as the time of benefit exhaustion approaches. Indeed, the chances of an unemployed person getting a job triples as the length of remaining benefits drops from six weeks to one week. Meyer suspects some of the jobless may have arranged to be recalled to previous work or to begin new work about the time their benefits expire. "If workers are bound to firms by implicit contracts, moving costs, specific human capital [education, experience, skills, etc.], or other reasons, firms have an incentive to base recall decisions on the length of UI [unemployment insurance] benefits," noted Meyer in a study done for the National Bureau of Economic Research.

Unionized firms tend to take greater advantage of this "layoff subsidy" than do nonunion establishments. And not surprisingly, given the incentives, layoffs are more common for those eligible for unemployment benefits than for those not eligible. If benefits are extended beyond twenty-six weeks, the unemployed tend to stay out of work nearly a day longer, on average, for each week of the extension.

Lawrence H. Summers, chief economist at the World Bank, and chief economic adviser to Democratic presidential candidate Michael Dukakis in 1988, reaches similar conclusions. Summers, along with Harvard economist Kim B. Clark, found that unemployment insurance almost doubles the number of unemployment spells lasting more than three months, thereby encouraging long-term joblessness. Summers and Clark suggest that unemployment insurance benefits cause many of the long-term unemployed to have high "reservation wages." Translation: to accept a job, these unemployed workers insist on getting a high wage, and if they aren't offered that wage, they stay on unemployment insurance as long as possible.

Economists have proposed various reforms to reduce the adverse effects of unemployment while still assisting people who lose their jobs. One of the more modest reforms suggested has been to reduce the minimum tax rate on employers and raise the maximum tax rate, so that the taxes they pay more closely reflect their layoff rates. A more extreme proposal, made by Robert Topel, is to experience-rate individual workers so that workers with a history of long unemployment spells pay higher tax rates. The federal government has already adopted one reform suggested by economists across the ideological spectrum. The 1986 Tax Reform Act eliminates the tax bias in favor of unemployment insurance by taxing unemployment benefits just like other income.

—**David R. Francis**

Biography: David R. Francis is an economic journalist with the *Christian Science Monitor*.

Further Reading

Becker, Joseph M. *Experience Rating in Unemployment Insurance: An Experiment in Competitive Socialism.* 1972.

Feldstein, Martin. "The Economics of the New Unemployment." *Public Interest* 33 (Fall 1973): 3–42.

Summers, Lawrence H. *Understanding Unemployment.* 1990.

Topel, Robert. "Unemployment and Unemployment Insurance." *Research in Labor Economics* 7 (1986): 91–135.

———. "Financing Unemployment Insurance: History, Incentives, and Reform." In *Unemployment Insurance: The Second Half Century,* edited by W. Lee Hansen and J. Byers. 1990.

CHAPTER FIVE

TAXES

Taxation, A Preface

Joseph J. Minarik

■ In recent years taxation has been one of the most prominent and controversial topics in economic policy. Taxation was a principal issue in three consecutive presidential elections—with a large tax cut as a winning issue in 1980, a tax increase a losing issue in 1984, and a pledge of "Read my lips: no new taxes" providing one of the enduring images of 1988. Taxation was also the subject of two major, and largely inconsistent, policy changes. It is still a source of ongoing debate.

Objectives

Economists specializing in public finance have long enumerated four objectives of tax policy: simplicity, efficiency, fairness, and revenue sufficiency. While these objectives are widely accepted, they often conflict, and different economists have different views of the appropriate balance among them.

Simplicity means that compliance by the taxpayer and enforcement by the revenue authorities be as easy as possible. Further, the ultimate tax liability should be certain. A tax whose amount is easily manipulated through decisions in the private marketplace (such as by investing in "tax shelters") can cause tremendous complexity for taxpayers, who attempt to reduce what they owe, and for revenue authorities, who attempt to maintain government receipts.

Efficiency means that taxation interferes as little as possible in the choices people make in the private marketplace. The tax law should not induce a businessman to invest in real estate instead of research and development—or vice versa. Further, tax policy should discourage work or investment, as opposed to leisure or consumption, as little as possible. Issues of efficiency arise from the fact that taxes always affect behavior. Taxing an activity (like earning a living) is similar to a price increase. With the tax in place, people will typically buy less of a good—or partake in less of an activity—than they would in the absence of the tax.

The most efficient tax system possible is one that few low-income people would want. That superefficient tax is a head tax, a tax on each person that is not affected by that person's income or by any of the person's characteristics. A head tax would not reduce the incentive to work, save, or invest. The problem with such a tax is that it would take the same amount from a high-income person as from a low-income person. It could even take the entire income of low-income people. Within the realm of what is practical, the goal of efficiency is to minimize the ways that taxes affect people's choices.

A major philosophical issue among economists is whether tax policy should purposefully deviate from efficiency in order to encourage taxpayers to pursue positive economic objectives (such as saving) or to avoid harmful economic activities (such as smoking). Most economists would accept some role for taxation in so steering economic choices, but economists disagree on two important points: how well policymakers can presume to know which objectives we should pursue (is discouraging smoking an infringement on personal freedom?), and the extent of our ability to influence taxpayer choices without unwanted side effects (will subsidies for saving merely reward those with the most discretionary income for saving no more than they would have without a subsidy?).

Fairness, to most people, requires that equally situated taxpayers pay equal taxes ("horizontal equity") and that better-off taxpayers pay more tax ("vertical equity"). Although these objectives seem clear enough, fairness is very much in the eye of the beholder. There is little agreement over how to judge whether two taxpayers are equally situated. For example, one taxpayer might receive income from labor while another receives the same income from inherited wealth. And even if one taxpayer is clearly better off than another, there is little agreement about how much more the better-off person should pay. Most people believe that fairness dictates that taxes be "progressive," meaning that higher-income taxpayers not only pay more, but proportionately more. However, a significant minority takes the position that taxes should be flat, with everyone paying the same proportion of their taxable incomes. Moreover, the idea of vertical equity (i.e., the "proper" amount of progressivity) often directly contradicts another notion of fairness, the

"benefit principle." According to this principle those who benefit more from the operations of government should pay more tax.

Revenue sufficiency might seem a fairly obvious criterion of tax policy. Yet the federal government's budget has been in enormous deficit for more than ten years. Part of the reason for the deficit is that revenue sufficiency may conflict with efficiency and with fairness. Economists who believe that income taxes strongly reduce incentives to work or save, and economists who believe that typical families already are unfairly burdened by heavy taxes, might resist tax increases that would move the federal budget toward balance.

Likewise, other objectives of tax policy conflict with one another. High tax rates for upper-income households are inefficient but are judged by some to make the tax system fairer. Intricate legal provisions to prevent tax sheltering and thus make taxes fairer would also make them more complex. Such conflicts among policy objectives are a constant constraint on the making of tax policy.

The U.S. Tax System

At the federal level total tax collections have hovered in a narrow range around 19 percent of the gross national product (GNP) since the end of the Korean War (see table 1). The individual income tax has provided just under half of that revenue over the entire period. The corporation income tax was the source of almost a third of total revenue at the beginning of the period but has declined dramatically to under 10 percent today. In mirror image the payroll tax for

TABLE 1

Federal Tax Revenues by Type of Tax—Percents of GNP, Fiscal Years

Year	Individual Income	Corporate Income	Social Security	Excise	Other	Total
1954	8.0%	5.7%	2.0%	2.7%	0.5%	18.9%
1959	7.6%	3.6%	2.4%	2.2%	0.7%	16.5%
1964	7.7%	3.7%	3.5%	2.2%	0.8%	17.9%
1969	9.4%	3.9%	4.2%	1.6%	1.0%	20.1%
1974	8.4%	2.7%	5.3%	1.2%	1.0%	18.6%
1979	8.9%	2.7%	5.7%	0.8%	0.8%	18.9%
1984	8.1%	1.5%	6.5%	1.0%	1.0%	18.1%
1989	8.7%	2.0%	7.0%	0.7%	0.9%	19.3%
1991	8.8%	1.7%	7.2%	0.8%	0.9%	19.4%

SOURCE: *Office of Management and Budget. 1991 figure is estimated.*

Social Security began at about 10 percent of total revenue, but it increased sharply to over 37 percent as the elderly population and inflation-adjusted Social Security benefits grew and as the Medicare program was added to the system. The relative contribution of excise taxes (primarily on alcohol, tobacco, gasoline, and telephone services) has declined significantly.

One little-recognized aspect of the development of federal taxes is the gradual decline of revenues other than those earmarked for the Social Security and Medicare programs. Although total federal taxes are a roughly constant percentage of GNP, the Social Security payroll tax has increased significantly while other taxes have been cut in approximately equal measure. The result has been that federal revenues available for programs other than

Social Security and Medicare have been squeezed—from about 17 percent of GNP in 1954 to about 12 percent today.

States rely primarily on sales taxes but increasingly on income taxes. Local governments rely most heavily on property taxes. Contrary to what many believe, the explosion in taxation has been in state and local taxes. Unlike federal taxes, state and local taxes have increased significantly—from about 7 percent of GNP in 1954 to about 12 percent now (see table 2).

Thus, although the level of federal taxes has been relatively constant for nearly thirty years, total taxes have increased because state and local taxes have increased. (The data in tables 1 and 2 are computed on different accounting procedures and years and thus cannot be added together; the general picture that they suggest is, however, accu-

TAXES

TABLE 2

State and Local Tax Revenues by Type of Tax—Percents of GNP

Year	Individual Income	Corporate Income	Property	Sales	Other	Total
1954	0.3%	0.2%	2.6%	1.7%	2.1%	7.0%
1959	0.4%	0.2%	3.0%	2.2%	2.1%	8.0%
1964	0.6%	0.3%	3.3%	2.5%	2.4%	9.1%
1969	1.0%	0.4%	3.4%	3.0%	2.7%	10.4%
1974	1.4%	0.5%	3.3%	3.3%	3.0%	11.5%
1979	1.5%	0.5%	2.6%	3.1%	3.2%	11.0%
1984	1.8%	0.5%	2.6%	3.2%	3.7%	11.8%
1989	2.0%	0.5%	2.7%	3.3%	3.7%	12.1%

SOURCE: *Department of Commerce, Bureau of Economic Analysis. Data are not comparable to those in table 1.*

rate.) The increase in state and local taxes has obviously added to the taxpayers' burden and has limited the federal government's ability to cut the federal deficit and to increase spending.

Recent Tax Policy Changes

Much of the recent interest in tax policy has focused on the federal individual and corporate income taxes. Advocates of "supply-side economics" (most prominently, Arthur Laffer) believed that income taxes had severely blunted incentives to work, save, and invest and that the income tax burden had become excessive. The income tax became a major issue in the 1980 presidential election, and Congress passed a substantial income tax cut in 1981. It provided for a cumulative across-the-board cut of 23 percent in the income tax rate, phased in over four years, along with significant tax inducements for business investment. In the face of a rapidly rising budget deficit, some of the investment incentives were repealed a year later.

An even more radical tax restructuring was passed in 1986. This new law, like the 1981 law, also significantly reduced income tax rates. It was, however, radically different from the 1981 tax cuts in a more meaningful sense, in that all of the tax rate cuts were "paid for" by the elimination of tax incentives—including the remaining business investment inducements from 1981. This tax "reform" made U.S. corporate and individual income tax rates the lowest in the industrialized world. It simplified the tax law in some respects but also included complicated provisions designed to prevent tax sheltering. The new law also provided significant tax relief for low-income taxpayers, especially families with children. And it transferred about $25 billion a year of the tax burden from the personal to the corporate income tax.

Tax scholars have observed the experience of the eighties closely to learn more about how taxes affect economic choices. While much controversy remains, certain results seem clear. First, as many economists expected, the reduction of tax rates in the eighties apparently did induce greater work effort, especially by married women. In 1988, according to Brookings economists Barry Bosworth and Gary Burtless, men between the ages of 25 and 64 worked 5.2 percent more hours than they would have under the pre-1981 tax code; women age 25 to 64 worked 5.8 percent more; and married women worked 8.8 percent more. These increased hours would translate into the equivalent of almost 5 million full-time jobs.

Second, household saving fell in the face of tax rate cuts and substantial targeted tax incentives for saving, strongly suggesting that taxes have a limited impact at best on saving. Studies by economists Steven F. Venti and David Wise have suggested that individual retirement accounts (IRAs) were successful in encouraging new saving, but another study by William Gale and John Karl Scholz indicated that much of the IRA deposits came from households that had already accumulated considerable wealth and could simply transfer it into the tax-favored accounts. And finally, while business investment did increase after the 1981–82 recession (as documented by Harvard's Martin Feldstein), other economists (notably Barry Bosworth of Brookings) argue

that this increase came primarily in assets (such as computers) that were not highly favored by the tax law. In fact, investment in equipment increased to a record percentage of GNP after the incentives were repealed in the 1986 tax reform, though Alan Auerbach and Kevin Hassett have argued that it would have increased even more strongly if investment incentives had been continued.

Distribution of the Tax Burden

Many economists judge the fairness of the tax system largely on how the tax burden is distributed among different income groups. Further, some economists used the distribution of the tax burden as a major criterion of the success or failure of the tax changes of the eighties. Despite considerable effort and innovative methods, however, estimates of the distribution of the tax burden are still limited by imperfect data and the differing perspectives of investigators.

Between 1980 and 1990 the percentage of income paid in federal tax increased for the 60 percent of families with the lowest incomes taken as a group, and decreased for the 40 percent with the highest incomes (see table 3). The decreases were largest for the families with the very highest incomes. Some economists have used these figures to claim that the changes of the eighties left the tax burden distributed less fairly. In fact, the 1986 tax reform taken by itself had the opposite effect when assessed by this methodology, but was outweighed by the 1981 tax cuts.

These figures are subject to challenge,

T A X E S

TABLE 3

Federal Taxes as a Percentage of Family Income, 1980 and 1990

Quintile of Families Ranked by Income	1980	1990	Change
Lowest	8.4%	9.7%	1.3%
Second	15.7%	16.7%	1.0%
Third	20.0%	20.3%	0.3%
Fourth	23.0%	22.5%	−0.5%
Highest	27.3%	25.8%	−1.5%
Top 10 percent	28.4%	26.4%	−2.0%
Top 5 percent	29.5%	26.7%	−2.8%
Top 1 percent	31.8%	27.2%	−4.6%
ALL	23.3%	23.0%	−0.3%

SOURCE: *Congressional Budget Office.*

however. They assume that half of the corporate income tax is borne by owners of business capital, and half by workers in the form of lower wages, and that the employer's share of the Social Security payroll tax is borne by workers, also through lower wages. If you assume that owners of businesses pay all the corporate income tax and the employer's share of Social Security, the tax burden would rest further up the income ladder. Also, although upper-income families paid a smaller percentage of their income in tax in 1990 than they did in 1980, they received a much larger share of total taxable income by the end of the decade. One reason the taxable income of upper-income families is higher is that changes in the tax law, particularly in 1986, caused many upper-income families to reallocate their portfolios from things like municipal bonds to assets that yield taxable income. But there also is evidence that the distribution of income simply became less equal. The net result is that upper-income families now pay a larger share of the total tax burden.

Current Tax Issues

Tax policy remains controversial, and some economists continue to argue for large-scale revision of the federal tax system. Some convervative economists, such as Charles McLure, and some liberals, such as Alice Rivlin, would like to see a broad-based federal tax on consumption, like the sales taxes imposed by the states or the value-added tax (VAT) widely used in Europe. The proceeds of the tax could be used to increase federal spending, to cut federal income taxes, or to reduce the deficit. Advocates argue that a tax on consumption would encourage saving; opponents claim that such a tax would unfairly burden low-income families.

Many economists, including Princeton's Alan Blinder, believe that the income tax should provide a comprehensive adjustment ("indexation") for inflation to eliminate the inflationary component of interest income and expense, depreciation of business investment, and capital gains. The case of capital gains is the clearest. A block of stock bought for $1,000 in 1978 and sold for $2,000 today would yield a $1,000 taxable capital gain. But the investor would have received no real increase in purchasing power because the price level has roughly doubled since then. The same problem, however, afflicts recipients of interest income. With inflation at 4 percent, only half of the interest on a bond yielding 8 percent is real income to the bondholder, but all of the interest is subject to income tax. An adjustment for inflation would be quite complex; it was considered and rejected for that reason in the debate on the 1986 tax reform. The merit of indexing for inflation might depend on the rate of inflation in the economy. In hyperinflation, indexation is essential. But at low rates of inflation—perhaps as high as 10 percent—the markets can offer higher interest rates to compensate lenders (and penalize borrowers) for the inexact taxation of their interest income (and deductions of business interest expense).

Some economists, including Martin Feldstein, argue for a targeted tax cut for capital gains (the profit from the sale of assets like corporate stock or real estate), or for reinstatement of targeted incentives for household saving (like the deductibility for all taxpayers of contributions to individual retirement accounts, or IRAs) Such initiatives are typically claimed to increase economic growth. Opponents, such as Brookings' Henry Aaron, believe that they would be ineffective and that they would unduly benefit upper-income groups who own the most capital assets and have the most discretionary income to save.

Finally, some economists (such as Robert Shapiro) and policymakers (most notably, Sen. Daniel Patrick Moynihan) believe that the Social Security payroll tax should be cut significantly. They argue that the growth of the payroll tax has been a major contributor to the shift in the tax burden toward lower-income families. Such a tax cut, however, would be intricately tied to the structure of the entire Social Security system and is accordingly extremely controversial.

—Joseph J. Minarik

Biography: Joseph J. Minarik is chief economist of the Office of Management and Budget. He has previously held positions with the Budget Committee of the U.S. House of Representatives, the Urban Institute, the Congressional Budget Office, and the Brookings Institution.

Further Reading

Auerbach, Alan, and Kevin Hassett."Investment, Tax Policy, and the Tax Reform Act of 1986." In *Do Taxes Matter? The Impact of the Tax Reform Act of 1986,* edited by Joel Slemrod. 1991.

Blinder, Alan. *Hard Heads, Soft Hearts.* 1987.

Bosworth, Barry P. "Taxes and the Investment Recovery." *Brookings Papers on Economic Activity*, no. 1 (1985): 1–38.

———, and Gary Burtless. "Effects of Tax Reform on Labor Supply, Investment, and Saving." Unpublished report prepared for the Brookings Institution.

Feldstein, Martin S., and Joosung Jun. "The Effects of Tax Rules on Nonresidential Fixed Investment: Some Preliminary Evidence from the 1980s." In *The Effects of Taxation on Capital Accumulation,* edited by Martin S. Feldstein. 1987.

Feldstein, Martin S., Joel Slemrod, and Shlomo Yitzhaki. "The Effects of Taxation on the Selling of Corporate Stock and the Realization of Capital Gains." *Quarterly Journal of Economics* 94 (June 1981): 777–91.

Gale, William, and John Karl Scholz. "Effects of IRAs on Household Saving." July 1992, mimeo.

Goode, Richard. *The Individual Income Tax.* 1976.

Lindsey, Lawrence. *The Growth Experiment.* 1990.

McLure, Charles E., Jr. *The Value-Added Tax: Key to Deficit Reduction?* 1987.

Minarik, Joseph J. *Making America's Budget Policy.* 1988.

———. "Capital Gains." In *How Taxes Affect Economic Behavior,* edited by Henry Aaron and Joseph A. Pechman. 1981.

Pechman, Joseph A. *Federal Tax Policy.* 1988.

Rivlin, Alice M. "Distinguished Lecture on Economics and Government: Strengthening the Economy by Rethinking the Role of Federal and State Governments." *Journal of Economic Perspectives* 5, no. 2 (Spring 1991): 3–13.

Slemrod, Joel, ed. *Do Taxes Matter?* 1991.

Venti, Steven F., and David Wise. "IRAs and Saving." In *The Effects of Taxation on Capital Accumulation,* edited by Martin S. Feldstein. 1987.

Capital Gains Taxes

Joseph J. Cordes

■ A capital gain or loss is the increase or decrease in the value of an asset (a share of corporate stock, some land, a house, an artwork, etc.) from the original purchase price. For example, a share of stock bought for forty dollars and sold one year later for fifty dollars would have a capital gain of ten dollars. If the same share were sold for thirty dollars, there would be a ten-dollar capital loss.

Changes in stock prices are one of the ways in which the market recognizes changes in the profitability of businesses. If a corporation becomes more profitable—by lowering production costs, for example, or by offering new or superior products—the corporation becomes more valuable and its stock price increases, resulting in capital gains for shareholders. Similarly, when a region of the country grows rapidly, rising demand for land and housing pushes up land and housing prices, providing capital gains to property owners. The opposite happens to share prices of corporations that become less profitable, or to land and housing prices in declining regions.

Capital gains and losses often are associated with risky investments. Investors in new businesses generally do not expect to earn dividend or interest payments. Rather, they hope to reap a capital gain from the increase in value of their initial stake in the company. Such investors may also suffer capital losses if the new venture is unprofitable.

The tax treatment of capital gains has recently attracted much political attention. Most people believe that if income is to be taxed, it follows that capital gains and losses should be treated like other forms of income in determining taxable income. Therefore, this logic goes, in arriving at a measure of a person's income, capital gains should be added to other sources of income, and capital losses should be subtracted.

But capital gains pose some nettlesome problems for the tax collector. One is how to treat capital gains and losses that exist on paper but are not actually "realized" into cash through sale of the asset. Another is what to do about changes in the asset values that reflect inflation of all prices instead of changes in the real value of assets. Economists and lawyers who specialize in taxation generally agree that a comprehensive measure of real income would include all capital gains and losses accrued during the relevant accounting period (e.g., one year), whether or not the underlying asset is sold. At the same time, taxable income should exclude inflationary gains that are due to price-level changes.

In practice the actual tax treatment of capital gains in industrial countries varies widely. Most countries tax capital gains much more lightly than the United States. Belgium, Italy, and the Netherlands exempt all capital gains from taxation, and Germany exempts capital gains on assets held for six months or more. Canada and Japan tax capital gains at lower rates than other income. France's tax rate on both short- and long-term gains is only 16 percent and is levied only on capital gains in excess of F272,000 (about $47,000). In many of these countries, however, other forms of income, such as wages and salaries, are taxed more heavily than in the United States.

Capital gains have been taxable in the United States since the enactment of the federal income tax in 1922. Several features of the tax on capital gains have remained constant throughout this period. Only capital gains and losses realized through the sale of an asset, not unrealized "paper" gains and losses, are recognized for tax purposes. The dollar amount of a taxable capital gain or loss is not adjusted for inflation. This means that some of the apparent capital gains that are taxed are actually phantom gains: they do not represent real gains in purchasing power. Also, capital losses are deductible in full against capital gains, but if the investor has no capital gains, the deduction for capital losses is limited to three thousand dollars per year. Lastly, capital gains held until death are not taxed at all (though the asset is subject to estate taxes).

The tax rate on capital gains has varied considerably over the years. The maximum tax rate on capital gains has ranged from a high of 49.1 percent in 1978 to a low of 20 percent between 1981 and 1986. Presently, the maximum rate is 28 percent. In 1989 about one out of fourteen taxpayers reported net capital gains on their tax returns. The total amount of net capital gains reported that year was $144.3 billion.

Until 1986 the tax rate on capital gains was below the tax rate on other income. This was mainly the result of excluding a fraction of long-term capital gains from taxable income, which effectively cut the tax rate by an amount equal to the percentage excluded. From November 1978 through 1986, for example, 60 percent of capital gains was excluded from taxable income. For a taxpayer in the 30 percent tax bracket, this lowered the effective tax rate on capital gains from 30 percent to 12 percent (.30 × [1 − .60]). The tax rate on capital gains was also capped at a maximum amount for taxpayers in the highest income tax brackets. Since the Tax Reform Act of 1986, capital gains have been taxed at the same rates as other income, although the 1990 Budget Agreement capped the maximum tax rate on capital gains at 28 percent, while raising the top statutory rate on other income to 31 percent.

The issue of whether to cut the capital gains tax rate has been the subject of an ongoing political debate in recent years. Advocates of lower rates believe that cutting them would provide a rough adjustment for the taxation of inflationary gains, encourage people to save more by allowing them to keep more of the total return earned on saving, and make savers more willing to provide equity capital to businesses. Opponents of lowering capital gains taxes counter that inflation can be dealt with more directly by indexing capital gains for inflation. They believe there is little evidence people will save more if the return to saving rises, and that people have adequate incentives under existing tax law to supply equity capital.

Advocates of lower capital gains taxes also believe that cutting the capital gains tax rate will bring in more tax revenue rather than less. They reason as follows: Because capital gains are not taxed unless an asset is sold, investors choose when to pay the tax by deciding when to sell assets. Payment of the tax can be delayed by holding on to an asset with a capital gain, which is financially worthwhile because the amount owed in taxes remains invested in the asset and continues to earn an investment return. Payment of capital gains can be avoided altogether if an asset is held until death. After weighing the advantages of not selling, a rational investor may conclude it is better to keep an asset rather than sell it. When this happens, the capital gain becomes ''locked in.'' No tax is collected because no capital gain is realized through sale. The gain from staying locked in is greater at higher tax rates, so that the volume of capital gains that are realized falls as the tax rate rises, and vice versa.

Thus, cutting the tax rate on capital gains has two opposite effects on tax collections. On the one hand, taxing each dollar of realized capital gain at a lower rate reduces revenue. On the other hand, a lower rate means there are more dollars of realized gains to tax because people have less reason to stay locked in. Cutting tax rates on capital gains thus can reduce, leave unchanged, or increase revenue. What actually happens depends on how many additional dollars of capital gains are realized annually when the tax rate is cut.

Economists have tried to determine how responsive capital gains realizations are to changes in the capital gains tax rate. There is general agreement on four points. First, lower tax rates on capital gains will measurably increase the volume of capital gains realizations. Second, the initial response to a cut in tax rates is likely to overstate the

long-term response. There is likely to be a short-term burst of realizations right after passage of the tax rate cut, which then subsides over the long term once taxpayers have adjusted fully to the rate cut. Third, cutting the tax rate on capital gains is more likely to stimulate sales of capital assets when the original tax rate is high. Cutting the tax rate from 50 percent to 40 percent, for example, would cause a bigger increase in sales than if the rate were cut from 30 percent to 20 percent. Fourth, cutting the tax rate on capital gains is more likely to stimulate sales among taxpayers in higher tax brackets. This means that the percentage revenue loss from low-income taxpayers is likely to exceed the percentage loss from high-income taxpayers.

Economists disagree, however, about whether realizations would rise by enough to permanently counter the effects of a lower tax rate. A key magnitude is what economists call the ''elasticity'' of capital gains realizations, or the percentage change in annual realizations of capital gains that results from a given percentage change in the tax rate. Roughly speaking, realizations will change by enough or more than enough to offset the effects of changing the tax rate when this elasticity has an absolute value of 1 or more. For example, a cut in the tax rate of 10 percent leaves tax collections unchanged if realizations of taxable capital gains rise by 10 percent. If the elasticity is 0.5, realizations will rise only 5 percent in response to a 10 percent rate cut.

Statistical studies have tried to pin down the size of this elasticity, with conflicting results. Studies of the correlation between realizations and tax rates over time generally find an elasticity well below 1. An elasticity below 1 implies that a cut in tax rates on capital gains would reduce tax revenue. But studies of the correlation between realizations and tax rates of different taxpayers at the same point in time generally find values above 1. This implies that a cut in tax rates on capital gains would increase tax revenue.

The lack of agreement about elasticity is reflected in differing estimates of how proposals for cutting the tax rate on capital gains affect tax revenue. In 1989 and 1990, for example, both the Office of Tax Analysis in the Treasury Department and the Congressional Joint Committee on Taxation estimated the effects on tax collections of excluding 30 percent of capital gains from taxable income (effectively cutting the tax rate by 30 percent). After reviewing the evidence, the Treasury Department concluded that a 30 percent capital gains exclusion would increase tax collections by $12.5 billion over a five-year period. The Joint Committee on Taxation estimated that the same exclusion would reduce tax revenues by $11.4 billion over the same time period.

Though it matters whether a capital gains tax cut is scored as a revenue loser or gainer, the difference between these revenue estimates is small. Total capital gains tax collections were estimated at $300 billion over the same five years with no change in the gains tax. In other words, both sides estimated that the capital gains tax cut would keep revenues within 4 percent of the baseline.

—Joseph J. Cordes

Biography: Joseph J. Cordes is a professor and chairman of the economics department at George Washington University in Washington, D.C. From 1980 to 1981 he was a Brookings Economics Policy Fellow in the U.S. Treasury Department, Office of Tax Analysis. From 1989 to 1991, he was deputy assistant director for tax analysis in the Congressional Budget Office.

Further Reading

Auten, Gerald E., and Joseph J. Cordes. "Cutting Capital Gains Taxes." *Journal of Economic Perspectives* 5 (Winter 1991): 181–92.

Congressional Budget Office. *How Capital Gains Tax Rates Affect Revenues: The Historical Evidence*. March 1986.

U.S. Department of the Treasury, Office of Tax Analysis. *Report to the Congress on the Capital Gains Reductions of 1978*. September 1985.

A Tax on Phantom Gains?

The U.S. economy has had inflation every year since 1940, except 1949. With inflation the value of capital rises in dollar terms even if the real value remains constant. Take a stock purchased for $100 in 1980. Between 1980 and 1991, the price level, measured by the GNP price deflator, rose by about 60 percent. This means that a stock would have had to sell for $160 in 1991 to retain its 1980 value. Assume that the stock was worth $160. Then the owner's true capital gain was zero. But if he sold for $160, the IRS would have claimed that he received a capital gain of $60. If he was in a 28 percent tax bracket, he would have paid the IRS 28 percent of that phantom gain, or $16.80.

—DRH

Consumption Tax

Al Ehrbar

■ For most of the twentieth century, the principal federal tax on individuals in the United States has been on income, whether it is earned from labor (wages and salaries) or capital (interest, dividends, and capital gains). But a growing number of economists and politicians have concluded that the United States should replace the income tax—partially or entirely—with a tax on consumption.

Most of the political debate over a consumption tax has centered on whether the United States should adopt a value-added tax (VAT) similar to the ones that European countries have. While a VAT definitely is a tax on consumption, it is not the kind that most consumption-tax advocates prefer. What's more, the debate over whether to add a VAT to the U.S. tax code has obscured the more basic issue of whether to tax income or consumption.

A consumption tax—also known as an expenditures tax, consumed-income tax, or cash-flow tax—is a tax on what people spend instead of what they earn. A VAT does that in the same way that a sales tax does. But a true consumption-tax system would entail something much different from simply layering a VAT on top of the current income tax. One way to think of a consumption-tax system is simply as an income tax that allows unlimited deductions for savings and that taxes all withdrawals from savings, much like independent retirement accounts (IRAs).

Proponents of a consumption tax argue that it is superior to an income tax because it achieves what tax economists call "temporal neutrality." A tax is "neutral" if it does not alter spending habits or behavior patterns and thus does not distort the allocation of resources. No tax is completely neutral, since taxing any activity will cause people to do less of it and more of other things. For instance, the income tax creates a "tax wedge" between the value of a person's labor (what employers are willing to pay) and what the person receives (after-tax income). As a result, people work less (and choose more leisure) than they would in a world with no taxes.

The theoretical case for a consumption tax actually is a case against the income tax. Champions of a consumption tax argue that the income tax does enormous long-term damage to the economy because it penalizes thrift by taxing away part of the return to saving. This tax wedge results in less saving, less investment, less innovation, and lower living standards than we would enjoy without a tax on saving. In other words, the income tax creates a bias in favor of current consumption at the expense of saving and future consumption.

Equally important, the result is less saving than society would choose in the absence of any taxes. The "social value" of saving is the market interest rate that borrowers are willing to pay for the use of resources now. (Economists are confident this is the value to society because it is the price society has established by bidding for savings, or offering savings to borrowers, in the marketplace.) If each potential saver could collect that market interest rate, the result would be an optimal amount of saving (that is, an optimal division of resources between present and future consumption). Optimal in this sense refers to the amount of saving that individuals, deciding freely on the basis of market prices, would choose to do on their own, rather than the amount of saving that a politician, social planner, or economist thinks they ought to do. But the income tax creates a wedge: the after-tax interest that savers receive is less than the pretax market interest that borrowers pay. So we get less than the optimal amount of saving.

In contrast, a properly constructed consumption tax can be neutral between consumption and saving. That is because taxes fall only on income that is consumed, not on income that is saved. The results are that the tax wedge on saving is zero and that total saving in the economy is much closer to the optimal amount.

To see how this works, first consider what happens with the income tax to a person with $10,000 of pretax income. Assume for simplicity that the only tax bracket is 25 percent, that the market (pretax) interest rate on bonds is 5 percent, and that inflation is zero. Under the income tax, the individual pays $2,500 in taxes no matter what he does, and then can consume $7,500 of goods and services now. Or he can save $7,500, investing it in bonds paying 5 percent interest. In the first year the individual earns $375 interest (5 percent of $7,500), pays 25 percent of that ($93.75) in taxes, and is left with $281.25 of after-tax interest income. Added to his original $7,500, he now can consume $7,781.25 of goods and services, or 3.75 percent more than a year ago. Note that the market paid the individual 5 percent to postpone consumption. But the income tax reduced what he received to 3.75 percent.

Now look at what happens under a consumption tax. If the individual consumes all his income, he pays the same $2,500 in taxes and has the same $7,500 to spend on goods and services. But if he saves all his income, he can invest $10,000 because he gets a deduction for all income saved. In the first year he earns $500 interest (5 percent of $10,000), leaving him with $10,500. If he wants to spend all of that now, he must pay taxes equal to 25 percent of the full $10,500, or $2,625. That is because all withdrawals from savings are taxable. After paying his taxes, the individual can consume $7,875 of goods and services. That is 5 percent more than the $7,500 he could have consumed a year earlier. The individual receives the full 5 percent market interest rate, and there is no tax distortion between present and future consumption.

Despite its allure of eliminating the current tax bias against saving, a true consumption tax runs into fervent opposition from some (mostly liberal) economists. The one objection to a consumption tax that is based on pure economics is that it would require a higher tax rate in order to raise the same revenue as the income tax. That is because

saved income is gone from the tax base. For this reason a consumption tax would be less neutral between work and leisure than an income tax. Advocates of a consumption tax maintain that the gains from additional saving and investment would outweigh the losses from less work effort. It is, however, impossible to know with certainty whether that is correct.

The practical objection to a consumption tax used to be that it is too complicated to monitor the amounts that people save or dissave each year. But that actually can be done quite easily, as we have learned with more than a decade of experience with IRAs. Moving to a complete consumption-tax system for the individual tax code would entail little more than allowing universal, unlimited IRAs and doing away with penalties for early withdrawals. That is, everyone would be able to contribute any amount he or she liked to an IRA or similar saving account and deduct the contribution from taxable income. Investment income would accumulate tax-free in the account, but all withdrawals, including principal, would be added to taxable income. People would not have to pay a penalty if they withdrew funds before waiting until age fifty-nine and a half, as they do now.

Another objection to a consumption tax is that it would be regressive (i.e., it would fall most heavily on those with the lowest incomes). The fear is that the tax burden would be shifted to labor because returns to saving and investments—which constitute a much larger share of income in the upper brackets—would not be taxed. That is partly true. IRAs, for example, have precisely the effect of making returns to saving tax-free. The objection, however, ignores two facts: income from existing capital would be tax exempt only if it was saved, and labor income that was saved would get the same exemption.

A similar objection is that people higher up the income spectrum save a larger portion of their incomes, and so would get a disproportionate share of the benefits from deducting IRA contributions. Advocates of a consumption tax respond with the argument that the middle class would have more parity with the wealthy than under the current system. As it stands now, people with substantial assets can let unrealized capital gains accrue untaxed (see CAPITAL GAINS TAXES), while wages and savings-account interest are taxed immediately.

Some supporters of a consumption tax actually see it as more equitable than the income tax. William Andrews, a Harvard law professor, makes the argument that taxing income—whether from labor or capi-

tal—taxes people on the basis of what they contribute to society. Taxing consumption, he argues, taxes what they take out.

IRAs were extremely popular during the eighties, when anyone could make deductible contributions to them of up to two thousand dollars a year. As attention has focused on the need for more saving and capital formation in the United States, bipartisan support for restoration of universal IRAs has been building in Congress. In addition, former President Bush and others have endorsed the idea of other special IRA-like savings accounts for such things as buying a first home and financing a college education. While a full consumption-tax system seems unlikely, there is a good chance that Congress will liberalize IRA rules again in the nineties.

—Al Ehrbar

Biography: Al Ehrbar is a journalist who writes about the economy for *The Wall Street Journal*. He has been a senior editor of *Fortune* magazine and editor of *Corporate Finance* magazine.

Corporate Taxation

Rob Norton

■ The corporate income tax is the most poorly understood of all the major methods by which the United States government collects money. Most economists concluded long ago that it is among the least efficient and least defensible of taxes. They have trouble agreeing on—much less measuring with any precision—who actually bears the burden of the corporate income tax, but there is wide agreement that it causes significant distortions in economic behavior. The tax is popular with the man in the street, who believes, incorrectly, that it is paid by corporations. Owners and managers of corporations often assume, just as incorrectly, that it is simply passed along to consumers. This very vagueness about who pays the tax accounts for its continued popularity among politicians.

The federal corporate income tax differs from the individual income tax in two major ways. First, it is a tax not on gross income, but on net income or profits, with permissible deductions for most costs of doing business. Second, it applies only to some businesses—those chartered as corporations—and not to partnerships or sole proprietorships. The federal tax is levied at three different rates on different brackets of income: 15 percent on taxable income under $50,000; 25 percent on income between $50,000 and $75,000; and 34 percent on income above that. The lower-bracket rates are beneficial to small corporations. Of the 3.2 million corporate tax returns filed in one

recent year, more than 90 percent were from corporations with assets of less than $1 million. The lower rates, however, had little economic significance. Nearly 94 percent of all corporate tax revenue came from the 8.8 percent of corporations with assets greater than $1 million.

States levy further income taxes on corporations, at rates ranging from 3 percent to 11.5 percent. Because states typically permit deductions for federal taxes paid, net rates range from 1.9 percent to 4.9 percent. Some localities tax corporations as well. A good reason that state and local corporate income taxes remain low is that corporations could easily relocate out of states that imposed unusually high taxes.

How the corporate income tax arose and how it has survived over the decades is a case study of the perniciousness of bad ideas, of why tax systems are often so much worse than they need be, and of how little influence the economics profession has over government policy. Except for emergency taxes in wartime, corporate profits were first taxed in 1909, when Congress enacted a 1 percent tax on corporation income. The rate had risen to 12.5 percent a decade later, and progressive rates were added in 1932. Surtaxes on corporate income were added for "excess profits" and "war profits" during both world wars. The highest peacetime rate, 52.8 percent, was reached in the sixties.

In the forties and early fifties the corporate income tax provided about a third of federal revenues, and as recently as 1966, the proportion was 23 percent. It declined steadily for the next twenty years, reaching a nadir of 6.2 percent in 1983. This was partly by design. The top corporate tax rates fell from 52.8 percent in 1969 to 46 percent in 1979. During much of that time, tax law permitted relatively generous deductions for capital expenditures, either through accelerated depreciation schedules or through such devices as investment tax credits, so that the average tax rate paid by corporations fell even more sharply. Recent research has found that an equally important reason for the relative decline in corporate tax revenue is that U.S. corporations became less profitable. Corporate profits as a percentage of corporate assets, which averaged nearly 11 percent during the sixties, were less than 5 percent from 1981 through 1985.

The Tax Reform Act of 1986 was designed to increase the share of federal revenues collected via the corporate income tax and to decrease the share from the individual income tax. While the top corporate tax rate, like the individual rate, was cut—to 34 percent—deductions for capital expenditures were severely curtailed, and the investment tax credit was repealed. As a result the effective tax rate for many corporations rose. The effort was somewhat successful. Corporate taxes as a share of total federal receipts climbed back to more than 10 percent in 1988 and 1989.

The central problem with the corporate income tax from an economic point of view is that, ultimately, only people can pay taxes. Economists have had great difficulty in assessing the incidence of the corporate tax—that is, on which groups of people the burden falls. As early as the seventeenth century, Sir William Petty, one of the progenitors of modern economics, argued that a tax on the production and sale of commodities would eventually be shifted by producers to consumers, who would pay it in the form of higher prices. Later classical economists disagreed, contending that the tax fell on owners, making it, in effect, a tax on capital. They thought it could not be shifted since, theoretically, a corporation already charging prices that produce maximum profits could not increase prices further without reducing the amount of its goods that people demanded.

Modern research has returned, in part, to Petty's view. A tax on corporate income will cause some firms to leave the business. This reduces the demand for labor, which reduces wages and reduces the supply of goods produced by corporations. With the supply of goods reduced, prices rise. Thus, part of the corporate income tax is paid by shareholders, part by workers through lower wages and fewer jobs, and part by consumers through higher prices.

Other than a general agreement that the corporate income tax has ramifications throughout the economy, economists have made little progress in measuring its incidence with any precision. Even if the basic problem were solved, such an exercise would need to allow for all the special provisions in the corporate tax code in order to measure the effects of the corporate tax in combination with all other taxes, and to assess the effects of international capital movements. Finally, any econometric approach seeking to measure the shifting of the corporate tax burden as a result of tax changes must first isolate the tax effects from the myriad nontax factors affecting business.

From an efficiency standpoint, however, most economists agree that the corporate income tax has two major flaws. First, it penalizes the corporate form of business organization because income is taxed first at the corporate level and then again when paid to stockholders as dividends. A traditional justification for singling out corporations is that they receive special benefits from the state and should pay for them. One problem with this rationale is that if it were true, then all corporations, not just profitable ones, should pay. Another problem is that current corporate tax rates seem disproportionately high for this purpose. But the fundamental problem with this traditional justification is that it harks back to the eighteenth century, when a corporate charter carried with it state-granted privileges such as monopoly power or exemption from specific laws. Today corporations are created by private contract, with the government acting merely as registry and tax collector.

Recent experience shows this disincentive to the corporate form of organization at work. U.S. companies with thirty-five or fewer shareholders can elect what is called Subchapter S status. So-called S corporations have taxable income passed through to the tax returns of the owners, as in a partnership, instead of paying the corporate income tax. In the five weeks surrounding year-end 1986, after enactment of the tax reform bill, which raised the effective rate of corporate taxes, 225,000 companies elected Subchapter S status, compared with 75,000 for all of 1985.

The second major flaw in the corporate income tax is that it misallocates capital by favoring the issuance of debt over equity, because interest payments are tax deductible while dividend payments are not. This favors investments in assets more readily financed by debt, such as buildings and structures (which can be used for many purposes and thus are more easily used as collateral for loans) over investments more logically financed by stock, such as specialized equipment or research and development. In addition, the deductibility of interest payments favors established companies over start-ups, because the former can more easily issue debt securities. Some economists, focusing on this last phenomenon, have argued that this feature makes the corporate income tax a tax on entrepreneurship. During the eighties U.S. corporations issued huge amounts of new debt. Corporate bonds outstanding increased from less than $500 billion outstanding in 1980 to $1.4 trillion in 1988. At the same time, many corporations reduced their outstanding equity by buying back their own shares. The increased emphasis on debt financing in the United States was much more pronounced than elsewhere.

The corporate income tax has survived all efforts to reform, repeal, or replace it, and there is little reason to expect a change in the near future. The simplest fix would be to equalize the treatment of interest and dividends, either by allowing corporations to deduct dividends or by granting an offsetting deduction or credit to stockholders. Most other large industrialized nations use the latter method. A more far-reaching reform, one recommended by economists for decades, would be to completely integrate the corporate and individual income taxes.

One way to do this would be to treat corporations as partnerships for tax purposes (that is, treat all corporations like S corporations), imputing all the profits to shareholders and taxing them under the individual income tax. The chief objection to this approach is that stockholders would face a tax liability for profits not distributed as dividends by the corporation. Several integration schemes have been proposed and rejected in the past.

The arguments in favor of leaving the corporate income tax alone are politically compelling. For one thing, the tax has a proven ability to raise revenue, an important consideration for a nation that has run chronic budget deficits. For another, the old aphorism that "an old tax is a good tax" has some validity. Any major change in the tax code changes expectations and imposes new costs and complications during the transition period. But the most compelling rationale for the corporate income tax is the difficulty in assessing its incidence. Since no political constituency sees itself as the primary payer of the tax, none is willing to lobby aggressively for change. Indeed, the art of taxation, as seventeenth-century French administrator Jean-Baptiste Colbert reportedly said, "consists in so plucking the goose as to obtain the largest possible amount of feathers with the smallest possible amount of hissing." Judged by this standard, the corporate income tax has worked well.

—**Rob Norton**

Biography: Rob Norton is an associate editor of *Fortune* magazine.

Further Reading

Eden, Lorraine, ed. *Retrospectives in Public Finance*. 1991.
Musgrave, Richard A., and Peggy B. Musgrave. *Public Finance in Theory and Practice*. 1989.
National Bureau of Economic Research. *Tax Policy and the Economy*. Vols. 1–5. 1987–91.
Stiglitz, Joseph E. *Economics of the Public Sector*. 1988.

Marginal Tax Rates

Alan Reynolds

■ The marginal tax rate is the rate on the last dollar of income earned. This is very different from the average tax rate, which is the total taxes paid as a percentage of total income earned. The seemingly arcane topic of marginal tax rates became the central theme of a revolution in economic policy that swept the globe in the eighties. By the end of the decade, more than fifty nations had significantly reduced their highest marginal tax rates (most of which are shown in table 1). Neither Karl Marx nor John Maynard Keynes had so much influence on so many countries in so little time.

Several economies that seemed on the verge of bankruptcy in the early eighties were suddenly revived once marginal tax rates were reduced. In 1983 to 1984, Turkey's marginal tax rates were slashed: the minimum rate dropped from 40 to 25 percent, the maximum from 75 to 50 percent. Real economic growth jumped to nearly 7 percent in the following four years and to 9 percent in 1990. Like Turkey, South Korea was deep in debt to international banks in 1980, when real output fell 2 percent. Korea subsequently cut tax rates and expanded deductions three times, and economic growth averaged 9.3 percent a year from 1981 to 1989. In the early eighties the African island of Mauritius faced an unemployment rate of 23 percent and massive emigration. Tax rates were cut from 60 percent to 35 percent, and the economy grew by 5.4 percent a year from 1981 through 1987. Egypt,

Jamaica, Colombia, Chile, Bolivia, and Mexico had similar experiences after slashing marginal tax rates.

The same pattern was repeated in most major industrial countries. Economic growth in Britain had averaged only 1.2 percent for a dozen years before tax rates were cut in 1984 and 1986. The British economy subsequently grew by 4 percent a year from 1985 to 1989. Economic growth in Japan from 1983 to 1987 had slowed to 3.9 percent—slower than the 4.3 percent growth in the United States. Japan cut higher tax rates by 15 to 20 percent in 1988, and economic growth and investment subsequently boomed. Even in the roaring eighties, economic growth had slipped to around 1.5 percent in Belgium, Austria, and the Netherlands before each country cut marginal tax rates. In the first year or two of tax reform, economic growth jumped to 4 percent in Austria, 4.1 percent in the Netherlands, and 4.3 percent in Belgium. The economies of Canada and West Germany likewise experienced brief booms when tax rates were reduced in 1988 and 1989 respectively, but Canada slipped into recession in early 1990 after reversing course with surtaxes and a new sales tax. Germany likewise added surtaxes and sales tax in mid-1991, with immediate adverse effects on the stock market and the value of its currency.

Despite widespread adoption of such policies, few seem to understand what mar-

TABLE 1

Maximum Marginal Tax Rates
on Individual Income

	1979	1990		1979	1990
Argentina	45	30	Italy	72	50
Australia	62	47	Jamaica	58	33
Austria	62	50	Japan	75	50
Belgium	76	55	Korea (South)	89	50
Bolivia	48	10	Malaysia	60	45
Botswana	75	50	Mauritius	50	35
Brazil	55	25	Mexico	55	35
Canada (Ontario)	58	47	Netherlands	72	60
Chile	60	50	New Zealand	60	33
Colombia	56	30	Norway	75	54
Denmark	73	68	Pakistan	55	45
Egypt	80	65	Philippines	70	35
Finland	71	43	Portugal	84	40
France	60	53	Puerto Rico	79	43
Germany (West)	56	53	Singapore	55	33
Greece	60	50	Spain	66	56
Guatemala	40	34	Sweden	87	65
Hungary	60	50	Thailand	60	55
India	60	50	Trinidad and Tobago	70	35
Indonesia	50	35	Turkey	75	50
Iran	90	75	United Kingdom	83	40
Ireland	65	56	United States	70	33
Israel	66	48			

SOURCE: *Price Waterhouse; International Bureau of Fiscal Documentation.*

ginal tax rates are and why they matter. In the United States, for example, it is commonly believed that the Reagan administration "slashed taxes," particularly for "the rich." Actually, real (that is, inflation-adjusted) federal receipts increased by one-third from 1980 to 1990. Moreover, the most affluent 5 percent of all taxpayers paid 45.9 percent of all federal income taxes in 1988—up from 37.6 percent in 1979. Apparent "tax cuts"—from a top marginal rate of 70 percent to 33 percent—became actual tax increases, particularly for "the rich." The explanation for this paradox lies in the critical distinctions between average and marginal tax rates, and between "static" effects right now and "dynamic" effects over years and decades. Dynamic effects include increased intensity and motivation of work effort, more efficient investment, and more innovation and risk taking.

Measuring the taxes that governments collect as a percentage of GNP, for example, is too static. It ignores the destructive effect that steep marginal rates have on both tax collections and GNP. Several African countries attempt to impose marginal tax rates of 60 to 85 percent on people whose income is equivalent to the U.S. poverty line. Yet receipts from such demoralizing income tax systems are usually less than 1 percent of GNP. Productive activity ceases, moves abroad, or vanishes into inefficient little "underground" enterprises. Taxes on sales, imports, payrolls, and profits also reduce the after-tax rewards to added investment and effort, of course. And just as "tax havens" attract foreign investment and immigrants, countries in which the combined marginal impact of taxes is to punish success invariably face "capital flight" and a "brain drain."

In the United States the concept of marginal tax rates is most familiar as tax brackets. Rapid inflation in the seventies pushed many skilled working couples up into the 50 percent tax bracket (then the highest rate on labor income). That did not mean that all of their income was taxed at a 50 percent rate. Instead, the first ten thousand dollars or so might be taxed at a 12 percent rate, the next ten thousand at a higher rate, and so on. Once the 50 percent bracket was

reached, though, the federal government really did expect to collect half of any additional earnings. Average federal income taxes—taxes divided by income—have rarely been much more than 25 percent even for the superrich, even when (in the fifties) marginal tax brackets rose as high as 90 percent. By keeping average taxes the same, while reducing marginal tax rates, it is possible to encourage people to earn and report more income. This is a "revenue neutral" tax reform, like the one in 1986.

The marginal tax on added earnings matters because it is easier to earn less than to earn more. To increase income, people have to study more, accept added risks and responsibilities, relocate, work late or take work home, tackle the dangers of starting a new business or investing in one, and so on. People earn more by producing more and better goods and services. If the tax system punishes added income, it must also punish added output—that is, economic growth.

Some economists used to argue that the incentive effect of lower marginal tax rates is ambiguous. Perhaps, they said, people will simply use the "tax cut" to enjoy more leisure, living just as well by working less. This argument again confuses average with marginal tax rates. With a "revenue neutral" cut in marginal tax rates, taxpayers do not automatically receive the increase in after-tax income that is alleged to make them work less. Since average tax rates remain unchanged, the only way to get this added income is to work harder and produce more.

More and more, theoretical and factual research on the sources of both long-term economic growth and short-term disturbances (recessions) has pointed to the level and variation of marginal tax rates. A comparison of sixty-three countries by Reinhard Koester and Roger Kormendi found that "holding average tax rates constant, a 10 percentage point reduction in marginal tax rates would yield a 15.2 percent increase in per capita income for LDCs [less developed countries]."

In 1990 Harvard economist Robert Barro and Paul Romer, then at the University of Chicago, surveyed the latest studies for the year-end report from the National Bureau of Economic Research. "Recent work on growth," they explained, "extends neoclassical markets so that all economic improvement can be traced to actions taken by people who respond to incentives." This approach leads to "very different predictions about how such policy variables as taxes can influence growth. . . . If government taxes or [regulatory] distortions discourage the activity that generates growth, growth will be slower."

What began in the early seventies as a topic that interested only a few quiet specialists in "optimal taxation," and a few noisy "supply-side" economists proposing a remedy for chronic stagflation, has now filtered into several textbooks—such as those written by Robert Barro and by James Gwartney and Richard Stroup. After decades of compulsive tinkering with budgets and money supplies to "manage demand," much of the world has rediscovered an insight as old as economics itself—namely, that cutting marginal tax rates encourages supply.

—Alan Reynolds

Biography: Alan Reynolds is director of economic research at the Hudson Institute in Indianapolis.

Further Reading

Barro, Robert. "Taxes and Transfers." In Barro, *Macroeconomics*. 1987.

Davies, David G. *United States Tax Policy*. 1986.

Koester, Reinhard B., and Roger C. Kormendi. "Taxation, Aggregate Activity and Economic Growth: Cross Country Evidence on Some Supply-Side Hypotheses." *Economic Inquiry* 27 (July 1989): 367–86.

McKenzie, Richard B., and Dwight R. Lee. *Quicksilver Capital*. Chap. 6. 1991.

Reynolds, Alan. "Some International Comparisons of Supply-Side Tax Policy." *Cato Journal* 5 (Fall 1985): 543–69.

Negative Income Tax

Jodie T. Allen

■ The idea of a negative income tax (NIT) is commonly thought to have originated with economist Milton Friedman, who advocated it in his 1962 book, *Capitalism and Freedom*. Others, notably the late Joseph Pechman, long-time tax dean of the Brookings Institution, credited the University of Wisconsin's Robert Lampman with at least simultaneous discovery and with bringing the concept to the attention of government policy planners in 1965.

In its purest form a NIT promised a revolution in American social policy. Gone would be the intrusive and costly welfare bureaucracy, the pernicious distinctions between "worthy" and "unworthy" recipients, the perverse disincentives for work effort and family formation. The needy would, like everyone else, simply file annual—or perhaps quarterly—income returns with the Internal Revenue Service. But unlike other filers who would make payments to the IRS, based on the amount by which their incomes exceeded the threshold for tax liability, NIT beneficiaries would receive payments ("negative taxes") from the IRS, based on how far their incomes fell below the tax threshold.

The NIT would thus be a mirror image of the regular tax system. Instead of tax liabilities varying positively with income according to a tax rate schedule, benefits would vary inversely with income according to a negative tax rate (or benefit-reduction) schedule. If, for example, the

threshold for positive tax liability for a family of four was, say, $10,000, a family with only $8,000 of annual income would, given a negative tax rate of 25 percent, receive a check from the Treasury worth $500 (25 percent of the $2,000 difference between its $8,000 income and the $10,000 threshold). A family with zero income would receive $2,500.

Very neat. So attractive that researchers in the Office of Economic Opportunity, the brain trust for Lyndon Johnson's Great Society in the midsixties, began planning a large-scale field experiment of the idea. Several sites in New Jersey were ultimately selected for the test, which was launched in 1968 with the University of Wisconsin's Institute for Research on Poverty in charge of the research and a Princeton-based firm, Mathematica Inc., in charge of field operations and data collection.

The primary purpose of the experiment was to address the concerns of labor-supply theorists. These labor economists worried that providing the working poor with a basic income guarantee if they quit work, and then reducing that guarantee at a fairly steep rate as income from work increased would damage work incentives and ultimately swell NIT costs. They feared that NIT would reduce work effort in two ways. First, by giving a family with no outside income a guaranteed minimum income, NIT might, at the extreme, discourage family members from working at all. And even if workers didn't quit entirely, they might work less since they could satisfy their basic needs with less work effort. Economists call this an income effect. Second, by reducing benefits some fraction of a dollar for every dollar earned, NIT would, along with payroll and state and local income taxes, reduce the net value of wages and induce recipients to "substitute" leisure for work. Economists call this a substitution effect.

Using a complicated model intended to minimize program costs for a given sample design, the New Jersey experimenters set out to measure the strength of these two effects. Potential participants were assigned to a variety of "treatment" cells, with the treatment being a particular combination of basic guarantee and negative tax rate. The sample included a "control" group of families not eligible for any experimental payments. Thus, a treatment might offer a guarantee equal to half the poverty line, which was then about $8,000 for a family of four, with benefits being reduced by 50 percent of the family's income. When income was zero, the family would receive the full $4,000 (50 percent of $8,000). When income reached $8,000, the benefit would be reduced to zero and the family would "break even" (i.e., neither receive negative taxes nor pay positive taxes).

The experimenters—and the planners in what was then called the Department of Health, Education, and Welfare (myself included) who drew upon their work in designing President Richard Nixon's Family Assistance Plan of 1969 (FAP)—quickly encountered a host of problems, both conceptual and administrative. These continue to haunt negative tax advocates to this day.

The first and most basic problem is that

it is currently fiscally—and perhaps administratively—impossible to construct an NIT that simultaneously

1. provides an income guarantee as generous as the cash and in-kind benefits already available to many welfare recipients in the United States,
2. provides an ostensible incentive to work (a far greater concern when benefits are to be extended beyond the traditional welfare population dominated by female-headed families), and
3. restricts coverage to any manageable proportion of the population—the so-called "break-even" problem.

These constraints are, in fact, irreconcilable as long as the median income remains within striking distance of the poverty line—a situation that has barely improved over the last two decades of slow average economic growth.

The McGovern plan proposed by the Democrats' 1972 presidential candidate starkly illustrated this problem. With a guarantee determined by the candidate's promise of $1,000 per person, and a benefit reduction rate limited to 33⅓ percent at the behest of economic advisers worried about imposing work disincentives on a sizable proportion of the labor force, the plan had a break-even of $12,000 for a family of four—roughly the median income at the time. Thus, it would have converted roughly half the population into federal tax beneficiaries while the other half of the population would have paid for these transfers along with the cost of all other federal activities.

The second problem with a NIT is that

the welfare system already provides a package of cash and in-kind benefits that, in many states, is worth considerably more than any likely NIT (though at the cost of excluding large groups of the poor—such as two-parent families—from eligibility). Political and humanitarian considerations prevent reducing these benefits, thus vitiating one of the NIT's attractions—the possibility of abolishing the welfare system.

Competition from welfare was a severe problem for the New Jersey experimenters. Many of the families in the study were actually receiving welfare benefits worth more than the experimental payments. Therefore, some experts questioned the experimenters' findings that the NIT had only a minimal effect on work incentives, and indeed questioned whether the experiment had really measured anything at all. HEW attempted to solve these problems by launching subsequent income-maintenance experiments in Seattle and Denver (SIME/DIME). These experiments more carefully integrated existing welfare programs and offered more generous NIT plans. But the generosity of most of the tested plans made them unlikely to be replicated on a national scale, and more complicated to analyze.

The Stanford Research Institute (SRI), which analyzed the SIME/DIME findings, found stronger work disincentive effects, ranging from an average 9 percent work reduction for husbands to an average 18 percent reduction for wives. This was not as scary as some NIT opponents had predicted. But it was large enough to suggest that as much as 50 to 60 percent of the transfers paid to two-parent families under a NIT might go to replace lost earnings. They also found an unexpected result: instead of promoting family stability (the presumed result of extending benefits to two-parent working families on an equal basis), the NITs seemed to increase family breakup.

The SRI researchers—Michael T. Hannah, Nancy B. Tuma, and Lyle P. Groeneveld—hypothesized that the availability of the income guarantee to some families reduced the pressure on the breadwinner to remain with the family, while the benefit-reduction rate also reduced the value to the family of keeping a wage earner in the unit. Other researchers, notably the University of Wisconsin's Glen G. Cain, disputed the analytical strength of these findings. But at the very least the results were discouraging to those who promoted an NIT as a boon to family stability.

A third set of problems is administrative. One is the matter of the appropriate income-accounting period, which spawned a whole literature (to which I contributed my share). If income for NIT purposes is measured over a year, as in the positive tax system, families in great, but temporary, need may be denied benefits. If the accounting period is shorter, say a month, as in the welfare system, and income reporting procedures are lax, potential costs and caseloads might be as much as 70 percent higher than those predicted by the annual income–based models used to estimate the costs of FAP and its early successors.

The income accounting and reporting analysis—backed up by an HEW administrative experiment in cooperation with the Denver welfare department—also drew attention to the fact that many negative tax participants cheat on income reports. To be sure, many taxpayers cheat too. But the irregularity of income sources and shifting family arrangements at the lower end of the distribution make it unlikely that the IRS could prevent widespread fraud unless it converted itself into a facsimile of the much-detested local welfare offices.

Some indication of the difficulty that the IRS might experience in administering a large-scale NIT is provided by the Earned Income Credit (EIC), a hybrid version of an NIT that was slipped into the tax code in 1975 by Finance Committee Chairman Russell Long. Long saw it as a way to offset the regressive effect of payroll taxes on low-income earners. The EIC works like this (using 1993 rules for a family with one qualifying child): For every dollar of earned income, the family receives a refundable tax credit of 18.5 percent, up to a maximum credit of $1,434 (not including additional credits for young children and health insurance costs) for a family with earnings of $7,750. The credit is phased out at a rate of 13.21 cents for every dollar of adjusted gross income (AGI) above $12,200, until it reaches a zero value for a family with AGI of $23,050.

One attraction of the EIC is that because its benefits rise positively with earnings up to the phase-out point, it has a positive rather than negative effect on work incentives for workers earning a very low income. In the phase-out range, however, its substitution effects are identical to those of a comparable NIT. More important, a 1990 IRS study revealed that owing in part to the complexity of the EIC rules, almost 40 percent of EIC benefits were paid to families who were not eligible for them. Yet the finding of such a high error rate did not deter

Congress from both enlarging and further complicating the EIC in the fall of 1990.

To these problems must be added the messy reality of the day-to-day stresses and strains of many of America's poor. Data from another HEW experiment revealed that many of the low-income population's problems are not readily addressed by the provision of an extra few hundred dollars in annual income. Indeed, recent revisionist social welfare thinking has questioned the central premise of the NIT planners—that a nonintrusive income-maintenance system is preferable. More recent policy has stressed direct interventions to improve family functioning and self-reliance, including eligibility rules that require work effort.

Nonetheless, the NIT is still popular among many researchers and politicians. Nixon's FAP, which compromised with both the conceptual and administrative problems by essentially retaining the current welfare system and grafting on to it a low-level income-maintenance benefit for the working poor, pleased neither academics nor welfare advocates. Nor did it please the big-city mayors and governors, who looked at welfare reform as primarily a way to reduce their share of the system's cost. (Sen. Daniel P. Moynihan's *Politics of a Guaranteed Income,* is the definitive text on this point.) The Ford administration floated a reworked version of FAP, but it foundered on the same concerns as FAP.

President Jimmy Carter set out to develop a welfare reform that would have zero additional cost. Although Carter's plan emphasized work alternatives to welfare, HEW's analysts quickly shifted the emphasis to a more generous reworking of the FAP concept. Forced to compromise with analysts at the Department of Labor—myself, by then, included—who were promoting a low-wage guaranteed job approach, the reformers ended up with the unwieldy Better Jobs and Income Plan (BJIP), which would have cost many billions more and pleased neither liberals nor conservatives in Congress.

The Reagan administration put its efforts into cutting back, rather than extending, income benefits, though the eighties witnessed both an expansion of earned-income tax credits and the 1988 welfare act, which tried, at so-far modest cost and effect, to direct more welfare recipients into jobs. More recently, some "middle-income tax relief" proposals floated in Congress in 1991 would convert the current positive tax personal exemption into a "refundable" credit, paid out in cash to families with incomes below the tax-liability threshold. These proposals, thus, would incorporate a full-bodied NIT into the Internal Revenue Code. The appeal of a negative income tax lives on. And so do its many problems.

—Jodie T. Allen

Biography: Jodie T. Allen is editor of the *Washington Post*'s "Sunday Outlook" section. Before joining the *Post* in 1980, she worked in several government departments and research institutions, analyzing costs and consequences of tax, transfer, and defense programs.

Further Reading

Allen, Jodie T. *Designing Income Maintenance Systems: The Income Accounting Problem*. 1973.
Browning, Edgar K. *Redistribution and the Welfare System*. 1975.
Friedman, Milton. *Capitalism and Freedom*. 1962.
Moynihan, Daniel P. *Politics of a Guaranteed Income*. 1973.
Munnell, Alicia H., ed. *Lessons from the Income Maintenance Experiments*. 1987.
Pechman, Joseph A., and P. Michael Timpane, eds. *Work Incentives and Income Guarantees: The New Jersey Negative Income Tax Experiment*. 1975.

Progressive Taxes

Joel B. Slemrod

■ If, as Oliver Wendell Holmes once said, taxes are the price we pay for civilized society, then the progressivity of taxes largely determines how that price varies among individuals. A progressive tax structure is one in which an individual or family's tax liability as a fraction of income rises with income. If, for example, taxes for a family with an income of $20,000 are 20 percent of income and taxes for a family with an income of $200,000 are 30 percent of income, then the tax structure over that range of incomes is progressive. One tax structure is more progressive than another if its average tax rate rises more rapidly with income.

Judged by the top income tax rates alone, tax progressivity in the United States declined markedly in the eighties. In 1980 the highest tax rate stood at 70 percent. The Economic Recovery Tax Act of 1981 reduced that rate to 50 percent, and the Tax Reform Act of 1986 further reduced it to 33 percent. Although the highest rate has since been nudged back up to around 34 percent, it is still less than half what it was in 1980. Other developed countries have emulated the United States in reducing their top rates, although usually by less.

Does the precipitous fall in the top tax rate represent a sea change in how the tax burden is distributed? No. The statutory tax rates misrepresent true progressivity for three reasons.

First, the tax base—the income that is taxed—is generally much less than total income due to a bewildering array of adjustments, deductions, omissions, and mismeasurements. Since the erosion of the tax base was more pronounced for upper-income taxpayers prior to the 1986 tax act, the tax system was much less progressive than the old tax rates implied, and possibly not progressive at all. Although the 1986 act lowered the top rate from 50 percent to 33 percent, it also eliminated the ability to exclude from taxable income 60 percent of long-term capital gains. Because capital gains comprise a large fraction of the taxable income of the most affluent taxpayers, the expansion of their tax base offset, on average, the decline in the tax rate applied to the base.

Second, the tax burden—the hurt caused by taxes—is not borne entirely by the people who write the checks to the Internal Revenue Service. To some extent many taxes are "shifted" to other members of society. For example, because highly progressive taxes discourage people from entering high-paying professions, salaries in these professions will be higher than otherwise. Therefore, the taxes paid by the upper-income taxpayers who do enter these professions overstate the true burden of taxation on them. Also burdened by these high taxes are the people who pay higher prices for the goods and services provided by the people with higher salaries.

To take another example, taxes paid by high-income people who take advantage of the federal tax exemption for interest on state and local government bonds understate their true burden. The reason is that the yield on these securities is already lower to reflect their tax-preferred status—7.25 percent for tax-exempts (according to the *Bond Buyer* municipal index) in mid-1991 compared to 9.10 percent for taxable bonds (according to the Merrill Lynch corporate bond index). The main beneficiaries of this tax exemption are not those who hold the securities, but the state and local governments that get to pay lower interest rates on the funds they borrow. Because interest from state and local government bonds was tax exempt before 1986 and still is, the tax burden for the well-to-do who hold these bonds was, and is, understated.

Third, the progressivity of the tax structure cannot be judged by looking at only one component of taxes. Federal income taxes are only about 25 percent of total revenues collected by all levels of government. In recent years the fastest-growing component of federal taxes has been the payroll tax, which is regressive (the opposite of progressive) in its impact, because it taxes at a flat rate only on wages below $63,400 (in 1991). The Social Security system, however, is progressive because it pays higher benefits—relative to taxes paid in—to lower-income workers.

Chart 1 illustrates the progressivity of the overall U.S. tax system in 1985 (the latest year for which this information is available), according to two different assumptions about the shifting of taxes. Under assumption A the average tax rate generally increased with income, suggesting a generally progressive tax. Under assumption B the average tax rate actually is lowest for families in the highest income decile. The key difference between the two results is that B assumes that half of the corporation income tax is shifted to consumers, in the form of higher prices, while A assumes that all of it is borne by shareholders, who are generally high-income taxpayers. Chart 1 illustrates both the importance of the shifting assumptions and the fact that, even though the federal income tax by itself is progressive, its progressivity is overwhelmed by less progressive levies such as sales taxes and, to a lesser extent, the payroll tax.

How progressive should income taxes be? The answer depends on prosaic issues like how taxpayers respond to high tax rates, and on profound issues like the proper role of government and how society should value a dollar in the hands of a low-income family versus a dollar in the hands of an upper-income family.

Traditionally, economists have taken three different approaches to this question. Under the benefit principle, taxes are thought of as a payment for services rendered by the government to individuals. Under this principle, revenue ought to be raised where possible by user fees. While this is a sensible policy for admission to national parks, it is not a feasible approach to financing other government activities such as national defense. It begs the question of how to measure the benefits any given taxpayer gains from such publicly provided goods as defense or the criminal justice system. Although the more affluent benefit more from the protection of that affluence, the precise relationship between their benefit and their income or wealth is undeterminable. Interestingly, reliance on

TAXES

CHART 1

Effective Tax Rate by Income Decile, 1985

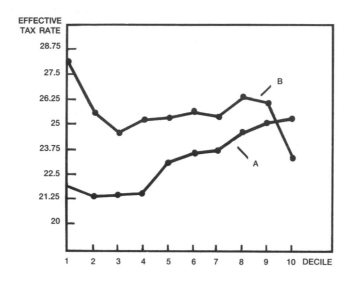

SOURCE: *Graph from Stiglitz, p. 348, based on Pechman, 1985.*

the benefit principle would prohibit the government from transferring wealth from one group to another. It therefore undermines the case for the welfare system and the vast number of other government programs whose explicit objective is to redistribute resources.

Under the ability-to-pay principle, tax burdens should be related not to what taxpayers receive from government, but rather to their ability to bear the tax burden—that is, to tolerate a sacrifice. Reasoning from the plausible, but unprovable, idea that paying a dollar is a lesser sacrifice for a well-to-do person than for a poor person, an equal sacrifice requires higher tax payments from the well-to-do person. But as with the bene-

fit principle, this reasoning does not point to a particular relationship between income and tax burden. A proportionate tax, whereby everyone pays the same percent of income, would take more from the rich person than from the poor person. Even a regressive tax, with everyone paying 25 percent on the first $20,000 of income, and 10 percent on all additional income, would take more from the rich than from the poor. Yet under other assumptions about sacrifice, a steeply progressive tax system is appropriate.

Under the utilitarian principle, tax burdens should be assigned to maximize social welfare. The nineteenth-century economist Francis Edgeworth showed that if from society's perspective a dollar is valued less as the income of the recipient rises, then social welfare would be maximized by a tax system that leveled all incomes, taxing away all income above a certain level and distributing the proceeds to those whose incomes would otherwise fall below the cutoff income. The problem, of course, is that a leveling tax system would destroy the incentive to work, save, invest, and innovate, so that the size of the economic pie to be divided equally would rapidly shrink.

The modern theory of optimal income tax progressivity begins with the utilitarian principle, but views the issue as a trade-off between the social benefits of a more equal distribution of after-tax income and the economic damage imposed by highly progressive taxes. The social benefits of equality are not a matter that economists can resolve—they are better left to the theologians and philosophers to debate. But the economic costs of progressive tax rates are, in principle, knowable, and economists have invested much effort in knowing. As of 1980 many prominent economists (such as Michael Boskin, later President Bush's chief economic adviser, and Harvard's Martin Feldstein) were arguing that these costs were quite high, and concluded that the tax system at the time was probably too progressive.

After a decade featuring two major tax changes, many economists now doubt that tax policy has much effect on investment or saving. Alan Auerbach of the University of Pennsylvania has concluded that the 1986 tax changes played a relatively unimportant role in explaining the level and especially the pattern of investment in equipment and structures since then. Also, the personal saving rate declined steadily from 1980 to 1987, despite lowered tax rates on the return to saving and liberalized IRAs, and began to recover in 1987, soon after new restrictions were put on IRA eligibility.

But according to Brookings economists Barry Bosworth and Gary Burtless, the reductions in marginal tax rates did cause a modest increase in labor supply of a magnitude that had been predicted in 1980 by mainstream economists. Bosworth and Burtless found that men between the ages of 25 and 64 worked 5.2 percent more hours than would have been predicted on the basis of past trends, that women age 25 and 64 work 5.8 percent more, and that married women worked 8.8 percent more. They conclude that tax policy was probably not the dominant factor influencing labor supply over the decade. One reason for their cautious conclusion about the role of tax cuts is that lower-income men increased their labor supply by a large amount even though their marginal tax rates were constant or even rising until 1987.

Also, upper-income taxpayers responded to sharply lower tax rates by changing the timing of their asset sales and by abandoning financial stratagems such as tax shelters that were attractive only because of the special tax treatment they were given. So marginal tax rates do matter, but perhaps not as much or not in the same way as many economists thought in 1980.

—Joel B. Slemrod

Biography: Joel B. Slemrod is an economics professor at the University of Michigan, and director of the Office of Tax Policy Research at the Michigan Business School. He was senior economist for tax policy in President Reagan's Council of Economic Advisers.

Further Readings

Pechman, Joseph A. *Who Paid the Taxes, 1966–1985?* 1985.
Slemrod, Joel B., ed. *Do Taxes Matter? The Impact of the Tax Reform Act of 1986.* 1990.
———. "Do We Know How Progressive the Income Tax System Should Be?" *National Tax Journal* 36, no. 3 (September 1983): 361–69.
Stiglitz, Joseph E. *Economics of the Public Sector*, 2d ed. 1988.

See also CORPORATE TAXATION; INVESTMENT; MARGINAL TAX RATES; SOCIAL SECURITY; SUPPLY-SIDE ECONOMICS; TAXATION, A PREFACE.

CHAPTER SIX

MONEY AND BANKING

Bank Runs

George G. Kaufman

■ A run on a bank occurs when a large number of depositors, fearing that their bank will be unable to repay their deposits in full and on time, try to withdraw their funds immediately. This creates a problem because banks keep only a small fraction of deposits on hand in cash; they lend out the majority of deposits to borrowers or use the funds to purchase other interest-bearing assets like government securities. When a run comes, a bank must quickly increase its liquidity to meet depositors' demands. It does so primarily by selling assets, frequently at fire-sale prices. Losses on these sales can make the bank insolvent.

The danger of bank runs has been overstated. For one thing, a bank run is unlikely to cause insolvency. Suppose that depositors, worried about their bank's solvency, start a run and switch their deposits to other banks. If their concerns about the bank's solvency are unjustified, other banks in the same market area would generally gain from recycling funds they receive back to the bank experiencing the run. They would do this by making loans to the bank or by purchasing the bank's assets at non-fire-sale prices. Thus, a run is highly unlikely to make a solvent bank insolvent.

Of course, if the depositors' fears are justified and the bank is economically insolvent, other banks would be unlikely to throw good money after bad by recycling their funds to the insolvent bank. As a result the bank could not replenish its liquidity

and would be forced into default. But the run would not have caused the insolvency; the insolvency had already been incurred, but not fully recognized. The recognition of the existing insolvency caused the run.

Runs are feared even more because of their potential spillover to other banks. The likelihood of this happening depends on what the "running" depositors do with their funds. They have three choices:

1. They can redeposit the money in banks that they think are safe, known as direct redeposit.
2. If they perceive no bank to be safe, they can buy Treasury securities in a "flight to quality." But what do the sellers of the securities do? If they deposit the proceeds in banks they believe are safe, as is likely, this is an indirect redeposit.
3. If neither the depositors nor the sellers of the Treasury securities believe any bank is safe, they would hold the funds as currency outside the banking system. A run on individual banks would then be transformed into a run on the banking system as a whole.

If the run is either type 1 or 2, no great harm is done. The deposits and reserves are reshuffled among the banks, possibly including overseas banks, but they do not leave the banking system. Temporary loan disruptions may occur because borrowers have to transfer from deposit-losing to deposit-gaining banks, and interest rates and exchange rates may change. But these costs are not the calamities that people often associate with bank runs.

Higher costs could occur in a type 3 run. Currency (an important component of bank reserves) would be removed from the banking system. This would cause a multiple contraction in aggregate money and credit, which would dampen economic activity in other sectors. In addition, almost all banks would sell assets to replenish their liquidity, and few banks would buy. Fire-sale losses would be large, and the number of bank failures would increase.

In practice, bank failures have been relatively infrequent. From the end of the Civil War through 1920 (after the Federal Reserve was established in 1913 but before the Federal Deposit Insurance Corporation in 1933), the bank failure rate was lower than that of nonbanks. The failure rate increased sharply in the twenties and again between 1929 and 1933, when nearly 40 percent of the nation's banks failed. Yet, from 1875 through 1933, losses from failures averaged only 0.2 percent of total deposits in the banking system annually. Losses to depositors at failed banks averaged only a fraction of the annual losses suffered by bondholders of failed nonbanking firms.

A survey of all failures of national banks from 1865 through 1936 by J. F. T. O'Con-

nor, who was comptroller of the currency from 1933 through 1938, concluded that runs were a contributing cause in less than 15 percent of the three thousand failures. The fact that the number of runs on individual banks was far greater than this means that most runs did not lead to failures.

The evidence suggests that most bank runs were type 1 or 2, and few were of the contagious type 3. Because a type 3 run— a run on the banking system—causes an outflow of currency, such a run can be identified by an increase in the ratio of currency to the money supply (most of the various measures of the money supply consist of currency in the hands of the public plus different types of bank deposits). Increases in this ratio have occurred in only four periods since the Civil War, and in only two— 1893 and 1929 to 1933—did an unusually large number of banks fail. Thus, market forces and the banking system on its own successfully insulated runs on individual banks in most periods. Moreover, even in the 1893 and 1929–33 incidents, the evidence is unclear whether the increase in bank failures caused the economic downturn or the economic downturn caused the bank failures.

—George G. Kaufman

Biography: George G. Kaufman is the John F. Smith Professor of Finance and Economics at Loyola University in Chicago. He is also a member of the Shadow Financial Regulatory Committee.

Further Reading

Benston, George J., Robert A. Eisenbeis, Paul M. Horvitz, Edward J. Kane, and George G. Kaufman. *Perspectives on Safe and Sound Banking*. 1986.

Carlstrom, Charles T. "Bank Runs, Deposit Insurance, and Bank Regulation," parts 1 and 2. *Economic Commentary*, Federal Reserve Bank of Cleveland, February 1 and 15, 1988.

Gorton, Gary. "Banking Panics and Business Cycles." *Oxford Economic Papers* 40 (December 1988): 751–81.

Kaufman, George G. "Bank Runs: Causes, Benefits and Costs." *Cato Journal* 2, no 3. (Winter 1988): 559–88.

———. "Banking Risk in Historical Perspective." In *Research in Financial Services,* vol. 1, edited by Kaufman. 1989.

Neuberger, Jonathan A. "Depositor Discipline and Bank Runs," Federal Reserve Bank of San Francisco weekly letter, April 12, 1991.

Tallman, Ellis. "Some Unanswered Questions about Bank Panics." *Economic Review*, Federal Reserve Bank of Atlanta, November/December 1988.

See also DEPOSIT INSURANCE, MONEY SUPPLY, SAVINGS AND LOAN CRISIS.

Competing Money Supplies

Lawrence H. White

■ What would be the consequences of applying the principle of laissez-faire to money? While the idea may seem strange to most people, economists have debated the question of competing money supplies off and on since Adam Smith's time. Most recently, trends in banking deregulation and important pockets of dissatisfaction with the performance of central banks (such as the Federal Reserve System in the United States) have made the question of competing money supplies topical again. Some leading economists have become sympathetic to laissez-faire in money, including Nobel Laureates Friedrich A. Hayek and Milton Friedman, as well as Eugene Fama of the University of Chicago, Neil Wallace of the University of Minnesota, and Leland B. Yeager of Auburn University.

Two sorts of monetary competition already exist today. First, private banks and financial firms compete in supplying different brands of checking accounts (also known as checkable deposits) and traveler's checks. Second, each national currency (like the U.S. dollar) competes with others (like pounds sterling, deutsche marks, and yen) to be the currency in which international contracts and portfolio assets are denominated. (Economists refer to paper money that is not convertible into an underlying asset like gold or silver as a "fiat" currency.)

Much more competition in money has existed in the past. Under "free banking" systems, private banks competitively issued their own paper currency notes, called "bank notes," that were redeemable for underlying "real," or "basic," monies like gold or silver. And competition among those basic monies pitted gold against silver and copper.

Today virtually all governments regulate and limit monetary competition. They maintain government monopolies over coinage and the issuance of paper currency, and to varying degrees restrict deposit banks and other financial firms, nationalize the interbank settlement system, restrict or place special taxes on holdings of gold or of foreign-currency assets, and refuse to enforce contracts denominated in alternative currencies. In developing countries, government banks sometimes monopolize the provision of checking accounts as well.

A significant number of economists would like to abolish many or even all of these legal restrictions. They attribute significant inefficiency and instability in the financial system to the legal restrictions on private banks and to poor central bank policy, and they view competition as a potential means for compelling the suppliers of money to be more responsive to the demands of money users. Many economists (most notably, monetarists) would like to restrict the discretion given to central banks, and the small but growing number of free-banking advocates would like to abolish central banks entirely. Most mainstream economists argue, on the other hand, that a return to free banking would bring more instability to the financial system.

Proponents of free banking have traditionally pointed to the relatively unrestricted monetary systems of Scotland (1716–1844), New England (1820–60), and Canada (1817–1914) as models. Other episodes of the competitive provision of bank notes took place in Sweden, Switzerland, France, Ireland, Spain, parts of China, and Australia. In total there have been more than sixty episodes of competitive note issue with varying amounts of legal restrictions. In all such episodes, the countries were on a gold or silver standard (except China, which used copper).

In a free banking system based on a gold standard, competing private banks would issue checking deposits and bank notes redeemable on demand for gold. In a system based on a frozen quantity of fiat dollars, as recently proposed by Milton Friedman and a few other economists, bank deposits and bank notes would be redeemable for paper dollars, as deposits are today.

Requiring private banks to redeem their deposits and bank notes for a fixed amount of gold or a fixed amount of paper currency issued by the government would rule out worries about "floating exchange rates" between rival banks. Citibank's ten-dollar notes, for example, would be redeemable for ten dollars in basic money, and so would notes issued by Chase Manhattan. What's more, competition among banks would compel all banks in the system to accept one another's bank notes at face value. Citibank, for example, would exchange one of its ten dollar bank notes for ten dollars in Chase notes or Chase deposits. The reason is that by accepting each other's notes at par, both Citibank and Chase would make their own money more useful and, therefore, more widely accepted. This is not just abstract theorizing. The same competitive considerations have led banks to form mutual par-acceptance networks for automatic teller machine cards, so that customers of one bank can get cash at another bank's machines.

What forms of money do households and business firms ordinarily use in a free banking system? When bank notes and checks issued by any bank in the system are accepted nearly everywhere, and when banks pay interest on deposits, the public seldom feels the need to handle basic money (gold or whatever is the asset for which bank money is redeemable). Bank notes and token coins serve the need for currency. Since bank notes do not bear interest, the competition among banks for a note-holding clientele is a nonprice competition.

Each bank in a free banking system is constrained to limit the quantity of its liabilities (the bank notes and deposits it has issued) to the quantity the public desires to hold. When one bank accepts another bank's notes or checks, it returns them to the issuer through a cooperative interbank clearing system for redemption in basic money or in claims on the clearinghouse. An issuing bank knows that it would suffer adverse clearings and a costly loss of reserves if too many of its liabilities came into the hands of its rivals. So banks would have to carefully manage their reserve positions (the funds they use to redeem their bank notes) even if there were no central bank setting minimum reserve requirements.

Most economists (and most everyone else) believe that a free banking system, especially one without government guarantees of deposits or bank notes, would be plagued by overissuance of bank notes, fraud, and suspensions of redeemability, all of which would give rise to runs on banks and, as a result, periodic financial panics. That would happen, the thinking goes, because the inability of any one bank to meet a run would cause runs to spread contagiously until the entire system collapsed.

The evidence from free banking systems in Scotland, Canada, Sweden, and other historical episodes does not support that conclusion. When free banking has existed, the interbank clearing system swiftly disciplined individual banks that issued more notes than their assets could support. In other words, redeemability restrained the system as a whole. Fraudulent and unsound bankers did not find it easy to get their notes into circulation. Rather, banks found that sound management was key to building a clientele. Clearinghouse associations policed the solvency and liquidity of their members. Runs on individual banks were not contagious; money withdrawn from those banks was redeposited in sounder ones. In the view of free banking proponents, the few historical episodes of contagious bank runs occurred in banking systems whose ill-advised legal restrictions blurred the distinctiveness of individual banks, so that troubles at one bank undermined public confidence in the entire system.

Proponents of competing money supplies have suggested several different institutional frameworks under which a competitive system could operate. A few monetary theorists, beginning with Benjamin Klein of UCLA and Friedrich Hayek, have contemplated private competition in the supply of nonredeemable ''fiat'' monies. We do not have any historical experience with such a regime, but it is doubtful that it would survive. If banks did not have to redeem their notes, they would face a strong temptation to issue money without limit. It would be too profitable for an issuer to break any promise not to overissue and depreciate its money. In contrast, where banks must redeem their notes for something, the holder of bank-issued money has a ''buy-back'' guarantee against depreciation.

Robert Greenfield and Leland B. Yeager, drawing on earlier work by Fischer Black, Eugene Fama, and Robert Hall, have proposed another kind of laissez-faire payments system that is supposed to maintain monetary equilibrium at a stable price level. Instead of redeeming their notes for gold, silver, or government-issued paper money, banks would have to redeem notes and checking-account deposits for a standard ''bundle'' of diverse commodities. Instead of a one-dollar or one-gram-of-gold note, for example, Citibank would have a note that could be redeemed for one unit of the

bundle. To avoid storage costs, people would redeem a one-bundle claim not for the actual goods comprising the bundle, but rather for financial assets (Treasury bonds, for example) equal to the current market value of one bundle. There would be no basic money, like the gold coin of old or the dollar bill of today, serving both as the accounting unit and as the redemption medium for bank liabilities. This regime also lacks historical precedent. Some critics have argued that it lacks the convenience of having a standard basic money as the medium of redemption and interbank settlement.

It is more likely that a deregulated and freely competitive payments system today would resemble free banking in the traditional sense. Bank money would be redeemable for a basic money produced outside the banks. To place all forms of money beyond government manipulation, the basic money could not continue to be government fiat paper unless its stock were permanently frozen (as Milton Friedman has suggested). The most plausible—and historically precedented—way to replace the government fiat dollar is to return to a private gold-coin or silver-coin monetary standard. But despite all the criticisms of current monetary systems, a return to the gold standard—or to any form of free banking—seems politically implausible today.

Even so, the move toward an economically integrated European Community has made the question of competing money supplies especially relevant. Proponents of a European ''monetary union'' want to establish a European central bank, perhaps modeled after the U.S. Federal Reserve System, that would issue a single European currency to replace the present national currencies. Advocates of currency competition, whose ranks have included former British prime minister Margaret Thatcher, are concerned that such a central bank could be very inflationary. With freedom to choose among competing national currencies, European citizens and firms can abandon high-inflation currencies like the Italian lira in favor of low-inflation currencies like the German deutsche mark. The threat that people will desert their currencies, thereby causing an embarrassing exchange-rate depreciation, imposes an anti-inflationary discipline on national central banks. No disciplinary pressure as strong would confront a pan-European central bank with a monopoly on supplying money.

—**Lawrence H. White**

Biography: Lawrence H. White is an associate professor of economics at the University of Georgia.

Further Reading

Dowd, Kevin. *The State and the Monetary System*. 1989.
Goodhart, Charles. *The Evolution of Central Banks*. 1988.
Hayek, Friedrich A. *Denationalisation of Money*, 2d ed. 1978.
Selgin, George A. *The Theory of Free Banking*. 1988.
White, Lawrence H. ''What Kinds of Monetary Institutions Would a Free Market Deliver?'' *Cato Journal* 9 (Fall 1989): 367–91.

Deposit Insurance

George G. Kaufman

■ No description of the savings and loan and banking crises of the eighties is complete without mention of federal deposit insurance. Deposit insurance gets mixed reviews. On the one hand it is credited with preventing a banking panic à la the Great Depression of the thirties, while on the other it is blamed for creating and magnifying the debacle. As a result federal deposit insurance reform has come under greater public scrutiny than at any time since its enactment in 1933.

Federal deposit insurance became law for commercial banks in 1933 as part of the Glass-Steagall Act, and for S&Ls in 1934. Although a number of state governments had provided deposit insurance before 1933, most state programs had failed and all had been disbanded by then. The federal program was enacted only after long debate.

The Federal Deposit Insurance Corporation (FDIC) and the Federal Savings and Loan Insurance Corporation (FSLIC) were both established in 1934. As initially conceived in the legislation, coverage was to be on a sliding scale, insuring 100 percent of the first $5,000 of deposits and progressively lower percentages of larger amounts. But this plan was never adopted, and 100 percent insurance was provided for only the first $2,500 per account. This was quickly increased to $5,000 in mid-1934 and, in a number of steps, to $100,000 per account in 1980. The insurance coverage was funded by a flat annual premium on banks,

initially set at 0.5 percent of insured deposits. That was lowered shortly thereafter to $\frac{1}{12}$ of 1 percent or less of total domestic deposits before being increased again in the late eighties to pay for the large losses then occurring.

The early advocates of federal deposit insurance argued that it would provide safety and liquidity for small depositors, would protect the smooth working of the national payments (check-clearing) system, and most important, would protect against bank runs. A bank run occurs when many depositors, fearing their bank's ability to make good on deposits, withdraw their money. No bank can refund all, or even a substantial portion, of its deposits at once. To meet the depositors' demands, therefore, the bank has to sell assets quickly and possibly suffer fire-sale losses that could lead to its failure.

Advocates of deposit insurance feared that such runs could spread to other banks, making solvent banks insolvent and reducing the amount of money in the economy. Sudden reductions in the supply of money can throw the economy into recession or even depression. Although the proponents of deposit insurance overstated the damage caused by bank runs (see BANK RUNS), insurance did reduce runs and bank failures. From the advent of deposit insurance until the late seventies, only rarely did more than ten banks fail in a year. Runs on troubled banks effectively disappeared for all but small, nonfederally insured institutions. If the government promised to make depositors whole, regardless of a bank's solvency, why bother removing deposits?

Opponents of deposit insurance argued, based in part on the experience of the state funds, that insurance would weaken the incentive for depositors to care whether their banks and S&Ls took excessive risks. Because the rates for deposit insurance were the same for the stodgy low-risk lender as they were for the high-flying, risk-taking lender, the low-risk banks and S&Ls would end up subsidizing the high-risk ones. As the S&L crisis and the bank crisis of the eighties and early nineties show, they were right. Over time the insurance-induced weakening of depositor discipline over banks caused a mostly unnoticed weakening of the financial condition of individual banks.

In the thirties, before deposit insurance, banks held capital of almost 15 percent of assets. (Capital, which consists of money put up by shareholders, is the "cushion" to absorb losses.) Moreover, bank owners had personal double liability. They were liable not only for the amount of their investment, but also for an additional amount up to the par value—the price at which the shares were initially offered—of their shares. By the late seventies bank capital ratios had fallen to only 6 percent of assets and double liability had been abolished. Banks also increased the riskiness of their loan portfolios by making more loans to less developed countries, to commercial real estate, and to corporations heavily indebting themselves to restructure. S&Ls increased their exposure both to credit risk and, by making long-term, fixed-rate mortgages financed by short-term deposits, to increases in interest rates. It would not take much of a shock to such portfolios to wipe out the low capital base. And in the eighties the shock happened, first to the S&Ls, from increases in interest rates, and then to both the S&Ls and the banks, from losses on loans.

Before deposit insurance, banks that were close to being insolvent would have experienced runs and would not have been able to attract replacement deposits. But deposit insurance prevented this self regulating mechanism. The FDIC made matters even worse by saying that it would often guarantee deposits even in excess of $100,000, especially for larger banks deemed "too large to fail." Insolvent institutions could thus remain in business and attract nearly all the funds they wanted by paying high interest rates on deposits. Runs occurred, but unlike the earlier ones, the new runs were from safer banks to riskier banks that offered higher rates on federally insured deposits. Without any capital of their own, the insolvent institutions frequently increased their risk exposures and incurred even larger losses. In effect, they were gambling with taxpayer money. If their risky loans paid off, they got to keep the profits. If the borrowers defaulted, the FDIC, the FSLIC, and ultimately the taxpayer got stuck with the loss.

If the losses that S&Ls incurred had been officially recognized when they happened, they would have depleted the reserves of the FSLIC by the early eighties. But officials at the FSLIC feared igniting runs at other S&Ls and even banks if they closed insolvent institutions too soon, felt political pressure from the industry, at times transmitted through members of Congress (e.g., the

"Keating five") to keep insolvent institutions open, and feared personal embarrassment from both admitting a large number of insolvencies and asking for additional industry contributions and taxes. Therefore, these officials did not recognize the losses formally. Instead, the FSLIC permitted insolvent S&Ls to continue operating and maintained a facade of solvency.

When interest rates shot up in the seventies and early eighties, many S&Ls were technically bankrupt. They had to pay higher short-term interest rates to attract deposits, but their interest income from long-term, fixed-rate mortgages was unchanged. In addition the market value of these mortgages had plummeted. Most appeared solvent (they had enough resources to pay interest and meet withdrawals) simply because they did not have to write down their mortgages to market value. The sharp decline in interest rates from 1982 through 1986 reversed S&L losses from interest rate risk. But many S&Ls, either through deliberate increases in risky loans or because they were in the energy belt centered in Texas or in other regions of the country that also suffered significant recessions, incurred large loan defaults that more than offset the gains from interest rate reductions. Industry losses increased sharply, and the negative economic net worth of insolvent S&Ls expanded rapidly from some $20 billion in 1985 to near $100 billion in 1988.

Belatedly, the FSLIC attempted to resolve the insolvencies but was short of funds. Therefore, it used expensive techniques to delay cash outlays to later periods and offered tax concessions to buyers of failing S&Ls that reduced revenues to the U.S. Treasury. The White House and Congress belatedly recognized both the seriousness of the problem and the need for federal funds to resolve insolvencies efficiently and make the depositors whole. In early 1989 President Bush introduced, and Congress enacted, the Financial Institutions Reform, Recovery, and Enforcement Act (FIRREA).

FIRREA punished the most visible villain by abolishing the FSLIC and its parent Federal Home Loan Bank Board and transferring its insurance powers over S&Ls to a new Savings Association Insurance Fund (SAIF) operated by the FDIC, which claimed that it could do better. Insurance premiums also increased sharply. Commercial banks were transferred to a new Bank Insurance Fund (BIF), also operated by the FDIC. Unfortunately, FIRREA was based on an underestimate of the cost of the bailout and on a mistaken view of the cause. It did little to correct the underlying faults in the structure of deposit insurance. Riskier banks and S&Ls still did not pay higher deposit insurance rates, and depositors still had little or no incentive to monitor the loan portfolios of their banks and S&Ls. Regulators still could delay resolving insolvencies.

Unfortunately, the FDIC has not done much better than the FSLIC. Mainly due to sharp declines in commercial real estate values in the late eighties and early nineties, the number of commercial bank failures increased sharply from around ten annually at the beginning of the decade to more than two hundred near the end. Many large banks failed, including nine of the ten largest banks in Texas. For many of the same reasons that motivated the FSLIC, the FDIC has repeated the FSLIC's pattern. It delayed recognizing many insolvencies, particularly for large banks it considered too large to fail, denied that it was encountering financial difficulties, and increasingly resolved insolvencies at a high cost to itself and to the U.S. Treasury.

Finally, in early 1991, the potential insolvency of the FDIC could no longer be disguised. Proposals for increasing the fund and for significantly reforming the insurance structure received serious public policy attention. Legislative proposals included reducing the amount of insurance coverage per account, particularly eliminating coverage of multiple accounts by the same depositor, to enhance depositor discipline; abolishing the "too-large-to-fail" doctrine; restricting insured banks to only safe investments (so-called "narrow" banks); allowing banks and S&Ls to broaden their product lines and to expand into other regions, in order to reduce risk through greater diversification; basing deposit premiums on bank risk; increasing capital requirements; and instituting earlier and progressively harsher regulatory intervention on a structured basis according to tiers, or zones, of bank capital in order to catch and recapitalize troubled institutions before they became insolvent.

The FDIC Improvement Act, which was passed at the end of 1991, gave the FDIC the power to intervene earlier in the affairs of insured institutions that are financially troubled. It also requires recapitalization of troubled institutions either by existing shareholders or by merger, sale, or liquidation before their capital is fully depleted. If the early intervention or the recapitalization succeeds, losses from failure are limited to the institution's shareholders and not spread to its depositors or the FDIC. The 1991 act also restricts the FDIC's ability to make uninsured depositors whole in too-big-to-fail resolutions and requires the FDIC to introduce risk-based premiums. These changes, if enforced, will reduce the flaws in deposit insurance and make the banking system safer.

—George G. Kaufman

Biography: George G. Kaufman is the John F. Smith Professor of Finance and Economics at Loyola University in Chicago. He also is a member of the Shadow Financial Regulatory Committee.

Further Reading

Benston, George J., et al. *Perspectives on Safe and Sound Banking.* 1986.
Federal Deposit Insurance Corporation. *The First Fifty Years.* 1984.
Kane, Edward J. *The Gathering Crisis in Federal Deposit Insurance.* 1985.
———. *The S&L Insurance Mess: How Did It Happen?* 1990.
Natter, Raymond. "History, Powers and Functions of the Federal Deposit Insurance Corporation." In *Research in Financial Services,* vol. 2, edited by George G. Kaufman. 1990.

See also BANK RUNS, COMPETING MONEY SUPPLIES, SAVINGS AND LOAN CRISIS.

Federal Reserve System

Manuel H. Johnson

■ The Federal Reserve System (the Fed) has been the central bank of the United States since it was created in 1913. The main purpose of a central bank is to regulate the supply of money and credit to the economy. The board of governors, the Fed's principal policy-making organization, plays a key role in this process.

The board has seven members, two of whom serve as chairman and vice chairman. Each governor is appointed to a fourteen-year term, while appointments to the roles of chairman and vice chairman are for four years. The president, with confirmation by the Senate, appoints all seven governors and designates which ones should also be confirmed as chairman and vice chairman. The terms of Federal Reserve governors are long (second only to lifetime appointments of federal judges) to insulate the members from political pressures and foster independent decisions.

The responsibility for regulating the nation's money supply requires the Federal Reserve to influence the amount of reserve funds available to banks and thus the level and direction of short-term interest rates. For example, whether banks and other financial institutions will make loans depends on the profit margin—the difference in the rate of interest they must pay to attract deposits or borrow funds and the interest rate they can charge customers for credit. The greater the profit margin that banks can realize on new loans, the more they will want to lend. To influence interest rates on deposits and interest rates that banks pay to borrow funds, the Fed uses its congressionally granted authority to create money. The Fed creates money in three ways.

First and most important, the Fed can purchase U.S. government securities from financial institutions by simply creating "funds" (credits) on their balance sheets in exchange for the securities. To the extent that these securities are purchased directly from banks, banks have new liquid reserves on their books immediately. When nonbank financial institutions deposit their proceeds from sales of securities, banks will see their reserves increase even more. As some banks become flush with extra reserves, they temporarily lend these funds to other banks overnight to earn interest. The increased supply of reserves relative to demand in the money market pushes down the overnight interest rate (called the federal funds rate). This decline in the cost of credit to banks increases the profitability of new loans to businesses and individuals and provides stronger incentives for banks to expand the amount of credit to the economy.

Fed purchases and sales of government securities to regulate money and credit are referred to as open-market operations. Decisions to conduct open-market operations are made by the Federal Open Market Committee (FOMC), where the board of governors holds a majority of the votes. The FOMC has twelve voting members: the seven members of the board of governors and five of the twelve presidents of the regional Federal Reserve operating banks. (All twelve bank presidents are members of the FOMC, but only five vote at a time. The president of the New York bank always has a vote because of the New York bank's central role as the system's major operating facility.) Each voting member of the FOMC has one vote, and a simple majority is required for a change in policy. FOMC meetings are held roughly every six weeks to decide the appropriate amount of reserves to provide the banking system and the desired level of short-term interest rates.

A second monetary policy tool available to the Federal Reserve is the discount rate, the interest rate the Fed charges on loans it makes to banks. By increasing or decreasing this rate, the Fed can discourage or encourage banks to borrow the funds it creates and, therefore, make more loans to the public. The board of governors (not the FOMC) sets the discount rate by majority vote. In deciding the rate, however, the board does consider the recommendations of the directors from the twelve regional reserve banks.

In the past, discount-rate lending has served a dual purpose: facilitating monetary policy as just described and providing emergency liquidity to troubled banks. The Fed's attempt to accomplish two different missions with the discount rate has prompted a debate over the rate's proper role. To stimulate the growth of credit in the economy via discount-rate lending, the Fed must set the discount rate below other prevailing short-term interest rates. Otherwise, banks have no incentive to borrow from the central bank. But if subsidized credit is also temporarily provided to troubled or failing banks,

borrowing from the Fed could become stigmatized, so that normal, healthy banks refrain from seeking discount-rate credit. Such behavior by healthy banks could defeat the overall credit growth objective of Fed monetary policy. This dilemma has led some analysts, both inside and outside the Fed, to recommend that the Fed discontinue use of the discount rate to affect overall credit, and instead, provide discount-rate lending solely to higher-risk banks for emergency liquidity purposes, and only at a penalty rate.

A third way in which the Fed operates monetary policy is by regulating the proportion of liquid reserves that banks must keep on hand. Obviously, the higher the reserve requirement, the less funds there are available to make new loans. The board of governors has the authority to determine reserve requirements above the legal minimum for all federally insured depository institutions. Reserve requirements may be changed by a simple majority vote of the board. In practice, however, reserve requirements are rarely changed because even small adjustments produce rather sweeping impacts on the quantity of required reserves.

The board of governors was not always the dominant policy-making body within the Federal Reserve System. The Federal Reserve Act that created the Fed in 1913 called for a highly decentralized system that empowered the twelve regional banks to conduct somewhat autonomous monetary policy actions based on regional economic considerations. Although the board of directors in Washington was to act in a supervisory capacity, it had limited authority to centrally manage monetary policy. Initially, the board consisted of five internal directors, one of whom served as governor. In addition, the secretary of the Treasury acted as chairman of the board and was an ex officio director along with the comptroller of the currency.

In the early days after the Federal Reserve Act, changes in the discount rate were the principal means of expanding credit growth in the regions. Because each regional reserve bank set its own separate discount rate, there often was no single prevailing Federal Reserve interest rate. As financial markets became more integrated, however, borrowers took advantage of the uneven discount rates by borrowing from the region offering the lowest rate. The ability of private banks to arbitrage between regional reserve bank rates constantly frustrated any attempt by Washington to centrally manage credit growth. This arbitrage eventually forced a standardized policy on the discount rate and brought into question the need for a decentralized Federal Reserve System. Also, during the twenties, Fed open-market operations were expanded into a general strategy for monetary policy under the leadership of Benjamin Strong, head of the Federal Reserve Bank of New York. Strong organized an informal policy committee that was the forerunner of the FOMC.

The Great Depression of the thirties shifted the Fed toward more central management of monetary affairs. Working with Marriner Eccles, a Utah banker, President Franklin Roosevelt fashioned the Banking Act of 1935, which concentrated the authority over monetary policy in Washington with the independent seven-member board of governors, and excluded the secretary of the Treasury and the comptroller of the currency. Eccles was appointed the first chairman of this new board, and a separate building was erected for its use on Constitution Avenue. Benjamin Strong's informal open-market group became a restructured, permanent Federal Open Market Committee in a provision of the banking act.

A trend of increasing board responsibility for the regulation and supervision of the banking system followed the shift in authority over monetary policy. Therefore, in addition to its primary function of managing U.S. monetary policy, today the board is also charged with the regulatory oversight of all bank holding companies, all state chartered banks that are members of the Federal Reserve System, and international activities of all U.S. banks. In addition, the board administers U.S. consumer banking laws and regulates margin requirements in the stock market.

—Manuel H. Johnson

Biography: Manuel H. Johnson is Koch Professor of International Economics at George Mason University and cochairman of Johnson Smick International, a consulting firm in Washington, D.C. He was vice chairman of the Federal Reserve Board from 1986 to 1990 and, previous to that, was assistant secretary of the Treasury for economic policy.

Further Reading

Board of Governors of the Federal Reserve System. *The Federal Reserve System: Purposes and Functions.* 1985.

Greider, William. *Secrets of the Temple.* 1987.

Jones, David M. *The Politics of Money: The Fed under Alan Greenspan.* 1991.

Kettl, Donald F. *Leadership at the Fed.* 1986.

Gold Standard

Michael D. Bordo

■ The gold standard was a commitment by participating countries to fix the prices of their domestic currencies in terms of a specified amount of gold. National money and other forms of money (bank deposits and notes) were freely converted into gold at the fixed price. England adopted a de facto gold standard in 1717 after the master of the mint, Sir Isaac Newton, overvalued the silver guinea and formally adopted the gold standard in 1819. The United States, though formally on a bimetallic (gold and silver) standard, switched to gold de facto in 1834 and de jure in 1900. In 1834 the United States fixed the price of gold at $20.67 per ounce, where it remained until 1933. Other major countries joined the gold standard in the 1870s. The period from 1880 to 1914 is known as the classical gold standard. During that time the majority of countries adhered (in varying degrees) to gold. It was also a period of unprecedented economic growth with relatively free trade in goods, labor, and capital.

The gold standard broke down during World War I as major belligerents resorted to inflationary finance and was briefly reinstated from 1925 to 1931 as the Gold Exchange Standard. Under this standard countries could hold gold or dollars or pounds as reserves, except for the United States and the United Kingdom, which held reserves only in gold. This version broke down in 1931 following Britain's departure from gold in the face of massive gold and capital outflows. In 1933 President Roosevelt nationalized gold owned by private citizens and abrogated contracts in which payment was specified in gold.

Between 1946 and 1971 countries operated under the Bretton Woods system. Under this further modification of the gold standard, most countries settled their international balances in U.S. dollars, but the U.S. government promised to redeem other central banks' holdings of dollars for gold at a fixed rate of $35 per ounce. However, persistent U.S. balance-of-payments deficits steadily reduced U.S. gold reserves, reducing confidence in the ability of the United States to redeem its currency in gold. Finally, on August 15, 1971, President Nixon announced that the United States would no longer redeem currency for gold. This was the final step in abandoning the gold standard.

Widespread dissatisfaction with high inflation in the late seventies and early eighties brought renewed interest in the gold standard. Although that interest is not strong today, it strengthens every time inflation moves much above 6 percent. This makes sense. Whatever other problems there were with the gold standard, persistent inflation was not one of them. Between 1880 and 1914, the period when the United States was on the "classical gold standard," inflation averaged only 0.1 percent per year.

How the Gold Standard Worked

The gold standard was a domestic standard, regulating the quantity and growth rate of a country's money supply. Because new production of gold would add only a small fraction to the accumulated stock, and because the authorities guaranteed free convertibility of gold into nongold money, the gold standard assured that the money supply and, hence, the price level would not vary much. But periodic surges in the world's gold stock, such as the gold discoveries in Australia and California around 1850, caused price levels to be very unstable in the short run.

The gold standard was also an international standard—determining the value of a country's currency in terms of other countries' currencies. Because adherents to the standard maintained a fixed price for gold, rates of exchange between currencies tied to gold were necessarily fixed. For example, the United States fixed the price of gold at $20.67 per ounce; Britain fixed the price at £3 17s. 10.5d. per ounce. The exchange rate between dollars and pounds—the "par exchange rate"—necessarily equaled $4.867 per pound.

Because exchange rates were fixed, the gold standard caused price levels around the world to move together. This comovement occurred mainly through an automatic balance-of-payments adjustment process called the price-specie-flow mechanism. Here is how the mechanism worked: Suppose a technological innovation brought about faster real economic growth in the United States. With the supply of money (gold) essentially fixed in the short run, this caused U.S. prices to fall. Prices of U.S. exports then fell relative to the prices of imports. This caused the British to demand more U.S. exports and Americans to demand fewer imports. A U.S. balance-of-payments surplus was created, causing gold (specie) to flow from the United Kingdom to the United States. The gold inflow increased the U.S. money supply, reversing the initial fall in prices. In the United Kingdom the gold outflow reduced the money supply and, hence, lowered the price level. The net result was balanced prices among countries.

The fixed exchange rate also caused both monetary and nonmonetary (real) shocks to be transmitted via flows of gold and capital between countries. Therefore, a shock in one country affected the domestic money supply, expenditure, price level, and real income in another country.

An example of a monetary shock was the California gold discovery in 1848. The newly produced gold increased the U.S. money supply, which then raised domestic expenditures, nominal income, and ultimately, the price level. The rise in the domestic price level made U.S. exports more expensive, causing a deficit in the U.S. balance of payments. For America's trading partners the same forces necessarily produced a balance of trade surplus. The U.S. trade deficit was financed by a gold (specie) outflow to its trading partners, reducing the monetary gold stock in the United States. In the trading partners the money supply increased, raising domestic expenditures, nominal incomes, and ultimately, the price level. Depending on the relative share of the U.S. monetary gold stock in the world total, world prices and income rose. Although the initial effect of the gold discovery was to increase real output (because wages and prices did not immediately increase), eventually the full effect was on the price level alone.

For the gold standard to work fully, central banks, where they existed, were supposed to play by the "rules of the game." In other words, they were supposed to raise their discount rates—the interest rate at which the central bank lends money to member banks—to speed a gold inflow, and lower their discount rates to facilitate a gold outflow. Thus, if a country was running a balance-of-payments deficit, the rules of the game required it to allow a gold outflow until the ratio of its price level to that of its principal trading partners was restored to the par exchange rate.

The exemplar of central bank behavior was the Bank of England, which played by the rules over much of the period between 1870 and 1914. Whenever Great Britain faced a balance-of-payments deficit and the Bank of England saw its gold reserves declining, it raised its "bank rate" (discount rate). By causing other interest rates in the United Kingdom to rise as well, the rise in the bank rate was supposed to cause holdings of inventories to decrease and other investment expenditures to decrease. These reductions would then cause a reduction in overall domestic spending and a fall in the price level. At the same time, the rise in the bank rate would stem any short-term capital outflow and attract short-term funds from abroad.

Most other countries on the gold standard—notably France and Belgium—did not, however, follow the rules of the game. They never allowed interest rates to rise enough to decrease the domestic price level. Also, many countries frequently broke the rules by "sterilization"—shielding the domestic money supply from external disequilibrium by buying or selling domestic securities. If, for example, France's central bank wished to prevent an inflow of gold from increasing its money supply, it would sell securities for gold, thus reducing the amount of gold circulating.

Yet the central bankers' breaches of the rules must be put in perspective. Although exchange rates in principal countries frequently deviated from par, governments rarely debased their currencies or otherwise manipulated the gold standard to support domestic economic activity. Suspension of convertibility in England (1797–1821, 1914–1925) and the United States (1862–1879) did occur in wartime emergencies. But as promised, convertibility at the original parity was resumed after the emergency passed. These resumptions fortified the credibility of the gold standard rule.

Performance of the Gold Standard

As mentioned, the great virtue of the gold standard was that it assured long-term price stability. Compare the aforementioned average annual inflation rate of 0.1 percent between 1880 and 1914 with the average of 4.2 percent between 1946 and 1990. (The reason for excluding the period from 1914 to 1946 is that it was neither a period of the classical gold standard nor a period during which governments understood how to manage monetary policy.)

But because economies under the gold standard were so vulnerable to real and monetary shocks, prices were highly unstable in the short run. A measure of short-term price instability is the coefficient of variation, which is the ratio of the standard deviation of annual percentage changes in the price level to the average annual percentage change. The higher the coefficient of variation, the greater the short-term instability. For the United States between 1879 and 1913, the coefficient was 17.0, which is quite high. Between 1946 and 1990 it was only 0.8.

Moreover, because the gold standard gives government very little discretion to use monetary policy, economies on the gold standard are less able to avoid or offset either monetary or real shocks. Real output, therefore, is more variable under the gold standard. The coefficient of variation for real output was 3.5 between 1879 and 1913, and only 1.5 between 1946 and 1990. Not coincidentally, since the government could not have discretion over monetary policy, unemployment was higher during the gold standard. It averaged 6.8 percent in the United States between 1879 and 1913 versus 5.6 percent between 1946 and 1990.

Finally, any consideration of the pros and cons of the gold standard must include a very large negative: the resource cost of producing gold. Milton Friedman estimated the cost of maintaining a full gold coin standard for the United States in 1960 to be more than 2.5 percent of GNP. In 1990 this cost would have been $137 billion.

Conclusion

Although the last vestiges of the gold standard disappeared in 1971, its appeal is still strong. Those who oppose giving discretionary powers to the central bank are attracted by the simplicity of its basic rule. Others view it as an effective anchor for the world price level. Still others look back longingly to the fixity of exchange rates. However, despite its appeal, many of the conditions which made the gold standard so successful vanished in 1914. In particular, the importance that governments attach to full employment means that they are unlikely to make maintaining the gold standard link and its corollary, long-run price stability, the primary goal of economic policy.

—**Michael D. Bordo**

Biography: Michael D. Bordo is a professor of economics at Rutgers University. From 1981 to 1982, he directed the research staff of the executive director of the U.S. Congressional Gold Commission.

Further Reading

Bordo, Michael D. "The Classical Gold Standard—Some Lessons for Today." *Federal Reserve Bank of St. Louis Review* 63, no. 5 (May 1981): 2–17.

———. "Financial Crises, Banking Crises, Stock Market Crashes, and the Money Supply: Some International Evidence, 1870–1933." In *Financial Crises and the World Banking System,* edited by Forrest Capie and Geoffrey E. Wood. 1986.

———, and A. J. Schwartz, eds. *A Retrospective on the Classical Gold Standard, 1821–1931.* Especially "The Gold Standard and the Bank of England in the Crisis of 1847," by R. Dornbusch and J. Frenkel. 1984.

———, and A. J. Schwartz. "Transmission of Real and Monetary Disturbances under Fixed and Floating Rates." *Cato Journal* 8, no. 2 (Fall 1988): 451–72.

Ford, A. *The Gold Standard, 1880–1914: Britain and Argentina.* 1962.

Officer, L. "The Efficiency of the Dollar-Sterling Gold Standard, 1890–1908." *Journal of Political Economy* 94 (1986): 1038–73.

Money Supply

Anna J. Schwartz

What Is the Money Supply?

The U.S. money supply comprises currency—dollar bills and coins issued by the Federal Reserve System and the Treasury—and various kinds of deposits held by the public at commercial banks and other depository institutions such as savings and loans and credit unions. On June 30, 1990, the money supply, measured as the sum of currency and checking account deposits, totaled $809 billion. Including some types of savings deposits, the money supply totaled $3,272 billion. An even broader measure totaled $4,066 billion.

These measures correspond to three definitions of money that the Federal Reserve uses: M1, a narrow measure of money's function as a medium of exchange; M2, a broader measure that also reflects money's function as a store of value; and M3, a still broader measure that covers items that many regard as close substitutes for money.

The definition of money has varied. For centuries physical commodities, most commonly silver or gold, served as money. Later, when paper money and checkable deposits were introduced, they were convertible into commodity money. The abandonment of convertibility of money into a commodity since August 15, 1971, when President Nixon discontinued converting U.S. dollars into gold at $35 per ounce, has made the U.S. and other countries' monies into fiat money—money that national monetary authorities have the power to issue without legal constraints.

Why Is the Money Supply Important?

Because money is used in virtually all economic transactions, it has a powerful effect on economic activity. An increase in the supply of money puts more money in the hands of consumers, making them feel wealthier, thus stimulating increased spending. Business firms respond to increased sales by ordering more raw materials and increasing production. The spread of business activity increases the demand for labor and raises the demand for capital goods. In a buoyant economy, stock market prices rise and firms issue equity and debt. If the money supply continues to expand, prices begin to rise, especially if output growth reaches capacity limits. As the public begins to expect inflation, lenders insist on higher interest rates to offset an expected decline in purchasing power over the life of their loans.

Opposite effects occur when the supply of money falls, or when its rate of growth declines. Economic activity declines and either disinflation (reduced inflation) or deflation (falling prices) results.

What Determines the Money Supply?

Federal Reserve policy is the most important determinant of the money supply. The Federal Reserve affects the money supply by affecting its most important component, bank deposits.

Here's how it works. The Federal Reserve requires commercial banks and other financial institutions to hold as reserves a fraction of the deposits they accept. Banks hold these reserves either as cash in their vaults or as deposits at Federal Reserve banks. In turn, the Federal Reserve controls reserves by lending money to banks and changing the ''Federal Reserve discount rate'' on these loans and by ''open-market operations.'' The Federal Reserve uses open-market operations to either increase or decrease reserves. To increase reserves, the Federal Reserve buys U.S. Treasury securities by writing a check drawn on itself. The seller of the Treasury security deposits the check in a bank, increasing the seller's deposit. The bank, in turn, deposits the Federal Reserve check at its district Federal Reserve bank, thus increasing its reserves. The opposite sequence occurs when the Federal Reserve sells Treasury securities: the purchaser's deposits fall and, in turn, the bank's reserves fall.

If the Federal Reserve increases reserves, a single bank can make loans up to the amount of its excess reserves, creating an equal amount of deposits. The banking system, however, can create a multiple expansion of deposits. As each bank lends and creates a deposit, it loses reserves to other banks, which use them to increase their loans and, thus, create new deposits, until all excess reserves are used up.

If the required reserve ratio is 20 percent, then starting with new reserves of, say, $1,000, the most a bank can lend is $800, since it must keep $200 as reserves against the deposit it simultaneously sets up. When the borrower writes a check against this amount in his bank A, the payee deposits it in his bank B. Each new demand deposit that a bank receives creates an equal amount of new reserves. Bank B will now have additional reserves of $800 of which it must keep $160 in reserves, so it can lend out only $640. The total of new loans granted by the banking system as a whole in this example will be five times the initial amount of excess reserve, or $4,000: 800 + 640 + 512.40 + 409.60, and so on.

In a system with fractional reserve requirements, an increase in bank reserves can support a multiple expansion of deposits, and a decrease can result in a multiple contraction of deposits. The value of the multiplier depends on the required reserve ratio on deposits. A high required-reserve ratio lowers the value of the multiplier. A low required-reserve ratio raises the value of the multiplier.

Even if there were no legal reserve requirements for banks, they would still maintain reserves with the Federal Reserve, whose ability to control the volume of deposits would not be impaired. Banks would continue to keep reserves to enable them to clear debits arising from transactions with other banks, to obtain currency to meet depositors' demands, and to avoid a deficit as a result of imbalances in clearings.

The currency component of the money

supply is far smaller than the deposit component. The Federal Reserve and the Treasury supply the banks with the currency their customers demand, and when their demand falls, accept a return flow from the banks. The Federal Reserve debits banks' reserves when it provides currency, and credits their reserves when they return currency. In a fractional reserve banking system, drains of currency from banks reduce their reserves, and unless the Federal Reserve provides adequate additional amounts of currency and reserves, a multiple contraction of deposits results, reducing the quantity of money.

Currency and bank reserves added together equal the monetary base, sometimes known as high-powered money. The Federal Reserve has the power to control the issue of both components. By adjusting the levels of banks' reserve balances, over several quarters it can achieve a desired rate of growth of deposits and of the money supply. When the public and the banks change the ratio of their currency and reserves to deposits, the Federal Reserve can offset the effect on the money supply by changing reserves and/or currency.

The Federal Reserve's techniques for achieving its desired level of reserves—both borrowed reserves that banks obtain at the discount window and nonborrowed reserves that it provides by open-market purchases—have changed significantly over time. At first the Federal Reserve controlled the volume of reserves and of borrowing by member banks mainly by changing the discount rate. It did so on the theory that borrowed reserves made member banks reluctant to extend loans, because their desire to repay their own indebtedness

to the Federal Reserve as soon as possible was supposed to inhibit their willingness to accommodate borrowers. In the twenties, when the Federal Reserve discovered that open-market operations also created reserves, changing nonborrowed reserves offered a more effective way to offset undesired changes in borrowing by member banks. In the fifties, the Federal Reserve sought to control what are called free reserves, or excess reserves minus member bank borrowing.

In recent decades the Federal Reserve has specified a narrow range for the federal funds rate, the interest rate on overnight loans from one bank to another, as the objective of open-market operations. It has interpreted a rise in interest rates as tighter monetary policy and a fall as easier monetary policy. But interest rates are an imperfect indicator of monetary policy. If easy monetary policy is expected to cause inflation, lenders demand a higher interest rate to compensate for this inflation, and borrowers are willing to pay a higher rate because inflation reduces the value of the dollars they repay. Thus, an increase in expected inflation increases interest rates. Between 1977 and 1979, for example, U.S. monetary policy was easy and interest rates rose. Similarly, if tight monetary policy is expected to reduce inflation, interest rates could fall.

From 1979 to 1982, the Federal Reserve tried to control nonborrowed reserves to achieve its monetary target. The procedure produced large swings in both money growth and interest rates. Forcing nonborrowed reserves to decline when above target led borrowed reserves to rise because the Federal Reserve allowed banks access to the discount window when they sought this alternative source of reserves. Since 1982 the Federal Reserve has targeted the borrowed reserves level but downgraded the importance of achieving monetary targets. In early 1991 it appeared to be paying attention once again to monetary growth rates.

If the Federal Reserve determines the magnitude of the money supply, what makes the nominal value of money in existence equal to the amount that people want to hold? One way to make that correspondence happen is for interest rates to change. A fall in interest rates increases the amount of money that people wish to hold; a rise in interest rates decreases the amount they want. Another way to make the money supply equal the amount demanded is for prices to change. When people hold more nominal dollars than they want, they spend them faster, causing prices to rise. These rising prices reduce the purchasing power of money until the amount people want equals the amount available. Conversely, when people hold less money than they want, they spend more slowly, causing prices to fall. As a result, the real value of money in existence just equals the amount people are willing to hold.

An Alternative View of Money Supply Determination

A different view is that the magnitude of the money supply is determined not by the Federal Reserve but by the decisions of the public and the banks. In this view banks supply only as much in deposits as the public wants to hold. Additional reserves cannot lead to an increase in the supply of deposits if the public does not want them. People will simply repay loans and shrink the money supply. According to this view a decline in the money supply is a response to a decline in people's demand to hold it, not an independent action by suppliers to reduce the quantity of money.

This alternative view, however, fails to account for the close relationship between bank reserves and deposits. If the alternative view were correct, we would observe discrepancies between movements of reserves and deposits over quarterly periods. We do not. Deposits cannot grow faster than reserves, given the required reserve ratio, no matter how avid the public's demand. Deposits may grow slower than reserves, but only if banks, fearing for their own safety in the absence of a reliable lender of last resort, want to accumulate excess reserves, as happened in the thirties. To hold excess reserves means they forgo the opportunity to hold earning assets. That is why banks usually hold minimal excess reserves.

History of the U.S. Money Supply

From the founding of the Federal Reserve in 1913 until the end of World War II, the money supply tended to grow at a higher rate than the growth of nominal GNP. This increase in the ratio of money supply to GNP shows an increase in the amount of money as a fraction of their income that people wanted to hold. From 1946 to 1980, nominal GNP tended to grow at a higher rate than the growth of the money supply, an indication that the public reduced its money balances relative to income. Until

1986, money balances grew relative to income; since then they have declined relative to income. Economists explain these movements by changes in price expectations, as well as changes in interest rates that make money holding more or less expensive. If prices are expected to fall, the inducement to hold money balances rises since money will buy more if the expectations are realized; similarly, if interest rates fall, the cost of holding money balances rather than spending or investing them declines. If prices are expected to rise or interest rates rise, holding money rather than spending or investing it becomes more costly.

The money supply has tended to rise more rapidly during business cycle expansions than during business cycle contractions. The rate of rise has tended to slow down before the peak in business and to accelerate before the trough.

Since 1914 an actual decline of the money supply has occurred during only three business cycle contractions, each of which was severe as judged by the decline in output and rise in unemployment: 1920 to 1921, 1929 to 1933, 1937 to 1938. The severity of the economic decline in each of these cyclical downturns, it is widely accepted, was a consequence of the reduction in the quantity of money, particularly so for the downturn that began in 1929, when the quantity of money fell by one-third, an unprecedented reduction.

The United States has experienced three major price inflations since 1914, and each has been preceded and accompanied by a corresponding increase in the rate of growth of the money supply: 1914 to 1920, 1939 to 1948, 1967 to 1980. An acceleration of money growth in excess of real output growth has invariably produced inflation—in these episodes and in many earlier examples in this country and elsewhere in the world.

To ignore the magnitude of money supply changes is to court monetary disorder. That is the lesson that the history of money supply teaches.

—Anna J. Schwartz

Biography: Anna J. Schwartz is an economist at the National Bureau of Economic Research in New York. She is a past president of the Western Economic Association.

Further Reading

Eatwell, John, Murray Milgate, and Peter Newman, eds. *The New Palgrave Money*. 1989.
Friedman, Milton, and Anna J. Schwartz. *A Monetary History of the United States, 1867–1960*. 1963.
McCallum, Bennett T. *Monetary Economics*. 1989.
Rasche, Robert H., and James M. Johannes. *Controlling the Growth of Monetary Aggregates. Rochester Studies in Economics and Policy Issues*. 1987.
Schwartz, Anna J. *Money in Historical Perspective*. 1987.

Savings and Loan Crisis

Bert Ely

■ The extraordinary cost of the S&L crisis is astounding to every taxpayer, depositor, and policymaker. The estimated present value cost of the bailout of the Federal Savings and Loan Insurance Corporation (FSLIC) is $175 billion or more. Present value means the dollar amount of a check written today that would pay the full cost of cleaning up the S&L mess.

The bankruptcy of FSLIC did not occur overnight; the FSLIC was a disaster waiting to happen for many years. Numerous public policies, some dating back to the thirties, created the disaster. Some policies were well-intended but misguided. Others lost whatever historical justification they might once have had. Yet others were desperate attempts to postpone addressing the reality of a rapidly worsening situation. All of these policies, however, greatly compounded the S&L problem and made its eventual resolution more difficult and much more expensive. When disaster finally hit the S&L industry in 1980, the federal government managed it very badly.

Fifteen public policies that contributed to the S&L debacle are summarized below.

Public Policy Causes with Roots before 1980

Federal deposit insurance, which was extended to S&Ls in 1934, was the root cause of the S&L crisis because deposit insurance was actuarially unsound from its inception. That is, deposit insurance provided by the federal government tolerated the unsound financial structure of S&Ls for years. No sound insurance program would have done that. Federal deposit insurance is unsound primarily because it charges every S&L the same flat-rate premium for every dollar of deposits, thus ignoring the riskiness of individual S&Ls. In effect, the drunk drivers of the S&L world pay no more for their deposit insurance than do their sober siblings.

Borrowing short to lend long was the financial structure that federal policy effectively forced S&Ls to follow after the Great Depression. S&Ls used short-term passbook savings to fund long-term, fixed-rate home mortgages. Although the long-term, fixed-rate mortgage may have been an admirable public policy objective, the federal government picked the wrong horse, the S&L industry, to do this type of lending since S&Ls always have funded themselves primarily with short-term deposits. The dangers inherent in this "maturity mismatching" became evident every time short-term interest rates rose. S&Ls, stuck with long-term loans at fixed rates, often had to pay more to their depositors than they were making on their mortgages. In 1981 and 1982 the interest rate spreads for S&Ls (the difference between the average interest rate on their mortgage portfolios and their average cost of funds) actually were −1.0 percent and −0.7 percent respectively.

Regulation Q, under which the Federal Reserve since 1933 had limited the interest rates banks could pay on their deposits, was extended to S&Ls in 1966. Regulation Q effectively was price-fixing, and like most efforts to fix prices (see PRICE CONTROLS), Regulation Q caused distortions far more costly than any benefits it may have delivered. Regulation Q created a cross-subsidy, passed from saver to home buyer, that allowed S&Ls to hold down their interest costs and thereby continue to earn, for a few more years, an apparently adequate interest margin on the fixed-rate mortgages they had made ten or twenty years earlier. Thus, the extension of Regulation Q to S&Ls was a watershed event in the S&L crisis: it perpetuated S&L maturity mismatching for another fifteen years, until it was phased out after disaster struck the industry in 1980.

Interest rate restrictions locked S&Ls into below-market rates on many mortgages whenever interest rates rose. State-imposed usury laws limited the rate lenders could charge on home mortgages until Congress banned states from imposing this ceiling in 1980. In addition to interest rate ceilings on mortgages, the due-on-sale clause in mortgage contracts was not uniformly enforceable until 1982. Before borrowers could transfer their lower-interest-rate mortgages to new homeowners when property was sold.

A federal ban on adjustable rate mortgages until 1981 further magnified the problem of S&L maturity mismatching by not allowing S&Ls to issue mortgages on which interest rates could be adjusted during times of rising interest rates. As mentioned above, during periods of high interest rates, S&Ls, limited to making long-term, fixed-rate mortgages, earned less interest on their loans than they paid on their deposits.

Restrictions on setting up branches and a restriction on nationwide banking prevented S&Ls, and banks as well, from expanding across state lines. S&Ls, unable to diversify their credit risks geographically, became badly exposed to regional economic downturns that reduced the value of their real estate collateral.

The dual chartering system permitted state-regulated S&Ls to be protected by federal deposit insurance. Therefore, state chartering and supervision could impose losses on the federal taxpayer if the state regulations became too permissive or if state regulators were too lax.

The secondary mortgage market agencies created by the federal government undercut S&L profits by using their taxpayer backing to effectively lower interest rates on all mortgages. This helped home buyers, but the resulting lower rates made S&L maturity mismatching even more dangerous, especially as interest rates became more volatile after 1966.

Public Policy Causes That Began in the Eighties

Disaster struck after Paul Volcker, then chairman of the Federal Reserve board, decided in October 1979 to restrict the growth of the money supply, which, in turn, caused interest rates to skyrocket. Between June 1979 and March 1980 short-term interest rates rose by over six percentage points, from 9.06 percent to 15.2 percent. In 1981 and 1982 combined, the S&L industry collectively reported almost $9 billion in losses. Worse, in mid-1982 all S&Ls combined had a negative net worth, valuing their mortgages on a market-value basis, of $100 billion, an amount equal to 15 percent of the industry's liabilities. Specific policy failures during the eighties are examined below.

An incomplete and bungled deregulation of S&Ls in 1980 and 1982 lifted restrictions on the kinds of investments that S&Ls could make. In 1980 and again in 1982, Congress and the regulators granted S&Ls the power to invest directly in service corporations, permitted them to make real estate loans without regard to the geographical location of the loan, and permitted them to lend up to 40 percent of their assets in commercial real estate loans. Congress and the Reagan administration naïvely hoped that if S&Ls made higher-yielding, but riskier, investments, they would make more money to offset the long-term damage caused by fixed-rate mortgages. However, the 1980 and 1982 legislation did not change how premiums were set for federal deposit insurance. Riskier S&Ls still were not charged higher rates for deposit insurance than their prudent siblings. As a result deregulation encouraged increased risk taking by S&Ls.

Capital standards were debased in the early eighties in an extremely unwise attempt to hide the economic insolvency of many S&Ls. The Federal Home Loan Bank Board (FHLBB), the now-defunct regulator of S&Ls, authorized accounting gimmicks that were not in accordance with generally accepted accounting principles. In one of the most flagrant gimmicks, firms that acquired S&Ls were allowed to count as goodwill the difference between the market value of assets acquired and the value of liabilities acquired. If a firm acquired an S&L with assets whose market value was $5 billion and whose liabilities were $6 billion, for example, the $1 billion difference was counted as goodwill, and the goodwill was then counted as capital. This "pushdown" accounting—losses were pushed down the balance sheet into the category of goodwill—and other accounting gimmicks permitted S&Ls to operate with less and less capital. Therefore, just as S&Ls, encouraged by deregulation, took on more risk, they had a smaller capital cushion to fall back on.

Inept supervision and the permissive attitude of the FHLBB during the eighties allowed badly managed and insolvent S&Ls to continue operating. In particular, the FHLBB eliminated maximum limits on loan-to-value ratios for S&Ls in 1983. Thus, where an S&L had been limited to lending no more than 75 percent of the appraised value of a home, after 1983 it could lend as much as 100 percent of the appraised value. The FHLBB also permitted excessive lending to any one borrower. These powers encouraged unscrupulous real estate developers and others who were unfamiliar with the banking business to acquire and then rapidly grow their S&Ls into insolvency. When the borrower and the lender are the same person, a conflict of interest develops. Also, because developers, by nature, are optimists, they lack the necessary counterbalancing conservatism of bankers.

Delayed closure of insolvent S&Ls greatly compounded FSLIC's losses by postponing the burial of already dead

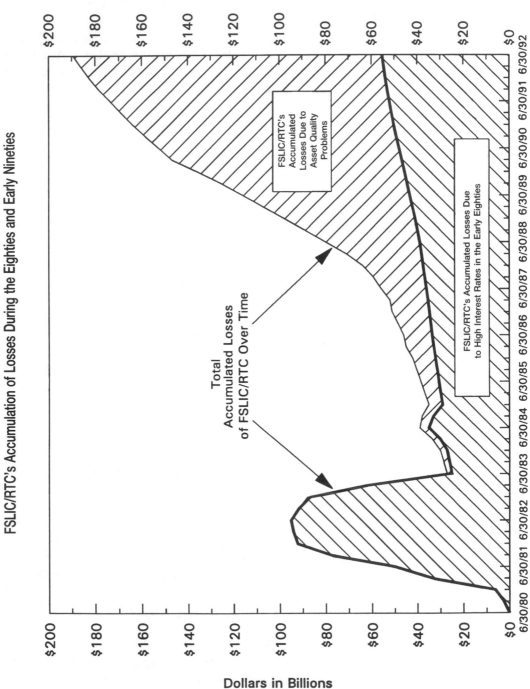

CHART 1

FSLIC/RTC's Accumulation of Losses During the Eighties and Early Nineties

Dollars in Billions

Total
Accumulated Losses
of FSLIC/RTC Over Time

FSLIC/RTC's
Accumulated
Losses Due to
Asset Quality
Problems

FSLIC/RTC's Accumulated Losses Due
to High Interest Rates in the Early Eighties

S&Ls. Chart 1 shows how losses in insolvent S&Ls grew during the eighties as the closure of insolvent S&Ls was delayed. Mid-1983 would have been the optimum time to close hopelessly insolvent S&Ls. Instead, Congress chose to put off the eventual day of reckoning, which only compounded the problem.

A lack of truthfulness in quantifying FSLIC's problems hid from the general public the size of the FSLIC's losses. Neither the FHLBB nor the General Accounting Office (GAO) provided realistic cost estimates of the problem as it was growing. On May 19, 1988, for example, Frederick Wolf of the GAO testified that the FSLIC bailout would cost $30 billion to $35 billion. Over the next eight months, the GAO increased its estimate by $46 billion.

Congressional and administration delay and inaction, due to an unwillingness to confront the true size of the S&L mess and anger politically influential S&Ls, prevented appropriate action from being taken once the S&L problem was identified. The 1987 FSLIC recapitalization bill provided just $10.8 billion for the cleanup, while it was clear at the time that much more, possibly as much as $40 billion, was needed. The first serious attempt at cleaning up the FSLIC mess did not come until Congress enacted the Financial Institutions Reform, Recovery, and Enforcement Act of 1989 (FIRREA). Even FIRREA, however, did not provide sufficient funds to completely clean up the S&L mess.

Flip-flops on real estate taxation first stimulated an overbuilding of commercial real estate in the early eighties and then accentuated the real estate bust when depreciation and ''passive loss'' rules were tightened in 1986. The flip-flop had a double-whammy effect: the 1981 tax law caused too much real estate to be built and the 1986 act then hurt the value of much of what had been built.

What Did Not Cause the S&L Disaster

Some highly publicized factors in the S&L debacle—criminality, a higher deposit-insurance limit, brokered deposits, and faulty audits of S&Ls—did not cause the mess. Instead, these factors are symptoms or consequences of it.

Crooks certainly stole money from many insolvent S&Ls. However, criminality costs the taxpayer money only when it occurs in an already insolvent S&L that the regulators had failed to close when it became insolvent. Delayed closure is the cause of the problem, and criminality is a consequence. In any event, criminality accounts for only $5 billion, or 3 percent, of the probable cost of the FSLIC bailout.

Raising the deposit-insurance limit in 1980 from $40,000 to $100,000 did not cause S&Ls to go haywire. All that raising the insurance limit did was make it slightly less expensive administratively to funnel money into insolvent S&Ls. Put another way, had the deposit-insurance limit been kept at $40,000, a depositor intent on putting $200,000 of insured funds into insolvent S&Ls paying high interest rates would have had to deposit his money, in $40,000 chunks, into five different S&Ls. Because of the higher limit, two $100,000 deposits would keep the $200,000 fully insured.

Brokered deposits became an important source of deposits for many S&Ls in the eighties. Brokered deposits allowed brokerage houses and deposit brokers to divide billions of dollars in customers' funds into $100,000 pieces, search the country for the highest rates being paid by S&Ls, and deposit these pieces into different S&Ls. Brokered deposits, though, were the regulators' best friend because this "hot money," always chasing high interest rates, kept insolvent S&Ls liquid, enabling regulators to delay closing these S&Ls. Regulators, therefore, were the true abusers of brokered deposits.

Certified public accountants (CPAs) have been blamed for not detecting failing S&Ls and reporting them to the regulators. However, CPAs were hired by S&Ls to audit their financial statements, not to backstop the regulators. Federal and state S&L examiners, working for the taxpayer, were supposed to be fully capable of detecting problems, and often did. Interestingly, CPA audit reports also disclosed many financial problems in S&Ls, including regulatory accounting practices that were at odds with generally accepted accounting principles. The regulators, however, often failed to act on these findings. The CPAs, in effect, are being used as scapegoats for known problems the regulators should have quickly acted upon.

Junk-bond investments by S&Ls are often cited in the press and by politicians as a major contributor to the industry's problems. In fact, junk bonds played a trivial role. (Junk bonds are securities issued by companies whose credit rating is below "investment grade," which includes the vast majority of corporations in the United States.) A GAO report issued just five months before the passage of FIRREA cited a study by a reputable research group that showed junk bonds to be the second most profitable asset (after credit cards) that S&Ls held in the eighties. The report also pointed out that only 5 percent of the nation's S&Ls owned any junk bonds at all. Total junk-bond holdings of all S&Ls amounted to only 1.2 percent of their total financial assets. Even so, Congress mandated in FIRREA that all S&Ls had to sell their junk-bond investments.

The Future of S&Ls

Rapid technological change is destroying the old structure of the financial services industry and replacing it with a new structure. Computerization has unbundled home mortgage financing into three distinct industries—mortgage origination, mortgage funding, and mortgage servicing. Thus, integrated, specialized housing lenders such as S&Ls are no longer needed. As more and more insolvent S&Ls fail and are merged into healthier institutions—both banks and S&Ls—the badly needed consolidation of the deposit-taking industry will accelerate. Eventually, S&Ls probably will cease to exist as a separately regulated industry.

—Bert Ely

Biography: Bert Ely is head of Ely and Company, a financial institutions consulting firm in Alexandria, Virginia. He was one of the first people to publicly predict FSLIC's bankruptcy.

Further Reading

Ely, Bert. "Technology, Regulation, and the Financial Services Industry in the Year 2000." *Issues in Bank Regulation* 12, no. 2 (Fall 1988): 13–19.

———, and Vicki Vanderhoff. *Lessons Learned from the S&L Debacle: The Price of Failed Public Policy.* 1991.

Fand, David. "The Savings and Loan Debacle." Paper presented at the George Edward Durell Foundation Conference, "American Money and Banking: Fiscal Fitness in the 1990s?" May 21–22, 1991.

Hector, Gary. "Where Did All Those Billions Go?" *Fortune,* September 10, 1990.

Kane, Edward J. *The Gathering Crisis in Federal Deposit Insurance.* 1985.

CHAPTER SEVEN

ECONOMIC REGULATION

Airline Deregulation

Alfred E. Kahn

■ The United States Airline Deregulation Act of 1978 was a dramatic event in the history of economic policy. It was the first thorough dismantling of a comprehensive system of government control since the Supreme Court declared the National Recovery Act unconstitutional in 1935. It also was part of a broader movement that, with varying degrees of thoroughness, transformed such industries as trucking, railroads, buses, cable television, stock exchange brokerage, oil and gas, telecommunications, financial markets, and even local electric and gas utilities.

Most disinterested observers agree that airline deregulation has been a success. The overwhelming majority of travelers have enjoyed the benefits that its proponents expected. Deregulation also has given rise to a number of problems, including congestion and a limited reemergence of monopoly power and, with it, the exploitation of a minority of customers. It would be a mistake, however, to regard these developments merely as failures of deregulation: in important measure they are manifestations of its success.

These problems drive home the lesson that the dismantling of comprehensive regulation should not be understood as synonymous with total government laissez-faire. The principal failures over the last fifteen years have been failures on the part of government to vigorously and imaginatively fulfill responsibilities that we, in deregulating the industry, never intended it to abdicate.

The Benefits of Deregulation

The two most important consequences of deregulation have been lower fares and higher productivity.

Fares. Between 1976 and 1990 average yields per passenger mile—the average of the fares that passengers actually paid—declined 30 percent in real, inflation-adjusted terms. Average yields were declining in the decades before deregulation as well, thanks largely to the introduction of jets and jumbo jets. The best estimates, however, are that deregulated fares have been 10 to 18 percent lower, on average, than they would have been under the previous regulatory formulas. The savings to travelers have been in the range of $5 billion to $10 billion per year.

The overwhelming majority of the traveling public has enjoyed these lower fares. In 1990, according to the Air Transport Association, 91 percent of all passenger miles traveled were on discount tickets, at an average discount of 65 percent from the posted coach fare. The benefits of the price competition unleashed by deregulation, however, have been unevenly distributed among travelers. That is because the intensity of competition varies from one market to another. Prices per mile are usually much higher on thinly traveled than on densely traveled routes. They also are higher for the minority of travelers who have to pay full coach fares because they are unwilling or unable to meet the typical conditions for discounts (advance purchase, nonrefundability, and staying over a weekend).

These differentials are not necessarily discriminatory. It genuinely costs more per passenger to provide service on thinner routes, largely because a seat-mile on small planes costs much more than on large planes. Short flights also cost more per mile than long ones. Similarly, it is costly to provide the frequent service preferred by business travelers.

Evidence accumulates, however, that full fares on routes served by only one or two airlines, particularly on flights originating or terminating at a so-called hub city dominated by a single airline, reflect some substantial amount of monopoly power. The Department of Transportation found in 1990, for example, that after adjusting for differences in the average length of trip and density of traffic, fares on routes served by the eight most concentrated hubs averaged 18.7 percent higher than for similar markets served by other airports.

Productivity. The other major accomplishment of deregulation has been the improvement in airline productivity. Deregulation fostered this improvement by removing the previous detailed restrictions on airline prices and on where they can fly. Decontrol of prices allowed airlines to fill their planes by offering large numbers of heavily discounted fares for seats that would otherwise go unused. Decontrol of routes permitted them to plan their operations as they see fit. And deregulation has com-

pelled improvements in efficiency through the intense pressures of the price competition it unleashed. Carriers have put more seats on their planes—the average went up from 136.9 in 1977 to 153.1 in 1988—and succeeded in filling a greater percentage of those seats—from an average of 52.6 percent in the ten years before 1978 to 61.0 percent in the twelve years after.

The dramatic move to hub-and-spoke operations (in which an airline routes its flights through one or several "hub" cities) has increased efficiency in a number of ways. It has allowed better adaptation of equipment to markets: small props and jet props for short hops and few passengers; big jets for dense, long-haul routes. It has also allowed the use of larger and more efficient planes, and the offer of a wider variety of destinations—albeit at the cost of a slight increase (estimated around 5 percent on average) in the circuity of routes. The industry's failure to realize the huge potential economies of hub-and-spoke operations under regulation is compelling evidence of the inefficiency of centralized government planning and the superiority of free competitive markets.

Tendencies to Increased Concentration and Price Discrimination

The recent wave of mergers and airline failures has made the industry more concentrated at the national level than it was before deregulation. The trend continues or threatens to do so, with the failure of Eastern Airlines, Midway, and Pan American, and the bankruptcy of carriers such as Continental, America West, and TWA. Most hubs will support only a single airline, and the superior efficiency of hubbing tends to insulate an airline from direct competition on short trips originating or terminating at its hub. All of this means that pricing may well become less competitive in the future.

On average and in the aggregate, however, it has not happened yet. That is mainly because concentration at the national level is not as important as concentration on individual routes. What passengers care about are the choices available to them between two particular points. By its detailed and pervasive restrictions on the routes that carriers could serve, regulation had substantially insulated each airline from the competition of the others. By wiping out all these restrictions and freeing carriers to enter any market, deregulation produced an estimated 25 percent increase in the average number of airlines per route despite the recent mergers.

For example, between 1979 and 1988 American Airlines increased the number of domestic airports it served from 50 to 173, and United Airlines from 80 to 169, both without major benefit of mergers. As of February 1992 a traveler between Boston and Phoenix could choose among six airlines; in 1977 there were only two. Again, back in 1979 only 27 percent of all passengers traveled on routes served by three or more competitors; by 1988 more than 55 percent enjoyed that kind of choice.

In this as in all other unregulated industries, there is always the possibility of anticompetitive behavior. That is why we have antitrust laws. The reconcentration of the industry reflects, in part, the failure of the Department of Transportation to disallow even one merger of direct competitors.

Also, some of the largest airlines have, at least in the past, used their computerized reservations systems to handicap their smaller competitors. Frequent-flyer programs, operating agreements and mergers with regional feeder airlines, and deeply discounted discriminatory fares have all put smaller competitors at a severe disadvantage and contributed to the demise of many of them. Like the hub-and-spoke system itself, these practices also have large efficiency advantages and so pose a familiar dilemma to scholars and practitioners of antitrust. Moreover, these potentially anticompetitive stratagems were scarcer before deregulation because they were unnecessary. Under that regime the government forced the airlines to operate as an effective cartel.

The instances of sharply increased price discrimination that deregulation has made possible are both a competitive and monopolistic phenomenon. They reflect intense competition for the travelers most likely to be attracted by price differences among competitors. They also have promoted economic efficiency in very important ways. The deeply discounted fares to discretionary air travelers have helped fill planes and, by doing so, helped make possible more frequent scheduling, which is particularly valuable to the full-fare travelers.

Still, the discrimination also reflects the exercise of monopoly power, no longer curbed by direct price regulation. The increasing sophistication with which the leading carriers practice what the industry euphemistically calls "yield management" enables them to take full advantage of that monopoly power, particularly in the unrestricted full fares paid by about 10 percent of the travelers. The continuing reconcentration of the industry threatens to extend that exploitation to an increasing proportion of the flying public in the future.

There are three possible ways in which government might respond to this dilemma. First, it could do nothing. After all, we put up with a great deal of competitive imperfection in industries that we would not think of regulating—very high profits on razor blades, discriminatory pricing by railroads and doctors, and automobile prices that go up when demand goes down. The high, unrestricted fares paid by the minority of passengers who cannot qualify for discounts may well be compensated for by frequent-flyer credits and by the improved convenience of schedules that the high fares and hubbing help make possible. The airline industry is far more competitive than it was; the benefits of that competition have been widely distributed; and industry profits have been lower, on average, since deregulation. In these circumstances it would be reasonable to conclude that no remedy was required.

Second, the government could actively attempt to make markets more competitive by assuming responsibilities that it has neglected. It could vigorously enforce the antitrust laws. It could also remove barriers to competition by expanding airport capacity enough to allow new competitors to operate on routes, by dissolving preferential arrangements between hub-dominating carriers and their hub airports, and above all, by allowing foreign airlines to compete for domestic traffic, either directly or by investing in American carriers.

Third, where restoration of more effective competition proves infeasible, price

ceilings could be reimposed to protect travelers subject to monopolistic exploitation.

My own strong preference—with which most economists would probably agree—is for the second approach. Once introduced, price controls have an almost irresistible tendency to breed further controls (see PRICE CONTROLS). Because airlines could adjust to price ceilings by reducing quality, price ceilings would have to be accompanied by regulations imposing minimum quality standards. It takes no imagination to see where that might lead: to prohibitions of reductions in frequent-flyer benefits, in scheduling, or in the frequency with which full-fare-paying customers are upgraded to first class, and to stipulations about the minimum quality of meals and maximum charges for headsets. These examples are not fanciful. All of them were adopted under regulation, in mirror image, to prevent competitive evasions of governmentally set price floors.

In any event it would be thoroughly irrational to restore regulation as it was practiced between 1938 and 1978. It would make no sense to respond to the limited reemergence of monopoly by reimposing a regime under which the government thoroughly and systematically suppressed all price competition.

Safety in the Skies

Air travel is unequivocally safer now than it was before deregulation. Accident rates during the twelve-year period from 1979 to 1990 were 20 to 45 percent (depending on the specific measures used) below their average levels in the six or twelve years before deregulation. Moreover, by taking intercity travelers out of cars, the low airfares made possible by deregulation have saved many more lives than the total number lost annually in air crashes.

Of course, the margin of safety may have narrowed. The skies have become more crowded and airlines may, under pressure of competition, have cut corners. If so, the proper remedy is not economic regulation, but more spending on policing safety, air traffic control, and airports.

The Quality of Service

The question of what has happened to the quality of service is more complicated.

First, service for small towns and rural communities has improved. They have, on average, experienced a 35 to 40 percent increase in the number of scheduled departures and, thanks to hub-and-spoke operations, have an increased number of destinations available to them. On the other hand, the planes serving them are, on average, smaller and less comfortable. Critics of deregulation note that 95 towns, net, lost uncertificated (that is, unregulated) service between February 1978 and February 1991. That is true. But 137 towns suffered a similar fate during the last decade of regulation.

Second, travelers have endured an undeniable increase in congestion, delays, and discomfort. But these are not, in themselves, a sign of failure. After deregulation, low-cost, aggressively competing airlines, such as People Express, offered the public low fares, with correspondingly lower-cost service—narrower seating, longer lines, and fewer amenities. The incumbents responded with very deep discounts, accompanied by similarly poorer service. The enormous response of travelers to the availability of these new options is a vindication of deregulation, not a condemnation, even though the quality of the air travel experience has deteriorated as a result.

Third, much of the congestion is the result of the failure of governments to do their job. When the demand for any service exceeds the available supply, it means two things. First, the service is probably being produced in inadequate quantity. Second, it is underpriced.

As for the supply side, the airline industry relies primarily on the federal government to provide sufficient air traffic control and on federal and local authorities for airports. The governments have not fulfilled those responsibilities. As for the demand side, the spectacle of airplanes filled with passengers, queued up on runways for an hour or more, proves that the price of access to airports and to the air traffic control system at those times and places is too low.

Most airports charge landing fees based primarily on the weight of the aircraft. The charge for landing at Washington National Airport, for example, is $1.34 per thousand pounds, with a minimum fee of $8.00. Thus, a small plane would pay only $8.00 while a Boeing 707 would pay under $300. With prices that low for access to some of the most precious real estate in the world, no wonder demand outruns supply. Highly congested airports might properly charge thousands of dollars for landings at peak hours, whether the planes are large or small. The consequence would be that travelers who place a high value on taking off and landing at peak times and on using convenient airports would pay higher fares in exchange for shorter delays. Travelers who value money more than convenience could be offered bargains to travel off-peak or to use uncrowded feeder airports.

Conclusion

Airline deregulation has worked. It would be ironic if, by misdiagnosing our present discontents, we were to return to policies of protectionism and centralized planning at the very time when countries as dissimilar as China, the Soviet Union, Chile, Australia, France, Spain, and Poland are all discovering the superiority of the free market.

—**Alfred E. Kahn**

Biography: Alfred E. Kahn is special consultant to National Economic Research Associates, and the Robert Julius Thorne Professor of Political Economy, Emeritus, at Cornell University. He was formerly an economic adviser to President Carter and chairman of the Civil Aeronautics Board. He wishes to thank Melanie Mauldin for her assistance.

Further Reading

Kahn, A. E. "Surprises of Airline Deregulation." *American Economic Review, Papers and Proceedings* 78, no. 2 (May 1988): 316–22.

McKenzie, Richard B. *Airline Deregulation and Air-Travel Safety: The American Experience*. July 1991.

Morrison, Steven A., and Clifford Winston. "Airline Deregulation and Public Policy." *Science,* August 1989, 707–11.

Transportation Research Board, National Research Council. *Winds of Change, Domestic Air Transport Since Deregulation*. Special report 230. 1991.

U.S. Department of Transportation. *Report of the Secretary's Task Force on Competition in the U.S. Domestic Airline Industry*. February 1990.

Antitrust

Fred S. McChesney

Origins

Before 1890 the only "antitrust" law was the common law. Contracts that allegedly restrained trade (price-fixing agreements, for example) often were not legally enforceable, but such contracts did not subject the parties to any legal sanctions. Nor were monopolies generally illegal. Economists generally believe that monopolies and other restraints of trade are bad because they usually have the effect of reducing total output and, therefore, aggregate economic welfare (see MONOPOLY). Indeed, the term "restraint" of trade indicates exactly why economists dislike monopolies and cartels. But the law itself did not penalize monopolies. The Sherman Act of 1890 changed all that. It outlawed cartelization (every "contract, combination . . . or conspiracy" that was "in restraint of trade") and monopolization (including attempts to monopolize).

The Sherman Act defines neither the practices that constitute restraints of trade nor monopolization. The second important antitrust statute, the Clayton Act, passed in 1914, is somewhat more specific. It outlaws, for example, certain types of price discrimination (charging different prices to different buyers), "tying" (making someone who wants to buy good A buy good B as well), and mergers—but only when the effects of these practices "may be substantially to lessen competition or to tend to create a monopoly." The Clayton Act also authorizes private antitrust suits and triple damages, and exempts labor organizations from the antitrust laws.

Economists did not lobby for the antitrust statutes, or even support them. Rather, their passage is generally ascribed to the influence of populist "muckrakers" such as Ida Tarbell, who frequently decried the supposed ability of emerging corporate giants ("the trusts") to increase prices and exploit customers by reducing production. One reason that most economists were indifferent to the law was their belief that any higher prices achieved by the supposed anticompetitive acts were more than outweighed by the price-reducing effects of greater operating efficiency and lower costs. Interestingly, Tarbell herself conceded that the trusts might be more efficient producers, as did "trustbuster" Teddy Roosevelt.

Only recently have economists looked at the empirical evidence (what has happened in the real world) to see whether the antitrust laws were needed. The popular view that cartels and monopolies were rampant at the turn of the century now seems incorrect to most economists. Thomas DiLorenzo has shown that the trusts against which the Sherman Act supposedly was directed were, in fact, expanding output many times faster than overall production was increasing nationwide; likewise, the trusts' prices were falling faster than those of all enterprises nationally. In other words, the trusts were doing exactly the opposite of what

385

economic theory says a monopoly or cartel must do to reap monopoly profits.

Anticompetitive Practices

In referring to contracts ''in restraint of trade,'' or to arrangements whose effects ''may be substantially to lessen competition or to tend to create a monopoly,'' the principal antitrust statutes are relatively vague. Little statutory guidance is provided for distinguishing benign from malign practices. Thus, judges have been left to decide for themselves which practices run afoul of the antitrust laws.

An important judicial question has been whether a practice should be treated as ''per se illegal'' (that is, devoid of redeeming justification and so automatically outlawed) or whether it should be judged by a ''rule of reason'' (its legality to depend on how it is used and on its effects in particular situations).

To answer such questions, judges sometimes have turned to economists for guidance. In the early years of antitrust, though, economists were of little help. They had not extensively analyzed arrangements like tying, information sharing, resale price maintenance, and other commercial practices challenged in antitrust suits. But as the cases exposed areas of economic ignorance or confusion about different commercial arrangements, economists turned to solving the various puzzles.

Indeed, analyzing the efficiency rationale for practices attacked in antitrust litigation has dominated the intellectual agenda of economists who study what is called industrial organization. Economic analysis of a challenged practice typically has proceeded in two phases. Initially, economists concluded that an unfamiliar commercial arrangement that was not explicable in a model of perfect competition must be anticompetitive. In the past thirty to forty years, however, economic evaluations of various practices have undergone a revolution. Economists now see that the perfect competition model relies on assumptions, such as everyone having perfect information and zero transaction costs, that are inappropriate for analyzing real-world production and distribution problems.

The use of more sophisticated assumptions in their models has caused economists to conclude that many practices previously deemed suspect are not typically anticompetitive. This change in evaluations has been reflected in the courts. Per se liability has increasingly been superseded by rule-of-reason analysis reflecting the procompetitive potential of a given practice. Under the rule of reason, courts have become increasingly sophisticated in analyzing information and transaction costs and the ways that contested commercial practices can reduce them. The sophistication of economists and judges has increased in several important areas.

Vertical contracts. Most antitrust practitioners used to believe that vertical mergers (that is, one company acquiring another that is either a supplier or customer) reduced competition. Today, most antitrust experts believe that vertical integration usually is not anticompetitive.

Progress in this area began in the fifties with work by Aaron Director and the Antitrust Project at the University of Chicago. Robert Bork, a scholar involved with this project (and later the federal judge whose unsuccessful nomination to the U.S. Supreme Court caused much controversy), showed that if firm A has monopoly power, vertically integrating with firm B (or acquiring B) does not increase A's monopoly power in its own industry. Nor does it give A monopoly power in B's industry if that industry was competitive in the first place.

Lester Telser, also of the University of Chicago, showed in a famous 1960 article that manufacturers used resale price maintenance ("fair trade") not to create monopoly at the retail level, but to stimulate nonprice competition among retailers. Since retailers operating under fair trade agreements could not compete by cutting price, noted Telser, they would instead compete by demonstrating the product to uninformed buyers. If the product is a sophisticated one that requires explaining to prospective buyers, resale price maintenance can be a rational— and competitive—action by a manufacturer. The same rationale can account for manufacturers' use of exclusive sales territories. This new learning about vertical contracts had had a large impact on judicial antitrust rulings.

Horizontal contracts. Changes in the assessment of horizontal contracts (agreements among competing sellers in the same industry) have come more slowly. Economists remain almost unanimous in condemning all horizontal price-fixing. Yet George Bittlingmaycr and Donald Dewey have indicated that price-fixing may actually be procompetitive in some situations, and Peter Asch and Joseph Seneca have shown empirically that price-fixers have not earned higher than normal profits. Other practices that some people believed make it easier for competitors to fix prices have been shown to have procompetitive explanations. Sharing of information among competitors, for example, may not necessarily be a prelude to price-fixing; it can, instead, have an independent efficiency rationale.

Perhaps the most important change in economists' understanding has occurred in the area of mergers. Particularly with the work of Joe Bain and of George Stigler in the fifties, economists (and courts) inferred that there was a lack of competition in markets simply from the fact that an industry had a high four-firm concentration ratio (the percentage of sales accounted for by the four largest firms in the industry). But later work by economists like Yale Brozen and Harold Demsetz demonstrated that correlations between concentration and profits either were transitory or were due more to superior efficiency than to anticompetitive conduct. Their work followed that of Oliver Williamson, who showed that even a merger that caused a large increase in monopoly power would be efficient if it produced only slight cost reductions. As a result of this new evidence and new thinking, economists and judges no longer assume that concentration alone indicates monopoly. The Department of Justice Merger Guidelines promulgated in the eighties have deemphasized concentration as a factor inviting government challenge of a merger.

Nonmerger monopolization. Worries about monopoly have generally been declining with the realization that various practices traditionally thought to be monopolizing devices (including vertical contracts, as discussed above) actually have procompetitive explanations. Likewise, belief in the efficacy of predatory pricing—cutting price below cost—as a monopolization device has diminished. Work begun by John McGee in the late fifties (also an outgrowth of the Chicago Antitrust Project) showed that firms are highly unlikely to use predatory pricing to create monopoly. That work is reflected in recent Supreme Court opinions expressing skepticism about predation as a rational strategy for achieving monopoly profits in most situations.

As older theories of monopolization have died, newer ones have hatched. In the eighties, economists began to lay out new monopolization models based on strategic behavior, often relying on game-theory constructs. They postulated that companies could monopolize markets by raising rivals' costs (sometimes called ''cost predation''). For example, if firm A competes with firm B and supplies inputs to both itself and B, A could raise B's costs by charging a higher price to B. It remains to be seen whether economists will ultimately accept the proposition that raising a rival's costs can be a viable monopolizing strategy, or how the practice will be treated in the courts. But courts have begun to impose antitrust liability on firms possessing supposedly ''essential facilities'' when they deny access to those facilities to competitors.

The recent era of antitrust reassessment has resulted in general agreement among economists that the most successful instances of cartelization and monopoly pricing have involved companies that enjoy the protection of government regulation of prices and government control of entry by new competitors. Occupational licensing and trucking regulation, for example, have allowed competitors to alter terms of com-petition and legally prevent entry into the market. Unfortunately, monopolies created by the federal government are almost always exempt from antitrust laws, and those created by state governments frequently are exempt as well. Municipal monopolies (e.g., taxicabs, utilities) may be subject to antitrust action but often are protected by statute.

The Effects of Antitrust

With the hindsight of better economic understanding, economists now realize that one undeniable effect of antitrust has been to penalize numerous economically benign practices. Horizontal and especially vertical agreements that are clearly useful, particularly in reducing transaction costs, have effectively been banned. A leading example is the continued per se illegality of resale price maintenance. Antitrust also increases transaction costs because firms must hire lawyers and often litigate to avoid antitrust liability.

One of the most worrisome statistics in antitrust is that for every case brought by government, private plaintiffs bring twenty. The majority of cases are filed to hinder, not help, competition. According to Steven Salop, formerly an antitrust official in the Carter administration, and Lawrence J. White, an economist at New York University, most private antitrust actions are filed by two groups. The most numerous private actions are brought by parties who are in a vertical arrangement with the defendant (e.g., dealers or franchisees) and who, therefore, are unlikely to have suffered from any truly anticompetitive offense.

Usually, such cases are attempts to convert simple contract disputes (compensable by ordinary damages) into triple-damage payoffs under the Clayton Act.

The second most frequent private case is that brought by competitors. Because competitors are hurt only when a rival is acting procompetitively by increasing its sales and decreasing its price, the desire to hobble the defendant's efficient practices must motivate at least some antitrust suits by competitors. Thus, case statistics suggest that the anticompetitive costs from "abuse of antitrust," as New York University economists William Baumol and Janusz Ordover refer to it, may actually exceed any procompetitive benefits of antitrust laws.

The case for antitrust does not get stronger when economists examine the kinds of antitrust cases brought by government. In a series of studies done in the early seventies, economists assumed that important losses to consumers from limits on competition existed, and constructed models to identify the markets where these losses would be greatest. Then they compared the markets where government was enforcing antitrust laws with the markets where governments should enforce the laws if consumer well-being were the government's paramount concern. The studies concluded unanimously that the size of consumer losses from monopoly played little or no role in government enforcement of the law.

Economists have also examined particular kinds of antitrust cases brought by the government to see whether anticompetitive acts in these cases were likely. The empirical answer usually is no. This is true even in price-fixing cases, where the evidence indicates that the companies targeted by the government either were not fixing prices or were doing so unsuccessfully. Similar conclusions arise from studies of merger cases and of various antitrust remedies obtained by government; in both instances results are inconsistent with antitrust's supposed goal of consumer well-being.

If public-interest rationales do not explain antitrust, what does? A final set of studies has shown empirically that, at least in part, patterns of antitrust enforcement are motivated by political pressures unrelated to aggregate economic welfare. For example, antitrust is useful to politicians in stopping mergers that would result in plant closings or job transfers in their home districts.

—**Fred S. McChesney**

Biography: Fred S. McChesney is the Robert T. Thompson Professor of Law and Business and a professor of economics at Emory University.

Further Reading

Asch, Peter, and J. J. Seneca. "Is Collusion Profitable?" *Review of Economics and Statistics* 53 (February 1976): 1–12.

Baumol, William J., and Janusz A. Ordover. "Use of Antitrust to Subvert Competition." *Journal of Law and Economics* 28 (May 1985): 247–65.

Bittlingmayer, George. "Decreasing Average Cost and Competition: A New Look at the Addyston Pipe Case." *Journal of Law and Economics* 25 (October 1982): 201–29.

Bork, Robert H. "Vertical Integration and the Sherman Act: The Legal History of an Economic Misconception." *University of Chicago Law Review* 22 (Autumn 1954): 157–201.

———. *The Antitrust Paradox: A Policy at War with Itself.* 1978.

Brozen, Yale. "The Antitrust Task Force Deconcentration Recommendation." *Journal of Law and Economics* 13 (October 1970): 279–92.

Coate, Malcolm B., Richard S. Higgins, and Fred S. McChesney. "Bureaucracy and Politics in FTC Merger Challenges." *Journal of Law and Economics* 33 (October 1990): 463–82.

Demsetz, Harold. "Industry Structure, Market Rivalry, and Public Policy." *Journal of Law and Economics* 16 (April 1973): 1–9.

Dewey, Donald. "Information, Entry and Welfare: The Case for Collusion." *American Economic Review* 69 (September 1979): 588–593.

DiLorenzo, Thomas J. "The Origins of Antitrust: An Interest-Group Perspective." *International Review of Law and Economics* 5 (June 1985): 73–90.

McGee, John S. "Predatory Price Cutting: The Standard Oil (N.J.) Case." *Journal of Law and Economics* 1 (1958): 137–69.

Shughart, William F., II, and Robert D. Tollison. "The Positive Economics of Antitrust Policy: A Survey Article." *International Review of Law and Economics* 5 (June 1985): 39–57.

Stigler, George J. "The Economists and the Problem of Monopoly." In Stigler. *The Economist as Preacher and Other Essays,* 38–54. 1982.

Telser, Lester G. "Why Should Manufacturers Want Fair Trade?" *Journal of Law and Economics* 3 (October 1960): 86–105.

Williamson, Oliver E. "Economies as an Antitrust Defense: The Welfare Tradeoffs." *American Economic Review* 58 (March 1968): 18–35.

Electric Utility Regulation

Robert J. Michaels

■ Most electricity in the United States is generated by steam from burning fossil fuels or from nuclear fission. Under pressure the steam turns a turbine, whose rotation induces an alternating current. In 1991, 68.2 percent of electricity was generated by fossil fuel, 21.6 percent in nuclear power plants, 9.8 percent by hydroelectric plants, and 0.4 percent from sources such as wind, solar, and biomass conversion. Newly generated power is transmitted at high voltage and distributed to residential and business users at lower voltage. These users spent $178.2 billion for it in 1990. Households consumed 34.6 percent of delivered electricity.

Two characteristics of electric power make utilities different from most other industries. First, both high-voltage transmission and low-voltage distribution are most economically performed by a single line or a single network of lines. Because a single high-capacity line minimizes both capital costs and losses to electrical resistance per unit of power carried, transmission and distribution are natural monopolies.

Second, because electricity cannot be stored cheaply, it must be produced instantaneously on demand. Failure to adjust production to demand can cause brownouts or blackouts over a large region. Reliable supply, therefore, requires operating generators to be backed up by "spinning reserve" units that can begin producing instantaneously. Generation must be operated as a network, centrally dispatched (usually by computer programs) to meet both predictable changes and unforeseen contingencies.

Not surprisingly, given these characteristics, the typical electricity supplier is a large integrated owner of generation, transmission, and distribution. It holds a monopoly granted by government in return for which it has a legal obligation as a public utility to serve all customers in an area. It (or several utilities) is responsible for the operation of a control area, within which it must maintain reliability and dispatch generation economically.

Most control areas are interconnected with adjacent control areas. These interconnections allow emergency support, coordination of operations, and purchases of low-cost power by higher-cost utilities. In 1990, 267 corporate utilities generated 76 percent of America's electricity (down from over 2,000 such firms in the twenties) and served 77 percent of final users. The remaining users were served by one of 2,011 municipal or 953 cooperatively owned entities. Some of these, such as Los Angeles and San Antonio, generate their own power, but most only resell power purchased from others.

Purchases and sales of high-voltage power between utilities, known as the bulk power market, have grown substantially since 1970. Facilitated by improved interconnections and control technologies, they have grown because of regional imbalances between production and demand, and because of price differences among fuels. In 1990, 17.5 percent of all power sales were for resale by others. Most bulk power transactions are based on long-term contracts rather than on day-to-day "spot" markets. Transactions may be for energy (power produced by another) or capacity (ownership interest in a plant) and may be firm (interruptible only in emergencies) or interruptible, with varying contract durations. Also included in bulk market transactions is the transmission of power by one utility for another, called wheeling.

State and federal governments extensively regulate corporate utilities. The states' power to regulate municipal utilities varies greatly. The federal government has almost no power to regulate municipal utilities, except as they are parties to certain contracts that must be filed with the Federal Energy Regulatory Commission (FERC).

Ideal regulation would pass the economies of natural monopoly and network reliability on to customers while providing shareholders with a fair return. At the state level an appointed or elected commission sets allowable rates upon application by the utility, with other affected parties allowed to present testimony. By law the utility must recover its cost of service, which includes "prudently" incurred expenses and a "fair" return on equity. Rates for customer classes are designed to cover the costs of serving each. Because allocating the costs of a utility-owned facility that jointly benefits several classes is an inherently arbitrary procedure, regulators face frequent claims that one class is subsidizing another.

The return on equity must be high enough to attract capital, but an inefficiently run utility may make less than the approved rate of return. Whether certain expenses are prudent is arguable, and regulators sometimes disallow unpopular ones (e.g., nuclear related) on these grounds in calculating recoverable costs.

At the federal level the Federal Energy Regulatory Commission (formerly the Federal Power Commission) regulates rates charged for sales of bulk power between utilities, even if they are in the same state. It also regulates the pricing and use of transmission for wheeling, and asset transfers, including mergers. Prior to the Comprehensive National Energy Policy Act of 1992, FERC's legal power to compel wheeling was modest. In the late eighties, it began to condition its approval of mergers and power marketing plans on transmission access commitments, although the Federal Power Act did not allow it to issue wheeling orders. The new law will permit power generators, including nonutilities, to request that FERC order utilities to wheel power they produce. The commission can order wheeling only if it finds that doing so is in the "public interest" and only if the charges recover the cost of the facilities used. The Nuclear Regulatory Commission oversees construction and operation of nuclear plants, and utilities are subject to the panoply of environmental and safety regulation.

Regulators have in some ways facilitated the growth of electricity markets. Although FERC requires cost justification, it generally approves bulk power and wheeling contracts if no third parties intervene. In other ways, the law does not give FERC sufficient power to foster the growth of markets. It has yet to deal with the serious technical problems of parallel or loop flows. Loop flow impedes the market because electricity does not flow solely over a contracted path from buyer to seller. Rather, it flows over all interconnected lines, including those of other utilities. This involuntary reduction in the victim's transmission capacity can foreclose beneficial transactions. Voluntary agreements on compensation for loop flows have been few and difficult to enforce.

Competition provides incentives for efficient production, but in electricity the coordination of operations also contributes to efficiency. Many utilities, for example, are members of regional power pools. Pooling agreements enable them to coordinate activities such as reserve scheduling, emergency service, maintenance, and sometimes the planning of new facilities. Regulators must frequently rule on the appropriate scope of coordination relative to competition, an issue that cannot be settled by appeal to economic theory alone.

In the past most utilities owned all of their own generating capacity, but competition is now rapidly transforming electricity generation. The Public Utility Regulatory Policies Act of 1978 (PURPA) requires utilities to purchase power from "qualifying facilities": small plants, owned by others, which generate electricity as a by-product of heat. The price must reflect the "avoided cost" of the utility-owned generation it replaces.

Further diversification of power sources will result from recent regulations in some states that require utilities to procure new generation by competitive bids. Bidders can include the utility itself, other utilities, and so-called independent power producers (IPPs), nonutilities that might also be industrial cogenerators. The Energy Policy Act of 1992 further facilitates entry into the market by relieving an important set of power producers from the onerous operating and reporting provisions of the Public Utility Holding Company Act of 1935. Over the next ten years, between 33 and 50 percent of new generating capacity will come from IPPs. As an alternative to new construction, some regulators now also entertain proposals for "demand-side management" programs ("negawatts"). These programs treat investments in conservation symmetrically with investments in generation for rate-making purposes.

Industry experts have some disagreements about the future roles of competition and regulation. As examples, they disagree on the amount of open access to transmission that is consistent with sound engineering practice. They disagree on the likely cost savings if bidding for IPP generation replaces centralized planning by regulated utilities. They debate whether large power users should be allowed to make their own bulk market transactions, which might adversely affect the bills of those smaller customers who remain "captives" of the utility.

Because certain laws intervene, we cannot always presume that an increase in bulk power trades will benefit all electricity consumers. For example, federal law stipulates that power generated at federal dam sites must be preferentially sold to municipal and cooperative utilities at low prices. There has been extensive litigation over the possible obligation of corporate utilities to wheel this power to municipals. This litigation results from the fact that such power is underpriced by law. If a municipal utility wins access to it, its customers gain at the expense of whoever lost access to it. Thus, adding the municipal to the bulk market leads to a zero-sum redistribution of benefits among subsets of consumers rather than an increase in benefits to consumers as a whole.

Utilities currently are not required to wheel power for individual customers (e.g., large industrial users and cogenerators) who wish to take service from others. These customers have sometimes found inexpensive external sources whose prices are less than those of the local utility. They have accordingly attempted to gain the use of transmission in the name of competition. But they have simultaneously asserted a right to return to the status of ordinary customers at regulated rates in the event that market prices turn against them.

Utilities claim that granting transmission access might leave them with "stranded investments" (useless facilities built in the anticipation of continued service to the departed customer). Their costs would have to be paid by the utility's remaining customers or borne as losses by shareholders. Customers who desire transmission service

minimize the importance of stranded investments, claiming that they are difficult to measure and will quickly be absorbed by normal utility growth. This problem promises to loom larger as independent power production grows.

The benefits of expanded bulk power markets have been substantial under the pre-1993 transmission regime, with its voluntary, albeit somewhat restrictive, access policy. The gains from further opening transmission are uncertain. According to some experts utilities are already competent at searching out economic opportunities, and therefore, few cheap sources of power are overlooked. Other experts believe that a monopoly utility could not possibly see all of the opportunities in the expanding bulk power sector, and that only a market will find the best of them. These experts accordingly prefer that new bulk power investments be evaluated by the market (to the extent engineering allows it), as they are in other competitive industries.

—Robert J. Michaels

Biography: Robert J. Michaels is an economics professor at California State University, Fullerton. He has advised corporate utilities and governments on electricity markets and regulation.

Further Reading

Joskow, Paul L. "Regulatory Failure, Regulatory Reform, and Structural Change in the Electrical Power Industry." *Brookings Papers on Economic Activity, Microeconomics 1989* (1989): 125–99.
Michaels, Robert J. "Deregulating Electricity: What Stands in the Way." *Regulation* 15 (Winter 1992): 38–47.
National Regulatory Research Institute. *Some Economic Principles for Pricing Wheeled Power*. 1987.

Pace, Joe D., and John H. Landon. "Introducing Competition into the Electric Utility Industry: An Economic Appraisal." *Energy Law Journal* 5, no. 1 (1982): 1–65.

"Transmission: A Special Report." *Public Utilities Fortnightly* 126 (July 19, 1990): 12–36.

U.S. Department of Energy. Energy Information Administration. *Financial Statistics of Selected Electric Utilities*. Publication no. DOE/EIA-0437. Annual.

U.S. Office of Technology Assessment. *Electric Power Wheeling and Dealing*. Publication no. OTA-E-409. 1989.

Industrial Concentration

Thomas W. Gilligan

■ Industrial concentration occurs when a small number of companies sell a large percentage of an industry's product. The most widely used measure of concentration is the so-called four-firm concentration ratio, which is the percentage of the industry's product sold by the four largest producers. If, for example, four firms each sell 10 percent of an industry's product, the four-firm concentration ratio for that industry is 40 percent.

Concentration in the United States

Concentration varies considerably across industries in the United States. In the household laundry equipment, breakfast cereal, and cigarette industries, the four largest companies produce well over 80 percent of the industry's product. At the other extreme the four largest firms in wooden household furniture, fur goods, and women's and misses' dresses sell well under 20 percent. For all U.S. industries the average four-firm concentration ratio is 37 percent. Weighted by industry sales, it is 36 percent. This average has been quite stable for a long time. In 1935 the average four-firm concentration ratio for U.S. industries was 40 percent; weighted by sales it was 37 percent. In 1977 the average was 37 percent, while the weighted average was 39 percent. In other words, there has been no discernible long-run trend toward concentration of industry since the Great Depression.

Effects of Concentration

Why does concentration matter? Economists used to fear that if only a few companies sold an industry's product, those few would collude to raise prices. Wrote conservative economist George Stigler in a 1952 *Fortune* article titled "The Case against Big Business": "When a small number of firms control most or all of the output of an industry, they can individually and collectively profit more by cooperation than by competition. . . . These few companies, therefore, will usually cooperate."

Some of the evidence supports this view. Economists who have compared the prices of a particular product or service across geographically separated markets have found that concentration increases prices. These same studies, however, show that the effect of concentration on prices, although statistically significant, is very small. A study of airline markets after deregulation found that airline fares in markets containing two equal-size competitors were 8 percent higher than the fares in similar markets with four equal-size competitors. In other cases, however, industrial concentration had a large effect on prices. One study found that the advertising rates of Irish provincial newspapers were 25 percent lower when three or more newspapers served a particular market area.

Of forty-six articles published before the early seventies on the relationship between concentration and profits (as opposed to prices), forty-two found that the more concentrated an industry, the higher were its profits. However, the correlation was statistically weak. Moreover, the implied effect of concentration on prices was found to be small: the average markup over long-run costs was only 1 to 5 percent higher in concentrated industries.

More recent—and more careful—studies find no statistically significant relationship between industrial concentration and profitability. This is true not only for U.S. industries but also for industries in other countries. This evidence has shifted most economists' viewpoints substantially. Concludes MIT economist Richard Schmalensee, a noted industrial organization scholar: "The relation, if any, between seller concentration and profitability is weak statistically, and the estimated concentration effect is usually small. The estimated relation is unstable over time and space and vanishes in many multivariate studies."

Causes of Concentration

Why are some industries concentrated and others not? One reason is economies of scale. If a company, for example, can lower its average costs by 3 percent by increasing its output by 10 percent, then it must be large to produce its product efficiently. The larger each company in the industry, the more concentrated the industry must be.

Industrial concentration can also be a natural result of competition. If some companies keep producing products that satisfy their customers more than their rivals' products do, consumers will "reward" these companies by buying more from them. The result is that concentration increases. Indirect evidence supports the view that competing successfully causes concentration. Economists have found that the profitability of the largest producers in U.S. industries is positively correlated to industrial concentration. But if a result of industrial concentration is to raise prices, the profits of small firms in an industry should also be correlated with industrial concentration. They are not. The most plausible conclusion, therefore, is that concentration is a reward for being successful.

Of course, horizontal mergers (that is, mergers of companies that produce the same product) are an obvious cause of concentration. Do mergers cause collusion? If they did, the rivals of the merged firms would benefit as well from diminished competition and higher prices. The stock prices of these rivals should then increase when an impending merger is announced. But they do not.

Merger and Antitrust Policy

Economists now understand that industrial concentration is unlikely to cause collusion and that concentration is a natural result of economies of scale and successful competition. This new understanding is now reflected in U.S. antitrust laws. Whereas antitrust officials used to disallow mergers that gave the top four firms a market share of less than 40 percent, they now often approve mergers that would give the top four firms a market share of over 70 percent. The merger of tire producers Michelin and Goodrich is one example. Charles F. Rule, formerly the Reagan administration's chief antitrust official, summed it up: "In the Sixties and Seventies [the evaluation of proposed mergers] was all based on concentration. In the Seventies, as an underpinning, it was wiped out. There

was a problem with just using concentration. [In the Eighties], we used it as a screen to tell us when to look further, say, into market operations, price discrimination, previous market share and loss of entry into the market by competitors.''

Another reason economists and antitrust officials are less concerned about industrial concentration is that so much competition is global. In 1980 MIT's Lester Thurow, a liberal economist, wrote in *The Zero-Sum Society*:

. . . With the growth of international trade it is no longer possible to determine whether an effective monopoly exists by looking at local market shares. Regardless of the share of domestic production held by General Motors, General Motors is part of a competitive industry and must deal with strong Japanese and European competitors. In markets where international trade exists or could exist, national antitrust laws no longer make sense. If they do anything, they only serve to hinder U.S. competitors who must live by a code that their foreign competitors can ignore.

In 1986, for example, just three companies—General Motors, Ford, and Chrysler—produced 95 percent of all cars manufactured in the United States. However, the big three accounted for only 70 percent of auto sales in the United States, the remainder being foreign imports. General Motors, Ford, and Chrysler produce only 30 percent of the world's automobiles.

Thurow himself questions antitrust laws

on this basis: "If competitive markets are desired, the appropriate policy should be to reduce barriers to free trade. . . . If one measures the potential gains to be made by enforcing the antitrust laws, as opposed to reducing real barriers to international trade, it is clear that the large gains exist in the area of more international competition."

—**Thomas W. Gilligan**

Biography: Thomas W. Gilligan is an associate professor of finance and business economics at the University of Southern California.

Further Reading

Less Technical
Bailey, Elizabeth E., David R. Graham, and Daniel P. Kaplan. *Deregulating the Airlines*. 1985.
Brozen, Yale. *Concentration, Mergers, and Public Policy*. 1982.
Thurow, Lester. *The Zero-Sum Society*. 1980.
More Technical
Eckbo, Espen. "Horizontal Mergers, Collusion, and Stockholder Wealth." *Journal of Financial Economics* 11 (1983): 241–73.
Gilbert, R. Alton. "Bank Market Structure and Competition: A Survey." *Journal of Money, Credit and Banking* 16 (1984): 617–45.
Smirlock, Michael, T. Gilligan, and William Marshall. "Tobin's q and the Structure-Performance Relationship." *American Economic Review* 74 (1984): 1051–60.

See also ANTITRUST, COMPETITION, MONOPOLY.

Monopoly

George J. Stigler

■ A monopoly is an enterprise that is the only seller of a good or service. In the absence of government intervention, a monopoly is free to set any price it chooses and will usually set the price that yields the largest possible profit. Just being a monopoly need not make an enterprise more profitable than other enterprises that face competition: the market may be so small that it barely supports one enterprise. But if the monopoly is in fact more profitable than competitive enterprises, economists expect that other entrepreneurs will enter the business to capture some of the higher returns. If enough rivals enter, their competition will drive prices down and eliminate monopoly power.

Before and during the period of the classical economics (roughly 1776 to 1850), most people believed that this process of monopolies being eroded by new competitors was pervasive. The only monopolies that could persist, they thought, were those that got the government to exclude rivals. This belief was well expressed in an excellent article on monopoly in the *Penny Cyclopedia* (1839; volume 15, page 741):

It seems then that the word monopoly was never used in English law, except when there was a royal grant authorizing some one or more persons only to deal in or sell a certain commodity or article. If a number of individuals were to unite for the purpose of producing any particular article or commodity, and if they should succeed in selling such article very extensively, and almost solely, such individuals in popular language would be said to have a monopoly. Now, as these individuals have no advantage given them by the law over other persons, it is clear they can only sell more of their commodity than other persons by producing the commodity cheaper and better.

Even today, most important enduring monopolies or near monopolies in the United States rest upon government policies. The government's support is responsible for fixing agricultural prices above competitive levels, for the exclusive ownership of cable television operating systems in any market, for the limit of two cellular telephone services in each market, for the exclusive franchises of public utilities and radio and TV channels, for the single postal service—the list goes on and on. Monopolies that exist independent of government support are likely to be due to smallness of markets (the only druggist in town) or to rest upon temporary leadership in innovation (the Aluminum Company of America until World War II).

Why do economists object to monopoly? The purely "economic" argument against monopoly is very different from what noneconomists might expect. Successful monopolists earn extralarge profits by raising prices above what they would be with competition, so that customers pay more and the monopolists (and perhaps their employees) gain. It may seem strange, but economists see no reason to criticize monopolies simply because they transfer wealth from customers to monopoly producers. That is because economists have no way of knowing who is the more worthy of the two parties—the producer or the customer. Of course, people (including economists) may object to the wealth transfer on other grounds, including moral ones. But the transfer itself does not present an "economic" problem.

Rather, the purely "economic" case against monopoly is that it reduces aggregate economic welfare (as opposed to simply making some people worse off and others better off by an equal amount). When the monopolist raises prices above the competitive level in order to reap his monopoly profits, customers buy less of the product, less is produced, and society as a whole is worse off. In short, monopoly reduces society's income. The following is a simplified example.

Consider the case of a monopolist who produces his product at a fixed cost (where "cost" includes a competitive rate of return on his investment) of $5 per unit. The cost is $5 no matter how many units the monopolist makes. The number of units he sells, however, depends on the price he charges. The number of units he sells at a given price depends on the following "demand" schedule:

Price	Quantity Demanded (units per year)
$7	200
$6	300
$5	420

The monopolist is best off when he limits production to 200 units, which he sells for $7 each. He then earns monopoly profits (what economists call "economic rent") of $2 per unit ($7 minus his $5 cost, which, again, includes a competitive rate of return on investment) times 200, or $400 a year. If he makes and sells 300 units at $6 each, he earns a monopoly profit of only $300 ($1 per unit times 300 units). If he makes and sells 420 units at $5 each, he earns no monopoly profit—just a fair return on the capital invested in the business. Thus, the monopolist is $400 richer because of his monopoly position at the $7 price.

Society, however, is worse off.

Customers would be delighted to buy 220 more units if the price were $5: the demand schedule tells us they value the extra 220 units at prices that do not fall to $5 until they have 420 units. Let us assume these additional 220 units have an average value of $6 for consumers. These additional 220 units would cost only $5 each, so the consumer would gain 220 × $1 of satisfaction if the competitive price of $5 were set. Because the monopolist would cover his costs of producing the extra 220 units, he would lose nothing. Producing the extra 220 units, therefore, would benefit society to the tune of $220. But the monopolist chooses not to produce the extra 220 units because to sell them at $5 a piece he would have to cut the price on the other 200 units from $7 to $5. The monopolist would lose $400 (200 units times the $2 per unit reduction in price), but consumers would gain the same $400. In other words, selling at a competitive price would transfer $400 from the monopolist to consumers and create an added $220 of value for society.

The desire of economists to have the state combat or control monopolies has undergone a long cycle. As late as 1890, when the Sherman antitrust law was passed, most economists believed that the only antimonopoly policy needed was to restrain government's impulse to grant exclusive privileges, such as that given to the British East India Company to trade with India. They thought that other sources of market dominance, such as superior efficiency, should be allowed to operate freely, to the benefit of consumers, since consumers would ultimately be protected from excessive prices by potential or actual rivals.

Traditionally, monopoly was identified with a single seller, and competition with the existence of even a few rivals. But economists became much more favorable toward antitrust policies as their view of monopoly and competition changed. With the development of the concept of perfect competition, which requires a vast number of rivals making the identical commodity, many industries became classified as oligopolies (i.e., ones with just a few sellers). And oligopolies, economists believed, surely often had market power—the power to control prices, alone or in collusion.

More recently, and at the risk of being called fickle, many economists (I among them) have lost both our enthusiasm for antitrust policy and much of our fear of oligopolies. The declining support for antitrust policy has been due to the often objectionable uses to which that policy has been put. The Robinson-Patman Act, ostensibly designed to prevent price discrimination (that is, companies charging different prices to different buyers for the same good) has often been used to limit rivalry instead of increase it. Antitrust laws have prevented many useful mergers, especially vertical ones. (A vertical merger is one in which company A buys another company that supplies A's inputs or sells A's output.) A favorite tool of legal buccaneers is the private antitrust suit in which successful plaintiffs are awarded triple damages.

How dangerous are monopolies and oligopolies? How much can they reap in excessive profits? Several kinds of evidence suggest that monopolies and small-number oligopolies have limited power to earn much more than competitive rates of return on capital. A large number of studies have compared the rate of return on investment with the degree to which industries are concentrated (measured by share of the industry sales made by, say, the four largest firms). The relationship between profitability and concentration is almost invariably loose: less than 25 percent of the variation in profit rates across industries can be attributed to concentration.

A more specific illustration of the effect that the number of rivals has on price was given in a study by Reuben Kessel of the underwriting of state and local government bonds. Syndicates of investment bankers bid for the right to sell an issue of bonds by, say, the state of California. The successful bidder might bid 98.5 (or $985 for a $1,000 bond) and, in turn, seek to sell the issue to investors at 100 ($1,000 for a $1,000 bond). In this case the underwriter "spread" would be 1.5 (or $15 per $1,000 bond).

In a study of thousands of bond issues, after correcting for size and safety and other characteristics of each issue, Kessel found the pattern of underwriter spreads to be as follows:

No. of Bidders	Underwriter Spread
1	$15.74
2	$12.64
3	$12.36
6	$10.71
10	$10.23

For twenty or more bidders, which is, effectively, perfect competition, the spread was ten dollars. Merely increasing the number of bidders from one to two was sufficient to halve the excess spread over what it would be at the ten-dollar competitive level. Thus, even a small number of rivals may bring prices down close to the competitive level. Kessel's results, more than any other single study, convinced me that competition is a tough weed, not a delicate flower.

If a society wishes to control monopoly—at least those monopolies that were not created by its own government—it has three broad options. The first is an antitrust policy of the American variety; the second is public regulation; and the third is public ownership and operation. Like monopoly, none of these is ideal.

Antitrust policy is expensive to enforce: the Antitrust Division of the Department of Justice had a budget of $54 million in 1991, and the Federal Trade Commission budget was $74 million. The defendants (who also face hundreds of private antitrust cases each year) probably spend ten or twenty times as much. Moreover, antitrust is slow moving. It takes years before a monopoly practice is identified, and more years to reach a decision; the antitrust case that led to the breakup of the American Telephone and Telegraph Company began in 1974 and was still under judicial administration in 1991.

Public regulation has been the preferred choice in America, beginning with the creation of the Interstate Commerce Commission in 1887 and extending down to municipal regulation of taxicabs and ice companies. Yet most public regulation has the effect of reducing or eliminating competition rather than eliminating monopoly. The limited competition—and resulting higher profits for owners of taxis—is the reason that New York City taxi medallions sold for more than $150,000 in 1991 (at one point in the seventies, a taxi medallion was worth more than a seat on the New York Stock Exchange). Moreover, regulation of "natural monopolies" (industries, usually utilities, in which the market can support only one firm at the most efficient size of operation) has mitigated some monopoly power but usually introduces serious inefficiencies in the design and operation of such utilities.

A famous theorem in economics states that a competitive enterprise economy will produce the largest possible income from a given stock of resources. No real economy meets the exact conditions of the theorem, and all real economies will fall short of the ideal economy—a difference called "market failure." In my view, however, the degree of "market failure" for the American economy is much smaller than the "political failure" arising from the imperfections of economic policies found in real political systems. The merits of laissez-faire rest less upon its famous theoretical foundations than upon its advantages over the actual performance of rival forms of economic organization.

—**George J. Stigler**

Biography: The late George J. Stigler was the Charles R. Walgreen Distinguished Service Professor, Emeritus, of Economics at the University of Chicago. He also was director of the Center for the Study of the Economy and the State. He won the Nobel Prize in economics in 1982.

Further Reading

Atkinson, Scott E., and Robert Halvorsen. ''The Relative Efficiency of Public and Private Firms in a Regulated Environment.'' *Journal of Public Economics* 29 (April 1986): 281–94.

Boardman, Anthony E., and Aidan R. Vining. ''Ownership and Performance in Competitive Environments.'' *Journal of Law and Economics* 32 (April 1989): 1–34.

Bork, Robert H. *The Antitrust Paradox.* 1978.

Kessel, Reuben. ''A Study of the Effects of Competition in the Tax-Exempt Bond Market.'' *Journal of Political Economy* 79 (July/August 1971): 706–38.

Shepherd, William G. ''Causes of Increased Competition in the U.S. Economy, 1939–80.'' *Review of Economics and Statistics* 64 (November 1982): 613–26.

Stigler, George J. *Memoirs of an Unregulated Economist.* Chap. 6. 1988.

Natural Monopoly

The main kind of monopoly that is both persistent and not caused by the government is what economists call a ''natural'' monopoly. A natural monopoly comes about due to economies of scale—that is, due to unit costs that fall as a firm's production increases. When economies of scale are extensive relative to the size of the market, one firm can produce the industry's whole output at a lower unit cost than two or more firms could. The reason is that multiple firms cannot fully exploit these economies of scale. Many economists believe that the distribution of electric power (but not the production of it) is an example of a natural monopoly. The economies of scale exist because another firm that entered would need to duplicate existing power lines, whereas if only one firm existed, this duplication would not be necessary. And one firm that serves everyone would have a lower cost per customer than two or more firms.

Whether, and how, government should regulate monopoly is controversial among economists. Most favor regulation to prevent the natural monopoly from charging a monopoly price. Other economists want no regulation because they believe that even natural monopolies must face some competition (electric utilities must compete with home generation of wind power, for example, and industrial customers can sometimes produce their own power or buy it elsewhere), and they want the natural monopoly to have a strong incentive to cut costs. Besides regulating price, governments usually prevent competing firms from entering an industry that is thought to be a natural monopoly. A firm that wants to compete with the local utility, for example, cannot legally do so. Economists tend to oppose regulating entry. The reason is as follows: If the industry really is a natural monopoly, then preventing new competitors from entering is unnecessary because no competitor would want to enter anyway. If, on the other hand, the industry is not a natural monopoly, then preventing competition is undesirable. Either way, preventing entry does not make sense.

—DRH

Natural Gas Regulation

Robert J. Michaels

■ Natural gas is methane in underground deposits, produced by the same geological processes as oil. As a relatively abundant and clean-burning fuel, gas has been touted as a means for achieving energy independence and environmental cleanliness. The 19.1 trillion cubic feet of gas used in the United States in 1991 accounted for 24.5 percent of total British thermal units (BTUs) consumed. Households consumed 26.3 percent of delivered gas and electric utilities used 16 percent to produce power.

Underground reserves of gas are difficult to project meaningfully because the amount of gas worth discovering and exploiting depends crucially on its expected future price.

Between the early sixties and the late seventies, federal regulations kept the price to producers low and discouraged exploration for new supplies. By the 1970–75 period annual additions to reserves had failed to keep pace with production, falling to less than half of their 1955–60 levels in the lower forty-eight states. With the decontrol of gas prices, which began in the late seventies, additions to reserves have stabilized and now roughly match production. Proved reserves are currently about ten years of production.

Before the development of high-pressure pipelines in the twenties, gas was either flared off as hazardous or consumed in the vicinity of its production. Today, interstate pipelines, usually owned by entities other than producers, link wells with consuming areas. Local distribution companies (LDCs), usually owned independently of pipelines and producers, deliver and sell gas to final users. Most distribution is by corporate LDCs, with the remainder by municipal governments. Two types of pipeline service are available to distributors. Under so-called sales, or system, supply the pipeline purchases gas from producers and resells the gas to the LDC. Under transport the LDC makes its own purchases directly from producers and uses the pipeline only as a transporter. Both sales and transport can either be firm (interruptible only in emergencies) or interruptible. Between 1984 and the first half of 1992, transport service grew from 4 percent to 87 percent of pipeline activity. More recently, some LDCs have also become transporters of gas purchased by their larger customers.

The markets faced by producers, pipelines, and distributors differ substantially. Because the average producer of gas is a small company—262,483 wells, owned by thousands of concerns, were operating in the United States at the end of 1989—production is intensely competitive. Because many gas fields are reachable by more than one pipeline and because pipelines are extensively interconnected, the buyers' side of the wellhead market is also competitive. Pipeline technology, however, has attributes of natural monopoly: the cheapest way to transport a given volume of gas is by a single pipeline. Furthermore, most consuming areas can be reached by only one or a very small number of pipelines. Because the cheapest technology for reli-

able local service is a single network of pipes under centralized control, distribution also has attributes of natural monopoly.

The regulation of the different stages of gas production is complex and has changed dramatically since the mideighties. Under the Natural Gas Wellhead Decontrol Act of 1989, the Federal Energy Regulatory Commission (FERC) ceased to regulate wellhead prices on Jan. 1, 1993. But in reality recent regulatory decisions and changes in market conditions made existing price controls irrelevant before that: prevailing market prices dropped below the maximum prices that the law allowed.

Interstate pipelines are also under FERC jurisdiction, whether they act as system suppliers or as transporters. Pipelines apply to the FERC for permission to set particular rates. The FERC then holds administrative hearings at which parties who are affected by the rates have legal standing to intervene and to question aspects of the application. Rates for each type of service and class of customer must cover the pipeline's cost of service, which is defined as "prudently" incurred expenses plus a "fair" rate of return on stockholders' equity. Neither prudence nor fairness is well defined, and pipelines and their customers may understandably differ over them. One reason for such differences is that when a facility simultaneously produces several services, there is no economically meaningful way of distributing its joint costs among customers. The inherent arbitrariness often leads some customers to allege that they are being forced to subsidize other customers.

State regulators set LDC rates by similar administrative procedures. Thus, competition effectively rules in the naturally competitive wellhead market, and regulation sets rates in the naturally monopolistic pipeline and LDC markets. The evolution of the gas industry is important both as history and as an illustration of the power of economic thinking to shape public policy. Only fifteen years ago, gas was a grossly misregulated industry. It reached its current, much-improved state as a result of legislation, regulations, and judicial decisions, many impelled by market forces that regulators could not control.

The Natural Gas Act of 1938 instituted pipeline regulation by the Federal Power Commission (FPC, reconstituted in 1977 as FERC) as a consequence of concern about monopoly. At the time, pipelines functioned only as resellers to LDCs of gas purchased from producers, and the FPC had jurisdiction over their resale rates. In its 1954 Phillips decision, the Supreme Court ruled that the commission also had jurisdiction over the prices at which producers sold gas to pipelines. The expansion in its regulatory task was tremendous: although there were fewer than a hundred pipelines, there were tens of thousands of gas wells. To make its task manageable, the FPC set ceiling prices by geographic areas, based on the premise that the cost of finding gas to replace exhausted wells would be about the same as exploration costs had been in the past.

As events unfolded, exploration costs rose dramatically, and a severe shortage of gas began to emerge in interstate commerce. However, because intrastate sales—sales of gas in the state where it was produced—were exempt from federal price controls, there was no shortage of gas in those markets. The FPC allowed some price increases in the interstate market, but these were not large enough to end the shortage. Faced with an obligation to deliver gas and a shortage at the wellhead, pipelines made ''take-or-pay'' contracts with producers, in which they obligated themselves to purchase certain amounts of gas. If they did not take the gas, they were still obligated to pay for the contracted amount.

As long as their LDC customers bought predictable amounts, the pipelines had a long-term asset (sales) that balanced a long-term liability (take-or-pay contracts). The predictability of LDC purchases, however, vanished in the midseventies. State regulators adjusted LDC rates so that industrial customers would bear relatively more of the burden of rising prices. These users responded by instituting conservation and fuel-switching capabilities, decreasing their consumption.

The Natural Gas Policy Act of 1978 (NGPA) attacked the shortage by a phased deregulation of wellhead prices. In the early eighties, however, the collapse of the world price of oil caused gas prices to fall as well. Supply and demand once again ruled, making the remaining price controls on natural gas largely irrelevant. Pipelines faced severe financial strains because take-or-pay contracts from the shortage period remained in force, committing them to purchase gas at higher prices than those at which they could resell it. They reacted by instituting ''special marketing programs'' (SMPs) to transport, rather than resell, gas to certain customers at discounted rates in exchange for forgiveness of take-or-pay obligations. In the 1985 Maryland People's Counsel cases, the U.S. Court of Appeals for the District of Columbia ruled that SMPs were unduly discriminatory, and that FERC would have to devise regulations that allowed all customers the option to use pipelines as transporters.

FERC devised such regulations, which were broadly approved by the same court in the 1987 Associated Gas Distributors case and some later decisions. Under them a pipeline could receive an "optional expedited certificate" for new service (thus bypassing a costly and tedious regulatory process) only if it agreed to be an "open access" transporter of gas for all customers who wished to switch from system supply to transport service. Take-or-pay obligations would be correspondingly credited. Within months every major pipeline had applied for and received open access status.

In April 1992, FERC Order 636 completed the transformation of the industry. Known as the Final Restructuring Rule, it mandates transportation "on a basis that is equal for all gas suppliers whether purchased from the pipeline or another seller." It requires the institution of "no-notice" transport service, liberalizes access to gas storage, increases a shipper's options to change receipt and delivery points, and increases downstream access to rights on upstream pipelines. The order reverses decades of inefficiency by requiring that a customer pay rates equal to the actual operating and capital costs that it imposes on the pipeline. Finally, a "capacity release" program requires each pipeline to set up an electronic bulletin board and to institute rules by which holders of unwanted transport capacity may take bids from others who

wish to lease or buy it. Somewhat oddly, Order 636 imposes price ceilings on the resale of capacity; these controls could cause shortages (see PRICE CONTROLS).

Despite economists' frequent criticisms of regulators and the courts, these were the prime forces that moved the gas industry from misregulation to competition. Converting pipelines into transporters allows customers the benefits of being able to search for attractive purchases, rather than obligating them to take whatever gas the pipeline chooses to buy. (The alternative of system supply remains.) Allowing customers to resell their pipeline rights further increases their options. The advent of open access transportation and a market in released capacity provided an important lesson in economics: although a pipeline is technologically a natural monopoly, a market is arising in which the services of that monopoly will be allocated competitively.

If LDCs can use pipelines as transporters, the next logical question is why final customers cannot use pipelines and LDCs to jointly transport gas for them. An industrial firm might buy gas from a producer, use an interstate pipeline to transport it to the city gate (currently legal), and then use LDC facilities for the final miles. Some state regulators have tried to prohibit such bypass of full LDC service, in hopes of perpetuating a rate regime in which industrial customers cross-subsidize residential customers. A growing number, however, now allow large users and associations of smaller users the option of using LDCs as transporters. An emerging gas brokerage industry now assembles groups of users, purchases their requirements from producers, and arranges for transport with pipelines and LDCs. Further limiting LDC powers, several U.S. appellate courts have, since 1989, ruled that state regulators cannot block residents from directly transacting with an interstate pipeline. As recently as 1988, FERC Chairman Martha Hesse called LDCs the only remaining islands of monopoly in a sea of competition. They may soon be submerged.

—Robert J. Michaels

Biography: Robert J. Michaels is an economics professor at California State University, Fullerton. He has served as consultant to gas producers and interstate pipelines.

Further Reading

Breyer, Stephen G., and Paul W. MacAvoy. *Energy Regulation by the Federal Power Commission*. 1974.

Michaels, Robert J. "The New Age of Natural Gas: How the Regulators Brought Competition." *Regulation* 16 (Winter 1993): 20–31.

Pierce, Richard J., Jr. "Reconstituting the Natural Gas Industry from Wellhead to Burnertip." *Energy Law Journal* 9, no. 1 (1988): 1–57.

Smith, Rodney T., Arthur S. DeVany, and Robert J. Michaels. "Defining a Right of Access to Interstate Natural Gas Pipelines." *Contemporary Policy Issues* 8 (April 1990): 142–58.

Traynor, William G. "Judicial Approval of Bypass Transportation: The Michcon Cases." *Wayne Law Review* 36 (Summer 1990): 1473–1506.

U.S. Department of Energy. Energy Information Administration. *Natural Gas Annual*, publication no. DOE/EIA-0131.

Occupational Licensing

S. David Young

■ Most Americans know that practicing medicine without a license is against the law. They also know that lawyers and dentists must have the state's approval before they can ply their trades. Few Americans, however, would guess that in some states falconers, ferret breeders, and palm readers are also subject to government regulation. Some regulations are relatively harmless, requiring little more of individuals than listing their names on official rosters. Sometimes, however, individuals must qualify for a state license to engage in a given trade or profession. At present, nearly five hundred occupations are licensed by at least one state. Indeed, it appears that every organized occupational group in America has tried at one time or another to acquire state licensure for its members. Today at least a fifth, and perhaps as much as a third, of the work force is directly affected by licensing laws.

The argument in favor of licensing always has been that it protects the public from incompetents, charlatans, and quacks. The main effect, however, is simply to restrict entry and reduce competition in the licensed occupation. Yet from the beginnings of the modern professional movement early in America's history until the seventies, the growth of licensing proceeded with little opposition. The possibility that licensing might be used to enhance professional income and power was considered incidental to serving the public interest.

A careful analysis of licensing's effects across a broad range of occupations reveals some striking, and strikingly negative, similarities. Occupational regulation has limited consumer choice, raised consumer costs, increased practitioner income, limited practitioner mobility, and deprived the poor of adequate services—all without demonstrated improvements in the quality or safety of the licensed activities.

Why have states required licensing of so many occupations if the results are so counter to consumer interests? Participants in any regulatory process must have a reason for getting involved. Because the number of potential political and legal battles is large, people tend to concentrate on those battles in which their personal stake is high. Because their per capita stakes in the licensing controversy are so much greater than those of consumers, it is professionals who usually determine the regulatory agenda in their domains. Crucial licensing decisions that can affect vast numbers of people are often made with little or no input from the public. If such a process serves the public interest, it is only by happenstance.

Licensing laws generally require candidates to meet four types of requirements: (1) formal schooling, (2) experience, (3) personal characteristics (such as citizenship and residence), and (4) successful completion of a licensing examination. The mechanism for enforcing these requirements and maintaining control over a licensed occupation is the state licensing board. The state legislature, in effect, grants a charter to the board, and the board's members, frequently drawn from the regulated profession itself, are appointed by the governor. Establishing licensure is only part of the story, of course. The tendency in all professions is to increase constraints on entry after licensing laws have been introduced, with existing members of the occupations protecting themselves with "grandfather clauses" that permit them to bypass the new entry requirements.

Many requirements found in licensing statutes and enforced by licensing boards are there by dint of custom or some arbitrary choice, not because the public is really served by them. Requirements are rarely based on the levels of knowledge, skill, ability, and other traits truly necessary to ensure adequate service. Apprenticeship requirements, for example, often bear little relation to the actual amount of time needed to acquire minimum competence. Until the courts called a halt to it, for example, it took longer in Illinois for an apprentice to become a master plumber than for a newly graduated physician to become a Fellow of the American College of Surgeons.

States also impose citizenship requirements on aspiring professionals. Defenders of such requirements argue that for certain professions, especially law, the practice of the profession is so closely associated with the country's history and traditions that licensees should be citizens. Others say that a person who wants to practice a licensed occupation and enjoy the benefits that licensure bestows ought to become a U.S. citizen within a reasonable period of time.

The courts have not accepted this line of reasoning, however. The Fourteenth Amendment provides that no state may deny equal protection of the law to any person within its jurisdiction; aliens, as well as citizens, are protected. This logic was used in 1981, when a federal court declared unconstitutional a Louisiana law requiring a person to be a U.S. citizen in order to practice dentistry. Similarly, many state laws requiring licensees to have lived in the state for a substantial period of time have been revoked in recent court cases. In 1985, for example, New Hampshire's residency requirement for lawyers was declared unconstitutional by the U.S. Supreme Court. Nevertheless, many residency provisions remain on the books and will continue to be enforced until challenged.

Although used ostensibly to help state licensing boards determine the fitness of candidates, most licensing exams require recall of a wide range of facts that may have little or nothing to do with good practice. For example, candidates taking California's architecture licensing exam have had to discuss the tomb of Queen Hatshepshut and the Temple of Apollo. The District of Columbia's cosmetology exam recently required applicants to do finger waves and pin curls—styles that have been out of fashion for decades (see sidebar). Even standardized national exams, now common in many professions, have rarely been more than superficially valid. Moreover, economists have found evidence that examination grading standards have sometimes been manipulated to reduce the number of applicants who pass the tests during tough economic times. In a study done for the U.S. Department of Labor, for example, economist Elton Rayack found that for ten of the twelve licensing exams he studied, failure rates were higher when unemployment rates were higher. My 1988 paper documents similar results for certified public accountants, although reforms mandating nationwide grading of the certification exam effectively ended the manipulation of failure rates.

Perhaps the most frequent criticism of licensing has been the failure of licensing boards to discipline licensees. A major cause is the reluctance of professionals to turn in one of their own. The in-group solidarity common to all professions causes members to frown on revealing unsavory activities of a fellow member to the public. Going public regarding infractions, no matter how grievous, is often viewed as disloyalty to the professional community.

Indeed, licensing agencies are usually more zealous in prosecuting unlicensed practitioners than in disciplining licensees. Even when action is brought against a licensee, harm done to consumers is unlikely to be the cause. Professionals are much more vulnerable to disciplinary action when they violate rules that limit competition. A 1986 report issued by the U.S. Department of Health and Human Services claims that despite the increasing rate of disciplinary actions taken by medical boards, few such actions are imposed because of malpractice or incompetence.

The evidence of disciplinary actions in other professions, such as law and dentistry, is no less disturbing than in medicine. According to Benjamin Shimberg's 1982 study, for example, as much as 16 percent of the California dental work performed in 1977 under insurance plans was so shoddy as to require retreatment. Yet in that year, the dental board disciplined only eight of its licensees for acts that had caused harm to patients.

Because licensing laws restrict entry, it is not surprising that such laws affect the income of licensees. William D. White's 1978 study of clinical laboratory personnel found that stringent licensing laws increased the relative wages of licensees by 16 percent. Lawrence Shepard's 1978 study compared average fees for dental services between states that recognize out-of-state licenses and those that do not. Controlling for other factors, he showed that the price of dental services and the average incomes of dentists were 12 to 15 percent higher in nonreciprocity states.

These higher costs might be acceptable if it could be shown that licensing enhances service quality. Most of the evidence on this issue, however, suggests that licensing has, at best, a neutral effect on quality and may even harm consumers. By making entry more costly, licensing increases the price of services rendered in the occupations and decreases the number of people employed in them. The result is a "Cadillac effect," in which consumers either purchase the services of high-quality practitioners at a high price or purchase no services at all. Some consumers, therefore, resort to do-it-yourself methods, which in some occupations has led to lower overall quality and less safety than if there were no licensing. The incidence of rabies is higher, for example, where there are strict limits on veterinary practice, and as Sidney Carroll and Robert Gaston documented, rates of electrocution are higher in states with the most restrictive licensing laws for electricians. Apparently, consumers often do their own electrical work in highly restrictive states rather than pay artificially high rates for professionals, with predictably tragic results. Carroll and Gaston also found, using data on retail sales of plumbing equipment, that plumbing restrictions increase the extent of do-it-yourself work.

Licensing laws have exerted a negative influence in many professions by inhibiting innovations in practice, training, education, and organization of services. The most prominent examples in recent years are the efforts of the organized medical profession to inhibit prepaid health plans and of lawyers to ban low-cost legal clinics.

In many fields advances have resulted from the very "crackpots," "quacks," and "outsiders" who have no standing in the profession and whom licensing seeks to eliminate. Thomas Edison, who had little formal education, could not be a licensed engineer under today's guidelines. Likewise, with the current education requirement, Mies van der Rohe and Frank Lloyd Wright would not qualify to sit for the architects' certifying examination. The leaders in the fight to establish inoculation as a cure for smallpox in colonial America were Cotton Mather and his fellow clergymen; their leading opponents were doctors. As Dennis

S. Lees wrote in *Economic Consequences of the Professions*: "Had retailing been organized like the professions, supermarkets with lower costs and prices . . . could never have emerged. Indeed, had the professions been dominant through manufacture and trade over the past two centuries, we would never have got to the horse-and-buggy stage, let alone beyond it."

The news is not all bad, however. The consumer movement of the seventies, along with a growing body of research that questions the social benefits of occupational regulation, has changed public attitudes about licensing. The result has been a slowdown in the growth of new regulation and, in a few isolated cases, the abolition of entire licensing boards. Some "sunset laws" have been enacted that require state agencies (including licensing boards) periodically to justify their existence or go out of business. Public representation on licensing boards has also become a popular way of improving accountability. Still, most professional groups have so far succeeded in thwarting serious deregulation.

—**S. David Young**

Biography: S. David Young is a professor at INSEAD (the European Institute of Business Administration) in France.

Further Reading

Carroll, Sidney L., and Robert J. Gaston. "Occupational Restrictions and the Quality of Service Received: Some Evidence." *Southern Economic Journal* 47 (1981): 959–76.

Gellhorn, Walter. "The Abuse of Occupational Licensing." *University of Chicago Law Review* 44 (Fall 1976): 6–27.

Lees, Dennis S. *Economic Consequences of the Professions.* 1966.

Lieberman, Jethro K. *Tyranny of the Experts.* 1970.

Maurizi, Alex. "Occupational Licensing and the Public Interest." *Journal of Political Economy* 82 (March/April 1974): 399–413.

Rayack, Elton. "An Economic Analysis of Occupational Licensure." Report prepared for the U.S. Department of Labor. 1976.

Shepard, Lawrence. "Licensing Restrictions and the Cost of Dental Care." *Journal of Law and Economics* 21 (April 1978): 187–201.

Shimberg, Benjamin. *Occupational Licensing: A Public Perspective.* 1982.

U.S. Department of Health and Human Services. Office of the Inspector General. "Medical Licensure and Discipline: An Overview." June 1986.

White, William D. "The Impact of Occupational Licensure on Clinical Laboratory Personnel." *Journal of Human Resources* 13 (Winter 1978): 91–102.

Young, S. David. *The Rule of Experts: Occupational Licensing in America.* 1987.

———. "The Economic Theory of Regulation: Evidence from the Uniform CPA Examination." *The Accounting Review* 63 (April 1988): 283–91.

Who Is Served?

Entrepreneur Taalib-Dan Abdul Uqdah runs Cornrows and Company, a Washington, D.C., salon that specializes in braiding the hair of black women. Starting with $500 in 1980, Uqdah had created a $500,000-a-year hair-care business by 1991. He refuses to use chemicals and, instead, weaves the hair into hundreds of tiny braids.

The District of Columbia government has tried at least four times to prosecute Uqdah for operating his shop without a license. Anyone who works with hair in D.C. must spend nine months in cosmetology school, at an out-of-pocket cost of about five thousand dollars. Yet such training would be useless for Uqdah and his employees because the schools do not teach his methods; because braiding does not use chemicals, it is not regarded as cosmetology.

Uqdah tried to get the law changed by having the D.C. Board of Cosmetology create a license for braiding, but the board refused. When he appealed to the City Council, the board successfully lobbied against him. The board recently fined him one thousand dollars for "operating an unlicensed beauty shop."

At this writing he faced the possibility of a prison sentence.

—DRH

Patents

David R. Henderson

■ A patent is the government grant of monopoly on an invention for a limited amount of time. Patents in the United States are granted for seventeen years from the date the patent is issued. Other countries grant patents for similar time periods. Italy and Mexico grant patents for fifteen years from the date of application; Japan grants them for fifteen years from the patent's publication; Germany grants for eighteen years from application. An invention is a new device or composition of matter, or a newly created technical method. In contrast, the discovery of a law of nature—the law of gravity, for example, is not an invention.

The economic justification for patents is straightforward. If there were no patents, then someone who invested time and money to create an invention would not necessarily get a return on even a very valuable invention. The reason is that others could imitate his or her invention. If imitators have the same production costs as the inventor, they could compete the price down so that the original inventor covers only production costs, but not invention costs. Potential inventors, knowing this, would be less likely to invest in inventing. But with a patent system in place, potential inventors are more likely to invest because they can expect to have a monopoly on their inventions for as long as seventeen years.

Although this argument is airtight, it is, in itself, an insufficient argument for patents. There are two main reasons.

First, there is a cost to the patent system. By creating a monopoly, it causes higher prices for consumers and thus a loss to them that outweighs the gain to producers (see MONOPOLY). One might argue that the loss is fictitious because without the patent the invention would not have been made. But many inventions would be made and have been made without patents. Sometimes such inventions occur intentionally, such as when the inventor thinks he can keep the invention secret long enough (but typically much less than seventeen years) to collect a monopoly return on it. Other times, the inventions occur by accident. Either way, one of the patent system's negative effects is to create monopolies in inventions that would have existed anyway.

Second, as British economist Arnold Plant argued in the thirties, the patent system diverts creative energy into the patentable inventions and away from the kinds of improvements that cannot be patented. An example of such an unpatentable improvement would be a new way of organizing shelf space in a supermarket. There is no assurance that this diversion creates net economic benefits for society.

One argument against patents, at one time thought to have merit, has been shown to be bogus. This is the argument that a monopolist who gets a patent on an improved product that costs no more to produce than his or her existing product would suppress it rather than use it. By so doing, goes the argument, the monopolist would avoid destroying the market for his current product. This idea has been so commonly held by noneconomists that it is the premise of a 1952 Alec Guinness comedy, *The Man in the White Suit*, and a more sinister 1980 movie titled *The Formula*. In the former a perpetually durable suit is suppressed, and in the latter a formula for synthetic fuel is suppressed. UCLA economist Jack Hirshleifer has shown that a rational monopolist would not suppress such inventions.

Consider, says Hirshleifer, a monopolist of light bulbs. He or she acquires the patent to a new light bulb that gives twice as many hours of use as his current bulbs, but that costs the same to produce. Hirshleifer points out that what the monopolist's customers care about is light hours. So, argues Hirshleifer, the monopolist could sell the same number of light hours at the same price per light hour by producing half as many as the new light bulbs as he or she was producing of the old ones, and charging twice the price. The monopolist would then earn the same revenue, but costs would be cut in half. Bottom line: higher profits from using the invention.

—David R. Henderson

Biography: David R. Henderson is the editor of this encyclopedia. He is a senior research fellow with Stanford's Hoover Institution and an associate professor of economics at the Naval Postgraduate School in Monterey, California. He was formerly a senior economist with the President's Council of Economic Advisers.

Further Reading

Hirshleifer, Jack. "Suppression of Inventions." *Journal of Political Economy* 79 (March/April 1971): 382–83.

Machlup, Fritz. "Patents." In *International Encyclopedia of the Social Sciences*, vol. 11, edited by David L. Sills. 1968.

Plant, Arnold. "The Economic Theory Concerning Patents for Inventions." *Economica* 1 (February 1934): 30–51.

Stigler, George J. "A Note on Patents." In Stigler. *The Organization of Industry*, chap. 11. 1968.

Price Controls

Hugh Rockoff

■ Governments have been trying to set maximum or minimum prices since ancient times. The Old Testament prohibited interest on loans, medieval governments fixed the maximum price of bread, and in recent years governments in the United States have fixed the price of gasoline, the rent on apartments in New York City, and the minimum wage, to name a few. At times governments go beyond fixing specific prices and try to control the general level of prices, as was done in the United States during both world wars, during the Korean War, and by the Nixon administration from 1971 to 1973.

The appeal of price controls is easy to divine. Even though they fail to protect many consumers and hurt others, controls hold out the promise of protecting groups of consumers who are particularly hard-pressed to meet price increases. Thus the prohibition against usury—charging high interest on loans—was intended to protect someone forced to borrow by desperation; the maximum price for bread was supposed to protect the poor, who depended on bread to survive; and rent controls were supposed to protect those who rented at a time when demand for apartments appeared to exceed the supply and landlords were able to "gouge" tenants.

But despite the frequent use of price controls, and despite the superficial logic of their appeal, economists are generally opposed to them, except perhaps for very brief periods during emergencies. The reason is

that controls on prices distort the allocation of resources. To paraphrase a remark by Milton Friedman, economists may not know much, but they do know how to produce a surplus or shortage. Price ceilings, which prevent prices from exceeding a certain maximum, cause shortages. Price floors, which prohibit prices below a certain minimum, cause surpluses. Suppose that the supply and demand for automobile tires are balanced at the current price, and that the government then fixes a lower ceiling price. The number of tires supplied will be reduced, but the number demanded will increase. The result will be excess demand and empty shelves. Although some consumers will be lucky enough to purchase tires at the lower price, others will be forced to do without.

Because controls prevent the price system from rationing the supply to those who demand it, some other mechanism will take its place. A queue or lineup, once a familiar sight in the controlled economies of Eastern Europe, is one possibility. When the U.S. government set maximum prices for gasoline in 1973 and 1979, dealers sold gas on a first-come–first-served basis, and drivers got a little taste of what life was like for people in the Soviet Union: they had to wait in long lines to buy gas. The true price of gas, which included both the cash paid and the time spent waiting in line, was often higher than if prices were not controlled at all. At one time in 1979, for example, the

U.S. government fixed the price of gasoline at about $1.00 per gallon. If the market price would have been $1.20, a driver who bought ten gallons apparently saved $.20 per gallon, or $2.00. But if the driver had to line up for thirty minutes to buy gas, and if her time was worth $8.00 per hour, the real cost to her was $10.00 for the gas and $4.00 for the time, an overall cost of $1.40 per gallon. Some gas, of course, was held for friends, long-time customers, the politically well-connected, or those who were willing to pay a little cash on the side.

The incentives to evade controls are ever present, and the forms that evasion can take are limitless. The precise form depends on the nature of the good or service, the organization of the industry, the degree of government enforcement, and so on. One of the simplest forms of evasion is quality deterioration. In the United States during World War II, fat was added to hamburger, candy bars were made smaller and of inferior ingredients, and landlords reduced their maintenance of rent-controlled apartments. The government can attack quality deterioration by issuing specific product standards (hamburger must contain so much lean meat, apartments must be painted once a year, and so on) and by government oversight and enforcement. But this means that the government bureaucracy controlling prices tends to get bigger, more intrusive, and more expensive.

Sometimes more subtle forms of evasion arise. One is the tie-in sale. During World War I, for example, in order to buy wheat flour at the official price, consumers were often required to purchase unwanted quantities of rye or potato flour. Forced up-trading is another. Consider a manufacturer that produces a lower-quality, lower-priced line sold in large volumes at a small markup, and a higher-priced, higher-quality line sold in small quantities at a high markup. When the government introduces price ceilings and causes a shortage of both lines, the manufacturer may discontinue the lower-priced line, forcing the consumer to "trade up" to the higher-priced line. In World War II, for this reason, the government made numerous attempts to force clothing manufacturers to continue lower-priced lines. Under the controls imposed by President Nixon in the early seventies, steel manufacturers eliminated a middle grade of steel sheet, allegedly with the intention of inducing buyers to purchase a more expensive grade.

Not only do producers have an incentive to raise prices, but at least some consumers have an incentive to pay them. The result may be payments on the side to distributors (a bribe for the superintendent of a rent-controlled building, for example) or it may be a full-fledged black market in which goods are bought and sold clandestinely. Prices in black markets may be above not only the official price, but even the price that would prevail in a free market, because the buyers are unusually desperate and because both buyers and sellers face penalties if their transactions are detected.

The obvious costs of queuing, evasion, and black markets often lead governments to impose some form of rationing. The simplest is a coupon issued to consumers entitling them to buy a fixed quantity of the controlled good. For example, each motorist might receive a coupon permitting the purchase of one set of new tires. Rationing solves some of the shortage problems created by controls. Producers no longer find it easy to divert supplies to the black market since they must have ration tickets to match their production; distributors no longer have as much incentive to accept bribes or demand tie-in purchases; consumers no longer have as much incentive to pay excessive prices since they are assured a minimum amount.

But rationing creates its own problems. The government must undertake the difficult job of adjusting rations to reflect fluctuating supplies and demands and the needs of individual consumers. While an equal ration for each consumer makes sense in a few cases—bread in a city under siege is the classic example—most rationing programs must face the problem that consumer needs vary widely. Some motorists drive a lot and buy a lot of gasoline, and others drive very little.

One solution is to tailor the ration to the needs of individual consumers. Physicians or salesmen can be given extra rations of gasoline. In World War II, community boards in the United States had the power to issue extra rations to particularly needy individuals. The danger of favoritism and corruption in such a scheme, particularly if continued after the spirit of patriotism has begun to erode, is obvious. One way of ameliorating some of the problems created by rationing is to permit a free market in ration tickets. The free exchange of ration tickets has the advantage of providing additional income for consumers who sell their extra tickets and also improves the well-being of those who buy. But the white market does nothing to encourage additional supplies, an end that can be accomplished only by removing price controls.

With all of the problems generated by controls, we can well ask why are they ever imposed, and why are they sometimes maintained for so long. The answer, in part, is that the public does not always see the links between controls and the problems they create. The elimination of lower-priced lines of merchandise may be interpreted simply as callous disregard for the poor rather than a consequence of controls. But price controls almost always benefit some subset of consumers, who may have a particular claim to public sympathy and who, in any case, have a strong interest in lobbying for controls. Minimum wage laws may create unemployment among the unskilled, but they do raise the income of poor workers who remain employed; rent controls make it difficult for young people to find an apartment, but they do hold down the price of rent for those who already have an apartment when controls are instituted (see RENT CONTROL).

General price controls—controls on prices of many goods—are often imposed when the public becomes alarmed that inflation is out of control. In the twentieth century, war has frequently been the reason for general price controls. Here, the case can be made that controls have a positive psychological benefit that outweighs, at least in the short run, the costs of shortages, bureaucracy, black markets, and rationing. Surging inflation may lead to panic buying, strikes, animosity toward racial or ethnic minorities that are perceived as benefiting from inflation, and so on. Price controls may make a positive contribution by calming these fears, particularly if patriotism can be counted on to limit evasion. However, such benefits are not likely to outlive the wartime emergency.

Moreover, most inflation, even in wartime, is due to inflationary monetary and fiscal policies rather than to panic buying. To the extent that wartime controls suppress price increases produced by monetary and fiscal policy, controls only postpone the day of reckoning, converting what would have been a steady inflation into a period of slow inflation followed by more rapid inflation. Also, part of the apparent stability of the price indices under wartime controls is an illusion. All of the problems with price controls—queuing, evasion, black markets, and rationing—raise the real price of goods to consumers, and these effects are only partly taken into account when the price indices are computed. When controls are removed, the hidden inflation is unveiled. During World War II, for example, measured inflation remained comparatively modest. But after controls were lifted the consumer price index jumped 18 percent between December 1945 and December 1946, the biggest one-year increase in this century.

Inflation is extremely difficult to contain through general controls, in part because some prices are inevitably left uncontrolled. At times the decision to leave some prices out is deliberate. The reason for controlling only some prices—those, say, of steel, wheat, and oil—is that these goods are strategic in the sense that controlling their prices is sufficient to control the whole price level. But demand tends to shift from the controlled to the uncontrolled sector, with the result that prices in the latter rise even faster than before. Resources follow prices, and supplies tend to rise in the uncontrolled sector at the expense of supplies in the controlled sector. Because the controlled sector was originally chosen to include goods thought to be crucial inputs for many production processes, the reduction in the amount of these inputs is particularly galling. Thus, if controls are kept in place for a long time, a government that begins by controlling prices on selected goods tends to replace them with across-the-board controls. This is what happened in the United States in World War II.

A second problem that afflicts general controls is the trade-off between the need to have a simple program generally perceived as fair and the need for sufficient flexibility to maintain a semblance of efficiency. Simplicity requires holding most prices constant, but efficiency requires making frequent changes. Adjustments of relative prices, however, subject the bureaucracy administering controls to a barrage of lobbying and complaints of unfairness. This conflict was brought out sharply by the American experience in World War II. At first, relative prices were changed frequently on the advice of economists who maintained that this was necessary to eliminate potential shortages and other distortions in specific markets. But mounting complaints that the program was unfair and was not stopping inflation led to President Roosevelt's famous "hold-the-line" order, issued in April 1943, that froze most prices. Whatever its defects as economic policy, the hold-the-line order was easy to explain and to sell to the public.

The case for imposing general controls in peacetime turns on the possibility that controls can ease the transition from high to low inflation. If, after a long period of inflation, a tight money policy is introduced to reduce inflation, some prices may continue to rise for a time at the old higher rate. Wages, in particular, may continue to rise because of long-term contracts or because workers fail to appreciate the extent of the change in policy. That, in turn, leads to high unemployment and reduced output. Price controls may limit these costs of disinflation by prohibiting wage increases that are out of line with the new trends in demand and prices. From this viewpoint restrictive monetary policy is the operation that cures inflation, and price and wage controls are the anesthesia that suppresses the pain.

While the logic is acceptable, the result often is not. In the eyes of the public, price controls free the monetary authority—the Federal Reserve in the United States—from responsibility for inflation. As a result the pressures on the Fed to avoid recession may lead to a continuation or even acceleration of excessive growth in the money supply. The painkiller is mistaken for the cure. Something very like this happened in the United States under the controls imposed by President Nixon in 1971. Although controls were justified on the grounds that they were being used to "buy time" while more fundamental cures for inflation were put in place, monetary policy continued to be expansionary, perhaps even more so than before.

The study of price controls teaches important lessons about free competitive markets. By examining cases in which controls have prevented the price mechanism from working, we gain a better appreciation of its usual elegance and efficiency. This does not mean that there are no circumstances in which temporary controls may be effective. But a fair reading of economic history shows just how rare those circumstances are.

—**Hugh Rockoff**

Biography: Hugh Rockoff is a professor of economics at Rutgers University in New Brunswick, New Jersey, and a research associate of the National Bureau of Economic Research.

Further Reading

Blinder, Alan S. *Economic Policy and the Great Stagflation.* 1979.
Clinard, Marshall Barron. *The Black Market: A Study in White Collar Crime.* 1952.
Galbraith, John Kenneth. *A Theory of Price Control.* 1952.
Grayson, C. Jackson. *Confessions of a Price Controller.* 1974.
Jonung, Lars. *The Political Economy of Price Controls: The Swedish Experience 1970–1987.* 1990.
Rockoff, Hugh. *Drastic Measures: A History of Wage and Price Controls in the United States.* 1984.
Schultz, George P., and Robert Z. Aliber, eds. *Guidelines: Informal Controls and the Market Place.* 1966.
Taussig, Frank W. "Price-Fixing as Seen by a Price-Fixer." *Quarterly Journal of Economics* 33 (1919): 205–41.

Rent Control

Walter Block

■ New York State legislators defend the War Emergency Tenant Protection Act—also known as rent control—as a way of protecting tenants from war-related housing shortages. The war referred to in the law is not the recent Gulf war, nor the Vietnam war. It is World War II. That is when rent control started in New York City. Of course, war has very little to do with apartment shortages. On the contrary, the difficulty is created by rent control, the supposed solution. Gotham is far from the only city to have embraced rent control—a form of housing socialism. Many others across the the United States have succumbed to the blandishments of this legislative "fix."

Rent control, like all other government-mandated price controls, is a law placing a maximum price, or a "rent ceiling," on what landlords may charge tenants. If it is to have any effect, the rent level must be set at a rate below that which would otherwise have prevailed. (An enactment prohibiting apartment rents from exceeding, say, $100,000 per month, would have no effect since no one would pay that amount in any case.) But if rents are established at less than their equilibrium levels, demand will necessarily exceed supply, and rent control will lead to a shortage of dwelling spaces. Absent controls on prices, if the amount of a commodity or service demanded is larger than the amount supplied, prices rise to eliminate the shortage (by both bringing

forth new supply and by reducing the amount demanded). But controls prevent rents from attaining market-clearing levels and shortages result.

With shortages in the controlled sector, this excess demand spills over onto the noncontrolled sector (typically, new upper-bracket rental units or condominiums). But this noncontrolled segment of the market is likely to be smaller than it would be without controls because property owners fear that controls may one day be slapped on them. The high demand in the noncontrolled segment along with the small supply, both caused by rent control, boost prices in that segment. Paradoxically, then, even though rents may be lower in the controlled sector, they rise greatly for uncontrolled units and may be higher for rental housing as a whole.

As in the case of other price ceilings, rent control causes shortages, diminution in the quality of the product, and queues. But rent control differs from other such schemes. With price controls on gasoline, the waiting lines worked on a first-come–first-served basis. With rent control, because the law places sitting tenants first in the queue, many of them can benefit.

The Effects of Rent Control

Economists are virtually unanimous in the conclusion that rent controls are destructive. In a late-seventies poll of 211 econo-

421

mists published in the December 1984 issue of *American Economic Review,* slightly more than 98 percent of U.S. respondents agreed that ''a ceiling on rents reduces the quantity and quality of housing available.'' Similarly, the June 1988 issue of *Canadian Public Policy* reported that over 95 percent of the Canadian economists polled agreed with the statement. The agreement cuts across the usual political spectrum, ranging all the way from Nobel Prize winners Milton Friedman and Friedrich Hayek on the ''right'' to their fellow Nobel Laureate Gunnar Myrdal, an important architect of the Swedish Labor Party's welfare state, on the ''left.'' Myrdal stated, ''Rent control has in certain Western countries constituted, maybe, the worst example of poor planning by governments lacking courage and vision.'' Fellow Swedish economist (and socialist) Assar Lindbeck, asserted, ''In many cases rent control appears to be the most efficient technique presently known to destroy a city—except for bombing.''

Economists have shown that rent control diverts new investment, which would otherwise have gone to rental housing, toward other, greener pastures—greener in terms of financial reward, but not in terms of consumer need. They have demonstrated that it leads to housing deterioration, to fewer repairs and less maintenance. For example, Paul Niebanck reports that 29 percent of rent-controlled housing in the United States is deteriorated, but only 8 percent of the uncontrolled units are in such a state of disrepair. Joel Brenner and Herbert Franklin cite similar statistics for England and France.

The economic reasons are straightforward. One effect of government oversight is to retard investment in residential rental units. Imagine that you have $5 million to invest and can place the funds in any industry you wish. In most businesses governments will place only limited controls and taxes on your enterprise. But if you entrust your money to rental housing, you must pass one additional hurdle: the rent-control authority, with its hearings, red tape, and rent ceilings. Under these conditions is it any wonder that you are less likely to build or purchase rental housing?

This line of reasoning holds not just for you, but for everyone else as well. As a result the supply of apartments for rent will be far smaller than otherwise. And not so amazingly, the preceding analysis holds true not only for the case where rent controls are in place, but even where they are only threatened. The mere anticipation of controls is enough to place a chilling effect on such investment. Instead, everything else under the sun in the real estate market has been built: condominiums, office towers, hotels, warehouses, commercial space. Why? Because such investments have never been subject to rent controls, and no one fears that they ever will be. It is no accident that these facilities boast healthy vacancy rates and only slowly increasing rental rates, while residential space suffers from a virtual zero vacancy rate and skyrocketing prices in the uncontrolled sector. Evidence for this is seen in the comparative vacancy rates for residential and commercial real estate; exceedingly small in the former case, reaching double-digit levels in the latter.

Although many rent-control ordinances specifically exempt new rental units from coverage, investors are too cautious (perhaps too smart) to put their faith in rental housing. In numerous cases housing units supposedly exempt forever from controls were nevertheless brought under the provisions of this law due to some "emergency" or other. New York City's government, for example, has three times broken its promise to exempt new or vacant units from control. So prevalent is this practice of rent-control authorities that a new term has been invented to describe it: "recapture."

Rent control has destroyed entire sections of sound housing in New York's South Bronx. It has led to decay and abandonment throughout the entire five boroughs of the city. Although hard statistics on abandonments are not available, William Tucker reports estimates that about thirty thousand New York apartments were abandoned annually from 1972 to 1982, a loss of almost a third of a million units in this eleven-year period. Thanks to rent control, and to potential investors' rational fear that rent control will become even more stringent, no sensible investor will build rental housing unsubsidized by government.

Effects on Tenants

Existing rental units fare poorly under rent control. Even with the best will in the world, the landlord cannot afford to pay his escalating fuel, labor, and materials bills, to say nothing of refinancing his mortgage, out of the rent increase he can legally charge. And under rent controls he lacks the best will; the incentive he had under free-market conditions to supply tenant services is severely reduced.

The sitting tenant is "protected" by rent control but, in many cases, receives no real rental bargain because of improper maintenance, poor repairs and painting, and grudging provision of services. The enjoyment he can derive out of his dwelling space ultimately tends to be reduced to a level commensurate with his controlled rent.

There are exceptions to this general rule. Many tenants, usually rich ones who are politically connected, or who were lucky enough to be in the right place at the right time, can gain a lot from rent control. Tenants in some of the nicest neighborhoods in New York City pay a scandalously small fraction of the market price of their apartments. Former mayor Ed Koch, for example, pays $441.49 for an apartment worth about $1,200 per month. Some people in this fortunate position use their apartments like a hotel room, visiting only a few times per year.

Then there is the "old lady effect." Consider the case of a two-parent, four-child family that has occupied a ten-room rental dwelling. One by one the children grow up, marry, and move elsewhere. The husband dies. Now the lady is left with a gigantic apartment. She uses only two or three of the rooms and, to save on heating and cleaning, closes off the remainder. Without rent control she would move to a smaller accommodation. But rent control makes that option unattractive. Needless to say, these practices further exacerbate the housing crisis. Repeal of rent control would free up thousands of rooms very quickly, dampening the impetus toward vastly higher rents.

What determines whether or not a tenant benefits from rent control? If the building in which he lives is in a good neighborhood, where rents would rise appreciably if rent control were repealed, then the landlord has an incentive to maintain the building against the prospect of that happy day. This incentive is enhanced if there are many decontrolled units in the building (due to "vacancy decontrol" when tenants move out) or privately owned condominiums for whom the landlord must provide adequate services. Then the tenant who pays the scandalously low rent may "free-ride" on his neighbors. But in the more typical case the quality of housing services tends to reflect rental payments. This, at least, is the situation that will prevail at equilibrium.

If government really had the best interests of tenants at heart and was for some reason determined to employ controls, it would do the very opposite of imposing rent restrictions: it would instead control the price of every other good and service available, apart from residential suites, in an attempt to divert resources out of all those other opportunities and into this one field. But that, of course, would bring about full-scale socialism, the very system under which the Eastern Europeans suffered so grimly. If the government wanted to help the poor and was for some reason constrained to keep rent controls, it would do better to tightly control rents on luxury unit rentals and to eliminate rent controls on more modest dwellings—the very opposite of present practice. Then, builders' incentives would be turned around. Instead of erecting luxury dwellings, which are now exempt, they would be led, "as if by an invisible hand," to create housing for the poor and middle classes.

Solutions

The negative consequences of rent legislation have become so massive and perverse that even many of its former supporters have spoken out against it. Instead of urging a quick termination of controls, however, some pundits would only allow landlords to buy tenants out of their controlled dwellings. That they propose such a solution is understandable. Because tenants outnumber landlords and are usually convinced that rent control is in their best interests, they are likely to invest considerable political energy in maintaining rent control. Having landlords "buy off" these opponents of reform, therefore, could be a politically effective way to end rent control.

But making property owners pay to escape a law that has victimized many of them for years is not an effective way to make them confident that rent controls will be absent in the future. The surest way to encourage private investment is to signal investors that housing will be safe from rent control. And the surest way to do that is to eliminate the possibility of rent control with an amendment to the state constitution that forbids it.

It may seem paradoxical to many people that the best way to help tenants is to grant economic freedom to landlords. But it's true.

—Walter Block

Biography: Walter Block is an economics professor at the College of the Holy Cross in Worcester, Massachusetts. He is also an adjunct scholar at the Fraser, Cato, and Mises institutes.

Further Reading

Block, Walter, and Edgar Olsen, eds. *Rent Control: Myths and Realities*. 1981.

Brenner, Joel F., and Herbert M. Franklin. *Rent Control in North America and Four European Countries*. 1977.

Niebanck, Paul L. *Rent Control and the Rental Housing Market in New York City*. 1968.

Tucker, William. *The Excluded Americans: Homelessness and Housing Policies*. 1990.

Rent Control: It's Worse Than Bombing

NEW DELHI—A "romantic conception of socialism" . . . destroyed Vietnam's economy in the years after the Vietnam war, Foreign Minister Nguyen Co Thach said Friday.

Addressing a crowded news conference in the Indian capital, Mr. Thach admitted that controls . . . had artificially encouraged demand and discouraged supply. . . .

House rents had . . . been kept low . . . so all the houses in Hanoi had fallen into disrepair, said Mr. Thach.

"The Americans couldn't destroy Hanoi, but we have destroyed our city by very low rents. We realized it was stupid and that we must change policy," he said.

> —from a news report in *Journal of Commerce,* quoted
> in Dan Seligman, "Keeping Up," *Fortune,* February 27, 1989.

Riskless Society

Aaron Wildavsky

■ Since the late fifties the regulation of risks to health and safety has taken on ever-greater importance in public policy debates—and actions. In its efforts to protect citizens against hard-to-detect hazards such as industrial chemicals and against obvious hazards in the workplace and elsewhere, Congress has created or increased the authority of the Food and Drug Administration, the Environmental Protection Agency, the Occupational Health and Safety Administration, the Consumer Protection Agency, and other administrative agencies.

Activists in the pursuit of a safer society decry the damage that industrial progress wreaks on unsuspecting citizens. Opponents of the "riskless society," on the other hand, complain that government is unnecessarily proscribing free choice in the pursuit of costly protection that people do not need or want. This article describes some facts about risk, along with some academic theories about why people on both sides of the risk debate take the positions they do.

The health of human beings is a joint product of their genetic inheritance (advice: choose healthy and long-lived parents), their way of life (the poor black person who eats regularly and in moderation, exercises, does not smoke or drink, is married, and does not worry overly much is likely to be healthier than the rich white person who does the opposite), and political economy (live in a rich, democratic, and technologi-cally advanced society). Contrary to common opinion, living in a rich, industrialized, technologically advanced country that makes considerable use of industrial chemicals and nuclear power is a lot healthier than living in a poor, nonindustrialized nation that uses little modern technology or industrial chemicals. That individuals in rich nations are far healthier, live far longer, and can do more of the things they want to do at corresponding ages than people in poor countries is a rule without exception.

Prosperous also means efficient. The most polluted nations in the world, many more times polluted than democratic and industrial societies, are the former communist countries of Central Europe and the Soviet Union. To produce one unit of output, communist countries use two to four times the amount of energy and material used in capitalist countries. Therefore, individuals unfortunate enough to live in an inefficient economy die younger and have more serious illnesses than in the Western and industrial democracies. A little richer is a lot safer. As Peter Huber demonstrated in *Regulation* magazine, "For a 45-year-old man working in manufacturing, a 15 percent increase in income has about the same risk-reducing value as eliminating all hazards—every one of them—from his workplace."

Among the many facts that might be observed from tables 1 and 2 is that longevity has increased dramatically (with only occasional downturns) since the middle of the

TABLE 1

Expectation of Life in the United States

Calendar period	Age	Calendar period	Age
WHITE MALES		ALL OTHER MALES[4]	
1850[3]	38.3	1900–1902[3]	32.54
1890[3]	42.50	1909–1911[3]	34.05
1900–1902[2]	48.23	1919–1921[3]	47.14
1909–1911[2]	50.23	1929–1931	47.55
1919–1921[3]	56.34	1939–1941	52.33
1929–1931	59.12	1949–1951	58.91
1939–1941	62.81	1959–1961[6]	61.48
1949–1951	66.31	1969–1971[4]	60.98
1959–1961[6]	67.55	1979–1981	65.63
1969–1971[6]	67.94	1985	67.2
1979–1981	70.82	1986	67.2
1985	71.9	1987	67.3
1986	72.0		
1987	72.2		
WHITE FEMALES		ALL OTHER FEMALES[4]	
1850[3]	40.5	1900–1902[2]	35.04
1890[3]	44.46	1909–1911[3]	37.67
1900–1902[3]	51.08	1919–1921[3]	46.92
1909–1911[3]	53.62	1929–1931	49.51
1919–1921[3]	58.53	1939–1941	55.51
1929–1931	62.67	1949–1951	62.70
1939–1941	67.29	1959–1961[3]	66.47
1949–1951	72.03	1969–1971[6]	69.05
1959–1961[3]	74.19	1979–1981	74.00
1969–1971[4]	75.49	1985	75.0
1979–1981	78.22	1986	75.1
1985	78.7	1987	75.2
1986	78.8		
1987	78.9		

1. Massachusetts only; white and nonwhite combined, the latter being about 1% of the total. 2. Original Death Registration dates. 3. Death Registration States of 1920. 4. Data for periods 1900–1902 to 1929–1931 relate to blacks only. 5. Alaska and Hawaii included beginning in 1959. 6. Deaths of nonresidents of the United States excluded starting in 1970. *Sources: Department of Health and Human Services, National Center for Health Statistics.*

SOURCE: The 1991 Information Please Almanac, *Boston: Houghton Mifflin, 1991, pp. 817, 820.*

TABLE 2

Mortality
Death Rates for Selected Causes

	Death Rates per 100,000						
Cause of Death	1989[3]	1988[3]	1985	1980	1950	1945–49	1920–24[4]	1900–04[4]
Typhoid fever	n.a.	n.a.	—	0.0	0.1	0.2	7.3	26.7
Communicable diseases								
of childhood	n.a.	n.a.	n.a.	0.0	1.3	2.3	33.8	65.2
Measles	0.0	—	—	0.0	0.3	0.6	7.3	10.0
Scarlet fever	n.a.	n.a.	1.0	0.0	0.2	0.1	4.0	11.8
Whooping cough	0.0	—	—	0.0	0.7	1.0	8.9	10.7
Diphtheria	n.a.	n.a.	—	0.0	0.3	0.7	13.7	32.7
Pneumonia and influenza	30.3	31.5	27.9	23.3	31.3	41.3	140.3	184.3
Influenza	0.5	0.8	0.8	1.1	4.4	5.0	34.8	22.8
Pneumonia	29.7	30.7	27.1	22.0	26.9	37.2	105.5	161.5
Tuberculosis	0.7	0.8	0.7	0.8	22.5	33.3	96.7	184.7
Cancer	199.9	198.2	191.7	182.5	139.8	134.0	86.9	67.7
Diabetes mellitus	18.7	16.1	16.2	15.0	16.2	24.1	17.1	12.2
Major cardiovascular								
diseases	375.3	394.5	410.7	434.5	510.8	493.1	369.9	359.5
Diseases of the heart	295.9	311.7	325.0	335.2	356.8	325.1	169.8	153.0
Cerebrovascular								
diseases	58.9	60.9	64.0	74.6	104.0	93.8	93.5	106.3
Nephritis and nephrosis	8.9	9.1	9.4	7.6	16.4	48.4	81.5	84.3
Syphilis	0.0	0.0	0.0	0.1	5.0	8.4	17.6	12.9
Appendicitis	0.2	0.2	0.2	0.3	2.0	3.5	14.0	9.4
Accidents, all forms	37.2	39.7	38.6	46.0	60.6	67.6	70.8	79.2
Motor vehicle accidents	18.9	20.4	18.8	23.0	23.1	22.3	12.9	n.a.
Infant mortality[3]	n.a.	9.9	10.6	12.5	29.2	33.3	76.7	n.a.
Neonatal mortality[3]	n.a.	6.4	7.0	8.4	20.5	22.9	39.7	n.a.
Fetal mortality[3]	n.a.	n.a.	7.9	9.2	19.2	21.6	n.a.	n.a.
Maternal mortality[3]	n.a.	n.a.	0.1	0.1	0.8	1.4	6.9	n.a.
All causes	868.1	883.9	890.8	883.4	960.1	1,000.6	1,157.4	1,621.6

1. Based on a 10% sample of deaths. 2. Rates per 1,000 live births. 3. Ratio per 1,000 births. 4. Includes only deaths occurring within the registration areas. Beginning with 1933, area includes the entire United States; Alaska included beginning in 1959 and Hawaii in 1960. Rates per 100,000 population residing in areas, enumerated as of April 1 for 1940, 1950, and 1980 and estimated as of July 1 for all other years. Due to changes in statistical methods, death rates are not strictly comparable. n.a. = not available. *Sources: Department of Health and Human Services, National Center for Health Statistics.*

SOURCE: The 1991 Information Please Almanac, *Boston: Houghton Mifflin, 1991, pp. 817, 820.*

last century. Black Americans and other minorities lag behind white Americans, but their life expectancy has also nearly doubled, albeit from a lower starting point. The most unequal relationship, though seldom commented upon, is the far greater longevity of females of all races compared to males (a 6.7-year advantage to white females, a 7.9 year advantage to black females). This female advantage is far greater than the lead in longevity of white men over nonwhite men (4.9 years) or of white women over nonwhite women (3.7 years).

Turning to death rates, note the decline by half since 1900 of deaths from all forms of accidents, and the spectacular declines in all sorts of diseases. The sixfold drop in deaths from pneumonia and influenza is par for the course. On the other side of the ledger, cancer continues to rise, though it has slowed down, and major cardiovascular diseases remain high. Why these discrepancies? Cancer is largely a disease of old age. When people died at roughly half the present life expectancy, they died before having an opportunity, if one may call it that, to get cancer. Of course, people must die of something. Lacking other information, it is usual to classify deaths due to heart failure, given that heart stoppage is one of the signs of death.

The most dangerous activities are precisely what we might think they are—sports such as motorcycling and parachuting and occupations such as fire fighting and coal mining. On the other hand, many of the risks that people have begun to worry about in recent years are far smaller than generally perceived. However low the risk of being killed by lightning (see table 3), the risk of getting cancer from drinking tap water

TABLE 3

Annual Fatality Rates per 100,000 Persons at Risk

Activity/Event	Death Rate
Motorcycling	2,000
Aerial acrobatics (planes)	500
Smoking (all causes)	300
Sport parachuting	200
Smoking (cancer)	120
Fire fighting	80
Hang gliding	80
Coal mining	63
Farming	63
Motor vehicles	24
Police work (nonclerical)	22
Boating	5
Rodeo performer	3
Hunting	3
Fires	2.8
1 diet drink per day (saccharin)	1.0
4 tbsp. peanut butter per day (aflatoxin)	0.8
Floods	0.06
Lightning	0.05
Meteorite	0.000006

SOURCE: Adapted from E. L. Crouch and R. Wilson, Risk/Benefit Analysis, Cambridge: Balinger, 1982. Reported in Paul Slovic, "Informing and Educating the Public about Risk," Risk Analysis, 6, no. 4 (1986): 407.

(chlorine forms chloroform, which is a weak carcinogen) is less than one-third of that, and the harm done by pesticides in food, based largely on animal studies, is even less. The lowest risk that statisticians have measured—getting killed by a falling meteorite—measures in at six-millionths of 1 percent.

In its regulations specifying maximum discharges of potentially harmful substances from factories, the Environmental Protection Agency (EPA) sets a safety threshold of one additional death in a million. How, we might ask, did the EPA arrive at one in a million? Well, let's face it, no real man tells his girlfriend that she is one in a hundred thousand. But the real root of "one in a million" can be traced to the Food and Drug Administration's (FDA) efforts to find a number that was essentially equivalent to zero.

Many experts argue that insisting on essentially zero risk is going too far. As Professor John D. Graham, director of the Harvard School of Public Health's Center for Risk Analysis, wrote, "No one seriously suggested that such a stringent risk level should be applied to a hypothetical maximally exposed individual." This mythical, "maximally exposed" human being is created by assuming that he or she lives within two hundred meters of the offending industrial plant, lives there for a full seventy years, remains outdoors day and night or at least all day, and will get cancers at the same level as rodents or other small animals that are bred to be especially susceptible to such cancers, and who are given doses running into the thousands of times larger than any person other than those who receive lifetime occupational exposures on the job.

The other assumption is that cancer causation is a linear process, meaning that there is no safe dose and that damage occurs at a constant rate as exposure increases. Yet scientific evidence increasingly shows that there are, indeed, threshold effects, and that the cancers animals develop as a result of being subjected to huge doses in short periods of time tell us essentially nothing about the reactions of human beings. To go from mouse to man, for instance, requires statistical adjustments for the hugely different weights of the two creatures and for the hugely different doses. Many statistical models fit the data that scientists have about risks. These models vary in their outcomes for risk by thousands of times over. And yet there is no scientifically approved way of choosing among them. Only if the mechanism by which a chemical causes cancer is well-known would it be possible to choose a good model. In short, current measures of risk from low-level exposures to industrial technology have no true validity whatsoever. This explains why health rates keep getting better and better while government estimates of risk keep getting worse and worse.

Why are some people frightened of risks and others not? Surveys of risk perception show that knowledge of the known hazards of a technology does not determine whether or to what degree an individual thinks a given technology is safe or dangerous. This holds true not only for laymen, but also for experts in risk assessment. Thus, the most powerful factors related to how people perceive risk apparently are "trust in institutions" and "self-rated liberal and conservative identification." In other words, these findings suggest strongly that people use a framework involving their opinion of the validity of institutions in order to interpret riskiness.

According to one cultural theory, people choose what to fear as a way to defend their way of life. The theory hypothesizes that adherents of a hierarchical culture will approve of technology, provided it is certified as safe by their experts. Competitive individualists will view risk as opportunity and, hence, be optimistic about technology. And egalitarians will view technology as part of the apparatus by which corporate capitalism maintains inequalities that harm society and the natural environment.

One recent study sought to test this theory by comparing how people rate the risks of technology compared to risks from social deviance (departures, such as criminal behavior, from widely approved norms), war, and economic decline. The results are that egalitarians fear technology immensely but think that social deviance is much less dangerous. Hierarchists, by contrast, think technology is basically good if their experts say so, but that social deviance leads to disaster. And individualists think that risk takers do a lot of good for society and that if deviants don't bother them, they won't bother deviants; but they fear war greatly because it stops trade and leads to conscription. Thus, there is no such thing as a risk-averse or risk-taking personality. People who take or avoid all risks are probably certifiably insane; neither would last long. Think of a protester against, say, nuclear power. She is evidently averse to risks posed by nuclear power, but she also throws her body on the line—i.e., takes risks in opposing it.

Other important literature pursues risk perception through what is known as cognitive psychology. Featuring preeminently the path-breaking work of Daniel Kahne-man and Amos Tversky, using mainly small group experiments in which individuals are given tasks involving gambling, this work demonstrates that individuals are very poor judges of probability. More important, perhaps, is their general conservatism: large proportions of people care more about avoiding loss than they do about making gains. Therefore, they will go to considerable lengths to avoid losses, even in the face of high probabilities of making considerable gains.

In regard to the consequences of technological risk, there are two major strategies for improving safety: anticipation versus resilience. The risk-averse strategy seeks to anticipate and thereby prevent harm from occurring. In order to make a strategy of anticipation effective, it is necessary to know the quality of the adverse consequence expected, its probability, and the existence of effective remedies. The knowledge requirements and the organizational capacities required to make anticipation an effective strategy—to know what will happen, when, and how to prevent it without making things worse—are very large.

A strategy of resilience, on the other hand, requires reliance on experience with adverse consequences once they occur in order to develop a capacity to learn from the harm and bounce back. Resilience, therefore, requires the accumulation of large amounts of generalizable resources, such as organizational capacity, knowledge, wealth, energy, and communication, that can be used to craft solutions to problems that the people involved did not know would occur. Thus, a strategy of resilience requires much less predictive capacity but much more growth, not only in wealth but also in knowledge. Hence it is not surprising that systems, like capitalism, based on incessant and decentralized trial and error accumulate the most resources. Strong evidence from around the world demonstrates that such societies are richer and produce healthier people and a more vibrant natural environment.

—Aaron Wildavsky

Biography: Aaron Wildavsky is the Class of 1940 Professor of Political Science and Public Policy at the University of California at Berkeley. He is the author of *Cultural Theory* (with Richard Ellis and Michael Thompson), *The Rise of Radical Egalitarianism,* and *Searching for Safety.*

Further Reading

Dake, Karl, and Aaron Wildavsky. ''Theories of Risk Perception: Who Fears What and Why?'' *Daedalus* 119, no. 4 (Fall 1990): 41–61.

Dietz, Thomas, and Robert Rycroft. *The Risk Professionals.* 1987.

Douglas, Mary, and Aaron Wildavsky. *Risk and Culture.* 1982.

Kahneman, Daniel, and Amos Tversky. ''Variants of Uncertainty.'' *Cognition* 11, no. 2 (March 1982): 143–57.

Kahneman, Daniel, Paul Slovic, and Amos Tversky, eds. *Judgment under Uncertainty: Heuristics and Biases.* 1982.

Keeney, Ralph L. ''Mortality Risks Induced by Economic Expenditures.'' *Risk Analysis* 10, no. 1 (1990): 147–59.

Moronwe, Joseph G., and Edward J. Woodhouse. *Averting Catastrophe.* 1986.

Schwarz, Michael, and Michael Thompson. *Divided We Stand: Redefining Politics, Technology and Social Choice.* 1990.

Wildavsky, Aaron. *Searching for Safety.* 1988.

Trucking Deregulation

Thomas Gale Moore

Regulation

The federal government has been regulating prices and competition in interstate transportation ever since Congress created the Interstate Commerce Commission (ICC) to oversee the railroad industry in 1887. Truckers were brought under the control of the ICC in 1935 after persistent lobbying by state regulators, the ICC itself, and especially, the railroads, which had been losing business to trucking companies.

The Motor Carrier Act of 1935 required new truckers to seek a "certificate of public convenience and necessity" from the ICC. Truckers already operating in 1935 could automatically get certificates, but only if they documented their prior service, and the ICC was quite restrictive in interpreting proof of service. New trucking companies, on the other hand, found it extremely difficult to get certificates.

The law required motor carriers to file all rates—also called tariffs—with the ICC thirty days before they became effective. Anyone, including a competitor, was allowed to inspect the filed tariffs. If the proposed tariffs were protested by another carrier (such as a trucker, a regulated water carrier, or a railroad), the ICC normally suspended the rates pending an investigation of their legality. In 1948 Congress authorized truckers to fix rates in concert with one another when it enacted, over President Truman's veto, the Reed-Bulwinkle Act, which exempted carriers from the antitrust laws.

From 1940 to 1980, new or expanded authority to transport goods was almost impossible to secure unless no one opposed an application. Even if the proposed service was not being offered by existing carriers, the ICC held that a certificated trucker who expressed a desire to carry the goods should be given the opportunity to do so; the new applicant was denied. The effect was to stifle competition from new carriers.

Purchasing the rights of an existing trucker became the only practical approach to entering a particular market. By the seventies the authority to carry certain goods on certain routes was selling for hundreds of thousands of dollars. Because the commission disapproved of "trafficking" in rights, it was hostile to mergers and purchases and attempted to restrict authority as much as possible. The result was often bizarre. For example, a motor carrier with authority to travel from Cleveland to Buffalo that purchased another carrier or the carrier's rights to go from Buffalo to Pittsburgh was required to carry goods destined for Pittsburgh through Buffalo, even though the direct route was considerably shorter. In some cases carriers had to go hundreds of miles out of their way, adding many hours or even days to the transport.

ICC regulation reduced competition and made trucking inefficient. Routes and the products that could be carried over them were narrowly specified. Truckers with authority to carry a product, such as tiles, from one city to another often lacked authority to haul anything on the return trip.

Regulation's Costs

Studies showed that regulation increased costs and rates significantly. Not only were rates lower without regulation, but service quality, as judged by shippers, also was better. Products exempt from regulation moved at rates 20 to 40 percent below those for the same products subject to ICC controls. For example, regulated rates for carrying cooked poultry, compared to unregulated charges for fresh dressed poultry (a similar product), were nearly 50 percent higher. Comparisons between heavily regulated trucking in West Germany and the United States and unregulated motor carriage in Great Britain, together with lightly regulated trucking in Belgium and the Netherlands, showed that charges in the highly regulated countries were 75 percent higher than in the nations with freer markets.

A number of economists were critical of the regulation of motor carriers right from the beginning. James C. Nelson, in a series of articles starting in 1935, led the attack. Walter Adams, a liberal Democrat, followed with a major critique in *American Economic Review*. Professors John R. Meyer of Harvard, Merton J. Peck of Yale, John Stenason, and Charles Zwick authored a very influential book, *The Economics of Competition in the Transportation Industries,* published in 1959.

In 1962 President John Kennedy became the first president to send a transportation message to Congress recommending a reduction in the regulation of surface freight transportation. In November 1975 President Gerald Ford called for legislation to reduce trucking regulation. He followed that by appointing to the ICC several commissioners who favored competition. By the end of 1976, these commissioners were speaking out for a more competitive policy at the ICC, a position rarely articulated in the previous eight decades of transportation regulation.

President Jimmy Carter followed Ford's lead by appointing strong deregulatory advocates and supporting legislation to reduce motor carrier regulation. After a series of ICC rulings that reduced federal oversight of trucking, and after the deregulation of the airline industry, Congress, spurred by the Carter administration, enacted the Motor Carrier Act of 1980. This act limited the ICC's authority over trucking.

Both the Teamsters Union and the American Trucking Associations strongly opposed deregulation and successfully headed off efforts to eliminate all economic controls. Supporting deregulation was a coalition of shippers, consumer advocates including Ralph Nader, and liberals such as Senator Edward Kennedy. Probably the most significant factor in forcing Congress to act was that the ICC commissioners appointed by Ford and Carter were bent on deregulating the industry anyway. Either Congress had to act or the ICC would. Congress acted in order to codify some of the commission changes and to limit others.

The Motor Carrier Act (MCA) of 1980 only partially decontrolled trucking. But together with a liberal ICC, it substantially freed the industry. The MCA made it significantly easier for a trucker to secure a certificate of public convenience and necessity. The MCA also required the commission to eliminate most restrictions on commodities that could be carried, on the routes that motor carriers could use, and on the geographical region they could serve. The law authorized truckers to price freely within a "zone of reasonableness," meaning that truckers could increase or decrease rates from current levels by 15 percent without challenge, and encouraged them to make independent rate filings with even larger price changes.

The Success of Deregulation

Deregulation has worked well. Between 1977, the year before the ICC started to decontrol the industry, and 1982, rates for truckload-size shipments fell about 25 percent in real, inflation-adjusted terms. The General Accounting Office found that rates charged by LTL (less-than-truckload) carriers had fallen as much as 10 to 20 percent, with some shippers reporting declines of as much as 40 percent. Revenue per truckload-ton fell 22 percent from 1979 to 1986. A survey of shippers indicates that they believe service quality improved as well. Some 77 percent of surveyed shippers favored deregulation of trucking. Shippers reported that carriers were much more willing to negotiate rates and services than prior to deregulation. Truckers have experimented with new price and service options. They have restructured routes, reduced empty return hauls, and provided simplified rate structures.

In arguing against deregulation, the American Trucking Associations predicted that service would decline and that small communities would find it harder to get any service at all under the new regime. In fact, service to small communities has improved and complaints by shippers have declined. The ICC has reported that in 1975 and 1976 it handled 340 and 390 complaints, respectively, against truckers; in 1980 it had to deal with only 23 cases, and just 40 in 1981. A 1982 ICC study of the effect of partial decontrol on small cities and remote parts of the country found that service quality had either been improved or remained unaffected by deregulation. Increased competition has bolstered the willingness of trucking firms to go off-route to pick up or deliver freight.

Deregulation has also made it easier for nonunion workers to get jobs in the trucking industry. This new competition has sharply eroded the strength of the drivers' union, the International Brotherhood of Teamsters. Before deregulation ICC-regulated truckers paid unionized workers about 50 percent more than comparable workers in other industries. Although unionized drivers still are paid a premium, by 1985 unionized workers were only 28 percent of the trucking work force, down from around 60 percent in the late seventies.

The number of new firms has increased dramatically. By 1990 the total number of licensed carriers exceeded forty thousand, considerably more than double the number authorized in 1980. The ICC had also awarded nationwide authority to about five thousand freight carriers. The value of operating rights granted by the ICC, once worth hundreds of thousands of dollars when such authority was almost impossible to secure from the commission, has plummeted to close to zero now that operating rights are easy to obtain.

Intermodal carriage has surged sharply since 1980: from 1981 to 1986, it grew 70 percent. The ability of railroads and truckers to develop an extensive trailer-on-flatcar network is a direct result of the MCA and the Staggers Act (1980), which partially freed the railroads.

The motor carrier industry has made little use of the rate zone provision and instead has opted for independent filings, which have increased sharply. These independent filings have increased price competition. Such filings by definition are not agreed on through rate bureaus. Truckers have been able to slash rates mainly by improving efficiency—reducing empty backhauls, eliminating circuities, pricing flexibly, and reducing by about 10 percent the proportion of employees who are drivers and helpers. At the same time, it has cut the pay of such employees by over 10 percent relative to wages of workers in the economy generally. In other words, although wages of drivers and helpers are still considerably higher than wages of comparable workers in other industries, the differential has shrunk.

Savings

One of the economy's major gains from trucking deregulation has been the substantial drop in the cost of holding and maintaining inventories. Because truckers are better able to offer on-time delivery service and more flexible service, manufacturers can order components just in time to be used and retailers can have them just in time to be sold. As a result inventories are leaner. Without the partial deregulation that resulted from the 1980 act, these changes would not have been possible. In 1981, inventories amounted to 14 percent of GNP; one study found that because of improved transportation services traceable to the Motor Carrier Act of 1980 and the Staggers Act, the total fell to 10.8 percent by 1987, for a saving of about $62 billion. A more conservative estimate by the Department of Transportation is that the gain to U.S. industry in shipping, merchandising, and inventories is between $38 and $56 billion per year.

Current Issues

Federal law still requires new carriers to apply for certificates of public convenience and necessity. All tariffs must be filed with the commission. Most states continue to enforce strict entry and price controls on intrastate carriers. These controls cause inefficiency. One result is that in some cases, shipping products from overseas is cheaper than shipping the same goods within the United States. Shipping blue jeans from El Paso, Texas, to Dallas, for example, costs about 40 percent more than shipping the identical jeans from Taiwan to Dallas.

The continuing obligation to file tariffs results in higher costs. Rates for shipping dog food, which are regulated, are 10 to 35 percent higher than the unregulated rates for other animal foods. Chicken, turkey, and fish TV dinners can be carried free of regulation, but a frozen dinner with a hamburger patty instead of a chicken leg requires trucking rates that are 20 to 25 percent higher. When the commission ruled that used beer bottles and kegs were exempt under the "used, empty shipping containers" provision, costs to haul the empties dropped 20 to 30 percent.

Even if the filing of tariffs did not lead to higher charges, the requirement adds to paperwork and confusion. For example, rates must be published for peanuts "roasted and salted in the shell," but a trucker carrying peanuts "shelled, salted, not roasted or otherwise" is exempt from any need to file. Truckers must submit tariffs for carrying show horses but not exhibit horses. Motor carriers must list their prices with the ICC to carry railroad ties cut lengthwise, but not if they are cut crosswise!

Current law also authorizes truckers to collude on tariff increases in rate bureaus. In any other industry such agreements would violate the antitrust laws. Although any single carrier can file separate rates, a rate bureau's filing for higher tariffs leads to pressures on all carriers to boost their prices.

Trucking deregulation is unfinished. According to one study, abolishing all remaining federal controls would save shippers about $28 billion per year. A Department of Transportation study done by researchers at the University of Pennsylvania's Wharton School estimated that abolishing state regulation would save another $5 billion to $12 billion.

—Thomas Gale Moore

Biography: Thomas Gale Moore is a senior fellow at the Hoover Institution at Stanford University. Between 1985 and 1989 he was a member of President Reagan's Council of Economic Advisers.

Further Reading

Moore, Thomas Gale. "Rail and Truck Reform: The Record So Far." *Regulation* (November/December 1988): 57–62.

Organization for Economic Cooperation and Development. International Conference. *Road Transport Deregulation: Experience, Evaluation, Research*. November 1988.

U.S. Congress. House. Committee on Government Operations. *Consumer Cost of Continued State Motor Carrier Regulation*. House Report 101–813, 101st Congress, 2d sess., October 5, 1990.

U.S. Congress. House. Committee on Public Works and Transportation. Subcommittee of Surface Transportation. *Hearings on Economic Regulation of the Motor Carrier Industry*. 100th Congress, 2d sess., March 16, 1988.

U.S. Department of Transportation. *Moving America: New Directions, New Opportunities. A Statement of National Transportation Policy; Strategies for Action*. February 1990.

CHAPTER EIGHT

ENVIRONMENTAL REGULATION

Environmentalism, A Preface

David R. Henderson

■ Many environmentalists see preserving the environment as a purely ethical issue that has no connection to economics. In fact, as MIT economist Lester Thurow wrote in *The Zero-Sum Society*, "Environmentalism is not ethical values pitted against economic values. It is thoroughly economic." What Thurow means is that preserving the environment is what economists call a good, and achieving that good uses up resources that could have produced other goods.

Environmental quality is what economists call a "normal" good. That is, people want more of it as their real incomes increase. As a result people with higher incomes tend to place a higher value on a clean environment, and wealthy nations tend to have more rigorous environmental laws than poorer nations. The cost of preserving the environment is inherently economic as well. Equipment and labor to clean air or water, for example, have an "opportunity" cost: they could be used to produce something else.

The economic approach to environmental issues does not make economists either pro- or anti-environment. They simply recognize that any given level of, say, clean air or water entails a cost. How clean the air should be is what economists call a normative issue: people's answers depend on their values.

What sets many economists apart in environmental debates is that they want to achieve environmental quality efficiently, and they tend to want an efficient (optimal) amount of environmental quality. Though figuring out the efficient amount of environmental quality is difficult, it theoretically is the point at which the value that people put on the last increment of cleanliness equals its cost. After that point additional cleanliness costs more than its value to society (see MARGINALISM). Some economists believe that air in much of the country is too dirty because the people who make it dirty do not have the right incentives to make it clean. Some of these same economists believe that air in other parts of the country is too clean. Why? Because the cost of achieving the last units of cleanliness outweighs the benefit to people of doing so.

—David R. Henderson

Biography: David R. Henderson is the editor of this encyclopedia. He is a senior research fellow with Stanford University's Hoover Institution and an associate professor of economics at the Naval Postgraduate School in Monterey, California. He was formerly a senior economist with the President's Council of Economic Advisers.

Environmentalism, Free-Market

Richard Stroup

■ Free-market environmentalism emphasizes markets as a solution to environmental problems. Proponents argue that free markets can be more successful than government—and have been more successful historically—in solving many environmental problems.

This new interest in free-market environmentalism is somewhat ironic because environmental problems have often been seen as a form of market failure (see PUBLIC GOODS AND EXTERNALITIES). In the traditional view many environmental problems are caused by decision makers who reduce their costs by polluting those who are downwind or downstream; other environmental problems are caused by private decision makers' inability to produce "public goods" (such as preservation of wild species) since no one has to pay to get the benefits of this preservation. While these problems can be quite real, growing evidence indicates that governments often fail to control pollution or to provide public goods at reasonable cost. Furthermore, the private sector is often more responsive than government to environmental needs. This evidence, which is supported by much economic theory, has led to a reconsideration of the traditional view.

Further interest in free-market environmentalism has been awakened, in part, by the failures of centralized government control in Eastern Europe and the Soviet Union. As *glasnost* lifted the veil of secrecy, press reports identified large areas where brown haze hung in the air, where people's eyes routinely burned from chemical fumes and where drivers had to use headlights in the middle of the day. In 1990 *The Wall Street Journal* quoted a claim by Hungarian doctors that 10 percent of the deaths in Hungary may be directly related to pollution. *The New York Times* reported that parts of the town of Merseburg, East Germany, were "permanently covered by a white chemical dust, and a sour smell fills people's nostrils."

For markets to work in the environmental field, as in any other, rights to each important resource must be clearly defined, easily defended against invasion, and divestible (transferable) by owners on terms agreeable to buyer and seller. Well-functioning markets, in short, require "3-D" property rights. When the first two are present—clear definition and easy defense of one's rights—no one is forced to accept pollution beyond the standard acceptable to the community. Each individual has a right against invasion of himself and his property, and the courts will defend that right. And when the third characteristic—divestibility—is present, each owner has an incentive to be a good steward: preservation of the owner's wealth (the value of his or her property) depends on good stewardship.

Environmental problems stem from the absence or incompleteness of these characteristics of property rights. When rights to resources are defined and easily defended against invasion, all individuals or corporations, whether potential polluters or potential victims, have an incentive to avoid pollution problems. When air or water pollution damages a privately owned asset, the owner whose wealth is threatened will gain by seeing that the threat is abated, in court if necessary. In England and Scotland, for example, unlike in the United States, the right to fish for sport and commerce is a privately owned, transferable right. This means that owners of fishing rights can obtain damages and injunctions against polluters of streams. Owners of these rights vigorously defend them, even though the owners are often small anglers' clubs whose members have modest means. They have formed an association that is ready to go to court when their fishing rights are violated by polluters. Such suits were successful well before Earth Day and before pollution control became part of public policy. Once rights against pollution are established by precedent, as these were many years ago, going to court is seldom necessary.

Thus, liability for pollution is a powerful motivator when a factory or other potentially polluting asset is privately owned. The case of the notorious waste dump, Love Canal, illustrates this point. As long as Hooker Chemical Company owned the Love Canal waste site, it was designed, maintained, and operated (in the late forties and fifties) in a way that met even the Environmental Protection Agency standards of 1980. The corporation wanted to avoid any damaging leaks, for which it would have to pay.

Only when the waste site was taken over by local government—under threat of emi-

nent domain, for the cost of one dollar, and in spite of warnings by Hooker about the chemicals—was the site mistreated in ways that led to chemical leakage. The government decision makers lacked personal or corporate liability for their decisions. They built a school on part of the site, removed part of the protective clay cap to use as fill dirt for another school site, and sold off the remaining part of the Love Canal site to a developer, without warning him of the dangers as Hooker had warned them. The local government also punched holes in the impermeable clay walls to build water lines and a highway. This allowed the toxic wastes to escape when rainwater, no longer kept out by the partially removed clay cap, washed them through the gaps created in the walls.

The school district owning the land had a laudable but narrow goal: it wanted to provide education cheaply for district children. Government decision makers are seldom held accountable for broader social goals in the way that private owners are by liability rules and potential profits. Of course, mistakes can be made by anyone, including private parties, but the decision maker whose private wealth is on the line tends to be more circumspect. The liability that holds private decision makers accountable is largely missing in the public sector.

Nor does the government sector have the long-range view that property rights provide, which leads to protection of resources for the future. As long as the third D, divestibility, is present, property rights provide long-term incentives for maximizing the value of property. If I mine my land and impair its future productivity or its groundwater, the reduction in the land's value reduces my current wealth. That is because land's current worth equals the present value of all future services (see PRESENT VALUE). Fewer services or greater costs in the future mean lower value now. In fact, on the day an appraiser or potential buyer first can see that there will be problems in the future, my wealth declines. The reverse also is true: any new way to produce more value—preserving scenic value as I log my land, for example, to attract paying recreationists—is capitalized into the asset's present value.

Because the owner's wealth depends on good stewardship, even a shortsighted owner has the incentive to act as if he or she cares about the future usefulness of the resource. This is true even if an asset is owned by a corporation. Corporate officers may be concerned mainly about the short term, but as financial economists such as Harvard's Michael Jensen have noted, even they have to care about the future. If current actions are known to cause future problems, or if a current investment promises future benefits, the stock price rises or falls to reflect the change. Corporate officers are informed by (and are judged by) these stock price changes.

This ability and incentive to engage in farsighted behavior is lacking in the political sector. Consider the example of Seattle's Ravenna Park. At the turn of the century, it was a privately owned park that contained magnificent Douglas firs. A husband and wife, Mr. and Mrs. W. W. Beck, had developed it into a family recreation area that brought in thousands of people a day. Concern that a future owner might not take proper care of it, however, caused the local government to "preserve" this beautiful place. The owners did not want to part with it, but following condemnation proceedings the city bought the park.

But since they had no personal property or income at stake, local officials allowed the park to deteriorate. In fact, the tall trees began to disappear soon after the city bought it in 1911. The theft of the trees was brought to official attention by a group of concerned citizens, but they continued to be cut. Gradually, the park became unattractive. By 1972 it was an ugly, dangerous hangout for drug users.

In contrast, private individuals and groups have preserved wildlife habitats and scenic lands in thousands of places in the United States. The sidebar lists more than fifty such state and local land trusts in Oregon and California alone. The 1980 National Directory of Conservation Land Trusts lists 748 local, state, and regional land trusts serving this purpose. Many other state and local groups have similar projects as a sideline, and national groups such as the Nature Conservancy and the Audubon Society have hundreds more. None of these are owned by the government. Using the market, such groups do not have to convince the majority that their project is desirable, nor do they have to fight the majority in choosing how to manage the site. The result, as the federal government's Council on Environmental Quality has reported, is an enormous and healthy diversity of approaches.

Even the lack of property rights today does not mean that a useful property rights solution is forever impossible. Property rights tend to evolve as technology, preferences, and prices provide added incentives and new technical options. Early in American history, property rights in cattle seemed impossible to establish and enforce on the Great Plains. But the growing value of such rights led to the use of mounted cowboys to protect herds and, eventually, barbed wire to fence the range. As economists Terry Anderson and Peter J. Hill have shown, the plains lost their status as commons and were privatized. Advances in technology may yet allow the establishment of enforceable rights to schools of whales in the oceans, migratory birds in the air, and—who knows?—even the ozone layer. Such is the hope of free-market environmentalism.

—**Richard Stroup**

Biography: Richard Stroup is an economics professor at Montana State University and senior associate at the Political Economy Research Center, both in Bozeman, Montana. From 1982 to 1984, he was director of the Office of Policy Analysis, U.S. Department of the Interior.

Further Reading

Anderson, Terry, and Donald Leal. *Free Market Environmentalism*. 1991.
Anderson, Terry, and Peter J. Hill. "The Race for Property Rights." *Journal of Law and Economics* 33, no. 1 (April 1990): 177–98.
Council on Environmental Quality. *The Fifteenth Annual Report of the Council on Environmental Quality*, chap. 9. 1984.
Jensen, Michael C. "Agency Costs of Free Cash Flow, Corporate Finance, and Takeovers." *American Economic Review* 76, no. 2 (May 1986): 324–29.
Kensinger, John W., and John D. Martin. "The Quiet Restructuring." *Journal of Applied Corporate Finance* 1, no. 1 (Spring 1988): 16–25.
Shaw, Jane S., and Richard L. Stroup. "Gone Fishin'." *Reason* 20, no. 4 (August/September 1988): 34–37.
———. "Pollution in Eastern Europe: What Can Be Done About It?" *Journal of Economic Growth* 4, no. 2 (Summer 1990): 17–21.
Zuesse, Eric. "The Truth Seeps Out" (story about Love Canal). *Reason* 12, no. 10 (February 1981): 16–33.

California and Oregon Conservation Land Trusts

Big Sur Land Trust
Bolinas Community Land Trust
Buena Vista Lagoon Foundation
Butte County Land Conservation Trust

California Institute of Man in Nature/Cross California
    Conservancy
California State Parks Foundation
Comptche Land Conservancy
Davis Rural Land Trust
Del Monte Forest Foundation
Desert Tortoise Preserve Committee
Elkhorn Slough Foundation
Fallbrook Land Conservancy
Homestead Valley Land Trust
Humboldt North Coast Land Trust
Land Trust for Santa
    Barbara County
Land Trust of Santa Cruz County
Lassen Land and Trails Trust
League to Save Lake Tahoe Charitable Trust
Los Penasquitos Lagoon Foundation
Mattole Restoration Council
Mattole Watershed Salmon Support Group
Mendocino Land Trust
Mill Creek Watershed Conservancy
Mission Creek Conservancy
Monterey County Agricultural and Historic Land
    Conservancy
Mountains Restoration Trust
Napa County Land Trust
North Coast Land Conservancy
Ojai Valley Land Conservancy
Oregon Parks Foundation
Oregon Women's Land Trust
Padua Hills Land Trust
Palos Verdes Peninsula Land Conservancy
Port Costa Conservation Society
Rancho Sante Fe Community Foundation
Riverside Land Conservancy
San Dieguito River Valley Land Conservancy
San Elijo Lagoon Foundation
San Joaquin River Parkway and Conservation Trust
Sanctuary Forest
Santa Catalina Island Conservancy
Santa Rosa Land Trust

Save Mount Diablo
Save-the-Redwoods League
Sempervirens Fund
Sequoya Challenge
Small Wilderness Area Preservation
Sonoma Land Trust
Southern Marin Land Trust
Symbiota Land Conservancy/Trust
Tamalpais Conservation
    Club
Ventura County Land Conservancy
Wetlands Conservancy
Yolo Land Conservation Trust

Greenhouse Effect

Thomas C. Schelling

What Is It?

The "greenhouse effect" is a complicated process by which the earth is becoming progressively warmer. The earth is bathed in sunlight, some of it reflected back into space and some absorbed. If the absorption is not matched by radiation back into space, the earth will get warmer until the intensity of that radiation matches the incoming sunlight. Some atmospheric gases absorb outward infrared radiation, warming the atmosphere. Carbon dioxide is one of these gases; so are methane, nitrous oxide, and the chlorofluorocarbons (CFCs). The concentrations of these gases are increasing, with the result that the earth is absorbing more sunlight and getting warmer.

This greenhouse phenomenon is truly the result of a "global common" (see THE TRAGEDY OF THE COMMONS). Because no one owns the atmosphere, no one has a sufficient incentive to take account of the change to the atmosphere caused by his or her emission of carbon. Also, carbon emitted has the same effect no matter where on earth it happens.

How Serious Is It?

The expected change in global average temperature for a doubling of CO_2 is 1.5 to 4.5 degrees centigrade. But translating a change in temperature into a change in climates is full of uncertainties. Meteorologists predict greater temperature change in the polar regions than near the equator. This change could cause changes in circulation of air and water. The results may be warmer temperatures in some places and colder in others, wetter climates in some places and drier in others.

Temperature is useful as an index of climate change. A band of about one degree covers variations in average temperatures since the last ice age. This means that climates will change more in the next one hundred years than in the last ten thousand. But to put this in perspective, remember that people have been migrating great distances for thousands of years, experiencing changes in climate greater than any being forecast.

The models of global warming project only gradual changes. Climates will ''migrate'' slowly. The climate of Kansas may become like Oklahoma's, but not like that of Oregon or Massachusetts. But a caveat is in order: the models probably cannot project discontinuities because nothing goes into them that will produce drastic change. There may be phenomena that could produce drastic changes, but they are not known with enough confidence to introduce into the models.

Carbon dioxide has increased about 25 percent since the onset of the industrial revolution. The global average temperature rose almost half a degree during the first forty years of this century, was level for the next forty, and rose during the eighties. Yet whether or not we are witnessing the greenhouse effect is unknown because other decades-long influences such as changes in solar intensity and in the atmosphere's particulate matter can obscure any smooth greenhouse trend. In other words, the increase in carbon dioxide will, by itself, cause the greenhouse effect, but other changes in the universe may offset it.

Even if we had confident estimates of climate change for different regions of the world, there would be uncertainties about the kind of world we will have fifty or a hundred years from now. Suppose the kind of climate change expected between now and, say, 2080 had already taken place, since 1900. Ask a seventy-five-year-old farm couple living on the same farm where they were born: would the change in the climate be among the most dramatic changes in either their farming or their lifestyle? The answer most likely would be no. Changes from horses to tractors and from kerosene to electricity would be much more important.

Climate change would have made a vastly greater difference to the way people lived and earned their living in 1900 than today. Today, little of our gross domestic product is produced outdoors, and therefore, little is susceptible to climate. Agriculture and forestry are less than 3 percent of total output, and little else is much affected. Even if agricultural productivity declined by a third over the next half-century, the per capita GNP we might have achieved by 2050 we would still achieve in 2051. Considering that agricultural productivity in most parts of the world continues to improve (and that many crops may benefit directly from enhanced photosynthesis due to increased carbon dioxide), it is not at all certain that the net impact on agriculture will be negative or much noticed in the developed world.

Its Effects on Developing Countries

Climate changes would have greater impact in underdeveloped countries. Agriculture provides the livelihoods of 30 percent or more of the population in much of the developing world. While there is no strong presumption that the climates prevailing in different regions fifty or a hundred years from now will be less conducive to food production, those people are vulnerable in a way that Americans and west Europeans are not. Nor can the impact on their health be dismissed. Parasitic and other vector-borne diseases affecting hundreds of millions of people are sensitive to climate.

Yet the trend in developing countries is to be less dependent on agriculture. If per capita income in such countries grows in the next forty years as rapidly as it has in the forty just past, vulnerability to climate change should diminish. This is pertinent to whether developing countries should make sacrifices to minimize the emission of gases that may change climate to their disadvan-

tage. Their best defense against climate change will be their own continued development.

Population is an important factor. Carbon emissions in developing countries rise with population. For instance, if China holds population growth to near zero for the next couple of generations, it may do as much for the earth's atmosphere as would a heroic anticarbon program coupled with 2 percent annual population growth. Furthermore, the most likely adverse impact of climate change would be on food production, and in the poorest parts of the world the adequacy of food depends on the number of mouths.

Why Should Developed Countries Do Anything?

Why might developed countries care enough about climate to do anything about it? The answer depends on how much people in developed countries care about people in developing countries and on how expensive it is to do something worthwhile. Abatement programs in a number of econometric models suggest that doing something worthwhile would cost about 2 percent of GNP in perpetuity. Two percent of the U.S. GNP is over $100 billion a year, and that is an annual cost that would continue forever.

One argument for doing something is that the developing countries are vulnerable, and we care about their well-being. But if the developed countries were prepared to invest, say, $200 billion a year in greenhouse gas abatement, explicitly for the benefit of developing countries fifty years or more from now, the developing countries would probably clamor, understandably, to receive the resources immediately in support of their continued development.

A second argument is that our natural environment may be severely damaged. This is the crux of the political debate over the greenhouse effect, but it is an issue that no one really understands. It is difficult to know how to value what is at risk, and difficult even to know just what is at risk. The benefits of slowing climate change by some particular amount are even more uncertain.

A third argument is that the conclusion I reported earlier—that climates will change slowly and not much—may be wrong. The models do not produce surprises. The possibility has to be considered that some atmospheric or oceanic circulatory systems may flip to alternative equilibria, producing regional changes that are sudden and extreme. A currently discussed possibility is in the way oceans behave. If the gulf stream flipped into a new pattern, the climatic consequences might be sudden and severe. (Paradoxically, global warming might severely cool western Europe.)

Is 2 percent of GNP forever, to postpone the doubling of carbon in the atmosphere, a big number or a small one? That depends on what the comparison is. A better question—assuming we were prepared to spend 2 percent of GNP to reduce the damage from climate change—is whether we might find better uses for the money.

I mentioned one such use—directly investing to improve the economies of the poorer countries. Another would be direct investment in preserving species or ecosystems or wilderness areas, if the alternative is to invest trillions in the reduction of carbon emissions.

What Solutions Are Proposed?

What can be done to reduce or offset carbon emissions? Reducing energy use and the carbon content of energy have received most of the attention. There are other possibilities. Trees store carbon. A new forest will absorb carbon until it reaches maturity; it then holds its carbon but does not absorb more. The area available for reforestation throughout the world suggests that reforestation can contribute, but not much.

Stopping or slowing deforestation is important for other reasons but is quantitatively more important than reforestation, partly because forest subsoils typically contain carbon greater than the amount in the trees themselves, and this carbon is subject to oxidation when the trees are removed.

Also, substances or objects can be put in orbit or in the stratosphere to reflect incoming sunlight. Some of these are as apparently innocuous as stimulating cloud formation and some as dramatic as huge mylar balloons in low earth orbit. If in decades to come the greenhouse impact confirms the more alarmist expectations, and if the costs of reducing emissions prove unmanageable, some of these "geoengineering" options will invite attention.

The main responses will be to adapt as the climate changes and to reduce carbon emissions. (CFCs are potent greenhouse gases and, if unchecked, might have rivaled carbon dioxide in decades to come. International actions to reduce or eliminate CFCs are making progress and are among the cheapest ways of reducing greenhouse emissions.)

It is improbable that the developing world, at least for the next several decades, will incur any significant sacrifice in the interest of reduced carbon, nor would it be advisable. Financing energy conservation, energy efficiency, and a switch from high-carbon to lower-carbon or noncarbon fuels in Asia and Africa would not only be a major economic enterprise, but also a complex effort in international diplomacy and politics. If successful, it would increase the costs to the developed world by at least another percent or two on top of the 2 percent I mentioned.

A universal carbon tax is a popular proposal among economists because it promises an efficient solution. A carbon tax set equally for all users worldwide would achieve a given reduction in the use of carbon at the lowest cost. If user A values his use of one ton of carbon at two thousand dollars more than its net-of-tax price, and if the tax is four hundred dollars per ton, he will continue to use the carbon because doing so is worthwhile. If user B values his use of one ton at only three hundred dollars more than the net-of-tax price, the tax will induce him to end his use. Thus the tax would eliminate the lowest-valued uses of carbon and would leave the highest-valued ones in place. A carbon tax would require no negotiation except over a tax rate and a formula for distributing the proceeds. But a tax rate that made a big dent in the greenhouse problem would have to be equivalent to around a dollar per gallon on motor fuel, and for the United States alone such a tax on coal, petroleum, and natural gas would currently yield close to half a trillion dollars

per year in revenue, almost 10 percent of our GNP. It is doubtful that any greenhouse taxing agency would be allowed to collect that kind of revenue, or that a treaty requiring the United States to levy internal carbon taxation at that level would be ratified.

Tradable permits have been proposed as an alternative to the tax. The main possibilities are estimating "reasonable" emissions country by country and establishing commensurate quotas, or distributing tradable rights in accordance with some "equitable" criterion. Depending on how restrictive the emission rights might be, the latter amounts to distributing trillions of dollars (in present value terms), an unlikely prospect. If quotas are negotiated to correspond to countries' currently "reasonable" emissions levels, they will surely be renegotiated every few years, and selling an emissions right will be perceived as evidence that a quota was initially too generous.

A helpful model for conceptualizing a greenhouse regime among the richer countries is the negotiations among the nations of Western Europe for distributing Marshall Plan aid after World War II. There was never a formula or explicit criterion, such as equalizing living standards, maximizing aggregate growth, or establishing a floor under levels of living. Baseline dollar-balance-of-payments deficits were a point of departure, but the negotiations took into account other factors such as investment needs and traditional consumption levels. The United States insisted that the recipients argue out and agree on shares. In the end they did not quite make it, the United States having to make the final allocation. But all the submission of data and open argument led, if not to consensus, to a reasonable appreciation of each nation's needs. Distribution of Marshall Plan funds is the only model of multilateral negotiation involving resources commensurate with the cost of greenhouse abatement. (In the first year Marshall Plan funds were about 1.5 percent of U.S. GNP and—adjusting for overvalued currencies—probably 5 percent of recipient countries' GNP.)

What the Marshall Plan model suggests is that the participants in a greenhouse regime would submit for each other's scrutiny and cross-examination plans for reducing carbon emissions. The plans would be accompanied by estimates of emissions, but any commitments would be to the policies, not the emissions.

The alternative is commitments to specific levels of emissions. Because target dates would be a decade or two in the future, monitoring a country's progress would be more ambiguous than monitoring the implementation of policies.

—**Thomas C. Schelling**

Biography: Thomas C. Schelling is a professor of economics at the University of Maryland in College Park. For most of his professional life he was an economics professor at Harvard University. In 1991 he was president of the American Economic Association. He is an elected member of the National Academy of Sciences.

Further Reading

Ausubel, Jesse. "Does Climate Still Matter?" *Nature* 350, April 25, 1991, 649–52.

Cline, William R. *The Greenhouse Effect: Global Economic Consequences.* 1992.

Congressional Budget Office. *Carbon Charges as a Response to Global Warming: The Effects of Taxing Fossil Fuels.* 1990.

Dornbush, Rudiger, and James M. Poterba. *Global Warming: Economic Policy Responses.* 1991.

Nordhaus, William D. "The Cost of Slowing Climate Change: A Survey." *Energy Journal* 12, no. 1 (1991): 37–66.

Pollution Controls

Robert W. Crandall

■ While there is general agreement that we must control pollution of our air, water, and land, various interest groups, public agencies, and experts have disputed just how we should control it. The pollution control mechanisms adopted in the United States have tended toward detailed regulation of technology. In 1970 popular concern about environmental degradation coalesced into a major political force, resulting in the creation of a federal Environmental Protection Agency (EPA) by President Nixon, and the first of the major federal attempts to regulate pollution directly—the Clean Air Act Amendments of 1970. Since then, the federal role in regulating pollution has grown immensely, unleashing a cascade of regulation upon the EPA, local governments, and the business community. But that has begun to change. Although the command-and-control approach is the norm, environmental lobbyists and legislators are beginning to consider market-based approaches to pollution control.

Regulatory Standards

In virtually every antipollution law, Congress has instructed the EPA to establish and enforce specific pollution standards for individual polluters. These standards are generally based on some notion of the "best available" technology for each source of pollution in each industry. Because each pollutant has many sources, the EPA often must set literally hundreds of maximum discharge standards for any single pollutant.

Existing pollution sources (such as old factories) are generally required to meet less onerous standards than those applicable for new sources, largely because it is considered more costly to retrofit an old factory than to build pollution control devices into a new one. And even the definition of "new" requires further regulations because EPA must distinguish, for example, among rebuilding a fossil-fuel-fired boiler, replacing it, or replacing the entire facility of which the boiler is only a part. Complicating matters further, standards for existing sources and new sources are often stricter in regions with a higher-quality environment (i.e., cleaner air, cleaner water, and so on).

The Cost of Pollution Controls

The way that pollution controls are often built into the production process makes any estimation of their cost extremely difficult. In addition, pollution controls often discourage new investment and production, but no one currently calculates such indirect costs as the value of what is not produced. The federal government has, however, estimated a subset of costs, namely direct expenditures on pollution controls. These expenditures cost governments and private entities an estimated $100 billion in 1988

453

alone. Some $40 billion was spent on air-pollution abatement, $40 billion on water-pollution controls, and $20 billion for a variety of solid-waste, hazardous-waste, and other programs.

The most costly and complex federal pollution control policy is the motor-vehicle program. In order to enforce automobile standards set by Congress, the EPA must test each model line of new cars and test and random sample vehicles already on the road. The Clean Air Act requires that emission controls work for at least the first fifty thousand miles driven. Direct expenditures for compliance with these vehicle standards totaled an estimated $14 billion in 1988, costs shouldered primarily by consumers.

Among the programs funded by the federal government, two are especially costly. The larger of these is the Municipal Sewage Treatment Construction Grant program begun in 1973. Through this program, the federal government directly underwrote grants totaling over $43 billion by 1983 to pay for municipal sewage treatment plants.

The second program is more well-known. In 1980 Congress established Superfund to finance the cleaning of hazardous waste sites. This program required private entities responsible for hazardous dumps to clean them up. But if these parties could not be found, the cleanup would be funded by the government, through general revenues and a tax on petroleum feedstocks. In 1986 a new statute—the Superfund Amendments and Reauthorization Act—levied a federal tax on all corporations with taxable income over $2 million to help fund these remedial actions. This new tax is expected to generate about $8.5 billion over five

years for waste cleanup. Thus, corporations that had nothing to do with old hazardous waste sites or that do not even generate toxic waste are required to pay for the pollution others left behind.

The Economic Effects of Pollution Controls

Pollution controls divert economic resources from other economic activities, thereby reducing the potential size of measured national output. As long as the increase in the value of the environment is at least one dollar for each additional dollar spent on controls, the total value of goods, services, and environmental amenities is not reduced. Unfortunately, that seldom happens, for at least three reasons.

First, the Congress or the EPA may decide to control the wrong substances or to control some discharges too strictly. Congress's own Office of Technology Assessment concluded, for example, that attempting to reach the EPA's goal for urban smog reduction could cost more than $13 billion per year, but result in less than $3.5 billion in improved health, agricultural, and amenity benefits.

Second, regulatory standards can result in very inefficient patterns of control. Some polluters may be forced to spend twenty-five thousand dollars per ton to control the discharge of a certain pollutant, while for others the cost is only five hundred dollars per ton. Obviously, shifting the burden away from the former polluter toward the latter would result in lower total control costs for society for any given level of pollution control.

Third, pollution controls can have deleterious effects on investment in two ways. First, by making certain goods—chemicals, paper, metals, motor vehicles—more expensive to produce in the United States, they raise the prices of these goods and thereby reduce the amount of each demanded. Second, because controls are generally more onerous for new sources than for older, existing ones, managers are more likely to keep an old plant in use rather than replace it with a new, more efficient facility, even though the new facility would produce the same goods as the old one.

The command-and-control approach is flawed in other ways, too. It does little to encourage compliance beyond what is mandated. Regulations are introduced only after noticeable damage has occurred. Polluters who manage to avoid legislative scrutiny continue to pollute. And regulations may be difficult to enforce.

Market-Based Approach to Pollution Control

Problems like these have led policymakers to look for more efficient means of cleaning up the environment. As a result, the 1990 Clean Air Act Amendments look very different from their predecessors of two decades earlier because they include market-based incentives to reduce pollution.

Market incentives are generally of two forms: pollution fees and so-called "marketable permits." Pollution fees are simply taxes on polluters that penalize them in proportion to the amount they discharge into an airshed, waterway, or local landfill. Such taxes are common in Europe but have not been used in the United States. Marketable permits are essentially transferable discharge licenses that polluters can buy and sell to meet the control levels set by regulatory authorities. These permits have been used in the United States because they do not impose large taxes on a small set of polluting industries, as would be the case with pollution fees.

The 1990 Clean Air Act allows the EPA to grant "emissions permits" for certain pollutants. These are, in effect, rights to pollute that can be traded among polluters. Imagine a giant bubble that encloses all existing sources of air pollution. Within that bubble some emitters may pollute over the control level as long as other polluters compensate by polluting less. The government or some other authority decides on the desired level of pollution and the initial distribution of pollution rights within an industry or for a geographic region—the "bubble" that encloses these sources. Purchases and sales of permits within the "bubble" should reduce the total level of pollution to the allowable limit at the lowest total cost.

For example, a St. Louis study found that the cost of reducing particulate emissions for a paper-products factory was $4 per ton, while the cost to a brewery was $600 per ton. The Clean Air Act could require St. Louis to reduce its emissions by a certain amount. Under the traditional approach, the brewery and the paper factory would each be required to cut emissions by, say, ten tons. The cost to the paper factory would be only $40, while the cost to the brewery would be $6,000. But with tradable permits, the brewery could pay the paper factory to cut emissions by twenty tons so that the brewery could continue to operate without reducing emissions at all. The net result is the same emission reduction of twenty tons as under the command-and-control approach, but the total cost to society of the reduction is only $80 instead of $6,040.

All this is not just speculative. A market for trading emissions permits was allowed by the EPA under the Carter administration in 1979. Said Douglas Costle, EPA chief at the time: "The bubble means less expensive pollution control, not less pollution control."

The tradable permits work. In 1981 General Electric had three months to meet the state of Kentucky's deadline for emissions control. To do it, GE paid $60,000 to International Harvester to lease several hundred tons of emissions reductions that International Harvester had "saved." Not only did GE meet the deadline, but it also saved $1.5 million in capital and $300,000 in operating costs. Up through 1984 bubbles approved by the EPA alone saved an estimated $300 million compared to what would have been spent to comply under traditional pollution controls. State-approved bubbles, like that used by GE, have saved millions more. Environmental economist Thomas H. Tietenberg estimates that marketable permits can reduce the cost of pollution control by as much as 75 percent. University of Maryland economist Wallace Oates estimates that a complete switch from command-and-control to marketable permits would reduce pollution control costs by at least one-third.

Marketable permits have also been used to phase down the use of chlorofluorocarbons in order to preserve the stratospheric ozone layer. This policy was instituted in 1990, and a number of trades had already taken place by mid-1991. Moreover, the Clean Air Act of 1990 includes a provision for allowing trading of pollution rights for sulfur oxides as part of a policy to reduce these emissions by nearly 50 percent by 2000. Allowing trading of these rights could make the cost of reducing sulfur dioxide as much as $4 billion per year less than the cost that would be required by the traditional pollution standards approach.

Protecting our environment does not have to put an end to economic progress. Free markets in permits to pollute, like free markets for other resources, can assure that pollution is controlled at the lowest cost possible.

—Robert W. Crandall

Biography: Robert W. Crandall is a senior fellow at the Brookings Institution in Washington, D.C. He served as acting director of the Council on Wage and Price Stability during the Carter administration and was previously an associate professor of economics at MIT.

Further Reading

Hahn, Robert W., and Gordon L. Hester. "Where Did All the Markets Go?" *Yale Journal on Regulation* 6, no. 1 (Winter 1989): 109–53.

Hahn, Robert W., and Roger G. Noll. "Environmental Markets in the Year 2000." *Journal of Risk and Uncertainty* 3, no. 4 (1990): 351–67.

Tietenberg, Thomas H. *Emissions Trading: An Exercise in Reforming Pollution Policy.* 1985.

U.S. Department of Energy. Office of Environmental Analysis, Assistant Secretary for Environmental Safety and Health. *A Compendium of Options for Government Policy to Encourage Private Sector Responses to Potential Climate Change.* October 1989.

Recycling

Jane S. Shaw

■ Recycling is the process of converting waste products into reusable materials. It differs from reuse, which simply means using a product again. According to the Environmental Protection Agency, about 13 percent of the nation's solid waste (that is, the waste that is normally handled through garbage collection systems) is recycled. This compares with 14 percent that is incinerated and 73 percent that goes into landfills.

Recycling is appealing because it seems to offer a way to simultaneously reduce the amount of waste disposed in landfills and to save natural resources. During the late eighties, as environmental concerns grew, public opinion focused on recycling as a key way to protect the environment. The EPA proposed increasing the percentage of recycled solid waste from 13 percent to 25 percent by 1992. Producers of plastics such as polystyrene, which traditionally has not been recycled in large quantities, set about doing so, and many companies began touting their use of recycled paper as a way to improve their image with consumers.

Recycling, however, is not always economically efficient or even environmentally helpful. The popular emphasis on recycling stems partly from two misconceptions: the view that landfills and incinerators are "bad," and the assumption that the nation is running out of landfill space. William Rathje, a University of Arizona archaeologist who specializes in studying garbage, says that landfills can be safely sited and designed, and there is still plenty of room for them in the United States, except for parts of the Northeast. Engineers have learned to avoid putting landfills in places that come into contact with water, such as sites on rivers and in wetlands, and have designed monitoring programs to ensure that any leakage is caught before it causes harm.

As for space for landfills, in the late eighties the state of New York commissioned a study of potential landfill sites. It found that two hundred square miles were available—a small part of the whole state, but still room for quite a few landfills. Community opposition to siting landfills (known as the "Not-in-my-backyard" syndrome) seems to have abated in recent years, too, as landfill operators learned that paying fees to communities would encourage acceptance. For example, *Waste Age* magazine reports that Charles City County, Virginia, will receive more than $1 million a year from the builder of a landfill, while a company in Madison, Wisconsin, expects to pay $6 million over twelve years for the right to build a landfill. Payments include the costs of guaranteeing the property values of all homeowners within a specified distance of the site, of rebuilding roads, and of operating a nearby park.

The Economics of Recycling

In the absence of government regulation, the economics of each material determines how much of it is recycled. For example, about 55 percent of all aluminum cans are recycled. This relatively high percentage reflects the fact that recycling aluminum is often cheaper than producing new aluminum. Recycling aluminum cans requires less than 10 percent of the energy required to produce aluminum from bauxite. The recycling of cans has grown along with the penetration of aluminum into the beverage can market. In 1964 only 2 percent of beverage cans were made of aluminum; by 1974 the share was nearly 40 percent, and by 1990 it was about 95 percent. In 1968 Reynolds Metals Company started a pilot can-recycling center. The chief motivation was to respond to public concerns about litter, reflected in proposed and actual laws requiring deposits on beverage containers. But it was the rapid rise in energy prices during the seventies, plus fears of energy cutoffs, that made recycling economically attractive.

Paper and cardboard, the largest components of municipal solid waste, are also extensively recycled. Because cardboard can be made from a wide variety of used paper, the costs of separating different kinds of paper are low, and because many places (such as grocery stores) use large quantities of corrugated boxes, collection can be efficient. As a result 45 percent of all corrugated boxes were recycled in 1988.

In contrast, the high costs of collecting and separating plastics have limited their recycling. People have not shown a willingness to clean and separate their discarded plastic. In fact, a study by the Plastics Recycling Foundation concluded that voluntary drop-off or buy-back centers will not bring in enough plastics to make nationwide recycling economically viable. Also, different plastic resins cannot be mixed together and reprocessed. (To deal with this problem, the plastics packaging industry has developed symbols for marking different kinds of resins, a step that could lower the costs in the future.) In spite of the limitations, 20 percent of plastic soft drink bottles are now recycled.

Ironically, recycling does not eliminate

environmental worries. Take newspapers, for example. First, recycled newspapers must be de-inked, often with chemicals, creating a sludge. Even if the sludge is harmless, it too must be disposed of, probably in a landfill. Second, recycling more newspapers will not necessarily preserve trees, because many trees are grown specifically to be made into paper. A study prepared for the environmental think tank Resources for the Future estimates that if paper recycling reaches 40 percent (compared with the present 30 percent), demand for virgin paper will fall by about 7 percent, and "some lands now being used to grow trees will be put to other uses," according to economist A. Clark Wiseman. The impact would not be large, but it is the opposite of what most people expect. Finally, curbside recycling programs usually require more trucks that use more energy and create more pollution.

Deterrents to Recycling

A major deterrent to recycling is that the prices of local garbage disposal rarely reflect the actual cost of disposal. Most collection systems are controlled or owned by governments, which assess a flat sum for garbage collection, sometimes as part of municipal taxes. The trash collector picks up whatever waste people leave at the curb, and people are not rewarded for discarding only a small amount or penalized for discarding a lot. Thus, they have no incentive to reduce their waste. In contrast, privately owned systems, operating without municipal price regulation, would have to accurately price garbage disposal to stay profitable. Accurate pricing—that is, high prices for people who generate more waste—would encourage people to reduce their waste.

Unfortunately, recycling has not taken the form of privatization or freeing up of municipal controls. Instead, more and more local governments have mandated curbside separation. A few cities, such as Seattle, have, however, experimented with charging for each trash can that has to be picked up. This has led 70 percent of Seattle residents to cut down on their waste. Such "per-can" charges provide an inducement to reduce waste, whether through recycling or other means. And it means that those who choose not to reduce their waste pay the full cost of the burden they place on the collection system.

Recycling is not a panacea for environmental problems. Instead, it is only one of several means for disposing of waste. It is widely used where the economics are favorable. Where they are not, government regulations may override the economics, but only by requiring actions, such as curbside recycling, that people will not do voluntarily. A fairer way to encourage recycling is to price the costs of disposal accurately.

—**Jane S. Shaw**

Biography: Jane S. Shaw is a senior associate at the Political Economy Research Center in Bozeman, Montana. She was formerly associate economics editor with *Business Week*.

Further Reading

Katz, Marvin G. "YIMBYism Is Coming, But . . ." *Waste Age,* January 1990, 40–41.

Rathje, William L. "Rubbish!" *The Atlantic Monthly,* December 1989, 99–109.

Scarlett, Lynn. "Make Your Environment Dirtier—Recycle." *The Wall Street Journal,* January 14, 1991, A14.

CHAPTER NINE

DISCRIMINATION AND LABOR ISSUES

Comparable Worth

June Ellenoff O'Neill

■ Should a truck driver earn more than a telephone operator, or an engineer more than a librarian? Questions like these are largely resolved in the labor market by the forces of supply and demand. Proponents of comparable worth, however, challenge the resulting pattern of wages by arguing that occupations dominated by female workers are paid less than comparable male-dominated jobs because of systematic discrimination against women. Under comparable worth, employers would be required to set wages to reflect differences in the "worth" of jobs, with worth largely determined by job evaluation studies, not by market forces. Advocates expect comparable worth to increase pay in jobs dominated by women and to sharply narrow the overall gender gap in wages.

The campaign for comparable worth policies has generated heated controversy. Advocates of the concept, who also refer to it as "pay equity," have won important political support. A policy that promises substantial pay increases for many women in the name of equity is bound to have popular appeal. Opponents, however, argue that comparable worth would reduce economic efficiency and would even reduce employment opportunities for women.

The issues are complex. Does the evidence on the male-female wage gap justify new and more radical methods for combating sex discrimination? How would a comparable worth policy actually operate? Would it ultimately benefit women and correct the inequities it is designed to remove?

The Wage Gap

In 1988 the ratio of women's to men's hourly earnings in the United States was around 70 percent. This ratio was close to 90 percent at 20 to 24 years of age and 80 percent at 25 to 34 years, but it was only 63 percent at 45 years of age and older. The extent to which these differentials reflect discrimination, and the form this discrimination takes, are issues central to the debate over comparable worth.

Proponents of comparable worth believe that most of the gender gap in wages is caused by discrimination. According to this view, employers, out of habit or prejudice, reduce the pay scale in traditionally female occupations to levels below the true worth of these jobs, even when the jobs are held by men. Discriminating against a whole occupation is not the same as unequal pay for equal work, or discriminatory hiring or promotion. The latter are widely considered unfair and are illegal under the Equal Pay Act of 1963 and Title VII of the Civil Rights Act of 1964. In the view of comparable worth supporters, however, equal-pay legislation is inadequate or even irrelevant because women tend to work in different occupations than men. Comparable worth is intended to address discrimination against the occupations in which women predominate.

Critics of comparable worth question whether the type of discrimination the policy seeks to remedy is important or even exists in a meaningful way in our economy. If firms with a large fraction of their work force in traditionally female jobs held wages below the value of the employees' services to the firm, they argue, profits would be high. The prospect of high profits would attract other firms to the industry. To fill the new female jobs created, new firms would offer higher wages, raising wages industrywide. The competition for workers could be thwarted only by collusion among employers. Most economists believe, however, that the prospect of collusion among literally thousands of firms is unrealistic because each firm has too strong an incentive to cheat on the collusive agreement by paying a little more in women's occupations. Moreover, critics of comparable worth point out that no evidence has been found that firms and industries with substantial employment in female jobs earn higher-than-average profits.

The critics question why workers in predominately female occupations do not leave the supposedly undervalued occupations to take the better-paid male or mixed-gender jobs if discrimination is the sole reason for lower wages. Some supporters of comparable worth have argued that women's mobility is limited because they are barred from entering nontraditional occupations. But this argument, which was valid in the past, has lost force over time as barriers have eroded. Moreover, if barriers to entry were the problem, the logical solution would be to remove the barriers, which are illegal under Title VII of the Civil Rights Act. Many comparable worth supporters, however, do not allude to barriers but instead simply argue that women who choose to work in traditionally female occupations should not be penalized for their choices.

Although pay in women's occupations is below pay in typically male occupations, many economists believe that this fact alone is not evidence of discrimination by employers. Other factors unrelated to discrimination can explain gender differences in occupations and in pay. One important factor is that women typically have primary responsibility for the care of home and children and, as a result, work outside the home for 40 percent fewer years than men. Anticipating a shorter and more uncertain career, therefore, women are less likely to invest in lengthy vocational schooling or training. Moreover, many women choose jobs that provide hours and other working conditions that are compatible with home demands.

The factors that limit their work reduce the wages women can earn in two ways. First, the occupations many women enter are paid less because they require less work experience and training and may impose costs on employers for providing the schedules and working conditions women value. Second, women are likely to earn less than men in the same occupation because they typically have less experience and, therefore, less skill on the job.

The situation described is by no means static, however. Younger women are working longer and taking shorter breaks for childbearing and child rearing. Because women expect to remain in the work force, they have greatly increased their representation in careers such as medicine and law, which require lengthy training periods. As a result the wage gap narrowed considerably during the eighties. The relatively high ratio of women's to men's earnings at younger ages partly reflects the increased experience and skill acquired by younger women.

Attempts by social scientists to measure the component of the wage gap accounted for by nondiscriminatory factors are inconclusive for two reasons. First, data on complete work-life histories are hard to obtain, and what economists call career attachment (basically, dedication to work) is even harder to quantify. Several studies have found that about half of the wage gap can be explained by fairly crude measures of years of experience and schooling, leaving the reasons for the other half of the gap unresolved. But when women and men with more similar backgrounds are compared—such as women and men with training in a particular field, or women and men who have never married—the pay gap tends to be much smaller than in the aggregate. For example, the pay gap between men and women with doctorates in economics is about 5 percent.

Discrimination almost certainly accounts for some of the gender gap. But the most likely form this discrimination takes is the restricted access of women to certain positions or promotions. Critics of comparable worth, who include most economists, argue that it would do nothing to address these problems.

Effects of Comparable Worth

Regardless of the sources of the gender gap, the proposed method for implementing comparable worth deserves attention in its own right. Under comparable worth, jobs within a firm or government would be rated, and points would be assigned according to characteristics such as necessary knowledge and skills, mental demands, accountability, and working conditions. Jobs scoring the same would then be paid the same, regardless of the pay differentials that might prevail in the market.

The evaluation procedure may appear objective, but it in fact is highly subjective. Although it makes sense for job attributes such as skills and working conditions to influence pay, there is no one correct method for determining the number of points to be assigned to each attribute, or for determining the weight each attribute should have in the overall worth of each job. Which takes the most skill, playing the violin, solving an engineering problem, translating a language, or managing a restaurant? How should skill be weighted relative to working conditions or accountability? Answers to these questions are bound to be subjective. Therefore, different job evaluation systems and different job evaluators are likely to assign different rankings to the same set of occupations.

Most economists would agree that the outcome is not likely to be efficient, since the procedure cannot incorporate the myriad factors that influence supply and demand in the market. One need only consider the economies of Eastern Europe to observe the results of replacing the market with administered and planned systems.

The imposition of comparable worth would likely raise pay in traditionally female jobs; appointing persons favorable to the concept to conduct the job evaluation would all but guarantee that result. But because the higher pay in female jobs would raise costs, employers would reduce the number of such jobs, by automating or by reducing the scale of operations, for example. Workers with the most skills would be more likely to keep their jobs, while those without the skills or experience to merit the higher pay would be let go. The ironic result is that fewer workers would be employed in traditionally female jobs. While the higher pay might induce more workers to seek these jobs, the reduced demand could not accommodate them. Less skilled women would lose out to more skilled women and, quite possibly, to men who would be attracted by the higher pay. What's more, some employers would respond to the higher wages by providing fewer of the non-monetary benefits (like flexible hours) that help accommodate the needs of someone who dovetails home responsibilities and a job.

The few instances where comparable worth has been implemented in the United States tend to support those conclusions. Thus far, comparable worth has been almost entirely confined to the civil service systems of about twenty state governments and a number of local governments. When Washington State implemented comparable worth, according to one study, the share of state government employment fell in those jobs that received comparable worth pay adjustments. The largest relative declines in employment were in the occupations that received the largest comparable worth pay boosts. Other studies have found that Minnesota's well-known comparable worth plan has reduced employment growth in female jobs relative to male jobs.

Comparable worth has not fared well in the courts. It suffered its biggest setback in 1985 when the Ninth Circuit Federal Court of Appeals rejected a comparable worth job evaluation as evidence of discrimination. In a case involving the government employees' union (AFSCME) versus the state of Washington, the court upheld the state's right to base pay on market wages rather than on a job evaluation, writing, "Neither law nor logic deems the free market system a suspect enterprise." The judge who wrote the decision was Anthony Kennedy, now a member of the U.S. Supreme Court. The state of Washington, despite its victory in court, found the political heat too great and implemented comparable worth anyway. But the momentum toward comparable worth appears to have slowed since the Ninth Circuit's ruling.

—June Ellenoff O'Neill

Biography: June Ellenoff O'Neill is an economics professor at the City University of New York's Baruch College, where she directs the Center for the Study of Business and Government. She was formerly director of the Office of Policy and Research at the U.S. Commission on Civil Rights, a senior research associate at the Urban Institute, and a senior economist with the president's Council of Economic Advisers.

Further Reading

Aaron, Henry J., and Cameron M. Lougy. *The Comparable Worth Controversy* (on the fence; neither pro nor con). 1986.

Paul, Ellen. *Equity and Gender* (in opposition). 1989.

Treiman, Donald, and Heidi Hartmann, eds. *Women, Work and Wages: Equal Pay for Jobs of Equal Value* (the bible of proponents). 1981.

U.S. Commission on Civil Rights. *Comparable Worth: Issue for the 80s,* vol. 1 (a collection of 16 articles on comparable worth, pro and con). June 1984.

Conscription

Christopher Jehn

■ Most nations, including the United States, have used military drafts at various times in their histories. Regardless of one's views on military or defense policy, a draft has many economic aspects that are inherently unfair (and inefficient) and repugnant to most economists. Hence, the question of whether to have a draft is whether any expected benefits outweigh those inequities.

A military draft forces people to do something they would not necessarily choose—serve in the military. With a draft in place, the military can pay lower wages than it would need to raise a force of willing volunteers of the same size, skills, and quality. This reduction in pay is properly viewed as a tax on military personnel. The amount of the tax is simply the difference between actual pay and the pay necessary to induce individuals to serve voluntarily. If, for example, pay would have to be $15,000 per year to attract sufficient volunteers, but these volunteers are instead drafted at $7,000 per year, the draftees pay a tax of $8,000 per year each.

Before the draft was abolished in the seventies some of its supporters argued that an all-volunteer force would be too expensive because the military would have to pay much higher wages to attract enlistees. But the draft does not really reduce the cost of national defense. Instead, the draft shifts part of the cost from the general public to junior military personnel (career personnel are not typically drafted). This tax is especially regressive: it falls on low-paid junior personnel who are least able to pay. Moreover, the tax is paid not just by draftees, but also by those who still volunteer despite the lower pay. In other words, it is a tax on military service, the very act of patriotism that a draft is sometimes said to encourage. The President's Commission on an All-Volunteer Force estimated that the draft tax during the Vietnam War was over $6 billion per year in 1991 dollars.

Every time a draft has been imposed, the result has been lower military pay. But even in the unlikely event that military pay is not reduced, a draft would force some unwilling people to serve in order to achieve "representativeness," or "equity." In recent years, for example, some have advocated a return to conscription because today's all-volunteer force supposedly has too few college graduates or too many blacks. How to decide which of today's volunteers to turn away is never addressed. The unwilling conscripts who replace the willing volunteers would bear a tax that no one bears in an all-volunteer force. Because these conscripts do not necessarily perform better than the volunteers they displace, this tax yields no "revenue." Because the conscripts are part of society, the tax they pay is simply a waste to the country as a whole. And some who are qualified and would like to enlist are denied and forced into jobs for which they are less well suited or that offer less opportunity.

To make matters worse, a draft also encourages the government to misuse resources. Because draftees and other junior personnel seem cheaper than they actually are, the government may "buy" more national defense than it should, and will certainly use people, especially high-skilled individuals and junior personnel, in greater numbers than is efficient. This means that a given amount of national defense is more costly to the country than it need be.

In 1988, for example, the U.S. General Accounting Office (GAO) studied the effects of reinstituting conscription and concluded that an equally effective force under a draft would be more expensive than the current force. With a draft a larger total force would be needed because draftees serve a shorter initial enlistment period than today's volunteers. Therefore, a larger fraction of the force would be involved in overhead activities such as training, supervising less experienced personnel, and traveling to a first assignment. The GAO estimated this would add $2 billion to $3 billion per year to the defense budget.

A draft forces some of the wrong people into the military—people who are more productive in other jobs or who have a strong distaste for military service. That has other serious consequences for the country: the military and society are both weaker. Society is weaker because a draft inevitably causes wasteful avoidance behavior like the unwanted schooling, emigration, early marriages, and distorted career choices of the fifties and sixties. The military is weaker because the presence of unwilling conscripts increases turnover (conscripts reenlist at lower rates than volunteers), lowers morale, and causes discipline problems.

U.S. experience since the end of the draft in 1973 validates all these arguments. Military personnel in the early nineties are the highest quality in the nation's history. Recruits are better educated and score higher on enlistment tests than their draft-era counterparts. In 1990, 95 percent of new recruits were high school graduates, compared to about 70 percent in the draft era. Fully 97 percent scored average or above on the Armed Forces Qualification Test, compared to 80 percent during the draft era. Because of that and because service members are all volunteers, the military has far fewer discipline problems, greater experience (because of less turnover), and hence more capability. So, for example, discipline rates—nonjudicial punishment and courts martial—are down from 184 per 1,000 in 1972 to just 76 per 1,000 in 1990, and more than half of today's force are careerists—people with more than five years' experience—as compared to only about one-third in the fifties and sixties.

Based on this experience, most military leaders are thoroughly convinced that a return to the draft could only weaken the armed forces. And a draft would not even reduce the budgetary costs of the military. While cutting pay of junior personnel can reduce budgetary costs, these "savings" would be offset by higher training costs and the costs of maintaining more military personnel to compensate for the lower experience of a drafted force.

In short, an all-volunteer force is both fairer and more efficient than conscription. The U.S. decision to adopt an all-volunteer force was one of the most sensible public policy changes in the last half of the twentieth century.

—Christopher Jehn

Biography: At the time of writing, Christopher Jehn was the assistant secretary of defense for force management and personnel. He was formerly director of the Marine Corps Operations Analysis Group at the Center for Naval Analyses in Alexandria, Virginia.

Further Reading

Anderson, Martin, ed. *Conscription: A Select and Annotated Bibliography*. 1976.
Bowman, William, Roger Little, and G. Thomas Sicilia, eds. *The All-Volunteer Force after a Decade*. 1986.
General Accounting Office. *Military Draft: Potential Impacts and Other Issues*. 1988.
The Report of the President's Commission on an All-Volunteer Armed Force. 1970.

Soldiers as Capital

The reluctance to view a man as capital is especially ruinous of mankind in wartime; here capital is protected, but not man, and in time of war we have no hesitation in sacrificing one hundred men in the bloom of their years to save one cannon.

In a hundred men at least twenty times as much capital is lost as is lost in one cannon. But the production of the cannon is the cause of an expenditure of the state treasury, while human beings are again available for nothing by means of a simple conscription order. . . .

When the statement was made to Napoleon, the founder of the conscription system, that a planned operation would cost too many men, he replied: ''That is nothing. The women produce more of them than I can use.''

—**German economist Johann Heinrich von Thünen, in *Isolated State*, 1850.**

Discrimination

Linda Gorman

■ Because government penalties against discrimination by business make headlines and market penalties do not, the popular wisdom holds that only government stands between individuals and unfair discrimination by business. In fact, governments may engage in much more unfair discrimination than private businesses. When business discriminates against individuals on any basis other than productivity, market mechanisms impose an inescapable penalty on profits. Over time this penalty acts with compelling force and has made profit-seeking business enterprises historically tenacious champions of fair treatment, even in the face of government disapproval and even when the people running individual businesses would prefer to discriminate. While governments practicing unfair discrimination face occasional losses only if their activities attract public disfavor, the losses incurred by businesses mount with each and every sale.

In part, the confusion about the effectiveness of market penalties for discrimination results from confusion about the meaning of the term *discrimination*. Although most people abhor discrimination on the basis of characteristics such as race and sex, they generally applaud those who discriminate against the lazy, the dishonest, and the unproductive by paying them lower wages, firing them, or refusing to hire them in the first place. The problem thus becomes one of distinguishing between unfair discrimination based on simple prejudice, which many people wish to prohibit, and productive discrimination based on merit, which most people wish to encourage. To understand how the market penalizes unfair discrimination while rewarding the productive kind, and why government often indiscriminately punishes both, one must first understand how markets constrain people's behavior.

To begin with, a business can afford to hire an additional employee only if the additional output made possible by hiring him sells for a price that equals or exceeds his wages. The employee's addition to output depends on the tools that he has to work with and on his ability. The price that the additional output sells for depends upon how much consumers are willing to pay. Suppose, for example, that a concessionaire at a baseball stadium decides to hire another hot-dog seller at a wage of $5.00 per hour. If hot dogs sell for $1.00 and cost $.90 to produce (excluding the seller's wage), the new salesman must sell at least fifty hot dogs an hour to cover the cost of paying

him. Because the concessionaire keeps any revenues from hot-dog sales in excess of his costs, he naturally prefers employees who can sell seventy hot dogs per hour to those who sell only the minimum fifty.

Employers wishing to maximize their profits attempt to hire people with the highest possible expected productivity. Suppose that the concessionaire notices that his highest producers have little body fat and wear road race T-shirts advertising marathons and ten kilometer runs. Suppose also that he has noticed that the majority of those who have failed to meet the standard of fifty hot dogs per hour were overweight smokers. Faced with a choice between a smoker and a marathon runner, a rational employer would hire the runner.

Of course, an exceptionally motivated smoker might outperform the average runner. Unfortunately, without requiring extensive physical examinations (the cost of which could wipe out all the profits from hot-dog sales and make any hiring moot), the manager cannot separate exceptional smokers from ordinary ones. So he must base his decision on his experience with smokers in general. As a result most of his employees will be lean and fit. An observer ignorant of the correlation between physical conditioning and productivity would condemn him for unfairly discriminating against overweight tobacco lovers.

In this example the correlation between personal habits and productivity makes it impossible for an outside observer to judge whether the employer discriminated fairly (for a bona fide business reason) or simply has a personal bias against smokers. In either case, because physical appearance and personal habits are correlated with productivity, overweight smokers will be underrepresented in the ranks of hot-dog salesmen. The employer's work force will look the same whether the manager discriminated fairly on the basis of real differences in productivity (no smoker will ever cover as much area as a marathon runner), fairly on the basis of incomplete information (the smoker was exceptionally fit but the manager did not know it), or unfairly on the basis of managerial taste (lean men are better looking than fat ones).

Correlations between personal characteristics and productivity abound in the real world, and their abundance makes it virtually impossible for outside observers to separate productive discrimination from unfair discrimination. On average, blacks with high school diplomas score much lower on achievement tests than whites or Hispanics. On average, recent immigrants have a worse command of English than natives. On average, women take more respites from continuous employment than men. Does the "underrepresentation" of blacks on college campuses stem from unfair discrimination or from their lower average academic achievement? Does the "underrepresentation" of recent immigrants in higher-paying jobs stem from bigotry or from the fact that in the United States fluent English substantially reduces the cost of communicating? Are women "overrepresented" in particular occupations because they are discriminated against or because women choose occupations that give them more flexibility to raise a family? An outsider cannot answer these questions.

The statistical measures of discrimination used by government agencies like the Equal Employment Opportunity Commission depend upon easily measurable individual characteristics, such as race, sex, and age. Although characteristics such as commitment, cooperativeness, motivation, and trustworthiness make large contributions to individual productivity, these same characteristics defy accurate quantitative measurement. For this reason they are often left out of the equation altogether. Evidence on the distortion that this causes suggests that the resulting estimates of discrimination are too unreliable for policy purposes. One study, for example, found that wages for women were either 61 percent lower or 19 percent higher than those of comparable men, depending on how one controlled for unobservable characteristics.

Leaving out the unobservables and basing government-imposed hiring guidelines on easily measured characteristics has the effect of basing hiring and promotion criteria on ethnic background, religion, and sex instead of merit. This punishes those innocent of discrimination along with the guilty and exacerbates social friction between favored and unfavored groups. To the extent that it substitutes less competent people for more competent ones and encourages defensive hiring, it also wastes resources and lowers the average standard of living. In extreme cases, hiring quotas based on caste membership in India and on Sinhalese extraction in Sri Lanka have provoked civil wars.

In contrast, the market mechanism penalizes only those who discriminate unfairly. Intolerant employers find their profits reduced, and bigoted customers must pay more for their shabby tastes. Suppose that black and white hot-dog salesmen are equally productive, but that the concessionaires at all of the stadiums want to hire whites rather than blacks. The stiffer competition for whites will force employers to pay more for a white worker than for an equally productive black one. In effect, employers insisting on white workers make themselves higher-cost producers. Unless customers are willing to pay more for a hot dog delivered by a white than a black, higher costs mean smaller profits. Concessionaires interested in maximum profit will hire blacks, make more money, and be able to underprice the bigots. Even if the white concessionaires collude in refusing to hire blacks, they could still be undercut by new black firms exploiting their lower operating costs. Competition will ultimately force a firm to hire people of either color unless the owner accepts a cut in his profits. As the more profitable equal-opportunity employers expand, the demand for black workers will increase and black wages will rise. Since a few owners may be willing and able to pay for their desire to discriminate against blacks, competition does not necessarily bankrupt all firms practicing unfair discrimination. But competition does make unfair discrimination expensive, thus ensuring that less will occur.

In South Africa in the early 1900s, for example, mine owners seeking profits laid off higher-priced white workers and hired lower-priced black workers, even in the face of penalties threatened by government and violence threatened by white workers. Only by lobbying for, and getting, extreme restriction on blacks' ability to work were the whites able to reserve higher-paying jobs for themselves (see APARTHEID). The profit motive also ameliorated the discrimination of the McCarthy era: profit-maximiz-

ing producers, in defiance of the Motion Picture Academy's blacklist, secretly hired blacklisted screenwriters.

Government, on the other hand, remains unconstrained by any considerations of profit and incurs no costs for discriminating on the basis of race or other factors so long as the discrimination is politically acceptable, which it often has been. At the turn of the century, blacks, who had been making progress since the Civil War, began to compete for previously all-white jobs. Racial animosity increased. Voting power was in the hands of whites and, as economist Thomas Sowell points out, civil service hiring rules were amended to require a photograph of the applicant and to allow the hiring official to choose between the three top performers on civil service tests. The number of blacks in federal employment plummeted. It remained low until the political repercussions of the civil rights movement resulted in affirmative action sixty years later. Although affirmative action changed the group discriminated against, the government continues to discriminate, now against white men. In contrast, private businesses in the South were less eager to discriminate against blacks even at the height of segregation (see sidebar).

Although the market makes people pay for unproductive discrimination, many of the restrictions that government imposes on markets blunt the market mechanisms that make discrimination expensive. Barriers to hiring and firing make employers less likely to try out types of people with whom they have little experience. Minimum wage laws and union wage scales, by keeping wages higher than market wages, reduce the number of people that employers wish to hire

while simultaneously attracting more applicants. With so many people to choose from,
the cost of turning away applicants who
meet the employer's productive require-

ments, but not his tastes, drops considerably.

—**Linda Gorman**

Biography: Linda Gorman is a free-lance economics journalist in Denver. She was previously an economics professor at the Naval Postgraduate School in Monterey, California.

Further Reading

(*indicates more advanced treatment*)
*Becker, Gary S. *The Economics of Discrimination*, 2d ed. 1971.
Friedman, Milton. *Capitalism and Freedom*. 1967.
Scanlon, James P. "Illusions of Job Segregation." *The Public Interest* 93 (Fall 1988): 54–69.
Sowell, Thomas. *Preferential Policies: An International Perspective*. 1990.
————. *Race and Economics*. 1975.

See also APARTHEID, COMPARABLE WORTH, GENDER GAP, LABOR UNIONS.

The Market Resists Discrimination

The resistance of southern streetcar companies to ordinances requiring them to segregate black passengers vividly illustrates how the market motivates businesses to avoid unfair discrimination. Before the segregation laws most streetcar companies voluntarily segregated tobacco users, not blacks. Nonsmokers of either race were free to ride where they wished, but smokers were relegated to the rear of the car or to the outside platform. The revenue gains from pleased nonsmokers apparently outweighed any losses from disgruntled smokers.

Streetcar companies refused, however, to discriminate against blacks because separate cars would have reduced their profits. They resisted even after the passage of turn-of-the-century laws requiring that they segregate blacks. One railroad manager complained that racial discrimination increased costs because it required that the company "haul around a good deal of empty space that is assigned to the colored people and not available to both races." Racial discrimination also upset some paying customers. Black customers boycotted the streetcar lines and formed competing hack (horse-drawn carriage) companies, and white customers often refused to move to the white section.

In Augusta, Savannah, Atlanta, Mobile, and Jacksonville, streetcar companies responded by refusing to enforce segregation laws for as long as fifteen years after their passage. The Memphis Street Railway "contested bitterly," and the Houston Electric Railway petitioned the Houston City Council for repeal. A black attorney leading a court battle against the laws provided an ironic measure of the strength of the streetcar companies' resistance by publicly denying that his group "was in cahoots with the railroad lines in Jacksonville." As pressure from the government grew, however, the cost of defiance began to outweigh the market penalty on profits. One by one, the streetcar companies succumbed, and the United States stumbled further into the infamous morass of racial segregation.

—LG

SOURCE: *Jennifer Roback, "The Political Economy of Segregation: The Case of Segregated Streetcars."* Journal of Economic History *56, no. 4 (December 1986): 893–917.*

Gender Gap

Claudia Goldin

■ When economists speak of the "gender gap," these days they usually are referring to systematic differences in the outcomes that men and women achieve in the labor market. These differences come in the percentages of men and women in the labor force, the types of occupations they choose, and the difference in the average incomes of men and women. These economic gender gaps have been a major issue in the women's movement and a major issue for economists.

The gender gap in U.S. labor force participation has been eroding steadily for 100 years (see chart 1). In 1890 the percentage of married white women who reported an occupation outside the home was extremely low—just 2.5 percent for the entire United States. The figure increased to 12.5 percent by 1940, 20.7 percent by 1950, and then by

CHART 1

Labor Force Participation Rates of Men and Women, 1890–1990

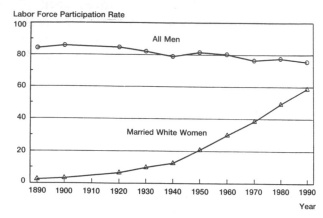

SOURCES: *Men: 1890 to 1970, U.S. Bureau of the Census,* Historical Statistics of the United States, Colonial Times to 1970. *Government Printing Office, 1975; and 1980 to 1990, U.S. Department of Labor, Bureau of Labor Statistics,* Employment and Earnings.

Women: C. Goldin, Understanding the Gender Gap: An Economic History of American Women, *table 2.1., 1990.*

about 10 percentage points for every decade since then. By 1990 the labor participation rate for all married women had climbed to almost 60 percent, versus 78 percent for married men. (By 1990 women made up 45 percent of the total labor force.) In the forties and fifties, increases were the greatest for older married women, and then for younger married women in the seventies and eighties. And the eighties witnessed an increase in labor force participation of the sole group that had resisted change in previous decades—women with infants.

The gender gap that gets the most attention, however, is in earnings. Although no comprehensive data exist for the period before 1950, evidence for certain sectors of the economy suggests that the gender gap in earnings narrowed substantially during

two earlier periods in U.S. history. Between about 1820 and 1850, the era known as the industrial revolution in America, the ratio of female to male full-time earnings rose from about 0.3, its level in the agricultural economy, to about 0.5 in manufacturing. That is, women's earnings rose from, on average, about 30 percent of what men made to about 50 percent. From about 1900 to 1930, when the clerical and sales sectors began their rise, the ratio of female to male earnings rose from 0.46 to 0.56. In neither period did married women's employment expand greatly. Yet between 1950 and 1980, when so many married women were entering the labor force, the ratio of female to male earnings for full-time, year-round employees was virtually constant at 60 percent.

What accounts for the differences in earnings between men and women? Observable factors that affect pay—such as education, job experience, hours of work, and so on—explain no more than 50 percent of the wage gap. The remainder—termed the residual—cannot be explained by observable factors. This residual could result from workers' choices or, alternatively, from economic discrimination. Surprisingly, only 10 percent to 33 percent of the difference in male and female earnings can be explained by the differing occupations of men and women. The remainder is due to differences within occupations, and part of that is due to the observable factors.

Many observers have noted the paradox that as married women entered the labor force in steadily increasing numbers between 1950 and 1980, their earnings and occupational status relative to men did not improve. Yet that is not so paradoxical as it might seem. Indeed, with so many new female entrants to the labor force, an economist would expect women's wages to fall (relative to men's) because of the huge increase in supply. In other words, the pay of women relative to men probably stayed constant not in spite of, but because of the increase in the female labor force.

As more and more women entered the labor market, many of the new entrants had very little job market experience and few skills. If women tend to stay in the labor force once they enter it, the large numbers of new entrants will continually dilute the average labor market experience of all employed women. Various data demonstrate that the average job experience of employed women did not advance much from 1950 to 1980 as participation rates increased sub-

stantially. Economists James P. Smith and Michael Ward found that among working women aged forty, for example, the average work experience in 1989 was 14.4 years, hardly any increase at all over the average experience of 14.0 years in 1950. Because earnings reflect the skills and experience of the employed, it is not surprising that the ratio of female to male earnings did not increase from 1950 to 1980.

The gender gap in earnings decreased substantially during the eighties. By 1989 the ratio of female to male earnings for those who work full-time throughout the year had climbed by about 8 percentage points to 68 percent. Thus, in the nine years from 1980 to 1989, 20 percent of the preexisting gender gap in pay had been eliminated. Moreover, the size of the gender gap has been overstated. That is because women working full-time work about 10 percent fewer hours than men. Per hour worked, women now earn about 75 percent of what men earn.

According to economists June O'Neill and Solomon Polachek, the ratio of women's to men's pay increased for virtually all ages, all levels of education, and all levels of experience in the labor market. For workers with less than a high school degree, they found, the increase was 6.1 percentage points. For those with at least a high school diploma but no college degree, it was 5.3 percentage points. For those with at least a college degree, it was 7.2 percentage points. (These statistics are for whites twenty-five to sixty-four years old during the period from 1978 to 1987.) What is more, the gains occurred across all age groups. Although women in their thirties had the greatest gains relative to men their own age, the pay of older women relative to older men rose almost as much.

In this sense the move to greater gender equality in the eighties was remarkable. It was not merely a reflection of increased opportunities for younger or more educated women in relation to comparable groups of men. Moreover, the increase did not occur only at the point of initial hire. It is not surprising, therefore, that conventional methods of explaining the decrease in the gender gap in earnings—those that rely on changing composition of the female work force by education, potential job experience, occupational skill, and industry—can account for, at most, 20 percent of the increase.

Just as the stability of the earnings gap between 1950 and 1980 was probably due to the large influx of inexperienced women into the labor force, the narrowing of the gap in the eighties may owe to the fact that female participation rates are now exceedingly high. Because a larger proportion of women currently employed were previously in the labor force, their skills and experience cannot be greatly diluted by those of new entrants.

Other changes also account for the decrease in the earnings gap. Educational advances, particularly among the college-educated, have placed more women on par with men. College-educated women now major in subjects that are very similar to those chosen by men. Whereas in 1960 male college graduates outnumbered female by five to three, by 1980 the number of female and male college graduates was equal. In the sixties, for every hundred male recipients of professional degrees, there were fewer than five female recipients. By 1990 almost sixty females earned professional degrees for every hundred males. Young women are now forming more realistic expectations of their own futures than was the case twenty years ago. In 1968 only 30 percent of fifteen- to nineteen-year-old women said that they would be in the labor force at age thirty-five; by 1979 more than 70 percent thought they would be. Because the 1968 group vastly underestimated their future participation rate, they may have "underinvested" in their skills by taking academic courses that left them less prepared to compete in the job market.

To what extent has legislation narrowed the gender gap? One piece of legislation is Title VII of the Civil Rights Act of 1964, which forbids discrimination on the basis of sex in hiring, promotion, and other conditions of employment. The other is affirmative action. There is only scant evidence that either law has had any effect on the gender gap in earnings or occupations, although not enough research on this has been done to justify strong conclusions one way or the other (see the discussion in Ehrenberg and Smith, 1988, p. 577).

The gender gap in employment, earnings, and occupations has narrowed in various ways during the twentieth century, but with increasing significance, it seems, in the eighties. Whether or not the gap will continue to narrow and eventually disappear is uncertain, and probably depends on the gender gap in time spent in child care and in the home.

—Claudia Goldin

Biography: Claudia Goldin is a professor of economics at Harvard University and program director and research associate at the National Bureau of Economic Research in Cambridge, Massachusetts.

Further Reading

Ehrenberg, Ronald G., and Robert S. Smith. *Modern Labor Economics: Theory and Public Policy,* 3d ed. 1988.

Goldin, Claudia. *Understanding the Gender Gap: An Economic History of American Women.* 1990.

O'Neill, June, and Solomon Polachek. ''An Analysis of Recent Trends in the Male-Female Wage Gap.'' Unpublished manuscript, 1991.

Smith, James P., and Michael Ward. ''Women in the Labor Market and in the Family.'' *Journal of Economic Perspectives* 3 (Winter 1989): 9–23.

See also COMPARABLE WORTH, DISCRIMINATION.

Human Capital

Gary S. Becker

■ To most people capital means a bank account, a hundred shares of IBM stock, assembly lines, or steel plants in the Chicago area. These are all forms of capital in the sense that they are assets that yield income and other useful outputs over long periods of time.

But these tangible forms of capital are not the only ones. Schooling, a computer training course, expenditures of medical care, and lectures on the virtues of punctuality and honesty also are capital. That is because they raise earnings, improve health, or add to a person's good habits over much of his lifetime. Therefore, economists regard expenditures on education, training, medical care, and so on as investments in *human* capital. They are called human capital because people cannot be separated from their knowledge, skills, health, or values in the way they can be separated from their financial and physical assets.

Education and training are the most important investments in human capital. Many studies have shown that high school and college education in the United States greatly raise a person's income, even after netting out direct and indirect costs of schooling, and even after adjusting for the fact that people with more education tend to have higher IQs and better-educated and richer parents. Similar evidence is now available for many years from over a hundred countries with different cultures and economic systems. The earnings of more educated people are almost always well above average, although the gains are generally larger in less developed countries.

Consider the differences in average earnings between college and high school graduates in the United States during the past fifty years. Until the early sixties college graduates earned about 45 percent more than high school graduates. In the sixties this premium from college education shot up to almost 60 percent, but it fell back in the seventies to under 50 percent. The fall during the seventies led some economists and the media to worry about "overeducated Americans." Indeed, in 1976 Harvard economist Richard Freeman wrote a book titled *The Overeducated American*. This sharp fall in the return to investments in human capital put the concept of human capital itself into some disrepute. Among other things it caused doubt about whether education and training really do raise productivity or simply provide signals ("credentials") about talents and abilities.

But the monetary gains from a college education rose sharply again during the eighties, to the highest level in the past fifty

years. Economists Kevin M. Murphy and Finis Welch have shown that the premium on getting a college education in the eighties was over 65 percent. Lawyers, accountants, engineers, and many other professionals experienced especially rapid advances in earnings. The earnings advantage of high school graduates over high school dropouts has also greatly increased. Talk about overeducated Americans has vanished, and it has been replaced by concern once more about whether the United States provides adequate quality and quantity of education and other training.

This concern is justified. Real wage rates of young high school dropouts have fallen by more than 25 percent since the early seventies, a truly remarkable decline. Whether because of school problems, family instability, or other factors, young people without a college or a full high school education are not being adequately prepared for work in modern economies.

Thinking about higher education as an investment in human capital helps us understand why the fraction of high school graduates who go to college increases and decreases from time to time. When the benefits of a college degree fell in the seventies, for example, the fraction of white high school graduates who started college fell, from 51 percent in 1970 to 46 percent in 1975. Many educators expected enrollments to continue declining in the eighties, partly because the number of eighteen-year-olds was declining, but also because college tuition was rising rapidly. They were wrong about whites. The fraction of white high school graduates who enter college rose steadily in the eighties, reaching 60 percent in 1988, and caused an absolute increase in the number of whites enrolling despite the smaller number of college-age people.

This makes sense. The benefits of a college education, as noted, increased in the eighties. And tuition and fees, although they rose about 39 percent from 1980 to 1986 in real, inflation-adjusted terms, are not the only cost of going to college. Indeed, for most college students they are not even the major cost. On average, three-fourths of the private cost—the cost borne by the student and by the student's family—of a college education is the income that college students give up by not working. A good measure of this "opportunity cost" is the income that a newly minted high school graduate could earn by working full-time. And during the eighties this forgone income, unlike tuition, did not rise in real terms. Therefore, even a 39 percent increase in real tuition costs translated into an increase of just 10 percent in the total cost to students of a college education.

The economics of human capital also account for the fall in the fraction of black high school graduates who went on to college in the early eighties. As Harvard economist Thomas J. Kane has pointed out, costs rose more for black college students than for whites. That is because a higher percentage of blacks are from low-income families and, therefore, had been heavily subsidized by the federal government. Cuts in federal grants to them in the early eighties substantially raised their cost of a college education.

According to the 1982 "Report of the Commission on Graduate Education" at the University of Chicago, demographic-based college enrollment forecasts had been wide of the mark during the twenty years prior to that time. This is not surprising to a "human capitalist." Such forecasts ignored the changing incentives—on the cost side and on the benefit side—to enroll in college.

The economics of human capital have brought about a particularly dramatic change in the incentives for women to invest in college education in recent decades. Prior to the sixties American women were more likely than men to graduate from high school but less likely to continue on to college. Women who did go to college shunned or were excluded from math, sciences, economics, and law, and gravitated toward teaching, home economics, foreign languages, and literature. Because relatively few married women continued to work for pay, they rationally chose an education that helped in "household production"—and no doubt also in the marriage market—by improving their social skills and cultural interests.

All this has changed radically. The enormous increase in the labor participation of married women is the most important labor force change during the past twenty-five years. Many women now take little time off from their jobs even to have children. As a result the value to women of market skills has increased enormously, and they are by-passing traditional "women's" fields to enter accounting, law, medicine, engineering, and other subjects that pay well. Indeed, women now comprise one-third or so of enrollments in law, business, and medical schools, and many home economics departments have either shut down or are emphasizing the "new home economics." Improvements in the economic position of black women have been especially rapid, and they now earn just about as much as white women.

Of course, formal education is not the only way to invest in human capital. Workers also learn and are trained outside of schools, especially on jobs. Even college graduates are not fully prepared for the labor market when they leave school, and are fitted into their jobs through formal and informal training programs. The amount of on-the-job training ranges from an hour or so at simple jobs like dishwashing to several years at complicated tasks like engineering in an auto plant. The limited data available indicates that on-the-job training is an important source of the very large increase in earnings that workers get as they gain greater experience at work. Recent bold estimates by Columbia University economist Jacob Mincer suggest that the total investment in on-the-job training may be well over $100 billion a year, or almost 2 percent of GNP.

No discussion of human capital can omit the influence of families on the knowledge, skills, values, and habits of their children. Parents affect educational attainment, marital stability, propensities to smoke and to get to work on time, as well as many other dimensions of their children's lives.

The enormous influence of the family would seem to imply a very close relation between the earnings, education, and occupations of parents and children. Therefore, it is rather surprising that the positive relation between the earnings of parents and children is not strong, although the relation between the years of schooling of parents and children is stronger. For example, if fathers earn 20 percent above the mean of

their generation, sons at similar ages tend to earn about 8 percent above the mean of theirs. Similar relations hold in Western European countries, Japan, Taiwan, and many other places.

The old adage of "from shirtsleeves to shirtsleeves in three generations" is no myth; the earnings of grandsons and grandparents are hardly related. Apparently, the opportunities provided by a modern economy, along with extensive public support of education, enable the majority of those who come from lower-income backgrounds to do reasonably well in the labor market. The same opportunities that foster upward mobility for the poor create an equal amount of downward mobility for those higher up on the income ladder.

The continuing growth in per capita incomes of many countries during the nineteenth and twentieth centuries is partly due to the expansion of scientific and technical knowledge that raises the productivity of labor and other inputs in production. And the increasing reliance of industry on sophisticated knowledge greatly enhances the value of education, technical schooling, on-the-job training, and other human capital.

New technological advances clearly are of little value to countries that have very few skilled workers who know how to use them. Economic growth closely depends on the synergies between new knowledge and human capital, which is why large increases in education and training have accompanied major advances in technological knowledge in all countries that have achieved significant economic growth.

The outstanding economic records of Japan, Taiwan, and other Asian economies in recent decades dramatically illustrate the importance of human capital to growth. Lacking natural resources—they import almost all their energy, for example—and facing discrimination against their exports by the West, these so-called Asian tigers grew rapidly by relying on a well-trained, educated, hardworking, and conscientious labor force that makes excellent use of modern technologies.

—Gary S. Becker

Biography: Gary S. Becker is a professor of economics and sociology at the University of Chicago and a senior fellow at Stanford's Hoover Institution. He was a pioneer in the study of human capital. He won the 1992 Nobel Prize in economics.

Further Reading

Becker, Gary S. *Human Capital*. 1975.

Freeman, Richard. *The Overeducated American*. 1976.

Kane, Thomas J. "College Entry by Blacks since 1970: The Role of Tuition, Financial Aid, Local Economic Conditions, and Family Background." Unpublished manuscript, 1990.

Murphy, Kevin M., and Finis Welch. "Wage Premiums for College Graduates: Recent Growth and Possible Explanations." *Educational Researcher* 18 (1989): 17–27.

"Report of the Commission on Graduate Education." *University of Chicago Record* 16, no. 2 (May 3, 1982): 67–180.

Immigration

George J. Borjas

■ Immigration is again a major component of demographic change in the United States. Since 1940 the number of legal immigrants has increased at a rate of 1 million per decade. By the eighties about 600,000 legal immigrants were being admitted each year, making for a rate of about 6 million per decade (see table 1). Large numbers of illegal aliens also enter the country. In 1986, for instance, the Border Patrol apprehended 1.8 million persons attempting to enter illegally, or more than three people per minute.

In the early 1900s, when immigration reached historically high levels, half of the growth in total U.S. population and in the labor force was due to immigration. In the seventies only about one-quarter of the growth in population and one-eighth of the growth in the labor force were due to immigration. In the eighties immigration was back up and accounted for just under 40 percent of the growth in population and for a quarter of all new labor market entrants. These proportions are approaching the earlier ones, not only because of the large number of immigrants, but also because of the declining fertility rate of American women.

Just as numbers of immigrants change, so has the means of selection. Between 1924 and 1965 immigrants were selected mainly on the basis of national origin. The United Kingdom and Germany received over 60 percent of the visas allocated outside the Western Hemisphere. (Visa applicants originating in North or South America were not subject to these quotas.) That all changed with the 1965 amendments to the Immigration and Nationality Act. Under the new system most visas are reserved for relatives of U.S. residents. By the late eighties 75 percent of immigrants were admitted because of family ties, and an additional 20 percent were refugees.

The 1965 amendments dramatically altered the mix of immigrants. In the fifties 53 percent of immigrants originated in Europe, 25 percent in Latin America, and 6 percent in Asia. By the eighties only 11 percent of immigrants originated in Europe, 42 percent in Latin America, and 42 percent in Asia.

Two major changes in immigration policy were enacted recently. First, the 1986 Immigration Reform and Control Act granted amnesty to 3 million illegal aliens and introduced penalties for employers who hire undocumented workers. Although the act's purpose was to stem the illegal flow, its effectiveness is already in doubt. The Border Patrol apprehended 1.2 million illegal aliens in 1990, the same number it apprehended in 1983. The second piece of legislation was the 1990 Immigration Act, which permits the entry of an additional 175,000 immigrants per year, with half of the extra visas reserved for skilled applicants.

Because of the increasing importance of immigration, the nineties will likely witness the renewal of the debate over the "immi-

TABLE 1

Flows of Immigrants Relative to Population and Labor Force

Period	Flow of Immigrants (in millions)	Immigrants as Percent of Change	
		In Population	In Labor Force
Legal Flows Only			
1901–10	8.8	55.0	
1911–20	5.7	41.6	51.4*
1921–30	4.1	24.0	26.0
1931–40	.5	5.6	4.0
1941–50	1.0	5.2	7.0
1951–60	2.5	8.9	14.5
1961–70	3.3	13.6	11.1
1971–80	4.5	19.8	9.3
1981–89	5.8	26.8	16.2
Legal and Illegal Flows			
1971–80	5.8	25.6	12.0
1981–89	8.4	38.2	23.1

*Average for 1901–10 and 1911–20.

SOURCES: *John M. Abowd and Richard B. Freeman,* Immigration, Trade, and the Labor Market, *1991: 4; U.S. Bureau of the Census,* Historical Statistics of the United States, Colonial Times to 1970, *1975: 105, 131.*

gration problem.'' This debate will be guided by three issues:

1. How well do immigrants adapt to the United States?
2. What is their impact on the labor market opportunities of natives?
3. What immigration policy is most beneficial for the country?

Immigrant Performance in the Labor Market

When immigrants enter the United States, they typically lack skills, such as proficiency in the English language, that American employers value. Hence, it is not surprising that new immigrants earn less than native workers. As immigrants acquire these skills, however, their economic status catches up to that of natives. But because the recent waves of immigrants are relatively less skilled than earlier ones, the wage disadvantage of newly arrived immigrants has worsened over time. Immigrants who arrived in the late fifties earned 12 percent less than natives at the time of arrival. This wage disadvantage upon arrival increased to 15 percent in the late sixties, to 25 percent in the late seventies, and to 27 percent in the late eighties. Because recent immigrants start so far behind, they cannot attain wage parity with natives even after two or three decades in the United States (see chart 1).

In 1980 newly arrived immigrants from India or Iran earned 20 percent less than natives; newly arrived Mexican or Haitian immigrants earned 50 percent less. Compare this to immigrants from Sweden or the United Kingdom, who earned about 20 percent more than natives.

The large disparity in earnings for various nationalities arises partly because skills acquired in advanced, industrialized economies (like the United Kingdom or Sweden) are more easily transferable to the American labor market. But another reason is that the typical worker who emigrates from, say, Sweden, differs substantially from the typical worker who leaves Mexico. The Swedish government taxes skilled workers heavily and subsidizes the unskilled. Hence Sweden suffers from what is called a brain drain: skilled Swedes migrate to the United States. In contrast, there is a great deal of income inequality in Mexico, where unskilled workers have few economic opportunities and skilled workers are well rewarded. Therefore, it is the unskilled who wish to emigrate. Because incomes are highly unequal in many of the less developed countries that are the source of U.S. immigrants today, current waves of immigrants are less skilled than earlier waves.

An important consequence of the shift toward a less skilled immigrant flow is a sizable increase in the costs associated with welfare use among immigrants. Between 1970 and 1980 the fraction of immigrant households on welfare rose by 3 percentage points (from 5.9 to 8.8 percent). Welfare recipiency among some national origin groups is disturbingly large. Some 11 percent of Filipino, 18 percent of Cuban, and 26 percent of households originating in the Dominican Republic receive public assistance, as compared to 7.9 percent of native households.

The Impact of Immigrants on Native Earnings

There are two opposing views about how immigrants affect the labor market opportunities of American natives. One view is that they have a harmful effect because immigrants and natives tend to have similar skills and compete for the same jobs, thus driving down the native wage. The other view is that the services of immigrants and natives are not interchangeable, but rather complement each other. For instance, some immigrant groups may be unskilled but particularly adept at harvesting crops. Immigration then increases native productivity and wages because natives can specialize in tasks for which they are better suited.

The first view is more likely correct. Economists who have rejected this view on the basis of evidence have looked at somewhat superficial data. These economists speculated that if the services of natives and immigrants are interchangeable, natives should earn less in cities where immigrants are in abundant supply, such as Los Angeles or New York, than in cities with few immigrants, such as Nashville or Pittsburgh. Although natives do earn somewhat less in cities that have large immigrant populations, the correlation between the native

CHART 1

Earnings over the Working Life for Immigrant and Native Men

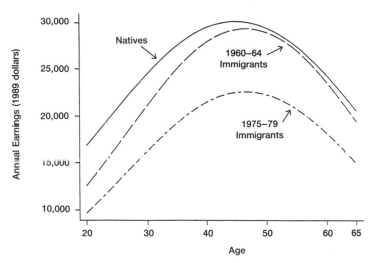

SOURCE: *Adapted from George J. Borjas,* Friends or Strangers: The Impact of Immigrants on the U.S. Economy, *1990: 114.*

wage and the presence of immigrants is weak. If one city has 10 percent more immigrants than another, the native wage in the city with the most immigrants is only 0.2 percent lower.

The results of the Mariel boatlift provide further evidence of how weak the correlation is. In April 1980, when Fidel Castro declared that Cubans wishing to emigrate could leave from the port of Mariel, 125,000 people accepted the offer. Miami's labor force suddenly grew by 7 percent. Yet the trends in wages and unemployment rates in Miami between 1980 and 1985, including those of black workers, resembled those observed in comparable cities.

But all this evidence is superficial. Why? Because it ignores the fact that labor and capital are mobile between cities. If an in-

flux of immigrant workers reduced wages substantially in a particular city, native workers and some immigrants would leave that city and find work elsewhere. And natives who had contemplated migrating to that city would choose another destination. Also, capital may "migrate" to cities with large numbers of unskilled immigrants, where capitalists can earn a greater return on their investment. Large-scale immigration, therefore, may not drive down wages in particular cities. Rather, its depressing effect on wages is nationwide.

Striking evidence for this aggregate effect of immigration is given by the deteriorating economic conditions for native workers with less than a high school education. During the eighties the wage of native high school dropouts fell by 10 percent relative to the wage of workers with more schooling. About a third of this decline is attributable to the increase of unskilled immigrants in the work force, who went from 13 percent of the high school–dropout work force in 1980 to 26 percent by 1988. Thus, a good case can be made that immigration reduced unskilled wages in the United States by about 3 percent (one-third of 10 percent).

Economic Impact of Immigration

Although the entry of immigrants reduces the wage of comparable native workers, it produces a slight increase in the income of U.S. natives overall. Using a well-known formula in economics, we can estimate that immigration increases the real income of natives, but only by about 0.1 percent. (This calculation is based on what is called the Harberger triangle.) That 0.1 percent increase translates to about a $5 billion a year gain from immigration for U.S. natives. Of course, not everyone benefits equally from immigration; workers with competing skills lose, while owners of land and capital gain.

Many people believe that because a comparatively large percentage of immigrants goes on welfare, the costs to native American taxpayers wipe out the gains from immigration. But this has not been the case in recent years. The numbers show why. The present value of cash welfare benefits (such as Aid to Families with Dependent Children) received by the typical immigrant family over its lifetime is $8,700. With 6.4 million immigrant households, the total cost of assistance programs for immigrants is about $56 billion.

But immigrants also pay taxes. The present value of lifetime earnings for the typical immigrant man is $380,000. With 7.6 million working immigrants (both men and women), total earnings of immigrants are at most $2.9 trillion, of which about 40 percent, or $1.2 trillion, are paid in taxes of all forms. Because 3 percent of total revenues are allocated to cash welfare benefits, immigrants pay about $36 billion ($1.2 trillion times .03) in taxes to fund welfare programs. Comparing the $36 billion that immigrants contribute to welfare to the $56 billion they consume, immigrants consume $20 billion more over their lifetimes than they contribute. Thus, the welfare system causes U.S. natives to lose about $1.1 billion per year (in present value terms). Subtracting this $1.1 billion from the $5 billion annual increase in national income, the United States benefits from immigration, but the economic gains are small.

The net benefit is even smaller when immigrants are relatively unskilled. For instance, suppose that all immigrants have the skill level of those who came in the late seventies. Lifetime welfare costs per household would then be $13,600, and the immigrant population would add $87 billion to welfare costs. These less skilled immigrants only earn $313,000 over their working lives, so that total earnings are about $2.4 trillion. They would then pay about $960 billion in taxes, of which $29 billion is allocated to funding cash benefit programs. The immigrants would drain the U.S. Treasury by about $58 billion over their lifetime, for a net loss of about $3.2 billion per year. Because national income increases by somewhat more, immigration is still beneficial. Note, however, that these calculations do not include the costs of other components of the welfare state, particularly health care. The introduction of these additional programs would further reduce the meager economic benefits associated with the immigration of less skilled workers.

Because the gains from immigration depend on the skill level of immigrants, other host countries (Australia and Canada, for instance) now use a "point system" to allocate visas. Applicants are graded on the basis of such factors as education and occupation, and only those applicants who "pass the test" are awarded entry visas. It is not surprising that people migrating to those countries are more skilled than those admitted by the United States. The United States, in effect, is losing the competition for skilled workers in the immigration market.

The evidence also suggests that a policy allowing unrestricted immigration will not necessarily increase the skill level of immigrants. A good example of unrestricted migration is the population flow between Puerto Rico and the United States. Despite the lack of any legal impediments, Puerto Ricans who migrated to the United States in the sixties and seventies are less skilled, on average, than those who remained in their birthplace. The typical Puerto Rican migrant residing in the United States has about 1.3 years less schooling than his compatriots back on the island. Because Puerto Rico's wage structure has substantial inequality and offers little opportunity for less skilled workers, it is not surprising to find that these are the workers who choose to leave, just as in the earlier example of Mexico.

Changes in immigration policy since 1965 greatly altered the number, national origin mix, and skill composition of immigrants. Importing unskilled workers helps fill menial jobs at low wages, but these immigrants also impose substantial costs, mainly by being disproportionately on welfare. Although U.S. natives benefit from immigration on net, the benefits are small.

—George J. Borjas

Biography: George J. Borjas is a professor of economics at the University of California, San Diego, and a research associate at the National Bureau of Economic Research. He was a member of the National Academy of Sciences Panel on Immigration Statistics.

Further Reading

Abowd, John M., and Richard B. Freeman, eds. *Immigration, Trade, and the Labor Market.* 1991.
Borjas, George J. "Self-Selection and the Earnings of Immigrants." *American Economic Review* 77 (September 1987): 531–53.
———. *Friends or Strangers: The Impact of Immigrants on the U.S. Economy.* 1990.
———, and Richard B. Freeman, eds. *Immigration and the Work Force: Economic Consequences for the United States and Source Areas.* 1992.

Borjas, George J., and Stephen J. Trejo. "Immigrant Participation in the Welfare System." *Industrial and Labor Relations Review* 44 (January 1991): 195–211.

Card, David. "The Impact of the Mariel Boatlift on the Miami Labor Market." *Industrial and Labor Relations Review* 43 (January 1990): 245–57.

Simon, Julian L. *The Economic Consequences of Immigration.* 1989.

Job Safety

W. Kip Viscusi

■ Many people believe that employers do not care whether their workplace conditions are safe. If the government were not regulating job safety, they contend, workplaces would be unsafe.

In fact, employers have many incentives to make workplaces safe. Since the time of Adam Smith, economists have observed that workers demand "compensating differentials" (that is, wage premiums) for the risks they face. The extra pay for job hazards in effect establishes the price that employers must pay for an unsafe workplace. Wage premiums paid to U.S. workers for risking injury are huge—they amount to about $120 billion annually, which is over 2 percent of the gross national product, and over 5 percent of total wages paid.

These wage premiums give firms an incentive to invest in job safety because an employer who makes his workplace safer can reduce the wages he pays. Employers have a second incentive because they must pay higher premiums for workers' compensation if accident rates are high. And the threat of lawsuits over products used in the workplace gives sellers of these products another reason to reduce risks.

Of course, the threat of lawsuits gives employers an incentive to care about safety only if they anticipate the lawsuits. In the case of asbestos litigation, for example, liability was deferred by several decades after the initial exposure to asbestos. Even if firms were cognizant of the extent of the health risk, which many were not, none of them could have anticipated the shift in legal doctrine that, in effect, imposed liability retroactively. Thus, it is for acute accidents rather than diseases that the tort liability system bolsters the safety incentives generated by the market for safety.

How well does the safety market work? For it to work well, workers must have some knowledge of the risks they face. And they do. One study of how 496 workers perceived job hazards found that the greater the risk of injury in an industry, the higher the proportion of workers in that industry who saw their job as dangerous. In industries with five or fewer disabling injuries per million hours worked, such as women's outerwear manufacturing and the communication equipment industry, only 24 percent of surveyed workers thought their jobs to be dangerous. But in industries with forty or more disabling injuries per million hours, such as logging camps and the meat products industry, 100 percent of the workers knew that their jobs were dangerous. That workers know the dangers makes sense. Many hazards, such as visible safety risks, can be readily monitored. Moreover, some dimly understood health risks are often linked to noxious exposures and dust levels that workers can monitor. Also, symptoms sometimes flag the onset of some more serious ailment. Byssinosis, for example, a disease that workers exposed to cotton dust often get, proceeds in stages.

Even when workers are not well informed, they do not necessarily assume that risks are zero. According to a large body of research, people systematically overestimate small risks and underestimate large ones. If workers overestimate the probability of an injury that occurs infrequently— for example, exposure to a highly publicized potential carcinogen, such as second-

hand smoke—then employers will have too great an incentive to reduce this hazard. The opposite is also true: when workers underestimate the likelihood of more frequent kinds of injuries, such as falling and motor vehicle accidents on the job, employers may invest too little in preventing those injuries.

The bottom line is that market forces have a powerful influence on job safety. The $120 billion in annual wage premiums referred to earlier is in addition to the value of workers' compensation. Workers on moderately risky blue-collar jobs, whose annual risk of getting killed is 1 in 10,000, earn a premium of $300 to $500 per year. The imputed compensation per "statistical death" (10,000 times $300 to $500) is therefore $3 million to $5 million. Even workers who are not strongly averse to risk and who have voluntarily chosen extremely risky jobs, such as coal miners and firemen, receive compensation on the order of $600,000 per statistical death.

These wage premiums are the amount that workers insist on being paid for taking risks. In other words, the wage premiums are the amount that workers would willingly forgo to avoid the risk. Employers will eliminate hazards only when it costs less to do so than what they will save in the form of lower wage premiums. For example, if eliminating a risk costs the employer $10,000 but allows him to pay $11,000 less in wages, he will do so. Costlier reductions in risk are not worthwhile to employees (since they would rather take the risk and get the higher pay) and are not voluntarily undertaken by employers.

Other evidence that the safety market

works comes from the decrease in the riskiness of jobs throughout the century. One would predict that as workers become wealthier they will be less desperate to earn money and will therefore demand more safety. The historical data show that that is what employees have done, and that employers have responded by providing more safety. As per capita disposable income per year rose from $1,085 (in 1970 prices) in 1933 to $3,376 in 1970, death rates on the job dropped from 37 per 100,000 workers to 18.

Despite this strong evidence that the market for safety works, not all workers are fully informed about the risks they face. They are particularly uninformed about little-understood health hazards that have not yet been called to their attention. But even where workers' information is imperfect, additional market forces are at work. Survey results indicate that of all workers who quit manufacturing jobs, over one-third do so when they discover that the hazards are greater than they initially believed. Losing employees costs money. Companies must train replacements, and production suffers while they do so. Companies, therefore, have an incentive to provide a safe work environment, or at least to inform prospective workers of the dangers. Although the net effect of these market processes does not always ensure the optimal amount of safety, the incentives for safety are substantial.

Beginning with the passage of the Occupational Safety and Health Act of 1970, the federal government has attempted to augment these safety incentives, primarily by specifying technological standards for workplace design. These government attempts to influence safety decisions formerly made by companies generated substantial controversy. In some cases, these regulations have imposed huge costs. A particularly extreme example is the 1987 OSHA formaldehyde standard, which imposed costs of $72 billion for each life that the regulation is expected to save. Because the U.S. Supreme Court has ruled that OSHA regulations cannot be subject to a formal cost-benefit test, there is no legal prohibition against regulatory excesses. However, OSHA sometimes takes account of costs while designing regulations.

Increases in safety from OSHA's activities have fallen short of expectations. According to some economists' estimates OSHA's regulations have reduced workplace injuries by at most 2 to 4 percent. Why such a modest impact on risks? One reason is that the financial incentives for safety imposed by OSHA are comparatively small. Although total penalties assessed by OSHA have increased dramatically since 1986, they have averaged less than $10 million per year for most years of the agency's operation. The $120 billion wage premium that workers "charge" for risk is over 1,200 times as large.

The workers' compensation system that has been in place in the United States throughout most of this century also gives companies strong incentives to make workplaces safe. Premiums for workers' compensation, which employers pay, exceed $50 billion annually. Particularly for large firms, these premiums are strongly linked to their injury performance. Statistical studies indicate that in the absence of the workers' compensation system, workplace death rates would rise by 27 percent. This estimate assumes, however, that workers' compensation would not be replaced by tort liability or higher market wage premiums. The strong performance of workers' compensation, particularly when contrasted with the command-and-control approach of OSHA regulation, has led many economists to suggest that an injury tax be instituted as an alternative to the current regulatory standards.

The main implication of economists' analysis of job safety is that financial incentives matter. The remaining task for society is to establish a reasonable balance in our quest for appropriate levels of workplace health and safety.

—W. Kip Viscusi

Biography: W. Kip Viscusi is the George G. Allen Professor of Economics at Duke University. While a student at Harvard he spent two summers working for Ralph Nader. Viscusi was also deputy director of President Carter's Council on Wage and Price Stability, which was responsible for White House oversight of major new regulations.

Further Reading:

Morrall, John F. "A Review of the Record." *Regulation* 10, no. 2 (1986): 13–24.
Viscusi, W. Kip. *Risk by Choice*. 1983.
———. *Fatal Tradeoffs*. 1991.

Labor Unions

Morgan O. Reynolds

■ For more than a century now, labor unions have been celebrated in folk songs and popular myth as fearless champions of the downtrodden working man, while "the bosses" are depicted as coldhearted exploiters of employees. But from the standpoint of economists—including many who are avowedly pro-union—unions are simply cartels that raise wages above competitive levels by capturing monopolies over who companies can hire and what they must pay.

Many unions have won higher wages and better working conditions for their members. In doing so, however, they have reduced the number of jobs available. That second effect is because of the basic law of demand: if unions successfully raise the price of labor, employers will purchase less of it. Thus, unions are the major anticompetitive force in labor markets. Their gains come at the expense of consumers, nonunion workers, the jobless, and owners of corporations.

According to Harvard economists Richard Freeman and James Medoff, who look favorably on unions, "Most, if not all, unions have monopoly power, which they can use to raise wages above competitive levels." The power that unions have to fix high prices for their labor rests on legal privileges and immunities that they get from government, both by statute and by nonenforcement of other laws. The purpose is to restrict others from working for lower wages. As anti-union economist Ludwig von Mises wrote in 1922, "The long and short of trade union rights is in fact the right to proceed against the strikebreaker with primitive violence."

Those unfamiliar with labor law may be surprised by the privileges that U.S. unions enjoy. The list is long. Labor cartels are immune from taxation and from antitrust laws. Companies are legally compelled to bargain with unions in "good faith." This innocent-sounding term is interpreted by the National Labor Relations Board to suppress such practices as Boulwarism, named for a former General Electric personnel director. To shorten the collective bargaining process, Lemuel Boulware communicated the "reasonableness" of GE's wage offer directly to employees, shareholders, and the public. Unions also can force companies to make their property available for union use.

Once the government ratifies a union's position as representing a group of workers, it represents them exclusively, whether particular employees want collective representation or not. Also, union officials can force compulsory union dues from employees, members and nonmembers alike, as a condition of keeping their jobs. Unions often use these funds for political purposes—political campaigns and voter registration, for example—unrelated to collective bargaining or to employee grievances. Unions are relatively immune from payment of tort damages for injuries inflicted in labor disputes, from federal court injunctions, and from many state laws under the "federal preemption" doctrine. Sums up Nobel Laureate Friedrich A. Hayek: "We have now reached a state where [unions] have become uniquely privileged institutions to which the general rules of law do not apply."

Labor unions cannot prosper in a competitive environment. Like other successful cartels, they depend on government patronage and protection. Worker cartels grew in surges during the two world wars and the Great Depression of the thirties. Federal interventions—the Railway Act of 1926 (amended in 1934), the Davis-Bacon Act of 1931, the Norris-LaGuardia Act of 1932, the National Labor Relations Act of 1935, the Walsh-Healy Act of 1936, the Fair Labor Standards Act of 1938, various War Labor Boards, and the Kennedy administration's encouragement of public-sector unionism in 1962—all added to unions' monopoly power.

Most unions in the private sector are in crafts and industries that have few companies or that are concentrated in one region of the country. This makes sense. Both factors—few employers or regionally concentrated employers—make organizing easier. Conversely, the large number of employers and the regional dispersion of employers sharply limit unionization in trade, services, and agriculture. A 1989 unionization rate of 35 percent in the public sector versus 12 percent in the private sector further demonstrates that unions do best in heavily regulated, monopolistic environments.

After nearly sixty years of government encouragement and protection of unions, what have been the economic consequences? A 1985 survey by H. Gregg Lewis of two hundred economic studies concluded that unions caused their members' wages to be, on average, 14 to 15 percent higher than wages of similarly skilled nonunion workers. Other economists—Harvard's Freeman and Medoff, and Peter Linneman and Michael Wachter of the University of Pennsylvania—claim that the union premium was 20 to 30 percent or higher during the eighties.

The wage premium varies by industry. Unions representing garment workers, textile workers, white-collar government workers, and teachers seem to have little impact on wages. But wages of unionized mine workers, building trades people, airline pilots, merchant seamen, postal workers, teamsters, rail workers, and auto and steel workers exceed wages of similarly skilled nonunion employees by 25 percent or more.

The wage advantage enjoyed by union members results from two factors. First, monopoly unions raise wages above competitive levels. Second, nonunion wages fall because workers priced out of jobs by high union wages move into the nonunion sector and bid down wages there. Thus, some of the gains to union members come at the expense of those who must shift to lower-paying or less desirable jobs or go unemployed.

Despite considerable rhetoric to the contrary, unions have blocked the economic advance of blacks, women, and other minorities. That is because another of their functions, once they have raised wages above competitive levels, is to ration the jobs that remain. And since they are monopolies, unions can indulge the prejudices of their leaders or members without the economic penalties that people in the competitive sector must face. In indulging those prejudices, unions have established a sordid history of racist and sexist practices.

Economist Ray Marshall, although a pro-union secretary of labor under President Jimmy Carter, made his academic reputation by documenting how unions excluded blacks from membership in the thirties and forties (see sidebar). Marshall also wrote of incidents in which union members assaulted black workers hired to replace them during strikes. During the 1911 strike against the Illinois Central, noted Marshall, whites killed two black strikebreakers and wounded three others at McComb, Mississippi. He also noted that white strikers killed ten black firemen in 1911 because the New Orleans and Texas Pacific Railroad had granted them equal seniority. Not surprisingly, therefore, black leader Booker T. Washington opposed unions all his life, and W. E. B. DuBois called unions the greatest enemy of the black working class. Another interesting fact: the "union label" was started in the 1880s to proclaim that a product was made by white rather than yellow (Chinese) hands. More generally, union wage rates, union-backed requirements for a license to practice various occupations, and union-backed labor regulations like the minimum wage law and the Davis-Bacon Act continue to reduce opportunities for black youths, females, and other minorities.

The monopoly success of private-sector unions, however, has brought their decline. The silent, steady forces of the marketplace continually undermine them. Linneman and Wachter, along with economist William Carter, found that the rising union wage premium was responsible for up to 64 percent of the decline in unions' share of employment in the last twenty years. The average union wage premium for railroad workers over similarly skilled nonrailroad workers, for example, increased from 32 percent to 50 percent between 1973 and 1987; at the same time, employment on railroads declined from 520,000 to 249,000. Increased wage premiums also caused declines in union employment in construction, manufacturing, and communications. As Rutgers economist Leo Troy concludes, "Over time, competitive markets repeal the legal protection bestowed by governments on unions and collective bargaining."

The degree of union representation of workers has declined in all private industries in the United States in recent decades. A major reason is that employees do not like unions. According to a Louis Harris poll commissioned by the AFL-CIO in 1984, only one in three U.S. employees would vote for union representation in a secret ballot election. The Harris poll found, as have other surveys, that nonunion employees, relative to union workers, are more satisfied with job security, recognition of job performance, and participation in decisions that affect their jobs. And the U.S. economy's evolution toward smaller companies, the South and West, higher-technology products, and more professional and technical personnel continues to erode union membership.

In the United States union membership in the private sector peaked at 17 million in 1970 and had fallen to 10.5 million by 1989. Moreover, the annual decline is accelerating. Barring new legislation, such as a recent congressional proposal to ban the hiring of nonunion replacement workers, private-sector membership will fall from 12 percent to about 7 percent by the year 2000, about the same percentage as a hundred years earlier. While the unionization rate in government jobs may decline slightly from 35 percent, public-sector unions are on schedule to claim an absolute majority of union members a few years after the year 2000, thereby transforming an historically private-sector labor movement into a primarily government one. Asked in the twenties what organized labor wanted, union leader Samuel Gompers answered, "More." Today's union leader would probably answer, "More government." That answer further exposes the deep, permanent conflict between union members and workers in general that inevitably arises when the first group is paid monopoly wage rates.

Assuming that unions continue to decline, what organizations might replace them? "Worker associations" that lack legal privileges and immunities and that must produce services of value to get members may fill the need. Such voluntary worker associations could negotiate labor contracts, serve as clearinghouses for workers to learn what their best alternatives are, monitor administration of fringe benefit plans, and administer training and benefit plans. Worker associations could also institute legal proceedings against collusion by employers, as the Major League Baseball Players' Association does so successfully for players who are free agents. Such services could be especially valuable to immigrant, minority, and female workers now dominating entry into the nineties' labor force.

—**Morgan O. Reynolds**

Biography: Morgan O. Reynolds is a professor of economics at Texas A&M University.

Further Reading

Epstein, Richard A. "A Common Law for Labor Relations: A Critique of the New Deal Labor Legislation." *Yale Law Journal* 92 (July 1983): 1357–1408.

Freeman, Richard B., and James L. Medoff. *What Do Labor Unions Do?* 1984.

Harvard Journal of Law and Public Policy 13 (Spring 1990). (Entire issue devoted to labor law.)

Hirsch, Barry T., and John T. Addison. *Economic Analysis of Labor Unions—New Approaches and Evidence.* 1986.

Hutt, William H. *The Strike-Threat System: The Economic Consequences of Collective Bargaining.* 1973.

Lewis, H. Gregg. *Union Relative Wage Effects.* 1985.

Linneman, Peter D., Michael L. Wachter, and William H. Carter. "Evaluating the Evidence on Union Employment and Wages." *Industrial and Labor Relations Review* 44 (October 1990): 34–53.

Lipset, Seymour Martin, ed. *Unions in Transition.* 1986.

Marshall, F. Ray. *The Negro and Organized Labor.* 1965.

Reynolds, Morgan O. *Making America Poorer: The Cost of Labor Law.* 1987.

Troy, Leo. "Is the U.S. Unique in the Decline of Private Sector Unionism?" *Journal of Labor Research* 11 (Spring 1990): 111–43.

Unions That Discriminated Against Blacks in 1930

American Federation of Express Workers (AFEW)
American Federation of Railway Workers (AFRW)
American Train Dispatchers Association (ATDA)
American Wire Weavers Protective Association (WWPA)
Boilermakers, Iron Shipbuilders and Helpers Union (BIS)
Brotherhood of Dining Car Conductors (BDCC)
Brotherhood of Locomotive Firemen and Enginemen (BLFE)
Brotherhood of Railroad Trainmen (BRT)
Brotherhood of Railway Carmen (BRC)
Brotherhood of Railway Conductors (ORC)
Brotherhood of Railway Station Employees and Clerks (BRSEC)
Brotherhood of Railway and Steamship Clerks (BRSC)
Commercial Telegraphers (CT)
International Association of Machinists (IAM)
National Organization of Masters, Mates and Pilots of North America (MMP)
Neptune Association (NA)
Order of Railway Expressmen (ORE)
Order of Railway Telegraphers (ORT)
Order of Sleeping Car Conductors (OSCC)
Railroad Yard Masters of America (RYA)
Railway Mail Association (RMA)
Switchmen's Union of North America (SNA)

SOURCE: *F. Ray Marshall.*

Minimum Wages

Linda Gorman

■ Minimum wage laws set legal minimums for the hourly wages paid to certain groups of workers. Invented in Australia and New Zealand with the admirable purpose of guaranteeing a minimum standard of living for unskilled workers, they have been widely acclaimed as both the bulwark protecting workers from exploitation by employers and as a major weapon in the war on poverty. Minimum wage legislation in the United States has increased the federal minimum wage from $.25 per hour in 1938 to $4.85 as of July 1992, and expanded its coverage from 43.4 percent of all private, nonsupervisory, nonagricultural workers in 1938 to over 87 percent by 1990. As the steady legislative expansion indicates, the minimum wage has had widespread political support enjoyed by few other public policies.

Unfortunately, neither laudable intentions nor widespread support can alter one simple fact: although minimum wage laws can set wages, they cannot guarantee jobs. In reality, minimum wage laws place additional obstacles in the path of the most unskilled workers who are struggling to reach the lowest rungs of the economic ladder. According to a 1978 article in *American Economic Review*, the American Economic Association's main journal, fully 90 percent of the economists surveyed agreed that the minimum wage increases unemployment among low-skilled workers. It also reduces the on-the-job training offered by employ-ers and shrinks the number of positions offering fringe benefits. To those who lose their jobs, their training opportunities, or their fringe benefits as a result of the minimum wage, the law is simply one more example of good intentions producing hellish results.

To understand why minimum wage policies have such pernicious effects, one must understand how wages are determined in the free market. Consider, for example, the owner-operator of a small diner. To stay in business, he has to make sufficient profits to provide adequate support for his family. The market dictates how much he can charge for his meals because people can choose to eat at other restaurants or prepare their meals at home. The market also dictates what he must pay for food, restaurant space, electricity, equipment, and other factors required to produce his meals. Although the restaurant owner has little control over either the prices he can charge for his meals or the prices that he must pay for the inputs needed to produce them, he can control his costs by changing the combinations of inputs that he uses. He can, for example, hire teenagers to wash and slice raw potatoes for french fries, or he can purchase ready-cut potatoes from a large company with an automated french-fry production process.

The combination of inputs used and the amount that the diner owner can afford to pay for each one depend both on the productivity of the input and on the price that customers will pay for the product. Suppose that a trainee french-fry cutter can peel, cut, and prepare ten orders of fries in an hour, and that the diner's customers order about ten orders of french fries an hour at $1.00 each. If the minimum profit required to keep the owner in business plus all costs except the cutter's labor amounts to $.80 for each order, then the owner can afford a wage of up to $2.00 per hour for one trainee. Legislating a minimum wage of $4.50 per hour means that the diner owner loses $2.50 an hour on the trainee. The owner will respond by firing the trainee. The minimum wage prices the trainee out of the labor market. Similarly, other employers will respond to the increased minimum wage by substituting skilled labor (which does not cost as much more than unskilled labor as it did before the minimum wage) for unskilled labor, by substituting machines for people, by moving production abroad, and by abandoning some types of production entirely.

Australia provided one of the earliest practical demonstrations of the harmful effects of minimum wages when, in 1921, the federal court institutionalized a real minimum wage for unskilled men. The court set the wage by estimating what employees needed, while ignoring what employers could afford to pay. As a result unskilled workers were priced out of the market. These laborers could find work only in occupations not covered by the law or with employers willing to break it. Aggressive reporting of violations by vigilant unions made evasion difficult, and the historical record shows that unemployment remained a particular problem for unskilled laborers throughout the rest of the decade.

The same type of thing happened in the United States when a hospital fired a group of women after the Minimum Wage Board in the District of Columbia ordered their wages raised to the legal minimum. Ironically, the women sued to halt enforcement of the minimum wage law. In 1923 the U.S. Supreme Court, in *Adkins* v. *Children's Hospital,* ruled that the minimum wage law was simple price-fixing and an unreasonable infringement on individuals' freedom to determine the price at which they would sell their services. Although the peculiar logic of the last seventy years has seen this line of reasoning completely abrogated, the battle over allowing people to work at whatever wage they choose continues.

One recent skirmish occurred in 1990 when the U.S. Department of Labor ordered the Salvation Army to pay the minimum wage to voluntary participants in its work therapy programs. The programs provide participants, many of them homeless alcoholics and drug addicts, a small weekly stipend and up to ninety days of food, shelter, and counseling in exchange for processing donated goods. The Salvation Army said that the expense of complying with the minimum wage order would force it to close the programs. Ignoring both the fact that the beneficiaries of the program could leave to take a higher-paying job at any time and the cash value of the food, shelter, and supervision, the Labor Department insisted that it was protecting workers' rights by enforcing the minimum wage. By the peculiar logic of the minimum wage laws, workers have the right to remain unemployed but not the right to get a job by selling their labor for less than the minimum wage.

In addition to affecting how many people

will be employed, minimum wage laws may also leave workers worse off by changing how they are compensated. For many low-wage employees fringe benefits such as paid vacation, free room and board, inexpensive insurance, subsidized child care, and on-the-job training (OJT) are an important part of the total compensation package. To avoid increasing total compensation, employers react to arbitrary boosts in money wages by cutting other benefits. In extreme cases, employers may convert low-wage full-time jobs with fringe benefits to high wage part-time jobs with reduced benefits and fewer hours. Employees who prefer working full time with benefits are simply out of luck.

The reduction in benefits may be substantial. Masanori Hashimoto used data from the 1967–68 U.S. minimum wage hike to calculate its effect on the value of on-the-job training received by white men. Hashimoto estimated that the 28 percent increase in the minimum wage reduced the value of OJT by 2.7 to 15 percent. Because OJT is an important source of education, particularly for those with limited formal schooling, Hashimoto's findings have ominous implications. By reducing OJT, the minimum wage law increases the number of dead-end jobs and effectively consigns some of the unskilled to a lifetime of reduced opportunity.

Estimates of the overall effect of increases in the minimum wage on total U.S. employment often focus on teenagers, who, as a group, contain the highest proportion of unskilled workers. Most studies suggest that a 10 percent increase in the minimum wage decreases teenage employment by 1 to 3 percent. Using these estimates to forecast

small increases in unemployment from future minimum wage increases is risky because most of the estimates rely on data from the sixties and early seventies, when minimum wage legislation applied to fewer occupations.

Raising the minimum wage when it applies to a relatively small proportion of occupations will not necessarily increase unemployment. Some people will lose their jobs in covered occupations and withdraw from the labor market entirely. These people are not included in the unemployment statistics. Others who lose their jobs or are offered fewer hours of work will seek jobs at lower pay in uncovered occupations. This labor influx drives down wages in the uncovered sector, but people do find jobs and unemployment remains constant. As minimum wage legislation expands to cover more occupations, however, the shrinking uncovered sector may not be able to absorb all of the people thrown out of work, and unemployment may increase. In the United States the 1989 minimum wage legislation brought this possibility one step closer by extending coverage to all workers engaged in interstate commerce regardless of employer size. Small businesses previously exempt from the minimum wage faced an 11.8 percent increase in money wages. If the repeal of the exemption that affected more than 6 percent of the nation's hourly workers substantially reduces the number of uncovered jobs, then overt unemployment caused by the minimum wage could become a more serious problem.

Estimates of the overall effect of minimum wage increases also tend to blur the regional and sectoral shifts that average together to produce the national result. A federal minimum wage of $4.85 an hour may have little effect in a large city where almost everyone earns more. But it may cause greater unemployment in a rural area where it substantially exceeds the prevailing wage. Regional and sectoral studies leave little doubt that substantial increases in the minimum in areas with lower wages can cause industries to shrink and can inhibit job creation. The growth of the textile industry in the South, for example, was propelled by low wages. Had the federal minimum wage been set at the wage earned by northern workers, the expansion might never have occurred.

This explains why unions, whose members seldom hold minimum wage jobs, encourage minimum wage legislation and, as in the Australian case, assiduously help enforce its provisions by reporting suspected violations. Unions have historically represented skilled, highly productive workers. As has been demonstrated in the construction industry, employers facing excessive wage demands from union members may find it less expensive to hire unskilled workers at low wages and to train them on the job. Unskilled workers often benefit: accepting lower wages in return for training increases their expected future income. With high minimum wages like those specified for government construction by the Davis-Bacon Act, the wages plus the training cost may exceed the total compensation that employers can afford. In that case the employer would prefer the union member to his unskilled competitor, and passage of a minimum wage law reduces the competition faced by union members.

In spite of evidence indicating that minimum wage laws reduce the number of jobs and distort compensation packages, some people still argue that their benefits outweigh their costs because they increase the incomes of the poor. This argument implicitly assumes that minimum wage workers are the sole earner in a family. This assumption is false. In 1988, for example, the vast majority of minimum wage workers were members of households containing other wage earners. Moreover, only 8 percent of all minimum wage workers were men or women who maintained families, and not all of those families were poor. The simple fact is that most minimum wage workers are young and work part-time. In 1988, 60 percent of minimum wage workers were sixteen to twenty-four years old, and about 70 percent worked part-time.

In view of what minimum wage laws actually do, their often uncritical acceptance as a major weapon in the war on poverty stands as one of the supreme ironies of modern politics. If a minimum wage set $.50 above the prevailing wage helps the working poor with no ill effects, why not eliminate poverty completely by simply legislating a minimum wage of $10.00? The problem, of course, is that pricing people out of a job does not reduce poverty. Neither does skewing compensation packages toward money wages and away from training, or encouraging employers to substitute skilled workers for unskilled workers, part-time jobs for full-time jobs, foreign labor for domestic labor, and machines for people. Minimum wage laws do all of these things and, in the process, almost surely do the disadvantaged more harm than good.

—Linda Gorman

Biography: Linda Gorman is a free-lance economics journalist in Denver. She was previously an economics professor at the Naval Postgraduate School in Monterey, California.

Further Reading

Brown Charles. "Minimum Wage Laws: Are They Overrated?" *Journal of Economic Perspectives* 2, no. 3 (1988): 133–45.

Eccles, Mary, and Richard B. Freeman. "What! Another Minimum Wage Study?" *American Economic Review* 94 (May 1982): 226–32.

Forster, Colin. "Unemployment and Minimum Wages in Australia, 1900–1930." *Journal of Economic History* 45, no. 2 (June 1985): 383–91.

Hashimoto, Masanori. "Minimum Wage Effects on Training on the Job." *American Economic Review* 72, no. 5 (1982): 1070–87.

Rottenberg, Simon, ed. *The Economics of Legal Minimum Wages.* 1981.

Welch, Finis. *Minimum Wages: Issues and Evidence.* 1978.

Wages and Working Conditions

Stanley Lebergott

■ CEOs of multinational corporations, exotic dancers, and children with lemonade stands have at least one thing in common. They all expect a return for their effort. Most workers get that return in a subtle and ever-changing combination of money wages and working conditions. This article describes how they changed for the typical U.S. worker during the twentieth century.

Working Conditions

Surely the single most fundamental working condition is the chance of death on the job. In every society workers are killed or injured in the process of production. While occupational deaths are comparatively rare overall in the United States today, they still occur with some regularity in ocean fishing, the construction of giant bridges and skyscrapers, and a few other activities.

For all United States workers the number of fatalities per dollar of real (inflation-adjusted) GNP dropped by 96 percent between 1900 and 1979. Back in 1900 half of all worker deaths occurred in two industries—coal mining and railroading. But between 1900 and 1979 fatality rates per ton of coal mined and per ton-mile of freight carried fell by 97 percent.

This spectacular change in worker safety resulted from a combination of forces that include safer production technologies, union demands, improved medical procedures and antibiotics, workmen's compensation laws, and litigation. Ranking the individual importance of these factors is difficult and probably would mean little. Together, they reflected a growing conviction on the part of the American people that the economy was productive enough to afford such change. What's more, the United States made far more progress in the workplace than it did in the hospital. Even though inflation-adjusted medical expenditures tripled from 1950 to 1970 and increased by 74 percent from 1975 to 1988, the nation's death rate declined in neither period. But industry succeeded in lowering its death rate, both by spending to improve health on the job and by discovering, developing, and adopting ways to save lives.

Data for injuries are scarcer and less reliable, but they probably declined as well. Agriculture has one of the highest injury rates of any industry; the frequent cuts and bruises can become infected by the bacteria in barnyards and on animals. Moreover, work animals and machinery frequently in-

jure farm workers. Since the proportion of farm workers in the total labor force fell from about 40 percent to 2 percent between 1900 and 1990, the U.S. worker injury rate would have fallen even if nothing else changed. The limited data on injuries in manufacturing also indicate a decline.

Another basic aspect of working conditions is exposure to the weather. In 1900 more than 80 percent of all workers farmed in open fields, maintained railroad rights of way, constructed or repaired buildings, or produced steel and chemicals. Their bosses may have been comfortably warm in the winter and cool in the summer, but the workers were not. A columnist of that era ironically described the good fortune of workers in Chicago steelworks, who could count on being warmed by the blast from the steel melt in freezing weather. Boys who pulled glass bottles from furnaces were similarly protected—when they didn't get burned. By 1990, in contrast, more than 80 percent of the labor force worked in places warmed in the winter and cooled in the summer.

Hours of work for both men and women were shorter in the United States than in most other nations in 1900. Women in Africa and Asia still spent two hours a day pounding husks off wheat or rice for the family food. American women bought their flour and cornmeal, or the men hauled it home from the mill. Women, however, still typically worked from dawn to dusk, or even longer by the light of oil or kerosene lamps. Caring for sick children lengthened those hours further. Charlotte Gilman, an early feminist leader, declared that cooking and care of the kitchen alone took forty-two hours a week. Early budget studies are consistent with that estimate. Men, too, worked dawn to dusk on the farm, and in most nonfarm jobs (about 60 percent of the total), men worked ten hours a day, six days a week.

By 1981 (the latest date available), women's kitchen work had been cut about twenty hours a week, according to national time-budget studies from Michigan's Institute of Survey Research. That reduction came about because families bought more restaurant meals, more canned, frozen, and prepared foods, and acquired an arsenal of electric appliances. Women also spent fewer hours washing and ironing clothes and cleaning house. Fewer hours of work in the home had little impact on women's labor force participation rate until the great increase after 1950.

Men's work hours were cut in half during the twentieth century. That decline reflected a cut of more than twenty hours in the scheduled work week. It also reflected the fact that paid vacations—almost nonexistent in 1900—had spread, and paid holidays multiplied.

In addition, the percentage of the labor force in the worst jobs has declined dramatically. Common laborers in most societies face the most arduous, dangerous, and distasteful working conditions. Their share of the U.S. labor force fell from about 30 percent to 5 percent between 1900 and 1990. Thousands of men in 1900 spent their lives shoveling coal into furnaces to power steam engines. Less than 5 percent of factory power came from electric motors. By 1990 nearly all these furnaces, and men, had been replaced—first by mechanical stokers and then by oil burners and electric motors. Tens of thousands of other men in 1900

laid railroad track and ties, shifting them by brute force, or shoveled tons of coal and grain into gondola cars and ships' holds. They too have given way to machines or now use heavy machinery to ease their toil.

The largest group of common laborers in 1900 was the men, women, and children who cultivated and harvested crops by hand (e.g., cotton, corn, beets, potatoes). Most blacks and many Asian and Mexican-American workers did so. These millions were eventually replaced by a much smaller group, generally using motorized equipment. New machinery also eased the lot of those who once spent their lives shoveling fertilizer, mixing cement, working in glueworks, carrying bundles of rags, waste paper, or finished clothing, and tanning hides.

Such tasks remain a miserable fact of life in many societies. But the expanding U.S. economy forced improvement as workers got the choice of better jobs on factory assembly lines, in warehouses, and in service establishments. Producers increasingly had to replace departing common labor with machinery. They substituted machinery for labor across the board. (Computer software even replaced some bank vice presidents.) But many more men who labored at difficult and boring jobs were replaced by machines tended by semiskilled workers. Between 1900 and 1990 the amount of capital equipment used by the typical American worked rose about 150 percent, taking all industries together.

Wages

Rock singers, movie stars, athletes, and CEOs stand at one end of the income distri-

TABLE 1

Nonfarm Employees Annual Earnings, 1900–80

Year	Money Earnings When Employed (dollars)	Real earnings (1914 dollars)		Consumer Price Index (1914 = 100)	Year	Money Earnings When Employed (dollars)	Real earnings (1914 dollars)		Consumer Price Index (1914 = 100)
		After Deduction for Unemployment (dollars)	When Employed (dollars)				After Deduction for Unemployment (dollars)	When Employed (dollars)	
1900	483	523	573	84.3	1940	1,438	812	1,032	139.4
1901	497	546	582	85.4	1941	1,593	931	1,088	146.4
1902	528	583	612	86.3	1942	1,877	1,080	1,159	162.0
1903	534	575	607	88.0	1943	2,190	1,239	1,273	172.0
1904	538	555	606	88.8	1944	2,370	1,331	1,354	175.0
1905	550	582	621	88.5	1945	2,460	1,338	1,375	179.0
1906	566	618	627	90.2	1946	2,575	1,253	1,326	194.2
1907	592	613	631	93.8	1947	2,802	1,194	1,262	222.1
1908	577	545	631	91.5	1948	3,067	1,216	1,281	239.4
1909	600	604	657	91.3	1949	3,088	1,190	1,303	237.0
1910	634	608	669	94.7	1950	3,276	1,272	1,368	239.4
1911	644	612	676	95.2	1951	3,560	1,317	1,378	258.3
1912	657	619	676	97.2	1952	3,777	1,375	1,431	263.9
1913	687	649	695	98.9	1953	3,986	1,442	1,499	265.9
1914	696	613	696	100.0	1954	4,110	1,427	1,538	267.3
1915	692	591	684	101.1	1955	4,318	1,529	1,621	266.3
1916	760	649	699	108.7	1956	4,557	1,597	1,686	270.3
1917	866	681	704	127.7	1957	4,764	1,608	1,702	279.9
1918	1,063	694	709	150.0	1958	4,956	1,574	1,724	287.5
1919	1,215	681	704	172.5	1959	5,217	1,674	1,800	289.8
1920	1,426	672	714	199.7	1960	5,402	1,706	1,834	294.5
1921	1,330	620	747	178.1	1961	5,584	1,719	1,877	297.5
1922	1,289	688	772	166.9	1962	5,829	1,804	1,938	300.8
1923	1,376	774	811	169.7	1963	6,045	1,847	1,986	304.4
1924	1,396	754	820	170.3	1964	6,327	1,921	2,052	308.4
1925	1,420	764	812	174.8	1965	6,535	1,968	2,083	313.7
1926	1,452	801	824	176.2	1966	6,860	2,028	2,126	322.7
1927	1,487	810	861	172.8	1967	7,156	2,058	2,155	332.0
1928	1,490	816	872	170.9	1968	7,675	2,126	2,219	345.9
1929	1,534	853	901	170.3	1969	8,277	2,165	2,257	364.5
1930	1,495	773	901	166.0	1970	8,821	2,155	2,285	386.1
1931	1,408	696	930	151.4	1971	9,423	2,181	2,340	402.7
1932	1,249	585	918	135.8	1972	10,066	2,265	2,420	416.0
1933	1,165	565	905	128.8	1973	10,767	2,303	2,437	441.9
1934	1,199	607	901	133.1	1974	11,632	2,521	2,372	490.4
1935	1,244	637	912	136.4	1975	12,702	2,148	2,373	535.2
1936	1,296	701	940	137.8	1976	13,727	2,216	2,425	566.1
1937	1,392	767	975	142.8	1977	14,743	2,256	2,447	602.6
1938	1,370	705	978	140.1	1978	15,847	2,279	2,443	648.7
1939	1,403	760	1,016	138.1	1979	17,183	2,229	2,381	721.8
					1980	18,861	2,114	2,300	820.0

SOURCE: *Lebergott, 1984.*

bution. At the other end are part-time workers and many of the unemployed. The differences in annual earnings only partly reflect hourly wages. They also reflect differences in how many hours a year workers spend on the job.

Thanks to increased income tax rates since 1936, today's workers attempt to reduce taxes by converting their earnings into other, nontaxable forms of income. Why use after-tax income to pay for medical care if you can get it as an untaxed fringe benefit? Why pay for the full cost of lunch if the company can subsidize meals at work? The proliferation of such "receipts in kind" has made it increasingly difficult to make meaningful comparisons of the distribution of income over time or of earnings in different social and occupational groups.

Comparing money wages over time thus offers only a partial view of what has happened to worker incomes. But what do the simple overall figures for earnings by the typical worker (before tax and ignoring "in kind" allowances) show? Table 1 reports how the average wage for nonfarm workers rose during this century. By 1980 real earnings of American nonfarm workers were about four times as great as in 1900. Government taxes took away an increasing share of the worker's paycheck. What remained, however, helped transform the American standard of living. In 1900 only a handful earned enough to enjoy such expensive luxuries as piped water, hot water, indoor toilets, electricity, and separate rooms for each child. But by 1990 workers' earnings had made such items common-place. Moreover, most Americans now have radios, TVs, automobiles, and medical care that no millionaire in 1900 could possibly have obtained.

Labor Productivity

The fundamental cause of this increase in the standard of living was the increase in productivity. What caused that increase? The tremendous changes in Korea, Hong Kong, and Singapore since World War II demonstrate how tenuous is the connection between productivity and such factors as sitting in classrooms, natural resources, previous history, or racial origins. Increased productivity depends more on national attitudes and on free markets, in the United States as in Hong Kong and Singapore.

Output per hour worked in the United States, which already led the world in 1900, tripled from 1900 to 1990. Companies competed away much of that cost savings via lower prices, thus benefiting consumers. (Nearly all of these consumers, of course, were in workers' families.) Workers also benefited directly from higher wages on the job.

The U.S. record for working conditions and real wages reveals impressive and significant advances, greater than in many other nations. But the quest for still higher wages and for less effort and boredom shows no sign of halting.

—Stanley Lebergott

Biography: Stanley Lebergott is professor of economics at Wesleyan University in Middletown, Connecticut. He was previously an economist with the U.S. Bureau of the Budget and the U.S.

Department of Labor. He was a member of the President's Commission on Federal Statistics in 1971 and president of the Economic History Association in 1984.

Further Reading

Goldin, Claudia. "The Work and Wages of Single Women, 1870–1920." *Journal of Economic History* 41 (1980): 81–89.

Lebergott, Stanley. *The American Economy: Income, Wealth, and Want.* 1976.

———. *The Americans: An Economic Record.* 1984.

CHAPTER TEN

INTERNATIONAL ECONOMICS

Balance of Payments

Herbert Stein

■ Few subjects in economics have caused so much confusion—and so much groundless fear—in the past four hundred years as the thought that a country might have a deficit in its balance of payments. This fear is groundless for two reasons: (1) there never is a deficit, and (2) it wouldn't necessarily hurt if there were.

The balance of payments accounts of a country record the payments and receipts of the residents of the country in their transactions with residents of other countries. If all transactions are included, the payments and receipts of each country are, and must be, equal. Any apparent inequality simply leaves one country acquiring assets in the others. For example, if Americans buy automobiles from Japan, and have no other transactions with Japan, the Japanese must end up holding dollars, which they may hold in the form of bank deposits in the United States or in some other U.S. investment. The payments of Americans to Japan for automobiles are balanced by the payments of Japanese to U.S. individuals and institutions, including banks, for the acquisition of dollar assets. Put another way, Japan sold the United States automobiles, and the United States sold Japan dollars or dollar-denominated assets such as Treasury bills and New York office buildings.

Although the totals of payments and receipts are necessarily equal, there will be inequalities—excesses of payments or receipts, called deficits or surpluses—in particular kinds of transactions. Thus, there can be a deficit or surplus in any of the following: merchandise trade (goods), services trade, foreign investment income, unilateral transfers (foreign aid), private investment, the flow of gold and money between central banks and treasuries, or any combination of these or other international transactions. The statement that a country has a deficit or surplus in its ''balance of payments'' must refer to some particular class of transactions. As table 1 shows, in 1991 the United States had a deficit in goods of $73.4 billion but a surplus in services of $45.3 billion.

Many different definitions of the balance of payments deficit or surplus have been used in the past. Each definition has different implications and purposes. Until about 1973 attention was focused on a definition of the balance of payments intended to measure a country's ability to meet its obligation to exchange its currency for other currencies or for gold at fixed exchange rates. To meet this obligation, countries maintained a stock of official reserves, in the form of gold or foreign currencies, that they could use to support their own currencies. A decline in this stock was considered an important balance of payments deficit because it threatened the ability of the country to meet its obligations. But that particular kind of deficit, by itself, was never a good indication of the country's financial position. The reason is that it ignored the

TABLE 1

The U.S. Balance of Payments, 1991
(billion dollars;
+ is surplus of receipts, − is deficit)

Merchandise trade	− 73.4
Services	+ 45.3
Investment income	+ 16.4
Balance on goods, services and income	− 11.7
Unilateral transfers	+ 8.0
Balance on current account	− 3.7
Nonofficial capital*	− 20.5
Official reserve assets	+ 24.2
Balance on capital account	+ 3.7
Total balance	0

*Includes statistical discrepancy.

SOURCE: *U.S. Department of Commerce,* Survey of Current Business.

likelihood that the country would be called upon to meet its obligation, and the willingness of foreign or international monetary institutions to provide support.

Interest in official reserve positions as a measure of balance of payments greatly diminished after 1973 as the major countries gave up their commitment to convert their currencies at fixed exchange rates. This reduced the need for reserves and lessened concern about changes in the size of reserves. Since 1973, discussions of "the" balance of payments deficit or surplus usually refer to what is called the current account. This account contains trade in goods and services, investment income earned abroad, and unilateral transfers. It excludes the capital account, which includes the acquisition or sale of securities or other property.

Because the current account and the capital account add up to the total account, which is necessarily balanced, a deficit in the current account is always accompanied by an equal surplus in the capital account, and vice versa. A deficit or surplus in the current account cannot be explained or evaluated without simultaneous explanation and evaluation of an equal surplus or deficit in the capital account.

A country is more likely to have a deficit in its current account the higher its price level, the higher its gross national product, the higher its interest rates, the lower its barriers to imports, and the more attractive its investment opportunities—all compared with conditions in other countries—and the higher its exchange rate. The effects of a change in one of these factors upon the current account balance cannot be predicted without considering the effect on the other causal factors. For example, if the U.S. government increases tariffs, Americans will buy fewer imports, thus reducing the current account deficit. But economic theory indicates that this reduction will occur only if one of the other factors changes to bring about a decrease in the capital account surplus. If none of these other factors changes, the reduced imports from the tariff increase will cause a decline in the demand for foreign currency (yen, deutsche marks, etc.) which in turn will raise the value of the U.S. dollar. The increase in the value of the dollar will make U.S. exports more expensive and imports cheaper, offsetting the effect of the tariff increase. The net result is that the tariff increase brings no change in the current account balance.

Contrary to the general perception, the existence of a current account deficit is not, in itself, a sign of bad economic policy or of bad economic conditions. If the United States has a current account deficit, all this means is that the United States is importing capital. And importing capital is no more unnatural or dangerous than importing coffee. The deficit is a response to conditions in the country. It may be a response to excessive inflation, to low productivity, or to inadequate saving. It may just as easily occur because investments in the United States are secure and profitable. Furthermore, the conditions to which the deficit responds may be good or bad and may be the results of good or bad policy, but if there is a problem, it is in the underlying conditions and not in the deficit per se.

During the eighties there was a great deal of concern about the shift of the U.S. current account balance from a surplus of $8 billion in 1981 to a deficit of $147 billion in 1987. This shift was accompanied by an increase of about the same amount in the U.S. deficit in goods. A common claim was that this shift in the international position was causing a loss of employment in the United States. But that was not true. In fact, between 1981 and 1987, the number of peo-ple employed rose by over 12 million, and employment as a percent of population rose from 60 percent to 62.5 percent.

Anxiety was also expressed over the other side of the accounts, the inflow of foreign capital that accompanied the current account deficit. Many people feared that the United States was becoming owned by foreigners. The inflow of foreign capital did not, however, reduce the assets owned by Americans. Instead, it added to the capital within the country. In any event the amount was small relative to the U.S. capital stock. Measurement of the net amount of foreign-owned assets in the United States (the excess of foreign assets in the United States over U.S. assets abroad) is very uncertain. At the end of 1988, however, it was surely much less than 4 percent of the U.S. capital stock and possibly even zero. Later, there was fear of what would happen when the capital inflow slowed down or stopped. But after 1987 it did slow down and the economy adjusted, just as it had adjusted to the big capital inflow earlier, by a decline in the current account and trade deficits.

—Herbert Stein

Biography: Herbert Stein is a senior fellow at the American Enterprise Institute in Washington, D.C., and is on the board of contributors of *The Wall Street Journal*. He was chairman of the Council of Economic Advisers under Presidents Nixon and Ford.

Further Reading

Dornbusch, Rudiger, and Stanley Fischer. *Macroeconomics*, 4th ed., 179–214. 1987. (For general concepts and theory.)

Economic Report of the President, 123–36. 1989 and subsequent years. (For recent developments and policies.)

Survey of Current Business, 34–55. March 1991 and subsequent issues. (For current data.)

Competitiveness

Robert Z. Lawrence

■ "Competitiveness," particularly with reference to an entire economy, is hard to define. Indeed, competitiveness, like love or democracy, actually has several meanings. And the question "Is America competitive?" has at least three interpretations: How well is the United States performing compared to other countries? How well has America performed in international trade? Are we doing the best we can?

How well is the United States performing compared to other economies? Note that this concept of competitiveness does not refer specifically to performance in trade. Although growth, inflation, unemployment, and income equality are all legitimate measures of performance, probably the most important indicator is living standards.

To evaluate competitiveness by this criterion, we need to decide how living standards should be measured. The most straightforward evaluations compare the buying power of residents in other countries with the market basket of goods and services that the average American's income can purchase. Of course, such a measure fails to capture some important qualitative aspects, such as the purity of the environment, the security of employment, and the quality of life. Nonetheless, the measure of purchasing power suggests that American living standards are higher than those in other major industrial economies. According to the Bureau of Labor Statistics, GDP (gross domestic product) per capita in

France, Germany, and Japan in 1989 were 85.9, 82.0, and 72.7 percent of that in the United States.

One reason U.S. living standards are high is that the share of the U.S. population in the labor force is higher than in most other countries. Primarily, however, high U.S. living standards reflect the productivity of the work force: output per worker in the United States exceeds that in other countries. Output per worker in U.S. manufacturing is, likewise, the world's highest.

What is striking, however, is how the relative position of the United States has changed. In 1960, GDP per employed person in France and Germany was less than 50 percent the U.S. level, while in Japan it was less than a quarter. But productivity growth in the United States has been slower than productivity growth elsewhere since then. As a result, foreign living standards and productivity levels are catching up with those of the United States.

This convergence of other economies with U.S. output levels has been the subject of much debate. Some believe that the burden of military spending (so-called "imperial overstretch") has been the chief cause of America's relative decline. But this argument presumes that if the United States had not spent as much on defense, it would have used the money for technological improvements and domestic investment. It seems more likely, however, that any dividend from reduced defense spending would have been spent in the same proportions as the rest of U.S. incomes—at least 90 percent would have been consumed and only a small proportion devoted to growth-enhancing investment.

Another view is that America's productivity growth has been slower because it has moved more rapidly out of the manufacturing sector (i.e., that it has deindustrialized). But judged by the quantity of goods it produces, the United States has not deindustrialized. The share of manufacturing in GNP was about the same in 1989 (i.e., 22.6 percent) as it was in 1979 (22.3 percent) and 1960 (20.3 percent).

A more viable reason for America's relatively slower productivity growth has been the relatively slower increase in U.S. investment in plant, equipment, and infrastructure. Americans have saved and invested lower shares of their incomes than citizens in other major industrial nations.

The most powerful explanation for America's slower productivity growth, however, is a simple fact of life: it is easier to copy than to innovate. As the country at the technological frontier, America has had to innovate to increase productivity growth. Foreigners, on the other hand, could increase productivity by adopting and copying U.S. practices.

Increasingly, however, foreigners have shifted from catching up to sharing the lead. U.S. productivity in overall manufacturing remains the world's highest. But in some industries (automobiles, electronics) and in some technologies, Japan has surpassed the United States in productivity. This change in relative technological advantage has been reflected in patterns of direct foreign investment. In the past, reflecting their technolog-

ical and managerial advantages, U.S. firms found opportunities to set up manufacturing and marketing operations abroad. Today, foreign firms increasingly find their technological capabilities afford them profitable opportunities for direct foreign investment in the United States.

It is important to recognize that this relative decline of the United States has differing implications for American power and for American living standards. The power of a nation (i.e., its ability to influence the actions of other nations) flows in large part from its relative economic capacity—the economic performance of the United States compared with other nations, particularly its adversaries. In this respect the power of the United States is less in a richer world economy. On the other hand, the welfare of a nation's citizens is largely a function of its absolute economic capacity. A nation's living standards are primarily based on its productivity and on its ability to exchange its products for those of others on international markets. Both of these effects are enhanced when increased innovation abroad provides U.S. consumers access to better products and U.S. manufacturers more opportunities to emulate foreign products and processes. The United States no longer has to carry the burden of global innovation alone—increasingly, American firms can learn from others.

In addition to providing benefits, however, the growing equalization of technological capabilities also increases competitive pressures on the United States. This equalization makes many nations close substitutes as locations for production. Thus, trade and investment flows are much more sensitive to differences in other factors that influence costs, including wages and skills and differences in national tax, regulatory, and trade policies. In this more competitive environment what once was thought of as purely domestic economic policy now has international consequences.

How well has America performed in international trade? First, it should be stressed that trade between economies is not like competition in sports. A sports contest is a zero-sum game. If one competitor does better, its opponents are, by definition, doing worse. However, because trade allows each nation to specialize in making the products it produces relatively well, trade simultaneously makes all nations better off.

How should trade performance be measured? It is tempting to use the trade balance (the difference between a nation's exports and imports) as a measure of trade competitiveness. But a nation's trade balance is more revealing of its spending patterns than of its products' attractiveness in world markets. The only way a country can consume more than it produces is to import the difference from abroad. Nations with trade deficits are spending more than their incomes. They must be borrowing from the rest of the world or selling domestic or foreign assets. Conversely, nations with trade surpluses accumulate claims on others or reduce others' claims on them. The U.S. trade deficit in the eighties, therefore, reflected American spending patterns. A big part of this pattern was the U.S. government's large budget deficits. If the government increases its borrowing, either the private sector must increase its lending or the country as a whole must borrow from abroad. For the private sector to lend more it must save more. In the eighties, however, when the govern-

ment increased its borrowing, the private sector's saving rate actually declined. Thus, the rise in the federal budget deficit was associated with an increase in overall borrowing from abroad—and therefore a larger trade deficit.

Are trade deficits good or bad? Just as with individual borrowing, it depends on how the borrowed money is used. If an individual borrows to fund education or to start a business, his spending will create income-earning assets that will aid in future repayment. Likewise, if a trade deficit reflects increased borrowing to fund investment, there could be no need for concern. The money would finance capital formation that would make workers more productive in the future.

The U.S. trade deficit in the eighties, however, reflected increased borrowing for consumption rather than investment. In 1990, gross fixed private investment was only 13.6 percent of GNP, versus 16 percent in 1980. Had Americans saved the same share of income in 1990 as in 1980—16.3 percent—they could have financed their investment and run a trade surplus of $148 billion!

Of course, simply running a trade surplus does not necessarily indicate that a nation is performing well. After all, some very poor countries have trade surpluses and some rich countries have deficits. What counts for competitiveness in trade, therefore, is not simply the level of the trade balance, but the living standards associated with it. Indeed, one widely accepted definition of competitiveness is "the ability of a country to sell its products in international markets, while enjoying rising living standards."

Everything else being equal, a nation's living standards will be higher, the higher the prices it receives for its exports and the lower the prices it pays for its imports. The level of living standards associated with a given trade balance will, therefore, depend on the terms of trade—the ratio of export to import prices. Since the early seventies the U.S. terms of trade have had a strong downward trend. To maintain any given trade balance, the prices of U.S. products relative to imports have had to fall.

One mechanism by which America's terms of trade have been lowered has been declines in the value of the dollar. If the dollar, measured in foreign currencies, falls, U.S. export prices tend to fall relative to the prices of foreign products. According to the Federal Reserve board, the dollar declined by 13.6 percent between 1973 and 1990, taking into account inflation differences in the United States and the rest of the world.

This discussion about the exchange rate highlights the difference between the perspective of American firms and that of the economy as a whole. A lower dollar makes American products more attractive to foreigners. In that sense American producers will be more competitive in world markets. On the other hand, a lower value of the dollar will, all other things equal, reduce the nation's international buying power—and thus its living standards. Thus, the nation becomes less competitive from the standpoint of workers and consumers.

The alternative, and more desirable, way of making a nation's products more attractive in world markets is to innovate and improve quality in products and production processes. In contrast to exchange rate depreciation, such technological improvements allow the nation simultaneously to sell more products in world markets and to raise living standards. Ultimately, therefore, both types of competitiveness depend on improved productivity.

Are we doing the best we can? Nations find themselves in different circumstances: some are richly endowed with natural and human resources while others are not. The most important concept of competitiveness is not, therefore, how national performances compare or even how well countries perform in international trade. The critical issue for each economy is whether it is making the best use of its resources.

Many people would argue that both the U.S. government and private sector could be more efficient than they are. In this sense, regardless of what other countries are doing, there is room for America to improve its competitiveness. The United States could learn much from practices in other countries. Ultimately, however, we must follow policies and practices that will work best in the American environment.

—Robert Z. Lawrence

Biography: Robert Z. Lawrence is an economics professor at the John F. Kennedy School of Government at Harvard University. He was formerly a senior fellow at the Brookings Institution. He has served as a consultant to the Federal Reserve Bank of New York, the World Bank, and the Organization for Economic Cooperation and Development. He writes a monthly column for the *Nikkei Financial Journal*.

Further Reading

Berger, Suzanne, Michael L. Dertouzos, Richard K. Lester, Robert M. Solow, and Lester Thurow. "Toward a New Industrial America." *Scientific American*, June 1989, 39–47. For further discussion see Dertouzos et al. *Made in America: Regaining the Productive Edge*. 1989.

Hatsopoulos, George N., Paul R. Krugman, and Lawrence Summers. "U.S. Competitiveness: Beyond the Trade Deficit." *Science* 15 (July 1988): 299–307.

Krugman, Paul. *The Age of Diminished Expectations*, chaps. 1–5. 1991.

Lawrence, Robert Z. *Can America Compete?* 1984.

———. "The International Dimension." Chap. 2 in *American Living Standards: Threats and Challenges*, edited by Robert E. Litan, Robert Z. Lawrence, and Charles L. Schultze. 1988.

———, and Barry P. Bosworth. "America's Global Role: From Dominance to Interdependence." In *Restructuring American Foreign Policy*, edited by John D. Steinbruner. 1988.

Lipsey, Robert E., and Irving B. Kravis. *Saving and Economic Growth: Is the United States Really Falling Behind?* The Conference Board research report no. 901. 1987.

Porter, Michael E. *The Competitive Advantage of Nations*. 1990.

Exchange Rates

Paul Krugman

■ Exchange rates between currencies have been highly unstable since the collapse of the Bretton Woods system of fixed exchange rates, which lasted from 1946 to 1973. Under the Bretton Woods system, exchange rates (e.g., the number of dollars it takes to buy a British pound or German mark) were fixed at levels determined by governments. Under the "floating" exchange rates we have had since 1973, exchange rates are determined by people buying and selling currencies in the foreign-exchange markets. The instability of floating rates has surprised and disappointed many economists and businessmen, who had not expected them to create so much uncertainty. The history of the pound sterling/U.S. dollar rate is instructive. From 1949 to 1966, that rate did not change at all. In 1967 the devaluation of the pound by 14 percent was regarded as a major economic policy decision. Since the end of fixed rates in 1973, however, the pound has, on average, either appreciated or depreciated by 14 percent every two years.

The instability of exchange rates in the seventies and eighties would not have surprised the founders of the Bretton Woods system, who had a deep distrust of financial markets. The previous experience with floating exchange rates (in the twenties) had been marked by massive instability. In an influential study of that experience, published in 1942, Norwegian economist Ragnar Nurkse argued that currency markets were subject to "destabilizing speculation," which created pointless and economically damaging fluctuations.

During the fifties and sixties, however, as stresses built on the system of fixed exchange rates, both economists and policymakers began to see exchange rate flexibility in a more favorable light. In a seminal paper in 1953, Milton Friedman argued that the fear of floating exchange rates was unwarranted. Unstable exchange rates in the twenties, he maintained, were caused by unstable policies, not by destabilizing speculation. Friedman went on to argue that profit-maximizing speculators would always tend to stabilize, not destabilize, the exchange rate. By the late sixties Friedman's view had become widely accepted within the economics profession and among many businessmen and bankers. Therefore, concern over the instability of floating exchange rates was replaced by an appreciation of the greater flexibility that floating rates would give to macroeconomic policy. The main advantage was that nations could pursue independent monetary policies and adjust easily to eliminate pay-

ments imbalances and offset changes in their international competitiveness. This change in attitude helped to prepare the way for the abandonment of fixed rates in 1973.

The instability of rates since 1973 has thus been a severe disappointment. Some of the changes in exchange rates can be attributed to differences in national inflation rates. But yearly changes in exchange rates have been much larger than can be explained by differences in inflation rates or in other variables such as different growth rates in various countries' money supplies.

Why are exchange rates so unstable? Economists have suggested two explanations. One, originally expressed in a celebrated 1976 paper by MIT economist Rudiger Dornbusch, is that even without destabilizing speculation, exchange rates will be highly variable because of a phenomenon that Dornbusch labeled "overshooting." Suppose that the United States increases its money supply. In the long run this must cause the value of the dollar to be lower; in the short run it will lead to a lower interest rate on dollar-denominated securities. But as Dornbusch pointed out, if the interest rate on dollar-denominated bonds falls below that on other assets, investors will be unwilling to hold them unless they expect the dollar to rise against other currencies in the future. How can the prospect of a long-run lower dollar and the need to offer investors a rising dollar be reconciled? The answer, Dornbusch asserted, is that the dollar must fall below its long-run value in the short run, so that it has room to rise. That is, if the U.S. money supply rises by 10 percent, which will eventually mean a 10 percent weaker dollar, the immediate impact will be a dollar depreciation of more than 10 percent—say 20 or 25 percent—"overshooting" the long-run value. The overshooting hypothesis helps explain why exchange rates are so much more unstable than inflation rates or money supplies.

In spite of the intellectual appeal of the overshooting hypothesis, many economists have returned to the idea that destabilizing speculation is the principal cause of exchange rate instability. If those who buy and sell foreign exchange are rational, then forward exchange rates—rates today for sale of dollars some months hence—should be the best predictors of future exchange rates. But a key study by the University of Chicago's Lars Hansen and Northwestern University's Robert Hodrick in 1980 found that forward exchange rates actually have no useful predictive power. Since that study many other researchers have reached the same conclusion.

At the same time, particular exchange rate fluctuations have seemed to depart clearly from any reasonable valuation. The run-up of the dollar in late 1984, for example, brought it to a level that priced U.S. industry out of many markets. The trade deficits that would have resulted could not have been sustained indefinitely, implying that the dollar would have to decline over time. Yet investors, by being willing to hold dollar-denominated bonds with only small interest premiums, were implicitly forecasting that the dollar would decline only slowly. Stephen Marris and I both pointed out that if the dollar were to decline as slowly as the market appeared to believe, growing U.S. interest payments to foreigners would outpace any decline in the trade deficit, implying an explosive and hence impossible growth in foreign debt. It was therefore apparent that the market was overvaluing the dollar. Overall, there is no evidence supporting Friedman's assumption that speculators would act in a rational, stabilizing fashion. And in several episodes Nurkse's fears of destabilizing speculation seem to ring true.

What are the effects of exchange rate instability? The effects on both the prices and volumes of goods and services in world trade have been surprisingly small. During the eighties real West German wages went from 20 percent above the U.S. level to 25 percent below, then back to 30 percent above. One might have expected this to lead to huge swings in prices and in market shares. Yet the effects, while there, were fairly mild. In particular, many firms seem to have followed a strategy of "pricing to market" (i.e., keeping the prices of their exports stable in terms of the importing country's currency). Significant examples are the prices of imported automobiles in the United States, which neither fell much when the dollar was rising nor rose much when it began falling. Statistical studies, notably by Wharton economist Richard Marston, have documented the importance of pricing to market, especially among Japanese firms.

The policy implications of unstable exchange rates remain a subject of great dispute. Refreshingly, this is not the usual debate between laissez-faire economists who trust markets and distrust governments, and interventionist economists with the opposite instincts. Instead, both camps are divided, and advocates of both fixed and floating rates find themselves with unaccustomed allies. Laissez-faire economists are divided between those who, like Milton Friedman, want stable monetary growth and therefore want to leave the exchange rate alone, and those who, like Columbia University's Robert Mundell, want the discipline of fixed exchange rates and even a return to the gold standard. Interventionists are divided between those who, like Yale's James Tobin, regard exchange rate instability as a price worth paying for the freedom to pursue an activist monetary policy, and those who, like John Williamson of the Institute for International Economics, distrust financial markets too much to trust them with determining the exchange rate.

In general, sentiment among both economists and policymakers has drifted away from belief in freely floating rates. On the one hand, exchange rates among the major currencies have been more erratic than anyone expected. On the other hand, the European Monetary System, an experiment in quasi-fixed rates, has proved surprisingly durable. Taking the long view, however, attitudes about exchange rate instability have repeatedly shifted, proving ultimately as poorly grounded in fundamentals as the rates themselves.

—Paul Krugman

Biography: Paul Krugman is a professor of economics at MIT. In 1991 he won the American Economic Association's John Bates Clark Medal, given every two years to ''that American economist under the age of 40 who is adjudged to have made a significant contribution to economic thought and knowledge.'' He has been a consultant to the International Monetary Fund, the World Bank, the United Nations, the Trilateral Commission, and the U.S. State Department. He was also on the staff of President Reagan's Council of Advisers. He was an adviser to Bill Clinton during the 1992 presidential campaign.

Further Reading

Dixit, Avinash. "Hysteresis, Import Penetration, and Exchange-Rate Pass-Through." *Quarterly Journal of Economics* 104 (1989): 205–28.

Dornbusch, Rudiger. "Expectations and Exchange Rate Dynamics." *Journal of Political Economy* 84 (1976): 1161–76.

Friedman, Milton. "The Case for Flexible Exchange Rates." In Friedman. *Essays in Positive Economics*. 1953.

Hansen, Lars, and Robert Hodrick. "Forward Exchange Rates as Optimal Predictors of Future Spot Rates: An Appraisal." *Journal of Political Economy* 88 (1980): 829–53.

Krugman, Paul. "Is the Strong Dollar Sustainable?" In Federal Reserve Bank of Kansas City. *The U.S. Dollar: Prospects and Policy Options*. 1985.

———. *Exchange Rate Instability*. 1988.

Lawrence, Robert Z. "U.S. Current Account Adjustment: An Appraisal." *Brookings Papers on Economic Activity*, no. 2 (1990): 343–92.

Marris, Stephen. *Deficits and the Dollar: The World Economy at Risk*. 1985.

Marston, Richard. "Pricing to Market in Japanese Manufacturing." *Journal of International Economics* 29 (1990): 217–36.

Nurkse, Ragnar. *International Currency Experience*. 1942.

•

Foreign Investment in the United States

Mack Ott

Introduction

In the short run, foreign capital invested in the United States raises U.S. gross domestic product (GDP). This means that U.S. residents are better off than they would be without foreign capital. Still, long-run scenarios of foreign ownership trouble many critics: What payment will foreigners exact for our use of their capital? Will sustained inflows of foreign capital give foreigners control of the U.S. capital stock, reduce job quality, or distort U.S. investment and research? Fortunately, these concerns can be dispelled by reviewing the extent of foreign investment in the U.S. economy vs. U.S. investment abroad, considering the motivations for foreign investment, and computing the negligible potential for foreign control.

Foreign Investment in the United States—How Much? Of What? By Whom?

Between 1982 and 1990 U.S. current account deficits—the amount by which imports of goods and services plus foreign aid exceeded U.S. exports of goods and services—totaled over $900 billion. The deficits were financed by net capital inflows—foreign investment in the United States less U.S. investment abroad. Although U.S. holdings of foreign assets rose, foreign holdings of U.S. assets rose by $900 billion more. U.S. assets abroad minus foreign assets in the United States went negative in 1985 for the first time since 1914.

These data, however, are based on historic cost, the cost at the time the investment was made. The proper measure of any investment is its current market value, not its historic cost. Recognizing this, the U.S. Commerce Department switched to market valuation in its June 1991 report. Measured by market values, the net foreign investment position of the United States remained positive until 1987, and reached minus $360.6 billion in 1990, about 40 percent smaller than the number computed on an historic cost basis.

At the end of 1990, about 16 percent of foreign assets in the United States were owned by foreign governments, while 84 percent were privately owned. (Similarly, 14 percent of foreign assets owned by the United States were official, and 86 percent were private.)

In contrast, as a share of total investment, U.S. direct investment abroad (comprising equity holdings of 10 percent or more of any firm) is substantially larger than foreign direct investment in the United States. U.S. direct investment abroad still exceeded foreign direct investment in the United States in 1990, and by a wider margin than in 1985—$184 billion versus $152 billion.

Despite the notoriety of Japanese investors, the British have the largest U.S. direct investment holding—with the Dutch not far behind—as has been the case since colonial times. In 1990 the United Kingdom held about 27 percent of foreign direct investment in the United States, significantly greater than Japan's 21 percent. The European Economic Community (EC) collectively holds about 57 percent. Moreover, according to research by Eric Rosengren, between 1978 and 1987, Japanese investors acquired only 94 U.S. companies, putting

them fifth behind the British (640), Canadians (435), Germans (150), and French (113).

Why Do Foreigners Invest in the United States?

With no restrictions on movements of labor or capital, each tends to flow to any host country where wages or returns are higher than at home. During the eighties laborers migrated to western Europe from eastern Europe, southern Europe, and Turkey, and to the Arab Gulf states from Africa and southern Asia because of higher wages. Capital migrated to the United States because of higher returns. The U.S. stock market's annual appreciation of over 15 percent (not counting dividends) was exceeded among the major Western industrial countries only by the Japanese stock market's rise of nearly 20 percent. In comparison, average stock market increases were 5 percent in Canada, about 11 percent in France, 12 percent in Germany, 14 percent in Italy, and 12 percent in the United Kingdom.

Tax differences also influence international capital flows. Both defenders and critics of the Reagan administration's 1981 tax cuts agree that they caused increased capital inflows during the eighties. Defenders argue that U.S. investments became more profitable after tax than non-U.S. investments, both to U.S. investors and to foreign investors, while critics argue that large federal deficits drew the capital inflows.

Consistent with the defenders' view, U.S. investors were selling off foreign assets in the early eighties to finance domestic investment. U.S. direct investment abroad, valued at historic cost, declined from 1981 to 1984; in market value it declined during 1983 and 1984. Correspondingly, U.S. nonresidential fixed investment rose substantially in 1983 and 1984 and peaked in 1985, following publication of the U.S. Treasury's tax reform proposals in the fall of 1984. In 1985 U.S. direct investment abroad began to rise again. Meanwhile, foreign investment in the United States grew somewhat faster in the early eighties than in the late eighties. Higher tax rates on capital gains became effective in 1986, and, from the end of 1985, the rise in U.S. foreign direct investment has exceeded that of foreign direct investment in the United States. Moreover, the pattern of the rise and fall of the U.S. dollar—appreciating between 1980 and 1985 and depreciating from 1985 to 1987—is also consistent with the defenders' view.

The United States attracts capital not only because of lower taxes, but also because of greater U.S. consumer wealth and labor productivity. At purchasing power parity—GDP adjusted for differences in exchange rates and prices—U.S. wealth (per capita GDP) was one-fourth greater than Japan's in 1990 and one-third greater than Germany's. Moreover, except for Japan the other main industrial countries did not narrow this margin between 1980 and 1990. On a production-per-employee basis, the message is the same: U.S. labor is the most productive in the world.

Is Foreign Investment Good or Bad?

Foreign investment increases the amount of capital—equipment, buildings, land, pa-

tents, copyrights, trademarks, and goodwill—in the host economy. The increase in the quantity and quality of tools for labor's use in converting one set of goods (labor and other inputs) into another (finished output) raises labor productivity and GDP. Because about two-thirds of GDP goes to labor as wages, salaries, and fringe benefits, rising output means higher wages or more employment. Thus, foreign investment raises labor productivity, income, and employment. Workers are better off with more capital than with less and are usually indifferent to the nationality of the investor.

Politicians generally overlook labor's benign attitude toward foreign capital, sometimes at their peril. In the 1988 presidential campaign the Democratic candidate, Michael Dukakis, told a group of workers at a St. Louis automotive parts plant: "Maybe the Republican ticket wants our children to work for foreign owners . . . but that's not the kind of a future Lloyd Bentsen and I and Dick Gephardt and you want for America." Dukakis's advance staff failed to tell him that the workers Dukakis was addressing had been employed by an Italian corporation for eleven years.

What Are the Long-Term Consequences of Foreign Investment in the United States?

The availability of foreign capital lowers the cost of capital to corporations. This makes additions to plant and equipment cheaper, permits some investment projects that otherwise would not be profitable, and raises the value of firms. Thus, even though most foreign capital inflows do not substantively alter the ownership of U.S. firms, they benefit asset owners as well as labor by lowering interest rates and the cost of capital.

Yet some critics, such as Martin and Susan Tolchin, warn of desperate long-run consequences from foreign capital even while conceding its short-run benefits. They worry about loss of skilled employment opportunities, loss of technological advantage, slower growth, and a declining standard of living. All of these worries are based on two implicit assumptions. First, they assume that foreigners will obtain control of the U.S. economy. Second, they assume that, unlike U.S. investors abroad, foreigners will use this control to systematically reduce the efficiency of the host economy. Both assumptions are false.

The probability of foreign investors obtaining control of the U.S. economy is negligible. Between 1982 and 1989, according to estimates by the U.S. Commerce Department, the U.S. stock of nonresidential capital rose from $5.9 trillion to $8.4 trillion. At the end of 1989, the U.S. net international investment position was estimated to be − $267.7 billion, or only 3.2 percent of this capital stock.

Even sustained net capital inflows of $100 billion per year, as happened during the mideighties, would not shift control of the U.S. capital stock to foreigners. At that rate foreign investors' share of the fixed U.S. capital stock would rise to about 8.4 percent in the year 2000, but decline to 7.8 percent in 2010 and to 2.8 percent in 2020.

The second concern is finessed by competitive forces in a market-based capitalist economy. If foreign owners of a U.S. firm reduced its efficiency by not using employees in the most advantageous way, the owners would lose wealth. They also would lose employees and, eventually, the firm. Labor, management, and technology would be hired away by other existing firms or by new firms eager to use them in the most profitable way feasible. The firm's decline in market value—due to the inefficiency of its incumbent management—also would make it an attractive takeover target, as its price would be lower than its value under efficient resource utilization. Either way, foreign owners could not subjugate an industry through perverse management, even if they were willing to sacrifice profits to do so.

—Mack Ott

Biography: Mack Ott is an economist with the U.S.–Saudi Arabia Joint Economic Commission in Riyadh. He was previously a research economist with the Federal Reserve Bank of St. Louis.

Further Reading

"Dukakis-Bensten-Gephardt." *The Wall Street Journal,* October 11, 1988, 22.

Ott, Mack. "Is America Being Sold Out?" *Federal Reserve Bank of St. Louis Review,* 71, no. 2 (March/April 1989): 47–63.

Rosengren, Eric S. ''Is the United States for Sale?'' *Federal Reserve Bank of Boston, New England Economic Review*, November/December 1988, 47–56.

Sinn, Hans-Werner. ''U.S. Tax Reform 1981 and 1986: Impact on International Capital Markets and Capital Flows.'' *National Tax Journal* 41, no. 3 (1988): 327–40.

Tolchin, Martin, and Susan Tolchin. *Buying into America—How Foreign Money Is Changing the Face of Our Nation*. 1988.

Free Trade

Alan S. Blinder

■ For more than two centuries, economists have steadfastly promoted free trade among nations as the best trade policy. Despite this intellectual barrage, many practical men and women of affairs continue to view the case for free trade skeptically, as an abstract argument made by ivory-tower economists with, at most, one foot on terra firma. Such people ''know'' that our vital industries must be protected from foreign competition.

The divergence between economists' beliefs and those of (even well-educated) men and women on the street seems to arise in making the leap from individuals to nations. In running our personal affairs, virtually all of us exploit the advantages of free trade and comparative advantage without thinking twice. For example, many of us have our shirts laundered at professional cleaners rather than wash and iron them ourselves. Anyone who advised us to ''protect'' ourselves from the ''unfair competition'' of low-paid laundry workers by doing our own wash would be thought looney. Common sense tells us to make use of companies that specialize in such work, paying them with money we earn doing something we do better. We understand intuitively that cutting ourselves off from specialists can only lower our standard of living.

Adam Smith's insight was that precisely the same logic applies to nations. Here is how he put it in 1776:

It is the maxim of every prudent master of a family, never to attempt to make at home what it will cost him more to make than to buy. . . . If a foreign country can supply us with a commodity cheaper than we ourselves can make it, better buy it of them with some part of the produce of our own industry, employed in a way in which we have some advantage.

The case for free trade among nations is no different. Spain, South Korea, and a variety of other countries manufacture shoes more cheaply than America can. They offer them for sale to us. Shall we buy them, as we buy the services of laundry workers, with money we earn doing things we do well—like writing computer software and growing wheat? Or shall we keep "cheap foreign shoes" out and purchase more expensive American shoes instead? It is pretty clear that the nation as a whole must be worse off if foreign shoes are kept out—even though the American shoe industry will be better off.

Most people accept this argument. But they worry about what happens if another country—say, Japan—can make everything, or almost everything, cheaper than we can. Will free trade with Japan then lead to unemployment for American workers, who will find themselves unable to compete with cheaper Japanese labor? The answer, which was provided by David Ricardo in 1810 (see RICARDO in Biographies section), is no. To see why, let us once again appeal to our personal affairs.

Some lawyers are better typists than their secretaries. Should such a lawyer fire his secretary and do his own typing? Not likely. Though the lawyer may be better than the secretary at both arguing cases and typing, he will fare better by concentrating his energies on the practice of law and leaving the typing to a secretary. Such specialization not only makes the economy more efficient, it also leaves both lawyer and secretary with productive work to do.

The same idea applies to nations. Suppose the Japanese could manufacture everything more cheaply than we can—which is certainly not true. Even in this worst-case scenario, there will of necessity be some industries in which Japan has an overwhelming cost advantage (say, televisions) and others in which its cost advantage is slight (say, chemicals). Under free trade the United States will produce most of the chemicals, Japan will produce most of the TVs, and the two nations will trade. The two countries, taken together, will get both products cheaper than if each produced them at home to meet all of its domestic needs. And what is also important, workers in both countries will have jobs.

Many people are skeptical about this argument for the following reason. Suppose the average American worker earns ten dollars per hour, while the average Japanese worker earns just six dollars per hour. Won't free trade make it impossible to defend the higher American wage? Won't there instead be a leveling down until, say, both American and Japanese workers earn eight dollars per hour? The answer, once again, is no. And specialization is part of the reason.

If there were only one industry and occupation in which people could work, then free trade would indeed force American wages close to Japanese levels if Japanese workers were as good as Americans (and who doubts that?). But modern economies are composed of many industries and occupations. If America concentrates its employment where it does best, there is no reason why American wages cannot remain far above Japanese wages for a long time—even though the two nations trade freely. A country's wage level depends fundamentally on the productivity of its labor force, not on its trade policy. As long as American workers remain more skilled and better educated, work with more capital, and use superior technology, they will continue to earn higher wages than their Japanese counterparts. If and when these advantages end, the wage gap will disappear. Trade is a mere detail that helps ensure that American labor is employed where, in Adam Smith's phrase, it has some advantage.

Those who are still not convinced should recall that Japan's trade surplus with the United States widened precisely as the wage gap between the two countries was disappearing. If cheap Japanese labor was stealing American jobs, why did the theft intensify as the wage gap closed? The answer, of course, is that Japanese productivity was growing at enormous rates. The remarkable upward march of Japanese productivity both raised Japanese wages relative to American wages and turned Japan into a ferocious competitor. To think that we can forestall the inevitable by closing our borders is to participate in a cruel self-deception.

Americans should appreciate the benefits of free trade more than most people, for we inhabit the greatest free trade zone in the world. Michigan manufactures cars; New York provides banking; Texas pumps oil and gas. The fifty states trade freely with one another, and that helps them all enjoy great prosperity. Indeed, one reason why the United States did so much better economically than Europe for two centuries is

that we had free movement of goods and services while the European countries "protected" themselves from their neighbors. To appreciate the magnitudes involved, try to imagine how much your personal standard of living would suffer if you were not allowed to buy any goods or services that originated outside your home state.

A slogan occasionally seen on bumper stickers argues, "Buy American, save your job." This is grossly misleading for two main reasons. First, the costs of saving jobs in this particular way are enormous. Second, it is doubtful that any jobs are actually saved in the long run.

Many estimates have been made of the cost of "saving jobs" by protectionism. While the estimates differ widely across industries, they are almost always much larger than the wages of the protected workers. For example, one study estimated that in 1984 U.S. consumers paid $42,000 annually for each textile job that was preserved by import quotas, a sum that greatly exceeded the average earnings of a textile worker. That same study estimated that restricting foreign imports cost $105,000 annually for each automobile worker's job that was saved, $420,000 for each job in TV manufacturing, and $750,000 for every job saved in the steel industry. Yes, $750,000 a year!

While Americans may be willing to pay a price to save jobs, spending such enormous sums is plainly irrational. If you doubt that, imagine making the following offer to any steelworker who lost his job to foreign competition: we will give you severance pay of $750,000—not annually, but just once—in return for a promise never to seek work in a steel mill again. Can you imagine any worker turning the offer down? Is that not sufficient evidence that our present method of saving steelworkers' jobs is mad?

But the situation is actually worse, for a little deeper thought leads us to question whether any jobs are really saved overall. It is more likely that protectionist policies save some jobs by jeopardizing others. Why? First, protecting one American industry imposes higher costs on others. For example, quotas on imports of semiconductors sent the prices of memory chips skyrocketing in the eighties, thereby damaging the computer industry. Steel quotas force U.S. automakers to pay more for materials, making them less competitive.

Second, efforts to protect favored industries from foreign competition may induce reciprocal actions in other countries, thereby limiting American access to foreign markets. In that case export industries pay the price for protecting import-competing industries.

Third, there are the little-understood, but terribly important, effects of trade barriers on the value of the dollar. If we successfully restrict imports, Americans will spend less on foreign goods. With fewer dollars offered for sale on the world's currency markets, the value of the dollar will rise relative to that of other currencies. At that point unprotected industries start to suffer because a higher dollar makes U.S. goods less competitive in world markets. Once again, America's ability to export is harmed.

On balance the conclusion seems clear and compelling: while protectionism is sold as job saving, it probably really amounts to job swapping. It protects jobs in some industries only by destroying jobs in others.

—Alan S. Blinder

Biography: Alan S. Blinder is a member of President Clinton's Council of Economic Advisers. He is on leave from Princeton University, where he is the Gordon S. Rentschler Memorial Professor of Economics at Princeton University. He wrote, from 1985 to 1992, a regular economics column for *Business Week* and is the coauthor of one of the best-selling textbooks on economics.

Further Reading

Baldwin, Robert E. *The Political Economy of U.S. Import Policy.* 1985.
Bhagwati, Jagdish. *Protectionism.* 1988.
Blinder, Alan S. *Hard Heads, Soft Hearts: Tough-Minded Economics for a Just Society.* 1987.
Dixit, Avinash. "How Should the U.S. Respond to Other Countries' Trade Policies?" In *U.S. Trade Policies in a Changing World Economy,* edited by Robert M. Stern. 1987.
Hufbauer, Gary C., Diane T. Berliner, and Kimberly A. Elliott. *Trade Protection in the United States: 31 Case Studies.* 1986.
Lawrence, Robert Z., and Robert E. Litan. *Saving Free Trade.* 1986.

See also FREE TRADE AGREEMENTS AND CUSTOMS UNIONS, PROTECTIONISM.

Free Trade Agreements and Customs Unions

Douglas A. Irwin

■ Ever since Adam Smith published *The Wealth of Nations* in 1776, the vast majority of economists have accepted the proposition that free trade among nations improves overall economic welfare. Free trade, usually defined as the absence of tariffs, quotas, or other governmental impediments to international trade, allows each country to specialize in the goods that it can produce cheaply and efficiently relative to other countries. Such specialization enables all countries to achieve higher real incomes.

Although free trade provides overall benefits, it hurts some people, most particularly the shareholders and employees of industries who lose money and jobs because they lose sales to imported goods. Some of the groups that are hurt by foreign competition wield enough political power to obtain protection against imports. Consequently, barriers to trade continue to exist despite their sizable economic costs. Although it has been estimated that the U.S. gain from removing trade restrictions on textile and apparel would have been over $12 billion for 1986 alone, for example, domestic textile producers have been able to persuade Congress to keep tariffs and quotas on imports.

While virtually all economists think free trade is desirable, they differ on how best to make the transition from tariffs and quotas to free trade. The three basic approaches to trade reform are unilateral, multilateral, and bilateral.

Some countries, such as Britain in the nineteenth century and Chile and South Korea in recent decades, have undertaken unilateral tariff reductions—reductions made independently and without reciprocal action by other countries. The advantage of unilateral free trade is that a country can reap the benefits of free trade immediately. Countries that lower trade barriers by themselves do not have to postpone reform while they try to persuade other nations to lower their trade barriers. The gains from such trade liberalization are substantial: a major study by the World Bank shows that income grows more rapidly in countries open to international trade than in those more closed to trade.

However, multilateral and bilateral approaches—dismantling trade barriers in concert with other countries—have two advantages over unilateral approaches. First, the economic gains from international trade are reinforced and enhanced when many countries or regions agree to a mutual reduction in trade barriers. By broadening markets, concerted liberalization of trade increases competition and specialization among countries, thus giving a bigger boost to efficiency and consumer incomes. Britain reaped additional benefits from unilaterally lowering its tariffs in the nineteenth century because its success with free trade prompted other countries to lower their barriers as well.

Second, multilateral reductions in trade barriers may reduce political opposition to frcc tradc in cach of thc countries involved. That is because groups that otherwise would be opposed or indifferent to trade reform might join the campaign for free trade if they see opportunities for exporting to the other countries in the trade agreement. Consequently, free trade agreements between countries or regions are a useful strategy for liberalizing world trade.

The best possible outcome of trade negotiations is a multilateral agreement that includes all major trading countries. Then free trade is widened to allow many participants to achieve the greatest possible gains from trade. The General Agreement on Tariffs and Trade (GATT), which the United States helped found after World War II, is an excellent example of a multilateral trade arrangement. The major countries of the world set up GATT in reaction to the waves of protectionism that crippled world trade during the Great Depression. With over 100 member countries, GATT is both an international agreement that sets the rules for world trade and an international institution that provides a forum for members to negotiate reductions in trade barriers.

As a multilateral trade agreement GATT requires its members to extend most-favored-nation (MFN) status to other trading partners participating in GATT. MFN status means that each member of GATT receives the same tariff treatment for its goods in foreign markets as that extended to the "most-favored" country competing in the same market, thereby ruling out preferences for, or discrimination against, any member country. Since GATT began, average tariffs set by member countries have fallen from about 40 percent shortly after World War II to about 5 percent today.

These tariff reductions helped stimulate the large expansion of world trade after World War II and the concomitant rise in real per capita incomes among developed and developing nations alike. The gain from removal of tariff and nontariff barriers to trade as a result of the Tokyo Round (1973 to 1979) of GATT negotiations has been put at over 3 percent of world GNP.

Although GATT embodies the principle of nondiscrimination in international trade, Article 24 of GATT permits the formation of "customs unions" among GATT members. A customs union is a group of countries that eliminate all tariffs on trade among themselves but maintain a common external tariff on trade with countries outside the union (thus technically violating MFN). This exception was designed in part to accommodate the formation of the European Economic Community (EC) in 1958. The EC, which has grown from six to a dozen participating countries, has gone beyond reducing barriers to trade among member states. It also coordinates and harmonizes each country's tax, industrial, and agricultural policies. The EC aims at even greater economic integration than in a customs union by moving toward a common market—an arrangement that eliminates impediments to the mobility of factors of production, such as capital and labor, between participating countries.

GATT also permits free trade areas (FTAs), such as the European Free Trade Area, which is composed primarily of Scandinavian countries. Members of FTAs eliminate tariffs on trade with each other but retain autonomy in determining their tariffs with nonmembers.

Unfortunately, GATT has encountered

difficulties in maintaining and extending the liberal world trading system in recent years. Discussions on trade liberalization often move slowly, and the requirement for consensus among GATT's many participants limits how far agreements on trade reform can go. While GATT successfully reduced tariffs on industrial goods, it has had much less success in liberalizing trade in agriculture, services, and other areas of international commerce. Moreover, slower growth of the world's economies in the seventies and eighties increased protectionist pressures worldwide. These pressures caused a proliferation of new trade barriers—such as voluntary limits on exports of steel and cars to the United States—not strictly covered by GATT regulations. Recent negotiations, such as the Uruguay Round of trade talks that began in 1986, aimed to extend GATT rules to new areas of trade. These negotiations, however, have run into problems, and their ultimate success is uncertain.

As a result many countries have turned away from GATT toward bilateral or regional trade agreements. One such agreement is the U.S.-Canada Free Trade Agreement (USCFTA), which went into effect in January 1989. The USCFTA eliminated all tariffs on U.S.-Canada merchandise trade and reduced restrictions on trade in services and foreign investment, categories not covered by GATT. Economists have estimated that the USCFTA will increase Canada's national income by anywhere from 0 to 8 percent, the particular estimate depending on the assumptions underlying the analysis. The total U.S. gain is roughly equivalent to the Canadian gain, but the percentage gains in U.S. income are much smaller because the U.S. economy is

about ten times the size of Canada's. The United States also has a free trade agreement with Israel and is, together with Canada, negotiating to bring Mexico into a North American Free Trade Agreement (NAFTA), and it has contemplated bilateral or regional trade agreements with other countries in Latin America, Asia, and the Pacific. Free trade zones have recently been established in parts of South America as well.

The advantage of such bilateral or regional arrangements is that they promote greater trade among the parties to the agreement. They may also hasten global trade liberalization if multilateral negotiations run into difficulties. Recalcitrant countries excluded from bilateral agreements, and hence not sharing in the increased trade they bring, may then be induced to join and reduce their own barriers to trade. But these advantages must be offset against a disadvantage: by excluding certain countries these agreements may shift the composition of trade from low-cost countries that are not party to the agreement to high-cost countries that are.

Suppose, for example, that Japan sells bicycles for $50, Mexico sells them for $60, and both face a $20 U.S. tariff. If tariffs are eliminated on Mexican goods, U.S. consumers will shift their purchases from Japanese to Mexican bicycles. The result is that Americans will purchase from a higher-cost source, and the U.S. government receives no tariff revenue. Consumers save $10 per bicycle, but the government loses $20. If a country enters such a "trade-diverting" customs union, economists have shown that the cost of this trade diversion may exceed the benefits of increased trade with the other members of the customs union. The net result is that the customs union could make the country worse off.

Another concern is that greater reliance on a bilateral or regional approach to trade liberalization may undermine and supplant, instead of support and complement, the multilateral GATT approach. Hence, the long-term result of bilateralism could be a deterioration of the world trading system into competing, discriminatory regional trading blocs, thereby stifling world trade. Just such a disastrous experience in the thirties prompted the creation of the current multilateral trading system and makes its repair and refurbishment today an urgent task.

—**Douglas A. Irwin**

Biography: Douglas A. Irwin is an economics professor at the University of Chicago's Graduate School of Business. He has formerly served on the staff of the President's Council of Economic Advisers and the Federal Reserve board.

Further Reading

Bhagwati, Jagdish. *The World Trading System at Risk.* 1991.

Coughlin, Cletus C. "What Do Economic Models Tell Us about the Effects of the U.S.-Canada Free Trade Agreement?" *Federal Reserve Bank of St. Louis Review* 72 (September/October 1990): 40–58.

Irwin, Douglas A. "Multilateral and Bilateral Trade Liberalization in the World Trading System: An Historical Perspective," in *New Dimensions in Regional Integration*, edited by Jaíme de Melo and Arvind Panagariya. 1993.

Lawrence, Robert Z., and Charles L. Schultze, eds. *An American Trade Strategy: Options for the 1990s.* 1990.

Schott, Jeffrey J., ed. *Free Trade Areas and U.S. Trade Policy.* 1989.

Tumlir, Jan. *Protectionism.* 1985.

World Bank. *World Development Report 1987.* 1987.

Mercantilism

Laura LaHaye

■ Mercantilism is economic nationalism for the purpose of building a wealthy and powerful state. Adam Smith coined the term "mercantile system" to describe the system of political economy that sought to enrich the country by restraining imports and encouraging exports. This system dominated western European economic thought and policies from the sixteenth to the late eighteenth century. The goal of these policies was, supposedly, to achieve a "favorable" balance of trade that would bring gold and silver into the country. In contrast to the agricultural system of the physiocrats, or the laissez-faire of the nineteenth and early twentieth centuries, the mercantile system served the interests of merchants and producers such as the British East India Company, whose activities were protected or encouraged by the state.

The most important economic rationale for mercantilism in the sixteenth century was the consolidation of the regional power centers of the feudal era by large competitive nation-states. Other contributing factors were the establishment of colonies outside Europe, the growth of European commerce and industry relative to agriculture, the increase in the volume and breadth of trade, and the increase in the use of metallic monetary systems, particularly gold and silver, relative to barter transactions.

During the mercantilist period, military conflict between nation-states was both more frequent and more extensive than at any time in history. The armies and navies of the main protagonists were no longer temporary forces raised to address a specific threat or objective, but were full-time professional forces. Each government's primary economic objective was to command a sufficient quantity of hard currency to support a military that would deter attacks by other countries and aid its own territorial expansion.

Most of the mercantilist policies were the outgrowth of the relationship between the governments of the nation-states and their mercantile classes. In exchange for paying levies and taxes to support the armies of the nation-states, the mercantile classes induced governments to enact policies that would protect their business interests against foreign competition.

These policies took many forms. Domestically, governments would provide capital to new industries, exempt new industries from guild rules and taxes, establish monopolies over local and colonial markets, and grant titles and pensions to successful producers. In trade policy the government assisted local industry by imposing tariffs, quotas, and prohibitions on imports of goods that competed with local manufacturers. Governments also prohibited the export of tools and capital equipment and the emigration of skilled labor that would allow foreign countries, and even the colonies of the home country, to compete in the production of manufactured goods. At the same time, diplomats encouraged foreign manufacturers to move to the diplomats' own countries.

Shipping was particularly important during the mercantile period. With the growth of colonies and the shipment of gold from the New World into Spain and Portugal, control of the oceans was considered vitally important to national power. Because ships could be used for merchant or military purposes, the governments of the era developed strong merchant marines. In France Jean-Baptiste Colbert, the minister of finance under Louis XIV from 1661 to 1683, increased port duties on foreign vessels entering French ports and provided bounties to French shipbuilders.

In England the Navigation Laws of 1650 and 1651 prohibited foreign vessels from engaging in coastal trade in England and required that all goods imported from the continent of Europe be carried on either an English vessel or a vessel registered in the country of origin of the goods. Finally, all trade between England and her colonies had to be carried in either English or colonial vessels. The Staple Act of 1663 extended the Navigation Act by requiring that all colonial exports to Europe be landed through an English port before being reexported to Europe. Navigation policies by France, England, and other powers were directed primarily against the Dutch, who dominated commercial marine activity in the sixteenth and seventeenth centuries.

During the mercantilist era it was often suggested, if not actually believed, that the principal benefit of foreign trade was the importation of gold and silver. According to this view the benefits to one nation were matched by costs to the other nations that exported gold and silver, and there were no net gains from trade. For nations almost constantly on the verge of war, draining one another of valuable gold and silver was thought to be almost as desirable as the direct benefits of trade.

Adam Smith refuted the idea that the wealth of a nation is measured by the size of the treasury in his famous treatise, *The Wealth of Nations*, a book rightly considered to be the foundation of modern economic theory. Smith made a number of important criticisms of mercantilist doctrine. First, he demonstrated that trade, when freely initiated, benefits both parties. In modern jargon it is a positive-sum game. Second, he argued that specialization in production allows for economies of scale, which improves efficiency and growth. Finally, Smith argued that the collusive relationship between government and industry was harmful to the general population. While the mercantilist policies were designed to benefit the government and the commercial class, the doctrines of laissez-faire, or free markets, which originated with Smith, interpreted economic welfare in a far wider sense of encompassing the entire population.

While *The Wealth of Nations* is generally considered to mark the end of the mercantilist era, the laissez-faire doctrines of free-market economics also reflect a general disenchantment with the imperialist policies of nation states. The Napoleonic Wars in Europe and the Revolutionary War in the United States heralded the end of the period of military confrontation in Europe and the mercantilist policies that supported it.

Despite these policies and the wars that they are associated with, the mercantilist period was one of generally rapid growth, particularly in England. This is partly because the governments were not very effective in enforcing the policies that they espoused. While the government could prohibit imports, for example, it lacked the resources to stop the smuggling that the prohibition would create. In addition, the variety of new products that were created during the industrial revolution made it difficult to enforce the industrial policies that were associated with mercantilist doctrine.

By 1860 England had removed the last vestiges of the mercantile era. Industrial regulations, monopolies, and tariffs were abolished, and emigration and machinery exports were freed. In large part because of her free trade policies, England became the dominant economic power in Europe. England's success as a manufacturing and financial power, coupled with the United States as an emerging agricultural powerhouse, led to the resumption of protectionist pressures in Europe and the arms race between Germany, France, and England, which ultimately resulted in World War I.

Protectionism remained important in the interwar period. World War I had destroyed the international monetary system based upon the gold standard. After the war manipulation of the exchange rate was added to the government's list of trade weapons. A country could simultaneously lower the international prices of its exports and increase the local currency price of its imports by devaluing its currency against the currencies of its trading partners. This "competitive devaluation" was practiced by many countries during the Great Depression of the thirties and led to a sharp reduction in world trade.

A number of factors led to the reemergence of mercantilist policies after World War II. The Great Depression created doubts about the efficacy and stability of free-market economies, and an emerging body of economic thought ranging from Keynesian countercyclical policies to Marxist centrally planned systems created a new role for governments in the control of economic affairs. In addition, the wartime partnership between government and industry in the United States created a relationship—the military-industrial complex, in Eisenhower's words—that also encouraged activist government policies. In Europe the shortage of dollars after the war induced governments to restrict imports and negotiate bilateral trading agreements to economize on scarce foreign exchange resources. These policies severely restricted the volume of intra-Europe trade and impeded the recovery process in Europe in the immediate postwar period.

The economic strength of the United States, however, provided the stability that permitted the world to emerge out of the postwar chaos into a new era of prosperity and growth. The Marshall Plan provided American resources that overcame the most acute dollar shortages. The Bretton Woods agreement established a new system of relatively stable exchange rates that encouraged the free flow of goods and capital. Finally, the signing of GATT (General Agreement on Tariffs and Trade) in 1947 marked the official recognition of the need to establish an international order of multilateral free trade.

The mercantilist era has passed. Modern economists accept Adam Smith's insight that free trade leads to international specialization of labor and, usually, to greater economic well-being for all nations. But some mercantilist policies continue to exist. Indeed, the surge of protectionist sentiment that began with the oil crisis in the midseventies and expanded with the global recession of the early eighties has led some economists to label the modern pro-export, anti-import attitude as "neomercantilism."

Although several rounds of multilateral trade negotiations have succeeded in reducing tariffs on most industrial goods to less than 5 percent, trade in agricultural goods remains heavily protected though tariffs or subsidies in Europe, Japan, and the United States. Countries have also responded to GATT by erecting various nontariff barriers to trade. The Long Term Arrangement on Cotton Textiles (1962) was the first major departure from the key GATT rule of non-discrimination. Discriminatory nontariff barriers are typically used by industrialized countries to protect mature industries from competition from Japan and newly industrialized countries like Brazil, Korea, and Taiwan. These nontariff barriers include voluntary export restraints, orderly marketing arrangements, health and safety codes, and licensing requirements. And the U.S. Jones Act, which prohibits shipment of goods between U.S. ports on foreign ships, is the modern counterpart of England's Navigation Laws.

Modern mercantilist practices arise from the same source as the mercantilist policies in the sixteenth to the eighteenth century. Groups with political power use that power to secure government intervention to protect their interests, while claiming to seek benefits for the nation as a whole.

Of the false tenants of mercantilism that remain today, the most pernicious is the idea that imports reduce domestic employment. This argument is most often made by American automobile manufacturers in their claim for protection against Japanese imports. But the revenue that the exporter receives must be ultimately spent on American exports, either immediately or subsequently when American investments are liquidated. Another mercantilist view that persists today is that a current account deficit is bad. When a country runs a current account deficit, it is borrowing capital from the rest of the world in order to purchase more goods and services than it sells. But this policy promotes economic wealth if the return on the capital borrowed exceeds the cost of borrowing. Many developing countries with high internal returns on capital have run current account deficits for extremely long periods, while enjoying rapid growth and solvency.

—Laura LaHaye

Biography: Laura LaHaye is an economist in Chicago. She was an economics professor at the University of Illinois in Chicago from 1981 to 1989 and was previously a research economist with the General Agreement on Tariffs and Trade in 1981.

Further Reading

Salvatore, Dominick, ed. *The New Protectionist Threat to World Welfare.* 1987.
Smith, Adam. *The Wealth of Nations,* Edwin Cannan edition. 1937.

See also FOREIGN INVESTMENT IN THE UNITED STATES, FREE TRADE, PROTECTIONISM.

Protectionism

Jagdish Bhagwati

■ The fact that trade protection hurts the economy of the country that imposes it is one of the oldest but still most startling insights economics has to offer. The idea dates back to the origin of economic science itself. Adam Smith's *The Wealth of Nations*, which gave birth to economics, already contained the argument for free trade: by specializing in production instead of producing everything, each nation would profit from free trade. In international economics it is the direct counterpart to the proposition that people within a national economy will all be better off if all people specialize at what they do best instead of trying to be self-sufficient.

It is important to distinguish between the case for free trade for oneself and the case for free trade for all. The former is an argument for free trade to improve one nation's own welfare (the so-called "national-efficiency" argument). The latter is an argument for free trade to improve every trading country's welfare (the so-called "cosmopolitan-efficiency" argument). Underlying both cases is the assumption that prices are determined by free markets. But government may distort market prices by, for example, subsidizing production, as European governments have done in aerospace, electronics, and steel in recent years, and as all industrial countries do in agriculture. Or governments may protect intellectual property inadequately, causing underproduction of new knowledge. In such cases production and trade, guided by distorted prices, will not be efficient.

The cosmopolitan-efficiency case for free trade is relevant to questions such as the design of international trade regimes. For example, the General Agreement on Tariffs and Trade oversees world trade among member nations, just as the International Monetary Fund oversees international macroeconomics and exchange rates. The national-efficiency case for free trade concerns national trade policies; it is, in fact, Adam Smith's case for free trade. Economists typically have the national-efficiency case in mind when they talk of the advantage of free trade and of the folly of protectionism.

This case, as refined greatly by economists in the postwar period, admits two theoretical possibilities in which protection could improve a nation's economic well-being. First, as Adam Smith himself noted, a country might be able to use the threat of protection to get other countries to reduce their protection against its exports. Thus, threatened protection could be a tool to pry open foreign markets, like oysters, with "a strong clasp knife," as Lord Randolph Churchill put it in the late nineteenth century. If the protectionist threat worked, then the country using it would gain doubly: from its own free trade and from its trading partners' free trade as well. However, both Smith and later economists in Britain feared that such threats would not work. They feared that the protection imposed as a threat would be permanent and that the threat would not lower the other countries' trade barriers.

The trade policy of the United States today is premised on a different assessment: that indeed U.S. markets can, and should, be closed as a means of opening new markets abroad. This premise underlies sections 301 through 310 of the 1988 Omnibus Trade and Competitiveness Act. These provisions permit, and sometimes even require, the U.S. government to force other countries into accepting new trade obligations by threatening tariff retaliation if they do not. But those "trade obligations" do not always entail freer trade. They can, for instance, take the form of voluntary quotas on exports of certain goods to the United States. Thus, they may simply force weak nations to redirect their trade in ways that strong nations desire, cutting away at the principle that trade should be guided by market prices.

The second exception in which protection could improve a nation's economic well-being is when a country has monopoly power over a good. Since the time of John Stuart Mill, economists have argued that a country that produces a large percentage of the world's output of a good can use an "optimum" tariff to take advantage of its latent monopoly power and, thus, gain more from trade. This is, of course, the same as saying that a monopolist will maximize his profits by raising his price and reducing his output.

Two objections to this second argument immediately come to mind. First, with rare exceptions such as OPEC, few countries seem to have significant monopoly power in enough goods to make this an important, practical exception to the rule of free trade. Second, other countries might retaliate against the optimum tariff. Therefore, the likelihood of successful (i.e., welfare-increasing) exploitation of monopoly power becomes quite dubious. Several economists have recently made their academic reputations by finding theoretical cases in which oligopolistic markets enable governments to use import tariffs to improve national welfare, but even these researchers have advised strongly against protectionist policies.

One may well think that any market failure could be a reason for protection. Economists did fall into this trap until the fifties. Economists now argue, instead, that protection would be an inappropriate way to correct for most market failures. For example, if wages do not adjust quickly enough when demand for an industry's product falls, as was the case with U.S. autoworkers losing out to foreign competition, the appropriate government intervention, if any, should be in the labor market, directly aimed at the source of the problem. Protection would be, at best, an inefficient way of correcting for the market failure.

Many economists also believe that even if protection were appropriate in theory, it would be "captured" in practice by special interests who would misuse it to pursue their own interests instead of letting it be used for the national interest. One clear cost of protection is that the country imposing it forces its consumers to forgo cheap imports. But another important cost of protection may well be the lobbying costs incurred by those seeking protection. These lobbying activities, now extensively studied by economists, are variously described as rent-seeking or directly unproductive profit-seeking activities. They are unproductive because they produce profit or income for those who lobby without creating valuable output for the rest of society.

Protectionism arises in ingenious ways. As free trade advocates squelch it in one place, it pops up in another. Protectionists seem to always be one step ahead of free traders in creating new ways to protect against foreign competitors.

One way is by replacing restrictions on imports with what are euphemistically called "voluntary" export restrictions (VERs) or "orderly" market arrangements (OMAs). Instead of the importing country restricting imports with quotas or tariffs, the exporting country restricts exports. The protectionist effect is still the same. The real difference, which makes exporting nations prefer restrictions on exports to restrictions on imports, is that the VERs enable the exporters to charge higher prices and thus collect for themselves the higher prices caused by protection.

That has been the case with Japan's voluntary quotas on exports of cars to the United States. The United States could have kept Japanese car imports in check by slapping a tariff on them. That would raise the price, so that consumers would buy fewer. Instead, Japan limits the number of cars shipped to the United States. Since supply is lower than it would be in the absence of the quotas, Japanese car makers can charge higher prices and still sell all their exports to the United States. The accrual of the resulting extra profits from the voluntary export restraint may also have helped the Japanese auto producers to find the funds to make investments that made them yet more competitive!

The growth of VERs in the eighties is a disturbing development for a second reason as well. They selectively target suppliers (in this case Japan) instead of letting the market decide who will lose when trade must be restricted. As an alternative, the United States could have provided just as much protection for domestic automakers by putting a quota or tariff on all foreign cars, letting consumers decide whether they wanted to buy fewer Japanese cars or fewer European ones. With VERs, in other words, politics replaces economic efficiency as the criterion determining who trades what.

Protectionism recently has come in another, more insidious form than VERs. Economists call the new form "administered protection." Nearly all industrialized countries today have what are called "fair trade" laws. The stated purpose of these laws is twofold: to ensure that foreign nations do not subsidize exports (which would distort market incentives and hence destroy efficient allocation of activity among the world's nations) and to guarantee that foreign firms do not dump their exports in a predatory fashion. Nations, therefore, provide for procedures under which, when subsidization or dumping is found to occur, a countervailing duty (CVD) against foreign subsidy or an antidumping (AD) duty can be levied. These two "fair trade" mechanisms are meant to complement free trade.

In practice, however, when protectionist pressures rise, "fair trade" is misused to work against free trade. Thus, CVD and AD actions often are started against successful foreign firms simply to harass them and coerce them into accepting VERs. Practices which are thoroughly normal at home are proscribed as predatory when foreign firms engage in them. As one trade analyst put it, "If the same anti-dumping laws applied to U.S. companies, every after-Christmas sale in the country would be banned."

Much economic analysis shows that in the eighties "fair trade" mechanisms turned increasingly into protectionist instruments used unfairly against foreign competition. U.S. rice producers got a countervailing duty imposed on rice from Thailand, for example, by establishing that the Thai government was subsidizing rice

exports by less than 1 percent—and ignoring the fact that Thailand also slapped a 5 percent tax on exports. We usually think a foreign firm is dumping when it sells at a lower price in our market than in its own. But the U.S. government took an antidumping action against Poland's exports of golf carts even though no golf carts were sold in Poland.

Therefore, economists have thought increasingly about how these "fair trade" mechanisms can be redesigned so as to insulate them from being "captured" and misused by special interests. Ideas include the creation of binational, as against purely national, adjudication procedures that would ensure greater impartiality, as in the U.S.-Canada Free Trade Agreement. Also, greater use of GATT dispute-settlement procedures, and readier acceptance of their outcomes, has been recommended.

Increasingly, domestic producers have labeled as "unfair trade" a variety of foreign policies and institutions. Thus, those who find Japanese commercial success hard to take have objected to its retail distribution system, its spending on infrastructure, and even its work habits. Opponents of the U.S.-Mexico Free Trade Agreement have claimed that free trade between the two nations cannot be undertaken because of differences in Mexico's environmental and labor standards. The litany of objections to gainful, free trade from these alleged sources of "unfair trade" (or its evocative synonym, "the absence of level playing fields") is endless. Here lies a new and powerful source of attack on the principles of free trade.

—Jagdish Bhagwati

Biography: Jagdish Bhagwati is the Arthur Lehman Professor of Economics and a professor of political science at Columbia University. He is also the economic policy adviser to the director general of the General Agreement on Tariffs and Trade. The *Financial Times* has called him "the doyen of economists working on international trade."

Further Reading

Bhagwati, Jagdish. *Protectionism.* 1988.
————. *The World Trading System at Risk* 1991.

Sanctions

Kimberly Ann Elliott and Gary Clyde Hufbauer

■ Throughout most of modern history, economic sanctions have preceded or accompanied war. Sanctions often have taken the form of a naval blockade intended to weaken the enemy during wartime. Only when the horrors of World War I prompted President Woodrow Wilson to call for new methods of dispute settlement were economic sanctions seriously considered as an alternative to war. Sanctions were incorporated as a tool of enforcement in each of the two collective security systems established in this century—the League of Nations between the two world wars and the United Nations since World War II. But individual countries, especially the United States, often use economic sanctions unilaterally.

Purposes of Economic Sanctions

Students of international law frequently argue that only economic measures deployed against states that have violated international standards or obligations may properly be classified as "sanctions." According to this view sanctions should be distinguished from national uses of economic power in pursuit of narrow national interests. But common usage of the term *economic sanctions* typically encompasses both types of actions. The broader meaning is used here. Specifically, economic sanctions are the deliberate, government-inspired withdrawal, or threat of withdrawal, of customary trade or financial relations.

("Customary" refers to the levels of trade or financial activity that would probably have occurred in the absence of sanctions.)

Although individual countries, as well as various ad hoc groups, have frequently imposed sanctions in response to perceived violations of international law, institutionally endorsed sanctions have been rare and have enjoyed mixed success. The League of Nations imposed or threatened to impose economic sanctions only four times in the twenties and thirties, twice successfully. But the league faded from history when its ineffectual response failed to deter Mussolini's conquest of Ethiopia in 1935 and 1936. The United Nations Security Council—divided because of the cold war—imposed sanctions only twice prior to the August 1990 embargo of Iraq. The first imposition was against Rhodesia beginning in 1966, the second an arms embargo against South Africa imposed in 1977. The British Commonwealth also imposed broader sanctions against South Africa (against the wishes of the United Kingdom).

The motives behind international uses of sanctions parallel the three basic purposes of national criminal law—to punish, to deter, and to rehabilitate. Like states that incarcerate criminals, international institutions that impose sanctions may find their hopes of rehabilitation unrealized, but they may be quite satisfied with whatever punishment and deterrence are accomplished.

Similarly, individual countries, particularly major powers, often impose economic sanctions even when the probability of forcing a change in the target country's policy is small. In addition to demonstrating resolve and signaling displeasure to the immediate transgressor and to other countries, politicians may also want to posture for their domestic constituencies. It is quite clear, for example, that U.S., European, and British Commonwealth sanctions against South Africa, as well as U.S., European, and Japanese sanctions against China in the wake of the T'ienanmen Square massacre, were designed principally to assuage domestic constituencies, to make a moral and historical statement, and to send a warning to future offenders of the international order. The effect on the specific target country was almost secondary. World leaders often decide that the most obvious alternatives to economic sanctions are unsatisfactory—military action would be too massive, and diplomatic protest too meager. Sanctions can provide a satisfying theatrical display, yet avoid the high costs of war. This is not to say that sanctions are costless, just that they are often less costly than the alternatives.

Types of Sanctions

A "sender" country tries to inflict costs on its target in two main ways: (1) with trade sanctions that limit the target country's exports or restrict its imports, and (2) with financial sanctions that impede finance (including reducing aid). Governments that impose limits on target countries' exports intend to reduce its foreign sales and deprive it of foreign exchange. Governments impose limits on their own exports to deny critical goods to the target country. If the sender country is important in world markets, this may also cause the target to pay higher prices for substitute imports. When governments impose financial sanctions by interrupting commercial finance or by reducing or eliminating government loans to the target country's government, they intend to cause the target country to pay higher interest rates, and to scare away alternative creditors. When a poor country is the target, the government imposing the sanction can use the subsidy component of official financing or other development assistance to gain further leverage.

Total embargoes are rare. Most trade sanctions are selective, affecting only one or a few goods. Thus, the economy-wide impact of the sanction may be quite limited. Because sanctions are often unilateral, the trade may only be diverted rather than cut off. Whether import prices paid by (or export prices received by) the target country increase (or decrease) after the sanctions are applied depends on the market in question. If there are many alternative markets and suppliers, the effects on prices may be very modest and the economic impact of the sanctions will be negligible.

For example, Australia cut off shipments of uranium to France from 1983 to 1986 because of France's refusal to halt testing of nuclear weapons in the South Pacific. In 1984, however, the price of uranium oxide dropped nearly 50 percent. France was able to replace the lost supply, and at a price lower than the one specified in its contract with the Australian mine. Because Australia was unable to find alternative buyers for all the uranium intended for France, the Australian government ultimately paid Queensland Mines $26 million in 1985 and 1986 for uranium it had contracted to sell to France.

In contrast, financial sanctions are usually more difficult to evade. Because sanctions are typically intended to foster or exacerbate political or economic instability, alternative financing may be hard to find and is likely to carry a higher interest rate. Private banks and investors are easily scared off by the prospect that the target country will face a credit squeeze in the future. Moreover, many sanctions involve the suspension or termination of official development assistance to developing countries—large grants of money or concessional loans from one government to another—which may be irreplaceable.

Another important difference between trade sanctions and financial sanctions lies in who are hurt by each. The pain from trade sanctions, especially export controls, usually is diffused through the target country's population. Financial sanctions, on the other hand, are more likely to hit the pet projects or personal pockets of government officials who shape local policy. On the sender's side of the equation, an interruption of official aid or credit is unlikely to create the same political backlash from business firms and allies abroad as an interruption of private trade. Finally, financial sanctions, especially involving trade finance, may interrupt trade even without the imposition of explicit trade sanctions. In practice, however, financial and trade sanctions are usually used in some combination with one another.

The ultimate form of financial and trade control is a freeze of the target country's foreign assets, such as bank accounts held in the sender country. In addition to imposing a cost on the target country, a key goal of an assets freeze is to deny an invading country the full fruits of its aggression. Such measures were used against Japan for that purpose just before and during World War II. In the 1990 Middle East crisis, the United States and its allies froze Kuwait's assets to prevent Saddam Hussein from plundering them.

Effectiveness of Sanctions

Senders usually have multiple goals and targets in mind when they impose sanctions, and simple punishment is rarely at the top of the list. Judging the effectiveness of sanctions requires sorting out the various goals sought, analyzing whether the type and scope of the sanction chosen was appropriate to the occasion, and determining the economic and political impact on the target country.

If governments that impose sanctions embrace contradictory goals, sanctions will usually be weak and ultimately ineffective. In such cases the country or group imposing sanctions will neither send a clear signal nor exert much influence on the target country. Thus, it may be the policy—not the instrument (sanctions)—that fails. For example, the Reagan and Bush administrations imposed economic sanctions against Panama beginning in 1987 in an effort to destabilize the Noriega regime. But because they wanted to avoid destroying their political allies in the Panamanian business and financial sectors, they imposed sanctions incrementally and then gradually weakened them with exemptions. In the end the sanctions proved inadequate, and military force was used to remove Noriega.

In many cases sanctions are imposed primarily for "signaling" purposes—either for the benefit of allies, other third parties, or a domestic audience. If the sanctions are not carefully targeted or if they entail substantial costs for the sender country, however, the intended signal may not be received. It may be overwhelmed by a cacophony of protests from injured domestic parties, which may force a premature reversal of the policy. For example, American farmers howled with outrage when President Carter embargoed grain sales to the Soviet Union following the invasion of Afghanistan. The protests, buttressed by candidate Reagan's promise to lift the embargo if elected—which he did within three months of his inauguration—undermined the seriousness of intent that Carter wanted to convey. Efforts to extend sanctions extraterritorially may produce similar effects abroad. Thus, sanctions imposed for symbolic or signaling purposes must be carefully crafted if they are to convey the intended signal.

Sanctions intended to change the behavior or government of a target country are even more difficult to design. In most cases, sanctions must be imposed as quickly and comprehensively as possible. A strategy of "turning the screws" gives the target time to adjust by finding alternative suppliers or markets, by building new alliances, and by mobilizing domestic opinion in support of its policies. Great Britain, followed by the United Nations, adopted a slow and deliberate strategy in response to Ian Smith's "unilateral declaration of independence" in Rhodesia in 1965. Aided by hesitation and delays, the Smith regime was able to use import substitution, smuggling, and other circumvention techniques to fend off the inevitable for over a decade.

Overall, based on an analysis of 116 case studies, beginning with World War I and going through the UN embargo of Iraq, economic sanctions tend to be most effective at modifying the target country's behavior under the following conditions:

1. When the goal is relatively modest: winning the release of a political prisoner versus ending South Africa's apartheid system, for example. Less ambitious goals may be achieved with more modest sanctions; this also lessens the importance of multilateral cooperation, which is often difficult to obtain. Finally, if the stakes are small, there is less chance that a rival power will step in with offsetting assistance.
2. When the target is much smaller than the country imposing sanctions, economically weak and politically unstable. The average sender's economy in the 116 cases studied was 187 times larger than that of the average target.
3. When the sender and target are friendly toward one another and conduct substantial trade. The sender accounted for 28 percent of the average target's trade in cases of successful sanctions, but only 19 percent in failures.
4. When the sanctions are imposed quickly and decisively to maximize impact. The average cost to the target as a percentage of GNP in success cases was 2.4 percent and in failures was only 1.0 percent, while successful sanctions lasted an average of only 2.9 years versus 8.0 years for failures.
5. When the sender avoids high costs to itself.

It is obvious from this list that effective sanctions, in the sense of coercing a change in target country policy, will be achieved only rarely. Economic sanctions were relatively effective tools of foreign policy in the first two decades after World War II: they achieved their stated goals in nearly half the cases. The evolution of the world economy, however, has narrowed the circumstances in which unilateral economic leverage can be effectively applied. For multilateral sanctions, increasing economic interdependence is a double-edged sword. It increases the latent power of economic sanctions because countries are more dependent on international trade and financial flows. But it also means wider sources of supply and greater access to markets, and thus the possibility that a greater number of neutral countries can undermine the economic impact of a sanctions effort should they choose to do so.

South Africa, Iraq, and the Future of Sanctions

What do the lessons of history tell us about the likely effectiveness of sanctions against Iraq and South Africa, and what do these cases portend for the future of sanctions as a tool of international diplomacy? Going against rule number one, both cases involved extremely difficult goals: forcing the removal of Iraqi troops from Kuwait in the first, and promoting the dismantling of the apartheid system in South Africa in the second. In the Iraq case, however, the level of international commitment and cooperation was unprecedented, trade and financial relations with Iraq were almost completely cut off, and the cost to the target probably approached half of GNP on an annual basis. Although the cost to the anti-Iraq coalition from boycotting Iraqi oil shipments could have been quite high, increased production of oil elsewhere within a few weeks lessened the impact. Thus, the embargo of Iraq had a high probability of achieving the stated UN goal of reversing Saddam Hussein's aggression, probably within a year to eighteen months, based on past history.

In the South Africa case, however, economic sanctions were applied piecemeal over a number of years, often halfheartedly, and at their height were far from comprehensive. The most significant sanctions, embodied in the U.S. Comprehensive Anti-Apartheid Act (CAAA) of 1986, were imposed only after Congress overrode a presidential veto, and administrative enforcement was reportedly weak. Even the CAAA, however, affected only some trade and financial relations, and except for the Nordic countries (Sweden, Norway, Finland, Iceland, and Denmark), other countries' sanctions were even less stringent. Thus, by the summer of 1991, the UN arms embargo had been in place for over a decade, an OPEC oil embargo for a similar number of years, and expanded U.S. sanctions for over five years. Yet the white government and the two major black opposition groups (the African National Congress and Inkatha)—though closer than previously—were still struggling to find common ground on which to begin constitutional negotiations. Assuming that reform is achieved and that South Africa does not degenerate into bloody civil war, sanctions will have made a modest contribution to the happy result.

The confluence of circumstances that resulted in the nearly unanimous condemnation and isolation of Iraq is unlikely to recur soon. Instead, future efforts at sanctions are likely to be plagued by the same economic, political, and diplomatic differences, both within and among countries, that long split the anti-apartheid coalition.

**—Kimberly Ann Elliott
and Gary Clyde Hufbauer**

Biography: Kimberly Ann Elliott is a research associate, and Gary Clyde Hufbauer a senior economist, with the Institute for International Economics in Washington, D.C.

Further Reading

Baldwin, David A. *Economic Statecraft*. 1985.
Carter, Barry E. *International Economic Sanctions: Improving the Haphazard U.S. Legal Regime*. 1988.
Doxey, Margaret P. *International Sanctions in Contemporary Perspective*. 1987.
Hufbauer, Gary Clyde, Jeffrey J. Schott, and Kimberly Ann Elliott. *Economic Sanctions Reconsidered*, rev. ed., 2 vols. 1990.

Knorr, Klaus. *The Power of Nations: The Political Economy of International Relations*. 1975.

Lenway, Stefanie Ann. ''Between War and Commerce: Economic Sanctions as a Tool of Statecraft.'' *International Organization* 42, no. 2 (Spring 1988): 397–426.

Malloy, Michael P. *Economic Sanctions and U.S. Trade*. 1990.

See also APARTHEID, OPEC.

CHAPTER ELEVEN

CORPORATIONS AND FINANCIAL MARKETS

Asset-Backed Securities

Phillip L. Zweig

■ Of the array of creative financing techniques that came of age in the eighties, one that emerged from that tumultuous decade with its reputation intact is asset securitization.

Asset-backed securities enable depository institutions, finance companies, and other corporations to "liquefy" their balance sheets (i.e., raise cash by borrowing against assets) and develop new sources of capital. Assets such as credit cards, automobile loans, and home equity loans are packaged as the collateral for intermediate-term (i.e., maturity of one to five years) securities and sold in the public markets or as private placements. Other assets that have been "securitized" in this way include loans for mobile homes, pleasure boats, and recreational vehicles.

Issuers reap many advantages by securitizing assets rather than keeping them on their books. By packaging their portfolios of credit card receivables as securities, major commercial banks, for example, have been able to reduce the amount of capital they would otherwise have to maintain under new, stringent capital guidelines mandated by bank regulators. As the leading bank issuer of credit cards, Citibank has also emerged as the largest issuer of securities backed by credit card receivables. Sears, Roebuck has also employed the technique aggressively. In 1991 it issued more than $5 billion in securities backed by the Discover card and retail-store credit card

receivables, as well as loans for recreational vehicles and autos. Led by the General Motors Acceptance Corporation (GMAC), the finance affiliates of the Big Three U.S. automakers have securitized billions in auto loans, giving the car companies an additional source of funds at attractive rates. Other corporations have converted trade and lease receivables into securities, though in much smaller volumes than the mainstay credit card and auto loan transactions.

Investor acceptance of asset-backed securities has grown as the market matured. Consequently, these securities now trade at interest-rate spreads over Treasury bills that make them a relatively low-cost source of funding for many companies. Credit card–backed securities, which in 1991 represented the largest single category of new issues (41 percent of the dollar volume), have settled into a trading range of 65 to 105 basis points (0.65 to 1.05 percentage points) over Treasurys with comparable maturities. Issues collateralized with auto debt, the second-biggest market component (30 percent), trade at a spread of just 60 to 80 basis points, while offerings supported by home equity loans, the third largest (21 percent) category, move in a range of 120 to 160 basis points.

Not surprisingly, asset-backed securities evolved out of the mortgage-backed securities market, which developed in the seventies when interest rates surged and thrift institutions found themselves saddled with residential mortgages that were earning less than what they were paying for deposits. Compared with mortgage-backed securities, asset-backed issues have been relatively unaffected by swings in interest rates. The reason is that the car loans and other loans backing the securities have shorter maturities than mortgages, and therefore people are less likely to refinance when interest rates fall. In that respect, asset-backed securities resemble noncallable bonds.

This new market was born in early 1985, when the Sperry Lease Finance Corporation, a special-purpose organization set up by Sperry Corporation (now Unisys), sold to institutional investors $192.4 million in fixed-rate notes collateralized by computer leases. Managed and structured by First Boston Corporation, that deal enabled Sperry to offset rising marketplace resistance to its conventional debt, which was hindering the company's efforts to lease new equipment. Another early milestone came in October 1986, when GMAC issued $4 billion in notes backed by automobile loans.

Although the legal devices used to package nonmortgage assets are very similar to those used for mortgage-backed securities, there are several key differences. For one thing, mortgage-backed securities are guaranteed by U.S. government agencies. In contrast, issuers of asset-backed securities typically gain a top investment-grade rating by selling the assets into a "bankruptcy-proof" entity, called a special-purpose company or trust, and cushioning investors against loss of principal with one or more kinds of credit support. This so-called "credit enhancement" takes a variety of

forms, including letters of credit from top-rated commercial banks, third-party guaranties, reserve funds, recourse to the parent company, and cash collateral accounts, which lately have overtaken letters of credit as the method of choice for major public transactions. So far, these securities have stood up extremely well on the rare occasions when issuers have run into rough financial seas. The concept passed a crucial test in mid-1991, when Miami's troubled Southeast Bank was forced to pay out early on a $300 million credit card issue. According to Walid Chammah, managing director of First Boston's asset finance unit, "Investors haven't been hurt in any transaction that was structured and rated."

Structuring these securities requires a careful analysis of complex tax, accounting, and legal issues. Generally, issuers seek to package the securities so that the receivables will be deemed to have been sold, rather than pledged, for purposes of bankruptcy, regulatory, and generally accepted accounting principles (GAAP). That way, issuers receive "off-balance-sheet" accounting and regulatory treatment, which is significantly more favorable than "on-balance-sheet" treatment.

The market enjoyed a banner year in 1991, but Wall Streeters think that year's results might represent the high-water mark, at least for the near term. According to *Asset Sales Report*, a trade newsletter, the volume of new public asset-backed debt reached a record $50.6 billion (106 issues) in 1991, up about 18 percent from the $42.8 billion (93 issues) level the year before. Among lead managers First Boston ranked first in dollar volume, with $13.9 billion

(22 issues), followed by Merrill Lynch with $11.7 billion (31 deals) and Salomon Brothers with $8.4 billion (10 issues).

Investment bankers do not expect this performance to continue. One reason is that so much credit card debt has already been securitized that not much unsold inventory is left. Moreover, the recession has slowed consumer borrowing and sparked concerns about increases in delinquencies. Citicorp, for one, expected its 1992 new issue volume to drop to less than $6 billion from the $9 billion level in 1991, according to *The Wall Street Journal*. To some extent, however, the expected decline in volume of credit card issues could be offset by growth in other, newer types of securities, such as those backed by home equity loans, "floor plan" loans used to finance automobile dealer inventories, and trade and lease receivables. With the collapse of the U.S. commercial real estate market, commercial banks and insurers, as well as the Resolution Trust Corporation, the government agency charged with disposing of the assets of failed thrifts, are beginning to securitize commercial real estate loans to get them off their books.

Investment bankers also think the fledgling but erratic overseas asset-backed securities market might eventually pick up some steam. In 1991, according to *Investment Dealers' Digest,* dollar volume of new European asset-backed issues fell by more than half, to $2.6 billion (nine issues) from $5.8 billion (eighteen issues) the year before. One reason for the slower development of the European market is that European banks are under less pressure than their American cousins to reduce leverage. Additionally, the legal and regulatory apparatus governing these transactions is still in its infancy.

—Phillip L. Zweig

Biography: Phillip L. Zweig is a New York–based business and financial writer. He is author of *Belly Up: The Collapse of the Penn Square Bank.* For his 1982 *American Banker* coverage of the failure of the Penn Square Bank of Oklahoma City, Zweig received the George Polk, Gerald Loeb, John Hancock, and Deadline Club awards.

Further Reading

Zweig, Phillip L. *Asset Securitization Handbook.* 1989.

Bonds

Clifford W. Smith

■ Bond markets are important components of capital markets. Bonds are fixed-income securities—securities that promise the holder a specified set of payments. The value of a bond (like the value of any other asset) is the present value of the income stream one expects to receive from holding the bond. This has several implications:

1. Bond prices vary inversely with market interest rates. Since the stream of payments usually is fixed no matter what subsequently happens to interest rates, higher rates reduce the present value of the expected payments, and thus the price.

2. Bonds are generally adversely affected by inflation. The reason is that higher expected inflation raises market interest rates and therefore reduces the present value of the stream of fixed payments. Some bonds (ones issued by the Israeli government, for example) are indexed for inflation. If, for example, inflation is 10 percent per year, then the income from the bond rises to compensate for this inflation. With perfect indexation the change in expected payments due to inflation exactly offsets the inflation-caused change in market interest rates, so that the current price of the bond is unaffected.

3. The greater the uncertainty about whether the payment will be made (the risk that the issuer will default on the promised payments), the lower the "expected" payment to bondholders and the lower the value of the bond.

4. Bonds whose payments are subjected to lower taxation provide investors with higher expected after-tax payments. Since investors are interested in after-tax income, such bonds sell for higher prices.

The major classes of bond issuers are the U.S. government, corporations, and municipal governments. The default risk and tax status differ from one kind of bond to another.

U.S. Government Bonds

The U.S. government is extremely unlikely to default on promised payments to its bondholders. Thus, virtually all of the variation in the value of its bonds is due to changes in market interest rates. That is why analysts use changes in prices of U.S. government bonds to compute changes in market interest rates.

Because the U.S. government's tax revenues rarely cover expenditures nowadays, it relies heavily on debt financing. Moreover, even if the government did not have a budget deficit now, it would have to sell new debt to obtain the funds to repay old debt that matures. Most of the debt sold by the U.S. government is marketable, meaning that it can be resold by its original purchaser. Marketable issues include Treasury bills, Treasury notes, and Treasury bonds. The major nonmarketable federal debt sold to individuals is U.S. Savings Bonds.

Treasury bills have maturities up to one year and are generally issued in denominations of $10,000. They are sold in bearer form—possession of the T-bill itself constitutes proof of ownership. And they do not pay interest in the sense that the government writes a check to the owner. Instead, the U.S. Treasury sells notes at a discount to their redemption value. The size of the discount determines the interest rate on the bill. For instance, a dealer might offer a bill with 120 days left until maturity at a yield of 7.48 percent. To translate this quoted yield into the price, one must "undo" this discount computation. Multiply the 7.48 by $120/_{360}$ (the fraction of the 360-day year) to obtain 2.493, and subtract that from 100 to get 97.506. The dealer is offering to sell the bond for $97.507 per $100 of face value.

Treasury notes and Treasury bonds differ from Treasury bills in several ways. First, their maturities generally are greater than one year. Notes have maturities of one to seven years. Bonds can be sold with any maturity, but their maturities at issue typically exceed five years. Second, bonds and notes specify periodic interest (coupon) payments as well as a principal repayment. Third, they are frequently registered, meaning that the government records the name and address of the current owner. When Treasury notes or bonds are initially sold, their coupon rate is typically set so that they will sell close to their face (par) value.

Yields on bills, notes, or bonds of different maturities usually differ. Because investors can invest either in a long-term note or in a sequence of short-term bills, expectations about future short-term rates affect current long-term rates. Thus, if the market expects future short-term rates to exceed current short-term rates, then current long-term rates would exceed short-term rates. If, for example, the current short-term rate for a one-year T-bill is 5 percent, and the market expects the rate on a one-year T-bill sold one year from now to be 6 percent, then the current two-year rate must exceed 5 percent. If it did not, investors would expect to do better by buying one-year bills today and rolling them over into new one-year bills a year from now.

Savings bonds are offered only to individuals. Two types have been offered. Series E bonds are essentially discount bonds; they pay no interest until they are redeemed. Series H bonds pay interest semiannually. Both types are registered. Unlike marketable government bonds, which have fixed interest rates, rates received by savings bond holders are frequently revised when market rates change.

Corporate Bonds

Corporate bonds promise specified payments at specified dates. In general, the interest received by the bondholder is taxed as ordinary income. An issue of corporate bonds is generally covered by a trust indenture, which promises a trustee (typically a bank or trust company) that it will comply with the indenture's provisions (or covenants). These include a promise of payment of principal and interest at stated dates, and other provisions such as limitations of the firm's right to sell pledged property, limitations on future financing activities, and limitations on dividend payments.

Potential lenders forecast the likelihood of default on a bond and require higher promised interest rates for higher forecasted default rates. One way that corporate borrowers can influence the forecasted default rate is to agree to restrictive provisions or covenants that limit the firm's future financing, dividend, and investment activities—making it more certain that cash will be available to pay interest and principal. With a lower anticipated probability of default, buyers are willing to offer higher prices for the bonds. Corporate officers must weigh the costs of the reduced flexibility from including the covenants against the benefits of lower interest rates.

Describing all the types of corporate bonds that have been issued would be difficult. Sometimes different names are employed to describe the same type of bond and, infrequently, the same name will be applied to two quite different bonds. Standard types include the following:

- Mortgage bonds are secured by the pledge of specific property. If default occurs, the bondholders are entitled to sell the pledged property to satisfy their claims. If the sale proceeds are insufficient to cover their claims, they have an unsecured claim on the corporation's other assets.
- Debentures are unsecured general obligations of the issuing corporation. The indenture will regularly limit issuance of additional secured and unsecured debt.
- Collateral trust bonds are backed by other securities (typically held by a trustee). Such bonds are frequently issued by a parent corporation pledging securities owned by a subsidiary.
- Equipment obligations (or equipment trust certificates) are backed by specific pieces of equipment (for example, railroad rolling stock or aircraft).
- Subordinated debentures have a lower priority in bankruptcy than unsubordinated debentures; junior claims are generally paid only after senior claims have been satisfied.
- Convertible bonds give the owner the option either to be repaid in cash or to exchange the bonds for a specified number of shares in the corporation.

Corporate bonds have differing degrees of risk. Bond rating agencies (for example, Moody's) provide an indication of the relative default risk of bonds with ratings that range from Aaa (the best quality) to C (the lowest). Bonds rated Baa and above are typically referred to as "investment grade." Below-investment-grade bonds are sometimes referred to as "junk bonds" (see JUNK BONDS). Junk bonds can carry promised yields that are 3 to 6 percent (300 to 600 basis points) higher than Aaa bonds.

Municipal Bonds

Historically, interest paid on bonds issued by state and local governments has been exempt from federal income taxes. Because investors are usually interested in returns net of tax, municipal bonds have therefore generally promised lower interest rates than other government bonds that have similar risk but that lack this attractive tax treatment. In 1991 the percentage difference between the yield on long-term U.S. government bonds and the yield on long-term municipals was about 15 percent. Thus, if an individual's marginal tax rate is higher than 15 percent, after-tax return would be higher from munis than from taxable government bonds.

Municipal bonds are typically designated as either general obligation bonds or revenue bonds. General obligation bonds are backed by the "full faith and credit" (and thus the taxing authority) of the issuing entity. Revenue bonds are backed by a specifically designated revenue stream, such as the revenues from a designated project, authority, or agency, or by the proceeds from a specific tax. Frequently, such bonds are issued by agencies that plan to sell their services at prices that cover their expenses, including the promised payments on the debt. In such cases the bonds are only as good as the enterprise that backs it. In 1983, for example, the Washington Public Power Supply System (nicknamed WHOOPS by Wall Street) defaulted on $2.25 billion on its number four and five nuclear power plants, leaving bondholders with much less than they had been promised. Finally, industrial development bonds are used to finance the purchase or construction of facilities to be leased to private firms. Municipalities have used such bonds to subsidize businesses choosing to locate in their area by, in effect, giving them the benefit of loans at tax-exempt rates.

—Clifford W. Smith

Biography: Clifford W. Smith is the Clarey Professor of Finance at the William E. Simon Graduate School of Business Administration, University of Rochester. He is editor of the *Journal of Financial Economics*, and associate editor of the *Journal of Financial Engineering*, the *Journal of Risk and Insurance*, and *Financial Management*.

Further Reading

Brealey, Richard A., and Stewart C. Myers. *Principles of Corporate Finance*. 1991.

Peavy, John W., and George H. Hempel. "The Effect of the WPPSS Crisis on the Tax-Exempt Bond Market." *Journal of Financial Research* 10, no. 3 (Fall 1987): 239–47.

Sharpe, William F., and Gordon J. Alexander. *Investments*. 1990.

Smith, Clifford W., Jr., and Jerold B. Warner. "On Financial Contracting: An Analysis of Bond Covenants." *Journal of Financial Economics* 7, no. 3 (June 1979): 117–61.

See also ASSET-BACKED SECURITIES.

Corporate Debt

Annette Poulsen

■ The eighties were the decade of corporate debt. Tremendous changes in corporate financing occurred. The phenomenal growth in the use of junk bonds, the onslaught of debt-financed hostile takeovers and leveraged buyouts, and massive corporate restructuring dominated news stories and discussions about U.S. business. Many commentators warned that these debt-bloated companies and an economic downturn could turn the nineties into the decade of bankruptcy.

In determining how much debt to use, corporate managers have reacted rationally to taxes. Indeed, the U.S. tax code may be the number one explanation for high debt levels. By allowing corporations to deduct interest payments from income before taxation, the U.S. government essentially subsidizes every dollar paid in interest. So instead of asking why the use of corporate debt has increased, perhaps the question should be why it has taken so long for the increase to occur.

For many financial economists the efforts of corporate managers to dramatically change the amount of debt on their balance sheets simply confirms the validity of a seminal 1958 paper by Franco Modigliani and Merton Miller. The paper is so well-known that financial economists now refer to the theory it elaborates as "the M&M theory." This paper arguably began the study of finance as its own discipline.

M&M showed that the value of a firm (and of its cash flows) is independent of the ratio of debt to equity used by the firm in financing its investments. This stunning conclusion was based on certain assumptions that are not true of the real world: there are no corporate or personal taxes; people have perfect information; individuals and corporations can borrow at the same rates; and how you pay for assets does not affect productivity. Still, it provides a jumping off point for a better understanding of corporate debt.

First, consider the assumption that how you pay for assets does not affect their productivity. In a simplified example, how you pay for a feather, a stone, and a vacuum chamber does not affect the basic law of physics that the stone and the feather will fall at the same rate in a vacuum. Whether the inputs are paid for with cash (equity) or credit (debt) cannot affect the results or the productivity of the inputs.

M&M extend this simple illustration with their famous arbitrage proof. Since we assume that capital structure cannot affect the productivity of assets, capital structure can affect the value of the firm only if investors are willing to pay more (or less) for the leveraged—highly indebted—firm. With the arbitrage proof M&M show that the leveraged and unleveraged firm must have the exact same value. An example shows why.

First, think of two firms that are identical in all respects except that one is financed completely with equity while the other uses some combination of equity and debt. Let Ms. E. buy 10 percent of the all-equity firm; she buys 10 percent of the outstanding shares. Mr. D. buys 10 percent of the leveraged firm; he buys 10 percent of the shares and 10 percent of the debt.

Now we want to determine what Ms. E. and Mr. D. get back for their investments. In the all-equity firm Ms. E. has a claim on 10 percent of the total profits of the firm. In the leveraged firm, however, the debt holders must receive their interest payments before the shareholders receive the remaining profits. Thus, for his share holdings, Mr. D. gets 10 percent of the profits after interest payments to debt holders are subtracted. But because Mr. D. also holds 10 percent of the bonds, he receives 10 percent of the profits that were paid out as interest payments. The net result for Mr. D? He receives 10 percent of the total profits, just as Ms. E. does.

This reasoning led M&M to argue that the leveraged firm and the all-equity firm must have the exact same value. The value of the all-equity firm is the value of the outstanding stock. The value of the leveraged firm is the value of the outstanding stock plus the value of the outstanding debt. Since the firms are identical in the level of total profits and identical in the cash payouts paid to the investors, Ms. E. and Mr. D. would pay identical amounts for their respective holdings. M&M went on to show that if the leveraged and all-equity firms do not have the exact same value, arbitragers can make a guaranteed risk-free profit by selling the overvalued firm and buying the undervalued firm.

The proposition that the ratio of debt to equity is irrelevant to the value of the company is known as the "irrelevance" proposition. Many commentators quickly rejected the irrelevance proposition because its restrictive assumptions separated it from the real world. In 1963 Modigliani and Miller modified their discussion of corporate debt to specifically recognize corporate taxes. Under current tax regulations, interest payments made to bondholders are deducted from corporate income before computation of taxes owed. In a real sense, therefore, the government subsidizes those interest payments. If the corporate tax rate is 34 percent, for every dollar paid in interest payments, 34 cents in corporate taxes is avoided, though those receiving the interest must pay taxes on it. In contrast, if income is paid out as dividends to shareholders, that income is taxed twice—once at the corporate level and once at the personal level. The implication, well-known to students of corporate finance, is that every corporation should minimize its taxes and maximize the cash available to bond- and stockholders by financing its investments with close to 100 percent debt.

This result was more controversial than the first. Casual empiricism shows that firms do not finance their investments with 100 percent debt and that there are clear patterns in financing decisions. Young firms in high-growth industries, for example, tend to use less debt, and firms in stable industries with large quantities of fixed assets tend to use more debt. The ensuing study of capital structure and corporate debt has focused on explaining these patterns and explaining why corporations are not 100 percent debt financed.

Financial economists have singled out three additional factors that limit the amount of debt financing: personal taxes, bankruptcy costs, and agency costs. In a 1977 article, Miller extended his earlier work with Modigliani to show that considering corporate taxes in isolation was incorrect.

Transferring interest payments to individuals to avoid corporate taxes does not make investors any better off if they then have to pay higher personal taxes on that income than the corporation and investors would have owed if the corporation had not used debt. Miller argues that because taxes owed on capital gains are (at many points in our history) lower than taxes owed on dividend and interest income, the firm might lower the total tax bill paid by the corporation and investor combined by not issuing debt. Moreover, taxes owed on capital gains can be deferred until the realization of those gains, further lowering the effective tax rate on capital gains.

The important thrust of Miller's argument is that one must look at the interaction of both corporate and personal taxes to determine the optimal level of corporate debt. Miller showed that because of this interaction, there is an optimal level of debt (less than 100 percent) for the economy as a whole. That said, however, he also showed that, for any given firm within the economy, the level of debt is again irrelevant as long as the economy-wide average is at the optimal level.

Financial distress or bankruptcy costs may also keep firms from loading up on debt. These financial distress costs take two forms—explicit and implicit. Explicit financial distress costs include the payments made to lawyers, accountants, and so on in filing for Chapter 11 protection from creditors or in liquidation of the firm. These costs can represent a significant portion of corporate assets. Corporations must also consider the indirect costs of bankruptcy. These include the costs of low inventories, higher costs of inputs from suppliers who fear the company might not pay its bills next month, and the loss of customers who desire a long-term relationship with the firm. The reluctance of travelers to buy airplane tickets from airlines in financial distress or Chapter 11 certainly illustrates these indirect costs.

The costs of financial distress are deadweight losses to the investors of the firm: they reduce the cash flows that will eventually be paid to the bondholders and stockholders. Clearly, investors would prefer that firms stay out of financial distress so that these losses are not incurred. As the firm takes on more and more debt, however, the probability of bankruptcy increases. The chance that the firm will not be able to meet interest payments in any given year and will be forced into default goes up as the amount of debt and corresponding interest increases. These costs prevent firms from maintaining exceptionally high levels of debt.

A third factor limiting the use of debt is "agency costs." Michael Jensen and William Meckling, in a 1976 article, noted differences between the firm that is 100 percent manager owned and one where the equity is owned partially by managers and partially by outsiders. The managers, in the latter case, act as agents for the outside shareholders. Agents should run the firm to maximize its value. But Jensen and Meckling recognize that managers may not be perfect agents and that they may make some decisions in their own interests rather than those of shareholders.

The concept of agency costs is readily applied to shareholder-bondholder relations also. The shareholders, through the managers, have the right to make most decisions about how to run the firm. The firm owes the bondholders fixed payments equal to the amount of money loaned to the firm and the interest payments going along with those payments. Shareholders may adopt policies that benefit themselves at the expense of the bondholders. The possibility for such self-serving behavior is strongest when it is not clear that the firm will have sufficient cash flow to cover its interest and principal loan payments.

The most obvious action shareholders might take to benefit themselves is to pay out all of the firm's assets as dividends to themselves, leaving an empty shell for the bondholders to claim when the firm is then unable to repay its debt. Shareholders might also follow more subtle strategies. One has been called ''risk shifting.'' A football analogy illustrates the risk-shifting concept. Woody Hayes, the legendary Ohio State University football coach known for grinding out yardage on the ground, used to say that three things can happen when you pass the ball, and two of them are bad. His philosophy is sound in a close game; in that case it is best to play conservatively and avoid the risk of incompletion or interception. But if you're down by three touchdowns in the fourth quarter, a conservative strategy will not get you back into the game quickly. Instead, you should throw a bomb—a long pass. True, the ball might be intercepted or fall incomplete, but if you were going to lose anyway, the downside is not that bad. On the upside is the chance of a big payoff—a touchdown.

How does this relate to shareholders and bondholders? If it looks as if the firm will not be able to cover its obligations and thus the equity claim is worthless, shareholders may throw the bomb, i.e., take on risky projects that have big payoffs but high probability of failure. If the project does fail, bondholders lose, but the shareholders are no worse off since their claims were worthless anyway. But if the project succeeds, the shareholders will be the major beneficiaries.

A third strategy that may be costly to bondholders is underinvestment on the part of stockholders. If the firm is close to being unable to meet its obligations to bondholders, shareholders may not be willing to put more equity into the firm to fund money-making projects. The reason is that any profits from the new projects are likely to go to bondholders rather than being returned to stockholders. While bondholders would be better off if the projects were undertaken, stockholders will not be willing to pay for them.

All three strategies—paying out large dividends, risk shifting, and underinvestment—are more likely the more indebted is the firm. Lenders know this. Therefore, those who organize the firm, wanting to attract lenders, rationally limit the debt.

Bond covenants exist to restrict these games that shareholders might play, but bond contracts cannot restrict against all eventualities. An interesting development of the eighties, however, was the development of the ''poison put.'' In reaction to the large leveraged buyouts of the eighties, many companies began to introduce these poison puts to protect bondholders in the event of a leveraged transaction. Bondholders generally have the right to "put" the bonds to the company and have them repurchased at face value or plus some small premium if the company takes on a lot of new debt that reduces the chance that the current bondholders will be paid off. These recent developments illustrate the dynamic nature of corporate finance.

There is no crystal ball to predict whether the increased levels of corporate debt of the eighties will be maintained. When junk bond king Michael Milken was convicted on charges of security-market manipulation, many feared that the absence of the man who had provided much of the important liquidity in the junk bond market would lead to lower levels of corporate debt. Recent news, however, suggests that the junk-bond market is reviving and other investment banking firms are providing the much-needed markets for these securities. The U.S. tax code still encourages the use of large amounts of debt, though the tendency to high debt is counterbalanced by bankruptcy and agency costs. Whether firms do have too much leverage and whether we are facing a decade of bankruptcy are questions that can be answered only in time. If there has been an "overleveraging" of corporate America and investors come to believe that corporate debt is too high, they will demand higher and higher interest rates until corporations can no longer afford to issue debt. In this way any overleveraging in an unregulated market will be self-correcting.

—Annette Poulsen

Biography: Annette Poulsen is an associate professor of finance at the University of Georgia. She was formerly acting chief economist at the Securities and Exchange Commission.

Further Reading

Jensen, Michael, and William Meckling. "Theory of the Firm: Managerial Behavior, Agency Costs and Ownership Structure." *Journal of Financial Economics* 3 (October 1976): 305–60.

Lehn, Kenneth, and Annette Poulsen. "Contractual Resolution of Bondholder-Stockholder Conflicts in Leveraged Buyouts." *Journal of Law and Economics* 34 (October 1991): 645–73.

Miller, Merton. "Debt and Taxes." *Journal of Finance* 32 (May 1977): 261–76.

———. "Leverage." *Journal of Finance* 46 (June 1991): 479–88.

Modigliani, Franco, and Merton Miller. "The Cost of Capital, Corporation Finance and the Theory of Investment." *American Economic Review* 48 (June 1958): 261–97.

———. "Corporate Income Taxes and the Cost of Capital: A Correction." *American Economic Review* 53 (June 1963): 433–43.

Warner, Jerold B. "Bankruptcy Costs: Some Evidence." *Journal of Finance* 32 (May 1977): 337–48.

Corporations

Robert Hessen

■ Corporations are easy to create but hard to understand. Because corporations arose as an alternative to partnerships, they can best be understood by comparing these competing organizational structures.

The presumption of partnership is that the investors will directly manage their own money, rather than entrusting that task to others. Partners are "mutual agents," meaning that each is able to sign contracts that are binding on all the others. Such an arrangement is unsuited for strangers or those who harbor suspicions about each other's integrity or business acumen. Hence the transfer of partnership interests is subject to restrictions.

In a corporation, by contrast, the presumption is that the shareholders will not personally manage their money. Instead, a corporation is managed by directors and officers who need not be investors. Because managerial authority is concentrated in the hands of directors and officers, shares are freely transferable unless otherwise agreed. They can be sold or given to anyone without placing other investors at the mercy of a new owner's poor judgment. The splitting of management and ownership into two distinct functions is the salient corporate feature.

To differentiate it from a partnership, a corporation should be defined as a legal and contractual mechanism for creating and operating a business for profit, using capital from investors that will be managed on their behalf by directors and officers. To lawyers, however, the classic definition is Chief Justice John Marshall's 1819 remark that "a corporation is an artificial being, invisible, intangible, and existing only in contemplation of law." But Marshall's definition is useless because it is a metaphor; it makes a corporation a judicial hallucination.

Recent writers who have tried to recast Marshall's metaphor into a literal definition say that a corporation is an entity (or a fictitious legal person or an artificial legal being) that exists independent of its owners. The entity notion is metaphorical too and violates Occam's Razor, the scientific principle that explanations should be concise and literal.

Attempts by economists to define corporations have been equally unsatisfactory. In 1917 Joseph S. Davis wrote: "A corporation [is] a group of individuals authorized by law to act as a unit." This definition is defective because it also fits partnerships and labor unions, which are not corporations. A contemporary economist, Jonathan Hughes, says that a corporation is a "multiple partnership" and that "the privilege of incorporation is the gift of the state to collective business ventures." Another, Robert Heilbroner, says a corporation is "an entity created by the state," granted a charter that enables it to exist "in its own right as a 'person' created by law."

But charters enacted by state legislatures

563

literally ceased to exist in the midnineteenth century. The actual procedure for creating a corporation consists of filing a registration document with a state official (like recording the use of a fictitious business name), and the state's role is purely formal and automatic. Moreover, to call incorporation a "privilege" implies that individuals have no right to create a corporation. But why is governmental permission needed? Who would be wronged if businesses adopted corporate features by contract? Whose rights would be violated if a firm declared itself to be a unit for the purposes of suing and being sued, holding and conveying title to property, or that it would continue in existence despite the death or withdrawal of its officers or investors, that its shares are freely transferable, or if it asserted limited liability for its debt obligations? (Liability for torts is a separate issue; see Hessen, pp. 18–21.) If potential creditors find any of these features objectionable, they can negotiate to exclude or modify them.

Economists invariably declare limited liability to be the crucial corporate feature. According to this view the corporation, as an entity, contracts debts in "its" own name, not "theirs" (the shareholders), so they are not responsible for its debts. But there is no need for such mental gymnastics because limited liability actually involves an implied contract between shareholders and outside creditors. By incorporating (that is, complying with the registration procedure prescribed by state law) and then by using the symbols "Inc." or "Corp.," shareholders are warning potential creditors that they do not accept unlimited personal liability, that creditors must look only to the corporation's assets (if any) for satisfaction of their claims. This process, known as "constructive notice," offers an easy means of economizing on transactions costs. It is an alternative to negotiating explicit limited-liability contracts with each creditor.

Creditors, however, are not obligated to accept limited liability. As Professor Bayless Manning observes; "As a part of the bargain negotiated when the corporation incurs the indebtedness, the creditor may, of course, succeed in extracting from a shareholder (or someone else who wants to see the loan go through) an outside pledge agreement, guaranty, endorsement, or the like that will have the effect of subjecting non-corporate assets to the creditor's claim against the corporation." This familiar pattern explains why limited liability is likely to be a mirage or delusion for a new, untested business, and thus also explains why some enterprises are not incorporated despite the ease of creating a corporation.

Another textbook myth is that limited liability explains why corporations were able to attract vast amounts of capital from nineteenth-century investors to carry out America's industrialization. In fact, the industrial revolution was carried out chiefly by partnerships and unincorporated joint stock companies, rarely by corporations. The chief sources of capital for the early New England textile corporations were the founders' personal savings, money borrowed from banks, the proceeds from state-approved lotteries, and the sale of bonds and debentures.

Even in the late nineteenth century, none of the giant industrial corporations drew equity capital from the general investment public. They were privately held and drew primarily on retained earnings for expansion. (The largest enterprise, Carnegie Brothers, was organized as a Limited Partnership Association in the Commonwealth of Pennsylvania, a status that did not inhibit its ability to own properties and sell steel in other states.)

External financing, through the sale of common stock, was nearly impossible in the nineteenth century because of asymmetrical information—that is, the inability of outside investors to gauge which firms were likely to earn a profit, and thus to calculate what would be a reasonable price to pay for shares. Instead, founders of corporations often gave away shares as a bonus to those who bought bonds, which were less risky because they carried underlying collateral, a fixed date of redemption, and a fixed rate of return. Occasionally, wealthy local residents bought shares, not primarily as investments for profit, but rather as a public-spirited gesture to foster economic growth in a town or region. The idea that limited liability would have been sufficient to entice outside investors to buy common stock is counterintuitive. The assurance that you could lose only your total investment is hardly a persuasive sales pitch.

No logical or moral necessity links partnerships with unlimited liability or corporations with limited liability. Legal rules do not suddenly spring into existence full grown; instead, they arise in a particular historical context. Unlimited liability for partners dates back to medieval Italy, when partnerships were family based, when personal and business funds were intermingled, and when family honor required payment of debts owed to creditors, even if

it meant that the whole debt would be paid by one or two partners instead of being shared proportionally among them all.

Well into the twentieth century, American judges ignored the historical circumstances in which unlimited liability became the custom and later the legal rule. Hence they repeatedly rejected contractual attempts by partners to limit their liability. Only near midcentury did state legislatures grudgingly begin enacting "close corporation" statutes for businesses that would be organized as partnerships if courts were willing to recognize the contractual nature of limited liability. These quasi-corporations have nearly nothing in common with corporations financed by outside investors and run by professional managers.

Any firm, regardless of size, can be structured as a corporation, a partnership, a limited partnership, or even one of the rarely used forms, a business trust or an unincorporated joint stock company. Despite textbook claims to the contrary, partnerships are not necessarily small scale or short-lived; they need not cease to exist when a general partner dies or withdraws. Features that are automatic or inherent in a corporation—continuity of existence, hierarchy of authority, freely transferable shares—are optional for a partnership or any other organizational form. The only exceptions arise if government restricts or forbids freedom of contract (such as the rule that forbids limited liability for general partners).

As noted, the distinctive feature of corporations is that investment and management are split into two functions. Critics call this phenomenon a "separation of ownership from control." The most influential indictment of this separation was presented in *The*

Modern Corporation and Private Property, written in 1932 by Adolf A. Berle, Jr., and Gardiner C. Means. Corporate officers, they claimed, had usurped authority, aided and abetted by directors who should have been the shareholders' agents and protectors.

But Berle and Means' criticism overlooked how corporations were formed. The "Fortune 500" corporations were not born as giants. Initially, each was the creation of one or a few people who were the prime movers and promoters of the business and almost always the principal source of its original capital. They were able to "go public"—sell shares to outsiders to raise additional equity—only when they could persuade underwriters and investors that they could put new money to work at a profit.

If these firms had initially been partnerships, then the general partners could have accepted outside investors as limited partners without running any risk of losing or diluting their control over decision making. (By law, limited partners cannot participate in management or exercise any voice or vote, or else they forfeit their claim to limited liability.) A far different situation applies to corporations. Shareholders receive voting rights to elect the board of directors, and the directors, in turn, elect the officers. Conceivably, new shareholders could play an active role in managing these corporations. But, in fact, this happens only rarely.

When a corporation is created, its officers, directors, and shareholders usually are the same people. They elect themselves or their nominees to the board of directors and then elect themselves as corporate officers.

When the corporation later goes public, the founders accept the possibility of a dilution of control because they value the additional capital and because they expect to continue to control a majority of votes on the board and thus to direct the company's future policy and growth.

That the board of directors is dominated by "insiders" makes sense. The founders are the first directors; later, their places on the board are filled by the executives they groomed to succeed them. This arrangement does not injure new shareholders. As outside investors they buy shares of common stock because they discover corporations whose record of performance indicates a competent managerial system. They do not want to interfere with it or dismantle it; on the contrary, they willingly entrust their savings to it. They know that the best safeguard for their investments, if they become dissatisfied with the company's performance, is their ability to sell instantly their shares of a publicly traded corporation.

Berle and Means challenged the legitimacy of giant corporations when they charged that corporate officers had seized or usurped control from the owners—the shareholders. But their underlying premise was wrong. In reality, investors make choices along a risk-reward continuum. Bondholders are the most risk-averse; then come those who buy the intermediate-risk, nonvoting securities (debentures, convertible bonds, and preferred shares); and then the least risk-averse investors, those who buy common shares and stand to gain (or lose) the most.

Just as one may assume that investors know the difference between being a general partner and a limited partner, so too they know that shareholders in a publicly traded corporation are the counterparts of limited partners, trust beneficiaries, those who make passbook deposits in a bank, or those who buy shares in a mutual fund. All hope to make money on their savings as a sideline to their regular sources of income.

To look askance at executives who supply little or none of the corporation's capital, as many of the corporation's critics do, is really to condemn the division of labor and specialization of function. Corporate officers operate businesses whose capital requirements far exceed their personal saving or the amounts they would be willing or able to borrow. Their distinctive contribution to the enterprise is knowledge of production, marketing, and finance, administrative ability in building and sustaining a business, in directing its growth, and in leading its response to unforeseen problems and challenges. But specialization—capital supplied by investors and management supplied by executives—should be unobjectionable as long as everyone's participation is voluntary.

Another technique used by critics to undermine the legitimacy of giant corporations is to equate them to government institutions and then to find them woefully deficient in living up to democratic norms (voting rights are based on number of shares owned, rather than one vote per person, for example). Thus shareholders are renamed "citizens," the board of directors is "the legislature," and the officers are "the executive branch." They call the articles of incorporation a "constitution," the bylaws "private statutes," and merger agreements "treaties."

But the analogy, however ingenious, is defective. It cannot encompass all the major groups within the corporation. If shareholders are called citizens or voters, what are other suppliers of capital called? Are bondholders "resident aliens" because they cannot vote? And are those who buy convertible debentures "citizens in training" until they acquire voting rights? A belabored analogy cannot justify equating business and government.

Those who cannot distinguish between a government and a giant corporation are also unable to appreciate the significance of the fact that millions of people freely choose to invest their savings in the shares of publicly traded corporations. It is farfetched to believe that shareholders are being victimized—denied the control over corporate affairs that they expected to exercise, or being shortchanged on dividends—and yet still retain their shares and buy new shares or bid up the price of existing shares. If shareholders were victims, corporations could not possibly raise additional capital through new stock offerings. Yet they do so frequently.

Particular corporations can be mismanaged. They are sometimes too large or too diversified to operate efficiently, too slow to innovate, overloaded with debt, top-heavy with high-salaried executives, or too slow to respond to challenges from domestic or foreign competitors. But this does not invalidate corporations as a class. Whatever the shortcomings of particular companies or whole industries, corporations are a superb matchmaking mechanism to bring savers (investors) and borrowers (workers and managers) together for their mutual benefit.

To appreciate the achievement of corporations, one has only to consider what the state of technology would be if workers or managers had to supply their own capital, or if industrialization were carried out under government auspices, using capital that was taxed or expropriated.

—**Robert Hessen**

Biography: Robert Hessen is a senior research fellow at the Hoover Institution.

Further Reading

Bromberg, Alan R. *Crane and Bromberg on Partnership.* 1968.
Conard, Alfred F. *Corporations in Perspective.* 1976.
Easterbrook, Frank, and Daniel Fischel. *The Economic Structure of Corporate Law.* 1991.
Hessen, Robert. *In Defense of the Corporation.* 1979.
Hovenkamp, Herbert. *Enterprise and American Law, 1836–1937.* 1991.
Manning, Bayless. *Legal Capital.* 1977.

Efficient Capital Markets

Steven L. Jones and Jeffry M. Netter

■ Shortly after the Constitution went into effect, Secretary of the Treasury Alexander Hamilton proposed that Congress redeem at face value securities that had been issued by the states and the federal government. At the time, these securities were selling for much less than face value because people were uncertain whether they would ever be redeemed. After Hamilton's proposal was made public but before it was adopted, however, congressmen and others who knew of the redemption plan made large profits by sending their agents into the countryside to buy the securities at depressed prices before most security holders heard of the plan.

Contrast this scenario with security markets today, in which the prices of securities react very quickly to new information about their value. In fact, the market often anticipates and reacts to news before it is officially made public. For example, General Motors announced a major restructuring in December 1991, closing twenty-one factories and cutting seventy-four thousand jobs. On the day of the announcement GM's stock price fell by only 0.4 percent because the market had already incorporated expectations about the restructuring into its price. The market reacted only to the difference between the anticipated news and what was actually announced.

To an economist the difference between the market in the late 1700s and today is that today's market is more "efficient" at incorporating information into security prices. Efficient capital markets are commonly thought of as markets in which security prices fully reflect all relevant information that is available about the fundamental value of the securities. Because a security is a claim on future cash flows, this fundamental value is the present value of the future cash flows that the owner of the security expects to receive. The cash flows anticipated for stocks consist of the stream of expected dividends paid to stockholders plus the expected price of the stock when sold. In the present value calculation, future cash flows are discounted by an interest rate that is a function of the riskiness of those cash flows. The riskier the cash flows, the higher is the rate used in discounting.

Theoretically, the profit opportunities represented by the existence of "undervalued" and "overvalued" stocks motivate competitive trading by investors that moves the prices of stocks toward the present value of the future cash flows. For example, new information about the fundamental values of securities will be reflected in prices through competitive trading. Thus, the search for mispriced stocks by investment analysts and their subsequent trading make the market efficient and make prices reflect fundamental values.

Due to technological innovation and organized markets such as the New York Stock Exchange, information is now relatively cheap to obtain and process. Thus, we can see why securities markets today are more efficient than in the late 1700s. It is in this environment of relatively low-cost information and active security analysis that the theory of efficient capital markets has developed.

The study of capital market efficiency examines how much, how fast, and how accurately available information is incorporated into security prices. Financial economists often classify efficiency into three categories based on what is meant as "available information"—the weak, semistrong, and strong forms. Weak-form efficiency exists if security prices fully reflect all the information contained in the history of past prices and returns. (The return is the profit on the security calculated as a percentage of an initial price.) If capital markets are weak-form efficient, then investors cannot earn excess profits from trading rules based on past prices or returns. Therefore, stock returns are not predictable, and so-called technical analysis (analyzing patterns in past price movements) is useless.

Under semistrong-form efficiency, security prices fully reflect all public information. Thus, only traders with access to nonpublic information, such as some corporate insiders, can earn excess profits. Under weak-form efficiency, some public information about fundamentals may not yet be reflected in prices. Thus, a superior analyst can profit from trading on the discovery of, or a better interpretation of, public information. Under semistrong-form efficiency, the market reacts so quickly to the release of new information that there are no profitable trading opportunities based on public information.

Finally, under strong-form efficiency, all information—even apparent company secrets—is incorporated in security prices; thus, no investor can earn excess profit trading on public or nonpublic information.

Why does informational efficiency matter? The capital markets channel funds from savers to firms, which use the funds to finance projects. Informational efficiency is necessary if funds, allocated through the capital market, are to flow to the highest-valued projects. Shareholders want management to maximize stock prices and thus will attempt to ensure that their managements undertake only projects (decisions) that increase the value of their stock. Management compensation packages tied to stock performance are one way in which stockholders align management's interests with their own. However, maximization of stock prices can result in the capital market directing funds to the most valuable projects only if stocks are efficiently priced, in the sense of accurately reflecting the fundamental value of all future cash flows. Thus, for example, if capital markets are efficient, there is no reason to expect managements to emphasize the short run at the expense of long-term projects. Additionally, efficient capital markets make it easier for firms to raise capital because the markets determine the prices at which existing and potential security holders are willing to exchange claims on a firm's future cash flows.

A related reason for caring about efficiency is that investors who do not have the time or the resources to do extensive analysis will be more willing to invest their savings in the market if they believe the securities they trade are accurately priced. This, in turn, helps the capital market to perform its function of translating savings into productive projects. Finally, there are policy implications of evidence on market efficiency. If capital markets are efficient, then the government's role in capital markets should be very limited. If security prices do not accurately reflect fundamentals, however, there might be a case for regulating both the operation of the securities markets and the capital-allocation process itself.

A large amount of empirical research has been directed at answering whether capital markets are efficient. Most research has used stock price data, for two reasons. First, stock prices are easily available. Second, the stock market is likely to be less efficient than other securities markets (such as the bond market) because cash flows paid to stockholders are relatively uncertain, and there is no terminal payoff as in a bond. Therefore, stocks are relatively difficult to value, and evidence of stock market efficiency would be compelling evidence of efficiency in securities markets in general.

An overwhelming amount of empirical evidence shows that stock prices react quickly, in the expected direction, to the release of information. Stock prices react within ten minutes to an earnings announcement, for example. This evidence is consistent with weak and semistrong efficiency. Such evidence, however, does not show that the amount of price reaction accurately reflects fundamentals or, by extension, that security prices accurately reflect the fundamental value of the securities. Other evidence shows that corporate insiders have earned excess profits trading on inside information. This evidence means that capital markets are not strong-form efficient. Today, the empirical debate on market efficiency centers on whether future returns are predictable.

The empirical tests of capital market efficiency began even before Eugene Fama of the University of Chicago offered a theory in 1970. The early tests hypothesized that if prices fully reflected available information, if information arrives randomly, and if expected returns are constant, then stock returns from one period to the next should be statistically independent. That is, they should follow what has loosely been referred to as a "random walk." This implies that historical returns are useless for predicting future returns, which is consistent with weak-form market efficiency.

The early tests, using various statistical methods, generally conclude that the past short-horizon (daily and weekly) returns of individual stocks are economically insignificant for predicting future returns. Consequently, the joint hypothesis of market efficiency and constant expected—but not actual—returns was generally accepted. Fama later refined the definition of capital market efficiency so that prices must not only fully, but correctly, reflect all available information. This implies that the market price should be a reasonable estimate of the rationally determined fundamentals.

By the early eighties the near consensus among academics in finance that capital markets are efficient started to fade for two reasons. First, researchers found anomalies in stock returns. One anomaly was that firms with low P/E ratios (ratios of stock prices to annual earnings per share) earn higher-than-normal returns. Researchers also found so-called January and day-of-the-week effects: stocks of small firms tend to earn excess returns in January, while Monday returns tend to be low. However, these anomalies could be due to misspecification of the models used in the tests, or to institutional factors (such as the impact of taxes), rather than market inefficiency. Consequently, they represent only an indirect attack on efficiency.

A second kind of evidence was a more direct challenge to market efficiency. Robert Shiller and others argued that the aggregate stock market has been much more volatile than can be justified by actual dividend changes (which represent fundamentals). Lawrence Summers shows that this evidence may indicate that stock prices take long slow swings away from fundamental values that would not be detectable in the early short-horizon return tests.

Shiller, Summers, and others assert that a deviation of prices from fundamental values may be caused by, or persist because of, fads or other manifestations of irrational behavior. In their models, unlike in traditional financial theory, the marginal trader who moves prices may not be rational or may not trade based on fundamentals. Therefore, competition does not necessarily eliminate mispricing because the rational trader cannot be certain that prices will converge on fundamental values, especially in the short term.

Consistent with these assertions, Fama and Kenneth French and, separately, James Poterba and Summers report that long-horizon (two- to ten-year) stock index returns tend to follow what is called a mean-reverting pattern through time. That is, periods of relatively high returns tend to be followed by periods of relatively low returns and vice versa. Summers, Poterba,

and Shiller conclude from this evidence that prices often move away from their fundamentals and that markets are, therefore, inefficient. But Fama and French suggest another explanation consistent with market efficiency—that actual returns are mean reverting because rationally determined expected returns are mean reverting.

The evidence of mean reversion—and therefore predictable long-term patterns—focuses on long-horizon index or portfolio returns rather than the returns of individual stocks. There is little evidence of mean reversion in the returns of individual stocks beyond what can be attributed to transaction costs. This suggests that mean-reverting return patterns are systematic across stocks, such that the general level of expected returns may change through time depending on macroeconomic conditions. During economic declines, for example, demanders of capital may need to offer higher levels of expected return to induce individuals to save. Consequently, the new evidence of predictability in index and portfolio returns amounts to a rejection of the constant expected returns model that was implicit in definitions of weak-form efficiency. Predictability in stock market indexes alone, however, is not enough evidence to reject the more basic implication of market efficiency that the market price should be a reasonable estimate of the rationally determined fundamentals.

Fama and French provide support for their argument with evidence on dividend yields and the "default spread." (The default spread is the premium that compensates for the risk of default.) They use dividend yields as a rough measure of expected returns on stocks, and the default spread as a rough measure of expected returns on bonds. They show that both are high during periods of economic decline and low during economic booms. In addition, the common variation in expected returns across securities, explained by the dividend yield and default spread, increases from low-risk to high-risk stocks and from low-grade to high-grade bonds, respectively. This is as would be anticipated in an efficient market, where expected returns vary with economic conditions. On the other hand, this common variation in expected returns may simply indicate that mispricing is systematic. For example, high dividend yields may indicate that stocks, in general, are temporarily undervalued rather than that expected returns are relatively high. Consequently, it may never be possible to precisely determine if the stock market rationally reflects fundamental values.

The main event that gained support for the view that capital markets are inefficient was the 22 percent drop in the Dow-Jones stock index on Monday, October 19, 1987. This happened even though little news about fundamentals was released over the weekend before the crash. The crash in the United States, however, actually began the Wednesday through Friday of the week before the Monday crash (October 14 through 16), when the Standard and Poor's 500 index had fallen 10.44 percent. This decline was the largest one-, two-, or three-day drop in the market in more than forty-five years (since May 13–14, 1940, when German tanks unexpectedly broke through French armies, sealing France's fate in World War II).

Mark Mitchell and Jeffry Netter present evidence that the large decline in the U.S. market from October 14 through 16 was largely a rational reaction to an unanticipated tax proposal by the House Ways and Means Committee limiting the deductibility of interest expense on corporate debt, especially in takeovers. This decline may have triggered portfolio insurance sales on October 19 that the exchanges were not prepared to handle. This liquidity crunch may have furthered depressed the market on that day. Thus, efficient markets theory is consistent with at least part of the market decline from October 14 through October 19, 1987. It may also be that the efficiency of capital markets varies through time. For instance, lessons learned in the 1987 crash by traders, regulators, and the exchanges may have resulted in more efficient capital markets.

The debate on how well security prices reflect fundamental values remains unsettled. There is, however, overwhelming evidence that on average the initial stock price response to new information is at least in the correct direction. This means that the theory of efficient capital markets provides a useful framework for analyzing many problems.

—Steven L. Jones and Jeffry M. Netter

Biography: Steven L. Jones is a finance professor at the University of Georgia. He was formerly a senior financial analyst at Amoco Corporation. Jeffry M. Netter is a finance professor and an adjunct law professor at the University of Georgia. He was formerly a senior financial economist with the U.S. Securities and Exchange Commission.

Further Reading

Ball, Ray. "What Do We Know about Stock Market Efficiency?" In *A Reappraisal of the Efficiency of Financial Markets*, edited by Rui Guimaraes. 1989.

Brealey, Richard, and Stewart Myers. *Principles of Corporate Finance*, 4th ed., 287–314. 1991.

Elton, Edwin, and Martin Gruber. *Modern Portfolio Theory and Investment Analysis*, 399–448. 1991.

Fama, Eugene. *Foundations of Finance*. 1976.

———. "Efficient Capital Markets II." *Journal of Finance* (1991): 1575–1617.

———, and Kenneth French. "Dividend Yields and Expected Stock Returns." *Journal of Financial Economics* 22 (1988): 3–25.

Gaines, Sally. "Founding Fathers, First Inside Traders," *Chicago Tribune*, May 17, 1987, 7-1.

Grossman, Sanford. *The Informational Role of Prices*. 1989.

Mitchell, Mark, and Jeffry Netter. "Triggering the 1987 Stock Market Crash: Antitakeover Provisions in the Proposed House Ways and Means Tax Bill?" *Journal of Financial Economics* 24 (1989): 37–68.

Patell, James M., and Mark Wolfson. "The Intraday Speed of Adjustment of Stock Prices to Earnings and Dividend Announcements." *Journal of Financial Economics* 13 (1984): 223–52.

Poterba, James, and Lawrence Summers. "Mean Reversion in Stock Prices: Evidence and Implications." *Journal of Financial Economics* 22 (1988): 27–59.

Shiller, Robert. *Market Volatility*. 1989.

Summers, Lawrence. "Does the Stock Market Rationally Reflect Fundamental Values?" *Journal of Finance* 41: 591–601.

See also BONDS, FUTURES AND OPTIONS MARKETS, STOCK PRICES.

Futures and Options Markets

Gregory J. Millman

■ In the late seventies and early eighties, radical changes in the international currency system and in the way the Federal Reserve managed the nation's money supply produced unprecedented volatility in interest rates and in currency exchange rates. As market forces shook the foundations of global financial stability, businesses wrestled with heretofore unimagined challenges. Between 1980 and 1985 Caterpillar, the Peoria-based maker of heavy equipment, saw exchange-rate shifts give its main Japanese competitor a 40 percent price advantage. Meanwhile, even the soundest business borrowers faced soaring, double-digit interest rates. Investors clamored for dollars as commodity prices collapsed, taking whole nations down into insolvency and ushering in the Third World debt crisis.

Stymied financial managers turned to Chicago, where the traditional agricultural futures markets had only recently invented techniques to cope with financial uncertainty. In 1972 the Chicago Mercantile Exchange established the International Monetary Market to trade the world's first futures contracts for currency. The world's first interest-rate futures contract was introduced shortly afterward, at the Chicago Board of Trade, in 1975. In 1982, futures contracts on the Standard and Poor's 500 index began to trade at the Chicago Mercantile Exchange. These radically new tools helped businesses manage in a volatile and unpredictable new world order.

How? Futures are standardized contracts that commit parties to buy or sell goods of a specific quality at a specific price, for delivery at a specific point in the future. They are not contracts directly between buyers and sellers of goods. The farmer who sells a futures contract and commits to deliver corn in six months does not make his commitment to a specific corn buyer, but rather to the clearinghouse of the futures exchange. The clearinghouse stands between buyers and sellers and, in effect, guarantees that both buyers and sellers will receive what they have contracted for.

Thanks to the clearinghouse, the farmer does not have to be concerned about the financial stability of the buyer of the futures contract, nor does the buyer need to be concerned about the progress of any particular farmer's crop. The clearinghouse monitors the credit of buyers and sellers. New information about changes in supply and demand causes the prices of futures contracts to fluctuate, sometimes moving them up and down many times in a trading day. For example, news of drought or blight that may reduce the corn harvest, cutting future supplies, causes corn futures contracts to rise in price. Similarly, news of a rise in interest rates or a presidential illness can cause stock-index futures prices to fall as investors react to the prospect of difficult or uncertain times ahead. Every day, the clearinghouse tallies up and matches all contracts bought or sold during the trading session. Parties holding contracts that have fallen in price during the trading session must pay the clearinghouse, a sort of security deposit called "margin." When the contracts are closed out, it is the clearinghouse that pays the parties whose contracts have gained in value. Futures trading is what economists call a zero-sum game, meaning that for every winner there is someone who loses an equal amount.

Because futures contracts offer assurance of future prices and availability of goods, they provide stability in an unstable business environment. Futures have long been associated with agricultural commodities, especially grain and pork bellies, but they are now more likely to be used by bankers, airlines, and computer makers than by farmers. By the end of the eighties, financial futures accounted for three-quarters of all futures volume, almost totally supplanting the agricultural commodities contracts that had been the futures industry's raison d'etre for over a hundred years.

Obviously, the idea of hedging against an unstable financial environment has great appeal. Companies like Caterpillar now protect themselves against currency shifts by buying and selling futures contracts or similar instruments. Investors use interest-rate, bond-futures, and stock-index contracts to protect against a decline in the value of their investments, just as farmers have long used futures to protect against a drop in the price of corn or beans.

Although the underlying risks have changed, the futures market operates much as it always has, with traders standing in a ring or a pit shouting buy and sell orders at each other, competing for each fraction of a cent. Futures exchanges are private, member-owned organizations. Members buy "seats" on the exchange and, depending on the kind of seat they buy, enjoy various trading rights. Since traders deal in contracts rather than actual commodities, they may not be expert in the oil or corn or stocks that underlie their contracts. Traders consider themselves experts on market movements rather than authorities on minerals and crops. This is why financial futures were relatively easy to introduce to markets originally designed for agricultural commodity futures. Full membership in the Chicago Mercantile Exchange, to pick just one example, now entitles a trader to deal in everything from pork bellies to European Currency Units.

In the nineteenth century Chicago's trading pits offered an organized venue in which farmers and other suppliers of agricultural commodities, such as warehouse owners and brokers, could remove the risk of price fluctuations from their business plans. Farmers who planted corn in the spring had no way of knowing what the price of their crop would be when they harvested in the fall. But a farmer who planted in the spring and sold a futures contract committed to deliver his grain in the fall for a definite price. Not only did he receive cash in the spring in return for his commitment, but he also received the contract price for his crop even if the market price subsequently fell because of an unexpected glut of corn. In exchange the farmer gave up the chance to get a higher price in the event of a drought or blight, receiving the same fixed price for which he had contracted. In the latter case, if the farmer had not sold the future, he would have netted more. However, most farmers preferred not to gamble on the corn market. Farming was risky enough, thanks to uneven rainfalls and unpredictable pests, without adding the risk of changes in market prices.

Farmers thus sought to lock in a value on their crop and were willing to pay a price for certainty. They gave up the chance of very high prices in return for protection against abysmally low prices. This practice of removing risk from business plans is called hedging. As a rule of thumb, about half of the participants in the futures markets are hedgers who come to market to remove or reduce their risk.

For the market to function, however, it cannot consist only of hedgers seeking to lay off risk. There must be someone who comes to market in order to take on risk. These are the "speculators." Speculators come to market to take risk, and to make money doing it. Some speculators, against all odds, have become phenomenally wealthy by trading futures. Interestingly, even the wealthiest speculators often report having gone broke one or more times in their career. Because speculation offers the promise of astounding riches with little apparent effort, or the threat of devastating losses despite even the best efforts, it is often compared to casino gambling.

The difference between speculation in futures and casino gambling is that futures market speculation provides an important social good, namely liquidity. If it were not for the presence of speculators in the market, farmers, bankers, and business executives would have no easy and economical way to eliminate the risk of volatile prices, interest rates, and exchange rates from their business plans. Speculators, however, provide a ready and liquid market

for these risks—at a price. Speculators who are willing to assume risks for a price make it possible for others to reduce their risks. Competition among speculators also makes hedging less expensive and ensures that the effect of all available information is swiftly calculated into the market price. Weather reports, actions of central banks, political developments, and anything else that can affect supply or demand in the future affects futures prices almost immediately. This is how the futures market performs its function of "price discovery."

There seems to be no limit to the potential applications of futures market technology. The New York Mercantile Exchange (NYMEX) began to trade heating oil futures in 1978. The exchange later introduced crude oil, gasoline, and natural gas futures. Airlines, shipping companies, public transportation authorities, home-heating-oil delivery services, and major multinational oil and gas companies have all sought to hedge their price risk using these futures contracts. In 1990 the NYMEX traded over 35 million energy futures and option contracts.

Meanwhile, international stock market investors have discovered that stock-index futures, besides being useful for hedging, also are an attractive alternative to actually buying stocks. Because a stock-index future moves in tandem with the prices of the underlying stocks, it gives the same return as owning stocks. Yet the stock-index future is cheaper to buy and may be exempt from certain taxes and charges to which stock ownership is subject. Some large institutional investors prefer to buy German stock-index futures rather than German stocks for this very reason.

Because stock-index futures are easier to

trade than actual stocks, the futures prices often change before the underlying stock prices do. In the October 1987 crash, for example, prices of stock-index futures in Chicago fell before prices on the New York Stock Exchange collapsed, leading some observers to conclude that futures trading had somehow caused the stock market crash that year. In fact, investors who wanted to sell stocks could not sell quickly and efficiently on the New York Stock Exchange and therefore sold futures instead. The futures market performed its function of price discovery more rapidly than the stock market (see PROGRAM TRADING).

Futures contracts have even been enlisted in the fight against air pollution and the effort to curb runaway health insurance costs. When the Environmental Protection Agency decided to allow a market for sulfur dioxide emission allowances under the 1990 amendments to the Clean Air Act, the Chicago Board of Trade developed a futures contract for trading what might be called air pollution futures. The reason? If futures markets provide price discovery and liquidity to the market in emission allowances, companies can decide on the basis of straightforward economics whether it makes sense to reduce their own emissions of sulfur dioxide and sell their emission allowance to others, or instead to sustain their current emission levels and purchase emission allowances from others.

Without a futures market it would be difficult to know whether a price offered or demanded for emissions allowances is high or low. But hedgers and speculators bidding in an open futures market will cause quick discovery of the true price, the equilibrium point at which buyers and sellers are both equally willing to transact. Similar reasoning led to the development of health insurance futures and options contracts, also at the Chicago Board of Trade. This contract may provide businesses, insurers, and other participants in the health care market with an effective mechanism to hedge themselves against the uncertain rise and fall of health insurance prices.

Options are one of the most important outgrowths of the futures market. Whereas a futures contract commits one party to deliver, and another to pay for, a particular good at a particular future date, an option contract gives the holder the right, but not the obligation, to buy or sell. Options are attractive to hedgers because they protect against loss in value but do not require the hedger to sacrifice potential gains. Most exchanges that trade futures also trade options on futures.

There are other types of options as well. In 1973 the Chicago Board of Trade established the Chicago Board Options Exchange to trade options on stocks. The Philadelphia Stock Exchange has a thriving business on currency options.

There is also a large, so-called over-the-counter (OTC) market in options. Participants in the OTC market include banks, investment banks, insurance companies, large corporations, and other parties. OTC options differ from exchange-traded options. Whereas exchange-traded options are standardized contracts, OTC options are usually tailored to a particular risk. If a corporation wants to hedge a stream of foreign currency revenue for five years, but exchange-traded options are available only out to six months, the corporation can use the OTC market. An insurance company or bank can design and price a five-year option on the currency in question, giving the company the right to buy or sell at a particular price during the five-year period.

Although users of the OTC options market do not access the futures exchange directly, the prices discovered on the futures exchanges are important data for determining the prices of OTC options. The liquidity and price discovery elements of futures help to keep the OTC market from getting far out of line with the futures market. When futures markets do not exist or cannot be used, hedgers pay steeply for the protection they seek.

—Gregory J. Millman

Biography: Gregory J. Millman is a journalist who writes about financial markets for *Barron's, Corporate Finance, Institutional Investor, Journal of Applied Corporate Finance,* and other financial journals. In 1992 he was awarded a fellowship by the Alicia Patterson Foundation to research and write about financial futures and options markets.

Further Reading

Ahn, Mark J. and William D. Falloon. *Strategic Risk Management.* 1991.
Miller, Merton H. *Financial Innovations and Market Volatility.* 1991.
Millman, Gregory J. *The Floating Battlefield: Corporate Strategies in the Currency Wars.* 1990.
Smith, Clifford W., Jr., and Charles W. Smithson. *The Handbook of Financial Engineering.* 1990.

Insider Trading

David D. Haddock

■ Since the depths of the Great Depression, the Securities and Exchange Commission (SEC) has tried to prevent insider trading in U.S. securities markets. Insiders—a firm's principal owners, directors, and management, as well as its lawyers, accountants, and similar fiduciaries—routinely possess information that is unavailable to the general public. Because some of that information will affect the prices of the firm's securities when it becomes public, insiders can profit by buying or selling in advance. Even before the thirties, insiders were liable under the common law if they fraudulently misled uninformed traders into accepting inappropriate prices. But the Securities Exchange Act of 1934 went further by forbidding insiders from even profiting passively from superior information.

One of the most famous instances of insider trading was Charles F. Fogarty's purchase of Texas Gulf Sulphur shares during 1963 and 1964. Fogarty, an executive vice president of Texas Gulf, knew that the company had discovered a rich mineral lode in Ontario that it could not publicize before concluding leases for mineral rights. In the meantime Fogarty purchased 3,100 Texas Gulf shares and earned \$125,000 to \$150,000 (in 1991 dollars).

The basic argument against insider trading is that insiders should not be permitted to earn such sums at the expense of uninformed traders. Yet in almost all other markets where information is important, insider trading is well established and widely accepted. For example, mineral leases are routinely bought by those better able than the sellers to evaluate a site's potential, as Texas Gulf Sulphur's behavior exemplified. Cattle buyers rely on superior estimates of what packers will pay when negotiating with ranchers. And so it goes, in markets for art, for real estate, for professional athletes—indeed in practically every market with substantial variations in prices. In all those markets a few buyers routinely profit from knowledge that most sellers do not possess, and a few sellers profit from knowledge that most buyers do not possess. Commentators rarely cast aspersions on such traders' ethics or contend that their transactions should be regulated because of the asymmetry in information. Why should securities markets be treated differently?

One reason frequently cited by policymakers and commentators is that insider trading undermines public confidence in the securities markets. If people fear that insiders will regularly profit at their expense, they will not be nearly as willing to invest. A similar argument is that companies prefer that their securities trade in "thick" markets—that is, markets with many traders, substantial capital available, and frequent opportunities to trade at readily observable prices. Efficient securities markets, it is argued, require a "level informational playing field" to avoid frightening away speculators, who contribute to securities market liquidity, and investors, who could invest their savings in markets with less risk of insider predation. Working on such a premise, over the last quarter-century the SEC has brought new and ever more stringent enforcement initiatives against insider trading.

Related to this argument is the harm that insider trading causes for "specialists." A specialist is someone whom the stock exchange appoints to ensure that a buyer of a particular security listed by the exchange can readily find a seller, and vice versa. These specialists must buy from or sell to any trader whose order cannot be offset against other orders arriving simultaneously. If, for example, a buyer wants a hundred shares of IBM, but no one wants to sell at that moment, the IBM specialist sells from his inventory of IBM stock. The specialist charges a "bid-ask spread" to cover the cost. A bid-ask spread implies that a slightly higher price is asked from someone who wishes to purchase a security than will be contemporaneously offered to someone who wishes to sell.

An inside trader, however, will sell securities to the specialist when only he knows that the securities will soon be worth less. After the price has fallen, the insider is free to repurchase the securities from the specialist for the lower price. If that occurs, the specialist loses money. If insider trading recurs, the security's specialist cannot continue indefinitely without recouping the funds being lost to informed traders. Therefore, specialists will insist on larger bid-ask spreads if insider trading is permitted and occurs often.

To investors, the bid-ask spread is a trading cost. If insider trading increased the spread but did nothing else, it would decrease a security's attractiveness relative to certificates of deposit, government bonds, and other assets. Raising new capital would, thus, be more costly for a firm whose securities were subjected to repeated insider trading. Hence, all else being equal, insider trading makes it harder for a firm to raise money when opportunities to undertake new projects arise.

But insider trading might also have offsetting benefits. Insider trading can be profitable only if securities prices move. Therefore, insiders hoping to trade on inside information may try to get the price to move by cutting the company's costs, seeking new products, and so on. While such actions benefit the insider, they also benefit the firm's security holders as a group.

Of course, insiders can also profit by borrowing and then selling securities when the price is apt to fall. Some argue that insider trading is more likely to harm companies because damage is easier to inflict. That argument, in turn, has been countered; major actions by a company require teams, not individuals. Efforts to damage a firm would likely be brought to the attention of higher management or shareholders by some ambitious team member looking to capitalize on the resulting gratitude. Unfortunately, no evidence has been presented to help resolve this debate.

A number of financial economists and law professors take the position that insider trading ought to be legal. They base their case on the proposition that insider trading makes the stock market more efficient. Presumably, the inside information will come out at some point. Otherwise, the insider would have no incentive to trade on the information. If insider trading was legal, this group argues, insiders would bid the prices of stocks up or down in advance of the information being released. The result is that the price would more fully reflect all information—both public and confidential—about a company at any given time.

Even if insider trading sometimes creates more harm than good, rules against it could be contractual (e.g., "employees of our company who trade on material, nonpublic information forfeit their pension rights") rather than mandated by government. Because the circumstances facing companies differ, insider trading might be advantageous for some companies and not for others. And if so, would it not be sensible to permit firms to "opt out" of insider trading enforcement? Interestingly, Texas Gulf insider Charles Fogarty was subsequently elevated to chief executive officer of his company. Moreover, following Fogarty's death, another insider, who was also known to have traded on the same information, was elevated to replace him. Clearly, Texas Gulf's board of directors and shareholders must not have found the trading completely reprehensible. Yet the law makes no provision for opting out, implicitly assuming that insider trading injures all companies. Policymakers never seriously ask who is harmed, who is helped (other than the insiders), and by how much.

Of course, insider trading can injure a firm if the trading elevates prices that the firm itself has to pay. For example, if Fogarty had purchased Ontario mineral rights before Texas Gulf Sulphur agents could acquire them, Texas Gulf would have been injured. Similarly, if Alpha, Inc., quietly tries to acquire control of Gamma Corp.,

unauthorized purchases of Gamma securities by Alpha's president could drive up Gamma's share price, thus making the acquisition more costly. But most litigated cases reflect trading in competition with ordinary participants in the securities markets, not with the insider's own firm.

Considered narrowly, most investors are on average neither hurt nor helped by insider trading because most investors are "time-function traders." That is, they buy securities (and other assets) when their income exceeds their expenditures, and sell securities when an emergency, the period of their life, or a propitious moment to initiate some project necessitates expenditures that exceed income. Hence, time-function traders do not try to "beat the market." Since statistical examinations show that insider trading affects securities prices even before nonpublic information is released, time-function traders can be harmed or helped by insiders. Suppose that an insider's trading has elevated a security price. Those time-function traders who, by chance, want to buy that security must pay a higher price for it, one closer to the price it will reach when the insider's information becomes public. But those time-function traders who chance to sell unwittingly realize a higher price as a result of the insider's action. Consequently, some time-function traders have lost, but others have gained. Over a time-function trader's lifetime, the reasonable expectation would be to break even.

Besides specialists the one group systematically injured by insider trading are "price-function traders"—those who trade securities because they believe the present price is inappropriate. If an insider secretly buys securities, the result is an increase in price. Because some price-function traders believe that the security is now overpriced, they sell, but soon regret their action. Few people, however, have the expertise to realize trading profits repeatedly. Those who "play the market" without such expertise soon lose their capital. Thus, few active investors—even the professionals who manage pension funds—are properly considered price-function traders.

Sometimes, through luck or effort, individuals with no formal relationship with a firm discover important nonpublic information about it. Like true insiders they can profit by trading prior to public awareness of the information. A peculiar feature of insider trading law is that informed trading is treated more leniently if the trader is such a "quasi insider" (often a market professional who holds a seat on an organized securities exchange) than if the trader is a true insider.

For example, in 1975 and 1976 Vincent Chiarella netted more than $60,000 (1991 dollars) by trading on important nonpublic information about firms other than his employer, a financial printing firm. Even though clients tried to mask sensitive information in documents that Chiarella's employer was hired to print, Chiarella was often able to "crack the code." By buying from uninformed individuals, Chiarella became a successful trader. Yet the Supreme Court ruled that Chiarella did not violate the insider trading regulations because he did not work for—and thus was not an insider of—any firm whose inside information he had discovered.

This decision is puzzling. Whether the benefits to companies from true insider trading outweigh the costs, at least there are potential benefits. Quasi-insider trading, in contrast, imposes many of the same costs on firms with no obvious benefits. Although there has been pressure to strengthen the rules against quasi insiders, the legal constraints on them are still not as stringent as those on true insiders.

One matter is clear. Because insider trading has little effect on time-function traders, they do not participate in the debate. Most proponents of stronger insider-trading laws are price-function traders—arbitragers, floor traders, investment bankers, and others who earn a living from the securities exchanges. Insiders are such traders' most potent competitors for trading profits from new information. Price-function traders benefit from laws curtailing insider trading whether or not firms, and hence common investors, do also.

Far from the clearly settled moral issue that naïve media pieces, movies, and novels would have it be, both the theory and the evidence of insider trading remain primitive and equivocal. Present rhetoric—and law—have far outrun present understanding.

—**David D. Haddock**

Biography: David D. Haddock, who holds a Ph.D. in economics from the University of Chicago, is a professor of law at Northwestern University, where he teaches corporation law. He previously worked in the Office of the General Counsel of the Ford Motor Company, where he was chief of economic studies for antitrust matters.

Further Reading

Benston, George J., and Robert L. Hagerman. ''Determinants of Bid-Ask Spreads in the Over-the Counter Market.'' *Journal of Financial Economics* 1 (1974): 353–64.

Carlton, Dennis W., and Daniel R. Fischel. ''The Regulation of Insider Trading.'' *Stanford Law Review* 35 (1983): 857–95.

Clark, Robert Charles. ''Insider Trading.'' In Clark. *Corporate Law*. 1986.

Dooley, Michael. ''Enforcement of Insider Trading Restrictions.'' *Virginia Law Review* 66 (1980): 1–83.

Easterbrook, Frank H. ''Insider Trading, Secret Agents, Evidentiary Privileges, and the Production of Information.'' *Supreme Court Review* (1981): 309–65.

———, and Daniel R. Fischel. ''Property Rights, Legal Wrongs in Insider Trading.'' *The American Enterprise* (October/September 1990): 57–63.

Fishman, Michael J., and Kathleen M. Hagerty, ''Insider Trading and the Efficiency of Stock Prices.'' *Rand Journal of Economics* 23 (Spring 1992): 106–22.

Haddock, David D., and Jonathan R. Macey. ''Regulation on Demand: A Private Interest Model, with an Application to Insider Trading Regulation.'' *Journal of Law and Economics* 30 (1987): 311–52.

Leland, Hayne E. ''Insider Trading: Should It Be Prohibited?'' *Journal of Political Economy* 100 (August 1992): 859–87.

Macey, Jonathan R. ''From Fairness to Contract: The New Directions of the Rules against Insider Trading.'' *Hofstra Law Review* 13 (1984): 9–64.

Manne, Henry G. *Insider Trading and the Stock Market*. 1966.

Seyhun, H. Nejat. ''Insiders' Profits, Costs of Trading, and Market Efficiency.'' *Journal of Financial Economics* 16 (1986): 189–212.

Interest

Paul Heyne

■ Interest is the price people pay to have resources now rather than later. Resources, of course, can be anything from college tuition to a big-screen TV. Interest is conventionally expressed as a percentage rate for a period of one year. If borrowers (those who want resources now) can obtain the resources from lenders (those who are willing to surrender current control) on the condition that they return 103 percent of the resources one year later, then the interest rate is 3 percent.

The standard procedure for calculating compound interest, under which the interest at the end of each year is added to the principal (the amount borrowed), requires borrowers who want to retain command for two years to repay 106.09 percent of the principal, assuming a 3 percent annual rate of interest. The formula for determining the amount to which the sum to be repaid will grow under compound interest is

$$P(1 + r)^n,$$

where P is the principal, r is the annual interest rate, and n is the number of years for which the principal is borrowed.

Compound interest is an incredibly powerful force. Just how powerful can be seen in the following example. If Thomas Jefferson had invested $10 at 3 percent compound interest to celebrate the signing of the Declaration of Independence, his heirs would have been entitled to almost $3,700 on the day in 1976 when the United States celebrated its two hundredth anniversary. At 6 percent compound interest, Mr. Jefferson's $10 investment would have grown to $1,150,000, or 311 times as much.

An immediate implication is that a quantity of resources available only at a future date has less value today (the present value) than the same quantity of resources available now. The difference in value is determined by the prevailing interest rate. If the annual rate of interest is 3 percent, 100 units of a resource to be received one year from now is equivalent in value to approximately 97.09 units at this time. The formula for determining the present value of future amounts (a process that is called discounting) is derived from the same formula for determining the amount to which present sums will grow in the future:

$$\text{Present value} = F/(1 + r)^n,$$

where F is the future amount and r and n are again the interest rate and the number of years, respectively.

The interest rate enters at least implicitly into all economic decisions, because economic decisions are made by comparing expected future benefits to costs. The only way to make the value of future benefits or costs comparable to one another is to discount them by their "temporal distance" from the present, using the relevant interest rate. The greater this temporal distance (that is, the further into the future the benefit or cost is), the smaller is the discounted, or present, value.

Interest rates quoted by lenders usually include much more than "pure" interest. To persuade a lender to surrender current control of resources, the borrower will have to pay, in addition to interest, an amount that compensates the lender for any costs incurred in arranging the transaction, usually including some kind of insurance premium against the risk of default by the borrower. Someone without an established credit rating who applies for an unsecured loan will typically be required to pay "interest" at an annual rate that is several times the prevailing rate of pure interest.

The interest rate is determined by demand and supply: the demand for present control of resources by those who do not have it, and the supply from those who do have control and are willing to surrender it for a price. The question of exactly why demand and supply yield a positive rate of interest is one of the most fiercely disputed questions in the history of economic theory. It is enough to point out that when an individual acquires present command of resources, his or her set of available opportunities expands. In short, the present command of resources is something that people want. Therefore, those who get it are willing to pay for it, and those who give it up insist that they be compensated for doing so.

The fact that loans are usually made by means of money leads to the mistaken belief that interest is a payment for the use of money. Money is usually what is lent because money offers a general command over resources. But interest also would exist in a pure barter economy where money was not used.

Calling interest "the price of money" mistakenly implies that the interest rate could be brought down by making more money available, in the same way that the price of wheat can be brought down by making more wheat available. This issue could get us into a discussion of monetary theory and policy. It is, however, sufficient to note that increasing the amount of money available tends to lower the purchasing power of money because it causes inflation. In countries that allow their money supplies to grow rapidly, interest rates typically rise because people come to expect inflation. When inflation is anticipated, lenders insist upon being compensated for the expected decline in the value of money over the period of the loan, and borrowers, expecting to make repayment in money of depreciated value, are willing to pay the compensation.

The real interest rate on money loans will be the stated (or nominal) rate minus the anticipated rate of inflation. In countries that are experiencing rapid growth in the amount of money available, interest rates will be very high. But these will be not be high real interest rates. Instead, they will be high nominal interest rates. If expected inflation is 10 percent, for example, and if the real interest rate is 5 percent, the nominal interest rate is 15 percent. But someone who lends money at 15 percent for a year will not be repaid with 15 percent more resources at the end of the year. Rather, the lender will be repaid with 15 percent more money and will be able to use that money to buy only 5 percent more resources.

The real interest rate, by determining the relative value of goods at different times in the future, has important effects on investment decisions. Lower interest rates increase the present value of distant returns, which encourages investors to expand projects that offer the prospect of large returns only at distant dates. Higher interest rates cause investors to concentrate on projects promising earlier returns.

The relationship is one of mutual determination, however. For reasons ranging from the psychological to the technological, people in one society may have a stronger desire for current availability of resources than people in another society. The stronger this desire for instant gratification is, the higher are interest rates.

—**Paul Heyne**

Biography: Paul Heyne is a senior lecturer in economics at the University of Washington in Seattle. He has a Ph.D. in ethics and society from the Divinity School of the University of Chicago.

Further Reading

Fisher, Irving. *The Theory of Interest*. 1930. Reprint. 1970.
Patinkin, Don. "Interest." *International Encyclopedia of the Social Sciences*, vol. 7. 1968.

Buyer Beware Consumer Reports

In a 1972 article on financing home appliances, *Consumer Reports* gives bad advice. It considers two financing options. Under one the appliance is purchased from a retail store for $675 with a two-year, 15 percent installment plan. Under the other the appliance is included as a standard feature for $450 in a home mortgaged over a twenty-seven-year period at 7.75 percent interest. Comparing those terms, *Consumer Reports* claims the store offers the better deal. Here are their figures:

	Cost from Store	Cost from Builder
Purchase price	$675	$ 450
Finance charge	110	625
Total	785	1,075

Consumer Reports goofed. It ignored the present value of money. Because financing charges are paid over time, not all at once, the total cost of both options is actually lower than the totals stated here. Since the builder's option includes interest paid in the distant future, it costs much less than *Consumer Reports* claims. The builder offers both a lower purchase cost and lower interest rate. Common sense would lead you to choose the builder's deal. Borrowing long-term at low interest rates can be good for your bank account. The present value of money shows why.

—DRH

Junk Bonds

Glenn Yago

■ Junk bonds, also known more respectfully as high-yield securities, are debt instruments that are issued by corporate borrowers and which the major bond-rating agencies say are less than "investment grade." A corporate bond is considered "junk" if it is rated as BaA or lower by Moody's or Ba3 or lower by Standard and Poor's bond-rating services. Bond ratings measure the riskiness of bonds (that is, the chance that the issuer will be unable to make interest payments or repay the principal). The riskier a bond, the lower its rating. Bonds with more A's are less risky than bonds with fewer A's, and the highest rating (for Standard and Poor's) is AAA, or triple-A.

Credit risk is based on a multitude of factors, many of which are linked to performance in the past. Some of the largest corporations, such as IBM and General Motors, and even the U.S. government were at times below investment-grade rating. Today many companies that are household names, including Time Warner and Duracell, fall into this category.

The bonds of 95 percent of U.S. companies with revenues over $35 million—and of all companies below that amount—are rated noninvestment grade or junk. This means that the companies must pay higher rates of interest on their bond issues than other corporations pay on investment-grade bonds. That is why non–investment-grade bonds also go by the name of high-yield bonds.

Until the late seventies all new bonds sold publicly to large groups of investors were investment grade. The only publicly traded junk bonds were ones that originally carried investment-grade ratings and had subsequently been "downgraded" because the financial strength of the issuing companies had deteriorated. Up until then, companies with ratings below investment grade raised new money by borrowing from banks or through what are called private placements. A private placement is the sale of bonds directly to an investor such as an insurance company. Because private placements are not registered with the Securities and Exchange Commission, the original purchasers cannot easily resell them to other investors. Interestingly, though, no one labeled such bonds as junk. Publicly issued bonds, on the other hand, can be traded freely.

The debt market in the United States changed dramatically after 1977, when Bear Stearns and Company, a New York investment house, underwrote the first original-issue junk bond (that is, the first public sale of new bonds with a junk rating). Soon thereafter, Drexel Burnham Lambert financed seven companies that had previously been shut out of the corporate bond market. By 1983 over a third of all corporate bond issues were non–investment grade, two-thirds of which were new issues.

What explains this explosion in the issue of junk bonds? For one thing, they held enormous appeal for borrowing companies because publicly issued bonds typically carry lower interest rates (because they are more easily resold) than private placements, and they also tend to impose fewer restrictions on the actions of the borrowers (known in the argot of finance as restrictive covenants). For another, research by economists showed that junk bonds ought to have great appeal to investors. W. Braddock Hickman, T. R. Atkinson, O. K. Burrell, and others examined the bond-rating systems and their impact on bond pricing. These academics were the first to quantify the actual risk premiums (the higher interest rates) paid to various bond investors. They were particularly struck by the fact that low-rated debt earned a high risk-adjusted rate of return. In other words, the interest-rate premium on low-rated debt was higher than was justified by the added risk of default. Therefore, someone who bought a diversified portfolio of these risky bonds would do better than someone who bought investment-grade bonds, even after deducting losses on the bonds that defaulted. Michael Milken of Drexel Burnham trumpeted these insights to his firm and his customers, with stunning success.

For many companies facing major structural economic changes in the eighties—foreign competition, technological shifts, deregulation—a missing element for economic adjustment was capital. Bank loans, restrictive private placements, or dilutive stock offerings were the only source of capital prior to the rise of the high-yield market. But suddenly the high-yield market was liquid enough to provide cost-effective funding alternatives.

That golden age of junk financing lasted roughly a decade and built to a virtual frenzy of new bond issues in 1988 and 1989. That resulted, in 1989 and 1990, in an unprecedented number of defaults by junk bond issuers and the bankruptcy of Drexel Burnham. Almost overnight the market for newly issued junk bonds disappeared, and no significant new junk issues came to market for more than a year.

In the wake of that shakeout and the scandals involving Drexel Burnham, junk bonds have been blamed for a broad range of troubles in the economy, including huge losses by commercial banks, the savings and loan crisis, high unemployment, low productivity growth, and almost everything else that seems amiss in the U.S. financial world. The facts do not support such assertions, but a handful of major bankruptcies of companies that went through leveraged buyouts or made acquisitions with junk bonds has fostered the general impression that they are responsible for many economic woes.

In fact, researchers have found that issuers of high-yield debt as a group have outperformed industrial averages in many important measures of industrial performance, including employment growth, productivity, sales, capital investment, and capital spending. Overall, high-yield firms increased employment at an average annual rate of 6.7 percent, compared with 1.4 percent for industry in general, from 1980 to 1987. High-yield firms also outperformed their industrial counterparts in productivity. In output per hour of labor, industries with higher utilization of high-yield securities were more productive. In sales per employee, high-yield firms averaged 3.2 percent growth annually, compared with an industrial average of 2.4 percent. The total invested capital of high-yield firms grew at an average annual rate of 12.4 percent, compared with 9.9 percent for industry in general. New capital expenditures for property and plant and equipment grew more than three times as fast among high-yield firms as they did for industry in general (10.6 percent vs. 3.8 percent).

The rise of high-yield securities accompanied the general growth of so-called debt securitization—the combining of loans into packages and the issuance of securities that represent claims on the interest and repayment of principal on those loans. Debt securitization has made marketable investment instruments out of such everyday borrowings as home mortgages and credit card debt. Studies indicate that throughout the eighties junk bonds were very profitable investments for S&Ls, second only to credit cards.

Why, then, have junk bonds gotten such a bad reputation? For one thing, top managers of investment-grade companies have been arguing for years that they are the em-

bodiment of reckless excess on Wall Street. They may take that position because junk bonds gave corporate raiders access to the public debt market and enabled them to mount assaults on the largest corporations in the United States. Less dramatically but also of importance, junk bonds make it possible for weaker companies to compete more successfully with investment-grade companies for financing. In addition, it is likely that a herd instinct on Wall Street helped make junk bonds anathema, at least for a while. By 1988 and 1989 Wall Street firms were financing deals that many observers said were bound to fail. But investors went on buying even the shakiest junk bonds. When the poorly structured deals did fail, investors shunned even the strongest junk bonds. But by the summer of 1991, it appeared that junk bonds were on their way back to filling a very useful role in financing U.S. business.

—Glenn Yago

Biography: Glenn Yago is an associate professor of management and policy at the Harriman School for Management and Policy, State University of New York, Stony Brook. He is also director of the school's Economic Research Bureau.

Further Reading

Altman, E. I., ed. *The High-Yield Debt Market: Investment Performance and Economic Impact*, 41–57. 1990.

Atkinson, T. R. *Trends in Corporate Bond Quality*. 1967.

Blume, Marshall E., and Donald R. Keim. "Low Grade Bonds: Their Risks and Returns." *Financial Analysts Journal* 43 (July/August 1987): 26–33.

Roach, Stephen. "Living with Corporate Debt." *Journal of Applied Corporate Finance* 2 (Spring 1989): 19–29.

Yago, Glenn. *Junk Bonds: How High Yield Securities Restructured Corporate America*. 1991.

Pensions

Henry McMillan

■ A private pension plan is an organized program to provide retirement income for a firm's workers. Private pension plans receive special tax treatment and are subject to eligibility, coverage, and benefit standards. Private pensions have become an important financial intermediary in the United States, with assets totaling nearly $1.9 trillion in 1989. By comparison, all New York Stock Exchange listed stocks and bonds totaled $4.4 trillion at year-end 1989. In other words, pension plan assets are large enough to purchase about 40 percent of all stocks and bonds listed on the NYSE.

For individuals, future pension benefits provided by employers substitute for current wages and personal saving. A person would be indifferent between pension benefits and personal saving for retirement if each provided the same retirement income at the same cost of forgone current consumption. Tax advantages, however, create a bias in favor of saving through organized pension plans administered by the employee's firm and away from direct saving.

For a firm, pension plans serve two primary functions. First, pension benefits substitute for wages. Second, pensions can provide firms with a source of financing because promised future pension benefits need not require current cash payments. The current U.S. tax code provides additional advantages for using pension plans to finance operations.

Basic Features of U.S. Pension Plans

Virtually all private pension plans satisfy federal requirements for favorable tax treatment. The tax advantages are three:

1. Pension costs of a firm are, within limits, tax deductible;
2. Investment income of a pension fund is tax exempt; and
3. Pension benefits are taxed when paid to retirees, not when earned by workers.

To qualify for these tax advantages, pension plan benefits must not discriminate in favor of highly compensated employees, and plan obligations must be satisfied through an organized funding program. (See McGill and Grubbs for further details on these and other institutional features.)

Benefits are calculated through formulas established in the pension plan. There are two primary plan types: defined contribution and defined benefit.

Defined Contribution Plans

Defined contribution plans specify (define) a firm's annual payment (contribution) to the pension fund. The funds are allocated to individual employees, much like a bank account or mutual fund shares. When the individual reaches retirement age, he or she usually can take the accumulated money as a lump-sum payment or use it to purchase a retirement annuity.

For example, suppose a defined contribution plan specifies that 5 percent of a worker's salary be contributed each year to a pension fund. Suppose the worker starts at age thirty, retires at age sixty, and earns $50,000 annually. Then the firm's annual contribution would be $2,500 (5 percent of $50,000). If the fund earns 8 percent annually, the worker would have $283,208 in the pension fund at retirement, which could purchase a twenty-year annuity paying $28,845 annually.

Defined Benefit Plans

A defined benefit plan specifies the monthly payment (benefit) to be received by a retiree instead of the annual contribution made by the employer. The benefit is typically specified in terms of years of service and percent of salary. For example, a plan might specify that a worker will receive an annual pension equal to 1.5 percent of his or her average salary in the last five years of service, times the years of service. If the worker began at thirty, retired at sixty, and earned an average of $50,000 in the last five years, the annual retirement payment would be $22,500. The worker's firm must pay the promised benefit, either by taking money from the pension fund annually or by purchasing an annuity for the worker from an insurance company. For the pension expense to be tax deductible, the firm must establish an ''actuarial funding program'' designed to accumulate enough assets to provide promised benefits.

An actuarial funding program combines data on plan specifications, employee characteristics, and pension fund size with assumptions about future interest, salary, turnover, death, and disability rates. Given these assumptions and data, an actuary estimates both the firm's future pension obligations and an annual payment schedule to satisfy those obligations. Different interest rate and salary assumptions can have a substantial effect on annual contributions. A rule of thumb is that raising the assumed interest rate by one percentage point will lower pension liabilities by 15 percent, holding all else constant.

Similarly, different actuarial funding methods can substantially affect required and allowable contributions in any given year, even with the same plan characteristics and actuarial assumptions. For example, when Financial Accounting Standard Board Statement No. 87 specified a particular actuarial method for financial disclosure, this raised pension expenses by $9 million for Firestone, but lowered expenses by $40 million for Goodyear when first applied in 1986. The latitude available in the choice of assumptions and in funding methods has been reduced by federal law, regulations, and accounting standards.

Plan Termination

Pension plans can be terminated. With defined contribution plans the employer merely passes the pension fund management to an insurance company and stops making contributions. Terminating a defined benefit plan is more complicated and controversial since pension fund assets do not necessarily equal the present value of promised benefits. If assets exceed promised benefits, the excess assets may revert to the employer. If a company fails and its pension assets fall short of obligations, deficiencies are partially insured by the Pension Benefit Guaranty Corporation (PBGC), a federal corporation established by the Employee Retirement Income Security Act of 1974 (ERISA).

Economic Issues

A basic premise of the extensive economic literature on pension policy in the United States is that pension benefits are not free goods: they are provided to workers as substitutes for current wages. Economists have found that the higher a person's marginal tax rate, the higher his pension is likely to be as a percent of his wage. This makes sense because pensions are, in part, a means of tax avoidance. Also, the higher an individual's income, the higher his pension benefit as a percent of current income. So if a person's income doubles, the pension portion of his current total compensation might rise from, say, 8 to 12 percent.

About 75 percent of all workers covered by pension plans are in defined benefit plans. Most large firms with unionized labor forces have defined benefit plans. Defined contribution plans are smaller on average, but more numerous (about 75 percent of all pension plans are defined contribution). Defined contribution plans have been growing more rapidly, possibly because government regulation has made defined benefit plans relatively more costly to operate, especially for small firms.

How do firms choose how much to fund pension plans and what kinds of assets to invest in? For defined contribution plans the first half of the question is simple: the employer has to make the promised contribution (e.g., 5 percent of salary or wages) each year and has no other funding decisions to make. So the only ongoing issue for a defined contribution plan is how to invest the assets. Standard portfolio theory suggests that workers would be best off with some well-diversified combination of stocks, bonds, and Treasury bills. The relative weights on the portfolios would depend on the worker's tolerance for risk: the more risk the worker wants to take, the higher the proportion in stock. Because attitudes toward risk differ among individuals and for any one individual as he or she ages, defined contribution plans frequently allow participants to select the allocation of their contributions among a handful of mutual funds.

For defined benefit plans the answers to both parts of the question are much more complex. In practice most pension plans are roughly ''fully funded'' (meaning that assets equal the present value of benefits already earned by workers) and the pension fund is split equally between stocks and bonds. Economists are not sure why this is so. They have come up with two possible explanations. The first assumes that the firm owns the pension fund. If so, the firm should choose the funding and portfolio strategy with the highest net present value to it. This leads to two polar-opposite solutions: underfund and buy risky assets, or overfund and buy high-grade bonds.

Why does the first strategy—underfunding and buying risky assets—make sense? Under federal law a firm can terminate its pension plan only if the pension fund is greater than accrued benefits or if the firm is bankrupt. In the latter case the PBGC pays the excess liability. The insurance premium that the firm pays the PBGC bears no relation to the riskiness of its pension fund investments. Therefore, the government's insurance plan gives the firm an incentive to fund the pension plan only to the minimum required, to substitute pension benefits for wages as much as workers will allow, and then to invest the fund in risky assets like stocks or junk bonds. If the investment works out, the firm gains. If the investment fails, the government and the firm's workers lose. Note the similarity to federal deposit insurance: both create an incentive to invest in exceptionally risky assets because the government (actually, the taxpayer) covers losses.

Now for the second strategy—overfunding and buying bonds. This makes sense as a way of reducing taxes for stockholders. Stockholders can reduce their taxes by shifting highly taxed assets out of their taxable personal portfolio and into the tax-exempt pension fund portfolio. This strategy works if stockholders own the pension fund and can claim those funds later. Furthermore, stockholders can increase their wealth by issuing debt on the corporate account (which is tax deductible at the corporate tax rate) and investing the proceeds in bonds owned by the pension fund. The overfunding strategy works best for ongoing plans because when plans terminate, the reversion of excess pension fund assets to the firm is subject to a stiff excise tax that ranges from 20 percent to 50 percent, depending on the circumstances.

Because one strategy leads to investment in stocks and junk bonds and the other leads to investment in low-risk bonds, firms might be following a mix of the two strategies. This could explain the roughly fifty-fifty split in pension plans' investments. Alternatively, the fifty-fifty split may simply reflect the "risk-averse" behavior of plan trustees as fiduciaries attempting to satisfy ERISA's "prudent man" investment standards.

Another explanation for this split is based on the idea that workers, as well as employers, implicitly own the pension fund by sharing in pension fund performance. How? While total pension benefits are allocated by a defined benefit formula, the size of total benefits implicitly depends on fund performance. In such a case, balanced investments serve workers' aggregate interests because they share in good and bad pension fund performance.

Why would firms allow workers to own the pension fund? One reason, in the case of salaried employees, would be to signal to the employees that it is safe for them to make a long-term commitment to the firm. For union employees the firm might be concerned that the union will hold out for high wages that, in the long run, will drive the firm out of business. The firm wants its workers to have a strong interest in its long-term survival. If their pension plan is underfunded, workers will have such an interest because they can collect their full benefits only if the firm survives. These incentives are weaker for overfunded defined benefit plans or for defined contribution plans (which must always be fully funded). This can explain why union plans have been almost exclusively of the defined benefit variety and were 30 percent less funded than nonunion plans prior to ERISA.

—Henry McMillan

Biography: Henry McMillan is the director of asset-liability management with Transamerica Occidental Life Insurance. He was previously an economist with the Securities and Exchange Commission and a business economics professor at the Graduate School of Management of the University of California at Irvine. His views do not necessarily reflect the views of Transamerica or its staff.

Further Reading

Alderson, Michael. "Corporate Pension Policy under OBRA, 1987." *Financial Management*, no. 4 (1990): 87–97.

Black, Fischer. "The Tax Consequences of Long-Run Pension Policy." *Financial Analysts Journal* 36 (July/August 1980): 21–28.

Blelberg, Steven. "Less Than Zero." *Financial Analysis Journal* 44 (March/April 1988): 13–15.

Bodie, Zvi. "Pensions as Retirement Income Insurance." *Journal of Economic Literature* 28, no. 1 (1990): 28–49.

Ghicas, Dimitrios. "Determinants of Actuarial Cost Method Changes for Pension Accounting and Funding." *Accounting Review* 65, no. 2 (1990): 384–405.

Ippolito, Richard. *Pensions, Economics, and Public Policy*. 1986.

McGill, Dan, and Donald Grubbs, Jr. *Fundamentals of Private Pensions*, 6th ed. 1989.

Sharpe, William. "Corporate Pension Funding Policy." *Journal of Financial Economics* 3, no. 2 (1976): 183–93.

Woodbury, Stephen. "Economic Issues in Employee Benefits." *Research in Labor Economics* 11 (1990): 271–96.

Present Value

David R. Henderson

■ Present value is the value today of an amount of money in the future. If the appropriate interest rate is 10 percent, then the present value of $100 spent or earned one year from now is $100/1.10, which is about $91. This simple example illustrates the general truth that the present value of a future amount is less than that actual future amount. If the appropriate interest rate is only 4 percent, then the present value of $100 spent or earned one year from now is $100/1.04, or about $96. This illustrates the fact that the lower the interest rate, the higher the present value. The present value of $100 spent or earned twenty years from now is, using an interest rate of 10 percent, $100/(1.10)^{20}$, or about $15. In other words, the present value of an amount far in the future is a small fraction of the amount.

The concept of present value is very useful. One interesting use is to determine what a lottery prize is really worth. The California state government, for example, advertises that one of its lottery prizes is $1 million. But that is not the value of the prize. Instead, the California government promises to pay $50,000 a year for twenty years. If the discount rate is 10 percent and the first payment is received immediately, then the present value of the lottery prize is only $468,246.

Some scientists say that millions of years from now the sun will burn out and the earth will die unless mankind discovers an alternative source of energy. Present value shows why this is not worth worrying about. Assume that 1 million years from now there are 10 billion people and that each person values his or her life at $100 trillion in 1992 dollars. (Economists typically find, by examining data on risk premiums for jobs, that Americans value their lives at no more than $3 million and that people in poorer countries place a lower value on their lives.) Then even with an unusually low interest rate of 2 percent, the present value of the loss from the sun burning out is less than 1¢.

—David R. Henderson

Biography: David R. Henderson is the editor of this encyclopedia. He is a senior research fellow at Stanford University's Hoover Institution and an associate professor of economics at the Naval Postgraduate School in Monterey, California. He was formerly a senior economist with the President's Council of Economic Advisers.

Program Trading

Dean Furbush

◼ Program trading, the subject of considerable controversy in recent years, is the simultaneous trading of a portfolio of stocks, as opposed to buying or selling just one stock at a time. The New York Stock Exchange defines program trading as any trade involving fifteen or more stocks with an aggregate value in excess of $1 million. Rudimentary program trading began in the seventies, with the trades in the program being walked around to the market maker's (specialist's) posts at the New York Stock Exchange. Since then the techniques have become much more sophisticated and efficient. Today, professional investment managers and brokers can send orders to buy or sell groups of stocks directly from their computers to computers at the exchange. On most days, program trading represents about 10 percent of overall trading on the NYSE.

In the eighties program trading became a popular culprit whenever stock prices moved quickly, especially when they moved down. Some people, including the regulators at the Securities and Exchange Commission, thought that program trading caused, or at least exacerbated, the October 1987 market crash. But most financial economists argue that the importance of program trading has been overblown.

Although it carries connotations of computers trading without supervision or human control, program trading need not have anything to do with computers. And even when they are involved, computers simply speed up the process. The actual decisions to buy and sell are made by people, not computers. In many cases people use computers to calculate algorithms that facilitate decisions, and in almost all cases computers help route trades to each individual stock in the program, but people make the trading decisions and implement them.

Program trading has developed because of three interrelated conditions. First, individual investors are learning that trading a diversified portfolio of securities eliminates some of the risks of investing in individual stocks. Second, institutions hold and trade a higher fraction of equity than ever before. These professional investors execute their diversified trades directly in the stock market as program trades or in the futures and options markets, where investors or speculators can trade contracts that are tied to changes in market indexes such as the Standard and Poor's 500. Third, technological advances have reduced trading costs.

Program trading has been associated with several trading strategies, including ones known as duration averaging, portfolio insurance, and index arbitrage. Understanding these strategies is important to understanding the role of program trading in our stock markets. People trade programs for just two reasons: either to accommodate an investment objective that includes several stocks, or for arbitrage purposes (i.e., to profit from price discrepancies between the stock market and so-called derivative markets such as the futures and options markets).

To understand the program trading that results from the pursuit of investment objectives, consider someone who invests, say, a thousand dollars in a mutual fund. When many investors make that decision, they collectively send a signal for the mutual fund to buy a portfolio of stocks—to make a program purchase. Similarly, a large number of mutual fund redemptions signals the fund to sell a portfolio of stocks. Both signals are, in effect, retail program trades that are efficiently channeled to the stock market through traditional program trades.

Several other, more complex investment strategies have been associated with program trading. Two notable investment strategies mentioned above are duration averaging and portfolio insurance. Both are used to decide how much of an investor's funds to invest in stocks versus other instruments such as bonds.

Duration averaging is based on an old idea that is easier said than done—buy low and sell high. A fund manager will shift assets into the stock portfolio—buy—when prices are low, and shift assets out of the stock portfolio—sell—when prices are high. This strategy is an effective one if prices stay within a particular trading range. But it leads to losses if prices fall below the range, and misses opportunities for profit if prices rise above the range. If duration averaging has any effect on price volatility, it reduces it. The reason is that duration averagers buy when prices fall and sell when prices rise, which tends to reduce the size of the move in either direction.

The purpose of portfolio insurance is to "insure" a minimum value for a stock portfolio in a falling market, while also allowing participation in a rising market. For instance, a portfolio insurer might buy a "put" option on the S&P 500, giving him the right to sell the index at a predetermined level. If the index falls below that level, the insurer "exercises" or sells the put. The profit on the put offsets some or all of the decline in the value of the stocks the insurer holds. If stocks in the index rise, all the insurer loses is what he paid for the put.

Another technique, called dynamic hedging, can be mathematically equivalent to buying a put option. In a dynamic hedging strategy a fund manager sells stocks as prices fall and buys stocks as prices rise. By one view dynamic hedging or portfolio insurance can increase volatility because both create extra selling pressure when prices fall and extra buying pressure when prices rise.

But two factors mitigate the effect of program trading on price volatility, whether the trading is for duration averaging or portfolio insurance. First, neither strategy is based on fundamental information regarding stock prices. If prices fall purely because of portfolio insurance trading, they have fallen below their "fundamental" level, and buying by other investors then becomes profitable. The same is true for any price movement engendered by a non–information-based trade. Second, duration averaging and portfolio insurance strategies are generally cheaper to implement using the futures and options markets rather than through program trades of the stocks themselves.

That brings us to index arbitrage between the stock market and the futures and options markets, which is the most controversial form of program trading. Because the financial products sold in the futures and options markets are derived from an underlying cash product—in this case stocks—their prices are mathematically related. This mathematical relation is no more mysterious than the relation between the price of a six-pack of root beer and the price of a single can. When one price falls relative to its mathematical relation to the other, index arbitragers can buy the cheaper product, sell the other one, and lock in a gain. That's what index arbitragers do whenever buying or selling by other traders causes futures or options prices to move too high or too low relative to underlying stock prices.

Thus, index arbitrage trading acts as a messenger, bringing the information impounded in prices from the futures market to the stock market. Suppose that prices are in a stable equilibrium, and the price of a futures contract is at its fair value in relation to stock prices. Now suppose there is good news about the economy. The news will be transmitted to the markets by buying in both the stock and futures markets, and prices will rise in both markets. For several reasons prices usually move faster in the futures market than in the stock market, so the futures price rises above its fair-value relation to the stock index. Enter index arbitrage, selling what has become relatively expensive—futures—and buying what has become relatively cheap—stocks. The effect is to bring prices back to their fair-value relation at the new, higher level caused by the good news. Thinking just about the stock side of the arbitrage, the program buy order was triggered by the price discrepancy, with index arbitragers not necessarily

knowing or caring what caused prices to move. But the effect of the buy order was to transfer the news in futures prices to the stock market.

Any complexity in this arbitrage strategy is purely due to unfamiliarity with the products involved. In fact, arbitrage is no big deal; everyone does it every day. Suppose you are standing in a long line at McDonald's and see a short line next to you. You quickly switch lines, "selling" the long line and "buying" the short one. When you do, the long line gets shorter and the short line gets longer. That's arbitrage: you get a gain for no pain while equalizing prices—or the length of lines.

Now suppose one line is next to the door, so people step naturally to that line first. When a busload of hungry travelers arrives, the door line gets longer before people realize they can save time by switching to the less accessible line. The travelers get their orders filled faster (liquidity is higher) if McDonald's allows line switching (arbitrage) from the door line (the futures market) to the short line (the stock market). In this analogy the futures market is the door line because prices move faster there; the door line lengthens first.

If McDonald's banned line switching, there would be two effects: one cash register would be calm relative to the other, and customers would be fed more slowly. If the success of McDonald's service was measured entirely by examining the level of calm or distress at the short-line cash register, McDonald's policy decision would be clear: discourage arbitrage because it makes the short line longer. If effectively imposed, the rule would slow service throughout the restaurant. But tomorrow the bus might go to Kentucky Fried Chicken instead. Actions that discourage liquidity lower the use of the market, as investors respond to the high cost of trading (illiquidity) by taking their business elsewhere.

My research has shown that the volume of index arbitrage is indeed positively related to price volatility. But for the most part index arbitrage seems to respond to volatility, not the other way around. Robert Neal of the University of Washington found much the same thing by examining the association of stock index returns with index arbitrage trades, after accounting for information effects. He found that index arbitrage has a statistically significant, but not economically significant, effect on volatility. That is, index arbitrage matters, but not much. An average index arbitrage trade moves the stocks in the index by less than half a cent.

Program trading and its principal subset, index arbitrage, rank among the most widely misunderstood financial terms. The growth of program trading is due to fundamental changes over the past twenty-five years in the way individuals hold stocks. Rather than trade a few stocks directly through a retail broker, investors are now more likely to hold stocks indirectly through a mutual fund or a pension fund. When institutions use program trading for their customers' accounts, the effect is to lower customer costs. When institutions use index arbitrage program trades, the effect is to link the markets and thus to enhance their overall liquidity.

—Dean Furbush

Biography: Dean Furbush is a senior economist for Economists Incorporated in Washington, D.C. He has served on the staff of the President's Council of Economic Advisers and at the Office of Economic Analysis of the U.S. Securities and Exchange Commission. He was also economic adviser to the chairman of the Commodity Futures Trading Commission.

Further Reading

Brennan, Michael, and Eduardo Schwartz. "Arbitrage in Stock Index Futures." *Journal of Business* 63 (1990): s7–s31.

Furbush, Dean. "Program Trading and Price Movement: Evidence from the October 1987 Market Crash." *Financial Management* 18 (1989): 68–83.

———. "Program Trading and Price Movements." Ph.D. diss., University of Maryland, 1990.

———, and Paul Laux. "The Price, Liquidity, and Volatility Response of Individual Stocks to Intermarket Trading: Is Index Arbitrage Special?" Working paper, University of Texas, Austin, 1993.

Fremault, Anne. "Stock Index Futures and Index Arbitrage in a Rational Expectations Model." *Journal of Business* 64 (1991): 523–47.

Harris, Lawrence, George Sofianos, and Jim Shapiro. "Program Trading and Intraday Volatility." NYSE working paper 90–03, 1992.

Miller, Jeffrey, Mara Miller, and Peter Brennan. *Program Trading: The New Age of Investing*. 1989.

Merton Miller, Jayaram Muthuswamy, and Robert Whaley. "Mean Reversion of S&P 500 Index Basis Changes: Arbitrage-Induced or Statistical Illusion?" Working paper no. 331, Graduate School of Business, University of Chicago, 1992.

Neal, Robert. "Direct Tests of Index Arbitrage Models." Working paper, Department of Finance, University of Washington, 1993.

Program Trading Did Not Cause 1987 Crash

Program trading did not cause the 508-point drop in the Dow-Jones industrial average that occurred on October 19, 1987. That was the conclusion of my 1988 study conducted for the Securities and Exchange Commission and issued by its Office of Economic Analysis. The evidence for the conclusion is that the five-minute intervals during which program-trading volume was heavy were not the times when prices fell the most. In fact, between 1:00 and 4:00 P.M. on that day, the typical relation between index arbitrage and price movement was reversed: above-average price changes tended to occur when index-arbitrage volume was below average. The Dow-Jones industrial average declined twice as fast in the afternoon as it had in the morning. The precipitous price declines occurred when the normal index-arbitrage relation was most disrupted, not when index arbitrage was prevalent.

—DF

Stock Prices

Jeremy J. Siegel

■ The price of a share of stock, like that of any other financial asset, equals the present value of the expected stream of future cash payments to the owner. The cash payments available to a shareholder are uncertain and subject to the earnings of the firm. This uncertainty contrasts sharply with cash payments to bondholders, the value of which is fixed by contractual obligation. Most of the cash payments to stockholders arise from dividends, which are paid out of earnings, and distributions resulting from the sale or liquidation of assets.

Over time most firms pay rising dividends. Rising dividends occur for two reasons. First, firms rarely pay out all their earnings as dividends, so that the difference, called retained earnings, is available to the firm to invest. This, in turn, often produces greater future earnings and hence higher prospective dividends. Second, the earnings of a firm will rise as the price of its output rises with inflation. Firms may also increase their dividends due to growth in the demand for their products and increased efficiencies of operation. These are the firms, of course, that investment advisers seek out when recommending stocks.

Cash payments to shareholders also result from the sale of some of the assets of the firm, outright liquidation, or a buyout. A firm may sell some of its operations, using the revenues from the sale to provide a lump-sum distribution to stockholders. When a firm sells all its operations and assets, this total liquidation results in a cash distribution after obligations to creditors are satisfied. Finally, if another firm or individual purchases the firm, existing shareholders may be eligible to receive cash payments or securities that can be sold in the open market for cash.

Some firms do not pay dividends but use their earnings to purchase their stock on the open market. Since this reduces the number of shares outstanding, the remaining shareholders each own a greater percentage interest in the assets of the firm. Therefore, the price of a stock can rise even if the firm does not pay a dividend and never intends to do so. If and when the assets of these firms are sold or liquidated, a cash distribution will be made and shareholders will realize a capital gain. Some firms pursue this policy to enable their shareholders to realize lower taxes, since taxes on capital gains are deferred and often paid at a lower rate.

The total return from owning stock arises from two sources: dividends and other cash distributions, and capital gains. A total return index for stocks can be computed by assuming that all cash distributions and capital gains are continually reinvested in the stock. This index would be akin to the accumulation of a pension plan that reinvested all dividends and capital gains in the stock (or group of stocks), or to the reinvestment of all distributions back into a mutual fund.

Over time, the total return on stocks has exceeded that of any other class of asset.

This is shown in chart 1, which compares the total returns to stocks, long- and short-term government bonds, gold, and commodities (measured by the consumer price index). One dollar invested in stocks in 1802 would have grown to $1,250,000 in 1991, in bonds to $6,920, in Treasury bills to $2,830, and in gold to $14.20. The consumer price index has risen by a factor of 10.4, almost all of it after World War II. One dollar invested in 1802 would have grown, in inflation-adjusted dollars, to $109,000 in stocks. $605 in bonds. $248 in Treasury bills, and $1.24 in gold.

The average compound rate of return on stocks from 1802 through 1991 was 7.7 percent per year: 5.8 percent from 1802 to 1870, 7.2 percent from 1871 to 1925, and 10.0 percent from 1926 to 1991. The increase in the rate of return of stocks over time has fully compensated the equity holder for the increased inflation that has occurred since World War II.

Stock prices are more variable than prices of most other assets, which means that the returns can change dramatically from year to year. In the postwar period annual stock returns have averaged about 12 percent, with a standard deviation of about 15 percent. This means that in about two-thirds of the years, stock returns should fall between − 3 percent and + 27 percent. In contrast, short-term government bonds have an annual return of 4.9 percent and a standard deviation of only 3 percent, so that in two-thirds of the years the return will be between 2 percent and 8 percent. Although on an annual basis stock returns are often lower

CHART 1

Total Returns
Cumulated Wealth from $1 Invested in 1802

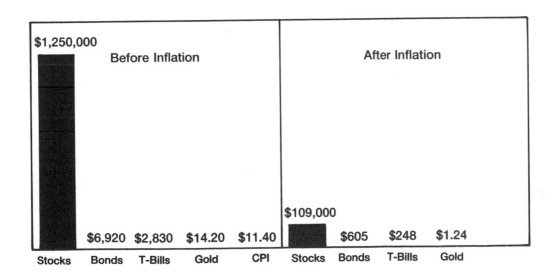

than returns on fixed-income assets, the higher average return on stocks virtually guarantees that stocks will outperform bonds in the long run. In every thirty-year period from 1872 to the present, and in every ten-year period from 1929 to the present, stocks have outperformed both long- and short-term government bonds.

The major determinants of stock prices are corporate earnings and interest rates. The stock market almost always falls before recessions. In fact, out of the forty-one recessions from 1802 through 1990, thirty-eight of them, or 93 percent, have been preceded or accompanied by declines of 8 percent or more in the stock returns index (the only exceptions were the 1829–30, 1945, and 1953 recessions). In the postwar period the peak of the stock market preceded the peak of the business cycle by between six and seven months.

The stock market is also prone to giving false alarms about oncoming recessions, and these false alarms appear to have increased in the postwar period. Excluding the war years, when declining stock markets have coincided with expanding war economies, there have been twelve episodes since 1802 when the cumulative returns index has fallen by 8 percent or more, but this has not been followed by a recession within the next twelve months. This occurred five times in the nineteenth century and seven times in the twentieth century. All those in this century have occurred since World War II (1946, 1956, 1962, 1966, 1978, 1984, and 1987).

The largest one-day drop in stock market history occurred on Monday, October 19, 1987, when the Dow-Jones industrial average fell 508 points, or 22.6 percent. No significant news event explains the decline, although rising interest rates and a falling dollar began to weigh on a market that had become tremendously overvalued after a five-year bull run. Once the decline gained momentum, selling begat more selling and a panic developed. Since a recession did not follow and stock prices subsequently recovered to new highs, many pointed to Black Monday as a confirmation of the "irrationality" of the stock market. Stock prices, however, are determined by expectations of the future, which must, by definition, be unknown. Shifts in sentiment and psychology can sometimes cause substantial changes in the valuation of the market. Despite false alarms the stock market is still considered an important indicator of future business conditions.

—**Jeremy J. Siegel**

Biography: Jeremy J. Siegel is a finance professor at the University of Pennsylvania's Wharton School.

Further Reading

Malkiel, Burton. *A Random Walk Down Wall Street*, 5th ed. 1990.
Siegel, Jeremy J. *Stocks for the Long-Run*. 1993.

————. "The Equity Premium: Stock and Bond Returns Since 1802." *Financial Analysts Journal* 48, no. 1 (January/February 1992): 28–38.

Teweles, Richard, and Edward Bradley. *The Stock Market*, 5th ed. 1987.

Takeovers and Leveraged Buyouts

Gregg A. Jarrell

■ Corporate takeovers became a prominent feature of the American business landscape during the seventies and eighties. A hostile takeover usually involves a public tender offer—a public offer of a specific price, usually at a substantial premium over the prevailing market price, good for a limited period, for a substantial percentage of the target firm's stock. Unlike a merger, which requires the approval of the target firm's board of directors as well as voting approval of the stockholders, a tender offer can provide voting control to the bidding firm without the approval of the target's management and directors.

Because it allows bidders to seek control directly from shareholders—by going "over the heads" of target management—the tender offer is the most powerful weapon available to the hostile bidder. Indeed, just the threat of a hostile tender offer can often bring a recalcitrant target management to the bargaining table, especially if the bidder already owns a substantial block of the target's stock (called a foothold block) and can demonstrably afford to finance a hostile offer for control. Although hostile bidders still need a formal merger to gain total control of the target's assets, this is easily accomplished once the bidder has purchased a majority of voting stock.

Hostile tender offers have been around for decades, but they were rare and generally involved small target firms until the midseventies. Then came the highly controversial multibillion-dollar hostile takeovers of very recognizable public companies. By the late eighties there were dozens of multibillion-dollar takeovers and their cousins, leveraged buyouts (LBOs). The largest acquisition ever was the $25 billion buyout of RJR Nabisco by Kolberg Kravis and Roberts in 1989.

Leveraged buyouts of small companies had also been common for decades, but in the eighties LBOs of large public companies became common. An LBO is a going-private transaction involving a tender offer for all of a firm's common stock, financed mostly by debt, made by a group usually involving some members of incumbent management. LBOs and leveraged cash-outs (first cousins of LBOs in which the target firm remains public because a small part of the compensation to selling shareholders is stock in the new, highly leveraged enterprise) rose to popularity for large public firms in the late eighties as a reaction to the hostile takeover activity. In essence the LBO was a way for management of a vulnerable public company to beat the hostile bidder to the punch, allowing management to buy out public shareholders at a premium and engage in the value-enhancing asset redeployments that otherwise would attract takeover entrepreneurs.

The vulnerability arises from a large "value gap"—which is the difference between a company's value as a going concern under the policies of incumbent management and the expected higher value of the stock, factoring in the value of redeploying the target's assets. Incumbent managements learned to tap the vast financial muscle of Wall Street in the late eighties and to engage in these control transactions to avoid being the victims of hostile attack. Indeed, many of the large leveraged restructurings were taken in direct defense after a hostile bid had been made.

Both economic and regulatory factors combined to spur the explosion in large takeovers and, in turn, large LBOs. The three regulatory factors were the Reagan administration's relatively laissez-faire policies on antitrust and securities laws, which allowed mergers the government would

have challenged in earlier years; the 1982 Supreme Court decision striking down state antitakeover laws (which were resurrected with great effectiveness in the late eighties); and deregulation of many industries, which prompted restructurings and mergers. The main economic factor was the development of the original-issue high-yield debt instrument. The so-called "junk bond" innovation, pioneered by Michael Milken of Drexel Burnham, provided many hostile bidders and LBO firms with the enormous amounts of capital needed to finance multibillion-dollar deals.

Managers of target companies in takeover battles have access to a variety of defensive tactics, many invented during the turbulent eighties. These defensive measures have always been controversial because they necessarily pose a conflict of interest for management. A top manager's own narrow interest is to save his job, which he often loses after a takeover. His legal obligation is to get a good deal for shareholders, which often means allowing the takeover. Not surprisingly, some managers go with self-interest.

The array of takeover defenses includes charter amendments that require supermajorities (i.e., votes of 70 percent or even 80 percent of shareholders) to approve a merger; dual-class restructurings that, by creating two classes of stock, concentrate voting control with management; litigation against the hostile suitor (usually alleging violations of antitrust and securities laws); and purchasing the hostile bidder's foothold stock at a premium to end the takeover threat (so-called green-mail payments). Although these particular defenses often are effective at delaying the hostile bidder, they rarely are enough to keep a target company independent. The two modern-day defensive weapons that can be "show-stoppers" are the poison pill and the state takeover laws.

The term "poison pill" describes a family of "shareholder rights" that are triggered by an event such as a hostile tender offer or the accumulation of voting stock above a designated threshold (usually 15 percent of outstanding stock) by an unfriendly buyer. When triggered, poison pills provide target shareholders (other than the hostile bidder) with rights to purchase additional shares or to sell shares to the target on very attractive terms. These rights impose severe economic penalties on the hostile acquirer and usually also dilute the voting power of the acquirer's existing stake in the firm.

Although poison pills are considered to be absolute deterrents to a hostile takeover, they can almost always be cheaply and quickly altered or removed by target management if they have not been irrevocably triggered. Therefore, they almost always are the subject of strenuous state-court litigation in takeover battles, and their practical effectiveness as an absolute deterrent has been decided in court more often than not. Today, the majority of large public companies are armed with poison pills of one type or another. State courts have allowed target managers to use pills to buy time (up to several months) to search for better third-party offers or develop value-creating corporate restructurings.

In the late eighties the Supreme Court upheld the constitutionality of state takeover laws, the most important being Delaware's merger moratorium law. This law prohibits a hostile acquirer from formally merging with the target for at least three years after buying a controlling interest. Widely regarded as a major deterrent, the Delaware law has an exception if the hostile bidder can acquire more than 85 percent of the target's stock, excluding shares held by inside managers and by certain kinds of employee stock-ownership plans. Since the law passed, Delaware-incorporated companies (which account for the majority of medium-size and large public companies in the United States) have engaged in various kinds of transactions to "lock up" more than 15 percent of stock in friendly hands, rendering these companies "bullet-proof" under Delaware law.

State antitakeover laws and the poison pill have dramatically reduced the scope for hostile tender offers in the U.S. market. Both defensive barriers can be overcome only by getting the target board of directors to approve the takeover. Therefore, hostile takeover activity has been moved directly into the boardroom, through the increasing use of proxy fights in conjunction with tender offers that are conditional on the bidder gaining control of the board or approval from the incumbent board. This hybrid proxy/tender offer approach is considerably more expensive, time-consuming, and risky than the hostile tender offer of the eighties. Consequently, hostile takeover activity has declined sharply, and the campaigns that have been waged were long, drawn-out proxy battles.

Was all this takeover and LBO activity good for the economy? The issue stirs strong emotions on both sides, but I believe the evidence shows that takeovers and buyouts are a good thing. Many published studies have documented the effects of tender offers and mergers on stock prices. The consensus is that these transactions confer large stock-price gains on target shareholders, averaging about 30 to 50 percent over preoffer prices during the eighties. The evidence on returns to bidders, however, is mixed. During the period from 1960 to 1980, the average stock-price gain to bidding firms was 3 to 5 percent. But during the eighties the returns to bidders began to erode, and some studies conclude that bidder firms suffered modest stock-price declines, on average, during the late eighties.

The principal reason for this erosion is the increased competition for targets. This increase in competition resulted from the target's greater effectiveness at dealing with the initial suitor and at getting rival bids, including bids from the targets' own management. The winning bidders in these auction contests of the late eighties frequently paid top dollar and saw their stock prices decline when the market learned that they had "won."

Nonetheless, the huge gains to target shareholders mean that takeovers and so-called highly leveraged transactions (HLTs) have created large net economic gains. Indeed, Harvard's Michael Jensen estimates that over the fourteen-year period from 1976 to 1990, the $1.8 trillion of tender offers, mergers, divestitures, and LBOs created over $650 billion in value for selling-firm shareholders. Moreover, this estimate does not include the additional large gains made by companies that restructured out of fear of being taken over.

Although this estimate excludes the gains and losses to shareholders of bidding firms, the empirical studies that find net losses for bidders also show that these losses—at 1 to 3 percent of the stock price—are minuscule compared with the enormous gains to target shareholders. These academic studies show clearly, on the basis of share prices, that hostile takeovers and highly leveraged transactions created huge increases in the values of companies. Moreover, several follow-up studies have shown that these stock-price gains are generally reliable predictors of real operating improvements and of increased corporate efficiency.

Critics of takeovers often complain that these share-price gains ignore the economic losses that takeovers and LBOs impose on other groups connected with the target firms. This intense debate has centered on the potential harm to corporate "stakeholders" other than shareholders, such as bondholders, employees, customers, suppliers, local communities, and taxpayers. Many takeovers in the airline industry, for example, have involved conflict between acquiring-firm management and the unionized labor of the target firm. These conflicts contributed to the popular view, shared by some economists, that shareholder premiums from takeovers come largely at the expense of labor's wages and benefits. But the empirical research has failed to show any reliable association between takeover activity and the income of workers. According to Joshua Rosett's recent study of over five thousand union contracts in over a thousand listed companies from 1973 to 1987, less than 2 percent of the premiums to shareholders can be attributed to wage reductions in the first six years following takeovers. In hostile takeovers the data show an *increase* in union wages in years following the control changes.

Another frequent complaint is that the constant threat of hostile takeovers forces nearly all corporate managers to stress short-term policies at the expense of more valuable long-term plans, thereby impairing the economic health and competitive vigor of their companies and the nation. Although rhetorically stirring, this theory has been studied thoroughly by economists and has received no empirical support. For example, the research shows no connection between takeover activity and public companies' expenditures on research and development. Studies also show that share prices generally respond positively to long-term investments by corporations. Also unsupported is the charge that losses to bondholders finance the shareholder gains from takeovers. Although some shareholder gains have come at the expense of bondholders, banks, and other creditors who financed these deals, Michael Jensen estimates that the aggregate amount of these losses between 1976 and 1990 is not likely to exceed $50 billion, a small fraction of the $650 billion gain to target shareholders.

There is some empirical basis for the idea that reducing taxes was at least a partial motive for takeovers, and especially LBOs. Some researchers estimate that for the typical leveraged buyout, tax savings (from deducting higher interest payments) accounted for about 15 percent of the premiums paid to sellers. Still, most mergers and tender offers were not motivated by tax savings. Also, Jensen has found that, contrary to popular assertion, LBOs have actually increased total tax payments to the U.S. Treasury. That is because selling shareholders pay taxes on their gains. All in all, the evidence shows that tax savings account for

only a small fraction, at most, of the huge gains to target shareholders and other selling firms.

In sum, although some individuals (incumbent management, for example) and some other groups obviously lose in any takeover, the empirical studies offer little or no support for the notion that the huge gains to shareholders reflect similarly large losses to other related parties. These zero-sum theories cannot begin to explain the large shareholder returns. The bottom line is that, on average, takeovers reflect wealth-enhancing and socially valuable redeployments of corporate resources.

Although several of these late-eighties LBOs and leveraged cash-outs ran into financial difficulties when the U.S. economy suffered a recession in the early eighties, there is much evidence that the LBO phenomenon also has been beneficial for our economy. Economists have found that the "free cash-flow" theory (developed by Michael Jensen) helps them to understand much of this activity. This theory postulates that high leverage can be a powerful disciplining device because it forces top management to undertake value-enhancing strategic changes. Companies with ample cash flow but few potentially profitable investment projects should pay out the excess cash to shareholders to maximize shareholder value.

According to this theory managements that fail to pay out excess cash, instead investing it in diversifying acquisitions or in low pay-off projects, will cause the stock price of their companies to be below their optimal value, creating a value gap. LBOs and other leveraged recapitalizations force managements to sell unprofitable divisions, avoid low pay-off investments, eliminate wasteful corporate expenses and diversifying acquisitions, and boost operating efficiency in order to meet the interest charges on the high level of debt. These forced efficiencies eliminate the value gap and create net economic gains for shareholders. Although this is a severe solution that exposes the firm to financial distress in the few years after the LBO, the evidence is that the LBOs and leveraged restructurings of the eighties created large net gains for shareholders.

In short, the U.S. market for corporate control witnessed unprecedented activity and change during the eighties as the largest public companies became frequent targets of hostile takeovers. Corporate managers reacted to this activity by lobbying hard for legal restrictions on the so-called raiders, and by restructuring and refocusing their companies while increasing debt levels and shareholder payouts.

—Gregg A. Jarrell

Biography: Gregg A. Jarrell is a professor of economics and finance and the director of the Bradley Policy Research Center at the University of Rochester's Simon School of Management. He was formerly chief economist at the U.S. Securities and Exchange Commission.

Further Reading

Jarrell, Gregg A., and Michael Bradley. "The Economic Effects of Federal and State Regulations of Cash Tender Offers." *Journal of Law and Economics* 23, no. 2 (October 1980): 371–407.

Jarrell, Gregg A., James Brickley, and Jeffry Netter. "The Market for Corporate Control: The Empirical Evidence Since 1980." *Journal of Economic Perspectives* 2, no. 1 (Winter 1988): 49–68.

Jensen, Michael, and Richard Ruback. "The Market for Corporate Control: The Scientific Evidence." *Journal of Financial Economics* 11 (March 1983): 5–50.

Rosett, Joshua G. "Do Union Wealth Concessions Explain Takeover Premiums? The Evidence on Contract Wages." *Journal of Financial Economics* 27 (1990): 263–82.

Shleifer, Andrei, and Robert Vishny. "The Takeover Wave of the 1980s." *Journal of Applied Corporate Finance* 4, no. 3 (Fall 1991): 49–56.

Smith, Roy C. *The Money Wars: The Rise and Fall of the Great Buyout Boom of the 1980s.* 1990.

Stewart, James B. *Den of Thieves.* 1991.

Vise, David, and Steve Coll. *Eagle on the Street.* 1991.

Weston, Fred J., Kwang S. Chung, and Susan E. Hoad. *Mergers, Restructuring and Corporate Control.* 1990.

CHAPTER TWELVE

THE MARKETPLACE

Advertising

George Bittlingmayer

■ Economic analysis of advertising dates to the thirties and forties, when critics attacked it as a monopolistic and wasteful practice. Defenders soon emerged who argued that advertising promotes competition and lowers the cost of providing information to consumers and distributing goods. Today, most economists side with the defenders most of the time.

There are many different types of advertising—the grocery ads that feature weekly specials, "feel-good" advertising that merely displays a corporate logo, ads with detailed technical information, and those that promise "the best." Critics and defenders have often adopted extreme positions, attacking or defending any and all advertising. But at the very least, it seems safe to say that the information that firms convey in advertising is not systematically worse than the information volunteered in political campaigns or when we sell a used car to a stranger.

Modern economics views advertising as a type of promotion in the same vein as direct selling by salespersons and promotional price discounts. This is because it is easier to understand why advertising is used in some circumstances and not in others by looking at the problems firms face in promoting their wares, rather than by focusing on advertising as an isolated phenomenon.

Scope

While advertising has its roots in the advance of literacy and the advent of inexpensive mass newspapers in the nineteenth century, modern advertising as we know it began at the turn of the century with two new products, Kellogg cereals and Camel cigarettes. What is generally credited as the first product endorsement also stems from this period: Honus Wagner's autograph was imprinted on the Louisville Slugger in 1905.

Advertising as a percentage of GNP has stayed relatively constant since the twenties at roughly 2 percent. More than half of that total is national, as opposed to local, advertising. In the eighties newspapers accounted for 26 percent of total advertising expenditures, magazines for 23 percent, television for 22 percent, radio for 7 percent, and miscellaneous techniques such as direct mail, billboards, and the Goodyear blimp for the remaining 22 percent. One popular argument in favor of advertising is, in fact, that it provides financial support for newspapers, radio, and television. In reply critics remark that advertiser-supported radio and television programming is of low quality because it appeals to those who are easily influenced by advertising. They also charge that advertiser-supported newspapers and magazines are too reluctant to criticize

TABLE 1

Advertising Expenditures (billions $)

	National	Local	Total	% of GNP
1940	1.2	0.9	2.1	2.11
1950	3.3	2.4	5.7	1.98
1960	7.3	4.7	12.0	2.32
1970	11.4	8.2	19.6	1.93
1980	29.8	23.7	53.5	1.96
1990	72.8	55.9	128.6	2.35

SOURCES: Statistical Abstract of the United States, *1987, 537*; U.S. Historical Statistics, Colonial Times to 1970, *Series T444; and* Advertising Age, *May 6, 1991, 16. Numbers may not add up due to rounding.*

products of firms that are actual or potential advertisers.

While aggregate expenditures on advertising have remained steady as a percentage of GNP, the intensity of spending varies greatly across firms and industries. Many inexpensive consumer items such as over-the-counter drugs, cosmetics, and razor blades are heavily advertised. Advertising-to-sales ratios also are high for food products such as soft drinks, breakfast cereals, and beer. And there is remarkable stability in this pattern from country to country. If a type of product is heavily advertised in the United States, it tends to be heavily advertised in Europe as well. Even within an industry, however, some firms will advertise more, others less. Among pharmaceutical manufacturers, Warner-Lambert's spending on advertising is over 30 percent of sales, while Pfizer's advertising-to-sales ratio is less than 7 percent.

The differences among industries, while stable, are deceptive. For example, auto-makers typically spend only 1 to 2 percent of sales on advertising, but their products are heavily promoted by the sales staffs in dealer showrooms. Similarly, industrial products are not heavily advertised because trade fairs and point-of-sale promotion are often more cost-effective than advertising. Products with relatively few customers may not be advertised at all, or advertised solely in specialized publications.

Economic Function

While persuasion and the creation of brand loyalty are often emphasized in discussions of advertising, economists tend to emphasize other, perhaps more important, functions. The rise of the self-service store, for example, was aided by consumer knowledge of branded goods. Before the advent of advertising, customers relied on knowledgeable shopkeepers in selecting products, which often were unbranded. To-

TABLE 2

Advertising-to-Sales Ratios, Top 10 Industries

Over-the-counter drugs	20.2
Perfumes, cosmetics	14.6
Soft drinks	13.8
Cutlery, razor blades	12.9
Breakfast cereals	11.4
Dog and cat food	11.0
Distilled liquors	11.0
Magazines and periodicals	10.3
Cigarettes	8.8
Soap and cleaning preparations	8.0

SOURCES: *Scherer and Ross,* Industrial Market Structure and Economic Performance, *3d ed., 573, quoting Federal Trade Commission,* Statistical Report, 1977. *(These data are based on the FTC's "Line of Business" data, which are no longer collected.)*

day, consumer familiarity with branded products is one factor that makes it possible for far fewer retail employees to serve the same number of customers.

Newly introduced products are typically advertised more heavily than established ones, as are products whose customers are constantly changing. For example, cosmetics, mouthwash, and toothpaste are marked by high rates of new product introductions because customers are willing to abandon existing products and try new ones. Viewed this way, consumer demand generates new products and the advertising that accompanies them, not the other way around.

In a similar vein "noninformative," or image, advertising (the Marlboro man, for example) can be usefully thought of as something that customers demand along with the product. When some customers are unwilling to pay for image, producers that choose not to advertise can supply them with a cheaper product. Often the same manufacturer will respond to these differences in customer demands by producing both a high-priced, labeled, heavily advertised version of a product and a second, low-priced line as an unadvertised house brand or generic product.

Advertising messages obviously can be used to mislead, but a heavily advertised brand name also limits the scope for deception and poor quality. A firm with a well-known brand suffers serious damage to an image that it has paid dearly to establish when a defective product reaches the consumer (see BRAND NAMES). Interestingly, officials in the Soviet Union encouraged the use of brand names and trademarks even under central planning as a way of monitoring which factories produced defective merchandise and as a way of allowing consumers to inform themselves about products available from various sources.

Monopoly

Economic debate in the fifties focused on whether advertising promotes monopoly by creating a "barrier to entry." Heavy advertising of existing brands, many economists thought, might make consumers less likely to try new brands, thus raising the cost of entry for newcomers. Other economists speculated that advertising made consumers less sensitive to price, allowing firms that advertise to raise their prices above competitive levels. The purported link between advertising and monopoly became so widely accepted that in the sixties the U.S. attorney general proposed a tax on advertising.

Economic researchers addressed this issue by examining whether industries marked by heavy advertising were also more concentrated or had higher profits. The correlation between advertising intensity and industry concentration turned out to be very low and erratic from sample to sample, and it is largely ignored today. What's more, early research found that high levels of advertising in an industry were associated with unstable market shares, consistent with the idea that advertising promoted competition rather than monopoly.

The idea that advertising creates monopoly received support from studies that found high rates of return in industries with high levels of advertising. As other economists pointed out, however, the accounting rates of return used to measure profits do not treat advertising as an asset. Consequently, measured rates of return—income divided by measured assets—will often overstate profit rates for firms and industries with heavy advertising. Subsequent work showed that when attention is restricted to industries with relatively small bias in the accounting numbers, the correlation disappears. A lucky by-product of the advertising-and-profits dispute were studies that estimated depreciation rates of advertising—the rates at which advertising loses its effect. Typically, estimated rates are about 33 percent per year, though some authors find rates as low as 5 percent.

Contrary to the monopoly explanation (and to the assertion that advertising is a wasteful expense), advertising often lowers prices. In a classic study of advertising restrictions on optometrists, Lee Benham found that prices of eyeglasses were twenty dollars higher (in 1963 dollars) in states banning advertising than in those that did not. Bans on price advertising but not on other kinds of advertising resulted in prices nearly as low as in the states without any restrictions at all. Benham argued that advertising allowed high-volume, low-cost retailers to communicate effectively with potential customers even if they could not mention price explicitly.

The importance of price advertising, however, apparently varies with the way the consumers typically obtain price information and make purchase decisions. An unpublished study by Al Ehrbar found that gasoline prices are significantly higher (about 6 percent, net of excise taxes) in communities that prohibit large price signs in gas stations.

Regulation

In the past many professions such as doctors, lawyers, and pharmacists succeeded in getting state legislatures to implement complete or partial bans on advertising, preventing either all advertising or advertising of prices. Recent court decisions have overturned these restrictions. At the federal level the U.S. Federal Trade Commission has jurisdiction over advertising by virtue of its ability to regulate ''deceptive'' acts or practices. It can issue cease-and-desist orders, require corrective advertising, and mandate disclosure of certain information in ads.

The regulation of cigarette advertising has been particularly controversial. The Federal Trade Commission has required cigarette manufacturers to disclose tar and nicotine content since 1970, although it had curiously prohibited precisely the same disclosure before that. The federal government also banned all radio and television advertising of cigarettes beginning January 1, 1971. While overall cigarette advertising expenditures dropped by more than 20 percent, per capita cigarette consumption remained unchanged for many years. Critics of the regulations maintain that it was the growing evidence of the harmful effects of smoking, rather than the reduction in advertising, that ultimately led to the smaller percentage of smokers in society. The critics also contend that the advertising ban may have slowed the rate at which low-tar cigarettes were introduced.

—George Bittlingmayer

Biography: George Bittlingmayer is an associate professor of economics and finance at the University of California at Davis. He was previously an economist with the Federal Trade Commission.

Further Reading

Benham, Lee. "The Effect of Advertising on the Price of Eyeglasses." *Journal of Law and Economics* 15 (October 1972): 337–52.

Borden, Neil H. *The Economic Effects of Advertising*. 1942.

Comanor, William S., and Thomas A. Wilson. "Advertising and Competition: A Survey." *Journal of Economic Literature* 17 (June 1979): 453–76.

Ekelund, Robert B., Jr., and David S. Saurman. *Advertising and the Market Process*. 1988.

Schmalensee, Richard. *The Economics of Advertising*. 1972.

Telser, Lester. "Advertising and Competition." *Journal of Political Economy* 72 (December 1964): 537–62.

———. "Some Aspects of the Economics of Advertising." *Journal of Business* 41 (April 1968): 166–73.

Brand Names

Benjamin Klein

■ Consumers always have incomplete information about product availability, quality, and alternative prices. Such "imperfect information" leads them to rely on brand names, which lessen the costs of acquiring product information. By relying on brand names and the company reputations associated with them, consumers can make reasonable purchases without searching or investigating products each time they buy.

Many economists have lamented the fact that consumers put so much reliance on brand names. The problem, as these economists see it, is that this consumer reliance gives companies with established brand names "market power" over the price they can charge. When companies "differentiate" their products with unique brand names and associated advertising and promotional campaigns, they can charge more than others for what these economists claim are "truly" identical products. Brand names lead consumers to make what these economists consider to be artificial distinctions between different products. Companies with respected brand names, therefore, can increase prices without losing significant sales.

The claim that brand names lead to unnecessarily high prices is often based on a comparison between the real world and a world of "perfect" consumer information, where every company in an industry is assumed to sell identical, unbranded ("homogeneous") products. These are the assumptions made in the model of "perfect competition," a simplifying construct sometimes employed by economists. Although imperfect information is completely natural and unavoidable, many economists find the unattainable ideal of perfect competition to be a desirable yardstick for policy. That is because under perfect competition no company has any power at all over the prices it charges. If a company raised its price even one cent above the market price, it would not sell anything. With perfect competition, therefore, no consumer would knowingly pay even one cent more for an identical product that could be obtained elsewhere at a lower price. Not surprisingly, the assumption that homogeneous products are the ideal leads to the incorrect implication that brand names that differentiate products decrease consumer welfare. That, in turn, leads to the policy, advocated by Harvard economist Edward H. Chamberlin in 1956, that trademarks should not be enforced.

More and more of the economics profession, however, has come to recognize the problem with assuming that brand name products are identical. One cannot understand the economic purpose served by brand names without dropping the assumption that we live in a world of perfect information where consumers are omniscient. Consumers, in fact, are not fully informed, and they know they are not. Therefore, they value company reputations—and they are willing to pay more for a product whose producer has a reputation for consistently supplying quality. By doing so, consumers are not acting irrationally. They are simply trying to protect themselves without having to devote huge amounts of time to learning all the details about each company's product. Reputations, and the brand names that go with them, are an efficient source of information for consumers.

Because consumers rely on and pay for reputations, companies have incentives to establish reputations by maintaining and improving the quality of their products. This incentive would be lost if all companies were required by law to sell indistinguishable, homogeneous products. If consumers could not identify the companies that produced the products they bought, individual companies would have no incentive to improve the quality of their products; in fact, each company would have an incentive to decrease the quality of its products. Economist Marshall Goldman has pointed out that this is exactly what occurred in the Soviet Union when brand names were eliminated after the 1917 communist revolution. That is why firms in the Soviet Union were required to identify their output with "production marks." When consumers cannot identify the company that produced what they buy, they have no recourse when they receive a product of low quality. Not only do consumers have no legal recourse, but more important, they have no economic recourse. Without brand names consumers do not know from current purchase experiences which products to buy—and which ones not to buy—in the future.

This repeat-purchase mechanism, where good past performance and a good reputation are rewarded with future profitable sales, and where poor performance is punished with the withdrawal of future profitable sales, provides companies with the incentive to perform in the marketplace. As a result, companies with superior reputations, representing good past performance and the likelihood of future profitable sales, have something to lose if they perform poorly. Their valuable brand names are a form of collateral that is at stake with every sale.

Consider, for example, the cost imposed upon Perrier in 1990 when it was discovered that the benzene used to clean its bottling machinery had contaminated some of its product. Perrier experienced a significant decrease in demand and had to spend large amounts of money on increased advertising, free samples, and other marketing and promotional expenditures in an attempt to recover its market share. Another recent newsworthy example was the image damage, lost sales, and greatly reduced profits suffered by Beech-Nut, the baby food company, when it was discovered in 1982 that its "apple juice" consisted of water, sugar, and flavoring. If brand names were not present in these cases, the large economic punishment imposed on the nonperforming companies would have been lost.

Because companies with valuable brand names that fail to perform have more to lose than companies without valuable brand names, consumers who buy brand name products are necessarily paying for something. They are buying the added assurance that the brand name company will have an increased incentive to take the necessary measures to protect its reputation for quality. For example, an established, profitable company such as Campbell's, with its huge share of canned soup sales, has more to lose if botulism is found in its product than a small marginal company such as Bon Vivant, which went bankrupt after botulism in its canned soup caused a death in 1971. Clearly, Campbell's has a higher stake in avoiding any occurrence of botulism in its product than did Bon Vivant. When consumers buy a brand name product, they are buying increased confidence and reliability.

Can the same be said for purchases of a "standardized" product such as aspirin, where most companies purchase the basic ingredient, acetylsalicylic acid, from the same manufacturer? If consumers are not ignorant or irrational, why would they buy an advertised, brand name product when they could get the exact same non-brand-name product at a lower price? The answer is that all aspirin is not exactly the same. Aspirins are not chemically equivalent. The filler ingredients, dissolve rate, and shelf life may differ from brand to brand. But more important, the higher-priced brand and the lower-priced "nonbrand" aspirins are not economically equivalent. In fact, to producers and consumers the products are necessarily different.

As the Perrier example vividly illustrates, even for a "simple" product, we live in an imperfect world where there is always a probability that something can go wrong. Because of the existence of a valuable brand name, the company selling the brand name aspirin has more to lose if something does go wrong. The company, therefore, has a greater economic incentive to take precautions. This added quality assurance is one of the things consumers of the brand name

product are purchasing when they knowingly pay the higher price.

The question, then, becomes not whether consumers are totally irrational when they pay the higher price for a brand name product, but whether they are paying too much for quality assurance. All consumers pay something for brand name assurance; it is merely the amount that consumers pay that varies across products. Even people who say "all aspirin is alike" spend some money on brand name assurance. They do not buy "nonbrand" aspirin off the back of a pickup truck at a swap meet. Instead, they may buy "lower" brand name aspirin, such as aspirin carrying the brand of a chain drugstore. Further, it is significant that consumers buy a much smaller share of such "lower" brand name aspirin in the children's aspirin segment of the market than in the adult segment. Many people decide, as evidenced by their behavior, that although they are willing to purchase less brand name assurance for themselves, they want the higher-quality assurance for their children.

Finally, it is important to recognize that brand names even operate in marketplaces where the government sets product quality standards. The obvious question is: why not rely entirely on government standards to assure company performance? There are two main answers. First, government standards often cannot easily capture some elements of performance. For example, although the government may grade agricultural commodities, such as vegetables, for color, size, and so on, they cannot define and grade characteristics such as taste that are quite important to consumers. Second, government agencies that rate and assure quality are far from perfect. For example, in 1989 the Food and Drug Administration found that several generic drug companies had faked or altered test results submitted to the FDA to get their drugs approved and that three FDA employees admitted accepting gifts from these generic companies. To assure the quality of the products they buy, consumers are right to rely not just on government standards, but also on brand names.

—Benjamin Klein

Biography: Benjamin Klein is an economics professor at the University of California in Los Angeles and is president of Economic Analysis Corporation.

Further Reading

Chamberlin, Edward. *The Theory of Monopolistic Competition,* 7th ed. 1956.

Goldman, Marshall. "Product Differentiation and Advertising: Some Lessons from the Soviet Experience." *Journal of Political Economy* 68 (1960): 346–57.

Klein, Benjamin, and Keith Leffler. "The Role of Market Forces in Assuring Contractual Performance." *Journal of Political Economy* 89 (1981): 615–41.

Competition

Jack High

■ "Competition," wrote Samuel Johnson, "is the act of endeavoring to gain what another endeavors to gain at the same time." We are all familiar with competition—from childhood games, from sporting contests, from trying to get ahead in our jobs. But our firsthand familiarity does not tell us how vitally important competition is to the study of economic life. Competition for scarce resources is the core concept around which all modern economics is built.

Adam Smith saw that competition would lead not to chaos, but to a spontaneous and productive social order. His insight gave birth to economics as a science. Economists have spent two centuries divining the myriad ways in which competition works its influences. What John Stuart Mill said in 1848 is still true today: "Only through the principle of competition has political economy any pretension to the character of a science."

The effects of competition permeate economic life. Prices, wages, methods of production, which products are produced and in what quantities, the size and organization of business firms, the distribution of resources, and people's incomes all result from competitive processes.

Consider market prices for consumer goods. The baker has on hand a stock of bread, a valuable good for which consumers are willing to compete by offering the baker a price. The baker wants to get the highest price possible, but he is constrained. If he sets his price too high, customers will not buy all that the baker has to sell. They will buy from another baker, or they will buy pizza or potatoes instead. So the baker sets a price that he thinks will "clear the market." That price is determined by the willingness of customers to compete for his product, and by the willingness of rivals to compete for his customers. In this way, competition determines the prices of houses and haircuts, beach chairs and Bibles, and the million-and-one other goods and services that we consumers desire.

An identical process occurs with producer goods. USX has on hand a supply of steel, for which automobile companies, appliance makers, and equipment manufacturers are willing to compete. The firm wants to get as much revenue as it can, taking into account the willingness of its customers to pay and the threat of lower offers from its rivals. The customers want to pay as little as possible, taking into account that rival customers may outbid them. This two-sided competition will again set a price that "clears the market."

The market-clearing price represents the lowest price that buyers of steel must pay, and the highest price that sellers of steel can receive, each without being outbid by rivals. This competitive process fixes the rates of all productive resources—from the prices of steel and semiconductors to the wages of busboys and brain surgeons.

At the same time that competitive bidding fixes prices in the market, it also determines incomes and allocates goods. The low wages earned by the busboy give him a relatively low income with which to go into the market and purchase consumer goods. The high wages earned by the doctor give him a relatively high income with which to purchase goods. Naturally, the doctor will be able to buy a larger share of consumer goods than will the preacher or busboy.

Purchases by consumers act as a kind of silent auction in which those who buy commodities bid them away from those who do not. If we could assemble gigantic snapshots of all the food in all the refrigerators in America, or all the furniture in all the rooms, or all cars in all the garages, we would see how competitive bidding allocates consumer goods.

The same kind of allocation occurs with producer goods. Automobile makers want steel for engines and auto bodies. Appliance manufacturers want it for washers, dryers, and refrigerators. Construction firms want it for reinforcement bars. Businessmen in all these industries compete for steel by placing orders to the manufacturers. Their purchases channel steel into its various uses in the economy. And what is true for steel is true for all resources used in production.

Competition acts as both stick and carrot in economic life. If the worker does not keep his hands to the machine, his employer will replace him. If the employer does not treat his employee as well as other employers would, the employee quits and goes somewhere else. If the manufacturer does not run his shop efficiently, his customers will go where they can find better service at the same price or equal service at a lower

price. All of us, as producers, are subject to replacement by those who are able and willing to do the job better or cheaper.

On the other side, if we do our jobs well, we are more likely to be rewarded. The successful manufacturer draws in more customers and increases his revenues. The productive worker moves up to higher wages and more responsibility. The incentives created by competition—or not created because of the lack of it—reveal themselves in the attitudes and activities of producers. Compare the listless indifference of the postal worker to the speed and efficiency of the United Parcel Service driver. Look at the shoddy workmanship in Eastern European goods as compared to their Western European counterparts. Now that firms in the two parts of Germany can openly compete, the Wartburg and Trabant have lost out to Opel and Volkswagen. Because producers are freer to compete by offering better products, and employees freer to compete by working harder, competent work is better rewarded in market economies than in planned or bureaucratic ones.

The carrot of successful market competition takes the form of profits. By introducing new goods, new technology, or new forms of organization, or by finding new markets or new sources of raw material, entrepreneurs can earn profits. The lure of profits inspires alertness, creativity, judgment, and risk taking. Similarly, workers who perform better will, all other things being equal, get bigger raises and more promotions.

The pursuit of profits, in the two hundred years since the industrial revolution, has unleashed what economist Joseph Schumpeter called a "gale of creative destruction." The horse and wagon have been replaced by the railroad, the automobile, and the airplane. The open-hearth fire has yielded to the electric stove and microwave oven. The washboard and clothesline have bowed to the washer and dryer. Novocaine and other modern drugs kill the pain that was formerly endured or drowned in whiskey. The telephone wire and the electromagnetic wave transmit news that previously traveled by ship or pony.

The competitive process that has wrought these enormous changes is governed by rules that, taken collectively, we call the market economy or the system of private property. This system recognizes the right of each person to use his property as he sees fit, and to keep the fruits of his labor. This leaves the worker free to pursue the occupations for which he thinks himself best suited. It leaves the entrepreneur free to explore new forms of production.

Many critics of capitalism and market economies contend that competition is one of the central evils of the system—that the pursuit of higher profits or higher wages pits people against one another, works to reduce cooperation within society, and makes some people better off only at the expense of others who are made worse off. Competition, however, is not the creation or even a by-product of a capitalist or market system. Competition exists everywhere in nature, and in all economic systems.

The difference in social systems is not the presence or absence of competition. Instead, one difference is the type of competition different systems unleash. For example, the rivalry to become a central planner in the Soviet Union was just as great as the rivalry to become a captain of industry in the United States. To succeed in becoming a planner, one must excel in bureaucratic politics; to succeed in becoming an entrepreneur, one must excel in productive efficiency.

Despite its importance to modern economic life, competition is not the be-all and end-all of economic activity. The modern market economy is as much a system of cooperation as it is a system of competition. Within the family and within the firm, between the customer and the supplier, we cooperate to achieve our ends. This cooperation is as vital as competition to a productive economy.

To a humane social order, the kind of competition matters far more than the amount. Competition that takes the form of violence and plunder destroys wealth; competition that takes the form of trying to be more productive creates wealth. One consequence of property, as the idea has been developed by Western philosophers and jurists over the past three centuries, has been to reduce plunder and to increase production. The result, while far from perfect, has been an economy that is more creative, and more humane, than any other system yet devised.

—Jack High

Biography: Jack High is associate professor of economics at George Mason University. He was Newcomen Fellow at Harvard University's Graduate School of Business Administration for the 1990–91 term and is acting editor of *Business History Review* for 1993–94.

Further Reading

Dennis, Kenneth G. *Competition in the History of Economic Thought*. 1977.

DiLorenzo, Thomas, and Jack High. "Antitrust and Competition, Historically Considered." *Economic Inquiry* 26 (July 1988): 423–35.

Hayek, Friedrich A. "The Meaning of Competition." In Hayek. *Individualism and Economic Order*. 1984.

———. "Competition as a Discovery Procedure." In Hayek. *New Studies in Philosophy, Politics, and Economics*. 1978.

McNulty, Paul. "A Note on the History of Perfect Competition." *Journal of Political Economy* 75 (August 1967): 395–99.

Schumpeter, Joseph. *Capitalism, Socialism, and Democracy*. 1942.

Stigler, George. "Perfect Competition, Historically Contemplated." *Journal of Political Economy* 65 (February 1957): 1–17.

See also CAPITALISM, FREE MARKET, MONOPOLY, PROFITS, SOCIALISM.

Disaster and Recovery

Jack Hirshleifer

■ Defeated in battle and ravaged by bombing in the course of World War II, Germany and Japan nevertheless made postwar recoveries that startled the world. Within ten years these nations were once again considerable economic powers. A decade later, each had not only regained prosperity but had also economically overtaken, in important respects, some of the war's victors.

The surprising swiftness of recovery was also noted in previous eras. John Stuart Mill commented on

". . . what has so often excited wonder, the great rapidity with which countries recover from a state of devastation; the disappearance, in a short time, of all traces of the mischiefs done by earthquakes, floods, hurricanes, and the ravages of war. An enemy lays waste a country by fire and sword, and destroys or carries away nearly all the moveable wealth existing in it: all the inhabitants are ruined, and yet in a few years after, everything is much as it was before."

Still, successful recovery is by no means universal. The ancient Cretan civilization may or may not have been destroyed by earthquake, and the Mayan civilization by disease, but in any case there was no recovery. Most famously, of course, a centuries-long Dark Ages followed the fall of Rome.

Sociologists, psychologists, historians, and policy planners have extensively studied the nature, sources, and consequences of disaster and recovery, but the professional economic literature is distressingly sparse. As a telling example, the four thick volumes of *The New Palgrave: A Dictionary of Economics* (1987) omit these topics entirely. The words *disaster* and *recovery* do not even appear in the index of that encyclopedic work. Yet disasters are natural economic experiments; they parallel the tests to destruction from which engineers and physicists learn about the strength of materials and machines. Much light would be thrown upon the normal everyday economy if we understood behavior under conditions of great stress.

The Historical Record

While everyday small-scale tragedies like auto accidents and disabling illnesses are disastrous enough for those personally involved, our concern here is with events of larger magnitude. It is useful to distinguish between community-wide (middle-scale) calamities, such as tornadoes, floods, or bombing raids, and society-wide (large-scale) catastrophes associated with widespread famine, destructive social revolution, or defeat and subjugation after total war. In community-wide disasters the fabric of the larger social order provides a safety net, whereas society-wide catastrophes threaten the very fabric itself. The former may involve hundreds or thousands of deaths; the latter, hundreds of thousands or millions. (As a special case, hyperinflations and great business depressions are society-wide events that do not directly generate massive casualties, yet still have calamitous consequences.)

Middle-scale, or community-wide, disasters are relatively frequent events, making empirical generalizations possible. In such disasters, it has been observed, individuals and communities adapt. Survivors are not helpless victims. Very soon after the shock they begin to help themselves and one another. In the immediate postimpact period community identification is strong, promoting cooperative and unselfish efforts aimed at rescue, relief, and repair. After the San Francisco earthquake of 1989, for example, inhabitants of a poor neighborhood spontaneously helped rescue motorists trapped by a freeway collapse. And after the Anchorage earthquake of 1964, local supermarkets kept the prices of necessities low while consumers generally cooperated by self-rationing.

On the other hand, there have been some serious instances of antisocial behavior. Notably, while goodwill and cooperation predominated in New York City during the 1965 electrical blackout, a second blackout in 1977 brought major violence and looting. Similar bad experiences have occurred more recently, for example after Hurricane Hugo struck the Virgin Islands in 1989. Nevertheless, as Russell Dynes and Thomas E. Drabek have shown, prosocial behavior has historically predominated. Instances to the contrary, while not rare, usually have fairly evident roots—where members of a community have a strong preexisting sense of grievance, for example. As an even more reliable generalization, a crisis almost always triggers a flow of support from outside the immediate impact area, a phenomenon that has become known as "convergence behavior." Surprisingly often, recovering communities even surpass previous rates of progress, owing to the emergence of new leaders, to enhanced social cohesion, and to the abolition of outmoded attitudes and regulations.

As a specific instance the fire-bomb raids on Hamburg in July and August of 1943 were highly intense community-wide disasters. People proved tougher than structures, as normally occurs in such situations. The raids destroyed about 50 percent of the buildings in the city, whereas the 40,000 people killed were under 3 percent of the population at risk. About half the survivors left the city. Some 300,000 returned in the recovery period, while around 500,000 were permanently evacuated to other areas throughout Germany. A "dead zone" of the city was closed off so that repairs could be concentrated in areas that were less seriously damaged. Electricity, gas, and telegraph were all adequate within a few days after the attacks ended. Water supply remained a difficult problem, however, and tank trucks had to be used. The transit system recovered only partially because of serious damage and abnormally heavy traffic, but mainline rail service was resumed in a few days. On the seventh day the central bank reopened, and business began to function normally. Hamburg was not a dead city. Within a few months, reported the

U.S. Strategic Bombing Survey, the city had recovered 80 percent of its former productivity.

Now consider a truly large-scale disaster: the Bolshevik attempt to impose "war communism" in Russia from 1917 to 1921, dispensing with markets and even the use of money. The Russian economy had already headed drastically downward during the preceding civil war. Industrial production fell to only 20 percent of the prewar level, and the cultivated area in agriculture to around 70 percent. But it was only after the final Red victory that the economy, instead of recovering, went into a total downspin. Baykov quotes Lenin:

On the economic front, in our attempt to pass over to Communism, we had suffered, by the spring of 1921, a more serious defeat than any previously inflicted on us by Kolchak, Denikin, or Pilsudsky. Compulsory requisition in the villages and the direct Communist approach to the problems of reconstruction in towns—this was the policy which . . . proved to be the main cause of a profound economic and political crisis. . . .

The explanation appears to be that, initially, the Bolsheviks had established direct control only over the "commanding heights" of industry (i.e., over a relatively small number of large factories located mainly in the major cities). Elsewhere, a variety of private and cooperative arrangement kept industry and trade functioning, at least minimally. Military victory permitted the communists to turn their attention to liquidating these remnants. In addition, many small capitalists who had stayed on in the hope of Soviet defeat finally decamped and abandoned their enterprises. Consequently, the paradox of economic collapse after political and military victory.

The shift in mid-1921 to the New Economic Policy (NEP), restoring monetary exchange and allowing considerable scope to private enterprise, led almost immediately to a substantial recovery. As a remarkable feature this very recovery, by creating a demand for currency as a means of exchange, permitted the Soviets to use the printing presses to acquire resources through a vast inflation of the money supply. The NEP allowed the economy a breathing space before the introduction of the Stalinist five-year plans, with their forced drive toward collectivization and industrialization.

Factors Helping and Hindering Recovery

One factor favorable to recovery is the inevitable shift of demand from less essential wants, which then frees resources for urgent rescue, repair, and rehabilitation. On the supply side, resource imports (gifts, insurance proceeds, commercial loans, and the like) will flow into damaged areas from outside support zones. More important, especially in the long run, is reserve productive capacity. Workers put in more hours, children leave school, and the elderly return from retirement. Machines and structures can be worked harder. Resource substitution—e.g., tents in place of houses, or trucks for buses and trains—enlarges the availability of essentials. Finally, stifling regulation of commerce and industry can be

relaxed or suspended, while socially dysfunctional activities such as crime and parasitical litigation can be placed under stricter rein.

For the middle-scale disasters the main problems have been technological and distributive (e.g., localized resource scarcities or the provision of fair compensation). But in large-scale calamities the survival of the social order itself is in question. Widespread famines, pandemics, destructive social revolutions, disastrous wars, and even severe business depressions and monetary hyperinflations—all of these threaten the network of arrangements supporting the elaborate division of labor that modern economies depend on.

Historically, the most immediately vulnerable aspect of this division of labor has been the money-mediated exchange of food and manufactured goods between rural and urban areas. Correspondingly, the most visible symptom of breakdown is a movement of population from the cities back to the countryside, as illustrated in ancient times by the emptying of cities in the declining Roman Empire. In modern times the populations of Moscow and Petrograd fell by over 50 percent between 1917 and 1920, during the Russian civil war. And similarly, though not to nearly so great a degree, the German and Japanese urban populations both declined substantially toward the end of and in the aftermath of World War II. And even in the United States, the 1929–35 depression saw a pause, and to some extent a reversal, of the long-run trend toward urbanization.

Under Russian war communism this breakdown of monetary exchange was due to an ideologically driven attempt to smash the system of private incentives that had previously served to feed the cities. For Japan and Germany a somewhat different "repressed inflation" process was at work, as had often occurred earlier, for example during the French Revolution and in the southern Confederacy during the American Civil War.

The process begins with military or economic stresses—such as territorial losses, transportation breakdowns, or inflationary war finance measures—that inevitably entail food scarcities. The crucial false step is the introduction of food price ceilings with the aim of "fair shares" or simply to hold down urban unrest. But the consequence is that farmers reduce their food deliveries to the cities. Unofficial mechanisms of distribution then emerge: black markets, barter, and trekking (day trips of city dwellers to the countryside), all involving losses due to higher transaction costs. As the cities begin to lose population, industrial production declines. The government may then attempt to confiscate the crops by military force. This threatens to cause a general breakdown of food production. At this point if not earlier, governments have historically given way, for example when the Bolshevik government was forced to introduce the NEP. In postwar Germany and Japan, fortunately, the downward spiral had not progressed nearly so far before the Erhard and Dodge reforms restored the functioning of the price system.

Policy Issues: The Role of Government

There is widespread agreement that government must take responsibility for maintaining and restoring the economic infrastructure—the system of law and order, plus public goods like essential transportation and communication links. For middle-scale, or community-wide, disasters the main policy question has been the extent to which government should engage in additional activities, at either the planning or the recovery stage, that might hamper or displace private efforts. Grants or subsidized loans subvert the motivation for private self-protection. For example, subsidized government flood insurance induces excessive construction in areas that are vulnerable to flood. Similarly, some forms of government relief hinder the recovery of normal business. Free food distribution, for example, may slow the restoration of regular marketing channels. Also debatable is the extent to which government should provide extra incentives for disaster preparations as well as a paternalistic safety net for those who were in a position to act but failed to do so. As reviewed by George Horwich, despite the government-created disincentives for private action, commercial disaster response firms have come into existence (e.g., Disaster Masters, Inc., of New York City) together with an industry newsletter, *Hazard Monthly*.

When it comes to the large-scale, or society-wide, disasters, however, private parties can scarcely protect themselves at all, except possibly by emigration. Historical experience suggests that recovery will hinge upon the ability of government to maintain or restore property rights together with a market system that will support the economic division of labor.

Taking a broader view, the subject of

disaster and recovery can be regarded as a special case within the general problem of economic development. As recent events have forcefully demonstrated, the doctrines of socialism, or at any rate the practices of socialist governments, have subjected the nations of Eastern Europe to a series of economic disasters from which they are now struggling to recover.

—Jack Hirshleifer

Biography: Jack Hirshleifer is an economics professor at the University of California, Los Angeles.

Further Reading

Anderson, J. L., and Eric L. Jones. "Natural Disasters and the Historical Response." *Australian Economic History Review* 28 (1988): 3–20.

Baykov, Alexander. *The Development of the Soviet Economic System.* 1947.

Dacy, Douglas C., and Howard Kunreuther. *The Economics of Natural Disasters.* 1969.

Douty, Christopher M. *The Economics of Localized Disasters.* 1977.

Drabek, Thomas E. *Human System Responses to Disaster.* 1986.

Dynes, Russell R. *Organized Behavior in Disasters.* 1970.

Fritz, Charles E. "Disaster." In *Contemporary Social Problems,* edited by R. K. Merton and R. A Nisbet. 1961.

Hirshleifer, Jack. *Economic Behaviour in Adversity.* 1987.

Horwich, George. "Disasters and Market Response." *Cato Journal* 9 (1990): 531–55.

Iklé, Fred Charles. *The Social Impact of Bomb Destruction.* 1958.

Mill, John Stuart. *Principles of Political Economy.* 1896.

Prince, Samuel Henry. *Catastrophe and Social Change.* 1920.

Sorokin, Pitirim A. *Man and Society in Calamity.* 1942.

Entrepreneurship

Mark Casson

■ The term *entrepreneur,* which most people recognize as meaning someone who organizes and assumes the risk of a business in return for the profits, appears to have been introduced by Richard Cantillon (1697–1734), an Irish economist of French descent. The term came into much wider use after John Stuart Mill popularized it in his 1848 classic, *Principles of Political Economy,* but then all but disappeared from the economics literature by the end of the nineteenth century.

The reason is simple. In their mathematical models of economic activity and behavior, economists began to use the simplifying assumption that all people in an economy have perfect information (see INFORMATION). That leaves no role for the entrepreneur. Although different economists have emphasized different facets of entrepreneurship, all economists who have written about it agree that at its core entrepreneurship involves judgment. But if people have perfect information, there is no need for judgment. Fortunately, economists have increasingly dropped the assumption of perfect information in recent years. As this trend continues, economists are likely to allow in their models for the role of the entrepreneur. When they do, they can learn from past economists, who took entrepreneurship more seriously.

According to Cantillon's original formulation, the entrepreneur is a specialist in taking on risk. He "insures" workers by buying their products (or their labor services) for resale before consumers have indicated how much they are willing to pay for them. The workers receives an assured income (in the short run, at least), while the entrepreneur bears the risk caused by price fluctuations in consumer markets.

This idea was refined by the U.S. economist Frank H. Knight (1885–1972), who distinguished between risk, which is insurable, and uncertainty, which is not. Risk relates to recurring events whose relative frequency is known from past experience, while uncertainty relates to unique events whose probability can only be subjectively estimated. Changes affecting the marketing of consumer products generally fall in the uncertainty category. Individual tastes, for example, are affected by group culture, which, in turn, depends on fashion trends that are essentially unique. Insurance companies exploit the law of large numbers to reduce the overall burden of risks by "pooling" them. For instance, no one knows whether any individual forty-year-old will die in the next year. But insurance companies do know with relative certainty how many forty-year-olds in a large group will die within a year. Armed with this knowledge, they know what price to charge for life insurance, but they cannot do the same when it comes to uncertainties. Knight observed that while the entrepreneur can "lay off" risks much like insurance companies do, he is left to bear the uncertainties himself. He is content to do this because his profit compensates him for the psychological cost involved.

If new companies are free to enter an industry and existing companies are free to exit, then in the long run entrepreneurs and capital will exit from industries where profits are low and enter ones where they are high. If uncertainties were equal between industries, this shift of entrepreneurs and of capital would occur until profits were equal in each industry. Any long-run differences in industry profit rates, therefore, can be explained by the different magnitudes of the uncertainties involved.

Joseph A. Schumpeter (1883–1950) took a different approach, emphasizing the role of innovation. According to Schumpeter, the entrepreneur is someone who carries out "new combinations" by such things as introducing new products or processes, identifying new export markets or sources of supply, or creating new types of organization. Schumpeter presented an heroic vision of the entrepreneur as someone motivated by the "dream and the will to found a private kingdom"; the "will to conquer: the impulse to fight, to prove oneself superior to others"; and the "joy of creating."

In Schumpeter's view the entrepreneur leads the way in creating new industries, which, in turn, precipitate major structural changes in the economy. Old industries are rendered obsolete by a process of "creative destruction." As the new industries compete with established ones for labor, materials, and investment goods, they drive up the price of these resources. The old industries cannot pass on their higher costs because demand is switching to new products. As the old industries decline, the new ones ex- pand because imitators, with optimistic profit expectations based on the innovator's initial success, continue to invest. Eventually, overcapacity depresses profits and halts investment. The economy goes into depression, and innovation stops. Invention continues, however, and eventually there is a sufficient stock of unexploited inventions to encourage courageous entrepreneurs to begin innovation again. In this way Schumpeter used entrepreneurship to explain structural change, economic growth, and business cycles, using a combination of economic and psychological ideas.

Schumpeter was concerned with the "high-level" kind of entrepreneurship that, historically, has led to the creation of railroads, the birth of the chemical industry, the commercial exploitation of colonies, and the emergence of the multidivisional multinational firm. His analysis left little room for the much more common, but no less important, "low-level" entrepreneurship carried on by small firms. The essence of this low-level activity can be explained by the Austrian approach of Friedrich A. Hayek and Israel M. Kirzner. In a market economy, price information is provided by entrepreneurs. While bureaucrats in a socialist economy have no incentive to discover prices for themselves (see SOCIALISM), entrepreneurs in a market economy are motivated to do so by profit opportunities. Entrepreneurs provide price quotations to others as an invitation to trade with them. They hope to make a profit by buying cheap and selling dear. In the long run, competition between entrepreneurs arbitrages away price differentials, but in the short run, such differentials, once discovered, generate a profit for the arbitrageur.

The difficulty with the Austrian approach is that it isolates the entrepreneur from the firm. It fits an individual dealer or speculator far better than it fits a small manufacturer or even a retailer. In many cases (and in almost all large corporations), owners delegate decisions to salaried managers, and the question then arises whether a salaried manager, too, can be an entrepreneur. Frank Knight maintained that no owner would ever delegate a key decision to a salaried subordinate, because he implicitly assumed that subordinates cannot be trusted. Uncertainty bearing, therefore, is inextricably vested in the owners of the firm's equity, according to Knight. But in practice subordinates can win a reputation for being good stewards, and even though salaried, they have incentives to establish and maintain such reputations because their promotion prospects depend upon it. In this sense, both owners and managers can be entrepreneurs.

The title of entrepreneur should, however, be confined to an owner or manager who exhibits the key trait of entrepreneurship noted above: judgment in decision making. Judgment is a capacity for making a successful decision when no obviously correct model or decision rule is available or when relevant data is unreliable or incomplete. Cantillon's entrepreneur needs judgment to speculate on future price movements, while Knight's entrepreneur requires judgment because he deals in situations that are unprecedented and unique. Schumpeter's entrepreneur needs judgment to deal with the novel situations connected with innovation.

The insights of previous economists can be synthesized. Entrepreneurs are specialists who use judgment to deal with novel and complex problems. Sometimes they own the resources to which the problems are related, and sometimes they are stewards employed by the owners. In times of major political, social, and environmental change, the number of problems requiring judgment increases and the demand for entrepreneurs rises as a result. For supply to match demand, more people have to forgo other careers in order to become entrepreneurs. They are encouraged to do so by the higher expected pecuniary rewards associated with entrepreneurship, and perhaps also by increases in the social status of entrepreneurs, as happened in the eighties.

The supply of entrepreneurs depends not only on reward and status, but also on personality, culture, and life experience. An entrepreneur will often find that his opinion is in conflict with the majority view. He needs the self-confidence that, even though in a minority, he is right. He must be persuasive, however, without disclosing too much information, because others may steal his ideas. Such shrewdness must, moreover, be combined with a reputation for honesty, because otherwise no one will wish to lend money to him for fear of deliberate default.

In identifying profitable opportunities the entrepreneur needs to synthesize information from different sources. Thus, the Schumpeterian innovator may need to synthesize technical information on an invention with information on customer needs and on the availability of suitable raw materials. A good education combined with wide-ranging practical experience helps the entrepreneur to interpret such varied kinds of information. Sociability also helps the entrepreneur to make contact with people who can supply such information second-hand. For low-level entrepreneurship, education and breadth of experience may be less important because information is less technical and more localized. Good social contacts within the local community are more important here. Key information is obtained by joining the local church, town council, residents' association, and so on.

The culture of a community may be an important influence on the level of entrepreneurship. A community that accords the highest status to those at the top of hierarchical organizations encourages "pyramid climbing," while awarding high status to professional expertise may encourage premature educational specialization. Both of these are inimical to entrepreneurship. The first directs ambition away from innovation (rocking the boat), while the second leads to the neglect of relevant information generated outside the limited boundaries of the profession. According high status to the "self-made" man or woman is more likely to encourage entrepreneurship.

There seems to be considerable inertia in the supply of entrepreneurs. One reason is that the culture affects the supply, and the culture itself changes only very slowly. Entrepreneurship is one of the major avenues of social and economic advancement, along with sport and entertainment. But the Horatio Alger myth that the typical entrepreneur has risen from rags to riches disguises the fact that as Frank Taussig and others have found, many of the most successful entrepreneurs are the sons of professionals and entrepreneurs. They owe much of their success to parental training and inherited family contacts. Thus, in most societies there is insufficient social mobility for entrepre-

neurial culture to change simply because of the changing origins of the entrepreneural elite. In any case, "self-made" entrepreneurs often adopt the culture of the elite, neglecting their business interests for social and political activities and even (in Britain) educating their children to pursue a more "respectable" career.

In the long run, though, changes can occur that have profound implications for entrepreneurship. In modern economies large corporations whose shares are widely held have replaced the family firm founded by the self-made entrepreneur. Corporations draw on a wider range of management skill than is available from any single family, and they avoid the problem of succession by an incompetent eldest son that has been the ruin of many family firms. Corporations plan large-scale activities using teams of professional specialists, but their efficiency gains are to some extent offset by the loss of employee loyalty that was a feature of many family firms. Loyal employees do not need close supervision, or complex bonus systems, to make them work, because they are self-motivated. Historically, family firms have drawn on two main sources of "cultural capital": the paternalistic idea that employees are adopted members of the founder's family, and the founder's own religious and moral values. The first is effective only within small firms.

A modern corporation that wishes to build up a family spirit must do so within its individual business units. These units can then be bonded together by a unifying corporate culture—the modern equivalent of the founder's system of values. The dissemination of corporate culture may be assisted by the charisma of the chairman or chief executive. This suggests that senior management in the modern corporation requires not only entrepreneurial skills, but also leadership skills—which means the ability to inspire trust and affection, rather than just fear, in subordinates. The need to combine entrepreneurial skills and leadership skills is, of course, universal, but its significance has increased as organizations have become larger and societies have abandoned traditional religions for secular values.

—**Mark Casson**

Biography: Mark Casson is an economics professor at the University of Reading in England.

Further Reading

Casson, Mark C. *The Entrepreneur: An Economic Theory.* 1982. Reprint. 1991.

———, ed. *Entrepreneurship.* Vol. 13, *International Library of Critical Writings in Economics.* 1990.

Evans, David S., and Linda S. Leighton. ''Some Empirical Aspects of Entrepreneurship.'' *American Economic Review* 79, no. 3 (1989): 519–35.

Kirzner, Israel M. *Perception, Opportunity and Profit.* 1979.

Rosenberg, Nathan, and L. E. Birdzell. *How the West Grew Rich: The Economic Transformation of the Industrial World.* 1986.

Taussig, Frank W., and C. S. Joslyn. *American Business Leaders: A Study in Social Origins and Social Stratification.* 1932.

Free Market

Murray N. Rothbard

■ *Free market* is a summary term for an array of exchanges that take place in society. Each exchange is undertaken as a voluntary agreement between two people or between groups of people represented by agents. These two individuals (or agents) exchange two economic goods, either tangible commodities or nontangible services. Thus, when I buy a newspaper from a newsdealer for fifty cents, the newsdealer and I exchange two commodities: I give up fifty cents, and the newsdealer gives up the newspaper. Or if I work for a corporation, I exchange my labor services, in a mutually agreed way, for a monetary salary; here the corporation is represented by a manager (an agent) with the authority to hire.

Both parties undertake the exchange because each expects to gain from it. Also, each will repeat the exchange next time (or refuse to) because his expectation has proved correct (or incorrect) in the recent past. Trade, or exchange, is engaged in precisely because both parties benefit; if they did not expect to gain, they would not agree to the exchange.

This simple reasoning refutes the argument against free trade typical of the "mercantilist" period of sixteenth- to eighteenth-century Europe, and classically expounded by the famed sixteenth-century French essayist Montaigne. The mercantilists argued that in any trade, one party can benefit only at the expense of the other, that in every transaction there is a winner and a loser, an "exploiter" and an "exploited." We can immediately see the fallacy in this still-popular viewpoint: the willingness and even eagerness to trade means that both parties benefit. In modern game-theory jargon, trade is a win-win situation, a "positive-sum" rather than a "zero-sum" or "negative-sum" game.

How can both parties benefit from an exchange? Each one values the two goods or services differently, and these differences set the scene for an exchange. I, for example, am walking along with money in my pocket but no newspaper; the newsdealer, on the other hand, has plenty of newspapers but is anxious to acquire money. And so, finding each other, we strike a deal.

Two factors determine the terms of any agreement: how much each participant values each good in question, and each participant's bargaining skills. How many cents will exchange for one newspaper, or how many Mickey Mantle baseball cards will swap for a Babe Ruth, depends on all the participants in the newspaper market or the baseball card market—on how much each one values the cards as compared to the other goods he could buy. These terms of exchange, called "prices" (of newspapers in terms of money, or of Babe Ruth cards in terms of Mickey Mantles), are ultimately determined by how many newspapers, or baseball cards, are available on the market in relation to how favorably buyers evaluate these goods. In shorthand, by the interaction of their supply with the demand for them.

Given the supply of a good, an increase in its value in the minds of the buyers will raise the demand for the good, more money will be bid for it, and its price will rise. The reverse occurs if the value, and therefore the demand, for the good falls. On the other hand, given the buyers' evaluation, or demand, for a good, if the supply increases, each unit of supply—each baseball card or loaf of bread—will fall in value, and therefore, the price of the good will fall. The reverse occurs if the supply of the good decreases.

The market, then, is not simply an array, but a highly complex, interacting latticework of exchanges. In primitive societies, exchanges are all barter or direct exchange. Two people trade two directly useful goods, such as horses for cows or Mickey Mantles for Babe Ruths. But as a society develops, a step-by-step process of mutual benefit creates a situation in which one or two broadly useful and valuable commodities are chosen on the market as a medium of indirect exchange. This money-commodity, generally but not always gold or silver, is then demanded not only for its own sake, but even more to facilitate a reexchange for another desired commodity. It is much easier to pay steelworkers not in steel bars, but in money, with which the workers can then buy whatever they desire. They are willing to accept money because they know from experience and insight that everyone else in the society will also accept that money in payment.

The modern, almost infinite latticework of exchanges, the market, is made possible by the use of money. Each person engages in specialization, or a division of labor, pro-

ducing what he or she is best at. Production begins with natural resources, and then various forms of machines and capital goods, until finally, goods are sold to the consumer. At each stage of production from natural resource to consumer good, money is voluntarily exchanged for capital goods, labor services, and land resources. At each step of the way, terms of exchanges, or prices, are determined by the voluntary interactions of suppliers and demanders. This market is "free" because choices, at each step, are made freely and voluntarily.

The free market and the free price system make goods from around the world available to consumers. The free market also gives the largest possible scope to entrepreneurs, who risk capital to allocate resources so as to satisfy the future desires of the mass of consumers as efficiently as possible. Saving and investment can then develop capital goods and increase the productivity and wages of workers, thereby increasing their standard of living. The free competitive market also rewards and stimulates technological innovation that allows the innovator to get a head start in satisfying consumer wants in new and creative ways.

Not only is investment encouraged, but perhaps more important, the price system, and the profit-and-loss incentives of the market, guide capital investment and production into the proper paths. The intricate latticework can mesh and "clear" all markets so that there are no sudden, unforeseen, and inexplicable shortages and surpluses anywhere in the production system.

But exchanges are not necessarily free. Many are coerced. If a robber threatens you with "Your money or your life," your payment to him is coerced and not voluntary, and he benefits at your expense. It is robbery, not free markets, that actually follows the mercantilist model: the robber benefits at the expense of the coerced. Exploitation occurs not in the free market, but where the coercer exploits his victim. In the long run, coercion is a negative-sum game that leads to reduced production, saving, and investment, a depleted stock of capital, and reduced productivity and living standards for all, perhaps even for the coercers themselves.

Government, in every society, is the only lawful system of coercion. Taxation is a coerced exchange, and the heavier the burden of taxation on production, the more likely it is that economic growth will falter and decline. Other forms of government coercion (e.g., price controls or restrictions that prevent new competitors from entering a market) hamper and cripple market exchanges, while others (prohibitions on deceptive practices, enforcement of contracts) can facilitate voluntary exchanges.

The ultimate in government coercion is socialism. Under socialist central planning the socialist planning board lacks a price system for land or capital goods. As even socialists like Robert Heilbroner now admit (see SOCIALISM), the socialist planning board therefore has no way to calculate prices or costs or to invest capital so that the latticework of production meshes and clears. The current Soviet experience, where a bumper wheat harvest somehow cannot find its way to retail stores, is an instructive example of the impossibility of operating a complex, modern economy in the absence of a free market. There was neither incentive nor means of calculating prices and costs for hopper cars to get to the wheat, for the flour mills to receive and process it, and so on down through the large number of stages needed to reach the ultimate consumer in Moscow or Sverdlovsk. The investment in wheat is almost totally wasted.

Market socialism is, in fact, a contradiction in terms. The fashionable discussion of market socialism often overlooks one crucial aspect of the market. When two goods are indeed exchanged, what is really exchanged is the property titles in those goods. When I buy a newspaper for fifty cents, the seller and I are exchanging property titles: I yield the ownership of the fifty cents and grant it to the newsdealer, and he yields the ownership of the newspaper to me. The exact same process occurs as in buying a house, except that in the case of the newspaper, matters are much more informal, and we can all avoid the intricate process of deeds, notarized contracts, agents, attorneys, mortgage brokers, and so on. But the economic nature of the two transactions remains the same.

This means that the key to the existence and flourishing of the free market is a society in which the rights and titles of private property are respected, defended, and kept secure. The key to socialism, on the other hand, is government ownership of the means of production, land, and capital goods. Thus, there can be no market in land or capital goods worthy of the name.

Some critics of the free-market argue that property rights are in conflict with "human" rights. But the critics fail to realize that in a free-market system, every person has a property right over his own person and his own labor, and that he can make free contracts for those services. Slavery violates the basic property right of the slave over his own body and person, a right that is the groundwork for any person's property rights over nonhuman material objects. What's more, all rights are human rights, whether it is everyone's right to free speech or one individual's property rights in his own home.

A common charge against the free-market society is that it institutes "the law of the jungle," of "dog eat dog," that it spurns human cooperation for competition, and that it exalts material success as opposed to spiritual values, philosophy, or leisure activities. On the contrary, the jungle is precisely a society of coercion, theft, and parasitism, a society that demolishes lives and living standards. The peaceful market competition of producers and suppliers is a profoundly cooperative process in which everyone benefits, and where everyone's living standard flourishes (compared to what it would be in an unfree society). And the undoubted material success of free societies provides the general affluence that permits us to enjoy an enormous amount of leisure as compared to other societies, and to pursue matters of the spirit. It is the coercive countries with little or no market activity, notably under communism, where the grind of daily existence not only impoverishes people materially, but deadens their spirit.

—Murray N. Rothbard

Biography: Murray N. Rothbard is an economics professor at the University of Nevada in Las Vegas.

Further Reading

Ballve, Faustino. *Essentials of Economics.* 1963.
Hazlitt, Henry. *Economics in One Lesson.* 1946.
Mises, Ludwig von. *Economic Freedom and Intervention*, edited by Bettina Greaves. 1990.
Rockwell, Llewellyn, Jr., ed. *The Free Market Reader.* 1988.
———, ed. *The Economics of Liberty.* 1990.
Rothbard, Murray N. *Power and Market: Government and the Economy*, 2d ed. 1977.
———. *What Has Government Done to Our Money?* 4th ed. 1990.

Game Theory

Avinash Dixit and Barry Nalebuff

■ Game theory is the science of strategy. It attempts to determine mathematically and logically the actions that "players" should take to secure the best outcomes for themselves in a wide array of "games." The games it studies range from chess to child rearing and from tennis to takeovers. But the games all share the common feature of interdependence. That is, the outcome for each participant depends upon the choices (strategies) of all. In so-called zero-sum games the interests of the players conflict totally, so that one person's gain always is another's loss. More typical are games with the potential for either mutual gain (positive sum) or mutual harm (negative sum), as well as some conflict.

Game theory was pioneered by Princeton mathematician John von Neumann. In the early years the emphasis was on games of pure conflict (zero-sum games). Other games were considered in a cooperative form. That is, the participants were supposed to choose and implement their actions jointly. Recent research has focused on games that are neither zero-sum nor purely cooperative. In these games the players choose their actions separately, but their links to others involve elements of both competition and cooperation.

Games are fundamentally different from decisions made in a neutral environment. To illustrate the point, think of the difference between the decisions of a lumberjack and those of a general. When the lumberjack decides how to chop wood, he does not expect the wood to fight back; his environment is neutral. But when the general tries to cut down the enemy's army, he must anticipate and overcome resistance to his plans. Like the general, a game player must recognize his interaction with other intelligent and purposive people. His own choice must allow for both conflict and for possibilities for cooperation.

The essence of a game is the interdependence of player strategies. There are two distinct types of strategic interdependence: sequential and simultaneous. In the former the players move in sequence, each aware of the others' previous actions. In the latter the players act at the same time, each ignorant of the others' actions.

A general principle for a player in a sequential-move game is to look ahead and reason back. Each player should figure out how the other players will respond to his current move, how he will respond in turn, and so on. The player anticipates where his initial decisions will ultimately lead, and uses this information to calculate his current best choice. When thinking about how others will respond, one must put oneself in their shoes and think as they would; one should not impose one's own reasoning on them.

In principle, any sequential game that ends after a finite sequence of moves can be "solved" completely. We determine each player's best strategy by looking ahead to every possible outcome. Simple games, such as tic-tac-toe, can be solved in this way and are therefore not challenging. For many other games, such as chess, the calculations are too complex to perform in practice—even with computers. Therefore, the players look a few moves ahead and try to evaluate the resulting positions on the basis of experience.

In contrast to the linear chain of reasoning for sequential games, a game with simultaneous moves involves a logical circle. Although the players act at the same time, in ignorance of the others' current actions, each must be aware that there are other players who, in turn, are similarly aware, and so on. The thinking goes: "I think that he thinks that I think. . . ." Therefore, each must figuratively put himself in the shoes of all and try to calculate the outcome. His own best action is an integral part of this overall calculation.

This logical circle is squared (the circular reasoning is brought to a conclusion) using a concept of equilibrium developed by the Princeton mathematician John Nash. We look for a set of choices, one for each player, such that each person's strategy is best for him when all others are playing their stipulated best strategies. In other words, each picks his best response to what the others do.

Sometimes one person's best choice is the same no matter what the others do. This is called a dominant strategy for that player. At other times, one player has a uniformly bad choice—a dominated strategy—in the sense that some other choice is better for him no matter what the others do. The search for an equilibrium should begin by looking for dominant strategies and eliminating dominated ones.

When we say that an outcome is an equilibrium, there is no presumption that each person's privately best choice will lead to a collectively optimal result. Indeed, there are notorious examples, such as the prisoners' dilemma (see below), where the players are drawn into a bad outcome by each following his best private interests.

Nash's notion of equilibrium remains an incomplete solution to the problem of circular reasoning in simultaneous-move games. Some games have many such equilibria while others have none. And the dynamic process that can lead to an equilibrium is left unspecified. But in spite of these flaws, the concept has proved extremely useful in analyzing many strategic interactions.

The following examples of strategic interaction illustrate some of the fundamentals of game theory:

- **The prisoners' dilemma.** Two suspects are questioned separately, and each can confess or keep silent. If suspect A keeps silent, then suspect B can get a better deal by confessing. If A confesses, B had better confess to avoid especially harsh treatment. Confession is B's dominant strategy. The same is true for A. Therefore, in equilibrium both confess. Both would fare better if they both stayed silent. Such cooperative behavior can be achieved in repeated plays of the game because the temporary gain from cheating (confession) can be outweighed by the long-run loss due to the breakdown of cooperation. Strategies such as tit-for-tat are suggested in this context. (See also PRISONERS' DILEMMA.)

- **Mixing moves.** In some situations of conflict, any systematic action will be discovered and exploited by the rival. Therefore, it is important to keep the rival guessing by mixing one's moves. Typical examples arise in sports—whether to run or to pass in a particular situation in football, or whether to hit a passing shot crosscourt or down the line in tennis. Game theory quantifies this insight and details the right proportions of such mixtures.

- **Strategic moves.** A player can use threats and promises to alter other players' expectations of his future actions, and thereby induce them to take actions favorable to him or deter them from making moves that harm him. To succeed, the threats and promises must be credible. This is problematic because when the time comes, it is generally costly to carry out a threat or make good on a promise. Game theory studies several ways to enhance credibility. The general principle is that it can be in a player's interest to reduce his own freedom of future action. By so doing, he removes his own temptation to renege on a promise or to forgive others' transgressions.

  For example, Cortés burned his own ships upon his arrival in Mexico. He purposefully eliminated retreat as an option. Without ships to sail home, Cortés would either succeed in his conquest or perish. Although his soldiers were vastly outnumbered, this threat to fight to the death demoralized the opposition; it chose to retreat rather than fight such a determined opponent. Polaroid Corporation used a similar strategy when it purposefully refused to diversify out of the instant photography market. It was committed to a life-or-death battle against any intruder in the market. When Kodak entered the instant photography market, Polaroid put all its resources into the fight; fourteen years later, Polaroid won a nearly billion-dollar lawsuit against Kodak and regained its monopoly market.

  Another way to make threats credible is to employ the adventuresome strategy of brinkmanship—deliberately creating a risk that if other players fail to act as one would like them to, the outcome will be bad for everyone. Introduced by Thomas Schelling in *The Strategy of Conflict*, brinkmanship "is the tactic of deliberately letting the situation get somewhat out of hand, just because its being out of hand may be intolerable to the other party and force his accommodation." When mass demonstrators confronted totalitarian governments in Eastern Europe and China, both sides were engaging in just such a strategy. Sometimes one side backs down and concedes defeat; other times, tragedy results when they fall over the brink together.

- **Bargaining.** Two players decide how to split a pie. Each wants a larger share, and both prefer to achieve agreement sooner rather than later. When the two take turns making offers, the principle of looking ahead and reasoning back determines the equilibrium shares. Agreement is reached at once, but the cost of delay governs the shares. The player more impatient to reach agreement gets a smaller share.

- **Concealing and revealing information.** When one player knows something that others do not, sometimes he is anxious to conceal this information (one's hand in poker), and at other times he wants to reveal it credibly (a company's commitment to quality). In both cases the general principle is that actions speak louder than words. To conceal information, mix your moves. Bluffing in poker, for example, must not be systematic. Recall Winston Churchill's dictum of hiding the truth in a "bodyguard of lies." To convey information, use an action that is a credible "signal," something that would not be desirable if the circumstances were otherwise. For example, an extended warranty is a credible signal to the consumer that the firm believes it is producing a high-quality product.

Recent advances in game theory have succeeded in describing and prescribing appropriate strategies in several situations of conflict and cooperation. But the theory is far from complete, and in many ways the design of successful strategy remains an art.

—Avinash Dixit and Barry Nalebuff

Biography: Avinash Dixit is the John J. Sherred Professor of Economics at Princeton University. Barry Nalebuff is a professor of economics and management at Yale University's School of Organization and Management.

Further Reading

Introductory
Ankeny, Nesmith. *Poker Strategy: Winning with Game Theory*. 1981.
Brams, Steven. *Game Theory and Politics*. 1979.
Davis, Morton. *Game Theory: A Nontechnical Introduction*, 2d ed. 1983.
Dixit, Avinash, and Barry Nalebuff. *Thinking Strategically: A Competitive Edge in Business, Politics, and Everyday Life*. 1991.
Luce, Duncan, and Howard Raiffa. *Games and Decisions*. 1957.
McDonald, John. *Strategy in Poker, Business and War*. 1950.
Porter, Michael. *Competitive Strategy*. 1982.
Raiffa, Howard. *The Art and Science of Negotiation*. 1982.
Riker, William. *The Art of Political Manipulation*. 1986.
Schelling, Thomas. *The Strategy of Conflict*. 1960.
Williams, J. D. *The Compleat Strategyst*, rev. ed. 1966.
Advanced
Neumann, John von, and Oskar Morgenstern. *Theory of Games and Economic Behavior*. 1947.
Ordeshook, Peter. *Game Theory and Political Theory*. 1986.
Shubik, Martin. *Game Theory in the Social Sciences*. 1982.

See also OPEC, PRISONERS' DILEMMA, THE TRAGEDY OF THE COMMONS.

CHAPTER THIRTEEN

THE ECONOMICS OF SPECIAL MARKETS

Agricultural Price Supports

Robert L. Thompson

■ Most governments around the world intervene actively in the operation of their agricultural markets. The ways they intervene and the reasons they do so depend in large part on the wealth of the country. Governments in poor Third World countries routinely impose price controls to keep food prices artificially low. They do so to gain favor with their more politically powerful urban residents. Though numerous (and partly because they are numerous), peasant farmers do not organize politically and therefore have much less political power than their urban brethren. The irony of this situation is that by artificially depressing the price of food, Third World governments reduce incentives for farmers to produce and reduce the availability of food from indigenous sources.

This has been particularly prevalent in Africa, the one continent to experience consistently declining per capita food production in the postcolonial period. In many African nations, state marketing boards are granted a legal monopoly to buy agricultural products from farmers and to resell them to domestic consumers and in export markets. Such boards often pay farmers only a third to half of the domestic consumer price or the export price. The result, according to the World Bank, is that after growing 0.2 percent per year in the sixties, per capita food production in sub-Saharan Africa fell at the rate of 0.9 percent per year from 1970 into the early eighties.

In highly developed countries, on the other hand, the opposite occurs. As development proceeds, the percentage of a nation's population employed in agriculture declines. The shrinking number of farmers makes organizing in interest groups easier. Furthermore, political redistricting often lags behind the shift in population to the cities. As a result, rural districts often have more legislative representatives and enjoy greater political power than their numbers would suggest. Farmers use this power to seek higher and more stable farm prices via legislation or fiat.

But good political organization is not the only reason that farmers succeed in getting governments to raise their prices. A second reason is that farmers are often viewed as disadvantaged. Rural communities lack many of the amenities that cities have. And because labor productivity is generally lower in agriculture than in manufacturing, wage rates are lower. Also, technological change tends to expand agricultural production faster than consumption, reducing the price of farm products. In 1870, for example, the price of wheat was over eleven dollars per bushel in 1991 dollars. Today, it is only about four dollars per bushel, a drop of over 60 percent. Although consumers gain by paying lower prices, the incomes of farmers drop. As labor leaves agriculture in search of higher income in the cities, the reduced supply of farmers causes the remaining farmers' incomes to rise back to their previous level. This can take years, however.

A third reason governments intervene to support farm prices is that they often are volatile. Weather conditions, over which farmers have no control, are an important determinant of how much a farmer harvests in a given year. The resulting variability of production in the face of relatively stable demand causes farm prices, and farmers' incomes, to vary from year to year. This may cause economic hardship for farm families in a bad year. It may also cause farmers to go bankrupt because modern farming requires large investments in specialized facilities and equipment.

Forms of Price Support

It is easiest to support the price of an agricultural product if a country's farmers do not produce enough of it to meet domestic consumption. The rest is made up through imports. In these cases the country simply imposes an import duty or quota until the domestic price rises to the desired level. Growers receive the higher price, and consumers pay the higher price for both imports and for domestic production. For example, in the mideighties, when the world market price of sugar was four cents per pound, United States import quotas were so limiting that the domestic wholesale price exceeded twenty cents per pound.

When a country grows more of a product than it consumes, supporting the price is more complex and requires a substantial bureaucracy. Legislating a minimum legal price below which a good cannot be sold rarely works. So instead of legislating mini-

mum prices, governments sometimes try to raise prices artificially by limiting production. Each farmer may be issued a quota that stipulates how much he can sell in a given year. This is done with peanuts in the United States and milk in Canada. Limiting supply can raise market prices as long as government inspectors monitor the market to ensure that no production beyond the quota is sold for a lower price. Limiting production effectively cartelizes the industry, and the government enforces the cartel.

While this policy raises prices, the only people who benefit are the individual farmers who receive the quotas when they are initially allocated. Because of their scarcity, the quotas immediately take on value. All future entrants must buy a quota to gain the right to sell the product. That raises the investment required to become a farmer and the cost of production. Once the original quotas are sold to new farmers, those farmers become a strong lobbying force against ever giving up quotas.

More common than issuing quotas is the practice of requiring (or paying) farmers to take land out of production. This "set-aside" approach rarely is very effective at supporting agricultural prices. Farmers are not stupid; they set aside their least productive land first. Furthermore, a policy that creates artificial scarcity of land induces farmers to intensify their production practices on each acre that remains in production, raising its yield. So unless very large reductions in acreage are required, set-asides alone rarely reduce production very much. Moreover, intensifying production often requires heavier doses of fertilizer and agricultural chemicals, with potentially adverse environmental consequences. For example, farmers in the European Economic Community (EC), where support prices for grain are higher than those in the United States, use more than twice as much fertilizer per acre than U.S. farmers. As a result a number of northern European countries are encountering elevated levels of fertilizer nutrients in their groundwater.

The most common U.S. approach to supporting the price of an exportable agricultural product is to create a government agency to buy any quantity of a product offered by the country's farmers at the guaranteed "support price."

That keeps market prices at or near the support price. Within the United States Department of Agriculture, this agency is called the Commodity Credit Corporation (CCC). Support prices must be accompanied by import quotas. Otherwise, foreign producers would sell their products in the U.S. market as long as the U.S. price exceeded the price they could get elsewhere. If that happened, the U.S. government would wind up guaranteeing the U.S. price to farmers around the world. A U.S. example is dairy products, which the CCC buys to support the farm price of milk. Quotas limit imports of dairy products to less than 3 percent of consumption. The CCC disposes of the commodities it buys in ways that will not displace market demand and depress the domestic market price. For example, dairy products are often given away to low-income people, in the school lunch program, and as foreign aid.

A variant of this policy is designed to stabilize market prices. The CCC buys grain at the support price, stores it, and releases it back into the market if the market price rises to a prescribed trigger level of,

say, 140 percent of the support price. In this manner the policy protects growers against the risk of low prices but also protects consumers against unusually high prices. This type of government program can provide some protection against wide swings in prices if the acquisition (support) price is set at about 75 percent of a five-year moving average of market prices (leaving the highest number and the lowest number out of the calculation). The markup between acquisition and release price should cover the cost of operating the buffer stock program.

Farm organizations, however, often lobby to raise the acquisition and release prices, so that "stabilization policy" becomes price support policy. When this happens, government inventories tend to rise without limit until the stabilization agency exhausts its budget for buying the product. This is exactly what happened when the Federal Farm Board, the predecessor of the CCC, tried to support the U.S. prices of wheat and cotton in 1929. At that point the agency has to subsidize the export of the inventories, with the taxpayers picking up the loss on the operation.

The United States currently uses a hybrid approach to price supports that also involves loans. At harvest the CCC gives grain farmers nine-month loans equal to their production times the support price. The support price is called the "loan rate." The CCC accepts the grain as collateral for the loan. If, during the term of the loan, the market price rises above the support price, farmers repay the loans with interest and sell the grain in the market. If the market price remains at or below the loan rate, farmers forfeit the grain to the CCC, keep the money, and have no further obligation. Such loans are called nonrecourse loans, meaning that the lender has no claim on the borrower beyond the collateral (in this case the crop).

Price Supports Cause Overproduction

By supporting prices above the market-clearing level, governments encourage farmers to expand production. To produce more, farmers apply more inputs per acre. They also compete against one another for the finite amount of farmland, bidding up its price. In this way the value of the price supports is capitalized (incorporated) into land prices. Thus, it is the owners of farmland, and not farmers per se, who are the principal beneficiaries of agricultural price supports. (See RICARDO.)

Price supports cause larger production and smaller consumption (since consumers will buy less of any good as its price rises), resulting in overproduction at the support price. The only way for the price support agency to get rid of its inventories is to use export subsidies to make them cheap enough that foreigners will buy them. The EC uses this approach for grains. From the midseventies to early eighties, internal EC grain prices were 150 to 200 percent of the prices at which other countries were willing to export their grain. Subsidies to agriculture account for over two-thirds of the total EC budget.

The United States takes a different approach for grains. With minor exceptions the United States does not make its domestic consumers pay more for grain than for-

eign buyers pay. Instead, the U.S. government combines price supports with income supports that are known as deficiency payments. In normal years the market price is above the support price, and the CCC accumulates few inventories. A so-called target price is then set at a somewhat higher level than the support price, usually through political bargaining between farm organizations and the federal government. The government then pays to producers, as an income supplement, the difference between the target price and the higher of the support price or the market price. To receive this income transfer, a farmer must set aside a prescribed fraction of his historical acreage planted in that crop, as documented in the county office of USDA's Agricultural Stabilization and Conservation Administration. The payment is made on only a finite volume of production equaling a prescribed fraction of the acreage planted each year times a fixed fraction of the historical yield per acre.

The deficiency payment was once paid on a farmer's full production. This encouraged farmers to intensify production and to plow up more land (often highly erodible) to qualify for larger government deficiency payments. As the program has evolved, the payments have been decoupled from production decisions. A farmer cannot gain larger deficiency payments from either planting more land or intensifying input use on the acres in production. In this sense the deficiency payments have moved far in the direction of becoming lump-sum income transfers that are not affected by current or future production decisions. But since the deficiency payment is made on a fraction of the historical acreage planted on a given farm, the land on farms with larger historical bases is worth more than land on farms with smaller bases. Once again, the value of the government payments is capitalized into the price of land.

Many people believe that the low income of farm families justifies price supports. The benefits of most farm programs, however, are distributed to farmers in proportion to the volume they produce or to the number of acres they own. In 1989, for example, 71 percent of the farmers in the United States each sold less than $40,000 worth of products. They received only 16 percent of government price-support payments. In contrast, 15 percent of all U.S. farmers each sold over $100,000 worth of products, and their average net cash income was $68,850. That 15 percent of the farm population received 62 percent of all government payments. One can conclude that farm program payments show little correlation with need.

Agricultural price supports often stimulate larger production, tax consumers, and impede international trade. They often transfer income from lower-income consumers to wealthier owners of farmland. Price supports do little to help farmers with below-average incomes because benefits are distributed in proportion to sales. A more efficient and equitable way to help low-income farmers would be to transfer income to them directly.

Although few commercial farmers have low incomes, their incomes are highly variable because variability in weather and in exports create instability in supply and demand. Nevertheless, there are ways to reduce this risk other than through government price supports. One is insurance. Farmers can purchase government-subsidized crop insurance against natural disasters. Farmers can also buy a form of price insurance in the futures markets. Commodity-futures options are really a form of price insurance for which a farmer pays a premium (the price of the option). Before planting his crop, a farmer can purchase a guarantee of a minimum price, without incurring the obligation to sell at that price should the market price be higher at harvest time. More sophisticated commercial farmers employ the full range of price insurance instruments available to reduce their market risk. But these instruments are used less by farmers than they would be if the government did not provide a subsidized form of price insurance through its price-support programs.

—**Robert L. Thompson**

Biography: Robert L. Thompson is dean of agriculture at Purdue University. He was formerly the assistant secretary for economics with the U.S. Department of Agriculture.

Further Reading

Council of Economic Advisers. "Food and Agriculture." In *Economic Report of the President 1984*, 112–44, 1984.

Economic Research Service. *The 1990 Farm Act and the 1990 Budget Reconciliation Act*. USDA/ERS misc. pub. no. 1489. 1990.

Johnson, D. Gale. *World Agriculture in Disarray*, 2d ed. 1990.

Knutson, Ronald D., J. B. Penn, and William T. Boehm. *Agricultural and Food Policy*, 2d ed. 1990.

Paarlberg, Don. *Farm and Food Policy: Issues of the 1980s*. 1980.

Thompson, Robert L. "U.S. Agriculture Policy: Components, Goals, and Possibilities for Change." *Food Policy* 15 (June 1990): 199–208.

Computer Industry

George Gilder

■ Most economic theory ignores or underplays the contributions of technological progress. Mostly relegated to the realm of "exogenous factors" unaffected by economic policy, innovation enters the accounts chiefly as an effect of capital formation—the accumulation of buildings and equipment. Yet the most careful studies of the sources of productivity growth—by such economists as Lord Peter Bauer, Robert Dennison, and Nobel Laureates Simon Kuznets and Robert Solow—assign only a small share to mere accumulation of capital. Somewhere between 55 and 90 percent of productivity gains spring from other factors, such as the advance of knowledge and innovation.

If economic growth feeds on knowledge and innovation, current advances stem largely from the computer industry, a force of innovation devoted chiefly to the generation and use of knowledge. During the mid-eighties, studies at the Brookings Institution by Robert Gordon and Martin Baily ascribed some two-thirds of all U.S. manufacturing productivity growth to advances in efficiency in making computers.

The history of the computer revolution is misunderstood by most people. Conventional histories begin with the creation of

Charles Babbage's analytical engine in the midnineteenth century and proceed through a long series of other giant mechanical calculating machines, climaxing with ENIAC at the University of Pennsylvania in the years after World War II. This is like beginning a history of space flight with a chronicle of triumphs in the production of wheelbarrows and horse-drawn carriages.

The revolution in information technology sprang not from any extension of Babbage's insights in computer science, but from the quantum revolution in physical science. Fundamental breakthroughs in solid-state physics led to the 1972 invention of the microchip. The microchip is a computer etched on a tiny sliver of silicon the size of a fingernail, containing scores of functioning logical devices in a space comparable not to the head of a pin, but to the point of a pin. This invention, not the ENIAC, ignited the real computer revolution.

As Robert Noyce, the key inventor of the microchip and father of the computer revolution, wrote in the early seventies:

Today's microcomputer, at a cost of perhaps $300, has more computing capacity than the first large electronic computer, the ENIAC. It is twenty times faster, has a larger memory, is thousands of times more reliable, consumes the power of a lightbulb rather than that of a locomotive, occupies 1/30,000th the volume and costs 1/10,000 as much.

Since Noyce wrote that, the cost-effectiveness of his invention has risen more than a millionfold in less than two decades.

An effect of entrepreneurial ingenuity and individual creativity, the microchip fueled a siege of innovations that further favored and endowed the values of individual creativity and freedom. Beginning with the computer industry, the impact of the chip reverberated across the entire breadth of the U.S. economy. It galvanized the overall U.S. electronics industry into a force with revenues that, today, exceed the combined revenues of all U.S. automobile, steel, and chemical manufacturers.

The United States dominated the computer industry in 1980, with 80 percent of the industry's revenues worldwide. Most of these revenues were produced by less than ten companies, with IBM as the leader. All of these firms, including IBM, however, lost ground during the ensuing decade, despite the facts that the computer industry grew three times in size and its cost-effectiveness improved some ten-thousand–fold.

This story carries profound lessons. Imagine that someone had told you in 1980 that even though the computer industry verged on extraordinary growth, all of the leading U.S. firms would suffer drastic losses of market share during the decade, and some would virtually leave the business. Would you have predicted that in 1990 U.S. companies would still command over 60 percent of world computer revenue? Probably not. Yet this is what happened. Despite other countries' lavish government programs designed to overtake the United States in computing, the U.S. industry held a majority of market share and increased its edge in revenues. The absolute U.S. lead over the rest of the world in revenues from computers and peripherals rose some 40 percent, from $35 billion in 1979 to $49 billion in 1989, while the U.S. lead in software revenues rose by a factor of 2.5. These numbers are not adjusted for inflation, but because prices in the computer industry dropped throughout this period, the unadjusted statistics understate the actual U.S. lead in real output.

What had happened was an entrepreneurial explosion, with the emergence of some fourteen thousand new software firms. These companies were the catalyst. The United States also generated hundreds of new computer hardware and microchip manufacturers, and they too contributed to the upsurge of the eighties. But software was decisive. Giving dominance to the United States were thousands of young people turning to the personal computer with all the energy and ingenuity that a previous generation had invested in its Model T automobiles.

Bill Gates of Microsoft, a high school hacker and Harvard dropout, wrote the BASIC language for the PC and ten years later was the world's only self-made thirty-five-year-old billionaire. Scores of others followed in his wake, with major software packages and substantial fortunes, which—like Gates'—were nearly all reinvested in their businesses.

During the eighties the number of software engineers increased about 28 percent per year, year after year. The new software firms converted the computer from the tool of data-processing professionals—hovering over huge, air-conditioned mainframes—into a highly portable, relatively inexpensive appliance that anyone could learn to use. Between 1977 and 1987 the percentage of the world's computer power commanded by large centralized computer systems with "dumb" terminals attached dropped from nearly 100 percent to under 1 percent. By 1990 there were over 50 million personal computers in the United States alone; per capita the United States has more than three times as much computer power as Japan.

In contrast to the American approach to the computer industry, European governments have launched a series of national industrial policies, led by national "champion" firms imitating a spurious vision of IBM. These firms mostly pursued memory microchips and mainframe systems as the key to the future. Their only modest successes came from buying up American firms in trouble. Following similar policies, the Japanese performed only marginally better until the late eighties, when they began producing laptop computers. By 1990 the Japanese had won a mere 4 percent of the American computer market.

Meanwhile, American entrepreneurs have launched a whole series of new computer industries, from graphics supercomputers and desktop workstations to transaction processors and script entry systems—all accompanied with new software. The latest U.S. innovation is an array of parallel supercomputers that use scores or even thousands of processors in tandem. Thinking that the game was supercomputers based on between two and eight processors, the Japanese mostly caught up in that field, but still find themselves in the wake of entrepreneurs who constantly change the rules.

Perhaps the key figure in the high-technology revolution of the eighties was a professor at the California Institute of Technology named Carver Mead. In the sixties he foresaw that he and his students would be able to build computer chips fabulously more dense and complex than experts at the time believed possible, or than anyone at the time could design by hand. Therefore, he set out to create programs to computerize chip design. Successfully developing a number of revolutionary design techniques, he taught them to hundreds of students, who, in turn, began teaching them to thousands on other campuses and bringing them into the industry at large.

When Mead began his chip design projects, only a few large computer and microchip firms were capable of designing or manufacturing complex new chips. By the end of the eighties, largely as a result of Mead's and his students' work, any trained person with a workstation computer costing only twenty thousand dollars could not only design a major new chip but also make prototypes on his desktop.

Just as digital desktop publishing programs led to the creation of some ten thousand new publishing companies, so desktop publishing of chip designs and prototypes unleashed tremendous entrepreneurial creativity in the microchip business. In just five years after this equipment came on line in the middle of the decade, the number of new chip designs produced in the United States rose from just under 10,000 a year to well over 100,000.

The nineties are seeing a dramatic acceleration of the progress first sown by the likes of Carver Mead. The number of transistors on a single sliver of silicon is likely to rise from about 20 million in the early nineties to over 1 billion by the year 2001. A billion-transistor chip might hold the central processing units of sixteen Cray

YMP supercomputers. Among the most powerful computers on the market today, these Crays currently sell for some $20 million. Based on the current rate of progress, the "sixteen-Cray" chip might be manufactured for under a hundred dollars soon after the year 2000, bringing perhaps a millionfold rise in the cost-effectiveness of computing hardware.

Just as the personal computer transformed the business systems of the seventies the small computers of the nineties will transform the electronics of broadcasting. Just as a few thousand mainframe computers were linked to hundreds of thousands of dumb terminals, today just over fourteen hundred television stations supply millions of dumb terminals known as television sets.

Many experts believe that the Japanese made the right decision ten years ago when they launched a multibillion-dollar program to develop "high-definition television." HDTV does represent a significant advance; the new sets will have a much higher resolution, larger screens, and other features such as windowing several programs at once. But all these gains will be dwarfed by the millionfold advance in the coming technology of the telecomputer: the personal computer upgraded with supercomputer powers for the processing of full-motion video.

Unlike HDTV, which is mostly an analog system using wave forms specialized for the single purpose of TV broadcast and display, the telecomputer is a fully digital technology. It creates, processes, stores, and transmits information in the nondegradable form of numbers, expressed in bits and bytes. This means the telecomputer will benefit from the same learning curve of steadily increasing powers as the microchip, with its billion-transistor potential, and the office computer with its ever-proliferating software.

The telecomputer is not only a receiver like a TV, but also a processor of video images, capable of windowing, zooming, storing, editing, and replaying. Furthermore, the telecomputer can originate and transmit video images that will be just as high-quality and much cheaper than those the current television and film industries can provide.

This difference replaces perhaps a hundred one-way TV channels with as many channels as there are computers attached to the network: millions of potential two-way channels around the world. With every desktop a possible broadcasting station, thousands of U.S. firms are already pursuing the potential market of a video system as universal and simple to use as the telephone is today.

Imagine a world in which you can dial up any theater, church, concert, film, college classroom, local sport event, or library anywhere and almost instantly receive the program in full-motion video and possibly interact with it. The result will endow inventors and artists with new powers, fueling a new spiral of innovation sweeping beyond the computer industry itself and transforming all media and culture.

—George Gilder

Biography: George Gilder was formerly semiconductors editor of *Release 1.0,* an industry newsletter. He is also a director of semiconductor and telecommunications equipment companies.

Further Reading

Gilder, George. *Microcosm: The Quantum Revolution in Economics and Technology*. 1989.
———. *Life after Television*. 1992.
Hillis, W. Daniel. *The Connection Machine*. 1985.
Malone, Michael. *The Big Score: The Billion-Dollar Story of Silicon Valley*. 1985.
Queisser, Hans. *The Conquest of the Microchip*. 1988.
Scientific American, September 1977. ''Microelectronics'' issue, including articles by Robert Noyce, Carver Mead, and others.

Crime

David D. Friedman

■ Economists approach the analysis of crime with one simple assumption—that criminals are rational people. A mugger is a mugger for the same reason I am an economist—because it is the most attractive alternative available to him. The decision to commit a crime, like any other economic decision, can be analyzed as a choice among alternative combinations of costs and benefits.

Consider, as a simple example, a point that sometimes comes up in discussions of gun control. Opponents of private ownership of handguns argue that in violent contests between criminals and victims, the criminals usually win. A professional criminal, after all, has far more reason to learn how to use a gun than a random potential victim.

The argument is probably true, but the conclusion—that permitting both criminals and victims to have guns will help the criminals—does not follow. To see why, imagine that the result of legal handgun ownership is that one little old lady in ten chooses to carry a pistol in her purse. Further suppose that, of those who do, only one in ten, if mugged, succeeds in killing the mugger—the other nine miss, or drop the gun, or shoot themselves in the foot.

On average, the muggers are winning. But also on average, each one hundred muggings of little old ladies produce one dead mugger. Very few little old ladies carry enough money to be worth one chance in a hundred of being killed. Economic theory suggests that the number of muggings will decrease—not because the muggers have all been killed, but because some of them have chosen to switch to safer professions.

If the idea that muggers are rational profit-maximizers seems implausible, consider who gets mugged. If a mugger's objective is to express machismo, to prove what a he-man he is, there is very little point in mugging little old ladies. If the objective is to get money at as low a cost as possible, there is much to be said for picking the most defenseless victims you can find. In the real world little old ladies get mugged a lot more often than football players.

This is one example of a very general implication of the economic analysis of conflict. In order to stop someone from doing something that injures you, whether robbing your house or polluting your air, it is not necessary to make it impossible for him to do it—merely unprofitable.

Economic analysis can also be used to help understand the nature of organized crime. Newspapers, prosecutors, and the FBI often make organized crime sound almost like General Motors or IBM—a hierarchical organization with a few kingpins controlling thousands of subordinates. What we know about the economics of organizations makes this an unlikely description of real criminal organizations. One major limitation on the size of firms is the problem of control. The more layers of hierarchy there are between the president and the factory worker, the harder it is for management to monitor and control the workers. That is one reason that small firms often are more successful than large ones.

We would expect this problem to be especially severe in criminal markets. Legitimate businesses can and do make extensive use of memos, reports, job evaluations, and the like to pass information from one layer of the hierarchy to another. The process is rather more difficult when the same information that is useful to a criminal trying to keep track of what his employees are doing is also useful to a district attorney trying to keep track of what the criminal is doing. What economists call "informational diseconomies of scale" are therefore a particularly serious problem in criminal firms, implying that the average size of such firms should tend to be smaller, not larger, than that of firms in other markets.

Criminal enterprises obviously are more difficult to study than ordinary ones. The work that has been done, however, such as that of Peter Reuter and Jonathan B. Rubinstein, seems to confirm what theory suggests. Criminal firms seem to be relatively small, and the organization of criminal industries relatively decentralized—precisely the opposite of the pattern described in novels, movies, and the popular press. It may well be that "organized crime" is not so much a corporation as a sort of Chamber of Commerce for the criminal market—a network of individuals and small firms that routinely do business with each other and occasionally cooperate in their mutual interest.

Economic analysis can also be used to predict the effectiveness of law enforcement measures. Consider the current "War on Drugs." From an economic standpoint, its objective is to reduce the supply of illegal drugs, thus raising their prices and reducing the amount people wish to consume. One enforcement strategy is to pressure countries such as Colombia to prevent the production of coca, the raw material used to make cocaine. Such a strategy, if successful, would shift coca production to whatever country is next best at producing it; since coca can be grown in many different places, this shift is not likely to result in a very large increase in cost.

Published estimates suggest that the cost of producing drugs abroad and transporting them to the United States represents only about 1 percent of their street price. So even if we succeed in doubling the cost of coca—which seems unlikely, given experience with elasticity of supply of other crops—the result would be only about a 1 percent increase in the price of cocaine, and a correspondingly small decrease in the amount consumed. Thus economic analysis suggests that pressuring other countries not to produce drugs is probably not a very effective way of reducing their use.

One interesting issue in the economic analysis of crime is the question of what legal rules are economically efficient. Loosely speaking, what rules maximize the total size of the economic pie? This is relevant both to broad issues such as whether theft should be illegal and to more detailed questions, such as how to calculate the optimal punishment for a particular crime.

Consider the question of laws against

theft. At first glance it might seem that, however immoral theft may be, it is not inefficient. If I steal ten dollars from you, I am ten dollars richer and you are ten dollars poorer, so the total wealth of society is unchanged. It seems that, if we judge laws solely on grounds of economic efficiency, there is no reason why theft should be illegal.

That seems obvious, but it is wrong. Opportunities to make money by stealing, like opportunities to make money in other ways, attract economic resources. If stealing is more profitable than washing dishes or waiting on tables, workers will be attracted out of those activities and into theft. As the number of thieves increases, the returns from theft fall, both because everything easy to steal has already been stolen and because victims defend themselves against the increased level of theft by installing locks, bars, burglar alarms, and guard dogs.

In equilibrium, the thief pays, with his time and effort, the price of what he steals. Thus the victim's loss is a net social loss— the thief has no equal gain to balance it. So the existence of theft makes society as a whole poorer, not because money has been transferred from one person to another, but because productive resources have been diverted out of the business of producing and into the business of stealing.

A full analysis of the cost of theft would be more complicated than this sketch, and the social cost of theft would no longer be exactly equal to the amount stolen. It would be less to the extent that people who are particularly skillful at theft earn more in that profession than they could in any other, giving them a net gain to partly balance the loss to their victims. It would be higher to the extent that theft results in additional costs, such as the cost of defensive precautions taken by potential victims. The central conclusion would, however, remain—that we will, on net, be better off if theft is illegal.

This conclusion must be qualified by the observation that to reduce theft we must spend resources catching and punishing thieves. Theft is inefficient—but spending a hundred dollars preventing a ten-dollar theft is still more inefficient. Reducing theft to zero would almost certainly cost more than it would be worth. What we want, from the standpoint of economic efficiency, is the optimal level of theft. We want to increase our expenditures on law enforcement only as long as one more dollar spent catching and punishing thieves reduces the net cost of theft by more than a dollar. Beyond that point, additional reductions in theft cost more than they are worth.

This raises a number of issues, both empirical and theoretical. The empirical issues involve an ongoing dispute about whether punishment deters crime, and if so, by how much. While economic theory predicts that there should be some deterrent effect, it does not tell us how large it should be. Isaac Ehrlich, in a widely quoted (and extensively criticized) study of the deterrent effect of capital punishment, concluded that each execution deters several murders. Other researchers have gotten very different results.

One interesting theoretical point is the question of how to choose the best combination of probability of apprehension and amount of punishment. One could imagine punishing theft by catching half the thieves and fining them a hundred dollars each, by catching a quarter and fining them two hundred each, or by catching one thief in a hundred and hanging him. How do you decide which alternative is best?

At first glance it might seem efficient always to impose the highest possible punishment. The higher the punishment, the fewer criminals you have to catch in order to maintain a given level of deterrence—and catching criminals is costly. One reason this is wrong is that punishing criminals is also costly. A low punishment can take the form of a fine; what the criminal loses the court gains, so the net cost of the punishment is zero. Criminals cannot pay large fines, so large punishments take the form of imprisonment or execution, which is less efficient—nobody gets what the criminal loses and someone has to pay for the jail.

A second reason we do not want maximum punishments for all offenses is that we want to give criminals an incentive to limit their crimes. If the punishments for armed robbery and murder are the same, then the robber who is caught in the act has an incentive to kill the witness. He may get away, and at worst they can hang him only once.

One final interesting question is why we have criminal law at all. In our legal system some offenses are called civil and prosecuted by the victim, while others are called criminal and prosecuted by the state. Why not have a pure civil system, in which robbery would be treated like trespass or breach of contract, with the victim suing the robber?

Such institutions have existed in some past societies. Indeed, our present system of having the state hire professionals to pursue criminals is actually a relatively recent development in the Anglo-American legal tradition, dating back only about two hundred years. Several writers, starting with Gary Becker and George Stigler, have suggested that a movement toward a pure civil system would be desirable, whereas others, most notably William Landes and Richard Posner, have argued for the efficiency of the present division between civil and criminal law.

—**David D. Friedman**

Biography: David D. Friedman is an Olin Fellow in Law and Economics at the University of Chicago Law School.

Further Reading

Becker, Gary S. "Crime and Punishment: An Economic Approach." *Journal of Political Economy* 76 (1968): 169–217.

———, & George J. Stigler. "Law Enforcement, Malfeasance, and Compensation of Enforcers." *Journal of Legal Studies* 3 (1974): 1–18.

Benson, Bruce. *The Enterprise of Law: Justice without the State.* 1990.

Ehrlich, Isaac. "The Deterrent Effect of Criminal Law Enforcement." *Journal of Legal Studies* 1 (1972): 259–76.

Friedman, David. "Private Creation and Enforcement of Law —A Historical Case." *Journal of Legal Studies* 8 (1979): 399–415.

———. "Efficient Institutions for the Private Enforcement of Law." *Journal of Legal Studies* 13 (1984): 379–97.

———. *The Machinery of Freedom.* 1971.

Landes, William M., and Richard A. Posner. "The Private Enforcement of Law." *Journal of Legal Studies* 4 (1975): 1–46.

Reuter, Peter, and Jonathan B. Rubinstein. "Fact, Fancy, and Organized Crime." *The Public Interest* 53 (Fall 1978): 45–67.

Defense

Benjamin Zycher

■ National defense is a public good. That means two things. First, consumption of the good by one person does not reduce the amount available for others to consume. Thus, all people in a nation must "consume" the same amount of national defense (the defense policy established by the government). Second, the benefits a person derives from a public good do not depend on how much that person contributes toward providing it. Everyone benefits, perhaps in differing amounts, from national defense, including those who do not pay taxes. Once the government organizes the resources for national defense, it necessarily defends all residents against foreign aggressors.

These two features of national defense cause an important "free-rider" problem. Because people benefit whether or not they contribute toward defense, each person has an incentive to wait for others to provide the public good and get a "free ride." Also, because a free-rider's consumption does not reduce the amount available for others to consume, even those who pay have little incentive to prevent free-riding by others.

As a result of free-riding, an individual acting alone to provide national defense would produce too little. Each person would provide defense until the incremental benefits to him equaled the incremental costs. But for society as a whole—that is, for all individuals—the incremental benefits exceed the incremental costs. That is because once an individual provides some of the public good, all people benefit from it and cannot be excluded. This free-rider behavior provides one of the important traditional arguments for government: by imposing taxes on all individuals and then providing public goods, government, in principle, eliminates free-rider behavior and can produce the ''right'' amount of national defense and other public goods.

How Can Government Be Induced to Provide the Optimal Amount of National Defense?

That traditional rationale for government taxation and spending on national defense is incomplete. It states that the government *can* eliminate free-rider behavior, but is silent on whether the government has the right incentives to do so. Just as economists have shown that individuals acting alone will provide too few public goods, public choice economists (see PUBLIC CHOICE THEORY) have shown that democratic government, acting under a majority decision rule, also will provide too few public goods. The reason is that the political majority can impose taxes on all citizens and then reduce spending on such public goods as national defense while increasing spending on private (that is, nonpublic) goods that benefit the majority but not the minority. Transfer payments such as Social Security and other subsidies such as price supports for farmers are examples of government spending on private goods.

If, however, the public goods provided by government can be transformed into private ones—that is, if provision of the public goods yields ancillary benefits that some majority coalition of voters views as private—then the problem of government underprovision of public goods can be offset, at least partially. National defense does yield ancillary benefits to special interests. Defense contractors, defense-related workers, and communities with military bases all benefit privately from defense spending.

These interests are located in a majority of congressional districts and in a majority of states. Their presence, therefore, offsets the bias toward too little defense spending. Ironically, therefore, the proliferation of military bases, geographic dispersion of defense contracts, and other seemingly ''wasteful'' aspects of defense spending actually may make government spending more efficient.

Optimal Taxation When the Government Provides National Defense

The traditional theory of optimal taxation states that the kinds of taxes used and the rates levied should minimize distortions. That is, they should interfere as little as possible with the choices taxpayers make in the private marketplace (see TAXATION, A PREFACE). But this traditional theory assumes implicitly that the size and composition of the government budget are independent of the kinds and magnitudes of the taxes imposed. That assumption is unrealistic. If government programs benefit one group of voters but arc financed by another, the beneficiaries will demand larger programs than if they were required to bear the tax burden themselves. A striking modern-day illustration of this is Congress's speedy 1989 repeal of compulsory catastrophic health insurance for the elderly. Congress did so at the behest of old people within months after these people realized that their taxes alone would pay for the program. In the area of defense, political processes are more likely to achieve the optimal amount of spending if each person pays taxes in proportion to the value he or she derives from the defense services provided.

National defense benefits everyone, but in different degrees. National defense defends against the threat that foreign aggressors will confiscate or destroy domestic property and destroy lives. It defends individual liberty, political freedom, and the domestic political system. It provides a foundation for foreign policy, which, presumably, serves the interests of all, but in differing amounts. In addition, the U.S. defense budget is used to support many foreign policy objectives and so is dedicated in part to protecting foreign people and assets. The post–World War II commitment to NATO is the best example.

Nevertheless, the protection of domestic wealth from foreign confiscation or destruction is an obvious and large part of the service provided by national defense. Accordingly, a substantial part of the demand for national defense can reasonably be ascribed to those U.S. residents who own assets threatened by foreign aggression. Some kinds of assets are more vulnerable than others: American-owned assets located overseas may be more vulnerable than identical ones in the United States, and civilian aircraft that can be moved may be more vulnerable to confiscation but less vulnerable to destruction than office buildings. In any event, a rough surrogate for individual valuation of this defense service is individual wealth. Thus, an important component of a tax system designed to yield appropriate democratic choices on the size of the defense sector is a tax on wealth. Taxes on incomes or consumption may provide good approximations to such a tax. Similarly, individual preferences for political freedom, for protection of the political system, and for foreign policy maneuverings are likely to be correlated positively with individual wealth. Again, taxes on wealth, income, or consumption may, therefore, be appropriate.

International Defense Alliances

Nations facing a common threat often pool their defense efforts in such alliances as NATO. While NATO is a formal alliance, nations can cooperate in informal alliances as well, sharing defense responsibilities and burdens without the trappings of an international organization. In principle, little communication between such informal partners is necessary: each nation can undertake given defense activities knowing that the other(s) will pursue complementary activities in response. Whatever the nature of the alliance, the defense (or other) efforts aimed at common goals are, again, a public good. Thus, nations, just like individuals, face the free-rider problem and the resulting underprovision of defense. Because larger nations like the United States are likely to value the collective defense effort more highly than smaller ones like Belgium, small nations may attempt to exploit larger ones by free-riding on the larger countries' defense efforts. Thus, members of alliances often bargain over "burden sharing," or the specific efforts to be made by each.

One problem with achieving an equitable and efficient sharing of burdens is knowing what the appropriate burdens are. Even if countries agree that they should contribute "proportionally," the question remains "proportional to what?" Population, GNP, per capita GNP, and physical proximity to the perceived threat all seem like plausible candidates. Furthermore, even if nations agree on what the effort should be proportional to, there are different measures of effort. One measure is military spending. But another reasonable measure is contribution of physical defense assets. Contributions of physical assets and manpower may not be proportional to spending because of differences in valuation or pricing, differences in efficiency, and a host of other factors. For example, U.S. defense spending in the mid-1980s was roughly 60 percent of the NATO total, while the United States provided about 46 percent of the main battle tanks and about 40 percent of the division-equivalent firepower. The German Federal Republic provided about 8 percent of NATO spending, but about 17 percent of the main battle tanks and 13 percent of division-equivalent firepower. Such indices are crude, but illustrate the difficulty of measuring relative contributions.

No definition of fairness in burden sharing is obviously correct, and this ambiguity inexorably creates tension within alliances. Furthermore, citizens of one nation may value the collective defensive effort less or more than citizens of another nation, and also may have different perceptions of how serious the threat is. That was the case in NATO for many years, as the United States and West Germany perceived a substantially greater threat than did Greece.

Dependence versus "Vulnerability" in Foreign Defense Procurement

Modern military forces combine many kinds of manpower and physical materiel. Inevitably, some of these inputs, such as rare metals and electronic components, are purchased from foreigners because doing so is necessary or at least cheaper than buying them at home. Many people worry that foreign procurement makes the United States vulnerable to a cutoff in items supplied by foreigners. They fear that cuts in foreign supplies may exceed, in both number and variety, potential cuts in supplies from domestic firms.

That view is misguided. Suppose that some defense good is purchased from foreign suppliers and that this arrangement is subject to easy but unpredictable cutoffs. Suppose, also, that such interruptions are easy to insure against (with stockpiles, alternative suppliers in other parts of the world, or excess production capacity in the United States). If so, then foreign dependence does not cause true vulnerability. The key question, therefore, is not the source of the defense goods, but rather the ease with which interruptions in supply—either foreign or domestic—can be insured against.

If domestic dependence is more difficult to insure against than foreign dependence, then ironically, domestic dependence causes greater vulnerability.

What could make insurance more difficult for domestic purchases than for foreign ones? One possibility is the expectation of price controls. Producers of defense-related goods know that the prices of such goods can rise dramatically when a government at war or preparing for war increases its purchases of those goods. These price increases serve an important function: they reward domestic producers for stockpiling goods, maintaining excess production capacity, and increasing production quickly. But domestic producers also know that governments, wanting goods on the cheap, often impose price controls on just such goods. The imposition of price controls on petroleum products during past wars is but one example. Taking anticipated price controls into account, domestic producers do not stockpile as much or maintain as much excess capacity. Nor do they increase production as much when price controls are actually imposed. But governments cannot impose price controls on foreign producers. Therefore, foreign producers have stronger incentives to stockpile and to maintain excess capacity.

Also, such government practices as cost-plus contracting may affect domestic suppliers of defense-related goods disproportionately. If cost-plus contracting is based upon historical or accounting cost instead of market value at the time of purchase, future prices paid by the government may not cover the market value (or opportunity cost) of many kinds of assets, thus causing a loss for suppliers. In short, the "vulnerability" issue is far more complex than the common foreign/domestic dependence view suggests.

Efficient Delivery of Defense Services

Now that the Soviet economic system is likely to be gradually replaced with free markets, the U.S. Department of Defense (DOD) may be the largest centrally planned economy in the world. And there is little reason to believe that central planning works better in the United States than elsewhere.

Central planning in DOD creates the same two problems that central planning always creates. First, DOD decision makers who design weaponry or who specify characteristics and performance features of equipment designed by contractors respond poorly to consumer preferences. The "consumers" of the weapons and equipment are the soldiers in the foxholes, the airmen facing dogfights and antiaircraft fire, and so on. A good proxy for these ultimate users may be the theater commanders charged with winning battles. But few institutions at DOD induce decision makers to conform their preferences to those of even the theater commanders. The absence of a profit motive weakens the incentive for DOD to adapt their decisions to the perceived preferences of users. The absence of competition in defense diminishes it even more.

As a result the DOD often has promoted weapons designs with dubious combat features and effectiveness. The air force's A-10 "Warthog" aircraft is a good example. The Warthog performed brilliantly in the 1991 Gulf War in support of army and marine ground operations. It was designed for that specific purpose. Yet the air force tried for years to eliminate funding for the A-10 precisely because it supports the other services and thus yields few bureaucratic benefits for the air force. The air force wanted to use F-16s and other more glamorous aircraft for ground support despite the fact that their great speed makes them much less suitable for such missions. One way to get weapons and other equipment that conform more to user demands is to give the users a larger voice or a direct veto in design decisions.

The absence of a profit motive, and of an individual or group with a claim to the economic benefits from reductions in costs, weakens the DOD's incentive to minimize the cost of achieving given objectives. Contracts for design and production of weaponry are often written on a cost-plus basis, under which the contractor receives a payment from the government equal to costs plus some predetermined "profit." Therefore, the contractors have little incentive to minimize costs. If, on the other hand, the contractor simply receives a fixed price for the output of defense goods, he has a strong incentive to minimize costs, but the contractor must bear the risk of increases in the prices of inputs and of other outcomes that cannot be predicted perfectly.

DOD itself has only a weak incentive to operate efficiently. Because the military services have sharply defined tasks with little overlap, each service is, in effect, a monopolist in its defined missions. The army, for example, is prevented from flying fixed-wing aircraft, thus giving the air force a near monopoly in providing close air support for ground operations. Because each service is likely to have better information than does Congress about the cost of providing given defense services, the efforts of the services to maximize their budgets can lead them to provide defense at a higher cost than necessary.

The services can be aided in this quest by such important interest groups as defense contractors in various congressional districts. This lobbying by private defense interests weakens the incentive for Congress to minimize the cost of obtaining a given package of defense output. An important way to reduce this inefficiency would be to have the services compete. The army and the Marine Corps could be required to compete on a much broader scale in "producing" ground combat operations. The army and the air force could compete in providing close air support for ground combat. The navy could be forced to compete on a much broader scale with the Coast Guard. Such competition, like competition in the private sector, would decrease the cost of defense.

The Defense Establishment and the Threat to the Polity

The existence of an armed defense establishment always threatens civilian governments and the rights and liberties enjoyed by individuals. The Founding Fathers recognized this threat. In August 1789, when Congress was considering the Bill of Rights, Congressman Elbridge Gerry wrote, "What, sir, is the use of militia? It is to prevent the establishment of a standing army, the bane of liberty." Therefore, they made two institutional arrangements. First, because the threat is posed mainly by ground forces, the ground forces are split into the army, the marines, and the states' national guards. That way, any service whose officers want a military coup must take into account the potential opposition posed by the other ground combat services.

Second, the Founding Fathers recognized from their own experience that an armed citizenry is more immune to the efforts of governments—of centralized military establishments—to impose dictatorship. Thus, they specified the "right of the people to keep and bear arms" in the Second Amendment to the Constitution. Unlike the First Amendment, which placed constraints only upon Congress, the Second Amend-ment decreed that the right to keep and bear arms "shall not be infringed."

Conclusion

National defense, while not a separate field of study within economics, raises a vast range of economic issues. Defense, like other areas of public policy, is suitable for the prescriptions yielded by economic analysis.

—Benjamin Zycher

Biography: Benjamin Zycher is vice president for research at the Milken Institute for Job and Capital Formation in Santa Monica, California, and is a visiting professor of economics at UCLA. He formerly was a senior economist at the Rand Corporation in Santa Monica, where he specialized in defense economics and Soviet military matters.

Further Reading

Cooper, Charles A., and Benjamin Zycher. "Perceptions of NATO Burden-Sharing." Rand Corporation paper no. R-3750-FF/RC, June 1989.

Enthoven, Alain C., and Wayne K. Smith. *How Much Is Enough? Shaping the Defense Program, 1961–1969.* 1971.

Halbrook, Stephen P. *That Every Man Be Armed: The Evolution of a Constitutional Right.* 1984.

Hitch, Charles J., and Roland N. McKean. *The Economics of Defense in the Nuclear Age.* 1970.

Thompson, Earl A. "Taxation and National Defense." *Journal of Political Economy* 82, no. 4 (1974): 755–82.

Zycher, Benjamin, Kenneth A. Solomon, and Loren Yager. "An 'Adequate Insurance' Approach to Critical Dependencies of the Department of Defense." Rand Corporation paper no. R-3880-DARPA, 1991.

Drug Lag

Daniel Henninger

■ The modern history of drug regulation in the United States has been marked by the simultaneous pursuit of two goals—safety and efficacy. Since passage of the 1962 amendments to the Food and Drug Act, most members of the medical and regulatory establishment have regarded those two goals as complementary. By the early seventies, however, critics had begun to charge that the Food and Drug Administration (FDA), in its pursuit of these goals, was delaying or preventing the timely introduction of promising new drugs for seriously ill patients.

With the 1962 amendments, Congress gave the FDA authority to judge a drug's efficacy—whether it produced the results for which it had been developed. Formerly the agency had monitored only safety. Indeed, from 1938 until 1962, the FDA had just sixty days to disapprove the application of a new drug. If it did not, the drug could be marketed. The system worked without significant incident. But in 1962 the thalidomide tragedy hit the world.

A sedative used to prevent miscarriage, thalidomide caused the birth of several thousand deformed babies in Europe. Thalidomide was not so major a tragedy in the United States, however, because the existing safety regulations allowed the FDA to catch it early. Ironically, the publicity generated by pictures of deformed newborns in Europe led Congress to amend the U.S. drug laws to add an efficacy require-

ment to the existing safety rules, even though the problem with thalidomide was safety, not efficacy. Congress gave the FDA the authority and latitude in judgment to decide whether a new drug did what it claimed it could do. It was not long after this expansion of regulatory responsibility that the phrase "drug lag" entered the lexicon.

Some critics charged that the efficacy requirement was extraneous to the agency's central mission to monitor safety. The often complicated procedures created for assessing a drug's efficacy added to the years required to get a new drug into general use. A 1974 study by University of Chicago economist Sam Peltzman concluded that since 1962 the new rules had reduced the rate of introduction of effective new drugs significantly—from an average of forty-three annually in the decade before the amendments to just sixteen annually in the ten years afterward. Peltzman also found that the regulations also made it difficult for companies to introduce drugs that competed with existing drugs, thus reducing competition in the industry.

The drug lag controversy intensified with the rise of the AIDS epidemic. On October 12, 1988, a large group of AIDS activists staged a demonstration at the FDA's headquarters in suburban Washington, chanting, "No more deaths!" They were protesting the snail's pace at which the FDA was approving new drugs to combat AIDS. These and other critics, who complained about the agency's handling of drugs to treat cancer and heart disease, posed a new and controversial question about drug delays: was not the federal agency charged by Congress with protecting ill Americans from harmful or useless drugs actually causing great harm to patients, precisely for exercising its congressional mandate?

Have patients in other countries gained access to new drugs sooner than patients in the United States? The Center for Drug Development at Tufts University studied forty-six new drugs approved by the United States in 1985 and 1986 and found that 72 percent were available on average 5.5 years earlier in foreign markets. Other studies, comparing drug approvals back to 1972, have suggested a similar time lag in the United States. Meanwhile, the costs of development rise. The cost of developing a new drug in the United States is estimated to have risen to $231 million today from $54 million in 1976 (all in 1987 dollars), with the approval time from earliest development to final marketing typically about twelve years.

The FDA responded to complaints about drug lag and the availability of promising experimental drugs by introducing a number of reforms. The most notable was "fast track" approval of the AIDS drug AZT, which was cleared for use within two years after it was discovered to be effective against the HIV virus. Other reforms allow patients access to promising experimental drugs. Unfortunately, to qualify to provide experimental drugs, administering physicians must meet burdensome paperwork requirements, such as the need to draft a "treatment protocol" for submission to an institutional review board, a practice more common to university-based clinical investigators. Also, because insurers will often resist payment for unapproved drugs, the rules limit the amount manufacturers may charge to "cost recovery," loosely defined as excluding charges that would constitute "commercialization" of the drug. Manufacturers, therefore, have little incentive to provide the drugs.

The severest criticism leveled at the drug lag is that without access to a drug available elsewhere, seriously ill patients will suffer or even die. Peltzman raised the subject in his 1974 study. He noted pharmacologist William Wardell's estimate that because the relatively safe hypnotic drug nitrazepam was not cleared for use in the United States until 1971, five years after it was available in Britain, more than 3,700 Americans may have died from less safe sedatives and hypnotics. After earning the Nobel Prize for chemistry in 1988, U.S. drug researcher George Hitchings of Burroughs Wellcome Company said of an antileukemia drug he helped develop before the 1962 amendments: "We went from synthesis to the commercial drug in three years. That is absolutely impossible today."

The issue of lost lives became more widely discussed with the controversy over the availability in the United States of drugs known as beta blockers. Beta blockers, administered to reduce risk to patients who have experienced a heart attack, were available in Europe in 1967 but not in the United States until 1976, primarily because of the FDA's concerns that long-term use might cause malignant tumors. When the agency ordered long-term animal studies to investigate this risk, critics argued that in risk-benefit terms, the agency's delay was unjustified, because beta blockers were estimated to save at least ten thousand lives annually. Similar arguments over delayed approvals have erupted over the FDA's handling of anticancer agents and drugs that dissolve blood clots in heart attack victims.

Those attempting to explain the FDA's cautious approach often cite one factor peculiar to the American system: politics. A 1972 remark by former FDA commissioner Alexander Schmidt aptly describes political pressures on the agency:

> The times when [congressional] hearings have been held to criticize our approval of new drugs have been so frequent that we aren't able to count them. . . . The message to FDA staff could not be clearer. Whenever a controversy over a new drug is resolved by its approval, the agency and the individuals involved likely will be investigated. . . . The congressional pressure for our negative action on new drug applications is, therefore, intense.

With the FDA facing such incentives, drug lag is inevitable.

To a great extent the FDA's caution in approving new drugs has reflected prevailing political and social attitudes toward risk in the United States. An analogous example of zero-risk policy-making in this period is the Delaney Amendment of 1958, which mandated the banning of any substance that caused cancer in one type of animal, even if the doses are extreme and the substance does not cause cancer in other animals.

In the eighties scientific and public attitudes toward risk began to change. Researchers, for example, developed more sophisticated methods of detecting levels of toxicity and carcinogenicity in chemicals, which, in turn, caused regulators to reassess the kind of absolute prohibitions imposed by Delaney. In 1986 the FDA said that based on state-of-the-art toxicological testing, it intended to reclassify certain dyes as safe to use in cosmetics. It noted that a scientific review panel of the U.S. Public Health Service had calculated the risk of cancer in humans from orange dye no. 17 to be, at worst, 1 in 19 billion. A court challenge from Public Citizen, an advocacy group founded by Ralph Nader, prevented the agency from following through with its plan, but the debate over zero-risk regulation continues. Studies by analysts such as Aaron Wildavsky (see RISKLESS SOCIETY) also have popularized the idea that in assessing the value of a drug, chemical, or technology, its benefits ought to be balanced against apparent risks.

The AIDS crisis forced the FDA and the rest of the medical establishment to consider these evolving attitudes toward risk. Many of the compounds under study to treat AIDS were unfamiliar, and some were known to be highly toxic. Under traditional regulatory practice the agency would have approached these therapies with time-consuming caution. Activist groups representing AIDS patients, however, argued that individuals with a terminal illness would willingly assume levels of risk higher than those normally allowed by the FDA. To press their claims, AIDS groups engaged in acts of civil disobedience, such as smuggling unapproved drugs into the United States from Mexico, disrupting important conferences of AIDS researchers, and picketing the FDA's headquarters. Press coverage, historically supportive of the agency's bias against risk, became supportive of these new concerns from patients.

This pressure led to a significant reassessment of the entire system of developing and approving drugs in the United States. AZT was approved in record time even though it was highly toxic and often produced severe side effects during clinical trials. Though the U.S. drug-approval system responded positively to the AIDS crisis, whether the system will undergo lasting, institutional change remains unknown. Patients' demands that they determine for themselves the risks they find acceptable often conflict with the FDA's long history of making decisions for patients in spite of their desires.

Moreover, even if regulators, patients, and researchers settle on a system that gives greater weight to benefits in setting acceptable levels of risk, the question of legal liability remains. FDA approval does not fully protect a drug manufacturer from liability claims, and however much society's sympathies may evolve in the direction of benefits, a single lawsuit on behalf of one plaintiff can expose manufacturers to enormous claims.

After settling 450 cases, G. D. Searle, in 1986, took its Copper-7 IUD off the market because the costs of defending a product ruled safe by the FDA had become prohibitive. Perhaps the most notorious case of a safe drug driven off the market by personal-injury litigation is Merrill Dow's Bendectin, a remedy for morning sickness in pregnant women. Though 33 million women had used the approved drug between 1956 and 1983, and though Merrill had never lost a case filed against it, the prospect of litigating some 700 cases filed by plaintiffs' attorneys caused the company to drop the drug.

Ultimately, the political process will decide whether U.S. regulatory practices should be changed to accommodate the desires of patients and to shorten the lag between approvals here and in Europe. Normally, political decisions about regulatory practice are made among a small community of specialists. Today, the intense interest in curing, or at least ameliorating, diseases such as cancer, AIDS, heart disease, arthritis, and Alzheimer's means that the outcome of the debate over the drug lag is likely to reflect the values of an unprecedentedly large community of public interests.

—Daniel Henninger

Biography: Daniel Henninger is the deputy editor of *The Wall Street Journal*'s editorial page. He has written most of the *Journal*'s editorials on drug regulation that have appeared in the last ten years.

Further Reading

Henninger, Daniel. "Will the FDA Revert to Type?" *The Wall Street Journal*, December 12, 1990, A16.

Kaitin, K. I., B. W. Richard, and Louis Lasagna. "Trends in Drug Development: The 1985–86 New Drug Approvals." *Journal of Clinical Pharmacology* 27 (August 1987): 542–48.

Kazman, Sam. "Deadly Overcaution: FDA's Drug Approval Process." *Journal of Regulation and Social Costs* 1, no. 1 (September 1990): 35–54.

Kessler, David A., M.D., J.D. "The Regulation of Investigational Drugs." *New England Journal of Medicine* 320, no. 5 (February 2, 1989): 281–88.

President's Cancer Panel. National Cancer Program of the National Cancer Institute. *Final Report of the National Committee to Review Current Procedures for Approval of New Drugs for Cancer and AIDS.* August 15, 1990.

Report of the Presidential Commission on the Human Immunodeficiency Virus Epidemic. February 1988.

Wildavsky, Aaron. *Searching for Safety.* 1988.

Energy

Robert A. Leone

■ Energy is not a single industry, but many industries tied into every facet of our economy, from transportation and manufacturing to home heating and lighting. As chart 1 shows, in 1990 over 40 percent of U.S. energy consumed was petroleum. Natural gas was about 23 percent of the energy mix and coal about 22 percent. Nuclear accounted for about 7 percent, and other sources ranging from hydroelectric to solar power to geothermal geysers accounted for the remaining 8 percent.

In most ways, energy is like any other economic commodity: when the price goes up, the quantity of energy used goes down. In some ways, though, energy is different, and energy markets do not reflect the true costs to society of energy use due to these differences. For example, the free-market price of energy does not adequately account for the burden on society of global warming or of urban air pollution. Some economists advocate a "carbon tax" so that those who use energy take account of their contribution to global warming. Urban air pollution from automobiles not only raises health care costs but affects our quality of life as well. Acid rain associated with electricity generation is estimated to cause more than $7 billion in materials corrosion damage annually throughout the seventeen eastern states in the United States. Economists point out, though, that a straight tax on energy is an inefficient way of dealing with pollution. A more efficient way is to tax the pollution directly. If governments taxed pollution rather than energy use per se, people would have incentives to produce and use energy in less-polluting ways.

Because of the environmental consequences of energy use and production, discussions of energy economics often are more emotional than rational. Such discussions are dominated by concerns about energy depletion and the limits to economic growth, the belief of many in the need for regulation of energy markets, and the exaggeration or misstatement of the political hurdles that must be overcome to address the real challenges of energy use in a global economy.

More dispassionate analyses give a different view of energy economics. There is little reason to believe, for example, that energy is a limiting factor in economic growth. Government statistics report that the United States has petroleum reserves that will provide the nation with oil for the next twenty-five years. It is a mistake to conclude from this, however, that in the twenty-sixth year there will be no gasoline. As old energy reserves are used up, new ones are discovered. In 1969, for example, total estimated U.S. oil reserves were about 30 billion barrels. More than twenty years later, after we had consumed 50 billion barrels of domestic oil, there are still almost 27 billion barrels of U.S. proved petroleum reserves.

Because industrial economies are so energy intensive, many people fear that limited energy supplies will limit economic growth. Again, the facts suggest otherwise. In 1960 the U.S. economy used over 26,000 BTUs of energy to produce each dollar of GNP. By 1988, due to technological improvements and increased energy conservation, the United States required only 20,000 BTUs of energy to produce the same real dollar of GNP. This 24 percent reduction in the energy intensity of the U.S. economy illustrates an economic truth called the law of demand: at a higher price, less of a good is used.

Another economic truth, however, is that higher income leads to higher demand for energy. While higher prices induced consumers to use less energy, higher incomes encouraged them to use more. The net result is that total energy use in the United States is still rising despite aggressive conservation efforts. From 1975 to 1990, GNP in the United States grew by 40 percent, while annual energy consumption rose 15 percent.

Some analysts take little solace in the U.S. statistics, citing the recent decline in domestic energy prices. From 1988 to 1990, the composite price of the three major energy fuels—crude oil, natural gas, and coal—was lower, in real dollars, than at any other time since 1975. These lower prices reduced the economic incentive to conserve energy.

Pessimistic analysts also cite the pent-up demand for energy in poor countries of the Third World. It is true that less developed nations will need to consume more energy as they industrialize. But there are grounds for optimism as well. There is much room left for well-developed countries to cut energy use. The world's largest energy user— the United States—still consumes twice as much energy per dollar of GNP as Japan or Germany. And even nations that today use much less energy per unit of output will be able to do still better as technology improves.

Aggregate statistics clearly show that energy use falls as the price rises. In spite of this evidence, many advocates of energy regulation still believe that energy consumers are insensitive to its price. This mistaken belief is reflected in the kinds of policies they advocate.

Consider gasoline consumption, one of the most emotional and visible issues. Those who believe that consumers do not adjust to changes in energy prices usually favor corporate average fuel economy (CAFE) regulations requiring that new cars meet prescribed fuel economy standards. Advocates of CAFE believe that cars get more miles per gallon because the CAFE laws were enacted in the midseventies. Advocates of a market-oriented energy policy believe that a major part of the increase in miles per gallon was due to gasoline prices that were much higher in the late seventies and early eighties than in the late sixties and early seventies. While there is likely some truth to the arguments of both groups, economic research indicates that the benefits of a market-driven approach to energy policy tend to be underestimated and the benefits of regulation exaggerated.

A case in point is a congressional proposal to require auto companies to make cars that get, on average, 40 miles per gallon (mpg), up from the current mandated average of 27.5. Absent an economic view, one might conclude that a fleet of vehicles averaging 40 mpg would consume one-third less gasoline than a fleet averaging 27.5 mpg. An economic view yields a different conclusion.

If gasoline is priced at $1.20 per gallon, gasoline costs 4.4¢ per mile in a vehicle averaging 27.5 mpg. This cost falls to 3¢ if the vehicle averages 40. In other words, the proposed regulatory initiative lowers the cost to drive a mile and, therefore, induces drivers to drive more miles. Empirical evidence shows that reducing the cost of driving a mile will encourage consumers to drive a little faster, purchase more pickup trucks instead of more fuel-economic passenger cars, and even drive cars slightly larger than they would have otherwise.

In addition, some consumers will be frustrated by less powerful and less safe 40-mpg vehicles and will keep their old cars longer, thus lengthening the amount of time it will take for the entire automobile fleet of used as well as new cars to achieve the 40-mpg average. All these economic responses by consumers reduce the energy savings anticipated by the proposed regulation. While each effect is small by itself, in the aggregate these consumer responses can offset perhaps half the anticipated savings from a 40-mpg regulatory requirement.

In contrast, a tax on gasoline would immediately affect the driving decisions of all drivers. The higher price would discourage driving additional miles, not encourage it. The higher price would also hasten, rather than stall, decisions to buy new vehicles that get better gasoline mileage. And a higher price would encourage consumers to drive fuel-economical passenger vehicles instead of trucks and utility vehicles. By one estimate, when all these factors are

CHART 1

Energy Use in the United States—1990

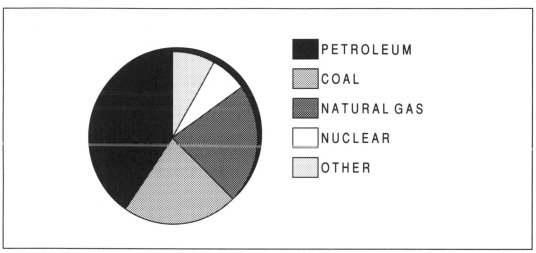

- ■ PETROLEUM
- ▨ COAL
- ◩ NATURAL GAS
- □ NUCLEAR
- ▦ OTHER

PETROLEUM 40.3%   COAL 22.2%   NATURAL GAS 22.5%   NUCLEAR 6.9%   OTHER 8.1%

SEE ALSO *Natural Resources, OPEC*

brought together, the United States could save as much gasoline over a ten-year period with a five-cent-a-gallon gasoline tax as it would by raising the CAFE mileage requirement from 27.5 mpg to 40 mpg.

The equivalent gasoline tax is so low, not because the consumer response to a nickel tax increase would be so large, but because the impact of the 40-mpg regulatory standard would be so small. The impact of regulation is so small because consumers adapt to even the best-conceived regulatory initiative in creative and unanticipated ways. That is simultaneously the virtue of energy markets and the reason why energy policy initiatives often accomplish less than their advocates intend.

Political debates over energy policy are inherently controversial because the stakes are so large and because the effects of policy changes fall unevenly across society. There may well be excessive controversy, however, because conventional views of the consequences of higher energy prices are not entirely accurate.

Many people believe, for example, that higher energy prices are especially harmful to people with low incomes. It is certainly true that low-income families spend a higher percentage of their income on gasoline than high-income families do. But that is not the end of the story. Low-income families are more likely to purchase used cars than new cars. Purchase prices for used, gas-guzzling cars fall as gasoline prices rise. So part of what low-income families pay in higher gasoline prices, they save by paying a lower price for their cars. Also, higher-income families engage in many more energy-intensive forms of consumption and recreation, such as boating, air travel, heating and cooling larger homes, and so on. When all these factors are combined, it is far less obvious that the poor spend proportionately more of their income on energy from all sources.

Moreover, if higher energy prices are caused by taxes on energy, the tax revenues generated would go to governments in the United States. Because these governments provide services consumed disproportionately by lower-income families (and assuming that the governments provide these services efficiently—a big assumption), the net effect of higher energy prices would be an increase in the real income of low-income families.

Because energy is so basic an economic commodity and because we produce it and consume it in so many different ways, even the most innovative regulator cannot anticipate all the ways that consumers will adapt to a changing energy market. A sound economy also requires full use of the creativity and responsiveness that markets can provide to changing energy realities.

—Robert A. Leone

Biography: Robert A. Leone is a professor of operations management at the Boston University School of Management. He was an energy economist with President Carter's Council of Economic Advisers.

Further Reading

Bohi, Douglas. *Energy Price Shocks and Macroeconomic Performance*. 1989.
Kaplan, Seymour. *Energy Economics: Quantitative Methods for Energy and Environmental Decisions*. 1983.
Ross, Marc. *Our Energy: Regaining Control*. 1981.

See also NATURAL RESOURCES, OPEC.

Health Care Industry

Patricia M. Danzon

■ Health care is one of the most rapidly growing sectors of the economy, with expenditures in 1988 totaling $539.9 billion, or 11.1 percent of GNP, up from 5.3 percent of GNP in 1960. For 1992, health care spending was projected to be over 13 percent of GNP. This amounts to $2,124 per capita, of which $1,882 was for personal health care—medical services and supplies for individuals. The rest was for research, construction, administration, and public health activities. Hospital expenditures accounted for 39 percent of the total spent for personal health care, physician services for 19 percent, nursing home care for 8 percent, and other personal health care for 22 percent.

Is Health Care Different?

Health care differs from other goods and services in important ways. The output of a shoe factory is shoes. But the output of the health care industry is less well defined. It is unpredictable and imperfectly understood by producers, and still less by consumers. Also, third-party payment and government intervention are pervasive. None of these characteristics is unique to health care, but their extent and their interaction are. Nevertheless, health care markets obey the fundamental rules of economics, and economic analysis is essential in appraising public policy.

The ultimate output of medical care is its effect on health. This effect can only be assigned probabilities before the care is provided and is difficult to measure even after the fact. Medical care is not the only determinant of health; others include nutrition, exercise, and other life-style factors. Efficient allocation of private and public budgets to health requires equating marginal benefit and marginal cost for each of these inputs (see MARGINALISM).

Risk and insurance. The risk of illness naturally leads people to demand health insurance. But in the United States the demand for health insurance is distorted by the fact that employer contributions are tax-exempt compensation to employees (see HEALTH INSURANCE). This implies an open-ended subsidy at the employee's marginal tax rate, including income and payroll taxes at the federal and state levels. This "tax expenditure," which does not appear in any government budget, was estimated at over $50 billion in 1990. Assuming an average marginal tax rate of 33 percent, this subsidy more than offsets the administrative expense built into insurance premiums. Consequently, the average employee is better off insuring even routine medical services.

Since 1960, third-party payment for health care has increased dramatically. The share paid directly out of pocket by consumers fell from 49 percent in 1960 to 21 percent in 1988. At the same time, public financing increased from 24.5 percent to

42.1 percent, and private health insurance increased from 22 percent to 32 percent.

Pervasive third-party payment profoundly affects the structure of the medical care industry and the quantity, cost, and quality of services offered. Because insurance companies pay a large percent of the cost of medical care, the insured consumer's point-of-purchase price is necessarily lower. If the doctor charges forty dollars and the insurance company pays 80 percent, for example, the consumer's price is only eight dollars. As in any market the quantity demanded increases when price falls.

A five-year randomized trial of alternative insurance plans for the nonelderly population conducted by the Rand Corporation found strong evidence of the responsiveness of demand to insurance coverage. Some patients in the experiment were given totally free care. Others were required to pay 95 percent of the cost of medical services, up to a stop-loss. (A stop-loss is a limit on out-of-pocket expenses. In the experiment, it was set at 5 to 15 percent of income, up to a maximum of a thousand dollars in 1976 dollars.) Beyond the stop-loss they too received free care. Total expenditures for the group given free care were 45 percent higher than for the group that paid 95 percent up to the stop-loss. Free care increased total expenditures by 23 percent relative to a plan in which patients made a 25 percent copayment up to a stop-loss. For the great majority of participants, the difference in expenditures had no measurable effect on health, whether judged by objective measures or by the patients themselves.

Far harder to measure is the effect of insurance on technological change and on the "quality" of services available. Insured consumers (or physicians on their behalf) have incentives to use any new medical service if the expected benefit exceeds their private out-of-pocket cost, which is less than the full social cost. Thus, medical technologies can be profitable even if their expected benefits are below their cost. Overinvestment in technology is reinforced by provider incentives to compete on nonprice dimensions of service in markets where consumers are insulated from prices. In recent years third-party payers have become more aggressive as cost-conscious purchasers on behalf of insured consumers (see below), but the tensions remain.

Asymmetric information. Consumers typically have less information than providers do about the risks and benefits of alternative treatments, and therefore rely on physicians to advise as well as treat them. Such mixed roles are common in many professional and other contexts. They are, however, more complex in medical care because the provider is an agent not only for the individual patient but also for the third-party payer, who in turn is ultimately the agent for policyholders/patients as a group. Each individual patient would like to consume any service that has any expected benefit at all if the out-of-pocket cost is zero. But in the long run patients as policyholders are better off if insurers control moral hazard (the increase in quantity and "quality" of services in response to insurance) because insurance premiums must ultimately rise to cover the costs.

Insurers compete by devising better ways of controlling moral hazard. Thus, devising contractual incentives for providers to make the right trade-offs between the short-run desires of individual patients and long-run insurer/policyholder interests is at the heart of the ongoing revolution in health care markets, both in forms of reimbursement and organizational structure. Preferred provider organizations (PPOs), health maintenance organizations (HMOs), and various forms of managed care give doctors incentives to control insurance-induced overutilization.

Government. Government is more pervasive in health care than in almost any other industry, though less so in the United States than in most other developed countries. Such interventions are rationalized on grounds of assuring either access or quality. Government is the largest insurer, through Medicare and Medicaid, and public hospitals act as provider of last resort for those who cannot pay for care. Licensure, accreditation, and other regulations either directly or indirectly affect entry of physicians, dentists, and other medical professionals, as well as hospitals, nursing homes, and other institutional providers. New pharmaceuticals and medical devices must first be approved by the Food and Drug Administration.

The Growth in Costs—Why, and Is It Worth It?

Health care expenditures as a percent of GNP have grown more rapidly in the United States than in other countries. How much value we get for these expenditures and whether governments should further intervene to control costs have become major issues in public debate.

The growth in real health care costs per capita, net of economy-wide inflation, can be split into three components: medical price increases (in excess of other prices); increases in volume of services per capita; and increases in intensity of resource use per unit of service. Intensity reflects changing technology, "quality," and other factors that make any given service, such as a diagnostic test, more resource-intensive than it was in the past. In practice it is virtually impossible to construct quality-adjusted and technology-adjusted price indexes that meaningfully separate pure medical price increases from increases in intensity. Moreover, even an accurate accounting for cost growth does not illuminate the underlying causes.

Nevertheless, technology appears to be the single most important factor driving health care costs currently. A standard economist's presumption, based on theory and evidence, is that technology is not introduced unless it produces benefits at least as great as the costs. This presumption does not necessarily apply to new medical technologies, however. The reason is that massive government subsidies, directly through tax-funded government insurance programs and indirectly through the tax subsidy to private health insurance, cause medical providers to use technology that consumers may value less than the cost.

Although other countries with more centralized government control over health budgets appear to have controlled costs more successfully, that does not mean that they have produced a more efficient result. In any case, reported statistics may be misleading. Efficient resource allocation requires that resources be spent on medical care as long as the marginal benefit exceeds the marginal cost. Marginal benefits are very hard to measure, but certainly include more subjective values than the crude measures of morbidity and mortality that are widely used in international comparisons.

In addition to forgone benefits, government health care systems have hidden costs. Any insurance system, public or private, must raise revenues, pay providers, control moral hazard, and bear some nondiversifiable risk. In a private insurance market such as in the United States, the costs of performing these functions can be measured by insurance overhead costs of premium collection, claims administration, and return on capital. Public monopoly insurers must also perform these functions, but their costs tend to be hidden and do not appear in health expenditure accounts. Tax financing entails deadweight costs that have been estimated at over seventeen cents per dollar raised—far higher than the 1 percent of premiums required by private insurers to collect premiums.

The use of tight physician fee schedules gives doctors incentives to reduce their own time and other resources per patient visit; patients must therefore make multiple visits to receive the same total care. But these hidden patient time costs do not appear in standard measures of health care spending.

Both economic theory and a careful review of the evidence that goes beyond simple accounting measures suggest that a government monopoly of financing and provision achieves a less efficient allocation of resources to medical care than would a well-designed private market system. The performance of the current U.S. health care system does not provide a guide to the potential functioning of a well-designed private market system. Cost and waste in the current U.S. system are unnecessarily high, because of tax and regulatory policies that impede efficient cost control by private insurers, while at the same time the system fails to provide for universal coverage (see below).

Industry Structure and Competition

Despite barriers to entry, the health care industry has become extremely competitive in recent years. This is because of the large number of firms in most market segments, a more aggressive role of public and private payers in attempting to control costs, and antitrust enforcement.

Hospitals. Prior to the eighties hospitals were paid largely on the basis of costs incurred. In 1983 Medicare introduced a system of "prospective" payment according to diagnosis-related groups (DRGs), whereby hospitals are paid a fixed fee per admission, based on the patient's diagnosis. In contrast to retrospective cost-based reimbursement, the hospital bears the marginal cost of all expenses incurred. In addition, employers and private insurers also have ceased to be passive payers; now, they actively attempt to control price and utilization through such strategies such as HMOs, selective contracting with PPOs for fixed, discounted fees, utilization review, and required second opinions. These attempts to reduce costs have been effective. Since 1981 the number of hospital admissions and the average length of stay have declined for both the over–sixty-five and under–sixty-five population, and average hospital occupancy fell from 75.9 percent in 1980 to 64.5 percent in 1988, despite a reduction in the number of beds. Changing technology has also contributed to the decline in length of stay, but aggressive buyers have certainly played a role.

The categories of customer for whom hospitals must compete have also increased. Traditionally, hospitals competed primarily for physicians who, as independent contractors with admitting privileges at multiple hospitals, have critical influence over the volume and cost of hospital admissions. Now, hospitals must also compete for contracts with third-party payers who restrict their policyholders' choice of facilities, and must market directly to patients, particularly for elective services, where patients choose the hospital. Moreover, technological advance has increased the number of surgical and major diagnostic procedures that can be performed on either an inpatient or outpatient basis. Hospitals, therefore, also compete with ambulatory surgery and diagnostic centers.

Physicians. The number of physicians active in patient care almost doubled from 237,500 in 1965 to 455,700 in 1987, or from 124 to 189 physicians per 100,000 population. This increase reflects the response of medical schools to federal subsidies introduced to increase the supply of physicians after the introduction of Medicare and Medicaid in 1965.

In competitive markets an increase in supply is expected to lead to lower prices and, hence, increased quantity. Total expenditures may increase or decrease, depending on whether demand is elastic or inelastic. Many commentators express concern that, in the medical context, more physicians means increased volume of "supplier-induced" services, rather than price reductions.

The evidence on this issue is mixed and likely to remain inconclusive. Many physicians have moved to rural areas that were previously unserved. Presumably, they would not have done so if they had unlimited ability to induce demand in cities. The increased willingness of physicians to accept alternatives to unconstrained fee-for-service payment is also consistent with increased competitive pressures. And many physicians have agreed to capitation (a fixed payment per patient per month, that puts the physician at risk for volume of services) and fixed-fee arrangements with utilization review. There is a persistent positive correlation between number of physicians per capita and frequency of physician visits or surgical procedures. While this is consistent with supplier-induced demand, it is however, also consistent with the commonsense idea that physicians tend to locate in areas where demand for their services is high.

Since the abolition of the antitrust immunity of physicians and other professions, antitrust has been applied to challenge such activities as maximum price schedules, preferred provider organizations, peer review, and denial of staff privileges. Similarly, antitrust has been applied to hospital mergers and contractual arrangements with physicians, medical supply companies, and insurers. Such cases require a delicate balancing of the need to protect against anticompetitive practice while at the same time permitting the contractual freedom needed to effectively control costs and quality in a market with pervasive insurance and asymmetric information.

Public Policy

Government intervention in the health care sector typically addresses either quality or access. Regulations to assure minimum quality can potentially enhance efficiency in markets with asymmetric information, infrequent purchase, and potential for catastrophic mistakes. But often the regulations take the form of licensing, which limits entry and therefore limits competition. For some professionals, replacing licensing with certification, so that consumers who want a minimum quality can be assured of it, might achieve quality control while interfering less with competition. Moreover, reputation and other market forces are increasingly powerful stimuli to quality (see BRAND NAMES). As the market evolves in the direction of competition among alternative medical plans that compete on all dimensions of quality (including technology, amenities, and choice of providers) as well as price, the appropriate role of government in setting minimum quality standards should be reassessed.

Government intervention to assure access includes public insurance and government subsidies to hospitals and clinics. Economic theory generally concludes that government intervention to stimulate the consumption of particular commodities is undesirable. People will consume, without subsidy, what they regard as the optimal amount of various items. A subsidy for consuming hamburgers, for example, causes people to consume too many hamburgers relative to

other goods. One exception to this rule is for goods whose consumption by some consumers confers benefits on others. If, for example, people would not get vaccinated against polio unless subsidized or required to do so, a strong case could be made for subsidizing or requiring polio vaccinations. But the great majority of health expenditures are now devoted to purely private services that benefit only the recipients of the services.

Another type of external effect, however, is often used to justify a public subsidy to health insurance for low-income individuals, rather than simply a cash transfer. Many view health care as a "merit" good. That is, people derive satisfaction from knowing that everyone has access to a minimum level of health care, and they therefore are unwilling to deny care to anyone in extreme need. Addressing this concern through private charity creates a free-rider dilemma: I have little incentive to give to the poor if I think you will take care of them. Moreover, the not-so-poor have little incentive to buy insurance if they expect to receive charity care should the need arise. In such cases government intervention can be efficient.

A strong public demand for some minimum medical safety net argues for assuring universal access to insurance, but this does not require public provision of either insurance itself or medical services. Universal access to insurance can be achieved through a system of vouchers with income-related subsidies. But subsidies may not be sufficient to assure that everyone buys coverage, unless the subsidies are set at a very high level. Subsidies high enough to induce everyone to buy insurance voluntarily would provide large benefits to those who would have bought coverage with a lower subsidy. And such subsidies would entail large deadweight costs of raising tax revenues. Subsidies alone are therefore an inefficient means of assuring universal coverage.

If the policy objective is universal coverage, then the simplest and most efficient approach is to make coverage compulsory, with income-related tax credits if necessary to assure affordability. Placing the requirement to obtain coverage on the individual entails less distortion of labor markets than the more widely discussed alternative, of mandating that employers provide coverage for employees. Mandating that employers provide coverage is equivalent to imposing a fixed tax per worker. Because insurance is a fixed cost per worker, the implicit tax rate is higher on low-wage and part-time workers. Unless wage rates of such workers fall to offset the cost of insurance to the employer, employment opportunities must fall. The cost of employer mandates will

therefore be borne largely by currently uninsured workers, many of whom are in low-wage jobs. Some costs may also fall on small employers. In either case, this approach to covering the uninsured entails unnecessarily high total costs.

By contrast, placing the requirement to obtain coverage on the individual does not preclude that employers provide insurance. Most insurance would probably continue to be obtained through employment because of the savings in administrative costs. But other sources of group insurance are more likely to develop than under the status quo, which distorts relative prices heavily in favor of providing insurance through employment. Despite the efficiency and equity arguments in favor of requiring individuals to obtain coverage, however, politicians favor employer mandates because the costs of such an approach, although higher, are largely hidden.

—Patricia M. Danzon

Biography: Patricia M. Danzon is Celia Moh Professor of Health Care Management and Insurance at the Wharton School in Philadelphia.

Further Reading

Danzon, Patricia M. "Hidden Overhead Costs: Is Canada's System Really Less Expensive?" *Health Affairs* (Spring 1992): 21–43.

Frech, H. Edward, III, ed. *Health Care in America: The Political Economy of Hospitals and Health Insurance.* 1988.

Manning, Willard, et al. "Health Insurance and the Demand for Medical Care: Evidence from a Randomized Experiment." *American Economic Review* 77, no. 3 (June 1987): 251–77.

Pauly, Mark, Patricia Danzon, Paul Feldstein, and John Hoff. "A Plan for 'Responsible National Health Insurance.' " *Health Affairs* (Spring 1991): 5–21.

See also DRUG LAG, HEALTH INSURANCE, INSURANCE.

Health Insurance

John C. Goodman

The Birth of the "Blues"

In the thirties and forties a competitive market for health insurance developed in many places in the United States. Typically, premiums tended to reflect risks, and insurers aggressively monitored claims to keep costs down and prevent abuses.

Following World War II, however, the market changed radically. Hospitals had created Blue Cross in 1939 and doctors started Blue Shield later. Under pressure from hospital and physician organizations, the "Blues" won competitive advantages from state governments and special discounts from medical providers. Once the Blues had used these advantages to gain a monopolistic position, the medical community was in a position to refuse to deal with commercial insurers unless they adopted many of the same practices followed by the Blues. Some of these practices were also later adopted by the federal government through the Medicare (for the elderly) and Medicaid (for the poor) programs.

Four characteristics of Blue Cross/Blue Shield health insurance fundamentally shaped the way Americans paid for health care in the postwar period.

First, hospitals were reimbursed on a cost-plus basis. If Blue Cross patients accounted for 40 percent of a hospital's total patient days, Blue Cross was expected to pay for 40 percent of the hospital's total costs. If Medicare patients accounted for one-third of patient days, Medicare paid one-third of the total costs. Other insurers reimbursed hospitals in much the same way. For the most part, physicians and hospital managers were free to incur costs as they saw fit. The role of insurers was to pay the bills, with few questions asked.

Second, the philosophy of the Blues was that health insurance should cover all medical costs—even routine checkups and diagnostic procedures. The early Blue plans had no deductibles and no copayments; insurers paid the total bill and patients and physicians made choices with little interference from insurers. Therefore, health insurance was not really "insurance." Instead, it was prepayment for the consumption of medical care.

Third, the Blues priced their policies based on what is called "community rating." In the early days this meant that everyone in a given geographical area was charged the same price for health insurance regardless of age, sex, occupation, or any other factor related to differences in real health risks. Even though a sixty-year-old can be expected to incur four times the health care costs of a twenty-five-year-old, for example, both paid the same premium. In this way higher-risk people were undercharged and lower-risk people were overcharged.

Fourth, instead of pricing their policies to generate reserves that would pay bills that weren't presented until future years (as life insurers and property and casualty insurers do), the Blues adopted a pay-as-you-go approach to insurance. This meant that each year's premium income paid that year's health care costs. If a policyholder developed an illness that required treatment over several years, in each successive year insurers had to collect additional premiums from all policyholders to pay those additional costs.

Even though most health care and most health insurance were provided privately, the U.S. health care system developed into a regulated, institutionalized market, dominated by nonprofit bureaucracies. Such a market is very different from a truly competitive market. Indeed, the primary reason that the medical community created the Blues was to avoid the consequences of a competitive market—including vigorous price competition and careful oversight of provider behavior by third-party payers.

One area where consumers become immediately aware that the medical marketplace is different is in the area of hospital prices. Even today, most patients cannot find out in advance what even routine surgical procedures will cost them. When discharged, they receive lengthy itemized bills that are difficult for even physicians to understand. Thus, the buyers (i.e., the patients) of hospital services cannot discover the price prior to buying and cannot understand the charge after the purchase has been made.

Under some reimbursement formulas in the cost-plus system, a hospital's reimbursement was partly determined by its charges. Hospitals discovered that by manipulating the charges, they could increase their total reimbursement. And because less than 10 percent of hospital bills were paid out of pocket by patients, artificial changes in the charges did little to affect the overall demand for hospital services. Even though the cost-plus system has been substantially dismantled, hospital charges still do not function as market prices that affect people's decisions and allocate resources. Instead, they are artifacts, arbitrarily manipulated to increase reimbursements from third-party payers.

One way to appreciate how much third-party payment has influenced the hospital marketplace is to contrast cosmetic surgery with other types of surgery. Because neither public nor private insurance any longer covers cosmetic surgery, patients pay with their own funds. And even though many parties are involved in supplying the service (physician, nurse, anesthetist, and the hospital), patients are quoted a single package price in advance. In other words, ordinary people, spending their own money, have been able to get advance price information that large employers, large insurance companies, and even federal and state governments generally have been unable to obtain for any other type of surgery.

Changes in the Eighties

The system of health insurance that prevailed from the forties through the seventies contained the seeds of its own destruction. Any system in which patients spend other people's money at the point of purchase and in which providers are reimbursed based on their costs and not on set fees, is a system in which health care costs will invariably rise.

Rising health care costs lead to higher health insurance premiums, giving the people who are being overcharged through the system of community rating greater incentives to find cheaper alternatives. New entrants into the health insurance market have incentives to supply those alternatives. And with increasing pressure to hold premiums down, diverse third-party payers have increasing incentives to find cheaper alternatives to the cost-plus system of hospital finance.

Thus, the system began to unravel in the seventies and eighties. Large employers began to manage their own health care plans, started paying hospitals based on set charges rather than costs, and negotiated price discounts. Through the Medicare program, the federal government began paying hospitals fixed prices for surgical procedures (the Prospective Payment System). Alternative prepaid programs, such as health maintenance organizations (HMOs) (under which total charges are fixed in advance) emerged as competitors to traditional fee-for-services medicine (under which charges rise with usage by people in the covered group). The system of community rating collapsed as individual insurers lowered their premium prices for lower-risk individuals and groups. The market for every medical service became more competitive.

The federal government also began to encourage competition in the health care sector. For example, it eliminated federal funding for, and encouragement of, health planning agencies. It also eliminated "certificate of need controls," under which hospitals had to have the government's permission to expand capacity or to buy expensive equipment. These changes strengthened the private sector's ability to solve many problems. Yet, the removal of the most obvious barriers to competition—while leaving more subtle barriers in place—has exacerbated three problems.

Lack of health insurance. One problem is that about 34 million Americans do not have health insurance, and their number has been rising. At least two government policies have contributed to this problem and made it much worse than it needs to be.

The first is the tax law. Most people who work for large companies receive health insurance as a fringe benefit. Because the health insurance premiums are deductible expenses for employers, many workers effectively avoid a 28 percent income tax, a 15.3 percent tax for Social Security (half of which is paid by employers), and a 2 to 9 percent state and local income tax. Thus, as much as fifty cents of every dollar spent on health insurance through employers is effectively paid by government. And we get what we subsidize. About 90 percent of the people who have private health insurance obtain it through an employer.

In contrast, the unemployed, the self-employed, and most employees of small businesses get little or no tax subsidy. If they have health insurance at all, they must first pay taxes and then purchase the insurance with what is left over. At the same time most of the 34 million people who have no health insurance pay higher tax rates to fund the $60 billion annual tax break for those who have employer-provided insurance.

A second source of the problem is state government regulations—specifically, laws that mandate what is covered under health insurance plans. Examples of mandated coverages include alcoholism, drug abuse, AIDS, mental illness, acupuncture, and in vitro fertilization.

In 1970 there were only thirty mandated health insurance benefit laws in the United States. Today there are at least one thousand. Coverage for heart transplants is mandated in Georgia, and for liver transplants in Illinois. Minnesota mandates coverage for hairpieces for bald people. Mandates cover marriage counseling in California, pastoral counseling in Vermont, and deposits to a sperm bank in Massachusetts.

There are more than 240 different health-related professions in the United States, ranging from chiropractors and naturopaths to athletic trainers. Every year, these special interest groups descend upon state legislatures demanding more and more regulations—and more and more mandated coverage. These regulations are driving up the cost of health insurance. The National Center for Policy Analysis estimates that as many as one out of every four people who lack health insurance has been priced out of the market by these costly regulations.

Not everyone is directly affected by state regulations. Federal law exempts federal government employees, Medicare enrollees, and employees of companies that manage their own health care plans. The last group employs more than half of all workers. State governments often exempt their own Medicaid patients and their own state employees. That means most of the burden of the mandates falls on employees of small businesses, the self-employed, and the unemployed. Yet these are the very groups that increasingly do without health insurance.

Rising health care costs. The second major problem is rising health care costs, a problem that also is exacerbated by federal tax law.

The primary reason health care costs are rising is that most spending on health care is done with someone else's money rather than the patient's. As a result patients avoid making tough choices between health care and other goods and services. The most wasteful kind of health insurance is insurance for small medical bills. These are the expenses over which patients exercise the most discretion and for which opportunities for waste and abuse are greatest. Moreover, by the time an insurance company gets through processing a twenty-five-dollar physician fee, the cost will be fifty dollars—thus doubling the cost of medical care.

The alternative to third-party insurance is individual self-insurance. The alternative to having third parties pay every medical bill is to have people pay most medical bills with their own money. The alternative to having large bureaucracies limit spending decisions with arbitrary rules and regulations is to let people make their own decisions.

Many economists who have studied the health insurance market believe that a more prudent approach would be to choose a high deductible and put the savings (from lower premiums) in individual medical savings accounts. In a short period of time, the vast majority of people would have accumulated savings far in excess of the annual deductible. If not spent, these funds could be used for postretirement medical expenses or as a supplement to retirement pensions. Singapore, for example, has built its entire health care system around individual self-insurance. Singapore workers are required to put 6 percent of their income into medical savings accounts every year.

In the United States we have moved in the opposite direction. Every dollar in premiums spent by employers for third-party health insurance receives a generous tax subsidy. Every dollar employees try to save is taxed.

Lack of actuarially priced insurance. The final problem is a lack of a real market for health insurance in which health risks are accurately priced. During the eighties most large companies realized that their premiums did not buy insurance. Instead, they were set to cover the employees' actual health costs each year. That is why most chose to self-insure, cut out the middleman (the insurance company), and pay health care bills directly. Today, about 80 percent of large companies use third-party insurers simply to process health care claims rather than to provide insurance services.

Ironically, however, most large companies continue to price health insurance internally (i.e., to employees) using the old Blue Cross method. Thus, if the average cost per employee is $3,300, and employees are asked to pay half that amount, all pay $1,650, regardless of their individual health risks. Because a sixty-year-old employee will generate about $5,280 in costs, on the average, older employees find health insurance underpriced and tend to bargain for more coverage for more items. To younger employees with expected costs of only $1,320, even one-half of the artificial premiums they face is often a bad buy, and their incentive is to forgo coverage.

In the market for small group and individual policies, the problem is even worse. Under the pay-as-you-go approach to premium pricing, insurers typically increase premiums each year to cover the continuing costs of people who contracted lengthy illnesses in past years. As a result healthier people and better risks find they can switch insurers and pay lower premiums for coverage or do without coverage altogether. That leaves the people who continue to buy coverage paying higher and higher premiums.

Today, most large insurers propose to deal with this problem by state or federal laws that would reimpose (to one degree or another) the old system of community rating. These proposals would, in effect, outlaw price cutting and force some insurers to share in the losses of others. The alternative is to adopt policies which encourage a market for real health insurance, in which risk is accurately priced. The first course requires laws and regulations designed to prevent the market from working. The alternative requires a legal environment that will allow the market to work.

—**John C. Goodman**

Biography: John C. Goodman is the president of the National Center for Policy Analysis, a Dallas-based think tank. In 1988 he won the Duncan Black Award for the best article in public choice economics.

Further Reading

Goodman, John C. *Regulation of Medical Care: Is the Price Too High?* 1980.
———, and Gerald L. Musgrave. *Patient Power: Solving America's Health Care Crisis.* 1992.
Herzlinger, Regina. *Creating New Health Care Ventures.* 1991.
Kessel, Reuben. "Price Discrimination in Medicine." *Journal of Law and Economics* 1 (October 1958): 20–53.
Starr, Paul. *The Social Transformation of American Medicine.* 1982.

See also HEALTH CARE INDUSTRY, INSURANCE.

Housing

Peter D. Salins

■ America's high standard of living is, by and large, equaled today in a growing number of other wealthy developed nations. But when it comes to housing, an essential component of that living standard, the United States still commands first place. By many objective standards Americans are the best-housed people in the world. Their homes are 20 to 40 percent larger than those of northern Europeans, and about 10 percent larger than those of their near peers, the Canadians and Australians. These larger homes shelter fewer residents than those of other countries. While the housing stock of Japan and the most prosperous of the European nations allocates, on average, one room per household member, American dwellings offer nearly two.

American homes also are considerably newer and more frequently equipped with the latest in modern mechanical equipment. Virtually all U.S. homes have refrigerators (not yet the norm in Europe or Japan), two-thirds of them self-defrosting. Not only are nearly all American dwellings centrally heated, but a third of them are centrally air-conditioned as well, while most of the rest have unit air conditioners. Unlike residents of other rich countries, American families are more likely to live in detached houses than apartments, and far more likely to own rather than rent them. And perhaps most distinctively, the typical American home is surrounded by a large private yard.

If U.S. housing standards look good in comparative international terms, they are equally impressive when viewed against American housing conditions of even the recent past. In 1960 the typical dwelling contained 1,200 square feet and was occupied by a household of 3.1 persons. By 1987 the average home had grown to over 1,600 square feet, while its occupancy had fallen to 2.4 persons. In 1960 over 13 percent of American homes lacked some component of a modern kitchen or bath; by 1987 that applied to only 2 percent. The proportion of all American homes with air-conditioning grew from 12 percent in 1960 to over 60 percent in 1987. During this same period the percentage of fully detached single-family homes fell from 77 percent in 1960 to 66 percent in 1987. Not so much an adverse development as a reflection of changes in American life-style, this marginal increase in the popularity of townhouse living moved the U.S. housing stock a little closer to the European model.

Of course, not all the U.S. housing facts are so benign. A visit to any American city will reveal conditions of housing squalor probably unmatched in other wealthy countries, although even America's worst dwellings are actually quite spacious and amenity-laden by international standards. The key to both the best and worst aspects of U.S. housing conditions is America's vastly greater reliance on the private market for the production and maintenance of housing.

America's singular housing conditions owe a great deal to the singular economics of the U.S. housing market. For one thing, the United States spends more on housing than any other nation, in both absolute and relative terms. As a percentage of GNP, America's 12.3 percent far exceeds the European and Japanese average of 9 percent, and even outpaces Canada and Australia's 11 percent. But in contrast to most other countries, developed and less developed alike, most American housing is built and financed by the private sector, without explicit subsidies.

The United States has somewhat over 2 million publicly owned or managed dwellings, which is a mere 2 percent of the housing stock. In Britain, by contrast, public housing makes up 30 percent of the total number of dwellings, and even in Canada it exceeds 10 percent. Not only is most U.S. housing privately owned, but most of it is owned by its occupants. Since 1950, approximately two-thirds of all U.S. homes have been owned rather than rented, with the current proportion slightly over 64 percent. Much has been written of the alleged inability of young couples today to afford home ownership. Yet the average first-time home buyer is still under thirty years old.

All of the positive features of the American housing scene must be viewed against a backdrop of considerable public hand-wringing about contemporary housing conditions. Media coverage and official reports constantly remind Americans of the outstanding examples of housing distress: physically devastated parts of inner-city neighborhoods that are invariably compared to war-torn Beirut; widespread homelessness invoking comparisons with Calcutta, and for the vast urban landscape where no manifest housing problems can be discerned, the purported scourge is lack of affordability.

Such critiques are not new. Nearly a century ago Jacob Riis spurred a housing reform movement by describing how "the other half lives." It was not until a half century later, when Franklin D. Roosevelt perceived that a third of the nation was ill housed, that people began looking to the government as the primary agent of housing amelioration. Ever since, successive generations of public officials and housing experts have proclaimed a "housing crisis" and proposed government action to end it. As a result a continuing stream of federal and state housing subsidy programs has been enacted since the passage of the National Housing Act of 1949, which promised "a decent home and suitable living environment for every American family."

The oldest and most direct of programmatic approaches, launched by the U.S. Housing Act of 1937, has depended on federal grants to underwrite the entire development cost of housing complexes owned and managed by local housing authorities, and since 1969, additional federal subsidization of roughly half their operating costs. While highly visible, especially in New York and some of the nation's other major cities, this "public housing" stock is available to only a small proportion of the urban poor.

By 1970 both its tenants and the general public were thoroughly disenchanted with this program, especially after journalists published a spate of highly critical accounts in the sixties of life in the public housing projects, showing large numbers of tenants abusing their new homes as well as their neighbors. Furthermore, direct public funding of new construction proved to be very costly, with modest apartments in bad sections of cities costing more than large private homes in the suburbs. Also, more and more people objected to having public housing in their neighborhoods. Thus, from the midsixties on, national, state, and local housing agencies have experimented with a wide variety of indirect subsidy approaches.

Although few old housing programs ever die completely, each presidential administration since the New Deal has promoted its own programmatic cure for the "housing crisis." Kennedy and Johnson favored mortgage subsidies. The Nixon and Ford administrations heavily promoted granting fifteen-year rental income guarantees to new or renovated housing developments tied to eligible tenants. The most recent Reagan and Bush administration policies represent a shift to consumer subsidies, including household rent supplements and the sale of housing authority apartments to their tenants. Parallel state and local efforts since the sixties have generally involved sponsorship and implementation of the changing menu of federal programs, or underwriting interest and tax abatement subsidies.

Whether the fifty-year effort of publicly funded housing assistance has made a great deal of difference in improving American housing conditions is hotly debated among housing specialists. Advocates of housing subsidies claim that the private sector can never build housing cheaply enough for the poor. On the other side, conservative housing policy analysts and a number of housing economists have published persuasive critiques of these programs, noting their high cost per household, the random distribution of their benefits by income class and region, and their likely role in displacing rather than supplementing the production of lower-priced homes by the private sector. In 1991 dollars few direct subsidy programs cost less than $80,000 per dwelling, and some cost more than $200,000, making most subsidized housing more expensive than privately built homes of comparable size. Because all housing programs are locally administered, they have been idiosyncratically implemented by place and time. And many of the beneficiaries of these programs have often been neither poor nor badly housed, but merely persistent or lucky.

Moreover, because the most egregious instances of housing squalor—broken windows and doors, graffiti, filthy streets and buildings, as well as distressing levels of neighborhood crime and vandalism—reflect the behavior of residents in poor urban neighborhoods rather than the physical deficiencies of their dwellings, they are not easily mitigated by dwelling-specific subsidies. At the same time, economists believe that most of the wholesale improvement in U.S. housing conditions since the depression is really due to a high rate of new housing production in the private market, which has permitted the retirement of the worst dwellings and reduced the quality-adjusted cost of all housing. In response, advocates of a continuing or growing role for the public sector allege that much of this "private" housing is indeed subsidized, by personal income tax deductions and public highways. (The deductibility of interest on home mortgages is indeed a subsidy—interest is not deductible in Canada, for example—and undoubtedly has contributed to the large private investment in housing.)

While this rhetorical debate between advocates of the private market and advocates of public subsidies rages on, at the practical level of policy implementation there continues to be an inexorable reduction in the level of government intervention in the U.S. housing market. In 1971 federal, state, and local programs subsidized the production of 483,000 homes. By 1981 the number had fallen to 211,000. Today, all government efforts together account for the construction and rehabilitation of no more than 100,000 dwellings per year.

With the decline in government's direct participation in subsidizing low-cost housing, the debate has shifted to the indirect effects of government policies. On one issue advocates of government subsidies to housing and their usual antagonists, conservative housing economists, agree. Both sides believe that among the greatest impediments to private market construction of "affordable" housing has been restrictive land-use regulation. With most new housing in the United States being built, of necessity, in the suburbs, local zoning, subdivision, and environmental regulations can increase housing prices, for new and older homes, by anywhere from 20 to 30 percent. The verbal protests of both the left and the right have provoked some court-mandated limits on the most restrictive local regulatory practices in New Jersey, Massachusetts, and a few other states. Yet protests against ''exclusionary zoning'' have not yet made much of a dent in suburban land-use policies.

—Peter D. Salins

Biography: Peter D. Salins is a professor of planning in the Urban Affairs and Planning Department of the City University of New York's Hunter College. He is also coeditor of the *Journal of the American Planning Association*.

Further Reading

Birch, Eugenie L., ed. *The Unsheltered Woman*. 1985.
Fannie Mae, Office of Housing Policy Research. *Housing Policy Debate* 2, no. 4 (1991).
Johnson, M. Bruce, ed. *Resolving the Housing Crisis*. 1982.
Rosenberry, Sara, and Chester Hartman, eds. *Housing Issues of the 1990s*. 1989.
Salins, Peter D., ed. *Housing America's Poor*. 1987.
———. ''Toward a Permanent Housing Problem.'' *The Public Interest* 85 (1986): 22–33.

See also RENT CONTROL.

Law and Economics

David D. Friedman

■ A legal rule has two consequences. The most immediate is to determine who pays what penalty to whom if the rule is broken. Thus, one might describe a law against speeding as a rule providing that anyone caught driving more than fifty-five miles an hour on the Dan Ryan Expressway must pay fifty dollars to the city of Chicago. Viewed this way, a speeding law is simply a way of raising revenue and a speeding ticket a rather peculiar sort of tax bill.

But that is not why we have most speeding laws. Their purpose is not to tax speeding, but to prevent it. We pass such laws because we believe that a driver is less likely to drive fast if one probable consequence of doing so is a fine.

The economic analysis of law deals with legal rules, whether made by legislatures or by courts, from this second viewpoint—not as a way of handing out rewards and punishments to those who deserve them, but as a system of incentives intended to affect behavior. Economic theory is used to predict how rational individuals will respond to such rules and what the consequences will be. This way of thinking about the law, and the conclusions it implies, are obvious in cases such as the speeding law. In other cases the analysis and the conclusions are much less obvious.

Consider a city ordinance restricting the terms of rental contracts. Suppose the government of Chicago forbids any apartment lease that permits the landlord to evict the tenant without giving him at least six months' notice. An obvious consequence is that tenants are better off, since they now have six months' security, while landlords are worse off, since it takes them longer to evict undesirable tenants.

While this is obvious, it is probably not true other than in the very short run. What the argument omits is the effect of the rule on the behavior of landlords and tenants. By increasing both the cost to landlords of providing apartments and the value to tenants of the apartments they rent, the rule increases the rent at which the number of apartments supplied by landlords equals the number demanded by tenants.

In the simplest case, where the costs of the additional security are the same for all landlords and the benefits are the same for all tenants, one can show that the law either has no effect or makes both sides worse off. If the benefits to tenants from the additional security exceed the costs to landlords, the rule has no effect. Landlords would offer the guarantee even without the rule, since tenants are willing to pay more for it than it costs the landlord. If the benefit of the additional security to the tenants is less than its cost to the landlords, the rule makes both sides worse off. Landlords receive more rent, but not enough to compensate them for the cost of providing security. Tenants receive security, but pay more for it than it is worth to them.

One can construct more complicated situuations where the restriction benefits tenants at the expense of landlords, or landlords at the expense of tenants, or some landlords (or tenants) at the expense of others, but there is no particular reason to expect any such effect. The typical result of such a restriction on the terms of contracts, for rental housing or other things, is a net cost plus some more or less random redistribution of wealth. It is like a law requiring all cars to be equipped with air-conditioning and stereo tape decks. The result is not that consumers get additional features for free, but that some get (and pay for) features they would have bought anyway, while others are forced to buy features worth less to them than they cost.

So one implication of economic analysis of law is a presumption in favor of freedom of contract—the legal rule permitting parties to a contract to set any terms mutually acceptable and have them enforced by the courts. This presumption is not always true. It is possible to construct economic arguments against freedom of contract in particular situations. But such arguments depend on the existence of some form of market failure, such as an externality (a situation in which A's contract with B imposes costs on C). Courts will not, for instance, enforce a contract to commit a crime.

In contract law, as in many other areas of law, economic analysis affects not only conclusions about what the law should be, but the whole form of the arguments on which such conclusions are based. In order for the noneconomist to decide for or against laws requiring "pro-tenant" terms in leases, he need only know whether he favors tenants or landlords. For the economist that is almost irrelevant, since once

the effect on rents of "pro-tenant" legal restrictions is taken into account, there is no reason to expect them to benefit tenants.

This is one example of the application of economics to the analysis of legal rules. Over the past twenty years economic arguments have been used to analyze the consequences of a wide variety of legal rules, including standards of proof, rules of evidence, damage rules for breach of contract, negligence rules for torts, and many others. An important—and controversial—element in much of this work is the claim that legal rules either are, or ought to be, designed to maximize economic efficiency— roughly speaking, to make the size of the economic pie as large as possible. (See EFFICIENCY.) Judge Richard Posner, for instance, has argued that the common law, the set of legal doctrines that has evolved out of decisions by judges, tends to be efficient—that many of the rules developed by the courts seem very much like those that would be proposed by an economist designing a legal system to maximize economic efficiency.

Consider, for example, the issue of negligence. Suppose I take some action that results in damage to you. In many, though not all, situations I will be required to pay for your damage only if my action was negligent. Under the definition of negligence proposed by Judge Learned Hand, I am negligent if I could have prevented the accident at a cost to me that is less than the expected benefit from preventing it. The expected benefit is the probability that the accident will occur times the damage that will be done.

Suppose that if I do not have my brakes checked there is a 10 percent chance my car will skid into yours and do $1,000 damage. If I have the brakes checked, the chance is reduced to zero, so the expected benefit is $.10 \times \$1,000 = \$100$. If the cost of the checkup is less than $100 then, under the Hand rule, I am negligent if I do not have the brakes checked, and will be liable for any accidents that result. If the cost is more than $100, then I am not negligent and will not be liable. This looks very much like a rule designed to produce the efficient outcome. If the cost of the precaution is greater than the benefit, then, on net, taking the precaution makes us worse off, so I should not be punished for not taking it—even if the result is an accident.

A similar analysis can be applied to the case of speeding tickets. I argued earlier that the purpose of speeding laws was not to collect money, but to prevent speeding. We could surely do so more effectively if we made the punishment more severe. If every speeder was hanged—or even if every speeder had his car confiscated—the number of speeders would rapidly approach zero.

One explanation of why we do not follow such a policy is that we do not wish to eliminate all speeding—just "inefficient" speeding. We punish speeding because it imposes a cost, in the increased likelihood of accidents, on other drivers. In some cases that cost may be worth paying. If we set the expected fine for speeding equal to the expected damage that the speeder does to other drivers, then each driver can decide for himself whether the benefit of getting where he is going a little sooner is worth the cost.

What these examples suggest is that many legal issues can be analyzed in economic terms, and that existing legal rules often make economic sense. Of course, a full economic analysis of either negligence or traffic fines, or a full description of the relevant law, would be much more complicated than the sketch given here.

Economics has made a substantial contribution to our understanding of the law, but the law has also contributed to our understanding of economics. Courts routinely deal with the reality of such economic abstractions as property and contract. The study of law thus gives economists an opportunity to improve their understanding of some of the concepts underlying economic theory. The most notable example is the work of University of Chicago economist Ronald Coase. Coase received the 1991 Nobel Prize in economics, in part for using ideas based on his study of the law of nuisance to revolutionize the corresponding area of economics—the theory of externalities.

—David D. Friedman

Biography: David D. Friedman is an Olin Fellow in Law and Economics at the University of Chicago Law School.

Further Reading

Calabresi, Guido, and A. Douglas Melamed. "Property Rules, Liability Rules, and Inalienability: One View of the Cathedral." *Harvard Law Review* 85 (1972): 1089–1128.

Coase, Ronald H. "The Problem of Social Cost." *Journal of Law and Economics* 3 (1960): 1–44.

Landes, William, and Richard Posner. *The Economic Structure of Tort Law*. 1987.

Posner, Richard. *Economic Analysis of Law*. 1986.

Shavell, Steven. *Economic Analysis of Accident Law*. 1987.

OPEC

Benjamin Zycher

■ Few people are aware of it today, but OPEC (the Organization of Petroleum Exporting Countries) was formed in response to the U.S. imposition of import quotas on oil. In 1959 the U.S. government established a Mandatory Oil Import Quota Program (MOIP) restricting the amount of crude oil (and refined products) that could be imported into the United States. The MOIP gave preferential treatment to oil imports from Mexico and Canada. This partial exclusion of the U.S. market to Persian Gulf producers depressed prices for their oil. As a result oil prices "posted" (paid to the selling nations) by the major oil companies were reduced in February 1959 and August 1960. In its early years the U.S.

import quota program also discriminated against oil from Venezuela.

In September 1960 four Persian Gulf nations (Iran, Iraq, Kuwait, and Saudi Arabia) and Venezuela formed OPEC, the purpose of which was to obtain higher prices for crude oil. By 1973 eight other nations (Qatar, Indonesia, Libya, the United Arab Emirates, Algeria, Nigeria, Ecuador, and Gabon) had joined OPEC. Ecuador withdrew on the last day of 1992.

OPEC was unsuccessful in its first decade. Real (that is, inflation-adjusted) world prices for crude oil continued to fall until 1971. In 1958 the real price was $10.85 per barrel (in 1990 dollars). By 1971 it had fallen to $7.46 per barrel. However, real prices began to rise slowly beginning in 1971, and then jumped dramatically in late 1973 and 1974 from roughly $8 per barrel to over $27 per barrel in the wake of the Arab-Israeli ("Yom Kippur") War.

Contrary to what many noneconomists believe, the 1973 price increase was not caused by the oil "embargo" (refusal to sell) directed at the United States and the Netherlands that year by the Arab members of OPEC. Instead, OPEC reduced its production of crude oil, thus raising world oil prices substantially. The embargo against the United States and the Netherlands had no effect whatever: both nations were able to obtain oil at the same prices as all other nations. The failure of this selective embargo was predictable. Oil is a fungible commodity that can easily be resold among buyers. Therefore, sellers who try to deny oil to buyer A will find other buyers purchasing more oil, some of which will be resold by them to buyer A.

Nor, as is commonly believed, was OPEC the cause of oil shortages and gasoline lines in the United States. Instead, the shortages were caused by price and allocation controls on crude oil and refined products, originally imposed in 1971 by President Nixon as part of the Economic Stabilization Program. By preventing prices from rising sufficiently, the price controls stimulated desired consumption above the quantities available at the legal maximum prices. Shortages were the inevitable result. Countries that avoided price controls, such as West Germany and Switzerland, also avoided shortages, queues, and the other perverse effects of the controls.

OPEC is a cartel—a group of producers that attempts to restrict output in order to keep prices higher than the competitive level. The heart of OPEC is the Conference, which comprises national delegations, usually at the level of oil minister. The Conference meets twice each year to assign output quotas, which are upper limits on the amount of oil each member is allowed to produce. The Conference may also meet in special sessions when deemed necessary, particularly when downward pressure on prices becomes acute.

OPEC faces the classic problem of all cartels: overproduction and cheating by members. At the higher cartel price, less oil is demanded. That is why OPEC assigns output quotas. Each member of the OPEC cartel has an incentive to produce more than its quota and "shave" (cut) this price because the cost of producing an additional barrel of crude is typically well below the cartel price. The methods available to shave official OPEC prices are numerous. Credit can be extended to buyers for periods longer than the standard thirty days. Higher grades (or blends) of oil can be sold for prices applicable to lower grades. Transportation credits can be given. Buyers can be offered side payments or rebates.

This tendency for individual producers to cheat on the cartel agreement is a longstanding feature of OPEC behavior. Individual producers usually have exceeded their production quotas, and so official prices have been unstable. But OPEC is an unusual cartel in that one producer—Saudi Arabia—is much larger than the others. That is why the Saudis are the "swing" producer. When prices start downward, they cut their production to keep prices up. One reason the Saudis have behaved that way is that departures from the official prices impose larger total losses on them than on other OPEC members in the short run. Because other producers have huge incentives to produce in excess of their quotas, the Saudis, in order to defend the official OPEC price, have had to reduce their sales dramatically at times. This erosion of Saudi production and sales has tended to reduce their revenues and profits substantially. In 1983 and 1984, for example, the Saudis found themselves producing only about 3.5 million barrels per day, despite their (then) production capacity almost three times that level.

How successful has OPEC been since the early seventies? Not as successful as many people perceive. Except in the wake of the 1979 Iranian revolution, and in anticipation of possible destruction of substantial reserves in the 1990–91 Persian Gulf conflict, real (inflation-adjusted) prices of crude oil have fallen since 1973. Prices began dropping very rapidly in the early eighties after the Saudis concluded that lower prices and higher production were in their best interests. Official prices fell from $34 (for the benchmark crude oil, Arabian light) to $29 in 1983, $24 in 1984, and about $18 in 1986 to 1988. Indeed, even prices unadjusted for inflation often have fallen. For example, prices fell from $35.10 per barrel ($49.10 in 1990 dollars) in 1981 to $16.69 ($18.69 in 1990 dollars) in 1987. (Price data are shown in table 1, and current reserves, production capacity, and production levels are shown in table 2.)

This downward trend has increased tensions between two rival groups within OPEC. The price ''hawks,'' usually nations with smaller crude oil reserves relative to population, argue for lower oil output and higher prices. The principal hawks within OPEC are Iran and Iraq. The price ''doves,'' usually nations with larger reserves relative to population, argue for higher output and lower prices to preserve, over the longer term, their oil markets and thus the economic value of their oil resources. The principal doves within OPEC are Saudi Arabia, Kuwait, and the United Arab Emirates.

Such relatively lower prices serve the interests of the doves because oil consumers have used less oil in response to prior price increases. For example, U.S. energy use per dollar of GNP (adjusted for inflation) was 27.49 thousand BTUs in 1970. By 1988, after the price increases of 1973 and 1979, it had decreased to 19.93 thousand BTUs. Thus, the price ''doves,'' led by Saudi Arabia, generally have resisted pressures for higher prices.

Over the long run, real prices of natural resources and commodities usually fall, largely because of technological advances. Crude oil is no exception. Technological advances in seismic exploration have dramatically reduced the cost of finding new reserves, thus increasing oil reserves greatly. Horizontal drilling and other new techniques have reduced the cost of recovering known reserves. Also, improvements in technology provide both substitutes for oil and ways to use less oil to achieve given ends.

Moreover, advances in technology will reduce prices for such substitute fuels as natural gas, thus exerting continuing downward pressure on crude oil prices. And increasing willingness to devote resources toward environmental improvement suggests that the market for crude oil will de-

TABLE 1

World Crude Oil Prices
(U.S. dollars per barrel)

Year	Nominal Price	In 1990 Dollars	Year	Nominal Price	In 1990 Dollars
1955	2.25	10.88	1973	3.27	8.69
1956	2.36	11.04	1974	11.17	27.20
1957	2.73	12.34	1975	11.57	25.66
1958	2.45	10.85	1976	12.41	25.86
1959	2.27	9.82	1977	13.33	26.05
1960	2.23	9.49	1978	13.43	24.46
1961	2.27	9.57	1979	20.19	33.78
1962	2.26	9.32	1980	32.27	49.52
1963	2.25	9.13	1981	35.10	49.10
1964	2.23	8.91	1982	32.11	42.22
1965	2.22	8.64	1983	27.73	35.10
1966	2.24	8.42	1984	27.44	33.50
1967	2.27	8.31	1985	25.83	30.63
1968	2.24	7.81	1986	12.52	14.47
1969	2.27	7.50	1987	16.69	18.69
1970	2.35	7.36	1988	13.25	14.36
1971	2.52	7.46	1989	16.89	17.59
1972	2.64	7.47	1990	20.42	20.42

SOURCE: *U.S. Departments of Energy, Commerce, and Labor.*

cline relative to those for such "cleaner" energy sources as natural gas and nuclear technology, unless other technical advances yield substantial improvement in the ability to use oil cleanly. Thus, the demand for crude oil is likely over the long term to decline relative to the demand for competing fuels. This has been the experience of mankind, as wood gradually gave way to coal, which in turn declined as the use of oil expanded. These facts suggest that the economic power of OPEC inexorably will erode.

—**Benjamin Zycher**

TABLE 2

OPEC Reserves, Production Capacity, and Production Levels

Nation	Reserves[a]	Capacity[b]	Production[c]
Algeria	9,200	800	750
Ecuador	1,514	330	280
Gabon	733	200	260
Indonesia	8,200	1,300	1,200
Iran	92,860	3,000	3,100
Iraq	100,000	3,500	3,100
Kuwait*	97,125	2,200	1,800
Libya	22,800	1,600	1,250
Neutral Zone	n.a.	600	300
Nigeria	16,000	1,700	1,700
Qatar	4,500	600	365
Saudi Arabia*	257,559	7,000	5,300
Un. Arab Em.	94,105	2,210	2,060
Venezuela	58,504	2,400	2,000
OPEC Total	763,100	27,440[d]	23,465
World Total	1,001,572	63,740[d]	60,320

[a] Millions of barrels on January 1, 1990.
[b] Maximum sustainable as of August 1990, thousands of barrels per day.
[c] Thousands of barrels per day as of May 1990, excluding natural gas liquids.
[d] Non-OPEC capacity for first quarter 1991, from internal Department of Energy/Energy Information Administration estimate.
* Includes one-half of the Neutral Zone.
n.a.—not available.

SOURCE: *U.S. Department of Energy, Central Intelligence Agency.*

Biography: Benjamin Zycher is vice president for research at the Milken Institute for Job and Capital Formation in Santa Monica, California. He also is a visiting professor of economics at the University of California at Los Angeles and an adjunct scholar at the Cato Institute in Washington. He was formerly a senior staff economist with President Reagan's Council of Economic Advisers.

Further Reading

Bohi, Douglas R., and Milton Russell. *Limiting Oil Imports: An Economic History and Analysis.* 1978.
Bradley, Robert L., Jr. *The Mirage of Oil Protection.* 1989.
Horwich, George, and David Leo Weimer, eds. *Responding to International Oil Crises.* 1988.
Glasner, David. *Politics, Prices, and Petroleum.* 1985.
Zycher, Benjamin. "The Silly Season for Energy Policy." *Regulation* (Spring 1991): 6–9.
———. "Emergency Management." In *Free Market Energy*, edited by S. Fred Singer. 1984.

See also ENERGY, NATURAL GAS REGULATION.

Public Schools

John E. Chubb

■ By most accounts America's schools are not performing very well. The average combined (verbal and mathematics) score on the Scholastic Aptitude Test was seventy-five points higher in 1963 than it was in 1990. A high school senior ranked at the 50th percentile on the SAT today would have ranked around the 33rd percentile in 1963. American students trail most of their international counterparts in mathematics and science achievement. Recent comparisons of industrialized countries place the United States between tenth and fifteenth in these economically vital fields. And excellence is not all that is missing. Performance among schools is quite inconsistent. Blacks score nearly two hundred points below whites on the SAT. Urban high schools, which serve disproportionately large numbers of poor families, fail to graduate nearly half of their students; high schools nationwide graduate about four-fifths of theirs.

To make matters worse, performance has stalled or fallen despite aggressive government efforts to turn it around. Since the launch of the Soviet Sputnik more than thirty years ago, school reform has been an ongoing enterprise. President Johnson signed the Elementary and Secondary Education Act, the cornerstone of his Great Society program and the beginning of aggressive federal efforts to upgrade the schools of children living in poverty. President Carter formed the Department of Education in order to raise the political profile of federal education policy. President Reagan's National Commission on Excellence in Education spurred nearly a decade of ambitious school reform when it warned, in a landmark report of the same name, that the United States is "A Nation at Risk." Most recently, President Bush introduced "America 2000," a comprehensive reform plan that, if implemented completely, would create an entirely new system of education.

All of this political attention has brought many changes. Annual inflation-adjusted expenditures per pupil have tripled since 1960, surpassing $5,500 in 1991. Over the same period class sizes were reduced by about 30 percent. Teachers have become much more experienced—fifteen years on average now versus eight years in 1971—and have acquired more formal education. Only a quarter of the nation's teachers held master's degrees in 1971, while more than half do today. Since 1980, virtually every state in the union has raised its high school graduation requirements, and students are now taking more academic courses than they did a decade ago.

To be sure, there have been some signs of improved performance. The average SAT score fell by ninety points between 1963 and 1980, but then rebounded by fifteen points during the early and mideighties. Black and other minority students improved their SAT scores during the seventies and eighties, slightly narrowing the chasm between their achievement and that of whites. During the eighties the percentage of students scoring at grade-appropriate levels on the National Assessment of Educational Progress—a test that is a better gauge of in-school learning than the SAT—was up several points. The dropout rate has improved by roughly 10 percentage points since the early seventies—if General Equivalency Diplomas are counted. Yet, as the National Assessment of Educational Progress reveals, most gains appear to have come in rote learning, computation, and basic skills, rather than in problem-solving and other higher-order skills. As of 1991, moreover, the nation's average SAT score had lost another ten points. By any standard, recent improvements have been exceedingly modest.

Why, then, despite great effort, are America's schools doing rather poorly? One possibility is that students have become more difficult and families less supportive. Yet scores of careful analyses have found little support for this hypothesis. The facts are these: drug use among schoolchildren has plummeted over the last decade; childhood poverty rates, though up and down, are the same today as in the late sixties; and student achievement began to decline in the early sixties—about ten years before divorce rates and female employment began their rapid ascents.

Hundreds of studies have also examined the relationship between major mainstream school reforms and student achievement, allowing for differences in the characteristics of students and families across schools and over time. The overwhelming majority of these studies have found the same thing. School performance is simply unrelated to conventional school "improvements," including higher expenditures per pupil, better educated or more experienced teachers, and smaller pupil–teacher ratios. School performance appears to be eroding or stagnating not because school problems are tougher (though this may be the explanation in some schools) but because the school "improvements" made by reformers do not have much influence on performance.

What, then, does influence school performance, and why haven't school reformers done the right things? Unfortunately, there is no simple recipe for school success. The "inputs" necessary to produce desirable educational "outputs" are not well understood, and this puts school reformers in a serious bind. Fortunately, some reform strategies do not depend so heavily on knowledge of which inputs really work. Rather, they rely on accountability for outputs (i.e., what students actually learn), incentives for performance, and ultimately, the market principles of school competition and parental choice. These strategies have given some reformers fresh hope of finally doing the right thing.

Experts increasingly agree that the qualities that distinguish America's best schools are very difficult to mandate. "Effective schools," as the best institutions are now often called, are distinguished by such attributes as a clear sense of purpose, strong leadership by principals toward shared educational goals, professionalism and teamwork on the part of teachers, and high academic expectations for all students. These attributes, which fall into the realm of attitudes and behavior, are beyond the direct control of school reformers. Educators can be told that they must work cooperatively, enthusiastically, creatively, and assiduously, but no one can guarantee that they will.

An alternative strategy that I and many others believe makes good educational as well as economic sense is for reformers to cease telling educators what to do and how to do it, and to start telling them what society expects from them as a finished product. This strategy would allow educators to exercise their professional judgment—in assembling a talented and dedicated teaching force, in selecting and designing interesting texts and curricular materials, in tailoring instructional techniques to fit the needs of the students and families being served, and in orienting the school around a theme or mission that captures the imagination of teachers and students alike. In exchange for such autonomy, the schools would be held accountable for results. Schools that use their autonomy productively would be rewarded. Nonproductive schools might even be punished.

Gradually, many educators and researchers are concluding that autonomy and accountability are the way to go. Various scholars and most of the organizations representing teachers and administrators claim that the system of public education has become too centralized and bureaucratized, and that the quality of schools has consequently suffered. As Terry M. Moe and I argue in *Politics, Markets, and America's Schools*, excessive regulation undermines the professionalism and vitality of teachers and principals, leading many good people to leave the schools. Those who remain tend to organize and lobby for regulatory protection from the growing number of authorities above them. Political conflict increases, and despite lots of good intentions, the system grows more bureaucratic, less manageable, and less successful.

The fact is, as school performance has eroded over the last several decades, bureaucracy has grown larger. Instructional expenditures account for a rapidly declining share—now less than 60 percent—of local school expenditures. Full-time classroom teachers account for less than half of local school employment, while administrators represent about 15 percent. The number of nonclassroom personnel is growing at seven times the rate of classroom teachers.

The system has also become more centralized, with the states surpassing local governments as the major source of school funds. An average state today pays for 50 percent of public elementary and secondary education; an average school district pays for 45 percent. In 1960, school districts averaged 60 percent, states only 35 percent. Although the federal share of school funding has actually fallen 3 percentage points since 1980, the number of special programs that the federal government implements has remained constant at roughly eighty, and the volume of regulation it promulgates has grown.

These developments have come under increasing attack. Numerous reformers are now calling for radical reductions in bureaucratic control. The chancellor of the New York City Public Schools, Joseph Fernandez, is the nation's leading advocate of a form of decentralization known as "school-based management," a strategy that he pioneered in Dade County, Florida. The Chicago Public School System was dramatically decentralized in 1989 by shifting much of the control over schools from a central board of education to hundreds of boards, each responsible for a single school. All across America, school-based management and variations on that theme have become the most popular reform strategies of the nineties.

It is too early to judge these recent reforms, and not surprisingly, the academic gains produced by them so far have been small or nonexistent. Indeed, there is good reason to believe that decentralization alone will not promote major improvement. The difficulty is that while decentralization attacks the problem of bureaucracy and affords schools professional freedom, it does not necessarily provide society with accountability for results. Unless there is some means for society to express its interest in schooling—to specify what results it wants—a decentralized system of schools may not produce the educational improvements society values.

Reformers are aware of the need for accountability. But except in very small public school systems, reformers have been unable to devise accountability mechanisms that do not entail yet another layer of bureaucracy. Most mechanisms involve much formality and detail about such indicators of performance as test scores, dropout rates, teacher attendance records, personnel evaluations, and so on, along with many specifications of the conditions under which schools may be rewarded or punished for changes in these indicators.

The dangers in such new bureaucracy are many. Schools may produce formal improvements on the indicators, but little genuine improvement in education. For example, schools may "baby-sit" students in order to reduce dropout rates, or teach students to take standardized tests rather than to think. The new bureaucracy may also interfere as much as the old bureaucracy with the legitimate needs of educators for professional autonomy. It is little wonder that one of the school reforms that is most popular with the general public—merit pay for teachers—has yet to be meaningfully implemented anywhere in the country.

How, then, do we get an autonomous school system that is accountable to the public? Some economists believe the most promising strategy is to reorganize the public education system according to the principles of competition and choice. The basic idea is to permit parents and students to choose their schools. Good schools, ones that provide the kinds of academic results that most parents want, would be rewarded and would flourish. Bad schools, schools that few want to attend, would not be propped up by interest groups that are able to influence the political process. They would be denied resources, go out of business, and be replaced. Opponents of this view argue, among other things, that it would further disadvantage poor students, whose parents are not as well equipped as wealthy parents to make informed choices.

For me and many others, however, the logic of educational choice holds great appeal. But there is more to recommend educational choice than its "survival-of-the-fittest" rationale. In particular, educational choice would create powerful disincentives for bureaucratic growth and powerful incentives for empowerment of professionals at the school level. In a marketplace where parent and student satisfaction are crucial to a school's longevity, schools must respond to diverse family wants and needs. This can

be accomplished only if the people closest to parents and students—namely, teachers and principals—have ample authority.

This is not just a matter of theoretical speculation. The New York City public schools, for example, employ more than 6,000 central office personnel—an administrator/student ratio of 1 to 150. The Catholic schools of the Archdiocese of New York, a smaller system than its public counterpart but nevertheless the twelfth largest school system in the country, employs only 30 central office personnel—a ratio of 1 to 4,000. Political control of schools encourages bureaucratization; market control dramatically discourages it. If reform aspires to create a school system that is based not only on accountability for results but on school autonomy and the professionalism of educators, a system organized around the principles of competition and choice is doubly desirable.

Of course, no market is perfect. For a system of educational choice to work efficiently and equitably, the government would need to play a significant role. Experts differ over precisely how this role would be played. But most agree that the government would need to fund the system and provide students from poor families the financial wherewithal to compete effectively with students from middle-class families for admission to schools of their choice. The government would need to ensure that all parents have ample and accurate information about how schools are performing so that students are not excluded from schools because of parental ignorance. The government might do this by operating parent information centers, mandating achievement tests, or like the Federal Trade Commission, regulating "truth in advertising" by schools. The government might also find private firms like Consumers Union offering all sorts of comparative assessments of schools, thereby reducing the need for government information.

The government would also need to design an admissions process that guarantees all students a school. Schools and students should be permitted to match up voluntarily as much as possible, but there must also be a safety net. Schools might be required, for example, to accept some mandatory placements from a lottery of students who do not find schools voluntarily. The government might also want to establish basic chartering criteria to guarantee that schools that participate in the system are nondiscriminatory, healthy, safe, and bona fide institutions of learning—not degree mills. If a system of educational choice is to make a real difference in the supply of schools, however, the government must also recognize the limits of its role and the need for market forces to operate. The government must trust and respect the professional judgment of teachers and principals, and the values, concerns, and intelligence of parents.

Increasingly, governments are doing just that. Most cities have introduced specialized "magnet" schools to motivate children and to bring together children of different races voluntarily. Several cities have fully "magnetized" their school systems, with encouraging results. Eight states now provide freedom of choice among most of their public schools.

A number of cities and towns also provide vouchers for students to attend private schools or colleges. Since 1986 Minnesota has had more than ten thousand juniors and seniors using vouchers to attend college instead of high school—a program that not only is popular with participants but that also has stimulated large increases in advanced placement classes in high schools threatened with college competition. Since 1990 Wisconsin has permitted low-income parents in Milwaukee to choose nonsectarian private schools. Despite court battles, opposition from the state and local education agencies, and great uncertainty about the program's future, roughly seven hundred families are happily (according to independent surveys) participating, and parents are much more involved in their children's education than they were before.

Of course, not all experiences with choice—public or private—are positive. Because public schools are often forced by government to be the same, parents have sometimes met public school "choice" with indifference. Because markets take time to weed out inferior products, the Milwaukee voucher program initially included one educationally dubious school that served its students poorly—before it closed and returned its students to the public schools. Nevertheless, choice was the keystone of the education strategy offered by former President Bush, and is the focus of school reform debates nationwide.

Public opinion polls indicate that the concept of educational choice is supported by a majority of Americans, especially poor Americans and racial minorities who are often trapped—without choice—in collapsing urban school systems. The business community is panicked about the quality of the work force and has grown impatient with traditional school reforms. As educators come to see that there is little hope for acquiring autonomy without also providing the accountability that choice allows, educators, too, may become supporters of the idea. In any event, choice will be the focus of educational debate over the next decade.

—**John E. Chubb**

Biography: John E. Chubb is a fellow with the Brookings Institution.

Further Readings

Boaz, David, ed. *Liberating Schools: Education in the Inner City.* 1991.

Chubb, John E., and Terry M. Moe. *Politics, Markets, and America's Schools.* 1990.

Coleman, James S., and Thomas Hoffer. *Public and Private High Schools: The Impact of Communities.* 1987.

Finn, Chester E., Jr. *We Must Take Charge: Our Schools and Our Future.* 1991.

Sizer, Theodore R. *Horace's Compromise: The Dilemma of the American High School.* 1985.

Sportometrics

Robert D. Tollison

■ Until recently, economists who analyzed sports focused on the such things as the antitrust exemption, the alleged cartel behavior of sports leagues, and the player draft (see SPORTS). Sportometrics is different. It is the application of economic theories to the behavior of athletes in the real world to see if we can explain what they do, and to see if what they do can help us explain the behavior of people in other professions. Instead of being about the "economics of sports," sportometrics introduces the idea of "sports as economics."

In other words, sportometricians view sports as an economic environment in which athletes behave according to incentives and constraints. Economists have, for example, shown how incentives and costs can explain how much effort runners exert in a footrace (see Higgins and Tollison). Using data from sprint events of the modern Olympics from 1896 to 1980, the cited study found that running times were faster when there were fewer contestants in a race. This makes sense. With fewer runners each runner's chance of winning is greater, and therefore, each runner's expected gain from putting out additional effort is greater. This cannot be attributed to decreased congestion: because each runner is given a lane, congestion does not diminish when the number of contestants falls.

The study also found that the harder an Olympic record is to break, the less effort contestants will expend to break it. Can any fan ever forget Carl Lewis's pass on a third attempt to break Bob Beamon's long-jump record in the 1984 Olympics? Horse racing is an even better contest to analyze, because there prerace odds were used to control for the differential abilities of the racers. The study found similar results: an increase in the number of competitors leads to an increase in average race times.

The economic activity called arbitrage also enters into sports. Arbitrage is what economists call the exploitation of price differences for the same commodity. For example, if wheat sells for $3.00 a bushel in Chicago and $3.30 in Indianapolis, and if it can be transported to Indianapolis for 20% per bushel, then an arbitrageur can make 10% on each bushel he buys in Chicago and sells in Indianapolis.

What does this have to do with professional basketball? A lot. Each player has an incentive to build up his individual performance statistics, particularly the number of points he scores. But a good coach enforces a regime in which shots are allocated—arbitraged—among players to maximize the probability that each shot taken will be made. Players who make a higher percentage of their shots should, thus, be given more chances to shoot. Using data from the National Basketball Association, Kevin Grier and I found that coaches who are better at enforcing such an allocation of shots—better arbitrageurs—are more likely to win games and to have longer tenure as head coaches. Among the better coaches, we found, was Cotton Fitzsimmons, the former coach of the Phoenix Suns. He became head coach of the Kansas City Kings in 1977 and, in his first full season, led the Kings to forty-eight wins and a shooting efficiency rating of 66 percent, which is very high.

In each case studied, economists gain insight not only on the behavior of athletes and coaches, but also on more general economic problems. The behavior of runners is analogous to that of bidders for a government contract: a bidder will expend more effort—lobbying and the like—the fewer competitors it has for a contract. Coaching a team is analogous to managing a company: within a company, managers ''arbitrage'' tasks among employees.

Analyzing sporting events, moreover, provides insights into the workings of all competition within well-defined rules—just as we see in our economy. Incentives and constraints are spelled out clearly; players behave as rational economic actors; sporting events and seasons can be seen as the operation of miniature economies—and so on. One of the first sportometrics analyses done (see McCormick and Tollison) showed, for example, that basketball players respond rationally when an additional monitor (referee) of their behavior is on the court. Using data on the Atlantic Coast Conference Basketball Tournament, the study found that, other things being equal, adding one referee reduced the number of fouls per game by about seventeen, a reduction of 34 percent! A more general application of this research is to the issue of how we can reduce the number of crimes by adding additional police.

Most economic analysis is based on the idea that when the incentive to do something increases, people will do more of it. Kenneth Lehn, chief economist at the Securities and Exchange Commission, showed that this idea applies even to the amount of time baseball players spend on the disabled list. After players were signed to multiyear, guaranteed contracts with no extra pay for each game played, their incentive to play diminished. Sure enough, Lehn found that the amount of time players spent on the disabled list increased from 4.7 days in the precontract period to 14.4 days after—an increase of 206 percent.

Sports data have been used to understand other interesting issues. Another study (see Fleisher, Goff, and Tollison), using data on how the National Collegiate Athletic Association (NCAA) enforces its rules, studied cartel behavior by colleges and universities. Although this study is closer to what I called the ''economics of sports,'' it produced the novel finding that the NCAA apparently enforces its rules to help the old-time football powers that have long controlled the organization. As other teams improve on the playing field, we found, they are put on probation as a way to protect the athletic success of old-time schools such as Notre Dame and Ohio State.

Yet another study (see Goff, Shughart, and Tollison) found that the structure of high school basketball competition affects the career longevity of NBA players. ''Open'' competition refers to situations where all schools compete for the state championship, as in the movie *Hoosiers*. Under ''classified'' competition, schools compete in divisions that are based on school size. We theorized that NBA players from the open states should be "fitter" and better "adapted" for survival in the NBA. Using a large sample of NBA players, that is exactly what we found. Players from open competition states, such as Indiana, have careers in the NBA that, on average, are 1 to 1.5 years longer than players from states with classified competition. Given an average tenure for NBA players of about five years, that is an increase of 20 to 30 percent.

—Robert D. Tollison

Biography: Robert D. Tollison is an economics professor at George Mason University in Fairfax, Virginia. He is a leader in using economic analysis to explain behavior of politicians and of athletes.

Further Reading

Fleisher, Arthur A., Brian L. Goff, and Robert D. Tollison. *The National Collegiate Athletic Association: A Study in Cartel Behavior*. 1992.

Goff, Brian L., William F. Shughart II, and Robert D. Tollison. "Homo Basketballus." In *Sportometrics*, edited by Goff and Tollison. 1990.

Goff, Brian L., and Robert D. Tollison, eds. *Sportometrics*. 1990.

Higgins, Richard S., and Robert D. Tollison. "Economics at the Track." In *Sportometrics*, edited by Goff and Tollison. 1990.

Lehn, Kenneth. "Property Rights, Risk Sharing, and Player Disability." *Journal of Law and Economics* 25 (October 1982): 343–66.

McCormick, Robert E., and Robert D. Tollison. "Crime on the Court." *Journal of Political Economy* 92 (April 1984)

Sports

Gerald W. Scully

■ Major league sports, as every reader of the sports pages knows, is a major league business. As a result economics has a lot to say about how players, teams, and leagues will act under different circumstances. But would you believe that economics can be used to predict which teams will win and which will lose? It can.

How good a professional sports team is depends, of course, on the quality of its players. Since teams compete for better players by offering higher salaries, how good a team is depends to a large extent on how strong it is financially. The financially stronger teams will, on average, be the better teams. And the financially stronger teams will, on average, be the ones in bigger cities.

A team's financial strength (its profitability) is its revenues minus costs. A team's main cost is player salaries. Because a given player will earn roughly the same no matter which team he plays for, each team's costs for a given-quality roster tend to be equal. But revenues derived from fielding a given-quality roster vary dramatically within a league. Teams earn revenue from ticket sales, concession income, and the sale of broadcast rights. All of these factors vary directly with market size. Therefore, all other things being equal, teams in large cities have higher revenues. For example, in 1990 the Los Angeles Dodgers drew 3 million fans to their home games while the Cleveland Indians drew only 1.2 million.

This is why teams in large cities tend to get better players than teams in small cities. Consider the baseball owner deciding how good a player roster to build. He or she will maximize profits when the revenue from one more win equals the cost of producing that win. The cost of a given win record (the quality of players on the team) is roughly the same for every team in a league. But the revenue from a win record varies with the size of the market. For example, if the win record of the New York Yankees rises by 10 percent, the owner of the Yankees will get, say, $10 million more in revenues from concession sales, ticket sales, and the value of broadcast rights. But if the win record of the Kansas City Royals rises by the same 10 percent, revenues would increase by only, say, $2 million.

Therefore, because the incremental revenue from a given increase in wins is higher for the Yankees, and the incremental cost is about the same, a rational owner of the Yankees should pay more for players and should, on average, do better than the Royals. Sure enough, professional sports teams in cities with large populations tend to have records above .500 while teams in cities with small populations tend to have records below .500. It is no accident that large-city teams historically have dominated as championship teams. It is easy to see why this is so in the era of free agents, when a star player can move to whichever team will pay him the most. But as I will explain below, it also was true when teams "owned" player contracts and players were not free to accept a higher offer.

One factor that matters for team revenues is the league's rule for dividing the gate receipts. In basketball and hockey the home team gets all of the gate receipts and the visitor gets nothing. In baseball the split is 85–15. In football the gate division is 60–40. When the home team gets to keep more of the gate receipts, the teams in bigger cities get more of the benefit from their inherent financial advantage. When the split is more equal, the financial advantage of being in a bigger market is less.

But in all sports, revenues from national television contracts have grown as a percent of total revenues, and these revenues are divided equally among the clubs. As a result the differences in the financial strength of teams have narrowed. Big-city domination, while not completely eliminated, has diminished.

By their very nature sports leagues are cartels that exclude competition from other companies. You cannot start a baseball team and hope to play the Yankees unless you can get Major League Baseball (the cartel) to grant you a franchise. The antitrust laws prohibit cartels, but professional sports is the only private business in the United States that is largely exempt from those laws. Ever since a 1922 court decision (*Federal Baseball Club of Baltimore* v. *National League et al.*), baseball has been totally exempt. No other sport enjoys such a blanket exemption from antitrust, but all

professional team sports have a labor exemption and, since the Sports Television Act of 1961, a broadcast exemption.

All of the leagues have collusive agreements that govern the selection, contractual arrangements, and distribution of players among the teams. Collectively, these agreements grant a degree of monopsony power (monopoly power over the right to buy something, in this case player services) to owners. The owners exploit this power by paying the players less than their incremental contribution to revenue.

Athletes enter most professional team sports through a drafting procedure. The common feature of the drafts is that they grant one team exclusive bargaining rights with each prospective player. Once drafted, the athlete negotiates with that team alone, and others cannot offer higher salaries to get him. These rules, weakened somewhat over the years, impede the competitive bidding for beginning players. Once the player has come to terms with the drafting team, he must sign a uniform player's contract. The contract allows him to sell his services only to the team holding the contract. Although player contracts vary from sport to sport, all contain some basic prohibitions against moves to other teams that are initiated by the player. That is, owners are free to "trade" (sell) players to other teams, but players are not totally free to offer their services to competing teams.

Owners claim that restrictions on player movement are necessary to maintain competitive balance and prevent financial powerhouses like the old Yankees from buying up all the best talent and totally dominating the sport. That, owners say, would make the sport duller for fans and hurt everyone. Economists have always been skeptical about the owners' motives—and about the evidence. There never was any disagreement that star players would wind up on big-city teams. But economists believe that this would happen regardless of whether leagues restrict moves initiated by players. If players were free to move between teams, then, assuming they were indifferent about location, they would play for the team that pays the most. The team that pays the most is the one that expects the largest increment in revenue from that player's performance. Since an increment in the win-loss record yields more revenue in, say, New York than in Kansas City, the best players go to New York rather than Kansas City.

This point, which is made by those who justify restrictions on mobility, is correct. But limiting the ability of players to initiate moves should not have any effect on where players end up playing. When players are not free to move, does a small-city team that acquired a star player in the draft keep him? For a small-city franchise the team holding the contract of the player expects him to contribute, say, $1 million in incremental revenue to the club. In a large city that same player's talents might contribute $3 million. Since the player is worth more to the big-city team in either case (and the big-city team will pay more for him), the small-city franchise has an incentive to sell the player's contract to the big-city team and thereby make more money than it could by keeping him. Thus, players should wind up allocated by highest incremental revenue, with or without restrictions on player-initiated movement.

The evidence supports that conclusion.

Since the advent of free agency, which made it easier for players to jump from one team to another, the total movement of players (trades, sales, minor league transfers) has been about the same as it was before. So although restrictions on player-initiated movement should not affect the allocation of player talent within a league, they dramatically affect the division of income between owners and players. Under free agency the players earn what they contribute to incremental revenue; under league restrictions on player-initiated transfers, the owners keep more of the revenues. The dramatic rise in player salaries since the midseventies, notably in baseball and basketball, is largely the result of the relaxation of restrictions on player-initiated transfers.

The most important antitrust issue in sports today relates to the formation of new leagues. The collusive arrangement in the allocation of broadcast rights between the television networks and the existing leagues constitutes a formidable barrier to entry for a new league. In particular, football programming is extremely valuable because football games attract large audiences. Large audiences mean high advertising revenues and, therefore, large network television revenues to the NFL. By allocating games to all three networks instead of just one, the NFL has become a partner with the networks in the broadcast enterprise. Further, the contract stipulates that no other professional football games can be broadcast by the networks within forty-eight hours of an NFL game. This relegates any competing league's games to midweek, which is hardly attractive to the networks.

Television, by building fan recognition and loyalty, builds attendance and gate receipts. Thus, a competing league may not be able to exist without access to television. The NFL has an exclusive, multiyear contract with the networks that is a barrier to entry for a competing league. Only when the network-NFL contract expires is there the possibility of a point of entry. But for that to happen, the networks would have to find a new league's games to be suitable substitutes for NFL games. Because teams in new leagues are inferior to established teams (the established teams already have the best stars), the networks have little incentive to substitute a new league's games for NFL games. Partly because of the broadcast exemption to antitrust laws, and partly because of the judicious expansion of the leagues in all of the professional team sports, fans are unlikely to see competing sports leagues rise.

—Gerald W. Scully

Biography: Gerald W. Scully is an economics professor at the University of Texas at Dallas.

Further Reading

El-Hodiri, Mohamed, and James Quirk. "An Economic Model of a Professional Sports League." *Journal of Political Economy* 79 (November/December 1971): 1302–19.
Noll, Roger G., ed. *Government and the Sports Business*. 1974.
Scully, Gerald W. *The Business of Major League Baseball*. 1989.
———. "Pay and Performance in Major League Baseball." *American Economic Review* 64 (December 1974): 915–30.

Telecommunications

John Haring

Introduction

Telecommunications is important for two reasons. First, it plays a vital role in the organization and operation of the modern global economy. Second, the problems associated with regulating and organizing the telecommunications industry have stimulated a great deal of economic analysis that is important in its own right and relevant to other sectors of the economy as well.

Telecommunications and the Information Age Economy

It would be difficult to overstate the significance of telecommunications in today's economy and virtually impossible to overstate its likely importance in the future. In the last quarter of the twentieth century, telecommunications has become the central nervous system of the economy. Just as the railroads once promoted economic growth and development, telecommunications is now globalizing markets, reducing transactions costs, expanding productivity, and directly increasing economic well-being.

An astounding array of technical advances is constantly reducing costs and expanding capabilities in telecommunications. The forces that are driving down costs and expanding supply capabilities involve advances in microelectronics, photonics, computer software, network architecture, high-definition television, and superconductivity. Many of these advances are simultaneously reducing the costs and expanding the capabilities of complementary goods and services (e.g., electronic data bases and the personal computers that interact with them). At the same time, we are raising a generation of computer-literate consumers and producers with a taste and propensity for interactive communication.

The use of telecommunications in the production and marketing of goods and services is ubiquitous. For many companies telecommunications has become an integral part of the production process and is itself becoming part of the product firms supply either as a value-added service or as part of the product itself. Telephonic order entry and credit validation make transacting business convenient. Customer-service telephone lines provide an excellent way to supply product information and guarantee customer satisfaction. General Electric now builds telecommunications capabilities right into the medical equipment it supplies to hospitals. GE's technicians can dial up the equipment from a central location, do remote monitoring and diagnosis, and implement a solution very rapidly if a problem develops or is anticipated.

Globalization of markets and businesses also relies upon intensive communication and extensive telecommunications capabilities. To bridge time-zone differences, companies are increasingly using video and teleconferencing services.

Economic Organization of the Telecommunications Industry

Time in the telecommunications industry is generally dated before and after the breakup of the Bell System on January 1, 1984. The breakup—AT&T had to divest the Bell operating companies resulted from a government antitrust suit. Before Ma Bell's breakup, most of the telecommunications industry in the United States was a unified, integrated monopoly, although the Bell System had always coexisted with a number of smaller operators. The Bell System's breakup was, in principle, designed to segregate the competitive portions of the telecommunications industry (telephone equipment and long-distance service) from the monopoly portions (local service). Competitive market forces would govern the equipment and long-distance segments, while government regulation of local service would continue.

Ironically, seven years after divestiture, the long-distance business remains heavily regulated while the market for local services has, in several notable respects, become significantly more competitive. While many key questions about which rules should govern competition in long-distance remain unresolved, competition at the local exchange is at hand and poses closely related policy issues and dilemmas.

To understand unfolding events in this dynamic sector of the economy, it is worth-

while to step back and focus on some salient features of the industry's technological and regulatory landscape. A telephone network is a big, lumpy asset. A substantial portion of the asset's costs are incurred up front, merely to build the network and provide the option of use, so to speak, rather than actual usage. The cost of actually using a telephone network is relatively small compared to the cost of the network investment.

The primary goal of government regulation of telephony has always been to promote telephone service for everyone. There is a potential economic justification for this government intervention grounded in the existence of what is called a consumption externality. That is, your presence on the network makes the network more valuable to me and vice versa. The existence of this (or any) kind of externality does not, by itself, justify intervention. It merely suggests that particular interventions could conceivably increase economic welfare.

The particular method that the government historically chose to achieve universal service was to set a low subscription fee for telephone service. The fee was sometimes below the actual cost of hooking subscribers up to the network and maintaining their network access. In sparsely populated rural areas, the cost of running a wire-pair to customer premises sometimes runs to many thousands of dollars. Low subscription fees were, moreover, offered to all, regardless of an individual customer's ability to pay. To cover the costs of building and operating the network, regulators charged high rates for long-distance service and business service.

This pricing had some interesting and

predictable economic consequences. One effect was to make phone service easy to get, but expensive to use. It was as if the government had decided that everyone should have high-quality automotive transport and so put a BMW in every garage, but paid for the cars by placing a very high tax on gasoline. Everyone has a nice car, but few can afford to drive far because gas is expensive. In telephony, access was cheap and high levels of subscriber penetration were achieved (above 90 percent), but long-distance calling was very expensive, with prices sometimes 60 to 80 percent above marginal costs.

A pricing regime that undercharges for one good by overcharging for another contains the seeds of its own destruction. Overcharges create a powerful profit incentive for new sellers to enter and supply the overpriced good at a lower price. Correspondingly, there is little incentive to enter and compete in a market in which the current producer undercharges for the good. Unless a potential entrant possesses superior skills or technology, actual entry would not be attractive.

Unsurprisingly, new telecommunications firms have entered in precisely those segments of the industry where prices are highest relative to costs of providing service. That is what happened historically in long-distance in the seventies. It is happening today in local telephone service as competitors using new technologies offer less expensive services to large corporate customers, who have traditionally paid disproportionately high rates for local service.

Competition has been highly salutary. It has forced a rebalancing of rates more in line with underlying costs, causing more

economically optimal rates of usage. The gains in economic welfare from more efficient telecommunications pricing have been estimated to be on the order of several billion dollars a year. Economist John T. Wenders estimates the potential gains from a move to fully efficient pricing to be tens of billions of dollars annually. At the same time, because the relevant markets are so large, very small taxes on service could, in principle, generate substantial amounts of revenue to finance subsidies to the poor and maintain universal service.

Public Policy Issues

The traditional method of regulating telephone rates has been to set them on the basis of average costs, including a "fair" return on invested capital. Most economists are highly critical of this approach. Even if prices reflected costs, customers would not be well served if costs were inflated. Costs are likely to be inflated, because if prices are based on costs, managers of regulated monopolies know that they can charge higher prices by having higher costs. At the same time, limitations on the amount of profit that may be earned limit incentives to reduce costs in order to increase profitability.

Costs of providing different services and service to different customers often vary significantly. Therefore, average-cost pricing overcharges some customers (those who are cheap to serve) and undercharges others (those who are expensive to serve). This promotes inefficient rates of use, with the overcharged customers using too little and the undercharged customers using too much. Overcharges may also lead some customers to seek lower-priced alternatives that are actually more costly to provide. Suppose a customer who is confronted with a $15 price for a service that costs $10 to supply turns to an alternative that is priced at $14 but costs $12 to supply. The customer saves a dollar on each unit purchased, but the cost of each unit is $2 higher than it need be. Inefficient pricing may thus promote an artificial industry structure not based on genuine differences in costs or in service quality.

Regulation that requires cost-based pricing may also give the regulated firm an incentive to allocate costs toward markets in which customers are captive (i.e., lack alternatives) and away from markets in which customers have alternatives. In this way the firm may restrain competition in potentially competitive ancillary markets.

One solution to these difficulties is for regulators to break the link between prices and costs and adopt a simple system of price caps. This is what regulators in the United Kingdom and the United States have recently tried to do. Under price cap regulation the regulated firm's ability to raise its prices is proscribed, but it is allowed to keep any additional profit it can earn by reducing its costs or introducing new services. Regulators monitor service quality to ensure that service is not degraded, and periodically reset the price caps to capture part of any cost savings for consumers on a forward-going basis. Because prices do not depend on cost allocations, incentives to misallocate costs and inhibit competition are reduced.

This type of regulatory reform works only if the government can make a credible commitment to allow regulated firms to keep some of the profits from their economizing. If it cannot—if as soon as a company economizes or innovates, the government attempts to cut prices—no incentives are created, and no such efforts will be undertaken. As price cap proposals have made their way through the regulatory and political process, they have often come to resemble traditional forms of regulation, with the promised opportunities to earn additional profits becoming increasingly weak. Nevertheless, small improvements have occurred in some jurisdictions. As experience with new forms of incentive regulation accrues, prospects for additional reforms should become brighter.

Finally, it should be noted that, in many respects, the old Bell System was like a sovereign state. By virtue of its monopoly, it had the power to tax and use the proceeds to perform all sorts of traditionally governmental functions, including the funding of basic scientific research and the establishment of industry technical standards. One frequently expressed fear was that divestiture would make inadequate provision for these kinds of public goods.

Actual experience offers a mixed picture. Funding of telecommunications-related research has increased in real terms since divestiture, but much of this research is oriented toward commercial applications. Whether sufficient funds are being directed toward fundamental research, only time will tell. The standards issue also presents a mixed picture. On the one hand, standards-setting processes are now clearly more open and less subject to strategic manipulation than they were before divestiture. On the other hand, the government supply of legal process has proven to be almost infinitely elastic, while the government's ability to resolve standards issues in a timely fashion remains unproven.

—**John Haring**

Biography: John Haring is a principal of Strategic Policy Research, Inc. He was previously the chief economist at the Federal Communications Commission and chief of the commission's Office of Plans and Policy.

Further Reading

Crandall, Robert W. *After the Breakup—U.S. Telecommunications in a More Competitive Era*. 1991.

Gilder, George. *Microcosm: The Quantum Revolution in Economics and Technology*. 1989.

Handler, G. J., ed. "The Special Section on Telecommunications: The Next Ten Years." *Proceedings of the IEEE*, September 1986.

Huber, Peter W. *The Geodesic Network—1987 Report on Competition in the Telephone Industry*. A report prepared for Department of Justice. 1987.

Temin, Peter. *The Fall of the Bell System*. 1987.

U.S. Federal Communications Commission. Office of Plans and Policy. Working paper series, various numbers.

Wenders, John T. *The Economics of Telecommunications: Theory and Policy*. 1987.

CHAPTER FOURTEEN

ECONOMIES OUTSIDE THE UNITED STATES

Capital Flight

Darryl McLeod

■ There is no widely accepted definition of *capital flight*. The classic use of the term is to describe widespread currency speculation, especially when it leads to cross-border movements of private funds that are large enough to affect national financial markets. The distinction between "flight" and normal capital outflows is thus a matter of degree, much like the difference between a "bank run" and normal withdrawals. The most common cause of capital flight is an anticipated devaluation of the home currency. No one wants to be caught holding assets that lose 20 or 30 percent of their value overnight, so everyone tries to buy gold or foreign currency. These episodes are usually short-lived, as the so-called "hot money" returns after the devaluation.

Capital flight is usually a symptom rather than a cause of financial crisis. Occasionally, however, rumors of a devaluation can trigger capital outflows. Expectations of devaluation can become self-fulfilling, as depletion of the central bank's reserves force it to devalue. In these cases capital flight becomes a source of financial instability, much as withdrawals by worried depositors can cause an otherwise sound bank to fail.

Not surprisingly, episodes of capital flight are most frequent when exchange rates are unstable. In the twenties and thirties the demise of the gold standard led to numerous speculative attacks on the French franc and German mark. When the Bretton Woods system of fixed exchange rates began to break apart in the late sixties, the United States tried to defend the dollar with capital controls and by refusing foreign banks' demands to convert dollars to gold. (U.S. citizens were already barred from owning gold.) After exchange rates were set free in 1973, the U.S. dollar replaced gold as the flight vehicle of choice. Convertible to most currencies, dollars also earn interest in convenient offshore or Eurodollar accounts.

Since the Third World debt crisis in the eighties, the term "capital flight" has been applied more broadly to capital outflows from residents of developing countries. One reason that capital fled the debtor countries is that domestic investors felt their government would give precedence to its foreign rather than its domestic debt obligations. This situation contrasts with the earlier experience with direct foreign investment, when domestically owned assets were considered safe from expropriation while foreign-owned assets were at risk.

Offshore holdings are notoriously difficult to measure, so economists simply subtract foreign currency payments for imports, debt service, and additions to official reserves from total sources of foreign exchange (exports, borrowing, investment by multinationals, etc.). The difference—unaccounted-for dollars—is called capital flight.

Using this broad measure, the International Monetary Fund estimates that citizens of developing countries amassed about $250 billion worth of foreign assets between 1975 and 1985 (compared to a total foreign debt of $800 billion). Although Mexico had the largest dollar total ($40 to $50 billion), Venezuela's and Argentina's holdings were a larger proportion of national income (nearly equal to their foreign debt). Indonesia, Nigeria, the Philippines, and even South Korea also had substantial capital outflows during this period.

This second type of capital flight superficially resembles the classic variety of currency speculation. It is often most intense during periods of currency overvaluation or just after an exchange rate crisis, for example. But unlike ''hot money'' these funds tend to remain abroad after the currency crisis ends. The driving force behind these outflows is generally a perceived decline in the return, or an increase in the riskiness, on long-term assets held in the country. A loss of confidence may be caused by an excessively large foreign debt burden, large fluctuations in commodity export prices, or chronic government mismanagement of the domestic economy. Interestingly, though, nationalization was not a major cause of rapid capital outflows. The reason is probably that most nationalizations were of foreign-owned assets rather than assets held by the country's residents.

This flight capital is held offshore until conditions improve or until the source of uncertainty is resolved. The tens of billions of dollars that fled Mexico in the early eighties, for example, did not begin to return until 1990, after Mexico got debt relief under the Brady Plan, committed itself to liberalizing trade and finance, and announced

it would sell the banks it nationalized in 1982. All of these measures helped to restore confidence in domestic financial markets and reduce fears of recurrent external debt crises.

While exporting countries often exaggerate the harmful consequences of capital flight, there are some legitimate areas of concern. Unlike movements of capital from Texas to New York, rapid international capital flows can disrupt financial markets and raise interest rates by causing unanticipated exchange rate movements, especially in small countries. Also, an unknown fraction of international funds transfers is due to tax evasion or to efforts to conceal illicit gains or embezzlement of public funds. The foreign holdings of the Philippines' Marcos family fall into this category. The use of offshore banks and Swiss accounts for tax evasion and money laundering taints all international capital flows to some degree.

Legitimate or not, once it starts there is no easy cure for capital flight, and preventive measures often have unpleasant side effects. Following the financial instability of the interwar period, currency speculation was reduced by fixing exchange rates and changing them very infrequently. The International Monetary Fund was set up to assist countries that ran into foreign exchange problems. This system fell apart in the early seventies, but some countries are still trying to return to fixed rates on a more modest scale (those joining the European Monetary System, for example).

When fixed exchange rates fail, governments often resort to capital controls, as the United States did in the sixties. Imposing controls during or just after a capital flight episode, however, is a little worse than closing the barn door after the horse has fled. Controls further reduce confidence in local financial markets and make capital that has flown less likely to return. Capital controls encourage black markets for foreign currency and other costly methods of evasion. Those who import or export goods can also export money by simply overstating the value of the goods they import or by understating their export earnings. Even the most draconian measures to limit capital flight often fail. Capital flight from the Weimar Republic continued in 1931, despite the fact that capital expatriation was made an offense punishable by death.

Another strategy that governments can use to limit capital flight is to make holding domestic currency more attractive by keeping it undervalued relative to other currencies or by keeping local interest rates high. The drawback to this approach is that raising interest rates and making imported equipment more expensive can reduce domestic investment. A more sophisticated defense against hot money flows, but one that is harder to execute, is for the central bank to occasionally turn the tables on speculators. A classic ''squeeze'' of this type was engineered by Lazard Frères for the French government in 1924. Using a $100 million loan from J. P. Morgan, they bid the franc from 124 to 61 per dollar in a few weeks. Speculators who had sold the franc short in the expectation that its value would fall were hit by big losses. Italy, the United States, and Sweden have also used this unexpected intervention tactic from time to time.

Yet another option is to reduce the tax benefits of capital flight by having rich and poor countries adopt new tax treaties and exchange data on income paid to foreigners. The U.S. government's termination in 1984 of the 30 percent withholding tax on U.S. portfolio income paid to foreigners and a similar lack of reporting by European governments are often blamed for encouraging capital outflows to those countries. But offshore tax havens and international competition for capital make new tax treaties unlikely.

In the end the most practical strategy for reducing capital flight is for governments to pursue fiscal and monetary policies that minimize the need for large changes in exchange rates. Agreements among countries and central banks can add to the credibility of these commitments. Tax evasion can be reduced by relying more on consumption or sales taxes and less on taxes on interest and profits. Developing countries in particular can also promote the development of domestic financial markets and trade in assets that offer investors a ''safe'' alternative to foreign assets. Brazil used this strategy with some success before 1988. Small countries with limited domestic financial markets and currencies that are more vulnerable to external shocks can hold a portfolio of foreign assets and try to diversify their exports over the longer term. During the seventies Indonesia, Kuwait, and tiny diamond-exporting Botswana, among others, used international financial markets to smooth their volatile revenues from commodity exports.

One encouraging sign is that private capital has begun to return to countries for whom future prospects have brightened. An estimated $10 billion has flowed back into Mexico since its successful 1989 anti-inflation, trade liberalization, and debt relief programs. To prevent future crises, Mexico set up a special contingency fund and uses futures markets to help stabilize its volatile oil earnings. Some combination of domestic reforms, debt relief, and improved foreign asset management may soon restore investor confidence in other countries as well.

—Darryl McLeod

Biography: Darryl McLeod is an economics professor at Fordham University in New York. He has been a consultant to the World Bank, the Organization of American States, and Mexico's Department of Commerce.

Further Reading

Cardoso, Eliana, and Rudiger Dornbusch. ''Foreign Private Capital Flows.'' In *Handbook of Development Economics,* edited by T. N. Srinivasan and Hollis Chenery. 1989.

Eaton, Jonathan. ''Public Debt Guarantees and Private Capital Flight.'' *World Bank Economic Review* 1 (1987): 377–95.

Kahn, Moshin S., and Nadeem Ul Haque. ''Capital Flight from Developing Countries.'' *Finance and Development* 24 (March 1987): 2–6.

Kindleberger, Charles P. *Manias, Panics and Crashes: A History of Financial Crisis.* 1989.

Lessard, Donald L., and John Williamson, eds. *Capital Flight and Third World Debt.* 1987.

See also EXCHANGE RATES, THIRD WORLD DEBT, THIRD WORLD ECONOMIC DEVELOPMENT.

Eastern Europe

David Lipton

■ In late 1989 the countries of Eastern Europe broke loose from the Soviet Union, threw off communism, and began to construct democratic institutions and market-oriented economies. This great transformation is founded on the idea that freedom and prosperity can best be advanced by adopting the institutions and practices that have proven successful in Western Europe since World War II. The people of the region want "to return to Europe." To do so, they plan to dismantle the remnants of the communist economic system and build market-oriented economies based on private ownership. While this is a daunting task, the transformation is well under way.

The Communist Inheritance

What complicates the process of economic transformation is the burden posed by the inheritance of the communist economic system. One Russian pundit, commenting on the communist legacy, explained that anyone can turn an aquarium into fish stew, but it is much harder to turn fish stew into an aquarium. The communist inheritance has had two important dimensions for Eastern Europe.

First, the laws, institutions, and ownership structure under communism are very different from what is needed for a modern, capitalist economy, so nearly all must be changed. Most important, the socialist own-ership structure placed industry, services, and (with the exception of Poland) agriculture mainly in state hands. State ownership and central planning produced poor decisions about how to use resources and led to greatly distorted economies. Every Eastern European government skewed investment toward heavy industry and capital goods at the expense of light industry, services, and consumer goods.

Moreover, attempts to subsidize certain economic activities left all the countries with heavily distorted pricing structures. Prices for energy and household necessities (mainly food and rent) were kept very low. Another factor that distorted prices was the overvalued domestic currency. It was kept so overvalued that it could not be converted into foreign currency. Instead, governments rationed the limited amount of foreign exchange available. Those not receiving official exchange usually had to pay much more to buy dollars in the black market. Therefore, most imported goods were severely rationed or available only at high black-market prices.

Second, after forty years the communist economic system failed to sustain itself, leaving utter industrial collapse, financial distress and chaos, and very low living standards.

Some countries in Eastern Europe sought to stave off collapse by replacing central planning with decentralized decision making. These communist-led reforms brought some improvement but did not lead to the emergence of normal competitive market relations. In the end each country in the region suffered an economic collapse and a cessation of sustained growth, and in some cases, acute shortages, balance of payments crises, and financial chaos.

The genesis of the financial crises came from deep within the system. Subsidies ballooned as governments tried to keep the prices of many consumer products and services low for households and tried to keep profits high in state enterprises (where managers were too willing to grant excessive wage increases). Credits to enterprises also ballooned in support of the huge appetite for investments on the part of state enterprises (where managers craved investment projects that might add to their power and prestige). Subsidies and credits were paid by printing money, which led to a steady buildup of demand throughout these economies. The ballooning of demand created shortages wherever price controls were inflexible, inflation wherever prices were allowed to rise, and external debt and balance of payments crises in most countries. The buildup of demand in Poland, for example, can be seen clearly in the gap between the black market exchange rate and the official one, which rose from 250 percent in early 1988 to 500 percent in mid-1989.

The collapse of living standards was broadly felt across Eastern Europe. Industrial production did not slow appreciably because strenuous efforts were made to channel the available resources to heavy industry. The result of this strategy was a decline in living standards for the population. While there were substantial differences among countries in the region, the people of Eastern Europe found goods increasingly unavailable at official prices, longer queues and bigger shortages, an absence of imported consumer goods, and in some cases, a deterioration in public services and basic utilities such as heat and hot water.

The Strategies for Economic Transformation

As the new governments of Eastern Europe surveyed the ruins of the communist system and prepared to transform their economies, they were initially preoccupied with the question of whether to free prices from centralized control quickly in order to cope with the shortages, high inflation, and scarcity of dollars. Alternatively, they could first reform the laws, institutions, and ownership structure to allow private property. Freeing prices from centralized control in the absence of private property seemed risky to many, because state enterprises would be granted too much market power and would operate in an unruly and unregulated environment. But was it possible to privatize enterprises, eliminate monopolies, restructure the banking system, reform the tax system, and build a social safety net in the absence of realistic prices and in the midst of a financial crisis?

Most governments concluded that reform was a seamless web, such that liberalization and structural reforms must be woven together simultaneously. The pattern of the web, however, has varied from country to country. In some the financial collapse was so acute that there was no room for maneuver. The Solidarity government in Poland, for example, inherited a hyperinflation so debilitating that immediate steps were necessary. But Czechoslovakia, where the financial situation was not as acute and the communist-led reform was limited, spent one year attempting to prepare the way for marketization.

Despite some differences in approach, on the whole prices have been freed from centralized control quickly. Meanwhile, the longer, and in many respects harder, job of rewriting laws, building capitalist institutions, modernizing and restructuring industry, and privatizing capital and land is under way but will take years, if not decades, to complete. Most countries are finding that the introduction of market relations greatly facilitates this harder job, by providing a more stable, more responsive market environment in which structural adjustment can be done more effectively. After all, how could industry be modernized, privatized, and restructured without market signals to guide the process?

The countries of Eastern Europe have three basic elements of economic transformation in common: stabilization, liberalization, and privatization.

Stabilization efforts in Eastern Europe have aimed at creating a stable financial environment that will foster the rapid growth of domestic business activity, international trade, and foreign direct investment. By reducing budget deficits, slowing the growth of the money supply, and establishing realistic exchange rates, Czechoslovakia, Hungary, and Poland have ended the chronic shortages that have plagued their economies and have achieved low rates of inflation and relatively stable exchange rates.

Economic liberalization includes permitting households and enterprises to conduct business freely, buying and selling at prices set by supply and demand. This has meant, among other things, a sweeping elimination of government price controls. In most countries liberalization has also been backed by changes in the legal framework aimed at allowing private gain, and deregulation to limit government interference in economic activities. The new governments also understand that the success of liberalization requires the protection of private property and the freedom to start private businesses. These freedoms are needed to foster a new private sector that strengthens competitive forces and channels resources into productive capital investments.

Because the countries of Eastern Europe are small and situated near the great market of the European Economic Community, another important component of liberalization has been the opening up of international trade. In the short run the opportunity to trade with the West has provided instant competition, greatly diminishing the domestic monopoly power of monolithic state enterprises. In the long run, international trade holds the key to the eventual integration of the economies of Eastern Europe with the economies of the West.

While the combination of liberalization and stabilization has helped restore the health of public finances and create a stable financial environment, these radical changes have also thrust the people of Eastern Europe into unfamiliar circumstances. Consumers accustomed to long lines and empty stores now face an abundance of goods, but at much higher prices. A journalistic account from Poland's 1990 liberalization records the reaction of a prominent editor: "I cry when I pay for gas, but one of the worst miseries of my existence—the endless hunting and queuing for fuel—is over. When I first filled up hassle-free in January, I was euphoric." (See Ziomecki.)

The elimination of price controls caused large initial jumps in consumer prices in Albania, Bulgaria, Czechoslovakia, and Poland. Because wages increased by a smaller percent, the measured real wage in each country has declined. This apparent decline in real wages, however, is misleading because few consumer goods had been available at the controlled prices. When prices rose after being freed from controls, shortages were eliminated and more goods were available. As one Polish journalist wrote, "Up to now, we have not been buying television sets because they were not available, whereas now, we are not buying them because they are too expensive." (See Skalski.)

The Eastern European economies are responding strongly to the opening up of international trade. Most countries in the region have increased exports, which will increase economic integration with the West. In Poland, for example, exports to the West rose from $8.5 billion in 1989 to about $13 billion in 1991, a period in which Poland's GDP was falling. Poland's ability to market its goods abroad has moderated the decline in living standards. The growth in Eastern European exports is vital to the modernization of the region because it provides the finance for needed imports of capital and technologies.

Liberalization of economic activity has also sparked the growth of private sector activity. The emergence of a new private sector has perhaps been greatest in Poland, where hundreds of thousands of new small businesses were opened in 1990, but Hungary and Czechoslovakia are not far behind. In Warsaw roughly 90 percent of retail shops are now in private hands. The service sector, long suppressed under the communist system, is mushrooming, and new private manufacturing activity is beginning, though still on a modest scale.

At the same time, the state enterprise sectors are declining in all Eastern European countries. Industrial production has fallen by 15 to 40 percent in these countries, and in some countries the decline may not be over. In part, these sectors must give way because their activities had been planned to suit the "communist production circle" mentioned earlier. In part, the decline has resulted from the collapse of the Soviet Union, which abruptly stopped trading with Eastern Europe at the beginning of 1991.

Continued state ownership has retarded the adjustment and restructuring needed to adapt the activities of state enterprises to markets. State enterprise managers no longer report to central planners or branch ministries, and are now all too free to manage state property for their own gain. Where labor unions have power, enterprise managers may also prefer to use enterprise profits to boost wages and buy calm in the workplace, rather than to undertake restructuring investments. This only worsens the international competitiveness of the sector. In addition, managers of state enterprise often appropriate state property. Some managers intentionally bankrupt government firms in order to buy them out cheaply. Others establish private firms that then receive preferential contracts with the state-owned enterprises. Still others accept unfavorable joint-venture and takeover offers that provide personal benefits.

Privatization is widely regarded by the new governments of Eastern Europe as a necessary step to making the best economic use of state property. It is well understood that much of the capital stock inherited from the past is dilapidated, based on outmoded technologies, and aimed at the now-collapsed Soviet market. The decisions of what to shut down, what to restructure, and what to modernize are best made by private owners with a true stake in the economic future of the firm.

The privatization challenge is enormous. The countries of Eastern Europe must privatize a wide range of property, including trucks, housing, shops, foreign trading firms, commercial banks, small manufacturing operations, and huge industrial concerns. Most countries have quickly privatized physical property and small shops. Auctions, leases, and other techniques have put a large proportion of retail trade and small service establishments in private hands in several countries. Because large industrial enterprises are more difficult to privatize, they are being privatized slowly.

Several countries initially flirted with the notion of adopting Western privatization techniques—such as public offerings of enterprise stock—for selling large industrial enterprises. These techniques have been too slow and too expensive. Margaret Thatcher's government privatized about two dozen firms in a decade; the countries of Eastern Europe have thousands of industrial enterprises to privatize. Efforts to prepare public offerings in Eastern Europe have come up against the facts that

1. selling enterprises requires valuation (which is impossible given the uncertainties surrounding these enterprises and these economies);
2. domestic investors in Eastern Europe do not have the financial resources to buy up their own industrial sectors; and
3. the purchase of too many large enterprises by foreigners is politically undesirable.

As a result, Eastern European countries have developed and implemented novel approaches. In Czechoslovakia citizens have purchased privatization vouchers that can be used to bid for enterprise shares. This approach is intended to allow all citizens the chance to gain from the privatization process. In Hungary enterprises are encouraged to prepare privatization plans, seek out investor groups, and make privatization proposals to the State Property Agency. In Poland some shares will be given directly to workers and managers. In addition, shares in large industrial enterprises will be distributed to newly created investment funds, which, as part owners, will exercise active control over enterprise managers by taking a role on boards of directors. Shares in the investment funds will be distributed to the population via some form of a voucher scheme. This approach is intended both to allow all Poles to gain from privatization and to generate a mechanism for investor scrutiny of enterprise management.

—David Lipton

Biography: David Lipton is a fellow at the Woodrow Wilson International Center for Scholars in Washington, D.C. He previously was on the staff of the International Monetary Fund.

Further Reading

Aghevli, Brjan, Edwardo Borenstein, and Tessavander Willigen. "Stabilization and Structural Reform in the Czech and Slovak Republic." Occasional paper no. 92, International Monetary Fund. 1992.

Boote, Anthony, and Janos Somogyi. "Economic Reform in Hungary." Occasional paper no. 83, International Monetary Fund. 1991.

Demekas, Dimitri, and Moshin Khan. "The Romanian Economic Reform." Occasional paper no. 89, International Monetary Fund. 1991.

Kornai, Janos. *The Road to a Free Economy, Shifting from a Socialist System: The Example of Hungary.* 1990.

Lipton, David, and Jeffrey Sachs. "Creating a Market Economy in Eastern Europe: The Case of Poland." *Brookings Papers on Economic Activity* 1 (1990): 75–133.

Shalski, Ernest. "The Idiot's Economy." *Gazeta International '90,* week 10: 6.

Williamson, John. "The Economic Opening of Eastern Europe." Policy analysis in international economics no. 31, Institute for International Economics. 1991.

Ziomecki, Mariusz. "After Years of Communist Rule, Poland Discovers the Miracle of Capitalism." *Detroit Free Press,* March 27, 1990.

See also GERMAN ECONOMIC "MIRACLE"

European Economic Community

Barry Eichengreen

■ The vast majority of economists agree that trade, by allowing specialization, enhances efficiency. But as Adam Smith observed, the division of labor (the degree of specialization) is limited by market size. International trade is an obvious way of increasing market size.

Since World War II, countries have reduced barriers to trade mainly through multilateral negotiations such as the General Agreement on Tariffs and Trade (GATT). A central premise of the GATT is nondiscrimination: countries should give all GATT members the same access to their markets. The main exemption to that rule is free trade areas. Partners to free trade agreements are allowed to exempt one another's goods from import duties while maintaining tariffs and/or quotas on products from other GATT countries.

The European Economic Community (EEC), the most prominent example of a free trade area, actually is what economists call a customs union. Whereas member nations in a free trade area remove all barriers to trade among themselves, in a customs union they also adopt uniform tariffs on goods and services from outside the union. The EEC is currently attempting to transform itself from a customs union to a true common market in which capital and labor, and not just goods, are allowed to flow freely from one country to another.

The EEC's impact has been significant. In 1960 more than 60 percent of the trade of the Community's twelve members was with other parts of the world. Now more than 60 percent stays within the European grouping. Where the EEC contented itself initially with removing internal barriers to trade, it has since expanded into the regulation of domestic markets and monetary unification.

Origins

The European Community is an amalgam of three separate communities: the European Coal and Steel Community, established by the Treaty of Paris in 1951 to regulate production and liberalize Europe's trade in coal and steel products; the European Atomic Energy Community, formed by the Treaty of Rome in 1957; and the European Economic Community, also created by the Treaty of Rome. All three were established to encourage political and economic cooperation among member countries, notably France and Germany, that had repeatedly warred with each other. By 1967 the institutions of the European Economic Community (or Common Market) became common to all three communities. Today it is conventional to refer to the European Community (aka the EC or the Community) in the singular, whether one means the Economic Community or all three initiatives.

The EC initially consisted of six Western European nations—Belgium, Luxembourg,

France, Italy, the Netherlands, and West Germany. Britain, Ireland, and Denmark were admitted in 1973. Three southern European countries were allowed to join once they installed democratic governments— Greece in 1981, Spain and Portugal in 1986. Other Western European countries (Austria, Finland, Sweden, and Switzerland) belong to the European Free Trade Association, or EFTA (as did Britain, Ireland, and Denmark before 1973). EFTA has traditionally concentrated on trade liberalization, in contrast to the EC's more ambitious agenda of economic and political integration.

Development

The EC's most important achievement has been its customs union. It was completed in 1968, when each of the six members abolished tariffs and quotas on goods from the other five member countries and adopted a common external tariff on goods from the rest of the world. The evolution from a free trade area to a customs union followed inevitably: had the participants maintained different external tariffs, exports from, say, Japan could have been imported through the low-tariff countries and transshipped to the others, circumventing the high tariffs. The customs union has propelled the growth of intra-Community trade from less than 40 percent to over 60 percent of the total trade of the participating countries.

As Jacob Viner pointed out in a classic analysis of trade, whether the participating countries benefit from their customs union depends on whether it creates additional trade or simply diverts trade away from the rest of the world. If EC countries continue to import petroleum from the Middle East, wheat from the United States, and stereo equipment from Asia but specialize further in their own production—if, for example, instead of producing both beer and wine, the British produce beer, the French produce wine, and they trade freely with one another—then trade is created and living standards rise. But if EC members now buy expensive German barley rather than cheap American wheat because of high external tariffs or low quotas, trade is diverted and European consumers are left worse off.

Which effect dominates depends on how similar the customs union participants are to one another. If similar, they will tend to produce many of the same things, and when internal trade barriers are removed, the additional imports will be items that the other participants produce even more efficiently than both the importing country and the rest of the world. Trade creation will dominate. But if the customs union participants have very different economic structures and specializations, damaging trade diversion may dominate instead.

To the naked eye, the twelve EC members resemble one another economically more than they resemble the rest of the world. It is not surprising, then, that most studies conclude that the European Community is a trade-creating customs union. But the benefits are surprisingly small, typically less than 1 percent of national income, or only five months' normal economic growth.

Why so small? One explanation is that these simple calculations miss dynamic gains from trade. Exposed to the chill winds of intra-European trade competition, European producers will work harder to come up with a better mousetrap. Innovation and productivity growth are thereby stimulated, producing growing efficiency gains over time. Another possibility is that the small estimate is correct, because the larger benefits potentially available are destroyed by the Community's Common Agricultural Policy (CAP). The CAP allows free trade in high-priced agricultural goods within the Community by excluding potential low-priced imports from outside. Community countries subsidize the domestic production of agricultural goods despite their comparative disadvantage. Consumers pay high prices as the twelve member countries collude to maintain trade-diverting tariffs on cheap imports from the rest of the world.

Thus, the CAP and the customs union show the two faces of the European Community, one that enhances efficiency by promoting competition and specialization, and one that sacrifices economic efficiency to help farmers.

The Single Market Program

In the eighties Western Europe suffered from persistent high unemployment. Productivity growth lagged behind other parts of the industrial world. The popular diagnosis was that Europe was suffering the effects of excessive government regulation and from the fragmentation of European labor and capital markets into a series of inefficiently small national markets. The disease was dubbed "Eurosclerosis," and the prescription, known as the Single Market Program, was a Community-wide initiative to deregulate and integrate national markets.

The Single Market Program was set out in a white paper published by the European Commission in 1985. It recommended nearly three hundred measures to remove obstacles to intra-European competition. The Single European Act (SEA) of 1986 committed EC members to implement those measures by the end of 1992.

The SEA will affect Europe's every nook and cranny. Trucks hauling merchandise will no longer have to stop at the border between EC countries, except for health and safety inspections. Governments may no longer discriminate in procurement or in awarding public works contracts. Every European country will have to recognize the product standards of the others. Remaining barriers to the movement of capital and labor across the EC's internal frontiers will be removed. EC residents will be able to shift their funds from one country to another without having to worry about capital controls, and will be able to work in another member country without having to secure a work permit or obtain local technical accreditation. National tax codes will be harmonized to simplify economic decision making.

Economic analyses suggest that the benefits are likely to be considerably larger than those derived from the customs union alone. The downside, however, is that regulation may well become more oppressive because the influence of intercountry competition, which tends to discourage costly regulation, is eliminated. Similarly, the harmonization of tax policy will prevent footloose factors of production (i.e., labor and capital) from fleeing to low-tax jurisdictions, thus removing an important constraint on spending by national governments.

Monetary Unification

In 1988, with European integration gathering momentum, the governments of the EC member states appointed a committee, chaired by Jacques Delors, president of the European Commission, to study the feasibility of complementing the single market with a single currency. After the Delors Report appeared, the EC governments appointed an Intergovernmental Conference to prepare amendments to the Treaty of Rome. The proposed amendments—the Treaty on Economic and Monetary Union—were presented at the Dutch town of Maastricht in December 1991.

The Maastricht Treaty proposes replacing the EC's twelve national currencies with a single currency and creating a European Central Bank (ECB). These goals are to be achieved in three stages. Stage I, which began in July 1990, is marked by the removal of capital controls (as already mandated by the SEA) and attempts to reduce differences in national inflation and interest rates and to make intra-European exchange rates more stable. In Stage II, to start in January 1994, national economic policies will converge further and a temporary entity, the European Monetary Institute, will coordinate member-country policies in the final phases of the transition. If the Council of Ministers, made up of ministers of economics or finance from each national government, decides during Stage II that a majority of member countries meet the preconditions for monetary union, it may recommend that the Council of Heads of State vote to inaugurate Stage III, establishing the ECB and giving it responsibility for monetary policy. To prevent Stage II from continuing indefinitely, however, the treaty requires the EC heads of state or government to meet before the end of 1996 to assess whether a majority of EC countries satisfy the conditions for monetary union. Stage III will begin in any case no later than January 1, 1999. In this case, Stage III may proceed with only a minority of EC countries participating.

When Stage III begins, exchange rates will be irrevocably fixed. The ECB will assume control of the monetary policies of the participating countries. It will decide how and when to replace the currencies of the participating countries with the new European currency. It may do so on the first day of Stage III, or it may instruct its operating arms, the national central banks, to intervene to stabilize the exchange rates among their national currencies until these are replaced by a single currency.

Monetary integration is more controversial than the Single Market Program. Denmark rejected the Maastricht Treaty in its June 1992 referendum, and France nearly did the same three months later.

No one questions that there are benefits from using one currency instead of twelve. For one thing, a single European currency will save on transactions costs: the EC's economists estimate the savings at 1 percent of EC GNP. And removing the uncertainty created by exchange-rate fluctuations will encourage additional intra-European trade and investment.

There is, however, no free lunch. Forcing all European countries to run the same monetary policy and to maintain the same interest rates will deprive Europe's national governments of a policy tool traditionally used to address their own macroeconomic problems. When Italy has had a recession not shared by other EC countries, its central bank (the Bank of Italy) has reduced interest rates, expanded the money supply, and devalued the exchange rate, with the goal of boosting domestic demand and moderating the recession. With no exchange rate to devalue and with monetary policy turned over to the ECB, this response will no longer be possible. Europe had a taste of this problem in 1991 and 1992, when high interest rates in Germany, together with the fixed exchange rates of the European Monetary System that already tied European monetary policies together, drove interest rates up throughout the EC.

As this experience reminds us, a monetary policy common to all twelve EC countries will be useful for moderating only those business cycle fluctuations that are common to the twelve countries. Insofar as European countries experience cyclical expansions and contractions at different times, their sacrifice of monetary autonomy may cost them a lot.

Barry Eichengreen

Biography: Barry Eichengreen is an economics professor at the University of California at Berkeley, a research associate of the National Bureau of Economic Research in Cambridge, Massachusetts, and a research fellow of the Centre for Economic Policy Research in London. He wrote this article while visiting the Institute for Advanced Study in Berlin.

Further Reading

Emerson, Michael, Michel Aujean, Michel Catinat, Philippe Goubet, and Alexis Jacquemin. ''The Economics of 1992.'' *European Economy* 35 (March 1988).
Kenen, Peter. *EMU after Maastricht*. 1992.
Tsoukalis, Loukas. *The New European Economy: The Politics and Economics of Integration*. 1991.
Viner, Jacob. *The Customs Union Issue*. 1950.

German Economic "Miracle"

David R. Henderson

■ After World War II the German economy lay in shambles. The war, along with Hitler's scorched-earth policy, had destroyed 20 percent of all housing. Food production per capita in 1947 was only 51 percent of its level in 1938, and the official food ration set by the occupying powers varied between 1,040 and 1,550 calories per day. Industrial output in 1947 was only one-third its 1938 level. Moreover, a large percentage of Germany's working-age men were dead. At the time, observers thought that Germany would have to be the biggest client of the U.S. welfare state. Yet twenty years later its economy was envied by most of the world. And less than ten years after the war people already were talking about the German economic miracle.

What caused the so-called miracle? The two main factors were a currency reform and the elimination of price controls, both of which happened over a period of weeks in 1948. A further factor was the reduction of marginal tax rates later in 1948 and in 1949.

Before

By 1948 the German people had lived under price controls for 12 years. Adolf Hitler had imposed them on the German people in 1936 so that his government could buy war materials at artificially low prices. (Roosevelt and Churchill also imposed price controls.) In November 1945 the Allied Control Authority, formed by the governments of the United States, Britain, France, and the Soviet Union, agreed to keep Hitler's price controls in place.

Each of the Allied governments controlled a ''zone'' of German territory. In the U.S. zone, a cost-of-living index in May 1948, computed at the controlled prices, was only 31 percent above its level in 1938. Yet in 1947, the amount of money in the German economy—currency plus demand deposits—was five times its 1936 level. With money a multiple of its previous level but prices only a fraction higher, there were bound to be shortages. And there were.

Price controls on food made the shortages so severe that some people started growing their own, and others made weekend treks to the countryside to barter for food. Yale University economist (and later Federal Reserve governor) Henry Wallich, in his 1955 book, *Mainsprings of the German Revival,* wrote:

> Each day, and particularly on weekends, vast hordes of people trekked out to the country to barter food from the farmers. In dilapidated railway carriages from which everything pilferable had long disappeared, on the roofs and on the running boards, hungry people traveled sometimes hundreds of miles at snail's pace to where they hoped to find something to eat.

They took their wares—personal effects, old clothes, sticks of furniture, whatever bombed-out remnants they had—and came back with grain or potatoes for a week or two.

Barter also was so widespread in business-to-business transactions that a new job title in many firms was that of "compensator." A compensator was a specialist who bartered his firm's output for needed inputs and often had to engage in multiple transactions to do so. In September 1947 U.S. military experts estimated that one-third to one-half of all business transactions in the bizonal area (the U.S. and British zones) were in the form of "compensation trade" (i.e., barter).

Barter was very inefficient compared to straight purchase of goods and services for money. German economist Walter Eucken wrote that barter and self-sufficiency were two things that were incompatible with an extensive division of labor. "The economic system," he wrote, "is reduced to a primitive condition." The numbers bear him out. In March 1948 bizonal production was only 51 percent of its level in 1936.

The Debate

Eucken was the leader of a school of economic thought based at Germany's University of Freiburg. The school was called Soziate Marktwirtschaft, the "socially conscious free market." Members of this school hated totalitarianism and had propounded their views at some risk during Hitler's regime. Wrote Henry Wallich: "During the Nazi period the school represented a kind of intellectual resistance movement, requiring great personal courage as well as independence of mind." The school's members believed in free markets, along with some slight degree of progression in the income tax system and government action to limit monopoly. (Cartels in Germany had been explicitly legal before the war.) The Soziate Marktwirtschaft was very much like the Chicago school, whose budding members Milton Friedman and George Stigler also believed in a heavy dose of free markets, slight government redistribution through the tax system, and antitrust laws to prevent monopoly.

Two members of the German school were Wilhelm Roepke and Ludwig Erhard. To clean up the postwar mess, Roepke advocated currency reform so that the amount of currency could be in line with the amount of goods, and abolition of price controls. Both were necessary, he thought, to end repressed inflation. The currency reform would end inflation. Price decontrol would end repression.

Ludwig Erhard agreed with Roepke. Erhard himself had written a memorandum during the war laying out his vision of a market economy. His memorandum made clear that he wanted the Nazis to be defeated.

The Social Democratic Party (SPD), on the other hand, wanted to keep government control. The SPD's main economic ideologue, Dr. Kreyssig, argued in June 1948 that decontrol of prices and currency reform would be ineffective. He argued instead for central government direction. Agreeing with the SPD were labor union leaders, the British authorities, most German manufacturing interests, and some of the American authorities.

The Change

Ludwig Erhard won the debate. Because the Allies wanted non-Nazis in the new German government, Erhard, whose anti-Nazi views were clear, was appointed Bavarian minister of finance in 1945. In 1947 he became the director of the bizonal Office of Economic Opportunity and, in that capacity, advised U.S. General Lucius D. Clay, military governor of the U.S. zone. Erhard advocated currency reform and price decontrol. After the Soviets withdrew from the Allied Control Authority, Clay, along with his French and British counterparts, undertook a currency reform on Sunday, June 20, 1948. The basic idea was to substitute a much smaller number of deutsche marks (DM), the new legal currency, for reichs marks. The money supply would, therefore, contract substantially so that even at the controlled prices, now stated in deutsche marks, there would be fewer shortages. The currency reform was highly complex, with many people taking a substantial reduction in their net wealth. The net result was about a 93 percent contraction in the money supply.

On that same Sunday the German Bizonal Economic Council adopted, at the urging of Ludwig Erhard and against the opposition of its Social Democratic members, a price decontrol ordinance. The new law allowed and encouraged Erhard to eliminate price controls.

Erhard had a fun summer. From June through August of 1948, wrote Fred Klopstock, an economist at the Federal Reserve Bank of New York, "directive followed directive removing price, allocation, and rationing regulations." Vegetables, fruit, eggs, and almost all manufactured goods were freed of controls. Ceiling prices on many other goods were raised substantially, and many remaining controls were no longer enforced. Erhard's motto could have been "Don't just sit there; undo something."

Along with currency reform and decontrol of prices, the government also cut tax rates. A young economist named Walter Heller, who was then with the U.S. Office of Military Government in Germany and who was later to be chairman of President Kennedy's Council of Economic Advisers, described the reforms in a 1949 article. To "remove the repressive effect of extremely high rates," wrote Heller, "Military Government Law No. 64 cut a wide swath across the German tax system at the time of the currency reform." The corporate income tax rate, which had ranged from 35 percent to 65 percent, was made a flat 50 percent. Although the top rate on individual income remained at 95 percent, it applied only to income above the level of DM250,000 annually. In 1946, by contrast, the Allies had taxed all income above 60,000 reichs marks (which translated into about DM6,000) at 95 percent. For the median-income German in 1950, with an annual income of a little less than DM2,400, the marginal tax rate was 18 percent. That same person, had he earned the reichs mark equivalent in 1948, would have been in an 85 percent tax bracket.

After

The effect on the German economy was electric. Wallich wrote: "The spirit of the country changed overnight. The gray, hungry, dead-looking figures wandering about the streets in their everlasting search for food came to life.''

Shops on Monday, June 21, were filled with goods as people realized that the money they sold them for would be worth much more than the old money. Walter Heller wrote that the reforms ''quickly reestablished money as the preferred medium of exchange and monetary incentives as the prime mover of economic activity.''

Absenteeism also plummeted. In May 1948 workers had stayed away from their jobs for an average of 9.5 hours per week, partly because the money they worked for was not worth much and partly because they were out foraging or bartering for money. By October average absenteeism was down to 4.2 hours per week. In June 1948 the bizonal index of industrial production was at only 51 percent of its 1936 level. By December the index had risen to 78 percent of its 1936 level. In other words, industrial production had increased by over 50 percent.

Output continued to grow by leaps and bounds after 1948. By 1958 industrial production was over four times its annual rate for the six months in 1948 preceding currency reform. Industrial production per capita was over three times as high.

Because Erhard's ideas had worked, the first chancellor of the new Federal Republic of Germany, Konrad Adenauer, appointed him as Germany's first minister of economic affairs. He held that post until 1963 when he became chancellor himself, a post he held until 1966.

The Marshall Plan

This account has not mentioned the Marshall Plan. Can't the German revival be attributed mainly to that? The answer is no. The reason is simple: Marshall Plan aid to Germany was not that large. Cumulative aid from the Marshall Plan and other aid programs totaled only $2 billion through October 1954. Even in 1948 and 1949, when aid was at its peak, Marshall Plan aid was less than 5 percent of German national income. Other countries that received substantial Marshall Plan aid had lower growth than Germany.

Moreover, while Germany was receiving aid, it was also making reparations and restitution payments that were well over $1 billion. Finally, and most important, the Allies charged the Germans DM7.2 billion annually ($2.4 billion) for their costs of occupying Germany. (Of course, these occupation costs also meant that Germany did not need to pay for its own defense.)

Conclusion

What looked like a miracle to many observers was really not a miracle. It was expected by Ludwig Erhard and by others of the Freiburg school who understood the damage that can be done by inflation coupled with price controls and high tax rates, and the large productivity gains that can be unleashed by ending inflation, removing controls, and cutting high marginal tax rates.

—David R. Henderson

Biography: David R. Henderson is the editor of this encyclopedia. He is a senior research fellow with Stanford University's Hoover Institution and an associate professor of economics at the Naval Postgraduate School in Monterey, California. He was formerly a senior economist with the President's Council of Economic Advisers.

Further Reading

Hazlett, Thomas W. "The German Non-Miracle." *Reason* 9 (April 1978): 33–37.

Heller, Walter W. "Tax and Monetary Reform in Occupied Germany." *National Tax Journal* 2, no. 3 (1949): 215–31.

Hirshleifer, Jack W. *Economic Behavior in Adversity*. 1987.

Klopstock, Fred H. "Monetary Reform in Western Germany." *Journal of Political Economy* 57, no. 4 (August 1949): 277–92.

Lutz, F. A. "The German Currency Reform and the Revival of the German Economy." *Economica* 16 (May 1949): 122–42.

Mendershausen, Horst. "Prices, Money and the Distribution of Goods in Postwar Germany." *American Economic Review* 39 (June 1949): 646–72.

Wallich, Henry C. *Mainsprings of the German Revival*. 1955.

See also MARGINAL TAX RATES, PRICE CONTROLS.

Japan and the Myth of MITI

David R. Henderson

■ At the end of World War II, Japan's economy was in tatters. Some 40 percent of its capital stock was destroyed during the war, and the Japanese standard of living was at pre–World War I levels. Today Japan has the second-largest economy in the world and its growth is the envy of most of the world. From 1952, when the American occupation ended, until 1991, Japan's real GNP grew at an average rate of 6.8 percent per year. During the period of greatest growth, from 1952 to 1971, real GNP grew at an average annual rate of 9.6 percent. Because of the miracle of compounding, Japan's GNP is now over thirteen times its 1952 level. In the United States from 1952 to 1991, by contrast, real GNP grew at an average rate of 2.9 percent, and only tripled over the whole period.

What caused the Japanese "miracle"? Answering that question is difficult. Economists, unlike physicists, cannot conduct controlled experiments in which they change one parameter, leaving all others unchanged, and then look for the effect of the change in this one parameter. Because Japan differs in many ways from other countries—particularly in its culture and its government policies—isolating the effect of any factor is especially difficult. Nevertheless, some major factors seem to be clear-cut causes of Japan's growth.

Sources of Growth

The most thorough study of the causes of Japan's twenty-year postwar growth spurt is a Brookings Institution study by Edward H. Denison and William K. Chung. They found that four factors contributed about two percentage points each to the 8.77 percent annual growth rate of national income between 1953 and 1971. The four, in order of importance, were: increases in capital (2.10 percentage points); advances in knowledge and factors not elsewhere classified (1.97); economies of scale (1.94); and increases in labor (1.85). Most of the remaining growth was accounted for by reallocation of resources away from the inefficient agricultural sector.

The major cause of Japan's large increase in capital was its large increases in investment. Gross private investment, which had been a healthy 17.2 percent of GNP from 1952 to 1954, increased almost continuously throughout the fifties and sixties. By 1970 and 1971 it was a whopping 30.5 percent of GNP. In other words, almost one out of every three yen of Japanese production in 1970 and 1971 was invested in capital. This private investment, in turn, was financed largely by Japanese saving. Gross private saving, half of which was by corporations and half by households, rose steadily from 16.5 percent of GNP between 1952 and 1954 and reached 31.9 percent of GNP in 1970 and 1971. In the United States between 1961 and 1971, by contrast, private saving averaged only 15.8 percent of GNP.

Economist Fumiyo Hayashi of the University of Pennsylvania cautions that comparisons between Japanese and U.S. savings rates are tricky because of the different ways that savings are measured in each country. Measuring savings the same way, he shows, reduces the gap between U.S. and Japanese savings rates. But a large gap still remains.

What accounts for the large Japanese savings rates? Economists are not agreed, but two factors are probably important. The first is low taxes. As Brookings economist Joseph Pechman wrote in 1976, "The fact that the tax burden is unusually low by the standards of other developed countries may alone be a significant factor in the explanation of the high rate of private saving and investment in Japan." From 1951 to 1970, while Japan's real GNP was growing at an average of 9 percent per year, total national and local taxes (excluding social security) fell from 22.4 percent of national income to 18.9 percent. This left more money for people to save and invest. Compare Japan's situation with the United States, where the proportion rose from 28.5 percent to 31.3 percent. Interestingly, Japan's two decades of greatest postwar growth were also its decades of lowest taxes. During the seventies, as Japan's taxes rose to 22.8 percent of national income in 1980, real GNP growth declined to only 4.8 percent. Higher taxes weren't the only reason for this deteriorating performance, of course; oil price increases also contributed.

The second probable cause of high Japanese saving is the incentive that Japan's tax code gives to savers. Since the early fifties, savers in Japan have been allowed to exempt large amounts of interest income from taxation. Employees who saved part of their wages in an employer-run savings plan paid no taxes on interest on the first x dollars of savings. In 1981, for example, x was $22,600. Interest on postal savings—in Japan the post office offers a limited range of financial services—is treated similarly. In 1981, for example, interest on the first $13,600 was tax free. Those without qualms about lawbreaking could theoretically hold one such account at each post office—there are more than twenty thousand—because postal savings officials tolerate multiple accounts. At one point, according to a study by the Hudson Institute, Japan had twice as many postal savings accounts as people. Also, capital gains from the sale of securities are untaxed.

The Myth of MITI

Early in the fifties, a small consumer-electronics company in Japan asked the Japanese government for permission to buy transistor-manufacturing rights from Western Electric. Permission was necessary because at the time foreign exchange was controlled by the tax and trade ministries. The Ministry of International Trade and Industry (MITI) refused, arguing that the technology wasn't impressive enough to justify the expenditure. Two years later, the company persuaded MITI to reverse its decision and went on to fame and fortune with the transistor radio. The company's name: Sony.

In the midfifties MITI exhorted a Japanese industry to develop a prototype "people's" model of its product so MITI could designate the winning firm as the single producer. In the 1960s MITI tried to force this industry's many firms to merge into just a few. Both times the companies rebuffed MITI, and today this industry is one of Japan's finest. Its product: cars.

Many people believe that Japan's outstanding growth is due in large part to MITI. They believe that MITI has decided what industries the Japanese should invest in, and that MITI persuaded other Japanese government agencies to use their coercive power to get companies to go along. But the evidence goes against this view. Although MITI plans for industry growth, and sometimes gets other agencies to use their powers to carry out the plans, the extent of MITI's control, and of government control generally, has been greatly exaggerated. Between December 1955 and February 1973, crucial years in Japan's growth, the government had six different National Economic Plans for economic growth. But without exception actual growth rates exceeded those required to fulfill the plan's targets. This is evidence that the plans themselves were not responsible. Moreover, had MITI succeeded in preventing Sony from developing the transistor radio, and in coercively limiting the auto industry, two of Japan's most successful industries would probably have been much less successful.

Between 1953 and 1955 MITI did persuade the government's Japanese Development Bank to lend money to four industries—electric power, ships, coal, and steel. Some 83 percent of JDB financing over that period went to those four industries. But even with hindsight, what has not been established is whether those were good investments.

The main book cited by those who argue that MITI is responsible for Japan's growth is *MITI and the Japanese Miracle,* by U.S. political scientist Chalmers Johnson. But Johnson's book actually contains little evidence that MITI has helped. Instead, he notes some of the policies, such as tariffs, that MITI persuaded other agencies to implement, and then attributes the large growth to these policies. But tariffs are a particularly unlikely cause of Japan's growth. Not even the Japanese have been able to repeal the law of comparative advantage. For Japan, as for other countries, tariffs, except in highly unusual circumstances, hinder growth. Most of Johnson's book is about MITI's structure and personnel and is not a sustained case for his belief that MITI is the cause of Japan's extraordinary economic performance.

Other Government Policies

A close look shows that in many ways, government in Japan is less interventionist than governments in most countries. By one reasonable measure—government spending as a percent of GNP—government's role in Japan is less than in any other major industrialized country. Another way Japan is less interventionist is in antitrust policy. Japan, unlike the United States, has no antitrust restrictions on joint research and development. This allows Japanese companies to avoid duplicating each other's research.

Japan's government also allows banks to own stock. America's Glass-Steagall Act prohibits this. Because Japanese banks own stock and because many bank officers sit on company boards, they can discipline managers. Also, banks in Japan, able to take equity positions in companies, are a source of venture capital.

A further advantage of allowing banks to own stock is that a bank confident of a company's future can back it when other creditors get scared. Later, if the company performs well, the bank profits because the company's share price increases. That happened in the case of Toyo Kogyo, the Japanese company that made Mazda autos. When the 1974 oil price increase made its fuel-inefficient Wankel engine uncompetitive, Toyo Kogyo almost went under. Sumitomo Bank, a large stockholder, assured Toyo Kogyo's creditors and suppliers that it stood behind the firm. Had the U.S. law prevailed in Japan, Sumitomo would have had much less to gain from lending to Toyo Kogyo.

Many economists and others who have written about Japan's high growth attribute it to a concern with quality production and to Japanese companies' treatment of their employees. These are certainly important factors in Japan's growth. But the Japanese government's only contribution to these factors is that it allowed them. Japan's growth is stunning evidence, not of the efficacy of government planning, but of the wonders that relatively free people can produce.

—David R. Henderson

Biography: David R. Henderson is the editor of this encyclopedia. He is a senior research fellow with Stanford University's Hoover Institution and an associate professor of economics at the Naval Postgraduate School in Monterey, California. He was formerly a senior economist with the President's Council of Economic Advisers.

Further Reading

Denison, Edward F., and William K. Chung. *How Japan's Economy Grew So Fast*. 1976.
Hayashi, Fumiyo. ''Why Is Japan's Saving Rate So Apparently High?'' In *NBER Macroeconomics Annual 1986*, edited by Stanley Fischer. 1986.
Henderson, David R. ''The Myth of MITI.'' *Fortune*, August 8, 1983. 113–16.
Johnson, Chalmers. *MITI and the Japanese Miracle*. 1982.
Ouchi, William. *The M-Form Society*. 1984.
Patrick, Hugh, and Henry Rosovsky. *Asia's New Giant: How the Japanese Economy Works*. 1976.

Perestroika

Marshall I. Goldman

■ To the outside world, the Soviet Union seemed little different in 1984 from what it had been for at least a decade. Except for a few skeptics, almost everyone agreed that the Soviet Union was the world's second-largest economy and, if not the most powerful military force in the world, then a very close second. It produced more machine tools, steel, oil, and natural gas than any other country, and its stock of nuclear and conventional weapons in Europe was at least double that of the United States.

Yet deep within the system, some had begun to question the reality of that apparent strength. In early 1983, for example, Tat'iana Zaslavskaia, a social scientist at the Siberian division of the Soviet Academy of Sciences, wrote a long study detailing the Soviet economy's shortcomings and its growing inability to compete in an age of high technology. As Zaslavskaia saw it, the central planning system had outlived its usefulness. According to her, central planning served reasonably well to acculturate illiterate peasants into an industrial, urban work force. But as the Soviet economy became more extensive and complex, the central planners could not maintain control over it. The control they did manage to exercise often served to stifle as much as it facilitated. Ludwig von Mises and Friedrich Hayek had pointed this out years earlier. People, they said, need a market to guide the millions of decisions that must be made each day about how, what, when, and for whom to produce. Without the market a planning commission like Gosplan, no matter how large, will find itself unable to react effectively.

Indeed, one of Zaslavskaia's criticisms was that the system was becoming more and more counterproductive. Increasingly, the Soviet industrial system was producing negative value added: the value of the inputs and components used in many production processes was worth more than the resulting final product. Thus, because of the wasteful use of metals in producing drilling equipment and pipelines, the expense of drilling and transporting petroleum often exceeded the value of the oil at its final destination. The slow growth rate that resulted from the inefficiencies made it impossible to provide a better life for the work force, which the government had promised would follow once an industrial foundation had been built.

By late 1984 Mikhail Gorbachev had joined the ranks of those who believed that the Soviet Union's economic system could not continue without far-reaching reforms. He was not to become the general secretary of the Communist Party of the Soviet Union until March 1985. He had, however, called in Zaslavskaia a few years earlier for a discussion about agricultural reform, and their discussion expanded to include an analysis of the overall economic system.

Gorbachev has described how, by December 1984, he had concluded "that it was impossible to live that way.'' This meant a change not only in the country's political and social life, but also in its economy. That same month, while speaking at a meeting of party officials, Gorbachev presented his version of what needed to be done. Although Konstantin Chernenko would be the nominal leader of the party for another three months, Gorbachev chose this speech to issue a call for ''perestroika''—for restructuring.

Although the exact meaning of Gorbachev's perestroika changed from year to year, in those early months he spoke of intensifying and accelerating production in the machine tool industry. Once elected general secretary, his concept of perestroika also came to include removing some decision making from the ministries and Gosplan, the state planning commission. This implied more reliance on market processes; at least there was a marked softening of the harsh rhetoric used to describe the market. But other than an experiment or two, he proposed no concrete measures to advance the use of markets. In fact, it sometimes looked as if the opposite was happening.

While Gorbachev closed down a large number of economic ministries, for example, he created superministries in their place. Thus, the resulting agricultural ministry (Gosagroprom) was even more dominant in determining agricultural production and ultimately became an obstacle to agricultural reform. Even more striking, in July 1986 the Soviet Union started a crackdown on all private trade. No individuals could sell anything that they themselves did not produce. This was a step back to the early thirties.

In 1987 Gorbachev concluded that he was headed in the wrong direction. In May of that year a new regulation authorized private and cooperative trade and even private manufacturing. Only pensioners and students were initially allowed to participate, but Gorbachev gradually opened the doors to everyone. About the same time, the Soviet government also announced that it would allow foreigners to open joint ventures on Soviet territory. As with private and cooperative trade, the joint ventures initially came with strict limitations (foreigners could not hold more than a 49 percent interest in such ventures). But by 1990, in theory at least, foreigners could own 100 percent of the shares, although none did.

Any meaningful move away from central planning, however, would also have to involve state industrial enterprises. One solution would be to privatize them or turn over all profit or loss responsibility to a group of private owners.

Gorbachev at first concluded that this was too radical a step, and so he introduced an ''Enterprise Law'' that called for a gradual reduction in the control that ministries exercised over enterprise operations. Beginning on January 1, 1988, enterprises producing 50 percent of the Soviet Union's industrial output would be required to set aside only about 80 percent of what they produced for allocation by central planning authorities.

Despite the best intentions, however, the Enterprise Law was a failure. The ministers did all they could to retain their controls, and the managers held back from exercising their new prerogatives. Without a wholesale market to help them find customers, selling on their own made their lives much more complicated. In addition, disposing of output outside of the central planning procedure carried with it the obligation to find inputs outside official state channels as well. The vast majority of managers decided that the risks and uncertainties outweighed the potential rewards, and refused to shift to the market.

Gorbachev carried on in this uncertain manner, experimenting a little here and a little there without any firm commitment to fundamental change. Recognizing that something more far-reaching was needed, he asked economists to design a more comprehensive approach. To one degree or another, these plans involved such measures as greater reliance on markets to set prices; free convertibility of the ruble into other currencies; ending subsidies to unprofitable enterprises; balanced state budgets; privatization of agriculture, trade, and industry; monetary reform; and demonopolization.

From October 1989 to mid-1991, the Soviet Union had at least eight such comprehensive plans, none of which seemed to meet Western prescriptions of what really was needed. But since Gorbachev seemed to be better at calling for new studies than at implementing them, the inadequacies of this or that proposal had no practical impact. Although Gorbachev never saw a proposal that he disliked, he never found one that he liked enough to implement. Each time a new proposal was completed, Gorbachev would approve it. But he also would recommend that it be amalgamated with some earlier proposals. In such an environment industry and shop managers, whether private entrepreneurs or state bureaucrats, find it difficult to plan and implement any long-term policies.

In all fairness to Gorbachev, no one has yet been able to figure out how to make a successful transition from a Stalinist, centrally planned economy to a market-oriented system in a relatively short time. The Soviet-type system developed in very different ways: the market atrophied, prices became distorted, individuals hesitated to assume initiatives, and profit making became associated with criminality and antisocial acts. Moreover, to prevent duplication the state purposefully created monopolies.

Undoing this damage is not easy. Some, such as Poland, have tried "shock therapy"—doing everything at once, including the move to a market for price determination, allowing currency reform, holding budget subsidies, and denationalizing and privatizing agriculture, industry, and services. Others say that moving too fast imposes too heavy a burden on the population. A more gradual approach, too, is criticized because it allows the opponents to gang up on the reformers and destroy them before they ever have a chance to succeed. Besides, the whole point of the market system is that it comes as a whole package. If there is no price flexibility, for example, then most likely there will have to be subsidies. This will cause budget deficits, which will cause inflation, which, even if it is suppressed, will nonetheless cause shortages.

In other words, moving from a planned to a market system is not easy. Joseph Berliner and Kenneth Boulding have likened the move from market to planned system to a forester chopping down a forest. If enough force is used, the procedure is relatively simple, even if it is destructive. Performing the reverse, however, is much more difficult. Planting a few trees does not make a forest. A forest encompasses a whole ecological system of insects, animals, and underbrush. In the same way, allowing a few private stores to open does not make a market.

Gorbachev knew what he wanted to change. His problem until he lost power in 1991—and indeed, one of the main reasons he lost power—was that he was unsure of what he wanted to change to. Moreover, neither he nor any other leader so far seems to know how to carry out that transformation. We Westerners sometimes forget that it took us several centuries to create our economic and political system, and even then, there are some who complain that we still don't have it right. The odds are that while perestroika may not require centuries to implement, it will not come quickly or painlessly.

—Marshall I. Goldman

Biography: Marshall I. Goldman is the Kathryn W. Davis Professor of Russian Economics at Wellesley College, and the associate director of the Russian Research Center at Harvard University.

Further Reading

Aganbegyan, Abel. *The Economic Challenge of Perestroika*. 1988.
———. *Inside Perestroika: The Future of the Soviet Economy*. 1989.
Desai, Padma. *Perestroika in Perspective*. 1989.
Goldman, Marshall I. *Gorbachev's Challenge: Economic Reform in the Age of High Technology*. 1987.
———. *What Went Wrong with Perestroika*. 1991.
Hewett, Edward A. *Reforming the Soviet Economy*. 1988.
Zaslavskaia, Tat'iana. *The Voice of Reform*. 1989.

Third World Debt

Kenneth Rogoff

■ By the end of 1990 the world's poor and developing countries owed more than $1.3 trillion to industrialized countries. Among the largest problem debtors were Brazil ($116 billion), Mexico ($97 billion), and Argentina ($61 billion). Of the total developing-country debt, roughly half is owed to private creditors, mainly commercial banks.

The rest consists of obligations to international lending organizations such as the International Monetary Fund (IMF) and the World Bank, and to governments and government agencies—export-import banks, for example. Of the private bank debt, the bulk has been incurred by middle-income countries, especially in Latin America. The world's poorest countries, mostly in Africa and South Asia, were never able to borrow substantial sums from the private sector and most of their debts are to the IMF, World Bank, and other governments.

Third World debt grew dramatically during the seventies, when bankers were eager to lend money to developing countries. Although many Third World governments defaulted on their debts during the thirties, bankers had put that episode out of their minds by the seventies. The mood of the time is perhaps best captured in the famous proclamation by the Citibank chairman at the time, Walter Wriston, that lending to governments is safe banking because sovereign nations do not default on their debts.

The loan pyramid came crashing down in August 1982, when the Mexican government suddenly found itself unable to roll over its private debts (that is, borrow new funds to replace loans that were due) and was unprepared to quickly shift gears from being a net borrower to a net repayer. Soon after, a slew of other sovereign debtors sought rescheduling agreements, and the "debt crisis" was officially under way. Though experts do not really understand why the crisis started precisely when it did, its basic causes are clear. The sharp rise in world interest rates in the early eighties greatly increased the interest burden on debtor countries because most of their borrowings were indexed to short-term interest rates. At the same time, export receipts of developing countries suffered as commodity prices began to fall, reversing their rise of the seventies. More generally, sluggish growth in the industrialized countries made debt servicing much more difficult.

Of course, the debtors were not simply hapless victims of external market forces. The governments of many of the seventeen nations referred to as Highly Indebted Countries (HICs) made the situation worse by badly mismanaging their economies. In many countries during the seventies, commercial bank or World Bank loans quickly escaped through the back door in the form of private capital flight (see CAPITAL FLIGHT). As table 1 shows, capital assets that "fled" abroad from the HICs were 103 percent of long-term public and publicly guaranteed debt. Loans intended for infra-

TABLE 1

Capital Flight
(in billions of 1987 dollars)

	Flight Capital Assets	As Percentage of Long-Term Public and Publicly Guaranteed Debt
Argentina	$ 46	111%
Bolivia	2	178
Brazil	31	46
Chile	2	17
Colombia	7	103
Ecuador	7	115
Ivory Coast	0	0
Mexico	84	114
Morocco	3	54
Nigeria	20	136
Peru	2	27
Philippines	23	188
Uruguay	4	159
Venezuela	58	240
Yugoslavia	6	79
Total	295	103

SOURCES: *Flight Capital, Morgan Stanley as cited in* The International Economy, *July/August 1989. Debt, World Debt Tables, 1988–89 edition. Data refer to external debt to private creditors. Reprinted from* Journal of Economic Perspectives, *4, no. 1 (Winter 1990): 37.*

structure investment at home were rerouted to buy condominiums in Miami. In a few countries, most notably Brazil, capital flight was not severe. But a great deal of the loan money was spent internally on dubious large-scale, government-directed investment projects. Though well intentioned, the end result was the same: not enough money was invested in productive projects that could be used to service the debt.

Not all of the debtor countries were plagued by mismanagement. South Korea, considered by many to be a problem debtor at the onset of the debt crisis, maintained a strong export-oriented economy. The resulting growth in real GNP—averaging 9.8 percent per year between 1982 and 1988—allowed South Korea to make the largest debt repayments in the world in 1986 and 1987. Korea's debt fell from $47 billion to $40 billion between the end of 1985 and the end of 1987.

But for most debtor countries, the eighties were a decade of economic stagnation. Loan renegotiations with bank committees and with government lenders became almost constant. While lenders frequently agreed to roll over a portion of interest due (thus increasing their loans), prospects for net new funds seemed to dry up for all but a few developing countries, located mostly in fast-growing Asia. In this context bankers and government officials began to consider many schemes for clearing away the developing-country debt problem.

In theory, loans by governments and by international lending organizations are senior to private debts—they must be repaid first. But private lenders are the ones who have been pressing to have their loans repaid. As a consequence, official creditors saw their share of problem-country debt double—to nearly half the total—during the first decade of the debt crisis.

Many Third World debtors, particularly in Latin America, chafe at being asked to pay down their large debts. Their leaders plead that debt is strangling their economies and that repayments are soaking away resources desperately needed to finance growth. Although these pleas evoke considerable sympathy from leaders of rich countries, opinions over what to do are widely divided.

A staggering range of "solutions" has been proposed. Some of the more ambitious plans would either force private creditors to forgive part of their debts or use large doses of taxpayer resources to sponsor a settlement, or both. Current official policy, which is based on the Brady Plan (after U.S. Treasury Secretary Nicholas Brady), is for governments of industrialized countries to subsidize countries where there is scope for negotiating large-scale debt-reduction agreements with the private commercial banks. In principle, countries must also demonstrate the will to implement sound economic policies, both fiscal and monetary, to qualify. A small number of Brady Plan deals have been completed to date, the most notable being Mexico's 1990 debt restructuring.

Toward the end of the eighties, a number of sovereign debtors began experimenting with so-called market-based debt-reduction schemes, in which countries repurchased their debts at a discount by paying cash or by giving creditors equity in domestic industries. On the surface these plans appear to hurt banks because debts are retired at a fraction of their full value. But a closer inspection reveals why the commercial banks responded so enthusiastically.

Consider the Bolivian buy-back of March 1988. When the Bolivian deal was first discussed in late 1986, Bolivia's government had guaranteed $670 million in debt to commercial banks. In world secondary markets this debt traded at six cents on the dollar.

That is, buyers of debt securities were willing to pay, and some sellers were willing to accept, only six cents per dollar of principal. Using funds that primarily were secretly donated by neutral third countries—rumored to include Spain, the Netherlands, and Brazil—Bolivia's government spent $34 million in March 1988 to buy back $308 million worth of debt at eleven cents on the dollar. Eleven cents was also the price that prevailed for the remaining Bolivian debt immediately after the repurchase. At first glance the buy-back might seem a triumph, almost halving Bolivia's debt. The fact that the price rose from six to eleven cents was interpreted by some observers as evidence that the deal had strengthened prospects for Bolivia's economy.

A more sober assessment of the Bolivian buy-back reveals that commercial bank creditors probably reaped most of the benefit. Before the buy-back, banks expected to receive a total of $40.2 million (.06 × $670 million). After the buy-back, banks had collected $34 million and their expected future repayments were still $39.8 million (.11 × $362 million). How did creditors manage to reap such a large share of the benefits? Basically, when a country is as deep in hock as Bolivia was, creditors attach a far greater likelihood to partial repayment than to full repayment. Having the face value of the debt halved did little to reduce the banks' bargaining leverage with Bolivia, and the chances that the canceled debt would have eventually been paid were low anyway. Similar problems can arise even in countries whose debt sells at much smaller discounts.

The fact that buy-backs tend to bid up debt prices presents difficulties for any plan in which funds taken from taxpayers in industrialized countries are used to promote debt restructurings that supposedly are for the sole benefit of people in the debtor countries. Banks will surely know of the additional resources available for repayment, and they will try to bargain for higher repayments and lower rollovers. The main focus of the Brady Plan is precisely to ensure that the lion's share of officially donated funds reaches debtors. But the fact that debt prices have been stronger in countries that have implemented Brady Plans than in non–Brady Plan countries suggests that the effort to limit the gain for banks has been only partially successful.

Aside from the question of such "leakage" to private banks, there are serious eq-uity concerns with any attempt to channel large quantities of aid relief to deal with private debt. Though poor by standards of Europe and the United States, countries such as Brazil, Mexico, and Argentina rank as middle-to upper-middle income in the broader world community. The average per capita income in the seventeen HICs was $1,430 in 1987. This compares with $470 in developing East Asia and $290 in South Asia. Even Bolivia, South America's basket case, has twice the per capita income of India. On a need basis, therefore, Africa and South Asia are stronger candidates for aid.

—Kenneth Rogoff

Biography: Kenneth Rogoff is an economics professor at Princeton University's Woodrow Wilson School. He has served on the staff of the International Monetary Fund and the Federal Reserve board and has been a visiting scholar at the World Bank.

Further Reading

Bulow, Jeremy, and Kenneth Rogoff. "The Buyback Boondoogle." *Brookings Papers on Economic Activity*, no. 2 (1988): 675–98.
———. "Cleaning Up Third-World Debt without Getting Taken to the Cleaners." *Journal of Economic Perspectives* 4 (Winter 1990): 31–42.
World Bank. *World Debt Tables: External Debt of Developing Countries*. 1990–91 edition.

Third World Economic Development

Clive Crook

■ The development experiences of Third World countries since the fifties have been staggeringly diverse—and hence very informative. Forty years ago the developing countries looked a lot more like each other than they do today. Take India and South Korea. By any standards, both countries were extremely poor: India's income per capita was about $150 (in 1980 dollars) and South Korea's was about $350. Life expectancy was about forty years and fifty years respectively. In both countries roughly 70 percent of the people worked on the land, and farming accounted for 40 percent of national income. The two countries were so far behind the industrial world that it seemed nearly inconceivable that either could ever attain reasonable standards of living, let alone catch up.

If anything, India had the edge. Its savings rate was 12 percent of GNP while Korea's was only 8 percent. India had natural resources. Its size gave its industries a huge domestic market as a platform for growth. Its former colonial masters, the British, left behind railways and other infrastructure that were good by Third World standards. The country had a competent judiciary and civil service, manned by a highly educated elite. Korea lacked all that. In the fifties the U.S. government thought it so unlikely that Korea would achieve any increase in living standards at all that its policy was to provide "sustaining aid" to stop them falling even further.

Less than forty years later—a short time in economic history—South Korea's extraordinary success is taken for granted. By the end of the eighties, its per capita income (in the same 1980 dollars) had risen to $2,900, an increase of nearly 6 percent a year sustained over more than three decades. None of today's rich countries, not even Japan, saw such a rapid transformation in the deep structure of their economies. In contrast, India's income per capita grew from $150 to $230, a rise of about 1.5 percent a year, between 1950 and 1980. India is widely regarded as a development failure. Yet over the past few decades even India has achieved more progress than today's rich countries did over similar periods and at comparable stages in their development.

This shows, first, that the setbacks the developing countries encountered in the eighties—high interest rates, debt-servicing difficulties, falling export prices—were an aberration, and that the currently fashionable pessimism about their future is greatly overdone. The superachievers of East Asia (South Korea and its fellow "dragons," Singapore, Taiwan, and Hong Kong) are by no means the only developing countries that are actually developing. Many others have also grown at historically unprecedented rates over the past few decades. As a group, the developing countries—134 of them, as conventionally defined, accounting for roughly three-quarters of the world's population—have indeed been catching up with the developed countries.

The comparison between India and South Korea shows something else. It no longer makes sense to talk of the developing countries as a homogeneous group. The East Asian dragons now have more in common with the industrial economies than with the poorest economies in South Asia and sub-Saharan Africa. Indeed, these subgroups of developing countries have become so distinct that one might think they have nothing to teach each other, that because South Korea is so different from India, its experience can hardly be relevant. That is a mistake. The diversity of experience among today's poor and not-so-poor countries does not defeat the task of analyzing what works and what doesn't. In fact, it is what makes the task possible.

Lessons of Experience

The hallmark of economic policy in most of the Third World since the fifties has been the rejection of orthodox free-market economics. The countries that failed most spectacularly (India, nearly all of sub-Saharan Africa, much of Latin America, the Soviet Union and its satellites) were the ones that rejected the orthodoxy most fervently. Their governments claimed that for one reason or another, free-market economics would not work for them. In contrast, the four dragons and, more recently, countries such as Chile, Colombia, Costa Rica, Ivory Coast, Malaysia, and Thailand have achieved growth ranging from good to remarkable by following policies based largely on market economics.

Among the most important ideas in orthodox economics is that countries prosper through trade. In the sixties and seventies the dragons participated in a boom in world trade. Because the dragons succeeded as exporters, they had abundant foreign exchange with which to buy investment goods from abroad. Unlike most other developing countries, the dragons had price systems that worked fairly well. So they invested in the right things, in ways that reflected their comparative advantage in cheap, unskilled labor.

Some economists still dismiss the dragons as special cases, but for reasons I find specious. They argue that Hong Kong and Singapore are small (hitherto smallness had been regarded as a disadvantage in development); that they are former colonies with traditions of excellence in public administration (like India and many others); that they have been generously provided with foreign capital (like Latin America). These economists also argue that Taiwan and South Korea received generous foreign aid (like many other developing countries), and have even argued that their lack of natural resources was an advantage. What was most unusual about these countries, in fact, was a relatively market-friendly approach to economic policy.

The countries that failed, often guided by "experts" in the industrialized world, are the ones that gave only a small role, if any, to private enterprise and to prices that are unregulated by government. Government planners concentrated on broad aggregates such as investment, consumption, and savings. Their priority was investment—the more, the better, regardless of its quality.

Most governments also thought that their

economies were inflexible and could not adjust to changing conditions. The export earnings of developing countries were regarded as fixed, for instance, and so was the import requirement for any given level of domestic production. The possibilities for substituting one good for another in response to a change in price were denied or ignored. The idea that workers respond to changes in incentives was likewise dismissed. This assumed lack of responsiveness led the planners to believe that prices, rather than providing signals for the allocation of resources, could serve other purposes instead. For instance, with direct controls they could be kept low to reduce inflation, or raised here and there to gather revenue for the government.

Taken to the limit, this "fixed-price" approach leads to regulation by input-output analysis. The idea is to tabulate the flow of primary, intermediate, and finished goods throughout the economy, on the assumption that each good requires inputs of other specific goods in fixed proportions. When all the cells in the table have been filled in, a government needs only to decide what it wants the economy to produce in order to know exactly what the country needs to import, good by good.

India went in for this sort of planning in a big way. More than a few of today's leading free-market economists have worked within India's planning system or have studied it in detail, and intimate contact with it leads them to one inescapable conclusion: government planning of the economy does not work. Professor Deepak Lal of London University, a leading proponent of market economics for the Third World, mentions his experience with India's planning commission in his book *The Poverty of Development Economics*. He calls the antimarket approach favored in so many countries the "dirigiste dogma."

From Peru to Ghana

In the noncommunist world, the most striking recent example of this dogma at work is Peru. When Alan Garcia's government came to power in the summer of 1985, Peru was already in a bad way, thanks largely to high tariffs and other import barriers, restrictive labor-protection laws, extensive credit rationing, high taxes, powerful trade unions, and an extraordinarily elaborate system of regulations to control the private sector. One result was Peru's justly celebrated black market, or "informal economy," described by Hernando de Soto in his modern classic, *The Other Path*. The other result was great vulnerability to adverse economic events. The early eighties delivered several, including a world recession, high interest rates, a drying up of external finance, and declining commodity prices.

Garcia's policy was based, he said, on two words: control and spend. After imposing price controls, he sharply increased public spending. The program succeeded at first. Gross domestic product (GDP) grew 9.5 percent in 1986 and 7 percent in 1987. But by the spring of 1988 inflation was running at 1,000 percent a year; by the end of the year it was 6,000 percent. After that, output and living standards collapsed. In 1990, the economy a wreck, Garcia was voted out of office.

The dirigiste dogma has proved equally

damaging in Africa. Take Ghana. When it became independent in 1957, it was the richest country in the region, with the best-educated population. It was the world's leading exporter of cocoa; it produced 10 percent of the world's gold; it had diamonds, bauxite, and manganese, and a flourishing trade in mahogany. Its income per capita was almost exactly equal to South Korea's at $490 (in 1980 dollars). By the early eighties, however, Korea's income per capita had risen fourfold, while Ghana's had actually fallen nearly 20 percent to $400 per head. Investment slumped from 20 percent of GDP in the fifties to 2 percent by 1982, and exports dropped from more than 30 percent of GDP to 4 percent.

The country's leader at independence, Kwame Nkrumah, was a spokesman for the newly independent Africa. He said the region needed to develop its own style of government, suited to its special circumstances. He spent vast sums on megaprojects. As economic troubles mounted, he nationalized companies and followed with capital repression. Under his regime capital flew abroad, and people with skills and money did the same. The kleptocrats (government officials who steal large amounts) ran the country into the ground. In the early eighties a new government came to power and at last began to steer the economy along orthodox lines. Until then, Ghana had been to Africa what Peru is to Latin America: a distillation of everything that has gone wrong with the continent's economies.

In the Third World, where so many people live off the land, agricultural development is crucial. Ghana provides a startling case study in how to wreck the farm sector. The means was the agricultural marketing board—a statutory monopoly that bought farmers' crops at controlled prices and resold them either at home or abroad. The prices paid to farmers were kept artificially low, on the assumption that farmers ignored price signals.

Between 1963 and 1979 the price of consumer goods went up by a factor of twenty-two in Ghana. The price of cocoa in neighboring countries went up by a factor of thirty-six. But the price paid by the cocoa marketing board to Ghana's farmers went up just sixfold. In real terms, therefore, the returns to cocoa farmers vanished. The country's supposedly price-insensitive farmers responded by switching to production of other crops for subsistence, and exports of cocoa collapsed. Peru and Ghana are extreme cases, but they show in the starkest way that prices do matter in the the Third World and that rejecting market economics carries extremely high costs.

The essential elements of a development strategy based on orthodox economics are macroeconomic stability, foreign trade, and strictly limited intervention in the economy. With policies under these three headings, governments can foster enterprise and entrepreneurship, the irreplaceable engines of capitalist growth.

The Macroeconomic Foundation

Experience shows that high and unstable inflation can harm growth. A noninflationary macroeconomic policy is, therefore, a prerequisite for rapid development. Control of government borrowing is the crucial element in such a policy. When public borrowing is excessive, governments are soon obliged to finance it by printing money, and rising inflation then follows. That is why the conventional approach to stabilization (a term that covers steps to reduce an unsustainable trade deficit as well as anti-inflation policies) usually advocates lower public spending and/or higher taxes. The International Monetary Fund has long made programs of this sort a precondition for financial assistance to countries in distress.

These so-called austerity programs have aroused two sorts of controversy. First, some economists question whether big changes in fiscal policy are really needed. In Latin America, for example, some governments sought ''heterodox'' policies to reduce inflation without the recession that the orthodox approach almost always brings on. The heterodox approach argues that in high-inflation countries, the budget deficit is caused mainly by inflation, not the other way round. The argument is twofold. First, because there is a lag between when people earn income and when they must pay taxes on it, high inflation reduces real tax revenues. Second, inflation increases the nominal interest rate (and hence the budgetary cost of servicing past government debt).

Hence the heterodox logic: reduce inflation with direct controls on prices and incomes and a currency reform, and the budget deficit will shrink of its own accord. This method has been tried repeatedly in Brazil and Argentina, where brief success has generally given way to a worse mess than at the outset, and in Israel, where the results were more encouraging. Israel shows that the heterodox can work—that falling inflation does cut public borrowing. What matters is whether the deficit that remains after the heterodox measures are in place is low enough to be noninflationary. In practice, the remaining deficit is almost always too high, and the program fails. Countering inflation almost always requires a dose of austerity.

The second controversy over austerity concerns the costs of this remedy. Many economists argue that orthodox programs put too much of the burden on the poorest parts of society. To cut their budget deficits, governments can either raise taxes or cut spending. Raising more revenue—even if that could be done without harming incentives—is hard because of weak tax administration. So stabilization nearly always involves cuts in public spending. If the cuts fall on food subsidies and welfare spending, goes this argument, they hurt the most vulnerable.

This argument sounds plausible, but in many countries it is wrong. A study by Guy Pfeffermann of the World Bank shows that the beneficiaries of social spending in the developing countries are not the poor. First, more public spending of any sort means more public employment. Bureaucracies in developing countries do not give many jobs to the landless rural poor, to small street traders, to unskilled manual workers, or to the urban unemployed. They recruit from the middle classes, who are, therefore, the first to benefit from public spending.

They often are the second and third to benefit as well. In some countries subsidies have amounted to more than 10 percent of GDP. These mainly go toward making electricity, gasoline, housing, and credit artificially cheaper for consumers. Quite apart from the massive microeconomic damage that these price distortions cause, such subsidies do not reach the poor. Many of the poor do not live in houses, which greatly reduces their need for electricity, and most do not own cars. (Gasoline subsidies alone in Ecuador and Venezuela have been equivalent to several percentage points of GDP.) Although some of the poor would benefit from credit, subsidized credit is not aimed at them and makes the unsubsidized kind harder to get and a lot more expensive. Spending on education is also, as a rule, heavily biased toward the middle classes. In some developing countries, spending per capita on university education exceeds spending per capita on primary education by a factor of thirty. Many of the poor lack access to even the most basic primary education, while the universities remain the publicly funded preserve of the middle class. And in most developing countries the coverage of heavily subsidized social security systems is strongly skewed against the poor. In Brazil in 1984, only 8 percent of workers in the poorest broad sector of the economy (farming) were covered by a social security system. Nearly 80 percent of workers in the most prosperous sector (transport and communications) were covered.

By and large, the scope for cutting public spending in developing countries without hurting the poor is more than enough for stabilization to succeed. In some cases (subsidized credit, for example) a reduction in public spending would actually help the poor directly, even before the broader benefits of macroeconomic stability began to flow back. Admittedly, this is not much help in political terms. It is easy to neglect the poor. That is precisely why this vast system of subsidies does not help them. But the middle classes can shout loudly when the economic distortions that help them are taken away. So the political barriers to getting economic policy right are formidable.

The Gains from Trade

For its *World Development Report* in 1987, the World Bank classified forty-one developing countries according to their openness to trade since the sixties. It classed economies as either inward looking (exports were discouraged) or outward looking (exports were not discouraged), with a further division according to the strength of any trade bias. The World Bank then plotted these groups against a variety of economic indicators.

Growth in income per capita was highest in the strongly outward-looking economies and lowest in the strongly inward-looking ones. The same was true for growth in total GDP and in value added in manufacturing, and for the standard measure of the efficiency of investment. On all these criteria the moderately outward-looking countries also outperformed inward-looking economies, although by a smaller margin. The failure of a strong inward orientation to promote domestic manufacturing—not just exports of manufactures—is particularly striking. The whole point of looking inward had been to industrialize faster.

The three strongly outward-oriented countries in the World Bank's report were Hong Kong, Singapore, and South Korea. Taiwan would have been the fourth if it had been included in the sample, and would have reinforced the message. The four dragons, however, have been more diverse in their policies than is usually assumed. Hong Kong's outward orientation is due to unalloyed free trade. The other three have been interventionist to varying degrees, using export incentives to offset the export-discouraging effects of domestic protection.

South Korea, by some measures the most interventionist dragon, is often cited as proof that intelligent dirigiste, rather than a broadly outward-looking trade policy, is the key to rapid development. This judgment is often based on the false premise that Korea has protected its domestic producers as much as if not more than the inward lookers have protected theirs, with the difference that it has then piled on a lot of incentives for exporters. This is incorrect. In reality, South Korea has had a moderate and declining degree of domestic protection with just enough export promotion to achieve broad neutrality in trade incentives.

Korea's growth surge began in the mid-sixties. Policy began to change in the late fifties. At that time Korea's government placed quantitative restrictions on almost all imports, but the restrictions were looser than in many other developing countries. The government began to provide export incentives to offset its protection for producers of import substitutes. At first this failed to work, perhaps because the currency was overvalued, leaving too great a bias against exports. In the early sixties the government dismantled its multiple exchange-rate system, devalued the currency, and (because devaluation helped exporters) reduced its export subsidies. These liberalizing reforms were the turning point. Exports began to grow rapidly.

In 1967 the government reformed its import control system, greatly reducing the number of imports subject to quotas and began to reduce its tariffs. So as the miracle proceeded in the late sixties and seventies, the background was not just outward orientation (domestic protection offset by export promotion), but a low average level of domestic protection, with relatively little variation in the rates of protection from one sector to another. Toward the end of the seventies, when Korea did increase its support for heavy industry, the economy began to run into trouble. Policymakers acknowledged their mistake and moved back toward liberalization.

The clear consensus among mainstream economists is that outward-looking trade policies are one of the keys to development. But why? The answer from orthodox economics is that trade allows countries to exploit their comparative advantage. Trade enables a country to consume a mix of goods that is different from the mix it produces—with prices in world markets acting as the mediator between the two. Conventional theory proves that trade, as a result, makes both partners unambiguously better off. So long as import barriers and other policies do not drive domestic prices too far away from world prices, market forces are enough to push production and consumption in the right direction. But trade does more than bring about the right mix of products. It also eliminates the inefficiencies in production caused by protection.

Protection may make some domestic producers monopolists or near monopolists, thus introducing an inefficiency directly (because monopolists exploit their market strength by producing less and charging more) and indirectly (because, lacking competition, they have no incentive to keep costs low).

Two of the world's top trade specialists, Professors Jagdish Bhagwati of Columbia University and Anne Krueger of Duke University, have emphasized yet another source of inefficiency pervasive in developing and industrial countries alike: "rent-seeking," or more generally, "directly unproductive profit-seeking." These spring from the efforts of businesses to exploit or evade the distortions caused by protection. For instance, import licensing may drive a wedge between the official price of an intermediate good and the price that a domestic producer is willing to pay.

This "rent" is a potential source of profit for somebody. Resources will be spent in trying to corner the market in licenses, or in bribing the bureaucrats who decide which firms will get them, or in lobbying governments to alter the pattern of protection in ways that favor the lobbyists. Worst of all, resources will be spent in trying to win an increase in the overall level of protection. A study of Turkey (see Grais et al.) found that the costs of rent-seeking in the late seventies were between 5 percent and 10 percent of GDP. Because the study made no allowance for the effect of protection on domestic monopoly power, this is an underestimate of the cost. A study by Joel Bergsman, which did take monopoly effects into account, found that the annual costs of protection were 7 percent of GDP in Brazil, 3 percent in Mexico, 6 percent in Pakistan, and 4 percent in the Philippines. Such results speak for themselves. The evidence shows that trade works; orthodox theory shows why.

Where to Intervene

It is often argued that all the dragons (except Hong Kong) have had highly interventionist governments. Even on the assumption that these interventions, by luck or judgment, left the economies with outward-looking trade regimes, this poses a question. Might their success be due to nothing more profound than the fact that good intervention is better than bad? It is not the extent of intervention that matters, the argument goes, but the skill with which it is done.

It is true that these countries, especially South Korea, have had interventionist governments. This they have in common with almost all developing countries. The difference is not only that they pursued an outward-looking approach to trade (broad lesson number one), but also that this approach molded the forms of intervention they undertook in the domestic economy (broad lesson number two). The net effect (broad lesson number three) was to leave the price system largely intact as a signaling device for the private sector.

More generally, an outward-looking approach to trade does not require laissez-faire (though laissez-faire does require an outward-looking approach to trade). The state has a vital role in development. Paradoxically, however, most of the Third World's highly interventionist governments neglect this role because they are too busy doing things they should not.

Government has several vital jobs to do and no spare resources to waste on other things. The cost of an effective legal system, for instance, is public money well spent. This means countries need rules that define property rights, contracts, liability, bankruptcy, and so on (which most developing countries already have). It also means enforcing those rules effectively (which fewer manage to do). Spending on physical and social infrastructure is essential, for there are good (orthodox) reasons to think that the private sector will provide too little. Numerous studies have shown that the economic returns to spending on primary education, especially for girls, are extremely high. Governments need to do more in such areas, not less, though none of these tasks requires the government to be a monopolist.

Governments have done too little in the areas where they can do some good because they have spread themselves too thin and been far too ambitious in areas where intervention is, at best, unnecessary. Instead of building roads, schools, and village health centers, Third World governments have built prestigious airports, universities, and big-city hospitals. Instead of letting businesses compete, they have created state-run industries and sheltered their extraordinary inefficiencies from foreign and domestic competition.

Advocates of state intervention often claim to be realists. Markets are not perfect, they say, so governments have to step in, especially in developing countries. They are right up to a point. The price system never works perfectly, least of all in developing countries. But it is important to be realistic about governments, too. The past forty years of development experience have shown that no resource is in scarcer supply than good government, and that nothing market forces could devise has done as much harm in the Third World as bad government.

Two Myths

A common argument is that many developing countries will be condemned to economic stagnation, regardless of the economic policies their governments pursue, by two factors beyond their control: their insupportable debts and their lack of homegrown entrepreneurs. Both ideas are wrong.

First, consider debt. The costs of the debt crisis of the eighties have indeed been great. At the margin, foreign capital matters a lot—not just in quantitative terms, but because of the foreign expertise that often comes with it. But the problem of debt, serious though it is, is by no means an insuperable obstacle to growth in the Third World. Even in good times, foreign capital has financed only a small part of the investment undertaken in developing countries. Debt needs to be kept in perspective.

In its *World Development Report 1989*, the World Bank compiled data on financial balances for a sample of fourteen developing countries (some now "highly indebted," others not) for which sufficiently detailed data were available. The figures suggest that the biggest source of capital, by far, in these economies during the seventies and eighties was household saving. This was equivalent, on average, to 13 percent of GDP in the countries in the sample. Businesses saved 9 percent of GDP. The domestic supply of capital—the sum of household saving and business saving—was 22 percent of GDP, while the inflow of foreign capital was only 2 percent of GDP.

After the debt myth comes the myth of the missing (especially African) entrepreneur. The idea that the Third World lacks the spirit of enterprise is laughable. Peasant farmers who switch to another crop in response to a change in their government's marketing arrangements are entrepreneurs. So are the unregistered taxi and minibus operators who keep most Third World cities moving. So are street vendors, perambulating water vendors, money changers, and informal credit brokers. So are the growers of illegal crops such as coca, who in many countries are denied the opportunity of making a decent living by legal means. So are the smugglers of just about anything that do such a roaring trade across Africa's borders, profiting from the massive price distortions that government policies create.

Entrepreneurship admittedly is partly a matter of skills—in choice of technique, in management, in finance, in the ability to read the label on a bag of fertilizer. Skills have to be learned, and in many developing countries they are in short supply. But this supply is not fixed. The success of the green revolution in India and elsewhere shows that farmers are willing to learn new skills when they can see an advantage in doing so. (The green revolution involved the introduction of high-yielding crop varieties that required different methods and more sophisticated inputs such as fertilizer and an assured water supply.)

To see what entrepreneurship in the Third World can achieve, consider the flowering of the garment export business in Bangladesh, one of the poorest countries in the world. This started with a collaboration between Noorul Quader, a bureaucrat-turned-entrepreneur, and the Daewoo Company of South Korea. Quader's new company, Desh, agreed to buy sewing machines from Daewoo and send workers to be trained in South Korea. Once Desh's factory started up, Daewoo would advise on production and handle the marketing in return for royalties of 8 percent of sales. Daewoo did not lend to Desh or take any stake in the business. But it showed Desh how to design a bonded warehouse system, which the government agreed to authorize. This was crucial. In effect, it made garment exporting a special economic zone—an island of free trade within a highly protected economy.

At the end of 1979, Desh's 130 trainees returned from South Korea with three Daewoo engineers to install the machines. Garment production began in April 1980 with 450 machines and 500 workers. In 1980 the company produced 43,000 shirts with a value of $56,000. By 1987 sales had risen to 2.3 million shirts and a value of $5.3 million—a growth rate of 92 percent a year.

Desh did so well that it canceled its collaboration agreement with Daewoo in June 1981, just eighteen months after the startup. It began to do its own marketing and bought its raw materials from other suppliers. It achieved most of its success on its own. Also, the company has suffered heavy defections of its Daewoo-trained staff. Of the initial batch of 130 who visited South Korea in 1980, 115 had left the company by 1987—to start their own garment-exporting businesses. From nothing in 1979, Bangladesh had seven hundred garment-export factories by 1985. They belonged to Desh, to Desh's graduates, or to others following their example.

There is no lack of entrepreneurship in the Third World. To release this huge potential, governments first need to do much less. Above all, they must stop trying to micromanage the process of industrialization, whether through trade policy, industrial licensing, or direct control of state-owned enterprises. But they also need to do more. They must strive to keep public borrowing and inflation in check, while investing adequately in physical and nonphysical infrastructure.

In the early nineties, spurred by the collapse of the socialist model in Eastern Europe, a growing number of developing countries are trying to reorder their economic priorities in this way. If they persevere, the coming decades will be a time of unprecedented advance in the developing world.

—**Clive Crook**

Biography: Clive Crook is the economics editor of *The Economist*.

Further Reading

Bergsman, Joel. "Commercial Policy, Allocative Efficiency and X-efficiency." *Quarterly Journal of Economics* 88, no. 3 (August 1974): 409–33.

Crook, Clive. "The Third World." *The Economist*, September 23, 1989.

Grais, W., et al. "A General Equilibrium Estimation of the Reduction of Tariffs and Quantitative Restrictions in Turkey in 1978." In *General Equilibrium and Trade Policy Modelling*, edited by T. N. Srinivasan and J. Whalley. 1984.

Lal, Deepak. *The Poverty of Development Economics*. 1985.

Pfeffermann, Guy. "Public Expenditure in Latin America: Effects on Poverty." World Bank discussion paper no. 5.

Soto, Hernando de. *The Other Path*. 1989.

World Bank. *World Development Report 1987*. 1987.

———. *World Development Report 1989*. 1989.

BIOGRAPHIES

Editor's note: Any choice of whom to include in biographies is inherently subjective. I tried to make it less so by using two criteria. First, all economists who won the Nobel Prize in economic science are included. The reason is that those who were judged by their peers in Sweden to be worthy of the Nobel Prize should be written up in any encyclopedia of economics. Second, I omitted all economists who were born after 1920 and still alive in June 1992 unless they had won the Nobel Prize. I chose this criterion because there are too many noteworthy younger economists to do them all justice in a book of this length. All biographies are written by me unless otherwise noted.

Nobel Memorial Prize Winners in Economic Science

■ The Nobel Prize was established by the will of Alfred Nobel (1833–96), the Swedish chemist who invented dynamite, to recognize humanitarian endeavors in physics, chemistry, physiology or medicine, literature, and peace. A prize in economics was introduced in 1969 after the Bank of Sweden donated funds for its monetary awards. In 1992 the economic prize carried a cash award of $1.2 million.

Nominations for the prize are solicited through invitation only, with over a thousand invitations per prize category, and require a written statement in support of the nomination. Committees then evaluate the nominees and make their recommendations to the appropriate prize-awarding organization. All the selection work for the Nobel Prize is conducted in secrecy. In economics the prize is awarded by the Royal Swedish Academy of Sciences. To date, twenty-one Americans have been honored with the prize.

The following individuals were awarded the Nobel Prize in economics:

Ragnar Frisch, Jan Tinbergen—1969
Paul Samuelson—1970
Simon Kuznets—1971
Kenneth Arrow, John Hicks—1972
Wassily Leontief—1973
Friedrich A. Hayek, Gunnar Myrdal—1974
Leonid Kantorovich, Tjalling C. Koopmans—1975
Milton Friedman—1976
James Meade, Bertil Ohlin—1977
Herbert Simon—1978
W. Arthur Lewis, Theodore Schultz—1979
Lawrence Klein—1980

James Tobin—1981
George Stigler—1982
Gerard Debreu—1983
Richard Stone—1984
Franco Modigliani—1985
James M. Buchanan—1986
Robert Solow—1987
Maurice Allais—1988
Trygve Haavelmo—1989
Harry Markowitz, Merton Miller, William Sharpe—1990
Ronald H. Coase—1991
Gary S. Becker—1992

Chairmen of the Council of Economic Advisers

■ The Council of Economic Advisers (CEA) is the most prestigious group of applied economists in the United States. The CEA, which was formed after World War II, advises the U.S. president on economic policy. Presidents tend to appoint the three members, including the chairman, from their own party. Yet the advice given is relatively nonpartisan. Below the chairman and the two members are the approximately 15 senior and junior economists. Economists at all levels are appointed for their expertise in policy economics. On macroeconomics, Democratic-appointed chairmen (the last one before the current chairman, Laura Tyson, was Charles Schultze, whose service ended when President Jimmy Carter left office) and members have believed that fiscal policy is more potent than monetary policy. Republican-appointed economists tend to believe that fiscal policy is relatively impotent and that monetary policy is much more powerful. On many microeconomic issues, CEA economists at all levels and in Republican and Democratic councils agree. They favor free trade and free markets and tend to oppose price controls and regulation, although current chairman Laura Tyson is a notable exception on free trade.

Council chairmen and their dates of service (with the president under whom they served in parentheses) are listed below.

Edwin G. Nourse (Truman)—1946–49
Leon H. Keyserling (Truman)—1950–53
Arthur F. Burns (Eisenhower)—1953–56
Raymond J. Saulnier (Eisenhower)—1956–61
Walter W. Heller (Kennedy, Johnson)—
    1961–64
Gardner Ackley (Johnson)—1964–68
Arthur M. Okun (Johnson)—1968–69
Paul W. McCracken (Nixon)—1969–71

Herbert Stein (Nixon)—1972–74
Alan Greenspan (Ford)—1974–77
Charles L. Schultze (Carter)—1977–81
Murray L. Weidenbaum (Reagan)—1981–82
Martin Feldstein (Reagan)—1982–84
Beryl W. Sprinkel (Reagan)—1985–89
Michael J. Boskin (Bush)—1989–93
Laura Tyson (Clinton)—1993–

Presidents of the American Economic Association

■ The American Economic Association is the largest organization of professional economists in the United States and in the world. It was organized at Saratoga, New York, on September 9, 1885. The title of president of the AEA is one of the highest honors that can be bestowed on an economist. The following are the past presidents of the AEA and their years of service (with their university or institute affiliations in parentheses).

Francis A. Walker (MIT)—1886–92
Charles F. Dunbar (Harvard)—1893
John B. Clark (Columbia)—1894–95
Henry C. Adams (Michigan)—1896–97
Arthur T. Hadley (Yale)—1898–99
Richard T. Ely (Wisconsin)—1900–01
Edwin R. A. Seligman (Columbia)—1902–03
Frank W. Taussig (Harvard)—1904–05
Jeremiah W. Jenks (Cornell)—1906–07
Simon N. Patten (Pennsylvania)—1908
Davis R. Dewey (MIT)—1909
Edmund J. James (Illinois)—1910
Henry W. Farnam (Yale)—1911
Frank A. Fetter (Princeton)—1912
David Kinley (Illinois)—1913
John H. Gray (Minnesota)—1914
Walter F. Willcox (Cornell)—1915
Thomas N. Carver (Harvard)—1916
John R. Commons (Wisconsin)—1917
Irving Fisher (Yale)—1918
Henry B. Gardner (Brown)—1919
Herbert J. Davenport (Cornell)—1920
Jacob H. Hollander (Johns Hopkins)—1921
Henry R. Seager (Columbia)—1922
Carl C. Plehn (California)—1923
Wesley C. Mitchell (Columbia)—1924
Allyn A. Young (Harvard)—1925
Edwin W. Kemmerer (Princeton)—1926
Thomas S. Adams (Yale)—1927
Fred M. Taylor (Michigan)—1928
Edwin F. Gay (Harvard)—1929

Matthew B. Hammond (Ohio State)—1930
Ernest L. Bogart (Illinois)—1931
George E. Barnett (Johns Hopkins)—1932
William Z. Ripley (Harvard)—1933
Harry A. Millis (Chicago)—1934
John M. Clark (Columbia)—1935
Alvin S. Johnson (New School)—1936
Oliver M. W. Sprague (Harvard)—1937
Alvin H. Hansen (Harvard)—1938
Jacob Viner (Chicago)—1939
Frederick C. Mills (Columbia)—1940
Sumner H. Slichter (Harvard)—1941
Edwin G. Nourse (Brookings)—1942
Albert B. Wolfe (Ohio State)—1943
Joseph S. Davis (Stanford)—1944
I. L. Sharfman (Michigan)—1945
E. A. Goldenweiser (Institute for Advanced Study)—1946
Paul H. Douglas (Chicago)—1947
Joseph A. Schumpeter (Harvard)—1948
Howard S. Ellis (California)—1949
Frank H. Knight (Chicago)—1950
John H. Williams (Harvard)—1951
Harold A. Innis (Toronto)—1952
Calvin B. Hoover (Duke)—1953
Simon Kuznets (Pennsylvania)—1954
John D. Black (Harvard)—1955
Edwin E. Witte (Wisconsin)—1956
Morris A. Copeland (Cornell)—1957
George W. Stocking (Vanderbilt)—1958
Arthur F. Burns (Columbia)—1959

Theodore W. Schultz (Chicago)—1960
Paul A. Samuelson (MIT)—1961
Edward S. Mason (Harvard)—1962
Gottfried Haberler (Harvard)—1963
George J. Stigler (Chicago)—1964
Joseph J. Spengler (Duke)—1965
Fritz Machlup (Princeton)—1966
Milton Friedman (Chicago)—1967
Kenneth E. Boulding (Colorado)—1968
William J. Fellner (Yale)—1969
Wassily Leontief (Harvard)—1970
James Tobin (Yale)—1971
John Kenneth Galbraith (Harvard)—1972
Kenneth J. Arrow (Harvard)—1973
Walter W. Heller (Minnesota)—1974
Robert Aaron Gordon (California)—1975
Franco Modigliani (MIT)—1976
Lawrence R. Klein (Pennsylvania)—1977

Jacob Marschak (California)—1978
Tjalling C. Koopmans (Yale)—1978
Robert M. Solow (MIT)—1979
Moses Abramovitz (Stanford)—1980
William J. Baumol (Princeton)—1981
Gardner Ackley (Michigan)—1982
W. Arthur Lewis (Princeton)—1983
Charles L. Schultze (Brookings)—1984
Charles P. Kindleberger (MIT)—1985
Alice M. Rivlin (Brookings)—1986
Gary S. Becker (Chicago)—1987
Robert Eisner (Northwestern)—1988
Joseph A. Pechman (Brookings)—1989
Gerard Debreu (California)—1990
Thomas C. Schelling (Maryland)—1991
William Vickrey (Columbia)—1992
Zvi Griliches (Harvard)—1993

Biographies

Alchian, Armen (1914–   )—Armen Alchian, an American economist born in Fresno, California, is in many ways like Ronald Coase (see COASE). Like Coase, Alchian has published only a few articles, but very few unimportant ones. Also, like Coase's articles, some of Alchian's are widely cited.

Many students and others who read economics are disturbed by economists' assumptions that companies maximize profits. One of their objections is that managers of companies do not know enough to be able to maximize profits. In 1950 Alchian presented a thoughtful response to this objection in his first major article, "Uncertainty, Evolution and Economic Theory." Alchian argued that even though all companies may not maximize profits, those that survive will be ones whose managers, by luck or by design, came close to maximizing profits. Therefore, those that we observe will have maximized profits. So for the long term at least, argued Alchian, for economists to derive the standard conclusions from the profit-maximization assumption, they do not need to show that all companies try to maximize profits.

While in the U.S. Army Air Forces during World War II, Alchian did some of the early work on the learning curve—the curve that relates unit costs to cumulative output. His article on the learning curve in aircraft production was based on statistical work he did during the war, but could not be published until 1963 because it was based on classified information.

Alchian is also known for his textbook, *University Economics* (now called *Exchange and Production*), coauthored with William R. Allen.

All biographies, except for those of Henry George and Karl Marx, are written by David R. Henderson.

That text is unique in economics. It is much more literary and humorous than any other modern economics textbook that deals with complex issues for an undergraduate audience. Example: "Since the fiasco in the Garden of Eden, most of what we get is by sweat, strain, and anxiety." It also welcomes controversy rather than shying away from it, in the process daring the reader to disagree. Take, for example, Alchian and Allen's discussion of violence:

> Before condemning violence (physical force) as a means of social control, note that its threatened or actual use is widely practiced and respected—at least when applied successfully on a national scale. Julius Caesar conquered Gaul and was honored by the Romans; had he simply roughed up the local residents, he would have been damned as a gangster. Alexander the Great, who conquered the Near East, was not regarded by the Greeks as a ruffian, nor was Charlemagne after he conquered Europe. Europeans acquired and divided—and redivided—America by force. Lenin is not regarded in Russia as a subversive. Nor is Spain's Franco, Cuba's Castro, Nigeria's Gowon, Uganda's Amin, China's Mao, our George Washington.

Because of its literary quality and complexity, their text generally did not work with undergraduate or even M.B.A. classes. But its impact was out of all proportion to its sales. Many graduate students, particularly at the University of California at Los Angeles, where Alchian has taught since 1964, and at the University of Washington (where Alchian student Steven Cheung taught), learned their basic economics from this book.

Some of the University of Washington students went on to write best-selling textbooks that made many of Alchian and Allen's insights more understandable to an undergraduate audience. Alchian and Allen's textbook was truly a public good, a good that created large benefits for which its creators could not charge. And while Alchian played the role of selfish cynic in his class, some who studied under him had the feeling that he put so much care and work into his low-selling text—and into his students—because of his concern for humanity.

Other than through his text, Alchian's largest impact was in the economics of property rights (he has written the article on property rights in this encyclopedia). Most of his work in property rights can be summed up in one sentence: you tell me the rules and I'll tell you what outcomes to expect. In their textbook, for example, Alchian and Allen ask why the organizers of the Rose Bowl refuse to sell tickets to the highest bidders and instead give up wealth by underpricing the tickets. Their answer is that the people who make the decision on ticket prices do not have property rights in the tickets, so the wealth that is given up by underpricing would not have accrued to them anyway. But the decision makers can give underpriced tickets to their friends and associates. This same line of reasoning has been used by Thomas Hazlett, former chief economist at the Federal Communications Commission, to explain why Rep. John Dingell has blocked the FCC's attempts to auction off the electromagnetic spectrum, and has instead favored giving it away.

Alchian also used the analysis of property rights to explain the incidence of discrimination. In a coauthored paper with Reuben Kessel, Alchian, who was himself subject to discrimination as an Armenian, pointed out that discrimination was more pervasive in private firms whose profits were regulated by the government. Alchian and Kessel explained that this is what the analysis of property rights would

predict. Discrimination is costly, not just to those discriminated against, but also to those who discriminate. The discriminators give up the chance to deal with someone with whom they could engage in mutually beneficial exchange. Therefore, argued Alchian and Kessel, discrimination would be more prevalent in situations where those who discriminate do not bear much of the cost from doing so. A for-profit company whose profits are not regulated would see the cost of discrimination in its bottom line in the form of lower profits. A company whose profits were limited and that was already at the limit would face no cost from discriminating. Alchian and Kessel used this analysis to explain why regulated utilities discriminated against Jews and why labor unions discriminated against blacks. This analysis explains why Alchian has never trusted government—but has trusted free markets—to reduce discrimination.

Before teaching at UCLA, Alchian was an economist with the RAND Corporation.

Selected Works

Economic Forces at Work. 1977.
(With W. R. Allen.) *Exchange and Production*. 1983.
"Some Economics of Property Rights." *Il Politico* 30 (1965): 816–29.
"Uncertainty, Evolution and Economic Theory." *Journal of Political Economy* 58 (June 1950): 211–21.

Allais, Maurice (1911–   )—In 1988 Maurice Allais became the first French citizen to win the Nobel Prize in economics. He won it for his contribution to the understanding of market behavior and the efficient use of resources. Allais also showed that his insights could be applied to help set efficient prices for state-owned monopolies, of which France had many. Allais' work paralleled, and sometimes preceded, similar work done by English-speaking economists

Sir John Hicks and Paul Samuelson. He also proved a result in growth theory in 1947 that had been credited to Edmund Phelps in 1961.

Allais did not get credit as early as his English counterparts because his work was in French. Commented Samuelson: "Had Allais' earliest writings been in English, a generation of economic theory would have taken a different course." Allais also helped revive the quantity theory of money (monetarism). In utility theory Allais discovered and resolved a paradox about how people behave when choosing between various risks; it is now called the Allais paradox.

From 1937 to 1944, Allais worked in the French state-owned mine administration. In 1944 he became a professor at the Ecole National Supérieure des Mines de Paris and is still there. He is also the research director at the National French Research Council. He was named an officer of the Legion of Honor in 1977.

Selected Works

"Growth and Inflation." *Journal of Money, Credit and Banking* 1, no. 3 (August 1969): 355–426.
"A Restatement of the Quantity Theory of Money." *American Economic Review* 56 (December 1966): 1123–57.
"The Role of Capital in Economic Development." In *The Econometric Approach to Development Planning*. 1965.

Arrow, Kenneth (1921–)—American economist Kenneth Arrow is probably known best for his Ph.D. dissertation (on which his book *Social Choice and Individual Values* was based). In it Arrow proved his famous "impossibility theorem." He showed that under certain assumptions about people's preferences between options, it is always impossible to find a voting rule under which one option emerges as the most preferred. The simplest example is Condorcet's paradox, named after an eigh-teenth-century French mathematician. Condorcet's paradox is as follows: There are three candidates for office; let's call them Bush (B), Clinton (C), and Perot (P). One-third of the voters rank them B, C, P. One-third rank them C, P, B. The final third rank them P, B, C. Then a majority will prefer Bush to Clinton, and a majority will prefer Clinton to Perot. It would seem, therefore, that a majority would prefer Bush to Perot. But in fact a majority prefers Perot to Bush. Arrow's more complicated proof is more general and is about political choice more than it is about economics.

Arrow went on to show, in a 1951 article, that a competitive economy in equilibrium is efficient and that any efficient allocation could be reached by having the government use lump-sum taxes to redistribute, and then letting the market work. One clear-cut implication of this finding was, and is, that the government should not control prices to redistribute income, but instead, if it redistributes at all, should do so directly. Arrow's insight is part of the reason economists are almost unanimously against price controls.

Arrow also showed, with coauthor Gerard Debreu, that under certain conditions an economy reaches a general equilibrium—that is, an equilibrium in which all markets are in equilibrium. Using new mathematical techniques, Arrow and Debreu showed that one of the conditions for general equilibrium is that there must be futures markets for all goods. Of course, we know that this condition does not hold—you cannot buy a contract for future delivery of a labor service, for example. This fact has led some economists to doubt the usefulness of Arrow's and Debreu's finding.

Arrow was also one of the first economists to note the existence of a learning curve. His basic idea was that as producers increase output of a product, they gain experience and become more efficient. Wrote Arrow: "The role of experience in increasing productivity has not gone unobserved, though the relation has yet to be absorbed into the main corpus of economic theory.'' Thirty years after Arrow's article, the learning curve insight has still not been fully integrated into mainstream economic analysis.

Arrow has also done excellent work on the economics of uncertainty. His work in that area is still a standard source for economists.

In 1972 Arrow, jointly with Sir John Hicks, won the Nobel Prize in economics. It was awarded for ''pioneering contributions to general equilibrium theory and welfare theory.''

Arrow has spent most of his professional life on the economics faculties of Stanford University (1949–68 and 1980–present) and Harvard University (1968–79).

Selected Works

''The Economic Implications of Learning by Doing.'' *Review of Economic Studies* 29 (June 1962): 155–73.
Essays in the Theory of Risk-Bearing. 1971.
(With Gerard Debreu.) ''Existence of a Competitive Equilibrium for a Competitive Economy.'' *Econometrica* 22, no. 3 (July 1954): 265–90.
(With Frank Hahn.) *General Competitive Analysis.* 1971.
Social Choice and Individual Values. 1951.

Bastiat, Frédéric (1801–50)—Joseph Schumpeter described Bastiat nearly a century after his death as ''the most brilliant economic journalist who ever lived.'' Orphaned at the age of nine, Bastiat tried his hand at commerce, farming, and insurance sales. In 1825, after he inherited his grandfather's estate, he quit working, established a discussion group, and read widely in economics.

Bastiat made no original contribution to economics, if we use ''contribution'' the way most economists use it. That is, we cannot associate one law, theorem, or path-breaking empirical study with his name. But in a broader sense Bastiat made a big contribution: his fresh and witty expressions of economic truths made them so understandable and compelling that the truths became hard to ignore.

Bastiat was supremely effective at popularizing free market economics. When he learned of Richard Cobden's campaign against the British Corn Laws (restrictions on the import of wheat, barley, rye, and oats), Bastiat vowed to become the ''French Cobden.'' He subsequently published a series of articles attacking protectionism that brought him instant acclaim. In 1846 he established the Association of Free Trade in Paris and his own weekly newspaper. He waged a witty assault against socialists and protectionists.

Bastiat's ''A Petition,'' usually referred to now as ''The Petition of the Candlemakers,'' displays his rhetorical skill and rakish tone, as this excerpt illustrates:

> We are suffering from the ruinous competition of a foreign rival who apparently works under conditions so far superior to our own for the production of light, that he is flooding the domestic market with it at an incredibly low price. . . . This rival . . . is none other than the sun. . . .
>
>   . . . We ask you to be so good as to pass a law requiring the closing of all windows, dormers, skylights, inside and outside shutters, curtains, casements, bull's-eyes, deadlights and blinds; in short, all openings, holes, chinks, and fissures. . . .

This reductio ad absurdum of protectionism was so effective that one of the most successful postwar economics textbooks, *Economics* by Paul A. Samuelson, quotes the candlemakers' petition at the head of the chapter on protectionism.

Bastiat also emphasized the unintended consequences of government policy (he called them the ''unseen'' consequences). Friedrich Hayek credits Bastiat with this important insight: if we judge economic policy solely by its immediate effects, we will miss all of its unintended and longer-run effects and will undermine economic freedom, which delivers benefits that are not part of anyone's conscious design. Much of Hayek's work, and some of Milton Friedman's, was an exploration and elaboration of this insight.

Selected Works

Economic Harmonies, translated by W. H. Boyers. 1964.

Economic Sophisms, translated by A. Goddard. 1964.

Selected Essays on Political Economy, translated by S. Caine. 1964.

Becker, Gary Stanley (1930–)—Gary S. Becker won the 1992 Nobel Prize in economics for ''having extended the domain of economic theory to aspects of human behavior which had previously been dealt with—if at all—by other social science disciplines such as sociology, demography and criminology.''

Becker's unusually wide applications of economics started early. In 1955 he wrote his doctoral dissertation at the University of Chicago on the economics of discrimination. Among other things, Becker successfully challenged the Marxist view that discrimination helps the person who discriminates. Becker pointed out that if an employer refuses to hire a productive worker simply because of his skin color, that employer loses out on a valuable opportunity. In short, discrimination is costly to the person who discriminates.

Becker showed that discrimination would be less pervasive in more competitive industries because companies that discriminated would lose market share to companies that did not. He also presented evidence that discrimination was more pervasive in more regulated and, therefore, less competitive industries. The idea that discrimination is costly to the discriminator is common sense among economists today, and that is due to Becker.

In the early sixties Becker moved on to the fledgling area of human capital. One of the founders of the concept (the other being Theodore Schultz), Becker pointed out what again seems like common sense but was new at the time: education is an investment. Education adds to our human capital just as other investments add to physical capital. (For more on this, see Becker's article, HUMAN CAPITAL, in this encyclopedia.)

One of Becker's insights was that a major cost of investing in education is one's time. Possibly that insight led him to his next major area, the study of the allocation of time within a family. Applying the economist's concept of opportunity cost, Becker showed that as market wages rose, the cost to married women of staying home would rise. They would want to work outside the home and economize on household tasks by buying more appliances and fast food.

Not even crime escaped Becker's keen analytic mind. In the late sixties he wrote a trailblazing article whose working assumption was that the decision to commit crime is a function of the costs and benefits of crime. From this assumption he concluded that the way to reduce crime is to raise the probability of punishment or to make the punishment more severe. His insights into crime, like his insights on discrimination and human capital, helped spawn a new branch of economics.

In the seventies Becker extended his insights on allocation of time within a family. He used the economic approach to explain the decisions to have children and to educate them, and the decisions to marry and to divorce.

Becker was a professor at Columbia University from 1957 to 1969. Except for that period, he has spent his entire career at the University of Chicago. He holds joint appointments in the departments of economics and sociology.

Becker won the John Bates Clark Award of the American Economic Association in 1967 and was president of that association in 1987.

Selected Works

"Crime and Punishment: An Economic Approach." *Journal of Political Economy* 76, no. 2 (March/April 1968): 169–217.
The Economics of Discrimination, 2d ed. 1971.
Human Capital, 2d ed. 1975.
"A Theory of the Allocation of Time." *Economic Journal* 40, no. 299 (September 1965): 493–508.
Treatise on the Family. 1981.

Bentham, Jeremy (1748–1832)—British economist Jeremy Bentham is most often associated with his theory of utilitarianism. Bentham's views ran counter to Adam Smith's vision of "natural rights." He believed in utilitarianism, or the idea that all social actions should be evaluated by the axiom "It is the greatest happiness of the greatest number that is the measure of right and wrong." Unlike Smith, Bentham believed that there were no natural rights to be interfered with.

Trained in law, Bentham never practiced, choosing instead to focus on judicial and legal reform. His reform plans went beyond rewriting legislative acts to include detailed administrative plans to implement his proposals. In his plan for prisons, workhouses, and other institutions, Bentham devised compensation schemes, building designs, worker timetables, and even new accounting systems. A guiding principle of Bentham's schemes was that incentives should be designed "to make it each man's interest to observe on every occasion that conduct which it is his duty to observe." Interestingly, Bentham's thinking led him to the conclusion, one he shared with Smith, that professors should not be salaried.

In his early years Bentham professed a free-market approach. He argued, for example, that interest rates should be free from government control. But by the end of his life, he had shifted to a more interventionist stance. He predated Keynes in his advocacy of expansionist monetary policies to achieve full employment and advocated a range of interventions, including the minimum wage and guaranteed employment.

His publications were few, but Bentham influenced many during his lifetime and lived to see some of his political reforms enacted shortly before his death in London at the age of eighty-four.

Selected Works

Defence of Usury. 1787.
An Introduction to the Principles of Morals and Legislation. 1789. Reprint, edited by J. H. Burns and H. L. A. Hart. 1970.
The Theory of Legislation. 1802. Reprint, edited by C. K. Ogden. 1931.

Böhm-Bawerk, Eugen von (1851–1914)—Eugen von Böhm-Bawerk was one of the leading members of the Austrian school of economics—an approach to economic thought founded by Carl Menger and augmented by Knut Wicksell, Ludwig von Mises, Friedrich A. Hayek, and Sir John Hicks. Böhm-Bawerk's work became so well known that before World War I, his Marxist contemporaries regarded the Austrians as their typical bourgeois, intellectual enemy. His theories of interest and capital were catalysts in the development of economics, but today little attention is paid to his original work.

Böhm-Bawerk gave three reasons why interest rates were positive. First, people's marginal utility of income will fall over time because they expect higher income in the future. Second, for psychological reasons the marginal utility of a good declines with time. For both reasons, which economists now call "positive time-preference," wrote Böhm-Bawerk, people were willing to pay positive interest rates to get access to resources in the present, and insisted on being paid interest to give up such access. Economists have accepted both as valid reasons for positive time-preference.

But Böhm-Bawerk's third reason—the "technical superiority of present over future goods"—was more controversial and harder to understand. Production, he noted, is "roundabout," meaning that it takes time. It uses capital, which is produced, to transform nonproduced factors of production—such as land and labor—into output. Roundabout production methods mean that the same amount of input can yield a greater output. Böhm-Bawerk reasoned that the net return to capital was the result of the greater value produced by roundaboutness.

An example helps illustrate the point. As the leader of a primitive fishing village, you are able to send out the townspeople to catch enough fish, with their bare hands, to ensure the village's survival for one day. But if you forgo consumption of fish for one day and use that labor to produce nets, hooks, and lines—capital—each fisherman can catch more fish the following day and the days thereafter. Capital is productive.

Further investment in capital, argued Böhm-Bawerk, increases roundaboutness, i.e., lengthens the production period. On this basis Böhm-Bawerk concluded that the net physical productivity of capital would lead to positive interest rates even if the first two reasons did not hold.

Although his theory of capital is one of the cornerstones of Austrian economics, modern mainstream economists pay no attention to Böhm-Bawerk's analysis of roundaboutness. Instead, they accept Irving Fisher's approach of just assuming that there are investment opportunities that make capital productive. Nevertheless, Böhm-Bawerk's approach helped to pave the way for modern interest theory.

Böhm-Bawerk was also one of the first economists to discuss Karl Marx's views seriously. He argued that interest does not exist due to exploitation of workers. Workers would get the whole of what they helped produce only if production were instantaneous. But because production is roundabout, he wrote, some of the product that Marx attributed to workers must go to finance this roundaboutness, i.e., must go to capital. Böhm-Bawerk noted that interest would have to be paid no matter who owned the capital. Mainstream economists still accept this argument.

Böhm-Bawerk was born in Vienna and studied law at the university there. After teaching at the University of Innsbruck and serving in the civil service, he was appointed minister of finance during the years 1895, 1897, and 1900. He left the ministry in 1904 and taught economics at the University of Vienna until his death in 1914.

Selected Works

Capital and Interest, vol. 1. 1884. Reprint. 1959. *Shorter Classics.* 1962.

Buchanan, James M. (1919–)—James Buchanan is the cofounder, along with Gordon Tullock, of public choice theory (see PUBLIC CHOICE THEORY). Buchanan entered the University of Chicago's graduate economics program as a "libertarian socialist." After six weeks of taking Frank Knight's course in price theory, recalls Buchanan, he had been converted into a zealous free marketer.

Buchanan's next big conversion came while reading an article in German by Swedish economist Knut Wicksell. The obscure 1896 article's message was that only taxes and government spending that are unanimously approved can be justified. That way, argued Wicksell, taxes used to pay for programs would have to be taken from those who benefited from those programs. Wicksell's idea contradicted the mainstream forties' view, still the mainstream view, that there need be no connection between what a taxpayer pays and what he receives in benefits. But Buchanan found it persuasive. He translated the essay into English and started thinking more along Wicksell's lines.

One of the products of his thinking was a book, coauthored with Gordon Tullock, titled *The Calculus of Consent.* They showed that the unanimity requirement is unworkable in practice. They then considered modifications to the rule, what they called "workable unanimity." Their book, along with Anthony Downs's *An Economic Theory of Democracy*, helped start the field of public choice and is now considered a classic. Together, Buchanan and Tullock also started the academic journal *Public Choice.*

Perhaps Buchanan's most important contribution to economics is his distinction between two levels of public choice—the initial level at which a constitution is chosen, and the postconstitutional level. The first is like setting rules of a game, and the second is like playing the game within the rules. Buchanan has proselytized his fellow economists to think more about the first level instead of mucking about as political players at the second level. To spread this way of thinking, Buchanan has even started a new journal called *Constitutional Economics.*

Buchanan also believes that because costs are subjective, much of welfare economics—cost-benefit analysis, and so on—is wrongheaded. He spells out these views in detail in *Cost and Choice*, an uncommonly impassioned economics book. Yet Buchanan has not persuaded most of his economist colleagues on this issue.

Buchanan was awarded the 1986 Nobel Prize in economics for "his development of the contractual and constitutional bases for the theory of economic and political decision making."

Buchanan is a southerner and proud of his heritage. He was born in Murfreeboro, Tennessee, and has spent most of his academic life in Virginia, first at the University of Virginia, then at Virginia Polytechnic Institute and State University, and most recently, at George Mason University. In 1969 Buchanan became the first director of the Center for the Study of Public Choice. He was president of the Southern Economic Association in 1963 and of the Western Economic Association in 1983 and 1984, and vice president of the American Economic Association in 1971.

Selected Works

(With Gordon Tullock.) *The Calculus of Consent: Logical Foundations of Constitutional Democracy.* 1962.
Cost and Choice. 1969.
The Demand and Supply of Public Goods. 1968.
Freedom in Constitutional Contract. 1977.
(With Robert P. Tollison.) *The Limits of Liberty.* 1975.
(With Geoffrey Brennan.) *The Power to Tax.* 1980.

Burns, Arthur Frank (1904–1987)—Arthur F. Burns is best known for having been chairman of the Federal Reserve System from 1970 to 1978. His appointment by President Richard Nixon capped a career of empirical studies of the economy and particularly of business cycles. In a 1934 study based on his Ph.D. dissertation, Burns had noted the almost universal tendency of industries to slow down after an initial growth spurt. Burns pointed out that this tendency did not imply slow growth for the whole economy because new industries continued to appear.

A later book, *Measuring Business Cycles*, coauthored with Wesley Mitchell, was a massive empirical study of previous business cycles. Burns and Mitchell distilled a large number of statistical indicators of recessions and expansions into one signal of turning points in the U.S. business cycle. Their book was published by the National Bureau of Economic Research, a private nonprofit research institute. The NBER is now the organization that announces when recessions begin and end. Much of NBER's approach is based on work done by Burns and Mitchell. Their book, more than any other single accomplishment, gave Burns a reputation as an expert in business cycle forecasting.

Burns earned all his degrees at Columbia University and did all his teaching there. From 1953 to 1956, he was chairman of President Eisenhower's Council of Economic Advisers. From 1957 to 1967, he was president of the NBER, and in 1959, president of the American Economic Association. From 1981 to 1985 Burns was the U.S. ambassador to the Federal Republic of Germany.

Selected Works

(With W. C. Mitchell.) *Measuring Business Cycles.* 1946.
Production Trends in the United States since 1870. 1934.

Cassel, Gustav (1866–1945)—Gustav Cassel, a Swedish economist, developed the theory of exchange rates known as purchasing power parity. He did so in some post–World War I memoranda for the League of Nations. The basic concept can be made clear with an example. If 2 U.S. dollars buy one bushel of wheat in the United States, and if 1.6 German marks exchange for 1 U.S. dollar, then the price of a bushel of wheat in Germany should be 3.2 German marks (2 × 1.6). In other words, there should be parity between the purchasing power of one U.S. dollar in the United States and the purchasing power of its exchange value in Germany.

Cassel believed that if an exchange rate was not at parity, it was in disequilibrium and that

either the exchange rate or the purchasing power would adjust until parity was achieved. The reason is arbitrage. If wheat sold for $2.00 in the United States and for DM4 ($2.50) in Germany, then arbitragers could buy wheat in the United States and sell it in Germany and would do so until the price differential was eliminated.

Economists now realize that purchasing power parity would hold if all of a country's goods were traded internationally. But most goods are not. If the price of a hamburger in the United States was $1.00 and in Germany was $1.50, arbitragers would not buy hamburgers in the United States and resell them in Germany. Transportation costs and storage costs would more than wipe out the gain from arbitrage. Nevertheless, economists still take seriously the concept of purchasing power parity. They often use it as a starting point for predicting exchange rate changes. If, for example, Israel's annual inflation rate is 20 percent and the U.S. inflation rate is 4 percent, chances are high that the Israeli shekel will lose value in exchange for the U.S. dollar.

Cassel was a professor of economics at the University of Stockholm from 1903 to 1936. His dying words were ''A world currency!''

Selected Works

The World's Monetary Problems. 1921. (A collection of two memoranda presented to the International Financial Conference of the League of Nations in Brussels in 1920 and to the Financial Committee of the League of Nations in September 1921.)

Coase, Ronald H. (1910–   )—Ronald Coase is an unusual economist for the twentieth century, and highly unusual for a Nobel Prize winner (he won in 1991). First, his writings are sparse. In a sixty-year career he wrote only about a dozen significant papers—and very few insignificant ones. Second, he uses little or no mathematics, disdaining what he calls "black-board economics." Yet his impact on economics has been profound. That impact stems almost entirely from two of his articles, one of which was published when he was twenty seven. The other was published twenty-three years later.

Coase conceived of the first article, "The Nature of the Firm," while still an undergraduate on a trip to the United States from his native Britain. At the time he was a socialist, and he dropped in on perennial presidential candidate of the Socialist party Norman Thomas. He also visited Ford and General Motors and came up with a puzzle: how could economists say that Lenin was wrong in thinking that the Russian economy could be run like one big factory, when some pretty big firms in the United States seemed to be run very well? In answering his own question, Coase came up with a fundamental insight about why firms exist. Firms are like centrally planned economies, he wrote, but unlike the latter, they are formed because of people's voluntary choices. But why do people make these choices? The answer, wrote Coase, is "marketing costs." (Economists now use the term "transactions costs.") If markets were costless to use, firms would not exist. Instead, people would make arm's-length transactions. But because markets are costly to use, the most efficient production process often takes place in a firm. His explanation of why firms exist is now the accepted one and has given rise to a whole literature on the issue. Coase's article was cited 169 times in academic journals between 1966 and 1980.

"The Problem of Social Cost," Coase's other widely cited article (661 citations between 1966 and 1980), was even more path-breaking. Indeed, it gave rise to the field called law and economics. Economists B.C. (Before Coase) of virtually all political persuasions had accepted British economist Arthur Pigou's idea that if, say, a cattle rancher's cows destroy his neighboring farmer's crops, the government should stop the rancher from letting his cattle roam free or should at least tax him for doing so. Otherwise, believed economists, the cattle would continue to destroy crops because the rancher would have no incentive to stop them.

But Coase challenged the accepted view. He pointed out that if the rancher had no legal liability for destroying the farmer's crops, and if transaction costs were zero, the farmer could come to a mutually beneficial agreement with the rancher under which the farmer paid the rancher to cut back on his herd of cattle. This would happen, argued Coase, if the damage from additional cattle exceeded the rancher's net returns on these cattle. If for example, the rancher's net return on a steer was two dollars, then the rancher would accept some amount over two dollars to give up the additional steer. If the steer was doing three dollars' worth of harm to the crops, then the farmer would be willing to pay the rancher up to three dollars to get rid of the steer. A mutually beneficial bargain would be struck.

Coase considered what would happen if the courts made the rancher liable for the damage caused by his steers. Economists B.C. had thought that the number of steers raised by the rancher would be affected. But Coase showed that the only thing affected would be the wealth of the rancher and the farmer; the number of cattle and the amount of crop damage, he showed, would be the same. In the above example, the farmer would insist that the rancher pay at least three dollars for the right to have the extra steer roaming free. But because the extra steer was worth only two dollars to the rancher, he would be willing to pay only up to two dollars. Therefore, the steer would not be raised, the same outcome as when the rancher was not liable.

This insight was stunning. It meant that the case for government intervention was weaker than economists had thought. Yet Coase's soulmates at the free-market-oriented University of

Chicago wondered, according to George Stigler, "how so fine an economist could make such an obvious mistake." So they invited Coase, who was then at the University of Virginia, to come to Chicago to discuss it. They had dinner at the home of Aaron Director, the economist who had founded the *Journal of Law and Economics*.

Stigler writes:

We strongly objected to this heresy. Milton Friedman did most of the talking, as usual. He also did much of the thinking, as usual. In the course of two hours of argument the vote went from twenty against and one for Coase to twenty-one for Coase. What an exhilarating event! I lamented afterward that we had not had the clairvoyance to tape it.

Stigler himself labeled Coase's insight the Coase Theorem.

Of course, because transaction costs are never zero and sometimes are very high, courts are still needed to adjudicate between farmers and ranchers. Moreover, strategic behavior by the parties involved can prevent them from reaching the agreement, even if the gains from agreeing outweigh the transactions costs.

So why were economists so excited by the Coase Theorem? The reason is that it made them look differently at many issues. Take divorce. University of Colorado economist H. Elizabeth Peters showed empirically that whether a state has traditional barriers to divorce or divorce on demand has no effect on the divorce rate. This is contrary to conventional wisdom but consistent with the Coase Theorem. If the sum of a couple's net gains from marriage, as seen by the couple, is negative, then no agreement on distributing the gains from the marriage can keep them together. All the traditional divorce law did was enhance the bargaining position of women. A husband who wanted out much more than his wife wanted him in could compensate his wife to let him out. Not surprisingly, divorce-on-demand laws have made women who get divorces financially worse off, just as the absence of liability for the rancher in our example made the farmer worse off.

Coase has also upset the apple cart in the realm of public goods. Economists often give the lighthouse as an example of a public good that only government can provide. They choose this example, not based on any information they have about lighthouses, but rather on their a priori view that lighthouses could not be privately owned and operated at a profit. Coase showed, with a detailed look at history, that lighthouses in nineteenth-century Britain were privately provided and that ships were charged for their use when they came into port.

Coase earned his doctorate from the University of London in 1951 and emigrated to the United States, where he was a professor at the University of Buffalo from 1951 to 1958, then at the University of Virginia from 1958 to 1964, and then at the University of Chicago from 1964 to 1979, when he retired. Today Coase is a senior fellow in law and economics at the University of Chicago.

Selected Works

"The Federal Communications Commission." *Journal of Law and Economics* 2 (October 1959): 1–40.
"The Lighthouse in Economics." *Journal of Law and Economics* 17, no. 2 (October 1974): 357–76.
"The Nature of the Firm." *Economica* 4 (November 1937): 386–405.
"The Problem of Social Cost." *Journal of Law and Economics* 3 (October 1960): 1–44.

Debreu, Gerard (1921–)—Gerard Debreu's contributions are in general equilibrium theory—highly abstract theory about whether and how each market reaches equilibrium. In a famous paper coauthored with Kenneth Arrow, published in 1954, Debreu proved that under fairly unrestrictive assumptions, prices exist that bring markets into equilibrium. In his 1959 book, *The Theory of Value*, Debreu introduced more general equilibrium theory. He used complex analytic tools from mathematics—set theory and topology—to prove his theorems. In 1983 Debreu was awarded the Nobel Prize for his work on general equilibrium economics.

A native of France, Debreu has spent most of his professional life at the University of California at Berkeley. In 1962 he started as a professor of economics and was appointed professor of mathematics in 1975. In 1976 Debreu was made a chevalier of the French Legion of Honor.

Selected Works

(With Kenneth Arrow.) "Existence of a Competitive Equilibrium for a Competitive Economy." *Econometrica* 22, no. 3 (1954): 205–90.
Mathametical Economics: Twenty Papers of G. Debreu, edited by W. Hildenbrand. 1981.
Theory of Value: An Axiomatic Analysis of Economic Equilibrium. 1959. Reprint. 1971.

Fisher, Irving (1867–1947)—Irving Fisher was one of America's greatest mathematical economists and one of the clearest economics writers of all time. He had the intellect to use mathematics in virtually all his theories and the good sense to introduce it only after he had clearly explained the central principles in words. And he explained very well. Fisher's *Theory of Interest* is written so clearly that graduate economics students, who still study it today, often find that they can read—and understand—half the book in one sitting. With other writings in technical economics, this is unheard of.

Although he damaged his reputation by insisting throughout the Great Depression that recovery was imminent, contemporary economic

models of interest and capital are based on Fisherian principles. Similarly, monetarism is founded on Fisher's principles of money and prices.

Fisher called interest "an index of a community's preference for a dollar of present [income] over a dollar of future income." He labeled his theory of interest the "impatience and opportunity" theory. Interest rates, Fisher postulated, result from the interaction of two forces: the "time preference" people have for capital now, and the investment opportunity principle (that income invested now will yield greater income in the future). This reasoning sounds very much like Böhm-Bawerk's. Indeed, Fisher's *Theory of Interest* was dedicated to "the memory of John Rae and of Eugen von Böhm-Bawerk, who laid the foundations upon which I have endeavored to build." But Fisher objected to Böhm-Bawerk's idea that roundaboutness necessarily increases production. Instead, argued Fisher, at a positive interest rate, no one would ever choose a longer period unless it were more productive. So if we look at processes selected, we do find that longer periods are more productive. But, he argued, the length of the period does not in itself contribute to productivity.

Fisher defined capital as any asset that produces a flow of income over time. A flow of income, said Fisher, was distinct from the stock of capital that generated it. Capital and income are linked by the interest rate. Specifically, wrote Fisher, the value of capital is the present value of the flow of (net) income that the asset generates. This still is how economists think about capital and income today.

Fisher also opposed conventional income taxation and favored a tax on consumption to replace it. His position followed directly from his capital theory. When people save out of current income and then use the savings to invest in capital goods that yield income later, noted Fisher, they are being taxed on the income that they used to buy the capital goods and then are being taxed later on the income that the capital generates. This, he said, is double taxation of saving, and biases the tax code against saving and in favor of consumption. Fisher's reasoning is still used by economists today in making the case for consumption taxes.

Fisher was a pioneer in the construction and use of price indexes. James Tobin of Yale has called Fisher "the greatest expert of all time on index numbers." Indeed, from 1923 to 1936, his own Index Number Institute computed price indexes from all over the world.

Fisher was also the first economist to distinguish clearly between real and nominal interest rates. He pointed out that the real interest rate is equal to the nominal interest rate (the one we observe) minus the expected inflation rate. If the nominal interest rate is 12 percent, for example, but people expect inflation of 7 percent, then the real interest rate is only 5 percent. Again, this is still the basic understanding of modern economists.

Fisher laid out a more modern quantity theory of money (i.e., monetarism) than had been done before. He formulated his theory in terms of the Equation of Exchange, which says that $MV = PT$, where M equals the stock of money; V equals velocity, or how quickly money circulates in an economy; P equals the price level; and T equals the total volume of transactions. Again, modern economists still draw on this equation, although they usually use the version $MV = Py$, where y stands for real income.

The equation can be a very powerful tool for checking the consistency of one's thinking about the economy. Indeed, Reagan economist Beryl Sprinkel, who was Treasury undersecretary for monetary affairs in 1981, used this equation to criticize his colleague David Stockman's economic forecasts. Sprinkel pointed out that the only way Stockman's assumptions about the growth of income, the inflation rate, and the growth of the money supply could prove true would be if velocity increased faster than it ever

had before. As it turned out, velocity actually declined.

Irving Fisher was born in upstate New York in 1867. He gained an eclectic education at Yale, studying science and philosophy. He published poetry and works on astronomy, mechanics, and geometry. But his greatest concentration was on mathematics and economics, the latter having no academic department at Yale. Nonetheless, Fisher earned the first Ph.D. in economics ever awarded by Yale. Upon graduation he stayed at Yale for the rest of his career.

A three-year struggle with tuberculosis beginning in 1898 left Fisher with a profound interest in health and hygiene. He took up vegetarianism and exercise and wrote a national best-seller titled *How to Live: Rules for Healthful Living Based on Modern Science,* whose value he demonstrated by living until age eighty. He campaigned for Prohibition, peace, and eugenics. He was founder or president of numerous associations and agencies, including the Econometric Society and the American Economic Association. He was also a successful inventor. In 1925 his firm, which held the patent on his "visible card index" system, merged with its main competitor to form what later was known as Remington Rand and then Sperry Rand. Although the merger made him very wealthy, he lost a large part of his wealth in the stock market crash of 1929.

Selected Works

The Nature of Capital and Income. 1906
The Purchasing Power of Money. 1911.
The Rate of Interest. 1907.
The Theory of Interest. 1930.

Friedman, Milton (1912–)—Milton Friedman is the twentieth century's most prominent economist advocate of free markets. He was born in 1912 to Jewish immigrants in New York City. He attended Rutgers University, where he received his B.A. at the age of twenty, then went on to earn his M.A. from the University of Chicago in 1933 and his Ph.D. from Columbia University in 1946. In 1951 Friedman won the John Bates Clark Medal honoring economists under age forty for outstanding achievement. In 1976 he won the Nobel Prize in economics for "his achievements in the field of consumption analysis, monetary history and theory, and for his demonstration of the complexity of stabilization policy." Before that time, he had served as an adviser to President Nixon and was president of the American Economic Association in 1967. Since retiring from the University of Chicago in 1977, Friedman has been a senior research fellow at the Hoover Institution at Stanford University.

Friedman established himself in 1945 with *Income from Independent Professional Practice,* coauthored with Simon Kuznets. In it he argued that state licensing procedures limited entry into the medical profession, thereby allowing doctors to charge higher fees than if competition were more open.

His landmark work of 1957, *A Theory of the Consumption Function,* took on the Keynesian view that individuals and households adjust their expenditures on consumption to reflect their current income. Friedman showed that, instead, people's annual consumption is a function of their expected lifetime earnings.

In *Capitalism and Freedom*, Friedman liberated the study of market economics from its ivory tower and brought it down to earth. He argued for, among other things, a volunteer army, freely floating exchange rates, abolition of licensing of doctors, a negative income tax, and education vouchers. (Friedman is a passionate foe of the military draft: he once stated that the abolition of the draft was the only issue on which he had personally lobbied Congress.) Although his book did not sell well, many of the young people who did read it were encouraged by it to study economics themselves. His

ideas spread worldwide with *Free to Choose* (coauthored with his wife, Rose Friedman), the best-selling nonfiction book of 1980, written to accompany a TV series on the Public Broadcasting System. This book made Milton Friedman a household name.

Although much of his trail-blazing work was done on price theory—the theory that explains how prices are determined in individual markets—Friedman is popularly recognized for monetarism. Defying Keynes and most of the academic establishment of the time, Friedman presented evidence to resurrect the quantity theory of money—the idea that the price level is dependent upon the money supply. In *Studies in the Quantity Theory of Money,* published in 1956, Friedman stated that in the long run, increased monetary growth increases prices but has little or no effect on output. In the short run, he argued, increases in the money supply cause employment and output to increase, and decreases in the money supply have the opposite effect.

Friedman's solution to the problems of inflation and short-run fluctuations in employment and real GNP was a so-called money supply rule. If the Federal Reserve board were required to increase the money supply at the same rate as real GNP increased, he argued, inflation would disappear. Friedman's monetarism came to the forefront when, in 1963, he and Anna Schwartz coauthored *Monetary History of the United States, 1867–1960.* In it they contend that the Great Depression was the result of ill-conceived monetary policies by the Federal Reserve. Upon receipt of the unpublished manuscript submitted by the authors, the Federal Reserve board responded internally with a lengthy critical review. Such was their agitation that the Fed governors discontinued their policy of releasing minutes from the board's meetings to the public. Additionally, they commissioned a counterhistory to be written (by Elmus R. Wicker) in the hope of detracting from *Monetary History.*

Although many economists disagree with Friedman's monetarist ideas, he has substantial influence on the profession. One measure of that influence is the change in the treatment of monetary policy given by MIT Keynesian Paul Samuelson in his best-selling textbook, *Economics*. In the 1948 edition Samuelson wrote dismissively that "few economists regard Federal Reserve monetary policy as a panacea for controlling the business cycle." But in 1967 Samuelson said that monetary policy had "an important influence" on total spending. The 1985 edition, coauthored with Yale's William Nordhaus, states, "Money is the most powerful and useful tool that macroeconomic policymakers have," adding that the Fed "is the most important factor" in making policy.

Throughout the sixties Keynesians—and mainstream economists generally—had believed that the government faced a stable long-run trade-off between unemployment and inflation—the so-called Phillips Curve. In this view the government could, by increasing the demand for goods and services, permanently reduce unemployment by accepting a higher inflation rate. But in the late sixties Friedman (and Columbia University's Edmund Phelps) challenged this view. Friedman argued that once people adjusted to the higher inflation rate, unemployment would creep back up. To keep unemployment permanently lower, he said, would require not just a higher, but a permanently accelerating inflation rate. (See PHILLIPS CURVE.)

The stagflation of the seventies—rising inflation combined with rising unemployment—gave strong evidence for the Friedman-Phelps view and swayed most economists, including many Keynesians. Again, Samuelson's text is a barometer of the change in economists' thinking. The 1967 edition indicated that policymakers faced a trade-off between inflation and unemployment. The 1980 edition said there was less of a trade-off in the long run than in the short run. The 1985 edition says there is no long-run trade-off.

No other economist since Keynes has reshaped the way we think about and use economics as much as Milton Friedman. By his scope of topics and magnitude of ideas, Friedman has not only laid a cornerstone of contemporary economic thought but has also built an entire construction.

Selected Works

Capitalism and Freedom. 1962.
An Economist's Protest: Columns on Political Economy. 1972.
Essays in Positive Economics. 1953.
(With Rose Friedman.) *Free to Choose*. 1980.
(With Simon Kuznets.) *Income from Independent Professional Practice*. 1945.
(With Anna J. Schwartz.) *A Monetary History of the United States, 1867–1960*. 1963.
Price Theory: A Provisional Text. 1962.
(Ed.) *Studies in the Quantity Theory of Money*. 1956.
A Theory of the Consumption Function. 1957.

Frisch, Ragnar (1895–1973)—In 1969 Norwegian Ragnar Frisch, along with Dutch economist Jan Tinbergen, received the first Nobel Prize for economics. Frisch received his prize for his pioneering work in econometric modeling and measurement. Indeed, Frisch invented the word "econometrics" to refer to the use of mathematical and statistical techniques to test economic hypotheses. Frisch founded the Econometric Society in 1930.

Frisch believed that econometrics would help establish economics as a science. But toward the end of his life, he had doubts about how econometrics was being used. He wrote: "I have insisted that econometrics must have relevance to concrete realities—otherwise it degenerates into something which is not worthy of the name econometrics, but ought rather to be called playometrics."

In a paper on business cycles, Frisch was the first to use the word "microeconomics" to refer to the study of single firms and industries and "macroeconomics" to refer to the study of the aggregate economy.

Frisch spent most of his professional life at the University of Oslo in Norway.

Selected Works

"Annual Survey of General Economic Theory: The Problem of Index Numbers." *Econometrica* 4, no. 1 (January 1936): 1–38.

"Econometrics in the World of Today." In *Induction, Growth and Trade; Essays in Honour of Sir Roy Harrod*, edited by W. A. Eltis, M. F. Scott, and J. N. Wolfe. 1970.

"Propagation Problems and Impulse Problems in Dynamic Economics." In *Economic Essays in Honor of Gustav Cassel*. 1933. Reprinted in *Readings in Business Cycles*, edited by R. A. Gordon and L. R. Klein. 1966.

Statistical Confluence Analysis by Means of Complete Regression Systems. 1934.

Galbraith, John Kenneth (1908–   )—John Kenneth Galbraith is one of the most widely read economists in the United States. One reason is that he writes so well. He turns a clever phrase that often makes those he argues against look foolish. Galbraith's first major book, published in 1952, was *American Capitalism: The Concept of Countervailing Power*. In it he argued that giant firms had replaced small ones to the point where the perfectly competitive model no longer applied to much of the American economy. But not to worry, he argued. The power of large firms was offset by the countervailing power of large unions, so that consumers were protected by competing centers of power.

Galbraith made his biggest splash with his 1958 book, *The Affluent Society*. In that volume he contrasted the affluence of the private sector

with the squalor of the public sector. Many people liked that book because of their view that Galbraith, like Veblen before him, attacked production that was geared to "conspicuous consumption." But that is not what Galbraith did. In fact, Galbraith argued that "an admirable case can still be made" for satisfying even consumer wants that "have bizarre, frivolous, or even immoral origins." His argument against satisfying all consumer demands was more subtle. Galbraith wrote: "If the individual's wants are to be urgent, they must be original with himself. They cannot be urgent if they must be contrived for him. And above all, they must not be contrived by the process of production by which they are satisfied. . . . One cannot defend production as satisfying wants if that production creates the wants."

Friedrich Hayek made the most fundamental criticism of Galbraith's argument (see HAYEK). Hayek conceded that most wants do not originate with the individual. Our innate wants, he wrote, "are probably confined to food, shelter, and sex." All other wants we learn from what we see around us. Probably all our aesthetic feelings—our enjoyment of music and literature, for example—are learned. So, wrote Hayek, "to say that a desire is not important because it is not innate is to say that the whole cultural achievement of man is not important."

Galbraith's magnum opus was his 1967 book, *The New Industrial State*. Galbraith argued that the American economy was dominated by large firms. "The mature corporation," wrote Galbraith, "had readily at hand the means for controlling the prices at which it sells as well as those at which it buys." Galbraith wrote: "Since General Motors produces some half of all the automobiles, its designs do not reflect the current mode, but are the current mode. The proper shape of an automobile, for most people, will be what the automobile makers decree the current shape to be."

The evidence has not been kind to Galbraith's

thesis. Even our largest firms lose money if they fail to produce a product that consumers want. The U.S. market share of GM, for example, one of Galbraith's favorite examples of a firm invulnerable to market forces, has fallen from about 50 percent when Galbraith wrote the book to about 30 percent today.

Galbraith was born in Canada and moved to the United States in the thirties. He earned his Ph.D. in agricultural economics at the University of California at Berkeley. He was one of the chief price controllers during World War II as head of the Price Section of the U.S. government's Office of Price Administration. Unlike almost all other economists, Galbraith defends permanent price controls. In 1943 Galbraith left the government to be on the editorial board of *Fortune*. After the war he directed the U.S. Strategic Bombing Survey. That survey's main finding was that saturation bombing of Germany was not very effective at slowing down German war production. In 1949 he became an economics professor at Harvard, where he had been briefly before the war. He is still at Harvard. Galbraith has also been politically active—an adviser to President Kennedy, Kennedy's ambassador to India, and president of Americans for Democratic Action. He was president of the American Economic Association in 1972.

Selected Works

The Affluent Society. 1958.
American Capitalism. 1952.
The New Industrial State. 1967.

George, Henry (1839–97)—Henry George is best remembered as a proponent of the "single tax" on land. The government should finance all of its projects, he argued, with proceeds from only one tax. This single tax would be on the unimproved value of land—the value that the land would have if it were in its natural state with no buildings, no landscaping, etc. George's idea was not new. It was largely borrowed from David Ricardo, James Mill, and John Stuart Mill.

In his heyday Henry George was very popular, with his ideas inspiring passionate debate among young intellectuals. After George published *Progress and Poverty* in 1879, a political movement grew in the United States around his work. He later narrowly missed being elected mayor of New York.

Most taxes, noted George, stifle productive behavior. A tax on income reduces people's incentive to earn income; a tax on wheat would reduce wheat production; and so on. But a tax on the unimproved value of land, claimed George, was different. The value of land comes from two components, its natural value and the value that is created by improving it (by building on it, for example). The value of a vacant lot in its natural state comes not from any sacrifice or opportunity cost borne by the owners of the land, but rather from demand for a fixed amount of land. Therefore, argued George, because the value of the unimproved land was unearned, neither the land's value nor a tax on the land's value could affect productive behavior. If land were taxed more heavily, the quantity available would not decline, as with other goods; nor would demand decline because of land's productive uses. By taxing the whole of the value of unimproved land, the government would drive the price of land to zero.

George was right that other taxes may have stronger disincentives. But economists now recognize that the single land tax is not innocent, either. Site values are created, not intrinsic. Why else would land in Tokyo be worth so much more than land in Mississippi? Why was land in Tokyo worth so much less years ago? A tax on the value of a site is really a tax on productive potential, which is a result of improvements to land in the area. Henry George's proposed tax on one piece of land, is, in effect, based on the improvements to the neighboring land.

And what if you are your "neighbor"? What if you buy a large expanse of land and raise the value of one portion of it by improving the surrounding land. Then you are taxed based on your improvements. This is not far-fetched. It is precisely what the Disney Corporation did in Florida. Disney bought up large amounts of land around the area where it planned to build Disneyworld, and then made this surrounding land more valuable by building Disneyworld. Had George's single tax on land been in existence, Disney might never have made the investment. So, contrary to George's reasoning, even a tax on unimproved land reduces incentives.

George's argument also assumes that in setting taxes, the government can separate the raw value of land from the value of its improvements—a difficult, if not impossible, task, especially for a politically motivated government. Can the government tax the "unimproved rental value" of the land under an office complex in Los Angeles without creating any disincentive for the owner to increase its improved value?

Objections aside, Henry George may have been arguing for what is really the least offensive tax. As Milton Friedman said almost a century after George's death: "In my opinion, the least bad tax is the property tax on the unimproved value of land, the Henry George argument of many, many years ago."

—**Charles Hooper** (Charles Hooper holds an M.S. in engineering–economic systems from Stanford University.)

Selected Works

Progress and Poverty. 1879.

Haavelmo, Trygve (1911–　)—In 1989 Norwegian economist Trygve Haavelmo was awarded the Nobel Prize for his pioneering work in the forties in econometrics. He made two main contributions in econometrics. The first was a 1943 article that showed some of the statistical implications of simultaneous equations. The second was a 1944 article that based econometrics more firmly on probability theory.

During the war years Haavelmo worked for the Norwegian government in the United States. He was a professor of economics at the University of Oslo from 1948 until his retirement in 1979.

Selected Works

"The Probability Approach in Econometrics." *Supplement to Econometrica* 12 (July 1944): S1–115.
"The Statistical Implications of a System of Simultaneous Equations." *Econometrica* 11 (January 1943): 1–12.
A Study in the Theory of Investment. 1960.

Harrod, Roy F. (1900–78)—Roy Harrod is credited with getting twentieth-century economists thinking about economic growth. Harrod built upon Keynes's theory of income determination. The model he built, which Evsey Domar also worked on independently, is called the Harrod-Domar model. A full explanation of Harrod's model can be found in *Towards a Dynamic Economics,* though Harrod's first version of the idea was published in "An Essay in Dynamic Theory."

Harrod introduced the concepts of warranted growth, natural growth, and actual growth. The warranted growth rate is the growth rate at which all saving is absorbed into investment. If, for example, people save 10 percent of their income, and the economy's ratio of capital to output is 4, the economy's warranted growth rate is 2.5 percent (10 divided by 4). This is the growth rate at which the ratio of capital to output would stay constant at 4.

The natural growth rate is the rate required to maintain full employment. If the labor force grows at 2 percent per year, then to maintain full employment, the economy's annual growth rate must be 2 percent.

Harrod's model showed that two kinds of problems could arise with growth rates. The first was that actual growth was determined by the rate of saving and that natural growth was determined by the growth of the labor force. There was no necessary reason for actual growth to equal natural growth and, therefore, no inherent tendency for the economy to reach full employment. This problem resulted from Harrod's assumptions that the wage rate is fixed and that the economy must use labor and capital in the same proportions. But most economists now believe that wage rates can fall when the labor force increases, although they disagree about how quickly. And virtually all mainstream economists agree that the ratio of labor and capital that businesses want to use depends on wage rates and on the price of capital. Therefore, one of the main problems implied by Harrod's model does not appear to be much of a problem after all.

The second problem implied by Harrod's model was unstable growth. If companies adjusted investment according to what they expected about future demand, and the anticipated demand was forthcoming, warranted growth would equal actual growth. But if actual demand exceeded anticipated demand, they would have underinvested and would respond by investing further. This investment, however, would itself cause growth to rise, requiring even further investment. Result: explosive growth. The same story can be told in reverse if actual demand fell short of anticipated demand. The result then would be a deceleration of growth. This property of Harrod's growth model became known as Harrod's knife-edge. Here again, though, this uncomfortable conclusion was the result of two unrealistic assumptions made by Harrod: first,

companies naïvely base their investment plans only on anticipated output, and second, investment is instantaneous. In spite of these limitations, Harrod's lasting contribution was to get economists thinking about the causes of growth as carefully as they had thought about other issues.

Harrod was a close colleague and official biographer of Keynes. *The Life of John Maynard Keynes* was a second, and only slightly less theoretical, product of Harrod's long association with Keynes.

Born in Norfolk, England, Roy Harrod graduated from New College, Oxford. After spending a term at King's College, Cambridge, where he came in contact with Keynes, Harrod returned to Oxford to administer and teach at Christ Church College until his retirement in 1967. Assar Lindbeck, the chairman of the Nobel Prize Committee, wrote that Harrod would have been awarded a Nobel Prize if he had lived longer. The backlog of other economists awarded the Nobel Prize caused Harrod to miss getting it.

Selected Works

"An Essay in Dynamic Theory." *Economic Journal* 49 (March 1939): 14–33.
The Life of John Maynard Keynes. 1951.
Towards a Dynamic Economics: Some Recent Developments of Economic Theory and Their Application to Policy. 1948.
The Trade Cycle: An Essay. 1936.

See also SOLOW.

Hayek, Friedrich August (1899–1992)—If any twentieth-century economist was a Renaissance man, it was Friedrich Hayek. He made fundamental contributions in political theory, psychology, and economics. In a field where the relevance of ideas often is eclipsed by expansions on an initial theory, many of his contributions are so remarkable that people still read them over forty years after they were written. Many graduate economics students today, for example, study his articles from the thirties and forties on economics and knowledge, deriving insights that some of their elders in the economics profession still do not totally understand. It would not be surprising if a substantial minority of economists still read and learn from his articles in the year 2050.

Hayek was the best-known advocate of what is now called Austrian economics. He was, in fact, the only major recent member of the Austrian school who was actually born and raised in Austria. After World War I Hayek earned his doctorates in law and political science at the University of Vienna. Afterward he, together with other young economists, Gottfried Haberler, Fritz Machlup, and Oskar Morgenstern, joined Ludwig von Mises's private seminar—the Austrian equivalent of Keynes's "Cambridge Circus." In 1927 Hayek became the director of the newly formed Austrian Institute for Business Cycle Research. In the early thirties, at the invitation of Lionel Robbins, he moved to the faculty of the London School of Economics, where he stayed for eighteen years. He became a British citizen in 1938.

Most of Hayek's work from the twenties through the thirties was in the Austrian theory of business cycles, capital theory, and monetary theory. Hayek saw a connection among all three. The major problem for any economy, he argued, is how people's actions are coordinated. He noticed, as Adam Smith had, that the price system—free markets—did a remarkable job of coordinating people's actions, even though that coordination was not part of anyone's intent. The market, said Hayek, was a spontaneous order. By spontaneous, Hayek meant unplanned—the market was not designed by anyone but evolved slowly as the result of human actions. But the market does not work perfectly. What causes the market, asked Hayek, to fail to coor-

dinate people's plans, so that at times, large numbers of people are unemployed?

One cause, he said, was increases in the money supply by the central bank. Such increases, he argued in *Prices and Production*, would drive down interest rates, making credit artificially cheap. Businessmen would then make capital investments that they would not have made had they understood that they were getting a distorted price signal from the credit market. But capital investments, noted Hayek, are not homogeneous. Long-term investments are more sensitive to interest rates than short-term ones, just as long-term bonds are more interest-sensitive than Treasury bills. Therefore, he concluded, artificially low interest rates not only cause investment to be artificially high, but also cause "malinvestment"—too much investment in long-term projects relative to short-term ones. He argued that the boom must turn into a bust. Hayek saw the bust as a healthy and necessary readjustment. The way to avoid the busts, he argued, was to avoid the booms that caused them.

Hayek and Keynes were building their models of the world at the same time. They were familiar with each other's views and battled over their differences. Most economists believe that Keynes's General Theory won the war. Hayek, until his dying day, never believed that, and neither do other members of the Austrian school. Hayek believed that Keynesian policies to combat unemployment would inevitably cause inflation, and that to keep unemployment low, the central bank would have to increase the money supply faster and faster, causing inflation to get higher and higher. Hayek's thought, which he expressed as early as 1958, is now accepted by mainstream economists (see PHILLIPS CURVE).

In the late thirties and early forties Hayek turned to the debate about whether socialist planning could work. He argued that it could not. The reason socialist economists thought central planning could work, argued Hayek, was that they thought planners could take the given economic data and allocate resources accordingly. But Hayek pointed out that the data are not "given." The data do not exist, and cannot exist, in any one mind or small number of minds. Rather, each individual has knowledge about particular resources and potential opportunities for using these resources that a central planner can never have. The virtue of the free market, argued Hayek, is that it gives the maximum latitude for people to use information that only they have. In short, the market process generates the data. Without markets, data are almost nonexistent.

Mainstream economists and even many socialist economists (see SOCIALISM) now accept Hayek's argument. Harvard economist Jeffrey Sachs has stated: "If you ask an economist where's a good place to invest, which industries are going to grow, where the specialization is going to occur, the track record is pretty miserable. Economists don't collect the on-the-ground information businessmen do. Every time Poland asks, Well, what are we going to be able to produce? I say I don't know."

In 1944 Hayek also attacked socialism from a very different angle. From his vantage point in Austria, Hayek had observed Germany very closely in the twenties and early thirties, and then moved to Britain. He noticed that many British socialists were advocating some of the same policies for government control of people's lives that he had seen advocated in Germany in the twenties. He had also seen that the Nazis really were National Socialists—that is, they were nationalists and socialists. So Hayek wrote *The Road to Serfdom* to warn his fellow British citizens of the dangers of socialism. His basic argument was that government control of our economic lives amounts to totalitarianism— total government control of our lives. Wrote Hayek: "Economic control is not merely control of a sector of human life which can be separated

from the rest; it is the control of the means for all our ends."

Surprisingly to some, John Maynard Keynes praised the book highly. On the book's cover, Keynes is quoted as saying: "In my opinion it is a grand book. . . . Morally and philosophically I find myself in agreement with virtually the whole of it; and not only in agreement with it, but in deeply moved agreement."

Although Hayek had intended *The Road to Serfdom* only for a British audience, it also sold well in the United States. Indeed, Reader's Digest condensed it. With that book Hayek established himself as the world's leading classical liberal, now called libertarian or market liberal. A few years later, along with Milton Friedman, George Stigler, and others, he formed the Mont Pelerin Society so that classical liberals could meet every two years and give each other moral support in what appeared to be a losing cause.

In 1950 Hayek became professor of social and moral sciences at the University of Chicago, where he stayed until 1962. During that time he worked on methodology, psychology, and political theory. In methodology Hayek attacked "scientism"—the imitation in social science of the methods of the physical sciences. His argument was that because social science, including economics, studies people and not objects, it can do so only by paying attention to human purposes. The Austrian school in the 1870s had already shown that the value of an item derives from its ability to fulfill human purposes. Hayek was arguing that social scientists more generally should take account of human purposes. His thoughts on the matter are in *The Counter-Revolution of Science: Studies in the Abuse of Reason*. In psychology Hayek wrote *The Sensory Order: An Inquiry into the Foundations of Theoretical Psychology*.

In political theory Hayek gave his view of the proper role of government in his book *The Constitution of Liberty*. He discussed the principles of freedom and based his policy proposals on those principles. His main objection to progressive taxation, for example, was not that it causes inefficiency but that it violates equality before the law. In the book's postscript, "Why I Am Not a Conservative," Hayek distinguished his classical liberalism from conservatism. Among his grounds for rejecting conservatism were that moral and religious ideals are not "proper objects of coercion" and that conservatism is hostile to internationalism and prone to a strident nationalism.

In 1962 Hayek returned to Europe as professor of economic policy at the University of Freiburg in Breisgau, West Germany, and stayed there until 1968. He then taught at the University of Salzburg in Austria until his retirement nine years later. His publications slowed substantially in the early seventies. In 1974 he shared the Nobel Prize with Gunnar Myrdal for his theories of money and his illumination of the "interdependence of economic, social, and institutional phenomena." This award seemed to breathe new life in him, and he began publishing again, both in economics and in politics.

Many people get more conservative as they age. Hayek became more radical. Although he had favored central banking for most of his life, in the seventies he began advocating denationalizing money. Private enterprises that issued distinct currencies, he argued, would have an incentive to maintain their currency's purchasing power. Customers could choose from among competing currencies, and whether they reverted to a gold standard was a question that Hayek was too much of a believer in spontaneous order to predict. With the collapse of communism in Eastern Europe, some economic consultants have considered Hayek's currency system as a replacement for fixed-rate currencies.

Hayek was still publishing at age eighty-nine. In his book *The Fatal Conceit*, he laid out some profound insights to explain the intellectuals'

attraction to socialism and then refuted the basis for their beliefs.

Selected Works

The Constitution of Liberty. 1960. Reprint. 1972.
The Counter-Revolution of Science: Studies on the Abuse of Reason. 1952.
Denationalization of Money. 1976.
"Economics and Knowledge." *Economica* NS4 (February 1937): 33–54.
The Fatal Conceit. 1988.
Individualism and Economic Order. 1948.
"Price Expectations, Monetary Disturbances, and Malinvestments." In Hayek. *Profits, Interest, and Investment*. 1939. Reprint. 1975.
Prices and Production, 2d ed. 1935. Reprint. 1975.
"The Use of Knowledge in Society." *American Economic Review* 35 (September 1945): 519–30.

Heller, Walter Wolfgang (1915–87)—Walter Heller's claim to fame stems from his years as chairman of the Council of Economic Advisers (CEA) from 1961 to 1964, under presidents John F. Kennedy and Lyndon B. Johnson. Before that, and after, he was an economics professor at the University of Minnesota.

As chairman of the CEA, Heller persuaded President Kennedy to cut marginal tax rates. This cut in tax rates, which was passed after Kennedy's death, helped cause a boom in the U.S. economy. Heller's CEA also developed the first "voluntary" (that is, enforced by veiled threats rather than by explicit laws) wage-price guidelines.

Heller's early academic work was on state and local taxation. In 1947 and 1948 he was tax adviser to the U.S. Military Government in Germany. He was involved in the currency and tax reforms that helped spur the German economic boom (see GERMAN ECONOMIC "MIRACLE"). In a 1950 article, Heller noted that the reduction in marginal tax rates helped "remove the repressive effect of extremely high rates."

According to tax economist Joseph Pechman, Heller was also one of the first economists to recognize that tax deductions and tax preferences narrowed the income tax base, thus requiring, for a given amount of revenue, higher marginal tax rates.

Selected Works

Monetary vs. Fiscal Policy (a dialogue with Milton Friedman). 1969.
New Dimensions of Political Economy. 1966.
"Tax and Monetary Reform in Occupied Germany." *National Tax Journal* 2, no. 3 (1949): 215–31.
"What's Right with Economics?" *American Economic Review* 65, no. 1 March (1975): 1–26.

Hicks, John R. (1904–1989)—A British economist, John Hicks is known for four contributions. The first was his introduction of the idea of the elasticity of substitution. While the concept is difficult to explain in a few words, Hicks used it to show, contrary to the Marxist allegation, that labor-saving technical progress—the kind that we generally have—does not necessarily reduce labor's share of national income.

His second major contribution was his invention of what is called the IS-LM model. The IS-LM model is a graphical depiction of the argument Keynes gave in the General Theory about how an economy could be in equilibrium with less than full employment. Hicks published it in a journal article the year after Keynes's book was published. It is reasonably certain that most economists became familiar with Keynes's argument by seeing Hicks's graph.

Hicks's third major contribution was his book *Value and Capital*. In it he showed that most of what economists understood and believed about value theory (the theory about why goods have value) can be derived without having to assume that utility is measurable. His book was also one of the first works on general equilibrium theory, the theory about how all markets fit together and reach equilibrium.

Hicks's fourth contribution was the idea of the compensation test. Before his test economists were hesitant to say that one particular outcome was preferable to another. The reason was that even a policy that benefited millions of people could hurt some people. Free trade in cars, for example, helps millions of American consumers at the expense of thousands of American workers and owners of stock in U.S. auto companies. How did an economist judge whether the help to some outweighed the hurt to others? Hicks asked, Could those helped compensate those hurt to the full extent of their hurt and still be better off? If the answer was yes, then the policy passed the "Hicks compensation test," even if the compensation was never paid, and was judged to be good. In the auto example economists can show that the dollar gains to car buyers far outweigh the dollar losses to workers and stockholders, and therefore, by Hicks's compensation test, free trade is good.

In 1972 John Hicks and Kenneth Arrow jointly received the Nobel Prize for economics. Hicks was recognized for his theories of welfare and resources allocation and his macroeconomic studies of general equilibrium. Educated at Balliol College, Oxford, John Hicks returned there as the Drummond Professor of Political Economy, a post he held until his retirement in 1965. In 1935 he married the economist Ursula Webb. He was knighted in 1964.

Selected Works

Capital and Growth. 1965.
Capital and Time: A Neo-Austrian Theory. 1973.
The Crisis in Keynesian Economics. 1974.

"The Foundations of Welfare Economics." *Economic Journal* 49 (December 1939): 696–712.

"Mr. Keynes and the 'Classics.' " *Econometrica* 5 (April 1937): 147–59.

"The Valuation of the Social Income." *Economica* 7 (May 1940): 105–24.

Value and Capital. 1939.

Hume, David (1711–76)—Though better known for his treatments of philosophy, history, and politics, the Scottish philosopher David Hume also made several essential contributions to economic thought. His empirical argument against British mercantilism formed a building block for classical economics. His essays on money and international trade published in *Political Discourses* strongly influenced his friend and fellow countryman Adam Smith.

British mercantilists believed that economic prosperity could be realized by limiting imports and encouraging exports in order to maximize the amount of gold in the home country. The American colonies facilitated this policy by providing raw materials that Britain manufactured into finished goods and reexported back to the colonial consumers in America. Needless to say, the arrangement was short-lived.

But even before the American Revolution intervened in mercantilistic pursuits, David Hume showed why net exporting in exchange for gold currency, hoarded by Britain, could not enhance wealth. Hume's argument was essentially the monetarist quantity theory of money: prices in a country change directly with changes in the money supply. Hume explained that as net exports increased and more gold flowed into a country to pay for them, the prices of goods in that country would rise. Thus, an increased flow of gold into England would not necessarily increase England's wealth substantially.

Hume showed that the increase in domestic prices due to the gold inflow would discourage exports and encourage imports, thus automati-

cally limiting the amount by which exports would exceed imports. This adjustment mechanism is called the price-specie-flow mechanism. Surprisingly, even though Hume's idea would have bolstered Adam Smith's attack on mercantilism and argument for free trade, Smith ignored Hume's argument. Although few economists accept Hume's view literally, it is still the basis of much thinking on balance-of-payments issues.

Considering Hume's solid grasp of monetary dynamics, his misconceptions about money behavior are all the more noteworthy. Hume erroneously advanced the notion of "creeping inflation"—the idea that a gradual increase in the money supply would lead to economic growth.

Hume made two other major lasting contributions to economics. One was his idea, later elaborated by Hayek in *The Road to Serfdom*, that economic freedom is a necessary condition for political freedom. The second was his assertion that "you cannot deduce ought from is"—that is, value judgments cannot be made purely on the basis of facts. Economists now make the same point by distinguishing between normative (what should be) and positive (what is).

Hume died the year *The Wealth of Nations* was published, and in the presence of its author, Adam Smith.

Selected Works

The Philosophical Works of David Hume, 4 vols, edited and annotated by T. H. Green and T. H. Grose. 1875.

Political Discourses. 1752.

Writings on Economics, edited by Eugene Rotwein. 1955.

See also GOLD STANDARD, SMITH.

Jevons, William Stanley (1835–82)—Jevons was one of three men to simultaneously advance the so-called "marginal revolution." Working in complete independence of one another—Jevons in Manchester, England; Leon Walras in Laussane, Switzerland; and Carl Menger in Vienna—each scholar developed the theory of marginal utility to understand and explain consumer behavior. The theory held that the utility (value) of each additional unit of a commodity—the marginal utility—is less and less to the consumer. When you are thirsty, for example, you get great utility from a glass of water. Thirst quenched, the second and third glass are less and less appealing. Feeling waterlogged, you will eventually refuse water altogether. "Value," said Jevons, "depends entirely upon utility."

This statement marked a significant departure from the classical theory of value, which stated that value derived from the labor used to produce a product or from the cost of production more generally. Thus began the neoclassical school, which is still the dominant one in economics today.

Jevons went on to define the "equation of exchange." This equation shows that for a consumer to be maximizing his or her utility, the ratio of the marginal utility of each item consumed to its price must be equal. If it is not, then he or she can, with a given income, reallocate consumption and get more utility.

Take, for example, a consumer whose marginal utility from oranges is 10 "utils," and from cookies 4 utils, when oranges and cookies are both priced at 50 cents each. The consumer's ratio of marginal utility to price for oranges is 10/$.50, or 20, and for cookies is 4/$.50, or 8. Jevons would have said (and modern economists would agree) that this does not satisfy the equation of exchange and, therefore, the consumer will change purchases. Specifically, the consumer could increase utility by spending 50 cents less on cookies and using the money to buy oranges. He would lose 4 utils on the cookies, but gain 10 on the oranges, for a net gain of

6 utils. He will have this incentive to reallocate purchases until the equation of exchange holds (that is, until the marginal utility of oranges falls and the marginal utility of cookies rises to a point where, as a ratio to their prices, they are equal).

Of course, as is true with most new developments in economic theory, one can always find earlier writers who said some of the same things. Jevons' role in the marginal revolution is no exception. Much of what he said was said earlier by Hermann Gossen in Germany, by Jules Dupuit and Antoine Cournot in France, and by Samuel Longfield in Britain. Yet historians of economic thought are sure that Jevons had never read them.

Jevons put much less thought into the production side of economics. It is ironic, therefore, that he became famous in Britain for his book *The Coal Question*. In it he wrote that Britain's industrial vitality depended on coal and, therefore, would decline as that resource was exhausted. As coal reserves ran out, he wrote, the price of coal would rise. This would make it feasible for producers to extract coal from poorer or deeper seams. He also argued that America would rise to become an industrial superpower. Although his forecast was right for both Britain and America, and he was right about the incentive to mine more costly seams, he was almost surely wrong that the main factor was the cost of coal. Jevons failed to appreciate the fact that as the price of an energy source rises, entrepreneurs have a strong incentive to invent, develop, and produce alternate sources. In particular, he did not anticipate oil or natural gas. Also, he did not take account of the incentive, as the price of coal rose, to use it more efficiently (see NATURAL RESOURCES).

Born in Liverpool, England, Jevons studied chemistry and botany at University College, London. Because of the bankruptcy of his father's business in 1847, Jevons left school to take up the position of assayer at the Mint in

Sydney, Australia. He remained there five years, resuming his studies at University College upon his return to England. He was later appointed to the post of chair in political economy at his alma mater and retired from there in 1880. Two years later, with a number of unfinished books in process, Jevons drowned while swimming. He was forty-six.

Selected Works

The Coal Question, 3d ed., revised and edited by A. W. Flux. 1906.
Investigations in Currency and Finance, edited and with an introduction by H. S. Foxwell. 1884.
A Serious Fall in the Value of Gold Ascertained, and Its Social Effects Set Forth. 1863. Reprinted in Jevons. *Investigations in Currency and Finance.* 1884.
"The Solar Period and the Price of Corn." 1875. First published in Jevons. *Investigations in Currency and Finance.* 1884.
The Theory of Political Economy. 1871. Reprint, edited by R. D. Collison Black. 1970.

Johnson, Harry Gordon (1923–77)—Harry Johnson, a Canadian, was one of the most active and prolific economists of all time. His main research was in the area of international trade, international finance, and monetary policy.

In international trade, one of Johnson's early articles showed that a country with monopoly power in some good could impose a tariff and be better off, even if other countries retaliated against the tariff. His proof was what is sometimes called a "possibility theorem." It showed that such a tariff *could* improve the country's well-being, not that it was likely to. Johnson, realizing the difference between what could be and what is likely to be, was a strong believer in free trade. Indeed, he often gave lectures in his native Canada excoriating the Canadian

government for its protectionist policies and arguing that Canada could eliminate some of the gap between Canadian and U.S. standards of living by implementing free trade.

In international finance Johnson's seminal 1958 paper named the growth in the money supply as one important factor that affects a country's balance of payments. Before then, economists had tended to focus on nonmonetary factors. Johnson's article began what is now called the monetary approach to the balance of payments.

In monetary economics Johnson made an early attempt to do for Britain what Milton Friedman and Anna Schwartz were doing for the United States: measure the money supply over time. Although he did not achieve as much in this area as Friedman and Schwartz, his work led to other more careful and detailed studies of the British money supply. In 1959, after having been a professor at the University of Manchester in England, Johnson moved to the University of Chicago as the token "Keynesian." But he learned a lot from monetarist Milton Friedman and others at Chicago, just as he had learned from Keynesians in England. Although never a monetarist himself, Johnson became increasingly sympathetic to monetarist views.

One of his classic articles, written in his early years at Chicago, was his 1962 survey, "Monetary Theory and Policy." The article is a graduate student's delight—tying together apparently disparate insights by other economists, pointing out their pitfalls, and laying out an agenda for future research—all in a clear, readable style that still managed not to sacrifice subtle distinctions.

In a relatively short career Johnson wrote 526 professional articles, 41 books and pamphlets, and over 150 book reviews. He also gave a prodigious number of speeches. According to Paul Samuelson, when Johnson died he had 18 papers in proof. (Commented Samuelson:

"That is dying with your boots on!") Johnson also earned many honors. In 1977, for example, he was named a Distinguished Fellow of the American Economic Association, and in 1976 the Canadian government named him an Officer of the Order of Canada. Johnson graduated from the University of Toronto in 1943 and earned his Ph.D. from Harvard in 1958.

Selected Works

"British Monetary Statistics." *Economica* 26 (February 1959): 1–17.
The Canadian Quandary: Economic Problems and Policies. 1963.
Essays in Monetary Economics, 2d ed. 1969.
Further Essays in Monetary Economics. 1972.
"The 'General Theory' after Twenty-five Years." *American Economic Review* 51 (May 1961): 1–17.
"The Keynesian Revolution and the Monetarist Counter-Revolution." *American Economic Review* 61 (May 1971): 1–14.
"Optimum Tariffs and Retaliation." *Review of Economic Studies* 21, no. 2 (1953): 142–53.

Kantorovich, Leonid Vitalievich (1912–86)—Leonid Kantorovich shared the 1975 Nobel Prize with Tjalling Koopmans "for their contributions to the theory of optimum allocation of resources." Kantarovich was born and died in Russia and did all his professional work there. His first major breakthrough came in 1938 when he was consulting to the Soviet government's Laboratory of the Plywood Trust. Asked to devise a technique for distributing raw materials to maximize output, Kantorovich saw that the problem was a mathematical one: to maximize a linear function subject to many constraints. The technique he developed is now known as linear programming.

In a 1939 book, *The Mathematical Method of Production Planning and Organization,* Kantor-ovich showed that all problems of economic allocation can be seen as maximizing a function subject to constraints. Across the world John Hicks in Britain and Paul Samuelson in the United States were reaching the same conclusion at around the same time. Kantorovich, like Samuelson, showed that certain coefficients in the equations could be regarded as the prices of each input.

Kantorovich's best-known book is *The Best Uses of Economic Resources*. In it he developed points made in his 1939 book. He showed that even centrally planned economies had to be concerned with using prices to allocate resources. He also made the point that socialist economies have to be concerned about trade-offs between present and future and, therefore, should use interest rates just as capitalist ones do. Unfortunately, Hayek has shown that the only way to use prices is to have a price system—that is, markets and private property.

Besides winning the Nobel Prize, Kantorovich won the Soviet government's Lenin Prize in 1965 and the Order of Lenin in 1967. From 1944 to 1960, Kantorovich was a professor at the University of Leningrad. In 1960 he became director of mathematical economic methods at the Siberian Division of the Soviet Academy of Sciences. In 1971 he was appointed laboratory chief of the Institute of National Economic Management in Moscow.

Selected Works

The Best Uses of Economic Resources. 1965.
"The Mathematical Method of Production Planning and Organization." *Management Science* 6, no. 4 (July 1960): 363–422.

Keynes, John Maynard (1883–1946)—So influential was John Maynard Keynes that an entire school of modern thought bears his name.

Many of his ideas were revolutionary; almost all are controversial. Keynesian economics serves as a sort of yardstick that can define virtually all economists who came after Keynes.

Keynes was born in Cambridge and attended King's College, Cambridge, where he earned his degree in mathematics in 1905. He remained there for another year to study under Alfred Marshall and Arthur Pigou, whose scholarship on the quantity theory of money led to Keynes's *Tract on Monetary Reform* many years later. After leaving Cambridge, Keynes took a position with the civil service in Britain. While there, he collected the material for his first book in economics, *Indian Currency and Finance,* in which he described the workings of India's monetary system. He returned to Cambridge in 1908 as a lecturer, then took a leave of absence to work for the British Treasury. He worked his way up quickly through the bureaucracy and, by 1919, was the Treasury's principal representative at the peace conference at Versailles. He resigned because he thought the Treaty of Versailles was overly burdensome to the Germans.

Upon resigning, he returned to Cambridge to resume teaching. Keynes was a prominent journalist and speaker, and one of the famous Bloomsbury Group of literary greats, which included Virginia Woolf and Bertrand Russell. At the 1944 Bretton Woods Conference, where the International Monetary Fund was established, Keynes was one of the architects of the postwar system of fixed exchange rates. In 1925 he married the Russian ballet dancer Lydia Lopokova. He was made a lord in 1942. Keynes died on April 21, 1946, survived by his father, John Neville Keynes, also a renowned economist in his day.

Keynes became a celebrity before becoming one of the most respected economists of the century. What gained him his celebrity status was his eloquent book *The Economic Consequences of the Peace*. Keynes wrote it to object to the punitive reparations payments imposed on Germany by the Allied countries after World War I. The amounts demanded by the Allies were so large, he wrote, that a Germany that tried to pay them would stay perpetually poor and, therefore, politically unstable. We now know that Keynes was right. Besides its excellent economic analysis of reparations, Keynes's book contained an insightful analysis of the Council of Four (Clemenceau of France, Prime Minister Lloyd George of Britain, President Woodrow Wilson of the United States, and Vittorio Orlando of Italy).

Keynes wrote: "The Council of Four paid no attention to these issues [which included making Germany and Austro-Hungary into good neighbors], being preoccupied with others,—Clemenceau to crush the economic life of his enemy, Lloyd George to do a deal and bring home something which would pass muster for a week, the President to do nothing that was not just and right."

In the twenties Keynes was a believer in the quantity theory of money (today called monetarism). His writings on the topic were essentially built upon the principles he had learned from his mentors, Marshall and Pigou. In 1923 he wrote *Tract on Monetary Reform,* and later he published *Treatise on Money,* both on monetary policy. His major policy view was that the way to stabilize the economy was to stabilize the price level, and that to do that the government's central bank must lower interest rates when prices tend to rise and raise them when prices tend to fall.

Keynes's ideas took a dramatic change, however, as unemployment in Britain dragged on during the interwar period, reaching levels as high as 20 percent. Keynes investigated other causes of Britain's economic woes, and *The General Theory of Employment, Interest and Money* was the result.

Keynes's General Theory revolutionized the way economists think about economics. It was path breaking in several ways. The two most important are, first, that it introduced the notion of aggregate demand as the sum of consumption, investment, and government spending. Second, it showed (or purported to show) that full employment could be maintained only with the help of government spending. Economists still argue about what Keynes thought caused high unemployment. Some think that Keynes attributed unemployment to wages that take a long time to fall. But Keynes actually wanted wages not to fall, and advocated in the General Theory that wages be kept stable. A general cut in wages, he argued, would decrease income, consumption, and aggregate demand. This would offset any benefits to output that the lower price of labor might have contributed.

Why shouldn't government, thought Keynes, fill the shoes of business by investing in public works and hiring the unemployed? General Theory advocated deficit spending during economic downturns to maintain full employment. Keynes's conclusion initially met with opposition. At the time, balanced budgets were standard practice with the government. But the idea soon took hold and the United States government put people back to work on public works projects. Of course, once policymakers had taken deficit spending to heart, they could not let it go.

Contrary to some of his critics' assertions, Keynes was a relatively strong advocate of free markets. It was Keynes, not Adam Smith, who said "there is no objection to be raised against the classical analysis of the manner in which private self-interest will determine what in particular is produced, in what proportions the factors of production will be combined to produce it, and how the value of the final product will be distributed between them." Keynes believed that once full employment was achieved by fiscal policy measures, the market mechanism could then operate freely. "Thus," continued Keynes, "apart from the necessity of central controls to bring about an adjustment between the propensity to consume and the inducement to invest, there is no more reason to socialize economic life than there was before."

Little of Keynes's original work survives in modern economic theory. Instead, his ideas have been endlessly revised, expanded, and critiqued. Keynesian economics today, while having its roots in *The General Theory*, is chiefly the product of work by subsequent economists including John Hicks, James Tobin, Paul Samuelson, Alan Blinder, Robert Solow, William Nordhaus, Charles Schultze, Robert Heller, and Arthur Okun. The study of econometrics was created, in large part, to empirically explain Keynes's macroeconomic models. Yet the fact that Keynes is the wellspring for so many outstanding economists is testament to the magnitude and influence of his ideas.

Selected Works

The Economic Consequences of Mr. Churchill. 1925. Reprinted in *Keynes, Collected Writings*, vol. 9.

The Economic Consequences of the Peace. 1919. Reprinted in *Keynes, Collected Writings*, vol. 2.

The General Theory of Employment, Interest and Money. 1936. Reprinted in *Keynes, Collected Writings*, vol. 7.

Indian Currency and Finance. 1913. Reprinted in *Keynes, Collected Writings*, vol. 1.

A Tract on Monetary Reform. 1923. Reprinted in *Keynes, Collected Writings*, vol. 4.

A Treatise on Money. Vol. 1: *The Pure Theory of Money*. 1930. Reprinted in *Keynes, Collected Writings*, vol. 5.

A Treatise on Money. Vol. 2: *The Applied Theory of Money*. 1930. Reprinted in *Keynes, Collected Writings*, vol. 6.

Klein, Lawrence Robert (1920–   )—Lawrence R. Klein received the Nobel Prize in 1980 for "the creation of economic models and their application to the analysis of economic fluctuations and economic policies." Klein began model building while still a graduate student. After getting his Ph.D. from MIT, he moved on to the Cowles Commission for Research in Economics, which was then at the University of Chicago. While there he built a model of the U.S. economy, using Jan Tinbergen's earlier model as a starting point. His purpose was to use the model to forecast economic conditions and to estimate the impact of changes in government spending, taxes, and other policies.

In 1946 the conventional wisdom was that the end of World War II would sink the economy into a depression for a few years. Klein used his model to counter the conventional wisdom. The demand for consumer goods that had been left unsatisfied during the war, he argued, plus the purchasing power of returning soldiers, would prevent a depression. Klein was right. Later he predicted correctly that the end of the Korean War would bring only a mild recession.

Klein moved to the University of Michigan, where he proceeded to build bigger and more complicated models of the U.S. economy. The Klein-Goldberger model, which he built with then graduate student Arthur Goldberger, dates from that time. But in 1954, after being denied tenure for having been a member of the Communist party from 1946 to 1947, Klein went to Oxford University. There he built a model of the British economy.

In 1958 Klein joined the Department of Economics at the University of Pennsylvania. He has been a professor of economics and finance at the university's Wharton School since 1968. There he built the famous Wharton model of the U.S. economy, which contains over a thousand simultaneous equations that are solved by computers.

In 1976 Klein was coordinator of Jimmy Carter's economic task force but turned down an invitation to join Carter's new administration. In 1977 he was president of the American Economic Association.

Selected Works

(With Gary Fromm.) *The Brookings Model*. 1975.
Economic Fluctuations in the United States, 1921–1941. 1950.
The Economics of Supply and Demand. 1983.
(With Arthur S. Goldberger.) *Econometric Model of the United States, 1929–52*. 1955.
The Keynesian Revolution, 2d ed. 1966.

Knight, Frank Hyneman (1885–1972)— Frank H. Knight was one of the founders of the so-called Chicago school of economics, of which Milton Friedman and George Stigler were the leading members from the fifties to the eighties. Knight made his reputation with his book *Risk, Uncertainty, and Profit*, which was based on his Ph.D. dissertation. In it Knight set out to explain why perfect competition would not necessarily eliminate profits. His explanation was ''uncertainty,'' which Knight distinguished from risk. According to Knight risk refers to a situation where the probability of an outcome could be determined, and therefore, the outcome could be insured against. Uncertainty, by contrast, referred to an event whose probability could not be known. Knight argued that even in long-run equilibrium, entreprenuers would earn profits as a return for their putting up with uncertainty. Knight's distinction between risk and uncertainty is still taught in economics classes today.

Knight made three other important contributions to economics. One was *The Economic Organization*, a set of lecture notes originally published in 1933. In it he lays out the circular flow model of the economy and emphasizes that investments will be made until the returns to investments in each use are equal at the margin. These elements still survive in textbooks today.

Another of Knight's contributions to economics was in his famous article ''Some Fallacies in the Interpretation of Social Cost,'' in which he took on Pigou's view that congestion of roads justified taxation of roads. Knight showed that if roads were privately owned, road owners would set tolls that would reduce congestion. Therefore, no government intervention was required.

Knight's final contribution was his work on capital theory in the thirties. Knight criticized Böhm-Bawerk's view that capital could be measured as a period of production (see BÖHM-BAWERK). Knight was seen to have won the debate over the Austrian concept of capital.

But Knight was much more than an economist. He was also a social philosopher, and most of his writings were in social philosophy rather than technical economics. A strong believer in freedom and a strong critic of social engineering, Knight worried that freedom would be undermined by increases in monopoly and in income inequality. George Stigler tells of Milton Friedman challenging Knight's view that inequality would increase, and Knight's relenting, only to take the same position at the next lunch.

Knight often despaired about whether even simple economic truths could be understood by the public. In his 1950 presidential address to the American Economic Association, Knight said:

> Of late I have a new and depressing example of popular economic thinking, in the policy of arbitrary price-fixing. Can there be any use in explaining, if it is needful to explain, that fixing a price below the free-market level will create a shortage and one above it a surplus? But the public oh's and ah's and yips and yaps at the shortage of residential housing and surpluses of eggs and potatoes as if these things presented problems any more than getting one's footgear soiled by deliberately walking in the mud.

Knight was an economics professor at the University of Chicago from 1927 until 1955, after which he was emeritus professor until his death.

Selected Works

The Economic Organisation. 1951.
The Ethics of Competition, and Other Essays. 1935.
Freedom and Reform: Essays in Economics and Social Philosophy. 1947. Reprint, edited by J. M. Buchanan. 1982.
Risk, Uncertainty and Profit. 1921.
''Some Fallacies in the Interpretation of Social Cost.'' *Quarterly Journal of Economics* 38 (1924): 582–606.

Koopmans, Tjalling Charles (1910–85)— Tjalling Koopmans shared the 1975 Nobel Prize with Leonid Kantorovich ''for their contributions to the theory of optimum allocation of resources.'' Koopmans, a native of the Netherlands, started in mathematics and physics, but in the thirties switched to economics because it was ''closer to real life.'' In 1938 he succeeded Jan Tinbergen at the League of Nations in Geneva and left in 1940 when Hitler invaded the Netherlands. In the United States Koopmans became a statistician with the Combined Shipping Adjustment Board in Washington. At that job he tried to solve the practical problem of how to reorganize shipping to minimize transportation costs. The problem was complex: the variables included thousands of merchant ships, millions of tons of cargo, and hundreds of ports. He solved it. The technique he developed to do so was called ''activity analysis'' and is now called linear programming. His first write-up of the analysis is in a 1942 memorandum. His techniques were very similar to those used by Kantorovich, whose work he discovered only much later.

Koopmans was also like Kantorovich in generalizing his approach from one sector of the economy to the economy as a whole. Koopmans showed the conditions required for economy-wide efficiency in allocating resources. He also, again like Kantorovich, used his activity-analysis techniques to derive efficient criteria for allocating between the present and the future.

Koopmans was an economist with the Cowles Commission at the University of Chicago between 1944 and 1955, and then moved with the Cowles Commission to Yale University, where he became professor of economics until he retired in 1981. Koopmans became an American citizen in 1946. He served as president of the American Economic Association in 1981.

Selected Works

"Exchange Ratios between Cargoes on Various Routes (Non-Refrigerating Dry Cargoes)." Memorandum for the Combined Shipping Adustment Board. 1942. Reprinted in Koopmans. *Scientific Papers.* 1970.
"Optimum Utilization of the Transportation System." Proceedings of the International Statistical Conferences, vol. 5 (1947): 136–45. Reprinted in *Supplement to Econometrica* 17 (July 1949): 136–46.
Scientific Papers of Tjalling C. Koopmans. 1970. (Contains a bibliography through September 1969.)
Three Essays on the State of Economic Science. 1957.

Kuznets, Simon (1901–85)—Simon Kuznets is best known for his studies of national income and its components. Prior to World War I, measures of GNP were rough guesses at best. No government agency collected data to compute GNP, and no private economic researcher did so systematically, either. Kuznets changed all that. With work that began in the thirties and stretched over decades, Kuznets computed na-

tional income back to 1869. He broke it down by industry, by final product, and by use. He also measured the distribution of income between rich and poor.

Although Kuznets was not the first economist to try this, his work was so comprehensive and meticulous that it set the standard in the field. His work was funded by the nonprofit National Bureau of Economic Research, which had been started in 1920. Kuznets later helped the U.S. Department of Commerce to standardize the measurement of GNP. In the late forties, however, he broke with the Commerce Department over its refusal to use GNP as a measure of economic well-being. He had wanted the department to measure the value of unpaid housework because this was an important component of production. The department refused, and still does.

Kuznets's development of measures of savings, consumption, and investment came along just as Keynes's ideas about how national income is determined created a demand for such measures. Thus, Kuznets helped advance the Keynesian revolution. Kuznets's measures also helped advance the study of econometrics established by Ragnar Frisch and Jan Tinbergen.

Kuznets approached his work with a strict adherence to fact and a desire to understand economic phenomena through quantitative measurement. He had started early in his native Russia: he was head of a statistical office in the Ukraine under the Bolsheviks before moving to the United States at age twenty-one.

Many economists believe that Kuznets got his 1971 Nobel Prize for his measurement in national income accounting, and certainly that was enough to merit the prize. But in fact, he got the prize for his empirical work on economic growth. In this work Kuznets identified a new economic era—which he called "modern economic growth"—that began in northwestern Europe in the last half of the eighteenth century. The growth spread south and east and by the end of the nineteenth century had reached Russia and Japan. In this era per capita income rose by about 15 percent or more each decade, something that had not happened in earlier centuries.

One of Kuznets's more startling findings was the effect of economic growth on income distribution. In poor countries, found Kuznets, economic growth increased the income disparity between rich and poor people. In wealthier countries, economic growth narrowed the difference. In addition, Kuznets analyzed and quantified the cyclical nature of production and prices in spans of fifteen to twenty years. Such trade cycles, while disputed, are often referred to as "Kuznets cycles."

Kuznets was a professor of economics at the University of Pennsylvania (1930–54), Johns Hopkins University (1954–60), and Harvard University (1960–71). He was president of the American Economic Association in 1954.

Selected Works

Economic Growth of Nations: Total Output and Production Structure. 1971.
Economic Growth and Structure: Selected Essays. 1965.
(With Milton Friedman.) *Income from Independent Professional Practice.* 1945.
Modern Economic Growth: Rate, Structure, and Spread. 1966.
National Income, 1929–1932. Senate document no. 124, 73d Congress, 2d session. 1934.
National Income and Capital Formation, 1919–1935. 1937.
(Assisted by Lillian Epstein and Elizabeth Jenks.) *National Product since 1869.* 1946.
(Assisted by Elizabeth Jenks.) *Shares of Upper Income Groups in Income and Savings.* 1953.

Lange, Oskar Ryszard (1904–65)—Polish economist Oskar Lange is best known for his contributions to the economics of socialism. His

views on the feasibility of socialism changed back and forth throughout his life.

While teaching at the University of Krakow in 1934, he outlined, with coauthor Marek Breit, a version of socialism in which the government owned all plants and in which each industry, called a public trust, was organized as a monopoly. Workers would have a large say in running each industry.

Lange left Europe in 1935 to teach at the University of Michigan. In 1936 and 1937 he entered the debate with Friedrich Hayek (see HAYEK) about the feasibility of socialism. He presented "market socialism," in which the government would own major industries and a central planning board (CPB) would set prices for those industries. The CPB would alter prices to reach equilibrium, raising them to get rid of shortages and lowering them to get rid of surpluses. Hayek pointed out that having government set prices to mimic competition, as Lange suggested, seemed inferior to having real competition. Whether in response to Hayek's criticism or for other reasons, Lange modified his proposal, advocating that only in industries with few firms would he have the government set prices.

In 1943 Lange moved to the University of Chicago. That same year he advocated that the Polish government socialize key industries, but that farms, shops, and many other small and medium-sized industries remain in private hands. A large private sector, wrote Lange, was necessary to preserve "the kind of flexibility, pliability and adaptiveness that private initiative alone cannot achieve."

In 1945, Poland's newly formed communist government appointed Lange ambassador to the United States and in 1946 Poland's delegate to the United Nations. When Stalinist orthodoxy was imposed in Poland in 1949, Lange was recalled to Poland and given a minor academic job. In 1953, with Poland still under Stalinist oppression, Lange reversed himself and wrote an article praising Stalin's totalitarian economic control.

In 1955, with the political oppression having lifted somewhat, Lange was made a professor at the University of Warsaw and chairman of the Polish State Economic Council.

Selected Works

"The Foundations of Welfare Economics." *Econometrica* 10, no. 3–4 (July–October 1942): 215–28.
"On the Economic Theory of Socialism, Part I." *Review of Economic Studies* 4, no.1 (October 1936): 53–71.
"On the Economic Theory of Socialism, Part II." *Review of Economic Studies* 4, no. 2 (February 1937): 123–42.
Working Principles of the Soviet Economy. 1943.

See also SOCIALISM.

Leontief, Wassily (1906–   )—Since he was a young man growing up in St. Petersburg, Wassily Leontief has devoted his studies to input-output analysis. When he left Russia at the age of nineteen to begin the Ph.D. program at the University of Berlin, he had already shown how Leon Walras's abstract equilibrium theory could be quantified. But it was not until many years later, in 1941, while a professor at Harvard, that Leontief calculated an input-output table for the American economy. It was this work, and later refinements of it, that earned Leontief the Nobel Prize in 1973.

Input-output analysis shows the extensive process by which inputs in one industry produce outputs for consumption or for input into another industry. The matrix devised by Leontief is often used to show the effect of a change in production of a final good on the demand for inputs. Take, for example, a 10 percent increase in the production of shoes. With the input-output ta-

ble, one can estimate how much additional leather, labor, machinery, and other inputs will be required to increase shoe production.

Most economists are cautious in using the table. The reason is that it assumes, to take the shoe example, that shoe production requires the inputs in the proportion they were used during the time period used to estimate the table. Therein lies the rub. Although the table is useful as a rough approximation of the inputs required, economists know from mountains of evidence that proportions are not fixed. Specifically, when the cost of one input rises, producers reduce their use of this input and substitute other inputs whose prices have not risen. If wage rates rise, for example, producers can substitute capital for labor and, by accepting more wasted materials, can even substitute raw materials for labor. That the input-output table is inflexible means that if used literally to make predictions, it will necessarily give wrong answers.

At the time of Leontief's first work with input-output analysis, all the required matrix algebra was done using, as inputs, hand-held calculators and sheer tenacity. Since then, computers have greatly simplified the process, and input-output analysis, now called "interindustry analysis," is widely used. Leontief's tables are commonly used by the World Bank, the United Nations, and the U.S. Department of Commerce.

Early on, input-output analysis was used to estimate the economy-wide impact of converting from war production to civilian production after World War II. It has also been used to understand the flow of trade between countries. Indeed, a 1954 article by Leontief showed, using input-output analysis, that U.S. exports were relatively labor-intensive compared to U.S. imports. This was the opposite of what economists expected at the time, given the high level of U.S. wages and the relatively high amount of capital per worker in the United States. Leontief's finding was termed the Leontief paradox. Since then, the paradox has been resolved. Economists have shown that in a country that produces more than two goods, the abundance of capital relative to labor does not imply that the capital intensity of its exports should exceed that of its imports.

Throughout his life Leontief has campaigned against "theoretical assumptions and nonobserved facts" (the title of a speech he delivered while president of the American Economic Association, 1970–71). According to Leontief too many economists were reluctant to "get their hands dirty" by working with raw empirical facts. To that end Wassily Leontief has done much to make quantitative data more accessible, and more indispensable, to the study of economics.

Selected Works

Essays in Economics: Theories and Theorizing. 1966.
The Structure of American Economy, 1919–1929. 1941.

Lerner, Abba Ptachya (1905–82)—Abba Lerner was the Milton Friedman of the left. Like Friedman, Lerner was a brilliant expositor of economics who was able to make complex concepts crystal clear. Also, Lerner was an unusual kind of socialist: he hated government power over people's lives. Like Friedman, he praised private enterprise on the ground that "alternatives to government employment are a safeguard of the freedom of the individual." Also like Friedman, Lerner loved free markets. He opposed minimum wage laws and other price controls because they interfered with the price system, which he called "one of the most valuable instruments of modern society."

Both his clear writing and his hatred of authority are illustrated in the following defense of consumer sovereignty, from "The Economics and Politics of Consumer Sovereignty":

One of the deepest scars of my early youth was etched when my teacher told me, "You do not want that," after I had told her that I did. I would not have been so upset if she had said that I could not have it, whatever it was, or that it was very wicked of me to want it. What rankled was the denial of my personality—a kind of rape of my integrity. I confess I still find a similar rising of my hackles when I hear people's preferences dismissed as not genuine, because influenced by advertising, and somebody else telling them what they "really want."

Lerner, like Friedman, had a sharp analytic mind that made him follow an argument to its logical conclusion. During World War II, for example, when John Maynard Keynes gave a talk at the Federal Reserve board in Washington, Lerner, who was in the audience, found Keynes's view of how the economy worked completely convincing and challenged Keynes for not carrying his own argument to its logical conclusion. Keynes denounced Lerner on the spot, but Keynes's colleague Evsey Domar, seated beside Lerner, whispered, "He ought to read *The General Theory*." A month later, wrote Lerner, Keynes withdrew his denunciation.

Lerner was born in Rumania and immigrated with his parents to Britain while still a child. He tried out several avocations: as tailor, Hebrew teacher, typesetter, and owner of a printing business that went bankrupt during the Great Depression. He turned to economics, enrolling in a night course at the London School of Economics in 1929, in order to discover why his business had failed. Lerner earned top honors and several scholarships for his logically reasoned essays, many of which were published while he was still an undergraduate. His appointment as assistant lecturer at the LSE in 1936 was the first of many teaching positions, the rest of which he held in the United States after 1937. Paul Samuelson, in a tribute to Lerner on his sixtieth birthday, wrote that Lerner's experience "tempts one to advise students in Economics A to quit college, fail in business, marry and raise a family, and resist being overpaid."

One of Lerner's first papers, published in 1934, was a clear diagrammatic exposition of international trade. Earlier, he had written, but not published, a proof of the conditions under which free trade in goods causes the prices of factors to be equal even when factors are mobile. Samuelson showed the same thing in an article much later. Samuelson wrote: "After I had enunciated the same result in 1948, Lord Robbins mentioned to me that he thought he had a seminar paper in his files by Lerner of a similar type. . . . He exhumed this gem, which appeared 17 years later in the 1950 *Economica*."

Probably Lerner's most well-known article was "The Concept of Monopoly and the Measurement of Monopoly Power." In it he laid out clearly why setting the price of a good equal to its marginal cost was important for efficiency. The amount by which the price exceeded marginal cost, then, was a measure of monopoly power in an industry. In 1964 Samuelson wrote: "Today this may seem simple, but I can testify that no one at Chicago or Harvard could tell me in 1935 exactly why $P = MC$ was a good thing."

Lerner's main contribution to macroeconomic policy was his concept of functional finance. Lerner's idea was that if governments wanted to increase aggregate demand so as to maintain employment, and if the federal budget was balanced, the government should run a deficit by increasing government spending or decreasing taxes. If, on the other hand, the government wanted to decrease aggregate demand, it should, if the budget was balanced, run a surplus by decreasing government spending or raising taxes. These thoughts are often attributed to Keynes, and they do follow from Keynes's rea-

soning. But Keynes never stated them. It took Lerner's clear thinking to get from Keynes's model of the economy to these policy conclusions. The reason Lerner's thoughts are attributed to Keynes is that textbook writers, wanting to make Keynes's thinking clear, were immediately drawn to Lerner's thinking. As economist David Colander has written, Keynes could be considered just as much a Lernerian as a Keynesian.

Lerner was active in economic analysis till the day he died. In 1980, for example, he laid out a plan for breaking OPEC. In an article titled "OPEC—A Plan—If You Can't Beat Them, Join Them," Lerner advocated that the United States and other governments of oil-consuming countries impose a 100 percent excise tax on the difference between OPEC's price and the pre-OPEC price adjusted for inflation. In 1980 OPEC charged $26 for a barrel of oil. The pre-OPEC price adjusted for inflation was $6. Therefore, at that price, the tax would have been 100 percent of $26 − $6, or $20. Lerner's plan, if followed, would have caused the price to consumers to rise $2 every time OPEC raised its price $1. More important, it would have caused the price to fall by $2 every time OPEC lowered its price by $1. Lerner's thinking, which was absolutely watertight, was that this plan would double consumers' elasticity of demand, causing them to demand less oil at higher prices and thus reduce the strength of the cartel. The plan was never adopted.

Lerner never developed a following. One reason, wrote Tibor Scitovsky of Stanford, was "Lerner's unrelenting logic," which "overruled whatever loyalties he started with" and "made him seem like a cold fish to just about everybody." Another reason was that Lerner rarely stayed in one university long, teaching at Columbia, the University of Virginia, Kansas City, Amherst, The New School for Social Research, Roosevelt, Johns Hopkins, Michigan State, and the University of California, Berkeley. Another reason was that although he made major contributions in so many areas, he did not have a specialty. Also, Lerner made his insights so clear and so apparently obvious that people who adopted his ideas forgot where they learned them. Probably because he lacked a following, Lerner never won the Nobel Prize, although many economists think he should have.

Selected Works

"The Concept of Monopoly and the Measurement of Monopoly Power." *Review of Economic Studies* 1 (June 1934). 157–75.

"The Diagrammatical Representation of Demand Conditions in International Trade." *Economica* NS 1 (August 1934): 319–34.

"The Economics and Politics of Consumer Sovereignty." *American Economic Review* (May 1972): 258–66.

The Economics of Control: Principles of Welfare Economics. 1944.

"Functional Finance and the Federal Debt." *Social Research* 10 (February 1943): 38–51.

"OPEC—A Plan—If You Can't Beat Them, Join Them." *Atlantic Economic Journal* (September 1980): 1–3.

"The Symmetry between Import and Export Taxes." *Economica* NS 3 (August 1936): 306–13.

Lewis, W. Arthur (1915–91)—In 1979, British citizen W. Arthur Lewis was awarded the Nobel Prize, along with Theodore Schultz, for "pioneering research into economic development . . . with particular consideration of the problems of developing countries." One of Lewis's major contributions to economics was a 1954 article that discussed his concept of a "dual economy" in a poor country. According to Lewis a poor country's economy could be thought of as containing two sectors, a small "capitalist" sector and a very large "traditional" (agricultural) sector. Employers in the capitalist sector hired people to make money.

Employers in the traditional sector, on the other hand, were not profit-maximizing and therefore hired too many people so that their productivity was very low. (The immediate question, of course, is why employers in the traditional sector would do this, and economists still debate what Lewis's reasons were for thinking this.) Lewis argued on this basis that the way to get development in poor countries is to shift labor into manufacturing, where it is more productive. Then the capitalists save out of their profits and use this saving to expand, which then adds to growth. Lewis assumed that workers in agriculture save nothing, so that the only source of saving is the capitalists in manufacturing.

Lewis used his model to explain the pattern of growth in countries in general. This was how he explained the inverted U-shape growth according to a country's per capita income. For very poor countries like Bangladesh, growth is slow because the manufacturing sector is small or nonexistent, and therefore there is no large source of savings. For middle-income countries like Korea and Taiwan, growth is high because the manufacturing sector is growing and pulling labor out of agriculture, where it is underemployed. For high-income countries with a large manufacturing sector, like the United States, growth is slower because the gains from diverting labor out of agriculture are almost all exploited.

In the same 1954 article Lewis made a separate argument for poor countries engaged in trade. He argued that poor countries would capture little or no benefit from increasing their exports. Instead, he claimed, they would confer benefits on consumers in the countries that import their exports. Take his example in which the richer countries produce steel (shorthand for manufactured goods) and food, and the poorer countries produce coffee (shorthand for exports of poor countries) and food. Assume that before exports are increased, ten pounds of coffee trade for one ton of steel. Now, because producers in the poor countries have a low opportunity cost of increasing exports of coffee (because the food that they could have produced is worth little), they will increase exports. But doing so will drive down the price of coffee. Say the exchange rate falls to twenty pounds of coffee per ton of steel. This is a good deal for coffee buyers, but not for coffee producers. In essence, Lewis was arguing that poorer countries had latent monopoly power in their exports that they were failing to exploit. These countries would do better, he argued, to divert their production into food and away from exports.

Lewis himself came from a poor British colony, St. Lucia in the West Indies. He entered the London School of Economics on a scholarship at age eighteen. Stated Lewis: "I wanted to be an engineer, but neither the colonial government nor the sugar plantations would hire a black engineer." So he decided to study economics. He earned his Ph.D. from the London School of Economics in 1940. He began working on problems of the world economy at the suggestion of Friedrich Hayek, then chairman of LSE's economics department. After World War II, when many former colonies became independent, Lewis began his study of economic development. Lewis had no sympathy for the view that poor countries should be run by dictators so that they could develop.

Lewis was a lecturer at the University of London from 1938 to 1948, then Stanley Jevons Professor of Political Economy at the University of Manchester from 1948 to 1958. He was vice chancellor of the University of West Indies from 1959 to 1963 and a professor of political economy at Princeton University from 1963 until his death.

Selected Works

"Economic Development with Unlimited Supplies of Labour." *Manchester School* 22 (May 1954): 139–91.
Economic Survey 1919–1939. 1949.

Politics in West Africa. 1965.
"The Slowing Down of the Engine of Growth." Nobel Lecture. Printed in *American Economic Review* 70, no. 4 (December 1980): 555–64.
The Theory of Economic Growth. 1955.

Locke, John (1632–1704)—Born in England, John Locke was a persistent champion of natural rights—the idea that each person owns himself and should have certain liberties that cannot be expropriated by the state or anyone else. When someone labors for a productive end, the results become that person's property, reasoned Locke. His conclusion that labor contributes far more than nature to the value of goods was the first step toward the labor theory of value, as articulated by David Ricardo and Karl Marx.

Locke also believed that governments should not regulate interest rates. In a pamphlet titled *Considerations of the Consequences of the Lowering of Interest,* Locke opposed a bill before Parliament to lower the maximum legal interest rate from 6 percent to 4 percent. Because interest was a price, and because all prices are determined by the laws of nature, he reasoned, ceilings on interest rates would be counterproductive. People would evade the ceiling, and the costs of evasion would drive interest rates even higher than they would have been without the ceiling, he wrote. Locke's reasoning on the subject, sophisticated for his era, has stood the test of time: economists make the same objection to controls on interest rates today. (See INTEREST, PRICE CONTROLS.)

Locke also sketched out a quantity theory of money, which held that the value of money was inversely related to the quantity of money in circulation. Locke erroneously believed that a country was in danger of falling into depression if its gold inflows from trade fell relative to those of its trade partners. What he did not realize, and what went unrealized until David Hume pointed it out, was that gold flows cannot get out of line with trade flows. If "too little" gold came into Britain relative to gold inflows to other countries, for example (Locke assumed that the supply of gold would grow relative to the volume of trade), then British goods would become cheap relative to other countries' goods, causing more gold to flow to England from other countries.

Selected Works

Several Papers Relating to Money, Interest and Trade, et cetera. 1696. Reprint. 1968.
Two Treatises of Government. 1690. Reprint, edited by Peter Laslett, 2d ed. 1953.

Machlup, Fritz (1902–83)—Born in Austria, Fritz Machlup moved to the United States in 1933. He worked in two main areas: industrial organization, with particular emphasis on the production and distribution of knowledge, and international monetary economics.

One of Machlup's most famous articles in industrial organization was a 1946 defense of the economist's standard assumption that firms maximize profits. Economist Richard Lester had argued that businessmen do not know enough about their demand and cost conditions to maximize profits. Machlup agreed but argued that the purpose of assuming profit maximization is not to predict everything a firm does, but instead to predict how it will react to changes in demand or in costs. For this purpose, argued Machlup, the assumption was appropriate. Machlup expanded on this argument in two later books, *The Economics of Sellers' Competition* and *The Political Economy of Monopoly.*

Another of Machlup's contributions to understanding the organization of industry was his 1949 book, *The Basing-Point System,* which is said to have influenced President Truman's decision to veto a bill that would have forced cement producers to charge the same price irrespective of their buyers' locations. Machlup also wrote at length about the economics of the patent system.

Machlup studied economics at the University of Vienna in the twenties under Ludwig von Mises and Friedrich Hayek. He wrote his doctoral dissertation under Mises on the gold-exchange standard. But from 1922 to 1932, he worked in his family's cardboard-manufacturing business. His interest in and insights into the economics of industry are often attributed to his experience in the family business. Machlup taught at the University of Buffalo from 1935 to 1947, moved to Johns Hopkins in 1947, and moved to Princeton in 1960. After retiring in 1971 he joined the faculty of New York University, where he was active until his death. Machlup was president of the American Economic Association in 1966.

Selected Works

The Basing-Point System. 1949.
An Economic Review of the Patent System. Study of the Subcommittee on Patents, Trademarks, and Copyrights of the Committee on the Judiciary, U.S. Senate, study no. 15. 1958.
The Economics of Sellers' Competition. 1952.
International Payments, Debts, and Gold, 2d ed. 1976.
The Political Economy of Monopoly. 1952.
The Production and Distribution of Knowledge in the United States. 1962.

Malthus, Thomas Robert (1766–1834)—Thomas Malthus studied philosophy and mathematics at St. John's College, Cambridge. Although he is known for his dire warnings against overpopulation, Malthus did not oppose population growth per se. Rather, he opposed growth that would outstrip the food supply. He predicted that population would grow geometrically, while the food supply would increase only arithmetically, resulting in mass starvation. His apocalyptic vision and his widely accepted subsistence theory of wages (wages will drop to the minimum required to sustain a worker because high wages induce population growth) helped stigmatize economics as the "dismal science."

Writing before the industrial revolution, Malthus could not fully appreciate the impact of technology (i.e., pesticides, refrigeration, mechanized farm equipment, and increased crop yields) on food production. Further discrediting his claims is the fact that life expectancy has nearly doubled, from forty years during his time to over seventy years today. Although starvation persists, it is more often political upheaval, not population growth, that keeps people hungry.

Although Malthus predicted disastrous undersupply of commodities in the long run, he believed there could be a general oversupply in the short run. These oversupplies, which he called "gluts," are now called recessions or depressions.

Selected Works

An Essay on the Principle of Population. 1798. Reprint. 1926.
"Pamphlets on the Bullion Question." *Edinburgh Review* 18 (August 1811): 448–70.
Principles of Political Economy. 1820.

Markowitz, Harry (1927–   )—In 1990, U.S. economists Harry Markowitz, William F. Sharpe, and Merton H. Miller shared the Nobel Prize for their contributions to financial economics. Their contributions, in fact, were what started financial economics as a separate field of study. In the early fifties Markowitz developed portfolio theory, which looks at how investment returns can be optimized. Economists had long understood the common sense of diversifying a portfolio; the expression "don't put all your eggs in one basket" has been around for a long time. But Markowitz showed how to measure the risk of various securities and how to combine them in a portfolio to get the maximum return for a given risk.

Say, for example, shares in Exxon and in General Motors have a high risk and a high return, but one share tends to go up when the other falls. This could happen because when OPEC raises the price of oil and, therefore, of gasoline, the prices of gasoline producers' shares rise and the prices of auto producers' shares fall. Then a portfolio that includes both Exxon and GM shares could earn a high return and have a lower risk than either share alone. Portfolio managers now routinely use techniques that are based on Markowitz's original insight.

Markowitz earned his Ph.D. at the University of Chicago. He has taught at Baruch College of the City University of New York since 1982.

Selected Works

"Portfolio Selection." *Journal of Finance* 7, no. 1 (March 1952): 77–91.
Portfolio Selection: Efficient Diversification of Investments. 1959. Reprint. 1970.

Marshall, Alfred (1842–1924)—Alfred Marshall was the dominant figure in British economics (itself dominant in world economics) from about 1890 until his death in 1924. His specialty was microeconomics—the study of individual markets and industries, as opposed to the study of the whole economy. His most important book was *Principles of Economics*. In it Marshall emphasized that the price and output of a good are determined by both supply and demand: the two curves are like scissor blades that intersect at equilibrium. Modern economists trying to understand why the price of a good changes still start by looking for factors that may have shifted demand or supply. They owe this approach to Marshall.

To Marshall also goes credit for the concept of price-elasticity of demand, which quantifies buyers' sensitivity to price.

Marshall also originated the concept of consumer surplus. He noted that the price is typically the same for each unit of a commodity that a consumer buys, but the value to the consumer of each additional unit declines. A consumer will buy units up the point where the marginal value equals the price. Therefore, on all units previous to the last one, the consumer reaps a benefit by paying less than the value of the good to himself. The size of the benefit equals the difference between the consumer's value of all these units and the amount paid for the units. This difference is called the consumer surplus, for the surplus value or utility enjoyed by consumers. Marshall also introduced the concept of producer surplus, the amount the producer is actually paid minus the amount that he would willingly accept. Marshall used these concepts to measure the changes in well-being from government policies such as taxation. Although economists have refined the measures since Marshall's time, his basic approach to what is now called welfare economics still stands.

Marshall wanted to understand how markets adjusted to changes in supply or demand over time. Therefore, he introduced the idea of three periods. First is the market period, the amount of time for which the stock of a commodity is fixed. Second, the short period is the time in which the supply can be increased by adding labor and other inputs but not by adding capital (Marshall's term was "appliances"). Third, the long period is the amount of time taken for capital ("appliances") to be increased.

To make economics dynamic rather than static, Marshall used the tools of classical mechanics, including the concept of optimization. With these tools he, like neoclassical economists who have followed in his footsteps, took

as givens technology, market institutions, and people's preferences. But Marshall was not satisfied with his approach. He once wrote that "the Mecca of the economist lies in economic biology rather than in economic dynamics." In other words, Marshall was arguing that the economy was an evolutionary process in which technology, market institutions, and people's preferences evolve along with people's behavior.

Rarely did Marshall attempt a statement or position without expressing countless qualifications, exceptions, and footnotes. Marshall showed himself to be an astute mathematician—he studied math at St. John's College, Cambridge—but limited his quantitative expressions so that he might appeal to the layman.

Marshall himself was born into a middle-class family in London and raised to enter the clergy. He defied his parents' wishes and became an academic in mathematics and economics.

Selected Works

Principles of Economics, vol. 1. 1890.

Marx, Karl (1818–83)—Karl Marx was communism's most zealous intellectual advocate. His comprehensive writings on the subject laid the foundation for later political leaders, notably V. I. Lenin and Mao Tse-tung, to impose communism on over twenty countries.

Marx was born in Trier, Prussia (now Germany), in 1818. He studied philosophy at universities in Bonn and Berlin, earning his doctorate in Jena at the age of twenty-three. His early radicalism, first as a member of the Young Hegelians, then as editor of a newspaper suppressed for its derisive social and political content, preempted any career aspirations in academia and forced him to flee to Paris in 1843. It was then that Marx cemented his lifelong friendship with Friedrich Engels. In 1849 Marx moved to London, where he continued to study and write, drawing heavily upon works by David Ricardo and Adam Smith. Marx died in London in 1883 in somewhat impoverished surroundings, never having held a job in England and relying on Engels for financial support.

At the request of the Communist League, Marx and Engels coauthored their most famous work, "The Communist Manifesto," published in 1848. A call to arms for the proletariat—"Workers of the world, unite!"—the manifesto set down the principles on which communism was to evolve. Marx held that history was a series of class struggles between owners of capital (capitalists) and workers (the proletariat). As wealth became more concentrated in the hands of a few capitalists, he thought, the ranks of an increasingly dissatisfied proletariat would swell, leading to bloody revolution and eventually a classless society.

It has become fashionable to think that Karl Marx was not mainly an economist but instead had integrated various disciplines—economics, sociology, political science, history, and so on. But Mark Blaug, a noted historian of economic thought, points out that Marx wrote "no more than a dozen pages on the concept of social class, the theory of the state, and the materialist conception of history." Marx, writes Blaug, wrote "literally 10,000 pages on economics pure and simple."

According to Marx capitalism contained the seeds of its own destruction. Communism was the inevitable end to the process of evolution begun with feudalism and passing through capitalism and socialism. Marx wrote extensively about the economic causes of this process in *Capital,* with volume one published in 1867 and the later two volumes, heavily edited by Engels, published posthumously in 1885 and 1894.

He was a masterful economist and his rigorous analysis of capitalism in *Capital* is testament to the twenty years of scholarship that led up

to its completion. The labor theory of value, decreasing rates of profit, and increasing concentration of wealth were key components of Marx's economic thought. His comprehensive treatment of capitalism stands in stark contrast, however, to his treatment of socialism and communism, which Marx handled only superficially. He declined to speculate on how those two economic systems would operate.

—**Janet Beales** (Janet Beales was assistant editor of this encyclopedia, on a summer fellowship with the Institute for Humane Studies. She is a policy analyst with the Reason Foundation.)

Selected Works

Capital, vol. 1. 1867. Reprint. 1976.
Contribution to the Critique of Political Economy. 1858. Reprint. 1970.
"Manifesto of the Communist Party." 1848. Reprinted in *Marx: The Revolutions of 1848.* 1973.
"Wages, Price and Profits." 1865. Reprinted in *Marx-Engels Selected Works,* vol. 2. 1969.

See also MARXISM, SOCIALISM.

Meade, James Edward (1907–)—James Meade, an Englishman, was corecipient of the Nobel Prize in 1977, along with Bertil Ohlin, for their "pathbreaking contribution to the theory of international trade and international capital movements." Much of Meade's work on international trade is in the two volumes of his *Theory of International Economic Policy,* which, writes Mark Blaug, "have become the bible of every trade economist." In the book's first volume, *The Balance of Payments,* Meade made the point that for each of its policy objectives, the government requires a policy tool. This was a principle developed by Dutch economist Jan Tinbergen. Meade advocated using fiscal policy to achieve full employment and monetary policy to achieve the government's target on balance of payments.

In the second volume, *Trade and Welfare,* Meade examined conditions under which free trade made a country better off and conditions under which it did not. Meade concluded that, contrary to previous beliefs, if a country was already protecting one of its markets from international competition, further protection of another market could be "second best." That is, although the ideal would be to eliminate all protection, if for some reason this was not feasible, then adding a carefully chosen dose of protectionism could improve the nation's economic well-being.

Like Milton Friedman in the United States, Meade wanted to use economics to help make the world a better place, and believed that government regulation often harmed an economy. Unlike Friedman, he believed that government should take strong measures to promote equality of income. Said Meade: "I have my heart to the left and my brain to the right."

Meade also helped prepare the British government's set of national income accounts during World War II. Meade was a professor of commerce at the London School of Economics from 1947 to 1957 and then moved to Cambridge University, where he taught until he retired in 1974.

Selected Works

A Geometry of International Trade. 1969.
The Theory of International Economic Policy. Vol. 1, *The Balance of Payments,* 1951; Vol. 2, *Trade and Welfare,* with "Mathematical Supplements."

Menger, Carl (1840–1921)—Carl Menger has the twin distinction of being the founder of Austrian economics and a cofounder of the marginal utility revolution. Menger worked separately from William Jevons and Leon Walras and reached similar conclusions by a different method. Unlike Jevons, Menger did not believe that goods provide "utils," or units of utility. Rather, he wrote, goods were valuable because they served various uses whose importance differed. For example, the first pails of water are used to satisfy the most important uses, and successive pails are used for less and less important purposes.

Menger used this insight to resolve the diamond-water paradox that had baffled Adam Smith (see MARGINALISM). He also used it to refute the labor theory of value. Goods acquired their value, he showed, not because of the amount of labor used in producing them, but because of their ability to satisfy people's wants. Indeed, Menger turned the labor theory of value on its head. If the value of goods is determined by the importance of the wants they satisfy, then the value of labor and other inputs of production (he called them "goods of a higher order") derived from their ability to produce these goods. Mainstream economists still accept this theory.

Menger used his "subjective theory of value" to arrive at one of the most powerful insights in economics: both sides gain from exchange, or in modern jargon, exchange is a positive-sum game. People will exchange something that they value less for something they value more. Because both trading partners do this, both gain. This insight led him to see that middlemen are highly productive: they facilitate transactions that benefit those they buy from and those they sell to. Without the middlemen these transactions either would not have taken place or would have been more costly.

Menger also came up with an explanation of how money develops that is still accepted today. If people barter, he pointed out, then they can rarely get what they want in one or two transactions. If they have lamps and want chairs, for example, they will not necessarily be able to trade lamps for chairs but must instead make a few intermediate trades. This is a hassle. But people notice that the hassle is much less when they trade what they have for some good that is widely accepted, and then use this good to buy what they want. The good that is widely accepted eventually becomes money. Indeed, the word *pecuniary* derives from the Latin *pecus*, meaning cattle, which in some societies served as money. Other societies have used cigarettes, cognac, salt, furs, or stones as money. As economies became more complex and wealthier, they began to use precious metals (gold, silver, and so on) as money.

Menger extended his analysis to other institutions. He argued that language, for example, developed for the same reason money developed—to make interaction between people easier. He noted that neither language nor money was developed by government. He called such developments "organic."

The Austrian school of economic thought first coalesced from Menger's writings and those of two young disciples, Eugen von Böhm-Bawerk and Friedrich von Wieser. Later Austrian economists Ludwig von Mises and Friedrich Hayek, used Menger's insights as a starting point, Mises with his work on money and Hayek with his idea of "spontaneous order."

Carl Menger was born in Galicia, part of Austro-Hungary (now southern Poland), to a prosperous family. He was one of three talented brothers; Anton was a legal philosopher and socialist historian, and Karl was a prominent mathematician. Carl earned his doctorate in law from the University of Krakow in 1867. As a result of publishing his *Principles of Economics* in 1871, he was given a lectureship and then a professorship at the University of Vienna, which he held until 1903. In 1876 he took a tutoring post for the Crown Prince Rudolf of Austria. In that capacity he traveled throughout Germany, France, Switzerland, and England.

Selected Works

"On the Origin of Money." *Economic Journal* 2 (June 1892): 239–55.
Principles of Economics. 1871. Translated by J. Dingwall and B. F. Hoselitz, with an introduction by Friedrich A. Hayek. 1981.

Mill, John Stuart (1806–73)—The eldest son of economist James Mill, John Stuart Mill was educated according to the rigorous expectations of his Benthamite father. He was taught Greek at age three and Latin at age eight. By the time he reached young adulthood, John Stuart Mill was a formidable intellectual, albeit an emotionally depressed one. After recovering from a nervous breakdown, he departed from his Benthamite teachings to shape his own view of political economy. He wrote *Principles of Political Economy,* which became the leading economics textbook for forty years after it was written. In it Mill elaborated on the ideas of David Ricardo and Adam Smith. He helped develop the ideas of economies of scale, opportunity cost, and comparative advantage in trade.

Mill was a strong believer in freedom, especially of speech and of thought. He defended freedom on two grounds. First, he argued, society's utility would be maximized if each person was free to make his or her own choices. (The "her" is particularly appropriate. Mill strongly believed, possibly due to the influence of his wife, Harriet Taylor, whom he idolized, that women were the equals of men. His book *The Subjection of Women* attacked the contemporary view of women's inherent inferiority.) Second, Mill believed that freedom was required for each person's development as a whole person. In his famous essay *On Liberty,* Mill enunciated the principle that "the sole end for which mankind are warranted, individually or collectively, in interfering with the liberty of action of any of their number, is self-protection." He wrote that we should be "without impediment from our fellow-creatures, so long as what we do does not harm them, even though they should think our conduct foolish, perverse, or wrong."

Surprisingly, though, Mill was not a consistent advocate of laissez-faire. His biographer, Alan Ryan, conjectures that Mill did not think of freedom of contract and property rights as being part of freedom. Mill favored inheritance taxation, trade protectionism, and regulation of employees' hours of work. Interestingly, although Mill favored mandatory education, he did not advocate mandatory schooling. Instead, he advocated a voucher system for schools and a state system of exams to ensure that people had reached a minimum level of learning.

Although Mill advocated universal suffrage, he suggested that the better-educated voters be given more votes. He emphatically defended this proposal from the charge that it was intended to let the middle class dominate. He argued that it would protect against class legislation and that anyone who was educated, including poor people, would have more votes.

Mill spent most of his working life with the East India Company. He joined it at age sixteen and worked there for thirty-eight years. He had little effect on policy, but his experience did affect his views on self-government.

Selected Works

Considerations on Representative Government. 1861.
On Liberty. 1859.
Principles of Political Economy, with Some of Their Applications to Social Philosophy, 2 vols. 1848.
The Subjection of Women. 1869.

Miller, Merton H. (1923–   )—In 1990, U.S. economists Merton H. Miller, Harry Markowitz, and William F. Sharpe shared the Nobel Prize for their contributions to financial econom-

ics. Miller's contribution was the Modigliani-Miller theorem, which he developed with Franco Modigliani while both were professors at Carnegie Institute of Technology. (Modigliani had earned the prize in 1985 for his life-cycle model of saving and for the Modigliani-Miller theorem.)

The Modigliani-Miller theorem says that under certain assumptions, the value of a firm is independent of the firm's ratio of debt to equity (see CORPORATE DEBT). Miller once gave a colorful analogy to try to simplify his and Modigliani's insight, which he relates in *Financial Innovations and Market Volatility*:

> Think of the firm as a gigantic tub of whole milk. The farmer can sell the whole milk as it is. Or he can separate out the cream, and sell it at a considerably higher price than the whole milk would bring. (Selling cream is the analog of a firm selling debt securities, which pay a contractual return.) But, of course, what the farmer would have left would be skim milk, with low butter-fat content, and that would sell for much less than whole milk. (Skim milk corresponds to the levered equity.) The Modigliani-Miller proposition says that if there were no cost of separation (and, of course, no government dairy support program), the cream plus the skim milk would bring the same price as the whole milk.

Miller is a strong defender of the view that the futures contracts are, just like other products, valuable to those who buy them. Therefore, he argues, government regulation of these contracts is likely to do more harm than good.

Miller earned his undergraduate degree at Harvard University in 1944 and went on to work as a tax expert at the Treasury Department. He later earned his Ph.D. in economics at Johns

Hopkins University. He taught at Carnegie from 1953 to 1961, and in 1961 became a professor at the University of Chicago's Graduate School of Business. He is now the Robert R. McCormick Distinguished Service Professor there. He became a public governor of the Chicago Mercantile Exchange in 1990.

Selected Works

(With Franco Modigliani.) "Corporate Income Taxes and the Cost of Capital." *American Economic Review* 53 (June 1963): 433–43.

(With Franco Modigliani.) "The Cost of Capital, Corporation Finance, and the Theory of Investment." *American Economic Review* 48 (June 1958): 261–97.

Financial Innovations and Market Volatility. 1991.

Mises, Ludwig Edler von (1881–1973)—Ludwig von Mises was one the last members of the original Austrian school of economics. He earned his doctorate in law and economics from the University of Vienna in 1906. One of his best works, *The Theory of Money and Credit*, was published in 1912. In that book, which was used as a money and banking textbook for the next two decades, Mises extended Austrian marginal utility theory to money. Money, noted Mises, is demanded for its usefulness in purchasing other goods, rather than for its own sake.

In that same book Mises also argued that business cycles were caused by the uncontrolled expansion of bank credit. In 1926 Mises founded the Austrian Institute for Business Cycle Research. His most influential student, who later developed Mises' business cycle theories, was Friedrich Hayek.

Another notable contribution by Mises was his claim that socialism must fail economically. In a 1920 article Mises argued that a socialist government could not make the economic calculations required to organize a complex economy efficiently. Although socialist economists Oskar Lange and Abba Lerner disagreed with Mises, modern economists agree that Mises' argument, combined with Hayek's elaboration of it, is correct (see SOCIALISM).

Mises believed that economic truths are derived from self-evident axioms and cannot be empirically tested. In his magnum opus, *Human Action*, and in other publications, Mises laid out these views. His view failed to persuade many economists outside the Austrian school. Mises was also a strong proponent of laissez-faire; he advocated that the government not intervene anywhere in the economy. Interestingly, though, even Mises made some striking exceptions to this view. For example, he believed that military conscription could be justified in wartime.

Mises was rare, for someone of his stature within the economics profession, in not having a paying academic job for much of his professional life. From 1913 to 1934 Mises was an unpaid professor at the University of Vienna. His salaried job from 1909 to 1934 was as an economist for the Vienna Chamber of Commerce, in which capacity he served as the principal economic adviser to the Austrian government. To avoid the Nazi influence in his Austrian homeland, in 1934 Mises left for Geneva, where he was a professor at the Graduate Institute of International Studies until 1940. In 1940 he emigrated to New York City. He was a visiting professor at New York University from 1948 until he retired in 1969. During those years his salary was paid by a private foundation.

Not only did Mises not have a regular tenure-track academic job, but his ideas—on economic reasoning and on economic policy—were out of fashion during the Keynesian revolution that took over American economic thinking from the midthirties to the sixties. Possibly both factors made Mises bitter from the late forties on, something that was not true early in his professional life. The contrast between his early view of himself as a mainstream member of his profession and his later view of himself as an outcast shows up starkly in *The Theory of Money and Credit*. The first section, written in 1912, is calmly argued; the last section, added in the forties, is strident.

Mises had a strong influence on young people. A resurgent Austrian school in the United States owes itself in no small part to Mises' persistence.

Selected Works

"Economic Calculation in the Socialist Commonwealth." 1920. Reprinted in *Collectivist Economic Planning: Critical Studies on the Possibilities of Socialism*, edited by Friedrich Hayek. 1935.
Human Action: A Treatise on Economics, 3d ed. 1966.
Omnipotent Government: The Rise of the Total State and Total War. 1944. Reprint. 1985.
The Theory of Money and Credit. 1912. 3d English ed. 1981.

Modigliani, Franco (1918–)—Franco Modigliani, an American born in Italy, won the 1985 Nobel Prize for two contributions. The first was "his analysis of the behavior of household savers." In the early fifties Modigliani, trying to improve on Keynes's consumption function, introduced his "life cycle" model of consumption. The basic idea was common sense, but no less powerful for that reason. Most people, he claimed, want to have a fairly stable level of consumption. If their income is low this year, for example, but expected to be high next year, they do not want to live like paupers this year and princes next. So in high-income years, Modigliani argued, people save. They spend more than their income (dissave) in low-income

years. Because income begins low for young adults just starting out, then increases in the middle years, and declines on retirement, said Modigliani, young people borrow to spend more than their income, middle-aged people save a lot, and old people run down their savings.

The second contribution that helped Modigliani win the Nobel Prize was the famous Modigliani-Miller theorem in corporate finance (see CORPORATE DEBT). Modigliani, together with Merton Miller, showed that under certain assumptions, the value of a firm is independent of its ratio of debt-to-equity. Although Modigliani claims his two articles with Miller were written tongue-in-cheek, that is not how Miller, the Nobel Prize Committee, or financial economists took their two articles. Their insight was a cornerstone in the field of corporate finance.

Modigliani also wrote one of the articles that started the rational expectations school of economics (see RATIONAL EXPECTATIONS). In a 1954 article he and coauthor Emile Grumburg pointed out that people may anticipate certain government policies and act accordingly. Modigliani strenuously objects, though, to how far the rational expectations school has run with this basic insight.

Modigliani considers himself a Keynesian. A cartoon on his office door in 1982 said: "With your permission, gentlemen, I'd like to offer a kind word on behalf of John Maynard Keynes." Modigliani left fascist Italy in 1939, because he was both Jewish and antifascist. He earned his Ph.D. from the New School of Social Research in 1944. Modigliani taught at the New School from 1944 to 1949 and was a research consultant to the Cowles Commission at the University of Chicago from 1949 to 1952. He was a professor at Carnegie Institute of Technology from 1952 to 1960, at Northwestern University from 1960 to 1962, and at MIT from 1962 to the present. He was president of the American Economic Association in 1976.

Selected Works

(With Merton Miller.) "Corporate Income Taxes and the Cost of Capital". *American Economic Review* 53 (June 1963): 433–43.

(With Merton Miller.) "The Cost of Capital, Corporation Finance, and the Theory of Investment." *American Economic Review* 48 (June 1958): 261–97.

"Fluctuations in the Saving-Income Ratio: A Problem in Economic Forecasting." In *Studies in Income and Wealth*, no. 11. 1949.

(With Albert Ando.) "The Life Cycle Hypothesis of Saving: Aggregate Implications and Tests." *American Economic Review* 53 (March 1963): 55–84.

(With Emile Grumburg.) "The Predictability of Social Events." *Journal of Political Economy* 62 (December 1954): 465–78.

(With Richard Brumberg.) "Utility Analysis and the Consumption Function." In *Post-Keynesian Economics*, edited by Kenneth Kurihara. 1954.

Morgenstern, Oskar (1902–77)—Oskar Morgenstern is best known for his book, coauthored with physicist John von Neumann, titled *Theory of Games and Economic Behavior* (see NEUMANN).

Morgenstern was also known for his skepticism about economic measurement. In a 1950 book, *On the Accuracy of Economic Observations*, Morgenstern challenged the easy use of data on national income to reach conclusions about the state of the economy and about appropriate policies. He cited Kuznets's finding that the measurement of national income was subject to a 10 percent margin of error. Morgenstern pointed out that economic policy advisers often proposed policies based on shifts in national income of 1 percent or less. Morgenstern reasoned that one cannot reach any conclusions based on small shifts that are well within the margin of error.

Morgenstern was born in Germany. After earning his doctorate, he became a professor at the University of Vienna in 1935. He was on leave in the United States in 1938 when the Nazis occupied Vienna. He was dismissed from the university because he was considered "politically unbearable." So Morgenstern became a professor at Princeton University, where he remained until his retirement in 1970.

Selected Works

On the Accuracy of Economic Observations, 2d ed. 1963.

(With John von Neumann.) *Theory of Games and Economic Behavior*, 3d ed. 1953.

Myrdal, Gunnar (1898–1987)—Gunnar Myrdal, a Swedish economist, made an international reputation with his 1944 book, *An American Dilemma*. The book was the end product of a study that the Carnegie Corporation had commissioned about what was then called the "Negro question." *An American Dilemma* is thought of as a classic in sociology. Indeed, Myrdal's damning critique of the "separate but equal" doctrine played a large role in the Supreme Court's 1954 ruling on *Brown* v. *Board of Education of Topeka*, which outlawed racial segregation in public schools. The book also contains solid economic reasoning. Myrdal, an egalitarian sympathetic to socialism, showed that Franklin Roosevelt's economic policies had badly hurt blacks. Myrdal singled out two New Deal policies in particular: restrictions on agricultural output and the minimum wage.

Myrdal opened a chapter titled "New Blows to Southern Agriculture during the Thirties: Trends and Policies" with the following:

Of all the calamities that have struck the rural Negro people in the South in recent decades—soil erosion, the infiltration of white tenants into plantation areas, the ravages of the boll weevil, the southwestern shift in cotton cultivation—none has had such grave consequences, or threatens to have such lasting effect, as the combination of world agricultural trends and federal agricultural policies initiated during the thirties.

In an attempt to stabilize farm income, wrote Myrdal, the government restricted the production of cotton, putting hundreds of thousands of mostly black sharecroppers out of work. Myrdal wrote: "It seems, therefore, that *the agricultural policies, and particularly the Agricultural Adjustment program (A.A.A.), which was instituted in May, 1933, was the factor directly responsible for the drastic curtailment in number of Negro and white sharecroppers and Negro cash and share tenants.*" (Italics in original.)

Myrdal also showed how minimum wage legislation, ostensibly to improve working conditions, actually worsened blacks' economic standing. Myrdal wrote:

During the 'thirties the danger of being a marginal worker became increased by social legislation intended to improve conditions on the labor market. The dilemma, as viewed from the Negro angle is this: on the one hand, Negroes constitute a disproportionately large number of the workers in the nation who work under imperfect safety rules, in unclean and unhealthy shops, for long hours, and for sweatshop wages; on the other hand, it has largely been the availability of such jobs which has given Negroes any employment at all. As exploitative working conditions are gradually being abolished, this, of course, must benefit Negro workers most, as they have been exploited most—but only if they are allowed to keep their employment. But it has

mainly been their willingness to accept low labor standards which has been their protection. When government steps in to regulate labor conditions and to enforce minimum standards, it takes away nearly all that is left of the old labor monopoly in the "Negro jobs."

As low wages and sub-standard labor conditions are most prevalent in the South, this danger is mainly restricted to Negro labor in that region. When the jobs are made better, the employer becomes less eager to hire Negroes, and white workers become more eager to take the jobs from the Negroes.

Myrdal's analysis predated George Stigler's classic 1946 article that showed the harmful effects caused by the minimum wage law. It supports the view that there truly is consensus among economists of various political persuasions when ideological loyalties are laid aside and clear economic analysis is allowed to prevail.

Myrdal's other major classic was *Asian Drama: An Inquiry into the Poverty of Nations.* Its major message was that the only way to bring about rapid development in Southeast Asia was to control population, have a wider distribution of agricultural land, and invest in health care and education.

In 1974 Myrdal, together with Friedrich Hayek, was awarded the Nobel Prize in economics "for their pioneering work in the theory of money and economic fluctuations and for their penetrating analysis of the interdependence of economic, social, and institutional phenomena."

Besides being an economist and a sociologist, Myrdal was also a politician. He was twice elected to Sweden's Parliament as senator (1934–36, 1942–46), was minister for trade and commerce (1945–47), and served as the executive secretary for the United Nations Economic Commission for Europe (1947–57).

Selected Works

An American Dilemma: The Negro Problem and Modern Democracy. 1944. Reprint. 1964.
Asian Drama: An Inquiry into the Poverty of Nations. 1968.

Neumann, John von (1903–57)—"There are two kinds of people in the world: Johnny von Neumann and the rest of us." This quote is attributed to Eugene Wigner, a physicist who won the Nobel Prize. John von Neumann, whom people called Johnny, was a brilliant mathematician and physicist who also made three fundamental contributions to economics.

First, a 1928 paper by von Neumann, written in German, established him as the father of game theory. Second was a 1937 paper, translated in 1945, that laid out a mathematical model of an expanding economy. This paper raised the level of mathematical sophistication in economics considerably. Third was a book coauthored with his Princeton colleague economist Oskar Morgenstern, titled *Theory of Games and Economic Behavior*. Morgenstern had convinced von Neumann that game theory applied to economics.

In their book, von Neumann and Morgenstern asserted that *any* economic situation could also be defined as the outcome of a game between two or more players. But the semicompetitive/semicooperative nature of most economic situations, in which the value of the outputs is greater than the value of the inputs, increased the complexity, and consequently, the two were unable to offer solutions. "Nash equilibrium" solutions have since been found, addressing the skepticism that some economists had about the applicability of game theory to economics.

In addition to game theory, their book gave birth to modern utility theory. Together, von Neumann and Morgenstern revived and mathematically structured the idea that individuals appear to be choosing among alternatives with probabilistic outcomes to maximize the expected amount of some measure of value termed "utility." This made clearer Knight's concept of risk. The definition of utility that they created led to the first coherent theory suggesting how we should make decisions when we know only the probabilities of some events.

The theory of games had been studied before, but after von Neumann and Morgenstern it received far more attention. Partly because of the enormous interest generated by their book, game theory has since been applied to economics, law, political science, and sociology.

Von Neumann was born in Hungary and published his first mathematical paper at age eighteen. He earned a degree in chemical engineering in Zurich and a doctorate in mathematics from the University of Budapest in 1926. In 1933 he joined the Institute for Advanced Study at Princeton. He was the youngest permanent professor of that institution and a colleague of Albert Einstein. In 1943 von Neumann was a consultant to the Manhattan Project at Los Alamos, New Mexico, in which the first atomic bomb was built. His work on the bomb later led to a presidential appointment to the Atomic Energy Commission in 1955. Von Neumann also helped develop the first electronic computer, the ENIAC, at the University of Pennsylvania.

Selected Works

"A Model of General Equilibrium." *Review of Economic Studies* 13 (1945–46): 1–9.
(With Oskar Morgenstern.) *Theory of Games and Economic Behavior,* 3d ed. 1953.

Ohlin, Bertil Gotthard (1899–1979)—Swedish economist Bertil Ohlin was corecipient of the Nobel Prize in 1977, along with James Meade, for his "pathbreaking contribution to the theory of international trade and international capital movements.'' In 1933 Ohlin published *Interregional and International Trade,* the book that won him his Nobel Prize. With a 1919 article by his former teacher Eli Heckscher as his starting point, Ohlin showed that both interregional and international trade occur because goods can move more easily than the labor, capital, and land that produce them. Therefore, showed Ohlin, a country with a relatively abundant factor of production should export goods that intensively use that abundant factor, and import those that intensively use the factor that is relatively scarce. Much later, economists showed that this was true only for a world with just two goods (see LEONTIEF).

In publications beginning in 1927 and ending in 1934, Ohlin also laid out theoretical reasoning and policy conclusions very similar to those in Keynes's 1936 classic, *The General Theory of Employment, Interest and Money.* Unfortunately, Ohlin's contributions were published in Swedish and never translated. Therefore, when he tried, in a 1937 article in a British journal, to get credit for these ideas, the Keynesians did not believe him. Much later, though, his originality in this area was recognized.

Ohlin earned his Ph.D. at Stockholm University in 1924. He taught at the University of Copenhagen from 1925 to 1930 and at the Stockholm School of Business Administration from 1930 to 1965. Ohlin was also a member of the Swedish parliament from 1938 to 1970 and the leader of the Liberal Party from 1944 to 1967.

Selected Works

Interregional and International Trade. 1933.
''Some Notes on the Stockholm Theory of Saving and Investment,'' 2 parts. *Economic Journal* 47 (March 1937): 53–69; (June 1937): 221–40. Reprinted in *Readings in Business Cycle Theory,* edited by G. Haberler. 1951.

''Transfer Difficulties, Real and Imagined.'' *Economic Journal* 37 (March 1929). Reprinted in *Readings in the Theory of International Trade,* edited by H. S. Ellis and L. Metzler. 1949.

Okun, Arthur M. (1928–80)—Arthur Okun is known mainly for Okun's Law, which describes a linear relation between percentage changes in unemployment and percent changes in gross national product. It states that for every percentage point that the unemployment rate falls, real GNP rises by 3 percent. Okun's Law was based on data from World War II to 1960. He cautioned that the law was good only within the range of unemployment rates—3 to 7.5 percent—experienced in that time period.

Like many economic laws, Okun's is an observation of an empirical (real-world) regularity that is not based on any strong economic reasoning. Nevertheless, it has held up well, within the appropriate range of unemployment rates, since Okun discovered it. Yale's James Tobin, who was Okun's colleague both at Yale and on President Kennedy's Council of Economic Advisers (CEA), has called Okun's Law ''one of the most reliable empirical regularities of macroeconomics.''

Okun discovered the law while he was a senior economist with Kennedy's CEA. The CEA wanted to convince Kennedy that the economy-wide gains of lowering unemployment from 7 to 4 percent were greater than previously imagined. Okun's Law was a major part of the empirical justification for Kennedy's tax cuts. At the end of President Johnson's admininstration, Okun was chairman of the CEA.

Okun believed that wealth transfers by taxation from the relatively rich to the relatively poor are an appropriate policy for government. But he recognized the loss of efficiency inherent in the redistribution process. In *Equality and Efficiency: The Big Tradeoff* Okun introduced the metaphor of the leaky bucket, which has become famous among economists. He wrote: ''The money must be carried from the rich to the poor in a leaky bucket. Some of it will simply disappear in transit, so the poor will not receive all the money that is taken from the rich.''

Okun attributed the losses to administrative costs of taxing and transferring, and to incentive effects. The poor who are receiving welfare or other transfer payments have less incentive to work because their transfer payments are reduced as they make more money. The rich have less incentive to work because high marginal tax rates take a large fraction of their additional income (top tax rates were between 50 and 70 percent at the time he was writing). The relatively rich also have more of an incentive to spend on tax-deductible items and on tax shelters as a way of avoiding taxes. ''High tax rates,'' wrote Okun, ''are followed by attempts of ingenious men to beat them as surely as snow is followed by little boys on sleds.'' For these insights, Okun can be considered one of the original supply-siders (see SUPPLY-SIDE ECONOMICS).

Selected Works

Economics for Policymaking: Selected Essays of Arthur M. Okun, edited by Joseph A. Pechman. 1983.
Equality and Efficiency: The Big Tradeoff. 1975.
The Political Economy of Prosperity. 1970.

Pareto, Vilfredo (1848–1923)—Pareto is best known for two concepts that are named after him. The first and most familiar is the concept of Pareto optimality. A Pareto-optimal allocation of resources is achieved when it is not possible to make anyone better off without making someone else worse off. The second is Pareto's law of income distribution. This law, which Pareto derived from British data on income, showed

a linear relationship between each income level and the number of people who received more than that income. Pareto found similar results for Prussia, Saxony, Paris, and some Italian cities. Although Pareto thought his law should be ''provisionally accepted as universal,'' he thought that exceptions were possible, and as it turns out, many exceptions have been found.

Pareto is also known for showing that the assumption that the utility of goods can actually be measured was not necessary for deriving any of the standard results in consumer theory. He showed that by simply being able to rank bundles of goods, consumers would act as economists had said they would.

In his later years Pareto shifted from economics to sociology. This reflected his own change in beliefs about how humans act. He came to believe that men act nonlogically, ''but they make believe they are acting logically.''

Born in Paris to Italian exiles, Pareto moved to Italy to complete his education in mathematics and literature. After graduating from the Polytechnic Institute in Turin in 1869, he applied his prodigious mathematical abilities as an engineer for the railroads. Throughout his life Pareto was an active critic of the Italian government's economic policies. He published pamphlets and articles denouncing protectionism and militarism, which he viewed as being the two greatest enemies of liberty. Although he was keenly informed on economic policy and frequently debated it, Pareto did not study economics seriously until he was forty-two. In 1893 he succeeded his mentor, Walras, as chair of economics at the University of Lausanne. His principal publications are *Cours d'économie politique* (1896–97), Pareto's first book, which he wrote at age forty-nine, and *Manual of Political Economy* (1906).

A self-described pacifist who disdained honors, Pareto was nominated in 1923 to a Senate seat in Mussolini's fledgling government but refused to become a ratified member. He died that year and was buried without fanfare in a small cemetery in Celigny.

Selected Works

"The New Theories of Economics." *Journal of Political Economy* 5: 485–502.

Pigou, Arthur Cecil (1877–1959)—Arthur C. Pigou, a British economist, is best known for his work in welfare economics. In his book *The Economics of Welfare* Pigou developed Alfred Marshall's concept of externalities (see PUBLIC GOODS AND EXTERNALITIES), costs imposed or benefits conferred on others that are not taken into account by the person taking the action. He argued that the existence of externalities was sufficient justification for government intervention. The reason was that if someone was creating a negative externality, such as pollution, he would engage in too much of the activity that generated the externality. Someone creating a positive externality, say, by educating himself and making himself more interesting to other people, would not invest enough in education because he would not perceive the value to himself as being as great as the value to society.

To discourage the activity that caused the negative externality, Pigou advocated a tax on the activity. To encourage the activity that created the positive externality, he advocated a subsidy. These are now called Pigovian taxes and subsidies.

Pigou's analysis was accepted until 1960, when Ronald Coase (see COASE) showed that taxes and subsidies were not necessary if the people affected by the externality and the people creating it could easily get together and bargain. Adding to the skepticism about Pigou's conclusions is the new view, introduced by public choice economists (see PUBLIC CHOICE THE-

ORY), that governments fail just as markets do. Nevertheless, most economists still advocate Pigovian taxes on pollution as a much more efficient way of dealing with pollution than government-imposed standards.

Pigou studied economics at Cambridge and lectured at Cambridge until World War II. In 1908 he was appointed to Marshall's chair in economics at the age of thirty. Pigou taught straight Marshallian economics, often insisting to his students that "it's all in Marshall." Pigou was throughout his life an avid free trader.

Selected Works

The Economics of Welfare, 4th ed. 1932.
Keynes's General Theory: A Retrospective View. 1950.
The Political Economy of War. 1921.
The Theory of Unemployment. 1933.
Unemployment. 1914.
Wealth and Welfare. 1912.

Quesnay, François (1694–1774)—François Quesnay was the leading figure of the Physiocrats, generally considered to be the first school of economic thinking. The name "Physiocrat" derives from the Greek words *phýsis*, meaning nature, and *kràtos*, meaning power. The Physiocrats believed that an economy's power derived from its agricultural sector. They wanted the government of Louis XV, who ruled France from 1715 to 1774, to deregulate and reduce taxes on French agriculture so that poor France could emulate wealthier Britain, which had a relatively laissez-faire policy. Indeed, Quesnay was the person who coined the term *"laissez-faire, laissez-passer."*

Quesnay himself did not publish until the age of sixty. His first work appeared only as encyclopedia articles in 1756 and 1757.

In *Tableau économique*, he detailed his famous zigzag diagram, a circular flow diagram of the economy that showed who produced what and who spent what. This table was Quesnay's way of trying to understand and explain the causes of growth. *Tableau* defined three classes: landowners, farmers, and others, called "sterile" classes, who consumed everything they produced and left no surplus for the next period. Quesnay believed that only the agricultural sector could produce a surplus that could then be used to produce more the next year and, therefore, help growth. Industry and manufacturing, thought Quesnay, were sterile. Interestingly, though, he did not reach this conclusion by consulting his table. Instead, Quesnay constructed the table to fit his belief. Indeed, he had to make his table inconsistent in order to fit his assumption that industry provided no surplus.

Although Quesnay was wrong about the sterility of the manufacturing sector, he was right in ascribing France's poverty to mercantilism, which he called Colbertisme (after Louis XV's finance minister, Colbert). The French government had protected French manufacturers from foreign competition, thus raising the cost of machinery for farmers, and had also sold to wealthy citizens the power to tax farmers. These citizens had then used this power to the limit.

Quesnay advocated reforming these laws by consolidating and reducing taxes, getting rid of tolls and other regulations that prevented trade within France, and generally freeing the economy from the government's stifling controls. These reforms were much more sensible than his theorizing about the sterility of industry. As Mark Blaug writes, "It was only the effort to provide these reforms with a watertight theoretical argument that produced some of the forced reasoning and slightly absurd conclusions that invited ridicule even from contemporaries."

Moreover, Quesnay's work paved the way for classical economics and, in particular, for Adam Smith, who latched on to Physiocratic notions of free trade and the preeminence of the agricultural sector.

That Quesnay had such a seminal influence on economics is all the more surprising in light of the fact that he served under Louis XV in Versailles, not as an economist, but as a medical doctor.

Selected Works

Tableau économique, 3d ed. 1759. Reprint, edited by M. Kuczynski and R. Meek. 1972.

See also MERCANTILISM.

Ricardo, David (1772–1823)—David Ricardo was one of those rare people who achieved tremendous success and lasting fame. After his family disinherited him for marrying outside his Jewish faith, Ricardo made a fortune as a stockbroker and a loan broker. When he died, his estate was worth over $100 million in today's dollars. At age twenty-seven, after reading Adam Smith's *The Wealth of Nations*, Ricardo got excited about economics. He wrote his first economics article at age thirty-seven and then spent only fourteen years—his last ones—as a professional economist.

Ricardo first gained notice among economists over the "bullion controversy." In 1809 he wrote that England's inflation was the result of the Bank of England's propensity to issue excess bank notes. In short, Ricardo was an early believer in the quantity theory of money, or what is known today as monetarism.

In his *Essay on the Influence of a Low Price of Corn on the Profits of Stock* (1815), Ricardo articulated what came to be known as the law of diminishing returns. One of the most famous laws of economics, it holds that as more and more resources are combined in production with a fixed resource—for example, as more labor and machinery are used on a fixed amount of land—the additions to output will diminish.

Ricardo also opposed the protectionist Corn Laws, which restricted imports of wheat. In arguing for free trade, Ricardo formulated the idea of comparative costs, today called comparative advantage. Comparative advantage—a very subtle idea—is the main basis for most economists' belief in free trade today. The idea is this: a country that trades for products that it can get at lower cost from another country is better off than if it had made the products at home.

Say, for example, that Poorland can produce one bottle of wine with five hours of labor and one loaf of bread with ten hours. Richland's workers, on the other hand, are more productive. They produce a bottle of wine with three hours of labor and a loaf of bread with one hour. One might think at first that because Richland requires fewer labor hours to produce either good, it has nothing to gain from trade.

Think again. Poorland's cost of producing wine, although higher than Richland's in terms of hours of labor, is lower in terms of bread. For every bottle produced, Poorland gives up half of a loaf, while Richland has to give up three loaves to make a bottle of wine. Therefore, Poorland has a comparative advantage in producing wine. Similarly, for every loaf of bread it produces, Poorland gives up two bottles of wine, but Richland gives up only a third of a bottle. Therefore, Richland has a comparative advantage in producing bread.

If they exchange wine and bread one-for-one, Poorland can specialize in producing wine and trading some of it to Richland, and Richland can specialize in producing bread. Both Richland and Poorland will be better off than if they hadn't traded. By shifting, say, ten hours of labor out of producing bread, Poorland gives up the one loaf that this labor could have produced. But the reallocated labor produces two bottles of wine, which will trade for two loaves of bread. Result: trade nets Poorland one additional loaf of bread. Nor does Poorland's gain come at Richland's expense. Richland gains also, or else it would not have traded. By shifting three hours out of producing wine, Richland cuts wine production by one bottle but increases bread production by three loaves. It trades two of these loaves for Poorland's two bottles of wine. Richland has one more bottle of wine than it had before, and an extra loaf of bread.

These gains come, Ricardo observed, because each country specializes in producing the good for which its comparative cost is lower.

Writing a century before Paul Samuelson and other modern economists popularized the use of equations, Ricardo is still esteemed for his uncanny ability to arrive at complex conclusions without any of the mathematical tools now deemed essential. As economist David Friedman put it in his 1990 textbook, *Price Theory,* "The modern economist reading Ricardo's *Principles* feels rather as a member of one of the Mount Everest expeditions would feel if, arriving at the top of the mountain, he encountered a hiker clad in T-shirt and tennis shoes."

One of Ricardo's chief contributions, arrived at without mathematical tools, is his theory of rents. Borrowing from Malthus, with whom Ricardo was closely, but often diametrically, associated, Ricardo explained that as more land was cultivated, farmers would have to start using less productive land. But because a bushel of corn from less productive land sells for the same price as a bushel from highly productive land, tenant farmers would be willing to pay more to rent the highly productive land. Result: the landowners, not the tenant farmers, are the ones who gain from productive land. This finding has withstood the test of time. Economists use Ricardian reasoning today to explain why agricultural price supports do not help farmers per se but do make owners of farmland wealthier.

Economists use similar reasoning to explain why the beneficiaries of laws that restrict the number of taxicabs are not cab drivers per se but rather those who owned the limited number of taxi medallions (licenses) when the restriction was first imposed.

Selected Works

The Works and Correspondence of David Ricardo, edited by Piero Sraffa, with the collaboration of M. H. Dobb, 11 vols. 1951–73.

Robbins, Lionel (1898–1984)—Although recognized equally for his contributions to economic policy, methodology, and the history of ideas, Lionel Robbins made his name as a theorist. In the twenties he attacked Alfred Marshall's concept of the "representative firm," arguing that the concept did not help one understand the equilibrium of the firm or of an industry. He also did some of the earliest work on labor supply, showing that an increase in the wage rate had an ambiguous effect on the amount of labor supplied.

Robbins' most famous book was *An Essay on the Nature and Significance of Economic Science,* one of the best-written prose pieces in economics. That book contains three main thoughts. First is Robbins' famous all-encompassing definition of economics that is still used to define the subject today: "Economics is the science which studies human behavior as a relationship between given ends and scarce means which have alternative uses." Second is the bright line Robbins drew between positive and normative issues. Positive issues are questions about what is; normative issues are about what ought to be. Robbins argued that the economist qua economist should be studying what is rather

than what ought to be. Economists still widely share Robbins' belief. Robbins' third major thought was that economics is a system of logical deduction from first principles. He was skeptical about the feasibility and usefulness of empirical verification. In this view he resembled the Austrians, not surprising since he was a colleague of the famous Austrian economist Friedrich Hayek, whom he had brought from Vienna in 1928.

In 1930, when Keynesianism was starting to take over in Britain, Robbins was the only member of the five-man Economic Advisory Council to oppose import restrictions and public works expenditures as a means of alleviating the depression. Instead, Robbins sided with the Austrian view that the depression was caused by undersaving (i.e., too much consumption), and he built upon this concept in *The Great Depression,* which exemplified his anti-Keynesian views. Although he remained an opponent of Keynesianism for the remainder of that decade, Robbins' views underwent a profound change after World War II. In *The Economic Problem in Peace and War* Robbins advocated Keynes's policies of full employment through control of aggregate demand.

The London School of Economics was home to Robbins for almost his entire adult life. He completed his undergraduate education there in 1923, taught as a professor from 1929 to 1961, and continued to be associated with the school on a part-time basis until 1980. During World War II he served briefly as an economist for the British government. Although Robbins was an advocate of laissez-faire, he made numerous ad hoc exceptions. His most famous was his view, known as the Robbins Principle, that the government should subsidize any qualified applicant for higher education who would not otherwise have the current income or savings to pay for it. His view was adopted in the sixties and led to an expansion of higher education in Britain in the sixties and seventies.

Selected Works

Autobiography of an Economist. 1971.
The Economic Basis of Class Conflict. 1939.
The Economic Causes of War. 1939.
The Economic Problem in Peace and War. 1947.
An Essay on the Nature and Significance of Economic Science. 1932.
The Great Depression. 1934.

Robinson, Joan Violet (1903–83)—British economist Joan Robinson was arguably the only woman born before 1940 who can be considered a great economist. She was in the same league as others who won the Nobel Prize; indeed, many economists expected her to win the prize in 1975. *Business Week* was so sure of it that it published a long article on her before that year's prize was announced. However, she never won the prize. Was the Swedish Royal Academy biased against giving the prize to Robinson? Many economists believe it was, but not because Robinson was a woman. Rather, her political views became more left-wing as she aged, to the point where she admired Mao Tse-tung's China and Kim Il Sung's North Korea. These extreme views, although they should not have affected her chances of getting an award for her intellectual contributions, probably did.

Robinson's first major book was *The Economics of Imperfect Competition.* In it she laid out a model of competition between firms, each of which had some monopoly power. Along with American economist Edward H. Chamberlin, whose *Theory of Monopolistic Competition* had appeared only a few months earlier, Robinson began what is known as the monopolistic competition revolution. Many economists believe that most industries are neither perfectly competitive nor complete monopolies. Robinson's and Chamberlin's books are what led them to that belief.

In her first book and with some early articles, Robinson showed a distinctive writing style. She was clear and analytic and managed to put complex mathematical concepts into words.

Later in the thirties Robinson became part of the "Cambridge Circus," a group of young economists that included later Nobel Prize–winner James Meade; Roy Harrod; Richard Kahn; her husband, Austin Robinson; and Piero Sraffa. These economists met regularly to discuss their work and especially to discuss Keynes's famous 1936 book *The General Theory,* both before and after it was published. Much of Robinson's own published work at the time, especially her *Introduction to the Theory of Employment,* clarified ideas that Keynes had not made clear. Robinson was the first to define macroeconomics, which became a separate field of inquiry only with Keynes's book, as the "theory of output as a whole."

In 1954 Robinson's article "The Production Function and the Theory of Capital" started what came to be called the Cambridge controversy. Robinson attacked the idea that capital can be measured and aggregated. This became the Cambridge, England, position. Across the Atlantic, Paul Samuelson and Robert Solow defended the by-then traditional neoclassical view that capital could be aggregated. Robinson won the battle. As historian Mark Blaug put it, Samuelson made a "declaration of unconditional surrender." Yet most economists still think that aggregating capital is useful and continue to do it anyway.

Whether or not Robinson's gender prevented her from winning the Nobel Prize, it seems to have slowed her advance in academia. She taught at Cambridge University from 1928 until retiring in 1971, but in spite of a very productive career, she did not become a full professor until 1965. Perhaps not coincidentally, this was the year her husband retired from Cambridge.

Selected Works

The Accumulation of Capital. 1956.
The Cultural Revolution in China. 1970.
Economic Heresies: Some Old-fashioned Questions in Economic Theory. 1971.
Economic Philosophy. 1962.
The Economics of Imperfect Competition, 2d ed. 1969.
An Essay on Marxian Economics. 1942.
Introduction to the Theory of Employment. 1937.

Samuelson, Paul Anthony (1915–   )—More than any other economist, Paul Samuelson raised the level of mathematical analysis in the profession. Until the late thirties, when Samuelson started his stunning and steady stream of articles, economics was typically understood in terms of verbal explanations and diagrammatic models. He wrote his first published article, "A Note on the Measurement of Utility," as a twenty-one-year-old doctoral student at Harvard. In a 1938 article Samuelson introduced the concept of "revealed preference." His goal was to be able to tell by observing a consumer's choices whether he or she was better off after a change in prices. Samuelson showed the circumstances under which one could tell. The consumer revealed by choices what his or her preferences were—hence the term "revealed preferences."

Samuelson's magnum opus, which did more than any other single book to spread the mathematical revolution in economics, was *Foundations of Economic Analysis,* based on his Harvard Ph.D. dissertation. In this book he showed how virtually all economic behavior could be understood as maximizing or minimizing subject to a constraint. Hicks had done something similar in his 1939 book, *Value and Capital.* But while Hicks relegated the math to appendices, "Samuelson," writes former Samuelson student Stanley Fischer, "flaunts his in the text."

Samuelson was one of the last generalists to be incredibly productive in a number of fields in economics. He has contributed fundamental insights in consumer theory and welfare economics, international trade, finance theory, capital theory, dynamics and general equilibrium, and macroeconomics.

Swedish economist Bertil Ohlin had argued that international trade would tend to equalize the prices of factors of production. Trade between India and the United States, for example, would narrow wage-rate differentials between the two countries. Samuelson, using mathematical tools, showed the conditions under which the differentials would be driven to zero. The theorem he proved is called the Factor Price Equalization Theorem.

In finance theory, which he took up at age fifty, Samuelson did some of the initial work that showed that properly anticipated futures prices should fluctuate randomly. Samuelson also did path-breaking work in capital theory, but his contributions are too complex to describe in just a few sentences.

Economists had long believed that there were goods that would be hard for the private sector to provide because of the difficulty of charging those who benefit from them. National defense is one of the best examples of such a good. Samuelson, in a 1954 article, was the first to attempt a rigorous definition of a public good.

In macroeconomics Samuelson demonstrated how combining the accelerator theory of investment with the Keynesian income determination model explains the cyclical nature of business cycles. He also introduced the concept of the neoclassical synthesis—a synthesis of the old neoclassical microeconomics and the new (in the fifties) Keynesian macroeconomics. According to Samuelson government intervention via fiscal and monetary policy is required to achieve full employment, but then at full employment the market works well, except at providing public goods and handling problems of externalities. James Tobin has called the neo-classical synthesis one of Samuelson's greatest contributions to economics.

In *Linear Programming and Economic Analysis* Samuelson and coauthors Robert Dorfman and Robert Solow applied optimization techniques to price theory and growth theory, thereby integrating these previously segregated fields.

Samuelson has been a prolific writer, averaging almost one technical paper a month for over fifty years. Some 338 of his articles are contained in the five-volume *Collected Scientific Papers* (1966–1986). He also has revised his immensely popular textbook, *Economics,* nearly every three years since 1948. This textbook, the best-selling one in the fifties, is translated into many languages. Samuelson once said, "Let those who will write the nation's laws if I can write its textbooks."

In 1970 Paul Samuelson became the first American to receive the Nobel Prize in economics. He won it "for the scientific work through which he has developed static and dynamic economic theory and actively contributed to raising the level of analysis in economic science."

Samuelson began teaching at the Massachusetts Institute of Technology in 1940 at the age of twenty-six, becoming a full professor six years later. He has remained there since. In addition to being honored with the Nobel Prize, Samuelson also earned the John Bates Clark Award in 1947—awarded for the most outstanding work by an economist under age forty. He was president of the American Economic Association in 1961.

Samuelson was born in Gary, Indiana. At age sixteen he enrolled at the University of Chicago, where he studied under Frank Knight, Jacob Viner, and other greats, and alongside fellow budding economists Milton Friedman and George Stigler, who were then graduate students. Samuelson went on to do his graduate work at Harvard University.

Samuelson, like Friedman, had a regular column in *Newsweek* from 1966 to 1981. But unlike Friedman, he did not and does not have a passionate belief in free markets or, for that matter, in government intervention in markets. His pleasure seemed to come from providing new proofs, demonstrating technical finesse, and turning a clever phrase.

Samuelson himself once said: "Once I asked my friend the statistician Harold Freeman, 'Harold, if the Devil came to you with the bargain that, in exchange for your immortal soul, he'd give you a brilliant theorem, would you do it?' 'No,' he replied, 'but I would for an inequality.' I like that answer."

Selected Works

Economics. 1948.
Foundations of Economic Analysis, 2d ed. 1982.
"Interactions between the Multiplier Analysis and the Principle of Acceleration." *Review of Economics and Statistics* (May 1939): 75–78.
"International Trade and the Equalization of Factor Prices." *Economic Journal* 58 (June 1948): 163–84.
(With Robert Dorfman and Robert Solow.) *Linear Programming and Economic Activity.* 1958.
"A Note on the Pure Theory of Consumers' Behavior." *Economica* NS 5 (February 1938): 61–71.
"The Pure Theory of Public Expenditure." *Review of Economics and Statistics* (November 1954): 387–89.

Say, Jean-Baptiste (1767–1832)—French economist J. B. Say is most commonly identified with Say's Law, which states that supply creates its own demand. Over the years Say's Law has been embroiled in two kinds of controversy. The first is over its authorship, the second over what it means, and given each meaning, whether it is true.

On the first controversy, it is clear that Say

did invent something like Say's Law. But the first person actually to use the words "supply creates its own demand" appears to have been James Mill, the father of John Stuart Mill.

Say's Law has various interpretations. The long-run version is that there cannot be overproduction of goods in general for a very long time because those who produce the goods, by their act of producing, produce the purchasing power to buy other goods. Say wrote: "How could it be possible that there should now be bought and sold in France five or six times as many commodities as in the miserable reign of Charles VI?" With this statement Say had the long run in mind. Certainly the long-run version is correct. Given enough time, supply does create its own demand. There can be no long-run glut of goods.

But Say also had a short-run version, that even in the short run there could be no overproduction of goods relative to demand. It was this version that Malthus attacked in the nineteenth century and that Keynes attacked in the twentieth century. They were right to attack it.

Say was the best-known expositor of Adam Smith's views in Europe and America. His *Traité d'économie politique* was translated into English and used as a textbook in England and the United States. But Say did not agree with Adam Smith on everything. In particular, he took issue with Smith's labor theory of value. Say was one of the first economists to have the insight that the value of a good derived from its utility to the user and not from the labor spent in producing it.

Say was born in Lyons. During his life he edited a journal, operated a cotton factory, and served as a member of the Tribunate under the Consulate of Napoleon. He was the first to teach a public course on political economy in France and continued his stay in academia first at the Conservatoire des Arts et Métiers, and then at the College de France in Paris. Say was a friend of Thomas Malthus and David Ricardo.

Selected Works

Traité d'économie politique, vol. 1. 1803.

Schultz, Theodore William (1902–   )—In 1979 Theodore Schultz was awarded the Nobel Prize along with W. Arthur Lewis for their "pioneering research into economic development . . . with particular consideration of the problems of developing countries." Schultz's focus was on agriculture, a natural interest for someone who had grown up on a South Dakota farm. In 1930 Schultz began teaching agricultural economics at Iowa State College (now Iowa State University). He left in protest in 1943 when the college's administration, bowing to political pressure from some of the state's dairy farmers, suppressed a report that recommended substituting oleomargarine for butter. Schultz moved to the University of Chicago's economics department, where he has been since.

Early on at Chicago, Schultz became interested in agriculture worldwide. In his 1964 book, *Transforming Traditional Agriculture,* Schultz laid out his view that primitive farmers in poor countries maximize the return from their resources. Their apparent unwillingness to innovate, he argued, was rational because governments of those countries often set artificially low prices on their crops and taxed them heavily. Also, governments in those countries, unlike in the United States, did not typically have agricultural extension services to train farmers in new methods. A persistent theme in Schultz's books is that rural poverty in poor countries persists because government policy in those countries is biased in favor of urban dwellers and against rural dwellers. Schultz is optimistic that, without this government hostility to agriculture, poor agricultural nations can develop. "Poor people in low-income countries," he has stated, "are not prisoners of an ironclad poverty equilibrium that economics is unable to break.''

Schultz is an empirical economist. When he travels to serve on commissions or to attend conferences, he visits farms. His visits to farms and interviews of farmers have led to new ideas, not the least of which was on human capital, which he pioneered along with Gary Becker and Jacob Mincer. After World War II, while interviewing an old, apparently poor farm couple, he noticed how contented they were. When he asked them why they were so contented even though poor, they answered that they were not poor because they had used up their farm to send four children to college and that these children would be productive because of their education. This led Schultz quickly to the concept of human capital, capital produced by investing in knowledge.

In 1960 Schultz was president of the American Economic Association. In 1972 he won the Francis A. Walker Medal, the highest honor given by that association.

Selected Works

The Economic Value of Education. 1963. (Translated into Spanish, Portuguese, Japanese, Greek.)
''Investment in Human Capital.'' American Economic Review 51 (March 1961): 1–17.
''Reflections on Poverty within Agriculture.'' Journal of Political Economy 43 (February 1950): 1–15.
Transforming Traditional Agriculture. 1964. Reprint. 1976. (Translated into Japanese, Korean, Portuguese, Spanish.)

Schumpeter, Joseph Alois (1883–1950)—

''Can capitalism survive? No. I do not think it can.'' Thus opens Schumpeter's prologue to a section of his 1942 book, Capitalism, Socialism and Democracy. One might think, on the basis of the quote, that Schumpeter was a Marxist. But the analysis that led Schumpeter to his conclusion differed totally from Karl Marx's. Marx believed that capitalism would be destroyed by its enemies (the proletariat), whom capitalism had purportedly exploited. Marx relished the prospect. Schumpeter believed that capitalism would be destroyed by its successes. Capitalism would spawn, he believed, a large intellectual class that made its living by attacking the very bourgeois system of private property and freedom so necessary for the intellectual class's existence. And unlike Marx, Schumpeter did not relish the destruction of capitalism. He wrote: ''If a doctor predicts that his patient will die presently, this does not mean that he desires it.''

Capitalism, Socialism, and Democracy was much more than a prognosis of capitalism's future. It was also a sparkling defense of capitalism on the grounds that capitalism sparked entrepreneurship. Indeed, Schumpeter was among the first to lay out a clear concept of entrepreneurship. He distinguished inventions from the entrepreneur's innovations. Schumpeter pointed out that entrepreneurs innovate, not just by figuring out how to use inventions, but also by introducing new means of production, new products, and new forms of organization. These innovations, he argued, take just as much skill and daring as does the process of invention.

Innovation by the entrepreneur, argued Schumpeter, led to gales of ''creative destruction'' as innovations caused old inventories, ideas, technologies, skills, and equipment to become obsolete. The question, as Schumpeter saw it, was not ''how capitalism administers existing structures, . . . [but] how it creates and destroys them.'' This creative destruction, he believed, caused continuous progress and improved standards of living for everyone.

Schumpeter argued with the prevailing view that ''perfect'' competition was the way to maximize economic well-being. Under perfect competition all firms in an industry produced the same good, sold it for the same price, and had access to the same technology. Schumpeter saw this kind of competition as relatively unimportant. He wrote: "[What counts is] competition from the new commodity, the new technology, the new source of supply, the new type of organization . . . competition which . . . strikes not at the margins of the profits and the outputs of the existing firms but at their foundations and their very lives."

Schumpeter argued on this basis that some degree of monopoly was preferable to perfect competition. Competition from innovations, he argued, was an "ever-present threat" that "disciplines before it attacks." He cited the Aluminum Company of America as an example of a monopoly that continuously innovated in order to retain its monopoly. By 1929, he noted, the price of its product, adjusted for inflation, had fallen to only 8.8 percent of its level in 1890, and its output had risen from 30 metric tons to 103,400.

Schumpeter never made completely clear whether he believed innovation was sparked by monopoly per se or, rather, by the prospect of getting a monopoly as the reward for innovation. Most economists accept the latter argument and, on that basis, believe that companies should be able to keep their production processes secret, have their trademarks protected from infringement, and obtain patents.

Schumpeter was also a giant in the history of economic thought. His magnum opus in the area was *History of Economic Analysis*, edited by his third wife, Elizabeth Boody, and published posthumously in 1954. In it Schumpeter made some controversial comparisons between economists, arguing that Adam Smith was unoriginal, that Alfred Marshall was confused, and that Leon Walras was the greatest economist of all time.

Born in Austria to parents who owned a textile factory, Schumpeter was very familiar with business when he entered the University of Vienna to study economics and law. He was one of the more promising students of Friedrich von Wieser and Eugen von Böhm-Bawerk, publishing at the age of twenty-eight his famous *Theory of Economic Development*. In 1911 Schumpeter took a professorship in economics at the University of Graz. He served as minister of finance in 1919. With the rise of Hitler, Schumpeter left Europe and the University of Bonn, where he was a professor from 1925 until 1932, and emigrated to the United States. In that same year he accepted a permanent position at Harvard, where he remained until his retirement in 1949. Schumpeter was president of the American Economic Association in 1948.

Selected Works

Business Cycles, 2 vols. 1939.
Capitalism, Socialism and Democracy, 5th ed. 1976.
History of Economic Analysis, edited by E. Boody. 1954.
Ten Great Economists. 1951.
The Theory of Economic Development. 1912. Translated by R. Opie, 1934. Reprint. 1961.

Sharpe, William F. (1934–)—In 1990 U.S. economists William F. Sharpe, Harry Markowitz, and Merton H. Miller shared the Nobel Prize for their contributions to financial economics. Their early contributions established financial economics as a separate field of study. In the sixties Sharpe, taking off from Markowitz's portfolio theory, developed the Capital Asset Pricing Model (CAPM). One implication of this model was that a single mix of risky assets fits in every investor's portfolio. Those who want a high return hold a portfolio heavily weighted with the risky asset; those who want a low return hold a portfolio heavily weighted with a riskless asset, such as an insured bank deposit. A measure of the portfolio risk that cannot be diversified away by mixing stocks is "beta." A portfolio with a beta of 1.5, for example, is likely to rise by 15 percent if the stock market rises by 10 percent and is likely to fall by 15 percent if the market falls by 10 percent.

One implication of Sharpe's work is that the expected return on a portfolio in excess of a riskless return should be beta times the excess return of the market. Thus, a portfolio with a beta of 2 should have an excess return that is twice as high as the market as a whole. If the market's expected return is 8 percent and the riskless return is 5 percent, the market's expected excess return is 3 percent (8 minus 5) and the portfolio's expected excess return is therefore 6 percent (twice the market's expected excess return of 3 percent). The portfolio's expected total return would then be 11 percent (6 plus the riskless return of 5).

Sharpe was a Ph.D. candidate at the University of California at Los Angeles and an employee of the Rand Corporation when he first met Markowitz, who was also employed at Rand. Sharpe chose Markowitz as his dissertation adviser, even though Markowitz was not on the faculty at UCLA. Sharpe taught first at the University of Washington in Seattle and then at the University of California at Irvine. In 1971 he became a professor of finance at Stanford University. In 1986 Sharpe founded William F. Sharpe Associates, a firm that consulted to foundations, endowments, and pension plans. He returned to Stanford as a professor of finance in 1993.

Selected Works

"Capital Asset Prices: A Theory of Market Equilibrium under Conditions of Risk." *Journal of Finance* 19 (September 1964): 425–42.
"The Capital Asset Pricing Model: A 'Multi-Beta' Interpretation." In *Financial Decision Making under Uncertainty,* edited by H. Levy and M. Sarnat. 1977.

Simon, Herbert Alexander (1916–   )—In 1978 American social scientist Herbert Simon was awarded the Nobel Prize in economics for his "pioneering research into the decision-making process within economic organizations." In a stream of articles, Simon, who trained as a political scientist, questioned the mainstream economists' view of economic man as a lightning-quick calculator of costs and benefits. Simon's proposed alternative view was of people's rationality as "bounded." Because getting information about alternatives is costly, and because the consequences of many possible decisions cannot be known anyway, argued Simon, people cannot act the way economists assume they act. Instead of maximizing their utility, he argued, they "satisfice." That is, they do as well as they think is possible. One way they do so is by devising rules of thumb (for example: save 10 percent of after-tax income every month) that economize on the cost of collecting information and on the cost of thinking.

Simon also questioned the economists' view that firms maximize profits. He proposed instead that because of their members' bounded rationality and often contradictory goals and perspectives, firms reach decisions that can only be described as satisfactory rather than the best.

Not surprisingly for one who believes that decision making is costly, Simon has also worked on problems of artificial intelligence.

After earning his Ph.D. in political science from the University of Chicago, Simon joined the school's faculty. In 1949 he left for Pittsburgh, where he helped start Carnegie-Mellon University's new Graduate School of Industrial Administration.

Selected Works

Administrative Behavior, 3d ed. 1967.
Models of Bounded Rationality and Other Topics in Economic Theory, 2 vols. 1982
Models of Man. 1957.

Organization. 1958.
The Sciences of the Artificial, 2d ed. 1981.

Smith, Adam (1723–90)—With *The Wealth of Nations* Adam Smith installed himself as the fountainhead of contemporary economic thought. Currents of Adam Smith ran through David Ricardo and Karl Marx in the nineteenth century, and through Keynes and Friedman in the twentieth.

Adam Smith was born in a small village in Kirkcaldy, Scotland. There his widowed mother raised him until he entered the University of Glasgow at age fourteen, as was the usual practice, on scholarship. He later attended Balliol College at Oxford, graduating with an extensive knowledge of European literature and an enduring contempt for English schools.

He returned home, and after delivering a series of well-received lectures, was made first chair of logic (1751), then chair of moral philosophy (1752), at Glasgow University.

He left academia in 1764 to tutor the young duke of Buccleuch. For over two years they lived and traveled throughout France and into Switzerland, an experience that brought Smith into contact with contemporaries Voltaire, Jean-Jacques Rousseau, François Quesnay, and Anne-Robert-Jacques Turgot. With the life pension he had earned in the service of the duke, Smith retired to his birthplace of Kirkcaldy to write *The Wealth of Nations*. It was published in 1776, the same year the American Declaration of Independence was signed and in which his close friend David Hume died. In 1778 he was appointed commissioner of customs. This job put him in the uncomfortable position of having to curb smuggling, which, in *The Wealth of Nations,* he had upheld as a legitimate activity in the face of "unnatural" legislation. Adam Smith never married. He died in Edinburgh on July 19, 1790.

Today Smith's reputation rests on his explanation of how rational self-interest in a free-market economy leads to economic well-being. It may surprise those who would discount Smith as an advocate of ruthless individualism that his first major work concentrated on ethics and charity. In fact, while chair at the University of Glasgow, Smith's lecture subjects, in order of preference, were natural theology, ethics, jurisprudence, and economics, according to John Millar, Smith's pupil at the time. In *The Theory of Moral Sentiments,* Smith wrote: "How selfish soever man may be supposed, there are evidently some principles in his nature which interest him in the fortune of others and render their happiness necessary to him though he derives nothing from it except the pleasure of seeing it."

At the same time, Smith had a benign view of self-interest. He denied the view that self-love "was a principle which could never be virtuous in any degree." Smith argued that life would be tough if our "affections, which, by the very nature of our being, ought frequently to influence our conduct, could upon no occasion appear virtuous, or deserve esteem and commendation from anybody."

To Smith sympathy and self-interest were not antithetical; they were complementary. "Man has almost constant occasion for the help of his brethren, and it is in vain for him to expect it from their benevolence only," he explained in *The Wealth of Nations*.

Charity, while a virtuous act, could not alone provide the essentials for living. Self-interest was the mechanism that could remedy this shortcoming. Said Smith: "It is not from the benevolence of the butcher, the brewer, or the baker, that we can expect our dinner, but from their regard to their own interest."

Someone earning money by his own labor benefits himself. Unknowingly, he also benefits society, because to earn income on his labor in a competitive market, he must produce something others value. In Adam Smith's lasting imagery, "By directing that industry in such a manner as its produce may be of greatest value, he intends only his own gain, and he is in this, as in many other cases, led by an invisible hand to promote an end which was no part of his intention."

The five-book series of *The Wealth of Nations* sought to reveal the nature and cause of a nation's prosperity. The main cause of prosperity, argued Smith, was increasing division of labor. Smith gave the famous example of pins. He asserted that ten workers could produce 48,000 pins per day if each of eighteen specialized tasks was assigned to particular workers. Average productivity: 4,800 pins per worker per day. But absent the division of labor, a worker would be lucky to produce even one pin per day.

Just how individuals can best apply their own labor or any other resource is a central subject in the first book of the series. Smith claimed that an individual would invest a resource, for example, land or labor, so as to earn the highest possible return on it. Consequently, all uses of the resource must yield an equal rate of return (adjusted for the relative riskiness of each enterprise). Otherwise reallocation would result. This idea, wrote George Stigler, is the central proposition of economic theory. Not surprisingly, and consistent with another Stigler claim that the originator of an idea in economics almost never gets the credit, Smith's idea was not original. French economist Turgot had made the same point in 1766.

Smith used this insight on equality of returns to explain why wage rates differed. Wage rates would be higher, he argued, for trades that were more difficult to learn, because people would not be willing to learn them if they were not compensated by a higher wage. His thought gave rise to the modern notion of human capital (see HUMAN CAPITAL). Similarly, wage rates would also be higher for those who engaged in dirty or unsafe occupations (see JOB SAFETY),

such as coal mining and butchering, and for those, like the hangman, who performed odious jobs. In short, differences in work were compensated by differences in pay. Modern economists call Smith's insight the theory of compensating wage differentials.

Smith used numerate economics not just to explain production of pins or differences in pay between butchers and hangmen, but to address some of the most pressing political issues of the day. In the fourth book of *The Wealth of Nations*—published, remember, in 1776—Smith tells Great Britain that her American colonies are not worth the cost of keeping. His reasoning about the excessively high cost of British imperialism is worth repeating, both to show Smith at his numerate best, and to show that simple clear economics can lead to radical conclusions:

A great empire has been established for the sole purpose of raising up a nation of customers who should be obliged to buy from the shops of our different producers all the goods with which these could supply them. For the sake of that little enhancement of price which this monopoly might afford our producers, the home-consumers have been burdened with the whole expense of maintaining and defending that empire. For this purpose, and for this purpose only, in the two last wars, more than a hundred and seventy millions has been contracted over and above all that had been expended for the same purpose in former wars. The interest of this debt alone is not only greater than the whole extraordinary profit, which, it ever could be pretended, was made by the monopoly of the colony trade, but than the whole value of that trade, or than the whole value of the goods, which at an average have been annually exported to the colonies.

Smith vehemently opposed mercantilism—the practice of artificially maintaining a trade surplus on the erroneous belief that doing so increased wealth. The primary advantage of trade, he argued, was that it opened up new markets for surplus goods and also provided some commodities at less cost from abroad than at home. With that, Smith launched a succession of free trade economists and paved the way for David Ricardo's and John Stuart Mill's theories of comparative advantage a generation later.

Adam Smith has sometimes been caricatured as someone who saw no role for government in economic life. In fact, he believed that government had an important role to play. Like most modern believers in free markets, Smith believed that the government should enforce contracts and grant patents and copyrights to encourage inventions and new ideas. He also thought that the government should provide public works, such as roads and bridges, that, he assumed, would not be worthwhile for individuals to provide. Interestingly, though, he wanted the users of such public works to pay in proportion to their use. One definite difference between Smith and most modern believers in free markets is that Smith favored retaliatory tariffs.

Retaliation to bring down high tariff rates in other countries, he thought, would work. "The recovery of a great foreign market," he wrote "will generally more than compensate the transitory inconvenience of paying dearer during a short time for some sorts of goods."

Some of Smith's ideas are testimony to his breadth of imagination. Today, vouchers and school choice programs are touted as the latest reform in public education. But it was Adam Smith who addressed the issue more than two hundred years ago:

Were the students upon such charitable foundations left free to choose what college they liked best, such liberty might contribute to excite some emulation among different colleges. A regulation, on the contrary, which prohibited even the independent members of every particular college from leaving it, and going to any other, without leave first asked and obtained of that which they meant to abandon, would tend very much to extinguish that emulation.

Smith's own student days at Oxford (1740–46), whose professors, he complained, had "given up altogether even the pretense of teaching," left Smith with lasting disdain for the universities of Cambridge and Oxford.

Smith's writings were both an inquiry into the science of economics and a policy guide for realizing the wealth of nations. Smith believed that economic development was best fostered in an environment of free competition that operated in accordance with universal "natural laws." Because Smith's was the most systematic and comprehensive study of economics up until that time, his economic thinking became the basis for classical economics. And because more of his ideas have lasted than those of any other economist, Adam Smith truly is the alpha and the omega of economic science.

Selected Works

An Inquiry into the Nature and Causes of the Wealth of Nations, edited by Edwin Cannan. 1976.
The Theory of Moral Sentiments, edited by D. D. Raphael and A. L. Macfie. 1976.

Solow, Robert Merton (1924–)—Robert Solow won the Nobel Prize in 1987 for his analysis of economic growth. His first major paper on growth was "A Contribution to the Theory of Growth." In it he presented a mathematical model of growth that was a version of the Harrod-Domar growth model (see HARROD).

The main difference between his model and the Harrod-Domar model was that Solow assumed that wages could adjust to keep labor fully employed. Out the window went the Harrod-Domar conclusion that the economy was on a knife edge.

Solow followed shortly after with another pioneering article, "Technical Change and the Aggregate Production Function." Before that article economists had believed that the main causes of economic growth were increases in capital and labor. But Solow showed that half of economic growth cannot be accounted for by increases in capital and labor. This unaccounted-for portion of economic growth—now called the "Solow residual"—he attributed to technological innovation. His article originated "sources-of-growth accounting," which economists use to estimate the separate effects on economic growth of labor, capital, and technological change.

Solow also was the first to develop a growth model with different vintages of capital. The idea was that because capital is produced based on known technology, and because technology is improving, new capital is more valuable than old capital.

A Keynesian, Solow has been a witty critic of economists ranging from interventionists like Marxist economists and John Kenneth Galbraith to noninterventionist economists such as Milton Friedman. Solow once wrote that Galbraith's disdain for ordinary consumer goods "reminds one of the Duchess who, upon acquiring a full appreciation of sex, asked the Duke if it were not perhaps too good for the common people." Of Milton Friedman, Solow wrote, "Everything reminds Milton of the money supply. Well, everything reminds me of sex, but I keep it out of the paper."

Solow earned his Ph.D. from Harvard, where he studied under Wassily Leontief, and has been an economics professor at MIT since 1950. From 1961 to 1963 he was a senior economist with President Kennedy's Council of Economic Advisers. In 1961 he won the American Economic Association's John Bates Clark Award, given to the best economist under age forty. In 1979 he was president of that association.

Selected Works

Capital Theory and the Rate of Return. 1963.
"A Contribution to the Theory of Economic Growth." *Quarterly Journal of Economics* 70 (February 1956): 65–94.
(With Robert Dorman and Paul Dorman Samuelson.) *Linear Programming and Economic Analysis* 1958.
"The New Industrial State or Son of Affluence." *The Public Interest* (Fall 1967): 108.
"Technical Change and the Aggregate Production Function." *Review of Economics and Statistics* 39 (August 1957): 312–20.

Stigler, George J. (1911–91)—George Stigler was the quintessential empirical economist. Paging through his classic microeconomics text *The Theory of Price*, one is struck by how many principles of economics are illustrated with real data rather than hypothetical examples. Probably more than any other economist, Stigler deserves credit for getting economists to look at data and evidence.

Stigler's two longest-held positions were at Columbia University (1947–58) and at the University of Chicago (1958–91). From the early fifties to the late sixties, most of his research was in a field called industrial organization. A typical Stigler article laid out a new proposition with clear reasoning and then presented amazingly simple but persuasive data to back up his argument.

Take, for example, Stigler's "A Note on Block Booking." Block booking of movies was the offer of a fixed package of movies to an exhibitor; the exhibitor could not pick and choose among the movies in the package. The Supreme Court banned the practice on the grounds that the movie companies were compounding a monopoly by using the popularity of the winning movies to compel exhibitors to purchase the losers.

Stigler disagreed and presented a simple alternative argument. If *Gone with the Wind* is worth $10,000 to the exhibitor and *Getting Gertie's Garter* is worth nothing, wrote Stigler, the distributor could get the whole $10,000 by selling *Gone with the Wind*. Throwing in a worthless movie would not cause the exhibitor to pay any more than $10,000. Therefore, reasoned Stigler, the Supreme Court's explanation seemed wrong.

But why did block booking exist? Stigler's explanation was that if exhibitors valued films differently from one another, the distributor could collect more by "bundling" the movies. Stigler gave an example in which exhibitor A is willing to pay $8,000 for movie X and $2,500 for Y, and B is willing to pay $7,000 for X and $3,000 for Y. If the distributor charges a single price for each movie, his profit-maximizing price is $7,000 for X and $2,500 for Y. The distributor will then collect $9,500 each from A and B, for a total of $19,000. But with block booking the seller can charge $10,000 (A and B each value the two movies combined at $10,000 or more) for the bundle and make $20,000. Stigler then went on to suggest some empirical tests of his argument and actually did one, showing that customers' relative tastes for movies, as measured by box office receipts, did differ from city to city.

Stigler's thinking on government regulation was even more influential than his work on industrial organization. Because of Stigler's research, economists view regulation much more skeptically than their counterparts of forty years ago. His first article on the topic, coauthored with long-time research assistant Claire

Friedland and published in 1962, was titled "What Can Regulators Regulate? The Case of Electricity." They found that regulation of electricity prices had only a tiny effect on those prices. But more important than this finding was their showing that one could examine the actual effects of regulation, and not just theorize about them.

Stigler devoted his entire 1964 presidential address to the American Economic Association to making this point. He argued that economists should study the effects of regulation and not just assume them. In his speech he twitted the great economists of the past who had given lengthy cases for and critiques of government regulation without ever trying to study its effects. In Stigler's view things were not much better in the twentieth century. "The economic role of the state," he said, "has managed to hold the attention of scholars for over two centuries without arousing their curiosity." Stigler added, "Economists have refused either to leave the problem alone or to work on it."

Many economists got the point. Since the midsixties, economists have used their sometimes awesome empirical tools to study the effects of regulation. Whole journals have been devoted to the topic. One is the *Journal of Law and Economics,* started at the University of Chicago in 1958. Another, the *Bell Journal of Economics and Management Science,* started in 1970. As a general rule economists have found that government regulation of industries harms consumers and often gives monopoly power to producers. Some of these findings were behind the widespread support of economists for the deregulation of transportation, natural gas, and banking, which gained momentum in the Carter administration and continued until halfway through the Reagan administration. Stigler was the single most important academic contributor to this movement.

Stigler was not content to examine the effects of regulation. He wanted to understand its causes. Did governments regulate industries, as many had believed, to reduce the harmful effects of monopoly? Stigler did not think so. In a seminal article, "The Theory of Economic Regulation," published in 1971, he presented and gave evidence for his "capture theory." Stigler argued that governments do not end up creating monopoly in industries by accident. Rather, he wrote, they regulate at the behest of producers who "capture" the regulatory agency and use regulation to prevent competition. Probably more important than the evidence itself was the fact that Stigler made this viewpoint respectable in the economics profession. It has now become the mainstream view.

For his earlier work on industrial organization and his work on the effects and causes of regulation, Stigler won the 1982 Nobel Prize for economics.

Stigler was an uncommonly clear and humorous writer. Economics from him never seemed like "the dismal science." Stigler, with his sometimes biting wit, could put a profound insight into one sentence. In discussing the benefits of capitalism, for example, Stigler wrote: "Professors are much more beholden to Henry Ford than to the foundation that bears his name and spreads his assets." (See box for more Stiglerisms.)

Not to be missed in a listing of Stigler's contributions is his research on information. His 1962 article "Information in the Labor Market" was a watershed for further studies on unemployment. According to Stigler, job seekers needed short periods of unemployment in order to search for a higher wage. Even in industries with a "going wage," variances in wage rates

still exist. Therefore, the unemployed are as much information seekers as job seekers. His theory is now called the theory of search unemployment.

Information is also a problem for firms when they collude, implicitly or explicitly, to set prices. They do not know whether their competitors are secretly undercutting them. This uncertainty can be reduced, wrote Stigler, by spending resources to gather information. Stigler applied this insight to show that collusion is less likely to succeed if there are more firms in a market.

Also highly regarded as an economic historian, Stigler wrote numerous articles on the history of ideas in the early years of his career. His Ph.D. dissertation on the history of neoclassical production and distribution theories was highly acclaimed as a critical link in the chain of economic thought. Some of his articles in the area are collected in *Five Lectures on Economic Problems* (1950) and *Essays in the History of Economics* (1965).

The entry on monopoly in this encyclopedia is one of Stigler's last published works.

Selected Works

The Citizen and the State: Essays on Regulation. 1975.
Essays in the History of Economics. 1965.
The Essence of Stigler, edited by Kurt R. Leube and Thomas Gale Moore. 1986.
Five Lectures on Economic Problems. 1950.
Memoirs of an Unregulated Economist. 1988.
The Organization of Industry. 1969.
The Theory of Price, 3d ed. 1966.

Straight Talk from Stigler

"Sears, Roebuck and Company and Montgomery Ward made a good deal of money in the process of improving our rural marketing structure, but I am convinced that they did more for the poor farmers of America than the sum total of the federal agricultural support programs of the last five decades."

"Am I to admire a man who injures me in an awkward and mistaken attempt to protect me, and to despise a man who to earn a good income performs for me some great and lasting service?"

"Smith's intellectual heirs did little to strengthen his case for laissez-faire, except by that most irresistible of all the weapons of scholarship, infinite repetition."

"Advertising itself is a completely neutral instrument and lends itself to the dissemination of highly contradictory desires. While the automobile industry tells us not to drink while driving, the bourbon industry tells us not to drive while drinking. . . . Our colleges use every form of advertising, and indeed the typical university catalog would never stop Diogenes in his search for an honest man."

"When a good comedian and a production of *Hamlet* are on rival channels, I wish I could be confident that less than half the professors were laughing."

Stone, John Richard Nicholas (1913–   )— British economist Richard Stone won the Nobel Prize in 1984 for his work in national income accounting. Stone started his work during World War II while in the British government's War Cabinet Secretariat. Stone and colleagues David Champernowne and James Meade were asked to estimate funds and resources available for the war effort. They did so, and their work was an important step toward full-blown national income accounts. Stone was by no means the first economist to produce national income accounts. Simon Kuznets, for example, had already done so for the United States. But Stone's distinct contribution was to integrate national income into a double-entry bookkeeping format. That way,

every income item on one side of the balance sheet had to be matched by an expenditure item on the other side. The result was that Stone's method ensured consistency. Stone's double-entry method has become the universally accepted way to measure national income.

Stone also did some important early work in measuring consumer behavior. He was the first person to use consumer expenditures, incomes, and prices to estimate consumers' utility functions.

Stone studied economics at Cambridge in the thirties. After leaving the government in 1945, he became director of the newly formed department of applied economics at Cambridge. He was a professor there until he retired in 1980. Stone was knighted in 1978.

Selected Works

"Balancing the National Accounts: The Adjustment of Initial Estimates." In *Demand, Equilibrium and Trade,* edited by A. Ingham and A. M. Ulph. 1984.

(With D. A. Rowe et al.) *The Measurement of Consumers' Expenditure and Behaviour in the United Kingdom, 1920–1938,* vol. 1. 1954.

(With David G. Champernowne and James E. Meade.) "The Precision of National Accounts Estimates." *Review of Economic Studies* 9 (1942): 111–25.

Quantity and Price Indexes in National Accounts. 1956.

Tinbergen, Jan (1903–   )—In 1969 Dutch economist Jan Tinbergen, along with Norwegian economist Ragnar Frisch, received the first Nobel Prize in economics. He received the award for his work in econometrics and economic measurement. Tinbergen, who earned a Ph.D. in physics, had become interested in economics while working on his dissertation. His 1929 dissertation was titled "Minimum Problems in Physics and Economics." He began to apply mathematical tools to economics, which, at the time, was relatively verbal and nonmathematical. In 1929 he joined a unit of the Dutch Central Bureau of Statistics to do research on business cycles. He stayed there until 1945, with a leave of absence from 1936 to 1938 to work for the League of Nations in Geneva.

Along with Frisch and others Tinbergen developed the field of econometrics, the use of statistical tools to test economic hypotheses. Tinbergen was one of the first economists to create multiequation models of economies. He produced a twenty-seven-equation econometric model of the Dutch economy. And in 1939 he published a book, *Business Cycles in the United States, 1919–1932,* which contained a forty-eight-equation model of the American economy that explained investment activity and modeled American business cycles.

Another of Tinbergen's major contributions was to show that a government with several economic targets—for both the unemployment rate and the inflation rate, for example—must have at least as many policy instruments, such as taxes and monetary policy.

Selected Works

Business Cycles in the United Kingdom, 1870–1914. 1951.

Business Cycles in the United States, 1919–1932. 1939.

On the Theory of Economic Policy. 1952.

Tobin, James (1918–   )—In 1981, U.S. economist James Tobin received the Nobel Prize for his "analysis of financial markets and their relations to expenditure decisions, employment, production, and prices." Many people regard Tobin as America's most distinguished Keynesian economist. Tobin's most important work has been on financial markets. He developed theories to explain how financial markets affect people's consumption and investment decisions.

Tobin argues that one cannot predict the effect of monetary policy on output and unemployment simply by knowing the interest rate or the rate of growth of the money supply. Monetary policy has its effect, claims Tobin, by affecting capital investment, whether in plant and equipment or in consumer durables. And although interest rates are an important factor in capital investment, they are not the only factor. Tobin introduced the concept of "Tobin's q" as a measure to predict whether capital investment would increase or decrease. The q is the ratio between the market value of an asset and its replacement cost. Tobin pointed out that if an asset's q is less than one—that is, the asset's value is less than its replacement cost—then new investment in similar assets is not profitable. If, on the other hand, q exceeds one, this is a signal for further investment in similar assets. Tobin's insight was also relevant to his ongoing debate with Milton Friedman and other monetarists. Tobin argued that his q, by predicting future capital investment, would be a good predictor of economy-wide economic conditions.

Another of Tobin's contributions was his portfolio-selection theory. He argued that investors balance high-risk, high-return investments with safer ones, so as to achieve a balance in their portfolios. Tobin's insights helped pave the way for further work in finance theory.

Tobin did his undergraduate and graduate work at Harvard University, with an interruption to serve in the U.S. Navy during World War II. Since 1950 he has been an economics professor at Yale University. He took a leave of absence to serve as a member of President Kennedy's Council of Economic Advisers from January 1961 to July 1962. Tobin is quite proud of the 1962 *Economic Report of the President* that he helped write. Tobin calls the report, which was mainly written by chairman Walter Heller, along with Tobin, Kermit Gordon, Robert Solow, and Arthur Okun, "the manifesto of our [Keynesian] economics, applied to the United States and world economic conditions of the day." Its counterpart in the Reagan years was the 1982 *Economic Report*. Always the partisan, although an honest and thoughtful one, Tobin says: "It is interesting to compare the two; we have nothing to fear."

Tobin was also an adviser to 1972 presidential candidate George McGovern. Tobin, like most other economists across the political spectrum, believes that government regulation often causes damage. Writes Tobin: "We should be especially suspicious of interventions that seem both inefficient and inequitable, for example, rent controls in New York or Moscow or Mexico City, or price supports and irrigation subsidies benefiting affluent farmers, or low-interest loans to well-heeled students."

In 1970 Tobin was president of the American Economic Association. He is also the author of this encyclopedia's article on monetary policy.

Selected Works

"On Improving the Economic Status of the Negro." *Daedalus* 94, no. 4 (Fall 1965): 878–97.
"One or Two Cheers for 'The Invisible Hand.' " *Dissent* (Spring 1990): 229–36.
"Liquidity Preference as Behavior towards Risk." *Review of Economic Studies*, 25 no. 67 (1958): 124–31.
National Economic Policy. 1966.
The New Economics One Decade Older. 1974.
(Edited with Murray Weidenbaum.) *Two Revolutions in Economic Theory, The First Economic Reports of Presidents Kennedy and Reagan.* 1988.

Turgot, Anne-Robert-Jacques (1727–81)— Turgot was the Frenchman's Adam Smith. His *Reflections on the Production and Distribution of Wealth*, which predated Smith's *The Wealth of Nations* by six years, argued against government intervention in the economic sector. Turgot recognized the function of the division of labor, investigated how prices were determined, and analyzed the origins of economic growth. Like Quesnay, Turgot was a leading Physiocrat and attempted to reform the most stifling of government economic policies.

Probably Turgot's most important contribution to economics was to point out that capital was necessary for economic growth, and that the only way to accumulate capital was for people not to consume all they had produced. Most capital, he believed, was accumulated by landowners who saved the surplus product after paying the cost of materials and of labor. Turgot agreed with Quesnay's notion of the circular flow of savings and investment, where savings in one period become investment in the next.

In *Reflections* Turgot analyzed the interdependence of different rates of return and interest among different investments. Interest is determined by the supply and demand for capital, said Turgot. Although the rates of return on each investment may vary, he argued, in a competitive free-market economy with capital mobility, rates of return on all investments will tend toward equality. Wrote Turgot: "As soon as the profits resulting from an employment of money, whatever it may be, increase or diminish, capitals turn in that direction or withdraw from other employments, or withdraw and turn towards other employments, and this necessarily alters in each of these employments, the relation between the capital and the annual product."

Turgot distinguished between a commodity's market price—determined by supply and demand—and its "natural" price, the price it would tend to if industries were competitive and resources could be reallocated. An increase in demand, for example, could increase a good's price, but if resources were free to enter that industry, the new supply would bring the price back down to its "natural" level. In this reasoning Turgot anticipated Adam Smith.

Turgot also predated Smith in recognizing the importance of the division of labor for an economy's prosperity. Turgot also was the first economist to recognize the law of diminishing returns in agriculture. Predating the Marginalists by a century, he argued that "each increase [in an input] would be less and less productive."

Turgot applied many of his laissez-faire economic beliefs during his thirteen-year appointment as chief administrator for the Limoges district (1761–74) under Louis XV and as minister of finance, trade, and public works from 1774 to 1776 under newly anointed Louis XVI. In the latter job one of his first measures was to abolish all restrictions on sales of grain within France, a measure that the Physiocrats had long advocated. He also ended the government's policy of conscripting labor to build and maintain roads, and replaced it with a more efficient tax in money. Milton Friedman has called the replacing of taxes in kind with taxes in money "one of the greatest advances in human freedom." Turgot also abolished the guild system left over from medieval times. The guild system, like occupational licensing today, prevented workers from entering certain occupations without permission. Turgot also argued against the regulation of interest rates.

Louis XVI did not welcome Turgot's reforms and dismissed him in 1776. Some historians claim that had Turgot's reforms been kept, the French revolution, which erupted thirteen years later, might have been averted.

Turgot himself never lived to witness the upheaval his own reforms might have helped thwart. He died in Paris of gout at age fifty-four.

Selected Works

Reflections on the Production and Distribution of Wealth. In Groenewegen, P. D. *The Economics of A. R. J. Turgot*. 1977.

Veblen, Thorstein (1857–1929)—Thorstein Veblen was odd man out in late-nineteenth and early-twentieth-century American economics. His position on the fringe started early. Veblen grew up in a Norwegian immigrant farming community in Wisconsin. He spoke only Norwegian at home and did not learn English until his teens. He studied economics under John Bates Clark, a leading neoclassical economist, but rejected his ideas. Later he did his graduate work at Johns Hopkins University under Charles Sanders Peirce, the founder of the pragmatist school in philosophy, and at Yale University under laissez-faire proponent William Graham Sumner. He repudiated their views as well.

Veblen is best known for his book *The Theory of the Leisure Class*. In it he introduced the term "conspicuous consumption." Conspicuous consumption was consumption undertaken to make a statement to others about one's class or accomplishments. This term, more than any other, is what Veblen is known for.

Veblen did not reject economists' answers to the questions they posed. Rather, he thought their questions were too narrow. Veblen wanted economists to try to understand the social and cultural causes and effects of economic changes. What social and cultural causes were responsible for the shift from hunting and fishing to farming, for example, and what were the social and cultural effects of this shift? Veblen was singularly unsuccessful at getting economists to focus on such questions. His failure may explain the sarcastic tone toward his fellow economists in his writing.

Veblen had to struggle to stay in academia. In the late nineteenth century many universities were affiliated in a substantial way with churches. Veblen's skepticism about religion and his rough manners and unkempt appearance made him unattractive to such universities. As a result, from 1884 to 1891 Veblen lived off his family and his wife's family. His big break came in 1892 when the newly formed University of Chicago hired his mentor, J. Laurence Laughlin. Laughlin took Veblen with him as a teaching assistant. Veblen later became managing editor of the *Journal of Political Economy*, which was and is edited at the University of Chicago. Veblen spent fourteen years at Chicago and the next three at Stanford. He died in obscurity in 1929.

Selected Works

The Theory of Business Enterprise. 1904.
The Theory of the Leisure Class. 1899.

Viner, Jacob (1892–1970)—Mark Blaug, an economic historian, calls Jacob Viner "the greatest historian of economic thought that ever lived." One of Viner's greatest accomplishments was his book *Studies in the Theory of International Trade*. This work is not just a history of the theory of international trade, but also a guidebook that tells where the early economists who studied trade were wrong and where they were right. In it Viner decisively refuted fallacies of mercantilism (see MERCANTILISM). Viner also wrote a famous 145-page introduction to an edition of John Rae's *Life of Adam Smith*.

Viner was an international trade theorist in his own right. His book *The Customs Union Issue* introduced the distinction between the trade-creating and the trade-diverting effects of customs unions (see FREE TRADE AGREEMENTS AND CUSTOMS UNIONS). His earliest book, *Dumping*, was a comprehensive analysis of the subject.

Viner was known for his view that the long run mattered. Some of his best articles are reprinted in a 1958 book, *The Long View and the Short*. Viner wrote: "No matter how refined and how elaborate the analysis, if it rests solely on the short view it will still be . . . a structure built on shifting sands." One of the articles published in this book, "Cost Curves and Supply Curves," laid out the short-run and long-run cost curves that still show up in microeconomics texts.

Viner, who grew up in Montreal, was an undergraduate student at McGill University, where he studied economics under famous Canadian humorist Stephen Leacock. He earned his Ph.D. at Harvard, writing his dissertation under international trade economist Frank W. Taussig. He was a professor at the University of Chicago from 1916 to 1917 and from 1919 until 1946. He moved to Princeton in 1946, where he taught until retiring in 1960. For many of his years at Chicago, Viner, along with Frank Knight, edited the *Journal of Political Economy*. Viner is not considered part of the Chicago school as he was much less sympathetic to free markets than his Chicago school colleagues.

Selected Works

The Customs Union Issue. 1950.
Dumping: A Problem in International Trade. 1923.
Guide to John Rae's "Life of Adam Smith." Introduction to Rae. *Life of Adam Smith.* 1965.
The Long View and the Short: Studies in Economic Theory and Policy. 1952.
Studies in the Theory of International Trade. 1937.

Walras, Leon (1834–1910)—Separately, but almost simultaneously with William Stanley Jevons and Carl Menger, French economist Leon Walras developed the idea of marginal utility and is thus considered one of the founders of the "marginal revolution." But Walras's biggest contribution was in what is now called general equilibrium theory. Before Walras, economists had made little attempt to show how a whole economy with many goods fits together and reaches an equilibrium. Walras's goal was to do this. He did not succeed, but he took some major first steps. First, he built a system of simultaneous equations to describe his hypothetical economy, a tremendous task. He then showed that, because the number of equations equaled the number of unknowns, the system could be solved to give the equilibrium prices and quantities of commodities. The demonstration that price and quantity were uniquely determined for each commodity is considered one of Walras's greatest contributions to economic science.

But Walras was aware that the mere fact that such a system of equations could be solved mathematically for an equilibrium did not mean that in the real world it would ever reach that equilibrium. So Walras's second major step was to simulate an artificial market process that would get the system to equilibrium. This process he called "*tâtonnement*" (French for groping). *Tâtonnement* was a trial-and-error process in which a price was called out and people in the market said how much they were willing to demand or supply at that price. If there was an excess of supply over demand, then the price would be lowered so that less would be supplied and more would be demanded. Thus would the prices "grope" toward equilibrium. To keep constant the equilibrium toward which prices were groping, Walras assumed, highly unrealistically, that no actual exchange were made until equilibrium was reached. If, for example, people who wanted to buy ketchup wanted more than sellers were willing to sell, then they would buy none at all. This assumption limits the usefulness of Walras's simulated process as an aid to understanding how real markets work.

Walras's sole academic job was as an economics professor at the University of Lausanne in Switzerland. This location was not ideal: because the dominant thinking in economics at the time was in Britain, it was difficult for Walras to affect the rest of the profession. Also, because his students were more interested in becoming lawyers than in becoming economists, Walras did not have disciples. Although his impact on economics was limited during his lifetime, it has been much greater since the thirties. Historian of economic thought Mark Blaug writes that Walras "may now be the most widely-read nineteenth century economist after Ricardo and Marx."

Walras's father, the French economist Auguste Walras, encouraged his son to pursue economics with a particular emphasis on mathematics. After sampling several careers—he was for a while a student at the School of Mines, a journalist, a lecturer, a railway clerk, a bank director, and a published romance novelist—Walras eventually returned to the study and teaching of economics. In that scientific discipline Walras claimed to have found "pleasures and joys like those that religion provides to the faithful." Walras retired in 1902 at age fifty-eight.

Selected Works

Elements of Pure Economics, translated and annotated by William Jaffe. 1954.

Weber, Max (1864–1920)—Max Weber was one of the founding fathers of sociology. In his most famous book, *The Protestant Ethic and the Spirit of Capitalism,* he found the seeds of capitalism in the Protestant work ethic.

But Weber was also an economist. To him, the distinctive feature of advanced capitalism, as in his pre–World War I Germany, was the extensive division of labor and a hierarchical administration that resembled the political bureaucracy. The two features together had created a new middle class whose position depended on neither physical capital nor labor, but on their human capital. Even in advanced capitalism, though, Weber thought the major source of progress to be risk taking by businessmen and entrepreneurs.

Weber accepted Ludwig von Mises's criticism of socialist economic planning (see MISES) and added his own argument. He believed that under socialism workers would still work in a hierarchy, but that now the hierarchy would be fused with government. Instead of dictatorship of the worker, he foresaw dictatorship of the official.

Weber, like David Hume before him, believed in the possibility of value-free social science. By that he meant that one could not draw conclusions about the way the world should be

simply from studying the way the world is. Weber did not rule out normative analysis as being feasible or worthwhile—he believed in rational discussion of values. He simply wanted economists to distinguish between facts and values.

Born in Germany, Weber studied law and went on to do graduate work with a dissertation on medieval trading companies in Italy and Spain. He was appointed to a chair in political economy at Freiburg in 1894, and to another chair in political economy at Heidelberg in 1896. He suffered a nervous breakdown in 1898 and did not continue his scholarly work until 1904. From 1904 on he was a private scholar, mostly in Heidelberg.

Selected Works

The Protestant Ethic and the Spirit of Capitalism. 1904.
"Socialism." 1918. Reprinted in *Weber Selections in Translation*, edited by W. G. Runciman. 1978.

Wicksell, Knut (1851–1926)—Economist Knut Wicksell made his name among the Swedish public with a series of provocative lectures on the causes of prostitution, drunkenness, poverty, and overpopulation. A Malthusian (see MALTHUS), the young Wicksell advocated birth control as the cure for these social ills. His image as a radical social reformer did much to attract the attention of the press and the Young Socialists with whom he sympathized. But his rejection of Marx and Marxism limited his popularity.

Wicksell was not so much an innovator as a synthesizer. His integration and refinement of existing microeconomic theories helped earn Wicksell recognition as the "economists' economist." In his 1893 book, *Value, Capital, and*

Rent, Wicksell analyzed and praised the Austrian theory of capital as elaborated by Böhm-Bawerk. In his *Lectures on Political Economy, I*, Wicksell concluded that Böhm-Bawerk's idea of roundaboutness (see BÖHM-BAWERK) did not make sense, and agreed with Irving Fisher (see FISHER) that waiting was a sufficient explanation for interest rates.

Wicksell also laid out marginal productivity theory, the theory that the payment to each factor of production equals that factor's marginal product. Economists Philip Wicksteed, Enrico Barone, and John Bates Clark had already elaborated this theory, but Wicksell's exposition of it was superior. Wicksell also emphasized that an efficient allocation of resources is not necessarily just, because the allocation depends crucially on the preexisting distribution of income, and nothing guarantees that this preexisting distribution is just.

Wicksell is best known for *Interest and Prices*, his contribution to the fledgling field now called macroeconomics. In this book and his 1906 *Lectures in Political Economy, II*, Wicksell sketched out his version of the quantity theory of money (monetarism). The standard view of the quantity theory before Wicksell was that increases in the money supply have a direct effect on prices—more money chasing the same amount of goods. Wicksell focused on the indirect effect. In elaborating this effect, Wicksell distinguished between the real rate of return on new capital (Wicksell called this the "natural rate of interest") and the actual market rate of interest. He argued that if the banks reduced the rate of interest below the real rate of return on capital, the demand for loan capital would increase and the supply of saving would fall. Investment, which equaled saving before the interest rate fell, would exceed saving at the lower rate. The increase in investment would increase overall spending, thus driving up prices. This "cumulative process" of inflation

would stop only when the banks' reserves had fallen to their legal or desired limit, whichever was higher.

In laying out this theory, Wicksell began the conversion of the old quantity theory into a full-blown theory of prices. The Stockholm school, of which Wicksell was the father figure, ran with this insight and developed its own version of macroeconomics. In some ways this version resembled later Keynesian economics. Among the young Swedish economists who learned from Wicksell were Bertil Ohlin (see OHLIN), Gunnar Myrdal (see MYRDAL), and Dag Hammarskjöld, later secretary general of the United Nations.

For much of his adult life, Wicksell depended on several small inheritances, grants, and the meager income earned through public lectures and publications. Not until 1886, when he was awarded a major grant, did he begin to pursue economics seriously. With financial support secured, Wicksell traveled to universities in London, Strasbourg, Vienna, Berlin, and Paris. By 1890 Wicksell had returned to Stockholm, but being "too notorious" and unqualified to teach—he held degrees in mathematics, but economics instructors were then required to have formal degrees in law and economics—he returned to free-lance writing and lecturing.

In 1900, when Wicksell was forty-eight years old, he was granted his first teaching position at the University of Lund, which he retained until retirement in 1916. His quirky habits, friendly demeanor, and willingness to actively defend his beliefs earned him respect and popularity among his students. Throughout his lifetime Wicksell never lost his penchant for radicalism. He forfeited a professorship by refusing to sign the application with the conventional "Your Majesty's most obedient servant." In 1910 he was jailed for two months by the Swedish government for a satirical public lecture he delivered on the Immaculate Conception. In spite of his disdain for ceremony and fanfare, his common-law widow consented to an extravagant funeral upon his death at age seventy-four.

Selected Works

Lectures on Political Economy, I. 1901. Translated by E. Classen. 1934.

Lectures on Political Economy, II. Translated by E. Classen. 1935.

Value, Capital and Rent. 1893. Translated by S. H. Frowein, 1954. Reprint. 1970.

INDEX

Boldface indicates articles in the book.

AAA *see* Agricultural Adjustment
  Act
Aaron, Henry, 315
Absenteeism, 741
Accountability, educational, 704,
  705
Acid rain, 672–673
Ackerman, Bruce, 49
Acquisitions, 267
Activity analysis *see* Linear
  programming
Actual growth, 790–791
Actuarial funding program, 592
Adams, Walter, 434
AD duty *see* Antidumping duty
Adenauer, Konrad, 741
Adkins v. *Children's Hospital*, 500
Adverse selection, 23–24
Advertising, 613–617
  brand loyalty, 614–615
  depreciation rate of, 616
  economic function of, 614–615
  expenditures, 614
  image, 615
  and information, 20
  and monopoly, 615–616
  as percent of GNP, 613
  price, 616
  ratio to sales, 615
  regulation of, 616–617
  scope of, 613–614
  see also Brand names
Advertising (Bittlingmayer),
  613–617
AFDC *see* Aid to Families with
  Dependent Children
Affirmative action, 473, 478
The Affluent Society (Galbraith),
  788
Africa, 647
  see also specific countries
African-Americans, 474–475,
  820–821
  and education, 481, 703
  poverty rate for, 57
  union discrimination against,
    495–496, 498
Afrikaners *see* Boers
Aged *see* Elderly; Retirement

Agency costs, 560–561
Agenda-setting, 153
Agent Orange, 28–29
The Age of Diminished Expectations
  (Krugman), 223
Aggregate demand, 118, 272, 801
  and deficits, 122
  externalities, 145–146
  and fiscal policy, 257–258,
    259–260
  and inflation, 214
Agricultural Adjustment Act
  (AAA), 201, 821
Agricultural economics, 35
Agricultural Price Supports
  (Thompson), 647–651
Agriculture, 52–53, 809
  and common laborers, 505
  under fascism, 116
  and futures trading, 576–577
  and Great Depression, 197
  and greenhouse effect, 448–449
  in India, 755
  injury rates in, 504
  loan rate, 649–650
  price supports, 647–651
    forms of, 648–650
    and overproduction, 650–651
    production, 647, 648
  reform in Soviet Union, 748
  research and development, 79
  restrictions on, 820–821
  and rural poverty, 832–833
  in South Korea, 755
  Third World development, 758
  transfer programs for, 295
Agriculture Department (U.S.), 649
AIDS, 668–669, 670–671
Aid to Families with Dependent
  Children (AFDC), 59, 60, 237
Airline Deregulation (Kahn),
  379–384
Air pollution, 76
  cost of abatement, 454
  emissions permits, 455
  and futures trading, 578
Albania, 730
Alchian, Armen, 108, 773–774
Alienation, 125–126

Allais, Maurice, 774–775
Allen, William R., 773–774
Allied Control Authority, 738, 740
Alperovitz, Gar, 113
Aluminum, 456
Aluminum Company of America,
  834
American Airlines, 381
*American Capitalism: The Concept
  of Countervailing Power*
  (Galbraith), 788
An American Dilemma (Myrdal),
  820–821
American Economic Association,
  771–772
American Economic Review
  (magazine), 499
American Telephone and Telegraph
  (AT&T), 402, 717
American Economic Association,
  771–772
American Trucking Association,
  434, 435
"America 2000," 703
Anchorage (Alaska), 626
Anderson, Terry, 445
Andrews, William, 324
Annuities, 231, 592
Anticipation, 431
Antidumping (AD) duty, 541
Antitakeover laws, 606, 607
Antitrust, 112, 381, 385–389
  anticompetitive practices,
    386–388
  in Austrian economics, 107–108
  and concentration, 397–398
  declining support for, 401
  effects of, 388–389
  enforcement of, 402
  government lawsuits, 389
  and health care, 681
  in Japan, 745
  origins of, 385–386
  private lawsuits, 388–389
  under Reaganomics, 291
  and sports, 713, 714–715
  and trucking industry, 433
  union exemption from, 494
  see also Monopolies

Antitrust (McChesney), 385–389
Apartheid, 97–103
  color bar, 98–101
  decline of, 102–103
  roots of, 97–98
  sanctions against, 103
Apartheid (Hazlett), 97–103
Apprenticeship, 410
Appropriations Committee (U.S.),
  244, 246
Arbitrage, 19, 781
  proof, 558–559
  in sports, 709–710
  see also Index arbitrage
Archdiocese of New York, 706
Argentina, 724, 754
  debt, 751
  heterodox policy, 759
  interest rates and depreciation,
  129
Arrow, Kenneth, 153, 775–776,
  784
Asbestos litigation, 28–29, 490
Asch, Peter, 387
Ashton, T. S., 13
Asian Drama: An Inquiry into the
  Poverty of Nations (Myrdal),
  821
Aspirin, 620
Asset-Backed Securities (Zweig),
  551–553
Assets freeze, 544–545
AT&T *see* American Telephone and
  Telegraph
A-10 Warthog (aircraft), 665–666
Audubon Society, 44
Auerbach, Alan, 313, 341
Austerity programs, 759
Australia, 499, 500, 544
Austria, 329
Austrian economics, 105–109, 792,
  816, 818
  and antitrust, 107–108
  basics of, 105–106
  and central planning, 108–109
  and entrepreneurship, 632–633
  history of, 105
  policy implications of, 107–108
Austrian Economics (Walker),
  105–109
Austrian Institute for Business
  Cycle Research, 818
Autarchy, 116
Auto loans, 551
Automatic stabilizers, 258
Automobiles
  emissions standards, 454
  mileage standards, 674
Autonomy, educational, 704

Axelrod, Robert, 63
AZT (drug), 671

Babbage, Charles, 653
Baden, John, 152
Baily, Martin, 652
Bain, Joe, 387
Balance of payments, 511–513, 815
  definitions of, 511–512
  Eastern European, 728
  and money supply, 798
  U.S., 512
The Balance of Payments (Meade),
  814
Balance of Payments (Stein),
  511–513
Bane, Mary Jo, 60
Bangladesh, 764–765
Banking Act of 1935 (U.S.), 358
Bank Insurance Fund (BIF; U.S.),
  354
Bank notes, 348, 349
Bank of England, 121, 361
Bank Runs (Kaufman), 345–346
Bankruptcy, 18
  and corporate debt, 560
Banks and banking, 18
  central, 272–278, 348, 350–351,
  361–362
  collapse during Great Depression,
  200
  failures, 346
  under fascism, 117
  free, 348–350, 794
  in Japan, 745–746
  and monetary competition,
  347–351
  under Reaganomics, 291
  reserve requirements, 275,
  277–278, 349, 353, 357,
  365–367
  runs on, 345–346, 349–350,
  352–353
  Third World debt, 751–754
  U.S. failures, 200
  see also Development banks;
  Federal Reserve System
Bargaining, 642
Barro, Robert, 122, 145, 158, 159,
  253, 298, 332
Barter, 209–210, 637, 738–739,
  815–816
Baseball, 713
The Basing-Point System
  (Machlup), 811
Basketball, 713
Bastiat, Frédéric, 776–777
Bauer, Peter, 652

Baumol, William J., 222, 223,
  262, 389
BCA *see* Benefit-cost analysis
BEA *see* Bureau of Economic
  Analysis
Bear Stearns and Company, 588
Beck, Mr. and Mrs. W. W., 444
Becker, Gary Stanley, 660,
  777–778, 833
Beech-Nut, 619
Belgium, 733
  capital gains tax, 317
  and gold standard, 361
  marginal tax rates, 329
Bell Journal of Economics and
  Management Science, 840
Bell System, 717, 719
Bendectin (drug), 671
Benefit-cost analysis (BCA), 3–6,
  780
  and marginalism, 31–32
  and public finance, 35
Benefit-Cost Analysis (Portney),
  3–6
Benefits
  and minimum wage, 499, 501
  see also Health insurance;
  Pensions
Bentham, Jeremy, 778
Bequests, 298–299
Bergsman, Joel, 762
Berle, Adolf A., Jr., 113, 566
Berliner, Joseph, 749
Bernheim, B. Douglas, 299
The Best Uses of Economic
  Resources (Kantorovich), 799
Beta blockers, 669–670
Better Jobs and Income Plan
  (BJIP), 337
Bewley, Truman, 159
Bhagwati, Jagdish, 762
Bid-ask spread, 581
BIF *see* Bank Insurance Fund
Birthrates, 51, 52
Bittlingmayer, George, 387
BJIP *see* Better Jobs and Income
  Plan
Black, Fischer, 350
Blackman, Sue Anne, 222, 223
Black market, 37
  and capital controls, 725
  exchange rate, 728
  Peruvian, 757
  and price controls, 417, 418
Blank, Rebecca, 58
Blaug, Mark, 814, 826
Blinder, Alan, 58, 315
Blue Cross/Blue Shield, 684–685
Bluestone, Barry, 266

Boers, 97
Böhm-Bawerk, Eugen von, 105, 778–779, 816
Bolivia
  debt buy-back, 753
  hyperinflation, 210
Bolsheviks, 627
Bondholders, 566
Bonds, 277, 554–557, 565
  corporate, 555–556
  covenants, 561–562
  municipal, 556–557
  and pensions, 594
  private placements, 588
  rating of, 588
  riskiness of, 588–589
  U.S. government, 554–555
  see also Securities; specific types of bonds, e.g., junk bonds
Bonds (Smith), 554–557
Bon Vivant (company), 620
Booms, 173, 174
Bork, Robert, 386–387
Boserup, Ester, 53
Boskin, Michael, 254, 299, 300
Bosworth, Barry, 313, 341
Botswana, 76, 725
Boulding, Kenneth, 749
Boulware, Lemuel, 494
Bounded rationality, 835
Brady Plan, 724, 753, 754
Brain drain, 331, 486
Brand names, 614–615, 618–621
Brand Names (Klein), 618–621
Brazil, 725, 754
  capital flight from, 752
  cost of protectionism, 762
  debt, 751
  heterodox policy, 759
  interest rates and depreciation, 129
  social security, 760
Breit, Marek, 805
Brenner, Joel, 422
Bresciani-Turroni, Costantino, 209
Bretton Woods agreement, 129, 132, 201, 360, 518, 536, 723, 800
Bribery, 417, 418
Brinksmanship, 642
Britain see Great Britain
British East India Company, 534
British Petroleum, 285
Brock, William A., 159
Broederbond (South African society), 102
Brown v. *Board of Education of Topeka*, 820
Brozen, Yale, 387

Buchanan, James, 32, 150, 153, 779–780
Budget see Federal budget
Building industry see Construction industry
Bulgaria, 730
Bulk power market, 391–394
Bundesbank (Germany), 131, 273
Bureaucracies, 49–50
  educational, 705–706
  incentives for, 152
  and socialism, 163–164
Bureau of Economic Analysis (BEA; U.S.), 204, 206–207
Bureau of Labor Statistics (U.S.), 212, 236
Bureau of Mines (U.S.), 40, 43
Burns, Arthur Frank, 173, 780–781
Burtless, Gary, 58, 313, 341
Bush, George, 703
Business cycles, 173–176, 217, 792, 818
  eliminating swings in, 175–176
  expectational error models of, 158–159
  and fiscal policy, 258–259
  inflation and unemployment over, 280
  and investment, 218
  and monetary policy, 272
  and money supply, 368
  in U.S., 174, 176
Business Cycles in the United States, 1919–1932 (Tinbergen), 843
Business Cycles (Romer), 173–176
Byssinosis (disease), 491

CAAA see Comprehensive Anti-Apartheid Act
CAFE regulations see Corporate average fuel economy regulations
Cain, Glen C., 335
The Calculus of Consent (Buchanan and Tullock), 153, 780
Cambridge controversy see Two Cambridges Capital Controversy
Campbell's, 620
Canada, 690
  capital gains tax, 317–318
  marginal tax rates, 329
Cancer, 429
Cantillon, Richard, 631
CAP see Common Agricultural Policy

Capacity utilization, 272
Capetown (South Africa), 97
Capital, 159, 214, 735, 784, 791
  account, 512
  controls, 724–725, 730, 735
  dilution, 53
  and economic growth, 844–845
  flight, 331, 723–726, 751–752, 758
  foreign, 756
  formation, 324
  growth model for different vintages of, 839
  human, 479–483, 777, 833
  inflow, 513
  and Japanese growth, 743
  migration, 523
  and production, 64
  and roundabout production, 779
  soldiers as, 470
  stock, 65
  theory, 792, 803
  see also Capital markets
Capital (Marx), 124, 814
Capital Asset Pricing Model (CAPM), 834–835
Capital consumption allowance, 65, 67
Capital Flight (McLeod), 723–726
Capital gains tax, 315, 317–320, 524, 602
  and corporate debt, 560
  effect on revenue, 318–320
  and elasticity of realizations, 319–320
  on phantom gains, 321
  and progressive taxes, 338
Capital Gains Taxes (Cordes), 317–320
Capitalism, 12, 110–114
  and apartheid, 101–102
  Marxist view of, 124–126, 814
  and Protestant work ethic, 848
  Schumpeter on demise of, 833
Capitalism and Freedom (Friedman), 333, 786
Capitalism (Hessen), 110–114
Capitalism, Socialism, and Democracy (Schumpeter), 833
Capital markets
  efficient, 569–573
  and information, 17–18
  see also Bonds; Securities; Stock market
Capital punishment, 659
Capitation, 681
CAPM see Capital Asset Pricing Model
Capture theory, 152, 841

Carbon emissions, 448, 450–451
Cardboard, 458
Cardosa, Eliana, 210
Career attachment, 465
Carnegie, Andrew, 112
Carroll, Sidney, 411–412
Cartels, 385, 698
    sports as, 713
    worker, 495
Carter, Jimmy, 336, 434, 545, 702
Carter, William, 496
"The Case Against Big Business"
    (Stigler), 396
Cassel, Gustav, 781
Castro, Fidel, 487
Caterpillar, 575
CCC see Commodity Credit
    Corporation
CEA see Council of Economic
    Advisors
Center for Drug Development
    (U.S.), 669
Center for Study of Public Choice,
    150
Central planning, 20–21, 638, 727,
    747–748, 793, 799, 805
    in Austrian economics, 108–109
    in U.S. Defense Department, 665
    see also Socialism
Certification, 682
    see also Licensing
Certified public accountants
    (CPAs), 374
Chamberlin, Edward H., 618, 829
Chamber of Mines (South Africa),
    98, 99, 100
Chamley, Christophe, 159
Chammah, Walid, 552
Champernowne, David, 842
Chernenko, Konstantin, 748
Chiarella, Vincent, 583
Chicago Board of Trade, 578
Chicago Mercantile Exchange, 575,
    576
Child labor, 111
Children, 57
Child Support Enforcement
    program, 246
Chile, 756
China, 543
Chlorofluorocarbons, 456
Chung, William K., 743
Churchill, Randolph, 539
Cigarette advertising, 616–617
Citibank, 551
Citicorp, 553
Citizenship, 410
Civilian Conservation Corps (U.S.),
    201

Civilized Labour Policy (South
    Africa), 99–100
Civil law, 660
Civil Rights Act of 1964 (U.S.),
    463, 464, 478
Clark, Colin, 82
Clark, John Bates, 845
Clark, Kim B., 304
Class consciousness, 201
Class struggle, 126
Clay, Lucius D., 740
Clayton Act (U.S.), 385
Clean Air Act (U.S.), 49, 150,
    453, 454, 455, 456
Climate change see Greenhouse
    effect
Coal, 504, 672
The Coal Question (Jevons), 797
Coase, Ronald, 696, 773, 781–783,
    825
Coase Theorem, 782–783
Coercion, 638
Cognitive psychology, 431
Colander, David, 808
Colbert, Jean-Baptiste, 328, 535
Collateral trust bonds, 556
Collective bargaining, 494
Collectivization, 161
Colleges and universities, research
    and development at, 78
Collusion, 62, 396, 437, 464, 713,
    841
Colombia, 756
Colonies, 534
Commerce Department (U.S.), 203,
    523
Commodity Credit Corporation
    (CCC; U.S.), 649
Common Agricultural Policy
    (CAP), 735
Commons, 88–91
    and budget deficit, 243–245,
    246
Common stock, 565, 566
Communications, 82–85
    decline in costs of, 84
    and disaster recovery, 629
    see also Telecommunications
Communism, 64, 727–728
"The Communist Manifesto"
    (Engels and Marx), 814
Community rating, 684
Comparable worth, 463–466
    effects of, 465–466
Comparable Worth (O'Neill),
    463–466
Comparative advantage, 827
Compensating wage differentials
    theory, 837

Compensation
    benefit-cost analysis, 4, 5–6
    product liability, 28
    test, 795
    see also Workers' compensation
Competing Money Supplies
    (White), 347–351
Competition, 45, 111–112,
    622–624, 639
    and concentration, 396, 397
    in defense procurement, 666
    and deregulation, 382
    in education, 706
    in health care, 680–682, 685,
    686
    international
       and concentration, 397–398
       and unemployment, 239
    and licensing, 409
    Marxist view of, 126
    nonprice, 387
    perfect, 107, 111–112, 386, 401,
    618, 833–834
    and property rights, 70
    and regulation, 402
    sports, 710
    in telecommunications industry,
    718
    in trucking industry, 433
    see also Antitrust
Competitiveness, 514–517
Competitiveness (Lawrence),
    514–517
Complements, 8
Compounding, 183
Comprehensive Anti-Apartheid Act
    (CAAA; U.S.), 547
Comprehensive National Energy
    Policy Act of 1992 (U.S.), 392
Computer Industry (Gilder),
    652–656
Computers, 217, 597, 652–656
    European industry, 654
    U.S. share of industry, 653–654
    see also Telecommunications
Concentration, 380–382, 395–398
    and advertising, 616
    causes of, 396–397
    effects of, 395–396
    four firm ratio, 395
    and profits, 387, 396, 401
    in U.S., 395
"The Concept of Monopoly and the
    Measure of Monopoly Power"
    (Lerner), 808
Condorcet's paradox, 775
Congressional Budget Office
    (CBO), 134, 169
Conscription, 467–469, 470

Conscription (Jehn), 467–469
Conservation Land Trusts (U.S.), 445–447
Conservatism, 794
Considerations of the Consequences of the Lowering of Interest (Locke), 810
Constitutional economics, 153
The Constitution of Liberty (Hayek), 793–794
Constraints, 710
Construction industry, 187–188
    commercial, 218
    and minimum wage, 502
    residential, 219
    and unions, 496
Consumer price index (CPI), 212
Consumer Reports (magazine), 587
Consumer spending, 203–204
Consumer surplus, 813
Consumption, 255, 804
    and competitiveness, 516
    conspicuous, 788, 846
    determinants of, 141
    during industrial revolution, 14
    nonrivalrous, 75
    permanent income theory of, 156–157
    and saving, 233, 234
    tax, 314–315, 321–324, 784–785
Consumption Tax (Ehrbar), 321–324
Contingent valuation method, 4
Contract law, 695, 817
"A Contribution to the Theory of Growth" (Solow), 838
Convergence behavior, 627
Convertible bonds, 556
Cooperation, 62–63, 624, 639
Copayments, 684
Copyrights, 72, 187
Corn Laws (U.K.), 827
Cornrows and Company, 413
Corporate average fuel economy (CAFE) regulations, 674
Corporate Debt (Poulsen), 558–562
Corporation income tax, 310, 312, 314, 325–328
    and debt, 558, 559
    integrating with individual income tax, 327–328
    in post-war Germany, 740
    and progressive taxes, 339
Corporations, 71, 113, 563–568, 788–789
    borrowing by, 276
    culture of, 634–635

debt, 558–562, 573, 817
    defining, 563–564
    earnings and stock prices, 604
    and environmentalism, 444
    profits as percentage of assets, 326
    Subchapter S status, 327
    see also Leveraged buyouts; Takeovers
Corporations (Hessen), 563–568
Corporation Taxation (Norton), 325–328
Corporative State (Italy), 115
Corporativism, 115–116
Corruption
    and price controls, 418
    see also Collusion; Crime
Cosmetic surgery, 685
Cost and Choice (Buchanan), 780
Costa Rica, 756
Cost-benefit analysis *see* Benefit-cost analysis
Costle, Douglas, 456
Cost of living, 14
Cost-plus contracting, 665, 666
Cost predation, 388
Costs
    calculations of, 4–5
    in marginalism, 32
    telecommunications, 718
    see also Benefit-cost analysis; Opportunity cost; Transaction costs
Council of Economic Advisors (CEA), 770, 823
Council of Four, 800
The Counter-Revolution of Science: Studies in the Abuse of Reason (Hayek), 793
Countervailing duty (CVD), 541
Cournot, Antoine, 797
Cours d'économie politique (Pareto), 824
CPAs *see* Certified public accountants
CPI *see* Consumer price index
Crafts, N. F. R., 13
Crandall, Robert, 49, 150, 268
Credibility, 642
Credit, 18, 199
    risk, 588
Credit cards, 551, 553
Crime, 657–660, 777
    and free market, 637–638
    organized, 657–658
    and savings and loan crisis, 373
Crime (Friedman), 657–660
Criminal law, 660

Currency, 277–278
    and bank runs, 346
    in circulation, 275
    component of money supply, 365–366
    Eastern European, 727
    European Community, 736
    and free banking, 348
    markets, 519
    options, 578
    reform in post-war Germany, 739–740
    speculation, 723–726
    see also Money
Current account, 512–513, 522, 537
Current Population Survey (CPS; U.S.), 177–178
The Customs Union Issue (Viner), 846
Customs unions, 530–533, 733–737
CVD *see* Countervailing duty
Czechoslovakia, 729, 730, 731

Daewoo Company, 764
Dairy industry, 649
Dalkon Shield, 28–29
Danziger, Sheldon, 57, 59
Davis, Joseph S., 563
Davis-Bacon Act, 496, 502
Death rate, occupational, 492
Debentures, 556
Debreu, Gerard, 775, 783–784
Debt, 327
    buy-backs, 753–754
    and capital flight, 723
    neutrality, 118, 122
    securitization, 590
    Third World, 751–757, 763
    see also Federal debt
Decision making *see* Information; Public choice theory
Deductibles, 684, 687
Default spread, 572–573
Defense, 661–667
    burden sharing in, 664
    and conscription, 467–469
    contractors, 666
    efficient delivery of, 665–666
    and foreign procurement, 664–665
    international alliances, 663–664
    optimal amount of, 662
    optimal taxation for, 662–663
    as public good, 661
    spending, 514–515

Defense (*cont.*)
  as threat to polity, 666–667
  U.S. spending on, 664
Defense Department (U.S.), 80,
  665
Defense (Zycher), 661–667
Deficiency payments, 650
Deficits, 205, 253–256, 516, 729
  average, 245
  and debt neutrality, 122
  and fiscal policy, 257
  in high-inflation countries, 759
  and industrial policy, 267–268
  measure of, 254
  relative to GNP, 243, 244
  and tax-smoothing, 158
Deficit spending *see* Federal budget
Defined benefit pension plans, 592,
  593
Defined contribution pension plans,
  591–592, 593
Deforestation, 450
Deindustrialization, 266
The Deindustrialization of America
  (Bluestone and Harrison), 266
De Klerk, F. W., 103
Delaney Amendment, 670
Delors, Jacques, 736
Demand, 7–8
  consumer, 112
  curve, 7, 86
  and growth, 791
  law of, 7
  management, 204
  price elasticity of, 813
  see also Aggregate demand;
    Supply and demand
Demand (Henderson), 7–8
Demographics
  and income distribution, 180
  and savings, 231–232
  see also Population
Demsetz, Harold, 108, 387
Denationalization, 285
Denison, Edward H., 224, 743
Denmark, 734, 736
Dennison, Robert, 652
Denzau, Arthur, 295
Deposit insurance, 201, 246,
  352–355
  and savings and loan crisis, 369,
  371, 373
Deposit Insurance (Kaufman),
  352–355
Deposits, 277–278, 364–368
  brokered, 373–374
Depreciation, 220
  accelerated, 218–219

Depressions, 174, 812
  European, 122
  Keynesian view of, 119
  see also Great Depression;
    Recessions
Deregulation, 291, 292
  airline, 379–384, 396
    benefits of, 379–380
    concentration and price
      discrimination, 380–382
    quality of service, 383–384
    safety, 382–383
  of savings and loans, 371
  and takeovers, 606
  of trucking industry, 435–436
  see also Regulation
Desh, 764–765
Design defect, 27
De Stefani, Alberto, 115
Devaluation, 723
Development, 809
  and population, 52–55
  Third World, 755–765
    experience in, 756–757
Development banks, 267, 269
Dewey, Donald, 387
DiLorenzo, Thomas, 385
Diocletian (Roman emperor), 211
Direct exchange, 637
Director, Aaron, 386, 783
Disaster and Recovery
  (Hirshleifer), 625–630
Disaster recovery, 625–630
  factors helping or hindering,
    628–629
  role of government, 629–630
Disaster response firms, 629
Discounting, 5
Discount rate, 199, 200, 275–276,
  357, 358, 361, 365
Discrimination, 470–475, 777,
  820–821
  and property rights, 70, 774
  by unions, 495–496
  against women, 463–464, 477
Discrimination (Gorman), 470–474
Disney Corporation, 790
Distortions, market, 36–37
Distribution, 89
Distribution of Income (Levy),
  177–182
Distribution theory, 135
Diversification of power sources,
  393
Divestiture, 717
Dividends, 561, 572–573, 602
Divorce, 60, 783
Doctors *see* Physicians

Dollarization, 210
Domar, Evsey, 790, 807
Dorfman, Robert, 831
Dornbusch, Rudiger, 519
Downs, Anthony, 151, 780
Drabeck, Thomas E., 626
Draft *see* Conscription
Dresher, Melvin, 62
Drexel Burnham Lambert, 588, 589
Drug Lag (Henninger), 668–671
Drugs, illegal, 658
  among children, 703
Drugs, prescription, 668–671
  cost of developing, 669
  efficacy of, 668
Dual economy, 809
DuBois, W. E. B., 496
Dukakis, Michael, 524
Dumping, 541
Dumping (Viner), 846
Dungell, John, 774
Dupuit, Jules, 3, 797
Duration averaging, 597, 598
Dynes, Russell, 626

Earned Income Credit (EIC), 336
Eastern Europe, 442, 727–731
  communist inheritance of,
    727–728
  strategies for transformation,
    728–731
Eastern Europe (Lipton), 727–731
EC *see* European Community
ECB *see* European Central Bank
Eccles, Marriner, 358
Eckstein, Otto, 143
Econometric models, 190–195
  accuracy of, 193–195
  errors in, 192–193
Econometrics, 787, 790
Economic and Monetary Union,
  Treaty on *see* Maastricht
  Treaty
*Economic and Philosophic
  Manuscripts of 1844* (Marx),
  125
Economic capacity, relative versus
  absolute, 515
*The Economic Consequences of the
  Peace* (Keynes), 800
*Economic Consequences of the
  Professions* (Lees), 412
Economic growth, 217, 790–791,
  809
  and capital, 844–845
  compound rates of, 183
  during mercantilist period, 536

and energy, 673
and gross domestic product, 204
and human capital, 482–483
and income distribution,
179–180, 805
and inflation, 215, 758–759
and innovation, 839
Japanese, 745
meta-ideas, 188–189
modern, 804–805
in per capita income, 184
and poverty, 58
recipes for, 184–185
research and development and,
186–189
and savings, 230, 231–232
Economic Growth (Romer),
183–189
Economic models, 801–802
The Economic Organization
(Knight), 802
*The Economic Problem in Peace
and War* (Robbins), 828
Economic quasi-rent, 87
Economic Recovery Act of 1981
(U.S.), 338
Economics (Samuelson), 787
"The Economics and Politics of
Consumer Sovereignty"
(Lerner), 807
*The Economics of Competition in
the Transportation Industry*
(Meyer, Peck, Stenason, and
Zwick), 434
*The Economics of Imperfect
Competition* (Robinson), 829
*The Economics of Sellers'
Competition* (Machlup), 811
The Economics of Welfare (Pigou),
825
Economic Stabilization Program,
698
An Economic Theory of Democracy
(Downs), 151, 780
Economies of scale, 396, 397, 403,
535, 743
Edgeworth, Francis Y., 137, 340
Edison, Thomas, 412
Education, 58, 186, 187, 480–482,
777, 817
accountability in, 704, 705
choice in, 706–708
and comparable worth, 465
decentralization in, 705
and gender gap, 478
and industrial policy, 267
and productivity, 225
public, 702–708

school choice, 706–708
South African, 101, 103
Third World, 760, 763
Education Department (U.S.),
702–703
EEC *see* European Economic
Community
Efficiency, 9–11
and antitrust, 386, 387
in Austrian economics, 106
and capital markets, 569–573
and corporate income tax, 327
and crime, 659–660
in defense, 665–666
and deregulation, 380, 381
electric utility, 393
and foreign investment in U.S.,
525
in health care, 679–680
of income transfer, 823–824
and information, 16–17
and law, 695–696
and pollution, 426
and price control, 419
taxation, 309–310
in Third World, 762
in trucking industry, 436
and trusts, 385
Efficiency (Heyne), 9–11
Efficiency wage theory, 17
Efficient Capital Markets (Jones
and Netter), 569–573
EFTA *see* European Free Trade
Association (EFTA)
Ehrbar, Al, 616
Ehrlich, Isaac, 658
Ehrlich, Paul, 54
Eichengreen, Barry, 198
Eisner, Robert, 254
Elasticity
of capital gains realizations,
319–320
of demand, 813
of substitution, 795
Elderly
poverty rate for, 57, 60
see also Pensions; Retirement
Electric Utility Regulation
(Michaels), 391–394
Elementary and Secondary
Education Act (U.S.),
702
Elephants, 76
Ellwood, David, 60
Embargoes, 544
Embezzlement, 724
Emissions permits *see* Marketable
permits

Employment, 214, 272
aggregate demand's impact on,
118
and balance of payment, 513
and comparable worth, 466
full, 174, 273, 791, 801
in high-yield firms, 589
and imports, 537
teenage, 501
see also Unemployment
Employment Act of 1946 (U.S.),
175
Employment Retirement Income
Security Act of 1974 (ERISA),
593
Energy, 40, 672–676
demand for, 673–674
and greenhouse effect, 450
U.S. consumption of, 673–674,
699
Energy (Leone), 672–676
Engels, Friedrich, 814
England *see* Great Britain
ENIAC (computer), 653
Enterprise Law (USSR), 748
Entrepreneurs, 64, 623, 631–635,
637, 833
and culture, 634
tax on, 327
Third World, 764–765
Entrepreneurship (Casson),
631–635
Entry
advertising as barrier to, 615–616
barriers, 464
and licensing, 409, 410, 411
regulating, 404
in sports, 714
and trucking industry
deregulation, 436
Environmentalism
free market, 442–445
policy, 441
benefit-cost analysis of, 3–6
and population, 54–55
and property rights, 72, 76
Environmentalism, A Preface
(Henderson), 441
Environmentalism, Free-Market
(Stroup), 442–445
Environmental Protection Agency
(EPA), 430, 453, 457
EPA *see* Environmental Protection
Agency
Equal Employment Opportunity
Commission, 472
*Equality and Efficiency: The Big
Tradeoff* (Okun), 823–824

Equal Pay Act of 1963 (U.S.), 463
Equation of Exchange, 785
Equilibrium, 641, 775
  see also General equilibrium
    theory
Equilibrium prices, 86
Equilibrium states, 106
Equipment obligations, 556
Equity, 327, 817
Equity markets, and information,
  17–18
Erhard, Ludwig, 739–741
ERISA see Employment Retirement
  Income Security Act of 1974
Error, 92
*Essay on the Influence of a Low
  Price of Corn on the Profits of
  Stock* (Ricardo), 825
*An Essay on the Nature and
  Significance of Economic
  Science* (Robbins), 828
Ethiopia, 116, 128
Eucken, Walter, 739
European Atomic Energy
  Community, 733
European Central Bank (ECB), 736
European Coal and Steel
  Community, 733
European Community (EC),
  350–351, 733–737
  development of, 734–735
  monetary unification, 736–737
  origins of, 733–734
  Single Market Program, 735
European Economic Community
  (EEC), 523, 531, 649, 650,
  733
European Economic Community
  (Eichengreen), 733–737
European Free Trade Area, 531
European Free Trade Association
  (EFTA), 734
European Monetary Institute, 736
European Monetary System, 122,
  521, 737
Evenson, Robert, 79
Exchange rates, 129, 133, 201,
  518–521, 536, 781, 800
  and balance of payments, 512
  black market, 728
  and capital flight, 723–725
  and competitiveness, 517
  in Eastern Europe, 728, 729
  effects of instability in, 520–521
  European Community, 736–737
  and fiscal policy, 258
  floating, 518–519
  forecasting, 132
  and futures, 575

and gold standard, 360–361
and monetary policy, 277
under Reaganomics, 291
Exchange Rates (Krugman),
  518–521
Excise tax, 311
Expansions, 227, 228
Expectations see Rational
  expectations
Expediters, 162
Experience, 465
  see also Education; Skills
Exploitation, 638
Exploratory synthesis, 185
Externalities, 74–77, 825
  consumption, 717

Factor Price Equalization Theory,
  830
Fairness
  in natural gas distribution, 405
  in taxation, 310, 313
Fair trade agreements, 387
Fair trade laws, 541
Fama, Eugene, 347, 350, 571, 572
Family, 482
  stability, 335
Family Assistance Plan (FAP;
  U.S.), 334, 336
Famine, 53
FAP see Family Assistance Plan
Fares (airline), 379–380
Farmers
  and apartheid, 101
  see also Agriculture
Fascism, 115–117
Fascism (Richman), 115–117
The Fatal Conceit (Hayek), 794
Favoritism, 418
FDA see Food and Drug
  Administration
FDIC see Federal Deposit Insurance
  Corporation
FDIC Improvement Act, 355
Federal budget, 243–247, 801
  decentralization in, 243–244, 246
  historical sketch of, 245–247
  intertemporal constraints,
    255–256
  and monetary policy, 274
  and problem of the commons,
    243–245, 246
  see also Deficits
Federal Budget (Cogan), 243–247
Federal debt, 248–252, 275
  alternative measures of, 249–250
  per capita, 251–252
  and private spending, 251

under Reaganomics, 292
  see also Debt
Federal Debt (Eisner), 248–252
Federal Deficit (Kotlikoff),
  253–256
Federal Deposit Insurance
  Corporation (FDIC), 352, 353,
  354–355
Federal Energy Regulatory
  Commission (FERC), 392,
  405, 407
Federal Farm Board, 649
Federal Home Loan Bank Board
  (FHLBB), 354, 371, 373
Federal Open Market Committee
  (FOMC), 275, 276, 278,
  356–357
Federal Reserve System
  (Johnson), 356–358
Federal Reserve System (U.S.),
  121, 197, 248, 356–358
  and bank failures during Great
    Depression, 198
  inflation rate predictions, 132
  monetary policy of, 175, 272–278
  and money supply, 365–367
  and price controls, 420
  response to Great Depression,
    199–200
Federal Savings and Loan Insurance
  Corporation (FSLIC; U.S.),
  90–91, 352, 353–354, 369,
  373
Federal Trade Commission (U.S.),
  402, 616
Fee schedules, 680
Feinstein, Charles, 14
Feldstein, Martin, 93, 213, 238,
  254, 298, 315
FERC see Federal Energy
  Regulatory Commission
Fernandez, Joseph, 705
Fertilizers, 648–649
FHLBB see Federal Home Loan
  Bank Board
Fiat money, 364
Final Restructuring Rule, 407
Financial distress, 560
*Financial Innovations and Market
  Volatility* (Miller), 817
Financial Institutions Reform,
  Recovery, and Enforcement
  Act (FIRREA), 354, 373
Firms, 190, 782
  see also Corporations; Small
    business
FIRREA see Financial Institutions
  Reform, Recovery, and
  Enforcement Act

First Amendment (U.S. Constitution), 667
First Boston Corporation, 552
First Colour Bar Act *see* Mines and Works Act of 1911 (South Africa)
Fiscal policy, 257–261, 282–283, 814–815
  discretionary, 259
  and hyperinflation, 209
  and monetary policy, 274–275
  obstacle to use of, 260–261
Fiscal Policy (Weil), 257–261
Fischer, Stanley, 121
Fisher, Irving, 137, 779, 784–785
Fitzsimmons, Cotton, 710
Flood, Merrill, 62
Flood insurance, 629
Fluctuations, economic *see* Business cycles
Fogarty, Charles F., 580, 582
FOMC *see* Federal Open Market Committee
Food and Drug Administration (FDA), 430, 621, 668, 679
Food stamps, 59, 180, 237, 246
Football, 714
Foothold stock, 605, 606
Forced-rider problem, 77
Forced up-trading, 417
Ford, Gerald, 434
Ford Motor Company, 29
Forecasting, 155, 190–195
  business cycle, 158–159
  and fiscal policy, 259
  and monetary policy, 131–132
  and Phillips curve, 283–284
Forecasting and Econometric Models (Hymans), 190–195
Foreign investment, 515, 522–525, 723
  long-term effect of, 524–525
Foreign Investment in the United States (Ott), 522–525
Foreign policy, 663
Forestry
  and greenhouse effect, 448
  see also Deforestation; Reforestation
Forest Service (U.S.), 152
Fort, Rodney, 152
Foundations of Economic Analysis (Samuelson), 830
France, 734, 736
  Australia's sanctions against, 544
  capital flight, 723, 725
  capital gains tax, 318
  during mercantilist period, 535
  and gold standard, 361–362

gross domestic product, 514
industrial policy, 268
privatization, 288
unemployment, 130
Franklin, Herbert, 422
Free agents, 713–714
Free cash-flow theory, 609–610
Freedom, 816
Freeman, Richard, 480, 494, 495
Free Market (Rothbard), 636
Free markets, 636–639, 792, 801
  and benefit-cost analysis, 3
  and information, 20–21
  Marxist view of, 125
  in Third World, 756–757
  see also Free trade
Free-rider problem, 46, 75
  in defense, 661–662, 663–664
  in health care, 682
Free to Choose (Friedman), 786
Free trade, 526–529, 536–537, 636, 827
  agreements, 530–533
  bilateral, 532–533
  multilateral, 530–531
  unilateral, 530
  see also Free markets; Protectionism
Free Trade Agreements and Customs Unions (Irwin), 530–533
Free trade areas (FTAs), 531, 733
Free Trade (Blinder), 526–529
Freiburg, University of, 739
French, Kenneth, 572
Frères, Lazard, 725
Friedland, Claire, 840
Friedman, David, 827
Friedman, Milton, 143, 239, 298, 739
  biography of, 785–787
  and competing money supplies, 347
  and exchange rates, 519, 521
  on Federal Reserve, 198, 200
  on gold standard, 362
  on inflation, 214
  and Keynesianism, 119, 121, 142
  and negative income tax, 333
  permanent income theory of consumption, 156–157
  and Phillips curve, 274, 280
Frisch, Ragnar, 787–788, 804
FSLIC *see* Federal Savings and Loan Insurance Corporation
FTAs *see* Free trade areas
Fundamental Theorem of Welfare Economics, 16

Futures and Options Markets (Millman), 575–579
Futures markets, 575–578, 726, 775, 817
  and agriculture, 651
  and program trading, 598–600
  see also Options markets

Galbraith, John Kenneth, 112, 266, 788–789
Gale, William, 313
Game theory, 636, 640–643, 822
Game Theory (Dixit and Nalebuff), 640–643
Garbage collection, 459
Garcia, Alan, 757
Gasoline, 674
  price control on, 416–417
  tax on, 674–675
Gaston, Robert, 411–412
Gate receipts, 713
Gates, Bill, 654
GATT *see* General Agreement on Tariffs and Trade
GDP *see* Gross domestic product
G. D. Searle and Company, 28, 671
Gender Gap (Goldin), 475–478
General Agreement on Tariffs and Trade (GATT), 531–532, 536, 539, 541, 733
General Electric, 456, 717
General equilibrium theory, 783–784, 795, 847
General Motors, 569, 788–789
General Motors Acceptance Corporation (GMAC), 551, 552
General obligation bonds, 557
General Revenue Sharing program, 246
The General Theory of Employment, Interest, and Money (Keynes), 139, 145, 800
Generational accounts, 255–256
Geological Survey (U.S.), 43
George, Henry, 789–790
Geothermal energy, 672
German Bizonal Economic Council, 740
German Economic "Miracle" (Henderson), 738–742
Germany, 200, 273, 623, 734, 800
  capital flight from, 723
  capital gains tax, 317
  disaster recovery, 625, 628–629
  gross domestic product, 514

Germany (*cont.*)
  hyperinflation, 208–210
  income distribution, 179
  industrial policy, 268
  marginal tax rates, 329
  monetary policy, 133
  money growth, 132
  NATO spending, 664
  post-war economic revival,
    738–742
  unemployment, 130
  wages, 520
Gerry, Elbridge, 666
Ghana, 758
Giersch, Herbert, 83
Giliomee, Herbert, 102
Gilman, Charlotte, 504
Glass-Steagall Act, 352, 745
Globalization, 84–85
Global warming *see* Greenhouse
  effect
GMAC *see* General Motors
  Acceptance Corporation
GNP *see* Gross national product
Gold, 98, 535, 810–811
Goldberger, Arthur, 802
Gold Exchange Standard, 359
Goldman, Marshall, 619
Gold standard, 216, 359–363, 536
  and capital flight, 723
  and free banking, 348, 350
  and Great Depression, 196–197,
    200
  performance of, 362
Gold Standard (Bordo), 359–363
Gompers, Samuel, 497
Goodrich, 397
Gorbachev, Mikhail, 163, 747–750
Gordon, David, 159
Gordon, Kermit, 844
Gordon, Robert, 121, 652
Gosplan, 161–162, 748
Gossen, Hermann, 797
Government, 83, 84
  coercion, 638
  and health care, 679, 682–683
  and information, 21
  investment, 217–218
  privatization, 285–289
  and public choice, 152
  role in disaster recovery,
    629–630
  spending and inflation, 214,
    262–264, 290
  Third World interventionist,
    762–763
  unions in, 497
Government Spending (Tullock),
  262–264

Gramm-Rudman law, 152, 301
Grandfather clauses, 410
Great Britain, 198, 200, 734
  free-market environmentalism,
    443
  and gold standard, 197, 359–362
  income distribution, 179
  investment in U.S., 523
  marginal tax rates, 329
  and mercantilism, 535, 536
  monetary policy, 132–133
  privatization, 285–289
  public housing, 690
  sanctions against Rhodesia, 545
  unemployment, 132
Great Depression, 17, 196–202, 536
  causes of, 198–200
  deficit spending during, 246
  and economic policy, 197
  and gold standard, 196–197, 200
  impact of World War I on,
    197–198
  production patterns, 197
  unemployment during, 239
The Great Depression (Robbins),
  828
Great Depression (Samuelson),
  196–202
Great Trek of 1835, 97
Greece, 734
Greenfield, Robert, 350
Greenhouse effect, 447–452, 672
  defined, 447–448
  and developed countries,
    449–450
  effect of, 449
  seriousness of, 448–449
  solutions to, 450–452
Greenhouse Effect (Schelling),
  447–452
Green-mail payments, 606
Green revolution, 764
Greenspan, Alan, 272
Grier, Kevin, 709
Griliches, Zvi, 224
Groeneveld, Lyle P., 335
Gross Domestic Product
  (Anderson), 203–207
Gross domestic product (GDP),
  143–144, 203–207
  base year for, 205–206
  data format, 204
  federal debt as percentage of,
    251–252
  federal spending and taxes as
    share of, 206, 290
  and fiscal policy, 258
  in Peru, 757
  and Reaganomics, 291

Gross national product (GNP),
  193–194, 804, 842
  and balance of payments, 512
  deficit relative to, 243, 244, 246
  growing government share of,
    262, 264
  and investment, 218, 220
  and monetary policy, 278
  and recessions, 226, 228
  and unemployment, 823
Group Areas Act (South Africa),
  101, 103
Growth *see* Economic growth
Grumburg, Emile, 819
Guaranteed Student Loan program,
  246
Guild system, 845
Gun control, 657
Gwartney, James, 332

Haavelmo, Trygve, 790
Haberler, Gottfried, 792
Hall, Robert E., 157, 158, 350
Hamburg (Germany), 627
Hamilton, Alexander, 569
Hand, Learned, 695
Hannah, Michael T., 335
Hansen, Lars, 520
Hardin, Garrett, 54
Harrington, Michael, 113
Harrison, Bennett, 266
Harrod, Roy F., 790–791
Harrod-Domar model, 790–791, 839
Harrod's knife edge, 791
Hart, Gary, 265
Hartwell, Max, 14
Hashimoto, Masanori, 501
Hassett, Kevin, 313
Hassler, William, 49
Haveman, Robert, 59, 296
Hawk Mountain Sanctuary
  Association, 10
Hayashi, Fumiyo, 744
Hayek, Friedrich, 105, 107, 108,
  632, 788, 816, 818
  biography of, 791–794
  on central control, 747
  and competing money supplies,
    347, 350
  on information, 20
  on labor unions, 495
  and socialism, 163
Hazard Monthly (newsletter), 629
Hazlett, Thomas, 774
HDTV *see* High-definition
  television
Head Start, 58
Head tax, 309

Health care, 51, 677–683
  expenditures, 504, 677
  growth in costs of, 679–680,
    687–688
  marginalism and, 32–33
  public policy in, 682–683
  risk and insurance in, 677–678
  structure and competition,
    680–682
  third-party payments for,
    677–678, 685
Health Care Industry (Danzon),
  677–683
Health, Education, and Welfare,
  Department of (U.S.), 334
Health insurance, 677–678, 680,
  684–688
  actuarially priced, 688
  community rating, 684, 686
  compulsory catastrophic, 663
  futures trading in, 578
  individual self, 687–688
  lack of, 686–687
  and self-employment, 686
  universal, 682–683
Health Insurance (Goodman),
  684–688
Health maintenance organizations
  (HMOs), 679, 680, 686
Heckscher, Eli, 823
Hedging, 577
  dynamic, 598
Heilbroner, Robert, 109, 563, 638
Heller, Walter Wolfgang, 740, 741,
  794–795, 844
Hesse, Martha, 408
Heterodox policies, 759
Hicks, John R., 775, 776, 795, 799
HICs *see* Highly Indebted Countries
High-definition television (HDTV),
  655
Highly Indebted Countries (HICs),
  751
Highly leveraged transactions
  (HLTs), 608
Hill, Peter J., 445
Hirshleifer, Jack, 415
History of Economic Analysis
  (Schumpeter), 834
Hitler, Adolf, 738
HLTs *see* Highly leveraged
  transactions
HMOs *see* Health maintenance
  organizations
Hobsbawm, Eric, 14
Hockey, 713
Hodrick, Robert, 520
Holidays, 505
Hollings, Ernest, 265

Home equity loans, 551, 553
Homelessness, 691
Hong Kong, 756, 760–761
Hooker Chemical Company, 443
Hoover, Herbert, 198
  response to Great Depression, 199
Horizontal contracts, 387
Horse racing, 709
Horwich, George, 629
Hospitals, 680–681, 684, 685
Households, 190
  capital gains for U.S., 234
  composition of, 56–58, 181
Housing, 689–693
  as percent of GNP, 690
  privatization of public, 287
  public, 690–692
  and rent control, 421–424
  value of, 234
  see also Mortgages
Housing (Salins), 689–693
Houston Electric Railway, 475
Hub-and-spoke operations, 380–381
Huber, Peter, 426
Hughes, Jonathan, 563
Human Action (Mises), 818
Human capital, 479–483, 777, 833
Human Capital (Becker), 479–483
Human rights, 638–639
  and property rights, 69, 73
  see also Natural rights
Hume, David, 796
Hungary, 729, 731
  hyperinflation in, 208
  private sector in, 730
Hurd, Michael, 300
Hurricane Hugo, 626
Hutterites, 90
Hydroelectric power, 672
Hyperinflation, 208–210, 315, 729
  causes of, 208
  effects of, 209–210
Hyperinflation (Salemi), 208–210
Hysteresis hypothesis, 284

IBM *see* International Business
  Machines
ICC *see* Interstate Commerce
  Commission
Ignorance, 92
Illegal aliens, 484
Illinois Central, 496
Immigration, 484–489
  economic impact of, 488–489
  impact on native earnings,
    486–488
  performance in labor market,
    485–486

relative to population and labor
    force, 484–485
Immigration and Nationality Act
  (U.S.), 484
Immigration (Borjas), 484–489
Immigration Reform and Control
  Act (U.S.), 484
Impossibility theorem, 775
Incentives, 694
  bureaucratic, 152
  created by competition, 623
  and fiscal policy, 260
  and marginal tax rates, 332
  and negative income tax, 333
  political, 151–152
  for research and development,
    186–188
  in sports, 710
  and supply-side economics, 160
  in Third World, 757
  and transfer programs, 296
Income, 8, 146
  and consumption, 141–142,
    156–157
  during industrial revolution, 13,
    15
  and education and training, 480
  effect, 334
  national *see* Gross national
    product
  South African, 103
  and supply-side economics, 165
  see also Wages
Income distribution, 137, 177–183,
    314, 507
  under alternative income
    definitions, 181
  and benefit-cost analysis, 5
  and economic growth, 805
  and family size, 181–182
  during industrial revolution, 13
  measurement of, 180–182
  Pareto's law of, 824
  transfer policies, 59–60
  transfer programs, 294–297
  and vanishing middle class,
    179–180
*Income from Independent
  Professional Practice*
  (Friedman and Kuznets), 786
Income tax, 310, 312, 312–315,
    322–324, 339
  and corporate debt, 560
  integrating with corporate income
    tax, 327–328
  negative, 333–337
  problems with, 334–336
  in post-war Germany, 740
  see also Corporation income tax

Independent power producers
(IPPs), 393
Index arbitrage, 597, 598–600
Index Number Institute, 785
India, 186, 764
  demand management, 204
  economic development, 755
  income growth per capita, 184
  per capita income, 755
  planning, 757
Indian Currency and Finance
  (Keynes), 800
Individual Retirement Accounts
  (IRAs), 234, 313, 323, 324
Indonesia, 724, 725
Industrial Concentration
  (Gilligan), 395–398
Industrial Conciliation Acts (South
  Africa), 100
Industrial democracy, 267
Industrial development bonds, 557
Industrial organization, 386, 811
Industrial policy, 265–271
  Democratic opposition to, 271
Industrial Policy (McKenzie),
  265–270
Industrial revolution, 12–15,
  111–112
**Industrial Revolution and the
  Standard of Living**
  (Nardinelli), 12–15
Inflation, 131, 132, 143, 176
  and bonds, 554
  and capital gains taxes, 317, 318,
    321
  causes of, 214–216
  costs of, 213
  defined, 211
  demand-pull, 214–215
  in Eastern Europe, 728
  and exchange rates, 519
  and federal debt, 251
  German fear of, 273
  and gold standard, 197, 360, 362
  and growth, 215, 758–759
  and housing investment, 219–220
  and interest rates, 129, 586
  and Keynesianism, 118, 120
  Latin American, 759
  and monetary growth, 128–130
  and monetary policy, 272–274
  and money supply, 368
  and output, 129–130
  and price control, 418–420
  and Reaganomics, 290, 292
  tax, 213, 315
  and unemployment, 121, 214,
    279–284, 787

welfare cost of, 213
  see also Hyperinflation
Inflation (Ranson), 211–216
Information, 16–21, 283, 386
  and bounded rationality, 835
  and capital markets, 569–573
  and central planning, 108, 793
  and efficiency, 16–17
  and entrepreneurship, 631–634
  full employment of resources,
    17–19
  and game theory, 643
  and health care, 678–679
  and insurance, 23–24
  and methodological
    individualism, 105
  motivation to act on, 164
  and perfect competition, 107
  under socialism, 163–164
  and uniform prices, 19
  see also Advertising; Brand
    names; Insider trading;
    Telecommunications
Information (Stiglitz), 16–21
Infrastructure, 54, 763
Innovation, 39–40, 41–43, 637,
  833–834
  and competitiveness, 515, 517
  and computer industry, 652
  economic growth, 839
  and entrepreneurs, 632
  product, 28
  and productivity, 224–225
  see also Research and
    development
Input errors, 192
Input-output analysis, 806
Insider trading, 571, 580–583
Insider Trading (Haddock),
  580–583
Insolvency *see* Bankruptcy
Installment lending, 199–200
Institute for Economic Research
  (U.S.), 333
Insurance, 22–26, 631
  agricultural, 651
  deposit, 201, 246, 352–355, 369
  equity issues in, 24–25
  identity and behavior of insured,
    23–24
  liability, 27, 29–30
  moral hazard, 24
  pension, 593–594
  portfolio, 597, 598
  and saving, 231
  underwriting cycle, 29
  see also Health insurance;
    Unemployment insurance

Insurance (Zeckhauser), 22–26
Interest and Prices (Wicksell), 849
Interest groups *see* Special interests
Interest (Heyne), 584–586
Interest rates, 64, 584–586,
  778–779, 810
  and balance of payments, 512
  and bonds, 554
  and business cycles, 175
  and capital flight, 724, 725
  and capital investment, 792, 843
  compound, 586–587
  and debt neutrality, 122
  during Great Depression, 200
  and federal debt, 251
  and federal deficit, 253
  and Federal Reserve System, 356
  Fisher's theory of, 784
  forecasting, 132
  and futures, 575
  and gold standard, 197
  and inflation, 129, 586
  and monetary policy, 276, 366
  and money supply, 586
  and present value, 585, 587, 596
  real versus nominal, 586, 785
  rigidity of, 18–19
  and savings and loan crisis, 354,
    369–371
  and single European currency,
    736–737
  and stock prices, 604
  and supply and demand, 585
  and Third World debt, 751
Intergenerational transfers, 255
Interindustry analysis, 806
Interior Department (U.S.), 44
Internal Revenue Service (U.S.),
  336
International Brotherhood of
  Teamsters *see* Teamsters
  Union
International Business Machines
  (IBM), 653
International economics, 35
International Harvester, 456
International Monetary Fund, 539,
  723–724, 759
International Monetary Market, 575
*Interregional and International
  Trade* (Ohlin), 823
Interstate Commerce Commission
  (ICC), 402, 433
*Introduction to the Theory of
  Employment* (Robinson), 829
Investment, 214, 217–221, 637,
  804
  accelerator model of, 218

and age distribution, 53
and balance of payments, 512
and business cycles, 218
business fixed, 217, 219
and capital flight, 725
and competitiveness, 515–516
and corporate debt, 559
and corporate income tax, 327
and cost of capital, 218–219
defined, 217–218
determinants of, 141, 219–220
Eastern European, 727
in Ghana, 758
interest rates and capital, 792
inventory, 217
Japanese, 743–744
and management, 113, 565–566
and pollution controls, 453, 455
and productivity, 224
and program trading, 598
rates of return on, 845
and rent control, 422
residential, 217, 219–220
and tax cuts, 143, 313
tax policy effect on, 341
Third World, 752, 756
in training, 482
in U.S., 220–221, 523, 524
see also Foreign investment
Investment (Auerbach), 217–221
Investment tax credit, 142–143,
218, 260, 326
IPPs see Independent power
producers
Iran, 699
Iraq, 546–547, 699
IRAs see Individual Retirement
Accounts
Ireland, 734
Irrelevance proposition, 559
IS-LM model, 795
Isolated State (von Thünen), 470
Israel, 532
heterodox policy, 759
income distribution, 179
Italy, 734
capital gains tax, 317
unemployment, 130
Ivory Coast, 756

Japan, 130, 186, 743–746
capital gains tax, 317–318
computer industry, 654
disaster recovery, 625, 628–629
government policy, 745–746
gross domestic product, 514
gross national product, 743

income growth per capita, 184
industrial policy, 268
investment, 220
investment in U.S., 523
marginal tax rates, 329
money growth, 132
privatization, 288
productivity, 515, 528
research and development,
187–188
sources of growth, 743–744
trade suplus, 528
voluntary export quotas, 540
Japanese Development Bank, 745
Jensen, Michael, 444, 560, 608,
609
Jevons, William Stanley, 137,
796–798
Job Corps (U.S.), 58
Job Safety (Viscusi), 490–493
Johnson, Chalmers, 745
Johnson, Harry Gordon, 798–799
Johnson, Lyndon, 211–212, 702
Johnson, Samuel, 622
Joint Committee on Taxation
(U.S.), 320
Joint ventures, 72, 748
Jones Act (U.S.), 537
Jorgenson, Dale W., 218, 224
Journal of Law and Economics,
840
Judgment, 631, 633
Junk bonds, 556, 588–590
and corporate debt, 562
and savings and loan crisis, 374
and takeovers and leveraged
buyouts, 606
Junk Bonds (Yago), 588
Justice Department (U.S.), 387

Kahn, Alfred, 271
Kahneman, Daniel, 431
Kane, Thomas J., 481
Kansas, 43
Kantorovich, Leonid Vitalievich,
799
Kennedy, Anthony, 466
Kennedy, Edward, 434
Kennedy, John, 434, 794
Kenya, 51, 76
Kessel, Reuben, 401–402, 774
Keynes, John Maynard, 18, 139, 145
biography of, 799–801
and Hayek, 792, 793
and rational expectations, 155
Keynesian Economics (Blinder),
118–122

Keynesianism, 118–122, 139
and business cycles, 175
and gross domestic product, 204
and investment tax credits,
142–143
and monetarism, 131–133,
272–273
monetary policy and
macroeconomic activity,
143–144
new, 145–149
and new classical economics,
139–144
and tax cuts, 141–142
see also New Keynesian
economics
Kindleberger, Charles, 198
Kirzner, Israel M., 107, 632
Klein, Benjamin, 350
Klein, Lawrence Robert, 801–802
Klein-Goldberger model, 802
Klemp, Katherine Hussman, 73–74
Kleptocrats, 758
Klopstock, Fred, 740
Knight, Frank Hyneman, 631, 633,
802–803
Koch, Ed, 423
Kodak, 642
Koester, Reinhard, 332
Kolberg Kravis and Roberts, 605
Koopmans, Tjalling Charles,
803–804
Korea, South, 724, 756, 760–761,
762
debt, 752
economic development, 755
marginal tax rates, 329
per capita income, 755
Kormendi, Roger, 332
Kreyssig, Dr., 739
Krueger, Anne, 762
Krugman, Paul R., 223
Kuwait, 699, 725
Kuznets, Simon, 652, 786,
804–805, 842
Kuznets cycles, 805

Labor, 84, 159
child, 111
costs, 98
decline in common laborers, 505
demand and unemployment, 239
division of, 107, 113, 567, 637,
837, 845, 848
economics, 35
farm workers as total of, 504
and Japanese growth, 743

Labor (*cont.*)
  market, 52
    immigrant performance in,
      485–486
    monopoly effect, 37–38
    participation rates, 476, 481–482
    power, 124–125
    productivity, 507
    and Single European Act, 735
    supply, 102
      and saving, 232
      and tax policy, 341
      wages and, 791
    see also Unions; Wages
Labor Department (U.S.), 500
Labor Unions (Reynolds),
  494–497
Laffer, Arthur, 166
Lal, Deepak, 757
Lampman, Robert, 33
Landes, William, 660
Landfills, 457–458
Landing fees, 383
Land-use regulation, 692–693
Lange, Oskar Ryszard, 163,
  805–806
Language, 816
Lapping, Brian, 102
Latin America
  hyperinflation, 210
  see also specific countries
Laughlin, J. Laurence, 846
Law
  and economics, 694–696, 782
  enforcement, 658
  Third World, 763
  see also Crime
Law of diminishing returns,
  826–827, 845
Law of Large Numbers, 23, 631
Law of the Single Price, 19
Lawson, Nigel, 133
Lawsuits *see* Litigation
Layoffs, 303–304
LBOs *see* Leveraged buyouts
LDCs *see* Local distribution
  companies
Leadership, 198
League of Nations, 542, 543
Learning curve, 775–776
Lectures on Political Economy
  (Wicksell), 849
Lees, Dennis S., 412
Legislation *see* Law
Legislators, 151
Lehn, Kenneth, 710
Lenin, V. I., 161, 627
Leontief, Wassily, 806–807
Leontief paradox, 806–807

Lerner, Abba Ptachya, 807–809
Lester, Richard, 811
Leveraged buyouts (LBOs),
  605–610
Leveraged cashouts, 606
Leviathan theory, 262
Levin, Lawrence, 299
Lewis, H. Gregg, 495
Lewis, W. Arthur, 809–810
Liability, 27–30
  and drug approval, 671
  limited, 564–565
  unlimited, 565
Liability (Viscusi), 27–30
Liberalization, 729
Licensing, 409–412, 413
  disciplining licensees, 411
  and health care, 679, 682
  import, 762
  and income, 411
  and quality, 411–412
Life-cycle saving, 230–231, 255,
  298–299, 819
Life expectancy, 426–429, 755,
  812
  in developed countries, 51
  during industrial revolution, 14
  and saving, 232
  and Social Security, 301
  in Soviet Union, 162–163
The Life of John Maynard Keynes
  (Harrod), 791
Lighthouses, 75–76, 783
Lindbeck, Assar, 422
Lindert, Peter, 14
Lindsey, Lawrence, 168
Linear programming, 799, 803
*Linear Programming and Economic
  Analysis* (Dorfman,
  Samuelson, and Solow), 831
Linneman, Peter, 495, 496
Lipton, Merle, 100
Liquidity, 219
  and futures, 577
  and program trading, 600
Literacy, 14
  see also Education
Litigation
  and job safety, 490–491
  product liability, 28–29, 30, 671
Living standards, 12–15, 182, 230,
  507
  and competitiveness, 514, 515
  Eastern European, 728
  and housing, 689–690
  in India and South Korea, 755
  and productivity, 222–223
  and trade balance, 516–517
Lloyd, William Forster, 88

Lobbying, 38, 540
  by defense contractors, 666
Local distribution companies
  (LDCs), 405–408
Locke, John, 92, 810–811
The Logic of Collective Action
  (Olson), 153
Log rolling, 151
Long, James, 168
Long, Russell, 336
Long, William F., 150
Longfield, Samuel, 797
Long Term Agreement on Cotton
  Textiles, 537
The Long View and the Short
  (Viner), 846
Loop flows, 392–393
Love Canal (NY), 443
Lucas, Robert, 142, 143, 145, 158,
  159
Luxembourg, 733

Maastricht Treaty, 736
Machlup, Fritz, 792, 811
Macroeconomics, 34
  monetary policy and
    performance, 277–278
  and poverty, 58
Madison, James, 89
Magnet schools, 707
Mainspring of the German Revival
  (Wallich), 738–739
Major League Baseball Players'
  Association, 497
Malaysia, 756
Malinvestment, 792
Malthus, Thomas Robert, 52,
  811–812
Management
  compensation packages, 570
  of corporations, 565–566
  and investment, 113
  and takeovers, 606
  and weak property rights, 71
Mandatory Oil Import Quota
  Program (MOIP), 697
Manning, Bayless, 564
Manual of Political Economy
  (Pareto), 824
Manufacturing, 204
  productivity in, 225
  and recessions, 228
Manville Corporation, 29
Marcuse, Herbert, 112
Marginalism, 31–34
Marginalism (Rhoads), 31–33
Marginal productivity theory,
  849

Marginal propensity to consume
    (MPC), 141–142
Marginal revolution, 135, 797, 815,
    847
Marginal Tax Rates (Reynolds),
    329–332
Mariel boatlift, 487
Marketable permits, 451, 455–456
Market-clearing price *see*
    Equilibrium prices
Markets, 45
    and discrimination, 474–475
    failure in, 402
    size of, 733
Markowitz, Harry, 812, 835
Marris, Stephen, 520
Marshall, Alfred, 800, 812–813
Marshall, John, 563
Marshall, Ray, 496
Marshall Plan, 451–452, 536, 741
Marston, Richard, 520
Marx, Karl, 111, 123–127, 161,
    813–814, 833
Marxism, 123–127
    alienation, 125–126
    appraisal of, 127
    labor theory of value, 124–125
Marxism (Prychitko), 123–127
Maryland People's Counsel cases,
    406–407
Mass toxic torts, 28–29
Mathematica Inc., 333
*The Mathematical Method of
    Production Planning and
    Organization* (Kantorovich),
    799
Mather, Cotton, 412
Mauritius, 329
Maximizing behavior, 36, 105,
    773, 811, 835
McGee, John, 388
McGovern plan, 334
McLure, Charles, 314
Mead, Carver, 654–655
Meade, James Edward, 814–815,
    842
Mean reversion, 572
Means, Gardiner C., 566
Measuring Business Cycles (Burns
    and Mitchell), 173, 780
Meckling, William, 560
Medicaid, 59, 180, 246, 679, 681,
    684, 687
Medical care *see* Health care
Medicare, 25, 59, 246, 294, 311,
    679, 681, 684, 686
Medoff, James, 494, 495
Mellon, Andrew, 167, 197
Memphis Street Railways, 475

Menger, Carl, 105, 797, 815–816
Menu costs, 145–146
Mercantilism, 534–537, 636, 638,
    796, 826
    policies of, 534–535
    Smith on, 838
Mercantilism (LaHaye), 534–537
Mergers, 267, 387, 392, 606
    and concentration, 397–398
    effect on stock prices, 608
    moratorium law, 607
    vertical, 401
    see also Acquisitions; Leveraged
        buyouts; Takeovers
Merit, 471
Merrill Dow, 671
Merrill Lynch, 553
Merton, Robert K., 92–93
Methodological individualism,
    105–106
Methodological subjectivism, 106
Mexico, 486, 724, 754
    and capital flight, 725–726
    cost of protectionism, 762
    debt, 751, 753
Meyer, Bruce D., 304
Meyer, John R., 434
MFN status *see* Most-favored-
    nation status
Miami (Florida), 487
Michelin, 397
Microchips, 653, 655
Microeconomics, 34–39
Microeconomics (Harberger),
    34–39
Microsoft (company), 654
Middle class, 179–180
Middlemen, 815
    and information economics, 20
Mies van der Rohe, Ludwig, 412
Milken, Michael, 562, 589, 606
Mill, James, 832
Mill, John Stuart, 622, 625, 631,
    816–817
Miller, James C., 152
Miller, Merton H., 558–559, 812,
    817–818
Mincer, Jacob, 482, 833
Mines and Works Act of 1911
    (South Africa), 99, 100
Mines and Works Act of 1926
    (South Africa), 100
Mine Workers' Union (South
    Africa), 99
"Minimum Problems in Physics
    and Economics" (Tinbergen),
    843
Minimum wage, 267, 418,
    499–502

and compensation packages, 501
and discrimination, 473–474,
    820–821
harmful effects of, 500, 820–821
and poverty, 499, 502
regional and sectoral effect of,
    501–502
and unions, 496, 502
Minimum Wages (Gorman),
    499–502
Mining, 504
Ministry of International Trade and
    Industry (MITI; Japan), 266,
    268, 744–745
Minnesota, 707
Minorities *see* African-Americans;
    Women
Mises, Ludwig von, 105, 816
    biography of, 818–819
    and central planning, 108, 163,
        747
    and labor unions, 494
Mitchell, Mark, 573
Mitchell, Wesley, 173, 780
MITI *see* Ministry of International
    Trade and Industry
MITI and the Japanese Miracle
    (Johnson), 745
Mobility, 84
Model errors, 192–193
*The Modern Corporation and
    Private Property* (Berle and
    Means), 113, 566
Modigliani, Franco, 230, 255,
    558–559, 817, 819
Modigliani-Miller theory, 817, 819
Moe, Terry M., 704
MOIP *see* Mandatory Oil Import
    Quota Program
Mokyr, Joel, 15
Mondale, Walter, 265, 267
Monetarism, 119, 128–134, 796,
    800, 810, 826
    and inflation, 215–216
    and Keynesians, 131–133,
        272–273
    and macroeconomic activity,
        143–144
    skepticism about, 133–134
    Wicksell's version of, 849
Monetarism (Meltzer), 128–134
Monetary aggregates, 277–278
Monetary base, 366
*A Monetary History of the United
    States, 1857–1960* (Friedman
    and Schwartz), 198, 786
Monetary policy, 118, 121–122,
    133, 272–278, 282–283, 420
    and balance of payments, 814–815

Monitary policy (*cont.*)
  and capital investment, 843–844
  European Community, 736–737
  expansionary, 273
  and Federal Reserve System,
    356–358
  and fiscal policy, 259, 274–275
  goals of, 277–278
  and gold standard, 362
  and hyperinflation, 208–209
  and interest rates, 366
  mechanics of, 275–276
  and money supply, 367
  operating procedures of, 276–277
  priorities for, 273–274
  under Reaganomics, 291
  and recessions, 228
  strategies, 274
  see also Money; Money supply
Monetary Policy (Tobin), 272–278
Monetary theory, 34, 792
"Monetary Theory and Policy"
  (Johnson), 798
Money, 107, 637
  development of, 815–816
  growth, 131
    and output, 130
    and recessions, 130
  high-powered, 366
  illusion, 281
  laundering, 724
  markets, 276
  quantity theory of *see*
    Monetarism
  velocity of, 278
  see also Monetary policy; Money
    supply
Money supply, 198, 290, 364–368,
  792
  and balance of payments, 798
  and business cycles, 368
  competing, 347–351
  defined, 364
  determination of, 365–367
  in Eastern Europe, 729
  and exchange rates, 519–520
  and gold standard, 360
  history of U.S., 367–368
  importance of, 364
  and interest rates, 586
  in post-war Germany, 738, 740
  ratio of currency to, 346
  reductions in, 352
  rule, 786
  and savings and loan crisis, 371
  see also Monetary policy; Money
Money Supply (Schwartz), 364–368
Monopolies, 37–38, 385, 399–402
  and advertising, 615–616

and central planning, 749
and deregulation, 380, 381–382
effect of labor, 37–38
over goods, 539
government support for, 399
and inflation, 214
Marxist inevitability of, 126
natural, 403, 405
nonmerger, 387–388
power of, 387
as preferable to perfect
  competition, 834
price premium of, 19
profit from, 65, 400
reduction of aggregate economic
  welfare, 400
regulating, 403–404
and research and development,
  79–80
telecommunications, 717
utilities as, 391
see also Antitrust; Concentration;
  Patents
Monopoly (Stigler), 399–402
Montaigne, Michel Eyquem, 636
Montgomery Ward, 112
Mont Pelerin Society, 793
Moral hazard, 24, 678–679
Morgan, J. P., 725
Morgenstern, Oskar, 792, 820, 822
Mortality rates, 428–429
Mortgages, 369
  adjustable rate, 370
  bonds, 556
  subsidies, 691
Moscow (Russia), 628
Most-favored-nation (MFN) status,
  531
Motor Carrier Act of 1935 (U.S.),
  433
Motor Carrier Act of 1980 (U.S.),
  434–435
MPC *see* Marginal propensity to
  consume
Multiplier effect, 118–119
Mundell, Robert, 521
Municipal Sewage Treatment
  Construction Grant, 454
Murphy, Kevin M., 480
Mussolini, Benito, 115–117
Muth, John F., 155, 157
Mutual funds, 72, 213, 598
Myrdal, Gunnar, 422, 820–821

Nader, Ralph, 434, 670
NAFTA *see* North American Free
  Trade Agreement
Nagle, Thomas, 8

NAIRU *see* Nonaccelerating
  inflation rate of unemployment
Nash, John, 641
National Academy of Sciences
  (U.S.), 28
National Assessment of Educational
  Progress (U.S.), 703
National Bureau of Economic
  Research (NBER; U.S.), 173,
  226, 228, 781, 804
National Center for Policy Analysis
  (U.S.), 687
National Collegiate Athletic
  Association (NCAA), 710
National Commission on Excellence
  in Education (U.S.), 703
National Council of Corporations
  (Italy), 116
National Directory of Conservation
  Land Trusts, 444
National Football League (NFL),
  714–715
National Housing Act of 1949
  (U.S.), 691
National Income and Product
  Accounts (U.S.), 203
Nationalism, 115, 794
Nationalization, 724
National Park Service (U.S.),
  49–50
National Recovery Act /
  Administration (NRA), 116,
  201
National Wool Act, 47–48
NATO *see* North Atlantic Treaty
  Organization
Natural gas, 404–408, 672
Natural Gas Act of 1938 (U.S.), 406
Natural Gas Policy Act of 1978
  (U.S.), 406
Natural Gas Regulation
  (Michaels), 404–408
Natural Gas Wellhead Decontrol
  Act of 1989 (U.S.), 405
Natural growth, 790–791
Natural resources *see* Resources
Natural Resources (Baumol and
  Blackman), 39–43
Natural rights, 810
  see also Human rights
Nature Conservancy (U.S.), 444
"The Nature of the Firm" (Coase),
  782
Navigation Laws (U.K.), 535
Nazism, 116, 793
NBER *see* National Bureau of
  Economic Research
NCAA *see* National Collegiate
  Athletic Association

Neal, Robert, 600
Negative Income Tax (Allen), 333–337
Negative-sum games, 640
Negative value added, 747
Negligence, 27, 695–696
Nelson, James C., 434
Neoclassical economics, 136–138
Neoclassical Economics (Weintraub), 135–138
Neoclassical synthesis, 830–831
Netherlands, 734
  capital gains tax, 317
  marginal tax rates, 329
Netter, Jeffry, 573
Neumann, John von, 640, 820, 822
New classical economics, 121–122
  and business cycles, 175
  and investment tax credits, 142–143
  monetary policy and macroeconomic activity, 143–144
  and tax cuts, 141–142
New Classical Economics (King), 139–144
New Deal, 200–201, 820
New Economic Policy, 161, 628
The New Industrial State (Galbraith), 788
New Keynesian economics, 145–149
  and business cycles, 175
  coordination failures, 147
  efficiency wages, 148
  menu costs and aggregate-demand externalities, 145–146
  policy implications of, 148–149
  staggering of prices, 146–147
  see also Keynesianism
New Keynesian Economics (Mankiw), 145–149
New Orleans and Texas Pacific Railroad, 496
The New Palgrave: A Dictionary of Economics, 626
Newspapers, 459
Newton, Isaac, 359
New York City, 626, 707
New York Mercantile Exchange (NYMEX), 577
New York State, 458
New York Stock Exchange (NYSE), 597
New Zealand, 499
The Next American Frontier (Reich), 265
NFL *see* National Football League
Niebank, Paul, 422

Nigeria, 724
Niskanen, William, 152
Nitrazepam (drug), 669
Nixon, Richard, 135, 212, 360, 698
Nkrumah, Kwame, 758
Nobel prize winners, 769
Nonaccelerating inflation rate of unemployment (NAIRU), 282–284
Nonexcludability, 74–75
Nonrivalrous consumption, 75
Nordhaus, William, 154, 787
North American Free Trade Agreement (NAFTA), 532
North Atlantic Treaty Organization (NATO), 663–664
Norway, 179
"A Note on Book Blocking" (Stigler), 839–840
"A Note on the Measurement of Utility" (Samuelson), 830
Noyce, Robert, 653
NRA *see* National Recovery Act/Administration
Nuclear energy, 672
Nuclear Regulatory Commission (U.S.), 392
Nurske, Ragnar, 519
NYMEX *see* New York Mercantile Exchange
NYSE *see* New York Stock Exchange

Oates, Wallace, 456
Occupational Licensing (Young), 409–412
Occupational Safety and Health Act (U.S.), 492
Oceans, 450
O'Connor, J. F. T., 346
Office of Economic Opportunity (U.S.), 333
Office of Technological Assessment (U.S.), 454
Ohlin, Bertil Gotthard, 822–823, 830
Oil, 41–44, 54, 672, 673
  real prices for, 697–698, 699, 700
  reserves, 699
  see also Gasoline; Organization of Petroleum Exporting Countries
Okun, Arthur, 296, 823–824, 844
Okun's Law, 823
Oligopolies, 401
Olson, Mancur, 153

OMAs *see* Orderly market arrangements
Omnibus Trade and Competitiveness Act (U.S.), 539
O'Neill, June, 477
On Liberty (Mill), 816
On the Accuracy af Economic Observation (Morgenstern), 820
OPEC *see* Organization of Petroleum Exporting Countries
"OPEC—A Plan—If You Can't Beat Them, Join Them" (Lerner), 808
OPEC (Zycher), 697
Opportunity cost, 20, 44–45
  of education, 481
  and environmentalism, 441
Opportunity Cost (Henderson), 44–45
Options markets, 578–579
  and program trading, 598–600
  see also Futures markets
Orange Free State (South Africa), 97
Orderly market arrangements (OMAs), 540
Ordover, Janusz, 389
The Organization of Industry (Stigler), 108
Organization of Petroleum Exporting Countries (OPEC), 41, 54, 697–701
  reserves and production, 701
OTC options *see* Over-the-counter options
The Other Path (Soto), 757
O'Toole, Randal, 152
Output
  aggregate demand's impact on, 118–119
  and fiscal policy, 258, 259, 260
  and inflation, 129–130
  per hour worked, 507, 514
  in post-war Germany, 741
  and productivity, 222
  and socialism, 162
  see also Input-output analysis
The Overeducated American (Freeman), 480
Overshooting, 519–520
Over-the-counter (OTC) options, 578–579
Ozone layer, 456

Packard, Vance, 112
Pain and suffering compensation, 28

Panama, 545
Paper, recycling, 458–459
Pareto, Vilfredo, 824–825
Pareto optimality, 824
Paris, Treaty of, 733
Parity prices, 37
Partnerships, 72, 563, 565, 566
Pass Laws (South Africa), 98, 101, 103
Patents, 72, 79, 187
  suppression of, 414–415
Patents (Henderson), 414–415
Pay equity *see* Comparable worth
Payroll tax, 310–311, 339
PBGC *see* Pension Benefit Guaranty Corporation
Peacock, Alan, 262
Pechman, Joseph, 333, 744, 795
Peck, Morton J., 434
Peirce, Charles Sanders, 845
Peltzman, Sam, 668, 669
Pension Benefit Guaranty Corporation (PBGC), 593, 594
Pensions, 51, 231, 301, 591–594
  basic features of U.S., 591
  defined benefit, 592, 593
  defined contribution, 591–592, 593
  economic issues, 593–594
  termination of, 592–593
  total assets of, 591
Pensions (McMillan), 591–594
Perestroika, 163, 747–750
  main obstacle to, 164
Perestroika (Goldman), 747–750
Perrier, 619
Peru, 757
  demand management, 204
  hyperinflation, 210
Peters, H. Elizabeth, 783
"The Petition of the Candlemakers" (Bastiat), 776
Petrograd (Russia), 628
Petroleum *see* Oil
Petty, William, 326
Pfeffermann, Guy, 759
Phelps, Edmund, 121, 143, 239, 280
Philippines, 724, 762
Phillips, A. W., 143, 274, 279
Phillips curve, 158, 274, 279–284, 787
  expectations-augmented, 282
  as policy guide, 280
Phillips Curve (Hoover), 279–284
Physicians, 681–682
Physiocrats, 825–826
Pigou, Arthur Cecil, 800, 825
Plant, Arnold, 414

Plastics, 458
Plastics Recycling Foundation, 458
Plotnick, Robert, 59
Poison pill, 607
Poison put, 561–562
Polachek, Solomon, 477
Poland, 728–730, 731, 749, 805
Polaroid Corporation, 642
Policy *see* specific policies, e.g., Fiscal policy
Policy ineffectiveness proposition, 159
Political Behavior (Stroup), 45–50
Political Discourses (Hume), 796
Political economy, 21
The Political Economy of Monopoly (Machlup), 811
Politics, 45–50
  and antitrust, 389
  citizen problems with, 48–49
  and drug approval, 670–671
  and transfer programs, 294–295
  voter ignorance, 48, 151
  see also Public choice theory; Public goods
Politics, Markets, and America's Schools (Chubb and Moe), 704
Pollution
  controls, 453–456
    cost of, 453–454
    economic effects of, 454–455
    market based, 455–456
  and efficiency, 426
  fees, 455
  and free-market environmentalism, 442
  liability for, 443
  standards, 453, 454
  tax on, 455, 673, 825
  see also Environmentalism; Greenhouse effect; specific types of pollution, e.g., Air pollution
Pollution Controls (Crandall), 453–456
Popov, Vladimir, 164
Population, 51–55, 811–812
  aging, 51–52
  decline in U.S. growth, 232
  and development, 52–55
  generation size, 52
  and greenhouse effect, 449
  see also Demographics
Population (Lee), 51–55
Population Registration Act (South Africa), 101, 103
Portfolio insurance, 597, 598
Portfolio theory, 812, 834, 844
Portugal, 734

Positive-sum games, 640, 815
Posner, Richard, 660, 695
Possibility theorem, 798
Poterba, James, 572
Poverty, 56–60
  and education, 703
  feminization of, 57
  impermanence of, 61
  line, 56
  and minimum wage, 499, 502
  rural, 832–833
  transfer programs' effect on, 295–297
Poverty in the United States (Sawhill), 56–60
The Poverty of Development Economics (Lal), 757
PPOs *see* Preferred provider organizations
Preferred provider organizations (PPOs), 679, 680
Present value, 585, 587, 596
Present Value (Henderson), 596
Price controls, 36–37, 87, 129, 382, 416–420
  agricultural, 647–651
  and defense, 665
  Eastern European, 727–728, 729–730
  on food, 629
  on oil, 698
  in Peru, 757
  post-war German, 738–740
  and property rights, 70
  and Reaganomics, 291
  Regulation Q, 370
  telecommunications, 719
  and trucking deregulation, 436
  see also Prices; Rent controls; Subsidies
Price Controls (Rockoff), 416–420
Price discrimination, 380–383, 385
Price-function traders, 582–583
Prices, 7–8, 636–637, 757
  black market, 417
  and brand names, 618
  and concentration, 396
  coordination failures, 147
  and corporate income tax, 326
  costs of adjusting, 145–146
  and deregulation, 379–380
  Eastern European, 727, 728–729
  effect of numerous rivals on, 401–402
  energy, 672, 673–676
  and entrepreneurs, 632
  equilibrium, 86
  and federal debt, 251
  and fiscal policy, 258

fixing, 87, 370, 387, 500
and gold standard, 360–361
high official, 37–38
information and uniform, 19
market-clearing, 145, 622
and monetary policy, 273–274
and money illusion, 281
and money supply, 367
monopoly, 19, 400
natural gas, 405, 406
natural versus market, 845
and new classical economics, 121
predatory, 388
and prisoners' dilemma, 62
producer, 212
and profit, 65
of resources, 40–41
response to supply and demand,
    119
rigidity of, 18–19, 118
as summary of information, 108
telecommunications, 717–719
see also Hyperinflation; Inflation;
    Price controls; Stock prices
Price-specie-flow mechanism,
    360–361, 796
Price theory, 34
Price Theory (Friedman), 827
Pricing to market, 520
Principles of Economics (Marshall),
    812
Principles of Economics (Menger),
    105
Principles of Political Economy
    (Mill), 631, 816
Principles of Political Economy
    (Ricardo), 124
Prisoners' dilemma, 61–63,
    641–642
    see also Game theory
Prisoners' Dilemma (Dixit and
    Nalebuff), 61–63
Private ownership *see* Property
    rights
Private placements, 588
Privatization, 285–289, 728–729,
    731, 748
Privatization (Pirie), 285–289
"The Problem of Social Cost"
    (Coase), 782
Producer surplus, 813
Product differentiation, 111–112
Product endorsement, 613
Production, 174, 637
    agricultural, 647–651
    and capital, 64
    in Eastern Europe, 730
    falling U.S. industrial, 268
    and Great Depression, 197

and innovation, 39–40
and pollution controls, 453
in post-war Germany, 741
restricting, 37
roundaboutness of, 779
and socialism, 162
see also Gross domestic product
"The Production Function and the
    Theory of Capital"
    (Robinson), 829
Productivity, 222–225, 272
    defined, 222
    and deregulation, 380
    European, 735
    and government spending, 262
    in high-yield firms, 589
    and innovation, 652
    labor, 507, 514
    in manufacturing, 225
    marginal theory, 849
    personal habits and, 471–472
    under Reaganomics, 291
    and technical advances, 482
    total factor, 222
    U.S. growth in, 515
    worldwide, 224
Productivity and American
    Leadership (Baumol,
    Blackman, and Wolff), 222
Productivity (Nasar), 222–225
Product standards, 417, 735
Profit, 64–68, 108
    and competition, 623–624
    and concentration, 387, 401
    Marxist view of, 124–125
    maximization, 773, 811, 835
    monopoly, 400
    as percentage of GNP, 67
    return on stockholders' equity, 66
Profits (Thurow), 64–68
Program trading, 597–600
    and 1987 stock crash, 601
Program Trading (Furbush),
    597–600
Progress and Poverty (George),
    789
Progressive Taxes (Slemrod),
    338–341
Prohibition of Mixed Marriages Act
    (South Africa), 103
Proletariat, 126
Property rights, 68, 69–74, 110,
    624, 638, 817
    in cattle, 445
    common ownership, 71
    commons, 88–91
    and disaster recovery, 629
    and discrimination, 70, 774
    in Eastern Europe, 728

and environmentalism, 442–445
and human rights, 69, 73
and *perestroika*, 164
private, 10–11, 69–70, 108
    basic elements of, 69–70
and public goods, 76
shared, 71–72
and socialism, 70–71
Property Rights (Alchian),
    69–73
Property tax, 311
Protectionism, 198, 201, 205, 536,
    537, 538–541, 776, 815
    administered, 541
    and employment, 528–529
    and industrial policy, 267, 269
    Third World, 761–762
    see also Free trade; Quotas;
    Tariffs
Protectionism (Bhagwati),
    538–541
The Protestant Ethic and the Spirit
    of Capitalism (Weber), 848
Proxy fights, 607
Public administration, 756
Public assistance programs, 59
Public Choice (journal), 780
Public choice theory, 150–154,
    779–780
Public Choice Theory (Shaw),
    150–153
Public Citizen (advocacy group),
    670
Public finance, 35
Public goods, 74–77, 783, 830
    defense as, 661, 662
    and government spending, 264
    research and development for,
    80–81
Public Goods and Externalities
    (Cowen), 74–77
Public Schools (Chubb),
    702–708
Public utilities, 391–394
Public Utility Holding Company
    Act of 1935 (U.S.), 393
Public Utility Regulatory Policies
    Act of 1978 (PURPA; U.S.),
    393
Public Works Administration
    (U.S.), 201
Puerto Rico, 489
Punishment, 659–660
Purchasing power, 514
    parity, 781
Puritan work ethic, 110
PURPA *see* Public Utility
    Regulatory Policies Act of
    1978

Quader, Noorul, 764
Quality
  and advertising, 615
  and brand names, 619–620
  health care, 682
  and licensing, 411–412
  and price controls, 382, 417
Quality of life *see* Living standards
Queensland Mines (Australia), 544
Quesnay, François, 825–826
Quotas, 93, 267, 530
  agricultural, 648
  for carbon emissions, 451
  European, 734
  Korean, 761
  on oil, 697

R&D *see* Research and
    development
Racial preferences, 100
Racism *see* Apartheid;
    Discrimination
Railroads, 433, 436, 496
  worker deaths on, 504
Rand Corporation, 678
Random walk theory, 156, 571
Rand Rebellion, 99
Rand River (Transvaal), 98
Ratchet effect, 262
Rathje, William, 457
Rational expectations, 120–121,
    155–160, 819
  efficient markets theory of stock
    prices, 156
  expectational error models of
    business cycle, 158–159
  macroeconomic policy design,
    159–160
  permanent income theory of
    consumption, 156–157
  and Phillips curve, 282–283
  and policy design, 159–160
  tax-smoothing models, 157–158
Rational Expectations (Sargent),
    155–160
Rationing, 417–418
Ravenna Park (Seattle), 444
Rayack, Elton, 410
Reagan, Ronald, 265, 290, 703
Reaganomics, 290–293
Reaganomics (Niskanen), 290–293
Real estate, 373
Recapture, 423
Recessions, 173, 174, 176,
    226–229, 812
  coordination failure as cause of,
    147

duration, depth, diffusion of,
    228, 229
  Federal Reserve as cause of, 272
  global nature of, 228
  Keynesian view of, 119
  and money growth, 130
  and new classical economics, 121
  and poverty, 58
  and stock market, 604
  and unemployment insurance,
    303
Recessions (Moore), 226–229
Reconstruction Finance Corporation
    (U.S.), 199, 267
Recovery *see* Disaster recovery
Recycling, 42, 457–459
  deterrents to, 459
  economics of, 458–459
Recycling (Shaw), 457–459
Redistribution of Income (Lee),
    294–297
Reed-Bulwinkle Act (U.S.), 433
*Reflections on the Production and
    Distribution of Wealth*
    (Turgot), 844
Reforestation, 450
Regulation, 114, 292, 402, 815,
    844
  of advertising, 616–617
  drug, 668
  educational, 704
  electric utility, 391–394, 840
  European, 735
  gas mileage, 674
  health care, 682
  health insurance, 686–687
  by input-output analysis, 757
  of insurance rates, 25
  land use, 692–693
  of monopolies, 403–404
  natural gas, 404–408
  of pollution, 453–456
  and Reaganomics, 290, 291
  Stigler on, 840, 840–841
  of telecommunications, 717, 719
  trucking industry, 433–435
  and unintended consequences, 92
  see also Deregulation; Licensing;
    Protectionism; types of
    regulation, e.g., Rent controls
Regulation Q, 370
Reich, Robert, 265, 266, 270
Rent Control (Block), 421–424
Rent controls, 70, 416, 418,
    421–424, 425
  effect of, 421–423
  effect on tenants, 423–424
  solutions, 424

Rents, economic, 87
Rent-seeking, 38, 85, 264, 540,
    762
Replacement ratio, 304
"Report of the Commission on
    Graduate Education," 481
Reputational equilibria, 159–160
Reputations, 19–20
  see also Advertising; Brand
    names
Research and Development
    (Levy), 78–81
Research and development (R&D),
    78–81
  beneficiaries of U.S., 81
  and economic growth, 185–189
  government, 78–81
  in Japan, 745
  meta-ideas, 188–189
  private, 78
  and productivity, 224–225
  and saving, 232
  special treatment for, 79–80
  and takeovers, 609
  see also Innovation
Research Seminar in Quantitative
    Economics (RSQE), 194
Resilience, 431
Resolution Trust Corporation
    (U.S.), 553
Resources, 39–43
  common ownership of, 71
  constraints of population, 52–53
  and economic growth, 184–185
  energy, 673
  forcible reallocation of, 72–73
  and Great Depression, 197
  increasing effective stock of,
    41–42
  information and full employment
    of, 17–19
  middlemen and allocation of, 20
  opportunity cost of, 44–45
  optimum allocation of, 798,
    803–804
  and population, 54–55
  prices, 40–41, 54
  productivity of, 39–40
  recycling, 457–459
  reserves and production of,
    40–41
Retirement, 51
  age, 256, 300
  length of, 232
  savings, 231
  see also Pensions
Reuter, Peter, 658
Revealed preference, 830

Revenue bonds, 557
Reynolds, Morgan, 296
Reynolds Metals Company, 458
Rhodesia, 543, 545
Ricardian Equivalence, 260
Ricardo, David, 124, 252, 253,
  527, 826–828
Rice, 541
Rights, 46
  see also Human rights; Property
  rights
Riis, Jacob, 691
The Rise and Decline of Nations
  (Olson), 153
Risk, 22–25, 822, 848
  and bonds, 554, 556
  and capital gains, 317
  credit, 588
  and deposit insurance, 353
  and drug approval, 669–671
  and entrepreneurs, 631
  and futures, 577
  and game theory, 642
  in health care, 677–678
  and information, 17–18
  and job safety, 490–493
  and liability, 29, 30
  and pension portfolios, 593
  perception, 430–431
  profit as return on, 64
  saving against, 231
  and savings and loans, 371
  shifting, 561
  in society, 426–432
  technological, 431
  see also Uncertainty
Riskless Society (Wildavsky),
  426–432
Risk, Uncertainty, and Profit
  (Knight), 802
Rivalry see Competition
Rivlin, Alice, 314
RJR Nabisco, 605
The Road to Serfdom (Hayek), 793
Robbery see Crime
Robbins, Lionel, 792, 828
Robbins Principle, 828
Robinson, Joan Violet, 137, 829
Robinson-Patman Act, 401
Rockefeller, John D., 112
Roepke, Wilhelm, 739
Roman Empire, 211, 628
Rome, Treaty of, 733
Romer, Paul, 332
Roosevelt, Franklin Delano, 116,
  200–201, 358, 359–360, 419,
  691, 820
Roosevelt, Theodore, 385

Rosengren, Eric, 523
Rosett, Joshua, 608
Ross, Christine, 57
Royal Dutch/Shell, 93
RSQE see Research Seminar in
  Quantitative Economics
Rubinstein, Jonathan B., 658
Rule, Charles F., 397
Ruttan, Vernon, 79
Ryan, Alan, 817

Sachs, Jeffrey, 71, 793
Safety, 490–493, 503–504
  and drug regulation, 668
  see also Risk
SAIF see Savings Association
  Insurance Fund
Sakoh, Katsuro, 268
Sales tax, 311, 314
Salomon Brothers, 553
Salop, Steven, 388
Salvation Army, 500
Samuelson, Paul Anthony, 137,
  143, 775, 787, 799, 808
  biography of, 830–831
  and Cambridge controversy, 137,
  829
  on industrial policy, 271
  and Phillips curve, 280
  and public choice theory, 154
Sanctions, 542–547
  against apartheid, 103
  effectiveness of, 545–546
  financial versus trade, 544
  future of, 546–547
  purposes of, 542–543
  types of, 543–545
Sanctions (Elliott and Hufbauer),
  542–547
San Francisco, 626
Sargent, Thomas J., 145, 209
Saudi Arabia, 698–699
Saving (Kotlokoff), 230–235
Savings, 33, 122, 230–235, 255,
  516, 637, 763–764, 804
  economic growth and
  demographic changes, 231–232
  explanations for decline in U.S.,
  233–234
  and fiscal policy, 259–260
  implications of baby boomers'
  low, 234–235
  and income tax, 322
  in India, 755
  individual medical, 687–688
  and individual retirement
  accounts, 324

and investment, 220–221
  Japanese, 743–744
  labor-supply decisions, 232
  motives for, 230–231
  and savings and loan crisis, 369
  Social Security's effect on,
  298–299
  in South Korea, 755
  and tax cuts, 313, 315, 341
Savings and loan crisis, 90–91,
  292, 353, 369–374
  causes of, 369–373
  delayed closure of insolvent,
  371–373
Savings and Loan Crisis (Ely),
  369–374
Savings Association Insurance Fund
  (SAIF), 354
Savings bonds, 555
Say, Jean-Baptiste, 831–832
Say's Law, 831–832
Scale effect, 90
Scarcity, 45
  see also Shortages
Schelling, Thomas, 642
Schlemmer, Lawrence, 102
Schmalensee, Richard, 396
Schmidt, Alexander, 670
Schofield, Roger S., 14
Scholz, John Karl, 313
Schooling see Education
Schramm, Richard, 150
Schultz, Theodore William,
  832–833
Schultze, Charles L., 109, 269, 271
Schumpeter, Joseph Alois, 80, 623,
  632, 833–834
Schwartz, Anna, 198, 200, 786
Scientism, 793
Scitovsky, Tibor, 808
Scotland, 443
SEA see Single European Act
Sears Roebuck, 112, 551
Seattle (Washington), 459
SEC see Securities and Exchange
  Commission
Second Amendment (U.S.
  Constitution), 667
Securities
  asset backed, 551–553
  high-yield see Junk bonds
  mortgage backed, 551–552
  see also Bonds; Capital markets
Securities and Exchange
  Commission (SEC), 201, 580,
  597
Securities Exchange Act of 1934
  (U.S.), 580

Segregation, 474, 820
Self-employment, 686
Self-interest, 62, 89, 110
 and public choice theory, 150
 Smith's view of, 836–837
Semistrong-form efficiency, 570
Seneca, Joseph, 387
Senior citizens see Elderly;
 Pensions; Retirement
*The Sensory Order: An Inquiry into
 the Foundations of Theoretical
 Psychology* (Hayek), 793
Sequential interdependence,
 640–641
Service industries, 228
Sesame Street Parent's Guide, 73
Setasides, 648–649
Sewage treatment, 454
Sexism see Discrimination; Women
Shareholders, 566–567
Sharing, 74
Sharpe, William F., 834–835
Shepard, Lawrence, 411, 812
Sherman Act of 1890 (U.S.), 385
Shiller, Robert, 572
Shimberg, Benjamin, 411
Shipping, 535, 803
Shortages, 416, 728, 730, 738
 housing, 421
Siles-Suazo, Hernan, 210
Silver, 535
Simon, Herbert Alexander, 835
Simon, Julian, 53, 54
Simultaneous interdependence,
 640–641
Singapore, 688, 756, 760
Single European Act (SEA), 735
Single Market Program, 735
Skills, 225, 764
 immigrant, 486
 and minimum wage, 500
 see also Education
Slavery, 638–639
 South African, 97
Small business, and minimum
 wage, 501
Smelev, Nikolai, 164
Smith, Adam, 92, 110, 539
 biography of, 836–838
 on competition, 622
 and free trade, 526–527
 and Hume, 796
 and labor theory of value, 124
 on mercantilism, 534, 535
 and total versus marginal utility,
  31
 and unintended conseqences, 92
Smith, Ian, 545
Smith, James P., 477

Smolensky, Eugene, 57, 296
Smoot-Hawley tariff, 198, 199
Smuggling, 536, 836
Social choice, 153
*Social Choice and Individual
 Values* (Arrow), 153
Social insurance programs, 59
Socialism, 111, 161–164, 630, 848
 collapse of, 127
 and government coercion, 638
 Hayek's view of, 792–793
 and individualism, 110
 Lange's view of, 805
 and management, 90
 Mises' view of, 818
 planning, 125–126
 problems with, 162–163
 and property rights, 70–71
 scientific, 126
 start of, 161–162
 western view of, 163–164
Socialism (Heilbroner), 161–164
Social sciences, 793
Social Security, 25, 246, 298–301
 advance funding idea, 300–301
 and decline in U.S. savings, 231,
  233
 and federal deficit, 254–255, 256
 as income redistribution, 294
 and labor force participation, 300
 payback period for, 299
 payroll tax for, 310–311, 314,
  315
 and poverty, 59
 as progressive tax system, 339
 and Reaganomics, 291
 total assets of, 300
 unintended consequences of, 93
Social Security Act of 1935 (U.S.),
 302
Social Security (Weaver), 298–301
Software (computer), 654
Solar energy, 672
Solow, Robert, 137, 143, 652, 831,
 844
 biography of, 838–839
 and Cambridge controversy, 137,
  829
 and Phillips curve, 280
Solow residual, 839
''Some Fallacies in the
 Interpretation of Social Cost''
 (Knight), 802–803
Sony Corporation, 744
Soto, Hernando de, 757
South Africa, 97–103, 473
 sanctions against, 543, 546–547
South African Labour Party
 (SALP), 99

South America see Latin America
South Korea see Korea, South
Soviet Union, 71, 162–163, 442
 agricultural reform, 748
 brand names, 619
 disaster recovery, 627–628
 grain embargo against, 545
 gross domestic product base year,
  205–206
 perestroika, 747–750
Sowell, Thomas, 473
Soziate marktwirtschaft (German
 economic school), 739
Spain, 734
Spatial economics, 82–85
Spatial Economics (Kasper),
 82–85
Special interests, 47–48, 151–152,
 153
 agricultural, 647
 and defense, 662
 and government spending, 264
 and health insurance, 687
 and protectionism, 540
Specialists, 581
Specialization, 107, 113, 222, 535,
 637
 and corporations, 567
 and free trade, 527, 530
 see also Labor, division of
Speculation, 198
 and exchange rates, 519, 520
 in futures, 577
Sperry Lease Finance Corporation,
 552
Sportometrics (Tollison), 709–711
Sports, 712–715
 as economics, 709–711
Sports (Scully), 712–715
Sports Television Act of 1961
 (U.S.), 713
Sprinkel, Beryl, 785
SRI see Stanford Research Institute
Stabilization, 119–120, 729,
 759–760
Stagflation, 787
Staggers Act of 1980 (U.S.), 436
Stalin, Joseph, 161
Standards, 620–621
Stanford Research Institute (SRI),
 335
Staple Act of 1663 (U.K.), 535
State ownership, 727
Statistics, economic, 203
Steel industry, 295
Stenason, John, 434
Stigler, George, 108, 660, 739,
 821, 842
 biography of, 839–841

on Coase, 783
on concentration, 396
and division of labor, 837
and information, 19
and law of demand, 7
and mergers, 387
Stinting, 89–90
Stock-index future, 577–578
Stockman, David, 785
Stock market
average increases in, 523
crash, 198–199
program trading on, 597–600
see also Bonds; Capital markets;
Securities
Stock prices, 571–573, 602–604
average return on, 603–604
corporate earning and interest
rates, 604
effect of tender offers and
mergers on, 608
efficient market theory of, 156
index arbitrage and volatility of,
599–600, 601
total return on, 602–603
Stock prices (Siegel), 602–604
Stokey, Nancy, 158, 159
Stone, John Richard Nicholas,
842–843
Strategy see Game theory
The Strategy of Conflict (Schelling),
642
Streetcar companies, 474–475
Strong, Benjamin, 200
Strong-form efficiency, 570
Stroup, Richard, 332
Studies in the Quantity Theory of
Money (Friedman), 786
Studies in the Theory of
International Trade (Viner),
846
Subchapter S status, 327
The Subjection of Women (Mill),
816
Subsidies, 36, 825
Eastern European, 727, 728
export, 541, 650, 761
health care, 679, 682–683
housing, 691–692
for industrial policy, 269, 270
insurance, 25
layoff, 303–304
Third World, 759–760
wool, 47–48
Substitutes, 8, 42, 795
Substitution effect, 334
Suffrage, 817
Sulfur oxides, 456
Sumitomo Bank (Japan), 746

Summers, Lawrence H., 231, 304,
572
Sumner, William Graham, 846
Sunset laws, 412
Superfund, 454
Superfund Amendments and
Reauthorization Act, 454
Supply and demand, 34–38, 637,
812–813
and airline deregulation, 383
equilibrium states, 106
and interest rates, 585
wage and price responses to
changes in, 119
see also Demand
Supply curve, 87
Supply (Ehrbar), 86–87
Supply-side economics, 165–169,
260
and gross domestic product, 204
Supply-Side Economics
(Gwartney), 165–169
Surpluses, 416
Sweden, 51
brain drain, 486
government spending, 263
income distribution, 179
Swift, Gustavus, 112
Switzerland, 132
Syndicalism, 115, 116

Tableau économique (Quesnay),
825–826
Taiwan, 756, 760
Takeovers, 605–610
defenses against, 606–607
see also Acquisitions; Leveraged
buyouts; Mergers
Takeovers and Leveraged
Buyouts (Jarrell), 605–610
Tanzania, 76
Tarbell, Ida, 385, 798
Tariffs, 201, 267, 530
European, 734
Japanese, 745
Korean, 761
reductions in, 531
retaliatory, 838
Tâtonnement (Walras), 847
Taussig, Frank, 634
Taxation, A Preface (Minarik),
309–315
Taxes, 35, 36, 192, 507, 779–780
ability-to-pay principle, 340
average versus marginal, 331
avoidance of, 165, 724, 725
base, 338
benefit principle, 339–340

and bonds, 554, 556
brackets, 331, 340
and budget deficit, 243, 759
burden, 338–339
capital, 159
and capital flight, 725
on carbon emissions, 451, 672
conscription, 467–468
consumption, 314–315,
321–324, 784–785
and debt neutrality, 122
and defense, 662–663
on energy, 673, 676
and federal debt, 252
and federal deficit, 255
federal revenue by type of, 311
and fiscal policy, 258, 260
and foreign investment in U.S.,
523
as government coercion, 638
and health insurance, 677, 686
hyperinflation as, 208–209
immigrant, 488
inflation as, 213
injury, 493
Japanese, 744
marginal rate, 33, 165–166, 234,
290, 329–332, 341, 795
middle-class cuts, 141–142
and pensions, 591, 594
as percentage of family income,
314
policy, 309–315
current issues, 314–315
European Community, 735
and investment, 217, 218–219,
341
and labor supply, 341
objectives of, 309–310
revenue sufficiency, 310
U.S., 310–315
burden distribution, 313–314
recent changes in, 312–313
pollution control, 455, 673, 825
in post-war Germany, 740
progressive, 338–341
rate reduction, 167–168
rates versus revenues, 166–168
and Reaganomics, 290–291,
292
real estate, 373
research and development credits,
80
and saving, 233
shelters, 165
smoothing models, 157–158, 159
Social Security, 300
state and local, 311–312
Superfund, 454

Taxes (*cont.*)
  and takeovers and leveraged
    buyouts, 609
  temporal neutrality in, 322
  unemployment insurance, 303,
    304–305
  on unimproved land, 789–790
  union exemption from, 494
  utilitarian principle, 340–341
  see also specific types of tax,
    e.g., Income tax; Payroll tax
Tax Reform Act of 1986 (U.S.),
  292, 305, 318, 326, 338
Taylor, John, 120–121
Teamsters Union, 434, 436
"Technical Change and the
  Aggregate Production
  Function" (Solow), 839
Technology
  health care, 678, 679
  progress in, 232
  see also Innovation; Research
    and development
Teenagers, 501
Telecommunications, 716–720
  economic organization of,
    717–718
  and information age economy,
    716–717
  public policy issues, 718–720
Telecommunications (Haring),
  716–720
Telecomputer, 655–656
Television, 655
  and sports, 713, 714–715
Telser, Lester, 387
Temin, Peter, 198
Tender offer, 605, 607, 608
Texas, 43, 239
Texas Gulf Sulphur, 580
Textile industry, 110, 530
Thach, Nguyen Co, 425
Thailand, 541, 756
Thalidomide, 668
"The Theory of Economic
  Regulation" (Stigler), 841
*Theory of Games and Economic
  Behavior* (Morgenstern and
  Neumann), 820, 822
Theory of Interest (Fisher), 784
*Theory of International Economic
  Policy* (Meade), 814
The Theory of Money and Credit
  (Mises), 818
The Theory of Moral Sentiments
  (Smith), 836
The Theory of Price (Stigler), 839
The Theory of the Leisure Class
  (Veblen), 846

The Theory of Value (Debreu), 784
Third World Debt (Rogoff),
  751–754
**Third World Economic
  Development** (Crook),
  755–765
Thomas, Norman, 782
Thurow, Lester, 266, 397–398, 441
Tie-in sale, 417, 418
Tietenberg, Thomas H., 456
Time-function traders, 585
Tinbergen, Jan, 787, 804, 843
Tobin, James, 521, 785, 823, 831,
  843–844
Tollison, Robert, 150
Topel, Robert, 303, 304
Totalitarianism, 793
Towards a Dynamic Economics
  (Harrod), 790
Toyo Kogyo, 746
Tract on Monetary Reform
  (Keynes), 800
Trade, 199, 515, 729–730, 733,
  798, 808, 809, 814–815
  balance, 516
    and fiscal policy, 258
  barriers, 113–114, 201, 267
    and balance of payments, 512
    nontariff, 537
    under Reaganomics, 291, 293
    and value of dollar, 529
  and capital movements, 823
  deficit, 205, 253, 516
  diversion, 532–533, 734
  and mercantilism, 535
  restraint of, 385
  terms of, 517
  Third World, 756, 760–762
  see also Free trade; Quotas;
    Tariffs
Trade and Welfare (Meade), 815
Trademarks, 615, 618
The Tragedy of the Commons
  (Hardin), 88–91
Training, 58, 267, 270, 480
  and minimum wage, 499, 501
  on-the-job, 482
  see also Education
Traité d'économie politique (Say),
  832
Transaction costs, 386, 388,
  782–783
*Transforming Traditional
  Agriculture* (Schultz), 832
Transportation, 82–85, 803
  decline in costs of, 84
  and disaster recovery, 629
  see also Trucking industry
Transvaal (South Africa), 97, 98

Treasury bills, 555
Treasury bonds, 555
Treasury Department (U.S.), 320
Treasury notes, 555
Treatise on Money (Keynes), 800
Tripartite councils, 267, 269
Troy, Leo, 496
Trucking Deregulation (Moore),
  433–437
Trucking industry, 433–437
  deregulation of, 435–436
    current issues in, 436–437
    saving of, 436
  regulation in, 433–434
    costs of, 434–435
  and Single European Act, 735
Tucker, Albert W., 62
Tucker, William, 423
Tullock, Gordon, 150, 152, 153,
  779, 780
Tuma, Nancy B., 335
Turgot, Anne-Robert-Jacques, 837,
  844–845
Turkey, 329, 762
The Turning Point (Smelev and
  Popov), 163–164
Tversky, Amos, 431
Two Cambridges Capital
  Controversy, 137, 829

Uganda, 76
"The Unanticipated Consequences
  of Purposive Social Action"
  (Merton), 92
Uncertainty, 106, 631–633, 802
  see also Risk
"Uncertainty, Evolution and
  Economic Theory" (Alchian),
  773
Underinvestment, 561
Unemployment, 17, 58, 176,
  236–240, 272, 801
  causes of long-term, 237–239
  costs to taxpayer, 238
  defined and measured, 236
  duration of, 236–237, 238
  and efficiency wages, 148
  European, 735
  in France, 130
  and gold standard, 362
  government intervention and,
    238–239
  in Great Britain, 132
  and gross national product, 823
  and health insurance, 686
  and inflation, 121, 214, 274,
    279–284, 787
  Keynesian view of, 119, 120

and minimum wage, 499,
501–502
natural rate of, 121, 239, 280,
282–284
and price controls, 418
prospects for nineties, 239–240
under Reaganomics, 291–292
structural, 58
theory of search, 841
Unemployment insurance, 59,
237–238, 239, 302–305
as automatic stabilizer, 258
extended benefits, 303
and recessions, 228
tax base for, 303
Unemployment Insurance
(Francis), 302–305
Unemployment (Summers),
236–240
Unintended consequences, 92–93,
776–777
Unintended Consequences
(Norton), 92–93
Unions, 38, 494–497
discrimination by, 495–496, 498
dues, 494
and hysteresis, 284
and inflation, 214
membership decline, 496–497
and minimum wage, 496, 502
monopoly power of, 494–495
and pensions, 594
South African, 99–100
and takeovers, 608
trucking, 435
and unemployment, 238
United Airlines, 381
United Arab Emirates, 699
United Nations, 542, 543, 545
United States
competitiveness, 514–517
federal budget, 243–247
federal debt, 248–252
foreign investment, 522–525
gross domestic product,
203–207
income distribution, 177–181
inflation, 129, 211–212, 214
investment, 220–221
national industrial policy,
265–271
poverty, 56–60
research and development, 79,
80–81, 187–188
saving, 230–235
tax rates, 213–214
Unit-value indexes, 212
Universities *see* Colleges and
universities

University Economics (Alchian and
Allen), 773
Uqdah, Taalib-Dan Abdu, 413
Urban underclass, 58–59
U.S.-Canada Free Trade Agreement
(USCFTA), 532, 541
User fees, 339
Usury, 416
Utilitarianism, 778
Utility
marginal, 797, 847
theory, 822
total versus marginal, 31

Vacations, 505
Value, 9–10, 31, 136, 797
Hicks' theory, 795
labor theory of, 124–125, 810
subjective theory of, 815
Value-added tax (VAT), 314, 321,
815
Value and Capital (Hicks), 795,
830
Value, Capital, and Rent
(Wicksell), 848–849
Value theory, 135
VAT *see* Value-added tax
Veblen, Thorstein, 845–846
Venezuela, 724
Venti, Steven F., 313
Vermont, 93
VERs *see* Voluntary export
restrictions
Versailles, Treaty of, 800
Vertical contracts, 386–387, 401
Vietnam, 425
Viner, Jacob, 734, 846–847
Violence, 773
Volcker, Paul, 272, 278, 292, 370
Voluntary export restrictions
(VERs), 540
Von Thünen, Johann Heinrich, 83,
470
Vote trading *see* Log rolling
Voting, 151, 153

Wachter, Michael, 495, 496
Wage Act (South Africa), 100
Wages, 145, 801
comparable worth, 463–466
compensating differentials, 837
and competition, 623
and conscription, 467
coordination failures, 147
and corporate income tax, 326
determination of, 499–500

during industrial revolution,
14–15
Eastern European, 730
effect of labor monopoly on,
37–38
efficiency, 148
and free trade, 527–528
gender gap, 475–478
for high school dropouts, 480,
487–488
immigrant, 485–488
and industrial policy, 268–269
and labor force, 791
and monetary policy, 273–274
and new classical economics, 121
nonfarm, 506
and Phillips curve, 280
premiums for hazardous work,
490, 491, 492
reservation, 237–238, 304
response to supply and demand,
119
rigidity of, 18–19
slowdown in growth of, 297
subsistence theory of, 812
takeovers and, 608
union, 494, 495–496, 608
for women, 472
and working conditions,
503–507
see also Minimum wage
Wages and Working Conditions
(Lebergott), 503–507
Waggoner, Paul, 79
Wagner, Adolph, 262
Wagner's law, 262
Wallace, Neil, 348
Wallich, Henry, 738–739,
740–741
Walras, Leon, 137, 797, 847–848
War, 418–420
Ward, Michael, 477
Wardell, William, 669
War Emergency Tenant Protection
Act (U.S.), 421
Warranted growth, 790–791
Warsaw Pact, 80
Washington, Booker T., 496
Washington National Airport, 383
Washington Public Power Supply
System, 557
Waste Age (magazine), 458
Water pollution, 454
Weak-form efficiency, 570
The Wealth of Nations (Smith),
124, 535, 836, 837
Weather, 504
Weber, Max, 110, 848
Welch, Finis, 480

Welfare
  economics, 35, 825
  and immigrants, 486, 488–489
  payments, 237
  policy, 59–60
  reform, 336–337
  see also Medicaid; Medicare;
    Unemployment insurance
Wenders, John T., 718
Western Electric, 744
Wharton model, 802
"What Can Regulators Regulate?
    The Case of Electricity"
    (Friedland and Stigler), 840
Wheeling, 392–394
White, Lawrence J., 388
White, William D., 411
Wicksell, Knut, 779–780, 848–850
Wieser, Friedrich von, 105, 816
Wigner, Eugene, 822
Williamson, Jeffrey, 14
Williamson, John, 521
Williamson, Oliver, 387
Wilson, Woodrow, 542
Wise, David, 313

Wiseman, A. Clark, 459
Wiseman, Jack, 262
Wolf, Frederick, 373
Wolff, Edward N., 222, 223
Women, 816
  African-American, 482
  and college education, 481
  comparable worth, 463–466, 472
  gender gap in wages, 475–478
  job experience, 477
  life expectancy, 429
  poverty rate for, 57
  and reduction of tax rates, 313
  and saving rate, 232
  union discrimination against,
    495
  work hours of, 504–505
Worker associations, 497
Workers' compensation, 490, 491,
    492–493
Working conditions
  hours, 504–505
  and wages, 503–507
Works Project Administration, 201
World Bank, 760, 763

World Development Report 1987
    (World Bank), 760
World Development Report 1989
    (World Bank), 763
The World in Depression
    (Kindleberger), 198
World War I, 197–198, 262, 359,
    536
World War II, 419
Wright, Frank Lloyd, 412
Wrigley, E. A., 14
Wriston, Walter, 751

Yeager, Leland B., 348, 350
Yugoslavia, 129

Zaslavskaia, Tat'iana, 747
Zero-sum games, 640
The Zero-Sum Society (Thurow),
    266, 397, 441
Zimbabwe, 76
Zoning, 692–693
Zwick, Charles, 434